A SHAKESPEAREAN GENEALOGY

This chart reflects Shakespeare's history plays and is thus not historically accurate. Many descendants of Henry II and Edward III are omitted. On occasion, Shakespeare combined or simply invented historical figures. These deviations from fact are explained in the notes.

In the chart, the names of Kings and Queens are printed in capitals, and the dates of their reigns are printed in bold. The names of characters appearing in the plays are underlined.

*Philip Faulconbridge, the bastard son of Richard I, had no historical existence. Such a character appears in the play *The Life and Death of King John* and is referred to in passing in Holinshed's *Chronicles*.

† In the character of Edmund Mortimer, Shakespeare combines two historical figures. The Edmund Mortimer who married Catrin, daughter of Owain Glyndŵr, was the grandson of Lionel, Duke of Clarence, and the younger brother of Roger, Earl of March. He died in 1409. Shakespeare combines him with his nephew, the Edmund Mortimer recognized by Richard II as his heir (d. 1424). This second Edmund was the brother of Anne Mortimer and the uncle of Richard Plantagenet.

‡ The character of the Duke of Somerset combines Henry Beaufort with his younger brother Edmund (d. 1471), who succeeded him as Duke.

Elizabeth Mortimer
("Kate")
m. Henry Percy
("Hotspur")
1364–1403

Henry, Earl of
Northumberland
1394–1455

EDWARD IV
1442–1483 (1461–83)
m. Elizabeth
Woodville d. 1492

EDWARD V
1470–1483 (1483)

Richard, Duke
of York 1472–1483

Elizabeth of York
1465–1503
m. HENRY VII
(below)

Edmund, Earl of
Rutland 1443–1460

Edmund Mortimer†

George, Duke of
Clarence 1449–1478
m. Isabel Neville
(below)

Anne Mortimer
m. Richard, Earl of
Cambridge (below)

Richard Plantagenet,
Duke of York
1411–1460
m. Cicely Neville
(below)

RICHARD III
1452–1485 (1483–85)
m. Anne Neville
(below)

Edward, Prince of Wales

HENRY V 1387–1422
(1413–22)
m. Catherine
1401–1437

HENRY VI 1421–1471
(1422–61)
m. Margaret of Anjou
d. 1482

Edward, Prince of
Wales 1453–1471
m. Anne Neville
(below)

Arthur
m. Catherine of
Aragon (below)

Thomas, Duke of
Clarence d. 1421

John of Lancaster,
Duke of Bedford
1389–1435

Margaret
m. James IV
of Scotland

James V
of Scotland
|
Mary, Queen of
Scots
|
JAMES I
1566–1625
(1603–25)

Humphrey, Duke of
Gloucester 1391–1447
m. Eleanor Cobham
d. 1454

John Beaufort, Duke
of Somerset
1403–1444

Margaret Beaufort
m. Edmund Tudor,
Earl of Richmond

HENRY VII 1457–1509
(1485–1509)
m. Elizabeth of York
(above)

HENRY VIII
1491–1547
(1509–47)
m. Catherine of
Aragon

MARY I 1516–1558
(1553–58)
m. Philip of Spain

Edmund Beaufort,
Duke of Somerset
1406–1455

Henry Beaufort,
Duke of Somerset
1436–1464‡

m. Anne Boleyn

ELIZABETH I
1533–1603
(1558–1603)

Isabel Neville
d. 1476
m. George, Duke
of Clarence
(above)

m. Jane Seymour

EDWARD VI
1537–1553
(1547–53)

Richard Neville,
Earl of Salisbury
1400–1460

Richard Neville,
Earl of Warwick
1428–1471

John Neville,
Marquess of
Montague d. 1471

Anne Neville
d. 1485
m. Edward, Prince
of Wales (above)

m. RICHARD III
(above)

m. Anne of Cleves

m. Katherine Howard

m. Katherine Parr

Cicely Neville
m. Richard
Plantagenet,
Duke of York (above)

Mary
m. Charles Brandon

Frances
|
Jane Grey
1537–1554

Humphrey, Duke of
Buckingham
1402–1460

Humphrey Stafford
d. 1455

Henry, Duke of
Buckingham
1454?–1483

Edward, Duke of
Buckingham
1478–1521

Richard II, 1377–99 Richard was the eldest son of Edward the Black Prince, himself the eldest son of King Edward III, who ruled England from 1327 to 1377. When the Black Prince died in battle in France in 1376, Richard became the legitimate heir to the throne. He ruled from Edward's death in 1377 until he was deposed in 1399 by Henry Bolingbroke, the eldest son of John of Gaunt, Duke of Lancaster. Because he was the fourth son of Edward III, Gaunt and his Lancastrian descendants had weaker hereditary claims to the throne than did Richard. When deposed, Richard had no children to succeed him, but he recognized Edmund Mortimer, Fifth Earl of March, as his heir presumptive. This Mortimer was descended from Lionel, Duke of Clarence, the third son of Edward III, and therefore also had stronger hereditary claims to the throne than did Bolingbroke. Shakespeare combined this Mortimer with his uncle Edmund Mortimer, who married Owain Glyndŵr's daughter.

Henry IV, 1399–1413 Henry Bolingbroke, eldest son of John of Gaunt, seized the throne from Richard II in 1399. When Henry died in 1413, he was succeeded by his eldest son, Prince Hal, who became Henry V.

Henry V, 1413–22 Henry V became king in 1413 and reigned until his death in 1422. He was succeeded by his son, Henry VI.

Henry VI, 1422–61 Henry VI was less than one year old when he succeeded his father, Henry V. In the young king's minority, his uncle Humphrey, Duke of Gloucester, was named Lord Protector, and the kingdom was ruled by an aristocratic council. Henry VI assumed personal authority in 1437. He was deposed in 1461 by his third cousin, who was crowned Edward IV. Henry was murdered in 1471.

Edward IV, 1461–83 Edward, the eldest son of Richard, Duke of York, seized the throne from Henry VI in 1461. His Yorkist claim to the throne derived from his grandmother, Anne Mortimer, who was descended from Lionel, third son of Edward III, and was sister to that Edmund Mortimer recognized by Richard II as his heir presumptive; Edward IV's grandfather, Richard, Earl of Cambridge, was the son of Edmund of Langley, fifth son of Edward III. Edward IV reigned until his death in 1483. His heir was his eldest son (Edward), but the throne was usurped by his brother Richard, Duke of Gloucester.

Richard III, 1483–85 Richard III was the youngeer brother of Edward IV. After the death of Edward IV in 1483, Richard prevented the coronation of Edward V with a claim of illegitimacy and succeeded to the throne himself. Edward and his younger brother, Richard, Duke of York, were murdered in the Tower of London. Richard III was killed at the Battle of Bosworth Field in 1485, and the kingdom fell to the victor, Henry Tudor, Earl of Richmond.

Henry VII, 1485–1509 Henry Tudor seized the throne from Richard III in 1485. He was descended from John of Gaunt by John's third marriage, with Catherine Swynford. He married Elizabeth, daughter of Edward IV, uniting the houses of Lancaster and York. He died in 1509 and was succeeded by his son, Henry VIII.

Henry VIII, 1509–47 Henry was the second son of Henry VII. His older brother, Arthur, died in 1502. Henry VIII's first wife was Catherine of Aragon, who bore his daughter Mary. His second wife, Anne Boleyn, was the mother of Elizabeth. His third wife, Jane Seymour, bore him a son, who succeeded to the throne as Edward VI after Henry VIII died in 1547.

Edward VI, 1547–53 Edward VI was nine years old when he became king. From 1547 to 1549, the realm was governed by a Lord Protector, the Duke of Somerset; power then passed to John Dudley, Duke of Northumberland. When Edward VI died in 1553, Northumberland attempted unsuccessfully to prevent the succession of Mary Tudor by installing as queen his daughter-in-law, Lady Jane Grey, a great-granddaughter of Henry VII.

Mary I, 1553–58 Mary, daughter of Henry VIII and his first wife, Catherine of Aragon, came to the throne in 1553. She married King Philip of Spain but died childless. She was succeeded by her half sister, Elizabeth.

Elizabeth I, 1558–1603 Elizabeth, the daughter of Henry VIII and his second wife, Anne Boleyn, became queen after the death of her half sister, Mary, in 1558. She ruled until her death in 1603. She was succeeded by her cousin James.

James I, 1603–1625 James VI of Scotland became James I of England in 1603. His claim to the throne of England derived from his great-grandmother, Margaret Tudor, a daughter of Henry VII who married James IV of Scotland. James ruled England and Scotland until his death in 1625; he was succeeded by his son, Charles I.

THE NORTON SHAKESPEARE

BASED ON THE OXFORD EDITION

SECOND EDITION

Comedies

The original Oxford Text on which this
edition is based was prepared by

Stanley Wells
Gary Taylor
General Editors

John Jowett
William Montgomery

The Norton Shakespeare, Second Edition, is based on *William Shakespeare: The Complete Works,*
Second Edition, and is published by arrangement with Oxford University Press,
with additional material from W. W. Norton & Company, Inc.

THE NORTON SHAKESPEARE

Based on the Oxford Edition

SECOND EDITION

Comedies

Stephen Greenblatt, *General Editor*
HARVARD UNIVERSITY

Walter Cohen
CORNELL UNIVERSITY

Jean E. Howard
COLUMBIA UNIVERSITY

Katharine Eisaman Maus
UNIVERSITY OF VIRGINIA

With an Essay on the Shakespearean stage
by Andrew Gurr

W · W · NORTON & COMPANY · NEW YORK · LONDON

W. W. Norton & Company has been independent since its founding in 1923, when William Warder Norton and Mary D. Herter Norton first published lectures delivered at the People's Institute, the adult education division of New York City's Cooper Union. The Nortons soon expanded their program beyond the Institute, publishing books by celebrated academics from America and abroad. By mid-century, the two major pillars of Norton's publishing program—trade books and college texts—were firmly established. In the 1950s, the Norton family transferred control of the company to its employees, and today—with a staff of four hundred and a comparable number of trade, college, and professional titles published each year—W. W. Norton & Company stands as the largest and oldest publishing house owned wholly by its employees.

Editor: Julia Reidhead
Manuscript editor: Carol Flechner
Electronic media editor: Eileen Connell
Editorial assistant: Rivka Genesen
Production manager: Diane O'Connor
Photo research: Rivka Genesen
Interior design: Antonina Krass
Managing editor, College: Marian Johnson

The Library of Congress has cataloged the one-volume edition as follows:

Shakespeare, William, 1564–1616.
The Norton Shakespeare / Stephen Greenblatt, general editor ; Walter Cohen, Jean E. Howard, Katharine Eisaman Maus [editors] ; with an essay on the Shakespearean stage by Andrew Gurr. — 2nd ed.
p. cm.
"Based on the Oxford edition."
Includes bibliographical references and index.
ISBN 978-0-393-92991-1
I. Greenblatt, Stephen, 1943–   II. Cohen, Walter, 1949–   III. Howard, Jean E. (Jean Elizabeth), 1948–   IV. Maus, Katharine Eisaman, 1955–   V. Gurr, Andrew.
VI. Title.
PR2754.G74   2008
822.3'3—dc22
2007046599

ISBN 978-0-393-93141-9

W. W. Norton & Company, Inc., 500 Fifth Avenue, New York, NY 10110
www.wwnorton.com

W. W. Norton & Company Ltd., Castle House, 75/76 Wells Street, London W1T 3QT

1 2 3 4 5 6 7 8 9 0

Contents

DOCUMENTS 993

TIMELINE 1016

Illustrations

Preface

Shakespeare's principal medium, the drama, was thoroughly collaborative, and it involved as well continual efforts at revision and renewal. It seems appropriate, then, that this edition of his works is itself the result of sustained collaboration and revision. Two lists of editors' names on the title-page spread hint at the collaboration that has brought to fruition the *Norton Shakespeare*. But the title page does not tell the full history of this project. The text on which the *Norton Shakespeare* is based was published in both modern-spelling and original-spelling versions by Oxford University Press, in 1986. Under the general editorship of Stanley Wells and Gary Taylor, the Oxford text was a thorough rethinking of the entire body of Shakespeare's works, the most far-reaching and innovative revision of the traditional canon in centuries. When many classroom instructors who wanted to introduce their students to the works of Shakespeare through a modern text expressed a need for the pedagogical apparatus they have come to expect in an edition oriented toward students, Norton negotiated with Oxford to assemble an editorial team of its own to prepare the necessary teaching materials around the existing Oxford text. Hence ensued a collaboration of two publishers and two editorial teams.

To what extent is this the *Norton Shakespeare* and to what extent the Oxford text? Introductions (both the General Introduction and those to individual plays and poems), footnotes, glosses, bibliographies, genealogies, annals, maps, documents, and illustrations have all been the responsibility of the Norton team. Andrew Gurr's much-admired essay on the London theater in Shakespeare's time, specially commissioned for the *Norton Shakespeare,* has been moved in this second edition to the front matter.

The textual notes and variants derive for the most part from the work of the Oxford team, especially as represented in *William Shakespeare: A Textual Companion* (Oxford University Press, 1987), a remarkably comprehensive explanation of editorial decisions that is herewith strongly recommended to instructors as a valuable companion to this volume. Several of the textual notes—those to *The First Part of Henry the Sixth,* Various Poems, *The Two Noble Kinsmen, The Merry Wives of Windsor, Troilus and Cressida,* The Sonnets and "A Lover's Complaint"—have been substantially updated in the current edition, and all Textual Variants are now gathered in an appendix.

The Oxford text is widely available and already well known to scholars. A few words here may help clarify the extent of our fidelity to that text and the nature of the collaboration that has brought about this volume. The Oxford editors have profited from the massive and sustained attention accorded their edition by Shakespeare scholars across the globe, and of course they have continued to participate actively in the ongoing scholarly discussion about the nature of Shakespeare's text. In the reprintings of the Oxford volumes and in various articles over the past years, the Oxford editors have made a number of refinements of the edition they originally published. Such changes have been incorporated silently here. A small number of other changes made by the Norton team, however, were not part of the Oxford editors' design and were only accepted by them after we reached, through lengthy consultation, a mutual understanding about the nature, purpose, and intended audience of this volume. In all such changes, our main concern was for the classroom; we wished to make fully and clearly available the scholarly innovation and freshness of the Oxford text, while at the same time making certain that this was a superbly useful teaching text. It is a pleasure here to record, on behalf of the Norton team, our gratitude for the personal and professional generosity of the Oxford editors in offering advice and entertaining arguments in our common goal of providing the best student Shakespeare for our times. The Norton changes to the Oxford text are various, but in only a few instances are they major. The following brief notes are sufficient to summarize all of these changes, which are also indicated in appropriate play introductions, footnotes, or textual notes.

1. The Oxford editors, along with other scholars, have strenuously argued—in both the Oxford text and elsewhere—that the now-familiar text of *King Lear*, so nearly omnipresent in our classrooms as to seem unquestionably authoritative but in reality dating from the work of Alexander Pope (1723) and Lewis Theobald (1733), represents a wrongheaded conflation of two distinct versions of the play: Shakespeare's original creation as printed in the 1608 Quarto and his substantial revision as printed in the First Folio (1623). The Oxford text, therefore, prints both *The History of King Lear* and *The Tragedy of King Lear*. Norton follows suit, but where Oxford presents these two texts sequentially, we print them on facing pages. While each version may be read independently, and to ensure this we have provided glosses and footnotes for each, the substantial points of difference between the two are immediately apparent and available for comparison. But even many who agree with the scholarly argument for the two texts of *Lear* nevertheless favor making available a conflated text, the text on which innumerable performances of the play have been based and on which a huge body of literary criticism has been written. With the reluctant acquiescence, therefore, of the Oxford editors, we have included a conflated *Lear*, a text that has no part in the Oxford canon and that has been edited by Barbara K. Lewalski of Harvard University rather than by Gary Taylor, the editor of the Oxford *Lears*.

The *Norton Shakespeare*, then, includes three separate texts of *King Lear*. The reader can compare them, understand the role of editors in constructing the texts we now call Shakespeare's, explore in considerable detail the kinds of decisions that playwrights, editors, and printers make and remake, witness firsthand the historical transformation of what might at first glance seem fixed and unchanging. The *Norton Shakespeare* offers extraordinary access to this supremely brilliant, difficult, compelling play.

2. Among several other plays, *Hamlet* offers similar grounds for objections to the traditional conflation, but both the economics of publishing and the realities of bookbinding—not to mention our recognition of the limited time in the typical undergraduate syllabus—preclude our offering three (or even four) *Hamlets* to match three *Lears*. What we have provided in this edition is a convenient selection of parallel passages that will enable teachers to convey some of the complex, often enigmatic issues, at once stylistic and conceptual, raised by the different texts of the play.

The Oxford text of *Hamlet* was based upon the Folio text, with an appended list of Additional Passages from the Second Quarto (Q2). These additional readings total more than two hundred lines, a significant number, among which are lines that have come to seem very much part of the play as widely received, even if we may doubt that they belong with all the others in any single one of Shakespeare's *Hamlets*. The Norton team, while following the Oxford text, has moved the Q2 passages from the appendix to the body of the play. But in doing so, we have not wanted once again to produce a conflated text. We have therefore indented the Q2 passages, printed them in a different typeface, and numbered them in such a way as to make clear their provenance. Those who wish to read the Folio version of *Hamlet* can thus simply skip over the indented Q2 passages, while at the same time it is possible for readers to see clearly the place that the Q2 passages occupy. We have adopted a similar strategy with several other plays: passages printed in Oxford in appendices are generally printed here in the play texts, though clearly demarcated and not conflated. In the case of *The Taming of the Shrew* and the related quarto text, *The Taming of a Shrew*, however, we have followed Oxford's procedure and left the quarto passages in an appendix, since we believe the texts reflect two distinct plays rather than a revision of one. We have similarly reproduced Oxford's brief appendices to A *Midsummer Night's Dream* and *Henry V,* enabling readers to consider alternative revisions of certain passages.

3. For reasons understood by every Shakespearean (and rehearsed at some length in this volume), the Oxford editors chose to restore the name "Sir John Oldcastle" to the character much better known as Falstaff in *1 Henry IV.* (They made comparable changes in the names of the characters known as Bardolph and Peto.) But for reasons understood by everyone who has presented this play to undergraduates or sampled the centuries of enthusiastic criticism, the Norton editors, with the Oxford editors' gracious agreement, have for this classroom edition opted for the familiar name "Falstaff " (and those of his boon companions), properly noting the change and its significance in the play's introduction.

4. The Oxford editors chose not to differentiate between those stage directions that appeared in the early editions up to and including the Folio and those that have been added by subsequent editors. Instead, in *A Textual Companion* they include separate lists of the original stage directions. These lists are not readily available to readers of the Norton text, whose editors opted instead to bracket all stage directions that derive from editions published after the Folio. Readers can thus easily see which stage directions derive from texts that may bear at least some relation to performances in Shakespeare's time, if not to Shakespeare's own authorship. The Norton policy is more fully explained in the General Introduction.

5. The Oxford editors have newly prepared complete texts of the multiauthored *King Edward III* and *Sir Thomas More,* in which Shakespeare may have had a hand as collaborator. The texts are available online at wwnorton.com/shakespeare. In addition, the *Norton Shakespeare,* Second Edition, continues to print, with a revised introduction, notes, and glosses, passages from *Sir Thomas More* that appear in the surviving manuscript to be in Shakespeare's own handwriting, and we include for the first time an introduction and bibliography to *King Edward III.*

The collaboration with Oxford was obviously essential to the creation of the *Norton Shakespeare.* But in preparing this Second Edition and making it something fresh and engaging, the critically important collaboration has been with the thousands of people who have used the book. Many of these, teachers and students alike, have generously offered helpful suggestions along with praise. Guided by their responses, as well as by recent developments in Shakespeare scholarship, we determined to look afresh at every detail and to make a wide range of changes. The General Introduction and the individual play introductions have been substantially revised, in some cases wholly rewritten, to make them clearer and more accessible. Textual notes throughout have been updated in response to new findings, and there are hundreds of new and fine-tuned notes and glosses, designed to make this edition an even better tool for learning and pleasure. The General Bibliography has been reorganized and extensively updated, with 7 new sections and over 350 new entries. The Selected Bibliographies, too, have been updated as well as newly annotated. A new introduction provides an illuminating guide to the array of maps, three of them archival and three new, showing places important to Shakespeare's plays. The genealogies have been revised, as has been the text/contexts Timeline. New annotated film lists, including over 50 films, now follow the play introductions. Instructors who emphasize films in their courses may wish to assign *Shakespeare and Film: A Norton Guide* by Samuel Crowl, available packaged with the *Norton Shakespeare.* Finally, in response to many requests, we are making the *Norton Shakespeare* available in three different formats: the familiar one-volume clothbound edition, new two-volume chronological splits (*Early Plays and Poems* and *Later Plays*), and four genre paperbacks, each with a new introduction.

With the Second Edition of the *Norton Shakespeare,* the publisher expands its extensive online resource, Norton Literature Online (wwnorton.com/literature). Students who activate the free password in each new copy of the book gain access to an array of general resources, among them a glossary of literary terms, advice on writing about literature and using MLA documentation style, an author portrait gallery, more than 100 maps, and over 90 minutes of recorded readings and musical selections, among them 80 songs by Shakespeare. With their passwords, students also gain access to a site specifically developed to support the *Norton Shakespeare* (wwnorton.com/shakespeare). Based on content prepared by Mark Rose, University of California, Santa Barbara, this Web site invites students to explore six of the most widely taught plays—*The Merchant of Venice, 1 Henry IV, Hamlet, Othello, King Lear,* and *The Tempest*—through different contextual lenses. For each of these plays, the Web site provides materials on the elements of theater, sources, stage history, and critical receptions, as well as the complete Oxford text. Audio clips and stills from classic productions, etchings, photographs, and costume-design illustrations help students appreciate performance aspects of the plays. The student Web site also includes the redesigned "Shakespearean Chronicle, 1558–1616," an illustrated timeline that interweaves three kinds of chronologies illuminating Shakespeare's life and times. As noted above, a password-protected section of the Web site also includes the complete texts of *The Book of Sir Thomas More* and *The Reign of King Edward the Third,* prepared by the editors of the *Oxford Shakespeare.*

The creation of this edition has drawn heavily on the resources, experience, and skill of its remarkable publisher, the independent, employee-owned company W. W. Norton. Our principal guide has been our brilliant editor Julia Reidhead, whose calm intelligence, common sense, and steady focus have been essential in enabling us to reach our goal. With this Second Edition, we were blessed with the characteristically thoughtful oversight of Marian Johnson, managing editor, college department; scrupulous manuscript editing by Carol Flechner; and the assistance of an extraordinary group of Norton staffers: editorial assistant Rivka Genesen, who, among many other things, coordinated the art program; production manager Diane O'Connor; designer Antonina Krass; editor of the *Norton Shakespeare* Web site Eileen Connell; and proofreaders Paula Noonan and Ann Warren.

The *Norton Shakespeare* editors have, in addition, had the valuable—indeed, indispensable—support of a host of undergraduate and graduate research assistants, colleagues, friends, and family. Even a partial listing of those to whom we owe our heartfelt thanks is very long, but we are all fortunate enough to live in congenial and supportive environments, and the edition has been part of our lives for a long time. We owe special thanks for sustained dedication and learning to our principal assistants: Tiffany Alkan, Lianne Habinek, and Emily Peterson. Particular thanks are due to Noah Heringman for his work on the texts assembled in the documents section and for the prefatory notes and comments on those texts; to Philip Schwyzer for preparing the genealogies and the glossary and for conceiving and preparing the (now online) "Shakespearean Chronicle"; and to Holger Schott Syme for reconceiving and extensively updating the General Bibliography. In addition, we are deeply grateful to Ezra Feldman, Francesca Mari, Douglas McQueen-Thomson, Jeffrey Patterson, and Benjamin Woodring. All of these companions, and many more besides, have helped us find in this long collective enterprise what the "Dedicatorie Epistle" to the First Folio promises to its readers: delight. We make the same promise to the readers of our edition and invite them to continue the great Shakespearean collaboration.

STEPHEN GREENBLATT
WALTER COHEN
JEAN E. HOWARD
KATHARINE EISAMAN MAUS

Acknowledgments

Among our many critics, advisers, and friends, the following were of special help in providing critiques for particular plays or of the project as a whole: Janet Adelman (University of California, Berkeley), Joel Altman (University of California, Berkeley), Rebecca Bach (University of Alabama at Birmingham), John Baxter (Dalhousie University), Edward I. Berry (University of Victoria), Timothy Billings (Middlebury College), Bruce Boehrer (Florida State University), Barbara Bono (University at Buffalo, SUNY), Gordon M. Braden (University of Virginia), Douglas Brooks (Texas A&M University), Stephen Buhler (University of Nebraska—Lincoln), Richard Burt (University of Florida), Joseph F. Ceccio (University of Akron), Julie Crawford (Columbia University), Christy Desmet (University of Georgia), Heather Dubrow (University of Wisconsin—Madison), Laurie Ellinghausen (University of Missouri—Kansas City), Chris Fitter (Rutgers, State University of New Jersey), Susan Fraiman (University of Virginia), Daniel Gil (University of Oregon), Miriam Gilbert (University of Iowa), Suzanne Gossett (Loyola University), Elizabeth Hanson (Queen's University), Jim Harner (Texas A&M University), Jonathan Gil Harris (George Washington University), Don Hedrick (Kansas State University), Roze Hentschell (Colorado State University), Clifford Huffman (Stony Brook University, SUNY), John Huntington (University of Illinois at Chicago), Sujata Iyengar (University of Georgia), Kimberly Johnson (Brigham Young University), Coppélia Kahn (Brown University), Sean Keilen (University of Pennsylvania), Theodore B. Leinwand (University of Maryland), Zachary Lesser (University of Pennsylvania), Naomi Liebler (Montclair State University), Joyce MacDonald (University of Kentucky), Leah Marcus (Vanderbilt University), Mark Matheson (University of Utah), Robert Matz (George Mason University), Kristen McDermott (Central Michigan University), Ted McGee (University of Waterloo), Scott McMillin (late of Cornell University), Gordon McMullan (King's College London), John Moore (Pennsylvania State University), Carol Neely (University of Illinois at Urbana-Champaign), Lori Newcomb (University of Illinois at Urbana-Champaign), Karen Newman (New York University), Hillary Nunn (University of Akron), Thomas G. Olsen (SUNY at New Paltz), Jim O'Rourke (Florida State University), Paul Parrish (Texas A&M University), Michael Payne (Bucknell University), Rebecca J. Pederin (University of Virginia), Curtis Perry (Arizona State University), Susan Phillips (Northwestern University), Tanya Pollard (Brooklyn College, CUNY), Kristen Poole (University of Delaware), Arnold Preussner (Truman State University), Phyllis Rackin (University of Pennsylvania), Peter L. Rudnytsky (University of Florida), Benjamin Saunders (University of Oregon), Barbara Sebek (Colorado State University), Tracey Sedinger (University of Northern Colorado), Jyotsna Singh (Michigan State University), Andrew Stott (University at Buffalo, SUNY), Garrett Sullivan (Pennsylvania State University), Ramie Targoff (Brandeis University), Henry Turner (University of Wisconsin—Madison), Martine van Elk (California State University, Long Beach), William N. West (University of Colorado at Boulder), Linda Woodbridge (Pennsylvania State University), Lingui Yang (Texas A&M University).

General Introduction
by
STEPHEN GREENBLATT

"He was not of an age, but for all time!"

The celebration of Shakespeare's genius, eloquently initiated by his friend and rival Ben Jonson, has over the centuries become an institutionalized rite of civility. The person who does not love Shakespeare has made, the rite implies, an incomplete adjustment not simply to a particular culture—English culture of the late sixteenth and early seventeenth centuries—but to "culture" as a whole, the dense network of constraints and entitlements, dreams and practices that links us to nature. Indeed, so absolute is Shakespeare's achievement that he has himself come to seem like great creating nature: the common bond of humankind, the principle of hope, the symbol of the imagination's power to transcend time-bound beliefs and assumptions, peculiar historical circumstances, and specific artistic conventions.

The near-worship that Shakespeare inspires is one of the salient facts about his art. But we must at the same time acknowledge that this art is the product of peculiar historical circumstances and specific conventions, four centuries distant from our own. The acknowledgment is important because Shakespeare the working dramatist did not typically lay claim to the transcendent, visionary truths attributed to him by his most fervent admirers; his characters more modestly say, in the words of the magician Prospero, that their project was "to please" (*The Tempest,* Epilogue, line 13). The starting point, and perhaps the ending point as well, in any encounter with Shakespeare is simply to enjoy him, to savor his imaginative richness, to take pleasure in his infinite delight in language.

"If then you do not like him," Shakespeare's first editors wrote in 1623, "surely you are in some manifest danger not to understand him." Over the years, accommodations have been devised to make liking Shakespeare easier for everyone. When the stage sank to melodrama and light opera, Shakespeare—in suitably revised texts—was there. When the populace had a craving for hippodrama, plays performed entirely on horseback, *Hamlet* was dutifully rewritten and mounted. When audiences went mad for realism, live frogs croaked in productions of *A Midsummer Night's Dream.* When the stage was stripped bare and given over to stark exhibitions of sadistic cruelty, Shakespeare was our contemporary. And when the theater itself had lost some of its cultural centrality, Shakespeare moved effortlessly to Hollywood and the soundstages of the BBC.

This virtually universal appeal is one of the most astonishing features of the Shakespeare phenomenon: plays that were performed before glittering courts thrive in junior-high-school auditoriums; enemies set on destroying one another laugh at the same jokes and weep at the same catastrophes; some of the richest and most complex English verse ever written migrates with spectacular success into German and Italian, Hindi, Swahili, and Japanese. Is there a single, stable, continuous object that underlies all of these migrations and metamorphoses? Certainly not. The global diffusion and long life of Shakespeare's works depend on their extraordinary malleability, their protean capacity to elude definition and escape secure possession. At the same time, they are not without identifiable shared features: across centuries and continents, family resemblances link many of the wildly diverse manifestations of plays such as *Romeo and Juliet, Hamlet,* and *Twelfth Night.* And if there is no clear limit or end point, there is a reasonably clear beginning: the

England of the late sixteenth and early seventeenth centuries, when the plays and poems collected in this volume made their first appearance.

An art virtually without end or limit but with an identifiable, localized, historical origin: Shakespeare's achievement defies the facile opposition between transcendent and time-bound. It is not necessary to choose between an account of Shakespeare as the scion of a particular culture and an account of him as a universal genius who created works that continually renew themselves across national and generational boundaries. On the contrary: crucial clues to understanding his art's remarkable power to soar beyond its originary time and place lie in the very soil from which that art sprang.

Shakespeare's World

Life and Death

Life expectancy at birth in early modern England was exceedingly low by our stan-dards: under thirty years old, compared with over seventy today. Infant mortality rates were extraordinarily high, and it is estimated that in the poorer parishes of London only about half the children survived to the age of fifteen, while the children of aristocrats fared only a little better. In such circumstances, some parents must have developed a certain detachment—one of Shakespeare's contemporaries writes of losing "some three or four children"—but there are many expressions of intense grief, so that we cannot assume that the frequency of death hardened people to loss or made it routine.

Still, the spectacle of death, along with that other great threshold experience, birth, must have been far more familiar to Shakespeare and his contemporaries than to our-selves. There was no equivalent in early modern England to our hospitals, and most births and deaths occurred at home. Physical means for the alleviation of pain and suffering were extremely limited—alcohol might dull the terror, but it was hardly an effective anesthetic—and medical treatment was generally both expensive and worthless, more likely to intensify suffering than to lead to a cure. This was a world without a concept of antiseptics, with little actual understanding of disease, with few effective ways of treating earaches or venereal disease, let alone the more terrible instances of what Shakespeare calls "the thousand natural shocks that flesh is heir to."

The worst of these shocks was the bubonic plague, which repeatedly ravaged England, and particularly English towns, until the third quarter of the seventeenth century. The plague was terrifyingly sudden in its onset, rapid in its spread, and almost invariably lethal. Physicians were helpless in the face of the epidemic, though they prescribed amulets,

Bill recording plague deaths in London, 1609.

preservatives, and sweet-smelling substances (on the theory that the plague was carried by noxious vapors). In the plague-ridden year of 1564, the year of Shakespeare's birth, some 254 people died in Stratford-upon-Avon, out of a total population of 800. The year before, some 20,000 Londoners are thought to have died; in 1593, almost 15,000; in 1603, 36,000, or over a sixth of the city's inhabitants. The social effects of these horrible visitations were severe: looting, violence, and despair, along with an intensification of the age's perennial poverty, unemployment, and food shortages. The London plague regulations of 1583, reissued with modifications in later epidemics, ordered that the infected and their households be locked in their homes for a month; that the streets be kept clean; that vagrants be expelled; and that funerals and plays be restricted or banned entirely.

The plague, then, had a direct and immediate impact on Shakespeare's own profession. City officials kept records of the weekly number of plague deaths; when these surpassed a certain number, the theaters were peremptorily closed. The basic idea was not only to prevent contagion but also to avoid making an angry God still angrier with the spectacle of idleness. While restricting public assemblies may in fact have slowed the epidemic, other public policies in times of plague, such as killing the cats and dogs, may have made matters worse (since the disease, as we now know, was spread not by these animals but by the fleas that bred on the black rats that infested the poorer neighborhoods). Moreover, the playing companies, driven out of London by the closing of the theaters, may have carried plague to the provincial towns.

Even in good times, when the plague was dormant and the weather favorable for farming, the food supply in England was precarious. A few successive bad harvests, such as occurred in the mid-1590s, could cause serious hardship, even starvation. Not surprisingly, the poor bore the brunt of the burden: inflation, low wages, and rent increases left large numbers of people with very little cushion against disaster. Further, at its best, the diet of most people seems to have been seriously deficient. The lower classes then, as throughout most of history, subsisted on one or two foodstuffs, usually low in protein. The upper classes disdained green vegetables and milk and gorged themselves on meat. Illnesses that we now trace to vitamin deficiencies were rampant. Some, but not much, relief from pain was provided by the beer that Elizabethans, including children, drank almost incessantly. (Home brewing aside, enough beer was sold in England for every man, woman, and child to have consumed 40 gallons a year.)

Wealth

Despite rampant disease, the population of England in Shakespeare's lifetime was steadily growing, from approximately 3,060,000 in 1564 to 4,060,000 in 1600 and 4,510,000 in 1616. Though the death rate was more than twice what it is in England today, the birthrate was almost three times the current figure. London's population in particular soared, from 60,000 in 1520 to 120,000 in 1550, 200,000 in 1600, and 375,000 half a century later, making it the largest and fastest-growing city not only in England but in all of Europe. Every year in the first half of the seventeenth century, about 10,000 people migrated to London from other parts of England—wages in London tended to be around 50 percent higher than in the rest of the country—and it is estimated that one in eight English people lived in London at some point in their lives. The economic viability of Shakespeare's profession was closely linked to this extraordinary demographic boom: between 1567 and 1642, a theater historian has calculated, the London playhouses were paid close to 50 million visits.

As these visits to the theater indicate, in the capital city and elsewhere a substantial number of English men and women, despite hardships that were never very distant, had money to spend. After the disorder and dynastic wars of the fifteenth century, England in the sixteenth and early seventeenth centuries was for the most part a nation at peace, and with peace came a measure of enterprise and prosperity: the landowning classes busied themselves building great houses, planting orchards and hop gardens, draining marshlands, bringing untilled "wastes" under cultivation. The artisans and laborers who actually accomplished these tasks, although they were generally paid very little, often managed to accumulate something, as did the small freeholding farmers, the yeomen, who are repeatedly celebrated in the period as the backbone of English national independence and well-being. William Harrison's *Description of England* (1577) lovingly itemizes the yeoman's precious possessions: "fair garnish of pewter on his cupboard, with so much more odd vessel going about the house, three or four featherbeds, so many coverlets and carpets of tapestry, a silver salt[cellar], a bowl for wine (if not a whole nest) and a dozen of spoons." There are comparable accounts of the hard-earned acquisitions of the city dwellers—masters and apprentices in small workshops, shipbuilders, wool merchants, clothmakers, chandlers, tradesmen, shopkeepers, along with lawyers, apothecaries, schoolteachers, scriveners, and the like—whose pennies from time to time enriched the coffers of the players.

The chief source of England's wealth in the sixteenth century was its textile industry, an industry that depended on a steady supply of wool. In *The Winter's Tale,* Shakespeare provides a warm, richly comic portrayal of a rural sheepshearing festival, but the increasingly intensive production of wool had in reality its grim side. When a character in Thomas More's *Utopia* (1516) complains that "the sheep are eating the people," he is referring to the practice of enclosure: throughout the sixteenth and early seventeenth centuries, many acres of croplands once farmed in common by rural communities were enclosed with fences by wealthy landowners and turned into pasturage. The ensuing misery, displacement, and food shortages led to repeated riots, some of them violent and bloody, along with a series of government proclamations, but the process of enclosure was not reversed.

The economic stakes were high, and not only for the domestic market. In 1565, woolen cloth alone made up more than three-fourths of England's exports. (The remainder consisted mostly of other textiles and raw wool, with some trade in lead, tin, grain, and skins.) The Company of Merchant Adventurers carried cloth to distant ports on the Baltic and Mediterranean, establishing links with Russia and Morocco (each took about 2 percent of London's cloth in 1597–98). English lead and tin, as well as fabrics, were sold in Tuscany and Turkey, and merchants found a market for Newcastle coal on the island of Malta. In the latter half of the century, London, which handled more than 85 percent of all exports, regularly shipped abroad more than 100,000 woolen cloths a year at a value of at least £750,000. This figure does not include the increasingly important and profitable trade in so-called New Draperies, including textiles that went by such exotic names as bombazines, calamancoes, damazellas, damizes, mockadoes, and virgenatoes. When the Earl of Kent in *King Lear* insults Oswald as a "filthy worsted-stocking knave" (2.2.14–15) or when the aristocratic Biron in *Love's Labour's Lost* declares that he will give up "taffeta phrases, silken terms precise, / Three-piled hyperboles" and woo henceforth "in russet yeas, and honest kersey noes" (5.2.406–07, 413), Shakespeare is assuming that a substantial portion of his audience will be alert to the social significance of fabric.

There is amusing confirmation of this alertness from an unexpected source: the report of a visit made to the Fortune playhouse in London in 1614 by a foreigner, Father Orazio Busino, the chaplain of the Venetian embassy. Father Busino neglected to mention the name of the play he saw, but like many foreigners, he was powerfully struck by the presence of gorgeously dressed women in the audience. In Venice, there was a special gallery for courtesans, but socially respectable women would not have been permitted to attend plays, as they could in England. In London, not only could middle- and upper-class women go to the theater, but they could also wear masks and mingle freely with male spectators and women of ill repute. The bemused cleric was uncertain about the ambiguous social situation in which he found himself:

> These theatres are frequented by a number of respectable and handsome ladies, who come freely and seat themselves among the men without the slightest hesitation. On the evening in question his Excellency and the Secretary were pleased to play me a trick by placing me amongst a bevy of young women. Scarcely was I seated ere a very

elegant dame, but in a mask, came and placed herself beside me. . . . She asked me for my address both in French and English; and, on my turning a deaf ear, she determined to honour me by showing me some fine diamonds on her fingers, repeatedly taking off not fewer than three gloves, which were worn one over the other. . . . This lady's bodice was of yellow satin richly embroidered, her petticoat of gold tissue with stripes, her robe of red velvet with a raised pile, lined with yellow muslin with broad stripes of pure gold. She wore an apron of point lace of various patterns: her head-tire was highly perfumed, and the collar of white satin beneath the delicately-wrought ruff struck me as extremely pretty.

Father Busino may have turned a deaf ear on this "elegant dame" but not a blind eye: his description of her dress is worthy of a fashion designer and conveys something of the virtual clothes cult that prevailed in England in the late sixteenth and early seventeenth centuries, a cult whose major shrine, outside the royal court, was the theater.

Imports, Patents, and Monopolies

England produced some luxury goods, but the clothing on the backs of the most fashionable theatergoers was likely to have come from abroad. By the late sixteenth century, the English were importing substantial quantities of silks, satins, velvets, embroidery, gold and silver lace, and other costly items to satisfy the extravagant tastes of the elite and of those who aspired to dress like the elite. The government tried to put a check on the sartorial ambitions of the upwardly mobile by passing sumptuary laws—that is, laws restricting to the ranks of the aristocracy the right to wear certain of the most precious fabrics. But the very existence of these laws, in practice almost impossible to enforce, only reveals the scope and significance of the perceived problem.

Sumptuary laws were in part a conservative attempt to protect the existing social order from upstarts. Social mobility was not widely viewed as a positive virtue, and moralists repeatedly urged people to stay in their place. Conspicuous consumption that was tolerated, even admired, in the aristocratic elite was denounced as sinful and monstrous in less exalted social circles. English authorities were also deeply concerned throughout the period about the effects of a taste for luxury goods on the balance of trade. One of the principal English imports was wine: the "sherris" whose virtues Falstaff extols in *2 Henry IV* came from Xeres in Spain; the malmsey in which poor Clarence is drowned in *Richard III* was probably made in Greece or in the Canary Islands (from whence came Sir Toby Belch's "cup of canary" in *Twelfth Night*); and the "flagon of rhenish" that Yorick in *Hamlet* had once poured on the Gravedigger's head came from the Rhine region of Germany. Other imports included canvas, linen, fish, olive oil, sugar, molasses, dates, oranges and lemons, figs, raisins, almonds, capers, indigo, ostrich feathers, and that increasingly popular drug from the New World, tobacco.

Joint-stock companies were established to import goods for the burgeoning English market. The Merchant Venturers of the city of Bristol (established in 1552) handled great shipments of Spanish sack, the light, dry wine that largely displaced the vintages of Bordeaux and Burgundy when trade with France was disrupted by war. The Muscovy Company (established in 1555) traded English cloth and manufactured goods for Russian furs, oil, and beeswax. The Venice Company and the Turkey Company—uniting in 1593 to form the wealthy Levant Company—brought silk and spices home from Aleppo and carpets from Istanbul. The East India Company (founded in 1600), with its agent at Bantam in Java, brought pepper, cloves, nutmeg, and other spices from east Asia, along with indigo, cotton textiles, sugar, and saltpeter from India. English privateers "imported" American products, especially sugar, fish, and hides, in huge quantities, along with more precious cargoes. In 1592, a privateering expedition principally funded by Sir Walter Ralegh captured a huge Portuguese carrack (sailing ship), the *Madre de Dios,* in the Azores and brought it back to Dartmouth. The ship, the largest that had ever entered any English port, held 536 tons of pepper, cloves, cinnamon, cochineal, mace, civet, musk, ambergris,

Cannoneer. From *Edward Webbe, . . . His Travailes* (1590).

and nutmeg, as well as jewels, gold, ebony, carpets, and silks. Before order could be established, the English seamen began to pillage this immensely rich prize, and witnesses said they could smell the spices on all the streets around the harbor. Such piratical expeditions were rarely officially sanctioned by the state, but the queen had in fact privately invested £1,800, for which she received about £80,000.

In the years of war with Spain, 1586–1604, the goods captured by the privateers annually amounted to 10 to 15 percent of the total value of England's imports. But organized theft alone could not solve England's balance-of-trade problems. Statesmen were particularly worried that the nation's natural wealth was slipping away in exchange for unnecessary things. In his *Discourse of the Commonweal* (1549), the prominent humanist Sir Thomas Smith exclaims against the importation of such trifles as mirrors, paper, laces, gloves, pins, inkhorns, tennis balls, puppets, and playing cards. And more than a century later, the same fear that England was trading its riches for trifles and wasting away in idleness was expressed by the Bristol merchant John Cary. The solution, Cary argues in "An Essay on the State of England in Relation to Its Trade" (1695), is to expand productive domestic employment. "People are or may be the Wealth of a Nation," he writes, "yet it must be where you find Employment for them, else they are a Burden to it, as the Idle Drone is maintained by the Industry of the laborious Bee, so are all those who live by their Dependence on others, as Players, Ale-House Keepers, Common Fiddlers, and such like, but more particularly Beggars, who never set themselves to work."

Stage players, all too typically associated here with vagabonds and other idle drones, could have replied in their defense that they not only labored in their vocation but also exported their skills abroad: English acting companies routinely traveled overseas and performed as far away as Bohemia. But their labor was not regarded as a productive contribution to the national wealth, and plays were in truth no solution to the trade imbalances that worried authorities.

The government attempted to stem the flow of gold overseas by establishing a patent system initially designed to encourage skilled foreigners to settle in England by granting them exclusive rights to produce particular wares by a patented method. Patents were granted for such things as the making of hard white soap (1561), ovens and furnaces (1563), window glass (1567), sailcloths (1574), drinking glasses (1574), sulphur, brimstone, and oil (1577), armor and horse harness (1587), starch (1588), white writing paper made from rags (1589), aqua vitae and vinegar (1594), playing cards (1598), and mathematical instruments (1598).

Although their ostensible purpose was to increase the wealth of England, encourage technical innovation, and provide employment for the poor, the effect of patents was often the enrichment of a few and the hounding of poor competitors by wealthy monopolists, a group that soon extended well beyond foreign-born entrepreneurs to the favorites of the monarch who vied for the huge profits to be made. "If I had a monopoly out" on folly, the Fool in *King Lear* protests, glancing at the "lords and great men" around him, "they would have part on't." The passage appears only in the quarto version of the play (*History of King Lear* 4.135–36); it may have been cut for political reasons from the Folio. For the issue of monopolies provoked bitter criticism and parliamentary debate for decades. In 1601, Elizabeth was prevailed upon to revoke a number of the most hated monopolies, including aqua vitae and vinegar, bottles, brushes, fish livers, the coarse sailcloth known as poldavis and mildernix, pots, salt, and starch. The whole system was revoked during the reign of James I by an act of Parliament.

Haves and Have-Nots

When in the 1560s Elizabeth's ambassador to France, the humanist Sir Thomas Smith, wrote a description of England, he saw the commonwealth as divided into four sorts of people: "gentlemen, citizens, yeomen artificers, and laborers." At the forefront of the class of gentlemen was the monarch, followed by a very small group of nobles—dukes, marquesses, earls, viscounts, and barons—who either inherited their exalted titles, as the eldest male heirs of their families, or were granted them by the monarch. Under Elizabeth, this aristocratic peerage numbered between 50 and 60 individuals; James's promotions increased the number to nearer 130. Strictly speaking, Smith notes, the younger sons of the nobility were only entitled to be called "esquires," but in common speech they were also called "lords."

Below this tiny cadre of aristocrats in the social hierarchy of gentry were the knights, a title of honor conferred by the monarch, and below them were the "simple gentlemen." Who was a gentleman? According to Smith, "whoever studieth the laws of the realm, who studieth in the universities, who professeth liberal sciences, and to be short, who can live idly and without manual labor, and will bear the port, charge and countenance of a gentleman, he shall be called master . . . and shall be taken for a gentleman." To "live idly and without manual labor": where in Spain, for example, the crucial mark of a gentleman was "blood," in England it was "idleness," in the sense of sufficient income to afford an education and to maintain a social position without having to work with one's hands.

For Smith, the class of gentlemen was far and away the most important in the kingdom. Below were two groups that had at least some social standing and claim to authority: the citizens, or burgesses, those who held positions of importance and responsibility in their cities, and yeomen, farmers with land and a measure of economic independence. At the bottom of the social order was what Smith calls "the fourth sort of men which do not rule." The great mass of ordinary people have, Smith writes, "no voice nor authority in our commonwealth, and no account is made of them but only to be ruled." Still, even they can bear some responsibility, he notes, since they serve on juries and are named to such positions as churchwarden and constable.

In everyday practice, as modern social historians have observed, the English tended to divide the population not into four distinct classes but into two: a very small empowered group—the "richer" or "wiser" or "better" sort—and all the rest who were without much social standing or power, the "poorer" or "ruder" or "meaner" sort. References to the "middle sort of people" remain relatively rare until after Shakespeare's lifetime; these people are absorbed into the rulers or the ruled, depending on speaker and context.

The source of wealth for most of the ruling class, and the essential measure of social status, was landownership, and changes to the social structure in the sixteenth and seventeenth centuries were largely driven by the land market. The property that passed into private hands as the Tudors and early Stuarts sold off confiscated monastic estates and then their own crown lands for ready cash amounted to nearly a quarter of all the land in England. At the same time, the buying and selling of private estates was on the rise throughout the period. Land was bought up not only by established landowners seeking to enlarge their estates but by successful merchants, manufacturers, and urban professionals; even if the taint of vulgar moneymaking lingered around such figures, their heirs would be taken for true gentlemen. The rate of turnover in landownership was great; in many counties, well over half the gentle families in 1640 had appeared since the end of the fifteenth century. The class that Smith called "simple gentlemen" was expanding rapidly: in the fifteenth century, they had held no more than a quarter of the land in the country; but by the later seventeenth century, they controlled almost half. Over the same period, the land held by the great aristocratic magnates held steady at 15 to 20 percent of the total.

Riot and Disorder

London was a violent place in the first half of Shakespeare's career. There were thirty-five riots in the city in the years 1581–1602, twelve of them in the volatile month of June 1595. These included protests against the deeply unpopular lord mayor Sir John Spencer, attempts to release prisoners, anti-alien riots, and incidents of "popular market regulation." There is an unforgettable depiction of a popular uprising in *Coriolanus*, along with many other glimpses in Shakespeare's works, including John Cade's grotesque rebellion in *The First Part of the Contention (2 Henry VI)*, the plebeian violence in *Julius Caesar*, and Laertes' "riotous head" in *Hamlet*.

The London rioters were mostly drawn from the large mass of poor and discontented apprentices who typically chose as their scapegoats foreigners, prostitutes, and gentlemen's servingmen. Theaters were very often the site of the social confrontations that sparked disorder. For two days running in June 1584, disputes between apprentices and gentlemen triggered riots outside the Curtain Theatre involving up to a thousand participants. On one occasion, a gentleman was said to have exclaimed that "the apprentice was but a rascal, and some there were little better than rogues that took upon them the name of gentlemen, and said the prentices were but the scum of the world." These occasions culminated in attacks by the apprentices on London's law schools, the Inns of Court.

The most notorious and predictable incidents of disorder came on Shrove Tuesday (the Tuesday before the beginning of Lent), a traditional day of misrule when apprentices ran riot. Shrove Tuesday disturbances involved attacks by mobs of young men on the brothels of the South Bank, in the vicinity of the Globe and other public theaters. The city authorities took precautions to keep these disturbances from getting completely out of control but evidently did not regard them as serious threats to public order.

Of much greater concern throughout the Tudor and early Stuart years were the frequent incidents of rural rioting against the enclosure of commons and wasteland by local landlords (and, in the royal forests, by the crown). This form of popular protest was at its height during Shakespeare's career: in the years 1590–1610, the frequency of anti-enclosure rioting doubled from what it had been earlier in Elizabeth's reign.

Although they often became violent, anti-enclosure riots were usually directed not against individuals but against property. Villagers—sometimes several hundred, often fewer than a dozen—gathered to tear down newly planted hedges. The event often took place in a carnival atmosphere, with songs and drinking, that did not prevent the participants from acting with a good deal of political canniness and forethought. Especially in the Jacobean period, it was common for participants to establish a common fund for legal defense before commencing their assault on the hedges. Women were frequently involved, and on a number of occasions wives alone participated in the destruction of the enclosure, since there was a widespread, though erroneous, belief that married women acting without the knowledge of their husbands were immune from prosecution. In fact, the powerful Court of Star Chamber consistently ruled that both the wives and their husbands should be punished.

Peddler. From Jost Amman, *The Book of Trades* (1568).

Although Stratford was never the scene of serious rioting, enclosure controversies there turned violent more than once in Shakespeare's lifetime. In January 1601, Shakespeare's friend Richard Quiney and others leveled the hedges of Sir Edward Greville, lord of Stratford manor. Quiney was elected bailiff of Stratford in September of that year but did not live to enjoy the office for long. He died from a blow to the head struck by one of Greville's men in a tavern brawl. Greville, responsible for the administration of justice, neglected to punish the murderer.

There was further violence in January 1615, when William Combe's men threw to the ground two local aldermen who were filling in a ditch by which Combe was enclosing common fields near Stratford. The task of filling in the offending ditch was completed the next day by the women and children of Stratford. Combe's enclosure scheme was eventually stopped in the courts. Although he owned land whose value would have been affected by this controversy, Shakespeare took no active role in it, since he had previously come to a private settlement with the enclosers insuring him against personal loss.

Most incidents of rural rioting were small, localized affairs, and with good reason: when confined to the village community, riot was a misdemeanor; when it spread outward to include multiple communities, it became treason, punishable by death. The greatest of the anti-enclosure riots, those in which hundreds of individuals from a large area participated, commonly took place on the eve of full-scale regional rebellions. The largest of these disturbances, Kett's Rebellion, involved some 16,000 peasants, artisans, and townspeople who rose up in 1549 under the leadership of a Norfolk tanner and landowner, Robert Kett, to protest economic exploitation. The agrarian revolts in Shakespeare's lifetime were on a much smaller scale. In the abortive Oxfordshire Rebellion of 1596, a carpenter named Bartholomew Steere attempted to organize a rising against enclosing gentlemen. The optimistic Steere promised his followers that "it was but a month's work to overrun England" and informed them "that the commons long since in Spain did rise and kill all gentlemen . . . and since that time have lived merrily there." Steere expected several hundred men to join him on Enslow Hill on November 21, 1596, for the start of the rising; no more than twenty showed up. They were captured, imprisoned, and tortured. Several were executed, but Steere apparently cheated the hangman by dying in prison.

Rebellions, most often triggered by hunger and oppression, continued into the reign of James I. The Midland Revolt of 1607, which may be reflected in *Coriolanus*, consisted of a string of agrarian risings in the counties of Northamptonshire, Warwickshire, and Leicestershire, involving assemblies of up to 5,000 rebels in various places. The best known of their leaders was John Reynolds, called "Captain Powch" because of the pouch he wore, whose magical contents were supposed to defend the rebels from harm. (According to the chronicler Edmund Howes, when Reynolds was captured and the pouch opened, it contained "only a piece of green cheese.") The rebels, who were called by themselves and others both "Levelers" and "Diggers," insisted that they had no quarrel with the king but only sought an end to injurious enclosures. But Robert Wilkinson, who preached a sermon against the leaders at their trial, credited them with the intention to "level all states as they leveled banks and ditches." Most of the rebels got off relatively lightly, but, along with other ringleaders, Captain Powch was executed.

The Legal Status of Women

Even though England was ruled for over forty years by a powerful woman, the great majority of women in the kingdom had very restricted social, economic, and legal standing. To be sure, a tiny number of influential aristocratic women, such as the formidable Countess of Shrewsbury, Bess of Hardwick, wielded considerable power. But, these rare exceptions aside, women were denied any rightful claim to institutional authority or personal autonomy. When Sir Thomas Smith thinks of how he should describe his country's social order, he declares that "we do reject women, as those whom nature hath made to keep home and to nourish their family and children, and not to meddle with matters abroad, nor to bear office in a city or commonwealth."

Then, with a kind of glance over his shoulder, he makes an exception of those few for whom "the blood is respected, not the age nor the sex": for example, the queen.

English women were not under the full range of crushing constraints that afflicted women in some countries in Europe. Foreign visitors were struck by their relative freedom, as shown, for example, by the fact that respectable women could venture unchaperoned into the streets and attend the theater. Single women, whether widowed or unmarried, could, if they were of full age, inherit and administer land, make a will, sign a contract, possess property, sue and be sued, without a male guardian or proxy. But married women had no such rights under the common law.

Early modern writings about women and the family constantly return to a political model of domination and submission, in which the father justly rules over wife and children as the monarch rules over the state. This conception of a woman's role conveniently ignores the fact that a *majority* of the adult women at any time in Shakespeare's England were not married. They were either widows or spinsters (a term that was not yet pejorative), and thus for the most part managing their own affairs. Even within marriage, women typically had more control over certain spheres than moralizing writers on the family cared to admit. For example, village wives oversaw the production of eggs, cheese, and beer, and sold these goods in the market. As seamstresses, pawnbrokers, secondhand clothing dealers, peddlers, and the like—activities not controlled by the all-male guilds—women managed to acquire some economic power of their own, and, of course, they participated as well in the unregulated, black-market economy of the age and in the underworld of thievery and prostitution.

Women were not in practice as bereft of property as, according to English common law, they should have been. Demographic studies indicate that the inheritance system called primogeniture, the orderly transmission of property from father to eldest male heir, was more often an unfulfilled wish than a reality. Some 40 percent of marriages failed to produce a son, and in such circumstances fathers often left their land to their daughters, rather than to brothers, nephews, or male cousins. In many families, the father died before his male heir was old enough to inherit property, leaving the land, at least temporarily, in the hands of the mother. And while they were less likely than their brothers to inherit land ("real property"), daughters normally inherited a substantial share of their father's personal property (cash and movables).

In fact, the legal restrictions upon women, though severe in Shakespeare's time, actually worsened in subsequent decades. The English common law, the system of law based on court decisions rather than on codified written laws, was significantly less egalitarian in its approach to wives and daughters than were alternative legal codes (manorial, civil, and ecclesiastical) still in place in the late sixteenth century. The eventual triumph of common law stripped women of many traditional rights, slowly driving them out of economically productive trades and businesses.

Limited though it was, the economic freedom of Elizabethan and Jacobean women far exceeded their political and social freedom—the opportunity to receive a grammar-school or university education, to hold office in church or state, to have a voice in public debates, or even simply to speak their mind fully and openly in ordinary conversation. Women who asserted their views too vigorously risked being perceived as shrewish and labeled "scolds." Both urban and rural communities had a horror of scolds. In the Elizabethan period, such women came to be regarded as a threat to public order, to be dealt with by the local authorities. The preferred methods of correction included public humiliation—of the sort Katherine endures in *The Taming of the Shrew*—and such physical abuse as slapping, bridling, and soaking by means of a contraption called the "cucking stool" (or "ducking stool"). This latter punishment originated in the Middle Ages, but its use spread in the sixteenth century, when it became almost exclusively a punishment for women. From 1560 onward, cucking stools were built or renovated in many English provincial towns; between 1560 and 1600, the contraptions were installed by rivers or ponds in Norwich, Bridport, Shrewsbury, Kingston-upon-Thames, Marlborough, Devizes, Clitheroe, Thornbury, and Great Yarmouth.

Such punishment was usually intensified by a procession through the town to the sound of "rough music," the banging together of pots and pans. The same cruel festivity accompanied the "carting" or "riding" of those accused of being whores. In some parts of the country, villagers also took the law into their own hands, publicly shaming women who married men much younger than themselves or who beat or otherwise domineered over their husbands. One characteristic form of these charivaris, or rituals of shaming, was known in the West Country as the Skimmington Ride. Villagers would rouse the offending couple from bed with rough music and stage a raucous pageant in which a man, holding a distaff, would ride backward on a donkey, while his "wife" (another man dressed as a woman) struck him with a ladle. In these cases, the collective ridicule and indignation was evidently directed at least as much at the henpecked husband as at his transgressive wife.

Women and Print

Books published for a female audience surged in popularity in the late sixteenth century, reflecting an increase in female literacy. (It is striking how many of Shakespeare's women are shown reading.) This increase is probably linked to a Protestant longing for direct access to the Scriptures, and the new books marketed specifically for women included devotional manuals and works of religious instruction. But there were also practical guides to such subjects as female education (for example, Giovanni Bruto's *Necessarie, Fit, and Convenient Education of a Young Gentlewoman*, 1598), midwifery (James Guillemeau's *Child-birth; or, The Happy Delivery of Women*, 1612), needlework (Federico di Vinciolo's *New and Singular Patterns and Workes of Linnen*, 1591), cooking (Thomas Dawson's *The Good Husewifes Jewell*, 1587), gardening (Pierre Erondelle's *The French Garden for English Ladyes and Gentlewomen to Walke In*, 1605), and married life (Patrick Hannay's *A Happy Husband; or, Directions for a Maide to Choose Her Mate*, 1619). As the authors' names suggest, many of these works were translations, and almost all were written by men.

Starting in the 1570s, writers and their publishers increasingly addressed works of recreational literature (romance, fiction, and poetry) partially or even exclusively to women. Some books, such as Robert Greene's *Mamillia, a Mirrour or Looking-Glasse for the Ladies of Englande* (1583), directly specified in the title their desired audience. Others, such as Sir Philip Sidney's influential and popular romance *Arcadia* (1590–93), solicited female readership in their dedicatory epistles. The ranks of Sidney's followers eventually included his own niece, Mary Wroth, whose romance *Urania* was published in 1621.

In the literature of Shakespeare's time, women readers were not only wooed but also frequently railed at, in a continuation of a popular polemical genre that had long inspired heated charges and countercharges. Both sides in the polemic generally agreed that it was the duty of women to be chaste, dutiful, shamefast, and silent; the argument was whether women fulfilled or fell short of this proper role. Ironically, then, a modern reader is more likely to find inspiring accounts of courageous women not in the books written in defense of female virtue but in attacks on those who refused to be silent and obedient.

The most famous English skirmish in this controversy took place in a rash of pamphlets at the end of Shakespeare's life. Joseph Swetnam's crude *Araignment of Lewd, Idle, Froward, and Unconstant Women* (1615) provoked three fierce responses attributed to women: Rachel Speght's *A Mouzell [Muzzle] for Melastomus*, Ester Sowernam's *Ester Hath Hang'd Haman*, and Constantia Munda's *Worming of a Mad Dogge*, all 1617. There was also an anonymous play, *Swetnam, the Woman-hater, Arraigned by Women* (1618), in which Swetnam, depicted as a braggart and a lecher, is put on trial by women and made to recant his misogynistic lies.

Prior to the Swetnam controversy, only one English woman, "Jane Anger," had published a defense of women (*Jane Anger, Her Protection for Women*, 1589). Learned women writers in the sixteenth century tended not to become involved in public debate but rather to undertake a project to which it was difficult for even obdurately chauvinistic

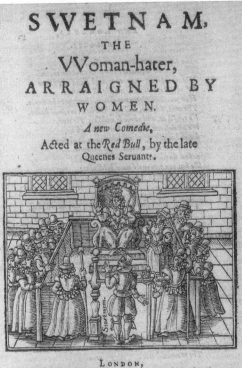

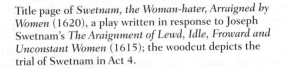

Title page of *Swetnam, the Woman-hater, Arraigned by Women* (1620), a play written in response to Joseph Swetnam's *The Araignment of Lewd, Idle, Froward and Unconstant Women* (1615); the woodcut depicts the trial of Swetnam in Act 4.

males to object: the translation of devotional literature into English. Thomas More's daughter Margaret More Roper translated Erasmus (*A Devout Treatise upon the Pater Noster,* 1524); Francis Bacon's mother, Anne Cooke Bacon, translated Bishop John Jewel (*An Apologie or Answere in Defence of the Churche of Englande,* 1564); Anne Locke Prowse, a friend of John Knox, translated the *Sermons of John Calvin* in 1560; and Mary Sidney, Countess of Pembroke, completed the metrical version of the Psalms that her brother Sir Philip Sidney had begun. Elizabeth Tudor (the future queen) herself translated, at the age of eleven, Marguerite de Navarre's *Miroir de l'âme pécheresse* (*The Glass of the Sinful Soul,* 1544). The translation was dedicated to her stepmother, Catherine Parr, herself the author of a frequently reprinted book of prayers.

There was in the sixteenth and early seventeenth centuries a social stigma attached to print. Far from celebrating publication, authors, and particularly female authors, often apologized for exposing themselves to the public gaze. Nonetheless, a number of women ventured beyond pious translations circulated in manuscript. Some, including Elizabeth Tyrwhitt, Anne Dowriche, Isabella Whitney, Mary Sidney, and Aemilia Lanyer, composed and published their own poems. Aemilia Lanyer's *Salve Deus Rex Judaeorum,* published in 1611, is a poem in praise of virtuous women, from Eve and the Virgin Mary to her noble patron, the Countess of Cumberland. "A Description of Cookeham," appended to the poem, may be the first English-country-house poem.

The first Tudor woman to translate a play was the learned Jane Lumley, who composed an English version of Euripides' *Iphigenia at Aulis* (c. 1550). The first known original play in English by a woman was by Elizabeth Cary, Viscountess Falkland, whose *Tragedie of Mariam, the Faire Queene of Jewry* was published in 1613. This remarkable play, which was not intended to be performed, includes speeches in defense of women's equality, though the most powerful of these is spoken by the villainous Salome, who schemes to divorce her husband and marry her lover. Cary, who bore eleven children, herself had a deeply troubled marriage, which effectively came to an end in 1625, when, defying her husband's staunchly Protestant family, she openly converted to Catholicism. Her biography was written by one of her four daughters, all of whom became nuns.

Henry VIII and the English Reformation

There had long been serious ideological and institutional tensions in the religious life of England, but officially, at least, England in the early sixteenth century had a single religion, Catholicism, whose acknowledged head was the pope in Rome. In 1517, drawing upon long-standing currents of dissent, Martin Luther, an Augustinian monk and professor of theology at the University of Wittenberg, challenged the authority of the pope and attacked several key doctrines of the Catholic Church. According to Luther, the Church, with its elaborate hierarchical structure centered in Rome, its rich monasteries and convents, and its enormous political influence, had become hopelessly corrupt, a conspiracy of venal priests who manipulated popular superstitions to enrich themselves and amass worldly power. Luther began by vehemently attacking the sale of indulgences—certificates promising the remission of punishments to be suffered in the afterlife by souls sent to purgatory to expiate their sins. These indulgences were a fraud, he argued; purgatory itself had no foundation in the Bible, which in his view was the only legitimate source of religious truth. Christians would be saved not by scrupulously following the ritual practices fostered by the Catholic Church—observing fast days, reciting the ancient Latin prayers, endowing chantries to say prayers for the dead, and so on—but by faith and faith alone.

This challenge, which came to be known as the Reformation, spread and gathered force, especially in northern Europe, where major leaders like the Swiss pastor Huldrych Zwingli and the French theologian John Calvin established institutional structures and elaborated various and sometimes conflicting doctrinal principles. Calvin, whose thought came to be particularly influential in England, emphasized the obligation of governments to implement God's will in the world. He advanced too the doctrine of predestination, by which, as he put it, "God adopts some to hope of life and sentences others to eternal death." God's "secret election" of the saved made Calvin uncomfortable, but his study of the Scriptures had led him to conclude that "only a small number, out of an incalculable multitude, should obtain salvation." It might seem that such a conclusion would lead to passivity or even despair, but for Calvin predestination was a mystery bound up with faith, confidence, and an active engagement in the fashioning of a Christian community.

The Reformation had a direct and powerful impact on those territories, especially in northern Europe, where it gained control. Monasteries were sacked, their possessions seized by princes or sold off to the highest bidder; the monks and nuns, expelled from their cloisters, were encouraged to break their vows of chastity and find spouses, as Luther and his wife, a former nun, had done. In the great cathedrals and in hundreds of smaller churches and chapels, the elaborate altarpieces, bejeweled crucifixes, crystal reliquaries holding the bones of saints, and venerated statues and paintings were attacked as "idols" and often defaced or destroyed. Protestant congregations continued, for the most part, to celebrate the most sacred Christian ritual, the Eucharist, or Lord's Supper, but they did so in a profoundly different spirit from that of the Catholic Church—more as commemoration than as miracle—and they now prayed not in the ancient liturgical Latin but in the vernacular.

"The Pope as Antichrist riding the Beast of the Apocalypse." From *Fierie Tryall of God's Saints* (1611; author unknown).

The Reformation was at first vigorously resisted in England. Indeed, with the support of his ardently Catholic chancellor, Thomas More, Henry VIII personally wrote (or at least lent his name to) a vehement, often scatological attack on Luther's character and views, an attack for which the pope granted him the honorific title "Defender of the Faith." Protestant writings, including translations of the Scriptures into English, were seized by officials of the church and state and burned. Protestants who made their views known were persecuted, driven to flee the country, or arrested, put on trial, and burned at the stake. But the situation changed drastically and decisively when in 1527 Henry decided to seek a divorce from his first wife, Catherine of Aragon, in order to marry Anne Boleyn.

Catherine had given birth to six children, but since only a daughter, Mary, survived infancy, Henry did not have the son he craved. Then as now, the Catholic Church did not ordinarily grant divorce, but Henry's lawyers argued on technical grounds that the marriage was invalid (and, therefore, by extension, that Mary was illegitimate and hence unable to inherit the throne). Matters of this kind were far less doctrinal than diplomatic: Catherine, the daughter of Ferdinand of Aragon and Isabella of Castile, had powerful allies in Rome, and the pope ruled against Henry's petition for a divorce. A series of momentous events followed, as England lurched away from the Church of Rome. In 1531, Henry charged the entire clergy of England with having usurped royal authority in the administration of canon law (the ecclesiastical law that governed faith, discipline, and morals, including such matters as divorce). Under extreme pressure, including the threat of mass confiscations and imprisonment, the Convocation of the English Clergy begged for pardon, made a donation to the royal coffers of over £100,000, and admitted that the king was "supreme head of the English Church and clergy" (modified by the rider "as far as the law of Christ allows"). On May 15 of the next year, the convocation submitted to the demand that the king be the final arbiter of canon law; on the next day, Thomas More resigned his post.

In 1533, Henry's marriage to Catherine was officially declared null and void, and on June 1 Anne Boleyn was crowned queen (a coronation Shakespeare depicts in his late play *All Is True*). The king was promptly excommunicated by the pope, Clement VII. In the following year, the parliamentary Act of Succession confirmed the effects of the divorce and required an oath from all adult male subjects confirming the new dynastic settlement. Thomas More and John Fisher, Bishop of Rochester, were among the small number who refused. The Act of Supremacy, passed later in the year, formally declared the king to be "Supreme Head of the Church in England" and again required an oath to this effect. In 1535 and 1536, further acts made it treasonous to refuse the oath of royal supremacy or, as More had tried to do, to remain silent. The first victims were three Carthusian monks who rejected the oath—"How could the king, a layman," said one of them, "be Head of the Church of England?"—and in May 1535, they were duly hanged, drawn, and quartered. A few weeks later, Fisher and More were convicted and beheaded. Between 1536 and 1539, the monasteries were suppressed and their vast wealth seized by the crown.

Royal defiance of the authority of Rome was a key element in the Reformation but did not by itself constitute the establishment of Protestantism in England. On the contrary, in the same year that Fisher and More were martyred for their adherence to Roman Catholicism, twenty-five Protestants, members of a sect known as Anabaptists, were burned for heresy on a single day. Through most of his reign, Henry remained an equal-opportunity persecutor, ruthless to Catholics loyal to Rome and hostile to some of those who espoused Reformation ideas, though many of these ideas gradually established themselves on English soil.

Even when Henry was eager to do so, it proved impossible to eradicate Protestantism, as it would later prove impossible for his successors to eradicate Catholicism. In large part this tenacity arose from the passionate, often suicidal heroism of men and women who felt that their souls' salvation depended on the precise character of their Christianity. It arose, too, from a mid-fifteenth-century technological innovation that made it almost impossible to suppress unwelcome ideas: the printing press. Early Protestants quickly grasped that with a few clandestine presses they could defy the Catholic authorities and flood the country with their texts. "How many printing presses there be in the world," wrote the Protestant polemicist John Foxe, "so many blockhouses there be against the high castle" of the pope in Rome, "so that either the pope must abolish knowledge and printing or printing at length will root him out." By the century's end, it was the Catholics who were using the clandestine press to propagate their beliefs in the face of Protestant persecution.

The greatest insurrection of the Tudor age was not over food, taxation, or land but over religion. On Sunday, October 1, 1536, stirred up by their vicar, the traditionalist parishioners of Louth in Lincolnshire, in the north of England, rose up in defiance of the ecclesiastical visitation sent to enforce royal supremacy. The rapidly spreading rebellion, which became known as the Pilgrimage of Grace, was led by the lawyer Robert Aske. The city of Lincoln fell to the rebels on October 6, and though it was soon retaken by royal forces, the rebels seized cities and fortifications throughout Yorkshire, Durham, Northumberland, Cumberland, Westmoreland, and northern Lancashire. Carlisle, Newcastle, and a few castles were all that were left to the king in the north. The Pilgrims soon numbered 40,000, led by some of the region's leading noblemen. The Duke of Norfolk, representing the crown, was forced to negotiate a truce, with a promise to support the rebels' demands that the king restore the monasteries, shore up the regional economy, suppress heresy, and dismiss his evil advisers.

The Pilgrims kept the peace for the rest of 1536, on the naive assumption that their demands would be met. But Henry moved suddenly early in 1537 to impose order and capture the ringleaders; 130 people, including lords, knights, heads of religious houses, and, of course, Robert Aske, were executed.

In 1549, two years after the death of Henry VIII, the west and the north of England were the sites of further unsuccessful risings for the restoration of Catholicism. The Western Rising is striking for its blend of Catholic universalism and intense regionalism among people who did not yet regard themselves as English. One of the rebels' articles, protesting against the imposition of the English Bible and religious service, declares, "We the Cornish men (whereof certain of us understand no English) utterly refuse this new English." The rebels besieged but failed to take the city of Exeter. As with almost all Tudor rebellions, the number of those executed in the aftermath of the failed rising was far greater than those killed in actual hostilities.

Henry VIII's Children: Edward, Mary, and Elizabeth

Upon Henry's death in 1547, his ten-year-old son, Edward VI, came to the throne, with his maternal uncle Edward Seymour named as Lord Protector and Duke of Somerset. Both Edward and his uncle were staunch Protestants, and reformers hastened to transform the English Church accordingly. During Edward's reign, Archbishop Thomas Cranmer formulated the forty-two articles of religion that became the core of Anglican orthodoxy and wrote the first Book of Common Prayer, which was officially adopted in 1549 as the basis of English worship services.

Somerset fell from power in 1549 and was replaced as Lord Protector by John Dudley, later Duke of Northumberland. When Edward fell seriously ill, probably of tuberculosis, Northumberland persuaded him to sign a will depriving his half sisters, Mary (the daughter of Catherine of Aragon) and Elizabeth (the daughter of Anne Boleyn), of their claim to royal succession. The Lord Protector was scheming to have his daughter-in-law, the Protestant Lady Jane Grey, a granddaughter of Henry VII, ascend to the throne. But when Edward died in 1553, Mary marshaled support, quickly secured the crown from Lady Jane (who had been titular queen for nine days), and had Lady Jane executed, along with her husband and Northumberland.

Queen Mary immediately took steps to return her kingdom to Roman Catholicism. Even though she was unable to get Parliament to agree to restore church lands seized under Henry VIII, she restored the Catholic Mass, once again affirmed the authority of the pope, and put down a rebellion that sought to depose her. Seconded by her ardently Catholic husband, Philip II, King of Spain, she initiated a series of religious persecutions that earned her (from her enemies) the name "Bloody Mary." Hundreds of Protestants took refuge abroad in cities such as Calvin's Geneva; almost three hundred less fortunate Protestants were condemned as heretics and burned at the stake.

The Family of Henry VIII: An Allegory of the Tudor Succession. By Lucas de Heere (c. 1572). Henry, in the middle, is flanked by Mary to his right, and Edward and Elizabeth to his left.

Mary died childless in 1558, and her younger half sister Elizabeth became queen. Elizabeth's succession had been by no means assured. For if Protestants regarded Henry VIII's marriage to Catherine as invalid and hence deemed Mary illegitimate, so Catholics regarded his marriage to Anne Boleyn as invalid and deemed Elizabeth illegitimate. Henry VIII himself seemed to support both views, since only three years after divorcing Catherine, he beheaded Anne Boleyn on charges of treason and adultery, and urged Parliament to invalidate the marriage. Moreover, though during her sister's reign Elizabeth outwardly complied with the official Catholic religious observance, Mary and her advisers were deeply suspicious, and the young princess's life was in grave danger. Poised and circumspect, Elizabeth warily evaded the traps that were set for her. As she ascended the throne, her actions were scrutinized for some indication of the country's future course. During her coronation procession, when a girl in an allegorical pageant presented her with a Bible in English translation—banned under Mary's reign—Elizabeth kissed the book, held it up reverently, and laid it to her breast; when the abbot and monks of Westminster Abbey came to greet her in broad daylight with candles (a symbol of Catholic devotion) in their hands, she briskly dismissed them with the telling words "Away with those torches! we can see well enough." England had returned to the Reformation.

Many English men and women, of all classes, remained loyal to the old Catholic faith, but English authorities under Elizabeth moved steadily, if cautiously, toward ensuring at least an outward conformity to the official Protestant settlement. Recusants, those who refused to attend regular Sunday services in their parish churches, were fined heavily. Anyone who wished to receive a university degree, to be ordained as a priest in the Church of England, or to be named as an officer of the state had to swear an oath to the royal supremacy. Commissioners were sent throughout the land to confirm that religious services were following the officially approved liturgy and to investigate any reported backsliding into Catholic practice or, alternatively, any attempts to introduce more radical reforms than the queen and her bishops had chosen to embrace. For the Protestant exiles who streamed back were eager not only to undo the damage Mary had done but to carry the Reformation much further. They sought to dismantle the church hierarchy, to purge the calendar of folk customs deemed pagan and the church service of ritual practices deemed superstitious, to dress the clergy in simple garb, and, at the extreme edge, to smash "idolatrous" statues, crucifixes, and altarpieces. Throughout her long reign, however, Elizabeth herself remained cautiously conservative and determined to hold in check what she regarded as the religious zealotry of Catholics, on the one side, and Puritans, on the other.

Shakespeare's plays tap into the ongoing confessional tensions: "Sometimes," Maria in *Twelfth Night* says of the sober, festivity-hating steward Malvolio, "he is a kind of puritan" (2.3.125). But they tend to avoid the risks of direct engagement: "The dev'l a puritan that he is, or anything constantly," Maria adds a moment later, "but a time-pleaser, an affectioned ass" (2.3.131–32). *The Winter's Tale* features a statue that comes to life—exactly the kind of magical image that Protestant polemicists excoriated as Catholic superstition and idolatry—but the play is set in pre-Christian world of the Delphic oracle. And as if this careful distancing might not be enough, the play's ruler goes out of his way to pronounce the wonder legitimate: "If this be magic, let it be an art / Lawful as eating" (5.3.110–11).

In the space of a single lifetime, England had gone officially from Roman Catholicism, to Catholicism under the supreme headship of the English king, to a guarded Protestantism, to a more radical Protestantism, to a renewed and aggressive Roman Catholicism, and finally to Protestantism again. Each of these shifts was accompanied by danger, persecution, and death. It was enough to make some people wary. Or skeptical. Or extremely agile.

The English Bible

Luther had undertaken a fundamental critique of the Catholic Church's sacramental system, a critique founded on the twin principles of salvation by faith alone (*sola fide*) and the absolute primacy of the Bible (*sola scriptura*). *Sola fide* contrasted faith with "works," by which was meant primarily the whole elaborate system of rituals sanctified, conducted, or directed by the priests. Protestants proposed to modify or reinterpret many of these rituals or, as with the rituals associated with purgatory, to abolish them altogether. *Sola scriptura* required direct lay access to the Bible, which meant in practice the widespread availability of vernacular translations. The Roman Catholic Church had not always and everywhere opposed such translations, but it generally preferred that the populace encounter the Scriptures through the interpretations of the priests, trained to read the Latin translation known as the Vulgate. In times of great conflict, this preference for clerical mediation hardened into outright prohibition of vernacular translation and into persecution and book burning.

Zealous Protestants set out, in the teeth of fierce opposition, to put the Bible into the hands of the laity. A remarkable translation of the New Testament, by an English Lutheran named William Tyndale, was printed on the Continent and smuggled into England in 1525; Tyndale's translation of the Pentateuch, the first five books of the Hebrew Bible, followed in 1530. Many copies of these translations were seized and burned, as was the translator himself, but the printing press made it extremely difficult for authorities to eradicate books for which there was a passionate demand. The English Bible was a force that could not be suppressed, and it became, in its various forms, the single most important book of the sixteenth century.

Tyndale's translation was completed by an associate, Miles Coverdale, whose rendering of the Psalms proved to be particularly influential. Their joint labor was the basis for the Great Bible (1539), the first authorized version of the Bible in English, a copy of which was ordered to be placed in every church in the kingdom. With the accession of Edward VI, many editions of the Bible followed, but the process was sharply reversed when Mary came to the throne in 1553. Along with people condemned as heretics, English Bibles were burned in great bonfires.

Marian persecution was indirectly responsible for what would become the most popular as well as most scholarly English Bible, the translation known as the Geneva Bible, prepared, with extensive, learned, and often fiercely polemical marginal notes, by English exiles in Calvin's Geneva and widely diffused in England after Elizabeth came to the throne. In addition, Elizabethan church authorities ordered a careful revision of the Great Bible, and this version, known as the Bishops' Bible, was the one read in the churches. The success of the Geneva Bible in particular prompted those Elizabethan Catholics who now in turn found themselves in exile to bring out a vernacular translation of their own in order to counter the Protestant readings and glosses. This Catholic translation, known as the Rheims Bible, may have been known to Shakespeare, but he seems to have been far better acquainted with the Geneva Bible, and he would also have repeatedly heard the Bishops' Bible read aloud. Scholars have identified over three hundred references to the Bible in Shakespeare's work; in one version or another, the Scriptures had a powerful impact on his imagination.

A Female Monarch in a Male World

In the last year of Mary's reign, 1558, the Scottish Calvinist minister John Knox thundered against what he called "the monstrous regiment of women." When the Protestant Elizabeth came to the throne the following year, Knox and his religious brethren were less inclined to denounce female rulers, but in England as elsewhere in Europe there remained a widespread conviction that women were unsuited to wield power over men. Many men seem to have regarded the capacity for rational thought as exclusively male; women, they assumed, were led only by their passions. While gentlemen mastered the arts of rhetoric and warfare, gentlewomen were expected to display the virtues of silence and good housekeeping. Among upper-class males, the will to dominate others was acceptable and, indeed, admired; the same will in women was condemned as a grotesque and dangerous aberration.

One of the Armada portraits (c. 1588). Note Elizabeth's hand on the globe.

Apologists for the queen countered these prejudices by appealing to historical precedent and legal theory. History offered inspiring examples of just female rulers, notably Deborah, the biblical prophetess who judged Israel. In the legal sphere, crown lawyers advanced the theory of "the king's two bodies." As England's crowned head, Elizabeth's person was mystically divided between her mortal "body natural" and the immortal "body politic." While the queen's natural body was inevitably subject to the failings of human flesh, the body politic was timeless and perfect. In political terms, therefore, Elizabeth's sex was a matter of no consequence, a thing indifferent.

Elizabeth, who had received a fine humanist education and an extended, dangerous lesson in the art of survival, made it immediately clear that she intended to rule in more than name only. She assembled a group of trustworthy advisers, foremost among them William Cecil (later named Lord Burghley, also known as Burleigh), but she insisted on making many of the crucial decisions herself. Like many Renaissance monarchs, Elizabeth was drawn to the idea of royal absolutism, the theory that ultimate power was properly concentrated in her person and, indeed, that God had appointed her to be His deputy in the kingdom. Opposition to her rule, in this view, was not only a political act but also a kind of impiety, a blasphemous grudging against the will of God. Apologists for absolutism contended that God commands obedience even to manifestly wicked rulers whom He has sent to punish the sinfulness of humankind. Such arguments were routinely made in speeches and political tracts and from the pulpits of churches, where they were incorporated into the *First* and *Second Book of Homilies*, which clergymen were required to read out to their congregations.

In reality, Elizabeth's power was not absolute. The government had a network of spies, informers, and agents provocateurs, but it lacked a standing army, a national police force, an efficient system of communication, and an extensive bureaucracy. Above all, the queen had limited financial resources and needed to turn periodically to an independent and often recalcitrant Parliament, which by long tradition had the sole right to levy taxes and to grant subsidies. Members of the House of Commons were elected from their boroughs, not appointed by the monarch, and although the queen had considerable influence over their decisions, she could by no means dictate policy. Under these constraints, Elizabeth ruled through a combination of adroit political maneuvering and imperious command, all the while enhancing her authority in the eyes of both court and country by means of an extraordinary cult of love.

"We all loved her," Elizabeth's godson Sir John Harington wrote, with just a touch of irony, a few years after the queen's death, "for she said she loved us." Ambassadors, courtiers, and parliamentarians all submitted to Elizabeth's cult of love, in which the queen's gender was transformed from a potential liability into a significant asset. Those who approached her generally did so on their knees and were expected to address her with extravagant compliments fashioned from the period's most passionate love poetry; she in turn spoke, when it suited her to do so, in the language of love poetry. The court moved in an atmosphere of romance, with music, dancing, plays, and the elaborate, fancy-dress entertainments called masques. The queen adorned herself in gorgeous clothes and rich jewels. When she went on one of her summer "progresses," ceremonial journeys through her land, she looked like an exotic, sacred image in a religious cult of love, and her noble hosts virtually bankrupted themselves to lavish upon her the costliest pleasures. England's leading artists, such as the poet Edmund Spenser and the painter Nicholas Hilliard, enlisted themselves in the celebration of Elizabeth's mystery, likening her to the goddesses and queens of mythology: Diana, Astraea, Gloriana. Her cult drew its power from cultural discourses that ranged from the secular (her courtiers could pine for her as a cruel Petrarchan mistress) to the sacred (the veneration that under Catholicism had been due to the Virgin Mary could now be directed toward England's semidivine queen).

There was a sober, even grim, aspect to these poetical fantasies: Elizabeth was brilliant at playing one dangerous faction off another, now turning her gracious smiles on one favorite, now honoring his hated rival, now suddenly looking elsewhere and raising an obscure upstart to royal favor. And when she was disobeyed or when she felt that her prerogatives had been challenged, she was capable of an anger that, as Harington put it, "left no doubtings whose daughter she was." Thus, when Sir Walter Ralegh, one of the queen's glittering favorites, married without her knowledge or consent, he found himself promptly imprisoned in the Tower of London. And when the Protestant polemicist John Stubbs ventured to publish a pamphlet stridently denouncing the queen's proposed marriage to the French Catholic Duke of Alençon, Stubbs and his publisher were arrested and had their right hands chopped off. (After receiving the blow, the now prudent Stubbs lifted his hat with his remaining hand and cried, "God save the Queen!")

The queen's marriage negotiations were a particularly fraught issue. When she came to the throne at twenty-five years old, speculation about a suitable match, already widespread, intensified and remained for decades at a fever pitch, for the stakes were high. If Elizabeth died childless, the Tudor line would come to an end. The nearest heir was her cousin Mary, Queen of Scots, a Catholic whose claim was supported by France and by the papacy, and whose penchant for sexual and political intrigue confirmed the worst fears of English Protestants. The obvious way to avert the nightmare was for Elizabeth to marry and produce an heir, and the pressure upon her to do so was intense.

More than the royal succession hinged on the question of the queen's marriage; Elizabeth's perceived eligibility was a vital factor in the complex machinations of international diplomacy. A dynastic marriage between the Queen of England and a foreign ruler would forge an alliance powerful enough to alter the balance of power in Europe. The English court hosted a steady stream of ambassadors from kings and princes eager to win the hand of the royal maiden, and Elizabeth, who prided herself on speaking fluent French and Italian (and on reading Latin and Greek), played her romantic part with exemplary skill, sighing and spinning the negotiations out for months and even years.

Most probably, she never meant to marry any of her numerous foreign (and domestic) suitors. Such a decisive act would have meant the end of her independence, as well as the end of the marriage game by which she played one power off against another. One day she would seem to be on the verge of accepting a proposal; the next, she would vow never to forsake her virginity. "She is a Princess," the French ambassador remarked, "who can act any part she pleases."

The Kingdom in Danger

Beset by Catholic and Protestant extremists, Elizabeth contrived to forge a moderate compromise that enabled her realm to avert the massacres and civil wars that poisoned France and other countries on the Continent. But menace was never far off, and there were constant fears of conspiracy, rebellion, and assassination. Many of the fears swirled around Mary, Queen of Scots, who had been driven from her own kingdom in 1568 by a powerful faction of rebellious nobles and had taken refuge in England. Her presence, under a kind of house arrest, was the source of intense anxiety and helped generate continual rumors of plots. Some of these plots were real enough, others imaginary, still others traps set in motion by the secret agents of the government's intelligence service under the direction of Sir Francis Walsingham. The situation worsened greatly after the St. Bartholomew's Day Massacre of Protestants (Huguenots) in France (August 24, 1572), after Spanish imperial armies invaded the Netherlands in order to stamp out Protestant rebels, and after the assassination there of Europe's other major Protestant leader, William of Orange (1584).

The queen's life seemed to be in even greater danger after Pope Gregory XIII's proclamation in 1580 that the assassination of the great heretic Elizabeth (who had been excommunicated a decade before) would not constitute a mortal sin. The immediate effect of the proclamation was to make existence more difficult for English Catholics, most of whom were loyal to the queen but who fell under grave suspicion. Suspicion was intensified by the clandestine presence of English Jesuits, trained at seminaries abroad and smuggled back into England to serve the Roman Catholic cause. When Elizabeth's spymaster Walsingham unearthed an assassination plot in the correspondence between the Queen of Scots and the Catholic Anthony Babington, the wretched Mary's fate was sealed. After vacillating, a very reluctant Elizabeth signed the death warrant in February 1587, and her cousin was beheaded.

The long-anticipated military confrontation with Catholic Spain was now unavoidable. Elizabeth learned that Philip II, her former brother-in-law and onetime suitor, was preparing to send an enormous fleet against her island realm. It was to sail to the Netherlands, where a Spanish army would be waiting to embark and invade England. Barring its way was England's small fleet of well-armed and highly maneuverable fighting vessels, backed up by ships from the merchant navy. The Invincible Armada reached English waters in July 1588, only to be routed in one of the most famous and decisive naval battles in European history. Then, in what many viewed as an act of God on behalf of Protestant England, the Spanish fleet was dispersed and all but destroyed by violent storms.

As England braced itself to withstand the invasion that never came, Elizabeth appeared in person to review a detachment of soldiers assembled at Tilbury. Dressed in a white gown and a silver breastplate, she declared that though some among her councillors had urged her not to appear before a large crowd of armed men, she would never fail to trust the loyalty of her faithful and loving subjects. Nor did she fear the Spanish armies. "I know I have the body of a weak and feeble woman," Elizabeth declared, "but I have the heart and stomach of a king, and of England too." In this celebrated speech, Elizabeth displayed many of her most memorable qualities: her self-consciously histrionic command of grand public occasion, her subtle blending of magniloquent rhetoric and the language of love, her strategic appropriation of traditionally masculine qualities, and her great personal courage. "We princes," she once remarked, "are set on stages in the sight and view of all the world."

The English and Otherness

Shakespeare's London had a large population of resident aliens, mainly artisans and merchants and their families, from Portugal, Italy, Spain, Germany, and, above all, France and the Netherlands. Many of these people were Protestant refugees, and they were accorded some legal and economic protection by the government. But they were not always welcome by the local populace. Throughout the sixteenth century, London was the site of repeated demonstrations and, on occasion, bloody riots against the communities of foreign artisans, who were accused of taking jobs away from Englishmen. There was widespread hostility as well toward the Welsh, the Scots, and especially the Irish, whom the English had for centuries been struggling unsuccessfully to subdue. The kings of England claimed to be rulers of Ireland, but in reality they effectively controlled only a small area known as the Pale, extending north from Dublin. The great majority of the Irish people remained stubbornly Catholic and, despite endlessly reiterated English repression, burning of villages, destruction of crops, and massacres, incorrigibly independent.

Shakespeare's *Henry V* (1598–99) seems to invite the audience to celebrate the conjoined heroism of English, Welsh, Scots, and Irish soldiers all fighting together as a "band of brothers" against the French. But such a way of imagining the national community must be set against the tensions and conflicting interests that often set these brothers at each other's throats. As Shakespeare's King Henry realizes, a feared or hated foreign enemy helps at least to mask these tensions, and, indeed, in the face of the Spanish Armada, even the bitter gulf between Catholic and Protestant Englishmen seemed to narrow significantly. But the patriotic alliance was only temporary.

Another way of partially masking the sharp differences in language, belief, and custom among the peoples of the British Isles was to group these people together in contrast to the Jews. Medieval England's Jewish population, the recurrent object of persecution, extortion, and massacre, had been officially expelled by King Edward I in 1290, but Elizabethan England harbored a tiny number of Jews or Jewish converts to Christianity who were treated with suspicion and hostility. One of these was Elizabeth's own physician, Roderigo Lopez, who was tried in 1594 for an alleged plot to poison the queen. Convicted and condemned to the hideous execution reserved for traitors, Lopez went to his death, in the words of the Elizabethan historian William Camden, "affirming that he loved the Queen as well as he loved Jesus Christ; which coming from a man of the Jewish profession moved no small laughter in the standers-by." It is difficult to gauge the meaning here of the phrase "the Jewish profession," used to describe a man who never, as far as we know, professed Judaism, just as it is difficult to gauge the meaning of the crowd's cruel laughter.

Elizabethans appear to have been fascinated by Jews and Judaism but uncertain whether the terms referred to a people, a foreign nation, a set of strange prac-

A Jewish man poisoning a well. From Pierre Boaistuau, *Certaine Secrete Wonders of Nature* (1569).

tices, a living faith, a defunct religion, a villainous conspiracy, or a messianic inheritance. Protestant Reformers brooded deeply on the Hebraic origins of Christianity; government officials ordered the arrest of those "suspected to be Jews"; villagers paid pennies to itinerant fortune-tellers who claimed to be descended from Abraham or masters of cabalistic mysteries; and London playgoers, perhaps including some who laughed at Lopez on the scaffold, enjoyed the spectacle of the downfall of the wicked Barabas in Christopher Marlowe's *Jew of Malta* (c. 1592) and the forced conversion of Shylock in Shakespeare's *Merchant of Venice* (1596–97). Few if any of Shakespeare's contemporaries would have encountered on English soil Jews who openly practiced their religion, though England probably harbored a small number of so-called Marranos, Spanish or Portuguese Jews who had officially converted to Christianity but secretly continued to observe Jewish practices. Jews were not officially permitted to resettle in England until the middle of the seventeenth century, and even then their legal status was ambiguous.

Shakespeare's England also had a small African population whose skin color was the subject of pseudoscientific speculation and theological debate. Some Elizabethans believed that Africans' blackness resulted from the climate of the regions in which they lived, where, as one traveler put it, they were "so scorched and vexed with the heat of the sun, that in many places they curse it when it riseth." Others held that blackness was a curse inherited from their forefather Chus, the son of Ham, who had, according to Genesis, wickedly exposed the nakedness of the drunken Noah. George Best, a proponent of this theory of inherited skin color, reported that "I myself have seen an Ethiopian as black as coal brought into England, who taking a fair English woman to wife, begat a son in all respects as black as the father was, although England were his native country, and an English woman his mother: whereby it seemeth this blackness proceedeth rather of some natural infection of that man."

As the word "infection" suggests, Elizabethans frequently regarded blackness as a physical defect, though the blacks who lived in England and Scotland throughout the sixteenth century were also treated as exotic curiosities. At his marriage to Anne of Denmark, James I entertained his bride and her family by commanding four naked black youths to dance before him in the snow. (The youths died of exposure shortly afterward.) In 1594, in the festivities celebrating the baptism of James's son, a "Black-Moor" entered pulling an elaborately decorated chariot that was, in the original plan, supposed to be drawn in by a lion. There was a black trumpeter in the courts of Henry VII and Henry VIII, while Elizabeth had at least two black servants, one an entertainer and the other a page. Africans became increasingly popular as servants in aristocratic and gentle households in the last decades of the sixteenth century.

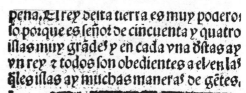

Man with head beneath his shoulders. From a Spanish edition of Sir John Mandeville's *Travels*. See *Othello* 1.3.144–45: "and men whose heads / Do grow beneath their shoulders." Such men were occasionally reported by medieval travelers to the East.

An Indian dance. From Thomas Hariot, *A Briefe and True Report of the New Found Land of Virginia* (1590 ed.).

Some of these Africans were almost certainly slaves, though the legal status of slavery in England was ambiguous. In Cartwright's case (1569), the court ruled "that England was too Pure an Air for Slaves to breathe in," but there is evidence that black slaves were owned in Elizabethan and Jacobean England. Moreover, by the mid-sixteenth century, the English had become involved in the profitable trade that carried African slaves to the New World. In 1562, John Hawkins embarked on his first slaving voyage, transporting some three hundred blacks from the Guinea coast to Hispaniola, where they were sold for £10,000. Elizabeth is reported to have said of this venture that it was "detestable, and would call down the Vengeance of Heaven upon the Undertakers." Nevertheless, she invested in Hawkins's subsequent voyages and loaned him ships.

English men and women of the sixteenth century experienced an unprecedented increase in knowledge of the world beyond their island, for a number of reasons. Religious persecution compelled both Catholics and Protestants to live abroad; wealthy gentlemen (and, in at least a few cases, ladies) traveled in France and Italy to view the famous cultural monuments; merchants published accounts of distant lands such as Turkey, Morocco, and Russia; and military and trading ventures took English ships to still more distant shores. In 1496, a Venetian tradesman living in Bristol, John Cabot, was granted a license by Henry VII to sail on a voyage of exploration; with his son Sebastian, he discovered Newfoundland and Nova Scotia. Remarkable feats of seamanship and reconnaissance soon followed: on his ship the *Golden Hind,* Sir Francis Drake circumnavigated the globe in 1579 and laid claim to California on behalf of the queen; a few years later, a ship commanded by Thomas Cavendish also completed a circumnavigation. Sir Martin Frobisher explored bleak Baffin Island in search of a Northwest Passage to the Orient; Sir John Davis explored the west coast of Greenland and discovered the Falkland Islands off the coast of Argentina; Sir Walter Ralegh ventured up the Orinoco Delta, in what is now Venezuela, in search of the mythical land of El Dorado. Accounts of these and other exploits were collected by a clergyman and promoter of empire, Richard Hakluyt, and published as *The Principal Navigations* (1589; expanded edition 1599).

"To seek new worlds for gold, for praise, for glory," as Ralegh characterized such enterprises, was not for the faint of heart: Drake, Cavendish, Frobisher, and Hawkins all died at sea, as did huge numbers of those who sailed under their command. Elizabethans sensible enough to stay at home could do more than read written accounts of their fellow countrymen's far-reaching voyages. Expeditions brought back native plants (including, most famously, tobacco), animals, cultural artifacts, and, on occasion, samples of the native peoples themselves, most often seized against their will. There were exhibitions in London of a kidnapped Eskimo with his kayak and of Virginians with their canoes. Most of these miserable captives, violently uprooted and vulnerable to European diseases, quickly perished, but even in death they were evidently valuable property: when the English will not give one small coin "to relieve a lame beggar," one of the characters in *The Tempest* wryly remarks, "they will lay out ten to see a dead Indian" (2.2.30–31).

Perhaps most nations learn to define what they are by defining what they are not. This negative self-definition is, in any case, what Elizabethans seemed constantly to be doing, in travel books, sermons, political speeches, civic pageants, public exhibitions, and theatrical spectacles of otherness. The extraordinary variety of these exercises (which include public executions and urban riots, as well as more benign forms of curiosity) suggests that the boundaries of national identity were by no means clear and unequivocal. Even peoples whom English writers routinely, viciously stigmatize as irreducibly alien—Italians, Indians, Turks, and Jews—have a surprising instability in the Elizabethan imagination and may appear for brief, intense moments as powerful models to be admired and emulated before they resume their place as emblems of despised otherness.

James I and the Union of the Crowns

Though under great pressure to do so, the aging Elizabeth steadfastly refused to name her successor. It became increasingly apparent, however, that it would be James Stuart, the son of Mary, Queen of Scots, and by the time Elizabeth's health began to fail, several of her principal advisers, including her chief minister, Robert Cecil, had been for several years in secret correspondence with him in Edinburgh. Crowned King James VI of Scotland in 1567 when he was but one year old, Mary's son had been raised as a Protestant by his powerful guardians, and in 1589 he married a Protestant princess, Anne of Denmark. When Elizabeth died on March 24, 1603, English officials reported that on her deathbed the queen had named James to succeed her.

Upon his accession, James—now styled James VI of Scotland and James I of England—made plain his intention to unite his two kingdoms. As he told Parliament in 1604, "What God hath conjoined then, let no man separate. I am the husband, and all of the whole isle is my lawful wife; I am the head and it is my body; I am the shepherd and it is my flock." But the flock was less perfectly united than James optimistically envisioned: English and Scottish were sharply distinct identities, as were Welsh and Cornish and other peoples who were incorporated, with varying degrees of willingness, into the realm.

Fearing that to change the name of the kingdom would invalidate all laws and institutions established under the name of England, a fear that was partly real and partly a cover for anti-Scots prejudice, Parliament balked at James's desire to be called "King of

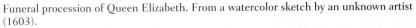

Funeral procession of Queen Elizabeth. From a watercolor sketch by an unknown artist (1603).

Great Britain" and resisted the unionist legislation that would have made Great Britain a legal reality. Although the English initially rejoiced at the peaceful transition from Elizabeth to her successor, there was a rising tide of resentment against James's advancement of Scots friends and his creation of new knighthoods. Lower down the social ladder, English and Scots occasionally clashed violently on the streets: in July 1603, James issued a proclamation against Scottish "insolencies," and in April 1604, he ordered the arrest of "swaggerers" waylaying Scots in London. The ensuing years did not bring the amity and docile obedience for which James hoped, and, though the navy now flew the Union Jack, combining the Scottish cross of St. Andrew and the English cross of St. George, the unification of the kingdoms remained throughout his reign an unfulfilled ambition.

Unfulfilled as well were James's lifelong dreams of ruling as an absolute monarch. Crown lawyers throughout Europe had long argued that a King, by virtue of his power to make law, must necessarily be above law. But in England, sovereignty was identified not with the King alone or with the people alone but with the "King in Parliament." Against his absolutist ambitions, James faced the crucial power to raise taxes that was vested not in the monarch but in the elected members of the Parliament. He faced as well a theory of republicanism that traced it roots back to ancient Rome and that prided itself on its steadfast and, if necessary, violent resistance to tyranny. Shakespeare's fascination with monarchy is apparent throughout his work, but in his Roman plays in particular, as well as in his long poem *The Rape of Lucrece*, he manifests an intense imaginative interest in the idea of a republic.

The Jacobean Court

With James as with Elizabeth, the royal court was the center of diplomacy, ambition, intrigue, and an intense jockeying for social position. As always in monarchies, proximity to the king's person was a central mark of favor, so that access to the royal bedchamber was one of the highest aims of the powerful, scheming lords who followed James from his sprawling London palace at Whitehall to the hunting lodges and country estates to which he loved to retreat. A coveted office, in the Jacobean as in the Tudor court, was the Groom of the Stool, the person who supervised the disposal of the king's wastes. The officeholder was close to the king at one of his most exposed and vulnerable moments, and enjoyed the further privilege of sleeping on a pallet at the foot of the royal bed and putting on the royal undershirt. Another, slightly less privileged official, the Gentleman of the Robes, dressed the king in his doublet and outer garments.

The royal lifestyle was increasingly expensive. Unlike Elizabeth, James had to maintain separate households for his queen and for the heir apparent, Prince Henry. (Upon Henry's death at the age of eighteen in 1612, his younger brother, Prince Charles, became heir, eventually succeeding his father in 1625.) James was also extremely generous to his friends, amassing his own huge debts in the course of paying off theirs. As early as 1605, he told his principal adviser that "it is a horror to me to think of the height of my place, the greatness of my debts, and the smallness of my means." This smallness notwithstanding, James continued to lavish gifts upon handsome favorites such as the Earl of Somerset, Robert Carr, and the Duke of Buckingham, George Villiers.

The attachment James formed for these favorites was highly romantic. "God so love me," the king wrote to Buckingham, "as I desire only to live in the world for your sake, and that I had rather live banished in any part of the earth with you than live a sorrowful widow's life without you." Such sentiments, not surprisingly, gave rise to widespread rumors of homosexual activities at court. The rumors are certainly plausible, even though the surviving evidence of same-sex relationships, at court or elsewhere, is extremely difficult to interpret. A statute of 1533 made "the detestable and abominable vice of buggery committed with mankind or beast" a felony punishable by death. (English law declined to recognize or criminalize lesbian acts.) The effect of the draconian laws against buggery and sodomy seems to have been to reduce actual prosecutions to the barest minimum: for the next hundred years, there are no known cases of trials resulting in a death sentence for homosexual activity alone. If the legal record is, therefore, unreliable as an index of the extent of homosexual relations, the literary record (including, most famously, the majority of Shakespeare's sonnets) is equally opaque. Any poetic avowal of male-male love may simply be a formal expression of affection based on classical models, or, alternatively, it may be an expression of passionate physical and spiritual love. The interpretive difficulty is compounded by the absence in the period of any clear reference to a homosexual "identity," even though there are many references to same-sex acts and feelings. What is clear is that male friendships at the court of James and elsewhere were suffused with a potential eroticism, at once delightful and threatening, that subsequent periods policed more anxiously.

In addition to the extravagant expenditures on his favorites, James was also the patron of ever more

James I. By John De Critz the Elder (c. 1606).

Two Young Men. By Crispin van den Broeck (c. 1590).

elaborate feasts and masques. Shakespeare's work provides a small glimpse of these in *The Tempest,* with its exotic banquet and its "majestic vision" of mythological goddesses and dancing nymphs and reapers. The actual Jacobean court masques, designed by the great architect, painter, and engineer Inigo Jones, were spectacular, fantastic, technically ingenious, and staggeringly costly celebrations of regal magnificence. With their exquisite costumes and their elegant blend of music, dancing, and poetry, the masques, generally performed by the noble lords and ladies of the court, were deliberately ephemeral exercises in conspicuous expenditure and consumption: by tradition, at the end of the performance, the private audience would rush forward and tear to pieces the gorgeous scenery. And although masques were enormously sophisticated entertainments, often on rather esoteric allegorical themes, they could on occasion collapse into grotesque excess. In a letter of 1606, Sir John Harington describes a masque in honor of the visiting Danish king in which the participants, no doubt toasting their royal majesties, had had too much to drink. A lady playing the part of the Queen of Sheba attempted to present precious gifts, "but, forgetting the steps arising to the canopy, overset her caskets into his Danish Majesty's lap. . . . His Majesty then got up and would dance with the Queen of Sheba; but he fell down and humbled himself before her, and was carried to an inner chamber and laid on a bed." Meanwhile, Harington writes, the masque continued with a pageant of Faith, Hope, and Charity, but Charity could barely keep her balance, while Hope and Faith "were both sick and spewing in the lower hall." This was, we can hope, not a typical occasion.

While the English seem initially to have welcomed James's free-spending ways as a change from the relative parsimoniousness of Queen Elizabeth, they were dismayed by its consequences. Elizabeth had died owing £400,000. In 1608, the royal debt had risen to £1,400,000 and was increasing by £140,000 a year. The money to pay off this debt, or at least to keep it under control, was raised by various means. These included customs farming (leasing the right to collect customs duties to private individuals); the highly unpopular impositions (duties on the import of nonnecessities, such as spices, silks, and currants); the sale of crown lands; the sale of baronetcies; and appeals to an increasingly grudging and recalcitrant Parliament. In 1614, Parliament demanded an end to impositions before it would relieve the king and was angrily dissolved without completing its business.

James's Religious Policy and the Persecution of Witches

Before his accession to the English throne, the king had made known his view of Puritans, the general name for a variety of Protestant sects that were agitating for a radical reform of the Church, the overthrow of its conservative hierarchy of bishops, and the rejection of a large number of traditional rituals and practices. In a book he wrote, *Basilikon Doron* (1599), James denounced "brainsick and heady preachers" who were prepared "to let King, people, law and all be trod underfoot." Yet he was not entirely unwilling to consider religious reforms. In religion, as in foreign policy, he was above all concerned to maintain peace.

On his way south to claim the throne of England in 1603, James was presented with the Millenary Petition (signed by 1,000 ministers), which urged him as "our physician" to heal the disease of lingering "popish" ceremonies. He responded by calling a conference on the ceremonies of the Church of England, which duly took place at Hampton Court Palace in January 1604. The delegates who spoke for reform were moderates, and there was little in the outcome to satisfy Puritans. Nevertheless, while the Church of England continued to cling to such remnants of the Catholic past as wedding rings, square caps, bishops, and Christmas, the conference did produce some reform in the area of ecclesiastical discipline. It also authorized a new English translation of the Bible, known as the King James Bible, which was printed in 1611, too late to have been extensively used by Shakespeare. Along with Shakespeare's works, the King James Bible has probably had the profoundest influence on the subsequent history of English literature.

Having arranged this compromise, James saw his main task as ensuring conformity. He promulgated the 1604 Canons (the first definitive code of canon law since the Reformation), which required all ministers to subscribe to three articles. The first affirmed royal supremacy; the second confirmed that there was nothing in the Book of Common Prayer "contrary to the Word of God" and required ministers to use only the authorized

The "swimming" of a suspected witch (1615).

services; the third asserted that the central tenets of the Church of England were "agreeable to the Word of God." There were strong objections to the second and third articles from those of Puritan leanings inside and outside the House of Commons. In the end, many ministers refused to conform or subscribe to the articles, but only about 90 of them, or 1 percent of the clergy, were deprived of their livings. In its theology and composition, the Church of England was little changed from what it had been under Elizabeth. In hindsight, what is most striking are the ominous signs of growing religious divisions that would by the 1640s burst forth in civil war and the execution of James's son Charles.

James seems to have taken seriously the official claims to the sacredness of kingship, and he certainly took seriously his own theories of religion and politics, which he had printed for the edification of his people. He was convinced that Satan, perpetually warring against God and His representatives on earth, was continually plotting against him. James thought, moreover, that he possessed special insight into Satan's wicked agents, the witches, and in 1597, while King of Scotland, he published his *Daemonology*, a learned exposition of their malign threat to his godly rule. Hundreds of witches, he believed, were involved in a 1590 conspiracy to kill him by raising storms at sea when he was sailing home from Denmark with his new bride.

In the 1590s, Scotland embarked on a virulent witch craze of the kind that had since the fifteenth century repeatedly afflicted France, Switzerland, and Germany, where many thousands of women (and a much smaller number of men) were caught in a nightmarish web of wild accusations. Tortured into lurid confessions of infant cannibalism, night flying, and sexual intercourse with the devil at huge, orgiastic "witches' Sabbaths," the victims had little chance to defend themselves and were routinely burned at the stake.

In England, too, there were witchcraft prosecutions, but on a much smaller scale and with significant differences in the nature of the accusations and the judicial procedures. Witch trials began in England in the 1540s; statutes against witchcraft were enacted in 1542, 1563, and 1604. English law did not allow judicial torture, stipulated lesser punishments in cases of "white magic," and mandated jury trials. Juries acquitted more than half of the defendants in witchcraft trials; in Essex, where the judicial records are particularly extensive, some 24 percent of those accused were executed, while the remainder of those convicted were pilloried and imprisoned or sentenced and reprieved. The accused were generally charged with *maleficium*, an evil deed—usually harming neighbors, causing destructive storms, or killing farm animals—but not with worshipping Satan.

After 1603, when James came to the English throne, he somewhat moderated his enthusiasm for the judicial murder of witches, for the most part defenseless, poor women resented by their neighbors. Although he did nothing to mitigate the ferocity of the ongoing witch hunts in his native Scotland, he did not try to institute Scottish-style persecutions and trials in his new realm. This relative waning of persecutorial eagerness principally reflects the differences between England and Scotland, but it may also bespeak some small, nascent skepticism on James's part about the quality of evidence brought against the accused and about the reliability of the "confessions" extracted from them. It is sobering to reflect that plays like Shakespeare's *Macbeth* (1606), Thomas Middleton's *Witch* (before 1616), and Thomas Dekker, John Ford, and William Rowley's *Witch of Edmonton* (1621) seem to be less the allies of skepticism than the exploiters of fear.

The Playing Field

Cosmic Spectacles

The first permanent, freestanding public theaters in England date only from Shakespeare's own lifetime: a London playhouse, the Red Lion, is mentioned in 1567, and James Burbage's playhouse, The Theatre, was built in 1576. (The innovative use of these new stages, crucial to a full understanding of Shakespeare's achievement, is, in this volume, the subject of a separate essay by the theater historian Andrew Gurr, pages 79–99.) But it is misleading to identify English drama exclusively with these specially constructed playhouses, for in fact there was a rich and vital theatrical tradition in England stretching back for centuries. Many towns in late medieval England were the sites of annual festivals that mounted elaborate cycles of plays depicting the great biblical stories, from the creation of the world to Christ's Passion and its miraculous aftermath. Most of these plays have been lost, but the surviving cycles, such as those from York, are magnificent and complex works of art. They are sometimes called "mystery plays," either because they were performed by the guilds of various crafts (known as "mysteries") or, more likely, because they represented the mysteries of the faith. The cycles were most often performed on the annual feast day instituted in the early fourteenth century in honor of the Corpus Christi, the sacrament of the Lord's Supper, which is perhaps the greatest of these religious mysteries.

The Feast of Corpus Christi, celebrated on the Thursday following Trinity Sunday, helped give the play cycles their extraordinary cultural resonance, but it also contributed to their downfall. For along with the specifically liturgical plays traditionally performed by religious confraternities and the "saints' plays," which depicted miraculous events in the lives of individual holy men and women, the mystery cycles were closely identified with the Catholic Church. Protestant authorities in the sixteenth century, eager to eradicate all remnants of popular Catholic piety, moved to suppress the annual procession of the Host, with its gorgeous banners, pageant carts, and cycle of visionary plays. In 1548, the Feast of Corpus Christi was abolished. Towns that continued to perform the mysteries were under increasing pressure to abandon them. It is sometimes said that the cycles were already dying out from neglect, but recent research has shown that many towns and their guilds were extremely reluctant to give them up. Desperate offers to strip away any traces of Catholic doctrine and to submit the play scripts to the authorities for their approval met with unbending opposition from the government. In 1576, the courts gave York permission to perform its cycle but only if

> in the said play no pageant be used or set forth wherein the Majesty of God the Father, God the Son, or God the Holy Ghost or the administration of either the Sacraments of baptism or of the Lord's Supper be counterfeited or represented, or anything played which tend to the maintenance of superstition and idolatry or which be contrary to the laws of God . . . or of the realm.

Such "permission" was tantamount to an outright ban. The local officials in the city of Norwich, proud of their St. George and the Dragon play, asked if they could at least parade the dragon costume through the streets, but even this modest request was refused. It is likely that as a young man Shakespeare had seen some of these plays: when Hamlet says of a noisy, strutting theatrical performance that it "out-Herods Herod," he is alluding to the famously bombastic role of Herod of Jewry in the mystery plays. But by the century's end, the cycles were no longer performed.

Early English theater was by no means restricted to these civic and religious festivals. Payments to professional and amateur performers appear in early records of towns and aristocratic households, although the terms—"ministralli," "histriones," "mimi," "lusores," and so forth—are not used with great consistency and make it difficult to distinguish among minstrels, jugglers, stage players, and other entertainers. Performers acted in town halls and the halls of guilds and aristocratic mansions, on scaffolds erected in town squares and marketplaces, on pageant wagons in the streets, and in inn yards. By the fifteenth century and probably earlier, there were organized companies of players traveling under noble patronage. Such companies earned a living providing amusement, while enhancing the prestige of the patron.

A description of a provincial performance in the late sixteenth century, written by one R. Willis, provides a glimpse of what seems to have been the usual procedure:

> In the City of Gloucester the manner is (as I think it is in other like corporations) that when the Players of Interludes come to town, they first attend the Mayor to

Panorama of London, showing two theaters, both
round and both flying flags: a flying flag indicated that
a performance was in progress. The Globe is in the
foreground, and the Beargarden or Hope is to the left.

inform him what nobleman's servant they are, and so to get licence for their public
playing; and if the Mayor like the Actors, or would show respect to their Lord and
Master, he appoints them to play their first play before himself and the Aldermen
and common Council of the City and that is called the Mayor's play, where everyone that will come in without money, the Mayor giving the players a reward as he
thinks fit to show respect unto them.

In addition to their take from this "first play," the players would almost certainly have
supplemented their income by performing in halls and inn yards, where they could pass
the hat after the performance or even on some occasions charge an admission fee. It
was no doubt a precarious existence.

The "Interludes" mentioned in Willis's description of the Gloucester performances
are likely plays that were, in effect, staged dialogues on religious, moral, and political
themes. Such works could, like the mysteries, be associated with Catholicism, but they
were also used in the sixteenth century to convey polemical Protestant messages, and
they reached outside the religious sphere to address secular concerns as well. Henry
Medwall's *Fulgens and Lucrece* (c. 1490–1501), for example, pits a wealthy but dissolute nobleman against a virtuous public servant of humble origins, while John Heywood's *Play of the Weather* (c. 1525–33) stages a debate among social rivals, including
a gentleman, a merchant, a forest ranger, and two millers. The structure of such plays
reflects the training in argumentation that students received in Tudor schools and, in
particular, the sustained practice in examining all sides of a difficult question. Some of
Shakespeare's amazing ability to look at critical issues from multiple perspectives may
be traced back to this practice and the dramatic interludes it helped to inspire.

Another major form of theater that flourished in England in the fifteenth century
and continued on into the sixteenth was the morality play. Like the mysteries, moralities addressed questions of the ultimate fate of the soul. They did so, however, not by
rehearsing scriptural stories but by dramatizing allegories of spiritual struggle. Typically,
a person named Human or Mankind or Youth is faced with a choice between a pious
life in the company of such associates as Mercy, Discretion, and Good Deeds and a dissolute life among riotous companions like Lust or Mischief. Plays like *Mankind* (c.
1465–70) and *Everyman* (c. 1495) show how powerful these unpromising-sounding
dramas could be, in part because of the extraordinary comic vitality of the evil character, or Vice, and in part because of the poignancy and terror of an individual's encounter
with death. Shakespeare clearly grasped this power. The hunchbacked Duke of
Gloucester in *Richard III* gleefully likens himself to "the formal Vice, Iniquity." And

when Othello wavers between Desdemona and Iago (himself a Vice figure), his anguished dilemma echoes the fateful choice repeatedly faced by the troubled, vulnerable protagonists of the moralities.

If such plays sound a bit like sermons, it is because they were. Clerics and actors shared some of the same rhetorical skills. It would be misleading to regard churchgoing and playgoing as comparable entertainments, but in attacking the stage, ministers often seemed to regard the professional players as dangerous rivals. The players themselves were generally too discreet to rise to the challenge; it would have been foolhardy to present the theater as the Church's direct competitor. Yet in its moral intensity and its command of impassioned language, the stage frequently emulates and outdoes the pulpit.

Music and Dance

Playacting took its place alongside other forms of public expression and entertainment as well. Perhaps the most important, from the perspective of the theater, were music and dance, since these were directly and repeatedly incorporated into plays. Many plays, comedies and tragedies alike, include occasions that call upon the characters to dance: hence Beatrice and Benedick join the other masked guests at the dance in *Much Ado About Nothing*; in *Twelfth Night*, the befuddled Sir Andrew, at the instigation of the drunken Sir Toby Belch, displays his skill, such as it is, in capering; Romeo and Juliet first see each other at the Capulet ball; the witches dance in a ring around the hideous caldron and perform an "antic round" to cheer Macbeth's spirits; and, in one of Shakespeare's strangest and most wonderful scenes, the drunken Antony in *Antony and Cleopatra* joins hands with Caesar, Enobarbus, Pompey, and others to dance "the Egyptian Bacchanals."

Moreover, virtually all plays in the period, including Shakespeare's, apparently ended with a dance. Brushing off the theatrical gore and changing their expressions from woe to pleasure, the actors in plays like *Hamlet* and *King Lear* would presumably have received the audience's applause and then bid for a second round of applause by performing a stately pavane or a lively jig. Indeed, jigs, with their comical leaping dance steps often accompanied by scurrilous ballads, became so popular that they drew not only large crowds but also official disapproval. A court order of 1612 complained about the "cutpurses and other lewd and ill-disposed persons" who flocked to the theater at the end of every play to be entertained by "lewd jigs, songs, and dances." The players were warned to suppress these disreputable entertainments on pain of imprisonment.

The displays of dancing onstage clearly reflected a widespread popular interest in dancing outside the walls of the playhouse as well. Renaissance intellectuals conjured up visions of the universe as a great cosmic dance, poets figured relations between men and women in terms of popular dance steps, stern moralists denounced dancing as an incitement to filthy lewdness, and, perhaps as significant, men of all classes evidently spent a great deal of time worrying about how shapely their legs looked in tights and how gracefully they could leap. Shakespeare assumes that his audience will be quite familiar with a variety of dances. "For hear me, Hero," Beatrice tells her friend, "wooing, wedding, and repenting is as a Scotch jig, a measure, and a cinquepace" (2.1.60–61). Her speech dwells on the comparison a bit, teasing out its implications, but it still does not make much sense if you do not already know something about the dances and perhaps occasionally venture to perform them yourself.

Closely linked to dancing and even more central to the stage was music, both instrumental and vocal. In the early sixteenth century, the Reformation had been disastrous for sacred music: many church organs were destroyed, choir schools were closed, the glorious polyphonal liturgies sung in the monasteries were suppressed. But by the latter part of the century, new perspectives were reinvigorating English music. Latin Masses were reset in English, and tunes were written for newly translated, metrical psalms. More important for the theater, styles of secular music were developed that emphasized music's link to humanist eloquence, its ability to heighten and to rival rhetorically powerful texts.

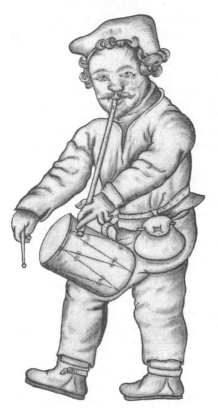

Richard Tarlton. Tarlton was the lead comedian of the Queen's Company from 1583, the year of its founding, until 1588, when he died.

This link is particularly evident in vocal music, at which Elizabethan composers excelled. Renowned composers William Byrd, Thomas Morley, John Dowland, and others wrote a rich profusion of madrigals (part songs for two to eight voices unaccompanied) and ayres (songs for solo voice, generally accompanied by the lute). These works, along with hymns, popular ballads, rounds, catches, and other forms of song, enjoyed immense popularity, not only in the royal court, where musical skill was regarded as an important accomplishment, and in aristocratic households, where professional musicians were employed as entertainers, but also in less exalted social circles. In his *Plaine and Easie Introduction to Practicall Musicke* (1597), Morley tells a story of social humiliation at a failure to perform that suggests that a well-educated Elizabethan was expected to be able to sing at sight. Even if this is an exaggeration in the interest of book sales, there is evidence of impressively widespread musical literacy, reflected in a splendid array of music for the lute, viol, recorder, harp, and virginal, as well as the marvelous vocal music.

Whether it is the aristocratic Orsino luxuriating in the dying fall of an exquisite melody or bully Bottom craving "the tongs and the bones," Shakespeare's characters frequently call for music. They also repeatedly give voice to the age's conviction that there was a deep relation between musical harmony and the harmonies of the well-ordered individual and state. "The man that hath no music in himself," warns Lorenzo in *The Merchant of Venice*, "nor is not moved with concord of sweet sounds, / Is fit for treasons, stratagems, and spoils" (5.1.82–84). This conviction, in turn, reflects a still deeper link between musical harmony and the divinely created harmony of the cosmos. When Ulysses, in *Troilus and Cressida*, wishes to convey the image of universal chaos, he speaks of the untuning of a string (1.3.109).

The playing companies must have regularly employed trained musicians, and many actors (like the actor who in playing Pandarus in *Troilus and Cressida* is supposed to accompany himself on the lute) must have possessed musical skill. Unfortunately, we possess the original settings for very few of Shakespeare's songs, possibly because many of them may have been set to popular tunes of the time that everyone knew and no one bothered to write down.

Alternative Entertainments

Plays, music, and dancing were by no means the only shows in town. There were jousts, tournaments, royal entries, religious processions, pageants in honor of newly installed civic officials or ambassadors arriving from abroad; wedding masques, court masques, and costumed entertainments known as "disguisings" or "mummings"; juggling acts, fortune-tellers, exhibitions of swordsmanship, mountebanks, folk healers, storytellers, magic shows; bearbaiting, bullbaiting, cockfighting, and other blood sports; folk festivals such as Maying, the Feast of Fools, Carnival, and Whitsun Ales. For several years, Elizabethan Londoners were delighted by a trained animal—Banks's Horse—that could, it was thought, do arithmetic and answer questions. And there was always the grim but compelling spectacle of public shaming, mutilation, and execution.

Most English towns had stocks and whipping posts. Drunks, fraudulent merchants, adulterers, and quarrelers could be placed in carts or mounted backward on asses and paraded through the streets for crowds to jeer and throw refuse at. Women accused of being scolds could be publicly muzzled by an iron device called a "brank" or tied to a cucking stool and dunked in the river. Convicted criminals could have their ears cut off, their noses slit, their foreheads branded. Public beheadings (generally reserved for the elite) and hangings were common. In the worst cases, felons were sentenced to be "hanged by the neck, and being alive cut down, and your privy members to be cut off, and your bowels to be taken out of your belly and there burned, you being alive."

Shakespeare occasionally takes note of these alternative entertainments: at the end of *Macbeth,* for example, with his enemies closing in on him, the doomed tyrant declares, "They have tied me to a stake. I cannot fly,/But bear-like I must fight the course" (5.7.1–2). The audience is reminded then that it is witnessing the human equivalent of a popular spectacle—a bear chained to a stake and attacked by fierce dogs—that they could have paid to watch at an arena near the Globe. And when, a few moments later, Macduff enters carrying Macbeth's head, the audience is seeing the theatrical equivalent of the execution of criminals and traitors that they could have also watched in the flesh, as it were, nearby. In a different key, the audiences who paid to see *A Midsummer Night's Dream* or *The Winter's Tale* got to enjoy the comic spectacle of a Maying and a Whitsun Pastoral, while the spectators of *The Tempest* could gawk at what the Folio list of characters calls a "salvage and deformed slave" and to enjoy an aristocratic magician's wedding masque in honor of his daughter.

An Elizabethan hanging.

The Enemies of the Stage

In 1624, a touring company of players arrived in Norwich and requested permission to perform. Permission was denied, but the municipal authorities, "in regard of the honorable respect which this City beareth to the right honorable the Lord Chamberlain," gave the players 20 shillings to get out of town. Throughout the sixteenth and early seventeenth centuries, there are many similar records of civic officials prohibiting performances and then, to appease a powerful patron, paying the actors to take their skills elsewhere. As early as the 1570s, there is evidence that the London authorities, while mindful of the players' influential protectors, were energetically trying to drive the theater out of the city.

Why should what we now regard as one of the undisputed glories of the age have aroused so much hostility? One answer, curiously enough, is traffic: plays drew large audiences—the public theaters could accommodate thousands—and residents objected to the crowds, the noise, and the crush of carriages. Other, more serious concerns were public health and crime. It was thought that numerous diseases, including the dreaded bubonic plague, were spread by noxious odors, and the packed playhouses were obvious breeding grounds for infection. (Patrons often tried to protect themselves by sniffing nosegays or stuffing cloves into their nostrils.) The large crowds drew pickpockets and other scoundrels. On one memorable afternoon, a pickpocket was caught in the act and tied for the duration of the play to one of the posts that held up the canopy above the stage.

The theater was, moreover, a well-known haunt of prostitutes and, it was alleged, a place where innocent maids were seduced and respectable matrons corrupted. It was darkly rumored that "chambers and secret places" adjoined the theater galleries, and in any case, taverns, disreputable inns, and whorehouses were close at hand.

There were other charges as well. Plays were performed in the afternoon and, therefore, drew people, especially the young, away from their work. They were schools of idleness, luring apprentices from their trades, law students from their studies, housewives from their kitchens, and potentially pious souls from the sober meditations to which they might otherwise devote themselves. Wasting their time and money on disreputable shows, citizens exposed themselves to sexual provocation and outright political sedition. Even when the content of plays was morally exemplary—and, of course, few plays were so gratifyingly high-minded—the theater itself, in the eyes of most mayors and aldermen, was inherently disorderly.

Syphilis victim in a tub. Frontispiece to the play *Cornelianum Dolium* (1638), possibly authored by Thomas Randolph. The tub inscription translates as "I sit on the throne of love, I suffer in the tub," and the banner as "Farewell O sexual pleasures and lusts."

The attack on the stage by civic officials was echoed and intensified by many of the age's moralists and religious leaders, especially those associated with Puritanism. While English Protestants earlier in the sixteenth century had attempted to counter the Catholic mystery cycles and saints' plays by mounting their own doctrinally correct dramas, by the century's end a fairly widespread consensus, even among those mildly sympathetic toward the theater, held that the stage and the pulpit were in tension with one another. After 1591, a ban on Sunday performances was strictly enforced, and in 1606, Parliament passed an act imposing a fine of £10 on any person who shall "in any stage-play, interlude, show, May-game, or pageant, jestingly or profanely speak or use the holy name of God, or of Christ Jesus, or of the Holy Ghost, or of the Trinity (which are not to be spoken but with fear and reverence)." If changes in the printed texts are a reliable indication, the players seem to have complied at least to some degree with the ruling. The Folio (1623) text of *Richard III*, for example, omits the Quarto's (1597) four uses of "zounds" (for "God's wounds"), along with a mention of "Christ's dear blood shed for our grievous sins"; "God's my judge" in *The Merchant of Venice* becomes "well I know"; "By Jesu" in *Henry V* becomes a very proper "I say"; and in all the plays, "God" from time to time metamorphoses to "Jove."

But for some of the theater's more extreme critics, these modest expurgations were tiny bandages on a gaping wound. In his huge book *Histriomastix* (1633), William Prynne regurgitates half a century of frenzied attacks on the "sinful, heathenish, lewd, ungodly Spectacles." In the eyes of Prynne and his fellow antitheatricalists, stage plays were part of a demonic tangle of obscene practices proliferating like a cancer in the body of society. It is "manifest to all men's judgments," he writes, that

> effeminate mixed dancing, dicing, stage-plays, lascivious pictures, wanton fashions, face-painting, health-drinking, long hair, love-locks, periwigs, women's curling, powdering and cutting of their hair, bonfires, New-year's gifts, May-games, amorous pastorals, lascivious effeminate music, excessive laughter, luxurious disorderly Christmas-keeping, mummeries . . . [are] wicked, unchristian pastimes.

Given the anxious emphasis on effeminacy, it is not surprising that denunciations of this kind obsessively focused on the use of boy actors to play the female parts. The enemies of the stage charged that theatrical transvestism excited illicit sexual desires, both heterosexual and homosexual.

Since cross-dressing violated a biblical prohibition (Deuteronomy 22:5), religious antitheatricalists attacked it as wicked regardless of its erotic charge; indeed, they often seemed to consider any act of impersonation as inherently wicked. In their view, the theater itself was Satan's domain. Thus a Cambridge scholar, John Greene, reports the sad fate of "a Christian woman" who went to the theater to see a play: "She entered in well and sound, but she returned and came forth possessed of the devil. Whereupon certain godly brethren demanded Satan how he durst be so bold, as to enter into her a Christian. Whereto he answered, that *he found her in his own house,* and therefore took possession of her as his own" (italic in original). When the "godly brethren" came to power in the mid-seventeenth century, with the overthrow of Charles I, they saw to it that the playhouses, temporarily shut down in 1642 at the onset of the Civil War, remained closed. The theater did not resume until the restoration of the monarchy in 1660.

Faced with enemies among civic officials and religious leaders, Elizabethan and Jacobean playing companies relied on the protection of their powerful patrons. As the liveried servants of aristocrats or of the monarch, the players could refute the charge that they were mere vagabonds, and they claimed, as a convenient legal fiction, that their public performances were necessary rehearsals in anticipation of those occasions when they would be called upon to entertain their noble masters. But harassment by the mayor and aldermen continued unabated, and the players were forced to build their theaters outside the immediate jurisdiction of the city authorities, either in the suburbs or in the areas known as the "liberties." A liberty was a piece of land within the City of London itself that was not directly subject to the authority of the lord mayor. The most significant of these from the point of view of the theater was the area near St. Paul's Cathedral called "the Blackfriars," where, until the dissolution of the monasteries in 1538, there had been a

Dominican monastery. It was here that in 1608 Shakespeare's company, then called the King's Men, built the indoor playhouse in which they performed during the winter months, reserving the open-air Globe in the suburb of Southwark for their summer performances.

Censorship and Regulation

In addition to those authorities who campaigned to shut down the theater, there were others whose task was to oversee, regulate, and censor it. Given the outright hostility of the former, the latter may have seemed to the London players equivocal allies rather than enemies. After all, plays that passed the censor were at least licensed to be performed and hence conceded to have some limited legitimacy. In April 1559, at the very start of her reign, Queen Elizabeth drafted a proposal that for the first time envisaged a system for the prior review and regulation of plays throughout her kingdom:

> The Queen's Majesty doth straightly forbid all manner interludes to be played either openly or privately, except the same be notified beforehand, and licensed within any city or town corporate, by the mayor or other chief officers of the same, and within any shire, by such as shall be lieutenants for the Queen's Majesty in the same shire, or by two of the Justices of Peace inhabiting within that part of the shire where any shall be played. . . . And for instruction to every of the said officers, her Majesty doth likewise charge every of them, as they will answer: that they permit none to be played wherein either matters of religion or of the governance of the estate of the commonweal shall be handled or treated upon, but by men of authority, learning and wisdom, nor to be handled before any audience, but of grave and discreet persons.

This proposal, which may not have been formally enacted, makes an important distinction between those who are entitled to address sensitive issues of religion and politics—authors "of authority, learning and wisdom" addressing audiences "of grave and discreet persons"—and those who are forbidden to do so.

The London public theater, with its playwrights who were the sons of glovers, shoemakers, and bricklayers and its audiences in which the privileged classes mingled with rowdy apprentices, masked women, and servants, was clearly not a place to which the government wished to grant freedom of expression. In 1581, the Master of the Revels, an official in the lord chamberlain's department whose role had hitherto been to provide entertainment at court, was given an expanded commission. Sir Edmund Tilney, the functionary who held the office, was authorized

> to warn, command, and appoint in all places within this our Realm of England, as well within franchises and liberties as without, all and every player or players with their playmakers, either belonging to any nobleman or otherwise . . . to appear before him with all such plays, tragedies, comedies, or shows as they shall in readiness or mean to set forth, and them to recite before our said Servant or his sufficient deputy, whom we ordain, appoint, and authorize by these presents of all such shows, plays, players, and playmakers, together with their playing places, to order and reform, authorize and put down, as shall be thought meet or unmeet unto himself or his said deputy in that behalf.

What emerged from this commission was in effect a national system of regulation and censorship. One of its consequences was to restrict virtually all licensed theater to the handful of authorized London-based playing companies. These companies would have to submit their plays for official scrutiny, but in return they received implicit, and on occasion explicit, protection against the continued fierce opposition of the local authorities. Plays reviewed and allowed by the Master of the Revels had been deemed fit to be performed before the monarch; how could mere aldermen legitimately claim that such plays should be banned as seditious?

The key question, of course, is how carefully the Master of the Revels scrutinized the plays brought before him either to hear or, more often from the 1590s onward, to peruse. What was Tilney, who served in the office until his death in 1610, or his successor, Sir George Buc, who served from 1610 to 1621, looking for? What did they insist be cut before they would release what was known as the "allowed copy," the only version licensed for performance? Unfortunately, the office books of the Master of the Revels in Shakespeare's time have been lost; what survives is a handful of scripts on which Tilney, Buc, and their assistants jotted their instructions. These suggest that the readings were rather painstaking, with careful attention paid to possible religious, political, and diplomatic repercussions. References, directly or strongly implied, to any living Christian prince or any important English nobleman, gentleman, or government official were particularly sensitive and likely to be struck. Renaissance political life was highly personalized; people in power were exceptionally alert to insult and zealously patrolled the boundaries of their prestige and reputation.

Moreover, the censors knew that audiences and readers were quite adept at applying theatrical representations distanced in time and space to their own world. At a time of riots against resident foreigners, Tilney read *Sir Thomas More,* a play in which Shakespeare probably had a hand, and instructed the players to cut scenes that, even though they were set in 1517, might have had an uncomfortable contemporary resonance. "Leave out the insurrection wholly," Tilney's note reads, "and the cause thereof and begin with Sir Thomas More at the Mayor's sessions, with a report afterwards of his good service done being sheriff of London upon a mutiny against the Lombards only by a short report and not otherwise at your own perils. E. Tilney." Of course, as Tilney knew perfectly well, most plays succeed precisely by mirroring, if only obliquely, their own times, but this particular reflection evidently seemed to him too dangerous or provocative.

The topical significance of a play depends in large measure on the particular moment in which it is performed and on certain features of the performance—for example, a striking resemblance between one of the characters and a well-known public figure—that the script itself will not necessarily disclose to us at this great distance or even to the censor at the time. Hence the Master of the Revels noted angrily of one play performed in 1632 that "there were diverse personated so naturally, both of lords and others of the court, that I took it ill." Hence, too, a play that was deemed allowable when it was first written and performed could return, like a nightmare, to haunt a different place and time. The most famous instance of such a return involves Shakespeare, for on the day before the Earl of Essex's attempted coup against Queen Elizabeth in 1601, someone paid the Lord Chamberlain's Men (the name of Shakespeare's company at the time) 40 shillings to revive their old play about the deposition and murder of Richard II. "I am Richard II," the queen declared. "Know ye not that?" However distressed she was by this performance, the queen significantly did not take out her wrath on the players: neither the playwright nor his company was punished, nor was the Master of the Revels criticized for allowing the play in the first place. It was Essex and several of his key supporters who lost their heads.

Evidence suggests that the Master of the Revels often regarded himself not as the strict censor of the theater but as its friendly guardian, charged with averting catastrophes. He was a bureaucrat concerned less with subversive ideas per se than with potential trouble. That is, there is no record of a dramatist being called to account for his heterodox beliefs; rather, plays were censored if they risked offending influential people, including important foreign allies, or if they threatened to cause public disorder by exacerbating religious or other controversies. The distinction is not a stable one, but it helps to explain the intellectual boldness, power, and freedom of a censored theater in a society in which the perceived enemies of the state were treated mercilessly. Shakespeare could have Lear articulate a searing indictment of social injustice—

> Robes and furred gowns hide all. Plate sin with gold,
> And the strong lance of justice hurtless breaks;
> Arm it in rags, a pygmy's straw does pierce it.
> (4.5.155–57)

—and evidently neither the Master of the Revels nor the courtiers in their robes and furred gowns protested. But when the Spanish ambassador complained about Thomas Middleton's anti-Spanish allegory *A Game at Chess,* performed at the Globe in 1624, the whole theater was shut down, the players were arrested, and the king professed to be furious at his official for licensing the play in the first place and allowing it to be performed for nine consecutive days.

In addition to the system for the licensing of plays for performance, there was also a system for the licensing of plays for publication. At the start of Shakespeare's career, such press licensing was the responsibility of the Court of High Commission, headed by the Archbishop of Canterbury and the Bishop of London. Their deputies, a panel of junior clerics, were supposed to review the manuscripts, granting licenses to those worthy of publication and rejecting any they deemed "heretical, seditious, or unseemly for Christian ears." Without a license, the Stationers' Company, the guild of the book trade, was not supposed to register a manuscript for publication. In practice, as various complaints and attempts to close loopholes attest, some playbooks were printed without a license. In 1607, the system was significantly revised when Sir George Buc began to license plays for the press. When Buc succeeded to the post of Master of the Revels in 1610, the powers to license plays for the stage and the page were vested in one man.

Theatrical Innovations

The theater continued to flourish under this system of regulation after Shakespeare's death; by the 1630s, as many as five playhouses were operating daily in London. When the theater reemerged after the eighteen-year hiatus imposed by Puritan rule, it quickly resumed its cultural importance, but not without a number of significant changes. Major innovations in staging resulted principally from Continental influences on the English artists who accompanied the court of Charles II into exile in France, where they supplied it with masques and other theatrical entertainments.

The institutional conditions and business practices of the two companies chartered by Charles after the Restoration in 1660 also differed from those of Shakespeare's theater. In place of the more collective practice of Shakespeare's company, the Restoration theaters were controlled by celebrated actor-managers who not only assigned themselves starring roles, in both comedy and tragedy, but also assumed sole responsibility for many business decisions, including the setting of their colleagues' salaries. At the same time, the power of the actor-manager, great as it was, was limited by the new importance of outside capital. No longer was the theater, with all of its properties from script to costumes, owned by the "sharers"—that is, by those actors who held shares in the joint-stock company. Instead, entrepreneurs would raise capital for increasingly fantastic sets and stage machinery that could cost as much as £3,000, an astronomical sum, for a single production. This investment, in turn, not only influenced the kinds of new plays written for the theater but helped to transform old plays that were revived, including Shakespeare's.

In his diary entry for August 24, 1661, Samuel Pepys notes that he has been "to the Opera, and there saw Hamlet, Prince of Denmark, done with scenes very well, but above all, Betterton did the prince's part beyond imagination." This is Thomas Betterton's first review, as it were, and it is typical of the enthusiasm he would inspire throughout his fifty-year career on the London stage. Pepys's brief and scattered remarks on the plays he voraciously attended in the 1660s are precious because they are among the few records from the period of concrete and immediate responses to theatrical performances. Modern readers might miss the significance of Pepys's phrase "done with scenes": this production of *Hamlet* was only the third play to use the movable sets first introduced to England by its producer, William Davenant. The central historical fact that makes the productions of this period so exciting is that public theater had been banned altogether for eighteen years until the Restoration of Charles II.

A brief discussion of theatrical developments in the Restoration period will enable us at least to glance longingly at a vast subject that lies outside the scope of this introduction: the rich performance history that extends from Shakespeare's time to our own, involving tens of thousands of productions and adaptations for theater, opera, Broadway musicals, and, of course, films. The scale of this history is vast in space as well as time: as early as 1607, there is a record of a *Hamlet* performed on board an English ship, HMS *Dragon,* off the coast of Sierra Leone, and troupes of English actors performed in the late sixteenth and early seventeenth centuries as far afield as Poland and Bohemia.

William Davenant, who claimed to be Shakespeare's bastard son, had become an expert on stage scenery while producing masques at the court of Charles I, and when the theaters reopened, he set to work on converting an indoor tennis court into a new kind of theater. He designed a broad open platform like that of the Elizabethan stage, but he replaced the relatively shallow space for "discoveries" (tableaux set up in an opening at the center of the stage, revealed by drawing back a curtain) and the "tiring-house" (the players' dressing room) behind this space with one expanded interior, framed by a proscenium arch, in which scenes could be displayed. These elaborately painted scenes could be moved on and off, using grooves on the floor. The perspectival effect for a spectator of one central painted panel with two "wings" on either side was that of three sides of a room. This effect anticipated that of the familiar "picture frame" stage, developed fully in the nineteenth century, and began a subtle shift in theater away from the elaborate verbal descriptions that are so central to Shakespeare and toward the evocative visual poetry of the set designer's art.

Another convention of Shakespeare's stage, the use of boy actors for female roles, gave way to the more complete illusion of women playing women's parts. The king issued a decree in 1662 forcefully permitting, if not requiring, the use of actresses. The royal decree is couched in the language of social and moral reform: the introduction of actresses will require the "reformation" of scurrilous and profane passages in plays, and this, in turn, will help forestall some of the objections that shut the theaters down in 1642. In reality, male theater audiences, composed of a narrower range of courtiers and aristocrats than in Shakespeare's time, met this intended reform with the assumption that the new actresses were fair game sexually; most actresses (with the partial exception of those who married male members of their troupes) were regarded as, or actually became, whores. But despite the social stigma and the fact that their salaries were predictably lower than those of their male counterparts, the stage saw some formidable female stars by the 1680s.

The first recorded appearance of an actress was that of a Desdemona in December 1660. Betterton's Ophelia in 1661 was Mary Saunderson (c. 1637–1712), who became Mrs. Betterton a year later. The most famous Ophelia of the period was Susanna Mountfort, who appeared in that role for the first time at the age of fifteen in 1705. The performance by Mountfort that became legendary occurred in 1720, after a disappointment in love, or so it was said, had driven her mad. Hearing that *Hamlet* was being performed, Mountfort escaped from her keepers and reached the theater, where she concealed herself until the scene in which Ophelia enters in her state of insanity. At this point, Mountfort rushed onto the stage and, in the words of a contemporary, "was in truth Ophelia herself, to the amazement of the performers and the astonishment of the audience."

That the character Ophelia became increasingly and decisively identified with the mad scene owes something to this occurrence, but it is also a consequence of the text used for Restoration performances of *Hamlet.* Having received the performance rights to a good number of Shakespeare's plays, Davenant altered them for the stage in the 1660s, and many of these acting versions remained in use for generations. In the case of *Hamlet,* neither Davenant nor his successors did what they so often did with other plays by Shakespeare—that is, alter the plot radically and interpolate other material. But many of the lines were cut or "improved." The cuts included most of Ophelia's sane speeches, such as her spirited retort to Laertes' moralizing; what remained made her part almost entirely an emblem of "female love melancholy."

Thomas Betterton (1635–1710), the prototype of the actor-manager, who would be the dominant figure in Shakespeare interpretation and in the theater generally through

The Spanish Tragedie:
OR,
Hieronimo is mad againe.

Containing the lamentable end of *Don Horatio*, and *Belimperia*; with the pittifull death of *Hieronimo*.

Newly corrected, amended, and enlarged with new Additions of the *Painters* part, and others, as it hath of late been diuers times acted.

LONDON,
Printed by W. White, for I. White and T. Langley, and are to be sold at their Shop ouer against the Sarazens head without New-gate. 1615.

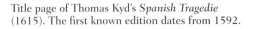

Title page of Thomas Kyd's *Spanish Tragedie* (1615). The first known edition dates from 1592.

the nineteenth century, made Hamlet his premier role. A contemporary who saw his last performance in the part (at the age of seventy-four, a rather old Prince of Denmark) wrote that to *read* Shakespeare's play was to encounter "dry, incoherent, & broken sentences," but that to see Betterton was to "prove" that the play was written "correctly." Spectators especially admired his reaction to the Ghost's appearance in the Queen's bedchamber: "his Countenance . . . thro' the violent and sudden Emotions of Amazement and Horror, turn[ed] instantly on the Sight of his fathers Spirit, as pale as his Neckcloath, when every Article of his Body seem's affected with a Tremor inexpressible." A piece of stage business in this scene, Betterton's upsetting his chair on the Ghost's entrance, became so thoroughly identified with the part that later productions were censured if the actor left it out. This business could very well have been handed down from Richard Burbage, the star of Shakespeare's original production, for Davenant, who had coached Betterton in the role, had known the performances of Joseph Taylor, who had succeeded Burbage in it. It is strangely gratifying to notice that Hamlets on stage and screen still occasionally upset their chairs.

Shakespeare's Life and Art

Playwrights, even hugely successful playwrights, were not ordinarily the objects of popular curiosity in early modern England, and few personal documents survive from Shakespeare's life of the kind that usually give the biographies of artists their appeal: no diary, no letters, private or public, no accounts of his childhood, almost no contemporary gossip, no scandals. Shakespeare's exact contemporary, the great playwright Christopher Marlowe, lived a mere twenty-nine years—he was murdered in 1593—but he left behind tantalizing glimpses of himself in police documents, the memos of high-ranking government officials, and detailed denunciations by sinister double agents. Ben Jonson recorded his opinions and his reading in a remarkable published notebook, *Timber; or, Discoveries Made upon Men and Matter,* and he also shared his views of the world (including some criticisms of his fellow playwright Shakespeare) with a Scottish poet, William Drummond of Hawthornden, who had the wit to jot them down for posterity. From Shakespeare, there is nothing comparable, not even a book with his name scribbled on the cover and a few marginal notes such as we have for Jonson, let alone working notebooks.

Yet Elizabethan England was a record-keeping society, and centuries of archival labor have turned up a substantial number of traces of its greatest playwright and his family. By themselves the traces would have relatively little interest, but in the light of Shakespeare's plays and poems, they have come to seem like precious relics and manage to achieve a considerable resonance.

Shakespeare's Family

William Shakespeare's grandfather Richard farmed land by the village of Snitterfield, near the small, pleasant market town of Stratford-upon-Avon, about 96 miles northwest of London. The playwright's father, John, moved in the mid-sixteenth century to Stratford, where he became a successful glover, landowner, moneylender, and dealer in wool and other agricultural goods. In or about 1557, he married Mary Arden, the daughter of a prosperous and well-connected farmer from the same area, Robert Arden of Wilmcote.

John Shakespeare was evidently highly esteemed by his fellow townspeople, for he held a series of important posts in local government. In 1556, he was appointed ale taster, an office reserved for "able persons and discreet," in 1558 was sworn in as a constable, and in 1561 was elected as one of the town's fourteen burgesses. As burgess, John served as one of the two chamberlains, responsible for administering borough property and revenues. In 1567, he was elected bailiff, Stratford's highest elective office and the equivalent of mayor. Although John Shakespeare signed all official documents with a cross or other sign, it is likely, but not certain, that he knew how to read and write. Mary, who also signed documents only with her mark, is less likely to have been literate.

According to the parish registers, which recorded baptisms and burials, the Shakespeares had eight children, four daughters and four sons, beginning with a daughter Joan born in 1558. A second daughter, Margaret, was born in December 1562 and died a few months later. William Shakespeare ("Gulielmus, filius Johannes Shakespeare"), their first son, was baptized on April 26, 1564. Since there was usually a few days' lapse between birth and baptism, it is conventional to celebrate Shakespeare's birthday on April 23, which happens to coincide with the feast of St. George, England's patron saint, and with the day of Shakespeare's death fifty-two years later.

William Shakespeare had three younger brothers, Gilbert, Richard, and Edmund, and two younger sisters, Joan and Anne. (It was often the custom to recycle a name, so the firstborn Joan must have died before the birth in 1569 of another daughter

"Southeast Prospect of Stratford-upon-Avon, 1746." From *The Gentleman's Magazine* (December 1792).

christened Joan, the only one of the girls to survive childhood.) Gilbert, who died in his forty-fifth year in 1612, is described in legal records as a Stratford haberdasher; Edmund followed William to London and became a professional actor, but evidently of no particular repute. He was only twenty-eight when he died in 1607 and was given an expensive funeral, perhaps paid for by his successful older brother.

At the high point of his public career, John Shakespeare, the father of this substantial family, applied to the Herald's College for a coat of arms, which would have marked his (and his family's) elevation from the ranks of substantial middle-class citizenry to that of the gentry. But the application went nowhere, for soon after he initiated what would have been a costly petitioning process, John apparently fell on hard times. The decline must have begun when William was still living at home, a boy of twelve or thirteen. From 1576 onward, John Shakespeare stopped attending council meetings. He became caught up in costly lawsuits, started mortgaging his land, and incurred substantial debts. In 1586, he was finally replaced on the council; in 1592, he was one of nine Stratford men listed as absenting themselves from church out of fear of being arrested for debt.

The reason for the reversal in John Shakespeare's fortunes is unknown. Some have speculated that it may have stemmed from adherence to Catholicism, since those who remained loyal to the old faith were subject to increasingly vigorous and costly discrimination. But if John Shakespeare was a Catholic, as seems quite possible, it would not necessarily explain his decline, since other Catholics (and Puritans) in Elizabethan Stratford and elsewhere managed to hold on to their offices. In any case, his fall from prosperity and local power, whatever its cause, was not absolute. In 1601, the last year of his life, his name was included among those qualified to speak on behalf of Stratford's rights. And he was by that time entitled to bear a coat of arms, for in 1596, some twenty years after the application to the Herald's office had been initiated, it was successfully renewed. There is no record of who paid for the bureaucratic procedures that made the grant possible, but it is likely to have been John's oldest son William, by that time a highly successful London playwright.

Education

Stratford was a small provincial town, but it had long been the site of an excellent free school, originally established by the Church in the thirteenth century. The main purpose of such schools in the Middle Ages had been to train prospective clerics; since many aristocrats could neither read nor write, literacy by itself conferred no special distinction and was not routinely viewed as desirable. But the situation began to change markedly in the sixteenth century. Protestantism placed a far greater emphasis upon lay literacy: for the sake of salvation, it was crucially important to be intimately acquainted with the Holy Book, and printing made that book readily available. Schools became less strictly bound up with training for the Church and more linked to the general acquisition of "literature," in the sense both of literacy and of cultural knowledge. In keeping with this new emphasis on reading and with humanist educational reform, the school was reorganized during the reign of Edward VI (1547–53). School records from the period have not survived, but it is almost certain that William Shakespeare attended the King's New School, as it was renamed in Edward's honor.

Scholars have painstakingly reconstructed the curriculum of schools of this kind and have even turned up the names and rather impressive credentials of the schoolmasters who taught there when Shakespeare was a student. (Shakespeare's principal teacher was Thomas Jenkins, an Oxford graduate, who received £20 a year and a rent-free house.) A child's education in Elizabethan England began at age four or five with two years at what was called the "petty school," attached to the main grammar school. The little scholars carried a "hornbook," a sheet of paper or parchment framed in wood and covered, for protection, with a transparent layer of horn. On the paper was written

The Cholmondeley sisters, c. 1600–10. This striking image brings to mind Shakespeare's fascination with twinship, both identical (notably in *The Comedy of Errors*) and fraternal (in *Twelfth Night*).

the alphabet and the Lord's Prayer, which were reproduced as well in the slightly more advanced *ABC with the Catechism*, a combination primer and rudimentary religious guide.

After students demonstrated some ability to read, the boys could go on, at about age seven, to the grammar school. Shakespeare's images of the experience are not particularly cheerful. In his famous account of the Seven Ages of Man, Jaques in *As You Like It* describes

> the whining schoolboy with his satchel
> And shining morning face, creeping like snail
> Unwillingly to school.
>
> (2.7.144–46)

The schoolboy would have crept quite early: the day began at 6:00 A.M. in summer and 7:00 A.M. in winter and continued until 5:00 P.M., with very few breaks or holidays.

At the core of the curriculum was the study of Latin, the mastery of which was in effect a prolonged male puberty rite involving much discipline and pain as well as pleasure. A late sixteenth-century Dutchman (whose name fittingly was Batty) proposed that God had created the human buttocks so that they could be severely beaten without risking permanent injury. Such thoughts dominated the pedagogy of the age, so that even an able young scholar, as we might imagine Shakespeare to have been, could scarcely have escaped recurrent flogging.

Shakespeare evidently reaped some rewards for the miseries he probably endured: his works are laced with echoes of many of the great Latin texts taught in grammar schools. One of his earliest comedies, *The Comedy of Errors*, is a brilliant variation on a theme by the Roman playwright Plautus, whom Elizabethan schoolchildren often performed as well as read; and one of his earliest tragedies, *Titus Andronicus*, is heavily indebted to Seneca. These are among the most visible of the classical influences that are often more subtly and pervasively interfused in Shakespeare's works. He seems to have had a particular fondness for *Aesop's Fables*, Apuleius's *Golden Ass*, and above all Ovid's *Metamorphoses*. His learned contemporary Ben Jonson remarked that Shakespeare had "small Latin and less Greek," but from this distance what is striking is not the limits of Shakespeare's learning but rather the unpretentious ease, intelligence, and gusto with which he draws upon what he must have first encountered as laborious study.

Traces of a Life

In November 1582, William Shakespeare, at the age of eighteen, married twenty-six-year-old Anne Hathaway, who came from the village of Shottery, near Stratford. Their first daughter, Susanna, was baptized six months later. This circumstance, along with the fact that Anne was eight years Will's senior, has given rise to a mountain of speculation, all the more lurid precisely because there is no further evidence. Shakespeare depicts in several plays situations in which marriage is precipitated by a pregnancy, but he also registers, in *Measure for Measure* (1.2.125ff.), the Elizabethan belief that a "true contract" of marriage could be legitimately made and then consummated simply by the mutual vows of the couple in the presence of witnesses.

On February 2, 1585, the twins Hamnet and Judith Shakespeare were baptized in Stratford. Hamnet died at the age of eleven, when his father was already living for much of the year in London as a successful playwright. These are Shakespeare's only known children, although the playwright and impressario William Davenant in the mid-seventeenth century claimed to be his bastard son. Since people did not ordinarily advertise their illegitimacy, the claim, though impossible to verify, at least suggests the unusual strength of the Shakespeare's posthumous reputation.

William Shakespeare's father, John, died in 1601; his mother died seven years later. They would have had the satisfaction of witnessing their eldest son's prosperity, and not only from a distance, for in 1597 William purchased New Place, the second largest house in Stratford. In 1607, the playwright's daughter Susanna married a successful and well-known physician, John Hall. The next year, the Halls had a daughter, Elizabeth, Shakespeare's first grandchild. In 1616, the year of Shakespeare's death, his daughter Judith married a vintner, Thomas Quiney, with whom she had three children. Shakespeare's widow, Anne, died in 1623, at the age of sixty-seven. His first-born, Susanna, died at the age of sixty-six in 1649, the year that King Charles I was beheaded by the parliamentary army. Judith lived through Cromwell's Protectorate and on to the Restoration of the monarchy; she died in February 1662, at the age of seventy-seven. By the end of the century, the line of Shakespeare's direct heirs was extinct.

Patient digging in the archives has turned up other traces of Shakespeare's life as a family man and a man of means: assessments, small fines, real-estate deeds, minor actions in court to collect debts. In addition to his fine Stratford house and a large garden and cottage facing it, Shakespeare bought substantial parcels of land in the vicinity. When in *The Tempest* the wedding celebration conjures up a vision of "barns and garners never empty," Shakespeare could have been glancing at what the legal documents record as his own "tithes of corn, grain, blade, and hay" in the fields near Stratford. At some point after 1610, Shakespeare seems to have begun to shift his attention from the London stage to his Stratford properties, although the term "retirement" implies a more decisive and definitive break than appears to have been the case. By 1613, when the Globe Theatre burned down during a performance of *All Is True* (*Henry VIII*), Shakespeare was probably residing for the most part in Stratford, but he retained his financial interest in the rebuilt playhouse and probably continued to have some links to his theatrical colleagues. Still, by this point, his career as a playwright was substantially over. Legal documents from his last years show his main concern to be the protection of his real-estate interests in Stratford.

Half a century after Shakespeare's death, a Stratford vicar and physician, John Ward, noted in his diary that Shakespeare and his fellow poets Michael Drayton and Ben Jonson "had a merry meeting, and it seems drank too hard, for Shakespeare died of a fever there contracted." It is not inconceivable that Shakespeare's last illness was somehow linked, if only coincidentally, to the festivities on the occasion of the wedding in February 1616 of his daughter Judith (who was still alive when Ward made his diary entry). In any case, on March 25, 1616, Shakespeare revised his will, and on April 23 he died. Two days later, he was buried in the chancel of Holy Trinity Church beneath a stone bearing an epitaph he is said to have devised:

> Good friend for Jesus' sake forbear,
> To dig the dust enclosed here:
> Blest be the man that spares these stones,
> And curst be he that moves my bones.

The verses are hardly among Shakespeare's finest, but they seem to have been effective: though bones were routinely dug up to make room for others—a fate imagined with unforgettable intensity in the graveyard scene in *Hamlet*—his own remains were undisturbed. Like other vestiges of sixteenth- and early seventeenth-century Stratford, Shakespeare's grave has for centuries been the object of a tourist industry that borders on a religious cult.

Shakespeare's will has been examined with an intensity befitting this cult; every provision and formulaic phrase, no matter how minor or conventional, has borne a heavy weight of interpretation, none more so than the bequest to his wife, Anne, of only "my second-best bed." Scholars have pointed out that Anne would in any case have been provided for by custom and that the terms are not necessarily a deliberate slight, but the absence of the customary words "my loving wife" or "my well-beloved wife" is difficult to ignore.

Portrait of the Playwright as Young Provincial

The great problem with the surviving traces of Shakespeare's life is not that they are few but that they are dull. Christopher Marlowe was a double or triple agent, accused of brawling, sodomy, and atheism. Ben Jonson, who somehow clambered up from bricklayer's apprentice to classical scholar, served in the army in Flanders, killed a fellow actor in a duel, converted to Catholicism in prison in 1598, and returned to the Church of England in 1610. Provincial real-estate investments and the second-best bed cannot compete with such adventurous lives. Indeed, the relative ordinariness of Shakespeare's social background and life has contributed to a persistent current of speculation that the glover's son from Stratford-upon-Avon was not in fact the author of the plays attributed to him.

The anti-Stratfordians, as those who deny Shakespeare's authorship are sometimes called, almost always propose as the real author someone who came from a higher social class and received a more prestigious education. Francis Bacon, the Earl of Oxford, the Earl of Southampton, even Queen Elizabeth, have been advanced, among many others, as glamorous candidates for the role of clandestine playwright. Several famous people, including Mark Twain and Sigmund Freud, have espoused these theories, though very few scholars have joined them. Since Shakespeare was quite well-known in his own time as the author of the plays that bear his name, there would need to have been an extraordinary conspiracy to conceal the identity of the real master who (the theory goes) disdained to appear in the vulgarity of print or on the public stage. Like many conspiracy theories, the extreme implausibility of this one only seems to increase the fervent conviction of its advocates.

To the charge that a middle-class author from a small town could not have imagined the lives of kings and nobles, one can respond by citing the exceptional qualities that Ben Jonson praised in Shakespeare: "excellent *Phantsie*; brave notions, and gentle expressions." Even in ordinary mortals, the human imagination is a strange faculty; in Shakespeare, it seems to have been uncannily powerful, working its mysterious, transforming effects on everything it touched. His imagination was intensely engaged by what he found in books. He seems throughout his life to have been an intense, voracious reader, and it is fascinating to witness his creative encounters with Raphael Holinshed's *Chronicles of England, Scotlande, and Irelande*, Plutarch's *Lives of the Noble Grecians and Romans*, Ovid's *Metamorphoses*, Montaigne's *Essays*, and the Bible, to name only some of his favorite books. But books were clearly not the only objects of Shakespeare's attention; like most artists, he drew upon the whole range of his life experiences.

To integrate some of the probable circumstances of Shakespeare's early years with the particular shape of the theatrical imagination associated with his name, let us indulge briefly in the biographical daydreams that modern scholarship is supposed to have rendered forever obsolete. The vignettes that follow are conjectural, but they may suggest ways in which his life as we know it found its way into his art.

1. THE GOWN OF OFFICE

Shakespeare was a very young boy—not quite four years old—when the Stratford council elected his father, John, to a year's term as bailiff (the equivalent of mayor). The office, the town's highest, was attended with considerable ceremony. The bailiff and his deputy were entitled to appear in public in furred gowns, attended by leather-clad sergeants bearing maces before them. On Rogation Days (three days of prayer for the harvest, before Ascension Day), they would solemnly pace out the parish boundaries, and they would similarly walk in processions on market and fair days. On Sundays, the sergeants would accompany the bailiff to church, where he would sit with his wife in a front pew, and he would have a comparable seat of honor at sermons in the Guild Chapel.

Public deference was a matter of law as well as custom: any inhabitant who spoke disrespectfully to the bailiff or other town officer was subject to the penalty of three days and three nights in the stocks. Newcomers who sought employment—notably including traveling players who hoped to stage performances—were obliged to obtain the bailiff's permission. In the year that John Shakespeare held office, two such professional playing companies arrived in Stratford. They must have proceeded to the bailiff's house on Henley Street and presented the letters of recommendation, with wax seals, that showed that they were not vagabonds. They would have spoken with more than ordinary deference, since it was the bailiff who would decide whether they would be sent packing or—as was the case—allowed to post their bills announcing the performances. The first of these performances was usually free to all comers. The bailiff would have been expected to attend, for it was his privilege to determine the level of the reward to be paid out of the city coffers; he would, presumably, have been given one of the best seats in the guildhall, where a special stage had been erected. It is impossible to know whether John Shakespeare took his family to these plays, but his little boy would certainly have been aware of what was happening.

On a precocious child (or even, for that matter, on an ordinary child), the effect of his father's office and the elaborate rituals that attended it would be at least threefold. First, the ceremony would convey irresistibly the power of clothes (the gown of office) and of symbols (the mace) to transform identity as if by magic. Second, it would invest the father with immense power, distinction, and importance, awakening what we may call a lifelong dream of high station. And third, pulling slightly against this dream, it would provoke an odd feeling that the father's clothes do not fit, a perception that the office is not the same as the man, and an intimate, firsthand knowledge that when the robes are put off, their wearer is inevitably glimpsed in a far different, less exalted light.

2. PROGRESSES AND ELECTIONS

This second biographical fantasy, slightly less plausible than the first but still quite likely, involves a somewhat older child witnessing two characteristic forms of Elizabethan political ceremony, both of which were well known in the provinces. Queen Elizabeth was fond of going on what were known as "progresses," triumphant ceremonial journeys around her kingdom. Let us imagine that the young Shakespeare—say, in 1574, when he was ten years old—went with his kinsfolk or friends to Warwick, some 8 miles distant, to witness a progress. He would thus have participated as a spectator in an elaborate celebration of charismatic power: the courtiers in their gorgeous clothes, the nervous local officials bedecked in velvets and silks, and at the center, carried in a special litter like a painted idol, the bejeweled queen. Let us imagine further that in addition to being struck by the overwhelming force of this charisma, the boy was struck, too, by the way this force depended paradoxically on a sense that the queen was after all quite human. Elizabeth was in fact fond of calling attention to this peculiar tension between near-divinization and human ordinariness. For example, on this occasion at Warwick (and what follows really happened), after the trembling Recorder, presumably a local civil official of high standing, had made his official welcoming speech, Elizabeth offered her hand to him to be kissed: "Come hither, little Recorder," she said. "It was told me that you would be afraid to look upon me or to speak boldly; but you were not so afraid of me as I was of you; and I now thank you for putting me in mind of my duty." Of course, the charm of this royal "confession" of nervousness depends on its manifest implausibility: it is, in effect, a theatrical performance of humility by someone with immense confidence in her own histrionic power.

A royal progress was not the only form of spectacular political activity that Shakespeare might well have seen in the 1570s; it is still more likely that he would have witnessed parliamentary elections, particularly since his father was qualified to vote. In 1571, 1572, 1575, and 1578, there were shire elections conducted in nearby Warwick, elections that would certainly have attracted well over a thousand voters. These were often memorable events: large crowds came together; there was usually heavy drinking and carnivalesque festivity; and, at the same time, there was enacted, in a very different register from that of the monarchy, a ritual of empowerment. The people, those entitled to vote by virtue of meeting the property and residence requirements, chose their own representatives by giving their votes—their voices—to candidates for office. Here, legislative sovereignty was conferred not by God but by the consent of the community, a consent marked by shouts and applause.

Recent cultural historians have been so fascinated by the evident links between the spectacles of the absolutist monarchy and the theater that they have largely ignored the significance of this alternative public arena, one that generated intense excitement throughout the country. A child who was a spectator at a parliamentary election in the 1570s might well have found the occasion enormously compelling. It is striking, in any case, how often the adult Shakespeare returns to scenes of acclamation and mass consent, and striking, too, how much the theater depends on the soliciting of popular voices.

3. EXORCISMS

A third and final fantasy is even more speculative than the second and involves a controversial claim, which has long been hotly debated— that Shakespeare either was a secret Catholic or was at least raised in a Roman Catholic household in a time of official suspicion and persecution of recusancy. A late seventeenth-century Anglican clergyman, Richard Davies, jotted down in some notes on Shakespeare that "he died a papist." In a modern biographical study, E. A. J. Honigmann convincingly linked several of the schoolmasters who taught in Stratford at the time that Shakespeare would have been a pupil to a network of Catholic families in Lancashire with whom one "William Shakeshafte," possibly a young schoolmaster or player, was connected in the late 1570s or early 1580s.

Exorcism: Nicole Aubry in the cathedral at Laon, 1566.

Catholics in Elizabethan England were not free to practice their religion—any more than Protestants, in Catholic countries, were free to practice theirs—and the beleaguered faithful, beset with spies, came together only at great risk to confess and receive Communion from clandestine priests. Under the circumstances, although a substantial portion of the population may have retained a residual inward loyalty to the traditional faith, the vast majority fell away from outward Catholic practice. After all, the churches, great and small, were now the places of Protestant worship; the innumerable local saints' shrines and pilgrimage sites had been systematically destroyed; the monasteries and convents had been abolished, their property bestowed on royal favorites or sold at bargain prices to local magnates. Seeking a spectacular way to demonstrate the enduring spiritual power and authenticity of the Roman Church, the embattled Counter-Reformers turned to an ancient ritual: exorcism. Devils who possessed the souls of troubled men and women had once been exorcised in public, but now the healing rite had to be conducted in secret, in a barn in a remote village, perhaps, or in the attic of the secluded house of a Catholic loyalist. The danger for those who presided was enormous—brutal interrogation, torture, and an unspeakably horrible execution was the usual fate of the missionary priests who were caught—but the vivid demonstration of the Church's triumph over evil was sufficiently compelling to warrant the risk. For despite the lynx-eyed alertness of the Protestant authorities, Catholics staged a surprising number of clandestine exorcisms, many of which drew substantial crowds.

Accepting for the moment that William Shakespeare was raised in the recusant faith of his father and mother, let us imagine that one day in the early 1580s the young man attended an exorcism of which he had learned through the secret network of the faithful. Here, based on an eyewitness account of such an occasion recently transcribed by Gerard Kilroy, is what he is likely to have seen. At the center of a large room, emptied of other furniture in order to accommodate the many observers, stood a bed. A young woman sat on the bed, and a priest, in clerical vestments, stood over her, preaching a sermon. As he spoke, the woman began to writhe and scream. At first the screams, uttered by a deep voice that could not have been the woman's although it came from her mouth, were not intelligible. Gradually, the bystanders began to make out some of the words, blasphemous oaths—"God's wounds! God's nails!"—followed by menaces, spoken as if by a rabid Protestant: "Popish priests, popish priests, to prison with them and hang them, hang them, hang them." The exorcist held up the Eucharist over the writhing woman, and the screams intensified. "Who are you?" he demanded. "I am Modu," the voice replied. "Depart, Modu!" shouted the priest, bringing the consecrated wafer closer to the demoniac. When that did not succeed in driving the devil out, the priest advanced a chafing dish of fire and brimstone, provoking more shouting and cursing, and then displayed a painting of the Blessed Virgin. "I will not behold or see her," screamed the demonic voice.

The longer the scene continued, the more there was confirmation of the contested tenets of the Catholic faith. The devil admitted that the Virgin Mary was a particularly efficacious intercessor, that purgatory existed, that the wafer, consecrated by the priest, actually was the body and blood of Christ. The devil also revealed that all Protestants were his followers. Finally, under the irresistible force of spiritual compulsion, he agreed to depart forever from the body of the possessed. The departure was difficult: again and again the tormented young woman gaped, as if her mouth were being torn open. She screamed in pain, rose up only to be cast down violently by invisible hands, cried out that she was being drowned, and called upon Jesus and his mother to save her. Only when a sacred relic was placed directly on her flesh did the devil finally leave her.

There is no way to know if William Shakespeare actually witnessed such a scene, but if he did, he would have carried away several indelible impressions: an awareness that strange, alien voices may speak from within ordinary, familiar bodies; an intimation of the immense, cosmic forces that may impinge upon human life; a belief in the possibility of making contact with these forces and compelling them to speak. These are, after all, the foundation stones of great tragedy.

Many years later, Shakespeare brooded about demonic possession when he was writing his greatest tragedy about the presence of evil in the world, *King Lear*. "This is the foul fiend Flibbertigibbet," shouts the madman, Poor Tom; "The Prince of Darkness is a gentleman. Modo he's called, and Mahu" (3.4.103, 127–28). But Poor Tom in that play is faking it; he is actually the noble Edgar, who has disguised himself as a madman in order to escape persecution. Did Shakespeare as a teenager already think that the whole compelling event, in all of its metaphysical weirdness, was a powerful theatrical fraud, a piece of pious propaganda? Perhaps. But if so, he also clearly understood that evil exists, that persecution is real, and that illusion has an irresistible force.

These imaginary portraits of the playwright as a young provincial introduce us to several of the root conditions of the Elizabethan theater. Biographical fantasies, though entirely speculative and playful, are useful in part because some people have found it difficult to conceive how Shakespeare, with his provincial roots and his restricted range of experience, could have so rapidly and completely mastered the central imaginative themes of his times. Moreover, it is sometimes difficult to grasp how seeming abstractions such as market society, monarchical state, and theological doctrine were actually experienced directly by peculiar, distinct individuals. Shakespeare's plays were social and collective events, but they also bore the stamp of a particular artist, one endowed with a remarkable capacity to craft lifelike illusions (what Jonson called "excellent *Phantsie*"), a daring willingness to articulate an original vision ("brave notions"), and a loving command, at once precise and generous, of language ("gentle expressions"). These plays are stitched together from shared cultural experiences, inherited dramatic devices, and the pungent vernacular of the day, but we should not lose sight of the extent to which they articulate an intensely personal vision, a bold shaping of the available materials. Four centuries of feverish biographical speculation, much of it foolish, bears witness to a basic intuition: the richness of these plays, their inexhaustible openness, is the consequence not only of the auspicious collective conditions of the culture but also of someone's exceptional skill, inventiveness, and courage at taking those conditions and making of them something rich and strange.

The Theater of the Nation

What precisely are the collective conditions highlighted by these vignettes? First, the growth of Stratford-upon-Avon, the bustling market town of which John Shakespeare was bailiff, is a small version of a momentous sixteenth-century development that made Shakespeare's career possible: the making of an urban "public." That development obviously depended on adequate numbers; the period experienced a rapid and still unexplained growth in population. With it came an expansion and elaboration of market relations: markets became less periodic, more continuous, and more abstract—centered, that is, not on the familiar materiality of goods but on the liquidity of capital and goods. In practical terms, this meant that it was possible to conceive of the theater not only as festive entertainment for special events—lord mayor's pageants, visiting princes, seasonal festivals, and the like—but as a permanent, year-round business venture. The venture relied on ticket sales—it was an innovation of this period to have money advanced in the expectation of pleasure rather than offered to servants afterward as a reward—and counted on habitual playgoing with a concomitant demand for new plays from competing theater companies: "But that's all one, our play is done," sings Feste at the end of *Twelfth Night* and adds a glance toward the next afternoon's proceeds: "And we'll strive to please you every day" (5.1.394–95).

Second, the royal progress is an instance of what the anthropologist Clifford Geertz has called the Theater State, a state that manifests its power and meaning in exemplary public performances. Professional companies of players, like the one Shakespeare belonged to, understood well that they existed in relation to this Theater State and would, if they were fortunate, be called upon to serve it. Unlike Ben Jonson, Shakespeare did not, as far as we know, write royal entertainments on commission, but his plays were frequently performed before Queen Elizabeth and then before King James and Queen Anne, along with their courtiers and privileged guests. There are many fascinating glimpses of these performances, including a letter from Walter Cope to Robert Cecil, early in James's reign. "Burbage is come," Cope writes, referring to the leading actor of Shakespeare's company, "and says there is no new play that the queen hath not seen, but they have revived an old one, called *Love's Labours Lost,* which for wit and mirth he says will please her exceedingly. And this is appointed to be played tomorrow night at my Lord of Southampton's." Not only would such theatrical performances have given great pleasure—evidently, the queen had already exhausted the company's new offerings—but they conferred prestige upon those who commanded them and those in whose honor they were mounted.

Monarchical power in the period was deeply allied to spectacular manifestations of the ruler's glory and disciplinary authority. The symbology of power depended on regal magnificence, reward, punishment, and pardon, all of which were heavily theatricalized. Indeed, the conspicuous public display does not simply serve the interests of power; on many occasions in the period, power seemed to exist in order to make pageantry possible, as if the nation's identity were only fully realized in theatrical performance. It would be easy to exaggerate this perception: the subjects of Queen Elizabeth and King James were acutely aware of the distinction between shadow and substance. But they were fascinated by the political magic through which shadows could be taken for substantial realities, and the ruling elite was largely complicit in the formation and celebration of a charismatic absolutism. At the same time, the claims of the monarch who professes herself or himself to be not the representative of the nation but its embodiment were set against the counterclaims of the House of Commons. And this institution, too, as we have glimpsed, had its own theatrical rituals, centered on the crowd whose shouts of approval, in heavily stage-managed elections, chose the individuals who would stand for the polity and participate in deliberations held in a hall whose resemblance to a theater did not escape contemporary notice.

Third, illicit exorcism points both to the theatricality of much religious ritual in the late Middle Ages and the Renaissance and to the heightened possibility of secularization. English Protestant authorities banned the medieval mystery plays, along with pilgrimages and other rituals associated with holy shrines and sacred images, but playing companies could satisfy at least some of the popular longings and appropriate aspects of the social energy no longer allowed a theological outlet. That is, official attacks on certain Catholic practices made it more possible for the public theater to appropriate and exploit their allure. Hence, for example, the plays that celebrated the solemn miracle of the Catholic Mass were banned, along with the most elaborate church vestments, but in *The Winter's Tale* Dion can speak in awe of what he witnessed at Apollo's temple:

> I shall report,
> For most it caught me, the celestial habits—
> Methinks I so should term them—and the reverence
> Of the grave wearers. O, the sacrifice—
> How ceremonious, solemn, and unearthly
> It was i'th' off'ring!
>
> (3.1.3–8)

And at the play's end, the statue of the innocent mother breathes, comes to life, and embraces her child.

The theater in Shakespeare's time, then, is intimately bound up with all three crucial cultural formations: the market society, the theater state, and the Church. But it is important to note that the institution is not *identified* with any of them. The theater may be a market phenomenon, but it is repeatedly and bitterly attacked as the enemy of diligent, sober, productive economic activity. Civic authorities generally regarded the theater as a pestilential nuisance, a parasite on the body of the commonwealth, a temptation to students, apprentices, housewives, even respectable merchants to leave their serious business and lapse into idleness and waste. That waste, it might be argued, could be partially recuperated if it went for the glorification of a guild or the entertainment of an important dignitary, but the only group regularly profiting from the theater were the players and their disreputable associates.

For his part, Shakespeare made a handsome profit from the commodification of theatrical entertainment, but he seems never to have written "city comedy"—plays set in London and more or less explicitly concerned with market relations—and his characters express deep reservations about the power of money and commerce: "That smooth-faced gentleman, tickling commodity," Philip the Bastard observes in King John, "wins of all, / Of kings, of beggars, old men, young men, maids" (2.1.574, 570–71). We could argue that the smooth-faced gentleman is none other than Shakespeare himself, for his drama famously mingles kings and clowns, princesses and panderers. But the mingling is set against a romantic current of social conservatism: in Twelfth Night, the aristocratic heiress Olivia falls in love with someone who appears far beneath her in wealth and social station, but it is revealed that he (and his sister Viola) are of noble blood; in The Winter's Tale, Leontes' daughter Perdita is raised as a shepherdess, but her noble nature shines through her humble upbringing, and she marries the Prince of Bohemia; the strange island maiden with whom Ferdinand, son of the King of Naples, falls madly in love in The Tempest turns out to be the daughter of the rightful Duke of Milan. Shakespeare pushes against this conservative logic in All's Well That Ends Well, but the noble young Bertram violently resists the unequal match thrust upon him by the King, and the play's mood is notoriously uneasy.

Similarly, Shakespeare's theater may have been patronized and protected by the monarchy—after 1603, his company received a royal patent and was known as the King's Men—but it was by no means identical in its interests or its ethos. To be sure, Richard III and Macbeth incorporate aspects of royal propaganda, but given the realities of censorship, Shakespeare's plays, and the period's drama as a whole, are surprisingly independent and complex in their political vision. There is, in any case, a certain inherent tension between kings and player kings: Elizabeth and James may both have likened themselves to actors onstage, but they were loath to admit their dependence on the applause and money, freely given or freely withheld, of the audience. The charismatic monarch insists that the sacredness of authority resides in the body of the ruler, not in a costume that may be worn and then discarded by an actor. Kings are not representations of power—or do not admit that they are—but claim to be the thing itself. The government institution that was actually based on the idea of representation, Parliament, had theatrical elements, as we have seen, but it significantly excluded any audience from its deliberations. And Shakespeare's oblique portraits of parliamentary representatives, the tribunes Sicinius Velutus and Junius Brutus in Coriolanus, are anything but flattering.

Finally, the theater drew significant energy from the liturgy and rituals of the late medieval Church, but as Shakespeare's contemporaries widely remarked, the playhouse and the Church were scarcely natural allies. Not only did the theater represent a potential competitor to worship services, and not only did ministers rail against prostitution and other vices associated with playgoing, but theatrical representation itself, even when ostensibly pious, seemed to many to empty out whatever it presented, turning substance into mere show. The theater could and did use the period's deep currents of religious feeling, but it had to do so carefully and with an awareness of conflicting interests.

Shakespeare Comes to London

How did Shakespeare decide to turn his prodigious talents to the stage? When did he make his way to London? How did he get his start? To these and similar questions we have a mountain of speculation but no secure answers. There is not a single surviving record of Shakespeare's existence from 1585, when his twins were baptized in Stratford church, until 1592, when a rival London playwright made an envious remark about him. In the late seventeenth century, the delightfully eccentric collector of gossip John Aubrey was informed that prior to moving to London the young Shakespeare had been a schoolteacher in the country. Aubrey also recorded a story that Shakespeare had been a rather unusual apprentice butcher: "When he killed a calf, he would do it in a high style, and make a speech."

These and other legends, including one that has Shakespeare whipped for poaching game, fill the void until the unmistakable reference in Robert Greene's *Groats-Worth of Witte, Bought with a Million of Repentance* (1592). An inspired hack writer with a university education, a penchant for self-dramatization, a taste for wild living, and a strong streak of resentment, Greene, in his early thirties, was dying in poverty when he penned his last farewell, piously urging his fellow dramatists Christopher Marlowe, Thomas Nashe, and George Peele to abandon the wicked stage before they were brought low, as he had been, by a new arrival: "For there is an upstart crow, beautified with our feathers, that with his 'Tiger's heart wrapped in player's hide' supposes he is as well able to bombast out a blank verse as the best of you, and, being an absolute *Johannes Factotum,* is in his own conceit the only Shake-scene in a country." If "Shake-scene" is not enough to identify the object of his attack, Greene parodies a line from Shakespeare's early play *Richard Duke of York* (3 *Henry VI*): "O tiger's heart wrapped in a woman's hide!" (1.4.138). Greene is accusing Shakespeare of being an upstart, a plagiarist, an egomaniacal jack-of-all-trades—and, above all perhaps, a popular success.

By 1592, then, Shakespeare had already arrived on the highly competitive London theatrical scene. He was successful enough to be attacked by Greene and, a few months later, defended by Henry Chettle, another hack writer who had seen Greene's manuscript through the press (or, some scholars speculate, had written the attack himself and passed it off as the dying Greene's). Chettle expresses his regret that he did not suppress Greene's diatribe and spare Shakespeare "because myself have seen his demeanor no less civil than he excellent in the quality he professes." Besides, Chettle adds, "divers of worship have reported his uprightness of dealing, which argues his honesty and his facetious [polished] grace in writing that approves his art." "Divers of worship": not only was Shakespeare established as an accomplished writer and actor, but he evidently had aroused the attention and the approbation of several socially prominent people. In Elizabethan England, aristocratic patronage, with the money, protection, and prestige it alone could provide, was probably a professional writer's most important asset.

This patronage, or at least Shakespeare's quest for it, is most visible in the dedications in 1593 and 1594 of his narrative poems *Venus and Adonis* and *The Rape of Lucrece* to the young nobleman Henry Wriothesley, Earl of Southampton. It may be glimpsed as well, perhaps, in the sonnets, with their extraordinary adoration of the fair youth, though the identity of that youth has never been determined. What return Shakespeare got for his exquisite offerings is likewise unknown. We do know that among wits and gallants, the narrative poems won Shakespeare a fine reputation as an immensely stylish and accomplished poet. An amateur play performed at Cambridge University at the end of the sixteenth century, *The Return from Parnassus,* makes fun of this vogue, as a foolish character effusively declares, "I'll worship sweet Mr. Shakespeare, and to honour him will lay his *Venus and Adonis* under my pillow." Many readers at the time may have done so: the poem went through sixteen editions before 1640, more than any other work by Shakespeare.

Patronage was crucially important not only for individual artists but also for the actors, playwrights, and investors who pooled their resources to form professional theater companies. The public playhouses had enemies, especially among civic and religious authorities, who wished greatly to curb performances or to ban them altogether. An act of 1572 included players among those classified as vagabonds, threatening them, therefore, with the horrible punishments meted out to those regarded as economic parasites. The players' escape route was to be nominally enrolled as the servants of high-ranking noblemen. The legal fiction was that their public performances were a kind of rehearsal for the command performances before the patron or the monarch.

When Shakespeare came to London, presumably in the late 1580s, there were more than a dozen of these companies operating under the patronage of various aristocrats.

We do not know for which of these companies, several of which had toured in Stratford, he originally worked, nor whether he began, as legend has it, as a prompter's assistant and then graduated to acting and playwriting. Shakespeare is listed among the actors in Ben Jonson's *Every Man in His Humour* (performed in 1598) and *Sejanus* (performed in 1603), but we do not know for certain what roles he played, nor are there records of any of his other performances. Tradition has it that he played Adam in *As You Like It* and the Ghost in *Hamlet,* but he was clearly not one of the leading actors of the day.

By the 1590s, the number of playing companies in London had been considerably reduced, in part through competition and in part through legislative restriction. (In 1572, knights and gentry lost the privilege of patronizing a troupe of actors; in 1598, justices of the peace lost the power to authorize performances.) By the early years of the seventeenth century, there were usually only three companies competing against one another in any season, along with two children's companies, which were often successful at drawing audiences away from the public playhouses. Shakespeare may initially have been associated with the Earl of Leicester's company or with the company of Ferdinando Stanley, Lord Strange; both groups included actors with whom Shakespeare was later linked. Or he may have belonged to the Earl of Pembroke's Men, since there is evidence that they performed *The Taming of a Shrew* and a version of *Richard Duke of York (3 Henry VI).* At any event, by 1594, Shakespeare was a member of the Lord Chamberlain's Men, for his name, along with those of Will Kemp (or Kempe) and Richard Burbage, appears on a record of those "servants to the Lord Chamberlain" paid for performance at the royal palace at Greenwich on December 26 and 28. Shakespeare stayed with this company, which during the reign of King James received royal patronage and became the King's Men, for the rest of his career.

Many playwrights in Shakespeare's time worked freelance, moving from company to company as opportunities arose, collaborating on projects, adding scenes to old plays, scrambling from one enterprise to another. But certain playwrights, among them the most successful, wrote for a single company, often agreeing contractually to give that company exclusive rights to their theatrical works. Shakespeare seems to have followed such a pattern. For the Lord Chamberlain's Men, he wrote an average of two plays per year. His company initially performed in The Theatre, a playhouse built in 1576 by an entrepreneurial carpenter, James Burbage, the father of the actor Richard, who was to perform many of

Edward Alleyn (1566–1626). Artist unknown. Alleyn was the great tragic actor of the Lord Admiral's Men (the principal rival to Shakespeare's company). He was famous especially for playing the great Marlovian heroes.

Shakespeare's greatest roles. When in 1597 their lease on this playhouse expired, the Lord Chamberlain's Men passed through a difficult and legally perilous time, but they formed a joint-stock company, raising sufficient capital to lease a site and put up a splendid new playhouse in the suburb of Southwark, on the south bank of the Thames. This playhouse, the Globe, opened in 1599. Shakespeare is listed in the legal agreement as one of the principal investors; and when the company began to use Blackfriars as their indoor playhouse around 1609, he was a major shareholder in that theater as well. The Lord Chamberlain's Men, later the King's Men, dominated the theater scene, and the shares were quite valuable. Then as now, the theater was an extremely risky enterprise—most of those who wrote plays and performed in them made pathetically little money—but Shakespeare was a notable exception. The fine house in Stratford and the coat of arms he succeeded in acquiring were among the fruits of his multiple mastery, as actor, playwright, and investor in the London stage.

The Shakespearean Trajectory

Even though Shakespeare's England was in many ways a record-keeping society, no reliable record survives that details the performances, year by year, in the London theaters. Every play had to be licensed by a government official, the Master of the Revels, but the records kept by the relevant officials from 1579 to 1621, Sir Edmund Tilney and Sir George Buc, have not survived. A major theatrical entrepreneur, Philip Henslowe, kept a careful account of his expenditures, including what he paid for the scripts he commissioned, but unfortunately Henslowe's main business was with the Rose and the Fortune theaters and not with the playhouses at which Shakespeare's company performed. A comparable ledger must have been kept by the shareholders of the Lord Chamberlain's Men, but it has not survived. Shakespeare himself apparently did not undertake to preserve for posterity the sum of his writings, let alone to clarify the chronology of his works or specify which plays he wrote alone and which with collaborators.

The principal source for Shakespeare's works is the 1623 Folio volume of *Mr. William Shakespeares Comedies, Histories, & Tragedies*. Most scholars believe that the editors were careful to include only those plays for which they knew Shakespeare to be the main author. Their edition does not, however, include any of Shakespeare's nondramatic poems, and it omits two plays in which Shakespeare is now thought to have had a significant hand, *Pericles, Prince of Tyre* and *The Two Noble Kinsmen*, along with his probable contribution to the multiauthored *Sir Thomas More*. (A number of other plays were attributed to Shakespeare, both before and after his death, but scholars have not generally accepted any of these into the established canon.) Moreover, the Folio edition does not print the plays in chronological order, nor does it attempt to establish a chronology. We do not know how much time would normally have elapsed between the writing of a play and its first performance, nor, with

IF YOV KNOW NOT ME,

You know no body.

OR,

The troubles of Queene ELIZABETH.

LONDON.

Printed by *B.A.* and *T.F.* for *Nathanaell Butter.* 1 6 3 2.

Title page of Thomas Heywood's *If You Know Not Me, You Know No Body; or, The Troubles of Queene Elizabeth* (1632 ed.).

a few exceptions, do we know with any certainty the month or even the year of the first performance of any of Shakespeare's plays. The quarto editions of those plays that were published during Shakespeare's lifetime obviously establish a date by which we know a given play had been written, but they give us little more than an end point, because there was likely to be a substantial though indeterminate gap between the first performance of a play and its publication.

With enormous patience and ingenuity, however, scholars have gradually assembled a considerable archive of evidence, both external and internal, for dating the composition of the plays. Besides actual publication, the external evidence includes explicit reference to a play, a record of its performance, or (as in the case of Greene's attack on the "upstart crow") the quoting of a line, though all of these can be maddeningly ambiguous. The most important single piece of external evidence appears in 1598 in *Palladis Tamia,* a long book of jumbled reflections by Francis Meres that includes a survey of the contemporary literary scene. Meres finds that "the sweet, witty soul of Ovid lives in melliflous and honey-tongued Shakespeare, witness his *Venus and Adonis,* his *Lucrece,* his sugered Sonnets among his private friends, etc." Meres goes on to list Shakespeare's accomplishments as a playwright as well:

> As Plautus and Seneca are accounted the best for Comedy and Tragedy among the Latins: so Shakespeare among the English is the most excellent in both kinds for the stage; for Comedy, witness his *Gentlemen of Verona,* his *Errors,* his *Love labors lost,* his *Love labours won,* his *Midsummers night dream,* & his *Merchant of Venice:* for Tragedy his *Richard the 2, Richard the 3, Henry the 4, King John, Titus Andronicus* and his *Romeo and Juliet.*

Meres thus provides a date by which twelve of Shakespeare's plays had definitely appeared (including one, *Love's Labour's Won,* that appears to have been lost or that we know by a different title). Unfortunately, Meres provides no clues about the order of appearance of these plays, and there are no other comparable lists.

Faced with the limitations of the external evidence, scholars have turned to a bewildering array of internal evidence, ranging from datable sources and topical allusions on the one hand to evolving stylistic features (ratio of verse to prose, percentage of rhyme to blank verse, colloquialisms, use of extended similes, and the like) on the other. Thus, for example, a cluster of plays with a high percentage of rhymed verse may follow closely upon Shakespeare's writing of the rhymed poems *Venus and Adonis* and *The Rape of Lucrece* and, therefore, be datable to 1594–95. Similarly, vocabulary overlap probably indicates proximity in composition, so if four or five plays share relatively "rare" vocabulary, it is likely that they were written in roughly the same period. Again, there seems to be a pattern in Shakespeare's use of colloquialisms, with a steady increase from *As You Like It* (1599–1600) to *Coriolanus* (1608), followed in the late romances by a retreat from the colloquial.

More sophisticated computer analysis should provide further guidance in the future, even though the precise order of the plays, still very much in dispute, is never likely to be settled to universal satisfaction. Still, certain broad patterns are now widely accepted. These patterns can be readily grasped in the *Norton Shakespeare,* which presents the plays in the chronological order proposed by the Oxford editors.

Shakespeare began his career, probably in the early 1590s, by writing both comedies and history plays. The attack by Greene suggests that he made his mark with the series of theatrically vital but rather crude plays based on the foreign and domestic broils that erupted during the unhappy reign of the Lancastrian Henry VI. Modern readers and audiences are more likely to find the first sustained evidence of unusual power in *Richard III* (c. 1592), a play that combines a brilliantly conceived central character, a dazzling command of histrionic rhetoric, and an overarching moral vision of English history.

At virtually the same time that he was setting his stamp on the genre of the history play, Shakespeare was writing his first—or first surviving—comedies. Here, there are even fewer signs than in the histories of an apprenticeship: *The Comedy of Errors*, one of his early efforts in this genre, already displays a rare command of the resources of comedy: mistaken identity, madcap confusion, and the threat of disaster, giving way in the end to reconciliation, recovery, and love. Shakespeare's other comedies from the early 1590s, *The Taming of the Shrew*, *The Two Gentlemen of Verona*, and *Love's Labour's Lost*, are no less remarkable for their sophisticated variations on familiar comic themes, their inexhaustible rhetorical inventiveness, and their poignant intimation, in the midst of festive celebration, of loss.

Successful as are these early histories and comedies, and indicative of an extraordinary theatrical talent, Shakespeare's achievement in the later 1590s would still have been all but impossible to foresee. Starting with *A Midsummer Night's Dream* (c. 1595), Shakespeare wrote an unprecedented series of romantic comedies—*The Merchant of Venice, The Merry Wives of Windsor, Much Ado About Nothing, As You Like It,* and *Twelfth Night* (c. 1602)—whose poetic richness and emotional complexity remain unmatched. In the same period, he wrote a sequence of profoundly searching and ambitious history plays—*Richard II, 1* and *2 Henry IV,* and *Henry V*—which together explore the death throes of feudal England and the birth of the modern nation-state ruled by a charismatic monarch. Both the comedies and histories of this period are marked by their capaciousness, their ability to absorb characters who press up against the outermost boundaries of the genre: the comedy *Merchant of Venice* somehow contains the figure, at once nightmarish and poignant, of Shylock, while the *Henry IV* plays, with their somber vision of crisis in the family and the state, bring to the stage one of England's greatest comic characters, Falstaff.

If in the mid to late 1590s Shakespeare reached the summit of his art in two major genres, he also manifested a lively interest in a third. As early as 1593, he wrote the crudely violent tragedy *Titus Andronicus*, the first of several plays on themes from Roman history, and a year or two later, in *Richard II*, he created in the protagonist a figure who achieves by the play's close the stature of a tragic hero. In the same year that Shakespeare wrote the wonderfully farcical "Pyramus and Thisbe" scene in *A Midsummer Night's Dream*, he probably also wrote the deeply tragic realization of the same story in *Romeo and Juliet*. But once again, the lyric anguish of *Romeo and Juliet* and the tormented self-revelation of *Richard II*, extraordinary as they are, could not have led anyone to predict the next phase of Shakespeare's career, the great tragic dramas that poured forth in the early years of the seventeenth century: *Hamlet, Othello, King Lear, Macbeth, Antony and Cleopatra,* and *Coriolanus*. These plays, written from 1601 to 1607, seem to mark a major shift in sensibility, an existential and metaphysical darkening that many readers think must have originated in a deep personal anguish, perhaps caused by the death of Shakespeare's father, John, in 1601.

Whatever the truth of these speculations—and we have no direct, personal testimony either to support or to undermine them—there appears to have occurred in the same period a shift as well in Shakespeare's comic sensibility. The comedies written between 1601 and 1604, *Troilus and Cressida, All's Well That Ends Well,* and *Measure for Measure*, are sufficiently different from the earlier comedies—more biting in tone, more uneasy with comic conventions, more ruthlessly questioning of the values of the characters and the resolutions of the plots—to have led many twentieth-century scholars to classify them as "problem plays" or "dark comedies." This category has recently begun to fall out of favor, since Shakespeare criticism is perfectly happy to demonstrate that *all* of the plays are "problem plays." But there is another group of plays, among the last Shakespeare wrote, that continue to constitute a distinct category. *Pericles, Cymbeline, The Winter's Tale,* and *The Tempest*, written between 1608 and 1611, when the playwright had developed a remarkably fluid, dreamlike sense of plot and a poetic style that could veer, apparently effortlessly, from the tortured to the ineffably sweet, are known as the "romances." These plays share an interest in the moral and emotional life less of the adolescents who dominate the earlier comedies than of their parents. The romances are deeply concerned with patterns of loss and recovery, suffering and redemption, despair and renewal. They have seemed to many critics to constitute a deliberate conclusion to a career that began in histories and comedies and passed through the dark and tormented tragedies.

One effect of the practice of printing Shakespeare's plays in a reconstructed chronological order, as this edition does, is to produce a kind of authorial plot, a progress from youthful exuberance and a heroic grappling with history, through psychological anguish and radical doubt, to a mature serenity built upon an understanding of loss. The ordering of Shakespeare's "complete works" in this way reconstitutes the figure of the author as the beloved hero of his own, lived romance. There are numerous reasons to treat this romance with considerable skepticism: the precise order of the plays remains in dispute, the obsessions of the earliest plays crisscross with those of the last, the drama is a collaborative art form, and the relation between authorial consciousness and theatrical representation is murky. Yet a longing to identify Shakespeare's personal trajectory, to chart his psychic and spiritual as well as professional progress, is all but irresistible.

The Fetishism of Dress

Whatever the personal resonance of Shakespeare's own life, his art is deeply enmeshed in the collective hopes, fears, and fantasies of his time. For example, throughout his plays, Shakespeare draws heavily upon his culture's investment in costume, symbols of authority, visible signs of status—the fetishism of dress he must have witnessed from early childhood. Disguise in his drama is often assumed to be incredibly effective: when Henry V borrows a cloak, when Portia dresses in a jurist's robes, when Viola puts on a young man's suit, it is as if each has become unrecognizable, as if identity resided in clothing. At the end of *Twelfth Night,* even though Viola's true identity has been disclosed, Orsino continues to call her Cesario; he will do so, he says, until she resumes her maid's garments, for only then will she be transformed into a woman:

> Cesario, come—
> For so you shall be while you are a man;
> But when in other habits you are seen,
> Orsino's mistress, and his fancy's queen.
> (5.1.372–75)

The pinnacle of this fetishism of costume is the royal crown, for whose identity-conferring power men are willing to die, but the principle is everywhere from the filthy blanket that transforms Edgar into Poor Tom to the coxcomb that is the badge of the licensed fool. Antonio, wishing to express his utter contempt, spits on Shylocks' "Jewish gaberdine," as if the clothing were the essence of the man; Kent, pouring insults on the loathsome Oswald, calls him a "filthy worsted-stocking knave"; and innocent Innogen, learning that her husband has ordered her murder, thinks of herself as an expensive cast-off dress, destined to be ripped at the seams:

> Poor I am stale, a garment out of fashion,
> And for I am richer than to hang by th' walls
> I must be ripped. To pieces with me!
> (*Cymbeline* 3.4.50–52)

What can be said, thought, felt, in this culture seems deeply dependent on the clothes one wears—clothes that one is, in effect, *permitted* or *compelled* to wear, since there is little freedom in dress. Shakespearean drama occasionally represents something like such freedom: after all, Viola in *Twelfth Night* chooses to put off her "maiden weeds," as does Rosalind, who declares, "We'll have a swashing and a martial outside" (*As You Like It* 1.3.114). But these choices are characteristically made under the pressure of desperate circumstances, here shipwreck and exile. Part of the charm of Shakespeare's heroines is their ability to transform distress into an opportunity for self-fashioning, but the plays often suggest that there is less autonomy than meets the eye. What looks like an escape from cultural determinism may be only a deeper form of constraint. We may take, as an allegorical emblem of this constraint, the transformation of the beggar Christopher Sly into a nobleman in the playful Induction to *The Taming of the Shrew*. The transformation seems to suggest that you are free to make of yourself whatever you choose to be—the play begins with the drunken Sly indignantly claiming the dignity of his pedigree ("Look in the Chronicles" [Induction 1.3–4])—but in fact he is only the subject of the mischievous lord's experiment, designed to demonstrate the interwovenness of clothing and identity. "What think you," the lord asks his huntsman,

> if he were conveyed to bed,
> Wrapped in sweet clothes, rings put upon his fingers,
> A most delicious banquet by his bed,
> And brave attendants near him when he wakes—
> Would not the beggar then forget himself?

To which the huntsman replies, in words that underscore the powerlessness of the drunken beggar, "Believe me, lord, I think he cannot choose" (Induction 1.33–38).

Petruccio's taming of Katherine is similarly constructed around an imposition of identity, an imposition closely bound up with the right to wear certain articles of clothing. When the haberdasher arrives with a fashionable lady's hat, Petruccio refuses it over his wife's vehement objections: "This doth fit the time, / And gentlewomen wear such caps as these." "When you are gentle," Petruccio replies, "you shall have one, too, / And not till then" (4.3.69–72). At the play's close, Petruccio demonstrates his authority by commanding his tamed wife to throw down her cap: "Off with that bauble, throw it underfoot" (5.2.126). Here as elsewhere in Shakespeare, acts of robing and disrobing are intensely charged, a charge that culminates in the trappings of monarchy. When Richard II, in a scene that was probably censored from the stage as well as the printed text during the reign of Elizabeth, is divested of his crown and scepter, he experiences the loss as the eradication of his name, the symbolic melting away of his identity:

> Alack the heavy day,
> That I have worn so many winters out
> And know not now what name to call myself!
> O, that I were a mockery king of snow,
> Standing before the sun of Bolingbroke
> To melt myself away in water-drops!
> (4.1.247–52)

When Lear tears off his regal "lendings" in order to reduce himself to the nakedness of the Bedlam beggar, he is expressing not only his radical loss of social identity but the breakdown of his psychic order as well, expressing, therefore, his reduction to the condition of the "poor bare forked animal" that is the primal condition of undifferentiated existence. And when Cleopatra determines to kill herself in order to escape public humiliation in Rome, she magnificently affirms her essential being by arraying herself as she had once done to encounter Antony:

> Show me, my women, like a queen. Go fetch
> My best attires. I am again for Cydnus
> To meet Mark Antony.
> (5.2.223–25)

Such scenes are a remarkable intensification of the everyday symbolic practice of Renaissance English culture, its characteristically deep and knowing commitment to illusion: "I know perfectly well that the woman in her crown and jewels and gorgeous gown is an aging, irascible, and fallible mortal—she herself virtually admits as much—yet I profess that she is the Virgin Queen, timelessly beautiful, wise, and just." Shakespeare understood how close this willed illusion was to the spirit of the theater, to the actors' ability to work on what the chorus in *Henry V* calls the "imaginary forces" of the audience. But there is throughout Shakespeare's works a counterintuition that, while it does not exactly overturn this illusion, renders it poignant, vulnerable, fraught. The "masculine usurp'd attire" that is donned by Viola, Rosalind, Portia, Jessica, and other Shakespeare heroines alters what they can say and do, reveals important aspects of their character, and changes their destiny, but it is, all the same, not theirs and not all of who they are. They have, the plays insist, natures that are neither transformed nor altogether concealed by their dress: "Pray God defend me," exclaims the frightened Viola. "A little thing would make me tell them how much I lack of a man" (*Twelfth Night* 3.4.268–69).

The Paradoxes of Identity

The gap between costume and identity is not simply a matter of what women supposedly lack; virtually all of Shakespeare's major characters, men and women, convey the sense of both a *self-division* and an *inward expansion*. The belief in a complex inward realm beyond costumes and status is a striking inversion of the clothes cult: we know perfectly well that the characters have no inner lives apart from what we see on the stage, and yet we believe that they continue to exist when we do not see them, that they exist apart from their represented words and actions, that they have hidden dimensions. How is this conviction aroused and sustained? In part, it is the effect of what the characters themselves say: "My grief lies all within," Richard II tells Bolingbroke,

> And these external manner of laments
> Are merely shadows to the unseen grief
> That swells with silence in the tortured soul.
> (4.1.285–88)

Similarly, Hamlet, dismissing the significance of his outward garments, declares, "I have that within which passeth show— / These but the trappings and the suits of woe" (1.2.85–86). And the distinction between inward and outward is reinforced throughout this play and elsewhere by an unprecedented use of the aside and the soliloquy.

The soliloquy is a continual reminder in Shakespeare that the inner life is by no means transparent to one's surrounding world. Prince Hal seems open and easy with his mates in Eastcheap, but he has a hidden reservoir of disgust:

> I know you all, and will a while uphold
> The unyoked humour of your idleness.
> Yet herein will I imitate the sun,
> Who doth permit the base contagious clouds
> To smother up his beauty from the world,
> That when he please again to be himself,
> Being wanted he may be more wondered at
> By breaking through the foul and ugly mists
> Of vapours that did seem to strangle him.
> (*1 Henry IV* 1.2.173–81)

"When he please again to be himself": the line implies that identity is a matter of free choice—you decide how much of yourself you wish to disclose—but Shakespeare employs other devices that suggest more elusive and intractable layers of inwardness. There is a peculiar, recurrent lack of fit between costume and character, in fools as in princes, that is not simply a matter of disguise and disclosure. If Hal's true identity is partially "smothered" in the tavern, it is not completely revealed either in his soldier's armor or in his royal robes, nor do his asides reach the bedrock of unimpeachable self-understanding.

Identity in Shakespeare repeatedly slips away from the characters themselves, as it does from Richard II after the deposition scene and from Lear after he has given away his land and from Macbeth after he has gained the crown. The slippage does not mean that they retreat into silence; rather, they embark on an experimental, difficult fashioning of themselves and the world, most often through role-playing. "I cannot do it," says the deposed and imprisoned Richard II. "Yet I'll hammer it out" (5.5.5). This could serve as the motto for many Shakespearean characters: Viola becomes Cesario, Rosalind calls herself Ganymede, Kent becomes Caius, Edgar presents himself as Poor Tom, Hamlet plays the madman that he has partly become, Hal pretends that he is his father and a highwayman and Hotspur and even himself. Even in comedy, these ventures into alternate identities are rarely matters of choice; in tragedy, they are always undertaken under pressure and compulsion. And often enough it is not a matter of role-playing at all, but of a drastic transformation whose extreme emblem is the harrowing madness of Lear and of Leontes.

There is a moment in *Richard II* in which the deposed King asks for a mirror and then, after musing on his reflection, throws it to the ground. The shattering of the glass serves to remind us not only of the fragility of identity in Shakespeare but of its characteristic appearance in fragmentary mirror images. The plays continually generate alternative reflections, identities that intersect with, underscore, echo, or otherwise set off that of the principal character. Hence, Desdemona and Iago are not only important figures in Othello's world, they also seem to embody partially realized aspects of himself; Falstaff and Hotspur play a comparable role in relation to Prince Hal, Fortinbras and Horatio in relation to Hamlet, Gloucester and the Fool in relation to Lear, and so forth. In many of these plays, the complementary and contrasting characters figure in subplots, subtly interwoven with the play's main plot and illuminating its concerns. The note so conspicuously sounded by Fortinbras at the close of *Hamlet*—what the hero might have been, "had he been put on"—is heard repeatedly in Shakespeare and contributes to the overwhelming intensity, poignancy, and complexity of the characters. This is a world in which outward appearance is everything and nothing, in which individuation is at once sharply etched and continually blurred, in which the victims of fate are haunted by the ghosts of the possible, in which everything is simultaneously as it must be and as it need not have been.

Are these antinomies signs of a struggle between contradictory and irreconcilable perspectives in Shakespeare? In certain plays—notably, *Measure for Measure, All's Well That Ends Well, Coriolanus,* and *Troilus and Cressida*—the tension seems both high and entirely unresolved. But Shakespearean contradictions are more often reminiscent of the capacious spirit of Montaigne, who refused any systematic order that would betray his sense of reality. Thus, individual characters are immensely important in Shakespeare—he is justly celebrated for his unmatched skill in the invention of particular dramatic identities, marked with distinct speech patterns, manifested in social status, and confirmed by costume and gesture—but the principle of individuation is not the rock on which his theatrical art is founded. After the masks are stripped away, the pretenses exposed, the claims of the ego shattered, there is a mysterious remainder; as the shamed but irrepressible Paroles declares in *All's Well That Ends Well,* "Simply the thing I am / Shall make me live" (4.3.310–11). Again and again, the audience is made to sense a deeper energy, a source of power that at once discharges itself in individual characters and seems to sweep right through them.

The Poet of Nature

In *The Birth of Tragedy,* Nietzsche called a comparable source of energy that he found in Greek tragedy "Dionysos." But the god's name, conjuring up Bacchic frenzy, does not seem appropriate to Shakespeare. In the late seventeenth and eighteenth centuries, it was more plausibly called Nature: "The world must be peopled," says the delightful Benedick in *Much Ado About Nothing* (2.3.213–14), and there are frequent invocations elsewhere of the happy, generative power that brings couples together—

Jack shall have Jill,
Naught shall go ill,
the man shall have his mare again, and all shall be well.
(*A Midsummer Night's Dream* 3.3.45–47)

—and the melancholy, destructive power that brings all living things to the grave: "Golden lads and girls all must, / As chimney-sweepers, come to dust" (*Cymbeline* 4.2.263–64).

But the celebration of Shakespeare as a poet of nature—often coupled with an inane celebration of his supposedly "natural" (that is, untutored) genius—has its distinct limitations. For Shakespearean art brilliantly interrogates the "natural," refusing to take for granted precisely what the celebrants think is most secure. His comedies are endlessly inventive in showing that love is not simply natural: the playful hint of bestiality in the line quoted above, "the man shall have his mare again" (from a play in which the Queen of the Fairies falls in love with an ass-headed laborer), lightly unsettles the boundaries between the natural and the perverse. These boundaries are called into question throughout Shakespeare's work, from the cross-dressing and erotic crosscurrents that deliciously complicate the lives of the characters in *Twelfth Night* and *As You Like It* to the terrifying violence that wells up from the heart of the family in *King Lear* or from the sweet intimacy of sexual desire in *Othello*. Even the boundary between life and death is not secure, as the ghosts in *Julius Caesar, Hamlet,* and *Macbeth* attest, while the principle of natural death (given its most eloquent articulation by old Hamlet's murderer, Claudius!) is repeatedly tainted and disrupted.

Disrupted, too, is the idea of order that constantly makes its claim, most insistently in the history plays. Scholars have observed the presence in Shakespeare's works of the so-called Tudor myth—the ideological justification of the ruling dynasty as a restoration of national order after a cycle of tragic violence. The violence, Tudor apologists claimed, was divine punishment unleashed after the deposition of the anointed king, Richard II, for God will not tolerate violations of the sanctified order. Traces of this propaganda certainly exist in the histories—Shakespeare may, for all we know, have personally subscribed to its premises—but a closer scrutiny of his plays has disclosed so many ironic reservations and qualifications and subversions as to call into question any straightforward adherence to a political line. The plays manifest a profound fascination with the monarchy and with the ambitions of the aristocracy, but the fascination is never simply endorsement. There is always at least the hint of a slippage between the great figures, whether admirable or monstrous, who stand at the pinnacle of authority and the vast, miscellaneous mass of soldiers, scriveners, ostlers, poets, whores, gardeners, thieves, weavers, shepherds, country gentlemen, sturdy beggars, and the like who make up the commonwealth. And the idea of order, though eloquently articulated (most memorably by Ulysses in *Troilus and Cressida*), is always shadowed by a relentless spirit of irony.

The Play of Language

If neither the individual nor nature nor order will serve, can we find a single comprehensive name for the underlying force in Shakespeare's work? Certainly not. The work is too protean and capacious. But much of the energy that surges through this astonishing body of plays and poems is closely linked to the power of language. Shakespeare was the supreme product of a rhetorical culture, a culture steeped in the arts of persuasion and verbal expressiveness. In 1512, the great Dutch humanist Erasmus published a work called *De copia verborum* that taught its readers how to cultivate "copiousness," verbal richness, in discourse. (Erasmus obligingly provides, as a sample, a list of 144 different ways of saying "Thank you for your letter.") Recommended modes of variation include putting the subject of an argument into fictional form, as well as the use of synonym, substitution, paraphrase, metaphor, metonymy, synecdoche, hyperbole, diminution, and a host of other figures of speech. To change emotional tone, he suggests trying *ironia, interrogatio, admiratio, dubitatio, abominatio*—the possibilities seem infinite.

In Renaissance England, certain syntactic forms or patterns of words known as "figures" (also called "schemes") were shaped and repeated in order to confer beauty or heighten expressive power. Figures were usually known by their Greek and Latin names, though in an Elizabethan rhetorical manual, *The Arte of English Poesie,* George Puttenham made a valiant if short-lived attempt to give them English equivalents, such as *"Hyperbole,* or the Overreacher," *"Ironia,* or the Dry Mock," and *"Ploce,* or the Doubler." Those who received a grammar-school education throughout Europe at almost any point between the Roman Empire and the eighteenth century probably knew by heart the names of up to one hundred such figures, just as they knew by heart their multiplication tables. According to one scholar's count, Shakespeare knew and made use of about two hundred.

As certain grotesquely inflated Renaissance texts attest, lessons from *De copia verborum* and similar rhetorical guides could encourage mere prolixity and verbal self-display. But even though he shared his culture's delight in rhetorical complexity, Shakespeare always understood how to swoop from baroque sophistication to breathtaking simplicity. Moreover, he grasped early in his career how to use figures of speech, tone, and rhythm not only to provide emphasis and elegant variety but also to articulate the inner lives of his characters. Take, for example, these lines from *Othello,* where, as scholars have noted, Shakespeare deftly combines four common rhetorical figures— *anaphora, parison, isocolon,* and *epistrophe*—to depict with painful vividness Othello's psychological torment:

> By the world,
> I think my wife be honest, and think she is not.
> I think that thou art just, and think thou art not.
> I'll have some proof.
> (3.3.388–91)

Anaphora is simply the repetition of a word at the beginning of a sequence of sentences or clauses ("I/I"). *Parison* is the correspondence of word to word within adjacent sentences or clauses, either by direct repetition ("think/think") or by the matching of noun with noun, verb with verb ("wife/thou"; "be/art"). *Isocolon* gives exactly the same length to corresponding clauses ("and think she is not/think thou art not"), and *epistrophe* is the mirror image of *anaphora* in that it is the repetition of a word at the end of a sequence of sentences or clauses ("not/not"). Do we need to know the Greek names for these figures in order to grasp the effectiveness of Othello's lines? Of course not. But Shakespeare and his contemporaries, convinced that rhetoric provided the most natural and powerful means by which feelings could be conveyed to readers and listeners, were trained in an analytical language that helped at once to promote and to account for this effectiveness. In his 1593 edition of *The Garden of Eloquence,* Henry Peacham remarks that *epistrophe* "serveth to leave a word of importance in the end of a sentence, that it may the longer hold the sound in the mind of the hearer," and in *Directions for Speech and Style* (c. 1599), John Hoskins notes that *anaphora* "beats upon one thing to cause the quicker feeling in the audience."

Shakespeare also shared with his contemporaries a keen understanding of the ways that rhetorical devices could be used not only to express powerful feelings but to hide them: after all, the artist who created Othello also created Iago, Richard III, and Lady Macbeth. He could deftly skewer the rhetorical affectations of Polonius in *Hamlet* or the pedant Holophernes in *Love's Labour's Lost.* He could deploy stylistic variations to mark the boundaries not of different individuals but of different social realms; in *A Midsummer Night's Dream,* for example, the blank verse of Duke Theseus is played off against the rhymed couplets of the well-born young lovers, and both in turn contrast with the prose spoken by the artisans. At the same time that he thus marks boundaries between both individuals and groups, Shakespeare shows a remarkable ability to establish unifying patterns of imagery that knit together the diverse strands of his plot and suggest subtle links among characters who may be scarcely aware of how much they share with one another.

One of the hidden links in Shakespeare's own works is the frequent use he makes of a somewhat unusual rhetorical figure called *hendiadys*. An example from the Roman poet Virgil is the phrase *pateris libamus et auro,* "we drink from cups and gold" (*Georgics* 2.192). Rather than serving as an adjective or a dependent noun, as in "golden cups" or "cups of gold," the word "gold" serves as a substantive joined to another substantive, "cups," by a conjunction, "and." Shakespeare uses the figure over three hundred times in all, and since it does not appear in ancient or medieval lists of tropes and schemes and is treated only briefly by English rhetoricians, he may have come upon it directly in Virgil. *Hendiadys* literally means "one through two," though Shakespeare's versions often make us quickly, perhaps only subliminally, aware of the complexity of what ordinarily passes for straightforward perceptions. When Othello, in his suicide speech, invokes the memory of "a malignant and a turbaned Turk," the figure of speech at once associates enmity with cultural difference and keeps them slightly apart. And when Macbeth speaks of his "strange and self-abuse," the *hendiadys* seems briefly to hold both "strange" and "self" up for scrutiny. It would be foolish to make too much of any single feature in Shakespeare's varied and diverse creative achievement, and yet this curious rhetorical scheme has something of the quality of a fingerprint.

But all of his immense rhetorical gifts, though rich, beautiful, and supremely useful, do not adequately convey Shakespeare's relation to language, which is less strictly functional than a total immersion in the arts of persuasion may imply. An Erasmian admiration for copiousness cannot fully explain Shakespeare's astonishing vocabulary of some 25,000 words. (His closest rival among the great English poets of the period was John Milton, with about 12,000 words, and most major writers, let alone ordinary people, have much smaller vocabularies.) This immense word hoard, it is worth noting, was not the result of scanning a dictionary; in the late sixteenth century, there were no English dictionaries of the kind to which we are now accustomed. Shakespeare seems to have absorbed new words from virtually every discursive realm he ever encountered, and he experimented boldly and tirelessly with them. These experiments were facilitated by the very fact that dictionaries as we know them did not exist and by a flexibility in grammar, orthography, and diction that the more orderly, regularized English of the later seventeenth and eighteenth centuries suppressed.

Owing in part to the number of dialects in London, pronunciation was variable, and there were many opportunities for phonetic association between words: the words "bear," "barn," "bier," "bourne," "born," and "barne" could all sound like one another. Homonyms were given greater scope by the fact that the same word could be spelled so many different ways—Christopher Marlowe's name appears in the records as Marlowe, Marloe, Marlen, Marlyne, Merlin, Marley, Marlye, Morley, and Morle—and by the fact that a word's grammatical function could easily shift, from noun to verb, verb to adjective, and so forth. Since grammar and punctuation did not insist on relations of coordination and subordination, loose, nonsyntactic sentences were common, and etymologies were used to forge surprising or playful relations between distant words.

It would seem inherently risky for a popular playwright to employ a vocabulary so far in excess of what most mortals could possibly possess, but Shakespeare evidently counted on his audience's linguistic curiosity and adventurousness, just as he counted on its general and broad-based rhetorical competence. He was also usually careful to provide a context that in effect explained or translated his more arcane terms. For example, when Macbeth reflects with horror on his murderous hands, he shudderingly imagines that even the sea could not wash away the blood; on the contrary, his bloodstained hand, he says, "will rather / The multitudinous seas incarnadine." The meaning of the unfamiliar word "incarnadine" is explained by the next line: "Making the green one red" (2.2.59–61).

What is most striking is not the abstruseness or novelty of Shakespeare's language but its extraordinary vitality, a quality that the playwright seemed to pursue with a kind of passionate recklessness. Perhaps Samuel Johnson was looking in the right direction when he complained that the "quibble," or pun, was "the fatal Cleopatra for which

[Shakespeare] lost the world, and was content to lose it." For the power that continually discharges itself throughout the plays, at once constituting and unsettling everything it touches, is the polymorphous power of language, language that seems both costume and that which lies beneath the costume, personal identity and that which challenges the merely personal, nature and that which enables us to name nature and thereby distance ourselves from it.

Shakespeare's language has an overpowering exuberance and generosity that often resembles the experience of love. Consider, for example, Oberon's description in *A Midsummer Night's Dream* of the moment when he saw Cupid shoot his arrow at the fair vestal: "Thou rememb'rest," he asks Puck,

> Since once I sat upon a promontory
> And heard a mermaid on a dolphin's back
> Uttering such dulcet and harmonious breath
> That the rude sea grew civil at her song
> And certain stars shot madly from their spheres
> To hear the sea-maid's music?
>
> (2.1.148–54)

Here, Oberon's composition of place, lightly alluding to a classical emblem, is infused with a fantastically lush verbal brilliance. This brilliance, the result of masterful alliterative and rhythmical technique, seems gratuitous—that is, it does not advance the plot, but rather exhibits a capacity for display and self-delight that extends from the fairies to the playwright who has created them. The rich music of Oberon's words imitates the "dulcet and harmonious breath" he is intent on recalling, breath that has, in his account, an oddly contradictory effect: it is at once a principle of order, so that the rude sea is becalmed like a lower-class mob made civil by a skilled orator, and a principle of disorder, so that celestial bodies in their fixed spheres are thrown into mad confusion. And this contradictory effect, so intimately bound up with an inexplicable, supererogatory, and intensely erotic verbal magic, is a key to *A Midsummer Night's Dream*, with its exquisite blend of confusion and discipline, lunacy and hierarchical ceremony.

The fairies in this comedy seem to embody a pervasive sense found throughout Shakespeare's work that there is something uncanny about language, something that is not quite human, at least in the conventional and circumscribed sense of the human that dominates waking experience. In the comedies, this intuition is alarming but ultimately benign: Oberon and his followers trip through the great house at the play's close, blessing the bridebeds and warding off the nightmares that lurk in marriage and parenthood. But there is in Shakespeare an alternative, darker vision of the uncanniness of language, a vision also embodied in creatures that test the limits of the human—not the fairies of *A Midsummer Night's Dream* but the weird sisters of *Macbeth*. When in the tragedy's opening scene the witches chant "Fair is foul, and foul is fair" (1.1.10), they unsettle through the simplest and most radical act of linguistic equation (x is y) the fundamental antinomies through which a moral order is established. And when Macbeth appears onstage a few minutes later, his first words unconsciously echo what we have just heard from the witches' mouths: "So foul and fair a day I have not seen" (1.3.36). What is the meaning of this linguistic "unconscious"? On the face of things, Macbeth presumably means only that the day of fair victory is also a day of foul weather, but the fact that he echoes the witches (something that we hear but that he cannot know) intimates an occult link between them, even before their direct encounter. It is difficult, perhaps impossible, to specify exactly what this link signifies—generations of emboldened critics have tried without notable success—but we can at least affirm that its secret lair is in the play's language, like a half-buried pun whose full articulation will entail the murder of Duncan, the ravaging of his kingdom, and Macbeth's own destruction.

Macbeth is haunted by half-buried puns, equivocations, and ambiguous grammatical constructions known as amphibologies. They manifest themselves most obviously in the words of the witches, from the opening exchanges to the fraudulent assurances that deceive Macbeth at the close, but they are also present in his most intimate and private reflections, as in his tortured broodings about his proposed act of treason:

> If it were done when 'tis done, then 'twere well
> It were done quickly. If th'assassination
> Could trammel up the consequence, and catch
> With his surcease success: that but this blow
> Might be the be-all and the end-all, here,
> But here upon this bank and shoal of time,
> We'd jump the life to come.
>
> (1.7.1–7)

The dream is to reach a secure and decisive end, to catch as in a net (hence "trammel up") all of the slippery, unforeseen, and uncontrollable consequences of regicide, to hobble time as one might hobble a horse (another sense of "trammel up"), to stop the flow ("success") of events, to be, as Macbeth later puts it, "settled." But Macbeth's words themselves slip away from the closure he seeks; they slide into one another, trip over themselves, twist and double back and swerve into precisely the sickening uncertainties their speaker most wishes to avoid. And if we sense a barely discernible note of comedy in Macbeth's tortured language, a discordant playing with the senses of the word "done" and the hint of a childish tongue twister in the phrase "catch / With his surcease success," we are in touch with a dark pleasure to which Shakespeare was all his life addicted.

Look again at the couplet from *Cymbeline:* "Golden lads and girls all must, / As chimney-sweepers, come to dust."

The playwright who insinuated a pun into the solemn dirge is the same playwright whose tragic heroine in *Antony and Cleopatra,* pulling the bleeding body of her dying lover into the pyramid, says, "Our strength is all gone into heaviness" (4.16.34). He is the playwright whose Juliet, finding herself alone on the stage, says, "My dismal scene I needs must act alone" (*Romeo and Juliet* 4.3.19), and the playwright who can follow the long, wrenching periodic sentence that Othello speaks, just before he stabs himself, with the remark "O bloody period!" (5.2.366). The point is not merely the presence of puns in the midst of tragedy (as there are stabs of pain in the midst of Shakespearean comedy); it is rather the streak of wildness that they so deliberately disclose, the sublimely indecorous linguistic energy of which Shakespeare was at once the towering master and the most obedient, worshipful servant.

The Dream of the Master Text

Shakespeare and the Printed Book

Ben Jonson's famous tribute to Shakespeare—"He was not of an age, but for all time!"—comes in one of the dedicatory poems to the 1623 First Folio of *Mr. William Shakespeares Comedies, Histories, & Tragedies.* This large, handsome volume, the first collection of Shakespeare's plays, was not, as far as we know, the product of the playwright's own design. We do not even know if he would have approved of the Folio's division of each play into five acts or its organization of the plays into three loose generic categories. Several of the plays grouped among the histories—*Richard Duke of York* (3 *Henry VI*), *Richard II,* and *Richard III*—had been printed separately during Shakespeare's lifetime as tragedies; one of the most famous of his tragedies had appeared as *The History of King Lear.* The Folio editors evidently decided to group together as "histories" only those plays which dealt with English history after the Norman Conquest; hence, *King Lear,* set in ancient Britain, appears with the "tragedies," and so, too, despite its happy ending, does *Cymbeline, King of Britain.* One play, *Troilus and Cressida,* was printed first as a "history," then printed in a second version with a preface that describes it as a "comedy," and then printed in the Folio as a "tragedy." As a fitting

Sixteenth-century printing shop. Engraving by Jan van der Straet. From *Nova Reperta* (1580).

emblem of the confusion, *Troilus and Cressida* does not appear in the Folio title page: apparently included only at the last minute, it was placed, unpaginated, after the last of the histories and the first of the tragedies. Modern readers, who remain perplexed by its genre, may take some consolation from the fact that for Shakespeare and his contemporaries generic boundaries were not hard and fast.

Published seven years after the playwright's death, the Folio was printed by the London printers William and Isaac Jaggard, who were joined in this expensive venture by Edward Blount, John Smethwicke, and William Aspley. It was edited by two of Shakespeare's old friends and fellow actors, John Heminges and Henry Condell, who claimed to be using "True Originall Copies" in the author's own hand. (None of these copies has survived, or, more cautiously, none has to date been found.) Eighteen plays included in the First Folio had already appeared individually in print in the small-format and relatively inexpensive texts called "Quartos" (or, in one case, the still smaller format called "Octavo"); to these, Heminges and Condell added eighteen others never before published: *All's Well That Ends Well, Antony and Cleopatra, As You Like It, The Comedy of Errors, Coriolanus, Cymbeline, All Is True (Henry VIII), Julius Caesar, King John, Macbeth, Measure for Measure, The Taming of the Shrew, The Tempest, Timon of Athens, Twelfth Night, The Two Gentlemen of Verona, The Winter's Tale,* and *1 Henry VI.** None of the

---

*This sketch simplifies several complex questions such as the status of the 1594 Quarto called *The Taming of a Shrew,* sufficiently distinct from the similarly titled Folio text as to constitute for many editors a different play.

plays included in the Folio has dropped out of the generally accepted canon of Shakespeare's works, and only two plays not included in the volume (*Pericles* and *The Two Noble Kinsmen*) have been allowed to join this select company, along with the nondramatic poems. Of the latter, *Venus and Adonis* (1593) and *The Rape of Lucrece* (1594) first appeared during Shakespeare's lifetime in Quartos with dedications from the author to the Earl of Southampton. *Shakespeare's Sonnets* (1609) were apparently printed without his authorization, as were his poems in a collection called *The Passionate Pilgrim* (1599).

Over the centuries, there have been many attempts to discover and authenticate additional works partly or entirely written by Shakespeare. An interesting case has been made for sections of a history play entitled *King Edward the Third* and for some small traces in the eighteenth-century tragicomedy *The Double Falsehood*, allegedly based on a manuscript of the lost Shakespearean play *Cardenio*. The *Norton Shakespeare* includes a poem, "Shall I die?" whose original inclusion in the 1988 *Oxford Shakespeare* provoked vigorous debate and much skepticism. Still more skepticism greeted the attribution to Shakespeare of a long poem called "A Funeral Elegy," printed in an appendix to *The Norton Shakespeare*'s first edition and now dropped in the wake of widespread consensus that the attribution was false. In the future, other claimants will no doubt come forward, but, with the very few additions already noted, the Folio will always remain the foundation of Shakespeare's dramatic canon.

The plays were the property of the theatrical company in which Shakespeare was a shareholder. It was not normally in the interest of such companies to have their scripts circulating in print, at least while the plays were actively in repertory: players evidently feared competition from rival companies and thought that reading might dampen playgoing. Plays were generally sold only when the theaters were temporarily closed by plague, or when the company was in need of capital (four of Shakespeare's plays were published in 1600, presumably to raise money to pay the debts incurred in building the new Globe), or when a play had grown too old to revive profitably. There is no evidence that Shakespeare himself disagreed with this professional caution, no sign that he wished to see his plays in print. Unlike Ben Jonson, who took the radical step of rewriting his own plays for publication in the 1616 folio of his *Works*, Shakespeare evidently was not interested in constituting his plays as a canon. If in the sonnets he imagines his verse achieving a symbolic immortality, this dream apparently did not extend to his plays, at least through the medium of print.

Moreover, there is no evidence that Shakespeare had an interest in asserting authorial rights over his scripts or that he or any other working English playwright had a public "standing," legal or otherwise, from which to do so. (Jonson was ridiculed for his presumption.) There is no indication whatever that he could, for example, veto changes in his scripts or block interpolated scenes or withdraw a play from production if a particular interpretation, addition, or revision did not please him. To be sure, in his advice to the players, Hamlet urges that those who play the clowns "speak no more than is set down for them," but—apart from the question of whether the Prince speaks for the playwright—the play within the play in *Hamlet* is precisely an instance of a script altered to suit a particular occasion. It seems likely that Shakespeare would have routinely accepted the possibility of such alterations. Moreover, he would of necessity have routinely accepted the possibility, and in certain cases the virtual inevitability, of cuts in order to stage his plays in the two to two and one-half hours that was the normal performing time. There is an imaginative generosity in many of Shakespeare's scripts, as if he were deliberately offering his fellow actors more than they could use on any one occasion and, hence, giving them abundant materials with which to reconceive and revivify each play again and again as they or their audiences liked it. The Elizabethan theater, like most theater in our own time, was a collaborative enterprise, and the collaboration almost certainly extended to decisions about selection, trimming, shifts of emphasis, and minor or major revision.

For many years, it was thought that Shakespeare himself did little or no revising. Some recent editors—above all the editors of the *Oxford Shakespeare*, whose texts the

Norton presents—have argued persuasively that there are many signs of authorial revision, even wholesale rewriting. But there is no sign that Shakespeare sought through such revision to bring each of his plays to its "perfect," "final" form. On the contrary, many of the revisions seem to indicate that the scripts remained open texts, that the playwright and his company expected to add, cut, and rewrite as the occasion demanded.

Ralph Waldo Emerson once compared Shakespeare and his contemporary Francis Bacon in terms of the relative "finish" of their work. All of Bacon's work, wrote Emerson, "lies along the ground, a vast unfinished city." Each of Shakespeare's dramas, by contrast, "is perfect, hath an immortal integrity. To make Bacon's work complete, he must live to the end of the world." Recent scholarship suggests that Shakespeare was more like Bacon than Emerson thought. Neither the Folio nor the quarto texts of Shakespeare's plays bear the seal of final authorial intention, the mark of decisive closure that has served, at least ideally, as the guarantee of textual authenticity. We want to believe, as we read the text, "This is the play as Shakespeare himself wanted it read," but there is no license for such a reassuring sentiment. To be "not of an age, but for all time" means in Shakespeare's case not that the plays have achieved a static perfection, but that they are creatively, inexhaustibly unfinished.

That we have been so eager to link certain admired scripts to a single known playwright is closely related to changes in the status of artists in the Renaissance, changes that led to a heightened interest in the hand of the individual creator. Like medieval painting, medieval drama gives us few clues as to the particular individuals who fashioned the objects we admire. We know something about the places in which these objects were made, the circumstances that enabled their creation, the spaces in which they were placed, but relatively little about the particular artists themselves. It is easy to imagine a wealthy patron or a civic authority in the late Middle Ages commissioning a play on a particular subject (appropriate, for example, to a seasonal ritual, a religious observance, or a political festivity) and specifying the date, place, and length of the performance, the number of actors, even the costumes to be used, but it is more difficult to imagine him specifying a particular playwright and still less insisting that the entire play be written by this dramatist alone. Only with the Renaissance do we find a growing insistence on the name of the maker, the signature that heightens the value and even the meaning of the work by implying that it is the emanation of a single, distinct shaping consciousness.

In the case of Renaissance painting, we know that this signature does not necessarily mean that every stroke was made by the master. Some of the work, possibly the greater part of it, may have been done by assistants, with only the faces and a few finishing touches from the hand of the illustrious artist to whom the work is confidently attributed. As the skill of individual masters became more explicitly valued, contracts began to specify how much was to come from the brush of the principal painter. Consider, for example, the Italian painter Luca Signorelli's contract of 1499 for frescoes in Orvieto Cathedral:

> The said master Luca is bound and promises to paint [1] all the figures to be done on the said vault, and [2] especially the faces and all the parts of the figures from the middle of each figure upwards, and [3] that no painting should be done on it without Luca himself being present. . . . And it is agreed [4] that all the mixing of colours should be done by the said master Luca himself.

Such a contract at once reflects a serious cash interest in the characteristic achievement of a particular artist and a conviction that this achievement is compatible with the presence of other hands, provided those hands are subordinate, in the finished work. For paintings on a smaller scale, it was more possible to commission an exclusive performance. Thus, the contract for a small altarpiece by Signorelli's great teacher, Piero della Francesca, specifies that "no painter may put his hand to the brush other than Piero himself."

There is no record of any comparable concern for exclusivity in the English theater. Unfortunately, the contracts that Shakespeare and his fellow dramatists almost certainly signed have not, with one significant exception, survived. But plays written for the professional theater are by their nature an even more explicitly collective art form than paintings; they depend for their full realization on the collaboration of others, and that collaboration may well extend to the fashioning of the script. It seems that some authors may simply have been responsible for providing plots that others then dramatized; still others were hired to "mend" old plays or to supply prologues, epilogues, or songs. A particular playwright's name came to be attached to a certain identifiable style—a characteristic set of plot devices, a marked rhetorical range, a tonality of character—but this name may refer in effect more to a certain product associated with a particular playing company than to the individual artist who may or may not have written most of the script. The one contract whose details do survive, that entered into by Richard Brome and the actors and owners of the Salisbury Court Theatre in 1635, does not stipulate that Brome's plays must be written by him alone or even that he must be responsible for a certain specifiable proportion of each script. Rather, it specifies that the playwright "should not nor would write any play or any part of a play to any other players or playhouse, but apply all his study and endeavors therein for the benefit of the said company of the said playhouse." The Salisbury Court players want rights to everything Brome writes for the stage; the issue is not that the plays associated with his name be exclusively *his* but rather that he be exclusively *theirs*.

Recent textual scholarship, then, has been moving steadily away from a conception of Shakespeare's plays as direct, unmediated emanations from the mind of the author and toward a conception of them as working scripts, composed and continually reshaped as part of a collaborative commercial enterprise in competition with other, similar enterprises. One consequence has been the progressive weakening of the idea of the solitary, inspired genius, in the sense fashioned by Romanticism and figured splendidly in the statue of Shakespeare in the public gardens in Germany's Weimar, the city of Goethe and Schiller: the poet, with his sensitive, expressive face and high domed forehead sitting alone and brooding, a skull at his feet, a long-stemmed rose in his crotch. In place of this projection of German Romanticism, we have now a playwright and sometime actor who is also (to his considerable financial advantage) a major shareholder in the company—the Lord Chamberlain's Men, later the King's Men—to which he loyally supplies for most of his career an average of two plays per year.

These developments are salutary insofar as they direct attention to the actual conditions in which the textual traces that the Folio calls Shakespeare's "Comedies, Histories, & Tragedies" came to be produced, reproduced, consumed, revised, and transmitted to future generations. They highlight elements that Shakespeare shared with his contemporaries, and they insistently remind us that we are encountering scripts written primarily for the stage and not for the study. They make us more attentive to such matters as business cycles, plague rolls, the cost of costumes, government censorship, and urban topography and less concerned with the elusive and enigmatic details of the poet's biography—his supposed youthful escapades and erotic yearnings and psychological crises.

All well and good. But the fact remains that in 1623, seven years after the playwright's death, Heminges and Condell thought they could sell copies of their expensive collection of Shakespeare's plays—"What euer you do," they urge their readers, "buy"— by insisting that their texts were "as he conceiued them." This means that potential readers in the early seventeenth century were already interested in Shakespeare's "conceits"—his "wit," his imagination, and his creative power—and were willing to assign a high value to the products of his particular, identifiable skill, one distinguishable from that of his company and of his rival playwrights. After all, Jonson's tribute praises Shakespeare not as the playwright of the incomparable King's Men but as the equal of Aeschylus, Sophocles, and Euripides. And if we now see Shakespeare's dramaturgy in the context of his contemporaries and of a collective artistic practice, readers continue to have little difficulty recognizing that most of the plays attached to his name tower over those of his rivals.

From Foul to Fair: The Making of the Printed Play

What exactly is a printed play by Shakespeare? Is it like a novel or a poem? Is it like the libretto or the score of an opera? Is it the trace of an absent event? Is it the blueprint of an imaginary structure that will never be completed? Is it a record of what transpired in the mind of a man long dead? We might say cautiously that it is a mechanically reproduced version of what Shakespeare wrote, but unfortunately, with the possible (and disputed) exception of a small fragment from a collaboratively written play called *Sir Thomas More*, virtually nothing Shakespeare actually wrote in his own hand survives. We might propose that it is a printed version of the script that an Elizabethan actor would have held in his hands during rehearsals, but here, too, no such script of a Shakespeare play survives; and besides, Elizabethan actors were evidently not given the whole play to read. To reduce the expense of copying and the risk of unauthorized reproduction, each actor received only his own part, along with the cue lines. (Shakespeare uses this fact to delicious comic effect in *A Midsummer Night's Dream* 3.1.80–88.) Nonetheless, the play certainly existed as a whole, either in the author's original manuscript or in the copy prepared for the government censor or for the company's prompter or stage manager, so we might imagine the text we hold in our hands as a printed copy of one of these manuscripts. But since no contemporary manuscript survives of any of Shakespeare's plays, we cannot verify this hypothesis. And even if we could, we would not have resolved the question of the precise relation of the printed text either to the playwright's imagination or to the theatrical performance by the company to which he belonged.

All of Shakespeare's plays must have begun their textual careers in the form of "foul papers," drafts presumably covered with revisions, crossings-out, and general "blotting." To be sure, Heminges and Condell remark that so great was the playwright's facility that they "have scarce received from him a blot in his papers." This was, however, a routine and conventional compliment in the period. The same claim, made for the playwright John Fletcher in an edition published in 1647, is clearly contradicted by the survival of Fletcher's far-from-unblotted manuscripts. It is safe to assume that, since Shakespeare was human, his manuscripts contained their share of second and third thoughts scribbled in the margins and between the lines. Once complete, this authorial draft would usually have to be written out again, either by the playwright or by a professional scribe employed by the theater company, as "fair copy."

In the hands of the theater company, the fair copy (or sometimes, it seems, the foul papers themselves) would be annotated and transformed into "the book of the play" or the "playbook" (what we would now call a "promptbook"). Shakespeare's authorial draft presumably contained a certain number of stage directions, though these may have been sketchy and inconsistent. The promptbook clarified these and added others, noted theatrical properties and sound effects, and on occasion cut the full text to meet the necessities of performance. The promptbook was presented to the Master of the Revels for licensing, and it incorporated any changes upon which the master insisted. As the editors of the *Oxford Shakespeare* put it, the difference between foul papers and promptbook is the difference between "the text in an as yet individual, private form" and "a socialized text."

But the fact remains that for Shakespeare's plays, we have neither foul papers nor fair copies nor promptbooks. We have only the earliest printed editions of these texts in numerous individual quartos and in the First Folio. (Quartos are so called because each sheet of paper was folded twice, making four leaves or eight pages front and back; folio sheets were folded once, making two leaves or four pages front and back.) From clues embedded in these "substantive" texts—substantive because (with the exception of *The Two Noble Kinsmen*) they date from Shakespeare's own lifetime or from the collected works edited by his associates using, or claiming to use, his own manuscripts—editors attempt to reconstruct each play's journey from manuscript to print. Different plays took very different journeys.

Of the thirty-six plays included in the First Folio, eighteen had previously appeared in quarto editions, some of these in more than one printing. Generations of editors have distinguished between "good Quartos," presumably prepared from the author's own draft or from a scribal transcript of the play (fair copy), and "bad Quartos." The latter category, first formulated as such by A. W. Pollard in 1909, includes, by widespread but not universal agreement, the 1594 version of *The First Part of the Contention (2 Henry VI)*, the 1595 *Richard Duke of York (3 Henry VI)*, the 1597 *Richard the Third*, the 1597 *Romeo and Juliet*, the 1600 *Henry the Fifth*, the 1602 *Merry Wives of Windsor*, the 1603 *Hamlet*, and *Pericles* (1609). Some editors also regard the 1591 *Troublesome Reign of King John*, the 1594 *Taming of a Shrew*, and the 1608 *King Lear* as bad Quartos, but others have strenuously argued that these are distinct rather than faulty texts, and the whole concept of the bad Quarto has come under increasingly critical scrutiny. The criteria for distinguishing between "good" and "bad" texts are imprecise, and the evaluative terms seem to raise as many questions as they answer. Nevertheless, the striking mistakes, omissions, repetitions, and anomalies in a number of the Quartos require some explanation beyond the ordinary fallibility of scribes and printers.

The explanation most often proposed for suspect Quartos is that they are the products of "memorial reconstruction." The hypothesis, first advanced in 1910 by W. W. Greg, is that a series of features found in what seem to be particularly flawed texts may be traced to the derivation of the copy from the memory of one or more of the actors. Elizabethan actors, Greg observed, often found themselves away from the London theaters—for example, on tour in the provinces during plague periods—and may not on those occasions have had access to the promptbooks they would ordinarily have used. In such circumstances, those in the company who remembered a play may have written down or dictated the text, as best they could, perhaps adapting it for provincial performance. Moreover, unscrupulous actors may have sold such texts to enterprising printers eager to turn a quick profit.

Memorially reconstructed texts tend to be much shorter than those prepared from foul papers or fair copy; they frequently paraphrase or garble lines, drop or misplace speeches and whole scenes, and on occasion fill in the gaps with scraps from other plays. In several cases, scholars think they can detect which roles the rogue actors played, since these parts (and the scenes in which they appear) are reproduced with greater accuracy than the rest of the play. Typically, these roles are minor ones, since the leading parts would be played by actors with a greater stake in the overall financial interest of the company and, hence, less inclination to violate its policy. Thus, for example, editors speculate that the bad Quarto of *Hamlet* (Q1) was provided by the actor playing Marcellus (and doubling as Lucianus). What is often impossible to determine is whether particular differences between a bad Quarto and a good Quarto or Folio text result from the actor's faulty memory or from changes introduced in performance, possibly with the playwright's own consent, or from both. Shakespearean bad Quartos ceased to appear after 1609, perhaps as a result of greater scrutiny by the Master of the Revels, who after 1606 was responsible for licensing plays for publication as well as performance.

The syndicate that prepared the Folio had access to the manuscripts of the King's Men. In addition to the previously published editions of eighteen plays, they made use of scribal transcripts (fair copies), promptbooks, and (more rarely) foul papers. The indefatigable labors of generations of bibliographers, antiquaries, and textual scholars have recovered an extraordinary fund of information about the personnel, finances, organizational structure, and material practices of Elizabethan and Jacobean printing houses, including the names and idiosyncrasies of particular compositors who calculated the page length, set the type, and printed the sheets of the Folio. This impressive scholarship has for the most part intensified respect for the seriousness with which the Folio was prepared and printed, and where the Folio is defective, it has provided plausible readings from the Quartos or proposed emendations to approximate what Shakespeare is likely to have written. But it has not succeeded, despite all its heroic efforts, in transforming the Folio, or any other text, into an unobstructed, clear window into Shakespeare's mind.

The dream of the master text is a dream of transparency. The words on the page should ideally give the reader unmediated access to the astonishing forge of imaginative power that was the mind of the dramatist. Those words welled up from the genius of the great artist, and if the world were not an imperfect place, they would have been set down exactly as he conceived them and transmitted to each of us as a precious inheritance. Such is the vision—at its core closely related to the preservation of the holy text in the great scriptural religions—that has driven many of the great editors who have for centuries produced successive editions of Shakespeare's works. The vision was not yet fully formed in the First Folio, for Heminges and Condell still felt obliged to apologize to their noble patrons for dedicating to them a collection of mere "trifles." But by the eighteenth century, there were no longer any ritual apologies for Shakespeare; instead, there was a growing recognition not only of the supreme artistic importance of his works but also of the uncertain, conflicting, and in some cases corrupt state of the surviving texts. Every conceivable step, it was thought, must be undertaken to correct mistakes, strip away corruptions, return the texts to their pure and unsullied form, and make this form perfectly accessible to readers.

Paradoxically, this feverishly renewed, demanding, and passionate editorial project has produced the very opposite of the transparency that was the dream of the master text. The careful weighing of alternative readings, the production of a textual apparatus, the writing of notes and glosses, the modernizing and regularizing of spelling and punctuation, the insertion of scene divisions, the complex calculation of the process of textual transmission from foul papers to print, the equally complex calculation of the effects that censorship, government regulation, and, above all, theatrical performance had on the surviving documents all make inescapably apparent the fact that we do not have and never will have any direct, unmediated access to Shakespeare's imagination. Every Shakespeare text, from the first that was published to the most recent, has been edited: it has come into print by means of a tangled social process and inevitably exists at some remove from the author.

Heminges and Condell, who knew the author and had access to at least some of his manuscripts, lament the fact that Shakespeare did not live "to have set forth and overseen his own writings." And even had he done so—or, alternatively, even if a cache of his manuscripts were discovered in a Warwickshire attic tomorrow—all of the editorial problems would not be solved, nor would all of the levels of mediation be swept away. Certainly, the entire textual landscape would change. But the written word has strange powers: it seems to hold on to something of the very life of the person who has written it, but it also seems to pry that life loose from the writer, exposing it to vagaries of history and chance independent of those to which the writer was personally subject. Moreover, with the passing of centuries, the language itself and the whole frame of reference within which language and symbols are understood have decisively changed. The most learned modern scholar still lives at a huge experiential remove from Shakespeare's world and, even holding a precious copy of the First Folio in hand, cannot escape having to read across a vast chasm of time what is, after all, an edited text. The rest of us cannot so much as indulge in the fantasy of direct access: our eyes inevitably wander to the glosses and the explanatory notes.

The Oxford Shakespeare

The shattering of the dream of the master text is no cause for despair, nor should it lead us to throw our hands up and declare that one text is as good as another. What it does is to encourage the reader to be actively interested in the editorial principles that underlie the particular edition that he or she is using. It is said that the great artist Brueghel once told a nosy connoisseur who had come to his studio, "Keep your nose out of my paintings; the smell of the paint will poison you." In the case of Shakespeare, it is increasingly important to bring one's nose close to the page, as it were, and sniff the ink. More precisely, it is important to understand the rationale for the choices that the editors have made.

The text of the *Norton Shakespeare* is, with very few changes, that published by the Oxford University Press in 1988 and, in a second edition, in 2005. The *Oxford Shakespeare* was the extraordinary achievement of a team of editors, Stanley Wells, Gary Taylor, John Jowett, and William Montgomery, with Wells and Taylor serving as the general editors. The Oxford editors approached their task with a clear understanding that, as we have seen, all previous texts have been mediated by agents other than Shakespeare; however, they regard this mediation not as a melancholy obstacle intervening between the reader and the "true" Shakespearean text but rather as a constitutive element of this text. The art of the playwright is thoroughly dependent on the craft of go-betweens.

Shakespeare's plays were not written to be circulated in manuscript or printed form among readers. They were written to be performed by the players and, as the preface to the Quarto *Troilus and Cressida* indelicately puts it, "clapper-clawed with the palms of the vulgar." The public was, thus, never meant to be in a direct relationship with the author but in a "triangular relationship" in which the players gave voice and gesture to the author's words. As we have seen, Shakespeare was the master of the unfinished, the perpetually open. And even if we narrow our gaze and try to find only what Shakespeare himself might have regarded as a textual resting point, a place to stop and go on to another play, we have, the Oxford editors point out, a complex task. For whatever Shakespeare wrote was meant from the start to be supplemented by an invisible "paratext" consisting of words spoken by Shakespeare to the actors and by the actors to each other concerning emphasis, stage business, tone, pacing, possible cuts, and so forth. To the extent that this paratext was ever written down, it was recorded in the prompt-book. Therefore, in contrast to standard editorial practice, the Oxford editors prefer, when there is a choice, copy based on the promptbook to copy based on the author's own draft. They choose the text immersed in history—that is, in the theatrical embodiment for which it was intended by its author—over the text unstained by the messy, collaborative demands of the playhouse. The closest we can get to Shakespeare's "final" version of a play—understanding that for him as for us there is no true "finality" in a theatrical text—is the latest version of that play performed by his company during his professional life—that is, during the time in which he could still oversee and participate in any cuts and revisions.

This choice does not mean that the Oxford editors are turning away from the very idea of Shakespeare as author. On the contrary, Wells and Taylor are deeply committed to establishing a text that comes as close as possible to the plays as Shakespeare wrote them, but they are profoundly attentive to the fact that he wrote them as a member of a company of players, a company in which he was a shareholder and an actor as well as a writer. "Writing" for the theater, at least for Shakespeare, is not simply a matter of setting words to paper and letting the pages drift away; it is a social process as well as an individual act. The Oxford editors acknowledge that some aspects of this social process may have been frustrating to Shakespeare: he may, for example, have been forced on occasion to cut lines and even whole scenes to which he was attached, or his fellow players may have insisted that they could not successfully perform what he had written, compelling him to make changes he did not welcome. But compromise and collaboration are part of what it means to be in the theater, and Wells and Taylor return again and again to the recognition that Shakespeare was, supremely, a man of the theater.

Is there a tension between the Oxford editors' preference for the performed, fully socialized text and their continued commitment to recovering the text as Shakespeare himself intended it? Yes. The tension is most visible in their determination to strip away textual changes arising from circumstances, such as government censorship, over which Shakespeare had no control. ("We have, wherever possible," they write, put "profanities back in Shakespeare's mouth.") It can be glimpsed as well in the editors' belief, almost a leap of faith, that there was little revision of Shakespeare's plays in his company's revivals between the time of his death and the publication of the Folio. But the tension is mainly a creative one, for it forces them (and, therefore, us) to attend to the play-wright's unique imaginative power as well as his social and historical entanglements.

The Oxford editors took a radical stance on a second major issue: the question of authorial revision. Previous editors had generally accepted the fact that Shakespeare practiced revision within individual manuscripts—that is, while he was still in the act of writing a particular play—but they generally rejected the notion that he undertook sub-stantial revisions from one version of a play to another (and, hence, from one manuscript to another). Wells and Taylor point out that six major works (*Hamlet, Othello, 2 Henry IV, King Lear, Richard II,* and *Troilus and Cressida*) survive in two independent substan-tive sources, both apparently authoritative, with hundreds of significant variant readings. Previous editors have generally sought to deny authority to one edition or another ("faced with two sheep," the Oxford editors observe wryly, "it is all too easy to insist that one *must* be a goat") or have conflated the two versions into a single text in an attempt to recon-struct the ideal, definitive, complete, and perfect version that they imagine Shakespeare must have reached for each of his plays. But if one doubts that Shakespeare ever con-ceived of his plays as closed, finished entities, if one recalls that he wrote them for the living repertory of the commercial playing company to which he belonged, then the whole concept of the single, authoritative text of each play loses its force. In a startling depar-ture from the editorial tradition, the *Oxford Shakespeare* printed two distinct versions of *King Lear,* quarto and Folio, and the editors glanced longingly at the impractical but allur-ing possibility of including two texts of *Hamlet, Othello,* and *Troilus.*

The *Oxford Shakespeare* was published in both old-spelling and modern-spelling editions. The former, the first of its kind ever published, raised some reviewers' eye-brows because the project, a critical edition rather than a facsimile, required the mod-ern editors to invent plausible Elizabethan spellings for their emendations and to add stage directions. The modern-spelling edition, which is the basis for Norton's text, is noteworthy for taking the principles of modernization further than they had generally been taken. Gone are such words as "murther," "mushrump," "vild," and "porpentine," which confer on many modern-spelling editions a certain cozy, Olde-English quaint-ness; Oxford replaces them with "murder," "mushroom," "vile," and "porcupine."

The inclusion of two texts of *King Lear* aroused considerable controversy when the *Oxford Shakespeare* first appeared, although by now the arguments for doing so have received widespread, though not unanimous, scholarly support. Other features remain controversial: "Ancients" Pistol and Iago have been modernized to "Ensigns"; *Henry VIII* has reverted to its performance title *All Is True*; demonic spirits in *Macbeth* sing lyrics written by Thomas Middleton. The white-hot intensity of the debates triggered by the *Oxford Shakespeare*'s editorial choices casts an interesting light on the place of Shake-speare not only in the culture at large but in the psyches of millions of individuals: any alteration, however minor, in a deeply familiar and beloved text, even an alteration based on thoughtful and highly plausible scholarly principles, arouses genuine anxiety. The anxiety in this case was intensified not only by the boldness of certain crucial emenda-tions but also by the fact that the editors' explanations, arguments, and justifications for all their decisions were printed in a separate, massive volume, *William Shakespeare: A Textual Companion.* This formidable, dense volume is an astonishing monument to the seriousness, scholarly rigor, and immense labor of the Oxford editors. Anyone who is interested in pursuing why Shakespeare's words appear as they do in the current edition, anyone who wishes insight into the editors' detailed reasons for making the thousands of decisions required by a project of this kind, should consult the *Textual Companion.*

The Norton Shakespeare

The primary task that the editors of the *Norton Shakespeare* set themselves was to present the modern-spelling Oxford *Complete Works* in a way that would make the text more accessible to modern readers. The *Oxford Shakespeare* prints little more than the text itself: along with one-page introductions to the individual works, it contains a short general introduction, a list of contemporary allusions to Shakespeare, and a brief glossary. But while it is possible to enjoy a Shakespeare play on stage or screen without any assistance beyond the actors' own art, many readers at least since the eighteenth century have found it far more difficult to understand and to savor the texts without some more substantial commentary.

In addition to writing introductions, textual notes, and brief bibliographies for each of the works, the Norton editors provide glosses and footnotes designed to facilitate comprehension. Such is the staggering richness of Shakespeare's language that it is tempting to gloss everything. But there is a law of diminishing returns: too much explanatory whispering at the margins makes it difficult to enjoy what the reader has come for in the first place. Our general policy is to gloss only those words that cannot be found in an ordinary dictionary or whose meanings have altered out of recognition. The glosses attempt to be simple and straightforward, giving multiple meanings for words only when the meanings are essential for making sense of the passages in which they appear. We try not to gloss the same word over and over—it becomes distracting to be told three times on a single page that "an" means "if"—but we also assume that the reader does not have a perfect memory, so after an interval we will gloss the same word again.

Marginal glosses generally refer to a single word or a short phrase. The footnotes paraphrase longer units or provide other kinds of information, such as complex plays on words, significant allusions, textual cruxes, historical and cultural contexts. Here, too, however, we have tried to check the impulse to annotate so heavily that the reader is distracted from the pleasure of the text, and we have avoided notes that provide interpretation, as distinct from information.

Following the works, the Norton editors have provided lists of textual variants. These are variants from the control text only—that is, they do not record all of the variants in all of the substantive texts, nor do they record all of the myriad shifts of meaning that may arise from modernization of spelling and repunctuation. Readers who wish to pursue these interesting, if complex, topics are encouraged to consult the *Textual Companion*, along with the old-spelling *Oxford Shakespeare*, the Norton facsimile of the First Folio, and the quarto facsimiles published by the University of California Press. The *Norton Shakespeare* does provide a convenient list for each play of the different ways the same characters are designated in the speech prefixes in the substantive texts. These variants (for example, Lady Capulet in *Romeo and Juliet* is called, variously, "Lady," "Mother," "Wife," "Old Woman," etc.) often cast an interesting light on the ways a particular character is conceived. Variants as they appear in this edition, as well as their line numbers, are printed in boldface; each is followed by the corresponding reading in the control text, and sometimes the source from which the variant is taken. Further information on readings in substantive texts is given in brackets.

Stage directions pose a complex set of problems for the editors of a one-volume Shakespeare. The printing conventions for the stage directions in sixteenth- and seventeenth-century plays were different from those of our own time. Often all of the entrances for a particular scene are grouped together at the beginning, even though some of the characters clearly do not enter until later; placement in any case seems at times haphazard or simply incorrect. There are moments when the stage directions seem to provide stunning insight into the staging of the plays in Shakespeare's time, other moments when they are absent or misleading. It is difficult to gauge how much the stage directions in the substantive editions reflect Shakespeare's own words or at least decisions. It would seem that he was often relatively careless about them, understanding perhaps that these decisions in any precise sense would be the first to be made and unmade by different productions.

The Oxford editors, like virtually all modern editors, necessarily altered and supplemented the stage directions in their control texts. They decided to mark certain of the stage directions with a special sign to indicate a dubious action or placement, but they did not distinguish between the stage directions that came from the substantive texts and those added in later texts, from the seventeenth century to the present. They referred readers instead to the *Textual Companion,* which provides lists of the exact wording of the stage directions in the substantive texts.

The editors of the *Norton Shakespeare* share a sense of the limitations of the early stage directions and share as well some skepticism about how many of these should be attributed even indirectly to Shakespeare. Hence, we do not routinely differentiate between quarto and Folio stage directions; we do so only when we think it is a significant point. But there is, it seems to us, a real interest in knowing which stage directions come from those editions of the plays published up to the 1623 Folio (and including *The Two Noble Kinsmen,* published shortly thereafter) and which were added when the editors were no longer in contact with Shakespeare's presence or his manuscripts. Therefore, we have placed brackets around all stage directions that were added after the First Folio. Unbracketed stage directions, then, all derive from editions up through the Folio.

The *Norton Shakespeare* has made several other significant departures from the Oxford text. The Oxford editors note that when *1 Henry IV* was first performed, probably in 1596, the character we know as Sir John Falstaff was called Sir John Oldcastle. But in the wake of protests from Oldcastle's descendants, one of whom, William Brooke, tenth Baron Cobham, was Elizabeth I's lord chamberlain, Shakespeare changed the name to "Falstaff" (and probably for similar reasons changed the names of Falstaff's companions, Russell and Harvey, to "Bardolph" and "Peto"). Consistent with their decision not to honor changes that Shakespeare was *compelled* to make by censorship or other forms of pressure, the Oxford editors changed the names back to their initial form. But this decision is a problem for several reasons. It draws perhaps too sharp a distinction between those things that Shakespeare did under social pressure and those he did of his own accord. More seriously, it pulls against the principle of a text that represents the latest performance version of a play during Shakespeare's lifetime: after all, even the earliest quarto title page advertises "the humorous conceits of Sir John Falstaff." And, of course, it asks the reader to ignore completely and radically centuries of response—elaboration, fascination, and love—all focused passionately on Sir John Falstaff. The response is not a modern phenomenon: it began with Shakespeare, who developed the character as Sir John Falstaff in *2 Henry IV* and *The Merry Wives of Windsor.* Norton thus restores the more familiar names.

Another major departure from the Oxford text is Norton's printing of the so-called Additional Passages, especially in *Hamlet.* Consistent with their decision not to conflate quarto and Folio texts, the Oxford editors adhere to their control text for *Hamlet,* the Folio, and print those passages that appear only in the Second Quarto in an appendix at the end of the play. As explained at length in the Textual Note to the play, the Norton editors decided not to follow this course, but instead chose a different way of demarcating the quarto and Folio texts (inserting the quarto passages, indented, in the body of the text), one that makes it easier to see how the quarto passages functioned in a version of the play that Shakespeare also authored.

The *Norton Shakespeare* follows Oxford in printing separate quarto and Folio texts of *King Lear,* to which we have added a conflated version of the play so that readers will have the opportunity to assess for themselves the effects of the traditional editorial practice. Moreover, we have departed from Oxford in printing the quarto and Folio texts of the plays on facing pages, so that their differences can be readily weighed. In the hundreds of changes, some trivial and other momentous, it is possible to glimpse, across what Prospero calls "the dark backward and abysm of time," a thrilling sight: Shakespeare at work.

The Shakespearean Stage
by
ANDREW GURR

Publication by Performance

The curt exchange between the sentries in the first six lines of *Hamlet* tells us that it is very late at night (" 'Tis now struck twelve") and that " 'tis bitter cold." This opening was staged originally at the Globe in London in broad daylight, at 2 o'clock probably on a hot summer's afternoon. The words required the audience, half of them standing on three sides of the stage platform and all of them as visible to one another as the players were, to imagine themselves watching a scene quite the opposite of what they could see and feel around them. The original mode of staging for a Shakespearean play was utterly different from the cinematic realism we are used to now, where the screen gives us close-ups on a simulacrum of reality, an even more privileged view of the actors' facial twitches than we get in ordinary life. Eloquence then was in words, not facial expressions.

The playgoers of Shakespeare's time knew the plays in forms at which we can only now guess. It is a severe loss. Shakespeare's own primary concept of his plays was as stories "personated" onstage, not as words on a page. He himself never bothered to get his playscripts into print, and more than half of them were not published until seven years after his death, in the First Folio of his plays published as a memorial to him in 1623. His fellow playwright Francis Beaumont called the printing of plays "a second publication"; the first was their showing onstage. Print recorded a set of scripts, written for the original players to teach them what they should speak in the ensemble of the play in production. The only technology then available to record the performances was the written word. If video recordings had existed at that time, our understanding of Shakespeare would be vastly different from what it is today.

Since the texts were composed only to be a record of the words the players were to memorize, we now have to infer how the plays were originally staged largely by guesswork. Shakespeare was himself a player and shareholder in his acting company, and he expected to be present at rehearsals. Consequently, the stage directions in his scripts are distinctly skimpy compared with some of those provided by his fellow playwrights. He was cursory even in noting entrances and exits, let alone how he expected his company to stage the more complex spectacles, such as heaving Antony up to Cleopatra on her monument. There are sometimes hints in the stage directions and more frequently in the words used to describe some of the actions, and knowing what the design of the theater was like is a help as well. Knowing more about how Shakespeare expected his plays to be staged can transform how we think about them. But gaining such knowledge is no easy matter. One of the few certainties is that Shakespeare's plays in modern performance are even more different from the originals than modern printed editions are from the first much-thumbed manuscripts.

The Shakespearean Mindset

The general mindset of the original playgoers, the patterns of thinking and expectation that Tudor culture imposed on Shakespeare's audiences, is not really difficult to identify.

It is less easy, though, to pin it down in the sort of detail that tells us what the original concept of staging the plays would have been like. We know that all the original playgoers paid for the privilege of attending the plays and committed themselves willingly to suspend their disbelief in what they were to see. They knew as we do that they were paying to be entertained by fictions. Beyond that, we need reminding today that going to open-air performances in daylight in Shakespeare's time meant being constantly aware that one was in a theater, a place designed to offer illusions. On the one hand, this consciousness of oneself and where one was meant that the players had to do more to hold attention than is needed now, when audiences have nothing but the stage to look at and armchairs to sit in. On the other hand, it made everyone more receptive to extratheatrical tricks, such as Hamlet's reference to "this distracted globe," or Polonius's claim in the same play to have taken the part of Julius Caesar at the university and been killed by Brutus. The regular playgoers at the Globe who recognized Polonius as the man who had played Caesar in Shakespeare's play of the year before, and who recognized Hamlet as the man who had played Brutus, would laugh at this theatrical in-joke. But two scenes later, when Hamlet kills Polonius, they would think of it again, in a different light.

Features of the original mindset such as these are readily identifiable. For others, though, we need to look further, into the design of the theaters and into the staging traditions that they housed and that Shakespeare exploited. Invisibility has a part to play in *A Midsummer Night's Dream* that we can easily underrate, for instance. Invisibility onstage is a theatrical in-joke, an obvious privileging of the audience, which is allowed to see what the characters onstage can't. The impresario Philip Henslowe's inventory of costumes used at the Rose theater in 1597, which lists "a robe for to go invisible," indicates a fictional device that openly expects the willing suspension of the audience's disbelief. In *A Midsummer Night's Dream*, the ostensible invisibility of all the visible fairies emphasizes the theatricality of the whole presentation while pandering to the audience's self-indulgent superiority, the feeling that it knows what is going on better than any character, whether he be Bottom or even Duke Theseus. That prepares us for the mockery of stage realism we get later, in the mechanicals' play in Act 5, and even for the doubt we as willing audience might feel over Theseus's own skepticism about the dangers of imagination that he voices in his speech at the beginning of Act 5.

More to the point, though, it throws into question our readiness to be an audience, since we have ourselves been indulging in just the games of suspending disbelief that the play staged by the mechanicals enters into so unsuccessfully. When Theseus disputes with Hippolyta about the credibility of the lovers' story, he voices the very skepticism—about the lover, the lunatic, and the poet—that any sensible realist in the audience would have been feeling for most of the previous three acts in the forest. The play starts and ends at the court in broad daylight, while the scenes of midsummer madness take place at night in a forest. At the early amphitheaters, all the plays were staged in broad daylight, between 2 and 5 o'clock in the afternoon, and without any persuasive scenery: the two stage posts served as trees onstage. So the play, moving as it does from daylight realism to nocturnal fantasy and back again, with a last challenge to credulity in the mechanicals' burlesque of how to stage a play, has already thoroughly challenged the willing suspension of the viewers' disbelief. *A Midsummer Night's Dream* is a play about nocturnal dreams and fictions that are accepted as truths in broad daylight. It was only a small extension of this game to have the women's parts played by boys, as well as plots in which the girls dressed as boys, to the point where in *As You Like It* Rosalind was played by a boy playing a girl pretending to be a boy playing a girl.

The Shakespeare plays were written for a new and unique kind of playhouse, the Elizabethan amphitheater, which had a distinctive design quite different from modern theaters. Elizabethans knew what the standard features in their theaters stood for, and Shakespeare drew on that knowledge for the staging of his plays. The physical features of the playhouses were a potent element in the ways that the plays were designed for the Elizabethan mindset. When Richard III, the archdeceiver and playactor, appears "aloft between two Bishops" to claim the crown in *Richard III* 3.7, his placing on the stage balcony literally above the crowd on the stage would, even without the accompanying priests, have signified his ironic claim to a social and moral superiority that ought to have matched his elevation. When Richard II comes down from the wall of Flint Castle to the "base court" in *Richard II* 3.3, Elizabethans would have seen his descent as a withdrawal from power and status. These theaters were still new when Shakespeare started to write for them, and their novelty meant that the plays were written more tightly to fit their specific design than the plays of later years, when theatergoing had become a more routine social activity and different kinds of theater were available.

London Playgoing and the Law

This heightened sense of theatricality, or "metatheater," in Shakespearean audiences was far from the only difference in their mindset from that of all modern audiences. Regular playgoing in London only started in the 1570s, and through Shakespeare's earlier years it was always a perilous and precarious activity. The Lord Mayor of London and the mayors of most of England's larger towns hated playgoing and tried to suppress it whenever and wherever it appeared. Playgoing was exciting not only because it was new but because it was dangerous. The hostility of so many authorities to plays meant that they were seen almost automatically as subversive of authority. Paradoxically, the first London companies were only able to establish themselves in London through the active support of Queen Elizabeth and her Privy Council, which tried hard, in the face of constant complaints from the Lord Mayor, to ensure that the best companies would be on hand every Christmas to entertain the Queen's leisure hours. Popular support for playgoing depended on royal protection for the leading companies.

London was by far the largest city in England. Within a few years of Shakespeare's death, it became the largest in Europe. It was generally an orderly place to live, especially in the city itself. Even in the suburbs, where the poorer people had to live, there were not many of the riots and other disorders that preachers always associated with the brothels, animal-baiting arenas, and playhouses clustering there. The reputation that the playhouses gained for promoting riots was not well justified. Any crowd of people was seen by the authorities as a potential riot, and playhouses regularly drew some of the largest crowds that London had yet seen. The city's government was not designed to control large crowds of people. There was no paid police force, and the Lord Mayor was held responsible by the Privy Council, the Queen's governing committee, for any disorders that did occur. So the city authorities found that playgoing challenged their control over their people.

The rapid growth of London did not help the situation. Officially, the city was governed by the Lord Mayor and his council. But he had authority only inside the city, and London now spread through a large suburban area in the adjacent counties of Middlesex to the north and Surrey across the river to the south. Because the court and the national government were housed in London, the Privy Council often intervened in city affairs in its own interests, as well as when orders were needed that covered broader zones than the city itself. The periodic outbreaks of bubonic plague were one clear instance of such a need, because the plague took no notice of parish or city boundaries. The intrusion of the professional companies to play in London provided another. In the early years, they were chronic travelers, and London was simply one of many stopovers. But the Queen enjoyed seeing plays at Christmas, and her council accordingly supported the best companies so that they could perform for her. It protected the playing companies against the hatred of successive Lord Mayors, except when a national emergency such as a plague epidemic erupted. The Privy Council took control then by ordering the 126 parishes in and around London to list all deaths from plague separately from ordinary deaths. Each Thursday, the parish totals were added together. When the total number of deaths from plague in these lists rose above 30 in any one week, the Privy Council closed all places of public assembly. This meant especially the playhouses, which created by far the largest gatherings. When the theaters were closed, the playing companies had to revert to their traditional practice of going on tour to play in the towns through the country, provided that the news of plague did not precede them.

Plague was not the only reason for the government to lay its controlling hand on the companies. From the time the post was inaugurated in 1578, the Master of the Revels controlled all playing. He was executive officer to the Lord Chamberlain, the Privy Council officer responsible for the annual season of royal entertainment and thus, by extension, for the professional playing companies. The Master of the Revels licensed each company and censored its plays. He was expected to cut out any references to religion or affairs of state, and he tried to prevent other offenses by banning the depiction of any living person onstage. After 1594, he issued licenses to the approved London playhouses, too. Later still, the printing of any playbook was allowed only if he gave authority for it. The companies had to accept this tight control because the government was its only protector against the hostile municipal authorities, who included not only the Lord Mayor of London but also the mayors of most of the major towns in the country.

Most mayors had the commercial interest of keeping local employees at work to justify their hostility to playgoing. But across the country, the hostility went much deeper. A large proportion of the population disliked the very idea of playacting. Their reasons, ostensibly religious, were that for actors to pretend to be characters they were unlike in life was a deception and that for boys to dress as women was contrary to what the Bible said. Somewhere beneath this was a more basic fear of pretense and deceit, of people not acting honestly. It put actors into the same category as con men, cheats, and thieves. That was probably one reason why companies of boys acting men's parts were thought rather more tolerable than men pretending to be other kinds of men. The deception involved in boys playing men was more transparent than when men played characters other than themselves. There was also a strong Puritan suspicion about shows of any kind, which looked too much like the Catholic ceremonial that the new Church of England had renounced. Playgoing found much better favor on the Catholic side of English society than on the Puritan side. Different preachers took different positions over the new phenomenon of playgoing. But few would speak in its favor, and most of them openly disapproved of it. Playgoing was an idle pastime, and the devil finds work for idle hands.

In the 1590s, when *Romeo and Juliet* and Shakespeare's histories and early comedies were exciting audiences, only two playhouses and two companies were officially approved by the Queen's Privy Council for the entertainment of London's citizens. The other main forms of paid entertainment were bear- and bullbaiting, which were much harder on the performers than was playing and so could be staged less frequently. The hostility to plays meant that the right to perform was confined to only a few of the most outstanding companies. These few companies were in competition with one another, and this led to a rapid growth in the quality of their offerings. But playacting was always a marginal activity. Paying to enter a specially built theater in order to see professional companies perform plays was still a new phenomenon, and it still met with great opposition from the London authorities. The open-air theaters like the Globe were built out in the suburbs. London as a city had no centrally located playhouses until after the civil war and the restoration of the monarchy, in 1661. And even playing in the city's suburbs, where they were free from the Lord Mayor's control, the companies had to work under the control of the Privy Council. All the great amphitheaters were built either in Middlesex or in Surrey. At the height of their success, in the years after Shakespeare's death, the Privy Council never licensed more than four or five playhouses in London.

Playgoing in London was viewed even by the playgoers as an idle occupation. The largest numbers who went to the Globe were apprentices and artisans taking time off from work, often surreptitiously, and law students from the Inns of Court doing the same. These fugitives were linked with the wealthier kind of idler, "gallants" or rich gentlemen and other men of property, along with soldiers and sailors on leave from the wars, people visiting London from the country on business or pleasure (usually both), and above all the women of London. Women were not expected to be literate, but one did not need to be able to read and write to enjoy hearing and seeing a play. A respectable woman had to make sure she was escorted by a man. He might be a husband or a friend, or her page if she was rich, or her husband's apprentice if she was a middle-class citizen. She might have a mask on, part of standard women's wear outdoors to protect the face against the weather and to assert modesty—and perhaps anonymity. Market women (applewives and fishwives) went to plays in groups. Whores were expected to be there looking for business, especially from the gallants, but they usually had male escorts, too.

The social range of playgoers at the two playhouses approved for use in 1594 was almost complete, stretching from the aristocracy to the poorest workmen and boys. Many people disapproved of plays, but at peak times up to 25,000 a week flocked to see the variety of plays being offered. Prices for playgoing remained much the same throughout the decades up to 1642, when the parliamentary government that was fighting the King closed all the theaters for eighteen years. Until then, one could get standing room at an amphitheater for 1 penny (1/240th of a modern pound, roughly 1 cent),

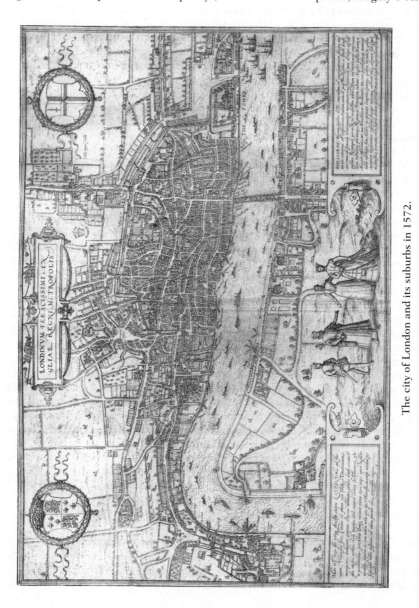

The city of London and its suburbs in 1572.

or a seat on a bench in the roofed galleries for twopence. A seat in a lord's room cost sixpence, which was not much less than a day's wage for a skilled artisan in 1600. The smaller roofed theaters that opened in 1599 were much more expensive. They were called "private" theaters to distinguish them from the "public" open-air amphitheaters, although the claim to privacy was mainly a convenient fiction to escape the controls imposed on the "public" theaters. At the Blackfriars hall theater, sixpence only gained you a seat in the topmost gallery, while a seat in the pit near the stage cost three times that amount and a seat in a box five times, or half a skilled worker's weekly wage.

It was not only the plays and players that were the sights at the playhouses. The richest lords and gallants went to be seen as much as they went to see. At the Globe, the costliest rooms were positioned alongside the balcony "above," over the stage. They were called "lords' rooms," and the playgoers who chose to sit there had a limited view of what went on beneath them. They saw no "discoveries," for instance, such as Portia's three caskets in *The Merchant of Venice,* which were uncovered underneath them inside the alcove in the center of the *frons scenae* (the wall at the back of the stage), or anything other than the backs of the players when they entered. But as audience, they were themselves highly visible, and that was what they paid for. In the hall, or "private," playhouses, with much higher admission prices than at the Globe, there were boxes flanking the stage for the gentry, which gave them a better view of the "discoveries." But at these "select" (because costlier) hall playhouses, where, unlike the Globe, everyone had a seat, some of the most colorful and exhibitionistic gallants could go one better. Up to fifteen gallants could pay for a stool to sit and watch the play on the stage itself, sitting in front of the boxes that flanked the stage. Each would enter from the players' dressing room (the "tiring-house") with his stool in hand before the play started. This gave them the best possible view of the play and easily the most conspicuous place in the audience's eye. Playgoing was a public occasion in which the visibility of audience members allowed them to play almost as large a part as the players.

Through the 1590s, the only permanent and custom-made playhouses were the large open-air theaters. Paying sixpence for a ferry across the river, as the richer playgoers did, or walking across London Bridge to the Rose or the Globe, or else trudging north through the mud of Shoreditch and Finsbury Fields or Clerkenwell to the Theatre or the Fortune in order to see a play, did not have great appeal when it was raining. Consequently, the companies were always trying to secure roofed halls nearer the city center. Up to 1594, they could use city inns, especially in winter, but the Lord Mayor's hostility to playing never made them reliable places for performing. Two constant problems troubled the players throughout these first years of professional theater in London: the city officials' chronic hatred of plays and the periodic visitations of the plague, which always led the government to close the theaters as soon as the number of plague deaths rose to dangerously high levels.

Playgoing was not firmly established in London until the Privy Council chose to protect it in 1594 and to approve specific playhouses for the two companies that it officially sanctioned. By then, Shakespeare had already made his mark. He became a player, a shareholder, and the resident playwright for one of these two companies. That status gained him a privileged place in the rapidly growing new world of playgoing. From then on, although his theater was still located only in the suburbs of the city, his work had the law behind it. That status was amply confirmed in 1603, when the new King made himself the company's patron. The King's Men held their status until the King himself lost power in 1642.

The Design of the Globe

The Globe was Shakespeare's principal playhouse. He put up part of the money for its construction and designed his best plays for it. It was built on the south side of the Thames in 1599, fashioned out of the framing timbers of an older theater. Essentially, it was a polygonal scaffold of twenty bays or sections, nearly 100 feet in outside diameter, making a circle of three levels of galleries that rose to more than 30 feet high, with wooden bench seating and cushions for those who could afford them. This surrounded an open "yard," into which the stage projected.

The yard was over 70 feet in diameter. Nearly half the audience stood on their feet to watch the play from inside this yard, closest to the stage platform. The stage extended out nearly to the middle of the yard, so the actors could stand in the center of the crowd. The uncertain privilege of having standing room in the open air around the stage platform could be bought with the minimal price for admission, 1 penny (about a cent). It had the advantage of proximity to the stage and the players; its disadvantage was keeping you on your feet for the two or three hours of the play, as well as leaving you subject to the weather. If you wanted a seat, or if it rained and you wanted shelter, you paid twice as much to sit in the three ranks of roofed galleries that circled behind the crowd standing in the yard. With some squeezing, the theater could hold over 3,000 people. It was an open-air theater because that gave it a larger capacity than a roofed hall. The drawback of its being open to the weather was more than outweighed by the gain in daylight that shone on stage and spectators alike.

The stage was a great square platform as much as 40 feet wide. It had over it a canopied roof, or "heavens," to protect the players and their expensive costumes from rain. This canopy was held up by two pillars rising through the stage. The stage platform was about 5 feet high and without any protective rails, so that the eyes of the audience in the yard were at the level of the players' feet. At the back of the stage, a wall—the *frons scenae*—stretched across the front of the players' tiring-house, the attiring or dressing room. It had a door on each flank and a wider curtained space in the center, which was used for major entrances and occasionally for set-piece scenes. Above these entry doors was a gallery or balcony, most of which was partitioned into rooms for the wealthiest spectators. A central room "above" was sometimes used in staging: for example, as Juliet's balcony, as the place for Richard III to stand between the bish-

The second Globe, from Wenceslaus Hollar's engraving of the "Long View" of London (1647). The two captions saying "The Globe" and "Beere bayting h." were accidentally transposed in the original. The Globe is the round structure in the center of the picture.

A photograph of the interior framework of the "new" Globe, on the south bank of the Thames in London, showing the general dimensions of the yard and the surrounding galleries.

ops, as the wall of Flint Castle in *Richard II*, and as the wall over the city gates of Harfleur in *Henry V*. After 1608, when Shakespeare's company acquired the Blackfriars consort of musicians, this central gallery room was turned into a curtained-off music room that could double as an "above" when required. Fewer than half of Shakespeare's plays need an "above."

The Original Staging Techniques

Shakespearean staging was emblematic. The "heavens" that covered the stage was the colorful feature from which gods descended to the earth of the stage platform. When Jupiter made his appearance in *Cymbeline*, in clouds of "sulphurous breath" provided by fireworks, he was mounted on an eagle being lowered through a trapdoor in the heavens. The other trapdoor, set in the stage platform itself, symbolized the opposite, a gateway to hell. The large stage trap was the place where the Gravedigger came to work at the beginning of Act 5 of *Hamlet*. It was the cell where Malvolio was imprisoned in *Twelfth Night*. The Shakespearean mindset accepted such conventions automatically.

Shakespeare inherited from Marlowe a tradition of using the stage trap as the dreaded hell's mouth. Barabbas plunges into it in *The Jew of Malta,* and the demons drag the screaming Faustus down it at the end of *Dr. Faustus*. Hell was not a fiction taken lightly by Elizabethans. Edward Alleyn, by far the most famous player of Faustus in the 1590s, wore a cross on his breast while he played the part, as insurance—just in case the fiction turned serious. Tracking the Elizabethan mindset about the stage trapdoor can give us a few warnings of what we might overlook when we come fresh to the plays today.

In the original staging of *Hamlet* at the Globe, the stage trap had two functions. Besides serving as Ophelia's grave, it was the distinctive entry point, not used by any other character, for the Ghost in Act 1. When he tells his son that he is "for the day confined to fast in fires," the first audiences would have already taken the point that he

The Globe as reconstructed in Southwark near the original site in London.

had come up from the underworld. His voice comes from under the stage, telling the soldiers to swear the oath of secrecy that Hamlet lays upon them. The connection between that original entry by the Ghost through the trap and the trap's later use for Ophelia is one we might easily miss. At the start of Act 5, the macabre discussion between the Gravediggers about whether she committed suicide and is, therefore, con-

The *frons scenae* of the new Globe.

A gesture using the language of hats, as shown by the man attending the brothers Browne.

signed to hell gets its sharpest edge from the association of the trap, here the grave being dug for her, with the Ghost's purgatorial fires. More to the point, though, Hamlet, as he eavesdrops on the curtailed burial ceremony, makes the same connection when he discovers that it is the body of Ophelia being so neglectfully interred. He remembers the other apparition that came up through the trap and springs forward in a grotesque parody of the Ghost, crying, "This is I, Hamlet the Dane!" It is a melodramatic claim to be acting a new role, that of his father the dead King. The first audiences would have remembered the ghost of dead King Hamlet using the stage trap at this point more readily than we do now. Hamlet's private knowledge of the Ghost and the trapdoor sets him, as so often happens in the play, at odds with his audience. Consequently, centuries of editors, like the characters onstage, have misread this claim as a declaration that young Hamlet ought to be King.

Since his own name is Hamlet, and since he alone could have made the connection between the Ghost and the trapdoor, he was all too likely to be misunderstood. In the next scene, Osric certainly shows that he understands Hamlet's graveside claim that he is his father's ghost to be a claim that he should now be King of Denmark. That explains why Osric insists on keeping his hat in his hand when he comes to invite Hamlet to duel with Laertes. With equals, an Elizabethan gentleman would doff his hat in greeting and then put it back on. Only in the presence of your master, or as a courtier in the presence of the King, did you keep it in your hand. Osric is trying tactfully to acknowledge what he thinks is Hamlet's lunatic claim to be King. He missed the private connection that Hamlet had made with the trapdoor and his father's ghost. Tudor body language, with its wordless gestures and signals that defined human relations, was an aspect of social life so widely understood that it needed no stage direction. The language of hats was a part of the Shakespearean mindset that we now have to register in footnotes.

Other signifiers are necessarily more elusive. We might take heart from the range of the comments made in *Much Ado About Nothing* 4.1 when Hero is accused and is seen to go red. Each of the viewers—Claudio, Leonato, and Friar Francis—gives a different reading (or "noting") of her blush. Different mindsets lead to visual indicators being read in different ways. Each reading tells as much about the observer as about the thing observed. We might add that since the blush is commented on so extensively, Shakespeare must have been concerned to save the boy playing Hero from the necessity of holding his breath long enough to produce the right visual effect.

Costume was a vital element in the plays, a mute and instant signifier of the scene. If a character entered carrying a candle and dressed in a gown with a nightcap on his head, he had evidently just been roused from bed. Characters who entered wearing cloaks and riding boots and possibly holding a whip had just ended a long journey. York,

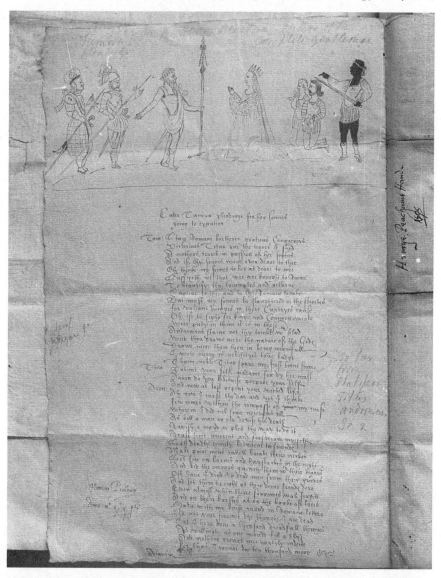

A sketch by Henry Peacham of an early staging of *Titus Andronicus* by Shakespeare's company (1595). Note the attempt at a Roman costume for Titus but not for his soldiers, who carry Tudor halberds, and note Aaron's makeup and wig.

entering in *Richard II* with a gorget (a metal neck plate, the "signs of war about his agèd neck" [2.2.74]), was preparing for battle. Even the women's wigs that the boys wore could be used to indicate the wearer's state of mind. Hair worn loose and unbound meant madness, whether in *Hamlet*'s Ophelia or *Troilus*'s Cassandra.

Comparable audience expectations could be roused by other visual features. Characters with faces blackened and wigs of curly black wool were recognized as Moors,

Johannes de Witt's drawing of the Swan Theatre in 1596, showing two boys playing women greeted by a chamberlain.

alien and dangerous non-Christians. Aaron the Moor in *Titus Andronicus* and the Prince of Morocco in *The Merchant of Venice* acquire that character as soon as they come in view. Othello, by Iago's report and by his own first appearance, takes on the same stereotype. By contrast, Iago is dressed like a simple and honest soldier. Only in the course of Act 1 does it become apparent that it is Othello who is the honest soldier, Iago the un-Christian alien. The play neatly reverses the visual stereotypes of Elizabethan staging. Twentieth-century playgoers miss most of these signals and the ways that the original players used them to show the discrepancy between outward appearance and inner person. As King Lear said, robes and furred gowns hide all.

For *The Merchant of Venice*, Shylock wore his "Jewish gabardine" and may also have put on a false nose, as Alleyn was said to have done for the title role in *The Jew of Malta*. Other national characteristics were noted by features of dress, such as the Irish "strait strossers" (tight trousers) that Macmorris would have worn in *Henry V*. The dress of the women in the plays, who were usually played by boys with unbroken voices, was always a special expense. The records kept by Philip Henslowe, owner of the Rose playhouse and impresario for the rival company to Shakespeare's, show that he paid the author less for the script of *A Woman Killed with Kindness* than he paid the costumer for the heroine's gown.

Women's clothing and the decorums and signals that women's costume contained were very different from those of men and men's clothing. Men frequently used their hats, doffing them to signal friendship and holding them in their hands while speaking to anyone in authority over them. Women's hats were fixed to their heads and were rarely if ever taken off in public. The forms and the language of women's clothes reflected the silent modesty and the quiet voices that men thought proper for women. Women had other devices to signal with, including handkerchiefs, fans, and face masks, and the boys playing the women's parts in the theaters exploited such accessories to the full. A lady out of doors commonly wore a mask to protect her complexion. When Othello is quizzing Emilia in 4.2 about his wife's behavior while she spoke to Cassio, he asks Emilia, who should have been chaperoning her mistress, whether Desdemona had not sent her away "to fetch her fan, her gloves, her mask, nor nothing?" There is little doubt that the boys would have routinely worn masks when they played gentlewomen onstage, and not just at the masked balls in *Romeo and Juliet*, *Love's Labour's Lost*, and *Much Ado About Nothing*.

Other features of the original staging stemmed from the actor–audience relationship, which differs radically in daylight, when both parties can see one another, from what we are used to in modern, darkened, theaters. An eavesdropping scene onstage, for instance, works rather on the same basis as the "invisible" fairies in *A Midsummer Night's Dream*, where the audience agrees to share the pretense. At the Globe, it also entailed adopting the eavesdropper's perspective. In *Much Ado*, the two games of eavesdropping played on Benedick and Beatrice are chiefly done around the two stage posts. In these scenes, the posts that held up the stage cover, or "heavens," near what we now think of as the front of the stage were round, like the whole auditorium, and their function was to allow things to be seen equally by all of the audience, wherever people might be standing or sitting. Members of the audience, sitting in the surrounding galleries or standing around the stage itself at the Globe or its predecessors, had the two tall painted pillars in their sight all the time, wherever they were in the playhouse. And since the audience was in a complete circle all around the stage, if the stage posts were used for concealment there was always a large proportion of the audience who could see the player trying to hide behind a post. It was a three-dimensional game in which the audience might find itself behind any of the game players, victims or eavesdroppers, complicit in either role.

The first of *Much Ado*'s eavesdropping scenes, 2.3, starts as usual in Shakespeare with a verbal indication of the locality. Benedick tells his boy, "Bring it hither to me in the orchard." So we don't need stage trees to tell us where we are supposed to be. He later hides "in the arbour" to listen to what Don Pedro and the others have set for him; this means concealing himself behind a stage post, closer to the audience than the playactors who are talking about him. Don Pedro asks, "See you where Benedick hath hid himself?" a self-contradiction that confirms the game. When it is Beatrice's turn in her arbor scene, 3.1, she slips into a "bower" behind "this alley," which again signals a retreat behind the prominent stage post. These games are played with both of the eavesdroppers hiding behind the post at the stage edge, while the others do their talking at center stage between the two posts.

Such games of eavesdropping, using the same bits of the stage structure, make a strong visual contrast with all that goes on at what we two-dimensional thinkers, used to the pictorial staging of the cinema, call the "back" of the stage, or upstage—where, for instance, the Friar starts the broken-off wedding and where Claudio and Don Pedro later figure at Leonato's monument. These events are more distant from the audience, less obviously comic and intimate. The close proximity of players to audience in such activities as eavesdropping strongly influenced the audience's feeling of kinship with the different groupings of players.

A multitude of other staging differences can be identified. Quite apart from the fact that the language idioms were more familiar to the playgoers at the original Globe than they are now, all playgoers in 1600, many of them illiterate, were practiced listeners. The speed of speech, even in blank verse, was markedly higher then than the recitation of Shakespeare is today. The original performances of *Hamlet,* if the Folio version reflects what was usually acted, would have run for not much more than two and a half hours (the time quoted by Ben Jonson for a play as long as *Hamlet*), compared with the more than four hours that the full Folio or 1605 quarto text with at least one intermission would take today. Quicker speaking, quicker stage action, no intermissions, and the audience's ability to grasp the language more quickly meant that the plays galloped along. The story, not the verse, carried the thrust of the action. Occasional set speeches, like Hamlet's soliloquies or Gaunt's "sceptred isle" speech in *Richard II,* would be heard, familiar as they already were to many in the audience, like a solo aria in a modern opera. In theory if not in practice, the business of hearing, as "audience" (from the Latin *audire,* "to hear"), was more important than the business of seeing, as "spectators" (from the Latin *spectare,* "to see"). The visual aspects of acting, like scenic staging, are inherently two-dimensional and do not work well when the audience completely surrounds the actors. Most of Shakespeare's fellow writers, notably Jonson, understandably set a higher priority on the audience's hearing their verse than on their seeing what the players did with the lines. The poets wanted listeners, although the players did try to cater to the viewers. Yet for all the games with magic tricks and devils spouting fireworks that were part of the Shakespearean staging tradition, spectacle was a limited resource on the scene-free Elizabethan stage. Shakespeare in this was a poet more than a player. Even in his last and most richly staged plays—*Cymbeline, The Winter's Tale,* and *The Tempest*—he made notably less use of such "spectacles" than did his contemporaries.

One piece of internal evidence about the original staging is Hamlet's advice to the visiting players. In 3.2, before they stage the *Mousetrap* play that he has rewritten for them, he lectures them on what a noble student of the theater then considered to be good acting. He objects first to overacting and second to the clown who ad libs with his own jokes and does not keep to the script. How far this may have been Shakespeare's own view it is impossible to say. Hamlet is an amateur lecturing professionals about how they should do their job. His views are what we would expect an amateur playwright with a liking for plays that are "caviar to the general" to hold. His objections to the clown are noteworthy, because once the original performances ended, the clown would conclude the afternoon's entertainment with a comic song-and-dance jig. Thomas Platter, a young German-speaking Swiss student, went to the Globe in 1599 to see *Julius Caesar.* He reported back home that

> on 21 September after lunch I and my party crossed the river, and there in the playhouse with the thatched roof witnessed an excellent performance of the tragedy of the first emperor Julius Caesar with a cast of about fifteen people. When the play

The hall screen in the Middle Temple Hall, built in 1574. Shakespeare's company staged *Twelfth Night* in this hall in February 1602.

was over they danced marvellously and gracefully together as their custom is, two dressed as men and two as women.[1]

The script for one jig survives, probably played by Will Kemp, who was the Shakespeare company clown until he left just before *Hamlet* came to the Globe. Its story is a bawdy knockabout tale of different men trying to seduce a shopkeeper's wife in rhyming couplets, hiding in a chest from her husband, and beating one another up. There is nothing to say what the audience reaction to such a jig might have been after they had seen a performance of *Julius Caesar* or *Hamlet*. It is possible that the Globe players stopped offering that kind of coda when they acquired the clown who played Feste in *Twelfth Night* in 1601. The song with which Feste ends that play might have become an alternative form of closure, replacing the traditional bawdy jig.

Vigorous and rapid staging was inevitable when the half of the audience closest to the stage had to stand throughout the performance. Shakespeare's plays were distinctive among the other plays of the time for their reliance on verbal sparkle over scenes of battle and physical movement, but even the soliloquies raced along. There was little occasion for long pauses and emoting. Dumb shows, like the players' prelude to the *Mousetrap* play in *Hamlet,* were the nearest that the players came to silent acting. There were no intermissions—apples, nuts, and drink were peddled in the auditorium throughout the performance—and the only "comfort stations" were, for the men, the nearest blank wall; for the women, whatever convenient pots or bottles they might be carrying under their long skirts.

Nor were there any pauses to change scenes. There was no static scenery apart from an emblematic candle to signify a night scene, a bed "thrust out" onto the stage, or the canopied chair of state on which the ruler or judge sat for court scenes. Usually any

1. *Thomas Platter's Travels in England* (1599), rendered into English from the German, and with introductory matter by Clare Williams (London: Cape, 1937), p. 166.

special locality would be signaled in the first words of a new scene, but unlocalized scenes were routine. Each scene ended when all the characters left the stage and another set entered. No act breaks appear in the plays before *The Tempest*. *Henry V* marked each act with a Chorus, but even he entered on the heels of the characters from the previous scene. Blue-coated stagehands were a visibly invisible presence onstage. They would draw back the central hangings on the *frons scenae* for a discovery scene, carry on the chair of state on its dais for courtroom scenes, or push out the bed with Desdemona on it for the last act of *Othello*. They served the stage like the house servants with whom the nobility peopled every room in their great houses, silent machines ready to spring into action when needed.

There has been a great deal of speculation about the tiring-house front at the rear of the stage platform: did it look more like an indoor set or an outdoor one, like the hall screen of a great house or palace or like a housefront exterior? In fact, it could easily be either. The upper level of the *frons*, the balconied "above," might equally represent a musicians' gallery, like those in the main hall of a great house, or a city wall under which the central discovery space served as the city gates, as it did for York in *Richard Duke of York* (*3 Henry VI*) 4.8, or *Henry V*'s Harfleur (3.3.78). The "above" could equally be an indoor gallery or an outdoor balcony. The appearance of the stage was everything and nothing, depending on what the play required. Players and playwrights expected the audience members to use their imagination, as they had to with the opening lines of *Hamlet*, or, as the Prologue to *Henry V* put it, to "piece out our imperfections with your thoughts."

Shakespeare's Companies and Their Playhouses

Shakespeare's plays were written for a variety of staging conditions. Until 1594, when he joined a new company under the patronage of the Lord Chamberlain, the Queen's officer responsible for licensing playing companies, poets had written their plays for any kind of playhouse. The Queen's Men, the largest and best company of the 1580s, is on record as playing at the Bell, the Bel Savage, and the Bull inns inside the city, and at the Theatre and the Curtain playhouses in the suburbs. Early in 1594, it completed this sweep of all the available London venues by playing at the Rose. But in that year, the system of playing changed. The Lord Mayor had always objected to players using the city's inns, and in May 1594 he succeeded in securing the Lord Chamberlain's agreement to a total ban. From then on, only the specially built playhouses in the suburbs were available for plays.

The Queen's Men had been set up in 1583, drawn from all the then-existing major companies with the best players. This larger and favored group at first monopolized playing in London. But it was in decline by the early 1590s, and the shortage of companies to perform for the Queen at Christmas led the Lord Chamberlain and his son-in-law, the Lord Admiral, to set up two new companies in its place as a duopoly in May 1594. Shakespeare became a "sharer," or partner, in one of these companies. As part of the same new establishment, his company, the Lord Chamberlain's Men, was allocated the Theatre to perform in, while its partner company in the duopoly, the Lord Admiral's Men, was assigned to the Rose. This was the first time any playing company secured a playhouse officially authorized for its use alone.

The Theatre, originally built in 1576 by James Burbage, father of the leading player of the Lord Chamberlain's company, was in Shoreditch, a suburb to the north of the city. The Rose, built in 1587 by Philip Henslowe, father-in-law of the Lord Admiral's leading player, Edward Alleyn, was in the suburb of Southwark, on the south bank of the Thames. Henslowe's business papers, his accounts, some lists of costumes and other resources, and his "diary," a day-by-day listing of each day's takings and the plays that brought the money in, have survived for the period from 1592 until well into the next decade. Together they provide an invaluable record of how one of the two major companies of the later 1590s, the only rival to Shakespeare's company, operated through these years.[2] Some of Shakespeare's earlier plays, written before he joined the Lord Chamberlain's Men, including *1 Henry VI* and *Titus Andronicus*, were performed at the Rose. After May 1594, the new company acquired all of his early plays; every Shakespeare play through the next three years was written for the Theatre. Its familiarity supplied one sort of resource to the playwright. But the repertory system laid heavy demands on the company.

Henslowe's papers give a remarkable record of the company repertory for these years. Each afternoon, the same team of fifteen or so players would stage a different play. With only two companies operating in London, the demand was for constant change. No play at the Rose was staged more than four or five times in any month, and it was normal to stage a different play on each of the six afternoons of each week that they performed. A new play would be introduced roughly every three weeks—after three weeks of transcribing and learning the new parts; preparing the promptbook, costumes, and properties; and rehearsing in the mornings—while each afternoon, whichever of the established plays had been advertised around town on the playbills would be put on. The leading players had to memorize on average as many as eight hundred lines for each afternoon. Richard Burbage, who played the first Hamlet in 1601, probably had to play Richard III, Orlando in *As You Like It,* and Hamlet on successive afternoons while at the same time learning the part of Duke Orsino and rehearsing the new *Twelfth Night*—and still holding at least a dozen other parts in his head for the rest of the month's program. In the evenings, he might be called on to take the company to perform a different play at court or at a nobleman's house in the Strand. The best companies made a lot of money, but not without constant effort.

The companies were formed rather like guilds, controlled by their leading "sharers." Each senior player shared the company's profits and losses equally with his fellows. Most of the plays have seven or eight major speaking parts for the men, plus two for the boys playing the women. A normal London company had eight or ten sharers, who collectively chose the repertory of plays to be performed, bought the playbooks from the poets, and put up the money for the main company resource of playbooks and costumes (not to mention the wagon and horses for touring when plague forced the London theaters to close). Shakespeare made most of his fortune from his "share," first in his company and later in its two playhouses.

As a playhouse landlord, Henslowe took half of the takings from the galleries each afternoon for his rent, while the players shared all the yard takings and the other half of the gallery money. From their takings, the sharers paid hired hands to take the walk-on parts and to work as stagehands, musicians, bookkeeper or prompter, and "gatherers" at the different entry gates. The leading players also kept the boys who played the women's parts, housing and feeding them as "apprentices" in an imitation of the London livery companies and trades, which ran apprenticeships to train boys to become skilled artisans, or "journeymen." City apprenticeships ran for seven years from the age of seventeen, but the boy players began much younger, because unbroken voices were needed. They graduated to become adult players at an age when the city apprentices were only beginning their training. Most of the "extras," apart from the playing boys, would be left in London whenever the company had to go on tour.

Because the professional companies of the kind that Shakespeare joined all started as traveling groups rather than as companies settled at a single playhouse in London, the years up to 1594 yielded plays that could be staged anywhere. The company might be summoned to play at court, at private houses, or at the halls of the Inns of Court as readily as at inns or innyards or the custom-built theaters themselves. They traveled the country with their plays, using the great halls of country houses, or town guildhalls and local inns, wherever the town they visited allowed them. Consequently, the plays could not demand elaborate resources for staging. In this highly mobile tradition of traveling

---

2. See *Henslowe's Diary,* ed. R. A. Foakes (Cambridge, Eng.: Cambridge University Press, 1961).

companies, they were written in the expectation of the same basic but minimal features being available at each venue. Besides the stage platform itself, the basic features appear to have been two entry doors, usually a trap in the stage floor, a pair of stage pillars, sometimes a discovery space, and very occasionally a heavens with descent machinery. Apart from these fixtures, properties such as chairs and a table, a canopied throne on a dais, and sometimes a bed were also in regular use, though in a pinch these could be as mobile as the players themselves. The only essential traveling properties were players, playbooks, and costumes.

Once the two authorized companies settled permanently at the Theatre and the Rose in 1594, they slowly lost some of this mobility. The demands of versatility and readiness to make rapid changes now had to be switched from the venues to the plays themselves. A traveling company needed very few plays, since the locations and audiences were always changing. When the venues became fixed, it was the plays that had to keep changing. The Henslowe papers record that the Lord Admiral's Men staged an amazingly varied repertory of plays at the Rose. Shakespeare's company must have been equally versatile. The practice of giving popular plays long runs did not begin until the 1630s, by which time the number of London playhouses had grown to as many as five, all offering their plays each afternoon. Shakespeare's company in London had only the one peer from 1594 until 1600; and only two from then until 1608, aside from the once-weekly plays by the two boy companies, the "little eyases" mentioned in *Hamlet*, that started with the new century.

From May 1594 to April 1597 at the Theatre, in addition to all his earlier plays that he brought to his new company, Shakespeare gave them possibly *Romeo and Juliet* and *King John*, and certainly *Richard II, A Midsummer Night's Dream, 1 Henry IV*, and *The Merchant of Venice*. But then they ran into deep trouble, because they lost the Theatre. In April 1597, its original twenty-one-year lease expired, and the landlord, who disliked plays, refused to let them renew it. Anticipating this, the company's impresario, James Burbage, had built a new theater for them, a roofed place in the Blackfriars near St. Paul's Cathedral. The Blackfriars precinct was a "liberty," free from the Lord Mayor's jurisdiction. But the plan proved a disaster. The rich residents of Blackfriars objected, and the Privy Council stopped the theater from opening. From April 1597, Shakespeare's company had to rent the Curtain, an old neighbor of their now-silent Theatre, and it was there that the next four of Shakespeare's plays—*2 Henry IV, Much Ado About Nothing, The Merry Wives of Windsor*, and probably *Henry V*—were first staged.

In December 1598, losing hope of a new lease for the old Theatre, the Burbage sons had it pulled down and quietly transported its massive framing timbers across the Thames to make the scaffold for the Globe on the river's south bank, near the Rose. Most of their capital was sunk irretrievably into the Blackfriars theater, and they could afford only half the cost of rebuilding. So they raised money as best they could. Some of the company's more popular playbooks were sold to printers, including *Romeo and Juliet, Richard III, Richard II*, and *1 Henry IV*. More to the point, the Burbage brothers raised capital for the building by cutting in five of the leading players, including Shakespeare, and asking them to put up the other half of its cost. The Globe, its skeleton taken from the old Theatre, thus became the first playhouse to be owned by its players, and, within the limits set by the old frame, the first one built to their own design.

For this theater, one-eighth of which he personally owned, Shakespeare wrote his greatest plays: *Julius Caesar, As You Like It, Hamlet, Twelfth Night, Othello, All's Well That Ends Well, Measure for Measure, King Lear, Macbeth, Pericles, Antony and Cleopatra, Coriolanus, Cymbeline, The Winter's Tale*, and most likely *Troilus and Cressida* and *Timon of Athens*. As the first playhouse to be owned by the players who expected to use it, its fittings must have satisfied all the basic needs of Shakespearean staging. At one time or another, the company staged every one of Shakespeare's plays there.

In 1600, a company consisting entirely of boys started using the Blackfriars playhouse that Richard Burbage's father had tried to open four years before. Companies of boy players had a higher social status than the adult professionals, and, playing only in halls, they commanded a more affluent clientele. The boys performed only once a week, and the relative infrequency of their crowds, plus their skills as trained singers (they were choir-school children turned to making money for their choirmasters), proved less offensive to the local residents than a noisy adult company with its drums and trumpets. Leasing the Blackfriars to the boy company made a minor profit for the Burbages, who took the rent for eight years.

In the longer run, though, this arrangement provided a different means for the Burbage–Shakespeare company to advance its career. The boys' eight years of playing in their rented hall playhouse eventually made it possible for the company of adult players to renew Burbage's old plan of 1596. Shakespeare's company had been made the King's Men when James came to the throne in 1603, and their new patron gave them a status that made it impossible for the residents of Blackfriars to prevent them from implementing the original plan. During a lengthy closure of all the theaters because of a plague epidemic in 1608, the boys' manager surrendered his lease of the hall playhouse to the Burbages. They then took possession for their own company of the playhouse that their father had built for them twelve years before. They divided the new playhouse property among the leading players as they had done in 1599 with the Globe.

A section from Wenceslaus Hollar's "Long View" of London, printed in 1644. Drawn from a standpoint on the tower of the church that is now Southwark Cathedral, Hollar's view shows the roof of the great hall in which the Blackfriars playhouse was built. It can be seen as the long angled roof with two central chimneys, below and to the east of St. Bride's Church.

They were the King's Men, the leading company in the country, and their status after ten years of playing at the Globe was matched by their wealth. By the time theaters reopened late in 1609, the company had established a new system of playing.

The King's Men now had two playhouses, a large open amphitheater and a much smaller roofed hall. Instead of selling or renting one out and using the other for themselves, they decided to use both in turn, for half of each year. It was a reversion to the old system with the city inns, where through the summer they played in the large open yards and in the winter played at inns with big indoor rooms. This time, though, the company owned both playhouses. Their affluence and their high status are signaled by the fact that they chose to keep one of their playhouses idle while they used the other, despite there now being a shortage of playhouses in London. That affluence was needed in 1613, when the Globe burned down at a performance of *All Is True (Henry VIII)* and the company chose the much more expensive option of rebuilding it instead of reverting to the Blackfriars for both winter and summer. That decision, in its way, was the ultimate gesture of affection for their original playhouse. It was a costly gesture, but it meant that the Globe continued in use by the company until all the theaters were closed down by Parliament in 1642.

In 1609, when they reopened after the closure for plague, Shakespeare's company had made several changes in their procedures. The restart was at the Blackfriars, and although they offered the same kind of plays, they began to alter their style of staging. Along with the Blackfriars playhouse, they acquired a famous consort of musicians who played on strings and woodwinds in a music room set over the stage. The new consort was a distinct enhancement of the company's musical resources, which until then had been confined to song, the occasional use of recorders or hautboys, and military drums and trumpets for the scenes with soldiery. In 1608, a central room on the Globe's stage balcony was taken over to serve as a music room like the one at the Blackfriars. From this time on, the King's Men's performances began with a lengthy overture or concert of music before the play.

With that change, the plays themselves now had music to back their singers and provide other sorts of atmospheric effects. Some of the songs and music that appear in the plays not printed until the First Folio of 1623, such as the song that Mariana hears in *Measure for Measure* 4.1, may have been added after Shakespeare's time to make use of this new resource. Shakespeare did use songs, sometimes with string accompaniment, quite regularly in the early plays, but instrumental music hardly ever appears. The last play that he wrote alone, *The Tempest,* was the only one in which he made full use of this new resource.

All the plays containing soldiers and battles used the military drums that in war conveyed signals to infantry formations, as well as the trumpets that were used for signaling to cavalry. These were usually employed for offstage noises, sound effects made from "within" (inside the dressing room or tiring-house behind the stage). Soldiers marching in procession, as in the dead march at the close of *Hamlet,* would have the time marked by an onstage drum. Shakespeare never calls for guns to be fired onstage, even though other writers did, but he did have other noises at his command. A small cannon or "chamber" might be used, fired from the gable-fronted heavens over the stage, as Claudius demands in *Hamlet* and as the Chorus to Act 3 of *Henry V* notes. It was wadding from a ceremonial cannon shot that set the gallery thatch alight at a performance of *All Is True* in July 1613 and burned the Globe to the ground. Stage battles such as Shrewsbury at the end of *1 Henry IV,* written for the Theatre, were accompanied by sword fights that were not the duels of *Hamlet*'s finale but exchanges with broadswords or "foxes" slammed against metal shields or "targets." That action guaranteed emphatic sound effects. The drums and trumpets, with clashes of swords and a great deal of to-ing and fro-ing onto and off the stage, were highlighted in between the shouted dialogue by some hard fighting between the protagonists. The leading players were practiced swordsmen, who knew they were being watched by experts. These were the scenes of "four or five most vile and ragged foils" that the fourth Chorus self-consciously derided in *Henry V* at the Curtain.

The second great reason for noise in the amphitheaters was to mark storm and tempest. Stagehands used the kind of device that Jonson mocked in the Prologue to *Every Man in His Humour*, written for its 1616 publication. His play, wrote Jonson, was free from choruses that wafted you over the seas, "nor rolled bullet heard / To say, it thunders; nor tempestuous drum / Rumbles, to tell you when the storm doth come." For centuries, lead balls rolling down a tin trough were a standard way of making thunder noises in English theaters. The tempest in Act 3 of *King Lear* is heralded several times in the text before a stage direction, "Storm and tempest" (Folio 2.2.450), tells us that it has at last arrived. In 2.2, Cornwall notes its coming twice (Folio 2.2.452, 473). Kent comments on the "Foul weather" in his first line in Act 3, prefaced by the entry stage direction for Act 3, "Storm still," which is repeated for 3.2. Such stage directions appear in both texts (Q has "Storm" for the equivalent Scenes 8, 9, and also at 11, F's 3.4, where F omits any further reference to these noises). These explicit signals indicate that the stagehands provided offstage noises, for all that Lear himself outstorms them with his violent speeches in 3.2.

The main question about the storm scenes in *King Lear* is this: with such consistent emphasis on storm in the language, what was the design behind the stage directions? In the centuries that *Lear* has been restaged, the tempest has been made to roar offstage in a wide variety of ways, often with so much effect that, in the face of complaints that the storm noises made it difficult for the audience to hear the words, some modern productions reduced the storm to solely visual effects, or even left Lear's own raging language to express it unsupported. But the two stage directions indicate that in the original performances the "storm in nature" was not left to Lear himself to convey. The two "Storm still" directions in the Folio suggest a constant rumbling, not the intermittent crashes that might allow Lear to conduct a dialogue with the occasional outbursts of storm noises, as some modern productions have done.

Shakespeare left regrettably few stage directions to indicate the special tricks or properties that he wanted. Curtained beds are called for in *Othello* 5.2 and *Cymbeline* 2.2, and there is the specification "Stocks brought out" in *King Lear* 2.2.132. Small and portable things like papers were a much more common device, from the letters in *The Two Gentlemen of Verona* 1.2.46, 1.3.44, and 2.1.95 to Lear's map at 1.1.35. Across the whole thirty-eight plays, though, there are very few such directions. Shakespeare's economy in preparing his scripts is a major impediment to the modern reader. He hardly ever bothered to note the standard physical gestures, such as kneeling or doffing a hat, and did little more to specify any special effects. Nonetheless, it is important not to imagine elaborate devices or actions where the text does not call for them. On the whole, the demands Shakespeare made of his fellows for staging his plays appear to have been remarkably modest. Since he was a company shareholder, his parsimony may have had a simple commercial motive. Stage properties cost the company money, and one had to be confident of a new play's popularity before investing much in its staging.

There may have been other reasons for avoiding extravagant staging spectacles. Shakespeare made little use of the discovery space until the last plays, for instance, for reasons that we can only guess at. The few definite discoveries in the plays include Portia's caskets in *The Merchant of Venice*, Falstaff sleeping off his sack in *1 Henry IV* 2.5.482, the body of Polonius in *Hamlet*, Hermione's statue in *The Winter's Tale* 5.3.20, and the lovers in *The Tempest* 5.1.173, who are found when discovered to be playing chess. The audience's shock when Hermione moves and comes out of the discovery space onto the main stage is rare in Shakespeare: in every other play, whether comedy or tragedy, the audience knows far more than the characters onstage about what is going on. Shakespeare matched this late innovation in *The Winter's Tale* with his last play, *The Tempest*. After the preliminary and soothing concert by the resident Blackfriars musicians, it opens with a storm at sea so realistic that it includes that peculiarly distinctive stage direction "Enter Mariners, wet" (1.1.46). That startling piece of stage realism turns out straightaway to be not real at all but a piece of stage magic.

COMEDIES

Shakespearean Comedy
by

KATHARINE EISAMAN MAUS

SLY   Is not a comonty
A Christmas gambol, or a tumbling trick?
BARTHOLOMEW   No, . . . it is a kind of history.
—*The Taming of the Shrew* Induction 2.132–135

When, after Shakespeare's death, his colleagues in his theater company, the King's Men, collected and printed his works in the First Folio, they organized them into three groups: comedies, tragedies, and histories. Since the late nineteenth century, several plays written late in Shakespeare's career—*Pericles, The Winter's Tale, Cymbeline,* and *The Tempest*—have been relegated (as they are in the *Norton Shakespeare*) to a separate group, the romances. With the romances subtracted, Shakespeare's comic output comes to twelve plays, plus *Troilus and Cressida* and the coauthored *Two Noble Kinsman,* which are sometimes classified as comedies and sometimes as tragedies.

Writing about 350 B.C.E., the Greek philosopher Aristotle speculated that comedy had originated in the *phallaka,* ribald songs that accompanied a fertility rite in which young men paraded a large model of an erect penis through a village to celebrate a bountiful grape harvest. The procession of youths who sang these songs was called a *komos,* from which the word *comedy* is perhaps derived. At this historical remove, it is impossible to recover exactly how "phallic songs" might have detached from their original performance circumstances and developed into staged drama. Yet many modern critics as well as Aristotle have remarked upon comedy's association with ancient myths of seasonal rebirth and renewal, and with festivities in which sexuality and fertility are celebrated, inhibitions loosened, bodily pleasures indulged, bounds of decorum overturned. Shakespeare's England was familiar neither with grape harvests nor with the *phallaka,* but it shared similar traditions with other European agrarian societies. May Day on May 1 and Midsummer Night at the summer solstice celebrated the effects of the burgeoning spring and fertile summer for plants, animals, and people. In late summer and fall, "harvest home" festivities marked the end of the arduous toil required to gather the year's crop in an age before mechanized farm equipment. The period between Christmas Eve and Epiphany, or Twelfth Night, was a time of revelry sometimes presided over by a "lord of misrule," who issued topsy-turvy edicts and encouraged playful role-playing and overindulgence in food and drink. Carnival—less elaborate in England than in southern Europe but still a period of feasting, mirth, and masquerade—took place just before Lent, the season of abstinence and penance, when the previous year's food supply was dwindling but the new year's crop was not yet available.

By the 1590s, rapid urbanization had begun to detach some English people, especially the Londoners who attended Shakespeare's theater, from the rhythms of planting and harvest that governed life in the countryside. Moreover, some Protestant reformers objected to all "holidays of indulgence" because of their pagan or Catholic origin. Yet the traditional holidays were still celebrated, and perhaps controversy sharpened Shakespeare's interest in them. Several of his comedies—*A Midsummer Night's*

An ancient Greek phallic procession. This drawing was made from a vase painting.

Dream, Twelfth Night, and *The Merry Wives of Windsor*—make overt references to such holidays or incorporate some of their rituals into the action. The dialogue between Spring and Winter in *Love's Labour's Lost* and many of the songs in *As You Like It* and *Twelfth Night* evoke the seasonal round which all these festivals commemorate and honor.

In addition, medieval and Renaissance England was home to a rich indigenous tradition of clowning, which flourished during holiday seasons but which was not necessarily tied to special occasions. Many medieval morality plays—dramas in which a religious or moral dilemma is allegorically represented—feature boisterously anarchic "Vices" or devil characters who comment irreverently on the action while sowing playful mayhem onstage. Wealthy men sometimes employed professional fools in their household, whose function was to amuse their employers with ridiculous banter. Although some written parts for Vice characters have survived, neither the "Vice" nor the professional fool necessarily tied his performance to a script. He was like a modern jazz performer, improvising ingeniously, rather than like a classical musician who aims to render a beautiful intepretation of a fully notated score. In *Twelfth Night,* the heroine Viola remarks upon the agile intelligence that the professional clown's spur-of-the-moment preposterousness requires:

> He must observe their mood on whom he jests,
> The quality of persons, and the time,
> And, like the haggard [hunting hawk], check at every feather
> That comes before his eye. This is a practice
> As full of labour as a wise man's art.
>
> (3.1.55–59)

Laborious, and perilous, too. The fool could not be funny if he refrained from obscene, satirical, or disrespectful remarks, and he was, therefore, permitted some liberty of speech. Still, his uninhibited, irreverent commentary risked offending those more powerful than himself. In Shakespeare's plays, every professional fool is threatened at some point with a whipping for having presumptuously overstepped his bounds. "The more pity that fools may not speak wisely what wise men do foolishly," remarks one of these fools, Touchstone, in *As You Like It* (1.2.72–73).

Once the public theaters opened in London in the 1570s, the stage became a place where professional clowns could entertain larger and more diverse audiences: Will Kempe, one of the members of Shakespeare's theater company in the 1590s, was famous for his witty jests and pranks both onstage and off. In *Hamlet,* Hamlet's advice to the acting company who visits him in Elsinore suggests both the scene-stealing appeal of improvisatory clowning and its potential to deform a carefully crafted play with random interpolations:

Will Kemp, the clown in Shakespeare's company, during the 1590s. From the title page of *Kempes Nine Daies Wonder . . .* (1600).

> And let those that play your clowns speak no more than is set down for them; for
> there be of them that will themselves laugh to set on some quantity of barren
> spectators to laugh too, though in the mean time some necessary question of the
> play be then to be considered. That's villainous, and shows a most pitiful ambi-
> tion in the fool that uses it.
>
> (3.2.34–40)

Yet scripted comedies retain some of the clown's typical focus upon what the fool Feste, in *Twelfth Night*, calls "present mirth" (2.3.44)—an emphasis on enjoyment in the here and now regardless of context or consequences.

In scripted drama, the word *comedy* can refer to anything from a short entertaining scene or improvisation to a whole play. Renaissance playwrights did not necessarily maintain strict demarcations between genres—they were prone to "mingling kings and clowns," as Shakespeare's contemporary Philip Sidney noted disapprovingly in *The Defence of Poesie*. Shakespeare's tragedies and history plays often contain comic episodes or subplots. In fact, Falstaff, arguably Shakespeare's greatest comic character, makes his most memorable appearances in the history plays, *1 Henry IV and 2 Henry IV*; in *Macbeth*, a drunken Porter staggers onstage to make obscene jokes immediately after Macbeth, offstage, has murdered Duncan; in *King Lear,* the Fool provides moments of extremely dark humor that blur the distinction between the tragic and the comically absurd.

Yet by Shakespeare's time, comedy, considered as a distinctive kind of play, was more than merely a series of jokes and funny sketches or a collection of festive customs. As Bartholomew informs the uncouth Christopher Sly in *The Taming of the Shrew,* a comedy "is a kind of history" (Induction 2.135)—that is, it has a plot. In the Renaissance, the most widely influential comic patterns were derived from the classical Roman dramatists Plautus and Terence, who were read in Latin, and sometimes performed or declaimed, in grammar schools of the kind Shakespeare attended as a boy in Stratford. Plautus and Terence had, in turn, appropriated plots and characters from Greek predecessors, most of whose works have since been lost. Their kind of drama is often called New Comedy to distinguish it from Old Comedy, an earlier Greek form that had satirized well-known living people and commented on current events.

Although, of course, individual New Comedies vary, they tend to follow a predictable pattern. A youth is in love with an apparently unsuitable maiden—often a slave girl. Various stock characters help or hinder his love: the "heavy father" or uncle, who prohibits the union and sometimes lusts after the maiden himself; the ingenious slave, who plots on the youth's behalf while remarking self-delightedly upon his own tricky skill; the stupid slave, who misconstrues the speech and action of other characters; the braggart soldier home from war, who exaggerates his exploits in battle but turns out to be a ridiculous coward. Sometimes the true identities of various characters are unclear, either because they have suffered some mishap that has obscured their family history or because they are in disguise. In the course of the play, one or both of the lovers find themselves in peril—"the course of true love never did run smooth" (1.1.134), as Shakespeare's Lysander remarks in *A Midsummer Night's Dream*—yet in the end nobody dies. Ultimately, confusions are sorted out and family members reunited and reconciled; often the maiden turns out to be freeborn and, therefore, marriage material. The couple may then be ushered to wedded bliss.

New Comedy registers the surprising triumph of the apparently weak over the apparently powerful: of youth over age, of love over property, of wit over authority, of pleasure-seekers over prudent calculators. At the same time, the end of the play channels the characters' unruly energies into a form that seems ultimately to reinforce rather than challenge the status quo. The tricky slave may hoodwink his masters, but he does not flee his household or agitate for the abolition of servitude. The lovers, though they flout their parents' authority, enter into marriage and prepare to become parents themselves in their turn. New Comedy implies that rebelliousness marks a phase of life; it is not a precursor to revolutionary social change. Human beings follow a predictable cycle just as the seasons do, with one life stage succeeding another in due course and the younger generation replacing the old.

Plautus's and Terence's plays were a treasure trove for later writers. The plots were easy to recycle because they were generalized rather than tied to particular people and to current events, as Old Comedy had been. New Comedy represents human eccentricities as perennial; absurd behavior apparently takes much the same form in ancient Greece or Rome as it does in Italy in the 1400s or in England in the 1590s. Moreover, New Comedy was well adapted to societies in which, like Shakespeare's England, censorship and slander laws prohibited the lampooning of powerful individuals and most public discussion of contemporary political affairs. The romance novella, adapting and recombining New Comic plot devices, flourished all over Renaissance Europe; Shakespeare knew versions from Italy, Spain, and France as well as, more immediately, romances written in the late sixteenth-century by such English writers as Thomas Lodge, Robert Greene, and Barnabe Riche. When, following age-old precedent, Shakespeare appropriates his plots from others, he sometimes adapts plot formulas directly from the classical originals and sometimes relies upon one of their mediated forms. In *The Comedy of Errors*, he goes straight to a classical source, Plautus's *Menaechmi*, but follows more recent renditions of New Comic devices for the plots of *The Two Gentlemen of Verona, The Merry Wives of Windsor, As You Like It, Twelfth Night, Much Ado About Nothing, Measure for Measure,* and *All's Well That Ends Well.*

The "marriage plot" of New Comedy is absolutely fundamental to Shakespeare's comic drama: most of his comedies involve multiple courtships and weddings. Sometimes, indeed, Shakespeare alters the expected formula, as in *Love's Labour's Lost,* in which the women defer the weddings for at least a year, or in *Measure for Measure,* in which most of the concluding marriages are apparently loveless ones. Yet in these cases, the familiarity of the pattern

A woodcut from a 1493 edition of Terence, showing a performance of *The Eunuch.*

means that characters as well as audiences register these changes as troubling departures from the norm. "Our wooing doth not end like an old play," complains Biron in *Love's Labour's Lost.* "Jack hath not Jill" (5.2.851–52). Many of Shakespeare's comedies also feature situations drawn from New Comic tradition: characters in disguise, separated family members reunited at the end of the play, smart-mouthed servant characters turning the tables on their masters, and (in *The Merry Wives of Windsor* and *All's Well That Ends Well*) cowardly braggart soldiers.

Aristotle and the Latin literary theorist Horace had maintained that comedy typically dealt with people worse, both in merit and in social class, than the audience, whereas tragedy dealt with people better than the audience. Following these authorities, some Renaissance critics likewise argued that comedy teaches spectators good behavior by holding bad behavior up to ridicule. This way of thinking about comic characters, which predicates the spectator's pleasure upon contempt, is inadequate to Shakespearean comedy. Many of Shakespeare's comic characters are empathetic, articulate, and self-aware. Moreover, and significantly in Shakespeare's hierarchy-conscious world, the central protagonists of his comedies are often of high rank. While classical New Comedies typically feature urban characters of the middling sort, the Renaissance romances derived from them move up the social scale so that the main characters are often kings and dukes, princesses and countesses. While Shakespeare's plays have plenty of lower-status characters in supporting roles, the marriage plots tend to retain this upscale orientation. In *Love's Labour's Lost,* a king and his nobles square off against a princess and her ladies; in *As You Like It,* the daughters of two dukes fall in love with noblemen brothers; *The Two Gentlemen of Verona, Twelfth Night, A Midsummer Night's Dream, Measure for Measure,* and *All's Well That Ends Well* all involve characters of high degree in the marriage plot. Countess Olivia, in *Twelfth Night,* suggests how indelible the markers of status were imagined to be. Olivia falls in love with a woman, Viola, disguised as a man, who is employed as a servant. When Olivia asks after her beloved's parentage, Viola replies that it is "above my fortunes. . . . I am a gentleman" (1.5.248–49). After Viola departs, Olivia soliloquizes:

> 'I am a gentleman.' I'll be sworn thou art.
> Thy tongue, thy face, thy limbs, actions, and spirit
> Do give thee five-fold blazon.
>
> (1.5.261–63)

Although unable to discern Viola's true sex, Olivia has no trouble at all accurately assessing Viola's class origins, which her behavior seems to set forth for all to view, as a gentleman's coat of arms, or "blazon," reveals his identity and family background. Even less exalted heroes and heroines, such as Katherine and Petruccio in *The Taming of the Shrew,* or the Antipholus twins in *The Comedy of Errors,* or the Page and Ford families in *The Merry Wives of Windsor,* live above the social line, critical in Shakespeare's time, that separated the landowning, professional, servant-employing classes from the vast majority who earned their living through manual toil.

Nonetheless, the emphasis in comedy tends to be on traits that all human beings share, not on those that elevate one person over another. Shakespeare's comedies tend not to focus upon the fate of a magnificent titular hero, as the tragedies do, but to feature a large collection of protagonists. Often, the different characters participate in several interlocking plots, a technique that originated in classical theater and was much elaborated in the middle ages and Renaissance. *The Two Gentlemen of Verona* follows the initially diverging but eventually reconnecting adventures of Valentine and of his faithless friend, Proteus. *The Taming of the Shrew* deals not only with Kate and Petruccio, but with Bianca and Lucentio, and Hortensio and the Widow; and this entire action is prefaced by a framing story about a practical joke on a drunken tinker, Christopher Sly. *Much Ado About Nothing* pairs the courtship of Claudio and Hero with the courtship of Beatrice and Benedick. *The Merry Wives of Windsor* combines Falstaff's attempt to seduce two middle-aged wives with a competition among several other men for the nubile daughter of one of the wives. *A Midsummer Night's Dream* attends to the wedding of Duke Theseus and Hippolyta, to the marital quarrels of Oberon and Titania, to the mishaps of four Athenian lovers lost in the woods, and to the attempts of a group of artisans to rehearse a play for the Duke's wedding.

The multiplot action encourages the audience to take a wide view, to make comparisons among various characters who often are doing more or less the same thing—for instance, falling in love—in different ways. No single story, no single individual, has a monopoly on the stage nor, implicitly, a monopoly on the truth, Often, the collisions among the various plotlines are surprising and funny: *The Comedy of Errors* is a tissue of such unlikely interpenetrations, as bewildered characters find themselves hijacked again and again into the wrong story. Not until the entire cast is assembled at the end of the play can the multiple farcical misunderstandings be sorted out. In most of Shakespeare's comedies the multiplot structure helps to foreground the importance of "hap," or fortune, in the outcome of the plot as apparently independent causal sequences intersect and react upon one another. In *A Midsummer Night's Dream,* the chance encounter of the fairies Oberon and Puck with the Athenian lovers in the woods proves unexpectedly fateful for the lovers. In *As You Like It,* an inexplicable twist of fate brings Orlando, roaming far from home, to the same forest to which his beloved Rosalind has fled, and then later brings Orlando's older brother to the same forest, where Orlando can happen upon him just in the nick of time to save him from being eaten by a lioness. In *Twelfth Night,* the lovesick Olivia, seeking to marry a man who is actually a woman in disguise, stumbles instead upon her beloved's identical twin brother, a shipwreck survivor who has just arrived in town that morning. For the audience, the pleasure of such plots depends upon an interplay between the completely predictable "happy ending" and the unforeseen, wildly fortuitous means by which the characters arrive there.

In the crowded comic world, the aggressively self-actualizing individual who tries to carve out his own destiny tends to make himself ridiculous. By contrast, those who surrender themselves to circumstances often benefit from the workings of accident or providence. *Twelfth Night* rewards Viola, the lucky survivor of a shipwreck who waits for time to untangle her dilemmas, but humiliates the unctuous steward Malvolio, who strives assiduously to better his social standing. Moreover, in a world in which rules of probability seem not to hold, laughably foolish characters often prove weirdly discerning: Bottom in *A Midsummer Night's Dream,* Lance in *The Two Gentlemen of Verona,* Dogberry in *Much Ado About Nothing,* Pompey in *Measure for Measure.* Another important source of insight is the professional fool with his honed expertise as an improviser of absurdity: *As You Like It's* Touchstone, *Twelfth Night's* Feste, or *All's Well's* Lavatch. These characters' crackpot misprisions and sly puns, bringing unrelated words and meanings into unanticipated conjunctions, are the verbal equivalents of the multilayered plot structure, in which apparently incompatible elements collide in productive chance encounters.

In an influential analysis, the critic Northrop Frye claimed that the comic world typically includes many characters and plots because comedy, as a genre, concerns itself with the renewal of an entire community, a renewal for which the concluding marriages are a kind of metaphor. As a practical matter, in order to perpetuate themselves, societies need their adult, fertile members to procreate—or, as Benedick comments in *Much Ado About Nothing,* "the world must be peopled" (2.3.213–14). The marriage of two people thus serves a social purpose beyond their individual gratification, as Shakespeare frequently reminds us by including some reference at the end of the play to the newlyweds' prospective children. Interestingly, the two genres with which Shakespeare is deeply involved as a young dramatist for a large swathe of the mid to late 1590s— chronicle history and comedy—both concern themselves with the construction of a community but consider the problem from different, even complementary, angles. While the history play is concerned with matters of state, with the fate of nations, and with a struggle for political power, comedy is concerned with domestic life and with the relations among family members and neighbors. Thus, features that seem marginal or supplemental in the history plays become central in the comedies, and vice versa. In the history plays, wars typically determine the outcome of events, so valor in battle is highly prized; in *2 Henry IV,* Prince Harry must renounce his association with the fat, pleasure-loving, admittedly cowardly Falstaff and embrace his own heroic destiny. In comedy, however, war is pushed to the margins. In *As You Like It,* the bad duke musters an army to defeat the good duke but, offstage, happens to meet a holy man who converts him to a hermit's life so that the threat of force simply evaporates. Moreover, bravery in battle is no longer a proxy for merit in other areas of life. As *Much Ado About Nothing* opens, a group of men are

Falstaff and Mistress Quickly, detail of the frontispiece to *The Wits; or, Sport upon Sport* (1662), a collection of short dramatic pieces, one of which featured Falstaff and his exploits.

returning from a military campaign: the soldier most remarked upon, who "hath borne himself beyond the promise of his age, doing in the figure of a lamb the feats of a lion" (1.1.11–12) is Claudio, whose ferocious misogyny eventually brings the play close to tragedy. In *All's Well That Ends Well,* Bertram likewise wins high honors on the battlefield but treats both his wife and his would-be lover shamefully.

One effect of this refocusing of perspective is that women, typically excluded from politics but central to domestic life, become likewise central to Shakespearean comedy. Whereas the young women in classical New Comedies tend to be fairly pallid—in some plays, the "love interest" does not even appear onstage—Shakespeare's comic women are highly realized and distinctive. He has a special partiality for vocal, opinionated heroines, who are dramatically much more compelling than the demure females held up for admiration by most Renaissance conduct books. In one of Shakespeare's first plays, *The Taming of the Shrew,* Kate, the "shrew" or overbearing woman of the title, puts up furious resistance to her marriage to the eccentric Petruccio, before finally testifying to her "taming" in a long public speech of flamboyantly abject submission that makes her once again the center of attention. In later plays, a clever woman—a softened, better-socialized version of the "shrew"—typically stage-manages some of the crucial action of the play. Beatrice, in *Much Ado About Nothing,* interrupts her raillery with Benedick to facilitate the rehabilitation of her cousin, who has been falsely accused of unchastity. In *As You Like It,* the talkative, quirky Rosalind presides over much of the action in male disguise, finally ushering in the marriage god Hymen to officiate at the weddings with which the play concludes. In *Twelfth Night,* the "fair shrew" Maria devises an elaborate practical joke on the killjoy Malvolio. In *Merchant of Venice,* Portia disguises herself as a young male lawyer and saves the life of her new husband's best friend in a stunning courtroom reversal. In *All's Well That Ends Well,* Helena is even more enterprising, first curing the King of a deadly malady and then following her caddish husband from France to Italy and arranging to get pregnant by him without his knowledge.

Despite their high-spiritedness, their frankness about their desires, their volubility, and, in some cases, their willingness to don transvestite disguise—all traits associated with promiscuity in Renaissance treatises about women—the premarital virginity of

OR,

The Man-Woman:

Being a Medicine to cure the Coltish Difeafe of
the Staggers in the *Mafculine-Feminines*
of our Times.

Expreft in a briefe Decla mation.

Non omnes poffumus omnes.

Miftris, will you be trim'd or truff'd?

London printed for J. T. and are to be fold at Chrift Church gate. 1620.

The title page of *Hic Mulier; or, The Man-Woman* (1620), a pamphlet denouncing the "unnatural" practice of women wearing men's clothing and adopting masculine styles (the women in this image are at a men's barber). *Hic Mulier* was answered by *Haec-Vir; or, The Womanish-Man* (also 1620).

Shakespeare's comic heroines is a nonnegotiable requirement, both for the men that love them and, apparently, for Shakespeare himself. The social value of chastity is suggested in *Measure for Measure* 5.1.170–77, when the Duke enumerates the categories of respectable women: they may be "maids" (that is, virgins) or "wives" or "widows." The only other category is "punk," or prostitute. Not surprisingly, then, Portia in *The Merchant of Venice* declares that if a husband does not claim her by passing the casket test devised by her father, she will live "chaste as Diana" (1.3.89–90), the goddess of virginity—taking a lover outside of marriage does not seem to occur to her as an option. In *A Midsummer Night's Dream,* when the eloping lovers Hermia and Lysander find themselves lost in the wood by night, Hermia insists that they sleep at some distance from one another: "Such separation as may well be said / Becomes a virtuous bachelor and a maid" (2.2.64–65). As a "virtuous bachelor," Lysander respects her scruples, but when the fairy Robin Goodfellow comes upon the sleeping couple, he misconstrues the situation: "Pretty soul, she durst not lie / Near this lack-love, this kill-courtesy" (2.2.282–83). Fairies, the play suggests, live by different rules of sexual conduct than mortals do. In other plays, the standards for servant women and for minor characters are considerably more relaxed than they are for the genteel heroines. In *Much Ado About Nothing,* when Hero is imagined to have talked out of the window at night with a man, her fiancé and father agree that she has so shamed herself that she might as well die. Yet her maid Margaret, for whom Hero was mistaken, apparently escapes without rebuke when the confusion becomes known. Similarly, Jaquenetta, the wench in *Love's Labour's Lost,* turns out to be pregnant by one of her two suitors at the end of the play; her evident consent to premarital intimacy contrasts with the behavior of the princess and her ladies-in-waiting, who engage their lovers in elegant mockery but at the same time carefully preserve their "maiden honour, yet as pure / As the unsullied lily" (5.2.351–52).

The wit of Shakespeare's heroines, then, is not simply anarchic or subversive: it coexists with implicit constraints upon their conduct. In Renaissance England, women's political and legal rights were severely restricted; yet Shakespeare's women, although often more intelligent and resourceful than the men with whom they are paired, only rarely chafe openly against their subordination or argue for a reconfiguration of gender roles. There are two different reasons for their acquiescence. One is that the comedies generally represent the restrictions upon women's freedom as easy to evade. In *The Merry Wives of Windsor,* Mistress Ford and Mistress Page, the merry wives of the title, will be ruined socially if their husbands discover that they are entertaining a man who is paying court to them. Twice, one of the husbands bursts in with a posse of neighbors to investigate their supposed adulterous scheming. Yet instead of being intimidated by this show of male authority or inveighing against the double standard for sexual behavior, the wives deliberately place themselves in risky situations, taking enormous pleasure in their narrow escapes and easily making fools of both the jealous husband and the would-be lover. In other comedies, faced with some restriction or impediment, women simply pass themselves off as men. In *As You Like It,* for instance, Celia and Rosalind know that two women traveling alone will be vulnerable to robbery and rape; so Rosalind disguises herself as a "youth," and they arrive at their destination safely. In *The Merchant of Venice,* Portia likewise disguises herself as a young man in order to gain access to the male preserve of the courtroom. In both cases, male disguise allows the heroine to combine her superior intelligence with the social privileges accorded to men.

Yet if the constraints of gender seem simple for a clever woman to renegotiate, they also, in many plays, do not seem especially onerous to those who must live within them. Shakespeare's heroines are not chaste because chastity needs to be imposed forcibly upon them, but because they accept their culture's notion of admirable conduct and take pride in their physical "purity." Moreover, many of Shakespeare's comic heroines associate erotic feeling with a happy acceptance of inferiority to the beloved man. In *A Midsummer Night's Dream,* Helena, desperate for Demetrius's affection, is especially abject:

> I am your spaniel, and, Demetrius,
> The more you beat me I will fawn on you.
> Use me but as your spaniel: spurn me, strike me,
> Neglect me, lose me; only give me leave,
> Unworthy as I am, to follow you.
>   (2.1.203–07)

Other women in Shakespeare's comedy possess more self-respect, but even Portia in *The Merchant of Venice,* who (disguised as a youthful lawyer) will shortly take masterful charge of a Venetian courtroom, professes to consider herself, in comparison to her intended husband, Bassanio, "an unlessoned girl, unschooled, unpractisèd" (3.2.159):

> Happiest of all is that her gentle spirit
> Commits herself to yours to be directed
> As from her lord, her governor, her king.
>   (3.2.163–65)

A married woman in Shakespeare's time could not own property in her own name: her estate was normally, upon marriage, at her husband's disposal. Portia alludes to this rule, called *couverture,* as her speech continues:

> But now I was the lord
> Of this fair mansion, master of my servants,
> Queen o'er myself; and even now, but now,
> This house, these servants, and this same myself
> Are yours, my lord's.
>   (3.2.167–71)

Portia is both cleverer and much wealthier than her intended; but instead of seeing the obligation to defer to her new husband as a degradation of her status, Portia embraces it, as if a willingness to relinquish her authority were an intrinsic part of her experience of love.

Shakespeare's comic heroines, then, triumph not in spite of, but because of, the restrictions placed upon them: in other words, they find constraint enabling. This paradox has generated a certain amount of disagreement among Shakespeare's critics. Some see him as a protofeminist because of the way his heroines challenge gender norms by donning transvestite disguises, devising "bed tricks," or distinguishing themselves in the male professions of law or medicine. Other critics emphasize the conservatism of the heroine's goal, marriage to a husband whom she accepts as her "lord." In fact, the heroine's preeminence in comedy seems of a piece with the almost magical conferral of power upon the ordinarily powerless that is an intrinsic aspect of the comic pattern. Often, her successes seem inexplicable by ordinary means: in *As You Like It*, Rosalind describes herself as a magician's disciple; and in *All's Well That Ends Well*, though "miracles are past" (2.3.1)—that is, the remarkable events described in the Bible no longer occur—Helen's cure of the king is called "the rarest argument of wonder that hath shot out in our latter times" (2.3.6–7).

In classical New Comedy, as I have already mentioned, an older authority figure, usually a father, refuses to permit the marriage of the young lovers, thus creating an obstacle that the action of the play has to overcome. Shakespeare sometimes uses this convention: in *A Midsummer Night's Dream*, Hermia flees Athens with her lover, Lysander, because her father, Egeus, backed by law, is trying to force her to marry Demetrius. In *The Merchant of Venice*, the Jewish Jessica must elope with Lorenzo, a Christian her father would never countenance. In *The Merry Wives of Windsor*, Anne and Fenton outwit both her parents, who have other matches for her in mind. Yet often in Shakespearean comedy, the young lovers woo without the interference, or even with the positive assistance, of parents and other older authority figures. In *The Two Gentlemen of Verona*, *Love's Labour's Lost*, and *Twelfth Night*, parents are elsewhere or dead. In *As You Like It*, Rosalind's father does not recognize her because she is in disguise, and he has nothing to do with her marriage plans. In *The Merchant of Venice*, Bassanio's father is apparently deceased; and while Portia's late father has devised an apparently arbitrary test for her suitors, it ends up selecting the man with whom she is already in love. In *Much Ado About Nothing*, Claudio asks his commanding officer, as his surrogate father, to help him arrange a marriage with Hero, whose father is likewise accommodating; in the same play, friends and relatives intervene to "undertake one of Hercules' labours, which is to bring Signor Benedick and the Lady Beatrice into a mountain of affection th'one with th'other" (2.1.317–19). In *All's Well That Ends Well*, the older generation is more enthusiastic about the union of the poor physician's daughter Helen and the aristocrat Bertram than are the young people themselves, generously dismissing the class difference between husband and wife, and ignoring property considerations as well.

By minimizing, in many plays, the importance of parental prohibition, Shakespeare focuses attention instead on the way that the young lovers create their own roadblocks to marriage. In their jubilant multiple weddings, the comedies generally celebrate the delights of heterosexual love, and Shakespeare seems to take as axiomatic that this celebration pleases the audience as well. Such titles as *Twelfth Night, or What You Will* and *As You Like It* suggest that Shakespeare sees his comedies as pleasurably gratifying his audience's wishful fantasies. The epilogues of several comedies invite the audience to share in the concluding festivities. In *A Midsummer Night's Dream*, after the lovers troop off to bed—to beget healthy children, we are told—Robin Goodfellow asks the audience to "give me your hands" (Epilogue.15): he both requests applause for the actor's performance and suggests that the world of the play and the world of the audience is continuous, and that the spectators of the play are part of the happy community of the comic conclusion. In *As You Like It*, even more explicitly, Rosalind's epilogue makes the connection between the comedy's onstage flirtations and a charged sexual atmosphere among the play's spectators: "I charge you, O women, for the love you bear to men, to like as much of this play as please you. And I charge you, O men, for the love you bear to women—as I perceive by your simpering none of you hates them—that between you and the women the play may please" (10–14).

Yet Shakespeare tempers this affirmative view of heterosexual attraction and gratification with some attention to inherently contradictory or recalcitrant aspects of sexuality. In fact, over the course of his career as a comic dramatist he seems to grow more pessimistic, so that in his last two comedies, *Measure for Measure* and *All's Well That Ends Well*, love's difficulties and disappointments come close to overwhelming its rewards. As we have seen, sexual congress is a social necessity—a community cannot survive unless its members procreate. Nonetheless, sexual passion figures, in Shakespearean comedy as in most Renaissance love poetry, as profoundly resistant to social control: a highly subjective, even solipsistic or isolating, experience.

> The lunatic, the lover, and the poet
> Are of imagination all compact.
> (*Midsummer Night's Dream* 5.1.7–8)

Again and again, Shakespeare stresses that, in love, there is no accounting for taste: beauty lies in the eye of the beholder, and socially mandated standards of beauty mean little to individual beholders. In *Love's Labour's Lost*, Biron's male friends tease him unmercifully for loving a "black," or dark-complexioned, woman, because the ideal female beauty in Shakespeare's day was fair-haired and white-skinned; but Biron staunchly defends his preference. In *Much Ado About Nothing*, when Claudio enthuses about Hero, "the sweetest lady that ever I looked on," Benedick replies that "I can see yet without spectacles, and I see no such matter" (1.1.151–54). In *A Midsummer Night's Dream*, Helena, unrequitedly in love with Demetrius, compares herself to Hermia, the woman Demetrius does love:

> Through Athens I am thought as fair as she.
> But what of that? Demetrius thinks not so.
> ....
> Love looks not with the eyes, but with the mind,
> And therefore is winged Cupid painted blind.
> (1.2.227–28, 233–34)

Yet at the same time as the lover's experience seems unshared by others, it also seems to come from outside the self, an alien invader. "What's this? What's this?" (2.2.167), asks the shocked Angelo in *Measure for Measure*, surprised by his sudden overpowering desire for Isabella. Both Biron, in *Love's Labour's Lost*, and Benedick, in *Much Ado About Nothing*, ridicule the follies of lovers until, unexpectedly, they fall in love themselves: "What? I love, I sue, I seek a wife?" (4.1.174), Biron asks himself incredulously. In *A Midsummer Night's Dream*, the fairies interfere with attachments between the human lovers by treating the humans' eyes with juice squeezed from a flower obtained by supernatural means from the other side of the globe. Yet ordinary sexual passion, generated from "within" the lover, apparently operates exactly the same way as the exotic flower juice operating from "without." In fact, Demetrius, one of the lovers, must remain permanently under the influence of the fairies' flower juice in order for the final pairing off to proceed.

How can this mysterious, giddy impulse be subjected to discipline? In particular, how can it be harnessed to what the Queen in *Love's Labour's Lost* calls the "world-without-end bargain" (5.2.771) of marriage, a bond that could not, in Shakespeare's time, be dissolved by divorce? "Tell me how long you would have her after you have possessed her?" the disguised Rosalind commands her lover, Orlando, who answers: "For ever and a day." "Say a day without the ever," Rosalind advises him (4.1.121–24). Shakespeare's plays are full of jokes about the brief half-life of erotic attraction, a desire that seems immense but will disappear as soon as its sexual goal is achieved. In *Much Ado About Nothing*, Balthasar sings:

> Sigh no more, ladies, sigh no more.
> Men were deceivers ever,
> One foot in sea, and one on shore,
> To one thing constant never.
> ....
> The fraud of men was ever so
> Since summer first was leafy.
> (2.3.56–59, 66–67)

Elsewhere, women are said to betray men, their infidelities imposing the shame of the "cuckold's horn" upon their husbands. In *Much Ado About Nothing*, Benedick worries that if he marries, he will inevitably "hang my bugle in an invisible baldric" (1.1.198) or horn belt; in *As You Like It*, the Duke's men, coming home from hunting the deer, sing a song that ends in a jolly insult to the listener and his presumed lineage:

> Take thou no scorn to wear the horn;
> It was a crest ere thou wast born.
> Thy father's father wore it,
> And thy father bore it.
> (4.2.14–17)

It is not surprising, then, that Shakespeare's comedies should be much concerned with the problem of constancy and with the making and breaking of vows, since a vow is essentially an assurance about the future. As the weaker parties to the love transaction, women are especially likely to insist upon the importance of the vow, since they have more to lose if it is breached. In *The Merchant of Venice*, as we have seen, Portia subjects herself and her estate to her new husband, Bassanio, but she does so conditionally:

> This house, these servants, and this same myself
> Are yours, my lord's. I give them with this ring,
> Which when you part from, lose, or give away,
> Let it presage the ruin of your love.
> (3.2.170–73)

In the event, Bassanio does give away the ring. In *The Two Gentlemen of Verona* and in *A Midsummer Night's Dream*, likewise some of the men, despite their professed ardor, do not remain faithful to the women they have courted. And in *Love's Labour's Lost*, the women warily impose a year's waiting period on the men in an attempt to test their dependability. If love is often instantly kindled, it must be perpetuated by promises, and the dependability of those promises rests upon the trustworthiness of the persons who make them.

Shakespeare's comedies thus hold in suspension two apparently disparate views of love: one highly idealized and idealizing, the other subjecting the idealism to critique and mockery. Shakespeare was certainly not the first to take a double view of "lover's follies": they had long generated much of the humor in New Comic plot situations. In many classical and Renaissance New Comedies, the enthusiastic young lover is laughably wholehearted and naive, the subject of his friends' sardonic commentary. Shakespeare often complicates this simple paradigm. Many of his most appealing characters deal with the complexities of sexual love neither by repudiating love nor by abandoning their capacity for critical detachment. Rather they fall in love but simultaneously remain entirely cognizant of their own absurdity; in other words, they combine the role of lover and love's critic. Biron in *Love's Labour's Lost* and Benedick in *Much Ado About Nothing* both play this double game, and in *As You Like It* Rosalind, in her disguise as "Ganymede," regales her lover, Orlando, with what she represents as sage advice. "Men have died from time to time, and worms have eaten

King Solomon *in flagrante delicto*, reproduced from *The Deceyte of Women* (1558?) by permission of The Huntington Library, San Marino, California.

them, but not for love," she assures him briskly in *As You Like It* 4.1.91–92; "men are April when they woo, December when they wed. Maids are May when they are maids, but the sky changes when they are wives" (lines 124–27). Yet after Orlando departs, Rosalind tells her cousin Celia: "O coz, coz, coz, my pretty little coz, that thou didst know how many fathom deep I am in love" (lines 175–76). Viola, in *Twelfth Night*, performs the same trick of detachment with less humor and more pathos, recounting her own story of apparently unrequited love to her beloved, Duke Orsino, as a story about her sister:

> ORSINO   And what's her history?
> VIOLA A blank, my lord. She never told her love,
>   But let concealment, like a worm i'th' bud,
>   Feed on her damask cheek. She pined in thought,
>   And with a green and yellow melancholy
>   She sat like patience on a monument,
>   Smiling at grief.
>
>   (2.4.108–14)

Whether this oblique utterance counts as "telling" her love is, of course, an open question, as uncertain, or "blank," as Viola perceives her own future to be. The self-aware lover, alert to the excesses of passionate sexual attachment but at the same time fully immersed in them, is a natural ally of the clown, with his professional expertise in ironic participation. Thus in *As You Like It*, the fool Touchstone throws in his lot with Rosalind and Celia, and Viola comments appreciatively upon Feste's skill in *Twelfth Night*.

If one problem for lovers is a temporal one—how to make a fleeting, if powerful, impulse the basis of a permanent relationship—another is how to reconcile the heterosexual, potentially procreative liaison with other kinds of relationship. While, compared to other comic dramatists, Shakespeare tends to play down generational strife, he again and again shows the emotional demands of heterosexual pairing in conflict with powerful same-sex loyalties. In the early *Two Gentlemen of Verona*, best friends Valentine and Proteus fall in love with the same woman: Proteus betrays his friend in an attempt to get Silvia for himself, and then Valentine (without consulting Silvia) cedes her to Proteus:

> And that my love may appear plain and free
> All that was mine in Silvia I give thee.
> (5.4.82–83)

The "love" to which Valentine refers here is not his love for his betrothed but his devotion to his male companion, which apparently trumps all other obligations. Another turn of the plot is required to return Silvia to Valentine and to pair Proteus with his original girlfriend, Julia. Shakespeare will not return to the depiction of so bald a rivalry between friends until the late, collaborative play *The Two Noble Kinsmen*, but in many other comedies a man's new love affair with a woman competes with his prior attachment to another man. In *Twelfth Night*, Sebastian owes his life to Antonio, a noble pirate who feels for him "desire / More sharp than filèd steel" (3.3.4–5). Following Sebastian to Illyria, where there is a price on his head, Antonio risks his life only to see Sebastian snatched away by the marriage-minded Olivia. In *The Merchant of Venice*, Bassanio must choose between his loyalty to Portia, whom he has just married, and his obligation to his friend Antonio—and initially chooses Antonio. In *A Midsummer Night's Dream*, it is the women—the fairy queen Titania and her Indian votress, and the mortal women Hermia and Helena—whose intimacies are ruptured by heterosexual passion. As the men quarrel over them and Hermia and Helena quarrel between themselves, Helena exclaims:

> O, is all quite forgot?
> All schooldays' friendship, childhood innocence?
> We, Hermia, like two artificial gods
> Have with our needles created both one flower,
> Both on one sampler, sitting on one cushion,
> Both warbling of one song, both in one key,
> As if our hands, our sides, voices, and minds
> Had been incorporate. So we grew together,
> Like to a double cherry: seeming parted,
> But yet a union in partition.
> (3.2.202–11)

Here, as in the other plays, Shakespeare leaves unspecified whether the emotional closeness between two persons of the same sex is ever physically consummated. But like marriage, female friendship as Helena describes it mysteriously makes one out of two: the word "incorporate," for instance, derives from a Latin word meaning "made into a single body." The implication is that whether or not such relationships are ever homosexually expressed, their intensity rivals that of heterosexual love.

Nonetheless, the potentially procreative marriages with which the comedy ends cannot occur if the characters sort permanently with persons of their own sex. Often, therefore, as here, idyllic moments of same-sex love are imagined retrospectively, as something already lost. At other times, same-sex attachment must be renounced. Thus, in *Much Ado About Nothing*, Beatrice requires her lover, Benedick, to challenge his friend, Claudio, to a duel for having slandered her cousin, Hero. Benedick initially recoils but then relents to her demand, a sign that his primary allegiance has shifted from his comrades-in-arms to the woman whom he will marry at the end of the play. In *The Merchant of Venice*, Portia forgives her husband, Bassanio, for having given away his wedding ring only after Bassanio's close friend Antonio pledges, essentially, that he will no longer claim priority in Bassanio's affections. In *A Midsummer Night's Dream*, the fairy queen Titania at first retains her Indian votress's child out of a sense of loyalty to the dead votress but ends up tamely relinquishing the child to her husband, Oberon.

Nonetheless, because Shakespeare portrays same-sex friendship as so rewarding and significant, some sense of loss as well as gain lingers over the happiness of the comic conclusion. Moreover some characters cannot—or refuse to be—included in the marital finale. Thus, in *Twelfth Night*, as so many of the main characters form heterosexual couples, the valiant Antonio is left isolated, an isolation the directors of some productions have emphasized by having him exit separately at the end of the play. In *As You Like It*, the "melancholy" Jaques simply declines to participate in the wedding revelry: "So, to your pleasures; / I am for other than for dancing measures" (5.4.181–82). Such characters make vivid the fact that not everybody is "the marrying kind" and that the inclusiveness of the comic conclusion has its limits.

Also left out of the comic conclusion or only shakily reintegrated are characters who might be considered scapegoats. The word *scapegoat* originates in an ancient ceremony in which a community ritually cleansed itself by delegating the responsibility for all its sins to a single person or animal—a goat in Israel, a slave or foreigner in ancient Greece—who was then punished and expelled. In modern parlance, a scapegoat is someone unfairly blamed as an individual for faults or crimes that are actually committed by a group. In many of his plays, Shakespeare manifests keen interest in the psychological mechanism by which people project their faults onto others and the way uniting against a despised "outsider" can help a community cohere more tightly. Thus, in *The Merchant of Venice*, the Christians revile the Jew Shylock, whose bald pursuit of self-interest and refusal to mix financial arrangements with friendship lay bare unwelcome truths about their own handling of money. Likewise the prim Malvolio, in *Twelfth Night*, is treated as a madman for having dared to imagine for himself the social advancement through marriage that the glamorous twins Sebastian and Viola actually achieve. The residents of Windsor humiliate Falstaff, in *The Merry Wives of Windsor*, for thinking that he can trade sex for money, even while Anne's parents plan to marry her off to one of her wealthy suitors rather than to the man she loves. Don John, the scheming bastard in *Much Ado About Nothing*, embodies the possibility of extramarital sexual activity, the prospect of which triggers so much of the suspicion and pain in the play. In all these cases, the scapegoat is indeed guilty, sometimes murderously so. Yet the community's investment in punishing him seems excessive in a way that exposes its own hypocrisy or blindness to its own motives.

In a few of the comedies, the scapegoat character remains completely beyond the pale at the end of the play: in *Much Ado About Nothing*, the Duke cheerfully anticipates devising "brave tortures" for his bastard brother Don John the day after the weddings. More often, there is some attempt at reconciliation, an effort to encircle the offender and keep him within the community after all. In *The Merry Wives of Windsor*, Falstaff is tormented but then invited to a feast; and in *All's Well That Ends Well*, the pretentious unscrupulous Paroles is first exposed as a liar and a coward, and then given a small pension. The attempt at reconciliation may seem profoundly hurtful, as when Shylock is given his life with the proviso that he convert to Christianity, a form of "mercy" that seems merely to substitute psychological for physical violence. Or the conciliatory gesture may be rejected: in *Twelfth Night*, despite Olivia's attempts to make peace, Malvolio storms off with a vow to "be revenged on the whole pack of you" (5.1.365).

Yet despite these darker notes, forgiveness and charity remain critically important in Shakespearean comedy. And since, as we have seen, the obstacles to happy love are so often self-imposed, not only the scapegoat characters are in need of it. A good deal of pain in the plays is the result of immature or unworthy young men behaving badly: Proteus in *The Two Gentlemen of Verona*, Demetrius in *A Midsummer Night's Dream*, Oliver in *As You Like It*, Bassanio in *The Merchant of Venice*, Claudio in *Much Ado About Nothing*, Angelo in *Measure for Measure*, Bertram in *All's Well That Ends Well*. All these characters, with greater or lesser motive and with more or less serious consequences, violate the bonds of relationship and must be forgiven at the end of the play. At times, indeed, they seem to get off too lightly—their efforts at repentance unconvincing, the pardons they are extended unmerited, and the women with whom they are matched too good for them. In Shakespeare's hands, however, comedy is not merely a genre that celebrates youth, abundance, and fertility, but one that represents for us, as we like it, the heartwarming possibility of getting more than we deserve.

SELECTED BIBLIOGRAPHY

Bamber, Linda. *Comic Women, Tragic Men: A Study of Gender and Genre in Shakespeare*. Stanford: Stanford University Press, 1982.

Barber, C. L. *Shakespeare's Festive Comedy: A Study of Dramatic Form and Its Relation to Social Custom*. Princeton: Princeton University Press, 1959.

Bradbrook, Muriel C. *The Growth and Structure of Elizabethan Comedy*. London: Chatto & Windus, 1955.

Frye, Northrop. *A Natural Perspective: The Development of Shakespearean Comedy and Romance*. New York: Columbia University Press, 1965.

———. *Anatomy of Criticism: Four Essays*. Princeton: Princeton University Press, 1957.

Miola, Robert S. *Shakespeare and Classical Comedy: The Influence of Plautus and Terence*. Oxford: Clarendon, 1994.

Wheeler, Richard. *Shakespeare's Development and the Problem Comedies: Turn and Counter-Turn*. Berkeley: University of California Press, 1981.

The Two Gentlemen of Verona

Readers and playgoers have often found both startling and disconcerting the events that conclude *The Two Gentlemen of Verona*. Proteus, a young man thwarted in his love for Silvia, who loves Proteus's friend Valentine, says that since wooing her with words has not worked, he will follow the soldier's path and "love you 'gainst the nature of love: force ye" (5.4.58). At that moment, Valentine steps out of hiding and stops the attempted rape by denouncing Proteus as a treacherous friend. Overcome with remorse for the betrayal of Valentine, though not explicitly for his attempted sexual violence, Proteus begs forgiveness. Generously, Valentine says he is content. He then announces that he will give Silvia to Proteus as a sign of the renewal of the friendship between the two men. A near rape and the blatant offer of a woman as an object of exchange between men—is this the stuff of comedy?

Apparently a number of directors, actors, and critics have thought not. In the mid-eighteenth century, it became common to cut Valentine's offer to give Silvia to his friend, a stage tradition that largely held until William Charles Macready, the famous actor and producer of Shakespeare's plays, reintroduced the lines in 1841. As late as 1952, however, Denis Carey's production at the Bristol Old Vic again deleted Valentine's offer. Some critics have been so certain Shakespeare could not have written the scene as it stands that they argued that it was altered in the playhouse. How is it that Shakespeare concluded his comedy with events that have seemed to many so distasteful and so disconcerting?

One answer might be that Shakespeare was simply a young dramatist not fully in control of his craft. *The Two Gentlemen of Verona* is, after all, one of his earliest plays, perhaps *the* earliest. It bears marks of its early date of composition. It has, for example, the smallest cast of any of the plays. Many scenes contain only two or three speakers, as if Shakespeare had not yet mastered the skill of orchestrating a full complement of stage voices and bodies. It is marked as well by a number of plot inconsistencies and confusing details. Valentine and Proteus leave Verona to go to the Emperor's court, for example, but end up attaching themselves to the Duke of Milan—an important nobleman, certainly, but not the Emperor. Likewise, the geographical placement of some scenes is vague. Verona, Milan, Mantua, and Padua are places of which characters speak, but the names often are used interchangeably and seem collectively to be Shakespeare's shorthand for "Italy" rather than distinct places.

In other ways, however, the play is both an accomplished theatrical piece and a genuine precursor of many aspects of Shakespeare's later comic techniques and structures. The contemporary film *Shakespeare in Love* takes this view, using scenes and speeches from *The Two Gentlemen of Verona* to indicate Shakespeare's youthful promise as a writer of romantic comedy and as a rival to Christopher Marlowe, the premier London dramatist of the early 1590s. The play features lovers whose fickle or thwarted passions lead them into all sorts of difficulties: treachery to friends, banishment, disguise. Strikingly, these difficulties get sorted out only after most of the drama's significant players decamp to a forest somewhere outside Milan. There, in a green world complete with a band of outlaws, the fickle Proteus reverts to his original love for Julia, Silvia's disapproving father forgoes his objections to Valentine, friendship is renewed between the two young men, the outlaws are pardoned and unworthy lovers dismissed. The utopian possibilities for social renewal in a world beyond the walls and customs of the city are celebrated in this play as they are later to be in *A Midsummer Night's Dream, As You Like It,* and other Shakespearean romantic comedies of the 1590s. *Two Gentlemen* also contains the first of Shakespeare's cross-dressed heroines, the faithful Julia, who follows her fickle lover from Verona to Milan and then, as his page, accompanies him into the woods in his pursuit of Silvia. Male disguise allows Julia a freedom of action and movement not normally granted to early modern women, but, as was often to be the case in later Shakespearean comedies, this freedom has as its ultimate goal the heroine's embrace of a mate and of marriage.

The excellence of much of the play, then, suggests that its disturbing ending may not be due to Shakespeare's relative inexperience as a playwright; rather, it may stem from the subject matter of the play itself—that is, from Shakespeare's ambitious attempt to probe the relationship between two kinds of human bonds: friendship between men and romantic love between a man and a woman. In the Renaissance, each of these was a privileged relationship, but their relative worth was a matter for debate and disagreement. In staging his exploration of the competing claims of love and friendship, Shakespeare drew on two different sources. The first was a Spanish prose romance published in 1542, Jorge de Montemayor's *Diana Enamorada*. Translated into French in 1578 and into English in the 1580s, it was published in English in 1598. Shakespeare, then, could have read the story in French or in the unpublished English version. He could also have learned of it from an anonymous court play of 1585, *The History of Felix and Philiomena*, now lost.

The Montemayor romance focuses on a man's unfaithfulness in love. Don Felix leaves Felismena for Celia; Felismena pursues him in the guise of a page; Celia falls in love with the page and conveniently dies when the page rejects her. Shakespeare retains much of this material in the Proteus-Silvia-Julia triangle but adds the Valentine plot, probably drawn from the story of two friends, Titus and Gisippus, told by Boccaccio and then recounted in Book 2, Chapter 12, of Thomas Elyot's *Book of the Governor* (1531).

Male friendship ("Steadfast is the love based on inclination"). From Richard Brathwaite, *The English Gentleman*, 2nd ed. (1633).

In this story, Titus falls in love with the woman Gisippus is to marry, and Gisippus gives the woman to his friend. Later, Gisippus takes upon himself the blame for a murder Titus is wrongly accused of committing. The story unabashedly advances the claims of heroic male friendship over other ties, including those of male-female love. Shakespeare's achievement in *The Two Gentlemen of Verona* is to join together aspects of these two stories. In his play, there are two pairs of lovers, not just a fickle Proteus figure moving between two women, and the close friendship between Valentine and Proteus is given a prominence equal to that of the male-female love stories.

In foregrounding the importance of male friendship, Shakespeare joined a long tradition of writers who celebrated such friendships, sometimes comparing them favorably with the presumably more dangerous relationships men could have with women. In *The Governor*, for example, Elyot praised male friendship in terms

that would be echoed in other early modern texts: "Verily it is a blessed and stable connection of sundry wills, making of two persons one in having and suffering. And therefore a friend is properly named of philosophers the other I. For that in them is but one
mind and one possession and that which more is, a man more rejoiceth at his friend's
good fortune than at his own" (Book 2, Chapter 11). By contrast, Sir Francis Bacon
(who also wrote an essay in praise of friendship) in his essay "Of Love" captures the fear
and disdain with which passionate love between men and women was often regarded:
"In life it doth much mischief, sometimes like a siren, sometimes like a fury. You may
observe that amongst all the great and worthy persons (whereof the memory
remaineth, either ancient or recent) there is not one that hath been transported to the
mad degree of love; which shows that great spirits and great business do keep out this
weak passion."

The Two Gentlemen of Verona participates both in the celebration of male friendship and to some extent in the comic deflation of male-female love. Several times male
characters speak of the strange transformations of the self that passion for a woman can
induce. Proteus, choosing to stay in Verona with Julia rather than follow his friend to
Milan for an education in courtiership, speaks of his own choice disdainfully. Of Valentine he says:

> He after honour hunts, I after love.
> He leaves his friends to dignify them more,
> I leave myself, my friends, and all, for love.
> Thou, Julia, thou hast metamorphosed me,
> Made me neglect my studies, lose my time,
> War with good counsel, set the world at naught;
> Made wit with musing weak, heart sick with thought.
> (1.1.63–69)

The play is one of Shakespeare's first explorations of what it means to be transformed,
or "metamorphosed," by love of a woman. Perhaps Shakespeare was taking his cue from
the Roman poet Ovid's vastly popular book the *Metamorphoses,* which contained numerous tales of people transformed by love. In Ovid, gods sometimes assume the shapes of
mortals or of animals to pursue their beloved; or women turn into trees or flowers in
their flight from unwanted amorous advances. In *The Two Gentlemen of Verona,* Proteus's name echoes that of the sea god who could change shape at will and who was thus
often associated with a fickle nature. It is Proteus who in the above passage first mentions being metamorphosed by love, but the play rings many changes on this idea. Sometimes the transformations wrought by love seem comic to others. Speed, for example,
has excellent fun laughing at the strange transformations of his master, Valentine, who,
in love with Silvia, begins to act like a perfect malcontent, "metamorphosed with a mistress" (2.1.26–27). A malcontent, here meaning someone made melancholy by love, was
a stock figure in Renaissance literature and the visual arts, sometimes rendered comic
by his disordered attire or his moody alienation from his fellow men.

Often, however, in this play, love is shown to have more positive consequences. It
leads to heroic feats such as Julia's daring cross-dressed journey in pursuit of Proteus
and to the outpouring of poetry and songs. However fickle Proteus's passion for Silvia
shows him to be, it also moves him to offer her the gorgeous song "Who is Silvia? What
is she, / That all our swains commend her?" (4.2.37–38). In *Shakespeare in Love,* this
lyricism is what compels Viola De Lesseps, the aristocratic heroine, to fall in love with
the youthful Shakespeare who wrote those verses. Valentine, under the influence of
love, is prepared to scale the walls of Silvia's tower to bear her, willingly, away. Clearly,
however, not all the metamorphoses wrought by love are either comic or admirable.
Love also makes men dangerous and hurtful. Under the influence of his fickle passions,
Proteus abandons one woman for another, betrays Valentine's marriage plans to Silvia's
father, and threatens to rape the woman he supposedly adores. As moralists warned, the
passion of man for woman can turn a man into a beast.

By contrast, friendship between men, though much compromised in this text, holds the promise of an ennobling intimacy. When Proteus and Valentine must part in the first scene, Proteus's language betrays the depth of his love for and dependence on his friend:

> Wilt thou be gone? Sweet Valentine, adieu.
> Think on thy Proteus when thou haply seest
> Some rare noteworthy object in thy travel.
> Wish me partaker in thy happiness
> When thou dost meet good hap; and in thy danger—
> If ever danger do environ thee—
> Commend thy grievance to my holy prayers;
> For I will be thy beadsman, Valentine.
>
> (1.1.11–18)

Here, the friend is imagined as "the other I," sharer of every joy, intimate of every thought. The delight with which Valentine later welcomes Proteus to the Duke's court and even his eventual offer of Silvia to his friend are signs of the potential depth of male bonds in the play.

But at what cost to women are the bonds between men to be privileged? By the way he creates the characters of Julia and Silvia, Shakespeare invites his audience to take them and their emotions seriously and makes it difficult to overlook the men's irresponsible and callous treatment of them. If Proteus can be faithful neither to his male friend nor to his female beloved, the women are models of constant affection. Each, moreover, risks a good deal for her beloved, and each is respectful of her female rival. Julia courts public scandal by dressing as a boy and following Proteus to Milan; Silvia flees her father's court to follow the banished Valentine into the forest. These are both bold and attractive women.

Julia, in particular, is a complex figure, proud and silly in the scene in which she pretends not to want to read the letter her maid has brought her from Proteus (1.2), but

The love melancholic. Isaac Oliver, *Edward, First Lord Herbert of Cherbury* (1617).

impressively dignified when, disguised as a male page, she is faced with the task of being Proteus's messenger to Silvia (4.4). Asked by Silvia to describe Julia, the disguised woman says that Julia is of her color and height. She knows this, she claims, because once she wore Julia's clothes "to play the woman's part" (4.4.152) in a holiday pageant. Moreover, the part she played

> 'twas Ariadne, passioning
> For Theseus' perjury and unjust flight;
> Which I so lively acted with my tears
> That my poor mistress, movèd therewithal,
> Wept bitterly; and would I might be dead
> If I in thought felt not her very sorrow.
> (4.4.159–64)

Ariadne, of course, is an archetype of the betrayed woman. She helped her lover, Theseus, escape the man-eating Minotaur in the labyrinth on Crete, but then was abandoned by him on the island of Naxos. The abandoned Julia, so transformed by love and grief that she no longer can lay claim to her own name, finds a point of identification in Ariadne's grief and in imagining what "Julia" would have felt to see the enactment of Ariadne's story. This is a wonderfully complicated moment, a representation of a woman's grief and self-alienation and also her empathetic engagement with the story of *another* woman's grief. It at once reveals the cost, to women, of men's inconstancy and makes it difficult to accept that women should simply become the objects of exchange between male friends.

The nearly tragic consciousness here granted to Julia is countered in this play by the boisterous comic voices of Speed and Lance, two of Shakespeare's earliest and liveliest clowns. Their presence helps suggest that however complicated Shakespeare's exploration of the tension between love and friendship becomes, the outcome will not be fully tragic. Speed is a clever clown, excellent at puns and wordplay, devastatingly accurate in his parodic imitation of Valentine's lovesick behavior and clever enough to see, when his master cannot, that Silvia has induced Valentine to write a love letter to himself. Lance, who may have been added to the play in the later stages of composition, is a doltish clown whose command of the English language is remarkable mainly for its deficiencies. If Speed specializes in puns, the witty play on the double meaning of words, Lance specializes in malapropisms, the linguistic blunders by which one word is mistaken for another. He can, for example, when leaving home to follow his master to Milan, say that he has received his "proportion, like the prodigious son" (2.3.3), by which he means that he has received his portion, or inheritance, like the prodigal son in the biblical story who received his inheritance and squandered it. In Lance's fractured English, nothing is communicated straightforwardly. He blunders into meaning, his linguistic mistakes turning the language of the learned and the witty on its head. In Lance's mouth, words become unfamiliar and unpredictable, always ready to yield up an obscene innuendo or to forge unlikely connections between different domains of meaning.

Lance's larger role in the play is as comically unsettling as his language. As was to be increasingly true of many of Shakespeare's low-life characters and subplots, his behavior mirrors and comments on the behavior of his "betters," but in a deflationary and unpredictable way. Lance's great love is for his dog, Crab. When he must leave for Milan, he is in an agony of grief because his dog, like a hard-hearted mistress, sheds no tears for his departure. "I think Crab, my dog, be the sourest-natured dog that lives. My mother weeping, my father wailing, my sister crying, our maid howling, our cat wringing her hands, and all our house in a great perplexity, yet did not this cruel-hearted cur shed one tear" (2.3.4–8). So deep is Lance's affection for his dog that when Crab, who in the end does accompany his master to Milan, disgraces himself by pissing under the Duke's table at a banquet, Lance takes the blame—and the subsequent punishment—upon himself. It is "the bit with the dog" that in *Shakespeare in Love* particularly wins the approval of Queen Elizabeth.

"I'll be sworn I have sat in the stocks for puddings he hath stolen" (4.4.25–26). From Geffrey Whitney, *A Choice of Emblemes* (1586).

The highborn lovers, Proteus and Valentine, do not always show an equal devotion to their human mistresses. Lance's attachment threatens to expose both the element of absurdity lurking inside every grand passion and also the falsity of the assumption that only the well-born are capable of self-sacrifice. Moreover, when Lance contemplates marriage, he is not very romantic. As Lance and Speed read a catalog of the qualities of Lance's beloved (3.1.269–351), Lance focuses on the practical: the woman's ability to fetch and carry, to sew and to milk. And her faults, which are manifold, pale in his eyes beside her wealth. Set against the rarified courtship rituals of his masters, Lance's pragmatism underscores the mundane aspects of the institution of marriage to which courtship will lead.

Together the two clowns do much to increase the hilarity and confusion that permeate this early comedy: a play in which letters are only with great difficulty delivered to their receivers, love tokens given to one mistress are rerouted to another, and masculine affection proves remarkably fickle and unsteady. When something like order descends on this society, it does so in a locale where Lance does not go—the forest outside Milan. The initial scenes in the forest are striking in that they have the fairy-tale quality of a Robin Hood story come to life. Banished from Milan, Valentine and Speed are beset by robbers in the forest; but these outlaws are so impressed with Valentine's bearing and his skill in languages that they make him captain of their forest band (4.1.61–64). Outside the town, living apart from women, the outlaws establish an alternative community where Valentine, despite his grief at being separated from Silvia, finds a measure of contentment. Several of Shakespeare's later comedies will depend on the contrast between the flawed life of town or court and the less fettered existence of rural spaces. *The Two Gentlemen of Verona* tries out this juxtaposition, contrasting to the betrayals and confusions of urban life and male-female courtship the straightforward male camaraderie of the forest.

The arrival of women and of Proteus, Valentine's friend-turned-rival, disrupts this harmonious male community as first Silvia appears, escorted by the timid Eglamour, and then Proteus, attended by Julia, disguised as his page. Suddenly, the potential for violence escalates as the frustrated Proteus threatens Silvia with rape, and the two men both lay claim to her affections. The disguised Julia can only watch. Just moments before Proteus, Silvia, and Julia had arrived, Valentine had made a speech that obliquely suggests one way their encounter might end. Alone in the woods, Valentine describes how he can

> sit alone, unseen of any,
> And to the nightingale's complaining notes
> Tune my distresses and record my woes.
> (5.4.4–6)

By mentioning the nightingale, Valentine evokes a horrific tale of sexual violence. In a story made famous by Ovid in the *Metamorphoses*, the beautiful Philomela was raped by her brother-in-law, Tereus, and eventually transformed into a nightingale. The bird's song is so melancholy because it is a perpetual lament for Philomela's lost chastity.

As it turns out, no one undergoes Philomela's fate in *The Two Gentlemen of Verona*. Silvia escapes rape, just as Julia avoids Ariadne's fate when the fickle Proteus returns his affections to her. But the close of this early comedy, through its mythic allusions and flirtation with sexual violence, hints at the tragic endings that have narrowly been averted. In this regard, the play is not unlike *A Midsummer Night's Dream,* in which there is a properly comic ending with lover wedded to lover. However, the last act of that play includes an unintentionally comic enactment of the tragic story of Pyramus and Thisbe, lovers whose passion ended in death, not marriage. Though *Two Gentlemen* ends comically, with two couples reunited and male friendship restored, the violent and unexpected turnabouts in the play's concluding moments indicate the difficulty of joining a tale of heroic male friendship to a tale of romantic love between men and women. Especially for the women, the "happy" ending comes at a cost. The two marriages are arranged only *after* male friendship has been renewed and Valentine has offered—without consulting Silvia—to give his beloved to his friend. Moreover, once that offer has been made, Silvia never speaks again in the play. Her response to all that has happened remains cloaked in silence, while Julia's male disguise, which she never removes, continues to remind the audience of the dangers she has faced because of Proteus's fickleness. As we have seen, this is an ending that since at least the eighteenth century has bothered readers and actors, perhaps because dominant culture has come to value love between men and women over other kinds of emotional bonds. In the Renaissance, the matter was not so settled, a reminder of the different ways in which Shakespeare both is and is not our contemporary.

JEAN E. HOWARD

TEXTUAL NOTE

The Two Gentlemen of Verona was first published in the 1623 First Folio (F), though it may have been written as early as 1590–91, making it perhaps the first of Shakespeare's theatrical compositions. F includes some unusual features, such as the listing at the beginning of each scene of all the characters in the scene no matter when they come onstage. This may have been done partly to imitate classical practice. The text also lacks any other stage directions except exits. These and other features lead editors to believe the play was transcribed by Ralph Crane, a professional scribe who seems to have been employed by Shakespeare's company to prepare several of his playscripts, including *The Two Gentlemen of Verona,* for publication in F.

The Folio text contains a number of confusing plot details and frequent inconsistencies as to the exact Italian setting in which various scenes occur. This suggests that Crane may have been working from Shakespeare's unrevised working papers. On the other hand, there is unusual consistency in regard to speech prefixes for characters' names, indicating that he may have worked from a script prepared for the playhouse or that he was unusually careful in attending to such detail. It is unclear whether the act and scene divisions in the text are Crane's additions or represent playhouse practice.

SELECTED BIBLIOGRAPHY

Brooks, Harold F. "Two Clowns in a Comedy (to Say Nothing of the Dog): Speed, Launce (and Crab) in 'The Two Gentlemen of Verona.'" *Essays and Studies: Collected for the English Association.* London: John Murray, 1963. 91–100. Examines how the clowns, Lance and Speed, contribute to the play's thematic unity by paralleling events and ideas involving the main characters.

Carroll, William C. "'And love you 'gainst the nature of love': Ovid, Rape, and *The Two Gentlemen of Verona.*" *Shakespeare's Ovid: "The Metamorphoses" in the Plays and Poems.* Ed. A. B. Taylor. Cambridge: Cambridge University Press, 2000. 49–65.

Argues that this seemingly genial comedy is darkened by an Ovidian view of male desire entailing possession and control of women.

Kiefer, Frederick. "Love Letters in *The Two Gentlemen of Verona.*" *Shakespeare Studies* 18 (1986): 65–85. Explores the role of letters in the negotiation of love in *Two Gentlemen,* which contains more letters than any of Shakespeare's other comedies.

Lindenbaum, Peter. "Education in *The Two Gentlemen of Verona.*" *Studies in English Literature 1500–1800* 15 (1975): 229–44. Discusses how the play achieves unity by its focus on the education of the protagonists, especially Proteus.

Masten, Jeffrey. "*The Two Gentlemen of Verona.*" Vol. 3 of *A Companion to Shakespeare's Works: The Comedies.* Ed. Richard Dutton and Jean E. Howard. 4 vols. Oxford: Blackwells, 2003. 266–88. Argues against the idea that *Two Gentlemen* is an immature play because of its focus on male friendship rather than heterosexual love and notes the persistence of intense male friendship throughout Shakespeare's writing career.

Rivlen, Elizabeth. "Mimetic Service in *The Two Gentlemen of Verona.*" *English Literary History* 72 (2005): 105–28. Focuses on the large number of servants in *Two Gentlemen* and the capacity of servants not just to mirror but to alter elite identities.

Sargent, Ralph M. "Sir Thomas Elyot and the Integrity of *The Two Gentlemen of Verona.*" *PMLA* 65 (1950): 1166–80. Explores Jorge de Montemayor's *Diana Enamorada* and Thomas Elyot's *The Book of the Governor* as sources for Shakespeare's investigation of the conflict between heterosexual love and male friendship.

Schlueter, June, ed. "*The Two Gentlemen of Verona*": *Critical Essays.* New York: Garland, 1996. Gathers together eighteenth- and nineteenth-century comments on the play along with essays by twentieth-century critics and reviews of notable theater and television productions.

Slights, Camille Wells. "*The Two Gentlemen of Verona* and the Courtesy Book Tradition.*" *Shakespeare Studies* 16 (1983): 13–31. Argues that the play explores the fashioning of a Renaissance gentleman.

Weimann, Robert. "Laughing with the Audience: 'The Two Gentlemen of Verona' and the Popular Tradition of Comedy." *Shakespeare Survey* 22 (1969): 35–42. Discusses the use of the play's two clowns to structure the audience's comic responses.

FILMS

The Two Gentlemen of Verona. 1983. Dir. Don Taylor. UK. 137 min. This BBC-TV version, in color, employs period music and elegant Italian settings in a performance that foregrounds the heterosexual love plot.

Shakespeare in Love. 1998. Dir. John Madden. UK. 123 min. Starring Gwyneth Paltrow and Joseph Fiennes. Includes scenes and speeches from *The Two Gentlemen of Verona* as examples of Shakespeare's early success with comedy and love lyric.

The Two Gentlemen of Verona

THE PERSONS OF THE PLAY

DUKE of Milan
SILVIA, his daughter
PROTEUS, a gentleman of Verona
LANCE, his clownish servant
VALENTINE, a gentleman of Verona
SPEED, his clownish servant
THURIO, a foolish rival to Valentine
ANTONIO, father of Proteus
PANTHINO, his servant
JULIA, beloved of Proteus
LUCETTA, her waiting-woman
HOST, where Julia lodges
EGLAMOUR, agent for Silvia in her escape
OUTLAWS
Servants, musicians

1.1

[*Enter*] VALENTINE[1] *and* PROTEUS[2]

VALENTINE   Cease to persuade, my loving Proteus.
   Home-keeping youth have ever homely° wits.   *dull*
   Were't not affection° chains thy tender° days   *love / young*
   To the sweet glances of thy honoured love,
5   I rather would entreat thy company
   To see the wonders of the world abroad
   Than, living dully sluggardized° at home,   *made very lazy*
   Wear out thy youth with shapeless° idleness.   *aimless*
   But since thou lov'st, love still,° and thrive therein—   *constantly*
10   Even as I would, when I to love begin.
PROTEUS   Wilt thou be gone? Sweet Valentine, adieu.
   Think on thy Proteus when thou haply° seest   *by chance*
   Some rare noteworthy object in thy travel.
   Wish me partaker in thy happiness
15   When thou dost meet good hap;° and in thy danger—   *fortune*
   If ever danger do environ° thee—   *surround*
   Commend° thy grievance to my holy prayers;   *Entrust*
   For I will be thy beadsman,[3] Valentine.
VALENTINE   And on a love-book[4] pray for my success?

1.1 Location: Presumably Verona, though we learn this only from the title.
1. St. Valentine is the patron saint of lovers. Valentine's name may thus indicate his role as faithful lover.
2. In classical mythology, a sea god who could change shape at will. The name suggests a fickle nature. In 1.1, it is pronounced with three syllables; elsewhere in the play, often with two. In F, the names of all the characters who appear in a given scene are listed as it opens, even if they enter at a later point. This edition marks entrances when characters actually appear onstage. In this scene, Speed enters at line 70, though in F his entrance is not marked and his name is listed with that of Proteus and Valentine at the beginning of the scene.
3. One who prays (counts the beads of a rosary) for another's spiritual welfare.
4. A book about love (instead of a prayer book). Valentine is twitting Proteus for making love his religion.

20 PROTEUS Upon some book I love I'll pray for thee.	
VALENTINE That's on some shallow story of deep love—	
How young Leander crossed the Hellespont.[5]	
PROTEUS That's a deep story of a deeper love,	
For he was more than over-shoes[6] in love.	
25 VALENTINE 'Tis true, for you are over-boots in love,	
And yet you never swam the Hellespont.	
PROTEUS Over the boots? Nay, give me not the boots.°	*do not mock me*
VALENTINE No, I will not; for it boots° thee not.	*profits*
PROTEUS What?	
VALENTINE To be in love, where scorn is bought with groans,	
30 Coy looks with heart-sore sighs, one fading moment's mirth	
With twenty watchful,° weary, tedious nights.	*wakeful*
If haply won, perhaps a hapless° gain;	*an unlucky*
If lost, why then a grievous labour won;	
However,° but a folly bought with wit,	*Either way*
35 Or else a wit by folly vanquishèd.	
PROTEUS So by your circumstance° you call me fool.	*lengthy discourse*
VALENTINE So by your circumstance° I fear you'll prove.	*situation*
PROTEUS 'Tis love you cavil at. I am not love.	
VALENTINE Love is your master, for he masters you,	
40 And he that is so yokèd by a fool	
Methinks should not be chronicled for wise.	
PROTEUS Yet writers say 'As in the sweetest bud	
The eating canker° dwells, so doting love	*harmful caterpillar*
Inhabits in the finest wits of all.'	
45 VALENTINE And writers say 'As the most forward bud	
Is eaten by the canker ere it blow,°	*blossom*
Even so by love the young and tender wit	
Is turned to folly, blasting° in the bud,	*withering*
Losing his verdure° even in the prime,°	*greenness / spring*
50 And all the fair effects of future hopes.'	
But wherefore waste I time to counsel thee	
That art a votary[7] to fond° desire?	*foolish*
Once more adieu. My father at the road°	*harbor*
Expects my coming, there to see me shipped.[8]	
55 PROTEUS And thither will I bring thee, Valentine.	
VALENTINE Sweet Proteus, no. Now let us take our leave.	
To Milan let me hear from thee by letters	
Of thy success° in love, and what news else	*fortune (good or bad)*
Betideth° here in absence of thy friend;	*Happens*
60 And I likewise will visit thee with mine.	
PROTEUS All happiness bechance to thee in Milan.	
VALENTINE As much to you at home; and so farewell. *Exit*	
PROTEUS He after honour hunts, I after love.	
He leaves his friends to dignify° them more,	*bring honor to*
65 I leave° myself, my friends, and all, for love.	*neglect*
Thou, Julia, thou hast metamorphosed° me,	*transformed*
Made me neglect my studies, lose° my time,	*waste*

---

5. In classical mythology, Leander drowned while swimming the Hellespont to visit his love, Hero. Shakespeare probably had read in manuscript Christopher Marlowe's poem "Hero and Leander."
6. So deep as to cover the shoes (or boots); recklessly or excessively.

7. One devoted to a particular pursuit; one bound by vows to a religious life.
8. Although Verona and Milan are inland, Shakespeare writes of Verona as if it were located, like London, on a tidal river leading to the sea.

War with good counsel, set the world at naught;
Made wit with musing weak, heart sick with thought.°   *melancholy ideas*
   [*Enter* SPEED]

70 SPEED   Sir Proteus, save° you. Saw you my master?   *God save (a greeting)*
   PROTEUS   But now he parted hence to embark for Milan.
   SPEED   Twenty to one, then, he is shipped already,
     And I have played the sheep[9] in losing him.
   PROTEUS   Indeed, a sheep doth very often stray,
75   An if° the shepherd be a while away.   *An if=If*
   SPEED   You conclude that my master is a shepherd, then, and
     I a sheep?
   PROTEUS   I do.
   SPEED   Why then, my horns are his horns,[1] whether I wake or
     sleep.
   PROTEUS   A silly answer, and fitting well a sheep.
80 SPEED   This proves me still a sheep.
   PROTEUS   True, and thy master a shepherd.
   SPEED   Nay, that I can deny by a circumstance.°   *argument*
   PROTEUS   It shall go hard but I'll prove it by another.[2]
   SPEED   The shepherd seeks the sheep, and not the sheep the
85   shepherd. But I seek my master, and my master seeks not me.
     Therefore I am no sheep.
   PROTEUS   The sheep for fodder follow the shepherd, the shepherd
     for food follows not the sheep. Thou for wages followest
     thy master, thy master for wages follows not thee. Therefore
90   thou art a sheep.
   SPEED   Such another proof will make me cry 'baa'.
   PROTEUS   But dost thou hear: gav'st thou my letter to Julia?
   SPEED   Ay, sir. I, a lost mutton,° gave your letter to her, a laced   *sheep*
     mutton,° and she, a laced mutton, gave me, a lost mutton,   *prostitute (slang)*
95   nothing for my labour.
   PROTEUS   Here's too small a pasture for such store° of muttons.   *abundance*
   SPEED   If the ground be overcharged,° you were best stick[3] her.   *overburdened*
   PROTEUS   Nay, in that you are astray. 'Twere best pound° you.   *empound; beat*
   SPEED   Nay sir, less than a pound shall serve me for carrying
100   your letter.
   PROTEUS   You mistake. I mean the pound, a pinfold.°   *pen for stray animals*
   SPEED   From a pound to a pin?[4] Fold it° over and over   *Multiply*
     'Tis threefold too little for carrying a letter to your lover.
   PROTEUS   But what said she?
105 SPEED [*nods, then says*] Ay.°   *Yes*
   PROTEUS   Nod-ay? Why, that's 'noddy'.°   *a fool*
   SPEED   You mistook, sir. I say she did nod, and you ask me if she
     did nod, and I say 'Ay'.
   PROTEUS   And that set together is 'noddy'.
110 SPEED   Now you have taken the pains to set it together, take it
     for your pains.
   PROTEUS   No, no. You shall have it for bearing the letter.
   SPEED   Well, I perceive I must be fain° to bear with you.   *willing*
   PROTEUS   Why, sir, how do you bear with me?

---

9. Been foolish, with a pun on "ship." "Ship" and "sheep" were pronounced similarly.
1. As Speed's master, Valentine owns Speed's horns. Traditionally, the horns signified the cuckold and were attributed to men whose wives were unfaithful.
2. It shall fare ill with me unless I prove my claim by using another argument.
3. Stab or slaughter the extra sheep, with a pun on "stick" as meaning "have sexual intercourse with."
4. Proverbially, pins have little value (e.g., "not worth a pin"). Speed fears he is going to be paid too little for carrying the letter to Julia.

115 SPEED   Marry,[5] sir, the letter very orderly,° having nothing but the   *dutifully*
    word 'noddy' for my pains.
   PROTEUS   Beshrew me° but you have a quick wit.   *Curse me (a mild oath)*
   SPEED   And yet it cannot overtake your slow purse.
   PROTEUS   Come, come, open the matter in brief. What said she?
120 SPEED   Open your purse, that the money and the matter may
    be both at once delivered.
   PROTEUS [*giving money*]   Well, sir, here is for your pains. What
    said she?
   SPEED   Truly, sir, I think you'll hardly win her.[6]
125 PROTEUS   Why? Couldst thou perceive so much from her?
   SPEED   Sir, I could perceive[7] nothing at all from her, no, not so
    much as a ducat[8] for delivering your letter. And being so hard°   *stingy; cold*
    to me, that brought your mind,° I fear she'll prove as hard to   *wishes*
    you in telling° your mind. Give her no token but stones,[9] for   *when you tell her*
130 she's as hard as steel.
   PROTEUS   What said she? Nothing?
   SPEED   No, not so much as 'Take this for thy pains'. To testify°   *attest to*
    your bounty, I thank you, you have testerned me;[1] in requital
    whereof, henceforth carry your letters yourself. And so, sir, I'll
135 commend you to my master.   [*Exit*]
   PROTEUS   Go, go, be gone, to save your ship from wreck,
    Which cannot perish having thee aboard,
    Being destined to a drier death on shore.[2]
    I must go send some better messenger.
140 I fear my Julia would not deign° my lines,   *graciously accept*
    Receiving them from such a worthless post.°   *Exit*   *messenger; blockhead*

1.2

Enter JULIA *and* LUCETTA
JULIA   But say, Lucetta, now we are alone—
    Wouldst thou then counsel me to fall in love?
LUCETTA   Ay, madam, so you stumble not unheedfully.°   *carelessly*
JULIA   Of all the fair resort° of gentlemen   *company*
5   That every day with parle° encounter me,   *talk*
    In thy opinion which is worthiest love?
LUCETTA   Please you° repeat their names, I'll show my mind   *If you will*
    According to my shallow simple skill.
JULIA   What think'st thou of the fair Sir Eglamour?[1]
10 LUCETTA   As of a knight well spoken, neat,° and fine,   *elegant*
    But were I you, he never should be mine.
JULIA   What think'st thou of the rich Mercatio?
LUCETTA   Well of his wealth, but of himself, so-so.
JULIA   What think'st thou of the gentle Proteus?
15 LUCETTA   Lord, lord, to see what folly reigns in us!
JULIA   How now? What means this passion° at his name?   *outburst of emotion*
LUCETTA   Pardon, dear madam, 'tis a passing° shame   *great*

---

5. A mild oath suggesting surprise, from the Virgin
Mary's name.
6. You'll have a hard time winning her.
7. Punning on an obsolete meaning of "perceive" as
"receive."
8. A coin worth about three shillings sixpence, a generous tip.
9. Precious stones; pebbles; perhaps also, testicles.
token: love gift.

1. Given me a testern, a coin worth much less than the
ducat Speed wanted.
2. *Which . . . shore*: alluding to the proverb "He that is
born to be hanged shall never be drowned."
1.2 Location: Out of doors, maybe in Julia's garden.
1. Not the same Eglamour who assists Silvia in 4.3.
The name is found in medieval romances and by the
1590s seems to have acquired comic associations.

That I, unworthy body as I am,
Should censure° thus on lovely gentlemen.   *pass judgment*
20 JULIA Why not on Proteus, as of all the rest?
LUCETTA Then thus: of many good, I think him best.
JULIA Your reason?
LUCETTA I have no other but a woman's reason:
I think him so because I think him so.
25 JULIA And wouldst thou have me cast my love on him?
LUCETTA Ay, if you thought your love not cast away.
JULIA Why, he of all the rest hath never moved° me.   *proposed marriage to*
LUCETTA Yet he of all the rest I think best loves ye.
JULIA His little speaking shows his love but small.
30 LUCETTA Fire that's closest kept° burns most of all.   *most enclosed*
JULIA They do not love that do not show their love.
LUCETTA O, they love least that let men know their love.
JULIA I would I knew his mind.
LUCETTA [*giving Proteus' letter*] Peruse this paper, madam.
35 JULIA 'To Julia'—say, from whom?
LUCETTA That the contents will show.
JULIA Say, say—who gave it thee?
LUCETTA Sir Valentine's page; and sent, I think, from Proteus.
He would have given it you, but I being in the way
40 Did in your name receive it.² Pardon the fault, I pray.
JULIA Now, by my modesty, a goodly broker.°   *go-between*
Dare you presume to harbour wanton lines?°   *receive love letters*
To whisper, and conspire against my youth?
Now trust me, 'tis an office of great worth,
45 And you an officer fit for the place.
There. Take the paper.
    [*She gives* LUCETTA *the letter*]
                    See it be returned,
Or else return no more into my sight.
LUCETTA To plead for love deserves more fee than hate.
JULIA Will ye be gone?
LUCETTA   That you may ruminate.°   *Exit*   *meditate*
50 JULIA And yet I would I had o'erlooked° the letter.   *examined*
It were a shame to call her back again
And pray her to° a fault for which I chid her.   *ask her to commit*
What fool is she, that knows I am a maid
And would not force the letter to my view,
55 Since maids in modesty say 'No' to that
Which they would have the profferer° construe 'Ay'.   *giver*
Fie, fie, how wayward is this foolish love
That like a testy° babe will scratch the nurse   *cranky*
And presently,° all humbled, kiss the rod.³   *immediately after*
60 How churlishly I chid Lucetta hence
When willingly I would have had her here.
How angerly I taught my brow to frown
When inward joy enforced my heart to smile.
My penance is to call Lucetta back
65 And ask remission for my folly past.

2. An inconsistency in the text. In 1.1, Speed said he delivered the letter to Julia. He may have mistaken Lucetta for Julia or may have lied to Proteus.

3. Children sometimes had to kiss the stick with which they were beaten.

What ho! Lucetta!
       [*Enter* LUCETTA]
LUCETTA   What would your ladyship?
JULIA   Is't near dinner-time?
LUCETTA   I would it were,
  That you might kill° your stomach° on your meat   *expend / hunger; rage*
  And not upon your maid.
       [*She drops and picks up the letter*][4]
JULIA   What is't that you
70   Took up so gingerly?°   *cautiously*
LUCETTA   Nothing.
JULIA   Why didst thou stoop then?
LUCETTA   To take a paper up that I let fall.
JULIA   And is that paper nothing?
75   LUCETTA   Nothing concerning me.
JULIA   Then let it lie for those that it concerns.
LUCETTA   Madam, it will not lie where it concerns,
  Unless it have a false interpreter.
JULIA   Some love of yours hath writ to you in rhyme.
80   LUCETTA   That I might sing it, madam, to a tune,
  Give me a note. Your ladyship can set.[5]
JULIA   As little by such toys° as may be possible.   *trifles*
  Best sing it to the tune of 'Light o' love'.[6]
LUCETTA   It is too heavy° for so light a tune.   *serious*
85   JULIA   Heavy? Belike it hath some burden,[7] then?
LUCETTA   Ay, and melodious were it, would you sing it.
JULIA   And why not you?
LUCETTA   I cannot reach so high.[8]
JULIA   Let's see your song.
       [*She tries to take the letter*][9]
           How now, minion![1]
LUCETTA   Keep tune° there still. So you will sing it out.[2]   *in tune; in good humor*
90   And yet methinks I do not like this tune.[3]
JULIA   You do not?
LUCETTA   No, madam, 'tis too sharp.°   *high-pitched; bitter*
JULIA   You, minion, are too saucy.
LUCETTA   Nay, now you are too flat,°   *low-pitched; blunt*
95   And mar the concord° with too harsh a descant.°   *harmony / melody*
  There wanteth but a mean to fill your song.[4]
JULIA   The mean is drowned with your unruly bass.°   *low notes; bad conduct*
LUCETTA   Indeed, I bid the base[5] for Proteus.
JULIA   This bauble° shall not henceforth trouble me.   *trifle (the letter)*
100   Here is a coil with protestation.°   *fuss about a love vow*
      [*She tears the letter and drops the pieces*]

4. There is no indication in F of when Lucetta drops the letter that she here picks up. Some directors and editors assume that she drops it, either advisedly or inadvertently, before leaving the stage at line 49. To have her drop and immediately retrieve the letter, as here, may suggest that Lucetta is trying once more to call her mistress's attention to this missive.
5. Set to music. Julia takes it to mean "set store by," or "give value to."
6. A popular song in Shakespeare's time.
7. Refrain; heavy load; perhaps punningly referring to the weight of a body during intercourse.
8. Sing so high a note, hope to win so high-ranking a lover.

9. Some editors and directors believe that Lucetta yields the letter at this point, but her refusal to do so seems to be what motivates Julia's anger in the ensuing lines. At some point before line 100, Julia must wrest the letter from her maid.
1. Hussy; with a possible pun on "minim," a musical term for a half note.
2. Finish singing it; come to the end of your anger.
3. Julia may have struck or threatened to strike Lucetta.
4. There lacks but a tenor to complete your song. Her implication is that Julia lacks a man to fulfill her desires.
5. I sang the bass part for; I acted in the interests of (a phrase from the game called prisoner's base).

Go, get you gone, and let the papers lie.
You would be fing'ring them to anger me.
LUCETTA [*aside*]   She makes it strange,° but she would be best   *pretends not to care*
    pleased
To be so angered with another letter.   [*Exit*]
105 JULIA   Nay, would I were so angered with the same.
O hateful hands, to tear such loving words;
Injurious wasps,[6] to feed on such sweet honey
And kill the bees that yield it with your stings.
I'll kiss each several° paper for amends.   *separate*
         [*She picks up some of the pieces of paper*]
110 Look, here is writ 'Kind Julia'—unkind Julia,
As° in revenge of thy ingratitude   *As if*
I throw thy name against the bruising stones,
Trampling contemptuously on thy disdain.
And here is writ 'Love-wounded Proteus'.
115 Poor wounded name, my bosom as a bed
Shall lodge thee till thy wound be throughly° healed;   *completely*
And thus I search° it with a sovereign° kiss.   *probe; cleanse / healing*
But twice or thrice was 'Proteus' written down.
Be calm, good wind, blow not a word away
120 Till I have found each letter in the letter
Except mine own name. That, some whirlwind bear
Unto a ragged, fearful, hanging° rock   *overhanging*
And throw it thence into the raging sea.
Lo, here in one line is his name twice writ:
125 'Poor forlorn Proteus', 'passionate Proteus',
'To the sweet Julia'—that I'll tear away.
And yet I will not, sith° so prettily   *since*
He couples it to his complaining names.
Thus will I fold them, one upon another.
130 Now kiss, embrace, contend, do what you will.
         [*Enter* LUCETTA]
LUCETTA   Madam, dinner is ready, and your father stays.°   *waits*
JULIA   Well, let us go.
LUCETTA   What, shall these papers lie like telltales here?
JULIA   If you respect° them, best to take them up.   *value*
135 LUCETTA   Nay, I was taken up° for laying them down.   *scolded*
Yet here they shall not lie, for° catching cold.   *for fear of*
JULIA   I see you have a month's mind° to them.   *strong desire*
LUCETTA   Ay, madam, you may say what sights you see.
I see things too, although you judge I wink.°   *close my eyes*
140 JULIA   Come, come, will't please you go?   *Exeunt*

1.3

Enter ANTONIO *and* PANTHINO
ANTONIO   Tell me, Panthino, what sad° talk was that   *serious*
Wherewith my brother held you in the cloister?°   *covered walk*
PANTHINO   'Twas of his nephew Proteus, your son.
ANTONIO   Why, what of him?
PANTHINO   He wondered that your lordship
5   Would suffer him to spend his youth at home
While other men, of slender° reputation,   *insignificant*

---

6. Referring to her hurtful fingers.   1.3 Location: Antonio's house in Verona.

Put forth° their sons to seek preferment° out— *Send / advancement*
Some to the wars, to try their fortune there,
Some to discover islands far away,
10 Some to the studious universities.
For any or for all these exercises
He said that Proteus your son was meet,° *fit*
And did request me to importune° you *beg*
To let him spend his time no more at home,
15 Which would be great impeachment to his age° *reproach in his old age*
In having known no travel in his youth.
ANTONIO Nor need'st thou much importune me to that
Whereon this month I have been hammering.° *thinking hard*
I have considered well his loss of time,
20 And how he cannot be a perfect° man, *complete*
Not being tried and tutored in the world.
Experience is by industry achieved,
And perfected by the swift course of time.
Then tell me, whither were I best to send him?
25 PANTHINO I think your lordship is not ignorant
How his companion, youthful Valentine,
Attends° the Emperor[1] in his royal court. *Waits upon*
ANTONIO I know it well.
PANTHINO 'Twere good, I think, your lordship sent him thither.
30 There shall he practise° tilts and tournaments, *take part in*
Hear sweet discourse, converse with noblemen,
And be in eye of° every exercise *witness*
Worthy his youth and nobleness of birth.
ANTONIO I like thy counsel. Well hast thou advised,
35 And that thou mayst perceive how well I like it,
The execution of it shall make known.
Even with the speediest expedition° *swiftness*
I will dispatch him to the Emperor's court.
PANTHINO Tomorrow, may it please you, Don Alfonso,
40 With other gentlemen of good esteem,
Are journeying to salute the Emperor
And to commend their service to his will.
ANTONIO Good company. With them shall Proteus go.
[*Enter* PROTEUS *with a letter. He does not see* ANTONIO
and PANTHINO]
And in good time.° Now will we break with him.[2] *at the right moment*
45 PROTEUS Sweet love, sweet lines, sweet life!
Here is her hand, the agent of her heart.
Here is her oath for love, her honour's pawn.° *pledge*
O that our fathers would applaud our loves
To seal our happiness with their consents.
50 O heavenly Julia!
ANTONIO How now, what letter are you reading there?
PROTEUS May't please your lordship, 'tis a word or two
Of commendations° sent from Valentine, *greetings*
Delivered by a friend that came from him.
55 ANTONIO Lend me the letter. Let me see what news.
PROTEUS There is no news, my lord, but that he writes
How happily he lives, how well beloved

---

1. One of several inconsistencies in the plot. Proteus of Milan, not at the Emperor's court.
and Valentine are later shown at the court of the Duke 2. Reveal the plan to him.

	And daily gracèd° by the Emperor,	*honored*
	Wishing me with him, partner of his fortune.	
60	ANTONIO And how stand you affected° to his wish?	*disposed*
	PROTEUS As one relying on your lordship's will,	
	And not depending on his friendly wish.	
	ANTONIO My will is something sorted with° his wish.	*in agreement with*
	Muse° not that I thus suddenly proceed,	*Wonder*
65	For what I will, I will, and there an end.	
	I am resolved that thou shalt spend some time	
	With Valentinus in the Emperor's court.	
	What maintenance° he from his friends° receives,	*money / family*
	Like exhibition° thou shalt have from me.	*The same allowance*
70	Tomorrow be in readiness to go.	
	Excuse it not,³ for I am peremptory.°	*resolved*
	PROTEUS My lord, I cannot be so soon provided.°	*equipped*
	Please you deliberate a day or two.	
	ANTONIO Look what° thou want'st shall be sent after thee.	*Whatever*
75	No more of stay. Tomorrow thou must go.	
	Come on, Panthino. You shall be employed	
	To hasten on his expedition. [*Exeunt* ANTONIO *and* PANTHINO]	
	PROTEUS Thus have I shunned the fire for fear of burning	
	And drenched me in the sea where I am drowned.	
80	I feared to show my father Julia's letter	
	Lest he should take exceptions° to my love,	*object*
	And with the vantage of mine own excuse⁴	
	Hath he excepted most° against my love.	*raised most obstacles*
	O, how this spring of love resembleth	
85	The uncertain glory of an April day,	
	Which now shows all the beauty of the sun,	
	And by and by a cloud takes all away.	
	[*Enter* PANTHINO]	
	PANTHINO Sir Proteus, your father calls for you.	
	He is in haste, therefore I pray you go.	
90	PROTEUS Why, this it is. My heart accords thereto,°	*agrees to it*
	And yet a thousand times it answers 'No'.⁵ *Exeunt*	

2.1

Enter VALENTINE [*and*] SPEED

SPEED [*offering* VALENTINE *a glove*]   Sir, your glove.

VALENTINE   Not mine.
My gloves are on.

SPEED   Why then, this may be yours, for this is but one.¹

VALENTINE   Ha, let me see. Ay, give it me, it's mine—
Sweet ornament, that decks a thing divine.

5   Ah, Silvia, Silvia!

SPEED   Madam Silvia, Madam Silvia!

VALENTINE   How now, sirrah?²

SPEED   She is not within hearing, sir.

VALENTINE   Why, sir, who bade you call her?

10   SPEED   Your worship, sir, or else I mistook.

---

3. Do not offer reasons why you should be excused
from this.
4. And by taking advantage of my lie (that the letter
came from Valentine).
5. *My . . . 'No'*: Suggesting that he is divided between

desire to go and desire to stay.
2.1 Location: Milan.
1. Punning on "one," which could be pronounced like
"on."
2. Fellow; a form of address to social inferiors.

VALENTINE Well, you'll still be° too forward.   *persist in being*
SPEED And yet I was last chidden for being too slow.
VALENTINE Go to,[3] sir. Tell me, do you know Madam Silvia?
SPEED She that your worship loves?
15 VALENTINE Why, how know you that I am in love?
SPEED Marry, by these special marks: first, you have learned,
like Sir Proteus, to wreath° your arms, like a malcontent;[4] to   *fold*
relish° a love-song, like a robin redbreast; to walk alone, like   *sing*
one that had the pestilence;° to sigh, like a schoolboy that   *plague*
20 had lost his ABC;° to weep, like a young wench that had buried   *primer; spelling book*
her grandam; to fast, like one that takes° diet; to watch,° like   *keeps to a / lie awake*
one that fears robbing; to speak puling,° like a beggar at Hal-   *whiningly*
lowmas.[5] You were wont, when you laughed, to crow like a
cock; when you walked, to walk like one of the lions. When
25 you fasted, it was presently° after dinner; when you looked   *immediately*
sadly, it was for want of money. And now you are metamor-
phosed with a mistress, that when I look on you I can hardly
think you my master.
VALENTINE Are all these things perceived in me?
30 SPEED They are all perceived without ye.°   *in your appearance*
VALENTINE Without me?[6] They cannot.
SPEED Without you? Nay, that's certain, for without° you were   *unless*
so simple, none else would.° But you are so without these fol-   *(perceive them)*
lies[7] that these follies are within you, and shine through you
35 like the water in an urinal,° that not an eye that sees you but   *glass jar for urine*
is a physician to comment on your malady.
VALENTINE But tell me, dost thou know my lady Silvia?
SPEED She that you gaze on so as she sits at supper?
VALENTINE Hast thou observed that? Even she I mean.
40 SPEED Why sir, I know[8] her not.
VALENTINE Dost thou know her by my gazing on her, and yet
know'st her not?
SPEED Is she not hard-favoured,° sir?   *ugly*
VALENTINE Not so fair, boy, as well favoured.°   *gracious; esteemed*
45 SPEED Sir, I know that well enough.
VALENTINE What dost thou know?
SPEED That she is not so fair as of you well favoured.°   *looked on with favor*
VALENTINE I mean that her beauty is exquisite but her favour°   *graciousness*
infinite.
50 SPEED That's because the one is painted° and the other out of   *wearing cosmetics*
all count.°   *unable to be counted*
VALENTINE How painted? And how out of count?
SPEED Marry, sir, so painted to make her fair that no man
counts° of her beauty.   *takes account; values*
55 VALENTINE How esteem'st thou me? I account of her beauty.
SPEED You never saw her since she was deformed.[9]
VALENTINE How long hath she been deformed?
SPEED Ever since you loved her.
VALENTINE I have loved her ever since I saw her, and still I see
60 her beautiful.

---

3. Expression of impatience.
4. A person made melancholy and discontented by love. Such people were often depicted with folded arms.
5. All Saints' Day, November 1, when it was customary to give charity to beggars.
6. Valentine has taken Speed to mean "They are all perceived when you are absent."
7. But you are so outwardly marked by these follies.
8. Punning on "know" as meaning "to be sexually familiar with."
9. Altered (Speed implies that Valentine's love for Silvia distorts his view of her).

SPEED   If you love her you cannot see her.

VALENTINE   Why?

SPEED   Because love is blind. O that you had mine eyes, or your
own eyes had the lights° they were wont to have when you   *power to see clearly*
65   chid at Sir Proteus for going ungartered.[1]

VALENTINE   What should I see then?

SPEED   Your own present folly and her passing° deformity; for he   *excessive*
being in love could not see to garter his hose, and you being in
love cannot see to put on your hose.

70   VALENTINE   Belike, boy, then you are in love, for last morning you
could not see to wipe my shoes.

SPEED   True, sir. I was in love with my bed. I thank you, you
swinged° me for my love, which makes me the bolder to chide   *beat*
you for yours.

75   VALENTINE   In conclusion, I stand affected to° her.   *in love with*

SPEED   I would you were set.[2] So your affection would cease.

VALENTINE   Last night she enjoined me to write some lines to one
she loves.

SPEED   And have you?

80   VALENTINE   I have.

SPEED   Are they not lamely writ?

VALENTINE   No, boy, but as well as I can do them. Peace, here she
comes.

    [*Enter* SILVIA]

SPEED [*aside*]   O excellent motion!° O exceeding puppet!° Now   *puppet show / (Silvia)*
85   will he interpret[3] to her.

VALENTINE   Madam and mistress, a thousand good-morrows.

SPEED [*aside*]   O, give° ye good e'en!° Here's a million of   *God give / evening*
manners.

SILVIA   Sir Valentine and servant,[4] to you two thousand.

90   SPEED [*aside*]   He should give her interest, and she gives it him.[5]

VALENTINE   As you enjoined me, I have writ your letter
Unto the secret, nameless friend of yours;
Which I was much unwilling to proceed in
But for my duty to your ladyship.
    [*He gives her a letter*]

95   SILVIA   I thank you, gentle servant. 'Tis very clerkly° done.   *like a scholar*

VALENTINE   Now trust me, madam, it came hardly off;°   *was not done easily*
For being ignorant to whom it goes
I writ at random, very doubtfully.

SILVIA   Perchance you think too much of so much pains?

100   VALENTINE   No, madam. So it stead° you I will write—   *help*
Please you command—a thousand times as much.
And yet . . .

SILVIA   A pretty period.° Well, I guess the sequel.°   *pause / what is next*
And yet I will not name it. And yet I care not.
And yet, take this again.
    [*She offers him the letter*]
105   And yet I thank you,
Meaning henceforth to trouble you no more.

---

1. Garters kept stockings from falling down. Going "ungartered" was a traditional sign of love melancholy.
2. Seated; satisfied. Speed has interpreted "stand" as carrying its bawdy connotation of "having an erection."
3. Provide commentary (as if in a puppet show).
4. In courtly love literature, a man devoted to a lady is called her servant.
5. He should surpass her in compliments, but she surpasses him.

SPEED [*aside*]   And yet you will, and yet another yet.

VALENTINE   What means your ladyship? Do you not like it?

SILVIA   Yes, yes. The lines are very quaintly° writ,   *skillfully*

110   But since unwillingly, take them again.

[*She presses the letter upon him*]

Nay, take them.

VALENTINE   Madam, they are for you.

SILVIA   Ay, ay. You writ them, sir, at my request,

But I will none of them. They are for you.

I would have had them writ more movingly.

115   VALENTINE   Please you, I'll write your ladyship another.

SILVIA   And when it's writ, for my sake read it over,

And if it please you, so. If not, why, so.

VALENTINE   If it please me, madam? What then?

SILVIA   Why, if it please you, take it for your labour.

120   And so good morrow, servant.   *Exit*

SPEED [*aside*]   O jest unseen, inscrutable, invisible

As a nose on a man's face or a weathercock on a steeple.

My master sues to her, and she hath taught her suitor,

He being her pupil, to become her tutor.

125   O excellent device!° Was there ever heard a better?—   *trick*

That my master, being scribe, to himself should write the letter.

VALENTINE   How now, sir—what, are you reasoning with your self?

SPEED   Nay, I was rhyming. 'Tis you that have the reason.

VALENTINE   To do what?

130   SPEED   To be a spokesman from Madam Silvia.

VALENTINE   To whom?

SPEED   To yourself. Why, she woos you by a figure.°   *device; indirect means*

VALENTINE   What figure?

SPEED   By a letter, I should say.

135   VALENTINE   Why, she hath not writ to me.

SPEED   What need she, when she hath made you write to
yourself? Why, do you not perceive the jest?

VALENTINE   No, believe me.

SPEED   No believing you indeed, sir. But did you perceive her

140   earnest?⁶

VALENTINE   She gave me none, except an angry word.

SPEED   Why, she hath given you a letter.

VALENTINE   That's the letter I writ to her friend.

SPEED   And that letter hath she delivered, and there an end.

145   VALENTINE   I would it were no worse.

SPEED   I'll warrant you, 'tis as well.

For often have you writ to her, and she in modesty

Or else for want of idle time could not again reply,

Or fearing else some messenger that might her mind discover,

150   Herself hath taught her love himself to write unto her lover.

—All this I speak in print,° for in print I found it.⁷ Why muse   *very precisely*

you, sir? 'Tis dinner-time.

VALENTINE   I have dined.°   *(on love)*

SPEED   Ay, but hearken, sir. Though the chameleon⁸ love can

---

6. To be serious. Valentine takes "perceive" to mean "receive," and takes "earnest" to mean "pledge" or "money given to seal a bargain."

7. Speed's reference to a printed speech probably shouldn't be taken literally. More likely, he is making

fun of Valentine's inability to understand Silvia's trick by stressing his own care with language.

8. A small lizard that can exist for long periods without food and was thought to feed on air.

155 feed on the air, I am one that am nourished by my victuals,
and would fain° have meat. O, be not like your mistress—be   *be eager to*
moved, be moved!⁹   *Exeunt*

2.2

Enter PROTEUS [*and*] JULIA

PROTEUS   Have patience, gentle Julia.

JULIA   I must where is no remedy.

PROTEUS   When possibly I can I will return.

JULIA   If you turn not,° you will return the sooner.   *are not unfaithful*

         [*She gives him a ring*]¹

5   Keep this remembrance for thy Julia's sake.

PROTEUS   Why then, we'll make exchange. Here, take you this.

         [*He gives her a ring*]

JULIA   And seal the bargain with a holy kiss.

         [*They kiss*]

PROTEUS   Here is my hand for my true constancy.

      And when that hour o'erslips° me in the day   *passes by*

10   Wherein I sigh not, Julia, for thy sake,

      The next ensuing hour some foul mischance

      Torment me for my love's forgetfulness.

      My father stays° my coming. Answer not.   *awaits*

      The tide is now. [JULIA *weeps*]   Nay, not thy tide of tears,

15   That tide will stay° me longer than I should.   *delay*

      Julia, farewell.   [*Exit* JULIA]

             What, gone without a word?

      Ay, so true love should do. It cannot speak,

      For truth hath better deeds than words to grace° it.   *adorn*

         [*Enter* PANTHINO]

PANTHINO   Sir Proteus, you are stayed for.

PROTEUS   Go, I come, I come.—

20   Alas, this parting strikes poor lovers dumb.   *Exeunt*

2.3

Enter LANCE¹ [*with his dog Crab*]²

LANCE [*to the audience*]   Nay, 'twill be this hour ere I have done
weeping. All the kind° of the Lances have this very fault. I have   *family; kin*
received my proportion,° like the prodigious³ son, and am   *portion*
going with Sir Proteus to the Imperial's° court. I think Crab, my   *(for "Emperor's")*
5   dog, be the sourest-natured dog that lives. My mother weeping,
my father wailing, my sister crying, our maid howling, our cat
wringing her hands, and all our house in a great perplexity, yet
did not this cruel-hearted cur shed one tear. He is a stone, a
very pebble-stone, and has no more pity in him than a dog.
10   A Jew would have wept to have seen our parting.⁴ Why, my
grandam, having no eyes,° look you, wept herself blind at   *being blind*
my parting. Nay, I'll show you the manner of it.⁵ This shoe is my
father. No, this left shoe is my father. No, no, this left shoe is

---

9. Be kind; be induced (to eat).

2.2 Location: probably Julia's house or garden.

1. The action in this scene resembles a betrothal ceremony, and thus in the Elizabethan period a legally binding agreement to marry.

2.3 Location: A street in Verona.

1. A shortened form of "Lancelot."

2. "Crab" may mean "crab apple" or a "crabbed, ill-

tempered person."

3. Lance frequently confuses one word with another.
His reference here is to the biblical parable of the
prodigal son, who wastes his inheritance but is welcomed home again (Luke 15:11–32).

4. Alluding to proverbs claiming that Jews and dogs
lack pity.

5. Taking off his shoes for demonstration.

my mother. Nay, that cannot be so, neither. Yes, it is so, it is so,
15 it hath the worser sole.[6] This shoe with the hole[7] in it is my
mother, and this my father. A vengeance on't, there 'tis.[8] Now,
sir, this staff is my sister, for, look you, she is as white as a lily
and as small° as a wand.° This hat is Nan our maid. I am the   *slender / small stick*
dog. No, the dog is himself, and I am the dog. O, the dog is me,
20 and I am myself. Ay, so, so. Now come I to my father. 'Father,
your blessing.' Now should not the shoe speak a word for weeping. Now should I kiss my father. Well, he weeps on. Now come
I to my mother. O that she could speak now, like a moved°   *full of emotion*
woman. Well, I kiss her. Why, there 'tis. Here's my mother's
25 breath[9] up and down.° Now come I to my sister. Mark the moan   *exactly*
she makes.[1]—Now the dog all this while sheds not a tear nor
speaks a word. But see how I lay the dust with my tears.
    [*Enter* PANTHINO]
PANTHINO   Lance, away, away, aboard. Thy master is shipped,
    and thou art to post° after with oars.° What's the matter? Why   *hurry / in a rowboat*
30 weep'st thou, man? Away, ass, you'll lose° the tide if you tarry   *miss*
    any longer.
LANCE   It is no matter if the tied[2] were lost, for it is the unkind-
    est tied that ever any man tied.
PANTHINO   What's the unkindest tide?
35 LANCE   Why, he that's tied here, Crab my dog.
PANTHINO   Tut, man, I mean thou'lt lose the flood,° and in los-   *miss the tide*
    ing the flood, lose thy voyage, and in losing thy voyage, lose
    thy master, and in losing thy master, lose thy service, and in
    losing thy service—
    [LANCE *puts his hand over Panthino's mouth*]
40 Why dost thou stop my mouth?
LANCE   For fear thou shouldst lose thy tongue.
PANTHINO   Where should I lose my tongue?
LANCE   In thy tale.
PANTHINO   In thy tail!°   *rear end*
45 LANCE   Lose the tide, and the voyage, and the master, and the
    service, and the tied? Why, man, if the river were dry, I am
    able to fill it with my tears. If the wind were down, I could
    drive the boat with my sighs.
PANTHINO   Come, come away, man. I was sent to call° thee.   *summon*
50 LANCE   Sir, call me what thou darest.
PANTHINO   Wilt thou go?
LANCE   Well, I will go.   *Exeunt*

2.4

Enter VALENTINE, SILVIA, THURIO, [*and*] SPEED
SILVIA   Servant!
VALENTINE   Mistress?
SPEED [*to* VALENTINE]   Master, Sir Thurio frowns on you.
VALENTINE   Ay, boy, it's for love.
5 SPEED   Not of you.

---

6. Punning on "soul" and alluding to medieval debates
about whether women had souls.
7. Punning on "hole" as "female genitalia."
8. Presumably Lance is now satisfied with his posi-
tioning of the shoes.
9. Comparing the smelly shoe to his mother's breath.

1. Perhaps Lance makes his staff "moan" by swishing
it in the air.
2. Taking "tide" for "tied," or one who is tied up, meaning Crab.
2.4 Location: The Duke's court in Milan.

VALENTINE Of my mistress, then.		
SPEED 'Twere good you knocked° him.	*struck*	
SILVIA [to VALENTINE] Servant, you are sad.		
VALENTINE Indeed, madam, I seem so.		

10   THURIO Seem you that you are not?

VALENTINE Haply° I do.   *Perhaps*

THURIO So do counterfeits.

VALENTINE So do you.

THURIO What seem I that I am not?

15   VALENTINE Wise.

THURIO What instance° of the contrary?   *evidence*

VALENTINE Your folly.

THURIO And how quote° you my folly?   *detect; observe*

VALENTINE I quote it in your jerkin.°   *short coat*

20   THURIO My 'jerkin' is a doublet.°   *jacket; couple or pair*

VALENTINE Well then, I'll double your folly.

THURIO How!

SILVIA What, angry, Sir Thurio? Do you change colour?

VALENTINE Give him leave, madam, he is a kind of chameleon.[1]

25   THURIO That hath more mind to feed on your blood than live
     in your air.[2]

VALENTINE You have said, sir.

THURIO Ay, sir, and done too, for this time.

VALENTINE I know it well, sir, you always end ere you begin.

30   SILVIA A fine volley of words, gentlemen, and quickly shot off.

VALENTINE 'Tis indeed, madam, we thank the giver.

SILVIA Who is that, servant?

VALENTINE Yourself, sweet lady, for you gave the fire.° Sir Thu-   *spark*
     rio borrows his wit from your ladyship's looks, and spends what

35   he borrows kindly° in your company.   *properly; naturally*

THURIO Sir, if you spend word for word with me, I shall make
     your wit bankrupt.

VALENTINE I know it well, sir. You have an exchequer° of words,   *treasury*
     and, I think, no other treasure to give your followers. For it

40   appears by their bare liveries[3] that they live by your bare° words.   *worthless*

SILVIA No more, gentlemen, no more. Here comes my father.

     [*Enter the* DUKE]

DUKE Now, daughter Silvia, you are hard beset.°   *set upon (by man)*
     Sir Valentine, your father is in good health,
     What say you to a letter from your friends
     Of much good news?

45   VALENTINE   My lord, I will be thankful
     To any happy messenger° from thence.   *bringer of happy news*

DUKE Know ye Don Antonio, your countryman?

VALENTINE Ay, my good lord, I know the gentleman
     To be of worth, and worthy estimation,

50   And not without desert so well reputed.

DUKE Hath he not a son?

VALENTINE Ay, my good lord, a son that well deserves
     The honour and regard of such a father.

DUKE You know him well?

---

1. Chameleons can change color, perhaps suggesting
that Thurio is fickle in love.
2. Chameleons were supposed to live on air (see note

to 2.1.154), but Thurio would rather drink Valentine's
blood.
3. By their threadbare clothing.

55	VALENTINE I knew him as myself, for from our infancy	
	We have conversed,° and spent our hours together.	kept company
	And though myself have been an idle truant,	
	Omitting° the sweet benefit of time	Neglecting
	To clothe mine age° with angel-like perfection,	adorn my years
60	Yet hath Sir Proteus—for that's his name—	
	Made use and fair advantage of his days:	
	His years but young, but his experience old;	
	His head unmellowed,° but his judgement ripe.	without gray hair
	And in a word—for far behind his worth	
65	Comes all the praises that I now bestow—	
	He is complete,° in feature° and in mind,	perfect / appearance
	With all good grace to grace a gentleman.	
	DUKE Beshrew me, sir, but if he make this good°	proves this to be true
	He is as worthy for an empress' love	
70	As meet° to be an emperor's counsellor.	fit
	Well, sir, this gentleman is come to me	
	With commendation from great potentates,°	rulers; men of power
	And here he means to spend his time awhile.	
	I think 'tis no unwelcome news to you.	
75	VALENTINE Should I have wished a thing° it had been he.	anything
	DUKE Welcome him then according to his worth.	
	Silvia, I speak to you, and you, Sir Thurio;	
	For Valentine, I need not cite° him to it.	urge
	I will send him hither to you presently. [Exit]	
80	VALENTINE This is the gentleman I told your ladyship	
	Had come along with me, but that his mistress	
	Did hold his eyes locked in her crystal looks.	
	SILVIA Belike that° now she hath enfranchised° them	Perhaps / freed
	Upon some other pawn for fealty.[4]	
85	VALENTINE Nay, sure, I think she holds them prisoners still.	
	SILVIA Nay, then he should be blind, and being blind	
	How could he see his way to seek out you?	
	VALENTINE Why, lady, love hath twenty pair of eyes.	
	THURIO They say that love hath not an eye at all.[5]	
90	VALENTINE To see such lovers, Thurio, as yourself.	
	Upon a homely object love can wink.°	close its eyes
	SILVIA Have done, have done. Here comes the gentleman.	
	[Enter PROTEUS]	
	VALENTINE Welcome, dear Proteus. Mistress, I beseech you	
	Confirm his welcome with some special favour.	
95	SILVIA His worth is warrant for his welcome hither,	
	If this be he you oft have wished to hear from.	
	VALENTINE Mistress, it is. Sweet lady, entertain him[6]	
	To be my fellow-servant to your ladyship.	
	SILVIA Too low a mistress for so high° a servant.	tall; distinguished
100	PROTEUS Not so, sweet lady, but too mean° a servant	lowly
	To have a look of° such a worthy mistress.	from
	VALENTINE Leave off discourse of disability.°	unworthiness
	Sweet lady, entertain him for your servant.	
	PROTEUS My duty will I boast of, nothing else.	
105	SILVIA And duty never yet did want his meed.°	lack his reward

4. *Upon . . . fealty*: Because of some other lover's pledge of faithful service.
5. Referring to the blindness of Cupid.
6. Take him into your service.

Servant, you are welcome to a worthless mistress.
PROTEUS   I'll die on° him that says so but yourself.   *die fighting*
SILVIA   That you are welcome?
PROTEUS   That you are worthless.
        [*Enter a* SERVANT][7]
SERVANT   Madam, my lord your father would speak with you.
SILVIA   I wait upon his pleasure.   [*Exit the* SERVANT]
110   Come, Sir Thurio,
    Go with me. Once more, new servant, welcome.
    I'll leave you to confer of° home affairs.   *talk about*
    When you have done, we look to hear from you.
PROTEUS   We'll both attend upon your ladyship.
                            [*Exeunt* SILVIA *and* THURIO]
115   VALENTINE   Now tell me, how do all from whence you came?
PROTEUS   Your friends are well, and have them much com-
    mended.°   *sent their regards*
VALENTINE   And how do yours?
PROTEUS   I left them all in health.
VALENTINE   How does your lady, and how thrives your love?
PROTEUS   My tales of love were wont to weary you.
120   I know you joy not in a love-discourse.
VALENTINE   Ay, Proteus, but that life is altered now.
    I have done penance for contemning° love,   *despising*
    Whose high imperious thoughts have punished me
    With bitter fasts, with penitential groans,
125   With nightly tears and daily heart-sore sighs.
    For in revenge of my contempt of love
    Love hath chased sleep from my enthrallèd° eyes,   *enslaved*
    And made them watchers of mine own heart's sorrow.
    O gentle Proteus, love's a mighty lord,
130   And hath so humbled me as° I confess   *that*
    There is no woe to° his correction,°   *equal to / punishment*
    Nor to his service no such joy on earth.
    Now, no discourse except it be of love.
    Now can I break my fast, dine, sup, and sleep
135   Upon the very naked name of love.
PROTEUS   Enough. I read your fortune in your eye.
    Was this the idol that you worship so?
VALENTINE   Even she; and is she not a heavenly saint?
PROTEUS   No, but she is an earthly paragon.
VALENTINE   Call her divine.
140   PROTEUS   I will not flatter her.
VALENTINE   O flatter me; for love delights in praises.
PROTEUS   When I was sick you gave me bitter pills,
    And I must minister the like to you.
VALENTINE   Then speak the truth by° her; if not divine,   *about*
145   Yet let her be a principality,°   *angel*
    Sovereign° to all the creatures on the earth.   *Superior*
PROTEUS   Except my mistress.
VALENTINE   Sweet, except not any,°   *make no exceptions*
    Except° thou wilt except against° my love.   *Unless / insult*
PROTEUS   Have I not reason to prefer° mine own?   *advance*

7. Even though F does not indicate the entrance of a   enter here to bring the message that Silvia's father
servant at this point and assigns the following line to   would speak with her.
Thurio, many editors have assumed that a servant must

150 VALENTINE　And I will help thee to prefer her, too.
　　　She shall be dignified with this high honour,
　　　To bear my lady's train, lest the base earth
　　　Should from her vesture° chance to steal a kiss　　　　　　　　*garments*
　　　And, of so great a favour growing proud,
155　Disdain to root° the summer-swelling flower,　　　　　　*receive the roots of*
　　　And make rough winter everlastingly.
　　PROTEUS　Why, Valentine, what braggartism° is this?　　　*excessive boasting*
　　VALENTINE　Pardon me, Proteus, all I can is nothing
　　　To her[8] whose worth makes other worthies nothing.
　　　She is alone.°　　　　　　　　　　　　　　　　　　　*unique*
160　PROTEUS　　　　Then let her alone.
　　VALENTINE　Not for the world. Why man, she is mine own,
　　　And I as rich in having such a jewel
　　　As twenty seas, if all their sand were pearl,
　　　The water nectar, and the rocks pure gold.
165　Forgive me that I do not dream on thee°　　　　　　*pay attention to you*
　　　Because thou seest me dote upon my love.
　　　My foolish rival, that her father likes
　　　Only for° his possessions are so huge,　　　　　　　　　　*because*
　　　Is gone with her along, and I must after;
170　For love, thou know'st, is full of jealousy.
　　PROTEUS　But she loves you?
　　VALENTINE　Ay, and we are betrothed. Nay more, our marriage hour,
　　　With all the cunning manner of our flight,
　　　Determined of:° how I must climb her window,　　　　　*Decided upon*
175　The ladder made of cords, and all the means
　　　Plotted and 'greed on for my happiness.
　　　Good Proteus, go with me to my chamber
　　　In these affairs to aid me with thy counsel.
　　PROTEUS　Go on before. I shall enquire you forth.°　　　　*seek you out*
180　I must unto the road,° to disembark　　　　　　　　　　　　*harbor*
　　　Some necessaries that I needs must use,
　　　And then I'll presently° attend you.　　　　　　　　　　　*at once*
　　VALENTINE　Will you make haste?
　　PROTEUS　I will.　　　　　　　　　　*Exit* [VALENTINE]
185　Even as one heat another heat expels,[9]
　　　Or as one nail by strength drives out another,
　　　So the remembrance of my former love
　　　Is by° a newer object quite forgotten.　　　　　　　　　*because of*
　　　Is it mine eye, or Valentine's praise,
190　Her true perfection, or my false transgression
　　　That makes me, reasonless,° to reason thus?　　　*wrongly; without cause*
　　　She is fair, and so is Julia that I love—
　　　That I did love, for now my love is thawed,
　　　Which like a waxen image 'gainst a fire
195　Bears no impression of the thing it was.
　　　Methinks my zeal° to Valentine is cold,　　　　　　　　　*affection*
　　　And that I love him not as I was wont.
　　　O, but I love his lady too-too much,
　　　And that's the reason I love him so little.

8. *all . . . her*: all I can say is nothing in comparison　　9. Referring to a popular belief that the application of
with her.　　　　　　　　　　　　　　　　　　　　　　　　heat takes away the pain of a burn.

<table>
<tr><td>200</td><td>How shall I dote on her with more advice,°</td><td>upon more deliberation</td></tr>
</table>

200 How shall I dote on her with more advice,°   *upon more deliberation*
That thus without advice begin to love her?
'Tis but her picture° I have yet beheld,   *outer appearance*
And that hath dazzled my reason's light.
But when I look on her perfections
205 There is no reason but° I shall be blind.   *doubt that*
If I can check my erring love I will,
If not, to compass° her I'll use my skill.   *Exit*   *win*

2.5

Enter SPEED *and* LANCE [*with his dog Crab*]

SPEED   Lance, by mine honesty, welcome to Milan.[1]

LANCE   Forswear° not thyself, sweet youth, for I am not wel-   *Perjure*
come. I reckon this always, that a man is never undone° till he   *ruined*
be hanged, nor never welcome to a place till some certain shot°   *tavern bill*
5   be paid and the hostess say 'Welcome'.

SPEED   Come on, you madcap. I'll to the alehouse with you
presently, where, for one shot of five pence, thou shalt have
five thousand welcomes. But sirrah, how did thy master part
with Madam Julia?

10 LANCE   Marry, after they closed[2] in earnest they parted very
fairly in jest.

SPEED   But shall she marry him?

LANCE   No.

SPEED   How then, shall he marry her?

15 LANCE   No, neither.

SPEED   What, are they broken?°   *no longer engaged*

LANCE   No, they are both as whole as a fish.[3]

SPEED   Why then, how stands the matter with them?

LANCE   Marry, thus: when it stands well with him[4] it stands well
20   with her.

SPEED   What an ass art thou! I understand thee not.

LANCE   What a block° art thou, that thou canst not! My staff[5]   *stupid person*
understands° me.   *comprehends; supports*

SPEED   What thou sayst?

25 LANCE   Ay, and what I do too. Look thee, I'll but lean, and my
staff under-stands me.

SPEED   It stands under thee indeed.

LANCE   Why, stand-under and under-stand is all one.

SPEED   But tell me true, will't be a match?

30 LANCE   Ask my dog. If he say 'Ay', it will. If he say 'No', it will.
If he shake his tail and say nothing, it will.

SPEED   The conclusion is, then, that it will.

LANCE   Thou shalt never get such a secret from me but by a
parable.°   *an indirect speech*

35 SPEED   'Tis well that I get it so. But Lance, how sayst thou[6] that
my master is become a notable lover?

LANCE   I never knew him otherwise.

SPEED   Than how?

2.5 Location: A street in Milan.
1. F reads "Padua," probably a first thought rejected but not canceled.
2. Came to an agreement; embraced.
3. Lance takes "broken" to mean "in pieces" and replies with a proverb.
4. When it goes well with him; when he has an erection.
5. A stick used when walking; also a euphemism for "penis." Lance may play with his staff during this dialogue.
6. What can you say about the fact.

	LANCE A notable lubber,° as thou reportest him to be.	*clumsy, stupid person*
40	SPEED Why, thou whoreson[7] ass, thou mistak'st° me.	*misunderstand*
	LANCE Why, fool, I meant not thee, I meant thy master.[8]	
	SPEED I tell thee my master is become a hot lover.	
	LANCE Why, I tell thee I care not, though he burn himself in	
	love. If thou wilt, go with me to the alehouse. If not, thou art	
45	an Hebrew, a Jew, and not worth° the name of a Christian.	*worthy*
	SPEED Why?	
	LANCE Because thou hast not so much charity in thee as to go	
	to the ale[9] with a Christian. Wilt thou go?	
	SPEED At thy service. *Exeunt*	

2.6

Enter PROTEUS

	PROTEUS To leave my Julia shall I be forsworn;°	*guilty of vow-breaking*
	To love fair Silvia shall I be forsworn;	
	To wrong my friend I shall be much forsworn.	
	And e'en that power° which gave me first my oath	*(love)*
5	Provokes me to this three-fold perjury.	
	Love bade me swear, and love bids me forswear.	
	O sweet-suggesting° love, if thou hast sinned	*sweetly seductive*
	Teach me, thy tempted subject, to excuse it.	
	At first I did adore a twinkling star,	
10	But now I worship a celestial sun.	
	Unheedful° vows may heedfully° be broken,	*Careless / advisedly*
	And he wants° wit that wants resolvèd will°	*lacks / determination*
	To learn° his wit t'exchange the bad for better.	*teach*
	Fie, fie, unreverent tongue, to call her bad	
15	Whose sovereignty so oft thou hast preferred°	*recommended*
	With twenty thousand soul-confirming° oaths.	*soul-confirmed; devout*
	I cannot leave° to love, and yet I do.	*cease*
	But there I leave to love where I should love.	
	Julia I lose, and Valentine I lose.	
20	If I keep them I needs must lose myself.	
	If I lose them, thus find I by their loss	
	For Valentine, myself, for Julia, Silvia.[1]	
	I to myself am dearer than a friend,	
	For love is still° most precious in itself,	*always*
25	And Silvia—witness heaven that made her fair—	
	Shows Julia but° a swarthy Ethiope.[2]	*to be merely*
	I will forget that Julia is alive,	
	Rememb'ring that my love to her is dead,	
	And Valentine I'll hold an enemy,	
30	Aiming at Silvia as a sweeter friend.	
	I cannot now prove constant to myself	
	Without some treachery used to Valentine.	
	This night he meaneth with a corded° ladder	*rope*
	To climb celestial Silvia's chamber-window,	
35	Myself in counsel his competitor.[3]	

---

7. Literally, "son of a whore." A term of abuse frequently used in jest.
8. Punning on "mistake." Lance understood Speed to mean "you misjudge me" or "you confuse me with someone else."
9. Referring to a church-ale, a charitable festival at which ale was sold in aid of the church or to relieve the poor.

2.6 Location: The Duke's court in Milan.
1. Proteus claims that to hold on to his selfhood and his love (Silvia), he must give up Julia and Valentine.
2. Ethiopian, or black African. The comparison rests on a European idealization of female fairness or whiteness.
3. Myself in on the secret as his partner.

Now presently I'll give her father notice
Of their disguising and pretended° flight,   *intended*
Who, all enraged, will banish Valentine;
For Thurio he intends shall wed his daughter.
40   But Valentine being gone, I'll quickly cross°   *thwart*
By some sly trick blunt Thurio's dull proceeding.
Love, lend me wings to make my purpose swift,
As thou hast lent me wit to plot this drift.°   *Exit*   *scheme*

2.7
Enter JULIA *and* LUCETTA

JULIA   Counsel, Lucetta. Gentle girl, assist me,
And e'en in kind love I do conjure° thee,   *entreat*
Who art the table° wherein all my thoughts   *notebook; tablet*
Are visibly charactered° and engraved,   *written*
5   To lesson° me, and tell me some good mean°   *teach / way*
How with my honour I may undertake
A journey to my loving Proteus.
LUCETTA   Alas, the way is wearisome and long.
JULIA   A true-devoted pilgrim is not weary
10   To measure° kingdoms with his feeble steps.   *make his way through*
Much less shall she that hath love's wings to fly,
And when the flight is made to one so dear,
Of such divine perfection as Sir Proteus.
LUCETTA   Better forbear till Proteus make return.
15   JULIA   O, know'st thou not his looks are my soul's food?
Pity the dearth that I have pinèd in
By longing for that food so long a time.
Didst thou but know the inly° touch of love   *inward*
Thou wouldst as soon go kindle fire with snow
20   As seek to quench the fire of love with words.
LUCETTA   I do not seek to quench your love's hot fire,
But qualify° the fire's extreme rage,   *lessen*
Lest it should burn above the bounds of reason.
JULIA   The more thou damm'st it up, the more it burns.
25   The current that with gentle murmur glides,
Thou know'st, being stopped, impatiently doth rage.
But when his fair course is not hinderèd
He makes sweet music with th'enamelled° stones,   *shiny*
Giving a gentle kiss to every sedge°   *plant*
30   He overtaketh in his pilgrimage.
And so by many winding nooks he strays
With willing sport to the wild ocean.
Then let me go, and hinder not my course.
I'll be as patient as a gentle stream,
35   And make a pastime of each weary step
Till the last step have brought me to my love.
And there I'll rest as after much turmoil
A blessèd soul doth in Elysium.[1]
LUCETTA   But in what habit° will you go along?   *clothing*
40   JULIA   Not like a woman, for I would prevent°   *forestall*
The loose encounters of lascivious men.

2.7 Location: Julia's house.   1. In Greek mythology, the final abode, after death, of blessed souls.

Gentle Lucetta, fit° me with such weeds°   *equip / clothing*
As may beseem some well-reputed page.
LUCETTA   Why then, your ladyship must cut your hair.
45   JULIA   No, girl, I'll knit° it up in silken strings   *bind*
With twenty odd-conceited° true-love knots.²   *strangely devised*
To be fantastic° may become a youth   *fanciful*
Of greater time° than I shall show° to be.   *age / appear*
LUCETTA   What fashion, madam, shall I make your breeches?
50   JULIA   That fits as well as 'Tell me, good my lord,
What compass° will you wear your farthingale?'³   *fullness*
Why, e'en what fashion thou best likes, Lucetta.
LUCETTA   You must needs have them with a codpiece,⁴ madam.
JULIA   Out, out,° Lucetta. That will be ill-favoured.°   *Not so / unbecoming*
55   LUCETTA   A round hose,⁵ madam, now's not worth a pin
Unless you have a codpiece to stick pins on.
JULIA   Lucetta, as thou lov'st me let me have
What thou think'st meet and is most mannerly.°   *seemly; modest*
But tell me, wench, how will the world repute me
60   For undertaking so unstaid° a journey?   *reckless*
I fear me it will make me scandalized.°   *disgraced*
LUCETTA   If you think so, then stay at home, and go not.
JULIA   Nay, that I will not.
LUCETTA   Then never dream on infamy, but go.
65   If Proteus like your journey when you come,
No matter who's displeased when you are gone.
I fear me he will scarce be pleased withal.°   *with it*
JULIA   That is the least, Lucetta, of my fear.
A thousand oaths, an ocean of his tears,
70   And instances of infinite° of love   *an infinity*
Warrant me° welcome to my Proteus.   *Assure me I will be*
LUCETTA   All these are servants to deceitful men.
JULIA   Base men, that use them to so base effect.
But truer stars did govern Proteus' birth.⁶
75   His words are bonds, his oaths are oracles,
His love sincere, his thoughts immaculate,
His tears pure messengers sent from his heart,
His heart as far from fraud as heaven from earth.
LUCETTA   Pray heaven he prove so when you come to him.
80   JULIA   Now, as thou lov'st me, do him not that wrong
To bear a hard opinion of his truth.
Only deserve my love by loving him,
And presently° go with me to my chamber   *at once*
To take a note of what I stand in need of
85   To furnish me upon my longing° journey.   *love-prompted*
All that is mine I leave at thy dispose,°   *in your care*
My goods, my lands, my reputation;
Only in lieu thereof dispatch me hence.°   *help me hurry away*
Come, answer not, but to it presently.
90   I am impatient of my tarriance.°   *Exeunt*   *delay*

---

2. Ornamental ribbons supposed to symbolize love.
3. Hooped petticoat.
4. A pouch attached to the front of men's breeches, covering the genital area. In the Elizabethan period, codpieces could be elaborately decorated, as with pins

(line 56).
5. Breeches fitting the legs and thighs tightly and puffed out at the hips.
6. The stars' position at one's birth supposedly determined one's character.

3.1

Enter DUKE, THURIO, [*and*] PROTEUS

DUKE   Sir Thurio, give us leave,° I pray, awhile.   *leave us alone*
We have some secrets to confer about.   [*Exit* THURIO]
Now tell me, Proteus, what's your will with me?
PROTEUS   My gracious lord, that which I would discover°   *reveal*
5   The law of friendship bids me to conceal.
But when I call to mind your gracious favours
Done to me, undeserving as I am,
My duty pricks° me on to utter that   *urges*
Which else no worldly good should draw from me.
10   Know, worthy prince, Sir Valentine my friend
This night intends to steal away your daughter.
Myself am one made privy to the plot.
I know you have determined to bestow her
On Thurio, whom your gentle daughter hates,
15   And should she thus be stol'n away from you
It would be much vexation to your age.
Thus, for my duty's sake, I rather chose
To cross° my friend in his intended drift°   *thwart / plan*
Than by concealing it heap on your head
20   A pack of sorrows which would press you down,
Being unprevented,° to your timeless° grave.   *unstopped / early*
DUKE   Proteus, I thank thee for thine honest care,
Which to requite° command me¹ while I live.   *repay*
This love of theirs myself have often seen,
25   Haply,° when they have judged me fast asleep,   *Perchance*
And oftentimes have purposed to forbid
Sir Valentine her company and my court.
But fearing lest my jealous aim might err,
And so unworthily disgrace the man—
30   A rashness that I ever yet have shunned—
I gave him gentle looks, thereby to find
That which thyself hast now disclosed to me.
And that thou mayst perceive my fear of this,
Knowing that tender youth is soon suggested,°   *tempted*
35   I nightly lodge her in an upper tower,
The key whereof myself have ever kept;
And thence she cannot be conveyed away.
PROTEUS   Know, noble lord, they have devised a mean°   *plan*
How he her chamber-window will ascend,
40   And with a corded ladder fetch her down,
For which the youthful lover now is gone,
And this way comes he with it presently,
Where, if it please you, you may intercept him.
But, good my lord, do it so cunningly
45   That my discovery° be not aimèd° at;   *disclosure / guessed*
For love of you, not hate unto my friend,
Hath made me publisher of this pretence.²
DUKE   Upon mine honour, he shall never know
That I had any light° from thee of this.   *information*
50   PROTEUS   Adieu, my lord. Sir Valentine is coming.   [*Exit*]

3.1 Location: The Duke's court in Milan.   2. Has caused me to make this plan public.
1. Ask anything of me.

[*Enter* VALENTINE]

DUKE   Sir Valentine, whither away so fast?[3]

VALENTINE   Please it° your grace, there is a messenger   *If it please*
  That stays° to bear my letters to my friends,   *waits*
  And I am going to deliver them.

55 DUKE   Be they of much import?

VALENTINE   The tenor° of them doth but signify   *general sense*
  My health and happy being at your court.

DUKE   Nay then, no matter. Stay with me awhile.
  I am to break with thee of° some affairs   *disclose to you*
60   That touch me near, wherein thou must be secret.
  'Tis not unknown to thee that I have sought
  To match my friend Sir Thurio to my daughter.

VALENTINE   I know it well, my lord; and sure the match
  Were° rich and honourable. Besides, the gentleman   *Would be*
65   Is full of virtue, bounty, worth, and qualities
  Beseeming° such a wife as your fair daughter.   *Suited to*
  Cannot your grace win her to fancy him?

DUKE   No, trust me. She is peevish, sullen, froward,°   *perverse*
  Proud, disobedient, stubborn, lacking duty,
70   Neither regarding° that she is my child   *taking into account*
  Nor fearing me as if I were her father.[4]
  And may I say to thee, this pride of hers
  Upon advice° hath drawn my love from her,   *After consideration*
  And where° I thought the remnant° of mine age   *whereas / remainder*
75   Should have been cherished by her child-like duty,
  I now am full resolved to take a wife,
  And turn her out to who will take her in.
  Then let her beauty be her wedding dower,
  For me and my possessions she esteems not.

80 VALENTINE   What would your grace have me to do in this?

DUKE   There is a lady of Verona[5] here
  Whom I affect,° but she is nice,° and coy,   *love / hard to please*
  And naught esteems° my agèd eloquence.   *does not value*
  Now therefore would I have thee to my tutor—
85   For long agone° I have forgot° to court,   *ago / forgotten how*
  Besides, the fashion of the time is changed—
  How and which way I may bestow° myself   *conduct*
  To be regarded in her sun-bright eye.

VALENTINE   Win her with gifts if she respect° not words.   *heeds*
90   Dumb jewels often in their silent kind°   *nature*
  More than quick words do move a woman's mind.

DUKE   But she did scorn a present that I sent her.

VALENTINE   A woman sometime scorns what best contents her.
  Send her another. Never give her o'er,
95   For scorn at first makes after-love the more.
  If she do frown, 'tis not in hate of you,
  But rather to beget more love in you.
  If she do chide, 'tis not to have you gone,
  Forwhy° the fools° are mad if left alone.   *Because / (women)*
100   Take no repulse, whatever she doth say:

---

3. Valentine may be crossing the stage without noticing
the Duke or starting to retreat on seeing him.
4. Nor respecting me as a father should be respected.

5. F reads "in Verona," another sign of inconsistency in
regard to the play's setting.

For° 'Get you gone' she doth not mean 'Away'.   *By*
Flatter and praise, commend, extol their graces;
Though ne'er so black,° say they have angels' faces.   *dark-complexioned*
That man that hath a tongue I say is no man
105   If with his tongue he cannot win a woman.
  DUKE   But she I mean is promised by her friends
Unto a youthful gentleman of worth,
And kept severely from resort of men,
That no man hath access by day to her.
110 VALENTINE   Why then I would resort to her by night.
  DUKE   Ay, but the doors be locked and keys kept safe,
That no man hath recourse to her by night.
  VALENTINE   What lets° but one may enter at her window?   *hinders*
  DUKE   Her chamber is aloft, far from the ground,
115 And built so shelving° that one cannot climb it   *projecting so far out*
Without apparent hazard of his life.
  VALENTINE   Why then, a ladder quaintly° made of cords   *skillfully*
To cast up, with a pair of anchoring hooks,
Would serve to scale another Hero's[6] tower,
120 So° bold Leander would adventure it.   *Provided*
  DUKE   Now as thou art a gentleman of blood,°   *well-born; passionate*
Advise me where I may have such a ladder.
  VALENTINE   When would you use it? Pray sir, tell me that.
  DUKE   This very night; for love is like a child
125 That longs for everything that he can come by.
  VALENTINE   By seven o'clock I'll get you such a ladder.
  DUKE   But hark thee: I will go to her alone.
How shall I best convey the ladder thither?
  VALENTINE   It will be light, my lord, that you may bear it
130 Under a cloak that is of any length.
  DUKE   A cloak as long as thine will serve the turn?
  VALENTINE   Ay, my good lord.
  DUKE   Then let me see thy cloak,
I'll get me one of such another length,
  VALENTINE   Why, any cloak will serve the turn, my lord.
135 DUKE   How shall I fashion me to wear° a cloak?   *get used to wearing*
I pray thee let me feel thy cloak upon me.
      [*He lifts Valentine's cloak and finds a letter and a rope-ladder*]
What letter is this same? What's here? 'To Silvia'?
And here an engine° fit for my proceeding.   *instrument (the ladder)*
I'll be so bold to break the seal for once.
      [*Reads*]
140 'My thoughts do harbour° with my Silvia nightly,   *dwell*
And slaves they are to me, that send them flying.
O, could their master come and go as lightly,
Himself would lodge where, senseless,° they are lying.   *without feeling*
My herald° thoughts in thy pure bosom rest them,   *message-bearing*
145 While I, their king, that thither them importune,°   *command*
Do curse the grace° that with such grace° hath blessed them,   *good fortune / favor*
Because myself do want° my servants' fortune.   *lack*
I curse myself for° they are sent by me,   *because*
That they should harbour where their lord should be.'
150 What's here?

---

6. See note to 1.1.22. Hero, Leander's beloved, lived in a tower.

'Silvia, this night I will enfranchise thee'?
'Tis so, and here's the ladder for the purpose.
Why, Phaëton,[7] for° thou art Merops' son   *since*
Wilt thou aspire to guide the heavenly car,
155   And with thy daring folly burn the world?
Wilt thou reach° stars because they shine on thee?   *grasp at*
Go, base intruder, over-weening° slave,   *presumptuous*
Bestow thy fawning smiles on equal mates,°   *mates of your own rank*
And think my patience, more than thy desert,
160   Is privilege for° thy departure hence.   *Allows*
Thank me for this more than for all the favours
Which, all too much, I have bestowed on thee.
But if thou linger in my territories
Longer than swiftest expedition°   *speed*
165   Will give thee time to leave our royal court,
By heaven, my wrath shall far exceed the love
I ever bore my daughter or thyself.
Be gone. I will not hear thy vain excuse,
But as thou lov'st thy life, make speed from hence.   **Exit**
170 VALENTINE   And why not death, rather than living torment?
To die is to be banished from myself,
And Silvia is my self. Banished from her
Is self from self, a deadly banishment.
What light is light, if Silvia be not seen?
175   What joy is joy, if Silvia be not by—
Unless it be to think that she is by,
And feed upon the shadow° of perfection.   *image; memory*
Except I be by Silvia in the night
There is no music in the nightingale.
180   Unless I look on Silvia in the day
There is no day for me to look upon.
She is my essence, and I leave° to be   *cease*
If I be not by her fair influence[8]
Fostered, illumined, cherished, kept alive.
185   I fly not death to fly his deadly doom.[9]
Tarry I here I but attend on° death,   *wait for*
But fly I hence, I fly away from life.
              [*Enter* PROTEUS *and* LANCE]
PROTEUS   Run, boy, run, run, and seek him out.
LANCE   So-ho, so-ho![1]
190 PROTEUS   What seest thou?
LANCE   Him we go to find. There's not a hair on's head but 'tis
a Valentine.[2]
PROTEUS   Valentine?
VALENTINE   No.
195 PROTEUS   Who then—his spirit?
VALENTINE   Neither.

7. Famous in Greek mythology for his reckless ambition, Phaëton set the world on fire when he tried to
drive the chariot of his father, Helios, the sun god.
Phaëton's mother, Clymene, was married to Merops,
not Helios, making Phaëton illegitimate. The rest of the
line, naming Merops as Phaëton's father, may question
Phaëton's status as the son of Helios (and so his ability
to drive the sun god's chariot) or may be an ironic
means of calling attention to his illegitimacy.

8. Alluding to the popular belief that the stars exert
power, or "influence," over individuals.
9. I cannot escape death by fleeing the Duke's death
sentence.
1. A cry in hare hunting and hawking.
2. Punning on "hare" and on Valentine's name. Every
part, down to the "hair," of the creature he sees suggests
a "valentine," or stereotypical lover.

PROTEUS   What then?

VALENTINE   Nothing.

LANCE   Can nothing speak?

[He threatens VALENTINE*]*

200   Master, shall I strike?

PROTEUS   Who wouldst thou strike?

LANCE   Nothing.

PROTEUS   Villain, forbear.

LANCE   Why, sir, I'll strike nothing. I pray you—

205   PROTEUS   Sirrah, I say forbear. Friend Valentine, a word.

VALENTINE   My ears are stopped, and cannot hear good news,
So much of bad already hath possessed them.

PROTEUS   Then in dumb silence will I bury mine,°   *(my news)*
For they are harsh, untuneable,° and bad.   *out of tune*

VALENTINE   Is Silvia dead?

210   PROTEUS   No, Valentine.

VALENTINE   No Valentine indeed, for sacred Silvia.
Hath she forsworn me?

PROTEUS   No, Valentine.

VALENTINE   No Valentine, if Silvia have forsworn me.
What is your news?

215   LANCE   Sir, there is a proclamation that you are vanished.°   *(for "banished")*

PROTEUS   That thou art banished. O that's the news:
From hence, from Silvia, and from me thy friend.

VALENTINE   O, I have fed upon this woe already,
And now excess of it will make me surfeit.°   *sicken*

220   Doth Silvia know that I am banishèd?

PROTEUS   Ay, ay; and she hath offered to the doom,°   *sentence*
Which unreversed stands in effectual force,[3]
A sea of melting pearl, which some call tears.
Those at her father's churlish feet she tendered,°   *offered*

225   With them, upon her knees, her humble self,
Wringing her hands, whose whiteness so became them
As if but now they waxèd° pale, for woe.   *turned*
But neither bended knees, pure hands held up,
Sad sighs, deep groans, nor silver-shedding tears[4]

230   Could penetrate her uncompassionate sire,
But Valentine, if he be ta'en, must die.
Besides, her intercession chafed him so
When she for thy repeal° was suppliant   *recall from exile*
That to close° prison he commanded her,   *tightly enclosed*

235   With many bitter threats of biding° there.   *staying permanently*

VALENTINE   No more, unless the next word that thou speak'st
Have some malignant power upon my life.
If so I pray thee breathe it in mine ear,
As ending anthem° of my endless dolour.°   *final hymn / grief*

240   PROTEUS   Cease to lament for that° thou canst not help,   *what*
And study° help for that which thou lament'st.   *devise*
Time is the nurse and breeder of all good.
Here if thou stay thou canst not see thy love.
Besides, thy staying will abridge thy life.

245   Hope is a lover's staff. Walk hence with that,
And manage it° against despairing thoughts.   *use it as a weapon*

---

3. Which, unless reversed, will be enforced.   4. Tears that flow like silver streams.

Thy letters may be here, though thou art hence,
Which, being writ to me, shall be delivered
Even in the milk-white bosom of thy love.
250 The time now serves not to expostulate.°   *complain; argue*
Come, I'll convey thee through the city gate,
And ere I part with thee confer at large°   *discuss at length*
Of all that may concern thy love affairs.
As thou lov'st Silvia, though not for thyself,
255 Regard thy danger, and along with me.
VALENTINE   I pray thee, Lance, an if° thou seest my boy   *an if=if*
Bid him make haste, and meet me at the North Gate.
PROTEUS   Go, sirrah, find him out. Come, Valentine.
VALENTINE   O my dear Silvia! Hapless Valentine.
            [*Exeunt* PROTEUS *and* VALENTINE]
260 LANCE   I am but a fool, look you, and yet I have the wit to think
            my master is a kind of a knave. But that's all one,° if he be but   *all right*
            one knave.[5] He lives not now that knows me to be in love, yet
            I am in love, but a team of horse shall not pluck that from me,
            nor who 'tis I love; and yet 'tis a woman, but what woman
265   I will not tell myself; and yet 'tis a milkmaid; yet 'tis not a
            maid,° for she hath had gossips;[6] yet 'tis a maid, for she is her   *virgin*
            master's maid, and serves for wages. She hath more qualities°   *abilities*
            than a water-spaniel,[7] which is much in a bare° Christian.   *mere*
            [*He takes out a paper*]
            Here is the catalogue of her conditions. '*Imprimis*,[8] she can
270   fetch and carry'—why, a horse can do no more. Nay, a horse
            cannot fetch, but only carry, therefore is she better than a
            jade.° '*Item*, she can milk.' Look you, a sweet virtue in a maid   *an inferior horse*
            with clean hands.
            [*Enter* SPEED]
SPEED   How now, Signor Lance, what news with your master-
275 ship?
LANCE   With my master's ship? Why, it is at sea.
SPEED   Well, your old vice still, mistake the word.[9] What news
            then in your paper?
LANCE   The blackest news that ever thou heard'st.
280 SPEED   Why, man, how 'black'?
LANCE   Why, as black as ink.
SPEED   Let me read them.
LANCE   Fie on thee, jolt-head,° thou canst not read.   *blockhead*
SPEED   Thou liest. I can.
285 LANCE   I will try thee. Tell me this: who begot thee?
SPEED   Marry, the son of my grandfather.
LANCE   O illiterate loiterer, it was the son of thy grandmother.
            This proves that thou canst not read.
SPEED   Come, fool, come. Try me in thy paper.
290 LANCE [*giving* SPEED *the paper*]   There: and Saint Nicholas[1] be
            thy speed.°   *protection*
SPEED   '*Imprimis*, she can milk.'

---

5. If he is only moderately a rascal; only a knave in one area (love).
6. Women who attended at childbirth; people who served as sponsors at the baptism of a newborn child.
7. A dog used for hunting waterfowl.
8. The paper employs the language of official docu-

ments. "*Imprimis*," Latin for "in the first place," was used to begin inventories. "*Item*" (line 272), meaning "also," was used to introduce subsequent articles in a list.
9. *your . . . word*: your customary fault of making blunders with language.
1. The patron saint of schoolchildren and scholars.

	LANCE	Ay, that she can.
	SPEED	'*Item*, she brews good ale.'
295	LANCE	And thereof comes the proverb 'Blessing of your heart, you brew good ale'.
	SPEED	'*Item*, she can sew.'
	LANCE	That's as much as to say 'Can she so?'
	SPEED	'*Item*, she can knit.'
300	LANCE	What need a man care for a stock° with a wench when she can knit him a stock?°
	SPEED	'*Item*, she can wash and scour.'
	LANCE	A special virtue, for then she need not be washed and scoured.²
305	SPEED	'*Item*, she can spin.'
	LANCE	Then may I set the world on wheels,° when she can spin for her living.
	SPEED	'*Item*, she hath many nameless° virtues.'
	LANCE	That's as much as to say 'bastard virtues', that indeed
310		know not their fathers, and therefore have no names.
	SPEED	Here follows her vices.
	LANCE	Close at the heels of her virtues.
	SPEED	'*Item*, she is not to be broken° with fasting, in respect of° her breath.'
315	LANCE	Well, that fault may be mended with a breakfast. Read on.
	SPEED	'*Item*, she hath a sweet mouth.'³
	LANCE	That makes amends for her sour breath.
	SPEED	'*Item*, she doth talk in her sleep.'
	LANCE	It's no matter for that, so she sleep not in her talk.
320	SPEED	'*Item*, she is slow in words.'
	LANCE	O villain, that set this down among her vices! To be slow in words is a woman's only virtue. I pray thee out with't, and place it for her chief virtue.
	SPEED	'*Item*, she is proud.'°
325	LANCE	Out with that, too. It was Eve's legacy,⁴ and cannot be ta'en from her.
	SPEED	'*Item*, she hath no teeth.'
	LANCE	I care not for that, neither, because I love crusts.
	SPEED	'*Item*, she is curst.'°
330	LANCE	Well, the best is, she hath no teeth to bite.
	SPEED	'*Item*, she will often praise° her liquor.'
	LANCE	If her liquor be good, she shall. If she will not, I will; for good things should be praised.
	SPEED	'*Item*, she is too liberal.'°
335	LANCE	Of her tongue she cannot, for that's writ down she is slow of. Of her purse she shall not, for that I'll keep shut. Now of another thing⁵ she may, and that cannot I help. Well, proceed.
	SPEED	'*Item*, she hath more hair than wit, and more faults than hairs, and more wealth than faults.'
340	LANCE	Stop there. I'll have her. She was mine and not mine twice or thrice in that last article. Rehearse° that once more.

Margin glosses:
- *dowry* (300)
- *stocking* (300–301)
- *take life easy* (306)
- *inexpressible* (308)
- *tamed* (313)
- *on account of* (314)
- *haughty; lascivious* (324)
- *shrewish* (329)
- *appraise (by tasting)* (331)
- *bold; wanton* (334)
- *Repeat* (341)

---

2. *washed and scoured:* slang for "knocked down and beaten."
3. A sweet tooth; a wanton nature.
4. In the Garden of Eden, Satan, in the form of a serpent, tempted Eve, wife of the first man, Adam, to eat fruit from the tree of Knowledge of good and evil, which God had forbidden humans to taste. Eve was thus guilty of the sin of pride for disobeying God and putting her will before his command. See Genesis 2:15–3:24.
5. "Purse" (line 336) and "another thing" (line 337) were colloquial terms for "female genitalia."

SPEED '*Item*, she hath more hair than wit'—

LANCE 'More hair than wit.' It may be. I'll prove it: the cover of
the salt° hides the salt, and therefore it is more° than the salt.   *saltcellar / greater*
345   The hair that covers the wit is more than the wit, for the
greater hides the less. What's next?

SPEED 'And more faults than hairs'—

LANCE That's monstrous. O that that were out!

SPEED 'And more wealth than faults.'

350   LANCE Why, that word makes the faults gracious.° Well, I'll   *pleasing*
have her, and if it be a match—as nothing is impossible—

SPEED What then?

LANCE Why then will I tell thee that thy master stays° for thee   *waits*
at the North Gate.

355   SPEED For me?

LANCE For thee? Ay, who art thou? He hath stayed for a better
man than thee.

SPEED And must I go to him?

LANCE Thou must run to him, for thou hast stayed so long that
360   going° will scarce serve the turn.   *walking*

SPEED Why didst not tell me sooner? Pox of⁶ your love letters!
[*Exit*]

LANCE Now will he be swinged° for reading my letter. An   *beaten*
unmannerly slave, that will thrust himself into secrets. I'll
after, to rejoice in the boy's correction.   *Exit*

3.2

Enter [the] DUKE *[and]* THURIO

DUKE Sir Thurio, fear not but that she will love you
Now Valentine is banished from her sight.

THURIO Since his exile she hath despised me most,
Forsworn my company, and railed at me,
5   That° I am desperate° of obtaining her.   *So that / hopeless*

DUKE This weak impress° of love is as a figure   *impression*
Trenchèd° in ice, which with an hour's heat   *Cut*
Dissolves to water and doth lose his form.
A little time will melt her frozen thoughts,
10   And worthless Valentine shall be forgot.
[*Enter* PROTEUS]
How now, Sir Proteus, is your countryman,
According to our proclamation, gone?

PROTEUS Gone, my good lord.

DUKE My daughter takes his going grievously?

15   PROTEUS A little time, my lord, will kill that grief.

DUKE So I believe, but Thurio thinks not so.
Proteus, the good conceit° I hold of thee—   *opinion*
For thou hast shown some sign of good desert—
Makes me the better° to confer with thee.   *the more willing*

20   PROTEUS Longer than I prove loyal to your grace
Let me not live to look upon your grace.

DUKE Thou know'st how willingly I would effect
The match between Sir Thurio and my daughter?

PROTEUS I do, my lord.

---

6. May disease take (a curse).   **3.2 Location:** The Duke's court in Milan.

25 DUKE And also, I think, thou art not ignorant
        How she opposes her° against my will?   *herself*
    PROTEUS She did, my lord, when Valentine was here.
    DUKE Ay, and perversely she persevers so.
        What might we do to make the girl forget
30   The love of Valentine, and love Sir Thurio?
    PROTEUS The best way is to slander Valentine
        With falsehood, cowardice, and poor descent,
        Three things that women highly hold in hate.
    DUKE Ay, but she'll think that it is spoke in hate.
35 PROTEUS Ay, if his enemy deliver° it.   *report*
        Therefore it must with circumstance° be spoken   *supporting detail*
        By one whom she esteemeth as his friend.
    DUKE Then you must undertake to slander him.
    PROTEUS And that, my lord, I shall be loath to do.
40   'Tis an ill office for a gentleman,
        Especially against his very° friend.   *true*
    DUKE Where your good word cannot advantage° him   *profit*
        Your slander never can endamage° him.   *harm*
        Therefore the office is indifferent,°   *neutral*
45   Being entreated to it by your friend.¹
    PROTEUS You have prevailed, my lord. If I can do it
        By aught that I can speak in his dispraise
        She shall not long continue love to him.
        But say this weed° her love from Valentine,   *uproot*
50   It follows not that she will love Sir Thurio.
    THURIO Therefore, as you unwind her love from him,
        Lest it should ravel and be good to none
        You must provide to bottom it on me;²
        Which must be done by praising me as much
55   As you in worth dispraise Sir Valentine.
    DUKE And Proteus, we dare trust you in this kind
        Because we know, on Valentine's report,
        You are already love's firm votary,°   *disciple*
        And cannot soon revolt, and change your mind.
60   Upon this warrant shall you have access
        Where you with Silvia may confer at large.
        For she is lumpish,° heavy, melancholy,   *low-spirited*
        And for your friend's sake will be glad of you;
        Where you may temper° her, by your persuasion,   *mold*
65   To hate young Valentine and love my friend.
    PROTEUS As much as I can do, I will effect.
        But you, Sir Thurio, are not sharp enough.
        You must lay lime³ to tangle° her desires   *capture*
        By wailful sonnets, whose composèd° rhymes   *well-crafted*
70   Should be full-fraught° with serviceable vows.⁴   *laden*
    DUKE Ay, much is the force of heaven-bred poesy.
    PROTEUS Say that upon the altar of her beauty
        You sacrifice your tears, your sighs, your heart.
        Write till your ink be dry, and with your tears
75   Moist it again; and frame some feeling line
        That may discover° such integrity;°   *reveal / sincerity*
        For Orpheus'⁵ lute was strung with poets' sinews,°   *nerves*

---

1. Being asked to do it by a friend like me.
2. To wind it like a skein of thread upon me.
3. Birdlime, a sticky substance used to trap birds.
4. Promises to be of service.
5. A figure in Greek mythology famous for his entrancing music.

Whose golden touch could soften steel and stones,
Make tigers tame, and huge leviathans°   *whales*
80   Forsake unsounded deeps to dance on sands.
After your dire-lamenting elegies,°   *love poems*
Visit by night your lady's chamber-window
With some sweet consort.° To their instruments   *band of musicians*
Tune° a deploring dump.° The night's dead silence   *Sing / sad melody*
85   Will well become such sweet-complaining grievance.
This, or else nothing, will inherit° her.   *win*
DUKE   This discipline° shows thou hast been in love.   *instruction*
THURIO   And thy advice this night I'll put in practice.
Therefore, sweet Proteus, my direction-giver,
90   Let us into the city presently
To sort° some gentlemen well skilled in music.   *select*
I have a sonnet that will serve the turn
To give the onset° to thy good advice.   *start*
DUKE   About it, gentlemen.
95   PROTEUS   We'll wait upon your grace till after supper,
And afterward determine our proceedings.
DUKE   Even now about it. I will pardon you.°   *excuse you from service*
Exeunt [THURIO *and* PROTEUS *at one door, and the* DUKE *at another*]

4.1

Enter [*the*] OUTLAWS
FIRST OUTLAW   Fellows, stand fast. I see a passenger.°   *traveler*
SECOND OUTLAW   If there be ten, shrink not, but down with 'em.
[*Enter* VALENTINE *and* SPEED]
THIRD OUTLAW   Stand,° sir, and throw us that° you have about ye. *Halt / that which*
If not, we'll make you sit, and rifle° you.   *search*
SPEED [*to* VALENTINE]   Sir, we are undone. These are the villains
5   That all the travellers do fear so much.
VALENTINE [*to the* OUTLAWS]   My friends.
FIRST OUTLAW   That's not so, sir. We are your enemies.
SECOND OUTLAW   Peace. We'll hear him.
THIRD OUTLAW   Ay, by my beard will we. For he is a proper° man. *handsome*
10   VALENTINE   Then know that I have little wealth to lose.
A man I am, crossed with adversity.
My riches are these poor habiliments,°   *clothes*
Of which if you should here disfurnish° me   *deprive*
You take the sum and substance that I have.
15   SECOND OUTLAW   Whither travel you?
VALENTINE   To Verona.
FIRST OUTLAW   Whence came you?
VALENTINE   From Milan.
THIRD OUTLAW   Have you long sojourned there?
20   VALENTINE   Some sixteen months,[1] and longer might have stayed
If crooked° fortune had not thwarted me.   *evil*
FIRST OUTLAW   What, were you banished thence?
VALENTINE   I was.
SECOND OUTLAW   For what offence?
VALENTINE   For that which now torments me to rehearse.°   *tell*

4.1 Location: A forest between Mantua and Milan.
1. A claim not consonant with the play's overall time
scheme. Either this is a textual inconsistency or Valentine is lying.

25	I killed a man,[2] whose death I much repent,	
	But yet I slew him manfully, in fight,	
	Without false vantage or base treachery.°	*unfair advantage*
	FIRST OUTLAW Why, ne'er repent it, if it were done so.	
	But were you banished for so small a fault?	
30	VALENTINE I was, and held me glad of such a doom.°	*sentence*
	SECOND OUTLAW Have you the tongues?°	*skill in languages*
	VALENTINE My youthful travel therein made me happy,°	*fortunate; skilled*
	Or else I had been often miserable.	
	THIRD OUTLAW By the bare scalp of Robin Hood's fat friar,°	*(Friar Tuck)*
35	This fellow were a king for our wild faction.°	*band*
	FIRST OUTLAW We'll have him. Sirs, a word.	

        [*The* OUTLAWS *confer*]

	SPEED [*to* VALENTINE] Master, be one of them.	
	It's an honourable kind of thievery.	
	VALENTINE Peace, villain.	
	SECOND OUTLAW Tell us this: have you anything to take to?[3]	
40	VALENTINE Nothing but my fortune.°	*luck*
	THIRD OUTLAW Know, then, that some of us are gentlemen	
	Such as the fury of ungoverned youth	
	Thrust from the company of aweful° men.	*respectable*
	Myself was from Verona banishèd	
45	For practising° to steal away a lady,	*plotting*
	An heir, and near allied unto the Duke.	
	SECOND OUTLAW And I from Mantua, for a gentleman	
	Who, in my mood,° I stabbed unto the heart.	*anger*
	FIRST OUTLAW And I, for suchlike petty crimes as these.	
50	But to the purpose, for we cite our faults	
	That they may hold excused our lawless lives.	
	And partly seeing you are beautified	
	With goodly shape, and by your own report	
	A linguist, and a man of such perfection	
55	As we do in our quality° much want—	*profession*
	SECOND OUTLAW Indeed because you are a banished man,	
	Therefore above the rest[4] we parley° to you.	*talk*
	Are you content to be our general,	
	To make a virtue of necessity	
60	And live as we do in this wilderness?	
	THIRD OUTLAW What sayst thou? Wilt thou be of our consort?°	*company*
	Say 'Ay', and be the captain of us all.	
	We'll do thee homage, and be ruled by thee,	
	Love thee as our commander and our king.	
65	FIRST OUTLAW But if thou scorn our courtesy, thou diest.	
	SECOND OUTLAW Thou shalt not live to brag what we have offered.	
	VALENTINE I take your offer, and will live with you,	
	Provided that you do no outrages	
	On silly° women or poor passengers.	*defenseless*
70	THIRD OUTLAW No, we detest such vile, base practices.	
	Come, go with us. We'll bring thee to our crews°	*bands of men*
	And show thee all the treasure we have got,	
	Which, with ourselves, all rest at thy dispose.° *Exeunt*	*disposal*

---

2. Why Valentine lies here is much debated. He may be protecting Silvia's reputation or trying to impress the outlaws.

3. Any way to support yourself.
4. For that above all other reasons.

4.2

Enter PROTEUS

PROTEUS   Already have I been false to Valentine,
    And now I must be as unjust to Thurio.
    Under the colour° of commending him   *pretext*
    I have access my own love to prefer.°   *advance*
5   But Silvia is too fair, too true, too holy
    To be corrupted with my worthless gifts.
    When I protest true loyalty to her
    She twits me with my falsehood to my friend.
    When to her beauty I commend my vows
10   She bids me think how I have been forsworn
    In breaking faith with Julia, whom I loved.
    And notwithstanding all her sudden quips,°   *sharp rebukes*
    The least whereof would quell a lover's hope,
    Yet, spaniel-like, the more she spurns my love,
15   The more it grows and fawneth on her still.
    But here comes Thurio. Now must we to her window,
    And give some evening music to her ear.
        [*Enter* THURIO *with Musicians*]
THURIO   How now, Sir Proteus, are you crept before us?
PROTEUS   Ay, gentle Thurio, for you know that love
20   Will creep° in service where it cannot go.°   *crawl / walk*
THURIO   Ay, but I hope, sir, that you love not here.
PROTEUS   Sir, but I do, or else I would be hence.
THURIO   Who, Silvia?
PROTEUS   Ay, Silvia—for your sake.
THURIO   I thank you for your own.° Now, gentlemen,   *own sake*
25   Let's tune, and to it lustily awhile.
        [*Enter the* HOST, *and* JULIA *dressed as a page-boy. They
        talk apart*]
HOST   Now, my young guest, methinks you're allycholly.° I pray   *melancholy*
    you, why is it?
JULIA   Marry, mine host, because I cannot be merry.
HOST   Come, we'll have you merry. I'll bring you where you
30   shall hear music, and see the gentleman that you asked for.
JULIA   But shall I hear him speak?
HOST   Ay, that you shall.
JULIA   That will be music.
HOST   Hark, hark.[1]
35 JULIA   Is he among these?
HOST   Ay. But peace, let's hear 'em.

Song[2]

    Who is Silvia? What is she,
        That all our swains° commend her?   *lovers*
    Holy, fair, and wise is she.
40   The heaven such grace did lend her
    That she might admirèd be.

4.2 Location: Outside the Duke's palace under Silvia's
window by moonlight.
1. Probably music plays.

2. Not ascribed to anyone in F. Julia's later comments
suggest that Proteus sings while playing a stringed
instrument.

        Is she kind as she is fair?
          For beauty lives with kindness.
        Love° doth to her eyes repair°   *(Cupid) / pay a visit*
45   To help° him of his blindness,   *cure*
        And, being helped, inhabits there.

        Then to Silvia let us sing
          That Silvia is excelling.
        She excels each mortal thing
50   Upon the dull earth dwelling.
        To her let us garlands bring.

HOST   How now, are you sadder than you were before? How do
     you, man? The music likes° you not.   *pleases*
JULIA   You mistake. The musician likes me not.
55 HOST   Why, my pretty youth?
JULIA   He plays false,[3] father.
HOST   How, out of tune on the strings?
JULIA   Not so, but yet so false that he grieves my very heart-strings.
HOST   You have a quick° ear.   *perceptive*
60 JULIA   Ay, I would I were deaf. It makes me have a slow° heart.   *heavy*
HOST   I perceive you delight not in music.
JULIA   Not a whit when it jars so.°   *is so discordant*
HOST   Hark what fine change° is in the music.   *modulation*
JULIA   Ay, that 'change' is the spite.
65 HOST   You would have them always play but one thing?
JULIA   I would always have one play but one thing. But host,
     doth this Sir Proteus that we talk on often resort unto this
     gentlewoman?
HOST   I tell you what Lance his man told me, he loved her out
70   of all nick.°   *excessively*
JULIA   Where is Lance?
HOST   Gone to seek his dog, which tomorrow, by his master's
     command, he must carry for a present to his lady.
JULIA   Peace, stand aside. The company parts.
75 PROTEUS   Sir Thurio, fear not you. I will so plead
     That you shall say my cunning drift° excels.   *scheme*
THURIO   Where meet we?
PROTEUS   At Saint Gregory's[4] well.
THURIO   Farewell.
         [Exeunt THURIO *and the Musicians]*
      [Enter SILVIA, *above]*°   *(at her window)*
PROTEUS   Madam, good even to your ladyship.
SILVIA   I thank you for your music, gentlemen.
80   Who is that that spake?
PROTEUS   One, lady, if you knew his pure heart's truth
     You would quickly learn to know him by his voice.
SILVIA   Sir Proteus, as I take it.
PROTEUS   Sir Proteus, gentle lady, and your servant.
85 SILVIA   What's your will?
PROTEUS   That I may compass yours.[5]

---

3. Is unfaithful; plays out of tune.
4. Patron saint of musicians and singers.

5. *compass:* win. Punning on "will." That I may win
your good will; that I may conquer your sexual desire.

SILVIA You have your wish. My will is even this,
    That presently you hie you home to bed.
    Thou subtle, perjured, false, disloyal man,
    Think'st thou I am so shallow, so conceitless°   *witless*
90   To be seducèd by thy flattery,
    That hast deceived so many with thy vows?
    Return, return, and make thy love amends.
    For me—by this pale queen of night[6] I swear—
    I am so far from granting thy request
95   That I despise thee for thy wrongful suit,
    And by and by intend to chide myself
    Even for this time I spend in talking to thee.
PROTEUS I grant, sweet love, that I did love a lady,
    But she is dead.
JULIA [*aside*]   'Twere false if° I should speak it,   *even if*
100   For I am sure she is not buried.
SILVIA Say that she be, yet Valentine, thy friend,
    Survives, to whom, thyself art witness,
    I am betrothed. And art thou not ashamed
    To wrong him with thy importunacy?°   *improper requests*
105 PROTEUS I likewise hear that Valentine is dead.
SILVIA And so suppose am I, for in his grave,
    Assure thyself, my love is buried.
PROTEUS Sweet lady, let me rake it from the earth.
SILVIA Go to thy lady's grave and call hers thence,
110   Or at the least, in hers sepulchre° thine.   *bury*
JULIA [*aside*] He heard not that.
PROTEUS Madam, if your heart be so obdurate,
    Vouchsafe me yet your picture for my love,
    The picture that is hanging in your chamber.
115   To that I'll speak, to that I'll sigh and weep;
    For since the substance of your perfect self
    Is else devoted,[7] I am but a shadow,°   *mere nothing*
    And to your shadow° will I make true love.   *image*
JULIA [*aside*] If 'twere a substance, you would sure deceive it
120   And make it but a shadow, as I am.
SILVIA I am very loath to be your idol, sir,
    But since your falsehood shall become you well°   *make you fit*
    To worship shadows and adore false shapes,
    Send to me in the morning, and I'll send it.°   *(the picture)*
    And so, good rest.   [*Exit*]
125 PROTEUS   As wretches have o'ernight,
    That wait for execution in the morn.   [*Exit*]
JULIA Host, will you go?
HOST By my halidom,° I was fast asleep.   *holy relic (an oath)*
JULIA Pray you, where lies° Sir Proteus?   *lodges*
130 HOST Marry, at my house. Trust me, I think 'tis almost day.
JULIA Not so; but it hath been the longest night
    That e'er I watched, and the most heaviest.°   [*Exeunt*]   *saddest*

6. The moon, imagined as Diana, goddess of chastity.   7. Is devoted to someone else.

4.3

Enter [Sir] EGLAMOUR

EGLAMOUR This is the hour that Madam Silvia
Entreated me to call, and know her mind.
There's some great matter she'd employ me in.
Madam, madam!

[*Enter* SILVIA *above*]

SILVIA Who calls?

EGLAMOUR Your servant, and your friend.
5 One that attends your ladyship's command.

SILVIA Sir Eglamour, a thousand times good morrow!

EGLAMOUR As many, worthy lady, to yourself.
According to your ladyship's impose° *command*
I am thus early come, to know what service
10 It is your pleasure to command me in.

SILVIA O Eglamour, thou art a gentleman—
Think not I flatter, for I swear I do not—
Valiant, wise, remorseful,° well accomplished. *compassionate*
Thou art not ignorant what dear good will
15 I bear unto the banished Valentine,
Nor how my father would enforce me marry
Vain Thurio, whom my very soul abhors.
Thyself hast loved, and I have heard thee say
No grief did ever come so near thy heart
20 As when thy lady and thy true love died,
Upon whose grave thou vowed'st pure chastity.
Sir Eglamour, I would° to Valentine, *would go*
To Mantua, where I hear he makes abode;
And for° the ways are dangerous to pass *because*
25 I do desire thy worthy company,
Upon whose faith and honour I repose.° *rely*
Urge not[1] my father's anger, Eglamour,
But think upon my grief, a lady's grief,
And on the justice of my flying hence
30 To keep me from a most unholy match,
Which heaven and fortune still° rewards with plagues. *always*
I do desire thee, even from a heart
As full of sorrows as the sea of sands,
To bear me company and go with me.
35 If not, to hide what I have said to thee
That I may venture to depart alone.

EGLAMOUR Madam, I pity much your grievances,
Which, since I know they virtuously are placed,
I give consent to go along with you,
40 Recking° as little what betideth° me *Caring / happens to*
As much I wish all good befortune° you. *befall*
When will you go?

SILVIA This evening coming.

EGLAMOUR Where shall I meet you?

SILVIA At Friar Patrick's cell,
Where I intend holy confession.
45 EGLAMOUR I will not fail your ladyship.

4.3 Location: The same place, the next morning.　　1. Do not offer as an excuse.

Good morrow, gentle lady.
SILVIA Good morrow, kind Sir Eglamour.   *Exeunt*

4.4

Enter LANCE [*and his dog Crab*]
LANCE [*to the audience*] When a man's servant shall play the
cur° with him, look you, it goes hard. One that I brought up   *act like a stupid dog*
of° a puppy, one that I saved from drowning when three or four   *from*
of his blind brothers and sisters went to it.° I have taught him,   *met their death*
5   even as one would say precisely 'Thus I would teach a dog'.
I was sent to deliver him as a present to Mistress Silvia from
my master, and I came no sooner into the dining-chamber but
he steps me to[1] her trencher° and steals her capon's leg. O, 'tis   *wooden plate*
a foul thing when a cur cannot keep° himself in all compa-   *behave*
10 nies. I would have, as one should say, one that takes upon him
to be a dog indeed, to be, as it were, a dog at° all things. If I had   *adept at*
not had more wit than he, to take a fault upon me that he did,
I think verily he had been hanged for't. Sure as I live, he had
suffered for't. You shall judge. He thrusts me himself into the
15 company of three or four gentleman-like dogs under the
Duke's table. He had not been there—bless the mark[2]—a
pissing-while[3] but all the chamber smelled him. 'Out with the
dog,' says one. 'What cur is that?' says another. 'Whip him out,'
says the third. 'Hang him up,' says the Duke. I, having been
20 acquainted with the smell before, knew it was Crab, and goes
me to the fellow that whips the dogs. 'Friend,' quoth I, 'you
mean to whip the dog.' 'Ay, marry do I,' quoth he. 'You do him
the more wrong,' quoth I, ''twas I did the thing you wot° of.' He   *know*
makes me no more ado, but whips me out of the chamber.
25 How many masters would do this for his servant? Nay, I'll be
sworn I have sat in the stocks[4] for puddings[5] he hath stolen,
otherwise he had been executed. I have stood on the pillory[6]
for geese he hath killed, otherwise he had suffered for't. (*To
Crab*) Thou think'st not of this now. Nay, I remember the trick
30 you served me when I took my leave of Madam Silvia. Did not
I bid thee still mark° me, and do as I do? When didst thou see   *watch*
me heave up my leg and make water against a gentlewoman's
farthingale?° Didst thou ever see me do such a trick?   *hooped petticoat*
         [*Enter* PROTEUS, *with* JULIA *dressed as a page-boy*]
PROTEUS [*to* JULIA] Sebastian[7] is thy name? I like thee well,
35 And will employ thee in some service° presently.   *work; sexual business*
JULIA In what you please. I'll do what I can.
PROTEUS I hope thou wilt.—How now, you whoreson peasant,
Where have you been these two days loitering?
LANCE Marry, sir, I carried Mistress Silvia the dog you bade me.
40 PROTEUS And what says she to my little jewel?

4.4 Location: The same place, somewhat later.
1. *he steps me to:* he (the dog) steps forward to Lance's
embarrassment or to his detriment. Here and in line
14, "thrusts me," Lance is describing the dog's actions
and their negative effect on himself.
2. An apology for offensive language.
3. Slang for "a very short time." Lance here employs it
literally.
4. An instrument of punishment in which the offender

sat with feet clamped between two wooden planks into
which ankle holes had been cut.
5. Dishes made of animal intestines or stomachs
stuffed with meat and spices.
6. An instrument of punishment similar to the stocks.
One stood with head and hands clamped between
wooden planks.
7. A name sometimes associated with male homoeroticism and the arrow-pierced body of St. Sebastian.

LANCE Marry, she says your dog was a cur, and tells you currish thanks is good enough for such a present.

PROTEUS But she received my dog?

LANCE No indeed did she not. Here have I brought him back
45 again.

PROTEUS What, didst thou offer her this from me?

LANCE Ay, sir. The other squirrel[8] was stolen from me by the
hangman° boys in the market place, and then I offered her   *fit for the hangman*
mine own, who is a dog as big as ten of yours, and therefore
50 the gift the greater.

PROTEUS Go, get thee hence, and find my dog again,
Or ne'er return again into my sight.
Away, I say. Stay'st thou to vex me here?
                              [*Exit* LANCE *with Crab*]
A slave, that still on end° turns me to shame.   *always*
55 Sebastian, I have entertainèd thee
Partly that I have need of such a youth
That can with some discretion do my business,
For 'tis no trusting to yon foolish lout,
But chiefly for thy face and thy behaviour,
60 Which, if my augury° deceive me not,   *fortune-telling skills*
Witness good bringing up, fortune, and truth.
Therefore know thou, for this I entertain thee.
Go presently, and take this ring with thee.
Deliver it to Madam Silvia.
65 She loved me well delivered° it to me.   *who gave*

JULIA It seems you loved not her, to leave° her token.   *part with*
She is dead belike?°   *perchance*

PROTEUS   Not so. I think she lives.

JULIA Alas.

PROTEUS Why dost thou cry 'Alas'?

70 JULIA I cannot choose but pity her.

PROTEUS Wherefore shouldst thou pity her?

JULIA Because methinks that she loved you as well
As you do love your lady Silvia.
She dreams on him that has forgot her love;
75 You dote on her that cares not for your love.
'Tis pity love should be so contrary,
And thinking on it makes me cry 'Alas'.

PROTEUS Well, give her that ring, and therewithal°   *along with it*
This letter. [*Pointing*] That's her chamber. Tell my lady
80 I claim the promise for her heavenly picture.
Your message done, hie home unto my chamber,
Where thou shalt find me sad and solitary.   [*Exit*]

JULIA How many women would do such a message?
Alas, poor Proteus, thou hast entertained
85 A fox to be the shepherd of thy lambs.
Alas, poor fool,[9] why do I pity him
That with his very heart despiseth me?
Because he loves her, he despiseth me.
Because I love him, I must pity him.
90 This ring I gave him when he parted from me,

8. A disparaging reference to the small dog Proteus   9. Julia is referring to herself.
intended to give Silvia.

To bind him to remember my good will.
And now am I, unhappy messenger,
To plead for that which I would not obtain;
To carry that which I would have refused;
95 To praise his faith, which I would have dispraised.
I am my master's true-confirmèd love,
But cannot be true servant to my master
Unless I prove false traitor to myself.
Yet will I woo for him, but yet so coldly
100 As, heaven it knows, I would not have him speed.°   *succeed*
          [*Enter* SILVIA]
Gentlewoman, good day. I pray you be my mean°   *agent, means*
To bring me where to speak with Madam Silvia.
SILVIA   What would you with her, if that I be she?
JULIA   If you be she, I do entreat your patience
105 To hear me speak the message I am sent on.
SILVIA   From whom?
JULIA   From my master, Sir Proteus, madam.
SILVIA   O, he sends you for a picture?
JULIA   Ay, madam.
110 SILVIA   Ursula, bring my picture there.
          [*An attendant brings a picture*]
Go, give your master this. Tell him from me
One Julia, that his changing thoughts forget,
Would better fit his chamber than this shadow.°   *portrait*
JULIA   Madam, please you peruse this letter.
          [*She gives* SILVIA *a letter*]¹
115 Pardon me, madam, I have unadvised°   *inadvertently*
Delivered you a paper that I should not.
          [*She takes back the letter and gives* SILVIA *another letter*]
This is the letter to your ladyship.
SILVIA   I pray thee, let me look on that again.
JULIA   It may not be. Good madam, pardon me.
120 SILVIA   There, hold. I will not look upon your master's lines.
I know they are stuffed with protestations,
And full of new-found° oaths, which he will break   *newly made*
As easily as I do tear his paper.
          [*She tears the letter*]
JULIA   Madam, he sends your ladyship this ring.
          [*She offers* SILVIA *a ring*]
125 SILVIA   The more shame for him, that he sends it me;
For I have heard him say a thousand times
His Julia gave it him at his departure.
Though his false finger have profaned the ring,
Mine shall not do his Julia so much wrong.
130 JULIA   She thanks you.
SILVIA   What sayst thou?
JULIA   I thank you, madam, that you tender° her.   *show concern for*
Poor gentlewoman, my master wrongs her much.
SILVIA   Dost thou know her?
135 JULIA   Almost as well as I do know myself.
To think upon her woes I do protest

---

1. Possibly the first letter is from Proteus to Julia. Whether Julia offers it to Silvia by mistake or deliberately (as she later seems deliberately to mistake two rings) is open to question.

That I have wept a hundred several times.
SILVIA Belike she thinks that Proteus hath forsook her?
JULIA I think she doth; and that's her cause of sorrow.
140 SILVIA Is she not passing° fair?   *exceedingly*
JULIA She hath been fairer, madam, than she is.
When she did think my master loved her well
She, in my judgement, was as fair as you.
But since she did neglect her looking-glass,
145 And threw her sun-expelling mask² away,
The air hath starved° the roses in her cheeks   *withered*
And pinched the lily tincture° of her face,   *white color*
That now she is become as black as I.
SILVIA How tall was she?
150 JULIA About my stature; for at Pentecost,³
When all our pageants of delight° were played,   *pleasing performances*
Our youth got me to play the woman's part,⁴
And I was trimmed° in Madam Julia's gown,   *dressed*
Which servèd me as fit, by all men's judgements,
155 As if the garment had been made for me;
Therefore I know she is about my height.
And at that time I made her weep agood,°   *in earnest*
For I did play a lamentable° part.   *pitiable*
Madam, 'twas Ariadne, passioning
160 For Theseus' perjury and unjust flight;⁵
Which I so lively° acted with my tears   *convincingly*
That my poor mistress, movèd therewithal,
Wept bitterly; and would I might be dead
If I in thought felt not her very sorrow.
165 SILVIA She is beholden to thee, gentle youth.
Alas, poor lady, desolate and left.
I weep myself to think upon thy words.
Here, youth. There is my purse. I give thee this
For thy sweet mistress' sake, because thou lov'st her.
170 Farewell.   [*Exit*]
JULIA And she shall thank you for't, if e'er you know her.—
A virtuous gentlewoman, mild, and beautiful.
I hope my master's suit will be but cold,°   *unsuccessful*
Since she respects 'my mistress' ' love so much.
175 Alas, how love can trifle with itself.
Here is her picture. Let me see, I think
If I had such a tire,° this face of mine   *headdress*
Were full as lovely as is this of hers.
And yet the painter flattered her a little,
180 Unless I flatter with myself too much.
Her hair is auburn, mine is perfect yellow.
If that be all the difference in his love,
I'll get me such a coloured periwig.
Her eyes are grey as glass, and so are mine.
185 Ay, but her forehead's low, and mine's as high.⁶

2. A mask to block the sun worn by upper-class En-
glishwomen to preserve their light complexions.
3. Religious days seven weeks after Easter, when plays
and theatrical pageants were staged in many English
towns.
4. Act the female role, as boys conventionally did in the
Elizabethan theater.
5. In Greek mythology, Ariadne hanged herself after
she was abandoned by her lover, Theseus. *passioning:*
sorrowing.
6. Mine's as high as hers is low. High foreheads were
considered a sign of beauty.

What should it be that he respects° in her   esteems
But I can make respective° in myself,   worthy of esteem
If this fond love were not a blinded god?
Come, shadow, come, and take this shadow up,[7]
For 'tis thy rival.
190   [She picks up the portrait]
                                     O thou senseless form,
Thou shalt be worshipped, kissed, loved, and adored;
And were there sense° in his idolatry   reason
My substance should be statue in thy stead.[8]
195 I'll use thee kindly, for thy mistress' sake,
That used me so; or else, by Jove I vow,
I should have scratched out your unseeing eyes,
To make my master out of love with thee.   Exit

5.1

Enter [Sir] EGLAMOUR

EGLAMOUR   The sun begins to gild the western sky,
   And now it is about the very hour
   That Silvia at Friar Patrick's cell should meet me.
   She will not fail; for lovers break not hours,°   appointments
5   Unless it be to come before their time,
   So much they spur their expedition.°   hasten their progress
       [*Enter* SILVIA]
   See where she comes. Lady, a happy evening!
SILVIA   Amen, amen. Go on, good Eglamour,
   Out at the postern° by the abbey wall.   back door or side door
10 I fear I am attended° by some spies.   followed
EGLAMOUR   Fear not. The forest is not three leagues off.
   If we recover° that, we are sure° enough.   Exeunt   reach / safe

5.2

Enter THURIO, PROTEUS, [*and*] JULIA [*dressed as a page-boy*]

THURIO   Sir Proteus, what says Silvia to my suit?
PROTEUS   O sir, I find her milder than she was,
   And yet she takes exceptions at° your person.   objects to
THURIO   What? That my leg is too long?
5 PROTEUS   No, that it is too little.
THURIO   I'll wear a boot, to make it somewhat rounder.
JULIA [*aside*]   But love will not be spurred to what it loathes.[1]
THURIO   What says she to my face?
PROTEUS   She says it is a fair one.
10 THURIO   Nay, then, the wanton lies. My face is black.
PROTEUS   But pearls are fair; and the old saying is,
   'Black men are pearls in beauteous ladies' eyes'.
JULIA [*aside*]   'Tis true, such pearls[2] as put out ladies' eyes,
   For I had rather wink° than look on them.   shut my eyes
15 THURIO   How likes she my discourse?
PROTEUS   Ill, when you talk of war.

---

7. Probably addressing herself as a "shadow," or mere nothing, Julia means "pick up Silvia's portrait" or "take up the challenge posed by this woman."
8. My person ("substance") should be an idol ("statue") to Proteus rather than Silvia's picture.
5.1 Location: An abbey in Milan.
5.2 Location: The Duke's court in Milan.

1. F assigns this line to Proteus and lines 13 and 14 to Thurio, but it makes more sense to assign them to the disguised Julia, whose covert comments on the words of Proteus and Thurio provide the scene with much of its humor.
2. Punning on the medical meaning of "pearl" as a thin film or cataract growing over the eye.

THURIO   But well when I discourse of love and peace.
JULIA [*aside*]   But better indeed when you hold your peace.
THURIO   What says she to my valour?
20   PROTEUS   O sir, she makes no doubt of that.
JULIA [*aside*]   She needs not, when she knows it cowardice.
THURIO   What says she to my birth?
PROTEUS   That you are well derived.°   *descended*
JULIA [*aside*]   True: from a gentleman to a fool.
25   THURIO   Considers she my possessions?
PROTEUS   O ay, and pities them.
THURIO   Wherefore?
JULIA [*aside*]   That such an ass should owe° them.   *own*
PROTEUS   That they are out by lease.°   *rented out*
JULIA   Here comes the Duke.
       [*Enter the* DUKE]
30   DUKE   How now, Sir Proteus. How now, Thurio.
    Which of you saw Eglamour of late?
THURIO   Not I.
PROTEUS   Nor I.
DUKE   Saw you my daughter?
PROTEUS   Neither.
DUKE   Why then, she's fled unto that peasant° Valentine,   *rascal*
    And Eglamour is in her company.
35   'Tis true, for Friar Laurence[3] met them both
    As he in penance wandered through the forest.
    Him he knew well, and guessed that it was she,
    But being masked, he was not sure of it.
    Besides, she did intend confession
40   At Patrick's cell this even, and there she was not.
    These likelihoods confirm her flight from hence;
    Therefore I pray you stand not to discourse,
    But mount you presently, and meet with me
    Upon the rising of the mountain foot
45   That leads toward Mantua, whither they are fled.
    Dispatch,° sweet gentlemen, and follow me.   [*Exit*]   *Hurry*
THURIO   Why, this it is to be a peevish° girl,   *silly; perverse*
    That flies her fortune when it follows her.
    I'll after, more to be revenged on Eglamour
50   Than for the love of reckless Silvia.   [*Exit*]
PROTEUS   And I will follow, more for Silvia's love
    Than hate of Eglamour that goes with her.   [*Exit*]
JULIA   And I will follow, more to cross that love
    Than hate for Silvia, that is gone for love.   *Exit*

5.3
    [*Enter the*] OUTLAWS [*with*] SILVIA [*captive*]
FIRST OUTLAW   Come, come, be patient. We must bring you to
  our captain.
SILVIA   A thousand more mischances than this one
    Have learned° me how to brook° this patiently.   *taught / endure*
5   SECOND OUTLAW   Come, bring her away.
FIRST OUTLAW   Where is the gentleman that was with her?°   (*Eglamour*)

---

3. Possibly a slip for "Friar Patrick," mentioned in the   friar in the forest.
preceding scene, although there may be more than one   **5.3** Location: At the frontiers of the Mantua forest.

THIRD OUTLAW   Being nimble-footed he hath outrun us;
But Moses and Valerius follow him.
Go thou with her to the west end of the wood.
10   There is our captain. We'll follow him that's fled.
The thicket is beset,° he cannot scape.   *surrounded*
            [*Exeunt the* SECOND *and* THIRD OUTLAWS]
FIRST OUTLAW [*to* SILVIA]   Come, I must bring you to our captain's cave.
Fear not. He bears an honourable mind,
And will not use a woman lawlessly.
15   SILVIA [*aside*]   O Valentine! This I endure for thee.   *Exeunt*

5.4

        Enter VALENTINE
VALENTINE   How use° doth breed a habit in a man!   *custom*
This shadowy desert,° unfrequented woods   *uninhabited spot*
I better brook° than flourishing peopled towns.   *endure*
Here can I sit alone, unseen of any,
5   And to the nightingale's¹ complaining notes
Tune my distresses and record my woes.
O thou° that dost inhabit in my breast,   *(addressing Silvia)*
Leave not the mansion² so long tenantless
Lest, growing ruinous, the building fall
10   And leave no memory of what it was.
Repair me with thy presence, Silvia.
Thou gentle nymph, cherish thy forlorn swain.
What hallooing and what stir is this today?
These are my mates, that make their wills their law,
15   Have° some unhappy passenger° in chase.   *Who have / traveler*
They love me well, yet I have much to do
To keep them from uncivil outrages.
Withdraw thee, Valentine. Who's this comes here?
        [*He stands aside.*
        Enter PROTEUS, SILVIA, *and* JULIA *dressed as a page-boy*]
PROTEUS   Madam, this service I have done for you—
20   Though you respect not aught your servant doth—
To hazard life, and rescue you from him
That would have forced your honour° and your love.   *violated your chastity*
Vouchsafe me for my meed° but one fair look.   *reward*
A smaller boon than this I cannot beg,
25   And less than this I am sure you cannot give.
VALENTINE [*aside*]   How like a dream is this I see and hear!
Love lend me patience to forbear awhile.
SILVIA   O miserable, unhappy that I am!
PROTEUS   Unhappy were you, madam, ere I came.
30   But by my coming I have made you happy.
SILVIA   By thy approach° thou mak'st me most unhappy.   *amorous advances*
JULIA [*aside*]   And me, when he approacheth to your presence.
SILVIA   Had I been seizèd by a hungry lion
I would have been a breakfast to the beast
35   Rather than have false Proteus rescue me.
O heaven be judge how I love Valentine,

5.4 Location: Another part of the forest.   a nightingale after Tereus raped her; her song is a lament.
1. In the classical mythology, Philomela was turned into   2. Referring to his body as Silvia's home.

Whose life's as tender° to me as my soul.   *precious*
And full as much, for more there cannot be,
I do detest false perjured Proteus.
40   Therefore be gone, solicit me no more.
PROTEUS   What dangerous action, stood it next to death,
Would I not undergo for one calm° look!   *gentle*
O, 'tis the curse in love, and still approved,°   *always confirmed*
When women cannot love where they're beloved.
45 SILVIA   When Proteus cannot love where he's beloved.
Read over Julia's heart, thy first, best love,
For whose dear sake thou didst then rend thy faith
Into a thousand oaths, and all those oaths
Descended into perjury° to love me.   *were forsworn*
50   Thou hast no faith left now, unless thou'dst two,³
And that's far worse than none. Better have none
Than plural faith, which is too much by one,
Thou counterfeit° to thy true friend.   *deceiver; false friend*
PROTEUS   In love
Who respects friend?
SILVIA   All men but Proteus.
55 PROTEUS   Nay, if the gentle spirit of moving words
Can no way change you to a milder form
I'll woo you like a soldier, at arm's end,°   *at swordpoint*
And love you 'gainst the nature of love: force ye.
SILVIA   O heaven!
PROTEUS [*assailing her*]   I'll force thee yield to my desire.
60 VALENTINE [*coming forward*]   Ruffian, let go that rude uncivil touch,
Thou friend of an ill fashion.
PROTEUS   Valentine!
VALENTINE   Thou common° friend, that's without faith or love,   *superficial*
For such is a friend now. Treacherous man,
Thou hast beguiled my hopes. Naught but mine eye
65   Could have persuaded me. Now I dare not say
I have one friend alive. Thou wouldst disprove me.
Who should be trusted, when one's right hand
Is perjured to the bosom?° Proteus,   *false to the heart*
I am sorry I must never trust thee more,
70   But count the world a stranger for thy sake.⁴
The private wound is deepest. O time most accursed,
'Mongst all foes that a friend should be the worst!
PROTEUS   My shame and guilt confounds me.
Forgive me, Valentine. If hearty sorrow
75   Be a sufficient ransom for offence,
I tender't° here. I do as truly suffer   *offer it*
As e'er I did commit.
VALENTINE   Then I am paid,
And once again I do receive thee° honest.   *accept you as*
Who by repentance is not satisfied
80   Is nor of heaven nor earth. For these are pleased;
By penitence th' Eternal's wrath's appeased.
And that my love may appear plain and free,

3. You have no faithfulness left now, unless you were to
have two lovers (Julia and Silvia).

4. But cut myself off from the world (in disillusionment) because of your treachery.

All that was mine in Silvia⁵ I give thee.

JULIA   O me unhappy!
           [*She faints*]

PROTEUS   Look to the boy.

VALENTINE   Why, boy!
85   Why wag,° how now? What's the matter? Look up. Speak.   *sweet boy*

JULIA   O good sir, my master charged me to deliver a ring to
       Madam Silvia, which out of my neglect was never done.

PROTEUS   Where is that ring, boy?

JULIA   Here 'tis. This is it.
           [*She gives* PROTEUS *the ring*]

90   PROTEUS   How, let me see!
       Why, this is the ring I gave to Julia.

JULIA   O, cry you mercy, sir, I have mistook.
           [*She offers* PROTEUS *another ring*]
       This is the ring you sent to Silvia.

PROTEUS   But how cam'st thou by this ring? At my depart
95   I gave this unto Julia.

JULIA   And Julia herself did give it me,
       And Julia herself hath brought it hither.

PROTEUS   How? Julia?

JULIA   Behold her that gave aim to° all thy oaths   *was the object of*
100 And entertained 'em deeply in her heart.
       How oft hast thou with perjury cleft the root?°   *bottom of her heart*
       O Proteus, let this habit° make thee blush.   *disguise*
       Be thou ashamed that I have took upon me
       Such an immodest raiment, if shame live
105 In a disguise of love.⁶
       It is the lesser blot, modesty finds,
       Women to change their shapes° than men their minds.   *appearances; clothes*

PROTEUS   Than men their minds! 'Tis true. O heaven, were man
       But constant, he were perfect. That one error
110 Fills him with faults, makes him run through all th' sins;
       Inconstancy falls off ere it begins.⁷
       What is in Silvia's face but I may spy
       More fresh in Julia's, with a constant° eye?   *faithful*

VALENTINE   Come, come, a hand from either.
115 Let me be blessed to make this happy close.°   *ending; union*
       'Twere pity two such friends should be long foes.
           [JULIA *and* PROTEUS *join hands*]

PROTEUS   Bear witness, heaven, I have my wish for ever.

JULIA   And I mine.
           [*Enter the* OUTLAWS *with the* DUKE *and* THURIO *as captives*]

OUTLAWS   A prize, a prize, a prize!

VALENTINE   Forbear, forbear, I say. It is my lord the Duke.
           [*The* OUTLAWS *release the* DUKE *and* THURIO]
120 [*To the* DUKE]   Your grace is welcome to a man disgraced,
       Banishèd Valentine.

DUKE   Sir Valentine!

THURIO   Yonder is Silvia, and Silvia's mine.

---

5. All my claims to Silvia; all that was mine, in the person of Silvia; all the love I gave to Silvia.
6. *if . . . love:* if a disguise one wears for the sake of love
can be considered shameful; if one who pretends to feel

love is capable of feeling shame.
7. The inconstant man begins to deceive, or "fall off,"
even before he swears constancy.

VALENTINE Thurio, give back,° or else embrace thy death.	*stand back*
Come not within the measure° of my wrath.	*reach*
125 Do not name Silvia thine. If once again,	
Verona⁸ shall not hold thee. Here she stands.	
Take but possession of her with a touch—	
I dare thee but to breathe upon my love.	
THURIO Sir Valentine, I care not for her, I.	
130 I hold him but a fool that will endanger	
His body for a girl that loves him not.	
I claim her not, and therefore she is thine.	
DUKE The more degenerate and base art thou	
To make such means° for her as thou hast done,	*efforts*
135 And leave her on such slight conditions.°	*trivial reasons*
Now by the honour of my ancestry	
I do applaud thy spirit, Valentine,	
And think thee worthy of an empress' love.	
Know then I here forget all former griefs,°	*grievances*
140 Cancel all grudge, repeal° thee home again,	*recall*
Plead a new state in thy unrivalled merit,⁹	
To which I thus subscribe:° Sir Valentine,	*bear witness*
Thou art a gentleman, and well derived.	
Take thou thy Silvia, for thou hast deserved her.	
145 VALENTINE I thank your grace. The gift hath made me happy.	
I now beseech you, for your daughter's sake,	
To grant one boon° that I shall ask of you.	*favor*
DUKE I grant it, for thine own, whate'er it be.	
VALENTINE These banishèd men that I have kept withal°	*lived with*
150 Are men endowed with worthy qualities.	
Forgive them what they have committed here,	
And let them be recalled from their exile.	
They are reformèd, civil, full of good,	
And fit for great employment, worthy lord.	
155 DUKE Thou hast prevailed. I pardon them and thee.	
Dispose of them as thou know'st their deserts.	
Come, let us go. We will include all jars°	*end all discord*
With triumphs,° mirth, and rare solemnity.°	*pageants / festivity*
VALENTINE And as we walk along I dare be bold	
160 With our discourse to make your grace to smile.	
What think you of this page, my lord?	
DUKE I think the boy hath grace in him. He blushes.	
VALENTINE I warrant you, my lord, more grace than boy.¹	
DUKE What mean you by that saying?	
165 VALENTINE Please you, I'll tell you as we pass along,	
That you will wonder° what hath fortunèd.°	*marvel at / happened*
Come, Proteus, 'tis your penance but to hear	
The story of your loves discoverèd.°	*revealed*
That done, our day of marriage shall be yours,	
170 One feast, one house, one mutual happiness. *Exeunt*	

---

8. Probably another slip for "Milan."
9. Argue (that there is) a new situation created by your
unparalleled merit.

1. He has more feminine charm ("grace") than male
gender (that is, "he" is really a girl).

The Taming of the Shrew

One of Shakespeare's first comedies—probably written in 1592 or earlier—*The Taming of the Shrew* is also one of his most controversial, focusing as it does on the battle between the sexes and on the process by which a strong-willed woman is made to submit to the control of her husband. In actuality, the play is more complex than such a bald description indicates. An early example of Shakespeare's extraordinary theatrical craftsmanship, it consists of two interwoven plots and a frame tale. This complex structure allows for contrasts and parallels in the development of the play's main themes, complicating how the audience thinks about the drama's examination of the relationship between the sexes and the possibility that people can change their social identities either as a result of choice or of coercion. Perhaps not surprisingly, the play has elicited wildly varying reactions from generations of readers, audiences, and theater practitioners.

In the frame story, a poor tinker, Christopher Sly, is made to believe that he is a nobleman with servants, a wife, fine food, and even erotic artwork at his command. This hoax, shown in the play's first two scenes (called Inductions), is engineered by a real Lord who has found Sly drunk and asleep outside a tavern. The Lord's trick leads to many jokes at Sly's expense. While the tinker likes playing the part of a nobleman, he doesn't do it very well. His language, especially, betrays him. For example, Sly doesn't know how to address a lady, anxiously inquiring of his servants what to call his elegant spouse and settling on the absurd title "Madam wife." The hilarity of this scene is compounded by the fact that Sly's "wife" is really the Lord's page, Bartholomew, dressed up to impersonate a woman. Sly thus mistakes the sex of the person he would take to bed. He is also ignorant of the tastes and customs of the nobility, asking for cheap ale when he should call for sack, the sweet wine favored by gentlemen.

While these blunders make Sly an object of humor, he is also the figure for whose viewing pleasure the main play's two central plots unroll. As a temporary lord, Sly has a troupe of actors to entertain him. At least until he falls asleep, Sly watches them enact a comedy about courtship and marriage in which the primary plot involves a strong-willed woman, Katherine Minola, who is "tamed" by a fortune-seeking suitor named Petruccio. In the other plot, Kate's seemingly demure sister, Bianca, is pursued by three adoring suitors and eventually elopes with one of them without her father's knowledge or consent. All three actions are united by themes of disguise and transformation. Snatched from the mud and given the clothes and the privileges of a lord, Sly is temporarily translated from one social class and identity to another, even though his behavior and the snickers of his "attendants" repeatedly remind the audience that he is not *really* a nobleman. In their pursuit of Bianca, several of her suitors also don disguises. One, Hortensio, poses as a teacher of music and mathematics; another, Lucentio, pretends to be Cambio, a language instructor; meanwhile, Lucentio's servant, Tranio, assumes his master's identity and in that disguise poses as yet another of Bianca's many admirers. Love makes men willing to transform themselves, although in this plot these changes are volitional and reversible. When the disguised gentlemen tire of acting as scholars-for-hire, they simply reclaim their houses, fortunes, and social positions and demote their servants.

In the main plot, more subtle questions of disguise arise. Petruccio, to teach Katherine that she must obey him, acts the part of "shrew tamer," a role in which he appears at his own wedding in outlandish and ragged clothes and, during a sojourn at his country house, turns the world on its head by denying Kate sleep, food, and any exercise of her own will. But if his servant Grumio is to be believed, this may not simply be a one-time disguise. Hearing of his master's plan to wed the rich and shrewish Katherine, Grumio says:

> O' my word, an she knew him as well as I do she would think scolding would do little good upon him. She may perhaps call him half a score knaves or so. Why, that's nothing; an he begin once he'll rail in his rope-tricks. I'll tell you what, sir, an she stand him but a little he will throw a figure in her face and so disfigure her with it that she shall have no more eyes to see withal than a cat. You know him not, sir.
> (1.2.104–10)

Grumio's words raise doubts about Petruccio's "real" nature. Is he temporarily adopting the role of a shrew tamer and verbal bully, or is that his customary mode of being or a role that he has previously adopted in dealing with servants and other social inferiors? And as Petruccio attempts to transform Kate from shrew to obedient spouse, new questions arise: is he forcing her to deform her nature or helping her experiment with a role that might bring out untapped aspects of her personality or lead to greater control of her social environment? Is there, in fact, anything like a "real self," or is personhood a succession of social roles adopted because of coercion, social expectations, material circumstances, or the drive for social mastery?

The multiple instances of disguise and transformation in the three plots certainly invite reflection on the sources of and possibilities for change both in people's behavior and in their social circumstances. From the play one might, for example, conclude that lords and gentlemen can play with their social roles with more success and less risk than can tinkers. Sly's transformation is thrust upon him; but his lack of wealth and education would in any case make it impossible for him to "pass" as nobility without the complicity of the Lord who found him asleep outside the tavern. His transformation is precarious, a mere dream from which he will have to awaken, no matter how much he might want to live on in his new circumstances. But for Lucentio, his role as a Latin master is nothing *but* a temporary stratagem, a part that his education allows him to play to perfection but that his social rank permits him to cast aside when he has won his bride. Similarly, the social fact of gender sets different limits on possible presentations and transformations of self. Petruccio's outrageous behavior—striking his servants and starving his wife—makes him admired by other men. Hortensio, for example, one of Bianca's suitors who eventually marries a wealthy widow, decides to model himself after Petruccio and to take lessons from him on how to tame a wife. But what is deemed to be Kate's outrageous behavior—striking a sister and defying a father and would-be husband—elicits only scorn and condemnation. Like class, gender limits one's permissible or possible range of action and the transformations of self one can effect. Unless she is willing to endure severe privation and penalties, Kate can only undergo one kind of transformation—toward greater docility and subservience to her husband. In such circumstances, it is difficult to determine—as many critics wish to do—whether Katherine finds her "real" self through her encounters with Petruccio. Like many characters in the play, she can only improvise a self in relation to the social constraints and possibilities available to her, and the constraints operating upon a tinker or a woman are very different from those affecting a university-educated gentleman or a lord.

The social hierarchies that shape the possibilities for personal transformations are, in the Sly frame tale, given a peculiarly English inflection. The Sly episodes refer repeatedly to the Warwickshire countryside that was Shakespeare's own birthplace. Sly mentions Greet, an actual village near Stratford, and Burton Heath (possibly Barton-on-the-Heath, another village close to Stratford), and the men enumerated as his tavern companions—Stephen Sly, John Naps, Peter Turf, and Henry Pimpernel—for the most part have homely English names. Moreover, the contrast between Sly and the Lord who carries him to his house mirrors the gap in sixteenth-century rural England between poor laborers, barely making a living at a succession of marginal jobs, and wealthy landowners. As arable and common land was fenced in or enclosed to increase the opportunities for grazing sheep, many landowners made huge profits, wool being one of England's most important exports. But enclosures, a number of which occurred in the Stratford region, also caused hardship for small tenant farmers forced off the enclosed land and, in some cases, driven into vagrancy.

Sly, simply called "Beggar" in the speech prefixes in the First Folio, is a poor man with a checkered employment history. He describes himself as "old Sly's son of Burton Heath, by birth a pedlar, by education a cardmaker, by transmutation a bearherd, and now by present profession a tinker" (Induction 2.17–19). A cardmaker makes the metal combs used to prepare wool for spinning; thus Sly has had some tangential involvement with the wool industry, although he seems primarily to have led an itinerant life mending pots, selling cheap goods from a pedlar's pack, and running up whatever tab he could at the local tavern. The Induction reveals the enormous gap in wealth and education separating this man from the leisured aristocrats who pick him up on the way home from hunting and use him for their evening's sport. The trick they play upon him is a fantastic one, but the details of the Lord's privilege and Sly's drunken poverty are evoked with vivid realism. For such a man as Sly, what hope is there of becoming a Lord?

By contrast, Bianca and her suitors exist in an Italian setting at many removes from Sly's English-countryside milieu. The events in this story line are drawn directly from George Gascoigne's *Supposes* (1566), itself an adaption of a work by Ariosto, *I Suppositi*, which employs the disguised identities, clever servants, and gullible fathers found in classical comedy. Wealth is also a crucial factor in this plot, for despite his speeches about the necessity for suitors to gain his daughters' love, Baptista is willing to give them to their wealthiest wooers. The suitors' money comes mostly from trade. Bianca's suitors testify to the number of ships they have at sea and to the luxury goods and property they have acquired through their ventures. In this world of prosperous urban merchants, Baptista can indulge his daughters with some training in the arts and languages, but he still expects to control their marriage choices. Kate he delivers to the frankly fortune-hunting Petruccio, but he ultimately has less luck with his supposedly compliant daughter, Bianca, whose name, meaning "white," implies her virtue and purity. Bianca not only elopes, but, in the play's final banquet scene, she refuses to come when her new husband summons her, suggesting that her earlier docility may have been a calculated pose. If her sister is gradually tamed, Bianca ultimately reveals her own considerable capacity to play the shrew, her education and social position having given her the wherewithal to manipulate the courtship process to her own advantage.

It is against this backdrop that the particular features of the main plot become apparent. The relationship between Kate and Petruccio has long been regarded as the play's most riveting story line. In fact, in the eighteenth century, the famous actor David Garrick produced a shortened version of the play simply called *Catharine and Petruchio*, which cut the Bianca plot and held the stage for nearly one hundred years. The interest in Kate and Petruccio is understandable, for Shakespeare created for them a story of taming at once enjoyable and deeply troubling. Though set in Italy, this plot line feels English, connected in subterranean ways to the world of Christopher Sly. For one thing, Petruccio is not just a creature of the city; he has a farmhouse that serves as this play's "green world," or place of transformations. Moreover, Petruccio is distinguished in many ways from the other Italian suitors. He has, for example, a sullen and quarrelsome servant, Grumio, in every respect the antithesis of the clever attendants, Tranio and Biondello, who help Lucentio win Bianca and, in fact, seem to do most of their master's thinking and plotting for him. This may be a kind of affectionate joke made at the expense of English domestic servants, who, despite their crude ways, at least aren't shown as mastering their masters. Moreover, while Hortensio, Gremio, and Lucentio woo Bianca with song and poetry, Petruccio woos Kate by contradicting her every word and taming her, like a hawk, by making her go hungry and sleepless. The language of

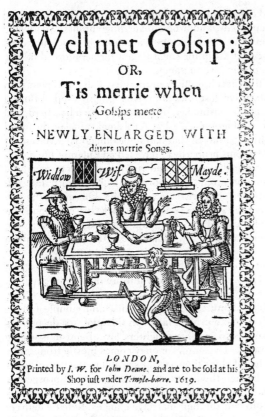

Well met Gofsip:
OR,
Tis merrie when
Gofsips meete

NEWLY ENLARGED WITH
divers merrie Songs.

Widdow   *Wif*   *Mayde.*

LONDON,
Printed by *I. W.* for *Iohn Deane.* and are to be fold at his
Shop iuft vnder *Temple-barre.* 1619.

"Gadding." Title page of Samuel Rowlands,
Tis Merrie When Gossips Meete (1619).

blood sport permeates both the Induction and the Petruccio scenes. The Lord who picks up Sly has just returned from hunting and speaks knowledgeably about the abilities of each of his hounds; Petruccio repeatedly compares the taming of a wife to the transformation of a wild hawk into a docile hunting falcon, aligning wife taming with other manly English sports.

Finally, of course, the source for the Petruccio-Kate plot is not an Italian comedy, as in the Bianca-Lucentio plot, but a folk story about taming a difficult wife, variants of which circulated throughout northern Europe in Shakespeare's day, including the vicious English ballad entitled "A Merry Jest of a Shrewd and Curst Wife Lapped in Morel's Skin for Her Good Behavior." In this ballad, a strong-willed wife is beaten bloody by her husband and then wrapped inside the salted skin of a dead horse named Morel. This mode of taming is more physically brutal than that employed by Petruccio, but both the play and the ballad assume that a husband can use extreme means to curb the will of a forward wife.

Despite his Italian name, then, Petruccio is in many ways an Englishman; and the play implicitly suggests that unlike his Italian counterpart, the true Englishman defines his manhood through the firm and, if necessary, cruel mastery of wife and servant. By contrast, the less assertive Lucentio takes direction from his servant, supplicates his betrothed on bended knee, and ends up with a wife he cannot master. Petruccio's bluff manliness constituted one of the period's privileged versions of English masculinity. In some respects he resembles the English military hero Talbot in *1 Henry VI*, a history play that Shakespeare had a hand in writing probably sometime not long after he composed *The Taming of the Shrew*. Petruccio also anticipates Shakespeare's portrait of England's great warrior king Henry V, the protagonist in a series of history plays that Shakespeare penned in the second half of the 1590s. Outspoken, commanding in battle or brawl, and adept at the blunt rhetorical and physical mastery of women, each of these male heroes in his own way helped define what distinguished a proper Englishman from what was French, Italian, or simply foreign.

This subtle Englishing of Kate and Petruccio may have heightened the original audience's interest in and even identification with them, as the play implicitly pits virile English wooing and wedding against the sophisticated ineffectiveness of Italian practices. Men and women, however, may not have been equally drawn to what they witnessed. In the wake of the modern women's movement, certainly, the very idea of "taming" a woman and curbing her tongue have seemed offensive to many readers and viewers. In *Taming of the Shrew*, language is a vehicle for domination. Sly cannot effectively play

Cucking stool, used to discipline scolds, shrews, and witches. From
T. N. Brushfield, *Chester Archaeological and Historic Society Journal*
(1855–62).

a lord because he has not mastered the language of the elite. Kate can be eloquent, but
because of her gender her verbal independence is read by her father and suitors as a
sign of shrewishness. In part, Petruccio tames Kate's tart tongue by aggressive use of
his own. A clear sign that he has succeeded occurs in 4.6, when, at her husband's
behest, Kate calls the sun the moon and an old man a budding virgin. Her words at this
point no longer express her own perceptions but her husband's blatantly willful reading of reality. In the play's last scene, she also makes a lengthy speech about a wife's
duty to obey her husband that conforms to the patriarchal ideology of the day and her
husband's wishes but is disturbingly far from her earlier expression of women's right to
independent speech and thought. Some directors have found this curbing of the female
tongue and will so intolerable that they have made production choices that downplay
the extent of Kate's submission to Petruccio or that mitigate the linguistic coercion and
physical cruelty that are part of his taming methods. For example, in many productions,
Kate delivers her last speech about wifely duty while signaling, by winks and gestures,
that she does not really believe it, or the director omits the lines in which Kate offers
to put her hand beneath her husband's foot as a token of submission. Such choices signal a desire to "save" Shakespeare from accusations that his play celebrates a crude
form of male dominance.

Even in Shakespeare's own day, it is not clear that everyone, including men, would
have found Petruccio's behavior entirely laudable. The proper relationship between husband and wife was a matter of discussion and debate. Many Protestant preachers
enjoined husbands to use no violence against their wives and to treat them as spiritual
equals and domestic helpmeets. They lauded marriage not merely as an economic
arrangement but as a union demanding mutual affection and respect from both parties.
At the same time, few disputed that in the last analysis husbands were masters of their
wives and that the household was "a little commonwealth," a realm in which the husband's supremacy over wife and children mirrored the supremacy of the monarch over
his subjects. Disorder in the domestic realm was treated as a serious matter, intimating
the possibility of a breakdown of order and hierarchy in the culture at large.

Strong-willed women were particularly apt to be labeled as disorderly in early modern towns and villages, even if their "crimes" involved nothing more than talkativeness.

Husband dominator. From a German playing card by Peter Flötner (1520).

A shrew, in fact, was commonly defined as a woman with a wagging tongue who, partly because of her garrulousness, was not properly submissive to her husband. The ideal wife, by contrast, was chaste, silent, and obedient. The talkativeness that could mark a woman as a shrew could also be interpreted as a sign of her sexual promiscuity, on the theory that one kind of looseness leads to another. Women deemed unruly were subject to various kinds of punishment. These could include being "cucked"—ducked into water on a "cucking stool"—or being fitted with a scold's bridle, a torturous harness that fitted around a woman's head with a metal bit that went into her mouth and prevented her from speaking and sometimes caused her to gag and her mouth to bleed or her teeth to be knocked loose. The husbands of disorderly and aggressive women could also be punished for failure to control their wives. Charivaris, or "rough ridings," were shaming rituals in which neighbors came to the house of a disorderly woman and made her or her husband ride backward through the town on a horse while bystanders shouted and played cacophonous music. This signaled that the world had been turned upside down and rendered inharmonious by her disorderliness and his inability to control his wife.

In *The Taming of the Shrew,* no man is submitted to a "rough riding" even though at the end of the play both Lucentio and Hortensio seem to have lost control of their wives. Instead, all the attention focuses on the taming of Kate and on the strategies employed by Petruccio to make her compliant with his will. On the eighteenth- and nineteenth-century stage, Petruccio often carried a whip, symbol of his power to control his wife and servants with physical force. Whether or not he *literally* carries a whip, Petruccio employs coercion—verbal, psychological, and physical—to control his wife, subjecting her to public humiliation and private deprivation in order to teach her proper submissiveness to the authority of her husband. In so doing, he reinforces the hierarchical principle upon which the entire Elizabethan social order was premised, warning not only unruly men but also servants and beggars that, except in jest, they cannot usurp the places of their masters. But is this account of *The Taming of the Shrew* adequate? Is the play as fiercely repressive as some critics assume? It is precisely on this point that readers, critics, and actors differ.

Some critics, for example, emphasize how Shakespeare mitigates the violence of many versions of the folktale on which the main plot is modeled. Kate is not, for example, beaten and wrapped in a salted horsehide, nor does Petruccio force her to sleep with him before their return to Padua. In his farmhouse, he keeps her awake by disordering the bed and talking at her, but only after their return to the relative safety and familiarity of her father's house does he speak of his intention to "bed" her. In short, sexual conquest does not seem to be part of his taming practices. Perhaps more importantly, many actors, audiences, and critics have seen in Kate and Petruccio's relationship an attractive mutuality and vitality they find difficult to reconcile with the idea that the play is simply a lesson in how to subordinate a woman. For example, when Petruccio first woos Kate in 2.1, the two of them engage in a verbal sparring match dazzling in its complexity and speed. Puns and insults fly back and forth, with Kate giving as good as she gets. The following exchange is typical:

PETRUCCIO   Come, come, you wasp, i'faith you are too angry.
KATHERINE   If I be waspish, best beware my sting.
PETRUCCIO   My remedy is then to pluck it out.
KATHERINE   Ay, if the fool could find it where it lies.
PETRUCCIO   Who knows not where a wasp does wear his sting?
    In his tail.
KATHERINE   In his tongue.
PETRUCCIO   Whose tongue?
KATHERINE   Yours, if you talk of tales, and so farewell.
PETRUCCIO   What, with my tongue in your tail? Nay, come again,
    Good Kate, I am a gentleman.
KATHERINE   That I'll try.
    She strikes him
PETRUCCIO   I swear I'll cuff you if you strike again.
                                        (2.1.207–16)

This is a beautifully orchestrated encounter, with Kate and Petruccio trading rapid-fire, one-line insults and deftly topping one another's puns. Their exchange has erotic intensity. These two are taking one another's measure, listening intently, struggling for advantage. Petruccio is not above talking dirty, and Katherine is not above making physical contact, albeit with a blow and not a caress. This is light years away from the vapid wooing of Lucentio and Bianca, hiding behind the screen of school Latin. On the stage, something vital and alive goes on between Katherine and Petruccio, and they have often been compared with Shakespeare's other witty couples, such as Benedick and Beatrice in *Much Ado About Nothing*, iconoclasts who seem more real and finally better and more equally matched than the more conventional couples with whom they are contrasted. Many critics, in fact, have argued that the real love story of the play belongs to Kate and Petruccio, and that his taming of her is merely a way of showing her the advantages of outwardly conforming to society's expectations so that she can have the husband, the home, and the social approval she surely must crave. Many argue that it is Kate's spirit that attracts Petruccio and that her spirit is never broken, just redirected, as in the final scene when Kate takes out her aggressions not against her husband but against the other wives, whom she lectures on their marriage duties.

The debate about how to interpret *The Taming of the Shrew* will surely continue. In performance, directors and actors sometimes emphasize the drama's playful and farcical elements, sometimes its dark, violent, and repressive potential. Critics and readers remain similarly divided as to what they see in this tale of woman tamed. Most agree, however, that *The Taming of the Shrew* deals with issues that deserve the thoughtful and sometimes heated critical debate the play has engendered. For example, while Kate's taming does not involve the kinds of physical brutality in the "Merry Jest" ballad, it is nonetheless true that in Petruccio's farmhouse Kate is deprived of sleep, food, and the protection of family and female companionship—techniques akin to modern methods of torture and brainwashing. As Kate says, she is "starved for meat, giddy for lack of sleep, / With oaths kept waking and with brawling fed" (4.3.9–10). This is horrifying, even if the horror is mitigated by the laughter-inducing techniques of knockabout farce. Grumio makes the audience laugh as he tantalizes Kate with one kind of food and then another, while ultimately withholding them all, but this does not erase the fact that Kate is hungry and that her hunger is used to starve her into complying with Petruccio's wishes. There is similar cruelty lurking behind the trick played on Sly in the Induction. The beggar is tantalized with the prospect of riches he can never retain. *The Taming of the Shrew* makes a joke out of the enormous gap between the poverty of a tinker and the privilege of a lord, comedy from the physical and psychic trials that lie in wait for a strong-willed woman.

It is perhaps appropriate to conclude by focusing again on the role of Sly. As he watches the play the actors perform for him, he at first makes comments on the action, but these stop after the first act, and he presumably falls asleep on stage. In another contemporary play, however, called *The Taming of a Shrew*, Sly makes interjections throughout, including a brief speech in which he vows to go home and tame his own wife, having learned from Petruccio how it is done. Scholars disagree about the relationship of *The Taming of the Shrew* and *The Taming of a Shrew*: they dispute which came first and whether Shakespeare had a hand in both (for a fuller discussion, see the Textual Note). Among the many differences between the two texts, however, is Sly's continuing stage prominence right to the end of *The Taming of a Shrew* and his final assertion that

> I'll to my
> Wife presently and tame her too,
> An if she anger me.
> (Additional Passages E.19–21)

No one knows for certain if Shakespeare wrote these lines or why they don't appear in *The Taming of the Shrew*. Like almost everything else connected to this play, they are subject to various interpretations. Perhaps because they are put in Sly's mouth they are discredited, taken as another example of the reductiveness of his responses to the pastimes of the cultural elite—in this case, to the play staged in the Lord's house by the traveling players. Maybe *only* a tinker would take this as the "message" of the play. On the other hand, perhaps Sly's response to what he has just watched indicates why this vital and attractive play seems to many readers to traffic in dangerous matters and to be easily used to justify the crudest kinds of male tyranny. It is a little disconcerting that *even* a downtrodden tinker can find comfort in the thought that while he is neither a lord nor a gentleman, he shares with them the same right to tame his wife "an if she anger me." Impoverished and ridiculed, Sly nonetheless feels entitled by virtue of his gender to dominate his spouse, perhaps thereby compensating for his powerlessness in other areas. In short, there is always something lower than a beggar—a beggar's wife. The play published in the First Folio omits Sly's speech, but in our day *The Taming of the Shrew* nonetheless remains, along with *The Merchant of Venice*, one of Shakespeare's most controversial plays: a spur to thought and to debate, a reminder of the serious matters that often lie at the heart of Shakespeare's "festive" comedies.

JEAN E. HOWARD

TEXTUAL NOTE

The Taming of the Shrew was first printed in the 1623 First Folio (F), the control text for this edition. Certain features of the text indicate that it was set from Shakespeare's "foul papers," or perhaps a scribal copy of them, rather than from a theatrical promptbook. Stage directions, exits, and entrances are not handled with the precision customary for a text that would have been used as the basis for an actual performance.

The greatest mystery surrounding the text is its relationship to another play, *The Taming of a Shrew*, entered in the Stationers' Register on May 2, 1594, and published the same year. This play bears many resemblances to Shakespeare's, and for years scholars have debated which preceded the other or whether, in fact, they both derived from a common original, now lost. Many editors have assumed that Shakespeare's play was the source for *The Taming of a Shrew*, though the subplots, in particular, differ substantially; and an interesting argument has been advanced by Leah Marcus that *A Shrew* is earlier than *The Shrew*, that it is at least partly by Shakespeare, and that, in her view, it inscribes an older version of patriarchy than that evident in *The Shrew*. Whatever one decides about order of composition, it is significant that *A Shrew* contains a number of passages involving Christopher Sly not found in *The Shrew,* passages in which Sly continues to comment on the play he watches and finally wakes from his "dream" announcing his intention to go home and tame his own wife. No one knows why these passages appear in one play and not the other. One possibility is that they were written by Shakespeare but for some reason deleted by him or by someone else from the manuscript that served as the basis for the Folio edition of the play, or were added by him at a date later than the composition of that manuscript. For their intrinsic interest, and because of their possible Shakespearean origin, these materials concerning Sly are printed at the end of this edition of *The Shrew* as Additional Passages.

The Oxford editors believe, on balance, that *A Shrew* imitates and is later than *The Shrew,* and this assumption affects their dating of Shakespeare's play, which would have to have been written before 1594, when *A Shrew* was published and designated as belonging to Pembroke's Men, a company that went bankrupt in 1593 and so must have had the play in their repertoire before that time. In addition, a stage direction in *A Shrew* refers to "Simon," who has been plausibly identified as Simon Jewell, an actor who was buried on August 21, 1592. This circumstantial evidence, along with stylistic features that mark the play as an early example of Shakespeare's art, suggests a date of composition of 1592 or earlier.

The Folio text of *The Taming of the Shrew* bears some marks of confusion or incomplete revision in the subplot, particularly in the handling of the character of Hortensio. Shakespeare may have decided rather late to make him one of Bianca's wooers. He is, for example, not included in the "bidding" for Bianca in which Tranio (disguised as Lucentio) and Gremio engage in 2.1. Other anomalies regarding his part are mentioned in the notes to this text, but in performance these issues seldom bother audiences.

In two instances, the present edition marks new scenes where most contemporary editions do not. The first is 3.3, which follows Petruccio's arrival in disheveled dress for his wedding. During this prenuptial scene, Lucentio has no speaking part, and there is no requirement that he be onstage. Consequently, the Oxford editors mark a new scene, 3.3, after everyone exits to attend the wedding and Lucentio comes onstage speaking with Tranio about Bianca before Gremio returns at 3.3.21 to describe the offstage wedding. Another new scene is marked after 4.4—that is, after the episode in which the Pedant, posing as Lucentio's father, meets Baptista and negotiates the marriage of Bianca and Lucentio. This edition makes a separate scene of the ensuing conversation between Biondello and Lucentio in which Biondello explains how Lucentio can elope with Bianca. This change is justified both because the stage has just been cleared before Lucentio's and Biondello's entry and also because there is plausibly a time gap between the two events. In addition, 4.4 shows signs of revision on Shakespeare's part, including indecision about whether or not to include Lucentio in that scene. Making Lucentio and Biondello's conversation a separate scene clarifies the different foci of the two episodes: the first concentrating on Tranio and the Pedant's tricking of Baptista, the second on Biondello's plans for Lucentio to elope.

SELECTED BIBLIOGRAPHY

Aspinall, Dana E., ed. *The Taming of the Shrew: Critical Essays.* New York: Routledge, 2002. A broad selection of twentieth-century critical essays about the play plus reviews of notable film, television, and stage versions.

Boose, Lynda. "Scolding Brides and Bridling Scolds: Taming the Woman's Unruly Member." *Shakespeare Quarterly* 42 (1991): 179–213. Draws on the research of nineteenth-century scholars to recover the early modern punishments, including iron gags and ducking stools, used against women accused of being shrews or scolds.

Haring-Smith, Tori. *From Farce to Metadrama: A Stage History of "The Taming of the Shrew," 1594–1983.* Westport, Conn.: Greenwood Press, 1985. A comprehensive stage history of the play and of some major adaptations from the late 1590s to the early 1980s.

Huston, J. Dennis. "Enter the Hero: The Power of Play in *The Taming of the Shrew.*" *Shakespeare's Comedies of Play.* New York: Columbia University Press, 1981. 58–93. Argues that Shakespeare playfully experiments with comic form in *The Taming of the Shrew* and creates a hero, Petruccio, who teaches Kate how to play with social roles in order to gain control over her environment.

Korda, Natasha. "Household Kates: Domesticating Commodities in *The Taming of the Shrew.*" *Shakespeare's Domestic Economies: Gender and Property in Early Modern England.* Philadelphia: University of Pennsylvania Press, 2002. 52–75. Explores the play as part of an historical shift that made women managers of domestic property and suggests that in taming Kate, Petruccio educates her about the proper management and consumption of household goods.

Marcus, Leah. "The Shakespearean Editor as Shrew-Tamer." *English Literary Renaissance* 22 (1992): 177–200. Examines and queries the historical process by which *The Taming of a Shrew* came to be regarded, not as a source for Shakespeare's *The Taming of the Shrew*, but as a debased derivative of it.

Newman, Karen. "Renaissance Family Politics and Shakespeare's *Taming of the Shrew.*" *Fashioning Femininity and English Renaissance Drama.* Chicago: University of Chicago Press, 1991. 33–50. Argues that Kate's linguistic freedom constitutes her main threat to male authority and that that freedom is never completely curtailed.

Orlin, Lena Cowen. "The Performance of Things in *The Taming of the Shrew.*" *Yearbook of English Studies* 23 (1993): 167–88. Notes the abundance of objects, especially household objects, in *The Taming of the Shrew* and analyzes their functions.

Smith, Amy L. "Performing Marriage with a Difference: Wooing, Wedding, and Bedding in *The Taming of the Shrew.*" *Comparative Drama* 36 (2002): 289–320. Uses Judith Butler's theories of performativity to argue that within Kate and Petruccio's self-conscious performance of courtship and marriage lies the potential for a critical reworking of gender norms, rather than outright submission to or resistance of them.

Walker, Kim. "Wrangling Pedantry: Education in *The Taming of the Shrew.*" *Shakespeare Matters: History, Teaching, Performance.* Ed. Lloyd Davis. Newark: University of Delaware Press, 2003. 191–208. Examines the importance of women's education in the play and in several adaptations of it and suggests that humanist education plays a role in Bianca's transformation into a shrew.

Films

The Taming of the Shrew. 1929. Dir. Samuel Taylor. USA. 63 min. One of the first "talkies," this black-and-white film, starring Douglas Fairbanks as Petruccio and Mary Pickford as Katherine, ends with Pickford's famous "wink" at the conclusion of her speech of submission.

Kiss Me Kate. 1953. Dir. George Sidney. USA. 109 min. Film version of the Cole Porter musical starring Howard Keel and Kathryn Grayson in which a group of actors is shown performing Shakespeare's play, the events of which mirror their own circumstances. Songs include "Brush Up Your Shakespeare" and "Where Is the Life That Late I Led?"

The Taming of the Shrew. 1967. Dir. Franco Zeffirelli. Italy/USA. 122 min. Broad-comedy performance starring the real-life couple of Elizabeth Taylor and Richard Burton as Katherine and Petruccio.

The Taming of the Shrew. 1980. Dir. Jonathan Miller. UK. 127 min. Intelligent BBC-TV version starring John Cleese as Petruccio and Sarah Badel as Katherine with sets modeled on Vermeer interiors.

10 Things I Hate About You. 1999. Dir. Gil Juner. USA. 97 min. Loose adaptation of Shakespeare's plot in which Julia Stiles plays a headstrong character, Kat Stratford, who comes to an accommodation with bad boy Heath Ledger as Patrick Verona.

The Taming of the Shrew

THE PERSONS OF THE PLAY

In the Induction

CHRISTOPHER SLY, beggar and tinker
A HOSTESS
A LORD
BARTHOLOMEW, his page
HUNTSMEN
SERVANTS
PLAYERS

In the play-within-the-play

BAPTISTA Minola, a gentleman of Padua
KATHERINE, his elder daughter
BIANCA, his younger daughter
PETRUCCIO, a gentleman of Verona, suitor of Katherine
GRUMIO ⎫ his servants
CURTIS ⎭
GREMIO, a rich old man of Padua, suitor of Bianca
HORTENSIO, another suitor, who disguises himself as Licio, a
  teacher
LUCENTIO, from Pisa, who disguises himself as Cambio, a
  teacher
TRANIO ⎫ his servants
BIONDELLO ⎭
VINCENTIO, Lucentio's father
A PEDANT (schoolmaster), from Mantua
A WIDOW
A TAILOR
A HABERDASHER
An OFFICER
SERVINGMEN, including NATHANIEL, PHILIP, JOSEPH, and PETER
Other servants of Baptista and Petruccio

Induction 1

Enter CHRISTOPHER SLY [*the*] *beggar, and* [*the*]
    HOSTESS

SLY I'll feeze you,° in faith.   *fix you; beat you*

HOSTESS A pair of stocks,[1] you rogue.

SLY You're a baggage.° The Slys are no rogues. Look in the   *whore*
    Chronicles[2]—we came in with Richard Conqueror,[3] therefore
5   *paucas palabras*,[4] let the world slide.° Sessa![5]   *go by*

Induction 1 Location: In front of a country tavern.
1. A threat to have him put in the stocks (an instrument of public punishment consisting of two wooden planks with semicircles carved into them; the criminal sat with his or her feet clamped between the planks).
2. Histories, especially histories of England such as

Raphael Holinshed's *Chronicles of England, Scotland, and Ireland* (2nd ed., 1587).
3. A blunder for "William the Conqueror," who took the English throne in 1066.
4. Misquoting *pocas palabras*, Spanish for "few words," a phrase from Thomas Kyd's *Spanish Tragedy* (c. 1587).
5. Probably equivalent to "Be quiet."

HOSTESS   You will not pay for the glasses you have burst?

SLY   No, not a denier. Go by, Saint Jeronimy![6] Go to thy cold
bed and warm thee.

HOSTESS   I know my remedy, I must go fetch the headborough.°   constable
                                    [*Exit*]

10   SLY   Third or fourth or fifth borough, I'll answer him by law. I'll
not budge an inch, boy.[7] Let him come, and kindly.°   *and welcome! (ironic)*
                    [*He*] *falls asleep.*
                Wind horns.° Enter a LORD *from hunting, with his train*   *Horns sound*
LORD   Huntsman, I charge thee, tender well° my hounds.   *care well for*
Breathe Merriman[8]—the poor cur is embossed°—   *exhausted*
And couple Clowder with the deep-mouthed brach.[9]
15   Saw'st thou not, boy, how Silver made it good
At the hedge corner, in the coldest fault?[1]
I would not lose the dog for twenty pound.
FIRST HUNTSMAN   Why, Belman is as good as he, my lord.
He cried upon it at the merest loss,[2]
20   And twice today picked out the dullest scent.
Trust me, I take him for the better dog.
LORD   Thou art a fool. If Echo were as fleet
I would esteem him worth a dozen such.
But sup° them well, and look unto them all.   *feed*
25   Tomorrow I intend to hunt again.
FIRST HUNTSMAN   I will, my lord.
LORD [*seeing* SLY]   What's here? One dead, or drunk? See, doth he breathe?
SECOND HUNTSMAN   He breathes, my lord. Were he not warmed with ale
This were a bed but cold to sleep so soundly.
30   LORD   O monstrous beast! How like a swine he lies.
Grim death, how foul and loathsome is thine image.[3]
Sirs, I will practise° on this drunken man.   *play a trick on*
What think you: if he were conveyed to bed,
Wrapped in sweet° clothes, rings put upon his fingers,   *scented*
35   A most delicious banquet by his bed,
And brave° attendants near him when he wakes—   *finely dressed*
Would not the beggar then forget himself?
FIRST HUNTSMAN   Believe me, lord, I think he cannot choose.°   *do otherwise*
SECOND HUNTSMAN   It would seem strange unto him when he waked.
40   LORD   Even as a flatt'ring° dream or worthless fancy.   *pleasing*
Then take him up, and manage well the jest.
Carry him gently to my fairest chamber,
And hang it round with all my wanton pictures.°   *erotic artworks*
Balm° his foul head in warm distillèd waters,   *Anoint*
45   And burn sweet wood to make the lodging sweet.[4]

---

6. Misquoting a popular line—"Hieronimo, beware! go
by, go by!"—from Kyd's *Spanish Tragedy* and confusing
Hieronimo, Kyd's hero, with Saint Jerome. *denier*:
French coin of little value.
7. Term of abuse applicable to either sex.
8. Give Merriman time to recover his breath.
9. And put Clowder on a leash with the female hound

("brach") who bays deeply.
1. When the scent was faintest.
2. When the scent had been completely lost.
3. Your likeness (invoking the common comparison
between sleep and death).
4. Aromatic woods like juniper were often burned to
make a room smell fragrant.

Procure me music ready when he wakes
To make a dulcet° and a heavenly sound,　　　　　　　　　　　*melodious*
And if he chance to speak be ready straight,°　　　　　　　　*at once*
And with a low submissive reverence°　　　　　　　　　　　*deep bow*
50　Say 'What is it your honour will command?'
Let one attend him with a silver basin
Full of rose-water and bestrewed with flowers;
Another bear the ewer,° the third a diaper,°　　　　　*water jug / towel*
And say 'Will't please your lordship cool your hands?'
55　Someone be ready with a costly suit,
And ask him what apparel he will wear.
Another tell him of his hounds and horse,
And that his lady mourns at his disease.
Persuade him that he hath been lunatic,
60　And when he says he is,° say that he dreams,　　　　　　*is indeed mad*
For he is nothing but a mighty lord.
This do, and do it kindly,° gentle sirs.　　　　　　　*naturally; fittingly*
It will be pastime passing° excellent,　　　　　　　　　*exceedingly*
If it be husbanded with modesty.°　　　　　　　　*prudently managed*
65　FIRST HUNTSMAN　My lord, I warrant you we will play our part
As he shall think by our true diligence
He is no less than what we say he is.
LORD　Take him up gently, and to bed with him;
And each one to his office° when he wakes.　　　　　　　*assigned role*
　　　　　　　　　　　[SERVINGMEN *carry* SLY *out*]
　　　Trumpets sound
70　Sirrah,[5] go see what trumpet 'tis that sounds.
　　　　　　　　　　　[*Exit a* SERVINGMAN]
Belike° some noble gentleman that means,　　　　　　　　*Perhaps*
Travelling some journey, to repose him here.
　　　Enter [a] SERVINGMAN
How now? Who is it?
SERVINGMAN　　　　　An't° please your honour, players　　　*If it*
That offer service to your lordship.
　　　Enter PLAYERS
75　LORD　Bid them come near. Now fellows, you are welcome.
PLAYERS　We thank your honour.
LORD　Do you intend to stay with me tonight?
A PLAYER　So please your lordship to accept our duty.°　　*services; respect*
LORD　With all my heart. This fellow I remember
80　Since once he played a farmer's eldest son.
'Twas where you wooed the gentlewoman so well.
I have forgot your name, but sure that part
Was aptly fitted° and naturally performed.　　　　*well suited (to you)*
ANOTHER PLAYER　I think 'twas Soto[6] that your honour means.
85　LORD　'Tis very true. Thou didst it excellent.
Well, you are come to me in happy time,°　　　　　　*at the right time*
The rather for° I have some sport in hand　　　　　　*Especially since*
Wherein your cunning° can assist me much.　　　　　　　　　*skill*

---

5. A form of address to social inferiors.
6. Possibly a reference to a character of this name in
John Fletcher's *Women Pleased*. Since that play was
first acted around 1620, the reference must be a late
addition to Shakespeare's text or else refer to a character in an earlier play, now lost.

There is a lord will hear you play tonight;

90　But I am doubtful of your modesties°　　　　　　　　　　*self-control*

Lest, over-eyeing of° his odd behaviour—　　　　　*noticing; staring at*

For yet his honour never heard a play—

You break into some merry passion,°　　　　　　　　*fit of laughter*

And so offend him; for I tell you, sirs,

95　If you should smile he grows impatient.

A PLAYER　Fear not, my lord, we can contain ourselves

Were he the veriest antic° in the world.　　　　*most eccentric fellow*

LORD [*to a* SERVINGMAN]　Go, sirrah, take them to the buttery[7]

And give them friendly welcome every one.

100　Let them want° nothing that my house affords.　　　　　　*lack*

Exit one with the PLAYERS

[*To a* SERVINGMAN] Sirrah, go you to Barthol'mew, my page,

And see him dressed in all suits° like a lady.　　　　*in every detail*

That done, conduct him to the drunkard's chamber

And call him 'madam', do him obeisance.°　　　　　*pay him respects*

105　Tell him° from me, as he will win my love,　　　(*Bartholomew, the page*)

He bear himself with honourable° action　　　　　　　*becoming*

Such as he hath observed in noble ladies

Unto their lords by them accomplishèd.°　　　　　　*performed*

Such duty to the drunkard let him do

110　With soft low tongue° and lowly courtesy,　　　　　　　*voice*

And say 'What is't your honour will command

Wherein your lady and your humble wife

May show her duty and make known her love?'

And then with kind embracements, tempting kisses,

115　And with declining head into his bosom[8]

Bid him shed tears, as being overjoyed

To see her noble lord restored to health,

Who for this seven years hath esteemèd him°　　*thought himself to be*

No better than a poor and loathsome beggar.

120　And if the boy have not a woman's gift

To rain a shower of commanded° tears,　　　　　*produced on demand*

An onion will do well for such a shift,°　　　　　　　*purpose*

Which, in a napkin being close conveyed,°　　　　*secretly carried*

Shall in despite[9] enforce a watery eye.

125　See this dispatched with all the haste thou canst.

Anon° I'll give thee more instructions.　　　　　　　　*Soon*

Exit a SERVINGMAN

I know the boy will well usurp° the grace,　　　　　　*assume*

Voice, gait, and action of a gentlewoman.

I long to hear him call the drunkard husband,

130　And how my men will stay themselves from laughter

When they do homage to this simple peasant.

I'll in to counsel them. Haply° my presence　　　　　　*Perhaps*

May well abate the over-merry spleen[1]

Which otherwise would grow into extremes.　　　　　[*Exeunt*]

---

7. Pantry, often used to store liquor as well as food.
8. And with his head bowing down into his chest.
9. In spite of an inability to cry.

1. May well lessen the impulse to laugh. Emotional outbursts, including laughter, were thought to originate in the spleen.

Induction 2

Enter aloft[1] [SLY,] *the drunkard, with attendants, some*
with apparel, basin, and ewer, and other appurte-
nances; and LORD

SLY For God's sake, a pot of small ale!°   *weak, cheap ale*

FIRST SERVINGMAN Will't please your lordship drink a cup of
sack?°   *costly imported wine*

SECOND SERVINGMAN Will't please your honour taste of these
conserves?°   *candied fruits*

THIRD SERVINGMAN What raiment will your honour wear today?

5 SLY I am Christophero Sly. Call not me 'honour' nor 'lordship'.
I ne'er drank sack in my life, and if you give me any conserves,
give me conserves of beef.° Ne'er ask me what raiment I'll   *salted beef*
wear, for I have no more doublets° than backs, no more stock-   *jackets*
ings than legs, nor no more shoes than feet—nay, sometime
10 more feet than shoes, or such shoes as my toes look through
the over-leather.

LORD Heaven cease this idle humour[2] in your honour.
O that a mighty man of such descent,
Of such possessions and so high esteem,
15 Should be infusèd with so foul a spirit.

SLY What, would you make me mad? Am not I Christopher
Sly—old Sly's son of Burton Heath,[3] by birth a pedlar, by
education a cardmaker,[4] by transmutation a bearherd,° and   *keeper of a tame bear*
now by present profession a tinker?° Ask Marian Hacket, the   *pot mender*
20 fat alewife[5] of Wincot, if she know me not. If she say I am
not fourteen pence on the score[6] for sheer° ale, score me up   *for nothing but*
for the lying'st knave in Christendom. What, I am not
bestraught;° here's—   *crazy*

THIRD SERVINGMAN O, this it is that makes your lady mourn.

25 SECOND SERVINGMAN O, this is it that makes your servants droop.

LORD Hence comes it that your kindred shuns your house,
As beaten hence by your strange lunacy.
O noble lord, bethink thee of thy birth.
Call home thy ancient° thoughts from banishment,   *former*
30 And banish hence these abject lowly dreams.
Look how thy servants do attend on thee,
Each in his office, ready at thy beck.°   *command*
Wilt thou have music?   *Music*
Hark, Apollo[7] plays,
And twenty cagèd nightingales do sing.
35 Or wilt thou sleep? We'll have thee to a couch
Softer and sweeter than the lustful bed

Induction 2 Location: A bedroom in the Lord's house.
1. Upon the gallery above the stage. Whether this long
and complex scene was in fact performed "aloft" is open
to question. At a later point (1.1.242–47), F has Sly
commenting from above on the play presented by the
traveling actors who arrive in Induction 1. If Induction 2
is played on the main stage, Sly must at some point
ascend to the gallery, or he must observe the entire play
from the side of the main stage.
2. Heaven put an end to this foolish fantasy. According
to Renaissance medical theory, humors, or bodily fluids,

determined one's disposition.
3. Possibly Barton-on-the-Heath, a village not far from
Stratford-upon-Avon.
4. Maker of metal combs used to prepare wool for
spinning.
5. Female proprietor of a tavern. Wincot is a small village near Stratford; individuals named Hacket were living there in 1591.
6. In debt. Accounts were originally kept by notching, or
"scoring," a stick, later by making marks on a wall or door.
7. Greek god of music, who played the lyre.

On purpose trimmed up for Semiramis.[8]
Say thou wilt walk, we will bestrew the ground.
Or wilt thou ride, thy horses shall be trapped,°   *fitted with adornments*
40 Their harness studded all with gold and pearl.
Dost thou love hawking? Thou hast hawks will soar
Above the morning lark. Or wilt thou hunt,
Thy hounds shall make the welkin° answer them   *sky*
And fetch shrill echoes from the hollow earth.
45 FIRST SERVINGMAN Say thou wilt course,° thy greyhounds are as swift   *hunt hares*
As breathèd° stags, ay, fleeter than the roe.[9]   *well-exercised*
SECOND SERVINGMAN Dost thou love pictures?[1] We will fetch thee straight
Adonis[2] painted by a running brook,
And Cytherea all in sedges° hid,   *water rushes*
50 Which seem to move and wanton° with her breath   *play amorously*
Even as the waving sedges play wi'th' wind.
LORD We'll show thee Io[3] as she was a maid,
And how she was beguilèd and surprised,
As lively° painted as the deed was done.   *realistically*
55 THIRD SERVINGMAN Or Daphne[4] roaming through a thorny wood,
Scratching her legs that one shall swear she bleeds,
And at that sight shall sad Apollo weep,
So workmanly° the blood and tears are drawn.   *skillfully*
LORD Thou art a lord, and nothing but a lord.
60 Thou hast a lady far more beautiful
Than any woman in this waning age.[5]
FIRST SERVINGMAN And till the tears that she hath shed for thee
Like envious° floods o'errun her lovely face   *spiteful*
She was the fairest creature in the world;
65 And yet° she is inferior to none.   *still*
SLY Am I a lord, and have I such a lady?
Or do I dream? Or have I dreamed till now?
I do not sleep. I see, I hear, I speak.
I smell sweet savours,° and I feel soft things.   *odors*
70 Upon my life, I am a lord indeed,
And not a tinker, nor Christopher Sly.
Well, bring our lady hither to our sight,
And once again a pot o'th' smallest° ale.   *weakest*
SECOND SERVINGMAN Will't please your mightiness to wash your hands?
75 O, how we joy to see your wit restored!
O that once more you knew but what you are!
These fifteen years you have been in a dream,
Or when you waked, so waked as if you slept.
SLY These fifteen years—by my fay,° a goodly nap.   *faith*
80 But did I never speak of° all that time?   *during*

---

8. Legendary Queen of Assyria, known for her great beauty and many sexual adventures.
9. Small deer proverbial for its swiftness.
1. Probably the "wanton pictures" referred to earlier (Induction 1.43). As described in the following lines, they are conventional erotic scenes, mostly derived from Ovid's *Metamorphoses*.
2. In classical mythology, a beautiful boy whom Aphrodite (Cytherea) loved. This scene shows Aphrodite spying on Adonis while he bathes in the brook.
3. Raped by Zeus, who concealed himself in a cloud or thick mist, she was then turned into a cow by Hera.
4. A nymph who was turned into a laurel tree as she fled from Apollo.
5. Alluding to the popular belief that the world had steadily degenerated from the perfection of paradise or the classical Golden Age.

FIRST SERVINGMAN O yes, my lord, but very idle words,
    For though you lay here in this goodly chamber
    Yet would you say ye were beaten out of door,
    And rail upon the hostess of the house,°   *tavern*
85   And say you would present° her at the leet°   *accuse / local court*
    Because she brought stone jugs and no sealed quarts.[6]
    Sometimes you would call out for Cicely Hacket.
SLY Ay, the woman's maid of the house.
THIRD SERVINGMAN Why, sir, you know no house, nor no such maid,
90   Nor no such men as you have reckoned up,
    As Stephen Sly, and old John Naps of Greet,[7]
    And Peter Turf, and Henry Pimpernel,
    And twenty more such names and men as these,
    Which never were, nor no man ever saw.
95 SLY Now Lord be thankèd for my good amends.°   *recovery*
   ALL Amen.
   SLY I thank thee. Thou shalt not lose by it.
        Enter [BARTHOLOMEW *the Page, as*] *Lady, with attendants*
   BARTHOLOMEW How fares my noble lord?
   SLY   Marry,[8] I fare° well,   *get on; feed*
    For here is cheer° enough. Where is my wife?   *food*
100 BARTHOLOMEW Here, noble lord. What is thy will with her?
   SLY Are you my wife, and will not call me husband?
    My men should call me lord. I am your goodman.[9]
   BARTHOLOMEW My husband and my lord, my lord and husband;
    I am your wife in all obedience.
   SLY I know it well. [*To the* LORD] What must I call her?
105 LORD   Madam.
   SLY Al'ce Madam or Joan Madam?[1]
   LORD Madam, and nothing else. So lords call ladies.
   SLY Madam wife, they say that I have dreamed,
    And slept above some fifteen year or more.
110 BARTHOLOMEW Ay, and the time seems thirty unto me,
    Being all this time abandoned° from your bed.   *banned*
   SLY 'Tis much. Servants, leave me and her alone.
        [*Exeunt* LORD *and attendants*][2]
    Madam, undress you and come now to bed.
   BARTHOLOMEW Thrice-noble lord, let me entreat of you
115   To pardon me yet for a night or two,
    Or if not so, until the sun be set,
    For your physicians have expressly charged,
    In peril to incur[3] your former malady,
    That I should yet absent me from your bed.
120   I hope this reason stands for my excuse.
   SLY Ay, it stands[4] so that I may hardly tarry° so long. But I would   *delay*

---

6. She served from unmarked stone jugs rather than from the officially measured and stamped ("sealed") quarts.
7. Greet is a small village not far from Stratford. The names may be those of Stratford citizens.
8. Mild oath, derived from the Virgin Mary's name.
9. Husband: a term normally not used by lords.
1. Misusing the usual title for a noblewoman. "Alice" and "Joan" are names rarely associated with the upper classes in Elizabethan texts.
2. F has no stage direction here, but those attending on Sly probably obey his command and leave the stage. It is unclear, however, whether the Lord leaves the stage with the other attendants at this point.
3. *In peril to incur:* Because of the risk of bringing on.
4. Punning on "stand" as meaning "to have an erection."

be loath to fall into my dreams again. I will therefore tarry in
despite of the flesh and the blood.
      Enter A MESSENGER
  MESSENGER   Your honour's players, hearing your amendment,
125   Are come to play a pleasant comedy,
      For so your doctors hold it very meet,°   *suitable*
      Seeing too much sadness hath congealed your blood,
      And melancholy is the nurse of frenzy.[5]
      Therefore they thought it good you hear a play
130   And frame your mind to mirth and merriment,
      Which bars° a thousand harms and lengthens life.   *prevents*
  SLY   Marry, I will let them play it. Is not a comonty°   *(for "comedy")*
      A Christmas gambol, or a tumbling trick?
  BARTHOLOMEW   No, my good lord, it is more pleasing stuff.
  SLY   What, household stuff?°   *furnishings; events*
135 BARTHOLOMEW   It is a kind of history.°   *story*
  SLY   Well, we'll see't. Come, madam wife, sit by my side
      And let the world slip. We shall ne'er be younger.
       [BARTHOLOMEW *sits*]

1.1

     Flourish.° Enter LUCENTIO *and his man,* TRANIO   *Fanfare of trumpets*
  LUCENTIO   Tranio, since for° the great desire I had   *because of*
      To see fair Padua, nursery of arts,[1]
      I am arrived fore° fruitful Lombardy,   *before*
      The pleasant garden of great Italy,
5   And by my father's love and leave am armed
      With his good will and thy good company,
      My trusty servant, well approved° in all,   *reliable*
      Here let us breathe,° and haply institute   *pause; rest*
      A course of learning and ingenious° studies.   *liberal; intellectual*
10   Pisa, renownèd for grave citizens,
      Gave me my being, and my father first°—   *before me*
      A merchant of great traffic° through the world,   *business*
      Vincentio, come of the Bentivolii.[2]
      Vincentio's son, brought up in Florence,
15   It shall become° to serve° all hopes conceived[3] *befit / fulfill*
      To deck° his fortune with his virtuous deeds.   *adorn*
      And therefore, Tranio, for the time I study,
      Virtue and that part of philosophy
      Will I apply° that treats of happiness   *pursue; study*
20   By virtue specially to be achieved.
      Tell me thy mind, for I have Pisa left
      And am to Padua come as he that leaves
      A shallow plash° to plunge him in the deep,   *pool*
      And with satiety seeks to quench his thirst.
25 TRANIO   *Mi perdonate,°* gentle master mine.   *Pardon me*
      I am in all affected° as yourself,   *inclined*
      Glad that you thus continue your resolve

---

5. According to Renaissance humoral theory, excessive
sadness could cause thickening of the blood and thus
delirium, or "frenzy." nurse: nourisher.
1.1 Location: A street in Padua.
1. A center for learning ("arts"). Padua's famous university attracted many English students in Shakespeare's
time.
2. Descended from the Bentivolii (perhaps a reference
to the famous Bentivoglio family of Bologna).
3. That is, by relatives and friends.

To suck the sweets of sweet philosophy.
Only, good master, while we do admire
30 This virtue and this moral discipline,
Let's be no stoics nor no stocks,[4] I pray,
Or so devote to Aristotle's checks[5]
As Ovid be an outcast quite abjured.[6]
Balk logic° with acquaintance that you have,   *Bandy words*
35 And practise rhetoric in your common talk.
Music and poesy use to quicken° you;   *revive; animate*
The mathematics and the metaphysics,
Fall to them as you find your stomach° serves you.   *appetite*
No profit grows where is no pleasure ta'en.
40 In brief, sir, study what you most affect.°   *like*
LUCENTIO   Gramercies,° Tranio, well dost thou advise.   *Thank you*
If, Biondello, thou wert come ashore,[7]
We could at once put us in readiness
And take a lodging fit to entertain
45 Such friends as time in Padua shall beget.
But stay a while, what company is this?
TRANIO   Master, some show to welcome us to town.
        Enter BAPTISTA *with his two daughters,* KATHERINE
           and BIANCA; GREMIO, *a pantaloon,*[8] HORTENSIO, *suitor*
           to Bianca. LUCENTIO, [*and*] TRANIO *stand by*
BAPTISTA   Gentlemen, importune me no farther,
For how I firmly am resolved you know:
50 That is, not to bestow° my youngest daughter   *give in marriage*
Before I have a husband for the elder.
If either of you both love Katherina,
Because I know you well and love you well
Leave shall you have to court her at your pleasure.
55 GREMIO   To cart her[9] rather. She's too rough for me.
There, there, Hortensio. Will you° any wife?   *Do you want*
KATHERINE [*to* BAPTISTA]   I pray you, sir, is it your will
To make a stale of me amongst these mates?[1]
HORTENSIO   'Mates', maid? How mean you that? No mates° for you   *husbands*
60 Unless you were of gentler, milder mould.°   *nature*
KATHERINE   I'faith, sir, you shall never need to fear.
Iwis it is not half-way to her heart,[2]
But if it were, doubt not her care should be
To comb your noddle° with a three-legged stool,   *hit your head*
65 And paint° your face, and use you like a fool.   *(with blood)*
HORTENSIO   From all such devils, good Lord deliver us.
GREMIO   And me too, good Lord.
TRANIO [*aside to* LUCENTIO]   Husht, master, here's some good
                pastime toward.°   *in view*

---

4. Wooden posts devoid of feeling. Punning on "stoics," the Greek philosophers who advocated both indifference to pleasure or pain and patient endurance.
5. Restraints. Aristotle defined virtue as a mean, the avoiding of excess (or deficiency).
6. *As . . . abjured:* That Ovid be renounced. Ovid was a Roman poet whose erotic writings were popular in the Renaissance. (His *Ars Amatoria* is mentioned by Lucentio at 4.2.8.)
7. Padua, an inland city, did not have a port. Shake-

speare's knowledge of Italian geography seems to have been shaky.
8. Foolish old man: a stock character from the Italian commedia dell'arte whose usual role was to hinder young lovers.
9. To carry her though the street in, or tied to, a cart. This was a common punishment for disorderly women.
1. To make me a laughingstock or a prostitute or a decoy (for Bianca) among these crude fellows.
2. Certainly, marriage does not even half interest her. (Kate speaks of herself in the third person here.)

That wench is stark mad or wonderful froward.°   *incredibly willful*

70 LUCENTIO [*aside to* TRANIO]   But in the other's silence do I see
Maid's mild behaviour and sobriety.
Peace, Tranio.

TRANIO [*aside to* LUCENTIO]   Well said, master. Mum, and gaze your fill.

BAPTISTA   Gentlemen, that I may soon make good

75 What I have said—Bianca, get you in.
And let it not displease thee, good Bianca,
For I will love thee ne'er the less, my girl.

KATHERINE   A pretty peat!° It is best   *pet; spoiled child*
Put finger in the eye,° an° she knew why.   *(to weep) / if*

80 BIANCA   Sister, content you° in my discontent.   *satisfy yourself*
[*To* BAPTISTA] Sir, to your pleasure° humbly I subscribe.°   *will / submit*
My books and instruments shall be my company,
On them to look and practise by myself.

LUCENTIO [*aside to* TRANIO]   Hark, Tranio, thou mayst hear
Minerva³ speak.

85 HORTENSIO   Signor Baptista, will you be so strange?°   *unnatural; cruel*
Sorry am I that our good will effects°   *causes*
Bianca's grief.

GREMIO   Why will you mew° her up,   *confine (like a falcon)*
Signor Baptista, for° this fiend of hell,   *because of*
And make her bear the penance° of her tongue?   *punishment*

90 BAPTISTA   Gentlemen, content ye. I am resolved.
Go in, Bianca.   [*Exit* BIANCA]
And for I know she taketh most delight
In music, instruments, and poetry,
Schoolmasters will I keep within my house

95 Fit to instruct her youth. If you, Hortensio,
Or, Signor Gremio, you know any such,
Prefer° them hither; for to cunning° men   *Recommend / skillful*
I will be very kind, and liberal
To mine own children in good bringing up.

100 And so farewell. Katherina, you may stay,
For I have more to commune with Bianca.   *Exit*

KATHERINE   Why, and I trust I may go too, may I not? What,
shall I be appointed hours, as though belike I knew not what
to take and what to leave? Ha!   *Exit*

105 GREMIO   You may go to the devil's dam.⁴ Your gifts are so good
here's none will hold° you. Their love⁵ is not so great, Horten-   *tolerate*
sio, but we may blow our nails° together and fast it fairly out.⁶   *wait patiently*
Our cake's dough on both sides.⁷ Farewell. Yet for the love I
bear my sweet Bianca, if I can by any means light on a fit man

110 to teach her that wherein she delights, I will wish° him to her   *recommend*
father.

HORTENSIO   So will I, Signor Gremio. But a word, I pray.
Though the nature of our quarrel yet never brooked parle,°   *permitted discussion*
know now, upon advice,° it toucheth° us both—that we may   *reflection / concerns*

115 yet again have access to our fair mistress and be happy rivals
in Bianca's love—to labour and effect one thing specially.

---

3. Roman goddess of wisdom.
4. The devil's mother, imagined as the stereotypical shrew and said to be worse than the devil himself.
5. Love of them (that is, of women).
6. And abstain as best we can.
7. Proverbial expression of failure.

GREMIO What's that, I pray?

HORTENSIO Marry, sir, to get a husband for her sister.

GREMIO A husband?—a devil!

120 HORTENSIO I say a husband.

GREMIO I say a devil. Think'st thou, Hortensio, though her
father be very rich, any man is so very° a fool to be married to   *completely*
hell?

HORTENSIO Tush, Gremio. Though it pass° your patience and   *exceeds*
125 mine to endure her loud alarums,° why, man, there be good   *calls to arms; scoldings*
fellows in the world, an a man could light on them, would take
her with all faults, and money enough.

GREMIO I cannot tell, but I had as lief° take her dowry with this   *would as willingly*
condition: to be whipped at the high cross[8] every morning.

130 HORTENSIO Faith, as you say, there's small choice in rotten
apples. But come, since this bar in law° makes us friends, it   *legal obstacle*
shall be so far forth friendly maintained[9] till by helping Bap-
tista's eldest daughter to a husband we set his youngest free for
a husband, and then have to't° afresh. Sweet Bianca! Happy   *begin the fight*
135 man be his dole.[1] He that runs fastest gets the ring.[2] How say
you, Signor Gremio?

GREMIO I am agreed, and would I had given him the best horse
in Padua to begin his wooing that would thoroughly woo her,
wed her, and bed her, and rid the house of her. Come on.

Exeunt [HORTENSIO *and* GREMIO]. *Manent*°   *Remain*
TRANIO *and* LUCENTIO

140 TRANIO I pray, sir, tell me: is it possible
That love should of a sudden take such hold?

LUCENTIO O Tranio, till I found it to be true
I never thought it possible or likely.
But see, while idly I stood looking on
145 I found the effect of love in idleness,[3]
And now in plainness do confess to thee,
That art to me as secret° and as dear   *intimate*
As Anna[4] to the Queen of Carthage was,
Tranio, I burn, I pine, I perish, Tranio,
150 If I achieve not this young modest girl.
Counsel me, Tranio, for I know thou canst.
Assist me, Tranio, for I know thou wilt.

TRANIO Master, it is no time to chide you now.
Affection is not rated° from the heart.   *driven out by scolding*
155 If love have touched you, naught remains but so—
Redime te captum quam queas minimo.[5]

LUCENTIO Gramercies,° lad. Go forward, this contents.   *Thanks*
The rest will comfort, for thy counsel's sound.

TRANIO Master, you looked so longly° on the maid   *persistently*
160 Perhaps you marked not what's the pith° of all.   *main point*

---

8. Cross set on a pedestal in the town center, the normal site for punishment in an English village.
9. *it . . . maintained*: we'll pursue the matter as
friends.
1. May the winner's fate be that of a happy man.
2. A proverb alluding to the ring that riders in a jousting match try to catch on their lances. Also punning on
"ring" as referring to both "wedding ring" and female
genitalia.
3. Punning on a flower known as "love-in-idleness,"
whose juice was thought to induce love. (See *A Midsummer Night's Dream* 2.1.166–68.)
4. Sister to Dido, Queen of Carthage. In both Virgil's
Aeneid and Christopher Marlowe's *Dido, Queen of
Carthage* (1594), Dido tells Anna of her secret love for
Aeneas.
5. Latin: Ransom yourself from captivity at the lowest
possible price. A phrase from Terence, quoted as it
appears in Lily's Latin grammar, a standard Elizabethan
school text.

LUCENTIO   O yes, I saw sweet beauty in her face,
　　　Such as the daughter of Agenor[6] had,
　　　That made great Jove to humble him to her hand
　　　When with his knees he kissed the Cretan strand.
165 TRANIO   Saw you no more? Marked you not how her sister
　　　Began to scold and raise up such a storm
　　　That mortal ears might hardly endure the din?
LUCENTIO   Tranio, I saw her coral lips to move,
　　　And with her breath she did perfume the air.
170 Sacred and sweet was all I saw in her.
TRANIO [aside]   Nay, then 'tis time to stir him from his trance.
　　　[To LUCENTIO] I pray, awake, sir. If you love the maid,
　　　Bend thoughts and wits to achieve her. Thus it stands:
　　　Her elder sister is so curst° and shrewd°   *quarrelsome / shrewish*
175 That till the father rid his hands of her,
　　　Master, your love must live a maid at home,
　　　And therefore has he closely mewed her up
　　　Because° she will not be annoyed with° suitors.   *So that / troubled with*
LUCENTIO   Ah, Tranio, what a cruel father's he!
180 But art thou not advised° he took some care   *aware*
　　　To get her cunning schoolmasters to instruct her?
TRANIO   Ay, marry am I, sir, and now 'tis plotted.
LUCENTIO   I have it, Tranio.
TRANIO   Master, for° my hand,   *by*
　　　Both our inventions° meet and jump° in one.   *schemes / agree*
LUCENTIO   Tell me thine first.
185 TRANIO   You will be schoolmaster
　　　And undertake the teaching of the maid.
　　　That's your device.°   *plan*
LUCENTIO   It is. May it be done?
TRANIO   Not possible; for who shall bear your part,
　　　And be in Padua here Vincentio's son,
190 Keep house, and ply his book,° welcome his friends,   *study*
　　　Visit his countrymen, and banquet them?
LUCENTIO   Basta,° content thee, for I have it full.°   *Enough / fully planned*
　　　We have not yet been seen in any house,
　　　Nor can we be distinguished by our faces
195 For man or master. Then it follows thus:
　　　Thou shalt be master, Tranio, in my stead;
　　　Keep house, and port,° and servants, as I should.   *social position*
　　　I will some other be, some Florentine,
　　　Some Neapolitan, or meaner° man of Pisa.   *poorer*
200 'Tis hatched, and shall be so. Tranio, at once
　　　Uncase° thee. Take my coloured hat and cloak.[7]   *Undress*
　　　When Biondello comes he waits on thee,
　　　But I will charm° him first to keep his tongue.   *persuade; use magic on*
TRANIO   So had you need.
　　　　　[They exchange clothes][8]
205 In brief, sir, sith° it your pleasure is,   *since*

---

6. **Europa.** Jove transformed himself into a bull and carried her across the sea to Crete to rape her.
7. The outfit of an Elizabethan gentleman. Servants usually wore uniforms, like the "blue coats" of Petruccio's servants (4.1.74).
8. F does not indicate at what point in this exchange

Lucentio and Tranio trade clothes; perhaps they begin during Lucentio's previous speech. This exchange of clothes, emphasizing the ease with which social identity is shifted, is an important visual enactment of one of the play's main preoccupations.

And I am tied to be obedient—
For so your father charged me at our parting,
'Be serviceable° to my son,' quoth he,   *diligent in service*
Although I think 'twas in another sense—
210   I am content to be Lucentio
Because so well I love Lucentio.
LUCENTIO   Tranio, be so, because Lucentio loves,
And let me be a slave t'achieve that maid
Whose sudden sight hath thralled° my wounded⁹ eye.   *enslaved*
     Enter BIONDELLO
215   Here comes the rogue. Sirrah, where have you been?
BIONDELLO   Where have *I* been? Nay, how now, where are *you?*
Master, has my fellow Tranio stolen your clothes, or you
stolen his, or both? Pray, what's the news?
LUCENTIO   Sirrah, come hither. 'Tis no time to jest,
220   And therefore frame your manners to the time.
Your fellow Tranio here, to save my life
Puts my apparel and my count'nance on,
And I for my escape have put on his,
For in a quarrel since I came ashore
225   I killed a man, and fear I was descried.°   *observed*
Wait you on him, I charge you, as becomes,°   *is fitting*
While I make way from hence to save my life.
You understand me?
BIONDELLO   I sir? Ne'er a whit.°   *Not at all*
LUCENTIO   And not a jot of Tranio in your mouth.
230   Tranio is changed into Lucentio.
BIONDELLO   The better for him. Would I were so too.
TRANIO   So could I, faith, boy, to have the next wish after—
That Lucentio indeed had Baptista's youngest daughter.
But sirrah, not for my sake but your master's I advise
235   You use your manners discreetly in all kind of companies.
When I am alone, why then I am Tranio,
But in all places else your master, Lucentio.
LUCENTIO   Tranio, let's go.
One thing more rests° that thyself execute°—   *remains / must do*
240   To make one among these wooers. If thou ask me why,
Sufficeth my reasons are both good and weighty.   *Exeunt*
     The presenters¹ above speak
FIRST SERVINGMAN   My lord, you nod. You do not mind° the play.   *pay attention to*
SLY   Yes, by Saint Anne² do I. A good matter, surely. Comes
there any more of it?
245   BARTHOLOMEW   My lord, 'tis but begun.
SLY   'Tis a very excellent piece of work, madam lady. Would
'twere done.
     They sit and mark°   *observe*

1.2

Enter PETRUCCIO *and his man,* GRUMIO
PETRUCCIO   Verona, for a while I take my leave
To see my friends in Padua; but of all

---

9. Wounded by Cupid's arrow.
1. Figures who introduce and comment on the action of a play for the audience.

2. A common oath. Saint Anne was the mother of the Virgin Mary and the patron saint of married women.
1.2 Location: In front of Hortensio's house in Padua.

My best-belovèd and approvèd friend
Hortensio, and I trow° this is his house.   *believe*
5   Here, sirrah Grumio, knock, I say.
GRUMIO   Knock, sir? Whom should I knock? Is there any man
has rebused[1] your worship?
PETRUCCIO   Villain, I say, knock me here[2] soundly.
GRUMIO   Knock you here, sir? Why, sir, what am I, sir, that I
10   should knock you here, sir?
PETRUCCIO   Villain, I say, knock me at this gate,
And rap me well or I'll knock your knave's pate.
GRUMIO   My master is grown quarrelsome. I should knock you first,
And then I know after who comes by the worst.[3]
15   PETRUCCIO   Will it not be?
Faith, sirrah, an° you'll not knock, I'll ring it.[4]   *if*
I'll try how you can sol-fa° and sing it.   *sing a scale*
          He wrings him by the ears. [GRUMIO kneels][5]
GRUMIO   Help, masters, help! My master is mad.
PETRUCCIO   Now knock when I bid you, sirrah villain.
          Enter HORTENSIO
20   HORTENSIO   How now, what's the matter? My old friend Grumio
and my good friend Petruccio? How do you all at Verona?
PETRUCCIO   Signor Hortensio, come you to part the fray?
Con tutto il cuore ben trovato,[6] may I say.
HORTENSIO   *Alla nostra casa ben venuto, molto onorato signor*
25   *mio Petruccio.[7]*
Rise, Grumio, rise. We will compound° this quarrel.   *settle*
          [GRUMIO *rises*]
GRUMIO   Nay, 'tis no matter, sir, what he 'leges° in Latin. If this   *alleges*
be not a lawful cause for me to leave his service—look you, sir:
he bid me knock him and rap him soundly, sir. Well, was it fit
30   for a servant to use his master so, being perhaps, for aught
I see, two-and-thirty, a pip out?[8]
Whom would to God I had well knocked at first,
Then had not Grumio come by the worst.
PETRUCCIO   A senseless villain. Good Hortensio,
35   I bade the rascal knock upon your gate,
And could not get him for my heart to do it.
GRUMIO   Knock at the gate? O heavens, spake you not these
words plain? 'Sirrah, knock me here, rap me here, knock me
well, and knock me soundly'? And come you now with
40   knocking at the gate?
PETRUCCIO   Sirrah, be gone, or talk not, I advise you.
HORTENSIO   Petruccio, patience. I am Grumio's pledge.°   *guarantor*
Why this' a heavy chance[9] 'twixt him and you,

---

1. Grumio regularly blunders and puns. Here he
means "abused" or "rebuked," or perhaps both.
2. Knock here for me: a conventional usage that Grumio misunderstands or pretends to understand as
"strike me." *Villain*: low-born man (often a contemptuous term of address).
3. *I should . . . worst*: You want me to give the first
blow, but then I know I'd have the worse of it.
4. I'll ring the bell; with a pun on "wring."
5. While F gives no stage direction indicating that
Grumio kneels at this point, at line 26 Hortensio
orders him to "rise." This may mean that he has been
brought to his knees when Petruccio wrings his ears at
line 17.
6. With all my heart, welcome (Italian).
7. Welcome to our house, my most honored Signor
Petruccio.
8. Drunk; a bit crazy. Probably alluding to the card
game one-and-thirty, in which the aim is to accumulate
exactly thirty-one points. To collect thirty-two means
the player has overshot or been excessive. A "pip" is a
spot on a card; hence "a pip out" means "off by one."
9. *Why . . . chance*: This is a sad occurrence.

Your ancient,° trusty, pleasant servant Grumio.   *long-standing*
45 And tell me now, sweet friend, what happy gale
  Blows you to Padua here from old Verona?
 PETRUCCIO Such wind as scatters young men through the world
  To seek their fortunes farther than at home,
  Where small experience grows. But in a few,°   *in short*
50 Signor Hortensio, thus it stands with me:
  Antonio, my father, is deceased,
  And I have thrust myself into this maze¹
  Happily to wive and thrive as best I may.
  Crowns° in my purse I have, and goods at home, *Five-shilling coins*
55 And so am come abroad to see the world.
 HORTENSIO Petruccio, shall I then come roundly° to thee *speak plainly*
  And wish thee to a shrewd, ill-favoured wife?
  Thou'dst thank me but a little for my counsel,
  And yet I'll promise thee she shall be rich,
60 And very rich. But thou'rt too much my friend,
  And I'll not wish thee to her.
 PETRUCCIO Signor Hortensio, 'twixt such friends as we
  Few words suffice; and therefore, if thou know
  One rich enough to be Petruccio's wife—
65 As wealth is burden° of my wooing dance— *refrain; chief theme*
  Be she as foul° as was Florentius' love,²   *ugly*
  As old as Sibyl,³ and as curst and shrewd
  As Socrates' Xanthippe⁴ or a worse,
  She moves° me not—or not° removes at least° *annoys / nor / at all*
70 Affection's edge° in me, were she as rough   *intensity*
  As are the swelling Adriatic seas.
  I come to wive it wealthily in Padua;
  If wealthily, then happily in Padua.
 GRUMIO [*to* HORTENSIO] Nay, look you, sir, he tells you flatly
75 what his mind is. Why, give him gold enough and marry him
  to a puppet or an aglet-baby,⁵ or an old trot° with ne'er a tooth *hag*
  in her head, though she have as many diseases as two-and-fifty
  horses. Why, nothing comes amiss so money comes withal.° *with it*
 HORTENSIO Petruccio, since we are stepped thus far in,
80 I will continue that° I broached in jest.   *what*
  I can, Petruccio, help thee to a wife
  With wealth enough, and young and beauteous,
  Brought up as best becomes a gentlewoman.
  Her only fault—and that is faults enough—
85 Is that she is intolerable curst,°   *shrewish*
  And shrewd and froward° so beyond all measure *willful*
  That, were my state° far worser than it is,   *fortune*
  I would not wed her for a mine of gold.
 PETRUCCIO Hortensio, peace. Thou know'st not gold's effect.
90 Tell me her father's name and 'tis enough,

1. This uncertain world; this unpredictable business of "wiving and thriving."
2. Florent, the knight in John Gower's *Confessio Amantis*, who had to marry the ugly old woman who had saved his life by answering a riddle he had been commanded to solve. On their wedding night, as a reward for his compliance, she became young and beautiful.

A version of this story also appears in Chaucer's *Wife of Bath's Tale*.
3. The Cumaean Sibyl, a prophetess in classical mythology, had immortality without eternal youth.
4. The philosopher's notoriously shrewish wife.
5. Small figure used as a tag or ornament on dresses, laces, and other goods.

For I will board[6] her though she chide as loud
As thunder when the clouds in autumn crack.

HORTENSIO   Her father is Baptista Minola,
An affable and courteous gentleman.
95 Her name is Katherina Minola,
Renowned in Padua for her scolding tongue.

PETRUCCIO   I know her father, though I know not her,
And he knew my deceasèd father well.
I will not sleep, Hortensio, till I see her,
100 And therefore let me be thus bold with you
To give you over° at this first encounter,   *leave you*
Unless you will accompany me thither.

GRUMIO   I pray you, sir, let him go while the humour° lasts.   *mood*
O' my word, an she knew him as well as I do she would think
105 scolding would do little good upon him. She may perhaps call
him half a score knaves or so. Why, that's nothing; an he begin
once he'll rail in his rope-tricks.[7] I'll tell you what, sir, an she
stand° him but a little he will throw a figure[8] in her face and   *withstand; arouse*
so disfigure her with it that she shall have no more eyes to see
110 withal than a cat. You know him not, sir.

HORTENSIO   Tarry, Petruccio, I must go with thee,
For in Baptista's keep° my treasure is.   *custody; stronghold*
He hath the jewel of my life in hold,
His youngest daughter, beautiful Bianca,
115 And her withholds from me and other more,°   *others besides*
Suitors to her and rivals in my love,
Supposing it a thing impossible,
For those defects I have before rehearsed,
That ever Katherina will be wooed.
120 Therefore this order hath Baptista ta'en:
That none shall have access unto Bianca
Till Katherine the curst have got a husband.

GRUMIO   Katherine the curst—
A title for a maid of all titles the worst.

125 HORTENSIO   Now shall my friend Petruccio do me grace,°   *a favor*
And offer me disguised in sober robes
To old Baptista as a schoolmaster
Well seen° in music, to instruct Bianca,   *skilled*
That so I may by this device at least
130 Have leave and leisure to make love to her,
And unsuspected court her by herself.

Enter GREMIO [*with a paper,*][9] *and* LUCENTIO *disguised*
[*as a schoolmaster*]

GRUMIO   Here's no knavery.[1] See, to beguile the old folks, how
the young folks lay their heads together. Master, master, look
about you. Who goes there, ha?

135 HORTENSIO   Peace, Grumio, it is the rival of my love.
Petruccio, stand by a while.

---

6. Woo aggressively; go aboard, as in a sea battle; have
sexual intercourse with.
7. An obscure phrase: "rope-tricks" may refer to rhetorical or sexual feats. Grumio's point seems to be that
when Petruccio "rails," he will be more aggressive than
Katherine.

8. A figure of speech.
9. Presumably Lucentio's list of books for Bianca's
studies.
1. Spoken sarcastically; perhaps referring to the plotting
of Petruccio and Hortensio rather than to that of Gremio
and Lucentio, whom Grumio may not yet have seen.

GRUMIO   A proper stripling,° and an amorous!   *handsome youth (ironic)*
    [PETRUCCIO, HORTENSIO, *and* GRUMIO *stand aside*]
GREMIO [*to* LUCENTIO]   O, very well—I have perused the note.°   *listing of books*
    Hark you, sir, I'll have them° very fairly bound—   *(the books)*
140   All books of love, see that at any hand°—   *in any case*
    And see you read no other lectures to her.
    You understand me. Over and beside
    Signor Baptista's liberality,
    I'll mend° it with a largess.° Take your paper, too,   *increase / gift*
145   And let me have them very well perfumed,
    For she is sweeter than perfume itself
    To whom they go to. What will you read to her?
LUCENTIO   Whate'er I read to her, I'll plead for you
    As for my patron, stand you so assured,
150   As firmly as yourself were still in place°—   *always present*
    Yea, and perhaps with more successful words
    Than you, unless you were a scholar, sir.
GREMIO   O this learning, what a thing it is!
GRUMIO [*aside*]   O this woodcock,[2] what an ass it is!
155 PETRUCCIO   Peace, sirrah.
HORTENSIO   Grumio, mum. [*Coming forward*] God save you, Signor Gremio.
GREMIO   And you are well met, Signor Hortensio.
    Trow° you whither I am going?   *Know*
    To Baptista Minola.
160   I promised to enquire carefully
    About a schoolmaster for the fair Bianca,
    And by good fortune I have lighted well
    On this young man, for learning and behaviour
    Fit for her turn,° well read in poetry   *use*
165   And other books—good ones, I warrant ye.
HORTENSIO   'Tis well, and I have met a gentleman
    Hath promised me to help me to another,
    A fine musician, to instruct our mistress.
    So shall I no whit be behind in duty
170   To fair Bianca, so beloved of me.
GREMIO   Beloved of me, and that my deeds shall prove.
GRUMIO [*aside*]   And that his bags° shall prove.   *money bags*
HORTENSIO   Gremio, 'tis now no time to vent° our love.   *express*
    Listen to me, and if you speak me fair°   *courteously*
175   I'll tell you news indifferent° good for either.   *equally*
    Here is a gentleman whom by chance I met,
    Upon agreement from us to his liking°   *If we accept his terms*
    Will undertake to woo curst Katherine,
    Yea, and to marry her, if her dowry please.
180 GREMIO   So said, so done, is well.
    Hortensio, have you told him all her faults?
PETRUCCIO   I know she is an irksome brawling scold.
    If that be all, masters, I hear no harm.
GREMIO   No, sayst me so, friend? What countryman?
185 PETRUCCIO   Born in Verona, old Antonio's son.
    My father dead, his fortune lives for me,°   *is mine*

---

2. Wild bird easily caught and so thought to be stupid.

And I do hope good days and long to see.
GREMIO   O sir, such a life with such a wife were strange.
    But if you have a stomach, to't, a'° God's name.　　　　　　　　　*in*
190　You shall have me assisting you in all.
    But will you woo this wildcat?
PETRUCCIO　　　　　　　　　　Will I live!
GRUMIO   Will he woo her? Ay, or I'll hang her.
PETRUCCIO   Why came I hither but to that intent?
    Think you a little din can daunt mine ears?
195　Have I not in my time heard lions roar?
    Have I not heard the sea, puffed up with winds,
    Rage like an angry boar chafèd with sweat?
    Have I not heard great ordnance° in the field,　　　　　　　　　*cannon*
    And heaven's artillery thunder in the skies?
200　Have I not in a pitchèd battle heard
    Loud 'larums,° neighing steeds, and trumpets' clang?　　　　*calls to arms*
    And do you tell me of a woman's tongue,
    That gives not half so great a blow° to hear　　　　　　　　*loud noise*
    As will a chestnut in a farmer's fire?
205　Tush, tush—fear° boys with bugs.°　　　　　*frighten / bogeymen*
GRUMIO   For he fears none.
GREMIO   Hortensio, hark.
    This gentleman is happily° arrived,　　　　　　　　　*fortunately*
    My mind presumes, for his own good and ours.
210　HORTENSIO   I promised we would be contributors,
    And bear his charge° of wooing, whatsoe'er.　　　　　　　*expense*
GREMIO   And so we will, provided that he win her.
GRUMIO   I would I were as sure of a good dinner.

     Enter TRANIO, *brave,*° [*as Lucentio,*] *and* BIONDELLO　　*richly dressed*

TRANIO   Gentlemen, God save you. If I may be bold, tell me, I
215　beseech you, which is the readiest way to the house of Signor
    Baptista Minola?
BIONDELLO   He that has the two fair daughters—is't he you
    mean?
TRANIO   Even he, Biondello.
220　GREMIO   Hark you, sir, you mean not her to—
TRANIO   Perhaps him and her, sir. What have you to do?[3]
PETRUCCIO   Not her that chides, sir, at any hand, I pray.
TRANIO   I love no chiders, sir. Biondello, let's away.
LUCENTIO [*aside*]   Well begun, Tranio.
HORTENSIO　　　　　　　　　　Sir, a word ere you go.
225　Are you a suitor to the maid you talk of—yea or no?
TRANIO   And if I be, sir, is it any offence?
GREMIO   No, if without more words you will get you hence.
TRANIO   Why, sir, I pray, are not the streets as free
    For me as for you?
GREMIO　　　　　　　　But so is not she.
230　TRANIO   For what reason, I beseech you?
GREMIO   For this reason, if you'll know—
    That she's the choice° love of Signor Gremio.　　　　*chosen; excellent*
HORTENSIO   That she's the chosen of Signor Hortensio.
TRANIO   Softly, my masters. If you be gentlemen,

---

3. What business is it of yours?

235   Do me this right,° hear me with patience.   *justice*
       Baptista is a noble gentleman
       To whom my father is not all unknown,
       And were his daughter fairer than she is
       She may more suitors have, and me for one.
240   Fair Leda's daughter⁴ had a thousand wooers;
       Then well one more may fair Bianca have,
       And so she shall. Lucentio shall make one,
       Though Paris came,⁵ in hope to speed° alone.   *succeed*
       GREMIO   What, this gentleman will out-talk us all!
245   LUCENTIO   Sir, give him head, I know he'll prove a jade.°   *worn-out horse*
       PETRUCCIO   Hortensio, to what end are all these words?
       HORTENSIO   Sir, let me be so bold as ask you,
       Did you yet ever see Baptista's daughter?
       TRANIO   No, sir, but hear I do that he hath two,
250   The one as famous for a scolding tongue
       As is the other for beauteous modesty.
       PETRUCCIO   Sir, sir, the first's for me. Let her go by.
       GREMIO   Yea, leave that labour to great Hercules,
       And let it be more than Alcides' twelve.⁶
255   PETRUCCIO   Sir, understand you this of me in sooth,°   *truth*
       The youngest daughter whom you hearken° for   *lie in wait; yearn*
       Her father keeps from all access of suitors,
       And will not promise her to any man
       Until the elder sister first be wed.
260   The younger then is free, and not before.
       TRANIO   If it be so, sir, that you are the man
       Must stead° us all, and me amongst the rest,   *help*
       And if you break the ice and do this feat,
       Achieve° the elder, set the younger free   *Win*
265   For our access, whose hap shall be° to have her   *he who is lucky enough*
       Will not so graceless be to be ingrate.
       HORTENSIO   Sir, you say well, and well you do conceive;°   *understand*
       And since you do profess to be a suitor
       You must, as we do, gratify° this gentleman,   *reward*
270   To whom we all rest generally beholden.
       TRANIO   Sir, I shall not be slack. In sign whereof,
       Please ye we may contrive° this afternoon,   *pass, spend (time)*
       And quaff carouses° to our mistress' health,   *toasts*
       And do as adversaries do in law—
275   Strive mightily, but eat and drink as friends.
       GRUMIO *and* BIONDELLO   O excellent motion!° Fellows, let's be gone.   *proposal*
       HORTENSIO   The motion's good indeed, and be it so.
       Petruccio, I shall be your *ben venuto.*°   *Exeunt*   *welcome (your host)*

2.1

Enter KATHERINE *and* BIANCA [*her hands bound*]
BIANCA   Good sister, wrong me not, nor wrong yourself
       To make a bondmaid and a slave of me.

---

4. Helen of Troy. In Marlowe's *Doctor Faustus*, her face
is said to have "launched a thousand ships."
5. Even if Paris (who stole Helen of Troy from her husband) were to come.
6. Hercules, the hero of classical mythology who suc-

cessfully performed twelve seemingly impossible tasks
("labours"), was also called Alcides (descendant of
Alcaeus).
2.1 Location: Baptista's house in Padua.

That I disdain, but for these other goods,°   *possessions*
Unbind my hands, I'll pull them off myself,
5   Yea, all my raiment to my petticoat,
Or what you will command me will I do,
So well I know my duty to my elders.

KATHERINE   Of all thy suitors here I charge thee tell
Whom thou lov'st best. See thou dissemble not.
10 BIANCA   Believe me, sister, of all the men alive
I never yet beheld that special face
Which I could fancy more than any other.

KATHERINE   Minion,° thou liest. Is't not Hortensio?   *Hussy*

BIANCA   If you affect° him, sister, here I swear   *love*
15   I'll plead for you myself but you shall have him.

KATHERINE   O then, belike you fancy riches more.
You will have Gremio to keep you fair.

BIANCA   Is it for him you do envy me so?
Nay, then, you jest, and now I well perceive
20   You have but jested with me all this while.
I prithee, sister Kate, untie my hands.

KATHERINE   If that be jest, then all the rest was so. *Strikes her*
            Enter BAPTISTA

BAPTISTA   Why, how now, dame, whence grows this insolence?
Bianca, stand aside.— Poor girl, she weeps.—
25   Go ply thy needle, meddle not with her.
[*To* KATHERINE] For shame, thou hilding° of a devilish spirit,   *worthless creature*
Why dost thou wrong her that did ne'er wrong thee?
When did she cross thee with a bitter word?

KATHERINE   Her silence flouts° me, and I'll be revenged.   *mocks*
            [*She*] *flies after* BIANCA
30 BAPTISTA   What, in my sight? Bianca, get thee in. *Exit* [BIANCA]

KATHERINE   What, will you not suffer me?° Nay, now I see   *let me have my way*
She is your treasure, she must have a husband.
I must dance barefoot on her wedding day,[1]
And for your love to her lead apes in hell.[2]
35   Talk not to me. I will go sit and weep
Till I can find occasion of revenge.   [*Exit*]

BAPTISTA   Was ever gentleman thus grieved as I?
But who comes here?
            Enter GREMIO, LUCENTIO [*as a schoolmaster*] *in the*
            habit of a mean man,° PETRUCCIO *with* [HORTENSIO *as*   *man of low social rank*
            a musician,] TRANIO [*as Lucentio*], *with* [BIONDELLO]
            his boy bearing a lute and books

GREMIO   Good morrow, neighbour Baptista.
40 BAPTISTA   Good morrow, neighbour Gremio. God save you,
gentlemen.

PETRUCCIO   And you, good sir. Pray, have you not a daughter
Called Katherina, fair and virtuous?

BAPTISTA   I have a daughter, sir, called Katherina.
45 GREMIO   You are too blunt. Go to it orderly.°   *properly*

PETRUCCIO   You wrong me, Signor Gremio. Give me leave.
[*To* BAPTISTA] I am a gentleman of Verona, sir,

---

1. Proverbially expected of older unmarried sisters.   2. *lead apes in hell:* the proverbial destiny of unmarried
women.

That hearing of her beauty and her wit,
Her affability and bashful modesty,
50　Her wondrous qualities and mild behaviour,
Am bold to show myself a forward° guest　　　　　　　　　*eager*
Within your house to make mine eye the witness
Of that report which I so oft have heard,
And for an entrance to my entertainment[3]
55　I do present you with a man of mine [*presenting* HORTENSIO]
Cunning in music and the mathematics
To instruct her fully in those sciences,
Whereof I know she is not ignorant.
Accept of him, or else you do me wrong.
60　His name is Licio, born in Mantua.
BAPTISTA　You're welcome, sir, and he for your good sake.
But for my daughter, Katherine, this I know:
She is not for your turn,° the more my grief.　　　　　　*will not suit you*
PETRUCCIO　I see you do not mean to part with her,
65　Or else you like not of my company.
BAPTISTA　Mistake me not, I speak but as I find.°　　　　　*as the facts stand*
Whence are you, sir? What may I call your name?
PETRUCCIO　Petruccio is my name, Antonio's son,
A man well known throughout all Italy.
70　BAPTISTA　I know him well.[4] You are welcome for his sake.
GREMIO　Saving° your tale, Petruccio, I pray　　　　　*With all respect to*
Let us that are poor petitioners speak too.
Baccare,° you are marvellous forward.　　　　　*Stand back (mock Latin)*
PETRUCCIO　O pardon me, Signor Gremio, I would fain be doing.[5]
75　GREMIO　I doubt it not, sir. But you will curse your wooing.
[*To* BAPTISTA] Neighbour, this is a gift[6] very grateful,° I am sure　　　*pleasing*
of it. To express the like kindness, myself, that have been more
kindly beholden to you than any, freely give unto you this
young scholar [*presenting* LUCENTIO] that hath been long
80　studying at Rheims,[7] as cunning in Greek, Latin, and other
languages as the other in music and mathematics. His name
is Cambio.[8] Pray accept his service.
BAPTISTA　A thousand thanks, Signor Gremio. Welcome, good
Cambio. [*To* TRANIO] But, gentle sir, methinks you walk like a
85　stranger. May I be so bold to know the cause of your coming?
TRANIO　Pardon me, sir, the boldness is mine own
That, being a stranger in this city here,
Do make myself a suitor to your daughter,
Unto Bianca, fair and virtuous.
90　Nor is your firm resolve unknown to me
In the preferment of the eldest sister.
This liberty is all that I request:
That upon knowledge of my parentage
I may have welcome 'mongst the rest that woo,
95　And free access and favour as the rest.
And toward the education of your daughters

---

3. And as an entrance fee for my reception ("entertainment") as a suitor.
4. Probably, I know him by reputation.
5. I am eager to get on with it (with a pun on "doing"

as meaning "have sexual intercourse").
6. That is, Petruccio's gift of Hortensio/Licio.
7. French city famous for its university.
8. Italian for "exchange"

I here bestow a simple instrument,
And this small packet of Greek and Latin books.
If you accept them, then their worth is great.

100 BAPTISTA   Lucentio is your name[9]—of whence, I pray?
TRANIO   Of Pisa, sir, son to Vincentio.
BAPTISTA   A mighty man of Pisa. By report
I know him well. You are very welcome, sir.
[To HORTENSIO] Take you the lute, [to LUCENTIO] and you the
set of books.
105 You shall go see your pupils presently.°   *immediately*
Holla, within!
            Enter a Servant
                        Sirrah, lead these gentlemen
To my daughters, and tell them both
These are their tutors. Bid them use them well.
            [*Exit Servant with* LUCENTIO *and* HORTENSIO,
                              BIONDELLO *following*]
[To PETRUCCIO] We will go walk a little in the orchard,°   *garden*
110 And then to dinner. You are passing° welcome—   *extremely*
And so I pray you all to think yourselves.
PETRUCCIO   Signor Baptista, my business asketh haste,
And every day I cannot come to woo.
You knew my father well, and in him me,
115 Left solely heir to all his lands and goods,
Which I have bettered rather than decreased.
Then tell me, if I get your daughter's love,
What dowry shall I have with her to wife?
BAPTISTA   After my death the one half of my lands,
120 And in possession° twenty thousand crowns.   *immediately*
PETRUCCIO   And for that dowry I'll assure her of
Her widowhood,[1] be it that she survive me,
In all my lands and leases whatsoever.
Let specialties° be therefore drawn between us,   *explicit contracts*
125 That covenants may be kept on either hand.
BAPTISTA   Ay, when the special thing is well obtained—
That is her love, for that is all in all.
PETRUCCIO   Why, that is nothing, for I tell you, father,
I am as peremptory as she proud-minded,
130 And where two raging fires meet together
They do consume the thing that feeds their fury.
Though little fire grows great with little wind,
Yet extreme gusts will blow out fire and all.[2]
So I to her, and so she yields to me,
135 For I am rough, and woo not like a babe.
BAPTISTA   Well mayst thou woo, and happy be thy speed.°   *fortune*
But be thou armed for some unhappy words.
PETRUCCIO   Ay, to the proof,[3] as mountains are for winds,
That shakes not though they blow perpetually.
            Enter HORTENSIO *with his head broke*
140 BAPTISTA   How now, my friend, why dost thou look so pale?

---

9. How Baptista knows this is unclear. He may read the name in one of the schoolbooks.
1. Widow's share of the estate.
2. Implying that those who have opposed Katherine so far have been too weak ("little wind") and that he will subdue her with his "extreme gusts."
3. In impenetrable armor. Proof armor was tested for its strength.

HORTENSIO For fear, I promise you, if I look pale.

BAPTISTA What, will my daughter prove a good musician?

HORTENSIO I think she'll sooner prove a soldier.
　　Iron may hold with° her, but never lutes.　　　　　　　　　*withstand*

145　BAPTISTA Why then, thou canst not break° her to the lute?　　*train*

HORTENSIO Why no, for she hath broke the lute to me.
　　I did but tell her she mistook her frets,⁴
　　And bowed° her hand to teach her fingering,　　　　　　　*bent*
　　When, with a most impatient devilish spirit,

150　　'Frets,⁵ call you these?' quoth she, 'I'll fume° with them,'　　*be in a rage*
　　And with that word she struck me on the head,
　　And through the instrument my pate made way,
　　And there I stood amazèd for a while,
　　As on a pillory,⁶ looking through the lute,

155　　While she did call me rascal, fiddler,
　　And twangling jack,° with twenty such vile terms,　　　　　*knave*
　　As° had she studied to misuse me so.　　　　　　　　　　*As if*

PETRUCCIO Now, by the world, it is a lusty° wench!　　　　　*lively*
　　I love her ten times more than e'er I did.

160　　O, how I long to have some chat with her!

BAPTISTA [*to* HORTENSIO] Well, go with me, and be not so
　　　　discomfited.
　　Proceed in practice° with my younger daughter.　　　*Continue your lessons*
　　She's apt to learn, and thankful for good turns.
　　Signor Petruccio, will you go with us,

165　　Or shall I send my daughter Kate to you?

PETRUCCIO I pray you, do.　　　*Exeunt. Manet*° PETRUCCIO　　*Remains*
　　　　　　　　　　　　I'll attend° her here,　　　　　　　　*await*
　　And woo her with some spirit when she comes.
　　Say that she rail, why then I'll tell her plain
　　She sings as sweetly as a nightingale.

170　　Say that she frown, I'll say she looks as clear
　　As morning roses newly washed with dew.
　　Say she be mute and will not speak a word,
　　Then I'll commend her volubility,
　　And say she uttereth piercing° eloquence.　　　　　　　　*moving*

175　　If she do bid me pack,° I'll give her thanks　　　　　　　*go away*
　　As though she bid me stay by her a week.
　　If she deny to wed, I'll crave° the day　　　　　　　　　*beg to know*
　　When I shall ask the banns,⁷ and when be marrièd.
　　But here she comes, and now, Petruccio, speak.
　　　　Enter KATHERINE

180　　Good morrow, Kate, for that's your name, I hear.

KATHERINE Well have you heard, but something° hard of hearing.　　*somewhat*
　　They call me Katherine that do talk of me.

PETRUCCIO You lie, in faith, for you are called plain Kate,
　　And bonny Kate, and sometimes Kate the curst,

185　　But Kate, the prettiest Kate in Christendom,

---

4. Placed her fingers upon the wrong bars ("frets") on the lute's fingerboard.
5. Kate plays on "frets" as also meaning "annoyances" or "vexations."
6. An instrument of public punishment in which the offender's head and hands were fastened in wooden clamps.
7. Have the banns read. Banns were required announcements in church of a forthcoming wedding.

Kate of Kate Hall,[8] my super-dainty Kate—
For dainties are all cates,[9] and therefore 'Kate'—
Take this of me, Kate of my consolation:
Hearing thy mildness praised in every town,
190 Thy virtues spoke of, and thy beauty sounded[1]—
Yet not so deeply as to thee belongs—
Myself am moved to woo thee for my wife.

KATHERINE   Moved? In good time.° Let him that moved you hither   *Indeed*
Re-move you hence. I knew you at the first
You were a movable.[2]

195 PETRUCCIO   Why, what's a movable?

KATHERINE   A joint-stool.[3]

PETRUCCIO   Thou hast hit it. Come, sit on me.

KATHERINE   Asses are made to bear,° and so are you.   *carry loads*

PETRUCCIO   Women are made to bear,[4] and so are you.

KATHERINE   No such jade° as you, if me you mean.   *worn-out horse*

200 PETRUCCIO   Alas, good Kate, I will not burden[5] thee,
For knowing° thee to be but young and light.[6]   *Because I know*

KATHERINE   Too light° for such a swain° as you to catch,   *quick / bumpkin*
And yet as heavy as my weight should be.[7]

PETRUCCIO   Should be?—should buzz.[8]

KATHERINE   Well ta'en, and like a buzzard.[9]

205 PETRUCCIO   O slow-winged turtle,° shall a buzzard take thee?   *turtledove*

KATHERINE   Ay, for a turtle, as he takes a buzzard.[1]

PETRUCCIO   Come, come, you wasp, i'faith you are too angry.

KATHERINE   If I be waspish, best beware my sting.

PETRUCCIO   My remedy is then to pluck it out.

210 KATHERINE   Ay, if the fool could find it where it lies.

PETRUCCIO   Who knows not where a wasp does wear his sting?
In his tail.

KATHERINE   In his tongue.

PETRUCCIO   Whose tongue?

KATHERINE   Yours, if you talk of tales,° and so farewell.   *gossip; genitals*

PETRUCCIO   What, with my tongue in your tail? Nay, come again,
Good Kate, I am a gentleman.

215 KATHERINE   That I'll try.°   *test*

She strikes him

PETRUCCIO   I swear I'll cuff you if you strike again.

KATHERINE   So may you lose your arms.[2]
If you strike me you are no gentleman,
And if no gentleman, why then, no arms.

---

8. Either an obscure allusion or an ironic reference to Kate's home as a place famous because she lives there.
9. For delicacies ("dainties") are called "cates."
1. Proclaimed; tested for depth.
2. Piece of furniture; changeable person.
3. Wooden stool made by a joiner.
4. Bear children; bear the weight of a lover.
5. Lie on you in sexual intercourse; make you pregnant; make accusations against you; accompany you with a musical refrain, or "burden."
6. Not heavy; wanton; lacking a musical accompaniment.
7. She is claiming social prominence ("weight") and

refusing the implication that she is wanton ("light") or like a coin that has been clipped so that it is lighter than it should be.
8. Punning on "be" and "bee," Petruccio suggests Kate should make a buzzing sound.
9. A hawk that cannot be trained to "take," or capture, prey; a fool.
1. Obscure line probably meaning that if a fool ("buzzard") mistakes me for a faithful love ("turtledove"), he'll be making as big a mistake as the turtledove makes when it captures a buzzing insect (another meaning of "buzzard").
2. Lose your claim to a coat of arms (sign of noble status); loosen your grip on me.

220	PETRUCCIO	A herald,° Kate? O, put me in thy books.³	*An authority on heraldry*
	KATHERINE	What is your crest⁴—a coxcomb?⁵	
	PETRUCCIO	A combless cock,⁶ so Kate will be my hen.	
	KATHERINE	No cock of mine. You crow too like a craven.°	*cock that won't fight*
	PETRUCCIO	Nay, come, Kate, come. You must not look so sour.	
225	KATHERINE	It is my fashion when I see a crab.°	*crab apple; sour person*
	PETRUCCIO	Why, here's no crab, and therefore look not sour.	
	KATHERINE	There is, there is.	
	PETRUCCIO	Then show it me.	
	KATHERINE	Had I a glass° I would.	*mirror*
	PETRUCCIO	What, you mean my face?	
230	KATHERINE	Well aimed,° of such a young one.	*A good guess*
	PETRUCCIO	Now, by Saint George,° I am too young for you.	*England's patron saint*
	KATHERINE	Yet you are withered.	
	PETRUCCIO	'Tis with cares.	
	KATHERINE	I care not.	
	PETRUCCIO	Nay, hear you, Kate. In sooth, you scape° not so.	*escape*
	KATHERINE	I chafe° you if I tarry. Let me go.	*annoy; inflame*
235	PETRUCCIO	No, not a whit. I find you passing gentle.	
		'Twas told me you were rough, and coy,° and sullen,	*disdainful*
		And now I find report a very liar,	
		For thou art pleasant, gamesome,° passing° courteous,	*playful / very*
		But slow in speech, yet sweet as springtime flowers.	
240		Thou canst not frown. Thou canst not look askance,°	*scornfully*
		Nor bite the lip, as angry wenches will,	
		Nor hast thou pleasure to be cross in talk,	
		But thou with mildness entertain'st thy wooers,	
		With gentle conference,° soft, and affable.	*conversation*
245		Why does the world report that Kate doth limp?	
		O sland'rous world! Kate like the hazel twig	
		Is straight and slender, and as brown in hue	
		As hazelnuts, and sweeter than the kernels.	
		O let me see thee walk. Thou dost not halt.°	*limp*
250	KATHERINE	Go, fool, and whom thou keep'st command.⁷	
	PETRUCCIO	Did ever Dian⁸ so become a grove	
		As Kate this chamber with her princely gait?	
		O, be thou Dian, and let her be Kate,	
		And then let Kate be chaste and Dian sportful.°	*playful; amorous*
255	KATHERINE	Where did you study all this goodly speech?	
	PETRUCCIO	It is extempore, from my mother-wit.°	*native intelligence*
	KATHERINE	A witty mother, witless else° her son.	*otherwise*
	PETRUCCIO	Am I not wise?	
	KATHERINE	Yes, keep you warm.⁹	
	PETRUCCIO	Marry, so I mean, sweet Katherine, in thy bed.	
260		And therefore setting all this chat aside,	
		Thus in plain terms: your father hath consented	
		That you shall be my wife, your dowry 'greed on,	

3. Heralds kept books listing gentlemen and their coats of arms.
4. Image on a coat of arms; a fleshy ridge or comb on a rooster's head.
5. Court fool's cap (resembling a cock's comb or crest).
6. A cock with its comb cut down (and thought, there-fore, to be gentle), with a pun on "cock" as "penis."
7. And command your servants (not me).
8. Goddess of the hunt and of chastity.
9. Alluding to the proverbial phrase "enough wit to keep oneself warm," implying that the person has few brains.

	And will you, nill you,° I will marry you.	*if you will or not*
	Now, Kate, I am a husband for your turn,°	*needs*
265	For by this light, whereby I see thy beauty—	
	Thy beauty that doth make me like thee well—	
	Thou must be married to no man but me,	

Enter BAPTISTA, GREMIO, [*and*] TRANIO [*as Lucentio*]

	For I am he am born to tame you, Kate,	
	And bring you from a wild Kate° to a Kate	*(punning on "wildcat")*
270	Conformable° as other household Kates.	*Submissive*
	Here comes your father. Never make denial.	
	I must and will have Katherine to my wife.	

BAPTISTA   Now, Signor Petruccio, how speed you with my daughter?

PETRUCCIO   How but well, sir, how but well?

	It were impossible I should speed amiss.	

BAPTISTA   Why, how now, daughter Katherine—in your dumps?°   *dejected*

KATHERINE   Call you me daughter? Now I promise you

	You have showed a tender fatherly regard,	
	To wish me wed to one half-lunatic,	
280	A madcap ruffian and a swearing Jack,	
	That thinks with oaths to face the matter out.°	*get his way brazenly*

PETRUCCIO   Father, 'tis thus: yourself and all the world

	That talked of her have talked amiss of her.	
	If she be curst, it is for policy,°	*part of a scheme*
285	For she's not froward,° but modest as the dove.	*willful*
	She is not hot, but temperate as the morn.	
	For patience she will prove a second Grissel,[1]	
	And Roman Lucrece[2] for her chastity.	
	And to conclude, we have 'greed so well together	
290	That upon Sunday is the wedding day.	

KATHERINE   I'll see thee hanged on Sunday first.

GREMIO   Hark, Petruccio, she says she'll see thee hanged first.

TRANIO   Is this your speeding?° Nay then, goodnight our part.[3]   *progress*

PETRUCCIO   Be patient, gentlemen. I choose her for myself.

	If she and I be pleased, what's that to you?	
	'Tis bargained 'twixt us twain, being alone,	
	That she shall still be curst in company.	
	I tell you, 'tis incredible to believe	
	How much she loves me. O, the kindest Kate!	
300	She hung about my neck, and kiss on kiss	
	She vied° so fast, protesting oath on oath,	*went me one better*
	That in a twink° she won me to her love.	*instant*
	O, you are novices. 'Tis a world° to see	*worth a world*
	How tame, when men and women are alone,	
305	A meacock° wretch can make the curstest shrew.	*timid*
	Give me thy hand, Kate. I will unto Venice,	
	To buy apparel 'gainst° the wedding day.	*in preparation for*
	Provide the feast, father, and bid the guests.	
	I will be sure my Katherine shall be fine.°	*richly dressed*
310	BAPTISTA I know not what to say, but give me your hands.	
	God send you joy, Petruccio! 'Tis a match.	

---

1. Griselda, proverbial for "wifely patience." Chaucer's *Clerk's Tale* offers one version of her story.
2. In Roman legend, a married woman who killed herself after being raped by Tarquin. Shakespeare's *Rape of Lucrece* recounts the story.
3. Good-bye to our chances (of gaining Bianca).

GREMIO *and* TRANIO   Amen, say we. We will be witnesses.

PETRUCCIO   Father, and wife, and gentlemen, adieu.
I will to Venice. Sunday comes apace.

315 We will have rings, and things, and fine array;
And kiss me, Kate. We will be married o' Sunday.

          Exeunt PETRUCCIO *and* KATHERINE [*severally*]°   *separately*

GREMIO   Was ever match clapped up° so suddenly?   *settled*

BAPTISTA   Faith, gentlemen, now I play a merchant's part,
And venture madly on a desperate mart.°   *risky bargain*

320 TRANIO   'Twas a commodity lay fretting by you.[4]
'Twill bring you gain, or perish on the seas.

BAPTISTA   The gain I seek is quiet in the match.

GREMIO   No doubt but he hath got a quiet catch.
But now, Baptista, to your younger daughter.

325 Now is the day we long have lookèd for.
I am your neighbour, and was suitor first.

TRANIO   And I am one that love Bianca more
Than words can witness, or your thoughts can guess.

GREMIO   Youngling, thou canst not love so dear° as I.   *deeply; expensively*

TRANIO   Greybeard, thy love doth freeze.

330 GREMIO   But thine doth fry.
Skipper,° stand back. 'Tis age that nourisheth.   *Irresponsible youth*

TRANIO   But youth in ladies' eyes that flourisheth.

BAPTISTA   Content you, gentlemen. I will compound° this strife.   *settle*
'Tis deeds must win the prize, and he of both°   *whichever of you*

335 That can assure my daughter greatest dower
Shall have my Bianca's love.
Say, Signor Gremio, what can you assure her?

GREMIO   First, as you know, my house within the city
Is richly furnishèd with plate and gold,

340 Basins and ewers to lave° her dainty hands;   *wash*
My hangings all of Tyrian[5] tapestry.
In ivory coffers I have stuffed my crowns,°   *coins*
In cypress chests my arras counterpoints,°   *tapestry bedcovers*
Costly apparel, tents° and canopies,   *bed curtains*

345 Fine linen, Turkey cushions bossed° with pearl,   *embossed*
Valance° of Venice gold in needlework,   *Fringe on bed drapery*
Pewter, and brass, and all things that belongs
To house or housekeeping. Then at my farm
I have a hundred milch-kine° to the pail,   *dairy cows*

350 Six score fat oxen standing in my stalls,
And all things answerable to° this portion.   *on the same scale as*
Myself am struck° in years, I must confess,   *advanced*
And if I die tomorrow this is hers,
If whilst I live she will be only mine.

355 TRANIO   That 'only' came well in. Sir, list to me.
I am my father's heir and only son.
If I may have your daughter to my wife
I'll leave her houses three or four as good,
Within rich Pisa walls, as any one

360 Old Signor Gremio has in Padua,

---

4. It (that is, Katherine) was a piece of merchandise deteriorating in value or a sexually available woman fretting with irritation while in your possession.

5. Crimson or purple. (The Mediterranean city of Tyre was famous for dye of this color.)

Besides two thousand ducats by the year
Of fruitful land,[6] all which shall be her jointure.°   *marriage settlement*
What, have I pinched° you, Signor Gremio?   *distressed*

GREMIO   Two thousand ducats by the year of land—
365   My land amounts not to so much in all.
That she shall have; besides, an argosy°   *a merchant ship*
That now is lying in Marseilles road.°   *harbor*
What, have I choked you with an argosy?

TRANIO   Gremio, 'tis known my father hath no less
370   Than three great argosies, besides two galliasses°   *large cargo ships*
And twelve tight° galleys. These I will assure her,   *watertight*
And twice as much whate'er thou off 'rest next.

GREMIO   Nay, I have offered all. I have no more,
And she can have no more than all I have.
375   If you like me, she shall have me and mine.

TRANIO   Why then, the maid is mine from all the world.
By your firm promise Gremio is out-vied.°   *outbid*

BAPTISTA   I must confess your offer is the best,
And let° your father make her the assurance,   *provided*
380   She is your own. Else, you must pardon me,
If you should die before him, where's her dower?

TRANIO   That's but a cavil. He is old, I young.

GREMIO   And may not young men die as well as old?

BAPTISTA   Well, gentlemen,
385   I am thus resolved. On Sunday next, you know,
My daughter Katherine is to be married.
[*To* TRANIO] Now, on the Sunday following shall Bianca
Be bride to you, if you make this assurance;
If not, to Signor Gremio.
390   And so I take my leave, and thank you both.

GREMIO   Adieu, good neighbour.   *Exit* [BAPTISTA]
            Now I fear thee not.
Sirrah, young gamester, your father were a fool
To give thee all, and in his waning age
Set foot under thy table.[7] Tut, a toy!°   *nonsense*
395   An old Italian fox is not so kind, my boy.   *Exit*

TRANIO   A vengeance on your crafty withered hide!
Yet I have faced it with a card of ten.[8]
'Tis in my head to do my master good.
I see no reason° but supposed Lucentio   *possible action*
400   Must get° a father called supposed Vincentio—   *beget; obtain*
And that's a wonder; fathers commonly
Do get their children, but in this case of wooing
A child shall get a sire, if I fail not of my cunning.   *Exit*

3.1

Enter LUCENTIO [*with books, as Cambio*], HORTENSIO
[*with a lute, as Licio*], *and* BIANCA

LUCENTIO   Fiddler, forbear. You grow too forward, sir.
Have you so soon forgot the entertainment

---

6. *Besides . . . land:* As well as fertile land that brings in an income of 2,000 ducats (Venetian gold coins) each year.
7. Become your dependent.

8. I have bluffed and won with a card of little value (a ten spot).
3.1 Location: Baptista's house in Padua.

Her sister Katherine welcomed you withal?°   *with*
HORTENSIO   But, wrangling pedant, this Bianca is,
5   The patroness of heavenly harmony.
Then give me leave to have prerogative,°   *precedence*
And when in music we have spent an hour
Your lecture° shall have leisure for as much.   *lesson*
LUCENTIO   Preposterous[1] ass, that never read so far
10   To know the cause why music was ordained!
Was it not to refresh the mind of man
After his studies or his usual pain?°   *labor*
Then give me leave to read philosophy,
And while I pause, serve in° your harmony.   *serve up (contemptuous)*
15 HORTENSIO   Sirrah, I will not bear these braves° of thine.   *insults*
BIANCA   Why, gentlemen, you do me double wrong
To strive for that which resteth in my choice.
I am no breeching[2] scholar in the schools.
I'll not be tied to hours nor 'pointed times,
20   But learn my lessons as I please myself;
And to cut off all strife, here sit we down.
[*To* HORTENSIO] Take you your instrument, play you the whiles.°   *in the meantime*
His lecture will be done ere you have tuned.
HORTENSIO   You'll leave his lecture when I am in tune?[3]
25 LUCENTIO   That will be never. Tune your instrument.
    [HORTENSIO *tunes his lute.* LUCENTIO *opens a book*]
BIANCA   Where left we last?
LUCENTIO   Here, madam.
    [*Reads*]   'Hic ibat Simois, hic est Sigeia tellus,
        Hic steterat Priami regia celsa senis.[4]
30 BIANCA   Construe them.°   *Translate the lines*
LUCENTIO   'Hic ibat', as I told you before—'Simois', I am
Lucentio—'hic est', son unto Vincentio of Pisa—'Sigeia tellus',
disguised thus to get your love—'hic steterat', and that Lucen-
tio that comes a-wooing—'Priami', is my man Tranio—'regia',
35   bearing my port°—'celsa senis', that we might beguile the old   *taking my social position*
pantaloon.°   *foolish old man*
HORTENSIO   Madam, my instrument's in tune.
BIANCA   Let's hear. [HORTENSIO *plays*] O fie, the treble jars.°   *is discordant*
LUCENTIO   Spit in the hole,[5] man, and tune again.
    [HORTENSIO *tunes his lute again*]
40 BIANCA   Now let me see if I can construe it. 'Hic ibat Simois',
I know you not—'hic est Sigeia tellus', I trust you not—
'hic steterat Priami', take heed he hear us not—'regia', presume
not—'celsa senis', despair not.
HORTENSIO   Madam, 'tis now in tune.
LUCENTIO   All but the bass.
45 HORTENSIO   The bass is right, 'tis the base knave that jars.
    [*Aside*] How fiery and forward our pedant is!

1. Literally, putting last what should come first; reversing the natural order of things.
2. Youthful (in breeches); liable to be whipped
(breeched).
3. When my lute is in the proper pitch. Lucentio
responds with a pun on "in tune" as meaning "in harmony" with Bianca.
4. Latin lines from Penelope's letter to her husband
Ulysses in Ovid's *Heroides:* "Here flowed the Simois;
here is the Sigeian land; here stood old Priam's lofty
palace."
5. Moisten the lute's peg hole (to aid tuning). Lucentio speaks contemptuously and may not be giving serious advice.

Now, for my life, the knave doth court my love.
Pedascule,° I'll watch you better yet.   *Little pedant*
BIANCA [*to* LUCENTIO]   In time I may believe; yet, I mistrust.
50   LUCENTIO   Mistrust it not, for sure Aeacides[6]
Was Ajax, called so from his grandfather.
BIANCA   I must believe my master, else, I promise you,
I should be arguing still upon that doubt.
But let it rest. Now Licio, to you.
55   Good master, take it not unkindly, pray,
That I have been thus pleasant with you both.
HORTENSIO [*to* LUCENTIO]   You may go walk and give me leave°   *allow me leisure*
awhile.
My lessons make no music in three parts.°   *for three voices*
LUCENTIO   Are you so formal,° sir? Well, I must wait.   *precise*
60   [*Aside*] And watch withal, for but° I be deceived   *unless*
Our fine musician groweth amorous.
HORTENSIO   Madam, before you touch the instrument
To learn the order of my fingering,
I must begin with rudiments of art,
65   To teach you gamut[7] in a briefer sort,°   *quicker way*
More pleasant, pithy, and effectual
Than hath been taught by any of my trade;
And there it is in writing, fairly drawn.
[*He gives a paper*]
BIANCA   Why, I am past my gamut long ago.
70   HORTENSIO   Yet read the gamut of Hortensio.
BIANCA [*reads*]
'*Gam-ut* I am, the ground° of all accord,   *lowest note; basis*
A—re—to plead Hortensio's passion.
B—mi—Bianca, take him for thy lord,
C—fa, ut—that loves with all affection.
75   D—sol, re—one clef, two notes[8] have I,
E—la, mi—show pity, or I die.'
Call you this gamut? Tut, I like it not.
Old fashions please me best. I am not so nice°   *capricious*
To change true rules for odd inventions.
Enter a MESSENGER
80   MESSENGER   Mistress, your father prays you leave your books
And help to dress your sister's chamber up.
You know tomorrow is the wedding day.
BIANCA   Farewell, sweet masters both. I must be gone.
LUCENTIO   Faith, mistress, then I have no cause to stay.
[*Exeunt* BIANCA, MESSENGER, *and* LUCENTIO]
85   HORTENSIO   But I have cause to pry into this pedant.
Methinks he looks as though he were in love.
Yet if thy thoughts, Bianca, be so humble°   *low*
To cast thy wand'ring eyes on every stale,°   *bait; lure*
Seize thee that list.[9] If once I find thee ranging,°   *unfaithful*
90   Hortensio will be quit with thee by changing.[1]   *Exit*

---

6. Aeacides, or Ajax, was named after his grandfather   8. Referring perhaps to his one love and two identities.
Aeacus. Lucentio pretends to continue the lesson.   9. Let anyone who wants you take you.
7. A musical scale, named after its lowest note,   1. Will get even with you or get rid of you by finding
"gamma-ut."   another love.

3.2

Enter BAPTISTA, GREMIO, TRANIO [AS LUCENTIO],
KATHERINE, BIANCA, AND OTHERS, ATTENDANTS[1]

BAPTISTA [*to* TRANIO] Signor Lucentio, this is the 'pointed day
That Katherine and Petruccio should be married,
And yet we hear not of our son-in-law.
What will be said, what mockery will it be,
5   To want° the bridegroom when the priest attends   *lack*
To speak the ceremonial rites of marriage?
What says Lucentio to this shame of ours?
KATHERINE   No shame but mine. I must forsooth be forced
To give my hand opposed against my heart
10   Unto a mad-brain rudesby° full of spleen,[2]   *unmannerly fellow*
Who wooed in haste and means to wed at leisure.
I told you, I, he was a frantic° fool,   *mad*
Hiding his bitter jests in blunt behaviour,
And to be noted for a merry man
15   He'll woo a thousand, 'point the day of marriage,
Make friends, invite them, and proclaim the banns,
Yet never means to wed where he hath wooed.
Now must the world point at poor Katherine
And say 'Lo, there is mad Petruccio's wife,
20   If it would please him come and marry her.'
TRANIO   Patience, good Katherine, and Baptista, too.
Upon my life, Petruccio means but well.
Whatever fortune stays° him from his word,   *incident keeps*
Though he be blunt, I know him passing wise;
25   Though he be merry, yet withal he's honest.[3]
KATHERINE   Would Katherine had never seen him, though.

                                    Exit weeping

BAPTISTA   Go, girl. I cannot blame thee now to weep.
For such an injury would vex a very saint,
Much more a shrew of thy impatient humour.

        Enter BIONDELLO

30 BIONDELLO   Master, master, news—old news, and such news as
you never heard of.
BAPTISTA   Is it new and old too? How may that be?
BIONDELLO   Why, is it not news to hear of Petruccio's coming?
BAPTISTA   Is he come?
35 BIONDELLO   Why, no, sir.
BAPTISTA   What then?
BIONDELLO   He is coming.
BAPTISTA   When will he be here?
BIONDELLO   When he stands where I am and sees you there.
40 TRANIO   But say, what to thine old news?
BIONDELLO   Why, Petruccio is coming in a new hat and an old
jerkin,° a pair of old breeches thrice-turned,[4] a pair of boots   *jacket*

3.2 Location: In front of Baptista's house.
1. Many editors include Lucentio, disguised as Cambio,
among the characters who enter at this point, though he
speaks no lines in the events leading up to and including
Petruccio's arrival for his wedding. The Oxford editors
feel that Lucentio only comes onstage when all the characters who enter at 3.2 leave to attend Katherine and
Petruccio's wedding (3.2.116–20). They then mark a
new scene, 3.3, when Lucentio enters with Tranio.

2. Caprice; impulsiveness. Contemporary medical theorists claimed that high and low spirits originated in the
spleen.
3. Some critics find Tranio's familiarity with Petruccio
improbable. Possibly these lines were originally meant
to be spoken by Hortensio.
4. Turned inside out three times (to make them last
longer).

that have been candle-cases,[5] one buckled, another laced, an
old rusty sword ta'en out of the town armoury with a broken
45 hilt, and chapeless,[6] with two broken points,[7] his horse hipped,°   *lame in the hips*
with an old mothy saddle and stirrups of no kindred,° besides,   *unmatched*
possessed with the glanders[8] and like to mose in the chine,[9]
troubled with the lampass,[1] infected with the fashions,° full   *farcins (small tumors)*
of windgalls,[2] sped with spavins,[3] rayed with the yellows,°   *disfigured by jaundice*
50 past cure of the fives,[4] stark spoiled with the staggers,[5] be-
gnawn with the bots,[6] weighed in the back° and shoulder-   *swaybacked*
shotten,[7] near-legged before[8] and with a half-cheeked° bit and   *improperly attached*
a headstall[9] of sheep's leather which, being restrained° to   *tightened*
keep him from stumbling, hath been often burst and now
55 repaired with knots, one girth° six times pieced,° and a woman's   *saddle strap / mended*
crupper of velour[1] which hath two letters for her name fairly set
down in studs, and here and there pieced with packthread.°   *twine*

BAPTISTA   Who comes with him?

BIONDELLO   O sir, his lackey, for all the world caparisoned° like   *outfitted*
60 the horse, with a linen stock° on one leg and a kersey boot-   *stocking*
hose[2] on the other, gartered with a red and blue list;° an old   *strip of cloth*
hat, and the humour of forty fancies pricked in't for a
feather[3]—a monster, a very monster in apparel, and not like a
Christian footboy or a gentleman's lackey.

65 TRANIO   'Tis some odd humour pricks° him to this fashion;   *incites, urges*
Yet oftentimes he goes but mean-apparelled.

BAPTISTA   I am glad he's come, howsoe'er he comes.

BIONDELLO   Why, sir, he comes not.

BAPTISTA   Didst thou not say he comes?

70 BIONDELLO   Who? That Petruccio came?

BAPTISTA   Ay, that Petruccio came.

BIONDELLO   No, sir. I say his horse comes with him on his back.

BAPTISTA   Why, that's all one.°   *the same thing*

BIONDELLO   Nay, by Saint Jamy,
75   I hold° you a penny,   *bet*
           A horse and a man
           Is more than one,
           And yet not many.

Enter PETRUCCIO *and* GRUMIO[*fantastically dressed*]

PETRUCCIO   Come, where be these gallants? Who's at home?

80 BAPTISTA   You are welcome, sir.

PETRUCCIO   And yet I come not well.

BAPTISTA   And yet you halt° not.   *limp*

---

5. In other words, discarded and used to store old candle ends.
6. Without the metal tip that protects the sword's point.
7. With two laces that don't hold up his hose; with two points (instead of one) on his broken sword.
8. The first in a catalogue of horse diseases, most of which are described in Gervase Markham's *Discourse of Horsemanship* (1593). The glanders caused swellings and nasal discharge.
9. Obscure phrase, probably meaning the horse was apt to suffer discharge from the nostrils, indicating the last stage of glanders.
1. A disease characterized by swellings in the mouth.
2. Soft tumors usually appearing on the fetlock, so

called because they were thought to contain air.
3. Rendered useless by swelling of the leg joints.
4. Swelling of glands below the ears.
5. A disease causing loss of balance.
6. Eaten by intestinal worms.
7. With sprained shoulders.
8. With knock-kneed forelegs.
9. The part of the bridle that fits around the horse's head. Sheepskin would be inferior to the animal skins normally used.
1. *crupper:* strap that passes under a horse's tail to keep the saddle straight, *velour:* velvet.
2. A coarse wool stocking.
3. Possibly an absurdly fanciful decoration attached to the hat instead of a feather.

TRANIO   Not so well apparelled as I wish you were.
PETRUCCIO   Were it not better I should rush in thus—
85   But where is Kate? Where is my lovely bride?
How does my father? Gentles,⁴ methinks you frown.
And wherefore gaze this goodly company
As if they saw some wondrous monument,
Some comet or unusual prodigy?
90   BAPTISTA   Why, sir, you know this is your wedding day.
First were we sad, fearing you would not come;
Now sadder that you come so unprovided.°   *unprepared*
Fie, doff this habit,° shame to your estate,°   *outfit / social place*
An eyesore to our solemn festival.
95   TRANIO   And tell us what occasion of import
Hath all so long detained you from your wife
And sent you hither so unlike yourself?
PETRUCCIO   Tedious it were to tell, and harsh to hear.
Sufficeth I am come to keep my word,
100   Though in some part enforcèd to digress,°   *deviate from my plan*
Which at more leisure I will so excuse
As you shall well be satisfied withal.
But where is Kate? I stay too long from her.
The morning wears, 'tis time we were at church.
105   TRANIO   See not your bride in these unreverent° robes.   *disrespectful*
Go to my chamber, put on clothes of mine.
PETRUCCIO   Not I, believe me. Thus I'll visit her.
BAPTISTA   But thus, I trust, you will not marry her.
PETRUCCIO   Good sooth,° even thus. Therefore ha' done with words.   *Yes indeed*
110   To me she's married, not unto my clothes.
Could I repair what she will wear° in me   *wear out (in sex)*
As I can change these poor accoutrements,
'Twere well for Kate and better for myself.
But what a fool am I to chat with you
115   When I should bid good morrow to my bride,
And seal the title with a lovely° kiss!   *Exit [with* GRUMIO]   *loving*
TRANIO   He hath some meaning in his mad attire.
We will persuade him, be it possible,
To put on better ere he go to church.   [*Exit with* GREMIO]
120   BAPTISTA   I'll after him, and see the event° of this.   *Exeunt*   *outcome*

3.3

[*Enter* LUCENTIO *as Cambio, and* TRANIO *as Lucentio*]
TRANIO   But, sir, to love concerneth us to add¹
Her father's liking, which to bring to pass,
As I before imparted to your worship,
I am to get a man—whate'er he be
5   It skills° not much, we'll fit him to our turn—   *matters*
And he shall be Vincentio of Pisa,
And make assurance here in Padua
Of greater sums than I have promisèd.

4. The polite term of address to men and women of the gentry.
3.3 Location: Scene continues.

1. To the love between Bianca and Lucentio it is necessary for us to add.

So shall you quietly enjoy your hope,°   *what you hope for*
10 And marry sweet Bianca with consent.
    LUCENTIO   Were it not that my fellow schoolmaster
    Doth watch Bianca's steps so narrowly,
    'Twere good, methinks, to steal our marriage,°   *elope*
    Which once performed, let all the world say no,
15 I'll keep mine own, despite of all the world.
    TRANIO   That by degrees we mean to look into,
    And watch our vantage° in this business.   *opportunity*
    We'll overreach the greybeard Gremio,
    The narrow-prying° father Minola,   *overly suspicious*
20 The quaint° musician, amorous Licio,   *skillful; crafty*
    All for my master's sake, Lucentio.
          Enter GREMIO
    Signor Gremio, came you from the church?
    GREMIO   As willingly as e'er I came from school.
    TRANIO   And is the bride and bridegroom coming home?
25 GREMIO   A bridegroom, say you? 'Tis a groom° indeed—   *crude, lower-class man*
    A grumbling groom, and that the girl shall find.
    TRANIO   Curster° than she? Why, 'tis impossible.   *More cantankerous*
    GREMIO   Why, he's a devil, a devil, a very fiend.
    TRANIO   Why, she's a devil, a devil, the devil's dam.°   *mother*
30 GREMIO   Tut, she's a lamb, a dove, a fool to him.²
    I'll tell you, Sir Lucentio: when the priest
    Should ask if Katherine should be his wife,
    'Ay, by Gog's woun's,'³ quoth he, and swore so loud
    That all amazed the priest let fall the book,
35 And as he stooped again to take it up
    This mad-brained bridegroom took° him such a cuff   *gave*
    That down fell priest, and book, and book, and priest.
    'Now take them up,' quoth he, 'if any list.'°   *choose*
    TRANIO   What said the vicar when he rose again?
40 GREMIO   Trembled and shook, forwhy° he° stamped and swore   *because / (Petruccio)*
    As if the vicar meant to cozen⁴ him.
    But after many ceremonies done
    He calls for wine. 'A health,' quoth he, as if
    He had been aboard,° carousing to his mates   *(a ship)*
45 After a storm; quaffed off the muscatel⁵
    And threw the sops all in the sexton's face,
    Having no other reason
    But that his beard grew thin and hungerly°   *sparsely; as if hungry*
    And seemed to ask him sops as he was drinking.
50 This done, he took the bride about the neck
    And kissed her lips with such a clamorous smack
    That at the parting all the church did echo,
    And I seeing this came thence for very shame,
    And after me, I know, the rout° is coming.   *crowd*
55 Such a mad marriage never was before.
          Music plays
    Hark, hark, I hear the minstrels play.

---

2. A good-natured innocent compared with him.
3. By God's (Christ's) wounds (a common oath).
4. Cheat (by not performing a legally binding ceremony).

5. Wine with small cakes, or "sops," soaked in it, traditionally drunk by the newly married couple and their
guests.

Enter PETRUCCIO, KATHERINE, BIANCA, HORTENSIO
[*as Licio*], BAPTISTA, [GRUMIO, *and others*, attendants]

PETRUCCIO Gentlemen and friends, I thank you for your pains.
I know you think to dine with me today,
And have prepared great store of wedding cheer.°   *food and drink*
60 But so it is my haste doth call me hence,
And therefore here I mean to take my leave.

BAPTISTA Is't possible you will away tonight?

PETRUCCIO I must away today, before night come.
Make° it no wonder. If you knew my business,   *Consider*
65 You would entreat me rather go than stay.
And, honest° company, I thank you all   *worthy*
That have beheld me give away myself
To this most patient, sweet, and virtuous wife.
Dine with my father, drink a health to me,
70 For I must hence; and farewell to you all.

TRANIO Let us entreat you stay till after dinner.

PETRUCCIO It may not be.

GREMIO   Let me entreat you.

PETRUCCIO It cannot be.

KATHERINE   Let me entreat you.

PETRUCCIO I am content.

KATHERINE   Are you content to stay?

75 PETRUCCIO I am content you shall entreat me stay,
But yet not stay, entreat me how you can.

KATHERINE Now, if you love me, stay.

PETRUCCIO   Grumio, my horse.

GRUMIO Ay, sir, they be ready. The oats have eaten the horses.⁶

KATHERINE Nay, then, do what thou canst, I will not go today,
80 No, nor tomorrow—not till I please myself.
The door is open, sir, there lies your way.
You may be jogging whiles your boots are green.⁷
For me, I'll not be gone till I please myself.
'Tis like you'll prove a jolly,° surly groom,   *an arrogant*
85 That take it on you at the first so roundly.⁸

PETRUCCIO O Kate, content thee. Prithee, be not angry.

KATHERINE I will be angry. What hast thou to do?⁹
Father, be quiet. He shall stay° my leisure.   *await*

GREMIO Ay, marry, sir. Now it begins to work.

90 KATHERINE Gentlemen, forward to the bridal dinner.
I see a woman may be made a fool
If she had not a spirit to resist.

PETRUCCIO They shall go forward, Kate, at thy command.
Obey the bride, you that attend on her.
95 Go to the feast, revel and domineer,°   *feast sumptuously*
Carouse full measure to her maidenhead.
Be mad and merry, or go hang yourselves.
But for my bonny Kate, she must with me.
Nay, look not big,° nor stamp, nor stare, nor fret.   *defiant*

---

6. Either Grumio gets it the wrong way around, or he is joking about the great quantity of oats the horses have eaten.
7. You can be off now while your boots are new ("green"). Proverbial expression for getting an early start or getting rid of an unwelcome guest.
8. That takes charge at the outset so outspokenly.
9. What business is it of yours?

100 I will be master of what is mine own.
She is my goods, my chattels. She is my house,
My household-stuff, my field, my barn,
My horse, my ox, my ass, my anything,
And here she stands, touch her whoever dare.[1]
105 I'll bring mine action on° the proudest he   attack; sue (in court)
That stops my way in Padua. Grumio,
Draw forth thy weapon, we are beset with thieves.
Rescue thy mistress if thou be a man.
Fear not, sweet wench. They shall not touch thee, Kate.
110 I'll buckler° thee against a million.   shield
            Exeunt PETRUCCIO, KATHERINE [*and* GRUMIO]
BAPTISTA   Nay, let them go—a couple of quiet ones!
GREMIO   Went they not quickly I should die with laughing.
TRANIO   Of all mad matches never was the like.
LUCENTIO   Mistress, what's your opinion of your sister?
115 BIANCA   That being mad herself she's madly mated.
GREMIO   I warrant him, Petruccio is Kated.[2]
BAPTISTA   Neighbours and friends, though bride and bridegroom wants°   *are missing*
For to supply° the places at the table,   *To fill*
You know there wants no junkets° at the feast.   *sweetmeats*
120 Lucentio, you shall supply the bridegroom's place,
And let Bianca take her sister's room.
TRANIO   Shall sweet Bianca practise how to bride it?
BAPTISTA   She shall, Lucentio. Come, gentlemen, let's go.
                                                            Exeunt

4.1

            Enter GRUMIO
GRUMIO   Fie, fie on all tired jades,° on all mad masters, and all   *worn-out horses*
foul° ways. Was ever man so beaten? Was ever man so rayed?°   *muddy / dirtied*
Was ever man so weary? I am sent before to make a fire, and
they are coming after to warm them. Now were not I a little
5 pot and soon hot,[1] my very lips might freeze to my teeth, my
tongue to the roof of my mouth, my heart in my belly ere
I should come by a fire to thaw me. But I with blowing the fire
shall warm myself, for considering the weather, a taller[2] man
than I will take cold. Holla! Hoa, Curtis!
            Enter CURTIS
10 CURTIS   Who is that calls so coldly?
GRUMIO   A piece of ice. If thou doubt it, thou mayst slide from
my shoulder to my heel with no greater a run but my head and
my neck. A fire, good Curtis!
CURTIS   Is my master and his wife coming, Grumio?
15 GRUMIO   O ay, Curtis, ay, and therefore fire, fire! Cast on no
water.[3]
CURTIS   Is she so hot a shrew as she's reported?

1. Petruccio warns others to leave Kate alone. In cata-
loguing the ways she is one of his possessions, he
alludes to the Tenth Commandment, which forbids
coveting a neighbor's wife or property.
2. Mated with a "Kate"; afflicted with Kate (imagined
as a disease).
4.1 Location: Petruccio's country house.

1. Proverbial for a small person who quickly becomes
angry.
2. Punning on "taller" as meaning "sturdier."
3. Alluding to the popular song "Scotland's Burning,"
in which the words "Fire, fire" are followed by "Cast on
water, cast on water."

GRUMIO She was, good Curtis, before this frost; but thou
know'st, winter tames man, woman, and beast, for it hath
20   tamed my old master, and my new mistress, and myself, fellow Curtis.
CURTIS Away, you three-inch° fool. I am no beast.   *short*
GRUMIO Am I but three inches? Why, thy horn[4] is a foot, and
so long am I, at the least. But wilt thou make a fire, or shall I
25   complain on thee to our mistress, whose hand—she being
now at hand—thou shalt soon feel to thy cold comfort, for
being slow in thy hot office.°   *fire-making duties*
CURTIS I prithee, good Grumio, tell me—how goes the world?
GRUMIO A cold world, Curtis, in every office but thine. And
30   therefore fire, do thy duty, and have thy duty,° for my master   *take your reward*
and mistress are almost frozen to death.
CURTIS There's fire ready, and therefore, good Grumio, the
news.
GRUMIO Why, 'Jack boy, ho boy!',[5] and as much news as wilt thou.
35   CURTIS Come, you are so full of cony-catching.[6]
GRUMIO Why, therefore fire, for I have caught extreme cold.
Where's the cook? Is supper ready, the house trimmed, rushes
strewed,[7] cobwebs swept, the servingmen in their new fustian,°   *coarse cloth*
the white stockings, and every officer° his wedding garment   *servant*
40   on? Be the Jacks fair within, the Jills fair without,[8] the carpets°   *table coverings*
laid, and everything in order?
CURTIS All ready, and therefore, I pray thee, news.
GRUMIO First, know my horse is tired, my master and mistress
fallen out.
45   CURTIS How?
GRUMIO Out of their saddles into the dirt, and thereby hangs a
tale.
CURTIS Let's ha't, good Grumio.
GRUMIO Lend thine ear.
50   CURTIS Here.
GRUMIO [*cuffing him*] There.
CURTIS This 'tis to feel a tale, not to hear a tale.
GRUMIO And therefore 'tis called a sensible tale,[9] and this cuff
was but to knock at your ear and beseech listening. Now I
55   begin. *Inprimis,*° we came down a foul° hill, my master riding   *First / muddy*
behind my mistress.
CURTIS Both of° one horse?   *on*
GRUMIO What's that to thee?
CURTIS Why, a horse.
60   GRUMIO Tell thou the tale. But hadst thou not crossed° me   *interrupted*
thou shouldst have heard how her horse fell and she under
her horse; thou shouldst have heard in how miry a place, how
she was bemoiled,° how he left her with the horse upon her,   *covered with mud*
how he beat me because her horse stumbled, how she waded
65   through the dirt to pluck him off me, how he swore, how she
prayed that never prayed before, how I cried, how the horses
ran away, how her bridle was burst, how I lost my crupper,

---

4. The proverbial sign of a cuckold; an erect penis.   which Grumio is fond. A cony is a rabbit.
Grumio implies that he is "long" enough to cuckold   7. Scattered on the floor.
Curtis.   8. Jacks and Jills were manservants and maidservants;
5. A line from another popular song.   also leather drinking vessels and metal drinking vessels.
6. Trickery, with a play on the "catches," or songs, of   9. Reasonable; capable of being felt.

with many things of worthy memory which now shall die in
oblivion, and thou return unexperienced° to thy grave.　　　　*ignorant; unknowing*
70　CURTIS　By this reckoning he is more shrew than she.

GRUMIO　Ay, and that thou and the proudest of you all shall find
when he comes home. But what° talk I of this? Call forth　　　　*why*
Nathaniel, Joseph, Nicholas, Philip, Walter, Sugarsop, and
the rest. Let their heads be sleekly combed, their blue coats[1]
75　brushed, and their garters of an indifferent° knit. Let them　　　　*ordinary; a matching*
curtsy with their left legs and not presume to touch a hair of
my master's horse-tail till they kiss their hands.[2] Are they all
ready?

CURTIS　They are.
80　GRUMIO　Call them forth.

CURTIS [*calling*]　Do you hear, ho? You must meet my master to
countenance[3] my mistress.

GRUMIO　Why, she hath a face of her own.

CURTIS　Who knows not that?
85　GRUMIO　Thou, it seems, that calls for company to countenance
her.

CURTIS　I call them forth to credit[4] her.
　　　　Enter four or five servingmen

GRUMIO　Why, she comes to borrow nothing of them.

NATHANIEL　Welcome home, Grumio!
90　PHILIP　How now, Grumio?

JOSEPH　What, Grumio?

NICHOLAS　Fellow Grumio!

NATHANIEL　How now, old lad!

GRUMIO　Welcome you, how now you, what you, fellow you, and
95　thus much for greeting. Now, my spruce° companions, is all　　　　*smartly dressed*
ready and all things neat?

NATHANIEL　All things is ready. How near is our master?

GRUMIO　E'en at hand, alighted by this, and therefore be not—
Cock's° passion, silence! I hear my master.　　　　*God's (a common oath)*
　　　　Enter PETRUCCIO *and* KATHERINE
100　PETRUCCIO　Where be these knaves? What, no man at door
To hold my stirrup nor to take my horse?
Where is Nathaniel, Gregory, Philip?

ALL SERVANTS　Here, here sir, here sir.

PETRUCCIO　Here sir, here sir, here sir, here sir!
105　You logger-headed° and unpolished grooms,　　　　*stupid*
What! No attendance! No regard! No duty!
Where is the foolish knave I sent before?

GRUMIO　Here, sir, as foolish as I was before.

PETRUCCIO　You peasant swain,° you whoreson,° malthorse　　　　*farm laborer / bastard*
drudge,[5]
110　Did I not bid thee meet me in the park[6]
And bring along these rascal knaves with thee?

GRUMIO　Nathaniel's coat, sir, was not fully made,
And Gabriel's pumps° were all unpinked° i'th' heel.　　　　*shoes / not ornamented*
There was no link[7] to colour Peter's hat,

---

1. The usual servant uniform.
2. A greeting signifying inordinate submissiveness.
3. Greet, pay respects to; with a pun in the next line on
"countenance" as meaning "face."
4. Honor, with pun in next line on "credit" as meaning
"offer financial assistance."

5. Stupid, menial worker. The slow, heavy malt horse
was used to grind malt by turning a treadmill.
6. A piece of ground comprising woodland and pasture
attached to a country house and used for recreation.
7. Torch, the smoke of which was used to blacken shoes.

115 And Walter's dagger was not come from sheathing.°   *having a sheath fixed*
There were none fine but Adam, Ralph, and Gregory.
The rest were ragged, old, and beggarly.
Yet as they are, here are they come to meet you.
PETRUCCIO   Go, rascals, go and fetch my supper in.
                         Exeunt servants
120   [*Sings*]   'Where is the life that late I led?
            Where are those—'⁸
Sit down, Kate, and welcome. Soud, soud, soud, soud.⁹
    Enter servants with supper
Why, when, I say?—Nay, good sweet Kate, be merry.—
Off with my boots, you rogues, you villains. When?
125   [*Sings*]   'It was the friar of orders gray,
            As he forth walkèd on his way.'¹
Out, you rogue, you pluck my foot awry.
[*Kicking a servant*] Take that, and mend the plucking of the other.
Be merry, Kate. [*Calling*] Some water, here. What, hoa!
    Enter one with water
130 Where's my spaniel Troilus? Sirrah, get you hence,
And bid my cousin Ferdinand come hither—
One, Kate, that you must kiss and be acquainted with.
[*Calling*] Where are my slippers? Shall I have some water?
Come, Kate, and wash, and welcome heartily.
    [*A servant drops water*]
135 You whoreson villain, will you let it fall?
KATHERINE   Patience, I pray you, 'twas a fault unwilling.
PETRUCCIO   A whoreson, beetle-headed,° flap-eared knave.   *thick-headed*
Come, Kate, sit down, I know you have a stomach.°   *an appetite; temper*
Will you give thanks, sweet Kate, or else shall I?
What's this—mutton?
FIRST SERVINGMAN   Ay.
PETRUCCIO   Who brought it?
140 PETER   I.
PETRUCCIO   'Tis burnt, and so is all the meat.
What dogs are these? Where is the rascal cook?
How durst you villains bring it from the dresser°   *cook; sideboard*
And serve it thus to me that love it not?
145 There, [*throwing food*] take it to you, trenchers,° cups, and all,   *plates*
You heedless jolt-heads° and unmannered slaves.   *careless blockheads*
What, do you grumble? I'll be with you straight.
    [*He chases the servants away*]
KATHERINE   I pray you, husband, be not so disquiet.
The meat was well, if you were so contented.
150 PETRUCCIO   I tell thee, Kate, 'twas burnt and dried away,
And I expressly am forbid to touch it,
For it engenders choler,² planteth anger,
And better 'twere that both of us did fast,
Since of ourselves° ourselves are choleric,   *by our natures*
155 Than feed it with such overroasted flesh.

---

8. Probably a fragment of a ballad, now lost, lamenting a newlywed's loss of freedom.
9. An expression of impatience.
1. Another fragment of a lost song, perhaps one of the many songs about a friar's seduction of a nun.
2. It causes anger. An excess of the choleric humor was believed to provoke anger.

Be patient, tomorrow't shall be mended,
And for this night we'll fast for company.°   together
Come, I will bring thee to thy bridal chamber.   *Exeunt*
    Enter servants severally
NATHANIEL   Peter, didst ever see the like?
160 PETER   He kills her in her own humour.[3]
    Enter CURTIS, *a servant*
GRUMIO   Where is he?
CURTIS   In her chamber,
Making a sermon of continency° to her,   on self-control
And rails, and swears, and rates,° that she, poor soul,   scolds
165 Knows not which way to stand, to look, to speak,
And sits as one new risen from a dream.
Away, away, for he is coming hither.   [*Exeunt*]
    Enter PETRUCCIO
PETRUCCIO   Thus have I politicly° begun my reign,   cunningly
And 'tis my hope to end successfully.
170 My falcon[4] now is sharp° and passing° empty,   hungry / extremely
And till she stoop[5] she must not be full-gorged,°   fully fed
For then she never looks upon her lure.°   falconer's bait
Another way I have to man my haggard,°   tame my female hawk
To make her come and know her keeper's call—
175 That is, to watch her° as we watch these kites°   keep her awake / hawks
That bate and beat,[6] and will not be obedient.
She ate no meat today, nor none shall eat.
Last night she slept not, nor tonight she shall not.
As with the meat, some undeservèd fault
180 I'll find about the making of the bed,
And here I'll fling the pillow, there the bolster,
This way the coverlet, another way the sheets,
Ay, and amid this hurly I intend°   will pretend
That all is done in reverent care of her,
185 And in conclusion she shall watch° all night,   stay awake
And if she chance to nod I'll rail and brawl
And with the clamour keep her still awake.
This is a way to kill a wife with kindness,
And thus I'll curb her mad and headstrong humour.
190 He that knows better how to tame a shrew,
Now let him speak. 'Tis charity to show.°   *Exit*   (his methods)

4.2

    Enter TRANIO [*as Lucentio,*] *and* HORTENSIO [*as Licio*]
TRANIO   Is't possible, friend Licio, that Mistress Bianca
Doth fancy any other but Lucentio?
I tell you, sir, she bears me fair in hand.°   leads me on
HORTENSIO   Sir, to satisfy you in what I have said,
5 Stand by, and mark the manner of his teaching.
    [*They stand aside.*]
    Enter BIANCA [*and* LUCENTIO *as Cambio*]
LUCENTIO   Now, mistress, profit you in what you read?
BIANCA   What, master, read you? First resolve° me that.   answer

---

3. He subdues her choleric humor by outdoing her in
bad temper.
4. In what follows, Petruccio likens his methods of dis-
ciplining Katherine to the training of a wild hawk.

5. Fly to the bait; submit to my authority.
6. That flutter and flap their wings (instead of settling
on the falconer's fist).
4.2 Location: Padua, in front of Baptista's house.

LUCENTIO I read that I profess,° *The Art to Love.*[1] *what I practice*
BIANCA And may you prove, sir, master of your art.
10 LUCENTIO While you, sweet dear, prove mistress of my heart.
    [*They stand aside*]
HORTENSIO Quick proceeders,[2] marry! Now tell me, I pray,
  You that durst swear that your mistress Bianca
  Loved none in the world so well as Lucentio.
TRANIO O despiteful° love, unconstant womankind! *cruel*
15 I tell thee, Licio, this is wonderful.° *astonishing*
HORTENSIO Mistake no more, I am not Licio,
  Nor a musician as I seem to be,
  But one that scorn to live in this disguise
  For such a one° as leaves a gentleman *(Bianca)*
20 And makes a god of such a cullion.° *base fellow*
  Know, sir, that I am called Hortensio.
TRANIO Signor Hortensio, I have often heard
  Of your entire° affection to Bianca, *sincere*
  And since mine eyes are witness of her lightness° *sexual infidelity*
25 I will with you, if you be so contented,
  Forswear Bianca and her love for ever.
HORTENSIO See how they kiss and court. Signor Lucentio,
  Here is my hand, and here I firmly vow
  Never to woo her more, but do forswear her
30 As one unworthy all the former favours
  That I have fondly° flattered her withal. *foolishly*
TRANIO And here I take the like unfeignèd oath
  Never to marry with her, though she would entreat.
  Fie on her, see how beastly° she doth court him! *lewdly*
35 HORTENSIO Would all the world but he had quite forsworn.[3]
  For me, that I may surely keep mine oath
  I will be married to a wealthy widow
  Ere three days pass, which hath as long loved me
  As I have loved this proud disdainful haggard.° *intractable woman; hawk*
40 And so farewell, Signor Lucentio.
  Kindness in women, not their beauteous looks,
  Shall win my love; and so I take my leave,
  In resolution as I swore before. [*Exit*]
TRANIO Mistress Bianca, bless you with such grace
45 As 'longeth° to a lover's blessèd case.° *belongs / state*
  Nay, I have ta'en you napping, gentle love,
  And have forsworn you with Hortensio.
BIANCA Tranio, you jest. But have you both forsworn me?
TRANIO Mistress, we have.
LUCENTIO   Then we are rid of Licio.
50 TRANIO I'faith, he'll have a lusty° widow now, *lively; lustful*
  That shall be wooed and wedded in a day.
BIANCA God give him joy.
TRANIO Ay, and he'll tame her.
BIANCA He says so, Tranio.
55 TRANIO Faith, he is gone unto the taming-school.

---

1. Ovid's *Ars Amatoria*, in which the poet calls himself the "Professor of Love" and treats erotic love as a science.
2. Taking up the allusion to a university degree implicit in Bianca's "master of your art," Hortensio puns on "proceeding" from a bachelor's to a master's degree.
3. I wish that everyone but Cambio had given her over (so that she will be left an old maid as she deserves; Hortensio apparently assumes that Bianca would never marry a poor musician).

BIANCA   The taming-school—what, is there such a place?
TRANIO   Ay, mistress, and Petruccio is the master,
        That teacheth tricks eleven-and-twenty long[4]
        To tame a shrew and charm her chattering tongue.[5]
            Enter BIONDELLO
60 BIONDELLO   O, master, master, I have watched so long
        That I am dog-weary, but at last I spied
        An ancient angel[6] coming down the hill
        Will serve the turn.
TRANIO   What is he, Biondello?
BIONDELLO   Master, a marcantant[7] or a pedant,°   schoolmaster
65   I know not what, but formal in apparel,
        In gait and countenance surely like a father.
LUCENTIO   And what of him, Tranio?
TRANIO   If he be credulous and trust my tale,
        I'll make him glad to seem° Vincentio   pretend to be
70   And give assurance to Baptista Minola
        As if he were the right Vincentio.
        Take in your love, and then let me alone.
                    [*Exeunt* LUCENTIO *and* BIANCA]
            Enter a PEDANT[8]
PEDANT   God save you, sir.
TRANIO   And you, sir. You are welcome.
        Travel you farre on, or are you at the farthest?
75 PEDANT   Sir, at the farthest for a week or two,
        But then up farther and as far as Rome,
        And so to Tripoli,[9] if God lend me life.
TRANIO   What countryman, I pray?
PEDANT   Of Mantua.
TRANIO   Of Mantua, sir? Marry, God forbid,
80   And come to Padua careless of your life!
PEDANT   My life, sir? How, I pray? For that goes hard.°   is difficult to deal with
TRANIO   'Tis death for anyone in Mantua
        To come to Padua. Know you not the cause?
        Your ships are stayed° at Venice, and the Duke,   detained
85   For private quarrel 'twixt your Duke and him,
        Hath published and proclaimed it openly.
        'Tis marvel, but that you are but newly come,
        You might have heard it else proclaimed about.[1]
PEDANT   Alas, sir, it is worse for me than so,°   my plight is even worse
90   For I have bills for money by exchange[2]
        From Florence, and must here deliver them.
TRANIO   Well, sir, to do you courtesy
        This will I do, and this I will advise you.
        First tell me, have you ever been at Pisa?
95 PEDANT   Ay, sir, in Pisa have I often been,

---

4. Who teaches tricks that are exactly appropriate or of just the right number. An allusion to the card game one-and-thirty, in which the object is to accumulate exactly thirty-one points. See note to 1.2.31.
5. Tranio's apparent knowledge of Hortensio's plans is puzzling and may be an indication that some text has been lost.
6. Worthy old man. Punning on "angel" as meaning both "valuable gold coin" and "divine messenger." The coin had a picture of the archangel Michael on it.

7. Biondello's version of *mercatante*, the Italian word for "merchant."
8. Because this character is said (at line 90) to have "bills for money," some editors have designated him a "merchant" like the corresponding character in George Gascoigne's comedy *Supposes* (1566).
9. The north African trading center or the city in Syria.
1. *but that . . . about:* if you hadn't just arrived, you would have heard it announced everywhere.
2. Promissory notes that the bearer could exchange for cash.

Pisa renownèd for grave citizens.

TRANIO   Among them know you one Vincentio?

PEDANT   I know him not, but I have heard of him,
A merchant of incomparable wealth.

100 TRANIO   He is my father, sir, and sooth to say,
In count'nance somewhat doth resemble you.

BIONDELLO [*aside*]   As much as an apple doth an oyster, and all
one.°   *but no matter*

TRANIO   To save your life in this extremity

105 This favour will I do you for his sake,
And think it not the worst of all your fortunes
That you are like to Sir Vincentio.
His name and credit° shall you undertake,°   *social status / assume*
And in my house you shall be friendly lodged.

110 Look that you take upon you° as you should.   *act your part*
You understand me, sir? So shall you stay
Till you have done your business in the city.
If this be courtesy, sir, accept of it.

PEDANT   O sir, I do, and will repute° you ever   *consider*

115 The patron of my life and liberty.

TRANIO   Then go with me to make the matter good.
This, by the way, I let you understand—
My father is here looked for every day
To pass assurance° of a dower in marriage   *convey legal guarantee*

120 'Twixt me and one Baptista's daughter here.
In all these circumstances I'll instruct you.
Go with me to clothe you as becomes you.   *Exeunt*

4.3

Enter KATHERINE *and* GRUMIO

GRUMIO   No, no, forsooth. I dare not, for my life.

KATHERINE   The more my wrong, the more his spite appears.[1]
What, did he marry me to famish me?
Beggars that come unto my father's door

5 Upon entreaty have a present° alms,   *immediate*
If not, elsewhere they meet with charity.
But I, who never knew how to entreat,
Nor never needed that I should entreat,
Am starved for meat, giddy for lack of sleep,

10 With oaths kept waking and with brawling fed,
And that which spites° me more than all these wants,   *vexes*
He does it under name of perfect love,
As who should say° if I should sleep or eat   *As if to say*
'Twere deadly sickness, or else present° death.   *instant*

15 I prithee, go and get me some repast.
I care not what, so it be wholesome food.

GRUMIO   What say you to a neat's foot?°   *ox foot or calf's foot*

KATHERINE   'Tis passing good. I prithee, let me have it.

GRUMIO   I fear it is too choleric° a meat.   *conducive to anger*

20 How say you to a fat tripe finely broiled?

KATHERINE   I like it well. Good Grumio, fetch it me.

GRUMIO   I cannot tell, I fear 'tis choleric.

4.3 Location: Petruccio's country house.
1. The more injustice I suffer, the more he seems to want me to suffer.

What say you to a piece of beef, and mustard?

KATHERINE A dish that I do love to feed upon.

25 GRUMIO Ay, but the mustard is too hot a little.

KATHERINE Why then, the beef, and let the mustard rest.

GRUMIO Nay, then I will not. You shall have the mustard,
Or else you get no beef of Grumio.

KATHERINE Then both, or one, or anything thou wilt.

30 GRUMIO Why then, the mustard without the beef.

KATHERINE Go, get thee gone, thou false, deluding slave,
        Beats him
That feed'st me with the very name° of meat.   *only the name*
Sorrow on thee and all the pack of you,
That triumph thus upon my misery.

35 Go, get thee gone, I say.
        Enter PETRUCCIO *and* HORTENSIO, *with meat*

PETRUCCIO How fares my Kate? What, sweeting,° all amort?°   *sweetheart / dejected*

HORTENSIO Mistress, what cheer?

KATHERINE   Faith, as cold as can be.

PETRUCCIO Pluck up thy spirits, look cheerfully upon me.
Here, love, thou seest how diligent I am

40 To dress° thy meat myself and bring it thee.   *prepare*
I am sure, sweet Kate, this kindness merits thanks.
What, not a word? Nay then, thou lov'st it not,
And all my pains is sorted to no proof.°   *are to no purpose*
Here, take away this dish.

KATHERINE   I pray you, let it stand.

45 PETRUCCIO The poorest service is repaid with thanks,
And so shall mine before you touch the meat.

KATHERINE I thank you, sir.

HORTENSIO Signor Petruccio, fie, you are to blame.
Come, Mistress Kate, I'll bear you company.

50 PETRUCCIO [*aside*] Eat it up all, Hortensio, if thou lov'st me.
[*To* KATHERINE] Much good do it unto thy gentle heart.
Kate, eat apace; and now, my honey love,
Will we return unto thy father's house,
And revel it as bravely as the best,

55 With silken coats, and caps, and golden rings,
With ruffs, and cuffs, and farthingales,² and things,
With scarves, and fans, and double change of bravery,°   *finery*
With amber bracelets, beads, and all this knavery.°   *tricks of dress*
What, hast thou dined? The tailor stays thy leisure,

60 To deck thy body with his ruffling° treasure.   *ornate (with ruffles)*
        Enter TAILOR [*with a gown*]
Come, tailor, let us see these ornaments.
Lay forth the gown.
        Enter HABERDASHER [*with a cap*]
            What news with you, sir?

HABERDASHER Here is the cap your worship did bespeak.

PETRUCCIO Why, this was moulded on a porringer°—   *porridge bowl*

65 A velvet dish.³ Fie, fie, 'tis lewd and filthy.
Why, 'tis a cockle° or a walnut-shell,   *mollusk shell*

---

2. *ruffs:* fashionable high collars made of starched linen or lace. *cuffs:* bands, often made of lace, sewn onto sleeves for ornament. *farthingales:* hooped petticoats.

3. It's merely a dish made of velvet. Velvet caps were often associated with prostitutes.

A knack,° a toy, a trick,° a baby's cap. *knickknack / trifle*
Away with it! Come, let me have a bigger.
KATHERINE   I'll have no bigger. This doth fit the time,° *suit current fashion*
70   And gentlewomen wear such caps as these.
PETRUCCIO   When you are gentle you shall have one, too,
And not till then.
HORTENSIO [*aside*]   That will not be in haste.
KATHERINE   Why, sir, I trust I may have leave to speak,
And speak I will. I am no child, no babe.
75   Your betters have endured me say my mind,
And if you cannot, best you stop your ears.
My tongue will tell the anger of my heart,
Or else my heart concealing it will break,
And rather than it shall I will be free
80   Even to the uttermost as I please in words.
PETRUCCIO   Why, thou sayst true. It is a paltry cap,
A custard-coffin,[4] a bauble, a silken pie.
I love thee well in that thou lik'st it not.
KATHERINE   Love me or love me not, I like the cap
85   And it I will have, or I will have none.   [*Exit* HABERDASHER]
PETRUCCIO   Thy gown? Why, ay. Come, tailor, let us see't.
O mercy, God, what masquing stuff[5] is here?
What's this—a sleeve? 'Tis like a demi-cannon.° *large cannon*
What, up and down carved like an apple-tart?[6]
90   Here's snip, and nip, and cut, and slish and slash,
Like to a scissor in a barber's shop.
Why, what i'° devil's name, tailor, call'st thou this? *in the*
HORTENSIO [*aside*]   I see she's like° to have nor cap nor gown. *likely*
TAILOR   You bid me make it orderly and well,
95   According to the fashion and the time.
PETRUCCIO   Marry, and did,° but if you be remembered *Indeed I did*
I did not bid you mar it to the time.
Go hop me[7] over every kennel° home, *gutter*
For you shall hop without my custom,° sir. *patronage; business*
100   I'll none of it. Hence, make your best of it.
KATHERINE   I never saw a better fashioned gown,
More quaint,° more pleasing, nor more commendable. *elegant*
Belike° you mean to make a puppet of me. *It seems*
PETRUCCIO   Why true, he means to make a puppet of thee.
105   TAILOR   She says your worship means to make a puppet of her.
PETRUCCIO   O monstrous arrogance! Thou liest, thou thread,
          thou thimble,
Thou yard, three-quarters, half-yard, quarter, nail,[8]
Thou flea, thou nit,° thou winter-cricket, thou. *egg of a louse*
Braved° in mine own house with° a skein of thread! *Defied; adorned / by*
110   Away, thou rag, thou quantity,° thou remnant, *fragment*
Or I shall so bemete° thee with thy yard° *measure; beat / ruler*
As thou shalt think on prating[9] whilst thou liv'st.
I tell thee, I, that thou hast marred her gown.

---

4. Pastry crust around a custard or open pie (perhaps
with a pun on "costard," slang for "head").
5. Extravagant clothing suitable for theatrical masques.
6. With slits like the top of an apple pie. The gown's
sleeves may have been designed so as to reveal fabric of
another color underneath.

7. You can go hopping.
8. Measure of cloth, a sixteenth of a yard; Petruccio is
literally belittling the tailor. "Yard" is slang for "penis."
9. You will think twice before you talk idly, with a pun
on "prat" as slang for "beat on the buttocks."

TAILOR	Your worship is deceived. The gown is made	
115	Just as my master had direction.	
	Grumio gave order how it should be done.	
GRUMIO	I gave him no order, I gave him the stuff.°	material
TAILOR	But how did you desire it should be made?	
GRUMIO	Marry, sir, with needle and thread.	
120 TAILOR	But did you not request to have it cut?	
GRUMIO	Thou hast faced° many things.	trimmed; defied
TAILOR	I have.	
GRUMIO	Face not me. Thou hast braved° many men. Brave°	dressed finely / Defy
	not me. I will neither be faced nor braved. I say unto thee	
125	I bid thy master cut out the gown, but I did not bid him cut it	
	to pieces. Ergo° thou liest.	Therefore
TAILOR	[showing a paper] Why, here is the note of the fashion,	
	to testify.	
PETRUCCIO	Read it.	
130 GRUMIO	The note lies in's throat if he° say I said so.	it
TAILOR	[reads] 'Imprimis,° a loose-bodied gown.'¹	First
GRUMIO	Master, if ever I said loose-bodied gown, sew me in the	
	skirts of it and beat me to death with a bottom° of brown	spool
	thread. I said a gown.	
135 PETRUCCIO	Proceed.	
TAILOR	[reads] 'With a small compassed° cape.'	flared
GRUMIO	I confess the cape.	
TAILOR	[reads] 'With a trunk° sleeve.'	wide
GRUMIO	I confess two sleeves.	
140 TAILOR	[reads] 'The sleeves curiously° cut.'	carefully; elaborately
PETRUCCIO	Ay, there's the villany.	
GRUMIO	Error i'th' bill,° sir, error i'th' bill. I commanded the	order (for the dress)
	sleeves should be cut out and sewed up again, and that I'll	
	prove upon thee though thy little finger be armed in a thimble.	
145 TAILOR	This is true that I say. An° I had thee in place where,°	If / in a suitable place
	thou shouldst know it.	
GRUMIO	I am for thee straight. Take thou the bill,² give me thy	
	mete-yard,° and spare not me.	yardstick
HORTENSIO	Godamercy, Grumio, then he shall have no odds.°	advantage
150 PETRUCCIO	Well, sir, in brief, the gown is not for me.	
GRUMIO	You are i'th' right, sir. 'Tis for my mistress.	
PETRUCCIO	[to the TAILOR] Go, take it up unto° thy master's use.	take it away for
GRUMIO	[to the TAILOR] Villain, not for thy life. Take up my	
	mistress' gown for thy master's use!°	sexual purposes
155 PETRUCCIO	Why, sir, what's your conceit° in that?	meaning
GRUMIO	O, sir, the conceit is deeper than you think for. 'Take	
	up my mistress' gown to his master's use'—O fie, fie, fie!	
PETRUCCIO	[aside] Hortensio, say thou wilt see the tailor paid.	
	[To the TAILOR] Go, take it hence. Be gone, and say no more.	
HORTENSIO	[aside to the TAILOR] Tailor, I'll pay thee for thy	
160	gown tomorrow.	
	Take no unkindness of his hasty words.	
	Away, I say. Commend me to thy master. Exit TAILOR	
PETRUCCIO	Well, come, my Kate. We will unto your father's	
	Even in these honest, mean habiliments.	

---

1. A loose-fitting dress. In the next line, Grumio takes this
to mean a dress suitable for a wanton, or loose, woman.

2. Grumio puns on "bill" as also meaning a "weapon" or
"halberd," a staff with a blade attached.

165 Our purses shall be proud, our garments poor,
For 'tis the mind that makes the body rich,
And as the sun breaks through the darkest clouds,
So honour peereth° in the meanest habit.   *can be seen*
What, is the jay more precious than the lark
170 Because his feathers are more beautiful?
Or is the adder better than the eel
Because his painted skin contents the eye?
O no, good Kate, neither art thou the worse
For this poor furniture° and mean array.   *clothing; attire*
175 If thou account'st it shame, lay it on me,°   *blame me*
And therefore frolic; we will hence forthwith
To feast and sport us° at thy father's house.   *amuse ourselves*
Go call my men, and let us straight to him,
And bring our horses unto Long Lane end.
180 There will we mount, and thither walk on foot.
Let's see, I think 'tis now some seven o'clock,
And well we may come there by dinner-time.°   *about noon*
KATHERINE   I dare assure you, sir, 'tis almost two,
And 'twill be supper-time° ere you come there.   *about 6 P.M.*
185 PETRUCCIO   It shall be seven ere I go to horse.
Look what I speak, or do, or think to do,
You are still crossing° it. Sirs, let't alone.   *contradicting*
I will not go today, and ere I do
It shall be what o'clock I say it is.
190 HORTENSIO [*aside*]   Why, so this gallant will command the sun.
                                                              [*Exeunt*]

4.4

Enter TRANIO [*as Lucentio,*] *and the* PEDANT *dressed
like Vincentio, booted and bare-headed*[1]

TRANIO   Sir, this is the house. Please it you that I call?
PEDANT   Ay, what else. And but[2] I be deceived,
Signor Baptista may remember me
Near twenty years ago in Genoa—
5 TRANIO   Where we were lodgers at the Pegasus.[3]—
'Tis well, and hold your own° in any case   *keep to your role*
With such austerity as 'longeth° to a father.   *belongs*
Enter BIONDELLO
PEDANT   I warrant you. But sir, here comes your boy.
'Twere good he were schooled.
10 TRANIO   Fear you not him. Sirrah Biondello,
Now do your duty throughly,° I advise you.   *thoroughly*
Imagine 'twere the right Vincentio.
BIONDELLO   Tut, fear not me.
TRANIO   But hast thou done thy errand to Baptista?
15 BIONDELLO   I told him that your father was at Venice
And that you looked for him this day in Padua.

4.4 Location: Padua. In front of Baptista's house.
1. In F, the Pedant is mistakenly given a second entry
at line 18, where he is described as "booted and bare-
headed," indicating that he is dressed for travel but has
taken off his hat, perhaps in deference to Baptista,
whom he is about to meet. The present stage direction

conflates F's two stage directions regarding the Pedant's
entrance.
2. Unless (the Pedant is rehearsing his speech to
Baptista).
3. Common name for an inn (marked by a sign of the
flying horse of classical mythology).

TRANIO [*giving money*] Thou'rt a tall° fellow. Hold thee° that   *worthy / Take*
    to° drink.   *for*
    Here comes Baptista. Set your countenance, sir.
        Enter BAPTISTA, *and* LUCENTIO [*as Cambio*]
TRANIO   Signor Baptista, you are happily met.
20   [*To the* PEDANT] Sir, this is the gentleman I told you of.
    I pray you stand good father to me now.
    Give me Bianca for my patrimony.
PEDANT   Soft,° son. [*To* BAPTISTA] Sir, by your leave, having   *Just a moment*
    come to Padua
    To gather in some debts, my son Lucentio
25   Made me acquainted with a weighty cause
    Of love between your daughter and himself,
    And for the good report I hear of you,
    And for the love he beareth to your daughter,
    And she to him, to stay him° not too long   *keep him waiting*
30   I am content in a good father's care⁴
    To have him matched, and if you please to like
    No worse than I, upon some agreement
    Me shall you find ready and willing
    With one consent to have her so bestowed,
35   For curious° I cannot be with you,   *overly particular*
    Signor Baptista, of whom I hear so well.
BAPTISTA   Sir, pardon me in what I have to say.
    Your plainness and your shortness please me well.
    Right true it is your son Lucentio here
40   Doth love my daughter, and she loveth him,
    Or both dissemble deeply their affections.
    And therefore if you say no more than this,
    That like a father you will deal with him
    And pass° my daughter a sufficient dower,   *grant*
45   The match is made, and all is done.
    Your son shall have my daughter with consent.
TRANIO   I thank you, sir. Where then do you know best
    We be affied,° and such assurance ta'en   *betrothed*
    As shall with either part's agreement stand?⁵
50 BAPTISTA   Not in my house, Lucentio, for you know
    Pitchers have ears,⁶ and I have many servants.
    Besides, old Gremio is heark'ning still,°   *always listening*
    And happily° we might be interrupted.   *perhaps*
TRANIO   Then at my lodging, an it like you.°   *if it please you*
55   There doth my father lie,° and there this night   *lodge*
    We'll pass° the business privately and well.   *settle*
    Send for your daughter by your servant here.
    My boy shall fetch the scrivener° presently.   *scribe; notary*
    The worst is this, that at so slender warning
60   You are like to have a thin and slender pittance.°   *scanty meal*
BAPTISTA   It likes me well. Cambio, hie° you home   *hurry*
    And bid Bianca make her ready straight,
    And if you will, tell what hath happened—
    Lucentio's father is arrived in Padua—

---

4. Content with the care that should be shown by a
good father.
5. As shall confirm the agreements of both parties.

6. Proverbial for "Someone may be eavesdropping."
The handles of a pitcher are its "ears."

65 And how she's like to be Lucentio's wife.   [*Exit* LUCENTIO][7]
BIONDELLO   I pray the gods she may with all my heart.
TRANIO   Dally not with the gods, but get thee gone.

Exit [BIONDELLO][8]

Signor Baptista, shall I lead the way?
Welcome. One mess° is like to be your cheer.°   dish / entertainment
70 Come, sir, we will better it in Pisa.
BAPTISTA   I follow you.   *Exeunt*

4.5

Enter LUCENTIO *and* BIONDELLO

BIONDELLO   Cambio.
LUCENTIO   What sayst thou, Biondello?
BIONDELLO   You saw my master wink and laugh upon you?
LUCENTIO   Biondello, what of that?
5 BIONDELLO   Faith, nothing, but he's left me here behind to
expound the meaning or moral of his signs and tokens.
LUCENTIO   I pray thee, moralize° them.   interpret
BIONDELLO   Then thus: Baptista is safe, talking with the deceiving father of a deceitful son.
10 LUCENTIO   And what of him?
BIONDELLO   His daughter is to be brought by you to the supper.
LUCENTIO   And then?
BIONDELLO   The old priest at Saint Luke's church is at your
command at all hours.
15 LUCENTIO   And what of all this?
BIONDELLO   I cannot tell, except they are busied about a coun-
terfeit assurance.° Take you assurance[1] of her *cum privilegio*   betrothal agreement
ad imprimendum solum[2]—to th' church take the priest, clerk,
and some sufficient honest witnesses.
20 If this be not that you look for, I have no more to say,
But bid Bianca farewell for ever and a day.
LUCENTIO   Hear'st thou, Biondello?
BIONDELLO   I cannot tarry, I knew a wench married in an afternoon as she went to the garden for parsley to stuff a rabbit,
25 and so may you, sir, and so adieu, sir. My master hath
appointed me to go to Saint Luke's to bid the priest be ready
t'attend against° you come with your appendix.[3]   *Exit*   by the time
LUCENTIO   I may and will, if she be so contented.
She will be pleased, then wherefore should I doubt?
30 Hap what hap may, I'll roundly go about her.[4]
It shall go hard° if Cambio go without her.   *Exit*[5]   be unfortunate

---

7. F does not mark an exit for Lucentio/Cambio here,
but it makes sense that he would follow Baptista's
order. If Lucentio exits here and Biondello at line 66 as
in F, or at line 67 as in this text, then their reentry a few
lines later can mark a new scene (see Textual Note).
Some editors assume Biondello and perhaps Lucentio
never leave the stage since Biondello says (at 4.5.5–6)
that he has been left behind by Tranio to explain things
to Lucentio. In that case, no scene break would be
introduced after Baptista exits.
8. F here has a mysterious stage direction: "Enter
Peter." Some editors have argued that this is the name
of an actor inadvertently introduced into the stage directions. Others assume it is the name of one of Lucentio's
servants, who enters to tell the disguised Tranio and
Baptista that their meal is ready; this possibility is not

entirely satisfactory, especially since Baptista and Tranio
still have to *proceed* to Lucentio's house for their meal.
Perhaps something has been lost or garbled in this portion of the scene.
4.5 Location: Scene continues.
1. Make yourself sure.
2. With the exclusive right to print (a Latin phrase used
by printers on the title pages of their books). Biondello
urges Lucentio to confirm his "exclusive right" to
Bianca and may be punning on "print" as meaning
"to father a child."
3. Appendage (the bride).
4. Come what may, I'll pursue her eagerly.
5. At the corresponding point in A *Shrew*, Sly, still
on-stage, comments on the action. See Additional Passages B.

4.6

Enter PETRUCCIO, KATHERINE, HORTENSIO [*and servants*]

PETRUCCIO   Come on, i' God's name. Once more toward our father's.
Good Lord, how bright and goodly shines the moon!

KATHERINE   The moon?—the sun. It is not moonlight now.

PETRUCCIO   I say it is the moon that shines so bright.

5   KATHERINE   I know it is the sun that shines so bright.

PETRUCCIO   Now, by my mother's son—and that's myself—
It shall be moon, or star, or what I list°   *please*
Or ere° I journey to your father's house.   *Before*
Go on, and fetch our horses back again.

10   Evermore crossed° and crossed, nothing but crossed.   *contradicted*

HORTENSIO [TO KATHERINE]   Say as he says or we shall never go.

KATHERINE   Forward, I pray, since we have come so far,
And be it moon or sun or what you please,
And if you please to call it a rush-candle[1]

15   Henceforth I vow it shall be so for me.

PETRUCCIO   I say it is the moon.

KATHERINE   I know it is the moon.

PETRUCCIO   Nay then you lie, it is the blessèd sun.

KATHERINE   Then God be blessed, it is the blessèd sun,

20   But sun it is not when you say it is not,
And the moon changes even as your mind.[2]
What you will have it named, even that it is,
And so it shall be still for Katherine.

HORTENSIO   Petruccio, go thy ways.° The field is won.   *do as you wish*

25   PETRUCCIO   Well, forward, forward. Thus the bowl should run,
And not unluckily against the bias.[3]
But soft, company is coming here.

        Enter [*old*] VINCENTIO

[*To* VINCENTIO] Good morrow, gentle mistress, where away?
Tell me, sweet Kate, and tell me truly too,

30   Hast thou beheld a fresher gentlewoman,
Such war of white and red within her cheeks?
What stars do spangle heaven with such beauty
As those two eyes become that heavenly face?
Fair lovely maid, once more good day to thee.

35   Sweet Kate, embrace her for her beauty's sake.

HORTENSIO   A° will make the man mad to make the woman of   *He*
him.°   *call him a woman*

KATHERINE   Young budding virgin, fair, and fresh, and sweet,
Whither away, or where is thy abode?

40   Happy the parents of so fair a child,
Happier the man whom° favourable stars   *to whom*
Allots thee for his lovely bedfellow.

PETRUCCIO   Why, how now, Kate, I hope thou art not mad.
This is a man, old, wrinkled, faded, withered,

45   And not a maiden as thou sayst he is.

KATHERINE   Pardon, old father, my mistaking eyes

4.6 Location: A road somewhere between Petruccio's
house and Padua.
1. Candle made from rush dripped in grease, thus giving poor light.
2. Implying that Petruccio is mad as well as fickle.

Lunatics and women were imagined to be governed by
the moon.
3. A metaphor from the game of bowls in which the
ball, or bowl, was weighted so that it ran along a "bias,"
or curving path.

That have been so bedazzled with the sun
That everything I look on seemeth green.°   *youthful*
Now I perceive thou art a reverend father.
50   Pardon, I pray thee, for my mad mistaking.
PETRUCCIO   Do, good old grandsire, and withal° make known   *in addition*
Which way thou travell'st. If along with us,
We shall be joyful of thy company.
VINCENTIO   Fair sir, and you, my merry mistress,
55   That with your strange encounter° much amazed me,   *greeting*
My name is called Vincentio, my dwelling Pisa,
And bound I am to Padua, there to visit
A son of mine which long I have not seen.
PETRUCCIO   What is his name?
VINCENTIO   Lucentio, gentle sir.
60   PETRUCCIO   Happily met, the happier for thy son.
And now by law as well as reverend age
I may entitle thee my loving father.
The sister to my wife, this gentlewoman,
Thy son by this hath married.⁴ Wonder not,
65   Nor be not grieved. She is of good esteem,
Her dowry wealthy, and of worthy birth,
Beside, so qualified° as may beseem   *with such qualities*
The spouse of any noble gentleman.
Let me embrace with old Vincentio,
70   And wander we to see thy honest son,
Who will of thy arrival be full joyous.
        [*He embraces* VINCENTIO]
VINCENTIO   But is this true, or is it else your pleasure
Like pleasant travellers to break a jest°   *crack a joke*
Upon the company you overtake?
75   HORTENSIO   I do assure thee, father, so it is.
PETRUCCIO   Come, go along, and see the truth hereof,
For our first merriment hath made thee jealous.°   *suspicious*
                Exeunt [*all but* HORTENSIO]
HORTENSIO   Well, Petruccio, this has put me in heart.
Have to my widow, and if she be froward,°   *difficult*
80   Then hast thou taught Hortensio to be untoward.° *Exit*   *unmannerly*

5.1

Enter BIONDELLO, LUCENTIO, *and* BIANCA. GREMIO
is out before°   *Gremio enters first*
BIONDELLO   Softly and swiftly, sir, for the priest is ready.
LUCENTIO   I fly, Biondello; but they may chance to need thee at
home, therefore leave us.
BIONDELLO   Nay, faith, I'll see the church a' your back¹ and then
5   come back to my master's as soon as I can.
            Exeunt [LUCENTIO, BIANCA, *and* BIONDELLO]²
GREMIO   I marvel Cambio comes not all this while.

---

4. By now has married. It is unclear how Petruccio and
Hortensio know this, especially since Hortensio has
heard "Lucentio" (Tranio) forswear Bianca (in 4.2).
The inconsistency may suggest textual alteration in the
role of Hortensio.
5.1 Location: Padua, in front of Lucentio's house.
1. At your back. Probably, I'll see the church as you

leave it after the wedding.
2. In F, Lucentio and Bianca exit first (after line 3)
and Biondello presumably follows after line 5, though
no exit is explicitly marked for him. Gremio, onstage
before this trio, apparently does not see them stealing
away to the church.

Enter PETRUCCIO, KATHERINE, VINCENTIO, GRUMIO,
with attendants

PETRUCCIO   Sir, here's the door. This is Lucentio's house.
My father's bears° more toward the market-place.   lies
Thither must I, and here I leave you, sir.

10   VINCENTIO   You shall not choose but drink before you go.
I think I shall command your welcome here,
And by all likelihood some cheer is toward.°   food is being prepared
[*He*] *knocks*

GREMIO   They're busy within. You were best knock louder.
[VINCENTIO *knocks again. The*] PEDANT *looks out
of the window*

PEDANT   What's he that knocks as he would beat down the gate?

15   VINCENTIO   Is Signor Lucentio within, sir?

PEDANT   He's within, sir, but not to be spoken withal.

VINCENTIO   What if a man bring him a hundred pound or two
to make merry withal?

PEDANT   Keep your hundred pounds to yourself. He shall need

20   none so long as I live.

PETRUCCIO [*to* VINCENTIO]   Nay, I told you your son was well
beloved in Padua. [*To the* PEDANT] Do you hear, sir, to leave
frivolous circumstances,° I pray you tell Signor Lucentio that   matters
his father is come from Pisa and is here at the door to speak

25   with him.

PEDANT   Thou liest. His father is come from Padua and here
looking out at the window.

VINCENTIO   Art thou his father?

PEDANT   Ay, sir, so his mother says, if I may believe her.

30   PETRUCCIO [*to* VINCENTIO]   Why, how now, gentleman? Why,
this is flat knavery, to take upon you another man's name.

PEDANT   Lay hands on the villain. I believe a° means to cozen°   he / cheat
somebody in this city under my countenance.°   name; person
Enter BIONDELLO

BIONDELLO [*aside*]   I have seen them in the church together,

35   God send 'em good shipping.° But who is here? Mine old mas-   fair sailing
ter, Vincentio—now we are undone and brought to nothing.

VINCENTIO [*to* BIONDELLO]   Come hither, crackhemp.[3]

BIONDELLO   I hope I may choose, sir.

VINCENTIO   Come hither, you rogue. What, have you forgot me?

40   BIONDELLO   Forgot you? No, sir, I could not forget you, for
I never saw you before in all my life.

VINCENTIO   What, you notorious villain, didst thou never see
thy master's father, Vincentio?

BIONDELLO   What, my old worshipful old master? Yes, marry,

45   sir, see where he looks out of the window.

VINCENTIO   Is't so indeed?
He beats BIONDELLO

BIONDELLO   Help, help, help! Here's a madman will murder me.
[*Exit*]

PEDANT   Help, son! Help, Signor Baptista!   [*Exit above*]

PETRUCCIO   Prithee, Kate, let's stand aside and see the end of

50   this controversy.
[*They stand aside.*]

---

3. Rogue (deserving to stretch the hangman's hemp rope).

Enter PEDANT *with servants,* BAPTISTA, TRANIO [*as Lucentio*]

TRANIO [*to* VINCENTIO] Sir, what are you that offer° to beat my   *presume*
servant?

VINCENTIO What am I, sir? Nay, what are you, sir? O immortal
gods, O fine villain, a silken doublet, a velvet hose, a scarlet

55   cloak, and a copintank° hat—O, I am undone, I am undone!   *high-crowned*
While I play the good husband at home, my son and my ser-
vant spend all at the university.

TRANIO How now, what's the matter?

BAPTISTA What, is the man lunatic?

60 TRANIO Sir, you seem a sober, ancient gentleman by your habit,
but your words show you a madman. Why sir, what 'cerns° it   *concerns*
you if I wear pearl and gold? I thank my good father, I am able
to maintain it.

VINCENTIO Thy father! O villain, he is a sailmaker in Bergamo.[4]

65 BAPTISTA You mistake, sir, you mistake, sir. Pray what do you
think is his name?

VINCENTIO His name? As if I knew not his name—I have
brought him up ever since he was three years old, and his
name is Tranio.

70 PEDANT Away, away, mad ass. His name is Lucentio, and he is
mine only son, and heir to the lands of me, Signor Vincentio.

VINCENTIO Lucentio? O, he hath murdered his master! Lay
hold on him, I charge you, in the Duke's name. O my son, my
son! Tell me, thou villain, where is my son Lucentio?

75 TRANIO Call forth an officer.
[*Enter an* OFFICER]
Carry this mad knave to the jail. Father Baptista, I charge you
see that he be forthcoming.°   *available when needed*

VINCENTIO Carry me to the jail?

GREMIO Stay, officer, he shall not go to prison.

80 BAPTISTA Talk not, Signor Gremio. I say he shall go to prison.

GREMIO Take heed, Signor Baptista, lest you be cony-catched°   *duped*
in this business. I dare swear this is the right Vincentio.

PEDANT Swear if thou dar'st.

GREMIO Nay, I dare not swear it.

85 TRANIO Then thou wert best say that I am not Lucentio.

GREMIO Yes, I know thee to be Signor Lucentio.

BAPTISTA Away with the dotard. To the jail with him.
Enter BIONDELLO, LUCENTIO, *and* BIANCA

VINCENTIO Thus strangers may be haled° and abused. O mon-   *dragged about*
strous villain!

90 BIONDELLO O, we are spoiled and—yonder he is. Deny him,
forswear him, or else we are all undone.
Exeunt BIONDELLO, TRANIO, *and* PEDANT, *as fast as may be*

LUCENTIO [*to* VINCENTIO] Pardon, sweet father.
[*He*] *kneels*

VINCENTIO Lives my sweet son?

BIANCA [*to* BAPTISTA] Pardon, dear father.

95 BAPTISTA How hast thou offended? Where is Lucentio?

LUCENTIO Here's Lucentio, right son to the right Vincentio,
That have by marriage made thy daughter mine,

---

4. An Italian town associated with Harlequin, the witty, resourceful servant of the Italian commedia dell'arte.

While counterfeit supposes[5] bleared thine eyne.°   *deceived your eyes*
GREMIO   Here's packing° with a witness,[6] to deceive us all.   *plotting*
100 VINCENTIO   Where is that damnèd villain Tranio,
That faced and braved° me in this matter so?   *defied*
BAPTISTA   Why, tell me, is not this my Cambio?
BIANCA   Cambio is changed into Lucentio.
LUCENTIO   Love wrought these miracles. Bianca's love
105 Made me exchange my state° with Tranio   *social position*
While he did bear my countenance in the town,
And happily I have arrived at the last
Unto the wishèd haven of my bliss.
What Tranio did, myself enforced him to.
110 Then pardon him, sweet father, for my sake.
VINCENTIO   I'll slit the villain's nose that would have sent me to
the jail.
BAPTISTA   But do you hear, sir, have you married my daughter
without asking my good will?
115 VINCENTIO   Fear not, Baptista. We will content you. Go to, but
I will in to be revenged for this villainy.   *Exit*
BAPTISTA   And I to sound the depth° of this knavery.   *Exit*   *discover the extent*
LUCENTIO   Look not pale, Bianca. Thy father will not frown.
                    Exeunt [LUCENTIO *and* BIANCA]
GREMIO   My cake is dough,[7] but I'll in among the rest, Out of
120 hope of all° but my share of the feast.   [*Exit*]   *With hope of nothing*
KATHERINE [*coming forward*]   Husband, let's follow to see the
end of this ado.
PETRUCCIO   First kiss me, Kate, and we will.
KATHERINE   What, in the midst of the street?
125 PETRUCCIO   What, art thou ashamed of me?
KATHERINE   No, sir, God forbid; but ashamed to kiss.
PETRUCCIO   Why then, let's home again. Come sirrah, let's away.
KATHERINE   Nay, I will give thee a kiss. Now pray thee love, stay.
                    [*They kiss*]
PETRUCCIO   Is not this well? Come, my sweet Kate.
130 Better once than never, for never too late.[8]   *Exeunt*

5.2

Enter BAPTISTA, VINCENTIO, GREMIO, *the* PEDANT,
LUCENTIO *and* BIANCA, [PETRUCCIO, KATHERINE,
and HORTENSIO,] TRANIO, BIONDELLO, GRUMIO, *and*
[*the*] WIDOW, *the servingmen with* TRANIO *bringing
in a banquet*[1]

LUCENTIO   At last, though long,° our jarring notes agree,   *after a long time*
And time it is when raging war is done
To smile at scapes° and perils overblown.   *escapes*
My fair Bianca, bid my father welcome,
While I with selfsame kindness welcome thine.
5   Brother Petruccio, sister Katherina,
And thou, Hortensio, with thy loving widow,
Feast with the best, and welcome to my house.

---

5. False ideas. Possibly an illusion to Gascoigne's *Sup-*
poses (1566), which was Shakespeare's main source for
the Bianca and Lucentio plot.
6. With clear evidence; without any doubt.
7. Proverbial expression for a failed project.

8. Two proverbs combined: "Better late than never"
and "It is never too late to mend."
5.2 Location: Lucentio's house in Padua.
1. Light meal of fruit, sweetmeats, and wine following
the main meal.

	My banquet is to close our stomachs up	
10	After our great good cheer.° Pray you, sit down,	*feast; happiness*
	For now we sit to chat as well as eat.	
	[*They sit*]	

PETRUCCIO Nothing but sit, and sit, and eat, and eat.

BAPTISTA Padua affords this kindness, son Petruccio.

PETRUCCIO Padua affords nothing but what is kind.

15 HORTENSIO For both our sakes I would that word were true.

PETRUCCIO Now, for my life, Hortensio fears[2] his widow.

WIDOW Then never trust me if I be afeard.°   *afraid*

PETRUCCIO You are very sensible, and yet you miss my sense.
I mean Hortensio is afeard of you.

20 WIDOW He that is giddy thinks the world turns round.[3]

PETRUCCIO Roundly° replied.   *Boldly*

KATHERINE Mistress, how mean you that?

WIDOW Thus I conceive by him.[4]

PETRUCCIO Conceives° by me! How likes Hortensio that?   *Becomes pregnant*

25 HORTENSIO My widow says thus she conceives her tale.[5]

PETRUCCIO Very well mended. Kiss him for that, good widow.

KATHERINE 'He that is giddy thinks the world turns round'—
I pray you tell me what you meant by that.

WIDOW Your husband, being troubled with a shrew,

30 Measures my husband's sorrow by his woe.
And now you know my meaning.

KATHERINE A very mean meaning.

WIDOW   Right, I mean you.

KATHERINE And I am mean indeed respecting you.[6]

PETRUCCIO To her, Kate!

35 HORTENSIO To her, widow!

PETRUCCIO A hundred marks[7] my Kate does put her down.°   *defeat her*

HORTENSIO That's my office.[8]

PETRUCCIO Spoke like an officer![9] Ha' to thee,° lad.   *Here's to you*
[*He*] *drinks to* HORTENSIO

BAPTISTA How likes Gremio these quick-witted folks?

40 GREMIO Believe me, sir, they butt together[1] well.

BIANCA Head and butt? An hasty-witted body
Would say your head and butt were head and horn.[2]

VINCENTIO Ay, mistress bride, hath that awakened you?

BIANCA Ay, but not frighted me, therefore I'll sleep again.

45 PETRUCCIO Nay, that you shall not. Since you have begun,
Have at° you for a better jest or two.   *I shall come at*

BIANCA Am I your bird? I mean to shift my bush,[3]
And then pursue me as you draw your bow.
You are welcome all.

Exit BIANCA [*with* KATHERINE *and the* WIDOW]

2. Is afraid of. The widow takes it to mean "frightens."
3. That is, people judge everything by their own experience, implying that Petruccio is afraid of his wife.
4. Thus I understand him.
5. Thus she understands or intends her remark, with a pun on "tail" as meaning "genitalia."
6. I am moderate (like the mathematical "mean") compared with you; I demean myself in dealing with you.
7. A substantial wager, since 1 mark was equivalent to 13 shillings and 4 pence, or two-thirds of a pound. An unskilled laborer might earn £6 to £8 in a year.

8. That's my job, with a pun on "put her down" as meaning "force or lay her down in sexual intercourse."
9. Like one who knows his duty.
1. They thrust their heads or horns together, with a pun on "butt" as meaning "buttocks."
2. Would say your butting head was a cuckold's horned head.
3. Alluding to the Elizabethan sport of shooting sitting birds with a bow and arrow. There may also be a bawdy pun on "bush" as meaning "pubic area" and the target of Petruccio's (phallic) arrow.

50 PETRUCCIO She hath prevented° me here, Signor Tranio.   *stopped; anticipated*
This bird you aimed at, though you hit her not.
Therefore a health to all that shot and missed.
TRANIO O sir, Lucentio slipped° me like his greyhound,   *unleashed*
Which runs himself and catches for his master.
55 PETRUCCIO A good swift° simile, but something currish.°   *witty/base; doglike*
TRANIO 'Tis well, sir, that you hunted for yourself.
'Tis thought your deer does hold you at a bay.[4]
BAPTISTA O, O, Petruccio, Tranio hits you now.
LUCENTIO I thank thee for that gird,° good Tranio.   *taunt*
60 HORTENSIO Confess, confess, hath he not hit you here?
PETRUCCIO A° has a little galled° me, I confess,   *He/wounded*
And as the jest did glance away from me,
'Tis ten to one it maimed you two outright.
BAPTISTA Now in good sadness,° son Petruccio,   *in all seriousness*
65 I think thou hast the veriest shrew of all.
PETRUCCIO Well, I say no.—And therefore, Sir Assurance,
Let's each one send unto° his wife,   *summon*
And he whose wife is most obedient
To come at first when he doth send for her
70 Shall win the wager which we will propose.
HORTENSIO Content.° What's the wager?   *Agreed*
LUCENTIO Twenty crowns.°   *coin worth 5 shillings*
PETRUCCIO Twenty crowns!
I'll venture so much of° my hawk or hound,   *on*
75 But twenty times so much upon my wife.
LUCENTIO A hundred, then.
HORTENSIO Content.
PETRUCCIO A match,° 'tis done.   *Agreed*
HORTENSIO Who shall begin?
80 LUCENTIO That will I.
Go, Biondello, bid your mistress come to me.
BIONDELLO I go.   *Exit*
BAPTISTA Son, I'll be your half Bianca comes.[5]
LUCENTIO I'll have no halves, I'll bear it all myself.
Enter BIONDELLO
How now, what news?
85 BIONDELLO   Sir, my mistress sends you word
That she is busy and she cannot come.
PETRUCCIO How? She's busy and she cannot come?
Is that an answer?
GREMIO   Ay, and a kind one, too.
Pray God, sir, your wife send you not a worse.
PETRUCCIO I hope, better.
90 HORTENSIO   Sirrah Biondello,
Go and entreat my wife to come to me forthwith.
Exit BIONDELLO
PETRUCCIO O ho, 'entreat' her—nay, then she must needs come.
HORTENSIO I am afraid, sir, do what you can,
Enter BIONDELLO
Yours will not be entreated. Now, where's my wife?

4. Your deer turns on you and holds you at a distance.   of any winnings) in wagering that Bianca will come
Punning on "deer" and "dear."   first.
5. I'll put up half the stake (and therefore collect half

95   BIONDELLO   She says you have some goodly jest in hand.
       She will not come. She bids you come to her.
       PETRUCCIO   Worse and worse! She will not come—O vile,
       Intolerable, not to be endured!
       Sirrah Grumio, go to your mistress.
100   Say I command her come to me.   *Exit* [GRUMIO]
       HORTENSIO   I know her answer.
       PETRUCCIO   What?
       HORTENSIO   She will not.
       PETRUCCIO   The fouler fortune mine, and there an end.[6]
         Enter KATHERINE
       BAPTISTA   Now by my halidom,° here comes Katherina.   *by all I hold sacred*
       KATHERINE [*to* PETRUCCIO]   What is your will, sir, that you send
         for me?
105   PETRUCCIO   Where is your sister and Hortensio's wife?
       KATHERINE   They sit conferring by the parlour fire.
       PETRUCCIO   Go, fetch them hither. If they deny° to come,   *refuse*
       Swinge me them soundly forth[7] unto their husbands.
       Away, I say, and bring them hither straight.   [*Exit* KATHERINE]
110   LUCENTIO   Here is a wonder, if you talk of wonders.
       HORTENSIO   And so it is. I wonder what it bodes.
       PETRUCCIO   Marry, peace it bodes, and love, and quiet life;
       An aweful° rule and right supremacy,   *inspiring awe*
       And, to be short, what not° that's sweet and happy.   *everything*
115   BAPTISTA   Now fair befall thee, good Petruccio,
       The wager thou hast won, and I will add
       Unto their losses twenty thousand crowns,
       Another dowry to another daughter,
       For she is changed as she had never been.[8]
120   PETRUCCIO   Nay, I will win my wager better yet,
       And show more sign of her obedience,
       Her new-built virtue and obedience.
         Enter KATHERINE, BIANCA, *and* [*the*] WIDOW
       See where she comes, and brings your froward° wives   *willful*
       As prisoners to her womanly persuasion.
125   Katherine, that cap of yours becomes you not.
       Off with that bauble, throw it underfoot.
         [KATHERINE *throws down her cap*]
       WIDOW   Lord, let me never have a cause to sigh
       Till I be brought to such a silly pass.
       BIANCA   Fie, what a foolish duty call you this?
130   LUCENTIO   I would your duty were as foolish, too.
       The wisdom of your duty, fair Bianca,
       Hath cost me a hundred crowns since supper-time.
       BIANCA   The more fool you for laying° on my duty.   *gambling*
       PETRUCCIO   Katherine, I charge thee tell these headstrong women
135   What duty they do owe their lords and husbands.
       WIDOW   Come, come, you're mocking. We will have no telling.
       PETRUCCIO   Come on, I say, and first begin with her.
       WIDOW   She shall not.

---

6. Worse luck for me (if you're right), and that's that.   8. As if she had never existed before; as if she had never
7. Beat them soundly for me, and bring them out.   been what she was before (a shrew).

PETRUCCIO I say she shall: and first begin with her.
140 KATHERINE Fie, fie, unknit that threat'ning, unkind brow,
    And dart not scornful glances from those eyes
    To wound thy lord, thy king, thy governor.
    It blots° thy beauty as frosts do bite the meads,°   *disfigures / meadows*
    Confounds thy fame° as whirlwinds shake fair buds,   *Ruins your reputation*
145 And in no sense is meet° or amiable.   *fitting*
    A woman moved° is like a fountain troubled,   *angry*
    Muddy, ill-seeming,° thick, bereft of beauty,   *ugly*
    And while it is so, none so dry or thirsty
    Will deign to sip or touch one drop of it.
150 Thy husband is thy lord, thy life, thy keeper,
    Thy head, thy sovereign, one that cares for thee,
    And for thy maintenance commits his body
    To painful labour both by sea and land,
    To watch the night in storms, the day in cold,
155 Whilst thou liest warm at home, secure and safe,
    And craves no other tribute at thy hands
    But love, fair looks, and true obedience,
    Too little payment for so great a debt.
    Such duty as the subject owes the prince,
160 Even such a woman oweth to her husband,
    And when she is froward, peevish,° sullen, sour,   *obstinate*
    And not obedient to his honest will,
    What is she but a foul contending rebel,
    And graceless traitor to her loving lord?
165 I am ashamed that women are so simple°   *foolish*
    To offer war where they should kneel for peace,
    Or seek for rule, supremacy, and sway
    When they are bound to serve, love, and obey.
    Why are our bodies soft, and weak, and smooth,
170 Unapt to° toil and trouble in the world,   *Unfitted for*
    But that our soft conditions° and our hearts   *dispositions*
    Should well agree with our external parts?
    Come, come, you froward and unable worms,°   *weak creatures*
    My mind hath been as big° as one of yours,   *proud*
175 My heart° as great, my reason haply more,   *spirit*
    To bandy word for word and frown for frown;
    But now I see our lances are but straws,
    Our strength as weak,° our weakness past compare,   *(as straws)*
    That seeming to be most which we indeed least are.
180 Then vail your stomachs, for it is no boot,⁹
    And place your hands below your husband's foot,
    In token of which duty, if he please,
    My hand is ready, may it do him ease.°   *give him comfort*
    PETRUCCIO Why, there's a wench! Come on, and kiss me, Kate.
        [*They kiss*]
185 LUCENTIO Well, go thy ways, old lad, for thou shalt ha't.¹
    VINCENTIO 'Tis a good hearing° when children are toward.²   *thing to hear*
    LUCENTIO But a harsh hearing when women are froward.
    PETRUCCIO Come, Kate, we'll to bed.

9. Then lower your pride, for it is of no profit.   2. Obedient (the opposite of "froward," line 187).
1. You shall have the prize.

We three are married, but you two are sped.°   *defeated*
190 'Twas I won the wager, though [*to* LUCENTIO] you hit the white,[3]
And being a winner,° God give you good night.   *since I am a winner*
Exit PETRUCCIO [*with* KATHERINE]
HORTENSIO Now go thy ways, thou hast tamed a curst shrew.
LUCENTIO 'Tis a wonder, by your leave, she will be tamed so.
[*Exeunt*][4]

Additional Passages

The Taming of a Shrew, printed in 1594 and believed to derive from Shakespeare's play as performed, contains episodes continuing and rounding off the Christopher Sly framework that may echo passages written by Shakespeare but not printed in the Folio. They are given below.

A. The following exchange occurs at a point for which there is no exact equivalent in Shakespeare's play. It could come before 2.1. The "two fine gentlewomen" to whom Sly refers in line 8 would thus be Katherine and Bianca. The "fool" of the first line is Sander, the counterpart of Grumio. "Sim" is short for Simon, the name of the Lord with whom Sly converses.

Then SLY *speaks*
SLY Sim, when will the fool come again?
LORD He'll come again, my lord, anon.
SLY Gi's° some more drink here. Zounds,[1] where's the tapster?°   *Give us / tavern keeper*
   Here, Sim, eat some of these things.
5 LORD So I do, my lord.
SLY Here, Sim, I drink to thee.
LORD My lord, here comes the players again.
SLY O brave, here's two fine gentlewomen.

B. This passage comes between 4.5 and 4.6. If it originates with Shakespeare, it implies that Grumio accompanies Petruccio at the beginning of 4.6. Ferando is the name of Petruccio's counterpart in *A Shrew*.

SLY Sim, must they be married now?
LORD Ay, my lord.
Enter FERANDO *and* KATE *and* SANDER
SLY Look, Sim, the fool is come again now.

C. Sly interrupts the action of the play-within-the-play. This could be inserted at 5.1.92 of Shakespeare's play, when Biondello, Tranio, and the Pedant all run away from the angry Vincentio. In *A Shrew*, the Duke (Vincentio's counterpart) has threatened to send to prison the people (Phylotus and Valeria) who have impersonated him and his son.

PHYLOTUS *and* VALERIA *runs away.*
Then SLY *speaks*
SLY I say we'll have no sending to prison.
LORD My lord, this is but the play. They're but in jest.
SLY I tell thee, Sim, we'll have no sending to prison, that's flat.°   *final*

---

3. Hit the target (with a pun on "Bianca," which means "white" in Italian).

4. In *A Shrew*, the Christopher Sly story concludes the

play. See Additional Passages E.

1. By God's wounds (a strong oath).

Why, Sim, am not I Don Christo Vary? Therefore I say they
5   shall not go to prison.
LORD   No more they shall not, my lord. They be run away.
SLY   Are they run away, Sim? That's well. Then gi's some more
   drink, and let them play again.
LORD   Here, my lord.
            SLY *drinks and then falls asleep*

D. Sly is carried off. This could be placed between 5.1 and 5.2 in Shakespeare's play.

                                    Exeunt omnes°   *They all exit*
            SLY *sleeps*
LORD   Who's within there? Come hither, sirs, my lord's
   Asleep again. Go take him easily° up   *gently*
   And put him in his own apparel again,
   And lay him in the place where we did find him
5   Just underneath the alehouse side below.
   But see you wake him not in any case.
BOY   It shall be done, my lord. Come help to bear him hence.
                                                              Exit

E. *The Taming of a Shrew* ends with the following episode.

            Then enter two bearing of SLY *in his own apparel again*
            and leaves him where they found him and then goes out.
            Then enter the TAPSTER
TAPSTER   Now that the darksome night is overpast
   And dawning day appears in crystal sky,
   Now must I haste abroad. But soft, who's this?
   What, Sly! O wondrous, hath he lain here all night?
5   I'll wake him. I think he's starved[1] by this,°   *this time*
   But° that his belly was so stuffed with ale.   *Except*
   What ho, Sly, awake, for shame!
SLY   Sim, gi's some more wine. What, 's all the players gone?
   Am not I a lord?
10 TAPSTER   A lord with a murrain![2] Come, art thou drunken still?
SLY   Who's this? Tapster? O Lord, sirrah, I have had
   The bravest° dream tonight that ever thou   *finest*
   Heardest in all thy life.
TAPSTER   Ay, marry, but you had best get you home,
15   For your wife will course° you for dreaming here tonight.   *trounce*
SLY   Will she? I know now how to tame a shrew.
   I dreamt upon it all this night till now,
   And thou hast waked me out of the best dream
   That ever I had in my life. But I'll to my
20   Wife presently and tame her too,
   An if° she anger me.   *An if=If*
TAPSTER   Nay, Tarry, Sly, for I'll go home with thee
   And hear the rest that thou hast dreamt tonight.
                                    Exeunt omnes

1. He'd have died from cold.
2. Pestilence or plague. "With a murrain" was often
used as an oath or expression of anger. The tapster
probably means "A plague on that" (Sly's dream of
being a lord).

The Comedy of Errors

In his essay "On Cripples," Shakespeare's great contemporary Montaigne alludes to a strange case of impersonation in a small rural community in southwestern France. There, a cunning imposter succeeded in assuming the identity of Martin Guerre, a man who had disappeared some years before. The imposter lived in the community for three years, sleeping with Guerre's wife and farming his land, until the real Martin Guerre unexpectedly returned. Convicted of fraud, the imposter confessed and was hanged.

Montaigne was dismayed by the execution, for he felt that the evidence was too murky, the imposture too convincing, and human identity too elusive a possession to justify capital punishment. The court, he writes, should have emulated the ancient Greek tribunal that, confronted by a similarly baffling case, ordered the parties to come back in a hundred years. Montaigne was not only advising judicial caution; he was urging his readers to take everyday life less automatically, to acknowledge the inevitability of ignorance and error, and to respond to their own existence with wonder. "I have seen no more evident monstrosity and miracle in the world than myself," he writes in the same essay in which he talks about Martin Guerre. "We become habituated to anything strange by use and time; but the more I frequent myself and know myself, the more my deformity astonishes me, and the less I understand myself."

Montaigne's reflections on Martin Guerre have no direct bearing on *The Comedy of Errors*, but they alert us to the play's wholesale unsettling of the familiar. The comfortable assumptions that condition a normal life—I know who I am; these things belong to me and not to someone else; these are the people I love, work for, do business with, or avoid—are undermined by the tangled interactions of two sets of identical (and identically named) twins. Antipholus of Syracuse and Antipholus of Ephesus, along with their servants, Dromio of Syracuse and Dromio of Ephesus, have been raised apart from one another in separate cities and are unaware that their paths are now unexpectedly crossing. Through a breathless succession of zany doublings and confusions, Shakespeare's comedy discloses the hidden strangeness of ordinary existence. An invitation to dinner, a simple transaction with a goldsmith, the operation of commercial and civil laws, the relation between master and servant, the bond between husband and wife (or mistress or sister-in-law)—all become unhinged, as if by sorcery. "There's not a man I meet but doth salute me," says Antipholus of Syracuse, "as if I were their well-acquainted friend, / And everyone doth call me by my name" (4.3.1–3). These are the practices of everyday life, but to this stranger who is, unbeknownst to him, being mistaken for his identical (and identically named) twin, they confirm the unsavory reputation of Ephesus as a place of "nimble jugglers," "Dark-working sorcerers," "Soul-killing witches," and "Disguisèd cheaters" (1.2.98–101).

The audience knows, of course, that Antipholus's uncanny experiences have been caused neither by witchcraft nor by the larcenous wiles that so astonished Montaigne. The wonder that seems to suffuse everything is the result of nothing more magical or malicious than twinship and a shared name, and hence, we could say, such wonder is spurious or misplaced, the result of misunderstandings. "This is the fairy land" (2.2.189), exclaims one of the Dromios, mystified by the succession of inexplicable events, and his similarly disoriented master invokes the notorious wiles of far-off Lapland. But in *The Comedy of Errors*, there is in reality only daylight and the familiar city

An Italian merchant pictured on a Florentine playing card.

street of Roman comedy, a street reassuringly adapted to the commercial world of Shakespeare's London. Disorientation and danger lurk, to be sure, in this conventional urban landscape—Antipholus of Syracuse thinks he is the victim of sorcery, Antipholus of Ephesus is treated as a madman, Adriana fears the loss of her husband's love, Luciana is convinced that her brother-in-law is trying to seduce her, the servants are constantly beaten, and poor Egeon is condemned to die at day's end. The pressure of time weighs heavily on virtually all of the characters, enmeshed as they are in humiliating, menacing, and apparently insoluble difficulties, but these confusions are neatly resolved by the appointed hour of 5:00 P.M.

Yet this comic resolution does not quite make wonder altogether evaporate from the play. Montaigne urged his readers to abandon their confident belief in the ordered rationality of life and to find the marvelous in the everyday. Identical twins are fairly commonplace and the fact that two people can bear the same name even more so, but Shakespeare's play calls attention to all that is potentially disorienting in the routine circumstances of life. The end of *The Comedy of Errors* seems to restore order and reason—to make the ordinary world ordinary again—but the closing gestures lightly unsettle this restoration. The abbess, who turns out to be Egeon's long-lost wife and the mother of the twin Antipholuses, finds a strange image, at once touching and grotesque, to describe her experiences: she declares that she has been pregnant for thirty-three years and has only now given birth. And the twin Dromios, unable to determine which of them is the elder and should therefore go first through the door, decide that they will draw lots for seniority; meanwhile, they will dispense with hierarchy and go through the door hand in hand.

More telling, perhaps, the questions raised by the strange case of Martin Guerre linger unresolved at the end of Shakespeare's comedy: What is the self? What are the guarantees of identity? Who possesses a name and by what right? How is individuality secured? How can one person represent another? The drama is the perfect medium for an exploration of these questions, for the form of the drama itself invites reflection on the extent to which it is possible for one person to assume the identity of another. From this perspective, *The Comedy of Errors* is not, as it is sometimes said to be, a simple and even simpleminded farce, the crude work of a novice playwright, but a remarkably subtle and acute deployment of the very conditions of the theater to engage with problems that haunted Shakespeare throughout his career.

While it is a mistake to view it as mere apprentice work, *The Comedy of Errors* is nonetheless one of the earliest of Shakespeare's plays (and it is also, perhaps not coincidentally, the shortest). Its exact date of composition and first performance are unknown; there was a performance at Gray's Inn, one of London's law schools, on December 28, 1594, but its thematic and stylistic resemblances to Shakespeare's other early comedies, *The Two Gentlemen of Verona, Love's Labour's Lost*, and *The Taming of the Shrew*, have led many scholars to conclude that he wrote it some years earlier. It was not printed until 1623, as part of the First Folio.

The anonymous recorder of the Gray's Inn performance—apparently something of a debacle because of the pushing and shoving of unexpectedly large crowds—noted the play's resemblance to an ancient comedy, the *Menaechmi*, written by the Roman playwright Plautus. Shakespeare probably read this much-admired play in Latin, since an English translation, by William Warner, was not printed until 1595. The *Menaechmi* is a brilliant, energetic farce, fast-paced, funny, and, as farces often are, cold at heart. A prologue carefully explains the premise: a Syracusan merchant took one of his twin sons, seven years old, on a business trip abroad. During a festival, he accidentally became separated from the son. The boy was found by a childless trader, who took him off to Epidamnum; the father, crazed with grief, died a few days later. When news of the catastrophe reached Syracuse, the remaining son was given the name of his missing brother.

The action of Plautus's play is set some years later, when Menaechmus of Syracuse, searching for his twin, finds himself in Epidamnum. Greeted warmly by perfect strangers, Menaechmus realizes that some mistake is being made, but he is not filled with dread. "I can lose nothing," he cheerfully tells his slave, as he accepts food, gifts, and sexual favors from a woman who has inexplicably confused him with someone else and imagines that she is his mistress. What most strikes him is that it is all free of charge. His twin, a prosperous citizen normally comfortable in an entourage that includes wife, household slaves, mistress, and an obnoxious hanger-on nicknamed the Sponge, is frustrated by the fact that everyone seems to have gone mad and becomes enraged when he himself is treated as a madman. The dizzying confusions steadily mount until the brothers find themselves face-to-face and, with delicious slowness, figure out that they are the long-separated identical twins. The brothers plan to return together to Syracuse, and the play ends with the announcement of the forthcoming auction of Menaechmus's property: "slaves, household effects, house, land, etcetera—and a wife, should there be any purchaser."

A scene in the street/the street as scene. Woodcut from a German edition of Terence's *Eunuchus* (1486).

Though he took over much of Plautus's farce, Shakespeare made highly revealing changes and additions. For a start, he shifted the setting from Epidamnum to Ephesus, a city associated with sorcery, exorcism, mystery cults, and early Christianity. As if to multiply the comic confusion generated by one set of identical twins, he added a second set—the servants, who, for reasons that are not really explained, bear like their masters a single name. (The device of the identical slaves is borrowed from another play by Plautus, the *Amphitruo*.) Shakespeare also chose in effect to double the plot by framing the main action with the anguished figure of the Syracusan merchant Egeon, caught up in his city's murderous commercial struggle with rival Ephesus. The melancholy personal history that Egeon relates is adapted not from the ancient comedy but from a medieval romance, the tale of Apollonius of Tyre as told by the fourteenth-century poet John Gower in his *Confessio Amantis* (a tale to which Shakespeare again turned many years later for the plot of *Pericles*). Egeon's fate quickly recedes from the audience's attention, but the threat to his life provides a somber context for the play's hilarity, and his return to the stage at the close, on the way to the place of execution, suddenly raises the stakes of the resolution. The closing scene highlights the romance elements that Shakespeare introduced into his frenetic scheme of mistaken identity: the reuniting of parents and children who had been tragically separated, the miraculous recovery of a beloved spouse long presumed dead, and a sense of wonder that does not entirely evaporate with the solving of the puzzle. Plautus's Epidamnum is a city full of rogues, parasites, and courtesans, a place where you can lose your cloak, your chain, and your money; Shakespeare's Ephesus is a place where you can lose—or regain—your life.

Egeon's story in *The Comedy of Errors* has a shape that merits attention: he is condemned to death through the operation of an inflexible law that even the sympathetic duke cannot mitigate, and then, through a wondrous turn of events, his life is spared, and he recovers the loved ones he thought he had lost forever. Even though the play is set in pagan antiquity, in this shape we may sense the psychic and moral rhythm of Christianity: the mortal penalty of the harsh law is wiped out, altogether unexpectedly and gratuitously, by a miraculous, loving dispensation. The farcical core of the play is at a considerable remove from this portentous rhythm, but Christianity's influence is not restricted to the frame. Since Shakespeare and his age were relatively indifferent to anachronism, Antipholus of Syracuse can say to his servant, "Now, as I am a Christian, answer me" (1.2.77), and the servant can call for his rosary beads and cross himself (2.2.188). The fear of demonic possession takes a specifically Christian form when Satan himself is exorcised by Doctor Pinch. And although pagan antiquity had shrines such as the Temple of Diana at Ephesus (where the tale of Apollonius of Tyre reaches it climax), the priory and its Abbess seem to belong in a Christian community, a community invoked by the very name of Ephesus, where St. Paul preached and to which he wrote an influential epistle.

A central concern of Paul's Epistle to the Ephesians is Christian marriage: men are urged to love their wives as their own bodies, while women are urged to submit themselves unto their husbands as unto the Lord. These strikingly asymmetrical admonitions make themselves felt throughout *The Comedy of Errors*. Where Plautus's Menaechmus cheerfully cheats on his wife, Shakespeare's married twin seems to have an inward principle of moral restraint. Antipholus is driven to the courtesan only when his wife, Adriana, seems to turn him away from his own house—and even then, protesting to his friends that his wife's suspicions are unfounded, he seems mainly interested in dinner and pleasant conversation. Where the nameless wife in Plautus is above all outraged that her husband has stolen from her a gown and a bracelet to bestow as presents on his mistress, Shakespeare's Adriana is obsessed with the possibility that her husband no longer loves her. It is this tormenting fear of marital estrangement that has driven her to a querulousness that only confirms her overwhelming craving for perfect union:

"I'll to the mart" (3.2.182). London's Royal Exchange, founded by Sir Thomas Gresham, 1565. Etching by Wenceslaus Hollar (1644).

> Ah, do not tear away thyself from me;
> For know, my love, as easy mayst thou fall
> A drop of water in the breaking gulf,
> And take unmingled thence that drop again
> Without addition or diminishing,
> As take from me thyself, and not me too.
> (2.2.124–29)

The oneness that is envisioned here, the poignant longing for wholeness, and the fear of pollution and self-loss have no place in the emotional register of the *Menaechmi*. Where Plautus's farce ends with a joke about offering the wife for sale, *The Comedy of Errors* ends with the characters, reconciled and reunited, entering the abbey for a feast.

Near the close of Shakespeare's play, the Abbess seems to reflect the spirit of St. Paul's admonition to wives when she observes that by robbing her husband of the "sweet recreation" that he should find at home, Adriana's "jealous fits" have driven him mad (5.1.69–87). This criticism echoes both Antipholus's own complaint that his wife is "shrewish" and the distinctly Pauline opinions voiced by Adriana's sister, Luciana. Luciana—a character for whom there is no precedent in Plautus—argues that males of every species are "masters to their females, and their lords" (2.1.24) and therefore that Adriana should patiently submit to her husband. Such views, similar to those expressed by the "reformed" Katherine in *The Taming of the Shrew*, are given considerable prominence in *The Comedy of Errors*, and yet they are neither unchallenged nor unequivocally endorsed. Adriana observes that her sister is single and hence that her views on marriage are untested by experience. And the Abbess's moralizing diagnosis—that Antipholus would not have mistreated Adriana or gone mad if she had reined in her tongue—turns out to be merely another of the mistaken conjectures that all of the characters incessantly advance in their attempts to account for the day's weird events.

There is a kind of laughter that functions as social regulation: comedy, writes Sir Philip Sidney in his *Defense of Poesie* (c. 1583), "is an imitation of the common errors of our life," which the dramatist represents "in the most ridiculous and scornful sort that may be, so as it is impossible that any beholder can be content to be such a one." The errors in *The Comedy of Errors* are ridiculous, but they are hardly common, and the audience's laughter seems something other than scornful or regulative. None of the explanatory accounts, not even the moral values and providential rhythm of Christianity with which Shakespeare has infused his pagan plot, seems entirely adequate as a response to the chain of mad mistakings. The characters are subject not to a divine plan or to the social order but to fortune. And if this fortune turns out to have the happy air of providence—epitomized by the reuniting of the divided and dispersed family—there seems to be no particularly uplifting lesson to be learned.

Shakespeare's play, to be sure, is cannily alert to social inequities—an innocent merchant is condemned to death for being in the wrong place at the wrong time; a husband is "master of his liberty," while a wife must "practise to obey" (2.1.7, 29); one set of twins is destined through poverty to be the servants, casually beaten and abused, of the other set—but it does not mount a strenuous protest or imagine a radical transformation. In the midst of the farcical confusions, characters repeatedly long for greater justice, equality, and emotional fulfillment, but *The Comedy of Errors* does not encourage us to believe that such an existence can be realized. There may be a happy resolution, but there is no escape from the pervasive, fundamentally inequitable social order and from the mercantile world based on credit, trade, exchange, bonds, and debt.

Several of Shakespeare's best-loved comedies are structured around alternative worlds: the familiar, daylit realm of the court or city is set against the magical realm of the woods and the enchanted night. But in *The Comedy of Errors*, there is only the single urban setting, a setting that would have reminded contemporary audiences of the bustling city that stretched out beyond the walls of the playhouse. In the sixteenth century, London had become the center of a commercial culture that Shakespeare deftly sketches with quick strokes. We learn that Antipholus keeps a purse of ducats locked "in the desk / That's covered o'er with Turkish tapestry" (4.1.103–4), that the courtesan considers a ring worth 40 ducats "too much to lose" (4.3.91), and that the goldsmith plans to discharge his overdue debt to a merchant with the money that Antipholus has promised to pay him for the gold chain. That gold chain functions as a convenient symbol of the interlinked network of obligations and exchanges in which the twins—who seem as like one another as two coins of equal value—are caught and which their uncontrolled interchangeability temporarily disrupts.

A closer look reveals that Antipholus of Ephesus and Antipholus of Syracuse are not perfectly interchangeable: the former is confident, well connected, and somewhat irascible; the latter is anxious, insecure, driven by restless longing:

> I to the world am like a drop of water
> That in the ocean seeks another drop,
> Who, falling there to find his fellow forth,
> Unseen, inquisitive, confounds himself.
> (1.2.35–38)

This poignant sense of self-loss, which anticipates the alienation and existential anxiety of the tragedies, is intensified by the mad confusions that follow: the events of *The Comedy of Errors* may be deliciously amusing to the audience, but to the characters they are mystifying and even nightmarish. Antonin Artaud, a modern writer who championed what he called the "Theater of Cruelty," praises the Marx Brothers' movies in terms that seem at least as relevant to Shakespeare's comedy: "In order to understand the powerful, total, definitive, absolute originality . . . of films like *Animal Crackers*," Artaud writes, "you would have to add to humor the notion of something disquieting and tragic, a fatality (neither happy nor unhappy, difficult to formulate) which would hover over it like the cast of an appalling malady upon an exquisitely beautiful profile." And yet it is not the nightmare that triumphs but laughter, laughter at what another sixteenth-century writer, George Gascoigne, called "supposes." Gascoigne defined a suppose as "a mistaking or imagination of one thing for another," and it is with a frantic succession of these supposes, all equally wide of the mark, that the baffled characters of *The Comedy of Errors* occupy themselves.

The "imagination of one thing for another" could serve as a definition of the theater. The spectators of Shakespeare's comedy have paid for the pleasure of watching identity slip away from the characters' grasp, as if in the home or the marketplace who you are is no more secure than it is onstage. They have paid too for the pleasure of watching identity serendipitously return, as if Shakespeare's theater had the magic power to restore the human family, however broken and scattered, and restore stability to the battered self. If neither the loss nor the recovery is altogether plausible, the delicious intertwining of the two seems designed to provoke what Montaigne urged upon his readers: a skeptical wonder.

STEPHEN GREENBLATT

TEXTUAL NOTE

The Comedy of Errors was first printed in the 1623 First Folio, which is therefore the only authoritative text of the play. Scholars generally believe that the text was based on Shakespeare's own autograph manuscript. Evidence for this belief centers on features of the stage directions and speech prefixes that are likely to derive from the playwright himself rather than a compositor or playhouse bookkeeper. For example, the stage direction before 4.4.36 calls for "a Schoole-master, call'd Pinch," although there is no mention in the dialogue that Pinch is a schoolmaster. Similarly, while the prompter's copy would normally call only for a particular character by name, the stage direction at 2.1.0 specifies that Adriana is "wife to Antipholis Sereptus." ("Sereptus" is from the Latin *surreptus*, "stolen away," an epithet applied several times by Plautus to the twin who corresponds to Antipholus of Ephesus. At his first appearance, Antipholus of Syracuse is referred to as "Antipholus Erotes"; some critics have conjectured that "Erotes" is a corruption of *erraticus*, "wandering," by analogy with *surreptus*.)

The Folio text indicates act divisions (and specifies "Scena Prima" at the beginning of Acts 1, 3, 4, and 5).

SELECTED BIBLIOGRAPHY

Baldwin, T. W. *Shakespere's Five-Act Structure: Shakespere's Early Plays on the Background of Renaissance Theories of Five-Act Structure from 1470*. Urbana: University of Illinois Press, 1947.

Christensen, Ann C. "'Because their business still lies out a' door': Resisting the Separation of the Spheres in Shakespeare's *The Comedy of Errors*." *Literature and History* 5 (1996): 19–37.

Frye, Northrop. "The Argument of Comedy." *English Institute Essays*. New York: AMS Press, 1948. 58–73.

Hunt, Maurice. "Slavery, English Servitude and *The Comedy of Errors*." *English Literary Renaissance* 27 (1997): 31–56.

Miola, Robert S., ed. *"The Comedy of Errors": Critical Essays*. New York: Routledge, 2001.

Parker, Patricia. "The Bible and the Marketplace: *The Comedy of Errors.*" *Shakespeare from the Margins: Language, Culture, Context.* Chicago: University of Chicago Press, 1996. 56–82.

Perry, Curtis. "Commerce, Community, and Nostalgia in *The Comedy of Errors.*" *Money and the Age of Shakespeare: Essays in New Economic Criticism.* Ed. Linda Woodbridge. New York: Palgrave Macmillan, 2003. 39–51.

Salgādo, Gāmini. "'Time's Deformed Hand': Sequence, Consequence, and Inconsequence in *The Comedy of Errors.*" *Shakespeare Survey* 25 (1972): 81–92.

Taylor, Gary. "Textual and Sexual Criticism: A Crux in *The Comedy of Errors.*" *Renaissance Drama* 19 (1988): 195–225.

Witmore, Michael. "The Avoidance of Ends in *The Comedy of Errors.*" *Culture of Accidents: Unexpected Knowledges in Early Modern England.* Stanford: Stanford University Press, 2001. 62–81.

FILM

The Comedy of Errors. 1983. Dir. James Cellan Jones. UK. 109 min. A BBC-TV production, with Roger Daltrey (lead singer of The Who) as the Dromios.

The Comedy of Errors

THE PERSONS OF THE PLAY

Solinus, DUKE of Ephesus
EGEON, a merchant of Syracuse, father of the Antipholus twins
ANTIPHOLUS OF EPHESUS ⎤
ANTIPHOLUS OF SYRACUSE ⎦ twin brothers, sons of Egeon
DROMIO OF EPHESUS ⎤ twin brothers, and bondmen of the
DROMIO OF SYRACUSE ⎦ Antipholus twins
ADRIANA, wife of Antipholus of Ephesus
LUCIANA, her sister
NELL, Adriana's kitchen-maid
ANGELO, a goldsmith
BALTHASAR, a merchant
A COURTESAN
Doctor PINCH, a schoolmaster and exorcist
MERCHANT OF EPHESUS, a friend of Antipholus of Syracuse
SECOND MERCHANT, Angelo's creditor
Emilia, an ABBESS at Ephesus
Jailer, messenger, headsman, officers, and other attendants

1.1

Enter [Solinus], the DUKE *of Ephesus, with* [EGEON] *the*
Merchant of Syracuse, JAILER, *and other attendants*

EGEON   Proceed, Solinus, to procure my fall,
  And by the doom° of death end woes and all.   *sentence*
DUKE   Merchant of Syracusa, plead no more.
  I am not partial° to infringe our laws.   *inclined*
5 The enmity and discord which of late
  Sprung from the rancorous outrage of your Duke
  To merchants, our well-dealing[1] countrymen,
  Who, wanting° guilders[2] to redeem° their lives,   *lacking / ransom*
  Have sealed° his rigorous statutes with their bloods,   *ratified*
10 Excludes all pity from our threat'ning looks.
  For since the mortal° and intestine jars°   *deadly / bitter strife*
  'Twixt thy seditious countrymen and us,
  It hath in solemn synods° been decreed,   *assemblies*
  Both by the Syracusians and ourselves,
15 To admit no traffic to[3] our adverse° towns.   *hostile*
  Nay more: if any born at Ephesus
  Be seen at Syracusian marts° and fairs;   *markets*
  Again, if any Syracusian born
  Come to the bay of Ephesus—he dies,

1.1 Location: A street in Ephesus. The setting of the entire play was probably modeled after that of ancient Roman comedy: a conjunction of city streets, with three doors to represent houses, each marked with a sign. The house of Antipholus of Ephesus, identified as the Phoenix, is flanked by the courtesan's house (marked with the sign of a porcupine) and the priory (perhaps marked anachronistically with a cross). When the action is not focused on these houses, the stage serves as a generalized urban space, most often called the "mart"—that is, the marketplace.
1. Honest-trading; more generally, civil or well-behaved.
2. Money, not specifically referring to Dutch or German coins.
3. To allow no trade between.

20   His goods confiscate to the Duke's dispose,°   *disposal*
      Unless a thousand marks[4] be levièd°   *raised*
      To quit° the penalty and ransom him.   *pay*
      Thy substance,° valued at the highest rate,   *goods*
      Cannot amount unto a hundred marks.
25   Therefore by law thou art condemned to die.
      EGEON   Yet this my comfort: when your words are done,
      My woes end likewise with the evening sun.
      DUKE   Well, Syracusian, say in brief the cause
      Why thou departed'st from thy native home,
30   And for what cause thou cam'st to Ephesus.
      EGEON   A heavier task could not have been imposed
      Than I° to speak my griefs unspeakable.   *Than for me*
      Yet, that the world may witness that my end
      Was wrought by nature,[5] not by vile offence,
35   I'll utter what my sorrow gives me leave.
      In Syracusa was I born, and wed
      Unto a woman happy but for me,[6]
      And by me° happy, had not our hap° been bad.   *by me made / luck*
      With her I lived in joy, our wealth increased
40   By prosperous voyages I often made
      To Epidamnum,[7] till my factor's° death,   *agent's*
      And the great care of goods at random° left,   *untended*
      Drew me from kind embracements of my spouse,
      From whom my absence was not six months old
45   Before herself—almost at fainting under
      The pleasing punishment that women bear°—   *(pregnancy)*
      Had made provision for her following me,
      And soon and safe arrivèd where I was.
      There had she not been long but she became
50   A joyful mother of two goodly sons;
      And, which was strange, the one so like the other
      As° could not be distinguished but by names.   *That they*
      That very hour, and in the selfsame inn,
      A mean-born woman° was deliverèd   *woman of low birth*
55   Of such a burden male, twins both alike.
      Those, for° their parents were exceeding poor,   *because*
      I bought, and brought up to attend my sons.
      My wife, not meanly° proud of two such boys,   *in no small degree*
      Made daily motions° for our home return.   *requests*
60   Unwilling, I agreed. Alas! Too soon
      We came aboard.
      A league from Epidamnum had we sailed
      Before the always-wind-obeying deep
      Gave any tragic instance° of our harm.   *sign*
65   But longer did we not retain much hope,
      For what obscurèd light the heavens did grant
      Did but convey unto our fearful minds
      A doubtful warrant° of immediate death,   *A fearsome confirmation*
      Which though myself would gladly have embraced,
70   Yet the incessant weepings of my wife—

---

4. A mark was two-thirds of a pound in English money, although there was no coin of this amount.
5. Was brought about by natural feeling: a father's love.
6. Fortunate except in her association with me.
7. Plautus's setting for the *Meneachmi*, now Durrës in Albania; Shakespeare's play, however, seems to treat it as if it were in Greece.

Weeping before° for what she saw must come— *in advance*
And piteous plainings° of the pretty babes, *cries*
That mourned for fashion, ignorant what to fear,[8]
Forced me to seek delays° for them and me. *reprieves*
75   And this it was—for other means was none:
The sailors sought for safety by our boat,° *lifeboat*
And left the ship, then sinking-ripe,[9] to us.
My wife, more careful° for the latter-born,° *anxious / younger*
Had fastened him unto a small spare mast
80   Such as seafaring men provide for storms.
To him one of the other twins was bound,
Whilst I had been like heedful of° the other. *equally attentive to*
The children thus disposed,° my wife and I, *placed*
Fixing our eyes on whom our care was fixed,
85   Fastened ourselves at either end the mast,
And floating straight,° obedient to the stream, *immediately*
Was carried towards Corinth, as we thought.
At length the sun, gazing upon the earth,
Dispersed those vapours° that offended° us, *clouds / harmed*
90   And by the benefit of his wishèd light
The seas waxed calm, and we discoverèd
Two ships from far, making amain° to us: *speeding*
Of Corinth that, of Epidaurus[1] this.
But ere they came—O let me say no more!
95   Gather the sequel by that went before.[2]
DUKE   Nay, forward, old man; do not break off so,
For we may pity though not pardon thee.
EGEON   O, had the gods done so, I had not now
Worthily° termed them merciless to us. *Justly*
100   For, ere the ships could meet by° twice five leagues, *come within*
We were encountered by a mighty rock,
Which being violently borne upon,
Our helpful ship° was splitted in the midst, *(the mast)*
So that in this unjust divorce of us
105   Fortune had left to both of us alike° *equally*
What° to delight in, what to sorrow for. *Something*
Her° part, poor soul, seeming as burdenèd *(My wife's)*
With lesser weight[3] but not with lesser woe,
Was carried with more speed before the wind,
110   And in our sight they three were taken up
By fishermen of Corinth, as we thought.
At length another ship had seized on us,° *hauled us up*
And, knowing whom it was their hap° to save, *luck*
Gave healthful welcome to their shipwrecked guests,
115   And would have reft° the fishers of their prey[4] *deprived*
Had not their barque° been very slow of sail; *vessel*
And therefore homeward did they bend their course.
Thus have you heard me severed from my bliss,
That by misfortunes was my life prolonged
120   To tell sad stories of my own mishaps.

8. That imitated the adults' lamentation without understanding it.
9. At the point of sinking; softened and ready to drop.
1. Either modern Dubrovnik, on the Adriatic and north of Durrës (Epidamnum), or the Greek city actually called Epidaurus, near Corinth.
2. Deduce what followed from that which I have already recounted.
3. Lighter than her husband and the other child.
4. Those whom they have fished out of the sea.

DUKE   And for the sake of them thou sorrow'st for,
    Do me the favour to dilate at° full   *relate in*
    What have befall'n of them and thee till now.
EGEON   My youngest boy,[5] and yet my eldest care,
125   At eighteen years became inquisitive
    After his brother, and importuned me
    That his attendant—so his case was like,[6]
    Reft of his brother, but retained his name[7]—
    Might bear him company in the quest of him;
130   Whom whilst I laboured of a love to see,[8]
    I hazarded the loss of whom I loved.
    Five summers have I spent in farthest Greece,
    Roaming clean through the bounds of Asia,
    And coasting° homeward came to Ephesus,   *sailing*
135   Hopeless to find,° yet loath to leave unsought   *find them*
    Or° that or any place that harbours men.   *Either*
    But here must end the story of my life,
    And happy were I in my timely death
    Could all my travels[9] warrant° me they live.   *assure*
140 DUKE   Hapless° Egeon, whom the fates have marked   *Unlucky*
    To bear the extremity of dire mishap,
    Now trust me, were it not against our laws—
    Which princes, would they, may not disannul[1]—
    Against my crown, my oath, my dignity,
145   My soul should sue as advocate for thee.
    But though thou art adjudgèd° to the death,   *sentenced*
    And passèd sentence may not be recalled
    But° to our honour's great disparagement,°   *Except / disgrace*
    Yet will I favour thee in what I can.[2]
150   Therefore, merchant, I'll limit° thee this day   *allot*
    To seek thy health° by beneficial help.   *deliverance*
    Try all the friends thou hast in Ephesus:
    Beg thou or borrow to make up the sum,
    And live. If no, then thou art doomed to die.
155   Jailer, take him to thy custody.
JAILER   I will, my lord.
EGEON   Hopeless and helpless doth Egeon wend,°   *go*
    But to procrastinate° his lifeless end.   *Exeunt*   *postpone*

1.2

Enter [from the bay] ANTIPHOLUS [OF SYRACUSE], MER-
CHANT [OF EPHESUS], *and* DROMIO [OF SYRACUSE]

MERCHANT OF EPHESUS   Therefore give out° you are of Epidamnum,   *say*
    Lest that your goods too soon be confiscate.
    This very day a Syracusian merchant
    Is apprehended for arrival here,
5   And, not being able to buy out° his life,   *ransom*
    According to the statute of the town
    Dies ere the weary sun set in the west.
    There is your money that I had to keep.°   *in my keeping*

---

5. An inconsistency of detail (see line 78).
6. *so . . . like:* in this way his situation was similar.
7. Bore the name of the brother from whom he was separated.
8. *Whom . . . see:* Since I longed to see my lost son.
9. Journeys; "travails," efforts.
1. *would . . . disannul:* even if they wished to, cannot cancel or make void.
2. Yet I will bend the law's strictness as much as I can.
1.2 Location: A street in Ephesus.

ANTIPHOLUS OF SYRACUSE [*to* DROMIO] Go bear it to the
　　　Centaur,[1] where we host,°　　　　　　　　　　　　　　　　*lodge*
10　And stay there, Dromio, till I come to thee.
　　　Within this hour it will be dinner-time.[2]
　　　Till that° I'll view the manners of the town,　　　　　　　　*then*
　　　Peruse° the traders, gaze upon the buildings,　　　　　　　*Observe*
　　　And then return and sleep within mine inn;
15　For with long travel I am stiff and weary.
　　　Get thee away.
DROMIO OF SYRACUSE　Many a man would take you at your word,
　　　And go indeed, having so good a mean.[3]　　　　　　*Exit*
ANTIPHOLUS OF SYRACUSE　A trusty villain,[4] sir, that very oft,
20　When I am dull° with care and melancholy,　　　　　　　*gloomy*
　　　Lightens my humour[5] with his merry jests.
　　　What,° will you walk with me about the town,　　　*Now then*
　　　And then go to my inn and dine with me?
MERCHANT OF EPHESUS　I am invited, sir, to certain merchants
25　Of whom I hope to make much benefit.
　　　I crave your pardon. Soon° at five o'clock,　　　　　　*Promptly*
　　　Please° you, I'll meet with you upon the mart,　　　*If it please*
　　　And afterward consort° you till bedtime.　　　　　　*accompany*
　　　My present business calls me from you now.
30　ANTIPHOLUS OF SYRACUSE　Farewell till then. I will go lose myself,
　　　And wander up and down to view the city.
MERCHANT OF EPHESUS　Sir, I commend you to your own
　　　content.°　　　　　　　　　　　　　　*Exit*　　*pleasures; peace*
ANTIPHOLUS OF SYRACUSE　He that commends me to mine own
　　　content
　　　Commends me to the thing I cannot get.
35　I to the world am like a drop of water
　　　That in the ocean seeks another drop,
　　　Who, falling there to find his fellow forth,[6]
　　　Unseen, inquisitive, confounds° himself.　　　　*mingles; destroys*
　　　So I, to find a mother and a brother,
40　In quest of them, unhappy, lose myself.
　　　　　　Enter DROMIO OF EPHESUS
　　　Here comes the almanac of my true date.[7]
　　　What now? How chance° thou art returned so soon?　　*What happened that*
DROMIO OF EPHESUS　Returned so soon? Rather approached too late.
　　　The capon burns, the pig falls from the spit.
45　The clock hath strucken twelve upon the bell;
　　　My mistress made it one[8] upon my cheek.
　　　She is so hot° because the meat is cold.　　　　　　　*angry*
　　　The meat is cold because you come not home.
　　　You come not home because you have no stomach.°　　*appetite*
50　You have no stomach, having broke your fast;°　　　*having eaten*
　　　But we that know what 'tis to fast and pray
　　　Are penitent[9] for your default° today.　　　　　　　*fault*

1. The name of an inn; taverns, inns, and shops were
frequently identified by a pictorial sign.
2. Noon, time for the midday meal.
3. Opportunity, but punning on "means" (wealth).
4. Servant or slave (villein); also rogue or scoundrel
(often used affectionately).
5. Mood, determined by the humors, bodily fluids that
formed the basis of Elizabethan medical psychology.

6. To locate a matching drop.
7. The measure of my exact age (because born on the
same date).
8. *made it one:* struck one o'clock.
9. Are doing penance in the ordinary way by prayer and
fasting (since the meal is delayed), and also through
being beaten.

ANTIPHOLUS OF SYRACUSE   Stop in your wind,° sir. Tell me this,   *Shut your mouth*
    I pray:
    Where have you left the money that I gave you?

55 DROMIO OF EPHESUS   O—sixpence that I had o' Wednesday last
    To pay the saddler for my mistress' crupper?[1]
    The saddler had it, sir; I kept it not.

ANTIPHOLUS OF SYRACUSE   I am not in a sportive humour now.
    Tell me, and dally not: where is the money?
60   We being strangers here, how dar'st thou trust
    So great a charge from° thine own custody?   *responsibility out of*

DROMIO OF EPHESUS   I pray you, jest, sir, as° you sit at dinner.   *when*
    I from my mistress come to you in post.°   *haste*
    If I return I shall be post[2] indeed,
65   For she will scour° your fault upon my pate.°   *score; flog / head*
    Methinks your maw,° like mine, should be your clock,   *stomach*
    And strike[3] you home without a messenger.

ANTIPHOLUS OF SYRACUSE   Come, Dromio, come, these jests are
    out of season.
    Reserve them till a merrier hour than this.
70   Where is the gold I gave in charge to thee?

DROMIO OF EPHESUS   To me, sir? Why, you gave no gold to me.

ANTIPHOLUS OF SYRACUSE   Come on, sir knave,[4] have done your
    foolishness,
    And tell me how thou hast disposed° thy charge.   *dealt with*

DROMIO OF EPHESUS   My charge was but to fetch you from the mart
75   Home to your house, the Phoenix,[5] sir, to dinner.
    My mistress and her sister stays° for you.   *wait*

ANTIPHOLUS OF SYRACUSE   Now, as I am a Christian,[6] answer me
    In what safe place you have bestowed my money,
    Or I shall break that merry sconce° of yours   *head*
80   That stands° on tricks when I am undisposed.°   *insists / not in the mood*
    Where is the thousand marks thou hadst of me?

DROMIO OF EPHESUS   I have some marks of yours upon my pate,
    Some of my mistress' marks upon my shoulders,
    But not a thousand marks between you both.
85   If I should pay your worship those again,°   *back*
    Perchance you will not bear them patiently.

ANTIPHOLUS OF SYRACUSE   Thy mistress' marks? What mistress,
    slave, hast thou?

DROMIO OF EPHESUS   Your worship's wife, my mistress, at the Phoenix:
    She that doth fast till you come home to dinner,
90   And prays that you will hie° you home to dinner.   *hasten*

ANTIPHOLUS OF SYRACUSE   What, wilt thou flout° me thus unto   *mock; disobey*
    my face,
    Being forbid? There, take you that, sir knave!
    [*He beats* DROMIO]

DROMIO OF EPHESUS   What mean you, sir? For God's sake,
    hold° your hands!   *stop*

---

1. A strap passed under a horse's tail to prevent the saddle from slipping forward.
2. Beaten, like a wooden doorpost on which tavern charges were tallied (scored).
3. Beat; ring time like a clock.
4. Ironic: "knave," like "villain," means both "servant" and "rogue."

5. Antipholus of Ephesus's house is, like the inn (line 9), identified by a sign, this one depicting the mythological bird that symbolized resurrection. Many Londoners lived above their places of business.
6. A common oath, though anachronistic in classical Greece.

Nay, an° you will not, sir, I'll take my heels.°   *Exit*   *if / run away*
95 ANTIPHOLUS OF SYRACUSE   Upon my life, by some device° or other   *trick*
The villain is o'er-raught° of all my money.   *cheated*
They say this town is full of cozenage,°   *deception*
As° nimble jugglers[7] that deceive the eye,   *Such as*
Dark-working[8] sorcerers that change the mind,
100 Soul-killing witches that deform[9] the body,
Disguisèd cheaters, prating mountebanks,°   *fast-talking quacks*
And many suchlike libertines of sin.[1]
If it prove so, I will be gone the sooner.
I'll to the Centaur to go seek this slave.
105 I greatly fear my money is not safe.   *Exit*

2.1

Enter [from the Phoenix] ADRIANA, *wife to* ANTIPHOLUS
[OF EPHESUS], *with* LUCIANA, *her sister*

ADRIANA   Neither my husband nor the slave returned
That in such haste I sent to seek his master?
Sure,° Luciana, it is two o'clock.   *Surely*
LUCIANA   Perhaps some merchant hath invited him,
5 And from the mart he's somewhere gone to dinner.
Good sister, let us dine, and never fret.
A man is master of his liberty.
Time is their mistress, and when they see time
They'll go or come. If so, be patient, sister.
10 ADRIANA   Why should their liberty than ours be more?
LUCIANA   Because their business still° lies out o' door.   *always*
ADRIANA   Look when I serve him so, he takes it ill.[1]
LUCIANA   O, know he is the bridle of your will.[2]
ADRIANA   There's none but° asses will be bridled so.   *Only*
15 LUCIANA   Why, headstrong liberty is lashed° with woe.   *beaten; tied down*
There's nothing situate under heaven's eye
But hath his bound° in earth, in sea, in sky.   *its limits*
The beasts, the fishes, and the wingèd fowls
Are their males' subjects and at their controls.°   *under their control*
20 Man, more divine,[3] the master of all these,
Lord of the wide world and wild wat'ry seas,
Indued with intellectual sense and souls,
Of more pre-eminence than fish and fowls,
Are masters to their females, and their lords.[4]
25 Then let your will attend on their accords.[5]
ADRIANA   This servitude makes you to keep unwed.
LUCIANA   Not this, but troubles of the marriage bed.[6]
ADRIANA   But were you wedded, you would bear some sway.°   *wield some power*
LUCIANA   Ere I learn love, I'll practise to obey.

---

7. Performers skilled in manipulating appearances; the term could mean either an actual sorcerer or a mere illusionist.
8. Operating secretly or producing darkness.
9. Injure, disfigure; change the shape of (like the enchantress Circe of Homer's *Odyssey*, who transformed Odysseus's men into swine).
1. Unrestrained sinners. F prints "Liberties," possibly referring to the district where many theaters of London (including Shakespeare's company) operated, just outside the city's legal jurisdiction.
2.1 Location: Before the house of Antipholus of Ephesus.

1. Whenever I treat him so, he takes it badly.
2. He is meant to restrain your desires.
3. Nearer to God (in the great hierarchy of all beings).
4. *Man . . . lords:* Man's dominion over the creatures of earth and water derives from Genesis 1:28–29; his rule over woman is expressed in Paul's epistles, especially 1 Corinthians 11:3ff. and Ephesians 5:22ff. ("Wives, submit yourselves unto your husbands, as unto the Lord").
5. *attend . . . accords:* serve their wishes.
6. Compare 1 Corinthians 7:28: "And if a virgin marry, she sinneth not: nevertheless such shall have trouble in the flesh."

30	ADRIANA How if your husband start° some otherwhere?°	strays; wanders / elsewhere
	LUCIANA Till he come home again, I would forbear.°	be patient
	ADRIANA Patience unmoved! No marvel though she pause:[7]	
	They can be meek that have no other cause.°	reason not to be
	A wretched soul, bruised with adversity,	
35	We bid be quiet when we hear it cry.	
	But were we burdened with like° weight of pain,	equal
	As much or more we should ourselves complain.	
	So thou, that hast no unkind mate to grieve thee,	
	With urging helpless° patience would relieve° me.	futile / comfort
40	But if thou live to see like right bereft,[8]	
	This fool-begged[9] patience in thee will be left.°	abandoned
	LUCIANA Well, I will marry one day, but to try.°	test

Enter DROMIO OF EPHESUS

	Here comes your man.° Now is your husband nigh.°	servant / near
	ADRIANA Say, is your tardy master now at hand?	
45	DROMIO OF EPHESUS Nay, he's at two hands with me, and that	
	my two ears can witness.[1]	
	ADRIANA Say, didst thou speak with him? Know'st thou his mind?	
	DROMIO OF EPHESUS I? Ay, he told[2] his mind upon mine ear.	
	Beshrew° his hand, I scarce could understand it.	Curse
50	LUCIANA Spake he so doubtfully° thou couldst not feel his meaning?	ambiguously
	DROMIO OF EPHESUS Nay, he struck so plainly I could too well	
	feel his blows, and withal so doubtfully° that I could scarce	dreadfully; stoutly
	under-stand° them.	stand under
	ADRIANA But say, I prithee,° is he coming home?	pray thee
55	It seems he hath great care to please his wife.[3]	
	DROMIO OF EPHESUS Why, mistress, sure my master is horn-mad.	
	ADRIANA Horn-mad,[4] thou villain?	
	DROMIO OF EPHESUS I mean not cuckold-mad, but sure he is stark mad.	
	When I desired him to come home to dinner,	
60	He asked me for a thousand marks in gold.	
	''Tis dinner-time,' quoth I. 'My gold,' quoth he.	
	'Your meat doth burn,' quoth I. 'My gold,' quoth he.	
	'Will you come home?' quoth I. 'My gold,' quoth he;	
	'Where is the thousand marks I gave thee, villain?'	
65	'The pig', quoth I, 'is burned.' 'My gold!' quoth he.	
	'My mistress, sir—' quoth I. 'Hang up° thy mistress!	Enough of
	I know thy mistress not. Out° on thy mistress!'	A curse
	LUCIANA Quoth who?	
	DROMIO OF EPHESUS Quoth my master.	
70	'I know', quoth he, 'no house, no wife, no mistress.'	
	So that my errand,° due unto my tongue,[5]	delivery; message
	I thank him, I bare° home upon my shoulders;	bore
	For, in conclusion, he did beat me there.	
	ADRIANA Go back again, thou slave, and fetch him home.	
75	DROMIO OF EPHESUS Go back again and be new° beaten home?	again

7. That she hesitates (to marry).
8. *like . . . bereft:* yourself similarly deprived of rights.
9. Declaredly foolish; to "beg a person for a fool" was to petition the Court of Wards for custody of a lunatic (and thus custody of all his possessions).
1. *he's . . . witness:* he boxed my ears with both of his hands.
2. Communicated, but playing on "struck" ("tolled").
3. Ironic: compare 1 Corinthians 7:32–33: "The unmar-

ried careth for the things of the Lord, how he may please the Lord: But he that is married careth for the things that are of the world, how he may please his wife."
4. Uncontrolled and wild as a horned beast (a common expression, as intended by Dromio); enraged at being made a cuckold, who by popular repute grew horns (as Adriana takes it).
5. *due . . . tongue:* which I should have carried back in words.

For God's sake, send some other messenger.
ADRIANA   Back, slave, or I will break thy pate across.
DROMIO OF EPHESUS   An he will bless that cross with other beating,[6]
   Between you I shall have a holy[7] head.
80   ADRIANA   Hence, prating peasant.° Fetch thy master home.   *babbling fellow*
   [*She beats* DROMIO]
DROMIO OF EPHESUS   Am I so round[8] with you as you with me,
   That like a football you do spurn° me thus?   *maltreat; kick*
   You spurn me hence, and he will spurn me hither.
   If I last in this service, you must case me in leather.[9]   [*Exit*]
85   LUCIANA [*to* ADRIANA]   Fie, how impatience loureth° in your face!   *frowns*
   ADRIANA   His company must do his minions grace,[1]
   Whilst I at home starve for a merry look.
   Hath homely age th'alluring beauty took
   From my poor cheek? Then he hath wasted it.[2]
90   Are my discourses dull? Barren my wit?
   If voluble and sharp° discourse be marred,   *witty*
   Unkindness blunts it more than marble hard.[3]
   Do their° gay vestments° his affections bait?[4]   *(the minions') / clothing*
   That's not my fault: he's master of my state.[5]
95   What ruins are in me that can be found
   By him not ruined?[6] Then is he the ground°   *cause*
   Of my defeatures.° My decayèd fair°   *disfigurement / beauty*
   A sunny look of his would soon repair.
   But, too unruly deer, he breaks the pale,[7]
100   And feeds from° home. Poor I am but his stale.[8]   *away from*
   LUCIANA   Self-harming jealousy! Fie, beat it hence.
   ADRIANA   Unfeeling fools can with such wrongs dispense.
   I know his eye doth homage otherwhere,
   Or else what lets° it but he would be here?   *prevents*
105   Sister, you know he promised me a chain.
   Would that alone o' love he would detain,[9]
   So° he would keep fair quarter° with his bed.   *If then / faith*
   I see the jewel best enamellèd
   Will lose her beauty. Yet the gold bides° still   *remains*
110   That others touch;[1] and often touching will
   Wear gold, and yet no man that hath a name°   *reputation*
   By falsehood and corruption doth it shame.[2]
   Since that my beauty cannot please his eye,
   I'll weep what's left away, and weeping die.
115   LUCIANA   How many fond° fools serve mad jealousy!   *infatuated*
              Exeunt [*into the Phoenix*]

6. If he will give me another beating (playing on
"across," a cross made by blows on my head, and
"bless," the French *blesser*, "to injure").
7. Blessed (because marked with the sign of the cross);
also, full of holes.
8. Blunt, disrespectful (with a play on "spherical," like
a football).
9. If I survive as your servant, you must cover me with
leather, like a football; with a play on "last," a wooden
model of a foot used in making leather shoes.
1. Must grace his paramours.
2. Caused it to waste away; squandered it.
3. More than hard marble would blunt a sharp tool.
4. Lure away (bait); lessen (abate) toward Adriana.
5. Estate or general condition, including clothes; also,

metaphorically, kingdom.
6. *What . . . ruined:* What deterioration can be found
in me that he is not responsible for?
7. He goes beyond the park boundary ("pale").
8. Lover held up to the ridicule of her rivals; prostitute.
9. *Would . . . detain:* I wish he would withhold that one
manifestation of love.
1. *touch:* test (the fineness of gold was tested by rubbing it on a touchstone); caress, referring to her husband's infidelities.
2. *I see . . . shame:* a difficult passage, possibly owing to
omitted lines. The general idea is that reputation, like
gold, withstands corruption and yet may be worn away.
Her husband's infidelities have not tarnished his name,
but they may diminish her substance.

2.2

Enter ANTIPHOLUS [OF SYRACUSE]

ANTIPHOLUS OF SYRACUSE   The gold I gave to Dromio is laid up
   Safe at the Centaur, and the heedful° slave   *careful*
   Is wandered forth in care to seek me out.
   By computation and mine host's report,[1]
5   I could not speak° with Dromio since at first   *could not have spoken*
   I sent him from the mart! See, here he comes.
       Enter DROMIO [OF] SYRACUSE
   How now, sir, is your merry humour altered?
   As you love strokes,° so jest with me again.   *blows*
   You know no Centaur? You received no gold?
10   Your mistress sent to have me home to dinner?
   My house was at the Phoenix?—Wast thou mad,
   That thus so madly thou didst answer me?
DROMIO OF SYRACUSE   What answer, sir? When spake I such a word?
ANTIPHOLUS OF SYRACUSE   Even now, even here, not half an hour since.
15 DROMIO OF SYRACUSE   I did not see you since you sent me hence
   Home to the Centaur with the gold you gave me.
ANTIPHOLUS OF SYRACUSE   Villain, thou didst deny the gold's
     receipt,°   *receiving the gold*
   And told'st me of a mistress and a dinner,
   For which I hope thou felt'st[2] I was displeased.
20 DROMIO OF SYRACUSE   I am glad to see you in this merry vein.°   *disposition*
   What means this jest? I pray you, master, tell me.
ANTIPHOLUS OF SYRACUSE   Yea, dost thou jeer and flout me in
     the teeth?°   *to my face*
   Think'st thou I jest? Hold,° take thou that, and that.   *Stop*
      [*He*] *beats* DROMIO
DROMIO OF SYRACUSE   Hold, sir, for God's sake—now your jest is earnest![3]
25   Upon what bargain[4] do you give it me?
ANTIPHOLUS OF SYRACUSE   Because that I familiarly sometimes
   Do use you for my fool,° and chat with you,   *jester*
   Your sauciness will jest upon my love,[5]
   And make a common[6] of my serious hours.
30   When the sun shines, let foolish gnats make sport,°   *play*
   But creep in crannies when he hides his beams.
   If you will jest with me, know my aspect,[7]
   And fashion your demeanour to° my looks,   *to match*
   Or I will beat this method° in your sconce.°   *rule / head*
35 DROMIO OF SYRACUSE   'Sconce'° call you it? So° you would leave   *Small fort / If*
   battering,[8] I had rather have it a head. An° you use these   *If*
   blows long, I must get a sconce° for my head, and ensconce° *protective screen / shelter*
   it too, or else I shall seek my wit° in my shoulders. But I pray,   *brains*
   sir, why am I beaten?
40 ANTIPHOLUS OF SYRACUSE   Dost thou not know?
DROMIO OF SYRACUSE   Nothing, sir, but that I am beaten.

2.2 Location: A street in Ephesus.
1. Based on a calculation of the time elapsed and the
innkeeper's account of Dromio's doings.
2. Perceived, with an allusion to the beating.
3. Serious, with a play on "earnest" as a deposit to
secure a business transaction.
4. Transaction (playing on the financial sense of
"earnest"); in this context, contention or quarrel.

5. *Your . . . love:* You impertinently assume the right to
joke because of my benevolence.
6. Land belonging to the whole community (Dromio
maintains an egalitarian spirit at inappropriate times).
7. Countenance, expression; (in astrology) the position
of a heavenly body, as the sun (lines 30–31).
8. Beating; here, with a play on "sconce," attacking
with a battering ram.

ANTIPHOLUS OF SYRACUSE   Shall I tell you why?

DROMIO OF SYRACUSE   Ay, sir, and wherefore;° for they say every _for what reason_
why hath a wherefore.

45 ANTIPHOLUS OF SYRACUSE   'Why' first: for flouting me; and then 'wherefore':
For urging° it the second time to me.   _repeating_

DROMIO OF SYRACUSE   Was there ever any man thus beaten out
of season,°   _unjustly_
When in the why and the wherefore is neither rhyme nor reason?—
Well, sir, I thank you.

ANTIPHOLUS OF SYRACUSE   Thank me, sir, for what?

50 DROMIO OF SYRACUSE   Marry,[9] sir, for this something that you
gave me for nothing.

ANTIPHOLUS OF SYRACUSE   I'll make you amends next, to give°   _by giving_
you nothing for something. But say, sir, is it dinner-time?

DROMIO OF SYRACUSE   No, sir, I think the meat wants that° I   _lacks what_
55 have.

ANTIPHOLUS OF SYRACUSE   In good time,[1] sir. What's that?

DROMIO OF SYRACUSE   Basting.[2]

ANTIPHOLUS OF SYRACUSE   Well, sir, then 'twill be dry.

DROMIO OF SYRACUSE   If it be, sir, I pray you eat none of it.

60 ANTIPHOLUS OF SYRACUSE   Your reason?

DROMIO OF SYRACUSE   Lest it make you choleric[3] and purchase
me another dry basting.°   _severe beating_

ANTIPHOLUS OF SYRACUSE   Well, sir, learn to jest in good time.[4]
There's a time for all things.

65 DROMIO OF SYRACUSE   I durst° have denied that before you were   _dared_
so choleric.

ANTIPHOLUS OF SYRACUSE   By what rule,° sir?   _principle_

DROMIO OF SYRACUSE   Marry, sir, by a rule as plain as the plain
bald pate of Father Time himself.[5]

70 ANTIPHOLUS OF SYRACUSE   Let's hear it.

DROMIO OF SYRACUSE   There's no time for a man to recover his
hair that grows bald by nature.

ANTIPHOLUS OF SYRACUSE   May he not do it by fine and
recovery?[6]

75 DROMIO OF SYRACUSE   Yes, to pay a fine° for a periwig, and   _fee_
recover the lost hair of another man.[7]

ANTIPHOLUS OF SYRACUSE   Why is Time such a niggard of hair,
being, as it is, so plentiful an excrement?°   _outward growth_

DROMIO OF SYRACUSE   Because it is a blessing that he bestows on
80 beasts, and what he hath scanted° men in hair he hath given   _given less to_
them in wit.°   _intellect_

ANTIPHOLUS OF SYRACUSE   Why, but there's many a man hath
more hair than wit.

DROMIO OF SYRACUSE   Not a man of those but he hath the wit to
85 lose his hair.[8]

9. By the Virgin Mary, a mild oath.
1. Indeed! (an expression of ironical acquiescence).
2. Punning on a second meaning, "beating."
3. Angry. Choler was the hot, dry humor (see note to
1.2.21); diet and climate were thought to affect the
humors sympathetically, so that overly dry meat might
lead to a choleric disposition.
4. Opportunely; in a merry or good-humored time.

5. Time was commonly depicted as a bald old man.
6. _fine and recovery_: the legal method of transferring
the ownership of property that could not normally be
sold, especially to break an entail.
7. _to pay . . . man_: to buy a wig made from someone
else's hair (as wigs usually were).
8. _wit . . . hair_: ironic—clever enough to catch syphilis
(which may cause hair loss).

ANTIPHOLUS OF SYRACUSE   Why, thou didst conclude hairy men
   plain dealers, without wit.[9]

DROMIO OF SYRACUSE   The plainer dealer,[1] the sooner lost. Yet
   he loseth it in a kind of jollity.°   *(sexual pleasure)*

90 ANTIPHOLUS OF SYRACUSE   For what reason?

DROMIO OF SYRACUSE   For two, and sound° ones too.   *strong*

ANTIPHOLUS OF SYRACUSE   Nay, not sound,° I pray you.   *healthy*

DROMIO OF SYRACUSE   Sure° ones, then.   *Certain*

ANTIPHOLUS OF SYRACUSE   Nay, not sure,° in a thing falsing.[2]   *trustworthy*

95 DROMIO OF SYRACUSE   Certain ones, then.

ANTIPHOLUS OF SYRACUSE   Name them.

DROMIO OF SYRACUSE   The one, to save the money that he
   spends in tiring;° the other, that at dinner they should not drop   *hairstyling*
   in his porridge.

100 ANTIPHOLUS OF SYRACUSE   You would all this time have proved
   there is no time for all things.

DROMIO OF SYRACUSE   Marry, and did, sir: namely, e'en° no time   *even; precisely*
   to recover hair lost by nature.

ANTIPHOLUS OF SYRACUSE   But your reason was not substantial,°   *firmly based*
105   why there is no time to recover.

DROMIO OF SYRACUSE   Thus I mend° it: Time himself is bald,   *improve*
   and therefore to the world's end will have bald followers.

ANTIPHOLUS OF SYRACUSE   I knew 'twould be a bald° conclusion.   *an inane*

Enter [from the Phoenix] ADRIANA *and* LUCIANA

   But soft—who wafts° us yonder?   *beckons*

110 ADRIANA   Ay, ay, Antipholus, look strange[3] and frown:
   Some other mistress hath thy sweet aspects.°   *loving looks*
   I am not Adriana, nor thy wife.
   The time was once when thou unurged wouldst vow
   That never words were music to thine ear,
115   That never object pleasing in thine eye,
   That never touch well welcome to thy hand,
   That never meat sweet-savoured in thy taste,
   Unless I spake, or looked, or touched, or carved to° thee.   *for*
   How comes it now, my husband, O how comes it
120   That thou art then estrangèd from thyself?—
   Thy 'self' I call it, being strange to me
   That, undividable, incorporate,°   *united in one body*
   Am better than thy dear self's better part.[4]
   Ah, do not tear away thyself from me;
125   For know, my love, as easy mayst thou fall°   *let fall*
   A drop of water in the breaking gulf,
   And take unmingled thence that drop again
   Without addition or diminishing,
   As take from me thyself, and not me too.[5]
130   How dearly° would it touch thee to the quick   *deeply*
   Shouldst thou but° hear I were licentious,   *only*
   And that this body, consecrate to thee,
   By ruffian lust should be contaminate?

---

9. *conclude . . . wit*: argue that hairy men were simple,
lacking in cunning and therefore honest (plain dealers).
1. With pun on "deal," have sex.
2. In a deceptive matter; perhaps punning on "thing"
as "sexual organ."
3. Look distant, but suggesting "without recognition,"
as if a foreigner—which he is.

4. Either his better qualities or his soul (which is better than his body). Adriana's plea depends on the doctrine of marriage as "one flesh" articulated in Genesis
2:23–24 and echoed in Paul's mystical view of the
church as wedded to God. Compare Ephesians
5:28–33.
5. *not me too*: not take me away from myself as well.

	Wouldst thou not spit at me, and spurn° at me,	*strike*
135	And hurl the name of husband in my face,[6]	
	And tear the stained skin[7] off my harlot brow,	
	And from my false hand cut the wedding ring,	
	And break it with a deep-divorcing vow?	
	I know thou canst, and therefore see° thou do it!	*make sure*
140	I am possessed with° an adulterate blot;[8]	*in possession of*
	My blood is mingled with the crime of lust.	
	For if we two be one, and thou play false,	
	I do digest the poison of thy flesh,	
	Being strumpeted° by thy contagion.	*made a whore*
145	Keep then fair league[9] and truce with thy true bed,	
	I live unstained, thou undishonourèd.	

ANTIPHOLUS OF SYRACUSE   Plead you to *me*, fair dame? I know you not.
In Ephesus I am but two hours old,
As strange unto your town as to your talk,
150   Who, every word by all my wit being scanned,°   *analyzed*
Wants° wit in all one word to understand.   *Lacks*

LUCIANA   Fie, brother,° how the world is changed with you!   *brother-in-law*
When were you wont to use° my sister thus?   *treat*
She sent for you by Dromio home to dinner.

155   ANTIPHOLUS OF SYRACUSE   By Dromio?

DROMIO OF SYRACUSE   By me?

ADRIANA   By thee; and this thou didst return° from him—   *bring back*
That he did buffet thee, and in his blows
Denied my house for° his, me for his wife.   *to be*

160   ANTIPHOLUS OF SYRACUSE   Did you converse, sir, with this gentlewoman?
What is the course and drift of your compact?[1]

DROMIO OF SYRACUSE   I, sir? I never saw her till this time.

ANTIPHOLUS OF SYRACUSE   Villain, thou liest; for even her very° words   *exact*
Didst thou deliver to me on the mart.

165   DROMIO OF SYRACUSE   I never spake with her in all my life.

ANTIPHOLUS OF SYRACUSE   How can she thus then call us by our
        names?—
Unless it be by inspiration.°   *divine revelation*

ADRIANA   How ill agrees it° with your gravity°   *does it suit / dignity*
To counterfeit° thus grossly° with your slave,   *dissemble / blatantly*
170   Abetting him to thwart me in my mood!
Be it my wrong you are from me exempt,[2]
But wrong not that wrong with a more contempt.[3]
Come, I will fasten on this sleeve of thine.
Thou art an elm, my husband; I a vine,[4]
175   Whose weakness, married to thy stronger state,°   *condition*
Makes me with thy strength to communicate.°   *share*
If aught possess thee from me,[5] it is dross,°   *worthless*
Usurping ivy, brier, or idle moss,
Who, all° for want of pruning, with intrusion°   *entirely / invasively*
180   Infect thy sap, and live on thy confusion.[6]

---

6. And bitterly confront me with my degraded marriage vow.
7. Mark of impure character, as if she had been legally branded as a harlot.
8. The stain, or disgrace, of adultery.
9. *Keep . . . league:* If you keep faithful alliance.
1. What is the purpose and meaning of your conspiracy?
2. *Be . . . exempt:* Grant that it is my fault that you are

alienated from me.
3. But do not add to that injury with mockery.
4. This image occurs both in Ovid's *Metamorphoses* 14.665–66 and in Psalm 128:3, included in the Elizabethan homily on marriage.
5. If anything takes possession of you away from (or apart from) me.
6. *live . . . confusion:* take life from your destruction.

ANTIPHOLUS OF SYRACUSE [*aside*]   To me she speaks, she moves°   *uses*
 me for her theme.°   *topic*
What, was I married to her in my dream?
Or sleep I now, and think I hear all this?
What error drives our eyes and ears amiss?
185 Until I know this sure uncertainty,
I'll entertain° the offered fallacy.°   *accept / delusion*
LUCIANA   Dromio, go bid the servants spread° for dinner.   *lay the table*
DROMIO OF SYRACUSE [*aside*]   O, for my beads!° I cross me[7] for°   *rosary beads / as*
 a sinner.
This is the fairy land. O spite of spites,
190 We talk with goblins, oafs,[8] and sprites.°   *spirits*
If we obey them not, this will ensue:
They'll suck our breath or pinch us black and blue.[9]
LUCIANA   Why prat'st° thou to thyself, and answer'st not?   *babble*
Dromio, thou drone,° thou snail, thou slug, thou sot.°   *idler / blockhead*
DROMIO OF SYRACUSE [*to* ANTIPHOLUS]   I am transformèd,
195 master, am not I?
ANTIPHOLUS OF SYRACUSE   I think thou art in mind, and so am I.
DROMIO OF SYRACUSE   Nay, master, both in mind and in my shape.
ANTIPHOLUS OF SYRACUSE   Thou hast thine own form.
DROMIO OF SYRACUSE   No, I am an ape.[1]
LUCIANA   If thou art changed to aught,° 'tis to an ass.   *anything*
DROMIO OF SYRACUSE [*to* ANTIPHOLUS]   'Tis true she rides° me,   *tyrannizes*
200 and I long for grass.[2]
'Tis so, I am an ass; else it could never be
But I should know her as well as she knows me.
ADRIANA   Come, come, no longer will I be a fool,
To put the finger in the eye and weep
205 Whilst man and master laughs my woes to scorn.[3]
[*To* ANTIPHOLUS] Come, sir, to dinner.—Dromio, keep the gate.—
Husband, I'll dine above with you today,
And shrive you of[4] a thousand idle pranks.—
Sirrah,[5] if any ask you for your master,
210 Say he dines forth,° and let no creature enter.—   *out*
Come, sister.—Dromio, play the porter well.
ANTIPHOLUS OF SYRACUSE [*aside*]   Am I in earth, in heaven, or in hell?
Sleeping or waking? Mad or well advised?°   *sane*
Known unto these, and to myself disguised!
215 I'll say as they say, and persever so,
And in this mist at all adventures° go.   *whatever occurs*
DROMIO OF SYRACUSE   Master, shall I be porter at the gate?
ADRIANA   Ay, and let none enter, lest I break your pate.°   *head*
LUCIANA   Come, come, Antipholus, we dine too late.
      Exeunt [*into the Phoenix*]

---

7. Make the sign of the cross (to ward off evil).
8. Changelings, goblin children left in the place of abducted human infants. F reads "owles," a possible reference to witchcraft.
9. Traditional recreations for fairies.

1. An imitation (of myself); a fool.
2. Freedom, as when a horse is put out to pasture.
3. *laughs . . . scorn:* make a mockery of my pain.
4. And act as your confessor to hear and pardon.
5. Standard term for addressing inferiors.

3.1

Enter ANTIPHOLUS OF EPHESUS, *his man* DROMIO,
ANGELO *the goldsmith, and* BALTHASAR *the merchant*

ANTIPHOLUS OF EPHESUS   Good Signor Angelo, you must excuse us all.
    My wife is shrewish° when I keep not hours.°   *ill tempered / am late*
    Say that I lingered with you at your shop
    To see the making of her carcanet,°   *jeweled necklace*
5   And that tomorrow you will bring it home.—
    But here's a villain that would face me down[1]
    He met me on the mart, and that I beat him,
    And charged him with[2] a thousand marks in gold,
    And that I did deny my wife and house.
10   Thou drunkard, thou, what didst thou mean by this?
DROMIO OF EPHESUS   Say what you will, sir, but I know what I know—
    That you beat me at the mart I have your hand[3] to show.
    If the skin were parchment, and the blows you gave were ink,
    Your own handwriting would tell you what I think.
ANTIPHOLUS OF EPHESUS   I think thou art an ass.
15 DROMIO OF EPHESUS   Marry, so it doth appear
    By the wrongs I suffer and the blows I bear.
    I should kick being kicked, and, being at that pass,°   *in that predicament*
    You would keep from my heels, and beware of an ass.
ANTIPHOLUS OF EPHESUS   You're sad,° Signor Balthasar. Pray   *serious*
    God our cheer°   *fare*
20   May answer° my good will, and your good welcome here.   *equal*
BALTHASAR   I hold your dainties cheap, sir, and your welcome dear.[4]
ANTIPHOLUS OF EPHESUS   O, Signor Balthasar, either at flesh or fish
    A table full of welcome makes scarce° one dainty dish.   *scarcely makes*
BALTHASAR   Good meat, sir, is common; that every churl° affords.   *peasant*
ANTIPHOLUS OF EPHESUS   And welcome more common, for
25   that's nothing but words.
BALTHASAR   Small cheer° and great welcome makes a merry feast.   *Little food*
ANTIPHOLUS OF EPHESUS   Ay, to a niggardly host and more spar-
    ing° guest.   *temperate*
    But though my cates° be mean,° take them in good part.   *provisions / poor*
    Better cheer may you have, but not with better heart.
30   But soft,[5] my door is locked. [*To* DROMIO] Go bid them let us in.
DROMIO OF EPHESUS [*calling*]   Maud, Bridget, Marian, Cicely, Gillian, Ginn!
    [*Enter* DROMIO OF SYRACUSE *within the Phoenix*]
DROMIO OF SYRACUSE [*within the Phoenix*]   Mome, malt-horse,
    capon, coxcomb, idiot, patch![6]
    Either get thee from the door or sit down at the hatch.[7]
    Dost thou conjure for° wenches, that thou call'st for such   *summon by spells*
    store°   *plenty*
35   When one is one too many? Go, get thee from the door.
DROMIO OF EPHESUS   What patch is made our porter? My mas-
    ter stays° in the street.   *waits*
DROMIO OF SYRACUSE [*within*]   Let him walk from whence he
    came, lest he catch cold on's° feet.   *on his*

3.1 Location: Before the house of Antipholus of Ephesus.
1. That would insist despite my denial that.
2. And accused him of possessing.
3. The mark of Antipholus's hand.
4. I value your welcome more highly than the delicacies of your table.
5. An exclamation of surprise.
6. Dolt, plodding oaf, eunuch, fool, idiot, clown.
7. Literally, sit down at the gate or half door, but playing on the proverbial phrase "set a hatch (gate) before
the door" of the tongue: keep silent.

ANTIPHOLUS OF EPHESUS Who talks within there? Ho, open the door!

DROMIO OF SYRACUSE [*within the Phoenix*] Right, sir, I'll tell
you when, an° you'll tell me wherefore.   *if*

40 ANTIPHOLUS OF EPHESUS Wherefore? For my dinner—I have not dined today.

DROMIO OF SYRACUSE [*within the Phoenix*] Nor today here you
must not. Come again when you may.

ANTIPHOLUS OF EPHESUS What art thou that keep'st me out
from the house I owe?°   *own*

DROMIO OF SYRACUSE [*within the Phoenix*] The porter for this
time,° sir, and my name is Dromio.   *for now*

DROMIO OF EPHESUS O villain, thou hast stol'n both mine
office° and my name.   *function*

45 The one ne'er got me credit, the other mickle blame.⁸

If thou hadst been Dromio today in my place,

Thou wouldst have changed thy pate° for an aim,⁹ or thy name   *exchanged your head*
for an ass.

Enter NELL [*within the Phoenix*]

NELL [*within the Phoenix*] What a coil° is there, Dromio? Who   *disturbance*
are those at the gate?

DROMIO OF EPHESUS Let my master in, Nell.¹

NELL [*within the Phoenix*]   Faith no, he comes too late;
And so tell your master.

50 DROMIO OF EPHESUS   O Lord, I must laugh.
Have at you² with a proverb: 'Shall I set in my staff?'³

NELL [*within the Phoenix*] Have at you with another—that's
'When? Can you tell?'⁴

DROMIO OF SYRACUSE [*within the Phoenix*] If thy name be
called Nell, Nell, thou hast answered him well.

ANTIPHOLUS OF EPHESUS [*to* NELL] Do you hear, you minion?°   *subordinate*
You'll let us in, I hope?

55 [   ]⁵

NELL [*within the Phoenix*] I thought to have asked you.

DROMIO OF SYRACUSE [*within*]   And you said no.°   *(already)*

DROMIO OF EPHESUS So, come help.

[*He and* ANTIPHOLUS *beat the door*]

Well struck! There was blow for blow.⁶

ANTIPHOLUS OF EPHESUS [*to* NELL] Thou baggage,° let me in.   *good-for-nothing*

NELL [*within the Phoenix*]   Can you tell for whose sake?

DROMIO OF EPHESUS Master, knock the door hard.

NELL [*within the Phoenix*]   Let him knock till it ache.

60 ANTIPHOLUS OF EPHESUS You'll cry for this, minion, if I beat the door down.

NELL [*within the Phoenix*] What needs all that, and a pair of stocks in the town?⁷

Enter ADRIANA [*within the Phoenix*]

ADRIANA [*within the Phoenix*] Who is that at the door that
keeps° all this noise?   *keeps up*

DROMIO OF SYRACUSE [*within the Phoenix*] By my troth, your
town is troubled with unruly boys.

---

8. My reputation ("name") has never brought me
credit, but in the course of my duties I have received
much reproof ("mickle").

9. A target or butt, punning on "a name."

1. In F, Nell is designated "Luce" throughout this scene.

2. A challenge or warning in a fight (as with a quarter
staff): Now I attack you.

3. Shall I take up residence? (proverbial).

4. Proverbial response of defiance.

5. Since line 54 has no rhyme in this consistently
rhymed passage, it seems likely that either "hope" should
be emended to "trow" (believe), or there is a line missing.

6. Blows to the door in response to verbal blows from
within.

7. Why should I worry when there is a legal punishment for such behavior? *stocks:* instrument of punishment in which a person was seated with his or her legs
locked in a wooden frame.

ANTIPHOLUS OF EPHESUS [*to* ADRIANA]   Are you there, wife? You
    might have come before.
ADRIANA [*within the Phoenix*]   Your wife, sir knave? Go, get you
65   from the door.   [*Exit with* NELL]
DROMIO OF EPHESUS [*to* ANTIPHOLUS]   If you went in pain, mas-
    ter, this knave would go sore.[8]
ANGELO [*to* ANTIPHOLUS]   Here is neither cheer, sir, nor wel-   *gladly*
    come; we would fain° have either.
BALTHASAR   In° debating which was best, we shall part° with   *After / depart*
    neither.
DROMIO OF EPHESUS [*to* ANTIPHOLUS]   They stand at the door,
    master. Bid them welcome hither.
ANTIPHOLUS OF EPHESUS   There is something in the wind,° that   *afoot*
70   we cannot get in.
DROMIO OF EPHESUS   You would say so, master, if your gar-
    ments were thin.°   *(taking "wind" literally)*
Your cake[9] here is warm within: you stand here in the cold.
It would make a man mad as a buck[1] to be so bought and sold.°   *betrayed*
ANTIPHOLUS OF EPHESUS   Go fetch me something. I'll break
    ope° the gate.   *open*
DROMIO OF SYRACUSE [*within the Phoenix*]   Break° any breaking   *Do*
75   here, and I'll break your knave's pate.
DROMIO OF EPHESUS   A man may break° a word with you, sir,   *speak*
    and words are but wind;
Ay, and break it in your face, so he break it° not behind.   *break wind*
DROMIO OF SYRACUSE [*within the Phoenix*]   It seems thou
    want'st breaking.[2] Out upon thee, hind!°   *slave; fellow*
DROMIO OF EPHESUS   Here's too much 'Out upon thee!' I pray
    thee, let me in.
DROMIO OF SYRACUSE [*within the Phoenix*]   Ay, when fowls have
80   no feathers, and fish have no fin.
ANTIPHOLUS OF EPHESUS   Well, I'll break in.—Go borrow me a crow.°   *crowbar*
DROMIO OF EPHESUS   A crow without feather? Master, mean you so?
For a fish without a fin, there's a fowl without a feather.
    [*To* DROMIO OF SYRACUSE]
If a crow help us in, sirrah, we'll pluck a crow° together.   *settle accounts*
85 ANTIPHOLUS OF EPHESUS   Go, get thee gone. Fetch me an iron crow.
BALTHASAR   Have patience, sir. O, let it not be so!
Herein you war against your reputation,
And draw within the compass of suspect°   *scope of suspicion*
Th'unviolated honour of your wife.
90 Once this:° your long experience of her wisdom,   *In brief*
Her sober virtue, years,° and modesty,   *maturity*
Plead on her part some cause° to you unknown;   *explanation; excuse*
And doubt not, sir, but she will well excuse°   *explain*
Why at this time the doors are made° against you.   *barred*
95 Be ruled by me. Depart in patience,
And let us to the Tiger[3] all to dinner,
And about evening come yourself alone
To know the reason of this strange restraint.°   *exclusion*
If by strong hand you offer° to break in   *attempt*
100 Now in the stirring passage° of the day,   *traffic*

8. If you, the master, get punished as a knave, so will I,   note).
the actual servant ("knave").   2. Need a beating; need to be "broken in," or tamed
9. Referring either to Adriana or to the meal.   like a horse.
1. Angry, with an allusion to cuckoldry (see 2.1.57 and   3. The name of an inn; see 1.2.9.

A vulgar° comment will be made of it,   *public; lewd*
And that supposèd° by the common rout°   *accepted / mob*
Against your yet ungallèd estimation,[4]
That may with foul intrusion enter in
105 And dwell upon your grave when you are dead.
For slander lives upon succession,°   *perpetuates itself*
For ever housed where once it gets possession.
ANTIPHOLUS OF EPHESUS You have prevailed. I will depart in quiet,
And in despite of mirth° mean to be merry.   *ridicule*
110 I know a wench of excellent discourse,
Pretty and witty; wild,° and yet, too, gentle.°   *lively / refined*
There will we dine. This woman that I mean,
My wife—but, I protest, without desert°—   *my deserving*
Hath oftentimes upbraided me withal.°   *scolded me about*
115 To her will we to dinner. [*To* ANGELO] Get you home
And fetch the chain. By this,° I know, 'tis made.   *this time*
Bring it, I pray you, to the Porcupine,
For there's the house.° That chain will I bestow—   *That is where she lives*
Be it for nothing but to spite my wife—
120 Upon mine hostess there. Good sir, make haste:
Since mine own doors refuse to entertain° me,   *welcome*
I'll knock elsewhere, to see if they'll disdain me.
ANGELO I'll meet you at that place some hour hence.
ANTIPHOLUS OF EPHESUS Do so.   [*Exit* ANGELO]
         This jest shall cost me some expense.
Exeunt [DROMIO OF SYRACUSE *within the*
Phoenix, and the others into the Porcupine]

3.2

Enter [*from the Phoenix*] LUCIANA *with* ANTIPHOLUS OF
SYRACUSE
LUCIANA And may it be that you have quite forgot
A husband's office?° Shall, Antipholus,   *duty*
Even in the spring of love thy love-springs° rot?   *young shoots of love*
Shall love, in building, grow so ruinous?[1]
5 If you did wed my sister for her wealth,
Then for her wealth's sake use° her with more kindness;   *treat*
Or if you like elsewhere, do it by stealth:
Muffle° your false love with some show of blindness.[2]   *Hide*
Let not my sister read it in your eye.
10 Be not thy tongue thy own shame's orator.
Look sweet, speak fair, become disloyalty;[3]
Apparel vice like virtue's harbinger.°   *herald*
Bear a fair presence,° though your heart be tainted: *Present a pleasant front*
Teach sin the carriage° of a holy saint.   *bearing*
15 Be secret-false. What° need she be acquainted?   *Why*
What simple thief brags of his own attaint?°   *crime*
'Tis double wrong to truant with° your bed,   *be unfaithful to*
And let her read it in thy looks at board.°   *table*
Shame hath a bastard fame, well managèd;°   *if properly handled*
20 Ill deeds is° doubled with an evil word.   *are*

---

4. *yet . . . estimation:* as yet uninjured reputation.
3.2 Location: Scene continues.
1. Shall love become a ruin at the time of its building?
2. Seem to blindfold yourself so that your glances do

not reveal your faithlessness.
3. *become disloyalty:* put an attractive face on your
unfaithfulness.

Alas, poor women, make us but believe—
    Being compact of credit⁴—that you love us.
Though others have the arm, show us the sleeve.⁵
    We in your motion turn,⁶ and you may move° us.   *control; touch*
25 Then, gentle brother, get you in again.
    Comfort my sister, cheer her, call her wife:
'Tis holy sport to be a little vain°   *false*
    When the sweet breath of flattery conquers strife.
ANTIPHOLUS OF SYRACUSE   Sweet mistress—what your name is else I know not,
30   Nor by what wonder you do hit of° mine.   *on*
Less in your knowledge and your grace you show not
    Than our earth's wonder,⁷ more than earth° divine.   *mortal flesh*
Teach me, dear creature, how to think and speak.
    Lay open to my earthy gross conceit,⁸
35 Smothered in errors, feeble, shallow, weak,
    The folded° meaning of your words' deceit.   *hidden*
Against my soul's pure truth why labour you
    To make it wander in an unknown field?
Are you a god? Would you create me new?°   *anew*
40   Transform me, then, and to your power I'll yield.
But if that I am I, then well I know
    Your weeping sister is no wife of mine,
Nor to her bed no homage° do I owe.   *duty*
    Far more, far more, to you do I decline.°   *incline; submit*
45 O, train° me not, sweet mermaid,⁹ with thy note   *entice*
    To drown me in thy sister's flood of tears.
Sing, siren, for thyself, and I will dote.°   *grow infatuated*
    Spread o'er the silver waves thy golden hairs,
And as a bed I'll take them, and there lie,
50   And in that glorious supposition° think   *(that the hair is a bed)*
He gains by death that° hath such means to die.¹   *who*
    Let love, being light,² be drownèd if she sink.
LUCIANA   What, are you mad, that you do reason so?
ANTIPHOLUS OF SYRACUSE   Not mad, but mated³—how, I do not know.
55 LUCIANA   It is a fault that springeth from your eye.°   *(from looking lustfully)*
ANTIPHOLUS OF SYRACUSE   For gazing on your beams,° fair sun,   *eyes*
    being by.
LUCIANA   Gaze where you should, and that will clear your sight.
ANTIPHOLUS OF SYRACUSE   As good to wink,° sweet love, as look   *shut one's eyes*
    on° night.   *at*
LUCIANA   Why call you me 'love'? Call my sister so.
ANTIPHOLUS OF SYRACUSE   Thy sister's sister.
LUCIANA   That's my sister.
60 ANTIPHOLUS OF SYRACUSE   No,
    It is thyself, mine own self's better part,
    Mine eye's clear eye, my dear heart's dearer heart,

---

4. Being made of credulity, gullible.
5. Although others have the reality of your love, present us the appearance.
6. We are subject to your influence (as heavenly bodies were believed to follow the rotations of concentric celestial spheres).
7. *Less . . . wonder:* You seem as wise and as gracious as the wonder of the world (probably an allusion to Queen Elizabeth, before whom the play may have been performed).

8. *earthy gross conceit:* clumsy mortal understanding.
9. Siren; in Greek legend, mermaids' singing lured sailors to their death (see line 47).
1. Perhaps with a pun on "to die" as the Elizabethan expression for "orgasm."
2. The line has two implications: only false love could sink, because true love is too light and buoyant; and love deserves drowning because it is giddy and wanton.
3. Amazed, confounded; in love; married.

My food, my fortune, and my sweet hope's aim,
My sole earth's heaven, and my heaven's claim.[4]

65 LUCIANA   All this my sister is, or else should be.

ANTIPHOLUS OF SYRACUSE   Call thyself sister, sweet, for I am thee.°   *thine*
Thee will I love, and with thee lead my life.
Thou hast no husband yet, nor I no wife.
Give me thy hand.

LUCIANA   O soft, sir, hold you still;
70   I'll fetch my sister to get her good will. *Exit* [*into the Phoenix*]
            Enter [*from the Phoenix*] DROMIO [OF] SYRACUSE

ANTIPHOLUS OF SYRACUSE   Why, how now, Dromio! Where
    runn'st thou so fast?

DROMIO OF SYRACUSE   Do you know me, sir? Am I Dromio? Am
    I your man? Am I myself?

75 ANTIPHOLUS OF SYRACUSE   Thou art Dromio, thou art my man,
    thou art thyself.

DROMIO OF SYRACUSE   I am an ass, I am a woman's man, and
    besides° myself.   *in addition*

ANTIPHOLUS OF SYRACUSE   What woman's man? And how
80   besides thyself?

DROMIO OF SYRACUSE   Marry, sir, besides myself I am due to a
    woman: one that claims me, one that haunts me, one that will
    have me.

ANTIPHOLUS OF SYRACUSE   What claim lays she to thee?

85 DROMIO OF SYRACUSE   Marry, sir, such claim as you would lay to
    your horse; and she would have me as a beast—not that, I being
    a beast, she would have me, but that she, being a very beastly
    creature, lays claim to me.

ANTIPHOLUS OF SYRACUSE   What is she?

90 DROMIO OF SYRACUSE   A very reverend° body; ay, such a one as a   *worthy*
    man may not speak of without he say 'sir-reverence'.[5] I have but
    lean luck in the match, and yet is she a wondrous fat marriage.

ANTIPHOLUS OF SYRACUSE   How dost thou mean, a fat marriage?

DROMIO OF SYRACUSE   Marry, sir, she's the kitchen wench,° and   *servant*
95   all grease; and I know not what use to put her to but to make
    a lamp of her, and run from her by her own light. I warrant°   *guarantee*
    her rags and the tallow in them will burn a Poland winter.[6] If
    she lives till doomsday, she'll burn a week longer than the
    whole world.[7]

100 ANTIPHOLUS OF SYRACUSE   What complexion is she of?

DROMIO OF SYRACUSE   Swart° like my shoe, but her face nothing   *Dark*
    like so clean kept. For why?°—She sweats a man may go over-   *How so?*
    shoes[8] in the grime of it.

ANTIPHOLUS OF SYRACUSE   That's a fault that water will mend.

105 DROMIO OF SYRACUSE   No, sir, 'tis in grain.° Noah's flood could   *ingrained*
    not do it.

ANTIPHOLUS OF SYRACUSE   What's her name?

DROMIO OF SYRACUSE   Nell, sir. But her name and three-
    quarters—that's an ell° and three-quarters—will not measure   *more than a yard*
110   her from hip to hip.

---

4. My only heaven on earth and only claim on heaven.
5. "Saving your reverence," an apology for a potentially offensive remark.
6. The length of a winter in Poland—a long time.

7. Than the rest of the world (the popular Christian belief being that the earth would end in fire).
8. She sweats so much a man may be up to his ankles.

ANTIPHOLUS OF SYRACUSE   Then she bears some breadth?

DROMIO OF SYRACUSE   No longer from head to foot than from
hip to hip. She is spherical, like a globe. I could find out°   *discover*
countries in her.

115 ANTIPHOLUS OF SYRACUSE   In what part of her body stands Ireland?

DROMIO OF SYRACUSE   Marry, sir, in her buttocks. I found it out
by the bogs.°   *peat marsh; sponginess*

ANTIPHOLUS OF SYRACUSE   Where Scotland?

DROMIO OF SYRACUSE   I found it by the barrenness, hard in the
120 palm of her hand.⁹

ANTIPHOLUS OF SYRACUSE   Where France?

DROMIO OF SYRACUSE   In her forehead, armed and reverted,¹
making war against her heir.²

ANTIPHOLUS OF SYRACUSE   Where England?

125 DROMIO OF SYRACUSE   I looked for the chalky cliffs,³ but I could
find no whiteness in them. But I guess it stood in her chin, by°   *judging by*
the salt rheum° that ran between France and it.   *mucus*

ANTIPHOLUS OF SYRACUSE   Where Spain?

DROMIO OF SYRACUSE   Faith, I saw it not, but I felt it hot in her
130 breath.⁴

ANTIPHOLUS OF SYRACUSE   Where America, the Indies?

DROMIO OF SYRACUSE   O, sir, upon her nose, all o'er embellished
with rubies, carbuncles, sapphires,⁵ declining their rich aspect⁶
to the hot breath of Spain, who sent whole armadas of car-
135 racks to be ballast⁷ at her nose.

ANTIPHOLUS OF SYRACUSE   Where stood Belgia, the Netherlands?

DROMIO OF SYRACUSE   O, sir, I did not look so low.⁸ To conclude,
this drudge or diviner° laid claim to me, called me Dromio,   *witch*
swore I was assured° to her, told me what privy° marks I had   *betrothed / private; secret*
140 about me—as the mark of my shoulder, the mole in my neck,
the great wart on my left arm—that I, amazed, ran from her
as a witch. And I think if my breast had not been made of faith,
and my heart of steel,⁹ she had transformed me to a curtal°   *tailless*
dog, and made me turn i'th' wheel.°   *turn a roasting spit*

ANTIPHOLUS OF SYRACUSE   Go, hie thee presently.° Post° to the   *now / Hasten*
145 road.°   *harbor*
An if° the wind blow any way from shore,°   *An if=If / out to sea*
I will not harbour in this town tonight.
If any barque put forth, come to the mart,
Where I will walk till thou return to me.
150 If everyone knows us, and we know none,
'Tis time, I think, to trudge,° pack, and be gone.   *depart*

DROMIO OF SYRACUSE   As from a bear a man would run for life,
So fly I from her that would be my wife.   *Exit [to the bay]*

ANTIPHOLUS OF SYRACUSE   There's none but witches do inhabit here,
155 And therefore 'tis high time that I were hence.
She that doth call me husband, even my° soul   *my very*

---

9. Hard with calluses and dry (a moist hand proverbially indicated fertility; hence a dry hand could con-
note barrenness).
1. In rebellion (perhaps referring to syphilitic sores).
2. A possible allusion to contemporary French politics;
a pun on "hair," which she is losing, probably on
account of venereal disease.
3. Teeth; an allusion to the white chalk cliffs of Dover.
4. As if she had been eating pungent food.

5. Glistening skin blemishes (as well as precious stones).
6. Casting their gaze down; paying tribute to.
7. *armadas . . . ballast:* fleets of galleons to be loaded.
8. The Netherlands and Belgium were also known as
the Low Countries.
9. Compare Ephesians 6:11ff.: "Put on the whole
armour of God, that ye may be able to stand against the
assaults of the devil. . . . having on the breast plate of
righteousness. . . . Above all, take the shield of faith."

Doth for a wife abhor. But her fair sister,
Possessed with such a gentle sovereign° grace,   *excellent*
Of such enchanting presence and discourse,
160 Hath almost made me traitor to myself.
But lest myself be guilty to° self-wrong,   *of*
I'll stop mine ears against the mermaid's song.
       Enter ANGELO *with the chain*
ANGELO   Master Antipholus.
ANTIPHOLUS OF SYRACUSE   Ay, that's my name.
ANGELO   I know it well, sir. Lo, here's the chain.
165 I thought to have ta'en° you at the Porcupine.   *overtaken*
The chain unfinished made me stay° thus long.   *delay*
ANTIPHOLUS OF SYRACUSE [*taking the chain*]   What is your will
    that I shall do with this?
ANGELO   What please° yourself, sir. I have made it for you.   *pleases*
ANTIPHOLUS OF SYRACUSE   Made it for me, sir? I bespoke° it not.   *ordered*
170 ANGELO   Not once, nor twice, but twenty times you have.
Go home with it, and please your wife withal,°   *with it*
And soon at supper-time I'll visit you,
And then receive my money for the chain.
ANTIPHOLUS OF SYRACUSE   I pray you, sir, receive the money now,
175 For fear you ne'er see chain nor money more.
ANGELO   You are a merry man, sir. Fare you well.   *Exit*
ANTIPHOLUS OF SYRACUSE   What I should think of this I cannot tell.
But this I think: there's no man is so vain°   *foolish*
That would refuse so fair an offered chain.
180 I see a man here needs not live by shifts,°   *his own efforts*
When in the streets he meets such golden gifts.
I'll to the mart, and there for Dromio stay.
If any ship put out, then straight° away!   *Exit*   *immediately*

4.1

      Enter [SECOND] MERCHANT, [ANGELO *the*] *goldsmith,*
      and an OFFICER
SECOND MERCHANT [*to* ANGELO]   You know since Pentecost[1] the sum is due,
And since I have not much importuned you;
Nor now I had not,° but° that I am bound   *I would not have / except*
To Persia, and want° guilders for my voyage.   *lack*
5 Therefore make present satisfaction,°   *immediate payment*
Or I'll attach° you by this officer.   *arrest*
ANGELO   Even just the sum that I do owe to you
Is growing° to me by Antipholus,   *owing*
And in the instant that I met with you
10 He had of me a chain. At five o'clock
I shall receive the money for the same.
Pleaseth you° walk with me down to his house,   *If it please you to*
I will discharge my bond, and thank you too.
      Enter ANTIPHOLUS [OF] EPHESUS, DROMIO [OF EPHESUS]
      from the Courtesan's [*house, the Porcupine*]
OFFICER   That labour may you save. See where he comes.

4.1 Location: A street in Ephesus.
1. Christian festival observed on the seventh Sunday after Easter, in commemoration of the descent of the Holy Ghost on the disciples on the day of the Jewish harvest holiday of Shavuoth.

ANTIPHOLUS OF EPHESUS [*to* DROMIO] While I go to the gold-
15   smith's house, go thou
And buy a rope's end.° That will I bestow°   *piece of rope / employ (as a whip)*
Among my wife and her confederates
For locking me out of my doors by day.
But soft,° I see the goldsmith. Get thee gone.   *wait*
20   Buy thou a rope, and bring it home to me.
DROMIO OF EPHESUS I buy a thousand pound a year, I buy a
  rope.[2]   *Exit*
ANTIPHOLUS OF EPHESUS [*to* ANGELO] A man is well holp up° *helped*
  that trusts to you!
I promisèd your presence and the chain,
But neither chain nor goldsmith came to me.
25   Belike° you thought our love° would last too long *Perhaps / friendship*
If it were chained together, and therefore came not.
ANGELO Saving° your merry humour, here's the note *Without offense to*
How much your chain weighs to the utmost carat,
The fineness of the gold, and chargeful fashion,° *costly craftsmanship*
30   Which doth amount to three odd ducats° more   *gold coins*
Than I stand debted° to this gentleman.   *indebted*
I pray you see him presently discharged,°   *paid off now*
For he is bound to sea, and stays but° for it.   *waits only*
ANTIPHOLUS OF EPHESUS I am not furnished with the present° money. *ready*
35   Besides, I have some business in the town.
Good signor, take the stranger to my house,
And with you take the chain, and bid my wife
Disburse the sum on the receipt thereof.
Perchance° I will be there as soon as you.   *Perhaps*
40 ANGELO Then you will bring the chain to her yourself?
ANTIPHOLUS OF EPHESUS No, bear it with you, lest I come not
  time° enough.   *soon*
ANGELO Well, sir, I will. Have you the chain about you?
ANTIPHOLUS OF EPHESUS An if I have not, sir, I hope you have;
  Or else you may return without your money.
45 ANGELO Nay, come, I pray you, sir, give me the chain.
Both wind and tide stays° for this gentleman,   *wait*
And I, to blame, have held him here too long.
ANTIPHOLUS OF EPHESUS Good Lord! You use this dalliance° to *trifling delay*
  excuse
Your breach of promise to° the Porcupine.   *to go to*
50   I should have chid you for not bringing it,
But like a shrew° you first begin to brawl.   *sour person*
SECOND MERCHANT [*to* ANGELO] The hour steals on. I pray you,
  sir, dispatch.°   *hurry*
ANGELO [*to* ANTIPHOLUS] You hear how he importunes me. The chain!
ANTIPHOLUS OF EPHESUS Why, give it to my wife, and fetch
  your money.
55 ANGELO Come, come, you know I gave it you even° now. *just*
Either send the chain, or send me by some token.[3]
ANTIPHOLUS OF EPHESUS Fie, now you run this humour out of
  breath.°   *exhaust this joke*
Come, where's the chain? I pray you let me see it.

---

2. Perhaps in exasperated contrast with Antipholus of 3. With some sign of yours (so that Adriana will know
Syracuse's earlier demand for a thousand marks (2.1.60). to pay me).

SECOND MERCHANT   My business cannot brook° this dalliance.   *tolerate*
60   Good sir, say whe'er° you'll answer° me or no;   *whether / repay*
     If not, I'll leave him to the officer.
ANTIPHOLUS OF EPHESUS   I answer you? What should I answer you?
ANGELO   The money that you owe me for the chain.
ANTIPHOLUS OF EPHESUS   I owe you none till I receive the chain.
65   ANGELO   You know I gave it you half an hour since.
ANTIPHOLUS OF EPHESUS   You gave me none. You wrong me much to say so.
ANGELO   You wrong me more, sir, in denying it.
     Consider how it stands upon° my credit.[4]   *affects*
SECOND MERCHANT   Well, officer, arrest him at my suit.
70   OFFICER [*to* ANGELO]   I do, and charge you in the Duke's name to obey me.
ANGELO [*to* ANTIPHOLUS]   This touches° me in reputation.   *injures*
     Either consent to pay this sum for me,
     Or I attach° you by this officer.   *arrest*
ANTIPHOLUS OF EPHESUS   Consent to pay thee that° I never had?   *for what*
75   Arrest me, foolish fellow, if thou dar'st.
ANGELO   Here is thy fee:[5] arrest him, officer.
     I would not spare my brother in this case
     If he should scorn me so apparently.°   *openly*
OFFICER [*to* ANTIPHOLUS]   I do arrest you, sir. You hear the suit.
80   ANTIPHOLUS OF EPHESUS   I do obey thee till I give thee bail.
     [*To* ANGELO] But, sirrah, you shall buy this sport as dear[6]
     As all the metal in your shop will answer.°   *amount to*
ANGELO   Sir, sir, I shall have law° in Ephesus,   *my legal rights*
     To your notorious shame, I doubt it not.
           Enter DROMIO [OF] SYRACUSE, *from the bay*
85   DROMIO OF SYRACUSE   Master, there's a barque of Epidamnum
     That stays but till her owner comes aboard,
     And then she bears away. Our freightage,° sir,   *luggage; goods*
     I have conveyed aboard, and I have bought
     The oil, the balsamum,[7] and aqua-vitae.
90   The ship is in her trim;° the merry wind   *ready to sail*
     Blows fair from land. They stay for naught° at all   *nothing*
     But for their owner, master, and yourself.
ANTIPHOLUS OF EPHESUS   How now? A madman? Why, thou
           peevish° sheep,[8]   *bleating*
     What ship of Epidamnum stays for me?
95   DROMIO OF SYRACUSE   A ship you sent me to, to hire waftage.°   *buy our passage*
ANTIPHOLUS OF EPHESUS   Thou drunken slave, I sent thee for a rope,
     And told thee to what purpose and what end.
DROMIO OF SYRACUSE   You sent me for a ropë's end° as soon.   *a beating*
     You sent me to the bay, sir, for a barque.
100 ANTIPHOLUS OF EPHESUS   I will debate this matter at more leisure,
     And teach your ears to list° me with more heed.   *listen to*
     To Adriana, villain, hie thee straight.°   *go immediately*
     Give her this key, and tell her in the desk
     That's covered o'er with Turkish tapestry
105 There is a purse of ducats. Let her send it.
     Tell her I am arrested in the street,
     And that shall bail me.° Hie thee, slave. Be gone!—   *pay my bail*

---

4. Financial standing; more generally, reputation.   7. A healing resin; alcoholic spirit.
5. Public officers were entitled to private payment.   8. Idiot, punning on "ship" in the next line (the words
6. You shall pay as dearly for this amusement.   were similarly pronounced).

On, officer, to prison, till it come.

Exeunt [all but DROMIO OF SYRACUSE]

DROMIO OF SYRACUSE   To Adriana. That is where we dined,
110   Where Dowsabel⁹ did claim me for her husband.
        She is too big, I hope, for me to compass.¹
        Thither I must, although against my will;
        For servants must their masters' minds° fulfil.   *Exit*   wishes

4.2

Enter [from the Phoenix] ADRIANA *and* LUCIANA

ADRIANA   Ah, Luciana, did he tempt thee so?
        Mightst thou perceive austerely in his eye¹
        That he did plead in earnest, yea or no?
        Looked he or° red or pale, or sad or merrily?   either
5   What observation mad'st thou in this case
        Of his heart's meteors tilting² in his face?
LUCIANA   First he denied you had in him no° right.   any
ADRIANA   He meant he did me none, the more my spite.°   grief
LUCIANA   Then swore he that he was a stranger here.
10   ADRIANA   And true he swore, though yet forsworn³ he were.
LUCIANA   Then pleaded I for you.
ADRIANA   And what said he?
LUCIANA   That love I begged for you, he begged of me.
ADRIANA   With what persuasion did he tempt thy love?
LUCIANA   With words that in an honest suit° might move.   courtship
15   First he did praise my beauty, then my speech.
ADRIANA   Didst speak him fair?°   encourage him
LUCIANA   Have patience, I beseech.
ADRIANA   I cannot, nor I will not, hold me still.°   silent
        My tongue, though not my heart, shall have his° will.   its
        He is deformèd, crookèd, old, and sere,°   withered
20   Ill-faced, worse-bodied, shapeless° everywhere,   ill shaped
        Vicious, ungentle, foolish, blunt, unkind,
        Stigmatical in making,⁴ worse in mind.
LUCIANA   Who would be jealous, then, of such a one?
        No evil lost is wailed when it is gone.
25   ADRIANA   Ah, but I think him better than I say,
        And yet would herein others' eyes were worse.⁵
        Far from her nest the lapwing⁶ cries away.
        My heart prays for him, though my tongue do curse.

Enter DROMIO [OF] SYRACUSE *running*

DROMIO OF SYRACUSE   Here, go—the desk, the purse! Sweet now, make haste!⁷
LUCIANA   How?⁸ Hast thou lost thy breath?
30   DROMIO OF SYRACUSE   By running fast.

---

9. English form of "Dulcibella," a generic name for a
sweetheart.
1. Embrace or gain; probably also alluding to her geographical extent (see 3.2.113–37).
4.2 Location: Before the house of Antipholus of Ephesus.
1. By the seriousness of his expression.
2. Conflicting emotions, as if heavenly bodies were
engaged in combat ("tilting").
3. *true . . . forsworn:* he is behaving like a stranger to
me, but he is lying and false to his marriage vows if he
claims to be one.

4. Deformed in his physical makeup.
5. And nevertheless wish others' eyes to be deceived
(and so think him ugly).
6. A bird (the peewit) that diverts attention away from
her nest to protect her young; Adriana wishes to turn
other women's attention from Antipholus's attractions.
7. Dromio is possibly speaking to himself as he rushes
in.
8. What's this? Although F treats Luciana's word as
one sentence, Dromio's answer is obviously a comic
misunderstanding.

ADRIANA   Where is thy master, Dromio? Is he well?

DROMIO OF SYRACUSE   No, he's in Tartar limbo,⁹ worse than hell.
    A devil in an everlasting¹ garment hath him,
    One whose hard heart is buttoned up with steel;
35   A fiend, a fairy,² pitiless and rough;
    A wolf, nay worse, a fellow all in buff;³
    A back-friend,⁴ a shoulder-clapper,° one that countermands°   arresting officer / prohibits
    The passages of alleys, creeks, and narrow launds;⁵
    A hound that runs counter,⁶ and yet draws dryfoot well;⁷
40   One that before the Judgement⁸ carries poor souls to hell.

ADRIANA   Why, man, what is the matter?

DROMIO OF SYRACUSE   I do not know the matter,° he is 'rested°   dispute / arrested
    on the case.⁹

ADRIANA   What, is he arrested? Tell me at whose suit.

DROMIO OF SYRACUSE   I know not at whose suit he is arrested well,
45   But is in a suit of buff which 'rested him, that can I tell.
    Will you send him, mistress, redemption—the money in his desk?

ADRIANA   Go fetch it, sister.   *Exit* LUCIANA [*into the Phoenix*]
                    This I wonder at,
    That he unknown to me should be in debt.
    Tell me, was he arrested on° a bond?   for breaking
50   DROMIO OF SYRACUSE   Not on a bond but on a stronger thing:
    A chain, a chain—do you not hear it ring?

ADRIANA   What, the chain?

DROMIO OF SYRACUSE   No, no, the bell. 'Tis time that I were gone:
    It was two ere I left him, and now the clock strikes one.¹

ADRIANA   The hours come back! That did I never hear.

DROMIO OF SYRACUSE   O yes, if any hour² meet a sergeant, a°   he
55   turns back for very fear.

ADRIANA   As if time were in debt. How fondly° dost thou reason!   foolishly

DROMIO OF SYRACUSE   Time is a very bankrupt, and owes more
    than he's worth to season.³
    Nay, he's a thief too. Have you not heard men say
    That time comes stealing on by night and day?
60   If a be in debt and theft, and a sergeant in° the way,   stands in
    Hath he not reason to turn back an hour in a day?
        Enter LUCIANA [*from the Phoenix, with the money*]

ADRIANA   Go, Dromio, there's the money. Bear it straight,°   quickly
    And bring thy master home immediately.   [*Exit* DROMIO]
    Come, sister, I am pressed° down with conceit:°   depressed / imaginings
65   Conceit, my comfort and my injury.
                Exeunt [*into the Phoenix*]

---

9. Hellish prison. "Tartar" is short for "Tartarus," the classical hell, but it also suggests the Tartars, central Asian people reputed by Elizabethans to be particularly savage. "Limbo" was common slang for "prison."
1. Term for the durable material used in the period for the uniform of prison officers; eternal, like hell's punishments.
2. Malevolent fairy, like the goblins in 2.2.190–92.
3. Stout leather used in uniforms.
4. False friend; also referring to the officer's hand on the culprit's back during an arrest.
5. The traffic through alleys, small passageways, and narrow pathways. *launds:* glades or clearings, pathways through woods.

6. Runs in the opposite direction to the prey; also perhaps alluding to the Counter, as several debtors' prisons in London were known.
7. *draws . . . well:* tracks game by the scent of its foot.
8. *before the Judgement:* in a court of law, with an allusion to the Day of Judgment.
9. *on the case:* in a legal action where the injury was not specifically addressed by precedent; by means of the officer's hand on his outer clothing ("case").
1. "On" and "one" were pronounced similarly.
2. Perhaps a pun on "ower" (debtor), or "whore."
3. "Seisin," a legal term for "possession"; opportunity; thus, there is too little time to make good the promises of the occasion.

4.3

Enter ANTIPHOLUS [OF] SYRACUSE [*wearing the chain*]

ANTIPHOLUS OF SYRACUSE   There's not a man I meet but doth salute° me   *greet*
 As if I were their well-acquainted friend,
 And everyone doth call me by my name.
 Some tender° money to me, some invite me,   *offer*
5 Some other give me thanks for kindnesses.
 Some offer me commodities to buy.
 Even now a tailor called me in his shop,
 And showed me silks that he had bought for me,
 And therewithal° took measure of my body.   *with that*
10 Sure, these are but imaginary wiles,°   *delusions*
 And Lapland sorcerers[1] inhabit here.

Enter DROMIO [OF] SYRACUSE [*with the money*]

DROMIO OF SYRACUSE   Master, here's the gold you sent me for.
 What, have you got redemption from the picture of old Adam
 new apparelled?[2]

ANTIPHOLUS OF SYRACUSE   What gold is this? What Adam dost
15 thou mean?

DROMIO OF SYRACUSE   Not that Adam that kept the Paradise,
 but that Adam that keeps the prison—he that goes in the calf's
 skin,[3] that was killed for the Prodigal;[4] he that came behind
 you, sir, like an evil angel, and bid you forsake your liberty.[5]

20 ANTIPHOLUS OF SYRACUSE   I understand thee not.

DROMIO OF SYRACUSE   No? Why, 'tis a plain case: he that went
 like a bass viol[6] in a case of leather; the man, sir, that when
 gentlemen are tired gives them a sob[7] and 'rests them; he, sir,
 that takes pity on decayed° men and gives them suits of   *ruined*
25 durance;[8] he that sets up his rest[9] to do more exploits with his
 mace° than a Moorish pike.   *staff of office*

ANTIPHOLUS OF SYRACUSE   What, thou mean'st an officer?

DROMIO OF SYRACUSE   Ay, sir, the sergeant of the band: he that
 brings any man to answer it° that breaks his bond; one that   *for it*
30 thinks a man always going to bed, and says 'God give you good
 rest.'°   *arrest*
   cease

ANTIPHOLUS OF SYRACUSE   Well, sir, there rest in° your foolery.
 Is there any ships puts forth tonight? May we be gone?

DROMIO OF SYRACUSE   Why, sir, I brought you word an hour
35 since that the barque *Expedition* put forth tonight, and then
 were you hindered by the sergeant to tarry for the hoy[1] *Delay*.
 Here are the angels[2] that you sent for to deliver you.

ANTIPHOLUS OF SYRACUSE The fellow is distraught,° and so am I,   *distracted; mad*
 And here we wander in illusions.
40 Some blessèd power deliver us from hence.

Enter a COURTESAN [*from the Porcupine*]

4.3 Location: A street in Ephesus.
1. Lapland was known for witches.
2. *from . . . apparelled*: from the sergeant in his leather
uniform. Old Adam is the figure of man's sinful nature,
dressed, after the Fall, in skins (Genesis 3:21). There is
also a possible reference to Ephesians 4:22–24 ("put
off . . . the old man, which is corrupt . . . put on the
new man, which after God is created in righteousness"). The text is emended from F: What have
you got the picture of old Adam new apparelled?
3. The buff of the officer's garments.
4. The prodigal son of Luke 15:11–32; his father killed

a calf for a feast on his return home.
5. *bid . . . liberty*: arrested you.
6. Large stringed instrument, like a cello (continuing
the jokes about the officer's leather uniform).
7. A rest (for tired horses) as well as a lament, picked
up in the following puns of "'rests" and "pity."
8. *suits of durance*: lawsuits or prosecutions ending in
imprisonment; clothes of hard-wearing material.
9. *sets up his rest*: gambles all (punning on "arrest").
1. A small, slow vessel used in coastal waters. The
names of the ships are Dromio's improvisations.
2. Gold coins bearing a figure of the archangel Michael.

COURTESAN   Well met, well met, Master Antipholus.
  I see, sir, you have found the goldsmith now.
  Is that the chain you promised me today?
ANTIPHOLUS OF SYRACUSE   Satan, avoid![3] I charge thee, tempt
    me not!

45 DROMIO OF SYRACUSE   Master, is this Mistress Satan?
ANTIPHOLUS OF SYRACUSE   It is the devil.
DROMIO OF SYRACUSE   Nay, she is worse, she is the devil's dam;°   *mother*
  and here she comes in the habit° of a light° wench. And thereof   *clothing / wanton*
  comes that the wenches say 'God damn me'—that's as much to
50 say, 'God make me a light wench.' It is written they appear to
  men like angels of light.[4] Light is an effect of fire, and fire will
  burn. Ergo,° light wenches will burn.[5] Come not near her.   *Therefore*
COURTESAN   Your man and you are marvellous merry, sir.
  Will you go with me? We'll mend° our dinner here.   *complete*
55 DROMIO OF SYRACUSE   Master, if you do, expect spoon-meat,[6]
  and bespeak° a long spoon.   *request*
ANTIPHOLUS OF SYRACUSE   Why, Dromio?
DROMIO OF SYRACUSE   Marry, he must have a long spoon that
  must eat with the devil.
ANTIPHOLUS OF SYRACUSE [*to* COURTESAN   Avoid, thou fiend!
60   What tell'st thou me of supping?
  Thou art, as you are all, a sorceress.
  I conjure° thee to leave me and be gone.   *order; charge*
COURTESAN   Give me the ring of mine you had at dinner,
  Or for my diamond the chain you promised,
65 And I'll be gone, sir, and not trouble you.
DROMIO OF SYRACUSE   Some devils ask but° the parings of one's nail,   *only*
  A rush,° a hair, a drop of blood, a pin,   *straw*
  A nut, a cherry-stone;
  But she, more covetous, would have a chain.
70 Master, be wise; an if° you give it her,   *an if=if*
  The devil will shake her chain,[7] and fright us with it.
COURTESAN [*to* ANTIPHOLUS]   I pray you, sir, my ring, or else the chain.
  I hope you do not mean to cheat me so?
ANTIPHOLUS OF SYRACUSE   Avaunt, thou witch!—Come, Dromio, let us go.
75 DROMIO OF SYRACUSE   'Fly pride' says the peacock.[8] Mistress, that you know.
                    Exeunt [ANTIPHOLUS OF SYRACUSE
                      and DROMIO OF SYRACUSE]
COURTESAN   Now, out of doubt, Antipholus is mad;
  Else would he never so demean° himself.   *conduct; debase*
  A ring he hath of mine worth forty ducats,
  And for the same he promised me a chain.
80 Both one and other he denies me now.
  The reason that I gather he is mad,
  Besides this present instance of his rage,
  Is a mad tale he told today at dinner
  Of his own doors being shut against his entrance.
85 Belike° his wife, acquainted with his fits,   *Probably*

---

3. Away. An echo of Jesus' words to Satan in Matthew
4:10: "Avoid Satan."
4. From 2 Corinthians 11:14: "Satan himself is transformed into an angel of light."
5. Will transmit venereal disease; will suffer in hell.
6. Soft food for babies or invalids, mentioned for the

sake of the proverb in lines 58–59.
7. Alluding to the binding of the devil in a chain in Revelation 20:1.
8. For the conniving courtesan to complain about
cheating is, in Dromio's view, analogous to a proud peacock decrying pride.

On purpose shut the doors against his way.°   *entrance*
My way is now to hie° home to his house,   *hasten*
And tell his wife that, being lunatic,
He rushed into my house, and took perforce°   *forcibly*
90   My ring away. This course I fittest choose,
For forty ducats is too much to lose.   [*Exit*]

4.4

Enter ANTIPHOLUS [OF] EPHESUS *with a Jailor* [*an*
OFFICER]

ANTIPHOLUS OF EPHESUS   Fear me not, man, I will not break away.
   I'll give thee ere I leave thee so much money
   To warrant thee° as I am 'rested for.   *As surety*
   My wife is in a wayward mood today,
5   And will not lightly° trust the messenger   *readily*
   That I should be attached° in Ephesus.   *arrested*
   I tell you 'twill sound harshly in her ears.
      Enter DROMIO [OF] EPHESUS *with a rope's end*
   Here comes my man. I think he brings the money.—
   How now, sir? Have you that I sent you for?
10 DROMIO OF EPHESUS   Here's that, I warrant you, will pay¹ them all.
ANTIPHOLUS OF EPHESUS   But where's the money?
DROMIO OF EPHESUS   Why, sir, I gave the money for the rope.
ANTIPHOLUS OF EPHESUS   Five hundred ducats, villain, for a rope?
DROMIO OF EPHESUS   I'll serve° you, sir, five hundred at the rate.°   *provide / for that price*
ANTIPHOLUS OF EPHESUS   To what end did I bid thee hie thee
15   home?
DROMIO OF EPHESUS   To° a rope's end, sir, and to that end am I   *For*
   returned.
ANTIPHOLUS OF EPHESUS   And to that end, sir, I will welcome you.²
      [*He beats* DROMIO]
OFFICER   Good sir, be patient.
DROMIO OF EPHESUS   Nay, 'tis for me to be patient: I am in adversity.³
20 OFFICER   Good now,° hold thy tongue.   *Please*
DROMIO OF EPHESUS   Nay, rather persuade *him* to hold° his   *hold off*
   hands.
ANTIPHOLUS OF EPHESUS   Thou whoreson,⁴ senseless villain!
DROMIO OF EPHESUS   I would I were senseless, sir, that I might
   not feel your blows.
25 ANTIPHOLUS OF EPHESUS   Thou art sensible in° nothing but   *responsive to*
   blows, and so is an ass.
DROMIO OF EPHESUS   I am an ass indeed. You may prove it by
   my long ears.⁵—I have served him from the hour of my nativity
   to this instant, and have nothing at his hands for my service
30   but blows. When I am cold, he heats me with beating. When
   I am warm, he cools me with beating. I am waked with it when
   I sleep, raised with it when I sit, driven out of doors with it when
   I go from home, welcomed home with it when I return. Nay, I
   bear it on my shoulders, as a beggar wont her brat,⁶ and I think

---

4.4 Location: Scene continues.
1. With a beating. (See 4.1.15–21.)
2. I will treat you to a rope's end (a beating).
3. In painful circumstances; alluding to Psalms 94:13.
4. Literally, son of a whore; more generally, a term of

contemptuous familiarity.
5. Playing on "ears/years," which were pronounced in
the same way.
6. *wont her brat*: is accustomed to carrying her child.

35 when he hath lamed me I shall beg with it[7] from door to door.

Enter ADRIANA, LUCIANA, COURTESAN, *and a schoolmas-*
ter called PINCH

ANTIPHOLUS OF EPHESUS Come, go along: my wife is coming
yonder.

DROMIO OF EPHESUS [*to* ADRIANA] Mistress, *respice finem*[8]—
respect your end—or rather, to prophesy like the parrot,[9]
'Beware the rope's end'.

ANTIPHOLUS OF EPHESUS Wilt thou still talk?

[*He*] *beats* DROMIO

40 COURTESAN [*to* ADRIANA] How say you now? Is not your husband mad?

ADRIANA His incivility confirms no less.—
Good Doctor Pinch, you are a conjurer.[1]
Establish him in his true sense[2] again,
And I will please you° what you will demand.   *repay you with*

45 LUCIANA Alas, how fiery and how sharp° he looks!   *fierce*

COURTESAN Mark how he trembles in his ecstasy.°   *frenzy*

PINCH [*to* ANTIPHOLUS] Give me your hand, and let me feel your pulse.

ANTIPHOLUS OF EPHESUS There is my hand, and let it feel your ear.

[*He strikes* PINCH]

PINCH I charge thee, Satan, housed within this man,
50 To yield possession to my holy prayers,
And to thy state of darkness hie thee straight:
I conjure thee by all the saints in heaven.

ANTIPHOLUS OF EPHESUS Peace, doting wizard, peace! I am not mad.

ADRIANA O that thou wert not, poor distressèd soul.

55 ANTIPHOLUS OF EPHESUS You minion,° you, are these your customers?   *hussy*
Did this companion° with the saffron° face   *rascal / yellow*
Revel and feast it at my house today,
Whilst upon me the guilty doors were shut,
And I denied to enter in my house?

60 ADRIANA O husband, God doth know you dined at home,
Where would you had remained until this time,
Free from these slanders° and this open shame.   *scandals*

ANTIPHOLUS OF EPHESUS Dined at home?

[*To* DROMIO]   Thou villain, what sayst thou?

DROMIO OF EPHESUS Sir, sooth to say,° you did not dine at home.   *to speak truly*

65 ANTIPHOLUS OF EPHESUS Were not my doors locked up, and I shut out?

DROMIO OF EPHESUS Pardie,° your doors were locked, and you   *By God (pardieu)*
shut out.

ANTIPHOLUS OF EPHESUS And did not she herself revile me there?

DROMIO OF EPHESUS Sans° fable, she herself reviled you there.   *Without*

ANTIPHOLUS OF EPHESUS Did not her kitchen-maid rail, taunt, and scorn me?

70 DROMIO OF EPHESUS Certes° she did. The kitchen vestal[3] scorned you.   *Certainly*

ANTIPHOLUS OF EPHESUS And did not I in rage depart from thence?

DROMIO OF EPHESUS In verity you did. My bones bears witness,
That since have felt the vigour of his rage.

---

7. I shall receive a beating (a frequent punishment for
begging).
8. A religious injunction to "think on your end," but
punning on *respice funem*, "think on the rope" (on
hanging).
9. Parrots were often taught to cry "rope," an exclamation or curse; the "prophecy" is that the hearer deserves
to be hanged.

1. Capable of exorcising devils; exorcism required a
"doctor"—a learned man—since it was thought that
devils needed to be addressed in Latin.
2. His right mind. Possession and lunacy were not necessarily medically distinct, since both involved the displacement of reason (by passion, sickness, or demons).
3. Ironic: a virgin priestess of the household goddess
Vesta's temple, responsible for keeping the fire burning.

ADRIANA [*aside to* PINCH] Is't good to soothe° him in these contraries? ——— *humor*
75 PINCH [*aside to* ADRIANA] It is no shame.° The fellow finds his vein, ——— *harm*
And, yielding to him, humours well his frenzy.
ANTIPHOLUS OF EPHESUS [*to* ADRIANA] Thou hast suborned° the ——— *induced*
goldsmith to arrest me.
ADRIANA Alas, I sent you money to redeem you,
By Dromio here, who came in haste for it.
80 DROMIO OF EPHESUS Money by me? Heart and good will you might,
But surely, master, not a rag° of money. ——— *farthing*
ANTIPHOLUS OF EPHESUS Went'st not thou to her for a purse of ducats?
ADRIANA He came to me, and I delivered it.
LUCIANA And I am witness with her that she did.
85 DROMIO OF EPHESUS God and the ropemaker bear me witness
That I was sent for nothing but a rope.
PINCH [*aside to* ADRIANA] Mistress, both man and master is possessed.
I know it by their pale and deadly° looks. ——— *deathlike*
They must be bound and laid in some dark room.⁴
ANTIPHOLUS OF EPHESUS [*to* ADRIANA] Say wherefore didst thou
90 lock me forth° today, ——— *out*
[*To* DROMIO] And why dost thou deny the bag of gold?
ADRIANA I did not, gentle husband, lock thee forth.
DROMIO OF EPHESUS And, gentle master, I received no gold.
But I confess, sir, that we were locked out.
95 ADRIANA Dissembling villain, thou speak'st false in both.
ANTIPHOLUS OF EPHESUS Dissembling harlot, thou art false in all,
And art confederate with a damnèd pack° ——— *conspiracy*
To make a loathsome abject scorn of me.
But with these nails I'll pluck out those false eyes,
100 That would behold in me this shameful sport.
[*He reaches for* ADRIANA; *she shrieks.*] *Enter three or*
four, and offer to bind him. He strives
ADRIANA O, bind him, bind him. Let him not come near me.
PINCH More company!° The fiend is strong within him. ——— *Get help*
LUCIANA Ay me, poor man, how pale and wan he looks.
ANTIPHOLUS OF EPHESUS What, will you murder me?—Thou, jailer, thou,
105 I am thy prisoner. Wilt thou suffer them
To make a rescue?⁵
OFFICER   Masters, let him go.
He is my prisoner, and you shall not have him.
PINCH Go, bind his man, for he is frantic too.
[*They bind* DROMIO]
ADRIANA What wilt thou do, thou peevish° officer? ——— *stupid*
110 Hast thou delight to see a wretched man
Do outrage and displeasure° to himself? ——— *harm*
OFFICER He is my prisoner. If I let him go,
The debt he owes will be required of me.
ADRIANA I will discharge° thee ere I go from thee. ——— *repay*
115 Bear me forthwith unto his creditor,
And, knowing how the debt grows,⁶ I will pay it.—
Good Master Doctor, see him safe conveyed
Home to my house. O most unhappy day!
ANTIPHOLUS OF EPHESUS O most unhappy strumpet!

4. An ordinary sixteenth-century treatment for insanity.   6. *knowing . . . grows*: when I know how the debt came
5. To release by force from legal custody.   about.

120 DROMIO OF EPHESUS Master, I am here entered in bond for you.
ANTIPHOLUS OF EPHESUS Out on thee, villain! Wherefore dost
   thou mad° me?   goad
DROMIO OF EPHESUS Will you be bound for nothing? Be mad, good master—
   Cry, 'The devil!'⁷
LUCIANA God help, poor souls, how idly do they talk!
125 ADRIANA Go bear him hence. Sister, go you with me.
        Exeunt [into the Phoenix, PINCH and others
        carrying off ANTIPHOLUS OF EPHESUS and DROMIO OF
        EPHESUS]. Manent° OFFICER, ADRIANA, LUCIANA, COURTESAN   Remain
        [*To the* OFFICER] Say now, whose suit is he arrested at?
OFFICER One Angelo, a goldsmith. Do you know him?
ADRIANA I know the man. What is the sum he owes?
OFFICER Two hundred ducats.
ADRIANA   Say, how grows it due?
130 OFFICER Due for a chain your husband had of him.
ADRIANA He did bespeak° a chain for me, but had it not.   order
COURTESAN Whenas your husband all in rage today
   Came to my house, and took away my ring—
   The ring I saw upon his finger now—
135 Straight after did I meet him with a chain.
ADRIANA It may be so, but I did never see it.
   Come, jailer, bring me where the goldsmith is.
   I long to know the truth hereof at large.°   in full
        Enter ANTIPHOLUS [OF] SYRACUSE [wearing the chain]
        with his rapier drawn, and DROMIO [OF] SYRACUSE [also
        with rapier]
LUCIANA God, for thy mercy, they are loose again!
140 ADRIANA And come with naked° swords. Let's call more help   drawn
   To have them bound again.
OFFICER   Away, they'll kill us!
        Run all out. Exeunt omnes,° as fast as may be, frighted.   all
        [ANTIPHOLUS *and* DROMIO *remain*]
ANTIPHOLUS OF SYRACUSE I see these witches are afraid of swords.
DROMIO OF SYRACUSE She that would be your wife now ran from you.
ANTIPHOLUS OF SYRACUSE Come to the Centaur. Fetch our stuff from thence.
145 I long that we were safe and sound aboard.
DROMIO OF SYRACUSE Faith, stay here this night. They will
   surely do us no harm. You saw they speak us fair, give us gold.
   Methinks they are such a gentle nation that, but for the
   mountain of mad flesh that claims marriage of me, I could
150 find in my heart to stay here still,° and turn witch.   always
ANTIPHOLUS OF SYRACUSE I will not stay tonight for all the town.
   Therefore away, to get our stuff aboard.   *Exeunt*

5.1
        Enter [SECOND] MERCHANT and [ANGELO] the goldsmith
ANGELO I am sorry, sir, that I have hindered you,
   But I protest he had the chain of me,
   Though most dishonestly he doth deny it.
SECOND MERCHANT How is the man esteemed here in the city?

7. A cry of exasperation; a direct address to the devil,   possessed.
which would lend support to the view that he is   5.1 Location: Before a priory.

5   ANGELO Of very reverend reputation, sir,
         Of credit infinite, highly beloved,
         Second to none that lives here in the city.
         His word might bear my wealth at any time.[1]
     SECOND MERCHANT Speak softly. Yonder, as I think, he walks.
             Enter ANTIPHOLUS [OF SYRACUSE, *wearing the chain,*]
             and DROMIO [OF SYRACUSE] *again*
10   ANGELO 'Tis so, and that self° chain about his neck   *same*
         Which he forswore° most monstrously to have.   *denied on oath*
         Good sir, draw near to me. I'll speak to him.—
         Signor Antipholus, I wonder much
         That you would put me to this shame and trouble,
15   And not without some scandal to yourself,
         With circumstance° and oaths so to deny   *detailed argument*
         This chain, which now you wear so openly.
         Beside the charge,° the shame, imprisonment,   *cost*
         You have done wrong to this my honest friend,
20   Who, but for staying on° our controversy,   *as a result of*
         Had hoisted sail and put to sea today.
         This chain you had of me. Can you deny it?
     ANTIPHOLUS OF SYRACUSE I think I had. I never did deny it.
     SECOND MERCHANT Yes, that you did, sir, and forswore it too.
25   ANTIPHOLUS OF SYRACUSE Who heard me to deny it or forswear it?
     SECOND MERCHANT These ears of mine, thou know'st, did hear thee.
         Fie on thee, wretch! 'Tis pity that thou liv'st
         To walk where any honest men resort.
     ANTIPHOLUS OF SYRACUSE Thou art a villain to impeach me thus.
30   I'll prove mine honour and mine honesty
         Against thee presently,° if thou dar'st stand.°   *now / defend yourself*
     SECOND MERCHANT I dare, and do defy thee for a villain.
             They draw. Enter ADRIANA, LUCIANA, COURTESAN, *and*
             others [*from the Phoenix*]
     ADRIANA Hold, hurt him not, for God's sake; he is mad.
         Some get within him,° take his sword away.   *his guard*
35   Bind Dromio too, and bear them to my house.
     DROMIO OF SYRACUSE Run, master, run! For God's sake take° a   *take cover in*
             house.
         This is some priory—in, or we are spoiled.°   *ruined*
             Exeunt ANTIPHOLUS [OF SYRACUSE *and*
                     DROMIO OF SYRACUSE] *to the priory*
             Enter [*from the priory*] *the Lady* ABBESS
     ABBESS Be quiet, people. Wherefore throng you hither?
     ADRIANA To fetch my poor distracted husband hence.
40   Let us come in, that we may bind him fast,
         And bear him home for his recovery.
     ANGELO I knew he was not in his perfect wits.
     SECOND MERCHANT I am sorry now that I did draw on him.
     ABBESS How long hath this possession held the man?
45   ADRIANA This week he hath been heavy, sour, sad,
         And much, much different from the man he was;
         But till this afternoon his passion°   *insanity*
         Ne'er brake° into extremity of rage.   *broke*
     ABBESS Hath he not lost much wealth by wreck at sea?

---

1. His word alone would be enough security to borrow all I have.

50 Buried some dear friend? Hath not else his eye
  Strayed° his affection in unlawful love—   *Led astray*
  A sin prevailing much in youthful men,
  Who give their eyes the liberty of gazing?
  Which of these sorrows is he subject to?
55 ADRIANA To none of these, except it be the last,
  Namely some love that drew him oft from home.
  ABBESS You should for that have reprehended him.
  ADRIANA Why, so I did.
  ABBESS   Ay, but not rough enough.
  ADRIANA As roughly as my modesty would let me.
60 ABBESS Haply° in private.   *Perhaps*
  ADRIANA And in assemblies too.
  ABBESS Ay, but not enough.
  ADRIANA It was the copy° of our conference.°   *theme/conversation*
  In bed he slept not for my urging it.
65 At board° he fed not for my urging it.   *table*
  Alone, it was the subject of my theme.
  In company I often glancèd° it.   *alluded to*
  Still° did I tell him it was vile and bad.   *Continually*
  ABBESS And thereof came it that the man was mad.
70 The venom° clamours of a jealous woman   *venomous*
  Poisons more deadly than a mad dog's tooth.
  It seems his sleeps were hindered by thy railing,
  And thereof comes it that his head is light.
  Thou sayst his meat was sauced with thy upbraidings.
75 Unquiet meals make ill digestions.
  Thereof the raging fire of fever bred,
  And what's a fever but a fit of madness?[2]
  Thou sayst his sports were hindered by thy brawls.
  Sweet recreation barred, what doth ensue
80 But moody and dull melancholy,
  Kinsman to grim and comfortless despair,
  And at her heels a huge infectious troop
  Of pale distemperatures° and foes to life? *illnesses; imbalances*
  In food, in sport, and life-preserving rest
85 To be disturbed would mad or° man or beast. *would make mad either*
  The consequence is, then, thy jealous fits
  Hath scared thy husband from the use of wits.
  LUCIANA She never reprehended him but mildly
  When he demeaned himself rough, rude, and wildly.
90 [*To* ADRIANA] Why bear you these rebukes, and answer not?
  ADRIANA She did betray me to my own reproof.—
  Good people, enter, and lay hold on him.
  ABBESS No, not a creature enters in my house.
  ADRIANA Then let your servants bring my husband forth.
95 ABBESS Neither. He took this place for sanctuary,[3]
  And it shall privilege him from your hands
  Till I have brought him to his wits again,
  Or lose my labour in essaying it.
  ADRIANA I will attend my husband, be his nurse,
100 Diet° his sickness, for it is my office,°   *Treat/duty*

2. Both are imbalances in the body's humors; see note
to 4.4.43.

3. Churches and other sacred buildings provided refuge
from legal prosecution until the seventeenth century.

And will have no attorney° but myself.   *proxy*
And therefore let me have him home with me.
ABBESS Be patient, for I will not let him stir
  Till I have used the approvèd° means I have,   *tested*
105 With wholesome syrups, drugs, and holy prayers
  To make of him a formal° man again.   *complete; sane*
  It is a branch and parcel° of mine oath,   *part*
  A charitable duty of my order.
  Therefore depart, and leave him here with me.
110 ADRIANA I will not hence, and leave my husband here;
  And ill it doth beseem your holiness
  To separate the husband and the wife.
ABBESS Be quiet and depart. Thou shalt not have him.
         [Exit into the priory]
LUCIANA *[to* ADRIANA*]* Complain unto the Duke of this indignity.
115 ADRIANA Come, go, I will fall prostrate at his feet,
  And never rise until my tears and prayers
  Have won his grace to come in person hither
  And take perforce my husband from the Abbess.
SECOND MERCHANT By this, I think, the dial point's at five.
120 Anon,° I'm sure, the Duke himself in person   *Soon*
  Comes this way to the melancholy vale,
  The place of death and sorry execution,
  Behind the ditches of the abbey here.
ANGELO Upon what cause?
125 SECOND MERCHANT To see a reverend Syracusian merchant,
  Who put unluckily into this bay
  Against the laws and statutes of this town,
  Beheaded publicly for his offence.
ANGELO See where they come. We will behold his death.
130 LUCIANA Kneel to the Duke before he pass the abbey.
    Enter [Solinus] DUKE *of Ephesus, and [*EGEON*] the mer-*
    chant of Syracuse, bareheaded, with the headsman° and *executioner*
    other officers
DUKE Yet once again proclaim it publicly:
  If any friend will pay the sum for him,
  He shall not die, so much we tender⁴ him.
ADRIANA *[kneeling]* Justice, most sacred Duke, against the Abbess!
135 DUKE She is a virtuous and a reverend lady.
  It cannot be that she hath done thee wrong.
ADRIANA May it please your grace, Antipholus my husband,
  Who I made lord of me and all I had
  At your important° letters⁵—this ill day   *urgent*
140 A most outrageous fit of madness took him,
  That desp'rately he hurried through the street,
  With him his bondman, all as mad as he,
  Doing displeasure to the citizens
  By rushing in their houses, bearing thence
145 Rings, jewels, anything his rage° did like. *he in his madness*
  Once did I get him bound, and sent him home,
  Whilst to take order for° the wrongs I went   *settle up*
  That here and there his fury had committed.

---

4. Offer; feel tender regard for.
5. Formal instructions. Adriana may have been the Duke's ward.

Anon, I wot° not by what strong° escape,   *know / forcible*

150   He broke from those that had the guard of him,

And with his mad attendant and himself,

Each one with ireful passion, with drawn swords,

Met us again, and, madly bent on us,

Chased us away; till, raising of more aid,

155   We came again to bind them. Then they fled

Into this abbey, whither we pursued them,

And here the Abbess shuts the gates on us,

And will not suffer us to fetch him out,

Nor send him forth that we may bear him hence.

160   Therefore, most gracious Duke, with thy command

Let him be brought forth, and borne hence for help.

DUKE [*raising* ADRIANA]   Long since, thy husband served me in my wars,

And I to thee engaged a prince's word,

When thou didst make him master of thy bed,

165   To do him all the grace° and good I could.—   *favor; patronage*

Go, some of you, knock at the abbey gate,

And bid the Lady Abbess come to me.

I will determine this before I stir.

        Enter a MESSENGER [*from the Phoenix*]

MESSENGER [*to* ADRIANA]   O mistress, mistress, shift° and save   *do what you can*

    yourself!

170   My master and his man are both broke loose,

Beaten the maids a-row,° and bound the Doctor,   *one after another*

Whose beard they have singed off with brands° of fire,   *torches*

And ever as it blazed they threw on him

Great pails of puddled° mire to quench the hair.   *foul*

175   My master preaches patience to him, and the while

His man with scissors nicks him like a fool;[6]

And sure—unless you send some present help—

Between them they will kill the conjurer.

ADRIANA   Peace, fool. Thy master and his man are here,

180   And that is false thou dost report to us.

MESSENGER   Mistress, upon my life I tell you true.

I have not breathed almost since I did see it.

He cries for you, and vows, if he can take you,

To scorch your face and to disfigure you.

        Cry within

185   Hark, hark, I hear him, mistress. Fly, be gone!

DUKE [*to* ADRIANA]   Come stand by me. Fear nothing. Guard

    with halberds!°   *spears with blades*

        Enter ANTIPHOLUS OF EPHESUS *and* DROMIO [OF]

        EPHESUS [*from the Phoenix*]

ADRIANA   Ay me, it is my husband! Witness you

That he is borne about invisible.

Even now we housed him in° the abbey here,   *chased him into*

190   And now he's there, past thought of human reason.

ANTIPHOLUS OF EPHESUS   Justice, most gracious Duke, O grant me justice,

Even for the service that long since I did thee,

When I bestrid thee[7] in the wars, and took

Deep scars to save thy life; even for the blood

195   That then I lost for thee, now grant me justice!

---

6. Cuts his hair in a foolish or fantastical fashion.   7. Stood over you (to defend you when you were down).

EGEON [*aside*]   Unless the fear of death doth make me dote,°   *grow senile*
   I see my son Antipholus, and Dromio.
ANTIPHOLUS OF EPHESUS   Justice, sweet prince, against that woman there,
   She whom thou gav'st to me to be my wife,
200   That hath abusèd and dishonoured me
   Even in the strength and height of injury.
   Beyond imagination is the wrong
   That she this day hath shameless thrown on me.
DUKE   Discover° how, and thou shalt find me just.   *Reveal*
205 ANTIPHOLUS OF EPHESUS   This day, great Duke, she shut the doors upon me
   While she with harlots° feasted in my house.   *scoundrels*
DUKE   A grievous fault!—Say, woman, didst thou so?
ADRIANA   No, my good lord. Myself, he, and my sister
   Today did dine together. So befall my soul
210   As this is false he burdens me withal.[8]
LUCIANA   Ne'er may I look on day nor sleep on night
   But° she tells to your highness simple truth.   *Unless*
ANGELO [*aside*]   O perjured woman! They are both forsworn.
   In this the madman justly chargeth them.
215 ANTIPHOLUS OF EPHESUS   My liege, I am advisèd° what I say,   *fully aware*
   Neither disturbed with the effect of wine,
   Nor heady-rash provoked with raging ire,
   Albeit my wrongs might make one wiser mad.
   This woman locked me out this day from dinner.
220   That goldsmith there, were he not packed° with her,   *conspiring*
   Could witness it, for he was with me then,
   Who parted with me to go fetch a chain,
   Promising to bring it to the Porcupine,
   Where Balthasar and I did dine together.
225   Our dinner done, and he not coming thither,
   I went to seek him. In the street I met him,
   And in his company that gentleman.
     [*He points to the* SECOND MERCHANT]
   There did this perjured goldsmith swear me down°   *contradict me in swearing*
   That I this day of him received the chain,
230   Which, God he knows, I saw not. For the which
   He did arrest me with an officer.
   I did obey, and sent my peasant° home   *servant*
   For certain ducats. He with none returned.
   Then fairly° I bespoke° the officer   *courteously / asked*
235   To go in person with me to my house.
   By th' way, we met my wife, her sister, and a rabble more
   Of vile confederates. Along with them
   They brought one Pinch, a hungry lean-faced villain,
   A mere anatomy,° a mountebank,°   *skeleton / quack*
240   A threadbare juggler,° and a fortune-teller,   *illusionist*
   A needy, hollow-eyed, sharp-looking° wretch,   *emaciated*
   A living dead man. This pernicious slave,
   Forsooth, took on him as° a conjurer,   *posed as*
   And gazing in mine eyes, feeling my pulse,
245   And with no face, as 'twere, outfacing me,[9]
   Cries out I was possessed. Then all together

---

8. *So . . . withal:* Let the fate of my soul depend on   9. And with his thin face staring me down.
whether what he charges me with is false.

They fell upon me, bound me, bore me thence,
And in a dark and dankish vault at home
There left me and my man, both bound together,
250 Till, gnawing with my teeth my bonds in sunder,°   *apart*
I gained my freedom, and immediately
Ran hither to your grace, whom I beseech
To give me ample satisfaction
For these deep shames and great indignities.
255 ANGELO My lord, in truth, thus far I witness with him:
That he dined not at home, but was locked out.
DUKE But had he such a chain of thee, or no?
ANGELO He had, my lord, and when he ran in here
These people saw the chain about his neck.
260 SECOND MERCHANT [*to* ANTIPHOLUS] Besides, I will be sworn these ears of mine
Heard you confess you had the chain of him,
After you first forswore it on the mart,
And thereupon I drew my sword on you;
And then you fled into this abbey here,
265 From whence I think you are come by miracle.
ANTIPHOLUS OF EPHESUS I never came within these abbey walls,
Nor ever didst thou draw thy sword on me.
I never saw the chain, so help me heaven,
And this is false you burden me withal.°   *with*
270 DUKE Why, what an intricate impeach° is this!   *complex charge*
I think you all have drunk of Circe's cup.[1]
If here you housed° him, here he would have been.   *cornered*
If he were mad, he would not plead so coldly.°   *rationally*
[*To* ADRIANA] You say he dined at home, the goldsmith here
275 Denies that saying. [*To* DROMIO] Sirrah, what say you?
DROMIO OF EPHESUS [*pointing out the* COURTESAN] Sir, he
dined with her there, at the Porcupine.
COURTESAN He did, and from my finger snatched that ring.
ANTIPHOLUS OF EPHESUS 'Tis true, my liege, this ring I had of her.
DUKE [*to* COURTESAN] Saw'st thou him enter at the abbey here?
280 COURTESAN As sure, my liege, as I do see your grace.
DUKE Why, this is strange. Go call the Abbess hither.
I think you are all mated,° or stark mad.   *bewildered*
Exit one to the ABBESS
EGEON [*coming forward*] Most mighty Duke, vouchsafe me speak a word.
Haply° I see a friend will save my life,   *Maybe*
285 And pay the sum that may deliver me.
DUKE Speak freely, Syracusian, what thou wilt.
EGEON [*to* ANTIPHOLUS] Is not your name, sir, called Antipholus?
And is not that your bondman Dromio?
DROMIO OF EPHESUS Within this hour I was his bondman,[2] sir,
290 But he, I thank him, gnawed in two my cords.
Now am I Dromio, and his man, unbound.
EGEON I am sure you both of you remember me.
DROMIO OF EPHESUS Ourselves we do remember, sir, by you;[3]
For lately we were bound as you are now.
295 You are not Pinch's patient, are you, sir?

---

1. The drink by means of which the enchantress Circe turned men into swine.
2. His indentured servant; tied up with him. (The pun continues in line 291.)
3. By looking at you, we remember how we were (bound).

EGEON Why look you strange° on me? You know me well.　　　　　*unknowingly*

ANTIPHOLUS OF EPHESUS I never saw you in my life till now.

EGEON O, grief hath changed me since you saw me last,
And careful° hours with time's deformèd° hand　　　　　　　*sorrowful / deforming*

300　　Have written strange defeatures° in my face.　　　　　　　*disfigurements*
But tell me yet, dost thou not know my voice?

ANTIPHOLUS OF EPHESUS Neither.

EGEON Dromio, nor thou?

DROMIO OF EPHESUS No, trust° me sir, nor I.　　　　　　　　*believe*

305　EGEON I am sure thou dost.

DROMIO OF EPHESUS Ay, sir, but I am sure I do not, and whatsoever a man denies, you are now bound to believe him.

EGEON Not know my voice? O time's extremity,
Hast thou so cracked and splitted my poor tongue

310　　In seven short years that here my only son
Knows not my feeble key of untuned cares?[4]
Though now this grainèd° face of mine be hid　　　　　　　　*lined*
In sap-consuming winter's drizzled snow,
And all the conduits of my blood froze up,

315　　Yet hath my night of life some memory,
My wasting lamps° some fading glimmer left,　　　　　　　　*failing eyes*
My dull deaf ears a little use to hear.
All these old witnesses, I cannot err,
Tell me thou art my son Antipholus.

320　ANTIPHOLUS OF EPHESUS I never saw my father in my life.

EGEON But° seven years since,° in Syracusa bay,　　　　　　　*Only / ago*
Thou know'st we parted. But perhaps, my son,
Thou sham'st to acknowledge me in misery.

ANTIPHOLUS OF EPHESUS The Duke, and all that know me in the city,

325　　Can witness with me that it is not so.
I ne'er saw Syracusa in my life.

DUKE [*to* EGEON] I tell thee, Syracusian, twenty years
Have I been patron to Antipholus,
During which time he ne'er saw Syracusa.

330　　I see thy age and dangers make thee dote.

　　　　　　　Enter [*from the priory*] *the* ABBESS, *with* ANTIPHOLUS
　　　　　　　[OF] SYRACUSE, [*wearing the chain,*] *and* DROMIO [OF]
　　　　　　　SYRACUSE

ABBESS Most mighty Duke, behold a man much wronged.
　　　　　　　All gather to see them

ADRIANA I see two husbands, or mine eyes deceive me.

DUKE One of these men is *genius*[5] to the other:
And so of these, which is the natural° man,　　　　　　　　*human; mortal*

335　　And which the spirit? Who deciphers them?

DROMIO OF SYRACUSE I, sir, am Dromio. Command him away.

DROMIO OF EPHESUS I, sir, am Dromio. Pray let me stay.

ANTIPHOLUS OF SYRACUSE Egeon, art thou not? Or else his ghost.

DROMIO OF SYRACUSE O, my old master, who hath bound him here?

340　ABBESS Whoever bound him, I will loose his bonds,
And gain a husband by his liberty.
Speak, old Egeon, if thou beest the man
That hadst a wife once called Emilia,

---

4. My weak voice born of harsh sorrows.
5. Attendant spirit. It was a classical belief that each
person had such a spirit, identical in appearance, allot-
ted to him at birth.

That bore thee at a burden° two fair sons.   *in one birth*
345   O, if thou beest the same Egeon, speak,
      And speak unto the same Emilia.
      DUKE   Why, here begins his morning story right:
      These two Antipholus', these two so like,
      And these two Dromios, one in semblance—
350   Besides his urging° of her wreck at sea.   *claim*
      These are the parents to these children,
      Which accidentally are met together.
      EGEON   If I dream not, thou art Emilia.
      If thou art she, tell me, where is that son
355   That floated with thee on the fatal° raft?   *ill-fated*
      ABBESS   By men of Epidamnum he and I
      And the twin Dromio all were taken up.
      But, by and by, rude° fishermen of Corinth   *harsh; boorish*
      By force took Dromio and my son from them,
360   And me they left with those of Epidamnum.
      What then became of them I cannot tell;
      I, to this fortune that you see me in.
      DUKE   [*to* ANTIPHOLUS OF SYRACUSE] Antipholus, thou cam'st
          from Corinth first.°   *originally*
      ANTIPHOLUS OF SYRACUSE   No, sir, not I. I came from Syracuse.
365   DUKE   Stay, stand apart. I know not which is which.
      ANTIPHOLUS OF EPHESUS   I came from Corinth, my most gracious lord.
      DROMIO OF EPHESUS   And I with him.
      ANTIPHOLUS OF EPHESUS   Brought to this town by that most famous warrior,
          Duke Menaphon, your most renownèd uncle.
370   ADRIANA   Which of you two did dine with me today?
      ANTIPHOLUS OF SYRACUSE   I, gentle mistress.
      ADRIANA   And are not you my husband?
      ANTIPHOLUS OF EPHESUS   No, I say nay to that.
      ANTIPHOLUS OF SYRACUSE   And so do I. Yet did she call me so;
375   And this fair gentlewoman, her sister here,
          Did call me brother. [*To* LUCIANA] What I told you then
          I hope I shall have leisure° to make good,   *opportunity*
          If this be not a dream I see and hear.
      ANGELO   That is the chain, sir, which you had of me.
380   ANTIPHOLUS OF SYRACUSE   I think it be, sir. I deny it not.
      ANTIPHOLUS OF EPHESUS [*to* ANGELO]   And you, sir, for this chain arrested me.
      ANGELO   I think I did, sir. I deny it not.
      ADRIANA [*to* ANTIPHOLUS OF EPHESUS]   I sent you money, sir, to be your bail,
          By Dromio, but I think he brought it not.
385   DROMIO OF EPHESUS   No, none by me.
      ANTIPHOLUS OF SYRACUSE [*to* ADRIANA]   This purse of ducats I received from you,
          And Dromio my man did bring them me.
          I see we still° did meet each other's man,   *constantly*
          And I was ta'en for him, and he for me,
390   And thereupon these errors are arose.
      ANTIPHOLUS OF EPHESUS   These ducats pawn I for my father here.
      DUKE   It shall not need. Thy father hath his life.
      COURTESAN   Sir, I must have that diamond from you.
      ANTIPHOLUS OF EPHESUS   There, take it, and much thanks for my good cheer.
395   ABBESS   Renownèd Duke, vouchsafe to take the pains
          To go with us into the abbey here,
          And hear at large discoursèd° all our fortunes,   *recounted in full*

And all that are assembled in this place,
That by this sympathizèd° one day's error   *shared*
400 Have suffered wrong. Go, keep us company,
And we shall make full satisfaction.
Thirty-three years have I but gone in travail°   *labor*
Of you, my sons, and till this present hour
My heavy burden ne'er deliverèd.
405 The Duke, my husband, and my children both,
And you the calendars of their nativity,[6]
Go to a gossips' feast,[7] and joy with me.
After so long grief, such festivity!
DUKE   With all my heart I'll gossip at° this feast.   *join in*

Exeunt omnes [into the priory]. Manent the two DROMIOS *and two*
brothers [ANTIPHOLUS]

DROMIO OF SYRACUSE [*to* ANTIPHOLUS OF EPHESUS]   Master,
410   shall I fetch your stuff from shipboard?
ANTIPHOLUS OF EPHESUS   Dromio, what stuff of mine hast thou
    embarked?°   *placed on board*
DROMIO OF SYRACUSE   Your goods that lay at host, sir, in the
    Centaur.
ANTIPHOLUS OF SYRACUSE   He speaks to me.—I am your master, Dromio.
    Come, go with us. We'll look to that anon.
415 Embrace thy brother there; rejoice with him.
                                    Exeunt [the brothers ANTIPHOLUS]
DROMIO OF SYRACUSE   There is a fat friend at your master's house,
    That kitchened me for you[8] today at dinner.
    She now shall be my sister, not my wife.
DROMIO OF EPHESUS   Methinks you are my glass° and not my brother.   *mirror*
420 I see by you° I am a sweet-faced youth.   *by means of you*
    Will you walk in to see their gossiping?°   *merrymaking*
DROMIO OF SYRACUSE   Not I, sir, you are my elder.[9]
DROMIO OF EPHESUS   That's a question. How shall we try° it?   *test*
DROMIO OF SYRACUSE   We'll draw cuts° for the senior. Till then,   *straws*
    lead thou first.
425 DROMIO OF EPHESUS   Nay, then thus:
    We came into the world like brother and brother,
    And now let's go hand in hand, not one before another.
                                            Exeunt [to the priory]

6. (Addressed to the Dromios): the two servants are a record of their masters' age, having been born at the same time.
7. A feast attended by the godparents ("gossips") to celebrate the christening of a child.
8. Who entertained me in the kitchen in mistake for you.
9. The elder customarily takes precedence and enters first.

Love's Labour's Lost

Love's Labour's Lost (1594–95) is an experimental play disguised as a conventional one. Its most striking feature—sexualized verbal wit—goes well with its aristocratic love plot. Yet the work is complicated by an unexpected concluding twist; challenges to hierarchies of gender, class, nation, and race; a scatological and homoerotic view of bodily function; and partly buried political and religious references. Without jettisoning the spirit of romantic comedy, then, *Love's Labour's Lost* offers a complex view of wooing and wedding with broader social implications.

Initially, Shakespeare telegraphs what is coming next. King Ferdinand of Navarre and his three courtiers—Biron, Dumaine, and Longueville—swear to shun women for three years to pursue the studious life of an ancient Greek or Renaissance Italian philosophical academy. Yet the arrival of a diplomatic embassy led by the Princess of France that includes three ladies-in-waiting—Rosaline, Catherine, and Maria—induces the men to fall in love. They are ridiculed for their about-face. In a multiple eavesdropping scene, they overhear each other confessing this change of heart and hypocritically denounce such oath breaking. In a court masque (a dramatic form where costumed aristocrats are the performers), they disguise themselves as Russians to advance their claims, but the ladies' own disguises lead each man to woo the wrong woman. Then, two hundred lines from the end, a messenger reports that the Princess's father, the King of France, has died. The world of romantic comedy—Navarre's rural retreat from the ordinary affairs of life—is invaded by death. When the men obliviously continue their wooing, the women, who all along have mistrusted their forsworn suitors, insist on a year's separation, which returns the plot to the opening rejection of heterosexual life.

From *Two Gentlemen of Verona* (1590–91) to *Twelfth Night* (1601), Shakespeare's young lovers marry off. *Love's Labour's Lost*'s open-ended conclusion thus sets its apart from the other romantic comedies, pointing instead to the problem plays, *Troilus and Cressida* (1601–02), *Measure for Measure* (1604), and *All's Well That Ends Well* (1604–05). Here, as Biron remarks with the work's typical dramaturgical self-consciousness, "Our wooing doth not end like an old play. / Jack hath not Jill" (5.2.851–52). Both the romantic plot and the deflating outcome are suggested by the concluding poetic dialogue between Spring, associated with fertility and love, and Winter, linked to coldness and suffering. Yet Spring also brings "unpleasing" cuckoldry and Winter "a merry note" (5.2.877, 893).

Before then, the aristocrats' verbal ingenuity dominates *Love's Labour's Lost*. No other Shakespearean play so emphasizes its own brilliance, so centrally concerns language itself, so heavily draws on bookishness, so revels in courtly style. *Love's Labour's Lost* possesses the highest ratio of rhyme to blank verse among the dramatic works—rivaled only by *A Midsummer Night's Dream* (1594–96). Shakespeare's most heavily rhymed tragedy, *Romeo and Juliet* (1595), and history, *Richard II* (1595), also date from these years, sometimes thought of as Shakespeare's lyrical period. Rhyming calls attention to the medium of language itself. By contrast, when Shakespeare seeks to render speech naturalistically, to make his language a neutral expression of thought, he characteristically resorts to blank verse or prose.

In *Love's Labour's Lost*, Shakespeare generally employs blank verse for serious moments in long speeches, while reserving rhyme for the witty repartee of love—itself a microcosm of the play's larger debate structure. In the opening scene, each male courtier discusses, in blank verse, the vow of abstinence from women before capping his speech with a concluding couplet (lines 1–48, couplets at 22–23, 26–27, 31–32,

47–48). But when the King and Biron then debate the plan, they switch to rhyme—usually rhymed pentameter couplets, sometimes known as heroic couplets. At times, Shakespeare shifts to quatrains rhymed *abab*. If such a passage is followed by a couplet (see, for example, 1.1.61–66), the result is the six-line stanza of Shakespeare's amatory narrative poem *Venus and Adonis* (1592–93), a work that meditates comically on gender reversal. If three quatrains are followed by a couplet, a sonnet is born (for instance, 1.1.80–93). Loosely speaking, there are at least seven sonnets in the play (also 1.1.160–74; 4.3.22–37 and 55–68; 5.2.274–89, 343–56, and 402–15). Six of the seven are romantic. In love with the peasant Jaquenetta, Armado from the subplot remarks, "I am sure I shall turn sonnet" (that is, sonneteer; 1.2.162–63). The boom of the English love sonnet begins in 1591 with the publication of Sidney's *Astrophil and Stella,* and Shakespeare is thought to have started his own sequence around 1592–93. Three of the lords' poems to the ladies were lifted from the 1598 quarto of the play for an unauthorized 1599 collection attributed to Shakespeare. Within the play, the sonnets function complexly. The ladies coolly receive their suitors' poetic protestations, the King deploys a sonnet to describe Armado, and the two sonnets in dialogue further extend the form while belittling the men. This turning of the sonnet upon itself achieves self-contradiction when Biron, having embraced plain speaking, avows his love to Rosaline—"O never will I . . . woo in rhyme" (5.2.402–05)—in what proves to be the opening of a sonnet.

This wooing rhetoric is also associated with male bonding. The lords begin by misogynistically excluding any woman from their company "'on pain of losing her tongue'" (1.1.122). Once in love, they switch to the Renaissance courtier's amatory style, derived from two influential Italian writers—the fourteenth-century lyric poet Petrarch, founder of the European sonnet craze, and the fifteenth-century Neoplatonic philosopher Ficino. But in the eavesdropping scene, their feelings are expressed not through direct address to the ladies but through intended soliloquies inadvertently delivered to each other. The scene enacts the rhetorical figure of chiasmus—common to many passages in the play—in which the second of two parallel structures inverts the order of the first. Here Biron, the King, Longueville, and Dumaine successively confess their love, whereupon Dumaine's oath breaking is denounced by Longueville, Longueville's by the King, and the King's by Biron. And just as Biron, who shares with Armado's page Mote the privilege of speaking directly to the audience, is the only courtier whose initial confession is not overheard, he alone denounces himself, albeit under compulsion. Thereafter, the courtiers imagine their wooing as collective sexual attack: "Advance your standards, and upon them, lords. / Pell-mell, down with them" (4.3.341–42). In short, the play casts a jaundiced eye on the sexual style of men in groups. Fittingly, then, the courtiers' year of isolation separates them not only from women but also from each other. As in *The Merchant of Venice* (1596–97), another play that punishes male lovers who break their vows, the dissolution of male bonds precedes durable heterosexual attachment.

But, of course, the language of *Love's Labour's Lost* is marked not just by the poetry of love but also by an often sexualized punning. Even though the men excel at this language of romantic combat, they are no match for the women. The following exchange occurs during the Russian masque:

CATHERINE What, was your visor made without a tongue?
LONGUEVILLE [*taking* CATHERINE *for Maria*] I know the reason, lady, why you ask.
CATHERINE O, for your reason! Quickly, sir, I long.
LONGUEVILLE You have a double tongue within your mask,
   And would afford my speechless visor half.
CATHERINE 'Veal', quoth the Dutchman. Is not veal a calf?
LONGUEVILLE A calf, fair lady?
CATHERINE   No, a fair lord calf.
LONGUEVILLE Let's part the word.

CATHERINE No, I'll not be your half.
Take all and wean it, it may prove an ox.
LONGUEVILLE Look how you butt yourself in these sharp mocks!
Will you give horns, chaste lady? Do not so.
CATHERINE Then die a calf before your horns do grow.
LONGUEVILLE One word in private with you ere I die.
CATHERINE Bleat softly, then. The butcher hears you cry.

(5.2.242–55)

Referring to the mouthpiece keeping the mask in place, Catherine evokes Longueville's silence ("without a tongue"). Longueville's second reply ("double tongue") accuses Catherine of punning, concealing her identity, being deceptive, and speaking enough for two, and then urges her to relinquish one tongue so he can speak and she will reveal her identity. Catherine's "Veal" combines Dutch for "well," German for "much," and a pun on "veil" with the end of her second comment ("long"). The result is "long-veal," veiled assertion of her interlocutor's identity. "Veal" also anticipates "calf" at line's end—source of the passage's remaining jokes. Catherine reverses Longueville's question, branding him "a fair lord calf," a dolt. Longueville's offer of compromise ("part the word") inspires Catherine's construal of "part" as "divide"; hence her refusal to "be your half" (better half, wife) and covert acknowledgment that the first half of the word ("ca") suggests her name. Longueville should raise the calf into an "ox," a castrated dolt with "horns," symbol of cuckoldry. This argument sullies her reputation, he warns, but Catherine tells him that to avoid cuckoldry he should drop dead. Longueville asks for a tête-à-tête "ere I die" (have an orgasm), to which Catherine agrees, while warning him of his impending doom.

The ladies also best the lords by critique of male verbal excess (*sans* is French for "without"):

BIRON My love to thee is sound, sans crack or flaw.
ROSALINE Sans 'sans', I pray you.

(5.2.415–16)

The men, Biron realizes, must drop their bookish language to approximate the women's norm: "Honest plain words best pierce the ear of grief" (5.2.735). Rosaline sentences him to a year of jesting among "the speechless sick and . . . groaning wretches" (5.2.828–29), where he will learn the value—or valuelessness—of wit. And the Princess usually exercises a dignified stylistic restraint that eludes the men. Yet the women's actual practice often repudiates their theory. Early on, Rosaline sympathetically evokes Biron's wit. The ladies then embrace the game of verbal one-upmanship and obscene punning, as the Catherine-Longueville exchange demonstrates. Thus they violate the principle Rosaline claims Biron has ignored:

A jest's prosperity lies in the ear
Of him that hears it, never in the tongue
Of him that makes it.

(5.2.838–40)

The women's self-contradictory avowal of wit and sobriety alike renders them romantically desirable in a fashion alien to the stereotypes of love poetry. Their possibly cynical economic mission may depend, as Boyet, their attending lord, suggests, on the Princess's ability to win the King's love. There are repeated jibes at their appearance as well as accusations of unchastity leveled at Rosaline by Biron, Boyet, and Catherine. The sexual innuendos in Catherine and Rosaline's exchange turn on "light" (bright, frivolous, or wanton), contrasted with both "heavy" (serious, overweight) and "dark" (black, obscure, wanton; 5.2.14–46, 4.3.228–78). While not erasing the ladies' moral superiority, these countertendencies justify modern productions that have treated them without idealism or sentimentality.

The subplot offers a different kind of critique. More a series of set pieces than a continuous story, it offers both structural parallel and social contrast to the main plot. The first eight scenes (in modern editions) alternate between main plot and subplot; the concluding, ninth scene unites the two sets of characters. In each plot, the characters are divided into two groups, one of which intrudes from the outside—the ladies in the main plot, Armado and Mote in the subplot. Such symmetries, which reinforce the work's formalized, dancelike structure and give it an aristocratic feel, recall the comedies that John Lyly wrote in the 1580s for boy actors. But this formalism acquires special force from the subplot's rootedness in popular culture, a culture reinvoked in the concluding speeches of Spring and Winter. Costard and Jaquenetta are from the rural lower classes; Dull, the constable, who anticipates Dogberry in *Much Ado About Nothing* (1598), barely stands above them. Mote is a page; Nathaniel, Holofernes, and Armado, although of higher rank, derive from the stock characters (minister, schoolmaster, braggart) of Italian commedia dell'arte, an originally popular, improvisational theater.

The juxtaposition of the two plots exalts and deflates the aristocrats. The subplot's fractured prose and doggerel verse sets off Biron's polished poetry to advantage. Holofernes is the leading practitioner of the popular characters' penchant for synonyms. An apple hangs in the "*caelo,* the sky, the welkin, the heaven, and . . . falleth . . . on . . . *terra,* the soil, the land, the earth" (4.2.5–6). Armado's forte is schematic syntax: "The time when? . . . Now for the ground which. . . . Then for the place where" (1.1.227–31). But if Armado's language is excessive, Biron's is only slightly less so. Similarly, Costard's violation of the edict against being "taken with a wench" (1.1.270–71) anticipates the failure of the aristocrats. This leveling continues when Armado's love letter to Jaquenetta is echoed by those of the lords. Armado and Biron both have their epistles delivered by Costard, whose confusion of the two exposes each writer to ridicule. The courtiers' Muscovite masque is paralleled by the popular pageant of the Nine Worthies, a scene resembling the humble theatricals of *A Midsummer Night's Dream.* Moreover, both masque and pageant anticipate the larger plot of *Love's Labour's Lost* in their failure to end as their performers wish.

Garden scene. From Thomas Hill, *The Gardener's Labyrinth* (1577).

Queen Elizabeth hunting. From George Gascoigne, *The Noble Art of Venerie or Hunting* (1575).

Costard's verbal sparring with the King and Princess, in which he holds his own, also reduces the sense of social superiority. His pointed response to dismissal by the forsworn courtiers—"Walk aside the true folk, and let the traitors stay" (4.3.209)—recalls his, but not their, honesty from the start. The lords' ridicule of the Nine Worthies prompts Holofernes' telling reply: "This is not generous, not gentle, not humble" (5.2.617). Although the aristocrats learn nothing from Mercadé's announcement of the death of the Princess's father, Armado, whom Costard has just accused of getting Jaquenetta pregnant, sees the need to reform. The lords accept their one-year sentences reluctantly, whereas his voluntary longer commitment echoes and reverses their opening oaths: "I am a votary, I have vowed to Jaquenetta / To hold the plough for her sweet love three year" (5.2.860–61). The oddity here is Biron. More than any other aristocratic character, he internalizes popular culture, moving from refined verse to colloquial and proverbial expression in what is one of Shakespeare's most proverb-rich plays. For instance, he is the only figure from the main plot with an extended prose speech (4.3.1–17). In Shakespeare, this sort of linguistic range is often integral to a character's unique ability to negotiate life's complexities for good or for ill. Yet Biron, despite his wit, intelligence, and insight, proves almost as hapless as his fellow suitors.

The subplot also reflects on the main plot through often scatological or homoerotic bodily imagery, which includes a series of terms for constipation and its release—"immured," "restrained," "bound," "purgation," "loose" (3.1.113–16)—as well as Armado's boast of intimacy with the King, who has a tendency "with his royal finger thus [to] dally with my excrement" (5.1.87–88). In the play of the Nine Worthies, Holofernes as Judas Maccabeus is reduced to Judas (Iscariot), betrayer of Jesus.

> BOYET   Therefore, as he is an ass, let him go.
>   And so adieu, sweet Jude. Nay, why dost thou stay?
> DUMAINE   For the latter end of his name.
> BIRON   For the ass to the Jude. Give it him. Jud-as, away.
>   (5.2.613–16)

Here, emphasis on "ass" activates the synonymous connotation of "end," which thus proves the end of his body as well as "of his name." This primarily popular material suggests that the main courtship plot is not the whole story. The romantic and sexual language of the aristocrats is balanced by a less exalted, more excremental view of the body. Such passages also exploit some of the possibilities of a transvestite theater, in which boys played the women's parts. Specifically, the normative heterosexuality of the main plot is answered by hints of homosexuality emanating from the subplot. In short, this verbal patterning expands the play's notions of the body and sexuality beyond what events themselves overtly offer.

This imagery also feeds into a consideration of religious, national, and racial xenophobia. Costard calls Mote "my incony [fine-quality] Jew" (3.1.124), where "incony" inspires "inkle" [tape] (3.1.127), which suggests "ingle" (catamite, a boy kept by a pederast; see also 1.2.7). When Judas Maccabeus is "clipped" of his surname, Jewish circumcision is apparently glanced at. As we have seen, Holofernes is expelled by the lords as "Jud-as"—sign of the age's association of Jews with both excrement and sodomy. Coming from "tawny Spain," "Dun"-colored Armado, "in all the world's new fashion planted" and hence perhaps associated with New World plantations, is also an alien figure (1.1.171, 4.3.195, 1.1.162). Yet he is less foreign than the Russians, much less their accompanying blackamoors, whose presence glances at racial subjugation. They could be based on a report of an earlier Tudor masque or on a contemporary amateur entertainment at one of London's law schools. Alternatively, the play and these two performances all may draw on the period's link of Russia with dark skin. Although Love's Labour's Lost dramatizes a practice of scapegoating foreigners, however, it does not ratify this practice. Holofernes as Judas issues a pointed rebuke to the aristocrats; Armado reveals a depth of commitment foreign to them; the Russian masque backfires. Just as the play undermines convention in the central love plot, here, too, it calls into question—without openly attacking—cultural norms.

But the aristocrats themselves, unlike most of the popular characters, are also foreign. Behind the play lie contemporary political events that assume importance, given the plot's lack of literary sources. The comedy's King of Navarre draws on King Henry of Navarre, who established a philosophical academy and was accused of withdrawing from life. His three courtiers are named for the historical king's aristocratic contemporaries, two of whom (the play's Biron and Dumaine) served him. The Princess may derive from Princess Marguerite de Valois, daughter of King Henry II of France. Marguerite was already Henry of Navarre's estranged wife when she led an embassy of reconciliation to him in 1578, accompanied by her famous ladies-in-waiting. As in Love's Labour's Lost, one topic of discussion was "Aquitaine, a dowry for a queen" (2.1.8). Negotiations proceeded amid rampant adultery that undermined the vows of reconciliation and, contemporaries believed, caused renewal of France's Wars of Religion (1562–98), the bloody conflict between Protestant and Catholic aristocrats arguably noticed in the play's "civil war of wits" (2.1.225). Boyet, Mercadé, and perhaps Mote also have prominent namesakes from these wars. To end the conflict and secure his claim on the French throne, Henry converted to Catholicism in 1593, a further oath breaking that provoked criticism in Protestant England. The sympathy and judgment directed toward the play's lords, the serious treatment of their repudiated vows, the current of threatening sexuality, the emphasis on conflict, the invasion of death into the festive aristocratic world—all are compatible with this background.

Foreignness and sexuality converge in the debate about the aristocrats' own colors. A 1984 production of the play cast a black actress as Rosaline. Although only Rosaline's hair and eyes are black, metaphorically the play cannot leave darkness alone. Unwillingly in love with Rosaline, Biron initially complains of her color (3.1.181–84, 4.3.2–3). But echoing Shakespeare's sonnets to the "dark lady," he later takes blackness as the standard of beauty:

> KING   By heaven, thy love is black as ebony
> . . . .
> BIRON   No face is fair that is not full so black.
> KING   O paradox! Black is the badge of hell.
>   (4.3.243, 249–50)

For the King, if black is beautiful, even "Ethiops," who presumably share his distaste for their appearance, "of their sweet complexion crack [boast]" (4.3.264). But it is not only the women whose faces evoke darkness. "Biron they call him," Rosaline remarks, "but a merrier man . . . I never spent an hour's talk withal" (2.1.66–68). The implied contrast is between "Merrier" and "Biron," punning on the brown in brown study, or seriousness. Before "the heavenly Rosaline," Biron imagines himself "a rude and savage man of Ind" (4.3.217–18), a claim that he repeats in her presence: "Vouchsafe to show the sunshine of your face / That we, like savages, may worship it" (5.2.200–01). The inclusion of the blackamoors thus accords with the play's unconventional association of its central and most attractive couple with blackness.

Love's Labour's Lost went unperformed from 1642 to 1839, remaining unpopular until the mid-twentieth century. But modern enthusiasm for wordplay and demonstrations of the comedy's theatrical potential have led to an upward revaluation. Perhaps today its significance lies in linguistic artifice that is and is not rejected, an upper class that learns its manners from the lower, a capacious sense of bodily and sexual experience, a sympathetic evocation of blackness, a plot that takes a clear-eyed but not dismissive view of romantic love, and a company of women who ride off into the sunset without their men.

WALTER COHEN

TEXTUAL NOTE

Although the date of *Love's Labour's Lost* is hard to pin down with much certainty, most scholars today locate the original and only composition of the play in 1594–95. Perhaps Shakespeare designed it for the Lord Chamberlain's Men, a recently formed professional company that worked in London's suburban, open-air, commercial theaters and of which he was an actor and a shareholder. The first printing of the play, in quarto, is lost. Another quarto, dated 1598 (Q), is the earliest extant printed version of a Shakespearean play that names its author. Q supposedly reproduces the play "as it was presented before her Highnes / this last Christmas." It is the basis for all modern editions. The title page calls the work *Loues labors lost,* a spelling that, in accord with the punning ethos of the play, leaves open various meanings, depending on where the apostrophe goes in the first word and whether there is an apostrophe—as a contraction for "is"—in the second. To complicate the semantic possibilities, *Loue labors lost* and *Loues Labour lost* are also among the early designations for the work.

Q derives from an authorial manuscript—either directly or, more probably, indi-

Berowne. Did not I dance with you in *Brabant* once?	*Berow.* Did not I dance with you in *Brabant* once?
Kather. Did not I dance with you in *Brabant* once?	*Rofa.* Did not I dance with you in *Brabant* once?
Ber. I know you did,	*Ber.* I know you did.
Kath. How needles was it then to aſke the queſtion?	*Rofa.* How needleſſe was it then to ask the queſtic
Ber. You muſt not be fo quicke.	*Ber.* You muſt not be fo quicke.
Kath. Tis long of you that ſpur me with ſuch queſtions,	*Rofa.* 'Tis long of you ý ſpur me with ſuch queſtioi
Ber. Your wit's too hot,it ſpeedes too faſt, twill tire.	*Ber.* Your wit's too hot,it ſpeeds too faſt, 'twill tii
Kath. Not till it leaue the rider in the mire,	*Rofa.* Not till it leaue the Rider in the mire.
Ber. What time a day?	*Ber.* What time a day ?
Kath. The houre that fooles ſhould aſke,	*Rofa.* The howre that fooles ſhould aske.
Ber. Now faire befall your maſke,	*Ber.* Now faire befall your maske.
Kath. Faire fall the face it couers.	*Rofa.* Faire fall the face it couers.
Ber. And ſend you manie louers,	*Ber.* And ſend you many louers,
Kath. Amen,fo you be none.	*Rofa.* Amen,fo you be none.
Ber. Nay then will I be gon.	*Ber.* Nay then will I be gone.

Biron's first flirtatious exchange with Catherine in Q (2.1.113–26) (left); revised to Rosaline in F (2.1.113–26) (right).

rectly via the lost quarto, which seems to have been printed from that manuscript. For an edition with an authorial manuscript behind it, it is extremely problematic, despite evidence that part of it was proofread. It is full of errors, uncorrected false starts, and the juxtaposition of original and revised versions of the same passages, although many of these are obvious and easily remedied. In this edition, the earlier renditions of subsequently rewritten text, beginning at 4.3.291, 5.2.130, and 5.2.798, are indented in the text. It is difficult to judge whether Q's foreign-language errors are Shakespeare's, the character's, or the compositor's. Here, they are usually corrected but occasionally attributed to the character. Q's speech prefixes often employ generic tags ("King," "Braggart," "Boy," "Page," "Princess," "Queen," "Lady 1–3," "Clown," "Maid," "Curate," "Pedant"). These tags function in various ways, but as a group they suggest that Shakespeare developed his characters out of stock dramatic, mainly comic, figures, especially from Italian commedia dell'arte (this legacy is discussed in the Introduction). *The Norton Shakespeare,* however, substitutes characters' names in the speech prefixes wherever possible, with the exception of Ferdinand of Navarre, who is identified as "King." At 4.2.60–97 and occasionally thereafter in the same scene, Q's speech prefixes attribute Nathaniel's lines to Holofernes and vice versa. These have been corrected. The biggest problem in Q involves the naming of the French ladies in 2.1, who are often referred to as "Lady," "Lady 1," "Lady 2," and "Lady 3." Most important, Catherine seems to be paired with Biron, Rosaline with Dumaine: Biron engages in witty exchanges first with Catherine (2.1.113–26) and then with Rosaline (2.1.178–92) before asking after Catherine (2.1.208–09), while Dumaine inquires about Rosaline (2.1.193–94). The remainder of the play reverses the pairings.

The version of *Love's Labour's Lost* printed in the First Folio of 1623 (F) is derived from either the lost or the extant quarto. F adds poorly conceived and mislabeled act divisions, which, along with scene divisions introduced by eighteenth-century editors, are reproduced here for ease of reference. F also introduces several new readings and speech attributions, at least some of them probably derived from manuscript annotations added to Q. Notably, it appends a new last line to the play, "You that way, we this way." Still more crucial is the replacement of Catherine by Rosaline in Biron's first flirtatious exchange (2.1.113–26). These shifts go much of the way toward aligning the scene's action with what happens thereafter, thus rejecting the apparent meaning of Q—that Biron and Dumaine each first express interest in one woman and then abruptly fall in love with another.

All subsequent editions of *Love's Labour's Lost,* even when based on Q, have followed F in this respect. Most current textual scholars believe that Q reveals Shakespeare's initial indecision about how to pair the men and women off, and that the annotations in the copy of Q on which F is based record a version of the text closer to performance than Q is. In short, F's linkage of Biron with Rosaline from the start is correct. But proponents of this position disagree among themselves on important points, disagreements that suggest the speculative character of the hypothesis. The fundamental problem is uncertainty about the source, nature, and authority of the annotations to Q that lie behind F: the available evidence is too frail and contradictory to inspire confidence.

Although the version printed here is based on the near consensus among recent textual scholars, an alternative position has existed since the eighteenth century. In a relatively recent essay, Manfred Draudt ("The 'Rosaline-Katherine Tangle' of *Love's Labour's Lost*," *The Library* 6 [1982]: 381–96) suggestively argues that Q 2.1 may provide the most accurate rendition available of the romantic relations in *Love's Labour's Lost*. Retaining Q's speech attributions would have various advantages. Biron's and Dumaine's feelings are not obvious in 2.1, and the abrupt switching of male love interest and the casual transfer of women between men have analogues in other Shakespearean plays of the period—*The Two Gentlemen of Verona, Romeo and Juliet,* and *A Midsummer Night's Dream*. The quarto readings are also closer to the events of the court of the historical Henry of Navarre than is the revised text. Further, if Biron and Dumaine are inconstant, it is easier to understand why in 5.2 Catherine and Rosaline attack each other in sexualized language so harsh the Princess has to intervene (lines 14–46); why Catherine accuses Dumaine of "hypocrisy" and Rosaline plans to "torture" Biron (51, 60), whereas the Princess and Maria criticize their suitors more mildly; why Catherine's and Rosaline's concluding promises to their lovers (lines 807, 840–46) are more equivocal than those of the Princess and Maria (lines 783–89, 810–11); and why Rosaline seems only recently to have met Biron (lines 818–19). Finally, the Quarto lends greater force to the ladies' disguises in 5.2, which trick the men into wooing the wrong women; to the women's skeptical, almost cruel treatment of the men throughout; and to the oft-noted near interchangeability of the aristocratic characters. The notes, therefore, list the rejected quarto readings in 2.1 to facilitate a running comparison of the two approaches to the text.

SELECTED BIBLIOGRAPHY

Archer, John Michael. "*Love's Labour's Lost.*" *A Companion to Shakespeare's Works*. Vol. 3: *The Comedies*. Ed. Richard Dutton and Jean E. Howard. Malden, Mass.: Blackwell, 2003. 320–37. Treats issues of race and nation in relation to language, gender, and sexuality.

Booth, Stephen. *King Lear, Macbeth, Indefinition, and Tragedy*. New Haven: Yale University Press, 1983. 69–82. The problem of the unexpected end, both of the plot and of the body.

Carroll, William C. *The Great Feast of Language in "Love's Labour's Lost."* Princeton: Princeton University Press, 1976. Wordplay, self-conscious theatricality, and poetic set pieces in relation to the larger debate structure of the play.

Elam, Keir. *Shakespeare's Universe of Discourse: Language-Games in the Comedies*. New York: Cambridge University Press, 1984. 289–308. Emphasis on the play's highly rhetorical critique of rhetoric.

Evans, Malcolm. *Signifying Nothing: Truth's True Contents in Shakespeare's Text*. Athens: University of Georgia Press, 1986. 50–65. The impact of writing on the speech of both aristocratic lovers and comic pedants.

Gilbert, Miriam. "*Love's Labour's Lost*": *Shakespeare in Performance*. Manchester: Manchester University Press, 1993. Survey of its topic, with detailed analysis of important recent performances.

Londré, Felicia Hardison, ed. "*Love's Labour's Lost*": *Critical Essays*. New York: Garland, 1997. Critical accounts of *Love's Labour's Lost,* both text and performance, 1598–1995, but primarily since World War II.

Maus, Katharine Eisaman. "Transfer of Title in *Love's Labour's Lost:* Language, Individualism, Gender." *Shakespeare Left and Right*. Ed. Ivo Kamps. New York: Routledge,

1991. 206–23. The relationship between the play's reversal of standard gender hierarchy and its questioning of the naturalness of meaningful language.

Mazzio, Carla. "The Melancholy of Print: *Love's Labour's Lost.*" *Historicism, Psychoanalysis, and Early Modern Culture.* Ed. Carla Mazzio and Douglas Trevor. New York: Routledge, 2000. 186–227. The intersection in the play of the speech(lessness) of love and early modern print culture, especially pedagogical manuals.

Parker, Patricia. "Preposterous Reversals: *Love's Labour's Lost.*" *Modern Language Quarterly* 54 (1993): 435–82. The centrality of wordplay, especially obscene bodily punning, to the work's dramatic structure and particularly to its challenge to class, gender, and sexual hierarchy.

FILM

Love's Labour's Lost. 2000. Dir. Kenneth Branagh. UK. 93 min. Musical comedy with 1930s songs and settings, half of Shakespeare's lines retained, and the play's events shadowed by the coming of World War II. Cast includes Branagh, Alicia Silverstone, and Nathan Lane.

Love's Labour's Lost

THE PERSONS OF THE PLAY

Ferdinand, KING of Navarre
BIRON ⎫
LONGUEVILLE ⎬ lords attending on the King
DUMAINE ⎭
Don Adriano de ARMADO, an affected Spanish braggart
MOTE, his page
PRINCESS of France
ROSALINE ⎫
CATHERINE ⎬ ladies attending on the
MARIA ⎭ Princess
BOYET ⎫
Two other LORDS ⎬ attending on the Princess
COSTARD, a clown
JAQUENETTA, a country wench
Sir NATHANIEL, a curate
HOLOFERNES, a schoolmaster
Anthony DULL, a constable
MERCADÉ, a messenger
A FORESTER

1.1

Enter Ferdinand, KING *of Navarre,* BIRON, LONGUEVILLE,
and DUMAINE[1]

KING Let fame, that all hunt after in their lives,
Live registered upon our brazen° tombs,   *brass; long-lasting*
And then grace° us in the disgrace° of death   *honor / disfigurement*
When, spite of cormorant° devouring time,[2]   *despite ravenous*
5 Th'endeavour of this present breath° may buy   *speech; life*
That honour which shall bate° his scythe's keen edge   *blunt*
And make us heirs of all eternity.
Therefore, brave conquerors—for so you are,
That war against your own affections°   *passions*
10 And the huge army of the world's desires—
Our late° edict shall strongly stand in force.   *recent*
Navarre shall be the wonder of the world.
Our court shall be a little academe,
Still° and contemplative in living art.[3]   *Peaceful*
15 You three—Biron, Dumaine, and Longueville—
Have sworn for three years' term to live with me
My fellow scholars, and to keep those statutes

1.1 Location: The action of the whole play takes place
in the King of Navarre's park.
1. For the historical background to these figures, see
the Introduction. Until Henry of Navarre's accession to
the French throne in 1589, Navarre was an independent
kingdom in southwestern France. "Biron" is pronounced
"Be-roon." The pronunciation of "Longueville" fluctu-
ates, rhyming with "ill" (4.3.120), "compile" (4.3.130),

and, by implication, "veal" (5.2.247).
2. Proverbial; one of many indications of the recourse
to proverbs in this play by aristocrats and commoners
alike.
3. The art of living (the term in this sense goes back to
ancient Stoic thought); learning invigorated by life.
academe (line 13): a philosophical academy of the sort
initiated by Plato and revived in the Renaissance.

That are recorded in this schedule° here.   *document*
Your oaths are passed;° and now subscribe° your names,   *pledged / sign*
20   That his own hand may strike his honour down
That violates the smallest branch° herein.   *clause*
If you are armed° to do as sworn to do,   *equipped*
Subscribe to your deep oaths, and keep it, too.[4]

LONGUEVILLE   I am resolved. 'Tis but a three years' fast.
25   The mind shall banquet, though the body pine.
Fat paunches have lean pates,° and dainty bits°   *heads / bites*
Make rich the ribs but bankrupt quite the wits.
          [*He signs*]

DUMAINE   My loving lord, Dumaine is mortified.°   *dead to worldliness*
The grosser manner of these world's delights
30   He throws upon the gross world's baser slaves.
To love, to wealth, to pomp I pine and die,
With all these[5] living in philosophy.
          [*He signs*]

BIRON   I can but say their protestation over.°   *again*
So much, dear liege,° I have already sworn: *lord*
35   That is, to live and study here three years.
But there are other strict observances,
As not to see a woman in that term,
Which I hope well is not enrollèd° there;   *listed*
And one day in a week to touch no food,
40   And but one meal on every day beside,
The which I hope is not enrollèd there;
And then to sleep but three hours in the night,
And not be seen to wink of° all the day,   *close my eyes during*
When I was wont to think no harm° all night,[6]   *it harmless (to sleep)*
45   And make a dark night too of half the day,
Which I hope well is not enrollèd there.
O, these are barren tasks, too hard to keep—
Not to see ladies, study, fast, not sleep.

KING   Your oath is passed to pass away from these.
50   BIRON   Let me say no, my liege, an if° you please.   *an if = if*
I only swore to study with your grace,
And stay here in your court, for three years' space.

LONGUEVILLE   You swore to that, Biron, and to the rest.

BIRON   By yea and nay,[7] sir, then I swore in jest.
55   What is the end of study, let me know?

KING   Why, that to know which else we should not know.

BIRON   Things hid and barred, you mean, from common sense.°   *ordinary perception*

KING   Ay, that is study's god-like recompense.

BIRON   Come on,[8] then, I will swear to study so
60   To know the thing I am forbid[9] to know,
As thus: to study where I well may dine
          When I to feast expressly am forbid;
Or study where to meet some mistress fine
          When mistresses from common sense are hid;

---

4. The first use of a couplet to cap a blank-verse
speech. See also 1.1.26–27, 31–32, 47–48, the last of
which begins the pattern of rhyming couplets. For an
abab quatrain followed by a couplet to form the six-line
Venus and Adonis stanza, see 1.1.61–66.
5. His three companions; the conditions prescribed in
the document; or the suggestion that philosophy is a
source or substitute for the worldly attractions of line 31.

6. Proverbial.
7. Earnestly (a solemn oath based on Matthew 5:37);
ambiguously.
8. Q has "Com'on," possibly indicating a pun on "common" (line 57).
9. Deliberately misinterpreting "should" (line 56) as
"ought" rather than "would."

65   Or having sworn too hard a keeping° oath,   *a too-demanding*
          Study to break it and not break my troth.
          If study's gain be thus, and° this be so,   *if*
          Study knows that which yet it doth not know.[1]
          Swear me to this, and I will ne'er say no.°   *(first rhyming triplet)*
70   KING   These be the stops° that hinder study quite,   *obstacles*
          And train° our intellects to vain delight.   *allure*
      BIRON   Why, all delights are vain, but that most vain
          Which, with pain° purchased, doth inherit pain;°   *labor / suffering*
          As° painfully to pore upon a book   *such as*
75   To seek the light of truth while truth the while
          Doth falsely° blind the eyesight of his look.°   *deceitfully / its vision*
           Light, seeking light, doth light of light beguile;[2]
          So ere you find where light in darkness lies
          Your light grows dark by losing of your eyes.
80   Study me[3] how to please the eye indeed
           By fixing it upon a fairer° eye,   *woman's*
          Who dazzling so,[4] that eye shall be his heed,°   *guard; what he heeds*
           And give him light that it° was blinded by.   *(his eye)*
          Study is like the heavens' glorious sun,
85   That will not be deep searched with saucy° looks.   *presumptuous; insolent*
          Small° have continual plodders ever won   *Little*
           Save base° authority from others' books.   *Except commonplace*
          These earthly godfathers of heaven's lights,°   *astronomers*
           That give a name to every fixèd star,
90   Have no more profit of their shining nights
           Than those that walk and wot° not what they are.   *know*
          Too much to know is to know naught but fame,°   *hearsay; reputation*
          And every godfather can give a name.°   *(as astronomers do)*
      KING   How well he's read, to reason against reading!
95   DUMAINE   Proceeded° well, to stop all good proceeding.[5]   *Argued*
      LONGUEVILLE   He weeds° the corn° and still lets grow the   *pulls up / wheat*
            weeding.°   *weeds*
      BIRON   The spring is near when green geese are a-breeding.[6]
      DUMAINE   How follows that?
      BIRON   Fit in his° place and time.   *its*
      DUMAINE   In reason nothing.
      BIRON   Something then in rhyme.[7]
100   KING   Biron is like an envious sneaping° frost,   *a malicious biting*
           That bites the first-born infants° of the spring.   *buds*
      BIRON   Well, say I am! Why should proud° summer boast   *splendid*
           Before the birds have any cause to sing?
          Why should I joy in any abortive° birth?   *premature*
105   At Christmas I no more desire a rose
          Than wish a snow in May's new-fangled shows,°   *displays of flowers*
          But like of° each thing that in season grows.   *But enjoy*
          So you to study, now it is too late,°   *(for us to be students)*

---

1. *If . . . know:* If study means experiencing the forbidden (line 60), study does indeed enable one to know what isn't yet known (line 56).
2. The eye, from too much study (reading), is blinded (as if from looking at a bright light).
3. Study, I say: the beginning of the first sonnet (lines 80–93; see also 1.1.160–74, 4.3.22–37, 4.3.55–68, 5.2.274–89, 5.2.343–56, 5.2.402–15). This is the earliest of Biron's claims that a man's spiritual enlightenment depends not on reading books but on gazing into a beautiful woman's eyes. This idea reached England

especially through the fourteenth-century Italian lyric poet Petrarch and the fifteenth-century Italian Neoplatonic philosopher Ficino.
4. The man (who does this) being thus bedazzled.
5. Toward a university degree.
6. When young geese are mating (as will the young lords, Biron implies). A goose is also a prostitute.
7. "In reason," it follows "nothing" (not at all); but in rhyme, "something" (somewhat)—an allusion to the proverbial phrase "neither rhyme nor reason" and perhaps to their own rhyming repartee.

Climb o'er the house to unlock the little gate.[8]

110 KING Well, sit you out.° Go home, Biron. Adieu.   *don't take part*

BIRON No, my good lord, I have sworn to stay with you.

And though I have for barbarism° spoke more   *on behalf of ignorance*

   Than for that angel knowledge you can say,

Yet confident I'll keep what I have sworn,

115   And bide the penance of each three years' day.°   *day of the three years*

Give me the paper. Let me read the same,

And to the strict'st decrees I'll write my name.

KING [*giving a paper*] How well this yielding rescues thee from

   shame!

BIRON [*reads*] 'Item: that no woman shall come within a mile of

120 my court.' Hath this been proclaimed?

LONGUEVILLE Four days ago.

BIRON Let's see the penalty. 'On pain of losing her tongue.'

   Who devised this penalty?

125 BIRON Sweet lord, and why?

LONGUEVILLE Marry,[9] that did I.

125 BIRON Sweet lord, and why?

LONGUEVILLE To fright them hence with that dread penalty.

BIRON A dangerous law against gentility.°   *courtesy*

   'Item: if any man be seen to talk with a woman within the term

of three years, he shall endure such public shame as the rest of

130 the court can possible° devise.'   *possibly*

This article, my liege, yourself must break;

   For well you know here comes in embassy

The French King's daughter with yourself to speak—

   A maid of grace and complete majesty—

135 About surrender-up of Aquitaine[1]

   To her decrepit, sick, and bedrid father.

Therefore this article is made in vain,

   Or vainly comes th'admirèd Princess hither.

KING What say you, lords? Why, this was quite forgot.

140 BIRON So study evermore is overshot.°   *wide of the mark*

While it doth study to have what it would,

It doth forget to do the thing it should;

And when it hath the thing it hunteth most,

'Tis won as towns with fire[2]—so won, so lost.

145 KING We must of force° dispense with this decree.   *necessity*

She must lie° here, on mere° necessity.   *lodge / absolute*

BIRON Necessity will make us all forsworn

   Three thousand times within this three years' space;

For every man with his affects° is born,   *passions*

150   Not by° might mastered, but by special grace.°   *by his own / (of God)*

If I break faith, this word° shall speak for me: *motto*

I am forsworn on mere necessity.

So to the laws at large° I write my name,   *in general*

   And he that breaks them in the least degree

155 Stands in attainder of° eternal shame.   *condemned to*

   [*He signs*]

Suggestions° are to other as to me,   *Temptations*

But I believe, although I seem so loath,

I am the last that will last° keep his oath.   *longest; least likely*

---

8. Set about things in a senseless, backward way—   1. A large area in southern France.
rather than climbing over the gate to unlock the house.   2. That is, destroyed in being captured.
9. Indeed (invocation of the Virgin Mary).

But is there no quick° recreation granted? | *lively*

160 KING Ay, that there is.° Our court, you know, is haunted[3] | *frequented*
With° a refinèd traveller of° Spain, | *By / from*
A man in all the world's new fashion planted,[4]
That hath a mint of phrases in his brain.
One who° the music of his own vain tongue | *whom*

165 Doth ravish like enchanting harmony;
A man of complements,° whom right and wrong | *fashion; attainments?*
Have chose as umpire of their mutiny.° | *discord*
This child of fancy,° that Armado hight,° | *absurd being / is called*
For interim° to our studies shall relate | *interlude*

170 In high-borne words the worth of many a knight
From tawny° Spain lost in the world's debate.° | *sunburned / warfare*
How you delight, my lords, I know not, I;
But I protest I love to hear him lie,
And I will use him for my minstrelsy.° | *entertainment*

175 BIRON Armado is a most illustrious wight,° | *person*
A man of fire-new° words, fashion's own knight. | *newly coined*
LONGUEVILLE Costard the swain[5] and he shall be our sport,
And so to study three years is but short.

Enter a constable [Anthony DULL] with a letter, with
COSTARD

DULL Which is the Duke's° own person? | *King's*

180 BIRON This, fellow. What wouldst?
DULL I myself reprehend° his own person, for I am his grace's | *(blunder for "represent")*
farborough.[6] But I would see his own person in flesh and blood.
BIRON This is he.
DULL Señor Arm—Arm—commends° you. There's villainy | *greets*

185 abroad. This letter will tell you more.
COSTARD Sir, the contempts[7] thereof are as touching me.
KING A letter from the magnificent Armado.[8]
BIRON How low soever the matter, I hope in God for high
words.

190 LONGUEVILLE A high hope for a low heaven.° God grant us | *a small blessing*
patience.
BIRON To hear, or forbear laughing?
LONGUEVILLE To hear meekly, sir, and to laugh moderately, or
to forbear both.

195 BIRON Well, sir, be it as the style shall give us cause to climb
in the merriness.[9]
COSTARD The matter° is to me, sir, as concerning Jaquenetta. | *(perhaps sexual)*
The manner of it is, I was taken with the manner.° | *caught red-handed*
BIRON In what manner?

200 COSTARD In manner and form[1] following, sir—all those three. I
was seen with her in the manor house, sitting with her upon
the form,° and taken following her into the park; which put | *bench*
together is 'in manner and form following'. Now, sir, for the
manner: it is the manner of a man to speak to a woman. For

205 the form: in some form.

---

3. The beginning of a sonnet that actually extends to fifteen lines (lines 160–74).
4. Established. *World's new fashion planted:* may also refer to Spanish New World plantations.
5. The costard is a large apple; the word is also used comically to refer to the head. *swain:* country lad.
6. Blunder for "thirdborough," a petty constable.
7. Blunder for "contents"; but also, inadvertently, "con-

tempt."
8. Phrase used of the Spanish Armada (1588).
9. *style . . . merriness:* stile=fence; the humble subject of "merriness" does not ordinarily lead one "to climb" to a high prose "style." A "style" is also a pen and, hence, perhaps a penis that will "climb" (swell) in "merriness" (pleasure).
1. Legal, then proverbial phrase.

BIRON For the 'following', sir?

COSTARD As it shall follow in my correction;° and God defend   *punishment*
the right.°   *(prayer before combat)*

KING Will you hear this letter with attention?

210 BIRON As we would hear an oracle.

COSTARD Such is the simplicity² of man to hearken after the
flesh.

KING [*reads*] 'Great deputy, the welkin's vicegerent° and sole   *heaven's deputy*
dominator of Navarre, my soul's earth's° god, and body's foster-   *earthly*
215 ing patron'—

COSTARD Not a word of Costard yet.

KING 'So it is'—

COSTARD It may be so; but if he say it is so, he is, in telling true,
but so.°   *truly only so-so*

220 KING Peace!

COSTARD Be to me and every man that dares not fight.

KING No words!

COSTARD Of other men's secrets, I beseech you.

KING 'So it is, besieged with sable-coloured° melancholy, I did   *black*
225 commend the black-oppressing humour° to the most whole-   *melancholy*
some physic° of thy health-giving air, and, as I am a gentleman,   *medicine*
betook myself to walk. The time when? About the sixth hour,
when beasts most graze, birds best peck, and men sit down to
that nourishment which is called supper. So much for the time
230 when. Now for the ground which—which, I mean, I walked
upon. It is yclept° thy park. Then for the place where—where,   *called (archaic)*
I mean, I did encounter that obscene° and most preposterous³   *disgusting; wanton*
event that draweth from my snow-white pen° the ebon-   *goose quill*
coloured° ink which here thou viewest, beholdest, surveyest, or   *black*
235 seest. But to the place where. It standeth north-north-east and
by east from the west corner of thy curious-knotted° garden.   *intricately patterned*
There did I see that low-spirited° swain, that base minnow° of   *base / shrimp*
thy mirth'—

COSTARD Me?

240 KING 'That unlettered,° small-knowing soul'—   *illiterate*

COSTARD Me?

KING 'That shallow vassal'°—   *base wretch; vessel*

COSTARD Still me?

KING 'Which, as I remember, hight Costard'—

245 COSTARD O, me!

KING 'Sorted° and consorted, contrary to thy established pro-   *Associated*
claimed edict and continent canon,° with, with, O with—but   *restraining law*
with this I passion° to say wherewith'—   *grieve*

COSTARD With a wench.

250 KING 'With a child of our grandmother Eve, a female, or for thy
more sweet understanding a woman. Him I, as my ever-
esteemed duty pricks⁴ me on, have sent to thee, to receive the
meed° of punishment, by thy sweet grace's officer Anthony   *reward*
Dull, a man of good repute, carriage, bearing, and estimation.'

255 DULL Me, an't° shall please you. I am Anthony Dull.   *if it*

KING 'For Jaquenetta—so is the weaker vessel° called—which I   *woman (I Peter 3:7)*
apprehended with the aforesaid swain, I keep her as a vessel of

---

2. Folly; Q has "sinplicitie"—perhaps a pun.
3. Unnatural; in reversed position—with "obscene"
(line 232) anatomically suggesting placement of the

rear, or posterior, in front. See 5.1.75, 77, 101.
4. Spurs (sexual). For other uses of the word, see
2.1.188; 4.1.128, 134; 4.2.11, 18, 45, 48, 53, 56.

thy law's fury, and shall at the least of thy sweet notice° bring   *as soon as you order*
her to trial.° Thine in all compliments of devoted and heart-   *(legally; sexually)*
260   burning heat of duty,

Don Adriano de Armado.'

BIRON   This is not so well as I looked for, but the best that ever I
heard.

KING   Ay, the best for° the worst. [*To* COSTARD]But, sirrah,⁵ what   *best example of*
265   say you to this?

COSTARD   Sir, I confess the wench.

KING   Did you hear the proclamation?

COSTARD   I do confess much of the hearing it, but little of the
marking of° it.   *paying attention to*

270   KING   It was proclaimed a year's imprisonment to be taken with
a wench.

COSTARD   I was taken with none, sir. I was taken with a damsel.

KING   Well, it was proclaimed 'damsel'.

COSTARD   This was no damsel, neither, sir. She was a virgin.

275   KING   It is so varied,° too, for it was proclaimed 'virgin'.   *covers that variation*

COSTARD   If it were, I deny her virginity. I was taken with a maid.

KING   This 'maid' will not serve your turn, sir.

COSTARD   This maid will serve my turn,° sir.   *(sexually)*

KING   Sir, I will pronounce your sentence. You shall fast a week
280   with bran and water.

COSTARD   I had rather pray a month with mutton and porridge.⁶

KING   And Don Armado shall be your keeper.
My lord Biron, see him delivered o'er,
And go we, lords, to put in practice that
285   Which each to other hath so strongly sworn.
[*Exeunt the* KING, LONGUEVILLE, *and* DUMAINE]

BIRON   I'll lay° my head to any good man's hat   *bet*
These oaths and laws will prove an idle scorn.
Sirrah, come on.

COSTARD   I suffer for the truth, sir; for true it is I was taken with
290   Jaquenetta, and Jaquenetta is a true° girl, and therefore, wel-   *an honest*
come the sour cup of prosperity, affliction⁷ may one day smile
again; and till then, sit thee down,° sorrow.   *Exeunt*   *stay with me*

1.2

Enter ARMADO *and* MOTE,¹ *his page*

ARMADO   Boy, what sign is it° when a man of great spirit grows   *what does it mean*
melancholy?

MOTE   A great sign, sir, that he will look sad.

ARMADO   Why, sadness is one and the selfsame thing,° dear imp.°   *(as melancholy)/child*

5   MOTE   No, no, O Lord, sir, no.

ARMADO   How canst thou part° sadness and melancholy, my   *distinguish between*
tender juvenal?²

MOTE   By a familiar° demonstration of the working,° my tough   *plain/their operation*
señor.°   *sir; senior*

10   ARMADO   Why 'tough señor'? Why 'tough señor'?

MOTE   Why 'tender juvenal'? Why 'tender juvenal'?

ARMADO   I spoke it, tender juvenal, as a congruent epitheton

---

5. Standard term for addressing social inferiors.
6. Mutton soup; "mutton" is also slang for "prostitute."
7. Blunder for reverse order: "affliction, prosperity."
1.2 Location: The King's park.

1. Q has "Moth," meaning "moth" or "mote" (speck). It
is pronounced like the latter word, and that sense may
be primary.
2. Youth; Juvenal, ancient Roman satirist.

appertaining to° thy young days, which we may nominate°   *suitable term for / call*
'tender'.

15   MOTE   And I, tough señor, as an appertinent° title to your old   *appropriate*
     time, which we may name 'tough'.

     ARMADO   Pretty and apt.

     MOTE   How mean you, sir? I 'pretty' and my saying 'apt'? Or I
     'apt' and my saying 'pretty'?

20   ARMADO   Thou 'pretty', because little.°   *(proverbial)*

     MOTE   Little pretty, because little. Wherefore 'apt'?

     ARMADO   And therefore 'apt' because quick.°   *quick-witted*

     MOTE   Speak you this in my praise, master?

     ARMADO   In thy condign° praise.   *well-deserved*

25   MOTE   I will praise an eel with the same praise.

     ARMADO   What—that an eel is ingenious?

     MOTE   That an eel is quick.°   *alive*

     ARMADO   I do say thou art quick in answers. Thou heatest my
     blood.°   *You make me angry*

30   MOTE   I am answered, sir.

     ARMADO   I love not to be crossed.

     MOTE [*aside*]   He speaks the mere° contrary—crosses³ love not
     him.   *absolute*

     ARMADO   I have promised to study three years with the Duke.

35   MOTE   You may do it in an hour, sir.

     ARMADO   Impossible.

     MOTE   How many is one, thrice told?°   *counted*

     ARMADO   I am ill at reckoning; it fitteth the spirit of a tapster.°   *bartender*

     MOTE   You are a gentleman and a gamester,° sir.   *gambler*

40   ARMADO   I confess both. They are both the varnish of a complete
     man.

     MOTE   Then I am sure you know how much the gross sum of
     deuce-ace° amounts to.   *a two and a one (dice)*

     ARMADO   It doth amount to one more than two.

45   MOTE   Which the base vulgar° do call three.   *common people*

     ARMADO   True.

     MOTE   Why, sir, is this such a piece° of study? Now here is 'three'   *masterpiece*
     studied ere ye'll thrice wink, and how easy it is to put 'years' to
     the word 'three' and study 'three years' in two words, the danc-
50   ing horse⁴ will tell you.

     ARMADO   A most fine figure.°   *verbal turn; number*

     MOTE [*aside*]   To prove you a cipher.°   *zero*

     ARMADO   I will hereupon confess I am in love; and as it is base°   *ignoble*
     for a soldier to love, so am I in love with a base° wench. If   *lowborn*
55   drawing my sword against the humour of affection° would   *inclination to love*
     deliver me from the reprobate thought of it, I would take desire
     prisoner and ransom him to any French courtier for a new-
     devised curtsy.° I think scorn° to sigh. Methinks I should out-   *bowing fashion / disdain*
     swear° Cupid. Comfort me, boy. What great men have been in   *renounce*
60   love?

     MOTE   Hercules, master.

     ARMADO   Most sweet Hercules! More authority, dear boy. Name
     more—and, sweet my child, let them be men of good repute
     and carriage.°   *behavior*

---

3. Coins (often imprinted with crosses).
4. Morocco, a performing horse trained to "count" with
its hooves, was a London sensation in 1591. Mote jok-
ingly takes "three years" as the object of "study" (line 34).

65 MOTE Samson, master; he was a man of good carriage, great
carriage, for he carried the town-gates on his back⁵ like a porter,
and he was in love.

ARMADO O well-knit Samson, strong-jointed Samson! I do excel
thee in my rapier as much as thou didst me in carrying gates. I
70 am in love, too. Who was Samson's love, my dear Mote?

MOTE A woman, master.

ARMADO Of what complexion?⁶

MOTE Of all the four, or the three, or the two, or one of the four.

ARMADO Tell me precisely of what complexion?

75 MOTE Of the sea-water green,⁷ sir.

ARMADO Is that one of the four complexions?

MOTE As I have read, sir; and the best of them, too.

ARMADO Green indeed is the colour of lovers, but to have a love
of that colour, methinks Samson had small reason for it. He
80 surely affected° her for her wit.°   *loved / intelligence*

MOTE It was so, sir, for she had a green wit.⁸

ARMADO My love is most immaculate white and red.

MOTE Most maculate° thoughts, master, are masked under such   *impure*
colours.°   *hues; pretexts*

85 ARMADO Define,° define, well-educated infant.   *Explain your meaning*

MOTE My father's wit and my mother's tongue assist me!

ARMADO Sweet invocation of a child!—most pretty and pathet-
ical.°   *touching*

MOTE If she be made° of white and red   *also "maid"*
90   Her faults will ne'er be known,
         For blushing cheeks by faults are bred
            And fears by pale white shown.
         Then if she fear or be to blame,
            By this you shall not know;
95   For still her cheeks possess the same
            Which native° she doth owe.°   *naturally / own*
A dangerous rhyme, master, against the reason of white and
red.

ARMADO Is there not a ballad, boy, of the King and the Beggar?⁹

100 MOTE The world was very guilty of such a ballad some three
ages since, but I think now 'tis not to be found; or if it were, it
would neither serve° for the writing nor the tune.   *be acceptable*

ARMADO I will have that subject newly writ o'er, that I may
example my digression° by some mighty precedent. Boy, I do   *justify my lapse*
105 love that country girl that I took in the park with the rational
hind¹ Costard. She deserves well.

MOTE [*aside*] To be whipped°—and yet a better love than my   *(as a prostitute)*
master.

ARMADO Sing, boy. My spirit grows heavy in love.

110 MOTE And that's great marvel, loving a light° wench.   *wanton*

ARMADO I say, sing.

MOTE Forbear till this company be past.

---

5. For the gates, see Judges 16:3. Love proved disastrous for both Hercules and Samson.
6. Temperament (Armado's meaning), as determined
by the balance of bodily humors: blood, phlegm, melancholy (from black bile), choler; skin coloring (Mote's
meaning).

7. Ill colored; evidence of chlorosis, an anemic condition affecting young women.
8. Immature understanding (proverbial).
9. The ballad concerns the love of King Cophetua for
the beggar maid Zenelophon. See also 4.1.65.
1. Peasant (or deer?) capable of reason.

Enter [COSTARD *the*] *clown, Constable* [DULL], *and* [JAQUENETTA, *a*] *wench*

DULL [*to* ARMADO] Sir, the Duke's pleasure is that you keep Costard safe, and you must suffer° him to take no delight, nor no penance,° but a° must fast three days a week. For this damsel, I must keep her at the park. She is allowed for the dey-woman.° Fare you well.

allow
(for "pleasance"?) / he
approved as dairymaid

ARMADO [*aside*] I do betray myself with blushing.—Maid.

JAQUENETTA Man.

ARMADO I will visit thee at the lodge.

JAQUENETTA That's hereby.[2]

ARMADO I know where it is situate.

JAQUENETTA Lord, how wise you are!

ARMADO I will tell thee wonders.

JAQUENETTA With that face?° *Really?*

ARMADO I love thee.

JAQUENETTA So I heard you say.° *You don't say so*

ARMADO And so farewell.

JAQUENETTA Fair weather after you.° *(proverbial)*

DULL Come, Jaquenetta, away. *Exeunt* [DULL *and* JAQUENETTA]

ARMADO Villain,° thou shalt fast for thy offences ere thou be pardoned. *Peasant; rascal*

COSTARD Well, sir, I hope when I do it I shall do it on a full stomach.° *well fed; bravely*

ARMADO Thou shalt be heavily punished.

COSTARD I am more bound to you than your fellows,° for they are but lightly rewarded. *servants*

ARMADO Take away this villain. Shut him up.

MOTE Come, you transgressing slave. Away!

COSTARD Let me not be pent up,° sir. I will fast, being loose.[3] *jailed; constipated*

MOTE No, sir. That were fast and loose.° Thou shalt to prison. *a cheating trick*

COSTARD Well, if ever I do see the merry days of desolation° that I have seen, some shall see. *(for "elation"?)*

MOTE What shall some see?

COSTARD Nay, nothing, Master Mote, but what they look upon. It is not for prisoners to be too silent in their words, and therefore I will say nothing. I thank God I have as little patience as another man, and therefore I can be quiet.

Exeunt [MOTE *and* COSTARD]

ARMADO I do affect° the very ground—which is base—where her shoe—which is baser—guided by her foot—which is basest—doth tread. I shall be forsworn—which is a great argument° of falsehood—if I love. And how can that be true love which is falsely attempted? Love is a familiar;° love is a devil. There is no evil angel but love. Yet was Samson so tempted, and he had an excellent strength. Yet was Solomon so seduced, and he had a very good wit. Cupid's butt-shaft° is too hard for Hercules' club, and therefore too much odds for a Spaniard's rapier. The first and second cause° will not serve my turn: the passado[4] he respects not, the duello° he regards not. His disgrace is to be called boy, but his glory is to subdue men. Adieu, valour; rust, rapier; be still, drum: for your manager° is in love; yea, he

love
proof
an attendant evil spirit
unbarbed arrow
(in the dueling code)
dueling code
wielder

2. Nearby; neither here nor there(?)
3. Being free; being loose in the bowels.
4. Fencing thrust.

loveth. Assist me, some extemporal° god of rhyme, for I am sure   *impromptu*
I shall turn sonnet.° Devise wit, write pen, for I am for whole   *sonneteer*
volumes, in folio.°   *Exit*   *largest size of book*

2.1

Enter the PRINCESS *of France with three attending ladies*
*[*MARIA, CATHERINE, *and* ROSALINE*] and three lords [one*
named BOYET*]*[1]

BOYET   Now, madam, summon up your dearest spirits.°   *utmost energies*
    Consider who the King your father sends,
    To whom he sends, and what's his embassy:
    Yourself, held precious in the world's esteem,
5   To parley with the sole inheritor°   *owner*
    Of all perfections that a man may owe,
    Matchless Navarre; the plea° of no less weight   *that which is claimed*
    Than Aquitaine, a dowry for a queen.
    Be now as prodigal of all dear grace
10   As nature was in making graces dear[2]
    When she did starve the general world beside°   *except (you)*
    And prodigally gave them all to you.
PRINCESS   Good Lord Boyet, my beauty, though but mean,°   *average*
    Needs not the painted flourish° of your praise.   *embellishment*
15   Beauty is bought by judgement of the eye,
    Not uttered[3] by base sale of chapmen's° tongues.   *salesmen's*
    I am less proud to hear you tell° my worth   *speak of; reckon up*
    Than you much willing to be counted wise
    In spending your wit in the praise of mine.
20   But now to task the tasker:[4] good Boyet,
    You are not ignorant all-telling fame°   *rumor*
    Doth noise abroad° Navarre hath made a vow   *spread the rumor that*
    Till painful° study shall outwear three years   *taxing*
    No woman may approach his silent court.
25   Therefore to's° seemeth it a needful course,   *to us*
    Before we enter his forbidden gates,
    To know his pleasure; and in that behalf,
    Bold° of your worthiness, we single you   *Confident*
    As our best-moving fair° solicitor.   *most eloquent and just*
30   Tell him the daughter of the King of France
    On serious business, craving quick dispatch,
    Importunes personal conference with his grace.
    Haste, signify so much while we attend,
    Like humble-visaged suitors, his high will.
35 BOYET   Proud of° employment, willingly I go.   *Honored with*
PRINCESS   All pride is willing pride,° and yours is so. *Exit* BOYET   *vanity*
    Who are the votaries,° my loving lords,   *vow takers*
    That are vow-fellows with this virtuous duke?
A LORD   Lord Longueville is one.
PRINCESS   Know you the man?
40 MARIA   I know him, madam. At a marriage feast
    Between Lord Périgord[5] and the beauteous heir

2.1 Location: Outside the gates of the King's court.
1. Pronounced "Boy-ett."
2. *dear grace . . . graces dear:* chiasmus, an *abba* rhetorical structure common to the aristocrats' speech and the larger movement of the play. See 4.3 and Introduc-

tion. The second "dear" means costly (because rare).
3. Not spoken; not offered for sale.
4. Impose a task on you who have given me one; chastise the task setter.
5. Not otherwise mentioned; Périgord was in Aquitaine.

Of Jaques Fauconbridge solemnizèd
In Normandy saw I this Longueville.
A man of sovereign parts° he is esteemed,   outstanding qualities
45 Well fitted in arts, glorious in arms.
Nothing becomes him ill that he would° well.   wishes to do
The only soil of° his fair virtue's gloss—   stain on
If virtue's gloss will stain with any soil—
Is a sharp wit matched with too blunt° a will,   rough; unfeeling
50 Whose edge hath power to cut, whose will still° wills   always
It should none spare that come within his° power.   its
PRINCESS   Some merry mocking lord, belike°—is't so?   probably
MARIA   They say so most that most his humours know.
PRINCESS   Such short-lived wits do wither as they grow.
55 Who are the rest?
CATHERINE[6]   The young Dumaine, a well-accomplished youth,
Of° all that virtue love for virtue loved.   By
Most power to do most harm, least knowing ill,[7]
For he hath wit to make an ill shape good,
60 And shape to win grace, though he had no wit.[8]
I saw him at the Duke Alençon's once,
And much too little° of that good I saw   short
Is my report to° his great worthiness.   my report compared with
ROSALINE[9]   Another of these students at that time
65 Was there with him, if I have heard a truth.
Biron[1] they call him, but a merrier man,
Within the limit of becoming° mirth,   decorous
I never spent an hour's talk withal.°   with
His eye begets occasion° for his wit,   finds opportunities
70 For every object that the one doth catch
The other turns to a mirth-moving jest,
Which his fair tongue, conceit's expositor,°   thought's expounder
Delivers in such apt and gracious words
That agèd ears play truant at° his tales,   neglect work to hear
75 And younger hearings are quite ravishèd,
So sweet and voluble° is his discourse.   fluent
PRINCESS   God bless my ladies, are they all in love,
That every one her own hath garnishèd
With such bedecking ornaments of praise?
A LORD   Here comes Boyet.
       Enter BOYET
80 PRINCESS   Now, what admittance,° lord?   reception
BOYET   Navarre had notice of your fair approach,
And he and his competitors° in oath   partners
Were all addressed° to meet you, gentle lady,   ready
Before I came. Marry, thus much I have learnt:
85 He rather means to lodge you in the field,

---

6. Q, F: 2 Lady. The remainder of the scene strongly suggests that Lady 2 is Rosaline, not Catherine. The last three acts imply that Lady 2 is Catherine, however. For the issues involved in this emendation and others in 2.1 (lines 64, 113–26, 178–92, 194, and 209), see the Textual Note.
7. Potentially dangerous by virtue of his very innocence; although he theoretically could do harm, he is free of all misdeeds.
8. *For . . . wit*: He is intelligent enough to make up for a displeasing appearance, if he had one (or perhaps to make something evil seem virtuous), and good-looking enough to win favor (from people or perhaps God), even if he lacked intelligence.
9. Q: 3 Lady; F: Rosaline. The remainder of the scene in Q strongly suggests that Lady 3 is Catherine, not Rosaline. The last three acts of Q imply that Lady 3 is Rosaline, however.
1. Probable pun on "Biron/brown." "Brown" was pronounced much like "Biron" ("Be-roon"); Q's spelling of "Biron" is "Berowne." "Brown" was associated with somberness or melancholy (as in a "brown study"), and is contrasted in this line with "merrier" by means of "but."

Like one that comes here to besiege his court,
Than seek a dispensation for his oath
To let you enter his unpeopled° house.   *servantless*

Enter NAVARRE, LONGUEVILLE, DUMAINE, *and* BIRON

Here comes Navarre.

90   KING   Fair Princess, welcome to the court of Navarre.
PRINCESS   'Fair' I give you back again, and welcome I have not
yet. The roof of this court° is too high to be yours, and welcome   *sky*
to the wide fields too base to be mine.
KING   You shall be welcome, madam, to my court.
95   PRINCESS   I will be welcome, then. Conduct me thither.
KING   Hear me, dear lady. I have sworn an oath—
PRINCESS   Our Lady help my lord! He'll be forsworn.
KING   Not for the world, fair madam, by my will.°   *willingly (mild oath)*
PRINCESS   Why, will° shall break it—will and nothing else.   *(sexual) desire*
100   KING   Your ladyship is ignorant what it is.
PRINCESS   Were my lord so his ignorance were wise,
Where now his knowledge must prove ignorance.
I hear your grace hath sworn out housekeeping.°   *repudiated hospitality*
'Tis deadly sin to keep that oath, my lord,
105   And sin to break it.
But pardon me, I am too sudden°-bold.   *rashly*
To teach a teacher ill beseemeth me.
Vouchsafe to read the purpose of my coming,
And suddenly resolve° me in my suit.   *immediately answer*

[*She gives him a paper*]

110   KING   Madam, I will, if suddenly I may.
PRINCESS   You will the sooner that I were away,°   *so that I'll go*
For you'll prove perjured if you make me stay.

[*Navarre reads the paper*]

BIRON [*to* ROSALINE]   Did not I dance with you in Brabant once?
ROSALINE[2]   Did not I dance with you in Brabant once?
BIRON   I know you did.
115   ROSALINE   How needless was it then
To ask the question!
BIRON   You must not be so quick.°   *sharp; hasty; witty*
ROSALINE   'Tis 'long of° you, that spur° me with such questions.   *due to / prod*
BIRON   Your wit's too hot, it speeds too fast, 'twill tire.
ROSALINE   Not till it leave the rider in the mire.
120   BIRON   What time o' day?
ROSALINE   The hour that fools should ask.
BIRON   Now fair befall° your mask.   *good luck to*
ROSALINE   Fair fall° the face it covers.   *befall*
BIRON   And send you many lovers.
125   ROSALINE   Amen, so you be none.
BIRON   Nay, then will I be gone.
KING [*to the* PRINCESS]   Madam, your father here doth intimate
The payment of[3] a hundred thousand crowns,
Being but the one-half of an entire sum
130   Disbursèd by my father in his° wars.   *(the King of France's)*
But say that he° or we—as neither have—   *(Navarre's father)*
Received that sum, yet there remains unpaid
A hundred thousand more, in surety of the which

---

2. Lines 114–25—Q: Catherine; F: Rosaline.   3. *intimate . . . of:* suggest he paid.

One part of Aquitaine is bound to us,
135 Although not valued° to the money's worth.   *equal in value*
If then the King your father will restore
But that one half which is unsatisfied,
We will give up our right in Aquitaine
And hold fair friendship with his majesty.
140 But that, it seems, he little purposeth,
For here he doth demand to have repaid°   *insists he has repaid*
A hundred thousand crowns, and not demands,°   *rather than offering*
On payment of a hundred thousand crowns,
To have his title live in Aquitaine,
145 Which we much rather had depart withal,°   *surrender*
And have the money by our father lent,
Than Aquitaine, so gelded° as it is.[4]   *reduced; castrated*
Dear Princess, were not his requests so far
From reason's yielding, your fair self should make
150 A yielding 'gainst some reason in my breast,
And go well satisfied to France again.
PRINCESS   You do the King my father too much wrong,
And wrong the reputation of your name,
In so unseeming° to confess receipt   *seeming unwilling*
155 Of that° which hath so faithfully been paid.   *200,000 crowns*
KING   I do protest I never heard of it,
And if you prove it I'll repay it back
Or yield up Aquitaine.
PRINCESS   We arrest° your word.   *seize as security*
Boyet, you can produce acquittances°   *receipts*
160 For such a sum from special officers
Of Charles, his° father.   *(Navarre's)*
KING   Satisfy me so.
BOYET   So please your grace, the packet is not come
Where that and other specialties° are bound.   *legal contracts*
Tomorrow you shall have a sight of them.
165 KING   It shall suffice me, at which interview
All liberal° reason I will yield unto.   *civilized*
Meantime receive such welcome at my hand
As honour, without breach of honour, may
Make tender of to thy true worthiness.
170 You may not come, fair princess, within my gates,
But here without° you shall be so received   *outside*
As you shall deem yourself lodged in my heart,
Though so denied fair harbour in my house.
Your own good thoughts excuse me, and farewell.
175 Tomorrow shall we visit you again.
PRINCESS   Sweet health and fair desires consort° your grace.   *accompany*
KING   Thy own wish wish I thee in every place.
                    Exit [with LONGUEVILLE *and* DUMAINE]
BIRON[5] [*to* ROSALINE]   Lady, I will commend you to mine own
heart.
180 ROSALINE   Pray you, do my commendations. I would be glad to
see it.[6]

---

4. Navarre says that of the 200,000 crowns he's owed,
the King of France falsely claims to have paid back half
and has given him Aquitaine as collateral for the other
half, even though it isn't worth that much. Navarre is
willing to return Aquitaine and forget the entire debt in
return for 100,000 crowns, but France wants Navarre
to pay that sum and keep Aquitaine.
5. Lines 178–92—Q: Biron; F: Boyet.
6. Know your real feelings; literally, behold your heart
and, hence, see you dead.

BIRON   I would you heard it groan.

ROSALINE   Is the fool° sick? *poor thing*

BIRON   Sick at the heart.

185 ROSALINE   Alack, let it blood.° *bleed it (medically)*

BIRON   Would that do it good?

ROSALINE   My physic° says 'Ay'. *medical knowledge*

BIRON   Will you prick't with your eye?[7]

ROSALINE   *Non point,*° with my knife. *Not at all; it's blunt*

190 BIRON   Now God save thy life.

ROSALINE   And yours, from long living.

BIRON   I cannot stay thanksgiving.[8]   *Exit*

      Enter DUMAINE

DUMAINE [*to* BOYET]   Sir, I pray you a word. What lady is that same?

BOYET   The heir of Alençon, Catherine[9] her name.

195 DUMAINE   A gallant lady. Monsieur, fare you well.   *Exit*

      [*Enter* LONGUEVILLE]

LONGUEVILLE [*to* BOYET]   I beseech you a word, what is she in the white?

BOYET   A woman sometimes, an° you saw her in the light. *if*

LONGUEVILLE   Perchance light in the light.° I desire her name. *wanton if seen clearly*

BOYET   She hath but one for herself; to desire that were a shame.

200 LONGUEVILLE   Pray you, sir, whose daughter?

BOYET   Her mother's, I have heard.

LONGUEVILLE   God's blessing on your beard!° *(insult)*

BOYET   Good sir, be not offended.

    She is an heir of Fauconbridge.

205 LONGUEVILLE   Nay, my choler° is ended. *anger*

    She is a most sweet lady.

BOYET   Not unlike,° sir. That may be.   *Exit* LONGUEVILLE *unlikely*

      Enter BIRON

BIRON   What's her name in the cap?

BOYET   Rosaline,[1] by good hap.

210 BIRON   Is she wedded or no?

BOYET   To her will, sir, or so.° *or something like that*

BIRON   O, you are welcome, sir. Adieu.

BOYET   Farewell to me, sir, and welcome to you.°   *Exit* BIRON *you're welcome to go*

MARIA   That last is Biron, the merry madcap lord.

    Not a word with him but a jest.

215 BOYET   And every jest but a word.

PRINCESS   It was well done of you to take him at his word.° *(literally; punningly)*

BOYET   I was as willing to grapple as he was to board.[2]

CATHERINE[3]   Two hot sheeps,[4] marry.

BOYET   And wherefore not ships?

    No sheep, sweet lamb, unless we feed on your lips.

220 CATHERINE[5]   You sheep and I pasture[6]—shall that finish the jest?

BOYET   So° you grant pasture for me. *So long as*

CATHERINE   Not so, gentle beast.

    My lips are no common, though several they be.[7]

BOYET   Belonging to whom?

---

7. "Eye" puns on "Ay" (line 187), suggesting a needle but also a vagina, impossibly serving as a penis.

8. Stay long enough to thank you (for that rude remark).

9. Q, F: Rosaline.

1. Q, F: Catherine.

2. Join ships ("grapple") for hand-to-hand combat ("board"): metaphor for competitive wordplay, with sexual overtones.

3. F: Maria.

4. "Sheeps" was pronounced like "ships."

5. Lines 220, 221, 223—Q, F: Lady.

6. Pun on "pastor" (shepherd).

7. My lips are not commonly owned grazing land, though they are pasture—they are privately owned, enclosed land (*several:* more than one; separate).

CATHERINE To my fortunes and me.

PRINCESS Good wits will be jangling;° but, gentles,° agree. *quarreling / gentlefolk*

225 This civil war of wits were much better used

On Navarre and his bookmen,° for here 'tis abused.° *scholars / misapplied*

BOYET If my observation, which very seldom lies,

By the heart's still rhetoric° disclosèd with eyes, *silent eloquence*

Deceive me not now, Navarre is infected.

230 PRINCESS With what?

BOYET With that which we lovers entitle 'affected'.° *being in love*

PRINCESS Your reason?

BOYET Why, all his behaviours did make their retire° *withdrawal*

To the court of his eye, peeping thorough° desire. *through*

235 His heart like an agate with your print impressed,[8]

Proud with his form,° in his eye pride expressed. *the Princess's image*

His tongue, all impatient to speak[9] and not see,

Did stumble with haste in his eyesight to be.

All senses to that sense did make their repair,° *resort*

240 To feel° only looking° on fairest of fair. *experience / by looking*

Methought all his senses were locked in his eye,

As jewels in crystal, for some prince to buy,

Who, tendering° their own worth from where they were *displaying*

glassed,° *encased in crystal*

Did point° you to buy them along as you passed. *direct*

245 His face's own margin[1] did quote° such amazes *indicate*

That all eyes saw his eyes enchanted with gazes.

I'll give you° Aquitaine and all that is his *bet you get*

An you give him for my sake but one loving kiss.

PRINCESS Come, to our pavilion. Boyet is disposed.° *(to be merry)*

250 BOYET But to speak that in words which his eye hath disclosed.

I only have made a mouth of his eye

By adding a tongue, which I know will not lie.

ROSALINE[2] Thou art an old love-monger, and speak'st skilfully.

MARIA He is Cupid's grandfather, and learns news of him.

255 CATHERINE Then was Venus° like her mother, for her father is *Cupid's mother*

but grim.° *not handsome*

BOYET Do you hear, my mad° wenches? *high-spirited*

MARIA No.

BOYET What then, do you see?

CATHERINE Ay—our way to be gone.

BOYET You are too hard for me.

Exeunt

3.1

Enter [ARMADO *the*] *braggart,*[1] *and* [MOTE] *his boy*

ARMADO Warble, child; make passionate° my sense of hearing. *responsive*

MOTE [*sings*] Concolinel.° *song title or opening*
  tune
ARMADO Sweet air!° Go, tenderness of years, take this key. Give

enlargement° to the swain. Bring him festinately° hither. I must *freedom / in a hurry*

5 employ him in a letter to my love.

---

8. Engraved with your image. Agates were engraved and set in rings.
9. Impatient at being able only to speak.
1. The part of a book in which comments were printed.
2. Lines 253, 254, 255, 256, 257: Q—Lady, Lady 2, Lady 3, Lady, Lady; F—Rosaline, Maria, Lady 2, Lady 1, Lady 2. It is uncertain which of the ladies should

speak these lines.
3.1 Location: The King's park.
1. The braggart soldier was a stock figure in the contemporary Italian commedia dell'arte, a theatrical form with popular roots. His theatrical ancestry can be traced back to ancient Roman comedy.

MOTE   Master, will you win your love with a French brawl?°   *dance*
ARMADO   How meanest thou—brawling in French?[2]
MOTE   No, my complete master; but to jig off a tune° at the   *sing a jiglike tune*
  tongue's end, canary° to it with your feet, humour° it with turn-   *dance / adapt to*
10 ing up your eyelids, sigh a note and sing a note, sometime
  through the throat as if you swallowed love with singing love,
  sometime through the nose as if you snuffed up love by smell-
  ing love, with your hat penthouse-like° o'er the shop of your   *like an awning*
  eyes, with your arms crossed° on your thin-belly[3] doublet like a   *(from love melancholy)*
15 rabbit on a spit, or your hands in your pocket like a man after°   *in the style of*
  the old painting, and keep not too long in one tune, but a snip°   *snatch*
  and away. These are complements, these are humours; these
  betray nice° wenches that would be betrayed without these,   *seduce wanton*
  and make them men of note—do you note? *men*—that most
20 are affected° to these.   *given*
ARMADO   How hast thou purchased this experience?
MOTE   By my penny of observation.
ARMADO   But O, but O—
MOTE   'The hobby-horse is forgot.'[4]
25 ARMADO   Call'st thou my love hobby-horse?
MOTE   No, master, the hobby-horse is but a colt,° and your love   *young horse; wanton*
  perhaps a hackney.° But have you forgot your love?   *riding horse; whore*
ARMADO   Almost I had.
MOTE   Negligent student, learn her by heart.
30 ARMADO   By heart and in heart, boy.
MOTE   And out of heart,° master. All those three I will prove.   *disheartened*
ARMADO   What wilt thou prove?
MOTE   A man, if I live; and this, 'by', 'in', and 'without', upon
  the instant: 'by' heart you love her because your heart cannot
35 come *by* her; 'in' heart you love her because your heart is *in*
  love with her; and 'out' of heart you love her, being *out* of heart
  that you cannot enjoy her.
ARMADO   I am all these three.
MOTE [*aside*]   And three times as much more, and yet nothing
40 at all.
ARMADO   Fetch hither the swain. He must carry me° a letter.   *for me*
MOTE [*aside*]   A message well sympathized°—a horse to be   *matched*
  ambassador for an ass.
ARMADO   Ha, ha! What sayst thou?
45 MOTE   Marry, sir, you must send the ass upon the horse, for he
  is very slow-gaited. But I go.
ARMADO   The way is but short. Away!
MOTE   As swift as lead, sir.
ARMADO   The meaning, pretty ingenious?
50 Is not lead a metal heavy, dull, and slow?
MOTE   *Minime,*° honest master—or rather, master, no.   *By no means*
ARMADO   I say lead is slow.
MOTE   You are too swift, sir, to say so.
  Is that lead slow which is fired from a gun?
ARMADO   Sweet smoke of rhetoric!

---

2. "Brawling" means "quarreling," but the phrase may also refer to popular rioting against immigrant French merchants and artisans.
3. Unpadded belly or lower part; also suggesting that Armado is wasting away for love.

4. A lament for the passing of the good old days; perhaps the refrain of a song. A hobbyhorse—a person costumed as a horse—was used in popular dancing; the word also meant "whore," perhaps suggested by the association between "O" (line 23) and "vagina."

55   He reputes me a cannon, and the bullet, that's he.
       I shoot thee at the swain.
    MOTE   Thump,° then, and I flee.   [*Exit*]   *Bang*
    ARMADO   A most acute juvenal—voluble° and free of grace.   *quick-witted*
       By thy favour, sweet welkin,° I must sigh in thy face.   *sky*
       Most rude melancholy, valour gives thee place.°   *gives way to you*
60   My herald is returned.
               Enter [MOTE *the*] *page, and* [COSTARD *the*] *clown*
    MOTE   A wonder, master—here's a costard broken in a shin.⁵
    ARMADO   Some enigma, some riddle; come, thy *l'envoi*.° Begin.   *explanation*
    COSTARD   No egma, no riddle, no *l'envoi*, no salve in the mail,⁶
       sir. O sir, plantain,° a plain plantain—no *l'envoi*, no *l'envoi*, no   *healing herb*
65   salve, sir, but a plantain.
    ARMADO   By virtue, thou enforcest laughter—thy silly thought
       my spleen.⁷ The heaving of my lungs provokes me to ridicu-
       lous° smiling. O pardon me, my stars! Doth the inconsiderate⁸   *mocking; absurd*
       take salve for *l'envoi*, and the word *l'envoi* for a salve?
70   MOTE   Do the wise think them other? Is not *l'envoi* a salve?
    ARMADO   No, page, it is an epilogue or discourse to make plain
       Some obscure precedence that hath tofore been sain.⁹
       I will example° it.   *give an example of*
             The fox, the ape, and the humble-bee°   *bumblebee*
75   Were still at odds,¹ being but three.
       There's the moral.° Now the *l'envoi*.   *lesson*
    MOTE   I will add the *l'envoi*. Say the moral again.
    ARMADO   The fox, the ape, and the humble-bee
           Were still at odds, being but three.
80   MOTE   Until the goose came out of door
           And stayed° the odds by adding four.°   *stopped / a fourth*
       Now will I begin your moral, and do you follow with my
       l'envoi.
             The fox, the ape, and the humble-bee
85   Were still at odds, being but three.
    ARMADO   Until the goose came out of door,
           Staying the odds by adding four.
    MOTE   A good *l'envoi*, ending in the goose.² Would you desire
       more?
90   COSTARD   The boy hath sold him a bargain—a goose,° that's flat.°   *made him a fool / certain*
       Sir, your pennyworth° is good an° your goose be fat.   *bargain / if*
       To sell a bargain well is as cunning as fast and loose.°   *cheating; (of bowels)*
       Let me see, a fat *l'envoi*—ay, that's a fat goose.°   *buttocks?*
    ARMADO   Come hither, come hither. How did this argument°   *topic*
95   begin?
    MOTE   By saying that a costard was broken in a shin.
       Then called you for the *l'envoi*.
    COSTARD   True, and I for a plantain. Thus came your argument°   *enema?*

5. A head with a cut shin (an anatomical impossibility that provokes Mote's amusement); disappointed in love or sex (alluding to Armado's triumph over Costard); taking a loan.
6. Costard takes Armado to be proposing remedies for his shin. "Egma" for "enigma" may be an error for an "egg" solution or "enema." *L'envoi* refers to a salve or ointment, perhaps by confusion with "lenify" (to soothe or purge). There is also a pun on the Latin *salve* (greetings), the opposite of *l'envoi*'s sense of "farewell." *mail:* traveling bag. In addition, a salve inserted in or an anal salvo discharged from the male.

7. Amusement: the spleen was regarded as the organ controlling laughter.
8. The thoughtless person.
9. *Some . . . sain:* What was obscurely said before. The couplet is in poulter's measure—fourteen syllables, then twelve.
1. Were always quarreling; were always an odd number.
2. Punning on the French *oie* (goose), the final sound in *envoi*, "ending in the goose" also because it is inserted in the end of the goose (prostitute, victim of venereal disease).

in. Then the boy's fat *l'envoi,* the goose that you bought, and
100   he ended the market.°   *bargaining*
ARMADO   But tell me, how was there a costard broken in a shin?
MOTE   I will tell you sensibly.°   *clearly; feelingly*
COSTARD   Thou hast no feeling of it. Mote, I will speak that
l'envoi.
105   I, Costard, running out, that was safely within,³
Fell over the threshold and broke my shin.
ARMADO   We will talk no more of this matter.
COSTARD   Till there be more matter° in the shin.   *pus; semen*
ARMADO   Sirrah Costard, I will enfranchise° thee.   *free*
110 COSTARD   O, marry me to one Frances!⁴ I smell some *l'envoi,*
some goose, in this.
ARMADO   By my sweet soul, I mean setting thee at liberty, enfree-
doming thy person. Thou wert immured,° restrained, capti-   *shut in*
vated, bound.°   *(of bowels)*
115 COSTARD   True, true, and now you will be my purgation° and let   *liberator; enema*
me loose.°   *(my bowels)*
ARMADO   I give thee thy liberty, set° thee from durance,° and in   *free/imprisonment*
lieu thereof impose on thee nothing but this: bear this signif-
icant° to the country maid, Jaquenetta.   *token*
120   [*Giving him a letter*] There is remuneration [*giving him
money*], for the best ward° of mine honour is rewarding my   *guard*
dependants. Mote, follow.   [*Exit*]
MOTE   Like the sequel, I. Signor Costard, adieu.   *Exit*
COSTARD   My sweet ounce of man's flesh, my incony Jew!⁵
125   Now will I look to his remuneration. Remuneration—O, that's
the Latin word for three-farthings.° Three-farthings—remuner-   *¾-pence coin*
ation. 'What's the price of this inkle?'⁶ 'One penny.' 'No, I'll give
you a remuneration.' Why, it carries it!° Remuneration! Why,   *carries the day*
it is a fairer name than French crown.⁷ I will never buy and
130   sell out of° this word.   *without using*
      Enter BIRON
BIRON   My good knave Costard, exceedingly well met.
COSTARD   Pray you, sir, how much carnation° ribbon may a man   *flesh-colored*
buy for a remuneration?
BIRON   What is a remuneration?
135 COSTARD   Marry, sir, halfpenny-farthing.°   *three farthings*
BIRON   Why, then, three-farthing-worth of silk.
COSTARD   I thank your worship. God be wi' you.
BIRON   Stay, slave, I must employ thee.
As thou wilt win my favour, good my knave,
140   Do one thing for me that I shall entreat.
COSTARD   When would you have it done, sir?
BIRON   This afternoon.
COSTARD   Well, I will do it, sir. Fare you well.
BIRON   Thou knowest not what it is.
145 COSTARD   I shall know, sir, when I have done it.
BIRON   Why, villain, thou must know first.

---

3. *running out . . . within:* possible reference to bodily
emissions.
4. Punning on "enfranchise" (line 109); "Frances" was
probably a common name for a prostitute.
5. Religious reference from the mishearing of "adieu"
(line 123); playful diminutive of "jewel" or "juvenal."
incony: fine, quality.

6. Linen tape, suggested by "incony" (line 124); near
homonym of "ingle," a catamite (boy kept by a pederast), and perhaps thereby evoking the period's association of the "Jew" (line 124) with sodomy.
7. A coin; syphilis (the "French disease") results in a
bald head ("crown").

COSTARD   I will come to your worship tomorrow morning.
BIRON   It must be done this afternoon. Hark, slave,
       It is but this:
150   The Princess comes to hunt here in the park,
       And in her train there is a gentle lady.
       When tongues speak sweetly, then they name her name,
       And Rosaline they call her. Ask for her,
       And to her white hand see thou do commend
       This sealed-up counsel.° There's thy guerdon° [*giving him a*   message / reward
155   *letter and money*], go.
COSTARD   Guerdon! O sweet guerdon!—better than remunera-
       tion, elevenpence-farthing better[8]—most sweet guerdon! I will
       do it, sir, in print.° Guerdon—remuneration.   *Exit*   to the letter
BIRON   And I, forsooth, in love—I that have been love's whip,
160   A very beadle[9] to a humorous° sigh,   moody
       A critic, nay, a night-watch constable,
       A domineering pedant° o'er the boy,°   schoolmaster / Cupid
       Than whom no mortal so magnificent.
       This wimpled,° whining, purblind,° wayward boy,   blindfolded / all-blind
165   This Signor° Junior, giant dwarf, Dan° Cupid,   Sir; senior / Master
       Regent of love-rhymes, lord of folded arms,
       Th'anointed sovereign of sighs and groans,
       Liege of all loiterers and malcontents,
       Dread prince of plackets, king of codpieces,[1]
170   Sole imperator° and great general   Absolute ruler
       Of trotting paritors[2]—O my little heart!
       And I to be a corporal of his field,°   field officer
       And wear his colours like a tumbler's hoop!°   (adorned with ribbons)
       What? I love, I sue, I seek a wife?—
175   A woman, that is like a German clock,
       Still° a-repairing, ever out of frame,°   Always / order
       And never going aright, being° a watch,   though
       But being° watched that it may still go right.   Except when
       Nay, to be perjured, which is worst of all,
180   And among three to love the worst of all—
       A whitely° wanton with a velvet° brow,   pale / smooth
       With two pitch°-balls stuck in her face for eyes—   tar black
       Ay, and, by heaven, one that will do the deed°   sexual act
       Though Argus[3] were her eunuch° and her guard.   harem guard
185   And I to sigh for her, to watch° for her,   stay awake at night
       To pray for her—go to,° it is a plague   come now
       That Cupid will impose for my neglect
       Of his almighty dreadful little might.
       Well, I will love, write, sigh, pray, sue, groan:
190   Some men must love my lady, and some Joan.°   [*Exit*]   lower-class woman

---

8. Biron has given Costard a "guerdon" of one shilling, or twelve pence, which is "elevenpence-farthing" (eleven pence and one farthing) "better than remuneration," defined earlier by Costard as "three-farthings" (where four farthings equal one pence; line 126).

9. Minor parish official who punished lesser offenses (for instance, by whipping).

1. The parts of clothes covering the male sexual organ (hence, penises, or men). *plackets*: slits in petticoats (hence, female genitalia, or women).

2. Officers who summoned sexual offenders to ecclesiastical courts.

3. Mythical watchman with a hundred eyes.

4.1

Enter the PRINCESS, *a* FORESTER, *her ladies* [ROSALINE,
MARIA, *and* CATHERINE] *and her lords* [*among them*
BOYET]

PRINCESS Was that the King that spurred his horse so hard
Against the steep uprising of the hill?

BOYET I know not, but I think it was not he.

PRINCESS Whoe'er a° was, a showed a mounting mind.   *he*
Well, lords, today we shall have our dispatch.

5   Ere Saturday we will return to France.
Then, forester my friend, where is the bush
That we must stand and play the murderer in?

FORESTER Hereby, upon the edge of yonder coppice°—   *thicket*
A stand° where you may make the fairest° shoot.   *hunter's station / best*

10 PRINCESS I thank my beauty, I am fair that shoot,
And thereupon thou speak'st 'the fairest shoot'.

FORESTER Pardon me, madam, for I meant not so.

PRINCESS What, what? First praise me, and again say no?
O short-lived pride! Not fair? Alack, for woe!

15 FORESTER Yes, madam, fair.

PRINCESS   Nay, never paint° me now.   *flatter*
Where fair° is not, praise cannot mend the brow.   *beauty*
Here, good my glass,° take this for telling true.   *my good mirror*
[*She gives him money*]
Fair payment for foul words is more than due.

FORESTER Nothing but fair is that which you inherit.°   *own*

20 PRINCESS See, see, my beauty will be saved by merit![1]
O heresy in fair,° fit for these days[2]—   *in regard to beauty*
A giving hand, though foul, shall have fair praise.
But come, the bow. Now mercy° goes to kill,   *the merciful Princess*
And shooting well is then accounted ill.°   *unmerciful*

25 Thus will I save my credit in the shoot,
Not wounding—pity would not let me do't.[3]
If wounding, then it was to show my skill,
That more for praise than purpose meant to kill.
And, out of question,° so it is sometimes—   *beyond doubt*

30 Glory° grows guilty of detested crimes   *The desire for glory*
When for fame's sake, for praise, an outward part,
We bend to that the working of the heart,
As I for praise alone now seek to spill
The poor deer's blood that my heart means no ill.

35 BOYET Do not curst° wives hold that self-sovereignty   *shrewish*
Only for praise' sake when they strive to be
Lords o'er their lords?

PRINCESS Only for praise, and praise we may afford
To any lady that subdues a lord.

40   *Enter* [COSTARD *the*] *clown*

BOYET Here comes a member of the commonwealth.°   *common people*

COSTARD God dig-you-de'en,° all. Pray you, which is the head   *give you good evening*
lady?

4.1 Location: A hunter's station in the King's park.
1. Desert; good works (her "payment").
2. Believing in salvation by faith, Protestants considered it a common "heresy" "these days" to think, as

Catholics did, that one could be "saved by merit."
3. *Thus . . . do't*: I will save my reputation as a hunter
by saying, if I miss, that pity for the deer caused me to
miss deliberately.

PRINCESS   Thou shalt know her, fellow, by the rest that have no
45   heads.[4]
COSTARD   Which is the greatest lady, the highest?
PRINCESS   The thickest and the tallest.
COSTARD   The thickest and the tallest—it is so, truth is truth.
   An your waist, mistress, were as slender as my wit
50   One o' these maids' girdles for your waist should be fit.
   Are not you the chief woman? You are the thickest here.
PRINCESS   What's your will, sir? What's your will?
COSTARD   I have a letter from Monsieur Biron to one Lady Rosaline.
PRINCESS   O, thy letter, thy letter! [*She takes it*] He's a good
   friend of mine.
55   [*To* COSTARD] Stand aside, good bearer. Boyet, you can carve.°   cut meat; act affected
   Break up° this capon.[5]   Cut up; open
         [*She gives the letter to* BOYET]
BOYET   I am bound to serve.
   This letter is mistook. It importeth° none here.   matters to
   It is writ to Jaquenetta.
PRINCESS   We will read it, I swear.
   Break the neck of the wax,° and everyone give ear.   seal; (capon)
60   BOYET [*reads*]   'By heaven, that thou art fair is most infallible,°   certain
   true that thou art beauteous, truth itself that thou art lovely.
   More fairer than fair, beautiful than beauteous, truer than truth
   itself, have commiseration on thy heroical vassal. The magnan-
   imous and most illustrate° King Cophetua set's° eye upon the   illustrious / set his
65   penurious and indubitate° beggar Zenelophon,[6] and he it was   undoubted
   that might rightly say "*Veni, vidi, vici*",[7] which to annothanize°   anatomize; annotate
   in the vulgar—O base and obscure vulgar!°—*videlicet*° "He   vernacular / namely
   came, see, and overcame." He came, one; see, two; overcame,
   three. Who came? The King. Why did he come? To see. Why
70   did he see? To overcome. To whom came he? To the beggar.
   What saw he? The beggar. Who overcame he? The beggar.
   The conclusion is victory. On whose side? The King's. The
   captive is enriched. On whose side? The beggar's. The catastro-
   phe° is a nuptial. On whose side? The King's—no, on both in   outcome
75   one, or one in both. I am the King—for so stands the comparison—thou the beggar, for so witnesseth thy lowliness. Shall I
   command thy love? I may. Shall I enforce thy love? I could.
   Shall I entreat thy love? I will. What shalt thou exchange for
   rags? Robes. For tittles?° Titles. For thyself? Me. Thus,   jots; specks
80   expecting thy reply, I profane my lips on thy foot, my eyes on
   thy picture, and my heart on thy every part.
         Thine in the dearest design of industry,°   gallantry?; diligence
                  Don Adriano de Armado.
   Thus dost thou hear the Nemean lion[8] roar
85   'Gainst thee, thou lamb, that standest as his prey.
   Submissive fall his princely feet before,
         And he from forage° will incline to play.   raging
   But if thou strive, poor soul, what art thou then?
   Food for his rage, repasture° for his den.'   food
90   PRINCESS   What plume of feathers° is he that indited° this   silly bird / wrote
         letter?

---

4. Part of the body, literalizing metaphorical use of   6. See 1.2.99.
"head" as "leader" (line 42); maidenhead.   7. Originally said by Julius Caesar.
5. Love letter; castrated male chicken.   8. Killed by Hercules as the first of his labors.

What vane?⁹ What weathercock?° Did you ever hear better?   *(example of showiness)*
BOYET   I am much deceived but I remember the style.
PRINCESS   Else your memory is bad, going o'er¹ it erewhile.
BOYET   This Armado is a Spaniard that keeps° here in court,   *dwells*
95   A phantasim,° a Monarcho,² and one that makes sport   *fantastic being*
To° the Prince and his bookmates.   *For*
PRINCESS [*to* COSTARD]   Thou, fellow, a word.
Who gave thee this letter?
COSTARD   I told you—my lord.
PRINCESS   To whom shouldst thou give it?
COSTARD   From my lord to my lady.
PRINCESS   From which lord to which lady?
100   COSTARD   From my lord Biron, a good master of mine,
To a lady of France that he called Rosaline.
PRINCESS   Thou hast mistaken his letter. Come, lords, away.
[*To* ROSALINE, *giving her the letter*]
Here, sweet, put up this, 'twill be thine another day.°   *your turn will come*
                    Exit [*attended*]
BOYET   Who is the suitor? Who is the suitor?°   *(with pun on "shooter")*
ROSALINE   Shall I teach you to know?
BOYET   Ay, my continent° of beauty.   *container of all*
105   ROSALINE   Why, she that bears the bow.
Finely put off.°   *evaded*
BOYET   My lady goes to kill horns, but if thou marry,
Hang me by the neck if horns that year miscarry.³
Finely put on.°   *applied*
ROSALINE   Well then, I am the shooter.
110   BOYET   And who is your deer?°   *prey; dear*
ROSALINE   If we choose by the horns, yourself come not near.⁴
Finely put on indeed!
MARIA   You still wrangle with her, Boyet, and she strikes at the
brow.⁵
BOYET   But she herself is hit lower⁶—have I hit her° now?   *found her out*
115   ROSALINE   Shall I come upon thee with an old saying that was a
man when King Pépin of France was a little boy,⁷ as touching
the hit it?⁸
BOYET   So I may answer thee with one as old that was a woman
when Queen Guinevere of Britain⁹ was a little wench, as
120   touching the hit it.
ROSALINE [*sings*]
            Thou canst not hit it, hit it, hit it,
                Thou canst not hit it, my good man.
BOYET [*sings*]
            An I cannot, cannot, cannot,
                An I cannot, another can.   *Exit* [ROSALINE]
125   COSTARD   By my troth, most pleasant! How both did fit it!°   *sing well; (bawdy)*
MARIA   A mark° marvellous well shot, for they both did hit it.   *target*

---

9. Weathervane, often in the form of a heraldic banner;
vanity.
1. Having read; having climbed (taking "style" in line
92 as "stile," "fence").
2. Pretentious person—from the nickname of an
eccentric Italian of Shakespeare's time who claimed to
be a monarch of the world.
3. If you do not soon cuckold your husband; possibly, if
penises fail or lead to a miscarriage. From here through
line 135, there are almost continuous sexual references.

4. Probably: If you want to be safe, don't come close,
because you have cuckold's horns.
5. Aims well; taunts you about your cuckold's horns.
6. In the heart; in the genitals.
7. Was already old when Charlemagne's father (d. 768)
was a little boy.
8. *the hit it:* bawdy popular round and the dance done
to it.
9. Notoriously unfaithful wife of the legendary King
Arthur.

BOYET   A mark—O mark but that mark! A mark, says my lady.
    Let the mark have a prick° in't to mete° at, if it may be.   *bull's-eye; penis / aim*
MARIA   Wide o' the bow hand[1]—i'faith, your hand is out.°   *out of practice*
COSTARD   Indeed, a must shoot nearer, or he'll ne'er hit the
130   clout.°   *bull's-eye; (bawdy)*
BOYET   An if my hand be out, then belike your hand is in.[2]
COSTARD   Then will she get the upshoot[3] by cleaving the pin.°   *center*
MARIA   Come, come, you talk greasily,° your lips grow foul.   *indecently*
COSTARD   She's too hard for you at pricks,° sir. Challenge her to   *archery; sex*
    bowl.
135 BOYET   I fear too much rubbing.[4] Goodnight, my good owl.[5]
           [*Exeunt* BOYET, MARIA, *and* CATHERINE]
COSTARD   By my soul, a swain, a most simple clown.
    Lord, Lord, how the ladies and I have put him down!
    O' my troth, most sweet jests, most incony° vulgar wit,   *fine-quality*
    When it comes so smoothly off, so obscenely,[6] as it were, so fit!
140   Armado o'th' t'other side°—O, a most dainty° man!—   *by contrast / elegant*
    To see him walk before a lady and to bear her fan!
    To see him kiss his hand, and how most sweetly° a will swear,   *stylishly*
    And his page o' t'other side, that handful of wit—
    Ah heavens, it is a most pathetical nit!°   *affecting little fellow*
        Shout° *within*   *Loud voice; shooting*
145 Sola, sola!°   *Exit*   *hunting cry*

4.2

Enter DULL, HOLOFERNES *the pedant,*[1] *and* NATHANIEL
[*the curate*]

NATHANIEL   Very reverend° sport, truly, and done in the testi-   *respectable*
    mony° of a good conscience.   *with the warrant*
HOLOFERNES   The deer was, as you know—*sanguis*[2]—in blood,°   *robust*
    ripe as the pomewater° who now hangeth like a jewel in the   *kind of apple*
5   ear of *caelo*, the sky, the welkin, the heaven, and anon° falleth   *soon after*
    like a crab° on the face of *terra*, the soil, the land, the earth.   *crab apple*
NATHANIEL   Truly, Master Holofernes, the epithets are sweetly
    varied, like a scholar at the least. But, sir, I assure ye it was a
    buck of the first head.[3]
10 HOLOFERNES   Sir[4] Nathaniel, *haud credo*.°   *I hardly think so*
DULL   'Twas not a 'auld grey doe', 'twas a pricket.[5]
HOLOFERNES   Most barbarous intimation!° Yet a kind of insinu-   *intrusion*
    ation, as it were *in via*, in way, of explication, *facere*,° as it were,   *to make*
    replication,° or rather *ostentare*, to show, as it were, his inclina-   *explanation*
15   tion after his undressed, unpolished, uneducated, unpruned,
    untrained, or rather unlettered, or ratherest unconfirmed,°   *inexperienced*
    fashion, to insert again° my '*haud credo*' for a deer.   *interpret*

---

1. Too far to the left side (a cry in archery).
2. If I'm out of practice (at archery, at sex), you're not.
3. Winning shot; ejaculation.
4. In the game of bowls, touching obstacles; sexual friction.
5. "Owl," a bird of night, is suggested by "Goodnight"; to "take owl" is to take offense; rhyming with "bowl," "owl" suggests "ole" (hole) in the sexual sense.
6. Inadvertently accurate; perhaps a blunder for "seemly."
4.2 Location: The King's park.
1. Holofernes—a character based on a warrior whose decapitation by the heroine of the apocryphal Book of Judith saves Jerusalem—was a familiar tyrant in medieval religious plays; also a doctor of theology and

tutor to Gargantua in Rabelais's *Gargantua and Pantagruel*. Like the braggart soldier, the pedant or schoolmaster was a stock character in commedia dell'arte (see Introduction); his prominence is due to the humanist-inspired, early Tudor educational reforms that presumably shaped Shakespeare's own formal education.
2. The Latin in this scene, some of it inaccurate, is translated only when the characters themselves fail to do so. It is often unclear whether an error is the character's or the printer's.
3. With his first head of antlers; in his fifth year.
4. Used generally of graduates, including priests (like "Reverend").
5. Buck in its second year, with a sexual hint.

DULL   I said the deer was not a 'auld grey doe', 'twas a pricket.
HOLOFERNES   Twice-sod simplicity, *bis coctus!*[6]
20   O thou monster ignorance, how deformed dost thou look!
NATHANIEL   Sir, he hath never fed of the dainties that are bred
   in a book.
He hath not eat paper, as it were, he hath not drunk ink. His
   intellect is not replenished, he is only an animal, only sensible°   *capable of feeling*
   in the duller parts,
And such barren plants are set before us that we thankful
25   should be,
Which we of taste and feeling are, for those parts that do fruc-
   tify° in us more than he.   *bear fruit*
For as it would ill become me to be vain, indiscreet, or a fool,
So were there a patch set on learning[7] to see *him* in a school.
But *omne bene*° say I, being of an old father's° mind: *all is well / sage's*
30   'Many can brook the weather that love not the wind.'[8]
DULL   You two are bookmen. Can you tell me by your wit
   What was a month old at Cain's birth that's not five weeks old
   as yet?
HOLOFERNES   *Dictynna*, Goodman° Dull, *Dictynna*, Goodman   *Yeoman*
   Dull.
35   DULL   What is '*Dictima*'?
NATHANIEL   A title to° Phoebe, to *luna*, to the moon.   *name for*
HOLOFERNES   The moon was a month old when Adam was no
   more,
And raught° not to five weeks when he came to five score.   *reached*
   Th'allusion holds in the exchange.[9]
40   DULL   'Tis true, indeed, the collusion° holds in the exchange.   *(for "allusion")*
HOLOFERNES   God comfort° thy capacity, I say th'allusion holds   *pity*
   in the exchange.
DULL   And I say the pollution[1] holds in the exchange, for the
   moon is never but a month old—and I say beside that 'twas a
45   pricket that the Princess killed.
HOLOFERNES   Sir Nathaniel, will you hear an extemporal epi-
   taph on the death of the deer? And to humour the ignorant call
   I the deer the Princess killed a pricket.
NATHANIEL   *Perge,*° good Master Holofernes, *perge,* so it shall   *Proceed*
50   please you to abrogate scurrility.[2]
HOLOFERNES   I will something affect the letter,[3] for it argues°   *shows*
   facility.
The preyful° Princess pierced and pricked a pretty pleasing   *desirous of prey*
   pricket.
Some say a sore,[4] but not a sore till now made sore with
   shooting.
The dogs did yell; put 'l' to 'sore', then 'sorel'° jumps from   *buck in its third year*
55   thicket—
Or° pricket sore, or else sorel. The people fall a-hooting.   *Either*

---

6. *Twice* . . . coctus: Twice-boiled folly, twice-cooked; "*coctus*" also continues the sexual innuendo of "pricket" (line 18) with the suggestion of "cock."
7. It would mean that a fool ("patch") had been put to his studies; there would be a black mark on learning.
8. Many can endure the weather while disliking some of its features (?); one must live with what one cannot change (proverbial).
9. The riddle works as well with Adam as with Cain.
1. Dull's blunder for "allusion" again, but in each case

a commentary on his interlocutors. "Collusion" can refer to a verbal trick designed to promote collusion in the sense of conspiracy; linguistic pollution occurs when one favors difficult foreign words over straight-forward English.
2. *Perge* . . . *scurrility:* proceed . . . avoid indecency. Nathaniel is probably worrying about "pricket"—justifiably, given line 53, below. "*Perge*" may suggest "purging."
3. I will to some extent aspire to alliteration.
4. Deer in its fourth year.

If sore be sore, then 'l'° to 'sore' makes fifty sores—O sore 'l'!   *Roman numeral for 50*
Of one sore I an hundred make by adding but one more 'l'.°   *50 more; moral*

NATHANIEL   A rare talent!°   *talon; ability*

60   DULL   If a talent be a claw, look how he claws° him with a talent.   *scratches; flatters*

HOLOFERNES   This is a gift that I have, simple, simple—a foolish
extravagant° spirit, full of forms, figures, shapes, objects, ideas,   *wandering*
apprehensions, motions,° revolutions.° These are begot in the   *impulses / reflections*
ventricle° of memory, nourished in the womb of *pia mater*,⁵ and   *part of the brain*
65   delivered upon the mellowing of occasion.° But the gift is good   *when the time is ripe*
in those in whom it is acute, and I am thankful for it.

NATHANIEL   Sir, I praise the Lord for you, and so may my parishioners; for their sons are well tutored by you, and their daughters profit very greatly under you.⁶ You are a good member of
70   the commonwealth.

HOLOFERNES   *Mehercle*,° if their sons be ingenious they shall   *By Hercules*
want° no instruction; if their daughters be capable, I will put it   *lack*
to them. But *Vir sapit qui pauca loquitur*;⁷ a soul feminine
saluteth us.

Enter JAQUENETTA, *and* [COSTARD] *the clown*

75   JAQUENETTA   God give you good-morrow, Master Parson.

HOLOFERNES   Master Parson, *quasi*° 'pierce one'?⁸ And if one   *as if*
should be pierced, which is the one?

COSTARD   Marry, Master Schoolmaster, he that is likeliest to° a   *most like*
hogshead.⁹

80   HOLOFERNES   'Of piercing a hogshead'°—a good lustre of con-   *getting drunk?*
ceit° in a turf of earth, fire enough for a flint, pearl enough for   *spark of imagination*
a swine¹—'tis pretty, it is well.

JAQUENETTA   Good Master Parson, be so good as read me this
letter. It was given me by Costard, and sent me from Don Arm-
85   ado. I beseech you read it.

[*She gives the letter to* NATHANIEL, *who reads it*]

HOLOFERNES [*to himself*]   '*Facile precor gelida quando pecas
omnia sub umbra ruminat*',² and so forth. Ah, good old Mantuan! I may speak of thee as the traveller doth of Venice:
         Venezia, Venezia,
90   *Chi non ti vede, chi non ti prezia.*³
Old Mantuan, old Mantuan— who understandeth thee not,
loves thee not. [*He sings*] Ut, re, sol, la, mi, fa.⁴ [*To* NATHANIEL]
Under pardon, sir, what are the contents? Or rather, as
Horace° says in his—what, my soul—verses?   *ancient Roman poet*
95   NATHANIEL   Ay, sir, and very learned.

HOLOFERNES   Let me hear a staff,° a stanza, a verse. *Lege,*   *stanza*
domine.°   *Read, sir*

---

5. Membrane surrounding the brain.
6. In conjunction with "member" (line 69), "capable" (line 72), and "put it to them" (lines 72–73), probably bawdy.
7. "That man is wise that speaketh few things or words" (Lily's Latin grammar, translating a common proverb).
8. Pronounced like "parson" or "person"; bawdy.
9. Large cask used for beer or wine; fool.
1. To "cast pearls before swine," a biblical phrase, was already proverbial.
2. "Easily, I pray, since you are getting everything wrong under the cool shade, it ruminates." A nonsensical mis-

quotation of the first line of a Latin poem by the Italian poet (1448–1516) Mantuan, a poem well known even to schoolboys in Shakespeare's time. The correct Latin means: "Faustus, I pray, since the whole herd are chewing their cud in the cool shade." The errors may be the printer's rather than Holofernes' or Shakespeare's.
3. Italian proverb, translated by John Florio as "Venice, who seeth thee not, praiseth thee not" (*First Fruits*, 1578).
4. Notes of the scale ("ut" is the modern "do"). If Holofernes sings them as a scale, he gets them in the wrong order; but they may represent a tune.

NATHANIEL [*reads*] 'If love make me forsworn, how shall I swear
 to love?[5]
  Ah, never faith could hold, if not to beauty vowed.
100 Though to myself forsworn, to thee I'll faithful prove.
  Those thoughts to me were oaks,[6] to thee like osiers° bowed. *willows*
 Study his bias leaves,° and makes his book thine eyes, *goes off course*
  Where all those pleasures live that art would comprehend.
 If knowledge be the mark,° to know thee shall suffice. *aim*
105 Well learnèd is that tongue that well can thee commend;
 All ignorant that soul that sees thee without wonder;
  Which is to me some praise that I thy parts° admire. *qualities*
 Thy eye Jove's lightning bears, thy voice his dreadful thunder,
  Which, not to anger bent, is music and sweet fire.
110 Celestial as thou art, O pardon, love, this wrong,
  That singeth heaven's praise with such an earthly tongue.'

HOLOFERNES You find not the apostrophus,° and so miss the *elision mark*
accent. Let me supervise° the canzonet.° Here are only num- *look over / little poem*
bers ratified,° but for the elegancy, facility, and golden cadence *correct meters*
115 of poesy—*caret*.° Ovidius Naso[7] was the man. And why indeed *it is lacking*
'Naso' but for smelling out the odoriferous flowers of fancy, the
jerks of invention?[8] *Imitari*° is nothing. So doth the hound his *To imitate*
master, the ape his keeper, the tired° horse his rider. But *domi-* *attired*
cella—virgin—was this directed to you?

120 JAQUENETTA Ay, sir.[9]

HOLOFERNES I will overglance the superscript.° 'To the snow- *address*
white hand of the most beauteous Lady Rosaline.' I will look
again on the intellect° of the letter for the nomination of the *meaning; contents*
party writing to the person written unto. 'Your ladyship's in all
125 desired employment, Biron.' Sir Nathaniel, this Biron is one of
the votaries with the King, and here he hath framed a letter to
a sequent° of the stranger° Queen's, which, accidentally or by *follower / foreign*
the way of progression,° hath miscarried. [*To* JAQUENETTA] Trip *in transit*
and go,[1] my sweet, deliver this paper into the royal hand of the
130 King. It may concern much. Stay not thy compliment, I forgive
thy duty.[2] Adieu.

JAQUENETTA Good Costard, go with me.—Sir, God save your
life.

COSTARD Have with thee,° my girl. *Exit* [*with* JAQUENETTA] *I'll come with you*

135 NATHANIEL Sir, you have done this in the fear of God very religiously, and, as a certain father° saith— *church father*

HOLOFERNES Sir, tell not me of the father; I do fear colourable
colours.[3] But to return to the verses—did they please you, Sir
Nathaniel?

140 NATHANIEL Marvellous well for the pen.° *penmanship*

---

5. The beginning of a sonnet (lines 98–111), with six
stresses per line. Like the poems of Longueville
(4.3.55–68) and Dumaine (4.3.97–116), it was
reprinted in *The Passionate Pilgrime* (1599), a collection attributed to Shakespeare on the title page but
actually containing poetry by various writers.
6. Those resolutions that seemed to me to be as strong
as oaks.
7. The full name of the ancient Roman poet Ovid was
Publius Ovidius Naso; *nasus* is Latin for "nose."
8. The strokes of imagination.
9. Q reads: "sir from one mounsier *Berowne*, one of the

strange Queenes Lordes." Jaquenetta has just said
(lines 84–85) that Armado wrote and Costard gave her
the letter, and she can't know that Biron, who is not a
"strange" (foreign) courtier, actually composed it.
Probably the errors are Shakespeare's.
1. A common expression, the title of a popular song
and dance.
2. Do not delay in order to take leave politely. I excuse
you from making a curtsy.
3. I do mistrust plausible—but specious—arguments
(a rejection of popishness?).

HOLOFERNES   I do dine today at the father's of a certain pupil of
mine where, if before repast it shall please you to gratify° the   *grace; please*
table with a grace, I will on my privilege I have with the parents
of the foresaid child or pupil undertake your *ben venuto*,[4]
145   where I will prove those verses to be very unlearned, neither
savouring of poetry, wit, nor invention. I beseech your society.
NATHANIEL   And thank you too, for society, saith the text,[5] is the
happiness of life.
HOLOFERNES   And certes° the text most infallibly concludes it.   *certainly*
150   [*To* DULL] Sir, I do invite you too. You shall not say me nay.
Pauca verba.° Away, the gentles are at their game,[6] and we will   *Few words*
to our recreation.   *Exeunt*

4.3

Enter BIRON *with a paper in his hand, alone*
BIRON   The King, he is hunting the deer. I am coursing° myself.   *pursuing*
They have pitched a toil,° I am toiling in a pitch[1]—pitch that   *set a snare*
defiles. Defile—a foul word. Well, set thee down,° sorrow; for   *stay with me*
so they say the fool said, and so say I, and I the fool. Well
5   proved, wit! By the Lord, this love is as mad as Ajax, it kills
sheep,[2] it kills me, I a sheep—well proved again o' my side. I
will not love. If I do, hang me; i'faith, I will not. O, but her
eye! By this light, but for her eye I would not love her. Yes, for
her two eyes. Well, I do nothing in the world but lie, and lie in
10   my throat.° By heaven, I do love, and it hath taught me to   *scandalously*
rhyme and to be melancholy, and here [*showing a paper*] is
part of my rhyme, and here [*touching his breast*] my melancholy. Well, she hath one o' my sonnets already. The clown
bore it, the fool sent it, and the lady hath it. Sweet clown,
15   sweeter fool, sweetest lady. By the world, I would not care a pin
if the other three were in.° Here comes one with a paper. God   *similarly involved*
give him grace to groan.°   *(out of love)*
He stands aside.[3] *The* KING *entereth* [*with a paper*]
KING   Ay me!
BIRON [*aside*]   Shot, by heaven! Proceed, sweet Cupid, thou hast
20   thumped him with thy birdbolt under the left pap.° In faith,   *your arrow in the heart*
secrets.
KING [*reads*]   'So sweet a kiss the golden sun gives not[4]
      To those fresh morning drops upon the rose
   As thy eyebeams when their fresh rays have smote
25   The night of dew° that on my cheeks down flows.   *nightly tears*
   Nor shines the silver moon one-half so bright
      Through the transparent bosom of the deep
   As doth thy face through tears of mine give light.
      Thou shin'st in every tear that I do weep.
30   No drop but as a coach doth carry thee,
      So ridest thou triumphing in my woe.
   Do but behold the tears that swell in me
      And they thy glory through my grief will show.

---

4. Undertake your welcome (Italian).
5. No convincing source has been identified.
6. The gentlefolk are at their sport (hunting).
4.3. Location: Scene continues.
1. In tar; in Rosaline's eyes(?)
2. At the Greek siege of Troy, when Agamemnon
awards Achilles' armor to Odysseus, Ajax goes mad with

rage and kills a flock of sheep, believing them to be the
Greek army.
3. At line 74, Biron says, "here sit I in the sky." At some
point before then—perhaps here—he mounts to a
higher level.
4. The beginning of a sonnet that actually extends to
sixteen lines (lines 22–37).

But do not love thyself; then thou wilt keep
35 My tears for glasses,° and still make me weep.   *mirrors*
O Queen of queens, how far dost thou excel,
No thought can think nor tongue of mortal tell.'
How shall she know my griefs? I'll drop the paper.
Sweet leaves, shade° folly. Who is he comes here?   *hide*

Enter LONGUEVILLE [*with papers*]. *The* KING *steps aside*

40 What, Longueville, and reading—listen, ear!
BIRON [*aside*]   Now in thy° likeness one more fool appear!   *(the King's)*
LONGUEVILLE   Ay me! I am forsworn.
BIRON [*aside*]   Why, he comes in like a perjure,° wearing papers.⁵   *perjurer*
KING [*aside*]   In love, I hope! Sweet fellowship in shame.
45 BIRON [*aside*]   One drunkard loves another of the name.
LONGUEVILLE   Am I the first that have been perjured so?
BIRON [*aside*]   I could put thee in comfort, not by two that I know.
Thou makest the triumviry,⁶ the corner-cap° of society,   *three-cornered cap*
The shape of love's Tyburn,⁷ that hangs up simplicity.°   *folly*
50 LONGUEVILLE   I fear these stubborn° lines lack power to move.   *rough*
O sweet Maria, empress of my love,
These numbers° will I tear, and write in prose.   *verses*
BIRON [*aside*]   O, rhymes are guards° on wanton Cupid's hose,   *decorative bands*
Disfigure not his slop.°   *breeches*
LONGUEVILLE   This same shall go.⁸

He reads the sonnet

55 'Did not the heavenly rhetoric of thine eye,
'Gainst whom the world cannot hold argument,
Persuade my heart to this false perjury?
Vows for thee broke deserve not punishment.
A woman I forswore, but I will prove,
60 Thou being a goddess, I forswore not thee.
My vow was earthly, thou a heavenly love.
Thy grace° being gained cures all disgrace in me.   *favor*
Vows are but breath, and breath a vapour is.
Then thou, fair sun, which on my earth dost shine,
65 Exhal'st° this vapour-vow; in thee it is.   *Draw up*
If broken then, it is no fault of mine.
If by me broke, what fool is not so wise
To lose an oath to win a paradise?'
BIRON [*aside*]   This is the liver vein,⁹ which makes flesh a deity,
70 A green goose° a goddess, pure, pure idolatry.   *silly girl; whore*
God amend us, God amend: we are much out o'th' way.°   *badly astray*

Enter DUMAINE [*with a paper*]

LONGUEVILLE [*aside*]   By whom shall I send this? Company? Stay.
[*He steps aside*]
BIRON [*aside*]   All hid, all hid—an old infant play.¹
Like a demigod here sit I in the sky,
75 And wretched fools' secrets heedfully o'er-eye.
More sacks to the mill!° O heavens, I have my wish.   *More to come!*
Dumaine transformed—four woodcocks° in a dish!   *fools*
DUMAINE   O most divine Kate!

5. Wearing a poem (lines 55–68). Convicted perjurers were exposed by having to wear papers that explained their guilt.
6. You complete the triumvirate (group of three rulers).
7. The common place of execution in London, here metaphorically for gallows, which were triangular.
8. Either he has hesitated before tearing the paper, or

he pieces it together, as if in response to Biron's aside.
9. Style of the lover (the liver was thought of as the seat of love).
1. Hide-and-seek ("play" means "game"); perhaps also a medieval religious play in which God views the actions from above, like Biron (line 74).

BIRON [*aside*]   O most profane coxcomb!°   *fool*

80   DUMAINE   By heaven, the wonder in a mortal eye!

BIRON [*aside*]   By earth, she is not, corporal;² there you lie.

DUMAINE   Her amber hairs for foul hath amber quoted.³

BIRON [*aside*]   An amber-coloured raven was well noted.⁴

DUMAINE   As upright as the cedar.

BIRON [*aside*]   Stoop,⁵ I say.

Her shoulder is with child.°   *bulging; bowed down*

85   DUMAINE   As fair as day.

BIRON [*aside*]   Ay, as some days; but then no sun must shine.

DUMAINE   O that I had my wish!

LONGUEVILLE [*aside*]   And I had mine!

KING [*aside*]   And I mine too, good Lord!

90   BIRON [*aside*]   Amen, so I had mine. Is not that a good word?⁶

DUMAINE   I would forget her, but a fever she

Reigns in my blood and will remembered be.

BIRON [*aside*]   A fever in your blood—why then, incision°   *bloodletting*

Would let her out in saucers⁷—sweet misprision.°   *misinterpretation*

95   DUMAINE   Once more I'll read the ode that I have writ.

BIRON [*aside*]   Once more I'll mark how love can vary° wit.   *inspire; impair*

DUMAINE *reads his sonnet*

DUMAINE   'On a day—alack the day—

Love, whose month is ever May,

Spied a blossom passing° fair   *surpassingly*

100   Playing in the wanton° air.   *playful*

Through the velvet leaves the wind

All unseen can° passage find,   *did*

That° the lover, sick to death,   *So that*

Wished himself the heavens' breath.

105   "Air", quoth he, "thy cheeks may blow;

Air, would I might triumph so.

But, alack, my hand is sworn

Ne'er to pluck thee from thy thorn—

Vow, alack, for youth unmeet,°   *inappropriate*

110   Youth so apt to pluck a sweet.

Do not call it sin in me

That I am forsworn for thee,

Thou for whom great Jove would swear

Juno but an Ethiop⁸ were,

115   And deny himself for° Jove,   *to be*

Turning mortal for thy love.' "

This will I send, and something else more plain,

That shall express my true love's fasting pain.

O, would the King, Biron, and Longueville

120   Were lovers too! Ill to example° ill   *be a precedent for*

Would from my forehead wipe a perjured note,⁹

For none offend where all alike do dote.

---

2. Officer in Cupid's army; perhaps, (she is merely) corporeal, or human. The possible application to both Dumaine and Catherine, but in different ways, is characteristic of Biron's asides here.
3. Her amber-colored hairs have caused amber itself to be regarded as foul by comparison.
4. Dumaine is an acute observer, Biron remarks ironically, in describing Catherine's black hair as amber. (Catherine is the raven, a black fowl, punningly suggested by "foul," line 82.)
5. She's stooped; come down to earth.
6. Isn't that a kind wish; isn't "Amen" a "good word"?
7. Into basins used to catch the blood; by the basinful.
8. Black African (used here in racist fashion to signify ugliness).
9. Inscription (and see Biron's description of Longueville, line 43).

LONGUEVILLE [*coming forward*]   Dumaine, thy love is far from
    charity,°   *Christian love*
  That in love's grief desir'st society.°   *company*

125   You may look pale, but I should blush, I know,
  To be o'erheard and taken napping so.
  KING [*coming forward*]   Come, sir, you blush. As his, your case
    is such.
  You chide at him, offending twice as much.
  You do not love Maria? Longueville
130   Did never sonnet for her sake compile,
  Nor never lay his wreathèd arms athwart[1]
  His loving bosom to keep down his heart?
  I have been closely° shrouded in this bush,   *secretly*
  And marked you both, and for you both did blush.
135   I heard your guilty rhymes, observed your fashion,
  Saw sighs reek° from you, noted well your passion.   *rise*
  'Ay me!' says one, 'O Jove!' the other cries.
  One, her hairs were gold; crystal the other's eyes.
  [*To* LONGUEVILLE] You would for paradise break faith and troth,
140   [*To* DUMAINE] And Jove for your love would infringe an oath.
  What will Biron say when that he shall hear
  Faith so infringèd, which such zeal did swear?
  How will he scorn, how will he spend his wit!
  How will he triumph, leap, and laugh at it!
145   For all the wealth that ever I did see
  I would not have him know so much by° me.   *about*
  BIRON [*coming forward*]   Now step I forth to whip hypocrisy.
  Ah, good my liege, I pray thee pardon me.
  Good heart, what grace hast thou thus to reprove
150   These worms for loving, that art most in love?
  Your eyes do make no coaches.° In your tears   *(see lines 31–32)*
  There is no certain princess that appears.
  You'll not be perjured, 'tis a hateful thing;
  Tush, none but minstrels like of sonneting!
155   But are you not ashamed, nay, are you not,
  All three of you, to be thus much o'ershot?°   *wide of the mark*
  [*To* LONGUEVILLE] You found his° mote, the King your mote   *(Dumaine's)*
    did see,
  But I a beam[2] do find in each of three.
  O, what a scene of fool'ry have I seen,
160   Of sighs, of groans, of sorrow, and of teen!°   *grief*
  O me, with what strict patience have I sat,
  To see a king transformèd to a gnat!
  To see great Hercules whipping a gig,°   *spinning a top*
  And profound Solomon to tune° a jig,   *play*
165   And Nestor[3] play at pushpin° with the boys,   *child's game*
  And critic Timon[4] laugh at idle toys!°   *foolish fancies*
  Where lies thy grief, O tell me, good Dumaine?
  And, gentle Longueville, where lies thy pain?
  And where my liege's? All about the breast.

---

1. Folded arms across. (Folded arms were a sign of love
melancholy.)
2. Larger defect: "And why beholdest thou the mote
that is in thy brother's eye, but considerest [or "per-
ceivest"] not the beam that is in thine own eye?"

(Matthew 7:3–5; Luke 6:41–42).
3. Homeric hero, a type figure of wise old age; later
portrayed in Shakespeare's *Troilus and Cressida*.
4. Cynical Greek misanthrope; later, the central character of Shakespeare's *Timon of Athens*.

A caudle,° ho!   *warm, healing drink*

170 KING   Too bitter is thy jest.
Are we betrayed thus to thy over-view?

BIRON   Not you to me, but I betrayed by you.
I that am honest, I that hold it sin
To break the vow I am engagèd in.

175 I am betrayed by keeping company
With men like you, men of inconstancy.
When shall you see me write a thing in rhyme,
Or groan for Joan, or spend a minute's time
In pruning me?° When shall you hear that I   *preening myself*

180 Will praise a hand, a foot, a face, an eye,
A gait, a state,° a brow, a breast, a waist,   *an attitude; bearing*
A leg, a limb?

KING   Soft, whither away so fast?
A true° man or a thief, that gallops so?   *an honest*

BIRON   I post° from love; good lover, let me go.   *hasten*

    Enter JAQUENETTA [*with a letter,*] *and* [COSTARD *the*]
    clown

JAQUENETTA   God bless the King!

185 KING   What present° hast thou there?   *writing; gift*

COSTARD   Some certain treason.

KING   What makes treason° here?   *is treason doing*

COSTARD   Nay, it makes nothing, sir.

KING   If it mar nothing neither,
The treason and you go in peace away together!

JAQUENETTA   I beseech your grace, let this letter be read.

190 Our parson misdoubts° it; 'twas treason, he said.   *suspects*

KING   Biron, read it over.

    [BIRON *takes and*] *reads the letter*

    [*To* JAQUENETTA] Where hadst thou it?

JAQUENETTA   Of Costard.

KING [*to* COSTARD]   Where hadst thou it?

195 COSTARD   Of Dun Adramadio,[5] Dun Adramadio.

    [BIRON *tears the letter*]

KING [*to* BIRON]   How now, what is in you? Why dost thou tear it?

BIRON   A toy, my liege, a toy. Your grace needs not fear it.

LONGUEVILLE   It did move him to passion, and therefore let's hear it.

DUMAINE [*taking up a piece of the letter*]   It is Biron's writing,
    and here is his name.

BIRON [*to* COSTARD]   Ah, you whoreson loggerhead,° you were   *foolish blockhead*
200   born to do me shame!
Guilty, my lord, guilty! I confess, I confess.

KING   What?

BIRON   That you three fools lacked me fool to make up the
    mess.°   *group of four at table*
He, he, and you—e'en you, my liege—and I

205 Are pickpurses° in love, and we deserve to die.   *cheaters*
O, dismiss this audience, and I shall tell you more.

DUMAINE   Now the number is even.

BIRON   True, true; we are four.
Will these turtles° be gone?   *turtledoves; lovers*

KING   Hence, sirs; away.

---

5. *Dun:* error for Don meaning "gray-brown," referring to skin color and recalling "tawny Spain" (1.1.171). *Adramadio:* error for Adriano that encompasses "drama," "mad," "amado" (loved).

COSTARD Walk aside the true folk, and let the traitors stay.

                [Exeunt COSTARD *and* JAQUENETTA]

210 BIRON Sweet lords, sweet lovers!—O, let us embrace.
     As true we are as flesh and blood can be.
     The sea will ebb and flow, heaven show his face.
     Young blood doth not obey an old decree.
     We cannot cross° the cause why we were born,   *oppose*
215   Therefore of all hands° must we be forsworn.   *in any case*
   KING What, did these rent° lines show some love of thine?   *torn*
   BIRON 'Did they', quoth you? Who sees the heavenly Rosaline
     That, like a rude° and savage man of Ind°   *an ignorant / India*
     At the first op'ning of the gorgeous east,
220   Bows not his vassal head and, strucken blind,
     Kisses the base ground with obedient breast?
     What peremptory° eagle-sighted eye[6]   *determined*
     Dares look upon the heaven of her brow
     That is not blinded by her majesty?
225 KING What zeal, what fury hath inspired thee now?
     My love, her mistress, is a gracious moon,
     She an attending star, scarce seen a light.°   *hardly visible*
   BIRON My eyes are then no eyes, nor I Biron.
     O, but for my love, day would turn to night.
230   Of all complexions the culled sovereignty°   *those chosen as best*
     Do meet as at a fair in her fair cheek,
     Where several worthies make one dignity,[7]
     Where nothing wants° that want° itself doth seek.   *lacks / desire*
     Lend me the flourish of all gentle tongues—
235   Fie, painted rhetoric! O, she needs it not.
     To things of sale a seller's praise belongs.
     She passes praise—then praise too short doth blot.[8]
     A withered hermit fivescore winters worn
     Might shake off fifty, looking in her eye.
240   Beauty doth varnish age as if new-born,
     And gives the crutch the cradle's infancy.
     O, 'tis the sun that maketh all things shine.
   KING By heaven, thy love is black as ebony.
   BIRON Is ebony like her? O word divine!
245   A wife of such wood were felicity.
     O, who can give an oath? Where is a book,°   *a Bible*
     That I may swear beauty doth beauty lack
     If that she learn not of her eye to look?[9]
     No face is fair that is not full so° black.   *just as*
250 KING O paradox! Black is the badge of hell,
     The hue of dungeons and the style[1] of night,
     And beauty's crest becomes the heavens well.[2]
   BIRON Devils soonest tempt, resembling spirits of light.[3]
     O, if in black my lady's brows be decked,
255   It mourns that painting and usurping hair°   *makeup and false hair*

---

6. The eagle, king of birds, was thought to be the only one able to look directly at the sun.
7. Various kinds of excellence together produce a single preeminent beauty.
8. Hence praise inevitably falls short and mars her reputation.
9. If beauty doesn't learn from Rosaline's eye how she (beauty) could look.
1. Title. Q, F: Schoole. The phrase "school of night" has been supposed to refer to a secret society of Shakespeare's time; alternatively, it may mean that night learns to be black in black's school.
2. (And yet, you say,) the badge of your dark beauty is heavenly (said incredulously); it is the sun, not your dark beauty, that is heavenly.
3. Fair beauties are not to be trusted, "for Satan himself is transformed into an angel of light" (2 Corinthians 11:14).

Should ravish doters with a false aspect,
   And therefore is she born to make black fair.
Her favour° turns the fashion of the days,   *appearance*
   For native blood° is counted painting now,   *natural red coloring*
60 And therefore red that would avoid dispraise
   Paints itself black to imitate her brow.
DUMAINE To look like her are chimney-sweepers black.
LONGUEVILLE And since her time are colliers counted bright.
KING And Ethiops of their sweet complexion crack.°   *boast*
65 DUMAINE Dark needs no candles now, for dark is light.
BIRON Your mistresses dare never come in rain,
   For fear their colours should be washed away.
KING 'Twere good yours did; for, sir, to tell you plain,
   I'll find a fairer face not washed today.
70 BIRON I'll prove her fair, or talk till doomsday here.
KING No devil will fright thee then° so much as she.   *(at doomsday)*
DUMAINE I never knew man hold vile stuff so dear.
LONGUEVILLE [*showing his foot*] Look, here's thy love—my foot
   and her face see.[4]
BIRON O, if the streets were pavèd with thine eyes
75   Her feet were much too dainty for such tread.
DUMAINE O vile! Then as she goes, what upward lies°   *(bawdy)*
   The street should see as she walked overhead.
KING But what of this? Are we not all in love?
BIRON Nothing so sure, and thereby all forsworn.
80 KING Then leave this chat and, good Biron, now prove
   Our loving lawful and our faith not torn.
DUMAINE Ay, marry there, some flattery° for this evil.   *excuse*
LONGUEVILLE O, some authority how to proceed,
   Some tricks, some quillets° how to cheat the devil.   *verbal tricks*
DUMAINE Some salve for perjury.°   *oath breaking; purging*
85 BIRON   O, 'tis more than need.
Have at you,° then, affection's° men-at-arms.   *Here goes / love's*
Consider what you first did swear unto:
To fast, to study, and to see no woman—
Flat treason 'gainst the kingly state of youth.
90 Say, can you fast? Your stomachs are too young,
And abstinence engenders maladies.[5]
291.1   *And where that° you have vowed to study, lords,*   *And whereas*
    In that[6] each of you have forsworn his book,
    Can you still dream, and pore, and thereon look?
    For when would you, my lord, or you, or you,
291.5   *Have found the ground of study's excellence*
    Without the beauty of a woman's face?
    From women's eyes this doctrine I derive.
    They are the ground, the books, the academes,
    From whence doth spring the true Promethean fire.
291.10 *Why, universal plodding poisons up*
    The nimble° spirits in the arteries,   *life-giving*
    As motion and long-during° action tires   *long-lasting*

---

4. You may see her face in my (black) shoes.
5. The following twenty-three indented lines (291.1–291.23) represent an unrevised version of parts of Biron's long speech, 4.3.285–91, 292–339. The first six lines form the basis of 292–97; the next three are revised at 4.3.324–28; the next four at 4.3.298–300; the last nine are less directly related to the revised version.
6. Inasmuch as; in that vow.

       The sinewy vigour of the traveller.
       Now, for not looking on a woman's face
291.15   *You have in that forsworn the use of eyes,*
       And study, too, thecause of your vow.
       For where is any author in the world
       Teaches such beauty as a woman's eye?
       Learning is but an adjunct to ourself,
291.20   *And where we are, our learning likewise is.*
       Then when ourselves we see in ladies' eyes
       With ourselves.
       Do we not likewise see our learning there?
      O, we have made a vow to study, lords,
      And in that vow we have forsworn our books;[7]
      For when would you, my liege, or you, or you
295   In leaden contemplation have found out
      Such fiery numbers° as the prompting eyes   *passionate verses*
      Of beauty's tutors have enriched you with?
      Other slow arts° entirely keep° the brain,   *disciplines / inhabit*
      And therefore, finding barren practisers,
300   Scarce show a harvest of their heavy toil.
      But love, first learnèd in a lady's eyes,
      Lives not alone immurèd° in the brain,   *only shut up*
      But with the motion of all elements[8]
      Courses as swift as thought in every power,°   *faculty*
305   And gives to every power a double power
      Above° their functions and their offices.°   *Beyond / normal duties*
      It adds a precious seeing to the eye—
      A lover's eyes will gaze an eagle blind.[9]
      A lover's ear will hear the lowest sound
310   When the suspicious head of theft is stopped.[1]
      Love's feeling is more soft and sensible°   *sensitive*
      Than are the tender horns of cockled snails.°   *snails with shells*
      Love's tongue proves dainty Bacchus° gross in taste.   *Greek god of wine*
      For valour, is not love a Hercules,
315   Still° climbing trees in the Hesperides?[2]   *Constantly*
      Subtle as Sphinx,[3] as sweet and musical
      As bright Apollo's° lute strung with his hair;   *Greek god of music*
      And when love speaks, the voice of all the gods
      Make heaven drowsy with the harmony.
320   Never durst poet touch a pen to write
      Until his ink were tempered with love's sighs.
      O, then his lines would ravish savage ears,
      And plant in tyrants mild humility.
      From women's eyes this doctrine I derive.
325   They sparkle still the right Promethean fire.[4]
      They are the books, the arts, the academes
      That show, contain, and nourish all the world,
      Else none° at all in aught proves excellent.   *Without them no one*
      Then fools you were these women to forswear,

---

7. Our true books, women's eyes.
8. Earth, air, fire, and water.
9. Can stare at the sun (here, the beloved woman) without injury longer than even an eagle can.
1. When even an alert thief (or someone listening for a thief) hears nothing.

2. Garden of golden apples that Hercules had to pick as his eleventh labor.
3. Monster in Greek mythology that killed travelers who failed to solve her riddle.
4. Divine fire. In Greek mythology Prometheus stole fire from heaven and gave it to humanity.

330 Or keeping what is sworn, you will prove fools.
For wisdom's sake—a word that all men love—
Or for love's sake—a word that loves[5] all men—
Or for men's sake—the authors of these women—
Or women's sake—by whom we men are men—
335 Let us once lose our oaths to find ourselves,[6]
Or else we lose ourselves to keep our oaths.
It is religion to be thus forsworn,
For charity itself fulfils the law,[7]
And who can sever love from charity?
340 KING   Saint Cupid, then, and, soldiers, to the field!
BIRON   Advance your standards,° and upon them, lords.   *(with a sexual sense)*
Pell-mell, down with them; but be first advised
In conflict that you get the sun of them.[8]
LONGUEVILLE   Now to plain dealing. Lay these glozes° by.   *verbal sophistries*
345 Shall we resolve to woo these girls of France?
KING   And win them, too! Therefore let us devise
Some entertainment for them in their tents.
BIRON   First, from the park let us conduct them thither;
Then homeward every man attach° the hand   *seize*
350 Of his fair mistress. In the afternoon
We will with some strange° pastime solace them,   *novel*
Such as the shortness of the time can shape,
For revels, dances, masques, and merry hours
Forerun° fair love, strewing her way with flowers.   *Run before*
355 KING   Away, away, no time shall be omitted
That will be time,° and may by us be fitted.°   *long enough / used well*
BIRON   *Allons, allons!*° Sowed cockle reaped no corn,[9]   *Come on*
And justice always whirls in equal measure.°   *acts impartially*
Light° wenches may prove plagues to men forsworn.   *Frivolous*
360 If so, our copper buys° no better treasure.   *[Exeunt]* *base coin deserves*

5.1

*Enter [*HOLOFERNES*] the pedant, [*NATHANIEL*] the
curate, and [Anthony]* DULL

HOLOFERNES   *Satis quid sufficit.*[1]
NATHANIEL   I praise God for you, sir. Your reasons° at dinner   *discourses*
have been sharp and sententious, pleasant without scurrility,
witty without affection,° audacious without impudency,   *affectation*
5 learned without opinion,° and strange° without heresy. I did   *arrogance / original*
converse this quondam day° with a companion of the King's   *the other day*
who is intituled, nominated, or called Don Adriano de
Armado.
HOLOFERNES   *Novi hominum tanquam te.*[2] His humour° is lofty,   *temperament*
10 his discourse peremptory,° his tongue filed,° his eye ambitious,   *overbearing / polished*
his gait majestical, and his general behaviour vain, ridiculous,

---

5. Meaning uncertain: is a friend to; values; pleases;
inspires with love; is lovable to.
6. "For whosoever will save his life shall lose it: and
whosoever will lose his life for my sake shall find it"
(Matthew 16:25).
7. "He that loveth another hath fulfilled the law"
(Romans 13:8). "Love worketh no ill to his neighbour:
therefore is love the fulfilling of the law" (Romans 13:10).
8. Get the sun in their eyes (get the advantage); also,
probably bawdy, playing on "beget the son."
9. Wheat ("corn") was never reaped where weeds

("cockle") were sown (proverbial): in other words, we
won't get something for nothing; we must make an effort.
5.1 Location: The King's park.
1. Should be *Satis est quod sufficit:* Enough is enough,
but recalling the English proverb "Enough is as good as
a feast." The Latin in this scene, some of it inaccurate,
again is translated only when the characters themselves
fail to do so. Here, too, it is often unclear whether the
error is the character's, the printer's, or Shakespeare's.
2. I know the man as well as I know you.

and thrasonical.[3] He is too picked,° too spruce, too affected,   *fastidious*
too odd, as it were, too peregrinate,° as I may call it.   *exotic*

NATHANIEL   A most singular and choice epithet.

    Draw[s] out his table-book°   *notebook*

15 HOLOFERNES   He draweth out the thread of his verbosity finer
than the staple of his argument.[4] I abhor such fanatical phan-
tasims,[5] such insociable and point-device° companions, such   *extremely precise*
rackers of orthography[6] as to speak 'dout', *sine*° 'b', when he   *without*
should say 'doubt'; 'det' when he should pronounce 'debt'—'d,
20 e, b, t', not 'd, e, t'. He clepeth° a calf 'cauf', half 'hauf',   *calls*
neighbour *vocatur*° 'nebour'—'neigh' abbreviated 'ne'. This is   *is called*
abhominable—which he would call 'abominable'. It insinu-
ateth me of *insanire*[7]—*ne intelligis, domine?*[8]—to make frantic,
lunatic.

25 NATHANIEL   *Laus deo, bone intelligo.*[9]

HOLOFERNES   *Bone? Bon, fort bon*—Priscian a little scratched[1]—
'twill serve.

    Enter [ARMADO *the*] *braggart,* [MOTE *his*] *boy* [*and* COS-
    TARD *the clown*]

NATHANIEL   *Videsne quis venit?*°   *Do you see who's coming?*

HOLOFERNES   *Video, et gaudio.*°   *I see, and rejoice*

30 ARMADO [*to* MOTE]   Chirrah.[2]

HOLOFERNES [*to* NATHANIEL]   *Quare*° 'chirrah', not 'sirrah'?   *Why*

ARMADO   Men of peace, well encountered.

HOLOFERNES   Most military sir, salutation!

MOTE [*aside to* COSTARD]   They have been at a great feast of lan-
35 guages and stolen the scraps.

COSTARD [*aside to* MOTE]   O, they have lived long on the alms-
basket[3] of words. I marvel thy master hath not eaten thee for a
word, for thou art not so long by the head as *honorificabilitu-*
dinitatibus.[4] Thou art easier swallowed than a flapdragon.[5]

40 MOTE [*aside to* COSTARD]   Peace, the peal° begins.   *jangling; babble*

ARMADO [*to* HOLOFERNES]   Monsieur, are you not lettered?°   *learned; literate*

MOTE   Yes, yes, he teaches boys the horn-book.° What is 'a, b'   *alphabet book*
spelled backward, with the horn on his head?°   *a cuckold*

HOLOFERNES   Ba, *pueritia,*° with a horn added.   *child(ishness)*

45 MOTE   Ba, most silly sheep, with a horn! You hear his learning.

HOLOFERNES   *Quis, quis,*° thou consonant?[6]   *Who*

MOTE   The last of the five vowels if you repeat them, or the
fifth° if I.   *"u"; you; ewe*

HOLOFERNES   I will repeat them: a, e, i—

50 MOTE   The sheep.[7] The other two concludes it: o, u.[8]

---

3. Boastful, bragging. From "Thraso," the braggart soldier in *Eunuchus,* by the Roman dramatist Terence.
4. He's wordy. (Unintentionally ironic, coming from
Holofernes; "staple" means "fiber," "argument" means
"subject matter.")
5. Extravagant, fantastic beings.
6. Tormentors of spelling. Holofernes speaks for those
educational theorists who urged, unsuccessfully, that
English words be spelled and pronounced like their
Latin roots.
7. Puts me in mind of madness; perhaps, drives me mad.
8. Don't you understand, master?
9. Praise God, I understand well.
1. Bone? Bon, fort bon: Well? Good, that's good
(French; ironical). *Priscian a little scratched:* imperfect
Latin (Priscian was a sixth-century Latin grammarian).
Holofernes is ridiculing Nathaniel's mistake of using

bone for *bene.*
2. Pseudo-Spanish or dialectal pronunciation of "Sirrah"; or garbled Greek for "Hail."
3. Basket in which the leftovers of a feast were collected for the poor.
4. Dative and ablative plural of a Latin word meaning
"honorableness," renowned for its length. *word:* "mote"
equals the French *mot,* which means "word."
5. A raisin floated on flaming brandy, which had to be
snapped up with the mouth and eaten in the game of
snapdragon.
6. Nonentity (because a consonant alone is soundless).
7. The Spanish for "sheep"—*oveja,* often spelled
oueia—seems to have been used as a device for memo-
rizing the vowels.
8. Proves what I say (or completes the list): oh, you.

ARMADO   Now by the salt° wave of the *Mediterraneum* a sweet   *salty; witty*
touch,° a quick venue° of wit; snip, snap, quick, and home.⁹ It   *hit / thrust*
rejoiceth my intellect—true wit.

MOTE   Offered by a child to an old man, which is 'wit-old'.¹

55   HOLOFERNES   What is the figure?° What is the figure?   *figure of speech*

MOTE   Horns.

HOLOFERNES   Thou disputes like an infant. Go whip thy gig.°   *spin your top*

MOTE   Lend me your horn to make one, and I will whip about
your infamy *circum circa*²—a gig of° a cuckold's horn.   *made of*

60   COSTARD   An° I had but one penny in the world, thou shouldst   *If*
have it to buy gingerbread. [*Giving money*] Hold, there is the
very remuneration I had of thy master, thou halfpenny° purse   *tiny*
of wit, thou pigeon-egg of discretion. O, an the heavens were
so pleased that thou wert but my bastard, what a joyful father
65   wouldst thou make me! Go to, thou hast it *ad dunghill*, at the
fingers' ends,° as they say.   *exactly; scatological*

HOLOFERNES   O, I smell false Latin—'dunghill' for *unguem*.°   *fingernail*

ARMADO   Arts-man, *preambulate*.³ We will be singled° from the   *separated*
barbarous. Do you not educate youth at the charge-house° on   *endowed school*
70   the top of the mountain?

HOLOFERNES   Or *mons*, the hill.

ARMADO   At your sweet pleasure, for the mountain.

HOLOFERNES   I do, sans° question.   *without*

ARMADO   Sir, it is the King's most sweet pleasure and affection°   *wish*
75   to congratulate° the Princess at her pavilion in the posteriors⁴   *greet*
of this day, which the rude multitude call the afternoon.

HOLOFERNES   The posterior of the day, most generous° sir, is lia-   *noble*
ble, congruent, and measurable° for the afternoon. The word   *suitable (synonyms)*
is well culled,⁵ choice, sweet, and apt, I do assure you, sir, I do
80   assure.

ARMADO   Sir, the King is a noble gentleman, and my familiar,° I   *close friend*
do assure ye, very good friend. For what is inward° between us,   *confidential*
let it pass. I do beseech thee, remember thy courtesy. I beseech
thee, apparel thy head.⁶ And, among other important and most
85   serious designs, and of great import indeed, too—but let that
pass,⁷ for I must tell thee it will please his grace, by the world,
sometime to lean upon my poor shoulder and with his royal
finger thus dally with my excrement,° with my mustachio. But,   *growth of hair; feces*
sweetheart, let that pass. By the world, I recount no fable. Some
90   certain special honours it pleaseth his greatness to impart to
Armado, a soldier, a man of travel, that hath seen the world.
But let that pass. The very all of all° is—but, sweetheart, I do   *sum of everything*
implore secrecy—that the King would have me present the
Princess—sweet chuck°—with some delightful ostentation,° or   *chick / spectacular show*
95   show, or pageant, or antic,° or firework. Now, understanding   *grotesque pageant*
that the curate and your sweet self are good at such eruptions°   *(scatological)*
and sudden breaking-out° of mirth, as it were, I have acquainted   *(scatological)*
you withal° to the end to crave your assistance.   *with it*

---

9. And to the target.
1. Mentally feeble; "wittol," a content cuckold.
2. Around and around.
3. Scholar, walk ahead, with a play on "arse."
4. End (temporal and anatomical).
5. With a play on "cul," French for backside.

6. *remember . . . head*: remember that you removed
your hat in courtesy (perhaps at line 33). I beseech you,
put it back on.
7. Suggestion of sodomy, developed in the repeated
phrase "but [butt] let that pass" (lines 85–86, 88–89,
92).

HOLOFERNES   Sir, you shall present before her the Nine Wor-
100   thies.[8] Sir Nathaniel, as concerning some entertainment of°   *way of spending*
      time, some show in the posterior of this day to be rendered by
      our assistance, the King's command, and this most gallant,
      illustrate,° and learned gentlemen before the Princess, I say   *illustrious*
      none so fit as to present the Nine Worthies.
105   NATHANIEL   Where will you find men worthy enough to present
      them?
      HOLOFERNES   Joshua, yourself;[9] myself, Judas Maccabeus; and
      this gallant gentleman, Hector. This swain, because of his great
      limb or joint, shall pass Pompey the Great;[1] the page, Hercules.
110   ARMADO   Pardon, sir, error! He is not quantity enough for that
      Worthy's thumb. He is not so big as the end of his club.
      HOLOFERNES   Shall I have audience?° He shall present Hercules   *attention*
      in minority.° His enter° and exit shall be strangling a snake,[2]   *childhood / entrance*
      and I will have an apology° for that purpose.   *explanatory speech*
115   MOTE   An excellent device! So, if any of the audience hiss, you
      may cry 'Well done, Hercules, now thou crushest the snake!'—
      that is the way to make an offence gracious, though few have
      the grace to do it.
      ARMADO   For the rest of the Worthies?
120   HOLOFERNES   I will play three myself.
      MOTE   Thrice-worthy gentleman!
      ARMADO   Shall I tell you a thing?
      HOLOFERNES   We attend.°   *listen*
      ARMADO   We will have, if this fadge° not, an antic. I beseech you,   *succeed*
125   follow.
      HOLOFERNES   Via,° goodman Dull! Thou hast spoken no word   *Come on*
      all this while.
      DULL   Nor understood none neither, sir.
      HOLOFERNES   Allons!° We will employ thee.   *Come on*
130   DULL   I'll make one° in a dance or so, or I will play on the tabor°   *join / small drum*
      to the Worthies, and let them dance the hay.°   *reel*
      HOLOFERNES   Most dull, honest Dull! To our sport, away.
                                                    Exeunt

5.2

Enter the [PRINCESS *and her*] *ladies* [ROSALINE, MARIA,
and CATHERINE]

PRINCESS   Sweethearts, we shall be rich ere we depart,
      If fairings° come thus plentifully in.   *gifts*
      A lady walled about with diamonds[1]—
      Look you what I have from the loving King.
5   ROSALINE   Madam, came nothing else along with that?
    PRINCESS   Nothing but this?—yes, as much love in rhyme
      As would be crammed up in a sheet of paper
      Writ o' both sides the leaf, margin and all,
      That he was fain to seal on Cupid's name.[2]

---

8. Famous conquerors often represented in folk plays
and pageants. Usually three pagans—Hector, Alexander,
Julius Caesar; three Jews—Joshua, David, Judas Maccabeus; and three Christians—Arthur, Charlemagne,
and Godfrey of Bouillon or Guy of Warwick. Of these,
only Alexander, Judas Maccabeus, and Hector appear in
the next scene; Shakespeare adds Pompey and Hercules.
9. In the event, Nathaniel plays Alexander.
1. *great . . . Great:* Costard's considerable size allows

him to "pass" for Pompey the Great, suggesting "penis"
through "limb" or "joint," and, through the jingle with
"pump" in "Pompey," both "penis" and "pudendum."
2. Hercules strangled two snakes sent by Juno to kill
him in his cradle.
5.2 Location: The ladies' lodgings in the King's park.
1. This describes the gift (a pendant or brooch).
2. So that he was obliged to obliterate Cupid's name
with his seal.

10	ROSALINE That was the way to make his godhead wax,°	*grow; sealing wax*
	For he hath been five thousand year° a boy.	*(age of the world)*
	CATHERINE Ay, and a shrewd unhappy gallows,³ too.	
	ROSALINE You'll ne'er be friends with him, a° killed your sister.	*he*
	CATHERINE He made her melancholy, sad, and heavy,	
15	And so she died. Had she been light like you,	
	Of such a merry, nimble, stirring spirit,	
	She might ha' been a grandam ere she died;	
	And so may you, for a light heart lives long.	
	ROSALINE What's your dark° meaning, mouse, of this light°	*covert / careless*
	word?	
20	CATHERINE A light° condition in a beauty dark.	*frivolous; wanton*
	ROSALINE We need more light to find your meaning out.	
	CATHERINE You'll mar the light by taking it in snuff,⁴	
	Therefore I'll darkly end the argument.	
	ROSALINE Look what° you do, you do it still i'th' dark.°	*whatever / (bawdy)*
25	CATHERINE So do not you, for you are a light wench.	
	ROSALINE Indeed I weigh not° you, and therefore light.	*weigh less than*
	CATHERINE You weigh me not? O, that's you care not for me.	
	ROSALINE Great reason, for past care is still past cure.	
	PRINCESS Well bandied, both; a set of wit well played.	
30	But Rosaline, you have a favour,° too.	*love token*
	Who sent it? And what is it?	
	ROSALINE I would you knew.	
	An if my face were but as fair as yours	
	My favour° were as great, be witness this.	*appearance*
	Nay, I have verses, too, I thank Biron,	
35	The numbers° true, and were the numb'ring,° too,	*meter / evaluation*
	I were the fairest goddess on the ground.	
	I am compared to twenty thousand fairs.°	*beauties*
	O, he hath drawn my picture in his letter.	
	PRINCESS Anything like?	
40	ROSALINE Much in the letters,° nothing in the praise.	*penmanship*
	PRINCESS Beauteous as ink°—a good conclusion.	*(that is, black)*
	CATHERINE Fair as a text° B in a copy-book.	*formally written black*
	ROSALINE Ware pencils,⁵ ho! Let me not die your debtor,°	*I'll pay you back*
	My red dominical,⁶ my golden letter.⁷	
45	O, that your face were not so full of O's!°	*pockmarks; pudendum*
	PRINCESS A pox of that jest; I beshrew° all shrews.	*wish mischief upon*
	But Catherine, what was sent to you from fair Dumaine?	
	CATHERINE Madam, this glove.	
	PRINCESS Did he not send you twain?	
	CATHERINE Yes, madam; and moreover,	
50	Some thousand verses of a faithful lover.	
	A huge translation° of hypocrisy	*expression*
	Vilely compiled, profound simplicity.°	*folly*
	MARIA This° and these pearls to me sent Longueville.	*(A chain)*
	The letter is too long by half a mile.	
55	PRINCESS I think no less. Dost thou not wish in heart	
	The chain were longer and the letter short?	

3. Ill-natured, pernicious gallows bird, deserving to be hanged.
4. Taking it amiss; snuffing a candle.
5. Beware of introducing the subject of brushes (used for cosmetic purposes as well as for drawing portraits).

6. Red letter marking Sundays and feast days in an almanac; reference to Catherine's ruddy complexion.
7. Also used to mark Sunday; reference to Catherine's fair hair.

MARIA   Ay, or I would these hands might never part.[8]

PRINCESS   We are wise girls to mock our lovers so.

ROSALINE   They are worse fools to purchase mocking so.

60   That same Biron I'll torture ere I go.

O that I knew he were but in by th' week!° —   *permanently caught*

How I would make him fawn, and beg, and seek,

And wait the season, and observe the times,°   *dance attendance*

And spend his prodigal wits in bootless° rhymes,   *fruitless*

65   And shape his service wholly to my hests,°   *commands*

And make him proud to make me proud that jests![9]

So pursuivant°-like would I o'ersway his state   *arresting officer*

That he should be my fool, and I his fate.

PRINCESS   None are so surely caught when they are catched

70   As wit turned fool. Folly in wisdom hatched

Hath wisdom's warrant, and the help of school,

And wit's own grace, to grace a learnèd fool.

ROSALINE   The blood of youth burns not with such excess

As gravity's° revolt to wantonness.   *a wise person's*

75   MARIA   Folly in fools bears not so strong a note°   *stigma*

As fool'ry in the wise when wit doth dote,°   *act foolishly*

Since all the power thereof it doth apply

To prove, by wit, worth in simplicity.°   *folly*

  Enter BOYET

PRINCESS   Here comes Boyet, and mirth is in his face.

80   BOYET   O, I am stabbed with laughter! Where's her grace?

PRINCESS   Thy news, Boyet?

BOYET   Prepare, madam, prepare.

Arm, wenches, arm. Encounters mounted are°   *An attack is prepared*

Against your peace. Love doth approach disguised,

Armèd in arguments. You'll be surprised.[1]

85   Muster your wits, stand in your own defence,

Or hide your heads like cowards and fly hence.

PRINCESS   Saint Denis to Saint Cupid![2] What are they

That charge° their breath against us? Say, scout, say.   *level (a weapon)*

BOYET   Under the cool shade of a sycamore

90   I thought to close mine eyes some half an hour

When lo, to interrupt my purposed rest

Toward that shade I might behold addressed°   *I could see approaching*

The King and his companions. Warily

I stole into a neighbour thicket by

95   And overheard what you shall overhear:°   *hear over again*

That by and by disguised they will be here.

Their herald is a pretty knavish page

That well by heart hath conned his embassage.°   *learned his message*

Action and accent° did they teach him there.   *Gesture and intonation*

100   'Thus must thou speak', and 'thus thy body bear'.

And ever and anon they made a doubt°   *expressed fear*

Presence majestical would put him out,[3]

'For', quoth the King, 'an angel shalt thou see,

Yet fear not thou, but speak audaciously.'

---

8. Perhaps she has twisted the chain around them; or, she'd never separate her hands to give one hand in marriage to so ungenerous a man.
9. And be pleased to praise the one who mocks him; and be glad to be ridiculed.

1. Overcome by a surprise attack.
2. St. Denis (the patron saint of France) against St. Cupid.
3. Would make him forget his lines.

105	The boy replied, 'An angel is not evil.	
	I should have feared her had she been a devil.'	
	With that all laughed and clapped him on the shoulder,	
	Making the bold wag by their praises bolder.	
	One rubbed his elbow⁴ thus, and fleered,° and swore	*grinned*
110	A better speech was never spoke before.	
	Another with his finger and his thumb°	*(snapping his fingers)*
	Cried '*Via*,° we will do't, come what will come!'	*Come on*
	The third he capered and cried 'All goes well!'	
	The fourth turned on the toe° and down he fell.	*did a pirouette*
115	With that they all did tumble on the ground	
	With such a zealous laughter, so profound,	
	That in this spleen° ridiculous appears,	*fit (of laughter)*
	To check their folly, passion's solemn tears.	

PRINCESS　But what, but what—come they to visit us?

120 BOYET　They do, they do, and are apparelled thus

[ ]⁵

Like Muscovites or Russians, as I guess.

Their purpose is to parley, to court and dance,

And every one his love-suit will advance

125	Unto his several° mistress, which they'll know	*particular*
	By favours several which they did bestow.	

PRINCESS　And will they so? The gallants shall be tasked,°　*put to the test*

For, ladies, we will every one be masked,

	And not a man of them shall have the grace,°	*luck*
130	Despite of suit,° to see a lady's face.⁶	*pleading; costume*
130.1	*Hold, Rosaline. This favour thou shalt wear,*	
	And then the King willcourt thee for his dear.	

[*To* ROSALINE] Hold, take thou this, my sweet, and give me thine.

So shall Biron take me for Rosaline.

[*She changes favours with* ROSALINE]

[*To* CATHERINE *and* MARIA]

And change you favours, too. So shall your loves

	Woo contrary, deceived by these removes.°	*exchanges*

[CATHERINE *and* MARIA *change favours*]

135	ROSALINE　Come on, then, wear the favours most in sight.°	*conspicuously*

CATHERINE　But in this changing what is your intent?

PRINCESS　The effect of my intent is to cross theirs.

	They do it but in mockery-merriment,°	*satirical mirth*
	And mock for mock is only my intent.	
140	Their several counsels° they unbosom shall	*confidences*
	To loves mistook, and so be mocked withal	
	Upon the next occasion that we meet	
	With visages displayed to talk and greet.	

ROSALINE　But shall we dance if they desire us to't?

145 PRINCESS　No, to the death we will not move a foot,

Nor to their penned speech render we no grace,

But while 'tis spoke each turn away her face.

BOYET　Why, that contempt will kill the speaker's heart,

And quite divorce his memory from his part.

---

4. Sign of satisfaction.
5. Absence of a rhyme for "guess" and a referent for "thus" suggests that a line describing the lords' costumes has been lost.

6. The following two indented lines (130.1–130.2), spoken by the Princess, seem to represent a first draft of 5.2.131–32.

150   PRINCESS   Therefore I do it; and I make no doubt
          The rest will ne'er come in if he be out.[7]
          There's no such sport as sport by sport o'erthrown,
          To make theirs ours, and ours none but our own.
          So shall we stay, mocking intended game,
155   And they well mocked depart away with shame.
              Sound trumpet
  BOYET   The trumpet sounds, be masked, the masquers come.
          [The ladies mask.]
          Enter blackamoors with music;[8] *the boy* [MOTE] *with a*
          speech; the [KING *and his*] *lords, disguised* [*as Russians*]
  MOTE   All hail, the richest beauties on the earth!
  BIRON [*aside*]   Beauties no richer than rich taffeta.°   *(masks of taffeta)*
  MOTE   A holy parcel° of the fairest dames—   *party*
          The ladies turn their backs to him
160   That ever turned their—backs to mortal views.
  BIRON   'Their eyes', villain, 'their eyes'!
  MOTE   That ever turned their eyes to mortal views.
          Out . . .
  BOYET   True, out° indeed!   *(of his part)*
165   MOTE   Out of your favours, heavenly spirits, vouchsafe°   *be willing*
          Not to behold—
  BIRON   'Once to behold', rogue!
  MOTE   Once to behold with your sun-beamèd eyes—
          With your sun-beamèd eyes—
170   BOYET   They will not answer to that epithet.
          You were best call it 'daughter-beamèd' eyes.
  MOTE   They do not mark° me, and that brings me out.   *listen to*
  BIRON   Is this your perfectness?° Be gone, you rogue!   *(in saying your lines)*
                       [Exit MOTE]
  ROSALINE [*as the Princess*][9]   What would these strangers?° Know   *foreigners*
          their minds, Boyet.
175   If they do speak our language, 'tis our will
          That some plain° man recount their purposes.   *plainspoken*
          Know what they would.
  BOYET   What would you with the Princess?
  BIRON   Nothing but peace and gentle visitation.°   *visiting*
  ROSALINE   What would they, say they?
180   BOYET   Nothing but peace and gentle visitation.
  ROSALINE   Why, that they have, and bid them so be gone.
  BOYET   She says you have it, and you may be gone.
  KING   Say to her we have measured° many miles   *paced*
          To tread a measure° with her on this grass.   *dance*
185   BOYET   They say that they have measured many a mile
          To tread a measure with you on this grass.
  ROSALINE   It is not so. Ask them how many inches
          Is in one mile. If they have measured many,
          The measure then of one is easily told.°   *counted*
190   BOYET   If to come hither you have measured miles,
          And many miles, the Princess bids you tell
          How many inches doth fill up one mile.

---

7. The rest of his prepared speech will be forgotten if
he's confused ("out" of his part).
8. Presumably nonspeaking musicians dressed as black
Africans to provide an exotic accompaniment (see

Introduction).
9. From here to line 229, Rosaline speaks as the
Princess.

BIRON   Tell her we measure them by weary steps.
BOYET   She hears herself.
ROSALINE   How many weary steps
195   Of many weary miles you have o'ergone
       Are numbered in the travel of one mile?
BIRON   We number nothing that we spend for you.
       Our duty is so rich, so infinite,
       That we may do it still° without account.°   *always / reckoning*
200   Vouchsafe to show the sunshine of your face
       That we, like savages, may worship it.
ROSALINE   My face is but a moon,[1] and clouded,° too.   *masked; dark*
KING   Blessed are clouds to do as such clouds do.
       Vouchsafe, bright moon, and these thy stars,° to shine,   *companions*
205   Those clouds removed, upon our watery eyne.°   *eyes*
ROSALINE   O vain petitioner, beg a greater matter.
       Thou now requests but moonshine in the water.°   *nothing*
KING   Then in our measure do but vouchsafe one change.[2]
       Thou bidd'st me beg; this begging is not strange.°   *odd; foreign*
ROSALINE   Play, music, then.
            [*Music plays*][3]
210   Nay, you must do it soon.
       Not yet?—no dance! Thus change I like the moon.
KING   Will you not dance? How come you thus estranged?
ROSALINE   You took the moon at full, but now she's changed.
KING   Yet still she is the moon, and I the man.°   *(in the moon)*
215   [   ][4]
       The music plays, vouchsafe some motion° to it.   *movement; response*
ROSALINE   Our ears vouchsafe it.
KING   But your legs should do it.
ROSALINE   Since you are strangers and come here by chance
       We'll not be nice.° Take hands. We will not dance.   *coy*
KING   Why take we hands, then?
220   ROSALINE   Only to part friends.
       Curtsy, sweethearts, and so the measure ends.
KING   More measure° of this measure, be not nice.   *A larger amount*
ROSALINE   We can afford no more at such a price.
KING   Price you yourselves. What buys your company?
ROSALINE   Your absence only.
225   KING   That can never be.
ROSALINE   Then cannot we be bought, and so adieu—
       Twice to your visor, and half once to you.[5]
KING   If you deny to dance, let's hold more chat.
ROSALINE   In private, then.
KING   I am best pleased with that.
            [*The* KING *and* ROSALINE *talk apart*]
       BIRON [*to the* PRINCESS, *taking her for Rosaline*]
230   White-handed mistress, one sweet word with thee.
PRINCESS   Honey and milk and sugar—there is three.
BIRON   Nay then, two treys,° an if you grow so nice°—   *threes (dice) / subtle*

---

1. Because it shines with a borrowed light.
2. Of the moon; of the figure in the dance, *measure:* dance.
3. It is not certain whether the music should start here or later.

4. A line rhyming with "man" seems to have dropped out.
5. Perhaps: your masked ("visor") (double) face deserves two farewells, but yourself less than one (for behaving so foolishly).

Metheglin, wort, and malmsey°—well run, dice!   *three sweet drinks*
There's half-a-dozen sweets.
PRINCESS   Seventh sweet, adieu.
235   Since you can cog,° I'll play no more with you.   *cheat*
BIRON   One word in secret.
PRINCESS   Let it not be sweet.
BIRON   Thou griev'st my gall.°   *chafe my sore place*
PRINCESS   Gall°—bitter!   *Liver bile*
BIRON   Therefore meet.°   *fitting; let's meet?*
     [BIRON *and the* PRINCESS *talk apart*]
DUMAINE [*to* MARIA, *taking her for Catherine*]
Will you vouchsafe with me to change a word?°   *exchange words*
MARIA   Name it.
DUMAINE   Fair lady—
MARIA   Say you so? Fair lord—
Take that for° your 'fair lady'.   *in exchange for*
240   DUMAINE   Please it you,
As much in private, and I'll bid adieu.
     [DUMAINE *and* MARIA *talk apart*]
CATHERINE   What, was your visor made without a tongue?[6]
LONGUEVILLE [*taking* CATHERINE *for Maria*]   I know the reason,
   lady, why you ask.
CATHERINE   O, for your reason! Quickly, sir, I long.
245   LONGUEVILLE   You have a double tongue within your mask,
And would afford my speechless visor half.[7]
CATHERINE   'Veal', quoth the Dutchman. Is not veal a calf?[8]
LONGUEVILLE   A calf, fair lady?
CATHERINE   No, a fair lord calf.°   *dolt*
LONGUEVILLE   Let's part the word.°   *compromise*
CATHERINE   No, I'll not be your half.[9]
250   Take all and wean° it, it may prove an ox.[1]   *raise*
LONGUEVILLE   Look how you butt° yourself in these sharp mocks!   *attack*
Will you give horns,[2] chaste lady? Do not so.
CATHERINE   Then die a calf before your horns do grow.
LONGUEVILLE   One word in private with you ere I die.°   *have an orgasm*
255   CATHERINE   Bleat softly, then. The butcher hears you cry.
     [LONGUEVILLE *and* CATHERINE *talk apart*]
BOYET   The tongues of mocking wenches are as keen
   As is the razor's edge invisible,
Cutting a smaller hair than may be seen,
   Above the sense of sense; so sensible[3]
260   Seemeth their conference.° Their conceits° have wings   *conversation / fancies*
Fleeter than arrows, bullets, wind, thought, swifter things.
ROSALINE   Not one word more, my maids. Break off, break off.

6. A projection within a mask permitting it to be held in place with the mouth. Catherine is also alluding to Longueville's silence.
7. *You . . . half:* You are double-tongued (masked; punning; deceptive; speaking enough for two) and ask about my silence because you'd be wise to give up half your speech by giving me one of the tongues (the one that keeps her mask on; this would reveal her identity).
8. *'Veal':* Well (ironic: Dutch pronunciation of "well" or German *viel,* meaning "much"; "Dutch" could mean "German"); veil (mask). Combined with Catherine's previous word, "long" (line 244), the result is "Longueville"—thus demonstrating that she knows the identity of her disguised suitor and had anticipated his "half" (line 246) by uttering half his name. *Veau,* French for "veal," does also mean "calf" (a dunce in Renaissance English).
9. Taking "part" as "divide": half of what you are the other half of; your better half (your wife); half of "calf" ("ca," for "Catherine").
1. Dolt; castrated male.
2. Butt with horns; equip with horns; cuckold.
3. *Above . . . sense:* Above the power of the senses to apprehend (perhaps with the ironic meaning of "nonsense"). *so sensible:* so acutely felt by the hearer.

BIRON   By heaven, all dry-beaten with pure scoff![4]
KING   Farewell, mad wenches, you have simple wits.

Exeunt [the KING, *lords, and blackamoors]*
[The ladies unmask]

265 PRINCESS   Twenty adieus, my frozen Muscovites.
Are these the breed of wits so wondered at?
BOYET   Tapers they are, with your sweet breaths puffed out.
ROSALINE   Well-liking° wits they have; gross, gross; fat, fat.   *Plump*
PRINCESS   O poverty in wit, kingly-poor flout![5]
270 Will they not, think you, hang themselves tonight,
Or ever but in visors show their faces?
This pert Biron was out of count'nance° quite.   *disconcerted; masked*
ROSALINE   Ah, they were all in lamentable cases.°   *states; outfits*
The King was weeping-ripe for° a good word.[6]   *near tears for lack of*
275 PRINCESS   Biron did swear himself out of all suit.[7]
MARIA   Dumaine was at my service, and his sword.
'*Non point*,'° quoth I. My servant straight was mute.   *Not at all; it's blunt*
CATHERINE   Lord Longueville said I came o'er his heart,
And trow you° what he called me?   *can you believe*
PRINCESS   'Qualm',[8] perhaps.
CATHERINE   Yes, in good faith.
280 PRINCESS   Go, sickness as thou art.
ROSALINE   Well, better wits have worn plain statute-caps.[9]
But will you hear? The King is my love sworn.
PRINCESS   And quick Biron hath plighted faith to me.
CATHERINE   And Longueville was for my service born.
285 MARIA   Dumaine is mine, as sure as bark on tree.
BOYET   Madam, and pretty mistresses, give ear.
Immediately they will again be here
In their own shapes,° for it can never be   *Undisguised*
They will digest° this harsh indignity.   *accept*
PRINCESS   Will they return?
290 BOYET   They will, they will, God knows,
And leap for joy, though they are lame with blows.
Therefore change favours, and when they repair,°   *return*
Blow° like sweet roses in this summer air.   *Bloom*
PRINCESS   How 'blow'? How 'blow'? Speak to be understood.
295 BOYET   Fair ladies masked are roses in their bud;
Dismasked, their damask sweet commixture[1] shown,
Are angels vailing° clouds, or roses blown.°   *letting fall / blooming*
PRINCESS   Avaunt, perplexity!° What shall we do   *Be off, riddler*
If they return in their own shapes to woo?
300 ROSALINE   Good madam, if by me you'll be advised,
Let's mock them still, as well known[2] as disguised.
Let us complain to them what fools were here,
Disguised like Muscovites in shapeless gear,°   *ill-cut clothes*
And wonder what they were, and to what end

---

4. Soundly beaten without bloodshed; battered by mocking words.
5. Reversed wordplay ("kingly-poor") on "well-li-king" (or like-king," line 268), criticizing Rosaline's "flout" (gibe) and perhaps the King's as well (line 264).
6. The beginning of a sixteen-line dialogue sonnet.
7. Avowed his passion—beyond all reason; out of character for his Russian "suit" (costume); in a mistaken "suit" at love (to the wrong woman).

8. Heartburn: perhaps punning on "came" (line 278) and picked up in "go" (line 280).
9. Cleverer people have been ordinary apprentices (whose headwear was regulated by statute); perhaps an allusion to fancy caps forming part of the lords' disguise.
1. Sweet red and white complexion.
2. Let's mock them just as much now that they are known for themselves.

305 Their shallow shows, and prologue vilely penned,
And their rough carriage° so ridiculous,   *awkward manner*
Should be presented at our tent to us.
BOYET   Ladies, withdraw. The gallants are at hand.
PRINCESS   Whip, to our tents, as roes° run over land!   *deer*

Exeunt [the ladies]
Enter the KING[, BIRON, DUMAINE, *and* LONGUEVILLE, *as themselves*]

310 KING   Fair sir, God save you. Where's the Princess?
BOYET   Gone to her tent. Please it your majesty
Command me any service to her thither?
KING   That she vouchsafe me audience for one word.
BOYET   I will, and so will she, I know, my lord.   *Exit*

315 BIRON   This fellow pecks up wit as pigeons peas,
And utters° it again when God doth please.   *speaks; sells*
He is wit's pedlar, and retails his wares
At wakes and wassails,° meetings, markets, fairs.   *festivals and revels*
And we that sell by gross,° the Lord doth know,   *wholesale*
320 Have not the grace to grace it with such show.
This gallant pins the wenches on his sleeve.°   *attracts all the girls*
Had he been Adam, he had° tempted Eve.   *would have*
A can carve³ too, and lisp,° why, this is he   *speak affectedly*
That kissed his hand away in courtesy.
325 This is the ape of form,° Monsieur the Nice,°   *good form / fastidious*
That when he plays at tables° chides the dice   *backgammon*
In honourable° terms. Nay, he can sing   *polite*
A mean most meanly,⁴ and in ushering°   *as a gentleman usher*
Mend° him who can. The ladies call him sweet.   *Improve on*
330 The stairs as he treads on them kiss his feet.
This is the flower that smiles on everyone
To show his teeth as white as whalës bone,°   *walrus ivory*
And consciences that will not die in debt
Pay him the due of 'honey-tongued' Boyet.
335 KING   A blister on his sweet tongue with my heart,
That put Armado's page out of his part!

Enter the ladies [and BOYET]

BIRON   See where it° comes. Behaviour,° what wert thou   *(Boyet) / Fine manners*
Till this madman° showed thee, and what art thou now?   *madcap*
KING   All hail, sweet madam, and fair time of day!
340 PRINCESS   'Fair' in 'all hail'° is foul, as I conceive.   *(as in "hailstorm")*
KING   Construe my speeches better, if you may.
PRINCESS   Then wish me better. I will give you leave.
KING   We came to visit you,⁵ and purpose now
To lead you to our court. Vouchsafe it, then.
345 PRINCESS   This field shall hold me, and so hold your vow.
Nor° God nor I delights in perjured men.   *Neither*
KING   Rebuke me not for that which you provoke.
The virtue° of your eye must break my oath.   *power*
PRINCESS   You nickname virtue.° 'Vice' you should have spoke,   *misname goodness*
350 For virtue's office° never breaks men's troth.   *action*
Now by my maiden honour, yet as pure
As the unsullied lily, I protest,

3. He can act with social grace, flirt.
4. *he . . . meanly:* he can sing an in-between vocal part
(tenor or alto) in the appropriate way (make himself

generally useful).
5. The beginning of another dialogue sonnet.

A world of torments though I should endure,
I would not yield to be your house's guest,
355 So much I hate a breaking cause° to be   cause of breaking
Of heavenly oaths, vowed with integrity.
KING   O, you have lived in desolation here,
Unseen, unvisited, much to our shame.
PRINCESS   Not so, my lord. It is not so, I swear.
360 We have had pastimes here, and pleasant game.
A mess of° Russians left us but of late.   group of four
KING   How, madam? Russians?
PRINCESS   Ay, in truth, my lord.
Trim gallants, full of courtship and of state.
ROSALINE   Madam, speak true.—It is not so, my lord.
365 My lady, to the manner of the days,°   in the present fashion
In courtesy gives undeserving praise.
We four indeed confronted were with four
In Russian habit. Here they stayed an hour,
And talked apace, and in that hour, my lord,
370 They did not bless us with one happy° word.   well-chosen
I dare not call them fools, but this I think:
When they are thirsty, fools would fain have drink.
BIRON   This jest is dry° to me. Gentle sweet,   barren (punningly)
Your wits makes wise things foolish. When we greet,
375 With eyes' best seeing, heaven's fiery eye,
By light we lose light.[6] Your capacity
Is of that nature that to° your huge store   compared to
Wise things seem foolish, and rich things but poor.
ROSALINE   This proves you wise and rich, for in my eye—
380 BIRON   I am a fool, and full of poverty.
ROSALINE   But that you take what doth to you belong
It were a fault to snatch words from my tongue.
BIRON   O, I am yours, and all that I possess.
ROSALINE   All the fool mine!
BIRON   I cannot give you less.
385 ROSALINE   Which of the visors was it that you wore?
BIRON   Where? When? What visor? Why demand° you this?   ask
ROSALINE   There, then, that visor, that superfluous case,°   mask
That hid the worse and showed the better face.
KING   [aside to the lords]   We were descried.° They'll mock us   uncovered
now, downright.
390 DUMAINE   [aside to the KING]   Let us confess, and turn it to a jest.
PRINCESS   Amazed, my lord? Why looks your highness sad?
ROSALINE   Help, hold his° brows, he'll swoon. Why look you pale?   (Biron's)
Seasick, I think, coming from Muscovy.
BIRON   Thus pour the stars down plagues for perjury.
395 Can any face of brass° hold longer out?   brazen shamelessness
Here stand I, lady. Dart thy skill at me—
Bruise me with scorn, confound me with a flout,
Thrust thy sharp wit quite through my ignorance,
Cut me to pieces with thy keen conceit,°   intelligence
400 And I will wish° thee nevermore to dance,   invite
Nor nevermore in Russian habit wait.°   attend on you
O, never will I trust to speeches penned,[7]

6. When we gaze intently at the sun, we go blind.   considering Biron's renunciation of literary effects.
7. The beginning of a sonnet (lines 402–15)—ironic,

Nor to the motion of a schoolboy's tongue,
Nor never come in visor to my friend,°   *sweetheart*
405   Nor woo in rhyme, like a blind harper's song.
Taffeta phrases, silken terms precise,
    Three-piled° hyperboles, spruce affectation,   *Rich velvet; Elaborate*
Figures° pedantical—these summer flies   *(of speech)*
Have blown me full of maggot ostentation.°   *laid maggot eggs in me*
410   I do forswear them, and I here protest,
    By this white glove—how white the hand, God knows!—
Henceforth my wooing mind shall be expressed
    In russet° yeas, and honest kersey° noes.   *homely / plain*
And to begin, wench, so God help me, law!°   *indeed (humble oath)*
415   My love to thee is sound, sans° crack or flaw.   *without*
ROSALINE   Sans 'sans', I pray you.
BIRON   Yet° I have a trick°   *Still / touch*
Of the old rage.° Bear with me, I am sick.   *fever*
I'll leave it by degrees. Soft, let us see.
Write 'Lord have mercy on us'[8] on those three.°   *(his companions)*
420   They are infected, in their hearts it lies.
They have the plague, and caught it of your eyes.
These lords are visited,° you are not free;   *afflicted by plague*
For the Lord's tokens° on you do I see.   *favors; plague spots*
PRINCESS   No, they are free[9] that gave these tokens to us.
425   BIRON   Our states are forfeit.[1] Seek not to undo us.[2]
ROSALINE   It is not so, for how can this be true,
That you stand forfeit, being those that sue?°   *sue at law; beg; woo*
BIRON   Peace, for I will not have to do° with you.   *deal; copulate*
ROSALINE   Nor shall not, if I do as I intend.
430   BIRON [*to the lords*]   Speak for yourselves. My wit is at an end.
KING   Teach us, sweet madam, for our rude transgression
Some fair excuse.
PRINCESS   The fairest is confession.
Were not you here but even now disguised?
KING   Madam, I was.
PRINCESS   And were you well advised?°   *in your right mind*
KING   I was, fair madam.
435   PRINCESS   When you then were here,
What did you whisper in your lady's ear?
KING   That more than all the world I did respect° her.   *value*
PRINCESS   When she shall challenge° this, you will reject her.   *assert her claim to*
KING   Upon mine honour, no.
PRINCESS   Peace, peace, forbear.
440   Your oath once broke, you force not° to forswear.   *find it easy*
KING   Despise me when I break this oath of mine.
PRINCESS   I will, and therefore keep it. Rosaline,
What did the Russian whisper in your ear?
ROSALINE   Madam, he swore that he did hold me dear
445   As precious eyesight, and did value me
Above this world, adding thereto moreover
That he would wed me, or else die my lover.

---

8. A common inscription on the doors of plague-visited houses.
9. Generous; at liberty; free of love; free of obligation.
1. (Denying the Princess's claim in line 424 that the men are "free"): Our estates are subject to confiscation; our condition as bachelors is ended; because we're in love, we've lost power over ourselves; as would-be husbands, we owe you our estates; we've acted dishonorably.
2. Don't undo our forfeiture (don't ruin us) by calling us "free" (by rejecting our love).

PRINCESS   God give thee joy of him! The noble lord
   Most honourably doth uphold his word.
450 KING   What mean you, madam? By my life, my troth,
   I never swore this lady such an oath.
ROSALINE   By heaven, you did, and to confirm it plain,
   You gave me this. But take it, sir, again.
KING   My faith and this the Princess I did give.
455   I knew her by this jewel on her sleeve.
PRINCESS   Pardon me, sir, *this* jewel did she wear,
   And Lord Biron, I thank him, is my dear.
   [*To* BIRON] What, will you have me, or your pearl again?
BIRON   Neither of either.° I remit° both twain.   *the two / surrender*
460   I see the trick on't.° Here was a consent,°   *of it / plot*
   Knowing aforehand of our merriment,
   To dash it like a Christmas comedy.
   Some carry-tale, some please-man, some slight zany,
   Some mumble-news, some trencher-knight, some Dick[3]
465   That smiles his cheek in years,° and knows the trick   *into wrinkles*
   To make my lady laugh when she's disposed,
   Told our intents before, which once disclosed,
   The ladies did change favours, and then we,
   Following the signs, wooed but the sign of she.°   *each mistress*
470   Now, to our perjury to add more terror,
   We are again forsworn, in will° and error.°   *willfully / mistakenly*
   Much upon this 'tis,[4] [*to* BOYET] and might not you
   Forestall° our sport, to make us thus untrue?   *Have undermined*
   Do not you know my lady's foot by th' square,[5]
475   And laugh upon the apple[6] of her eye,
   And stand between her back, sir, and the fire,°   *keep the heat from her*
      Holding a trencher,° jesting merrily?   *serving plate*
   You put our page out. Go, you are allowed.°   *privileged (as a fool)*
   Die when you will, a smock[7] shall be your shroud.
480   You leer° upon me, do you? There's an eye   *look malevolently at*
   Wounds like a leaden sword.°   *harmless stage sword*
BOYET   Full merrily
   Hath this brave manège, this career been run.
BIRON   Lo, he is tilting straight.[8] Peace, I have done.
      Enter [COSTARD *the*] *clown*
   Welcome, pure wit. Thou partest a fair fray.
485 COSTARD   O Lord, sir, they would know
   Whether the three Worthies shall come in or no.
BIRON   What, are there but three?
COSTARD   No, sir, but it is vara° fine,   *very*
   For everyone pursents° three.   *(re)presents*
BIRON   And three times thrice is nine.
COSTARD   Not so, sir, under° correction, sir, I hope it is not so.   *subject to*
   You cannot beg us,° sir. I can assure you, sir, we know what   *show we're fools*
490   we know.

3. *carry-tale:* talebearer. *please-man:* toady. *zany:* clownish, rustic servant in commedia dell'arte. *mumble-news:* gossip. *trencher-knight:* parasite, who dines from his lord's dish ("trencher") or who has a lordly appetite. *Dick:* low fellow.
4. It happened very much like this.
5. Know how to please your mistress. *square:* a carpenter's rule (Boyet "has her measure"); possible pun on "squire" (an "apple-squire" was a pimp; see "apple," line 475 and note).
6. Pupil. Boyet can wittily catch the Princess's eye; he is on intimate terms with her.
7. Woman's garment (either a charge of effeminacy or equivalent to "women will be the death of you").
8. Jousting (linguistically) at once. *manège* (line 482): feat of horsemanship. *career:* short gallop at full speed.

I hope, sir, three times thrice, sir—

BIRON   Is not nine?

COSTARD   Under correction, sir, we know whereuntil° it doth   *to what*
    amount.

BIRON   By Jove, I always took three threes for nine.

495   COSTARD   O Lord, sir, it were pity you should get your living by
    reck'ning,⁹ sir.

BIRON   How much is it?

COSTARD   O Lord, sir, the parties themselves, the actors, sir, will
    show whereuntil it doth amount. For mine own part, I am, as
500   they say, but to parfect° one man in one poor man, Pompion¹   *present; perfect*
    the Great, sir.

BIRON   Art thou one of the Worthies?

COSTARD   It pleased them to think me worthy of Pompey the
    Great. For mine own part, I know not the degree° of the Wor-   *rank*
505   thy, but I am to stand for him.

BIRON   Go, bid them prepare.

COSTARD   We will turn it finely off, sir. We will take some care.
                                                                         Exit

KING   Biron, they will shame us. Let them not approach.

BIRON   We are shame-proof, my lord, and 'tis some policy°   *clever strategy*
510   To have one show worse than the King's and his company.

KING   I say they shall not come.

PRINCESS   Nay, my good lord, let me o'errule you now.
    That sport best pleases that doth least know how.
    Where zeal strives to content, and the contents
515   Dies in the zeal of that which it presents,²
    There form confounded makes most form in mirth,³
    When great things labouring° perish in their birth.   *(to be born)*

BIRON   A right description of our sport,° my lord.   *(the Russian masque)*
                Enter [ARMADO *the*] *braggart*

ARMADO [*to the* KING]   Anointed, I implore so much expense of
520   thy royal sweet breath as will utter a brace° of words.   *pair*
                [ARMADO *and the* KING *speak apart*]

PRINCESS   Doth this man serve God?

BIRON   Why ask you?

PRINCESS   A° speaks not like a man of God his° making.   *He / (God's)*

ARMADO   That is all one, my fair sweet honey monarch,° for, I   *King or Princess?*
525   protest, the schoolmaster is exceeding fantastical, too-too vain,
    too-too vain. But we will put it, as they say, to *fortuna de la*
    guerra.° I wish you the peace of mind, most royal couplement.   *the fortune of war*
                                                                         Exit

KING   Here is like to be a good presence of Worthies. He pres-
    ents Hector of Troy, the swain Pompey the Great, the parish-
530   curate Alexander, Armado's page Hercules, the pedant Judas
    Maccabeus,
    And if these four Worthies in their first show thrive,
    These four will change habits° and present the other five.   *costumes*

BIRON   There is five in the first show.

535   KING   You are deceived, 'tis not so.

BIRON   The pedant, the braggart, the hedge-priest,° the fool,   *illiterate priest*
    and the boy,

---

9. It would be a shame if you had to earn your living by
arithmetic.
1. Pumpkin (blunder for "Pompey").

2. *and . . . presents:* and the enthusiasm of those who
present the play is fatal to the substance.
3. Artistry defeated produces the greatest comic effect.

Abate throw at novum[4] and the whole world again
Cannot pick out five such, take each one in his vein.°   *characteristic manner*
KING   The ship is under sail, and here she comes amain.°   *at full speed*
    Enter [COSTARD *the clown as*] *Pompey*
COSTARD [*as Pompey*]   I Pompey am—
540   BIRON   You lie, you are not he.
COSTARD [*as Pompey*]   I Pompey am—
BOYET   With leopard's head on knee.[5]
BIRON   Well said, old mocker. I must needs be friends with thee.
COSTARD [*as Pompey*]   I Pompey am, Pompey surnamed the Big.°   *(sexual)*
DUMAINE   'The Great'.
545   COSTARD   It is 'Great', sir—
    [*As Pompey*] Pompey surnamed the Great,
    That oft in field with targe° and shield did make my foe to sweat,[6]   *shield*
    And travelling along this coast I here am come by chance,
    And lay my arms before the legs° of this sweet lass of France.—   *(bawdy)*
550   If your ladyship would say 'Thanks, Pompey', I had done.
PRINCESS[7]   Great thanks, great Pompey.
COSTARD   'Tis not so much worth, but I hope I was perfect.° I   *I recited correctly*
    made a little fault in 'great'.
BIRON   My hat to a halfpenny° Pompey proves the best Worthy.   *I'll bet anything*
    [COSTARD *stands aside.*]
    Enter [NATHANIEL *the*] *curate* [*as*] *Alexander*
NATHANIEL [*as Alexander*]   When in the world I lived I was the
555   world's commander.
    By east, west, north, and south, I spread my conquering
      might.
    My scutcheon° plain° declares that I am Alisander.   *coat of arms / clearly*
BOYET   Your nose says no, you are not, for it stands too right.[8]
BIRON [*to* BOYET]   Your nose smells 'no'[9] in this, most tender-
    smelling° knight.   *sensitive-to-smell*
560   PRINCESS   The conqueror is dismayed. Proceed, good Alexander.
NATHANIEL [*as Alexander*]   When in the world I lived I was the
    world's commander.
BOYET   Most true, 'tis right, you were so, Alisander.
BIRON [*to* COSTARD]   Pompey the Great.
COSTARD   Your servant, and Costard.
565   BIRON   Take away the conqueror, take away Alisander.
COSTARD [*to* NATHANIEL]   O, sir, you have overthrown Alisander
    the Conqueror. You will be scraped out of the painted cloth[1]
    for this. Your lion that holds his pole-axe sitting on a close-stool
    will be given to Ajax.[2] He will be the ninth Worthy. A con-
570   queror and afeard to speak? Run away for shame, Alisander.
                        Exit [NATHANIEL *the*] *curate*
There, an't° shall please you, a foolish mild man, an honest   *if it*
man, look you, and soon dashed. He is a marvellous good

---

4. Barring a lucky chance in the dice game of novum (in which the main throws were five and nine—like the five actors playing the Nine Worthies).
5. Embossed either on the knee piece of his armor or on his shield, which he might then be holding upside down.
6. The first of three lines in fourteeners (14-syllable lines)—an archaic meter by the 1590s, like most of those used by the nonaristocratic characters.
7. Q gives the line to "Lady": perhaps Costard kneels to the wrong woman.
8. Straight (alluding to Alexander's reputed crooked neck).

9. Implying that Nathaniel smells bad; according to the Greek biographer Plutarch, Alexander was reputed to have "a marvellous good savour" (Thomas North's translation).
1. Referring to the practice of representing the Worthies on wall hangings.
2. Alexander's arms, which showed a lion holding a battle-ax (or penis) and seated (a "close-stool" is a toilet), will be given to another warrior, Ajax (punning on "a jakes," a toilet), a Greek hero from the Trojan War who coveted the armor of Achilles. See 4.3.6 and note.

neighbour, faith, and a very good bowler, but for Alisander—
alas, you see how 'tis—a little o'erparted.° But there are Wor-   *given too hard a role*
575 thies a-coming will speak their mind in some other sort.
PRINCESS Stand aside, good Pompey.
    *Enter [*HOLOFERNES *the] pedant [as] Judas, and the boy*
    [MOTE *as] Hercules*
HOLOFERNES Great Hercules is presented by this imp,°   *child*
    Whose club killed Cerberus, that three-headed *canus*,³
    And when he was a babe, a child, a shrimp,
580   Thus did he strangle serpents in his *manus*.°   *hands; (play on "anus")*
    Quoniam° he seemeth in minority,°   *Since / a child*
    Ergo° I come with this apology.   *Therefore*
    [*To* MOTE] Keep some state° in thy exit, and vanish.   *dignity*
                          Exit [MOTE]
HOLOFERNES [*as Judas*] Judas I am—
585 DUMAINE A Judas?
HOLOFERNES Not Iscariot, sir.
    [*As Judas*] Judas I am, yclept° Maccabeus.   *named*
DUMAINE Judas Maccabeus clipped° is plain Judas.   *shortened; circumcised*
BIRON A kissing traitor.⁴ How art thou proved Judas?
590 HOLOFERNES [*as Judas*] Judas I am—
DUMAINE The more shame for you, Judas.
HOLOFERNES What mean you, sir?
BOYET To make Judas hang himself.
HOLOFERNES Begin,° sir. You are my elder.   *You go first*
595 BIRON Well followed—Judas was hanged on an elder.°   *(tree)*
HOLOFERNES I will not be put out of countenance.°   *be upset*
BIRON Because thou hast no face.°   *countenance*
HOLOFERNES What is this?⁵
BOYET A cittern-head.°   *guitar*
600 DUMAINE The head of a bodkin.°   *hairpin; small dagger*
BIRON A death's face° in a ring.   *death's head*
LONGUEVILLE The face of an old Roman coin, scarce seen.°   *worn down*
BOYET The pommel° of Caesar's falchion.°   *handle / sword*
DUMAINE The carved-bone face on a flask.°   *gunpowder horn*
605 BIRON Saint George's half-cheek° in a brooch.   *profile*
DUMAINE Ay, and in a brooch of lead.°   *(indicating low rank)*
BIRON Ay, and worn in the cap of a tooth-drawer.⁶ And now for-
    ward, for we have put thee in countenance.°   *depicted you*
HOLOFERNES You have put me out of countenance.
610 BIRON False, we have given thee faces.
HOLOFERNES But you have outfaced° them all.   *mocked*
BIRON An thou wert a lion, we would do so.
BOYET Therefore, as he is an ass,⁷ let him go.
    And so adieu, sweet Jude. Nay, why dost thou stay?
615 DUMAINE For the latter end of his name.
BIRON For the ass to the Jude. Give it him. Jud-as, away.⁸
HOLOFERNES This is not generous,° not gentle,° not humble.°   *noble / courteous / kind*
BOYET A light for Monsieur Judas. It grows dark, he may stumble.
                     [*Exit* HOLOFERNES]

---

3. In classical mythology, the three-headed watchdog ("canis") of Hades.
4. Alluding to the kiss with which Judas Iscariot betrayed Jesus, with a pun on "clipped" (embraced, kissed), itself punning on "yclept."
5. Indicating his face. The replies refer to ornamental faces on objects.

6. Worn by a lowly dentist as a sign of his trade.
7. An ass disguises himself as a lion in one of Aesop's tables—only to have his own nature undo him. "Ass" in the sense of "backside" is punningly evoked by "end" (line 615).
8. *As*, in "Jud-as," is "the latter end of his name" (line 615), but "end" also means "ass."

PRINCESS Alas, poor Maccabeus, how hath he been baited!
     *Enter [*ARMADO *the] braggart [as Hector]*
620 BIRON Hide thy head, Achilles,⁹ here comes Hector in arms.
DUMAINE Though my mocks come home by° me, I will now be   *later rebound on*
   merry.
KING Hector was but a Trojan¹ in respect of° this.   *in comparison with*
BOYET But is this Hector?
625 KING I think Hector was not so clean-timbered.°   *well built*
LONGUEVILLE His leg is too big for Hector's.
DUMAINE More calf,° certain.   *part of the leg; fool*
BOYET No, he is best endowed in the small.°   *leg below the calf*
BIRON This cannot be Hector.
630 DUMAINE He's a god, or a painter, for he makes faces.°   *grimaces; creates life*
ARMADO [*as Hector*] The armipotent° Mars, of lances the   *powerful in arms*
   almighty,
   Gave Hector a gift—
DUMAINE A gilt nutmeg.²
BIRON A lemon.
635 LONGUEVILLE Stuck with cloves.
DUMAINE No, cloven.
ARMADO Peace!
   [*As Hector*] The armipotent Mars, of lances the almighty,
   Gave Hector a gift, the heir of Ilion,°   *Troy*
640 A man so breathèd° that certain he would fight, yea,   *fit*
   From morn till night, out of his pavilion.°   *jousting tent*
   I am that flower—
DUMAINE   That mint.
LONGUEVILLE   That colombine.
ARMADO Sweet Lord Longueville, rein thy tongue.
LONGUEVILLE I must rather give it the rein, for it runs° against   *jousts; races; speaks*
645 Hector.
DUMAINE Ay, and Hector's a greyhound.³
ARMADO The sweet war-man is dead and rotten. Sweet chucks,
   beat not the bones of the buried. When he breathed he was a
   man. But I will forward with my device.° [*To the* PRINCESS]   *performance*
650 Sweet royalty, bestow on me the sense of hearing.
      BIRON *steps forth*
PRINCESS Speak, brave Hector, we are much delighted.
ARMADO I do adore thy sweet grace's slipper.
BOYET Loves her by the foot.
DUMAINE He may not by the yard.°   *penis (slang)*
655 ARMADO [*as Hector*] This Hector far surmounted Hannibal.⁴
   [   ]⁵
ARMADO The party is gone.°   *Hector is dead*
COSTARD Fellow Hector, she is gone, she is two months on her
   way.⁶

9. Leading Greek hero in the Trojan War; Hector's
chief opponent and slayer in Homer, but his inferior
and a coward in *Troilus and Cressida*.
1. An ordinary guy (slang).
2. A nutmeg glazed with egg yolk, used, like "lemon"
and "cloves" (lines 634, 635), to flavor drinks. A common lover's gift, the "gilt nutmeg" may also allude to
Armado's makeup. "Lemon" perhaps puns on "leman"
(lover, sweetheart), in which case "cloven" (line 636)
would have a sexual innuendo.
3. Famous as a runner; "Hector" was a common name
for a greyhound.

4. Surpassed Hannibal, leader of Carthage against
Rome (with the unintentional homosexual innuendo of
"surmounted").
5. An interjection may be missing here.
6. Jaquenetta is two months pregnant. Since at most only
a few days seem to have passed in the aristocratic plot, it
is possible to infer that Costard is the actual father; but
this may be an example of Shakespearean double time.
The stage direction "Biron steps forth" following line 650
may indicate that he urges Costard to make this declaration. Alternatively, he may merely be trying to prevent
Armado from speaking, an effort the Princess thwarts.

660 ARMADO What meanest thou?

COSTARD Faith, unless you play the honest Trojan the poor wench is cast away. She's quick.° The child brags in her belly already. 'Tis yours.° *pregnant / (because it brags)*

ARMADO Dost thou infamonize° me among potentates? Thou *defame (a coinage)*
665 shalt die.

COSTARD Then° shall Hector be whipped for Jaquenetta that is *In that case* quick by him, and hanged for Pompey that is dead by him.[7]

DUMAINE Most rare Pompey!

BOYET Renowned Pompey!

670 BIRON Greater than great—great, great, great Pompey, Pompey the Huge.° *(bawdy)*

DUMAINE Hector trembles.

BIRON Pompey is moved. More Ates,° more Ates—stir them on, *goddess of discord* stir them on!

675 DUMAINE Hector will challenge him.

BIRON Ay, if a° have no more man's blood in his belly than will *he* sup° a flea. *feed*

ARMADO By the North Pole, I do challenge thee.

COSTARD I will not fight with a pole, like a northern° man. I'll *an uncivilized (Scot)*
680 slash, I'll do it by the sword. I bepray you, let me borrow my arms° again. *(from the Princess)*

DUMAINE Room for the incensed Worthies.

COSTARD I'll do it in my shirt.

DUMAINE Most resolute Pompey.

685 MOTE [*aside to* ARMADO] Master, let me take you a button-hole lower.[8] Do you not see Pompey is uncasing° for the combat? *undressing* What mean you? You will lose your reputation.

ARMADO Gentlemen and soldiers, pardon me. I will not combat in my shirt.

690 DUMAINE You may not deny it, Pompey hath made the challenge.

ARMADO Sweet bloods,° I both may and will. *men of fiery spirit*

BIRON What reason have you for't?

ARMADO The naked truth of it is, I have no shirt. I go woolward
695 for penance.[9]

MOTE True, and it was enjoined him in Rome° for want of *center of Catholicism* linen, since when I'll be sworn he wore none but a dish-clout° *dishcloth* of Jaquenetta's, and that a wears next his heart, for a favour.

Enter a messenger, Monsieur MERCADÉ[1]

MERCADÉ God save you, madam.

PRINCESS   Welcome, Mercadé,
700 But that thou interrupt'st our merriment.

MERCADÉ I am sorry, madam, for the news I bring Is heavy in my tongue. The King your father—

PRINCESS Dead, for° my life. *upon*

MERCADÉ   Even so. My tale is told.

BIRON Worthies, away. The scene begins to cloud.

705 ARMADO For mine own part, I breathe free breath. I have seen

---

7. Whom Armado has killed; whose hopes of Jaque- netta Armado has killed.
8. Help you to take off your doublet; take you down a peg or two; (both proverbial).
9. He has no linen between his wool outer garments and his skin—a form of Catholic self-punishment.
1. Possibly Mercury, the classical messenger of the gods and guide of souls to the underworld; perhaps also Mar-Arcadia, a reminder that death enters even the pastoral, Arcadian world of Navarre's park.

the day of wrong through the little hole of discretion, and I will
right myself like a soldier.[2]   *Exeunt Worthies*

KING   How fares your majesty?°   *(her new title)*
QUEEN   Boyet, prepare. I will away tonight.
710   KING   Madam, not so, I do beseech you stay.
QUEEN   Prepare, I say. I thank you, gracious lords,
For all your fair endeavours, and entreat,
Out of a new-sad soul, that you vouchsafe
In your rich wisdom to excuse or hide°   *overlook*
715   The liberal° opposition of our spirits.   *unrestrained*
If overboldly we have borne ourselves
In the converse of breath,° your gentleness°   *conversation / courtesy*
Was guilty of it. Farewell, worthy lord.
A heavy heart bears not a nimble tongue.
720   Excuse me so coming too short of thanks,
For my great suit so easily obtained.[3]
KING   The extreme parts of time extremely forms
All causes to the purpose of his speed,[4]
And often at his very loose° decides   *the last moment*
725   That which long process could not arbitrate.
And though the mourning brow of progeny
Forbid the smiling courtesy of love
The holy suit which fain it would convince,°   *give proof of*
Yet since love's argument was first° on foot,   *already*
730   Let not the cloud of sorrow jostle it
From what it purposed, since to wail friends lost
Is not by much so wholesome-profitable
As to rejoice at friends but newly found.
QUEEN   I understand you not. My griefs are double.[5]
735   BIRON   Honest plain words best pierce the ear of grief,
And by these badges° understand the King.   *signs; words*
For your fair sakes have we neglected time,
Played foul play with our oaths. Your beauty, ladies,
Hath much deformed us, fashioning our humours
740   Even to the opposèd end of our intents,[6]
And what in us hath seemed ridiculous—
As love is full of unbefitting strains,°   *impulses*
All wanton° as a child, skipping and vain,   *careless*
Formed by the eye and therefore like the eye,
745   Full of strange shapes, of habits and of forms,
Varying in subjects as the eye doth roll
To every varied object in his glance;
Which parti-coated° presence of loose° love   *foolish / unrestrained*
Put on by us, if in your heavenly eyes
750   Have misbecomed° our oaths and gravities,   *been unbecoming to*
Those heavenly eyes that look into these faults
Suggested° us to make them. Therefore, ladies,   *Tempted*
Our love being yours, the error that love makes
Is likewise yours. We to ourselves prove false
755   By being once false for ever to be true

2. I have enough sense to acknowledge my wrongdoing
and will honorably put myself in the right.
3. Even though there is no mention of the suit after
2.1, we must assume that it was settled.
4. *The extreme . . . speed:* Final moments enforce rapid

decisions.
5. Doubled because I cannot understand you.
6. *fashioning . . . intents:* distorting our behavior into
the opposite of what we intended.

To those that make us both—fair ladies, you.
And even that falsehood, in itself a sin,
Thus purifies itself and turns to grace.
QUEEN   We have received your letters full of love,
760   Your favours the ambassadors of love,
And in our maiden council rated them
At° courtship, pleasant jest, and courtesy,   *As*
As bombast[7] and as lining to the time.
But more devout° than this in our respects°   *serious / consideration*
765   Have we not been, and therefore met your loves
In their own fashion, like a merriment.
DUMAINE   Our letters, madam, showed much more than jest.
LONGUEVILLE   So did our looks.
ROSALINE   We did not quote° them so.   *interpret*
KING   Now, at the latest minute of the hour,
Grant us your loves.
770   QUEEN   A time, methinks, too short
To make a world-without-end° bargain in.   *an everlasting (biblical)*
No, no, my lord, your grace is perjured much,
Full of dear° guiltiness, and therefore this: *grievous; precious*
If for my love—as there is no such cause[8]—
775   You will do aught,° this shall you do for me: *anything*
Your oath I will not trust, but go with speed
To some forlorn and naked hermitage
Remote from all the pleasures of the world.
There stay until the twelve celestial signs°   *(of the zodiac)*
780   Have brought about the annual reckoning.
If this austere, insociable life
Change not your offer made in heat of blood;
If frosts and fasts, hard lodging and thin weeds°   *clothes*
Nip not the gaudy blossoms of your love,
785   But that it bear this trial and last° love,   *remain*
Then at the expiration of the year
Come challenge° me, challenge me by these deserts,   *claim*
And, by this virgin palm now kissing thine,
I will be thine, and till that instance° shut   *instant*
790   My woeful self up in a mourning house,
Raining the tears of lamentation
For the remembrance of my father's death.
If this thou do deny, let our hands part,
Neither entitled in the other's heart.
795   KING   If this, or more than this, I would deny,
To flatter up° these powers of mine with rest   *pamper*
The sudden hand of death close up mine eye.
Hence, hermit,° then. My heart is in thy breast.[9]   *I'm off to be a hermit*
     [*They talk apart*]
798.1   BIRON   *And what to me, my love? And what to me?*
ROSALINE   *You must be purgèd, too. Your sins are rank.*
     You are attaint° with faults and perjury.   *dishonored; infected*
     Therefore if you my favour mean to get
798.5   *A twelvemonth shall you spend, and never rest*
     But seek the weary beds of people sick.

---

7. Wool stuffing for clothes; inflated rhetoric.   9. The following six indented lines (798.1–798.6) rep-
8. No reason why you should feel obliged to do so.   resent a draft version of 5.2.814–31.

DUMAINE [*to* CATHERINE]   But what to me, my love? But what
       to me?
800   A wife?
CATHERINE   A beard,[1] fair health, and honesty.
       With three-fold love I wish you all these three.
DUMAINE   O, shall I say 'I thank you, gentle wife'?
CATHERINE   Not so, my lord. A twelvemonth and a day
805   I'll mark no words that smooth-faced wooers say.
       Come when the King doth to my lady come;
       Then if I have much love, I'll give you some.
DUMAINE   I'll serve thee true and faithfully till then.
CATHERINE   Yet swear not, lest ye be forsworn again.
       [*They talk apart*]
LONGUEVILLE   What says Maria?
810 MARIA   At the twelvemonth's end
       I'll change my black gown for a faithful friend.°   *lover*
LONGUEVILLE   I'll stay° with patience; but the time is long.   *wait*
MARIA   The liker you—few taller are so young.[2]
       [*They talk apart*]
BIRON [*to* ROSALINE]   Studies my lady?° Mistress, look on me.   *Are you preoccupied*
815   Behold the window of my heart, mine eye,
       What humble suit attends° thy answer there.   *waits for*
       Impose some service on me for thy love.
ROSALINE   Oft have I heard of you, my lord Biron,
       Before I saw you; and the world's large tongue
820   Proclaims you for a man replete with mocks,
       Full of comparisons° and wounding flouts,   *satirical similes*
       Which you on all estates° will execute   *classes of people*
       That lie within the mercy of your wit.
       To weed this wormwood° from your fruitful brain,   *bitterness*
825   And therewithal to win me if you please,
       Without the which I am not to be won,
       You shall this twelvemonth term from day to day
       Visit the speechless sick and still converse°   *always associate*
       With groaning wretches, and your task shall be
830   With all the fierce° endeavour of your wit   *forceful*
       To enforce the painèd impotent° to smile.   *sick*
BIRON   To move wild laughter in the throat of death?—
       It cannot be, it is impossible.
       Mirth cannot move a soul in agony.
835 ROSALINE   Why, that's the way to choke a gibing spirit,
       Whose influence is begot of that loose grace°   *uncritical acceptance*
       Which shallow laughing hearers give to fools.
       A jest's prosperity lies in the ear
       Of him that hears it, never in the tongue
840   Of him that makes it. Then if sickly ears,
       Deafed with the clamours of their own dear groans,
       Will hear your idle scorns, continue then,
       And I will have you and that fault withal.°   *as well*
       But if they will not, throw away that spirit,
845   And I shall find you empty of that fault,
       Right joyful of your reformation.

---

1. Implying that he looks immature; perhaps also that
as a hermit he'll grow a beard.

2. The more like you—although tall ("long"), you are
still young.

BIRON   A twelvemonth? Well, befall what will befall,
I'll jest a twelvemonth in an hospital.
QUEEN [*to the* KING]   Ay, sweet my lord, and so I take my leave.
850 KING   No, madam, we will bring° you on your way.   *escort*
BIRON   Our wooing doth not end like an old play.
Jack hath not Jill. These ladies' courtesy
Might well have made our sport a comedy.
KING   Come, sir, it wants° a twelvemonth an' a day,   *lacks*
And then 'twill end.
855 BIRON   That's too long for a play.
        Enter [ARMADO *the*] *braggart*
ARMADO [*to the* KING]   Sweet majesty, vouchsafe me.
QUEEN   Was not that Hector?
DUMAINE   The worthy knight of Troy.
ARMADO   I will kiss thy royal finger and take leave.
860 I am a votary, I have vowed to Jaquenetta
To hold the plough° for her sweet love three year. But, most   *To farm (bawdy)*
esteemed greatness, will you hear the dialogue° that the two   *debate*
learned men³ have compiled in praise of the owl and the
cuckoo? It should have followed in the end of our show.
865 KING   Call them forth quickly, we will do so.
ARMADO   Holla, approach!
        Enter [HOLOFERNES, NATHANIEL, COSTARD, MOTE, DULL,
        JAQUENETTA, *and others*]
                      This side is Hiems, winter,
This Ver, the spring, the one maintained° by the owl,   *supported*
The other by the cuckoo. Ver, begin.
SPRING [*sings*]
                When daisies pied° and violets blue,⁴   *multicolored*
870   And lady-smocks,° all silver-white,   *cuckoo flowers*
           And cuckoo-buds° of yellow hue   *buttercups?*
                Do paint the meadows with delight,
           The cuckoo then on every tree
           Mocks married men, for thus sings he:
875   Cuckoo!
           Cuckoo, cuckoo—O word of fear,⁵
           Unpleasing to a married ear.
           When shepherds pipe on oaten straws,
                And merry larks are ploughmen's clocks;
880   When turtles tread,° and rooks and daws,   *turtledoves mate*
                And maidens bleach their summer smocks,
           The cuckoo then on every tree
           Mocks married men, for thus sings he:
                Cuckoo!
885   Cuckoo, cuckoo—O word of fear,
           Unpleasing to a married ear.
WINTER [*sings*]
                When icicles hang by the wall,
                And Dick the shepherd blows his nail,⁶
           And Tom bears logs into the hall,
890   And milk comes frozen home in pail;
           When blood is nipped,° and ways° be foul,   *chilled / pathways*

---

3. Holofernes and Nathaniel(?)
4. The dialogue is in iambic tetrameter, a song meter.
5. Because it sounds like "cuckold."
6. Blows on his hands to keep warm; is idle.

Then nightly sings the staring owl:
Tu-whit, tu-whoo!⁷—a merry note,
While greasy Joan doth keel° the pot.   *stir to cool*
895   When all aloud the wind doth blow,
And coughing drowns the parson's saw,°   *moralizing*
And birds sit brooding in the snow,
And Marian's nose looks red and raw;
When roasted crabs° hiss in the bowl,°   *crab apples / (of ale)*
900   Then nightly sings the staring owl:
Tu-whit, tu-whoo!—a merry note,
While greasy Joan doth keel the pot.
ARMADO   The words of Mercury are harsh after the songs of
Apollo.⁸ You that way, we this way.⁹   *Exeunt [severally]°*   *separately*

---

7. Perhaps: to it (a hunting cry, with possible sexual overtones), to woo.
8. Presumably the love poetry of the King and courtiers. *words of Mercury*: probably referring to Mercadé's somber message. (See note to the stage direction following line 698.)

9. This line may distinguish the audience ("you") from the actors ("we"), the aristocratic from the humbler characters, the French ladies from the inhabitants of Navarre, or even the actor playing Spring from the one playing Winter.

Love's Labour's Won

In 1598, Francis Meres called as witnesses to Shakespeare's excellence in comedy 'his *Gẽtlemẽ of Verona*, his *Errors*, his *Loue labors lost*, his *Loue labours wonne*, his *Midsummers night dreame*, & his *Merchant of Venice*'. This was the only evidence that Shakespeare wrote a play called *Love's Labour's Won* until the discovery in 1953 of a fragment of a bookseller's list that had been used in the binding of a volume published in 1637/8. The fragment itself appears to record items sold from 9 to 17 August 1603 by a book dealer in the south of England. Among items headed '[inte]rludes & tragedyes' are

> marchant of vennis
> taming of a shrew
> knak to know a knave
> knak to know an honest man
> loves labor lost
> loves labor won

No author is named for any of the items. All the plays named in the list except *Love's Labour's Won* are known to have been printed by 1600; all were written by 1596–97. Taken together, Meres's reference in 1598 and the 1603 fragment appear to demonstrate that a play by Shakespeare called *Love's Labour's Won* had been performed by the time Meres wrote and was in print by August 1603. Conceivably the phrase served as an alternative title for one of Shakespeare's other comedies, though the only one believed to have been written by 1598 but not listed by Meres is *The Taming of the Shrew*, which is named (as *The Taming of a Shrew*) in the bookseller's fragment. Otherwise we must suppose that *Love's Labour's Won* is the title of a lost play by Shakespeare, that no copy of the edition mentioned in the bookseller's list is extant, and that Heminges and Condell failed to include it in the 1623 Folio.

None of these suppositions is implausible. We know of at least one other lost play attributed to Shakespeare (see *Cardenio*, below), and of many lost works by contemporary playwrights. No copy of the first edition of *Titus Andronicus* was known until 1904; for *I Henry IV* and *The Passionate Pilgrim* only a fragment of the first edition survives. And we now know that *Troilus and Cressida* was almost omitted from the 1623 Folio (probably for copyright reasons) despite its evident authenticity. It is also possible that, like most of the early editions of Shakespeare's plays, the lost edition of *Love's Labour's Won* did not name him on the title-page, and this omission might go some way to explaining the failure of the edition to survive, or (if it does still survive) to be noticed. *Love's Labour's Won* stands a much better chance of having survived, somewhere, than *Cardenio*: because it was printed, between 500 and 1,500 copies were once in circulation, whereas for *Cardenio* we know of only a single manuscript.

The evidence for the existence of the lost play (unlike that for *Cardenio*) gives us little indication of its content. Meres explicitly states, and the title implies, that it was a comedy. Its titular pairing with *Love's Labour's Lost* suggests that they may have been written at about the same time. Both Meres and the bookseller's catalogue place it after *Love's Labour's Lost*; although neither list is necessarily chronological, Meres's does otherwise agree with our own view of the order of composition of Shakespeare's comedies.

THE OXFORD EDITORS

A Midsummer Night's Dream

Imagine an aristocratic wedding in a grand English country house. Imagine that after the solemnities and the wedding supper, the newlyweds and their distinguished guests—including the most distinguished guest of all, Queen Elizabeth I—are treated to a private entertainment, a play written especially for them. Imagine that the play is Shakespeare's *A Midsummer Night's Dream*, a comedy that culminates not only in three marriages but in a play, *Pyramus and Thisbe*, performed for the newlyweds with delicious incompetence by well-meaning, hopelessly bumbling artisans. Their inept performance amuses the happy couples and helps to "wear away this long age of three hours," as the amorously impatient Duke Theseus puts it, "between our after-supper and bedtime" (5.1.33–34). At the end of the play within the play, the stage brides and grooms exit to consummate their marriages—"Sweet friends, to bed"—and so, too, amid the blessings and sly jokes of their guests, the real newlyweds retire to bed.

Scholars have told and retold this story of the aristocratic wedding for which Shakespeare wrote his most enchanting comedy until it has come to seem like an established truth, one of the few things we actually know about the composition of the plays. But while the story is both charming and plausible, there is not a shred of actual evidence that *A Midsummer Night's Dream* was ever performed at, let alone written expressly for, such a wedding. What we do know is that this play was performed on the London stage: the title page of the First Quarto says that it "hath been sundry times publikely acted" by the Lord Chamberlain's Men and that it was written by William Shakespeare.

The precise date that *A Midsummer Night's Dream* was written and first performed is unknown; the Elizabethan writer Francis Meres mentions it admiringly in 1598, and certain of its stylistic features have led many scholars to place it around 1594–96, the probable period of the comparably lyrical *Romeo and Juliet* and *Richard II*. Attempts to find more precise coordinates by locating an allusion to a particular Royal Progress in Oberon's lines about the "fair vestal thronèd by the west" (2.1.158) or to a particular wet season in Titania's lines about the miserable weather (2.1.88ff.) have been defeated by the frequency of both Queen Elizabeth's travels and English rainstorms.

What accounts, then, for all the speculation about the wedding ceremony, complete with royal attendance? In part, the answer lies in the comedy's thematic focus on love consummated in marriage. The final ritual blessing of the bride beds—the fairies' version of a traditional Catholic practice deemed superstitious by zealous Protestants—can be seen as the culmination of the elaborate festivities, including song, music, dancing, and plays, that often accompanied upper-class Elizabethan marriages. In part, imagining a specific historical occasion helps to highlight an uncertainty, at once pleasurable and disturbing, about the borderline between reality and illusion: as in a hall of mirrors, the real-life newlyweds whiling away the hours before bedtime by watching a play would see onstage other newlyweds whiling away the hours before bedtime by watching a play.

But, as four centuries of readers and playgoers have found, you do not need to see *A Midsummer Night's Dream* on your wedding day, nor do you need to be an aristocrat, to savor its delights. There have, to be sure, been a few dissenters: the diarist Samuel Pepys wrote after seeing a production in 1662 that "it is the most insipid ridiculous play that ever I saw in my life," although he took note of "some good dancing and some handsome women." Most audiences have been vastly more enthusiastic. The play has inspired a succession of musical adaptations and settings, along with famously lavish productions. By the nineteenth century, Shakespeare's bare stage had given way to

Cupid and his victims. From Gilles Corrozet, *Hecatomgraphie* (1540).

gorgeous sets, with twinkling lights, fairies rising on midnight mushrooms, the moon shining over the Acropolis, and live rabbits hopping across carpets of flowers. Film is, of course, well suited to such fantasies, as a series of famous motion pictures have shown, but *A Midsummer Night's Dream* has proved equally at home in the simplest of settings. Generations of schoolchildren have romped through cardboard forests, while in Peter Brook's influential 1970 production for the Royal Shakespeare Company the actors performed (often on trapeze) in a three-sided, brightly lit, bare white box.

Working its magic on the imagination, Shakespeare's visionary poetic drama appeals to an unusually broad spectrum of spectators. The play may induce fantasies of aristocratic or private pleasure, but it does so with the resources of the public stage. If it mocks working-class artisans (skilled craftsmen who are simply called "the rabble" in one quarto stage direction), it also laughs at well-born young lovers. Its language reflects an unusually high incidence of the tropes familiar to those who had received rhetorical and literary training, but you do not have to learn the Greek names for these tropes—*anaphora, isocolon, epizeuxis,* and the like—to enjoy their effects. Take, for example, the exchange between Lysander and Hermia in the wake of Egeus's attempt to block their betrothal:

> LYSANDER   The course of true love never did run smooth,
>   But either it was different in blood—
> HERMIA   O cross!—too high to be enthralled to low.
> LYSANDER   Or else misgrafted in respect of years—
> HERMIA   O spite!—too old to be engaged to young.
> LYSANDER   Or merit stood upon the choice of friends—
> HERMIA   O hell!—to choose love by another's eyes.
>   (1.1.134–40)

The alternation of single lines, called *stichomythia,* is a scheme that Shakespeare borrowed from the Roman playwright Seneca and used in different ways in many of his plays. The effect here is to convey the lovers' mutual anguish, tinging it slightly perhaps with a gently ironic distance that evaporates in the poignant lament that follows (lines 141–49). The rhetorical devices, along with the subtle modulations from blank verse to rhymed couplets to boisterous comic prose, are so deftly handled that their pleasures are accessible to the learned and unlearned alike. This breadth also reflects the very wide range of cultural materials that the playwright has cunningly woven together, from the classical heritage of the educated elite to popular ballads and folk customs, from refined and sophisticated entertainments to the coarser delights of farce.

The exquisite lyricism of much of the play, the celebration of aristocratic pastimes such as the hunt, and a vision of courtly glamour conjure up an upper-class milieu. There is no single literary source for Shakespeare's depiction of this world, or indeed for the play as a whole, but he is indebted for the legendary Theseus and Hippolyta to Thomas North's translation (1579) of Plutarch's *Lives of the Noble Grecians and Romanes,* and still more to Chaucer's *Knight's Tale.* The *Dream* repeatedly echoes Chaucer's references to observing "the rite of May," a folk custom still current in Elizabethan England and quite possibly known to Shakespeare personally. To the dismay of Puritans, who regarded the celebration as a lascivious remnant of paganism, young men and women of all classes would go out into the woods and fields to welcome the

Pyramus and Thisbe. From George Wither, *A Collection of Emblemes* (1635).

May with singing and dancing. Shakespeare's title associates this custom with another occasion for festive release: Midsummer Eve (June 23), when the solstice was marked not only by holiday license but by tales of fairy spells and temporary madness.

Some Elizabethan aristocrats kept theatrical troupes as liveried servants, along with young pages who could sing and perform, and powerful magnates, both secular and religious, often had plays, masquerades, and elaborate shows staged in their houses. From this milieu, Shakespeare derives a vision of what we can call the revels of power, performances designed to entertain, gratify, and reflect the values of those at the top. From this milieu too Shakespeare absorbs a sense of social hierarchy: a distinction between Duke Theseus, at once imperious and genteel, and Egeus, wealthy but distinctly lower in rank and harping on what is his by law, along with a more marked distinction between these characters and the artisans, loyal members of the lower orders, regarded by their social superiors with condescending indulgence.

The artisans—or "rude mechanicals," as they are called—enable Shakespeare to introduce wonderful swoops into earthy prose, snatches of jigs, a comical taste for the grotesque, a glimpse of a world that usually resides beyond the horizon of courtly vision. The lovers at the pinnacle of the play's society do not know the names and trades of the "hard-handed men that work in Athens here" (5.1.72) who have come to offer them entertainment, but we the audience do, and we even know something of their hopes and dreams. As with the Pageant of the Nine Worthies in *Love's Labour's Lost,* we are invited at once to join in the mockery of the inept performers and to distance ourselves from the mockers. That is, the audience of *A Midsummer Night's Dream* is not simply mirrored in the play's upper classes: the real audience is given a broader perspective, a more capacious understanding than anyone onstage.

This understanding is signaled not only in our ability to take in both the courtly and popular dimensions of the play, but also in our ability to see what escapes both aristocrats and artisans: the world of the fairies. But what are the fairies? From what social milieu do they spring? It is tempting to reply that they are denizens of the country—that is, characters drawn from the semipagan folklore of rural England. This is at least partially true: Reginald Scot, who wrote a brilliant attack on witchcraft persecutions (*The Discoverie of Witchcraft*, 1584), suggests that Robin Goodfellow, the mischievous spirit also called a Puck, was once feared by villagers, but was now widely recognized to be a figure of mere "illusion and knaverie." Yet intensive scholarly research over several generations has suggested that Shakespeare's fairies are quite unlike those his audience might have credited, half-credited, or—as Scot hoped—discredited.

The fairies of Elizabethan popular belief were often threatening and dangerous, while those of *A Midsummer Night's Dream* are generally benevolent. The former steal human infants, perhaps to sacrifice them to the devil, while the latter, even when they quarrel over the possession of a young boy, do so to bestow love and favor upon him; the former leave deformed, emaciated children in place of those they have stolen, while the latter trip nimbly through the palace blessing the bride beds and warding off deformities. Shakespeare's fairies have some of the menacing associations of "real" fairies—Puck speaks of shrouds and gaping graves, while the quarrel between Oberon and Titania has disrupted the seasons and damaged the crops, as wicked spirits were said to do. But the fairies we see are, as Oberon says, "spirits of another sort." Oberon and Titania (whose names Shakespeare took from the French romance *Huon of Bordeaux* and from Ovid, respectively) repeatedly demonstrate their good will toward mortals, though they have very little good will toward each other. The fairy king and queen are distressed at the unintended consequences of their quarrel, and each is involved, with romantic generosity, in the happiness of Theseus and Hippolyta. This generosity extends beyond the immediate range of their interests: in the midst of plotting to humiliate Titania, Oberon attempts to intervene on behalf of the spurned Helena, and though this intervention proves, through Puck's mistake, to lead to hopeless confusion, the fairies make amends.

Indeed, if Puck takes mischievous delight in the discord he has helped to sow among the four young lovers—"Lord, what fools these mortals be!" (3.2.115)—he is not the originator of that discord, and he is the indispensable agent for setting things right. In his role as both mischief-maker and matchmaker, Puck resembles the crafty slave in comedies by the Latin playwrights Plautus and Terence, a stock character who sometimes seems to enjoy and contribute to the plot's tangles but who manages in the end to remove the obstacles that stand in the way of the young lovers.

This resemblance brings us to yet another of the cultural elements that Shakespeare cunningly interweaves in the plot of *A Midsummer Night's Dream*. From the classical literary tradition, which he must have first encountered in grammar school, Shakespeare derives the ancient Greek setting, the story of Pyramus and Thisbe as told in Ovid's *Metamorphoses*, the comic transformation of a man into an ass as told in Apuleius's *Golden Ass*, and, above all, the basic plot device of young lovers contriving to escape the rigid will of a stern father. This device was one of the staples of the New Comedy of ancient Greece and was a mainstay as well in Roman comedy. The literary convention corresponds to certain aspects of actual life in Shakespeare's England, where lawsuits provide records of parents trying to compel children to marry against their will. But the historical problem of marital consent has a complex relation to its artistic representation. Not only does the play exaggerate the actual punitive power of the father—Egeus threatens his disobedient daughter with death (to which Theseus offers, as a grim alternative, the nunnery)—but it also exaggerates the release from this power by staging the giddy possibility of a marriage based entirely on love and desire rather than parental will.

In *A Midsummer Night's Dream*, this release, a highly implausible dream for any Elizabethan member of the middle or upper classes, is brought about by a further plot device: the escape from the court or city to the "green world" of the forest. This the-atrical structure is not characteristic of the New Comedy, but it somewhat resembles the Saturnalian rhythms of the Old Comedy of Aristophanes, with its festive release from the discipline and sobriety of everyday life, and, still more perhaps, it reflects cer-tain English folk customs, such as Maying. When Theseus comes upon the four exhausted lovers asleep in the woods, he thinks that "they rose up early to observe / The rite of May" (4.1.129–30).

But, of course, Theseus is wrong. The lovers were not out a-Maying, but had spent the night stumbling through the woods in a confused state of fear, anger, and desire. When it enters the charmed, moonlit space of *A Midsummer Night's Dream*, "the rite of May," along with the other rituals and representations Shakespeare stitched together in creating his play, is transformed; to use Peter Quince's term for the metamorphosed Bottom, the rites and rituals are "translated." Folk customs, the revels of power, the classical tradition as taught in schools, all are displaced from their points of origin, their enabling institutions and assumptions, and brought into a new space, the space of the Shakespearean stage.

This "translation" has, in every case, the odd effect of simultaneous elevation and enervation, celebration and parody. Thus the minor Ovidian tale of Pyramus and Thisbe is greatly elaborated but also travestied; the popular realm is at once lovingly repre-sented and mercilessly ridiculed; the revels of power are reproduced but also ironically distanced.

Some of the play's most wonderful moments spring from the zany conjunction of distinct and even opposed theatrical modes (a conjunction characteristically parodied in the oxymoronic title of the artisans' play, "A tedious brief scene of young Pyramus / And his love Thisbe: very tragical mirth" [5.1.56–57]). Thus, for example, exquisite love poetry and low comedy meet in the wonderful moment in which the queen of fairies awakens to become enraptured at the sight of the most flatulently absurd of the mechanicals, Bottom. Bottom has been transformed with perfect appropriateness into an ass, yet it is he who is granted the play's most exquisite vision of delight and who articulates, in a comically confused burlesque of St. Paul (1 Corinthians 2:9), the deep-est sense of wonder: "The eye of man hath not heard, the ear of man hath not seen, man's hand is not able to taste, his tongue to conceive, nor his heart to report what my dream was" (4.1.204–07).

It would be asinine, the play suggests, to try to expound this dream, but we can at least suggest that, whatever its meaning, its existence is closely linked to the nature of

A fairy hill. From Olaus Magnus, *Historia de Gentibus Septentrionalibus* (1555).

the theater itself. Puck suggests as much when he proposes in the Epilogue that the audience imagine that it has all along been slumbering: the play it has seen has been a collective hallucination. The play, then, is a dream about watching a play about dreams. Fittingly, the comedy devotes much of its last act to a parody of a theatrical performance, as if its most enduring concern were not the fate of the lovers but the possibility of performing plays. The entire last act of *A Midsummer Night's Dream* is unnecessary in terms of the plot: by Oberon's intervention and Theseus's fiat, the plot complications have all been resolved at the end of Act 4. Knots that had seemed almost impossible to untangle—Theseus had declared in Act 1 that he was powerless to overturn the ancient privilege of Athens invoked by Egeus—suddenly dissolve. The absurdly easy resolution of an apparently hopeless dilemma characterizes not only the lovers' legal but also their emotional condition, a blend of mad confusion and geometric logic that is settled, apparently permanently, with the aid of the fairies' magical love juice.

But this diagrammatic settling of affairs sits uncomfortably with all that the lovers have experienced in the woods. Both critics and directors have given different weight to this experience. Some treat the lovers as mindless comic puppets, jerked by the playwright's invisible strings, while others take more seriously the darkness that shadows their words and actions. This darkness includes emotional violence and masochism, the betrayal of friendship, the radical fickleness of desire. It extends to the play's sexual politics. Under the strain of the night's adventures, the friendship between Hermia and Helena begins to crack apart, while Lysander and Demetrius become bitter rivals. Although they are eventually reconciled, it is as if the heterosexual couplings can only be formed by painfully sundering the intimate same-sex bonds that preceded them. Shakespeare had begun to reflect on this problem as early as *The Two Gentlemen of Verona,* possibly his first play, and throughout his career he returned to it repeatedly, including in what is possibly his last play, *The Two Noble Kinsmen.* For the most part, the broken friendships are repaired, but, as with Antonio and Sebastian in *Twelfth Night* and Leontes and Polixenes in *The Winter's Tale,* there is usually a lingering sense of loss, from which even the sunnier *Midsummer Night's Dream* is not completely exempt.

In another very early play, *The Taming of the Shrew,* Shakespeare had also begun his lifelong reflection on the struggle between men and women, a struggle frequently focused on the male desire to dominate and subdue the female. In *A Midsummer Night's Dream,* tension flares in the case of the fairies into open conflict over the Indian boy, the locus of Oberon's assertion of patriarchal power and Titania's claim to independence. In the human world of the play, this tension is less immediately apparent, but in the first scene Theseus alludes to his military conquest of the Amazon queen Hippolyta, and there are other brief glimpses of cruelty, indifference, and rage. Those who see *A Midsummer Night's Dream* as lighthearted entertainment must somehow laugh off this darkness; those who wish to emphasize the play's more troubling and discordant notes must somehow neutralize the comic register in which such notes are sounded. For example, the brutal insults hurled at Hermia by the young man who had loved her and with whom she has eloped might well seem extremely painful, but the fantastic language in which these insults are expressed—

> Get you gone, you dwarf,
> You *minimus* of hind'ring knot-grass made,
> You bead, you acorn
>
> (3.2.329–31)

—distances audiences from the pain and generates laughter.

Audiences for most productions tend to oscillate between engagement and detachment. In the young lovers' choices and sufferings, we encounter a situation where the final outcome doesn't matter greatly to us but matters greatly to them. And while we see the characters from a distance—although Hermia and Helena are distinct enough, even attentive readers occasionally find it difficult to remember which is Lysander and which Demetrius—we also experience at least glancingly *their* sense of how important the difference is, how unbearable to be matched against one's consent, how painfully difficult to make a match that corresponds to one's desires.

Desires in *A Midsummer Night's Dream* are intense, irrational, and alarmingly mobile. This mobility, the speed with which desire can be detached from one object and attached to a different object, does not diminish the exigency of the passion, for the lovers are convinced at every moment that their choices are irrefutably rational and irresistibly compelling. But there is no security in these choices, and the play is repeatedly haunted by a fear of abandonment. The emblem, as well as agent, of a dangerously mobile desire is the fairies' love juice. No human being in the play experiences a purely abstract, objectless desire; when you desire, you desire *someone*. But the love juice is the distilled essence of erotic mobility itself, and it is appropriately in the power of the fairies. For the fairies seem to embody the principle of what we might call polytropic desire—that is, desire that can instantaneously alight on any object, including an ass-headed man, and that can with equal instantaneousness swerve away from that object and on to another. Oberon and Titania have, we learn, long histories of amorous adventures; they are aware of each other's wayward passions; and, endowed with an extraordinary, eroticizing rhetoric, they move endlessly through the spiced, moonlit night.

If there is a link between the fairies and the erotic, there is a still more powerful link between the fairies and the imagination. Theseus makes the connection explicit when he rejects the stories that the lovers have told him: "I never may believe / These antique fables, nor these fairy toys." In a famous speech (5.1.2–22), he accounts for such fables and toys as products of the imagination. The speech reflects Theseus's misplaced confidence in his own sense of waking reality, a reality that does not include fairies. Yet paradoxically, in dismissively categorizing the lunatic, the lover, and the poet as "of imagination all compact," he manages to articulate insights that the play seems to uphold. Those in the grip of a powerful imagination may be loosed from the moorings of reason and nature, and they may inhabit a world of wish fulfillment and its converse, nightmare. But the poet whose imagination "bodies forth / The forms of things unknown" (5.1.14–15) has created *A Midsummer Night's Dream*, giving his fantasies— including the fantasy called "Theseus"—"a local habitation and a name." Finally, it is the imagination that enables giddy, restless, changeable mortals to attach their desires to a particular person.

For Theseus, the imagination is the agent of delusion—and there is much in the play that would seem to support this conclusion. But his account is not complete without Hippolyta's insistence that the story the four young lovers tell seems to have something that goes beyond delusion. Their minds, she observes, have been "transfigured" together, and this shared transfiguration bears witness to "something of great constancy; / But howsoever, strange and admirable" (5.1.26–27). It is as if we were all to wake up one morning and discover we had had the same dream.

And, of course, *we* in the audience have, as Puck's epilogue suggests, had just this experience: the experience of the theater. In the theater, we confront a living representation of the complex relation between transfiguration and delusion, a relation explored with fantastic, anxious literalness in the artisans' performance of *Pyramus and Thisbe*. In reassuring the ladies that the lion is only Snug the Joiner, that nothing is what it claims to be, the players simultaneously burlesque the stage and call attention to the basic elements from which any performance is made: rudimentary scenery, artisans, language, imagination, desire.

There is precious little evidence, to be sure, of either imagination or desire in the artisans' performance of *Pyramus and Thisbe*. Their absence is part of the comical awfulness of the play within the play, the reason in effect that it does not become the Shakespearean tragedy it so strikingly resembles, *Romeo and Juliet*. And yet, as Theseus says, "The best in this kind are but shadows, and the worst are no worse if imagination amend them." "It must be your imagination, then," Hippolyta points out, "and not theirs" (5.1.208–10). But that is true of performances far greater than that of which the artisans are capable. If we are to see fairies onstage in *A Midsummer Night's Dream*, and not simply flesh-and-blood actors (probably boy actors in Shakespeare's theater), it must be our imagination that makes amends. So too if we are to believe in the lovers' desire and sympathize with their predicament, it must be *our* desire that animates their words.

Such, at least, is the vision of the theater suggested by the play that Bottom and company offer to the newlyweds. There is nothing really out there, their performance implies, except what the audience graciously consents to dream. Yet in the closing moments of the play, when the fairies emerge from the woods and venture into Theseus's mansion to bless the bride beds, a quite different vision of theater is suggested, one in which the dreams and desires that we have are determined by forces over which we have no control, forces that only a playwright's love juice can make visible under an imaginary moon.

Stephen Greenblatt

TEXTUAL NOTE

A Midsummer Night's Dream was entered in the Stationers' Register on October 8, 1600, and printed that same year in quarto:

> A Midsommer nights dreame. As it hath beene sundry times pub*lickely acted, by the Right honourable,* the Lord Chamberlaine his *seruants. Written by William Shakespeare.* Imprinted at London, for *Thomas Fisher,* and are to be soulde at his shoppe, at the Signe of the White Hart, in *Fleetestreete.* 1600.

This quarto (Q1) was evidently prepared from a manuscript in Shakespeare's hand. A second quarto (Q2), printed in 1619 (though falsely dated 1600), corrects some errors in Q1, but it also introduces new errors. This second quarto was used as the basis for the 1623 First Folio text of the play (F), though the Folio editors also had recourse to a theatrical manuscript, probably a promptbook in the possession of Shakespeare's company, the King's Men. Evidence for this manuscript includes a Folio stage direction before 5.1.126: "Tawyer with a Trumpet before them." "Tawyer" presumably refers to William Tawyer, a musician employed by the King's Men.

From this theatrical manuscript evidently derived several alterations in stage directions and in speech prefixes, the most notable of which is the substitution in Act 5 of Egeus for Philostrate as the master of ceremonies. The substitution may simply be a mistake: in an early performance, the same actor may have played the parts of both Egeus and Philostrate, and this doubling may have led to an error in the speech prefix. But it is also possible that the play was revised in order to integrate the disgruntled Egeus more fully into the festive conclusion.

Act and scene divisions all derive from F; there are none in the quarto text. Traditionally, Act 3, Scene 2 continues to the end of the act, but since the stage is apparently cleared at 3.2.413, this edition marks a break (perhaps indicating a gap in time and place) by dividing the scene in two and designating a third scene. In F, at the end of Act 3 there is a stage direction, "They sleepe all the Act," which indicates that the four lovers remain asleep onstage during the interval customary between acts and that the action that resumes in the next act is understood to be continuous.

On the basis of mislined verses in 5.1.1–84, scholars have conjectured that Shakespeare may have revised Theseus's speech as originally conceived and added lines in the margin of his copy. Since these revisions may give us a glimpse of Shakespeare's process of composition, this book appends a reconstruction of what would have been the original speech.

The control text for this edition of *A Midsummer Night's Dream* is Q1 (1600). But in keeping with the Oxford editors' principle of basing their text on the most theatrical early version of each play—that is, the version closest to the play as performed by Shakespeare's company during the playwright's own lifetime—changes in speech prefixes and other substantive variants have been adopted from F.

SELECTED BIBLIOGRAPHY

Barber, C. L. "May Games and Metamorphoses on a Midsummer's Night." *Shakespeare's Festive Comedy: A Study of Dramatic Form and Its Relation to Social Custom*. Princeton: Princeton University Press, 1959. 119–62. *A Midsummer Night's Dream* combines folk customs, Ovidian fancy, and Elizabethan pageantry to produce a clarifying release of imagination.

Bate, Jonathan. *Shakespeare and Ovid*. New York: Oxford University Press, 1993. *A Midsummer Night's Dream* indirectly dramatizes Ovid, gathering themes of myth, metamorphosis, and love into a mixed mode typical of sixteenth-century mythography.

Briggs, K. M. *The Anatomy of Puck: An Examination of Fairy Beliefs Among Shakespeare's Contemporaries and Successors*. London: Routledge and Kegan Paul, 1959. A survey of early modern notions about fairies, especially in English literary tradition, describing also the influence of Shakespeare's innovations.

Dash, Irene G. *Women's Worlds in Shakespeare's Plays*. London: Associated University Presses, 1997. Looks at *A Midsummer Night's Dream* in performance, arguing that traditional staging practices have tended reductively to simplify Shakespeare's women.

Girard, René. "Myth and Ritual in Shakespeare: *A Midsummer Night's Dream*." *Textual Strategies: Perspectives in Post-Structuralist Criticism*. Ed. Josué V. Harari. Ithaca, N.Y.: Cornell University Press, 1979. 189–212. This play presents a genetic theory of myth, charting a collective mental transformation.

Loomba, Ania. "The Great Indian Vanishing Trick—Colonialism, Property, and the Family in *A Midsummer Night's Dream*." *A Feminist Companion to Shakespeare*. Ed. Dympna Callaghan. Malden, Mass.: Blackwell, 2000. 163–87. Argues that the Indian boy represents the shaping dialectic between non-European practices and Western domestic ideology.

Montrose, Louis. *The Purpose of Playing: Shakespeare and the Cultural Politics of the Elizabethan Theatre*. Chicago: University of Chicago Press, 1996. Examines the play's relationship to Elizabethan ideology through discourses of gender, physiology, social rank, and royal iconography.

Traub, Valerie. *The Renaissance of Lesbianism in Early Modern England*. Cambridge: Cambridge University Press, 2002. Observes how renovated classical idioms and new scientific knowledge made female-female desire intelligible in the Renaissance.

Williams, Gary Jay. *Our Moonlight Revels: "A Midsummer Night's Dream" in the Theatre*. Iowa City: University of Iowa Press, 1997. The major stage, film, and opera adaptations, understood in relation to the cultures that produced them.

Young, David P. *Something of Great Constancy: The Art of "A Midsummer Night's Dream."* New Haven: Yale University Press, 1966. Extensive, variegated study covering sources, structure, performance, and contexts.

FILMS

A Midsummer Night's Dream. 1935. Dir. William Dieterle and Max Reinhardt. USA. 133 min. Sumptuous production, with balletic fairies, a serpentine Hippolyta, an elaborate Mendelssohn score, and Mickey Rooney as Puck.

A Midsummer Night's Dream. 1968. Dir. Peter Hall. UK. 124 min. Noted for its miniskirted sensuality, body paint, and extremely gnarled and muddy forest. With Diana Rigg and Helen Mirren.

A Midsummer Night's Dream. 1996. Dir. Adrian Noble. UK. 105 min. Theseus and Hippolyta double as Oberon and Titania, with a frame device of a boy dreaming the play. Starring Lindsay Duncan and Alex Jennings.

A Midsummer Night's Dream. 1999. Dir. Michael Hoffman. USA. 116 min. In Victorian costume against the Tuscan backdrop, this dreamy and erotic version amplifies Bottom's role. With Kevin Kline and Michelle Pfeiffer.

A Midsummer Night's Dream

THE PERSONS OF THE PLAY

THESEUS, Duke of Athens
HIPPOLYTA, Queen of the Amazons, betrothed to Theseus
PHILOSTRATE, Master of the Revels to Theseus
EGEUS, father of Hermia
HERMIA, daughter of Egeus, in love with Lysander
LYSANDER, loved by Hermia
DEMETRIUS, suitor to Hermia
HELENA, in love with Demetrius
OBERON, King of Fairies
TITANIA, Queen of Fairies
ROBIN GOODFELLOW, a puck
PEASEBLOSSOM ⎫
COBWEB ⎪
⎬ fairies
MOTE ⎪
MUSTARDSEED ⎭
Peter QUINCE, a carpenter
Nick BOTTOM, a weaver
Francis FLUTE, a bellows-mender
Tom SNOUT, a tinker
SNUG, a joiner
Robin STARVELING, a tailor
Attendant lords and fairies

1.1

Enter THESEUS, HIPPOLYTA, [*and* PHILOSTRATE,] *with others*

THESEUS   Now, fair Hippolyta, our nuptial hour
Draws on apace. Four happy days bring in
Another moon—but O, methinks how slow
This old moon wanes! She lingers° my desires   *delays fulfillment of*
5   Like to a stepdame° or a dowager   *stepmother*
Long withering out a young man's revenue.[1]
HIPPOLYTA   Four days will quickly steep° themselves in night,   *plunge*
Four nights will quickly dream away the time;
And then the moon, like to a silver bow
10   New bent in heaven, shall behold the night
Of our solemnities.
THESEUS   Go, Philostrate,
Stir up the Athenian youth to merriments.
Awake the pert and nimble spirit of mirth.
Turn melancholy forth to funerals—
15   The pale companion is not for our pomp. [*Exit* PHILOSTRATE]
Hippolyta, I wooed thee with my sword,
And won thy love doing thee injuries.[2]

1.1 Location: Theseus's palace in Athens.
1. *a dowager . . . revenue:* a widow using up the inheritance that will go to her husband's (young) heir on her
death.
2. Theseus captured Hippolyta in his military conquest
of the Amazons.

But I will wed thee in another key—
With pomp, with triumph,° and with revelling.   *public festivity*

Enter EGEUS[3] *and his daughter* HERMIA, *and* LYSANDER
and DEMETRIUS

20 EGEUS   Happy be Theseus, our renownèd Duke.

THESEUS   Thanks, good Egeus. What's the news with thee?

EGEUS   Full of vexation come I, with complaint
Against my child, my daughter Hermia.—
Stand forth Demetrius.—My noble lord,
25 This man hath my consent to marry her.—
Stand forth Lysander.—And, my gracious Duke,
This hath bewitched the bosom of my child.
Thou, thou, Lysander, thou hast given her rhymes,
And interchanged love tokens with my child.
30 Thou hast by moonlight at her window sung
With feigning[4] voice verses of feigning love,
And stol'n the impression of her fantasy[5]
With bracelets of thy hair, rings, gauds,° conceits,°   *trinkets / clever gifts*
Knacks,° trifles, nosegays,° sweetmeats—messengers   *Knickknacks / bouquets*
35 Of strong prevailment° in unhardened youth.   *persuasiveness*
With cunning hast thou filched my daughter's heart,
Turned her obedience which is due to me
To stubborn harshness. And, my gracious Duke,
Be it so° she will not here before your grace   *If*
40 Consent to marry with Demetrius,
I beg the ancient privilege of Athens:
As she is mine, I may dispose of her,
Which shall be either to this gentleman
Or to her death, according to our law
45 Immediately° provided in that case.   *Expressly*

THESEUS   What say you, Hermia? Be advised, fair maid.
To you your father should be as a god, — Simile
One that composed° your beauties, yea, and one   *fashioned*
To whom you are but as a form in wax,
50 By him imprinted,[6] and within his power
To leave° the figure or disfigure° it.   *maintain / destroy*
Demetrius is a worthy gentleman.

HERMIA   So is Lysander.

THESEUS   In himself he is,
But in this kind,° wanting your father's voice,[7]   *respect*
55 The other must be held the worthier.

HERMIA   I would my father looked but with my eyes.

THESEUS   Rather your eyes must with his judgement look.

HERMIA   I do entreat your grace to pardon me.
I know not by what power I am made bold,
60 Nor how it may concern° my modesty   *befit*
In such a presence here to plead my thoughts,
But I beseech your grace that I may know
The worst that may befall me in this case
If I refuse to wed Demetrius.

---

3. Pronounced "Ege-us," accented on the second syllable.
4. A triple pun: desiring; feigning; soft (in music).
5. *stol'n . . . fantasy:* by craftily impressing your image
on her imagination, like a seal in wax, you have stolen

her love.
6. *you are . . . imprinted:* you are a wax impression of
his seal.
7. Lacking your father's consent or vote.

65	THESEUS Either to die the death,° or to abjure	*be executed*
	For ever the society of men.	
	Therefore, fair Hermia, question your desires.	
	Know° of your youth, examine well your blood,°	*Inquire / passions*
	Whether, if you yield not to your father's choice,	
70	You can endure the livery° of a nun,[8]	*habit*
	For aye° to be in shady cloister mewed,°	*ever / caged in*
	To live a barren sister all your life,	
	Chanting faint hymns to the cold fruitless moon.[9]	
	Thrice blessèd they that master so their blood	
75	To undergo such maiden pilgrimage;°	*life as a virgin*
	But earthlier happy is the rose distilled[1]	
	Than that which, withering on the virgin thorn,	
	Grows, lives, and dies in single blessedness.°	*celibate*
	HERMIA So will I grow, so live, so die, my lord,	
80	Ere I will yield my virgin patent[2] up	
	Unto his lordship whose unwishèd yoke	
	My soul consents not to give sovereignty.	
	THESEUS Take time to pause, and by the next new moon—	
	The sealing day betwixt my love and me	
85	For everlasting bond of fellowship—	
	Upon that day either prepare to die	
	For disobedience to your father's will,	
	Or else to wed Demetrius, as he would,	
	Or on Diana's altar to protest°	*vow*
90	For aye austerity and single life.	
	DEMETRIUS Relent, sweet Hermia; and, Lysander, yield	
	Thy crazèd title° to my certain right.	*unsound claim*
	LYSANDER You have her father's love, Demetrius;	
	Let me have Hermia's. Do you marry him.	
95	EGEUS Scornful Lysander! True, he hath my love;	
	And what is mine my love shall render him,	
	And she is mine, and all my right of her	
	I do estate° unto Demetrius.	*settle; bestow*
	LYSANDER [*to* THESEUS] I am, my lord, as well derived° as he,	*descended*
100	As well possessed.° My love is more than his,	*endowed with wealth*
	My fortunes every way as fairly ranked,	
	If not with vantage,° as Demetrius;	*superiority*
	And—which is more than all these boasts can be—	
	I am beloved of beauteous Hermia.	
105	Why should not I then prosecute° my right?	*pursue*
	Demetrius—I'll avouch it to his head°—	*face*
	Made love to Nedar's daughter, Helena,	
	And won her soul, and she, sweet lady, dotes,	
	Devoutly dotes, dotes in idolatry	
110	Upon this spotted and inconstant[3] man.	
	THESEUS I must confess that I have heard so much,	
	And with Demetrius thought to have spoke thereof;	
	But, being over-full of self affairs,°	*my own concerns*
	My mind did lose it. But, Demetrius, come;	
115	And come, Egeus. You shall go with me.	

[handwritten annotation: —metaphor]

8. Orders of nuns were established in the Christian Middle Ages, but Elizabethans used the term as well for women devoted to a religious life in classical antiquity.
9. The emblem of Diana, goddess of chastity.

1. Made use of (roses were distilled to make perfumes). *earthlier happy:* happier on earth.
2. My right to remain a virgin.
3. *spotted and inconstant:* stained with fickleness.

I have some private schooling° for you both.　　　　　　　*advice*
For you, fair Hermia, look you arm° yourself　　　　　　*prepare*
To fit your fancies° to your father's will,　　　　　　　　*desires*
Or else the law of Athens yields you up—
120　Which by no means we may extenuate°—　　　　　　*mitigate*
To death or to a vow of single life.
Come, my Hippolyta; what cheer, my love?—
Demetrius and Egeus, go along.
I must employ you in some business
125　Against° our nuptial, and confer with you　　　　*In preparation for*
Of something nearly that⁴ concerns yourselves.
EGEUS　With duty and desire we follow you.
　　　　　　Exeunt. Manent° LYSANDER *and* HERMIA　　　*Remain*
LYSANDER　How now, my love? Why is your cheek so pale?
How chance the roses there do fade so fast?
130　HERMIA　Belike° for want of rain, which I could well　　*Probably*
Beteem° them from the tempest of my eyes.　　　*Afford; grant*
LYSANDER　Ay me, for aught that I could ever read,
Could ever hear by tale or history,
The course of true love never did run smooth,
135　But either it was different in blood°—　　　　*hereditary rank*
HERMIA　O cross!°—too high to be enthralled to low.　　*vexation*
LYSANDER　Or else misgrafted° in respect of years—　　*badly matched*
HERMIA　O spite!—too old to be engaged to young.
LYSANDER　Or merit stood° upon the choice of friends°—　*rested / kin*
140　HERMIA　O hell!—to choose love by another's eyes.
LYSANDER　Or if there were a sympathy° in choice,　　*an agreement*
War, death, or sickness did lay siege to it,
Making it momentany° as a sound,　　　　　　*momentary*
Swift as a shadow, short as any dream,
145　Brief as the lightning in the collied° night,　　*coal-black*
That, in a spleen,° unfolds° both heaven and earth,　*swift impulse / reveals*
And, ere a man hath power to say 'Behold!',
The jaws of darkness do devour it up.
So quick⁵ bright things come to confusion.
150　HERMIA　If then true lovers have been ever° crossed,　*always*
It stands as an edict in destiny.
Then let us teach our trial patience,⁶
Because it is a customary cross,
As due to love as thoughts, and dreams, and sighs,
155　Wishes, and tears, poor fancy's° followers.　　　*love's*
LYSANDER　A good persuasion.° Therefore hear me, Hermia.　*principle; doctrine*
I have a widow aunt, a dowager
Of great revenue, and she hath no child,
And she respects° me as her only son.　　　　　*regards*
160　From Athens is her house remote seven leagues.
There, gentle Hermia, may I marry thee,
And to that place the sharp Athenian law
Cannot pursue us. If thou lov'st me then,
Steal forth thy father's house tomorrow night,
165　And in the wood, a league without° the town,　　*outside*
Where I did meet thee once with Helena

---

4. *nearly that:* that closely.　　　　6. Let us teach ourselves to be patient in this trial.
5. Quickly (adverb); vital, lively (adjective).

To do observance to a morn of May,°   *celebrate May Day*
There will I stay for thee.

HERMIA   My good Lysander,
I swear to thee by Cupid's strongest bow,
170   By his best arrow with the golden head,[7]
By the simplicity° of Venus' doves,[8]   *innocence*
By that which knitteth souls and prospers loves,
And by that fire which burned the Carthage queen
When the false Trojan under sail was seen;[9]
175   By all the vows that ever men have broke—
In number more than ever women spoke—
In that same place thou hast appointed me
Tomorrow truly will I meet with thee.

LYSANDER   Keep promise, love. Look, here comes Helena.

     Enter HELENA

180   HERMIA   God speed, fair[1] Helena. Whither away?

HELENA   Call you me fair? That 'fair' again unsay.
Demetrius loves your fair—O happy fair!°   *fortunate beauty*
Your eyes are lodestars,° and your tongue's sweet air°   *guiding stars / melody*
More tuneable° than lark to shepherd's ear   *tuneful*
185   When wheat is green, when hawthorn buds appear.
Sickness is catching. O, were favour° so!   *looks; charms*
Your words I catch, fair Hermia; ere I go,
My ear should catch your voice, my eye your eye,
My tongue should catch your tongue's sweet melody.
190   Were the world mine, Demetrius being bated,°   *excepted*
The rest I'd give to be to you translated.°   *transformed*
O, teach me how you look, and with what art
You sway the motion° of Demetrius' heart.   *desire*

HERMIA   I frown upon him, yet he loves me still.
195   HELENA   O that your frowns would teach my smiles such skill!

HERMIA   I give him curses, yet he gives me love.

HELENA   O that my prayers could such affection move!

HERMIA   The more I hate, the more he follows me.

HELENA   The more I love, the more he hateth me.

200   HERMIA   His folly, Helen, is no fault of mine.

HELENA   None but your beauty; would that fault were mine!

HERMIA   Take comfort. He no more shall see my face.
Lysander and myself will fly this place.
Before the time I did Lysander see
205   Seemed Athens as a paradise to me.
O then, what graces in my love do dwell,
That he hath turned a heaven unto a hell?

LYSANDER   Helen, to you our minds we will unfold.
Tomorrow night, when Phoebe° doth behold   *Diana (the moon)*
210   Her silver visage in the wat'ry glass,
Decking with liquid pearl the bladed grass—
A time that lovers' sleights doth still° conceal—   *always*
Through Athens' gates have we devised to steal.

HERMIA   And in the wood where often you and I
215   Upon faint° primrose beds were wont° to lie,   *pale / accustomed*

---

7. Cupid's sharp golden arrow was said to create love;
his blunt lead arrow caused dislike.
8. Said to draw Venus's chariot.
9. *fire . . . seen:* Dido, Queen of Carthage, burned herself

on a funeral pyre when her lover, Aeneas, sailed away.
1. The dialogue plays on the meanings "blonde,"
"beautiful," "beauty." Helena is presumably fair-haired
and Hermia (called a "raven" at 2.2.120) a brunette.

Emptying our bosoms of their counsel sweet,
There my Lysander and myself shall meet,
And thence from Athens turn away our eyes
To seek new friends and stranger companies.°   *the company of strangers*
220   Farewell, sweet playfellow. Pray thou for us,
And good luck grant thee thy Demetrius.—
Keep word, Lysander. We must starve our sight
From lovers' food till morrow deep midnight.
LYSANDER   I will, my Hermia.   *Exit* HERMIA
Helena, adieu.
225   As you on him, Demetrius dote on you.   *Exit*
HELENA   How happy some o'er other some² can be!
Through Athens I am thought as fair as she.
But what of that? Demetrius thinks not so.
He will not know what all but he do know.
230   And as he errs, doting on Hermia's eyes,
So I, admiring of his qualities.
Things base and vile, holding no quantity,°   *shape; proportion*
Love can transpose to form and dignity.
Love looks not with the eyes, but with the mind,³
235   And therefore is winged Cupid painted blind. *Helena*
Nor hath love's mind of any judgement taste;°   *any trace of judgment*
Wings and no eyes figure° unheedy haste.   *symbolize*
And therefore is love said to be a child
Because in choice he is so oft beguiled.
240   As waggish° boys in game° themselves forswear,   *playful / sport; play*
So the boy Love is perjured everywhere.
For ere Demetrius looked on Hermia's eyne°   *eyes*
He hailed down oaths that he was only mine,
And when this hail some heat from Hermia felt,
245   So he dissolved,° and showers of oaths did melt.   *broke faith; melted*
I will go tell him of fair Hermia's flight.
Then to the wood will he tomorrow night
Pursue her, and for this intelligence°   *information*
If I have thanks it is a dear expense.⁴
250   But herein mean I to enrich my pain,
To have his sight thither and back again.   *Exit*

1.2

Enter QUINCE *the carpenter, and* SNUG *the joiner, and*
BOTTOM *the weaver, and* FLUTE *the bellows-mender, and*
SNOUT *the tinker, and* STARVELING *the tailor*¹
QUINCE   Is all our company here?
BOTTOM   You were best to call them generally,² man by man,
according to the scrip.°   *script; list*
QUINCE   Here is the scroll of every man's name which is thought

---

2. *o'er other some:* in comparison with others.
3. Love is promoted not by the evidence of the senses, but by the fancies of the mind.
4. Costly (because of the betrayal of secrecy and because it leads Demetrius to Hermia); or welcome (because the potential return is Demetrius's love regained).
1.2 Location: Somewhere in the city of Athens.
1. The artisans' names recall their occupations. Quince's name is probably derived from "quoins," wooden wedges used by carpenters who made buildings

such as houses and theaters. The name "Snug" evokes well-finished wooden furniture made by joiners. A bottom was the piece of wood on which thread was wound; Bottom's name also connotes "ass" and "lowest point." As Flute's name suggests, domestic bellows whistle through holes when needing repair. Snout's name may refer to the spouts of the kettles he repairs, or to his nose. Tailors, as Starveling's name recalls, were proverbially thin.
2. Bottom's error for "individually" (he frequently mistakes words in this manner).

5 fit through all Athens to play in our interlude° before the Duke   *brief play*
and the Duchess on his wedding day at night.

BOTTOM   First, good Peter Quince, say what the play treats on;
then read the names of the actors; and so grow to a point.[3]

QUINCE   Marry,° our play is *The Most Lamentable Comedy and*   *By the Virgin Mary*
10 *Most Cruel Death of Pyramus and Thisbe.*[4]

BOTTOM   A very good piece of work, I assure you, and a merry.
Now, good Peter Quince, call forth your actors by the scroll.
Masters, spread yourselves.

QUINCE   Answer as I call you. Nick Bottom, the weaver?

15 BOTTOM   Ready. Name what part I am for, and proceed.

QUINCE   You, Nick Bottom, are set down for Pyramus.

BOTTOM   What is Pyramus? A lover or a tyrant?

QUINCE   A lover, that kills himself most gallant for love.

BOTTOM   That will ask some tears in the true performing of it. If
20 I do it, let the audience look to their eyes. I will move stones.
I will condole,° in some measure. To the rest.—Yet my chief   *lament; arouse pity*
humour° is for a tyrant. I could play 'erc'les[5] rarely,° or a part   *inclination / excellently*
to tear a cat° in, to make all split.°   *rant / go to pieces*

> The raging rocks
25 > And shivering shocks   } alliteration
> Shall break the locks
>   Of prison gates,
> And Phibus' car[6]
> Shall shine from far
30 > And make and mar
>   The foolish Fates.

This was lofty. Now name the rest of the players.—This is
'erc'les' vein, a tyrant's vein. A lover is more condoling.

QUINCE   Francis Flute, the bellows-mender?

35 FLUTE   Here, Peter Quince.

QUINCE   Flute, you must take Thisbe on you.

FLUTE   What is Thisbe? A wand'ring knight?°   *knight-errant*

QUINCE   It is the lady that Pyramus must love.

FLUTE   Nay, faith, let not me play a woman.[7] I have a beard
40 coming.

QUINCE   That's all one.° You shall play it in a mask,[8] and you   *irrelevant*
may speak as small° as you will.   *high-pitched; shrill*

BOTTOM   An° I may hide my face, let me play Thisbe too. I'll   *If*
speak in a monstrous° little voice: 'Thisne, Thisne!'[9]—'Ah   *exceptionally*
45 Pyramus, my lover dear, thy Thisbe dear and lady dear.'

QUINCE   No, no, you must play Pyramus; and Flute, you Thisbe.

BOTTOM   Well, proceed.

QUINCE   Robin Starveling, the tailor?

STARVELING   Here, Peter Quince.

50 QUINCE   Robin Starveling, you must play Thisbe's mother. Tom
Snout, the tinker?

SNOUT   Here, Peter Quince.

QUINCE   You, Pyramus' father; myself, Thisbe's father. Snug the

---

3. *grow to a point*: draw to a conclusion.
4. Parodying titles such as that of Thomas Preston's *Cambyses: A Lamentable Tragedy Mixed Full of Pleasant Mirth* . . . (c. 1570).
5. Hercules (a stock ranting role in early plays).
6. The chariot of Phoebus Apollo, the sun god (the odd spelling may represent Bottom's pronunciation).

7. On the Elizabethan stage, women's parts were played by boys and young men.
8. Elizabethan ladies regularly wore masks for anonymity and to protect their complexions.
9. Probably intended as a pet name for Thisbe; or it may mean "in this manner."

joiner, you the lion's part; and I hope here is a play fitted.°   *(well) cast*

55   SNUG   Have you the lion's part written? Pray you, if it be, give it
me; for I am slow of study.

QUINCE   You may do it extempore, for it is nothing but roaring.

BOTTOM   Let me play the lion too. I will roar that I will do any
man's heart good to hear me. I will roar that I will make the

60   Duke say 'Let him roar again; let him roar again'.

QUINCE   An you should do it too terribly you would fright the
Duchess and the ladies that they would shriek, and that were
enough to hang us all.

ALL THE REST   That would hang us, every mother's son.

65   BOTTOM   I grant you, friends, if you should fright the ladies out
of their wits they would have no more discretion but to hang us,
but I will aggravate° my voice so that I will roar you as gently   *(for "moderate")*
as any sucking dove.[1] I will roar you an 'twere° any nightingale.   *as though it were*

QUINCE   You can play no part but Pyramus; for Pyramus is a

70   sweet-faced man; a proper° man as one shall see in a summer's   *handsome*
day; a most lovely, gentlemanlike man. Therefore you must
needs play Pyramus.

BOTTOM   Well, I will undertake it. What beard were I best to
play it in?

75   QUINCE   Why, what you will.

BOTTOM   I will discharge° it in either your straw-colour beard,   *perform*
your orange-tawny[2] beard, your purple-in-grain° beard, or your   *very deep red*
French-crown-colour° beard, your perfect yellow.   *gold-coin-colored*

QUINCE   Some of your French crowns have no hair at all,[3] and

80   then you will play bare faced.° But masters, here are your   *beardless; undisguised*
parts,[4] and I am to entreat you, request you, and desire you to
con° them by tomorrow night, and meet me in the palace wood   *memorize*
a mile without the town by moonlight. There will we rehearse;
for if we meet in the city we shall be dogged with company,

85   and our devices° known. In the meantime I will draw a bill°   *plans / list*
of properties such as our play wants. I pray you fail me not.

BOTTOM   We will meet, and there we may rehearse most
obscenely[5] and courageously. Take pains; be perfect.[6] Adieu.

QUINCE   At the Duke's oak we meet.

90   BOTTOM   Enough. Hold, or cut bowstrings.[7]   *Exeunt*

2.1

Enter a FAIRY *at one door and* ROBIN GOODFELLOW [*a*
puck][1] *at another*

ROBIN   How now, spirit, whither wander you?

FAIRY   Over hill, over dale,
       Thorough° bush, thorough brier,   *Through*
       Over park, over pale,°   *enclosure; fence*

5   Thorough flood, thorough fire:
       I do wander everywhere

---

1. Bottom confuses "sitting dove" and "sucking lamb."
2. Dark yellow, a recognized name for the dye. (Bottom the weaver shows his professional knowledge.)
3. Referring to the baldness caused by venereal disease ("the French disease").
4. Literally; an Elizabethan actor was generally given only his own lines and cues.
5. A comic blunder, possibly for "out of sight" (from the scene or from being seen).
6. Letter perfect in learning your parts.
7. *Hold, or cut bowstrings* (from archery): Keep your word, or be disgraced (?).
2.1 Location: A wood near Athens.
1. A puck is a devil or an imp; in Elizabethan folklore, Robin Goodfellow (also known as Puck) was a mischievous spirit who would do housework if well treated.

Swifter than the moonës sphere,[2]
And I serve the Fairy Queen
To dew her orbs[3] upon the green.
10 The cowslips tall her pensioners° be.   *royal bodyguards*
In their gold coats spots you see;
Those be rubies, fairy favours;°   *gifts*
In those freckles live their savours.°   *scent*
I must go seek some dewdrops here,
15 And hang a pearl in every cowslip's ear.
Farewell, thou lob° of spirits; I'll be gone.   *country bumpkin*
Our Queen and all her elves come here anon.
ROBIN   The King doth keep his revels here tonight.
Take heed the Queen come not within his sight,
20 For Oberon is passing fell and wroth[4]
Because that she, as her attendant, hath
A lovely boy stol'n from an Indian king.
She never had so sweet a changeling;[5]
And jealous Oberon would have the child
25 Knight of his train, to trace° the forests wild.   *range*
But she perforce° withholds the lovèd boy,   *forcibly*
Crowns him with flowers, and makes him all her joy.
And now they never meet in grove, or green,
By fountain° clear, or spangled starlight sheen,°   *spring / shining starlight*
30 But they do square,° that all their elves for fear   *quarrel*
Creep into acorn cups, and hide them there.
FAIRY   Either I mistake your shape and making° quite   *form*
Or else you are that shrewd° and knavish sprite   *mischievous*
Called Robin Goodfellow. Are not you he
35 That frights the maidens of the villag'ry,°   *villages*
Skim milk, and sometimes labour in the quern,°   *hand mill*
And bootless° make the breathless housewife churn,   *in vain*
And sometime° make the drink to bear no barm°—   *at times / froth on ale*
Mislead night wanderers, laughing at their harm?
40 Those that 'hobgoblin' call you, and 'sweet puck',
You do their work, and they shall have good luck.
Are not you he?
ROBIN   Thou speak'st aright;
I am that merry wanderer of the night.
I jest to Oberon, and make him smile
45 When I a fat and bean-fed horse beguile,°   *trick*
Neighing in likeness of a filly foal;
And sometime lurk I in a gossip's° bowl   *an old woman's*
In very likeness of a roasted crab,[6]
And when she drinks, against her lips I bob,
50 And on her withered dewlap° pour the ale.   *loose skin on neck*
The wisest aunt° telling the saddest° tale   *old woman / most serious*
Sometime for three-foot stool mistaketh me;
Then slip I from her bum. Down topples she,
And 'tailor' cries,[7] and falls into a cough,
55 And then the whole choir° hold their hips, and laugh,   *company*

2. Each planet, including the moon, was thought to be fixed in a transparent hollow globe revolving round the earth. *moonës:* the obsolete genitive of "moon."
3. Sprinkle her fairy rings (circles of dark grass).
4. *passing fell and wroth:* exceedingly fierce and angry.
5. Usually a child left by fairies in exchange for one stolen, but here the stolen child.
6. Crab apple ("lamb's wool," a winter drink, was made with roasted apples and warm ale).
7. Possibly the old woman cries this because she ends up cross-legged on the floor as tailors sat to work or because she falls on her "tail."

And waxen° in their mirth, and sneeze, and swear   increase
A merrier hour was never wasted there.—
    Enter [OBERON] King of Fairies at one door, with his
    train, and [TITANIA] Queen at another, with hers
But make room, fairy: here comes Oberon.
FAIRY   And here my mistress. Would that he were gone.

60 OBERON   Ill met by moonlight, proud Titania.
TITANIA   What, jealous Oberon?—Fairies, skip hence.
I have forsworn his bed and company.
OBERON   Tarry, rash wanton.° Am not I thy lord?   impetuous creature
TITANIA   Then I must be thy lady; but I know

65 When thou hast stol'n away from fairyland
And in the shape of Corin[8] sat all day,
Playing on pipes of corn, and versing love[9]
To amorous Phillida. Why art thou here
Come from the farthest step° of India,   limit

70 But that, forsooth, the bouncing° Amazon,   vigorous
Your buskined° mistress and your warrior love,   wearing hunting boots
To Theseus must be wedded, and you come
To give their bed joy and prosperity?
OBERON   How canst thou thus for shame, Titania,

75 Glance at my credit° with Hippolyta,   Question my good name
Knowing I know thy love to Theseus?
Didst not thou lead him through the glimmering night
From Perigouna whom he ravishèd,
And make him with fair Aegles[1] break his faith,

80 With Ariadne and Antiopa?[2]
TITANIA   These are the forgeries of jealousy,
And never since the middle summer's spring°   beginning of midsummer
Met we on hill, in dale, forest, or mead,
By pavèd fountain or by rushy[3] brook,

85 Or in° the beachèd margin° of the sea   on / shore
To dance our ringlets° to the whistling wind,   circular dances
But with thy brawls thou hast disturbed our sport.
Therefore the winds, piping to us in vain,
As in revenge have sucked up from the sea

90 Contagious fogs which, falling in the land,
Hath every pelting° river made so proud   paltry
That they have overborne their continents.°   banks
The ox hath therefore stretched his yoke in vain,
The ploughman lost his sweat, and the green corn°   grain

95 Hath rotted ere his youth attained a beard.
The fold stands empty in the drownèd field,
And crows are fatted with the murrain° flock.   dead of disease
The nine men's morris[4] is filled up with mud,
And the quaint mazes in the wanton green[5]

100 For lack of tread are undistinguishable.

---

8. Corin and Phillida are typical names for a shepherd and shepherdess in pastoral poetry.
9. Making or reciting love poetry. *pipes of corn:* musical instruments made of oat stalks.
1. Perigouna and Aegles were previous mistresses of Theseus (taken from Plutarch's *Life of Theseus*).
2. Taken from Plutarch; some writers used "Antiopa" as an alternative name for the Amazonian queen Theseus married, although here it seems to refer to a different

woman. Ariadne helped Theseus kill the Minotaur and escape from his labyrinth on Crete; she fled with Theseus, but he deserted her on Naxos.
3. Fringed with reeds. *pavèd:* pebbled.
4. The playing area for this outdoor game (traditionally, a board game played with nine pebbles or pegs) was cut in turf.
5. Luxuriant grass. *quaint mazes:* intricate arrangements of paths (kept visible by use).

The human mortals want° their winter cheer.[6]   *lack*
No night is now with hymn or carol blessed.
Therefore[7] the moon, the governess of floods,
Pale in her anger washes° all the air,   *moistens; wets*
105   That rheumatic[8] diseases do abound;
And thorough this distemperature° we see   *bad weather; disturbance*
The seasons alter: hoary-headed frosts
Fall in the fresh lap of the crimson rose,
And on old Hiems'° thin and icy crown   *winter's*
110   An odorous chaplet° of sweet summer buds   *wreath*
Is, as in mock'ry, set. The spring, the summer,
The childing° autumn, angry winter change   *fruitful*
Their wonted liveries,[9] and the mazèd° world   *bewildered*
By their increase° now knows not which is which;   *crop yield*
115   And this same progeny of evils comes
From our debate,° from our dissension.   *quarrel*
We are their parents and original.°   *origin*

OBERON   Do you amend it, then. It lies in you.
Why should Titania cross her Oberon?
120   I do but beg a little changeling boy
To be my henchman.°   *page of honor*

TITANIA   Set your heart at rest.[1]
The fairyland buys not the child of me.
His mother was a vot'ress[2] of my order,
And in the spicèd Indian air by night
125   Full often hath she gossiped by my side,
And sat with me on Neptune's yellow sands,
Marking th'embarkèd traders° on the flood,°   *merchant ships / tide*
When we have laughed to see the sails conceive
And grow big-bellied with the wanton° wind,   *playful; amorous*
130   Which she with pretty and with swimming[3] gait
Following,° her womb then rich with my young squire,   *Copying*
Would imitate, and sail upon the land
To fetch me trifles, and return again
As from a voyage, rich with merchandise.
135   But she, being mortal, of that boy did die;
And for her sake do I rear up her boy;
And for her sake I will not part with him.

OBERON   How long within this wood intend you stay?
TITANIA   Perchance till after Theseus' wedding day.
140   If you will patiently dance in our round,
And see our moonlight revels, go with us.
If not, shun me, and I will spare° your haunts.   *avoid*
OBERON   Give me that boy and I will go with thee.
TITANIA   Not for thy fairy kingdom.—Fairies, away.
145   We shall chide° downright if I longer stay.   *quarrel*
Exeunt [TITANIA *and her train*]
OBERON   Well, go thy way. Thou shalt not from° this grove   *go from*
Till I torment thee for this injury.°—   *insult*
My gentle puck, come hither. Thou rememb'rest

---

6. Winter cheer would include the hymns and carols of
the Yuletide. But Q, F reading: here.
7. As in lines 88 and 93 above, referring to the consequences of their quarrel.
8. Characterized by rheum: colds, coughs, etc.

9. Customary clothing.
1. Proverbial expression for "Abandon that idea."
2. Woman who has taken a vow to serve (often religious).
3. As though gliding through the waves.

	Since° once I sat upon a promontory	*When*
150	And heard a mermaid on a dolphin's back	
	Uttering such dulcet° and harmonious breath°	*sweet / voice; song*
	That the rude° sea grew civil at her song	*rough*
	And certain stars shot madly from their spheres°	*orbits*
	To hear the sea-maid's music?	
	ROBIN I remember.	
155	OBERON That very time I saw, but thou couldst not,	
	Flying between the cold moon and the earth	
	Cupid, all armed. A certain aim he took	
	At a fair vestal thronèd by the west,⁴	
	And loosed his love-shaft° smartly from his bow	*golden arrow*
160	As° it should pierce a hundred thousand hearts.	*As though*
	But I might° see young Cupid's fiery shaft	*could*
	Quenched in the chaste beams of the wat'ry moon,	
	And the imperial vot'ress passèd on,	
	In maiden meditation, fancy-free.°	*free of love thoughts*
165	Yet marked I where the bolt° of Cupid fell.	*arrow*
	It fell upon a little western flower—	
	Before, milk-white; now, purple with love's wound—	
	And maidens call it love-in-idleness.⁵	
	Fetch me that flower; the herb I showed thee once.	
170	The juice of it on sleeping eyelids laid	
	Will make or° man or woman madly dote	*either*
	Upon the next live creature that it sees.	
	Fetch me this herb, and be thou here again	
	Ere the leviathan⁶ can swim a league.	
175	ROBIN I'll put a girdle° round about the earth	*circle*
	In forty minutes. *Exit*	
	OBERON Having once this juice	
	I'll watch Titania when she is asleep,	
	And drop the liquor° of it in her eyes.	*juice*
	The next thing then she waking looks upon—	
180	Be it on lion, bear, or wolf, or bull,	
	On meddling monkey, or on busy ape—	
	She shall pursue it with the soul of love.	
	And ere I take this charm from off her sight—	
	As I can take it with another herb—	
185	I'll make her render up her page to me.	
	But who comes here? I am invisible,	
	And I will overhear their conference.	
	Enter DEMETRIUS, HELENA *following him*	
	DEMETRIUS I love thee not, therefore pursue me not.	
	Where is Lysander, and fair Hermia?	
190	The one I'll slay, the other slayeth me.	
	Thou told'st me they were stol'n unto this wood,	
	And here am I, and wood° within this wood	*insane*
	Because I cannot meet my Hermia.	
	Hence, get thee gone, and follow me no more.	
195	HELENA You draw me, you hard-hearted adamant,⁷	

---

4. To the west of India; in England. *vestal:* virgin (a compliment to Queen Elizabeth, the Virgin Queen, and possibly an allusion to a specific entertainment in her honor, such as the water pageant at Elvetham in 1591).
5. Pansy. (Classical legend describes how the mulberry turned purple with Pyramus's blood and the hyacinth with Hyacinthus's, but does not mention the pansy.)
6. Biblical sea monster, identified with the whale.
7. Very hard stone supposed to have magnetic properties. *draw me:* the magnetic power of attraction.

But yet you draw not iron; for my heart
Is true as steel.[8] Leave you° your power to draw,   *Relinquish*
And I shall have no power to follow you.
DEMETRIUS   Do I entice you? Do I speak you fair?[9]
200   Or rather do I not in plainest truth
Tell you I do not nor I cannot love you?
HELENA   And even for that do I love you the more.
I am your spaniel, and, Demetrius,
The more you beat me I will fawn on you.
205   Use me but as your spaniel: spurn me, strike me,
Neglect me, lose me; only give me leave,
Unworthy as I am, to follow you.
What worser place can I beg in your love—
And yet a place of high respect with me—
210   Than to be usèd as you use your dog?
DEMETRIUS   Tempt not too much the hatred of my spirit;
For I am sick when I do look on thee.
HELENA   And I am sick when I look not on you.
DEMETRIUS   You do impeach° your modesty too much,   *call into question*
215   To leave the city and commit yourself
Into the hands of one that loves you not;
To trust the opportunity of night,
And the ill counsel of a desert° place,   *deserted*
With the rich worth of your virginity.
220   HELENA   Your virtue is my privilege,° for that°   *protection / because*
It is not night when I do see your face;
Therefore I think I am not in the night,
Nor doth this wood lack worlds of company;
For you in my respect° are all the world.   *As far as I am concerned*
225   Then how can it be said I am alone,
When all the world is here to look on me?
DEMETRIUS   I'll run from thee, and hide me in the brakes,°   *thickets*
And leave thee to the mercy of wild beasts.
HELENA   The wildest hath not such a heart as you.
230   Run when you will. The story shall be changed:
Apollo flies, and Daphne holds the chase.[1]
The dove pursues the griffin,[2] the mild hind°   *doe*
Makes speed to catch the tiger: bootless° speed,   *useless*
When cowardice pursues, and valour flies.
235   DEMETRIUS   I will not stay thy questions.[3] Let me go;
Or if thou follow me, do not believe
But I shall do thee mischief in the wood.
HELENA   Ay, in the temple, in the town, the field,
You do me mischief. Fie, Demetrius,
240   Your wrongs do set a scandal on my sex.[4]
We cannot fight for love as men may do;
We should be wooed, and were not made to woo.
I'll follow thee, and make a heaven of hell,
To die upon the hand I love so well.

---

8. Hermia contrasts the base metal iron with steel, which holds its temper.
9. Do I speak kindly to you?
1. A reversal of the traditional myth in which the nymph Daphne, flying from Apollo, was transformed into a laurel tree to escape him.

2. Fabulous monster with a lion's body and an eagle's head and wings.
3. I will not wait here any longer to hear you talk.
4. Your injustice to me causes me to behave in a way that disgraces my sex (by wooing him rather than being wooed).

Exit [DEMETRIUS, HELENA *following him*]

245 OBERON   Fare thee well, nymph. Ere he do leave this grove
Thou shalt fly him, and he shall seek thy love.
Enter [ROBIN GOODFELLOW *the*] *puck*
Hast thou the flower there? Welcome, wanderer.

ROBIN   Ay, there it is.

OBERON   I pray thee give it me.
I know a bank where the wild thyme blows,
250 Where oxlips⁵ and the nodding violet grows,
Quite overcanopied with luscious woodbine,°   *honeysuckle*
With sweet musk-roses,⁶ and with eglantine.°   *sweetbrier, a type of rose*
There sleeps Titania sometime of the night,
Lulled in these flowers with dances and delight;
255 And there the snake throws° her enamelled skin,   *throws off ; casts*
Weed° wide enough to wrap a fairy in;   *Garment*
And with the juice of this I'll streak° her eyes,   *anoint*
And make her full of hateful fantasies.
Take thou some of it, and seek through this grove.
260 A sweet Athenian lady is in love
With a disdainful youth. Anoint his eyes;
But do it when the next thing he espies
May be the lady. Thou shalt know the man
By the Athenian garments he hath on.
265 Effect it with some care, that he may prove
More fond° on her than she upon her love;   *doting*
And look thou meet me ere the first cock crow.⁷

ROBIN   Fear not, my lord. Your servant shall do so.
Exeunt [*severally*]°   *separately*

2.2

Enter TITANIA, *Queen of Fairies, with her train*

TITANIA   Come, now a roundel° and a fairy song,   *circular dance*
Then for the third part of a minute¹ hence:
Some to kill cankers° in the musk-rose buds,   *caterpillars*
Some war with reremice° for their leathern wings   *bats*
5 To make my small elves coats, and some keep back
The clamorous owl, that nightly hoots and wonders
At our quaint° spirits. Sing me now asleep;   *dainty*
Then to your offices, and let me rest.
[*She lies down.*] FAIRIES *sing*

FIRST FAIRY   You spotted snakes with double° tongue,   *forked*
10   Thorny hedgehogs, be not seen;
               Newts and blindworms,² do no wrong;
               Come not near our Fairy Queen.

CHORUS [*dancing*]   Philomel³ with melody,
               Sing in our sweet lullaby;
15   Lulla, lulla, lullaby; lulla, lulla, lullaby.
               Never harm
               Nor spell nor charm

---

5. Hybrid between primrose and cowslip.
6. Large rambling white roses.
7. Some spirits were thought unable to bear daylight (compare *Hamlet* 1.1.28–36).
2.2 Location: The wood.
1. The fairies are quick enough to do their tasks in

twenty seconds.
2. Newts (water lizards) and blindworms were thought to be poisonous, as were spiders (line 20).
3. Philomel, the nightingale (in classical mythology, a woman who, raped by her sister's husband, was transformed into a bird).

		Come our lovely lady nigh.	
		So good night, with lullaby.	
20	FIRST FAIRY	Weaving spiders, come not here;	
		Hence, you long-legged spinners, hence;	
		Beetles black, approach not near;	
		Worm nor snail do no offence.	
	CHORUS [*dancing*]	Philomel with melody,	
25		Sing in our sweet lullaby;	
		Lulla, lulla, lullaby; lulla, lulla, lullaby.	
		Never harm	
		Nor spell nor charm	
		Come our lovely lady nigh.	
30		So good night, with lullaby.	

[TITANIA] *sleeps*

SECOND FAIRY Hence, away. Now all is well.
One aloof° stand sentinel.   *at a distance*
           [*Exeunt all but* TITANIA *and the sentinel*]
           Enter OBERON. [*He drops the juice on Titania's eyelids*]
OBERON What thou seest when thou dost wake,
           Do it for thy true love take;
35   Love and languish for his sake.
           Be it ounce,° or cat, or bear,   *lynx*
           Pard,° or boar with bristled hair,   *Leopard*
           In thy eye that shall appear
           When thou wak'st, it is thy dear.
40   Wake when some vile thing is near.   [*Exit*]
           Enter LYSANDER *and* HERMIA
LYSANDER Fair love, you faint with wand'ring in the wood,
           And, to speak truth, I have forgot our way.
           We'll rest us, Hermia, if you think it good,
           And tarry for the comfort of the day.
45 HERMIA Be it so, Lysander. Find you out a bed;
           For I upon this bank will rest my head.
           [*She lies down*]
LYSANDER One turf shall serve as pillow for us both;
           One heart, one bed; two bosoms, and one troth.°   *pledged faith*
HERMIA Nay, good Lysander; for my sake, my dear,
50   Lie further off yet; do not lie so near.
LYSANDER O, take the sense,° sweet, of my innocence!   *true meaning*
           Love takes the meaning in love's conference[4]—
           I mean that my heart unto yours is knit,
           So that but one heart we can make of it.
55   Two bosoms interchainèd with an oath;
           So, then, two bosoms and a single troth.
           Then by your side no bed-room me deny;
           For lying so, Hermia, I do not lie.[5]
HERMIA Lysander riddles very prettily.
60   Now much beshrew[6] my manners and my pride
           If Hermia meant to say Lysander lied.
           But, gentle friend, for love and courtesy,
           Lie further off, in humane° modesty.   *courteous*

---

4. Love enables lovers truly to understand one another.   6. Curse (used in a mild sense).
5. Deceive; punning on "lie down."

Such separation as may well be said
65 Becomes a virtuous bachelor and a maid,
So far be distant; and good night, sweet friend.
Thy love ne'er alter till thy sweet life end.
LYSANDER   Amen, amen, to that fair prayer say I;
And then end life when I end loyalty.
70 Here is my bed; sleep give thee all his rest.
          [*He lies down*]
HERMIA   With half that wish the wisher's eyes be pressed.[7]
          They sleep [apart.]
          *Enter [*ROBIN GOODFELLOW the] *puck*
ROBIN   Through the forest have I gone,
But Athenian found I none
On whose eyes I might approve°   test
75 This flower's force in stirring love.
Night and silence. Who is here?
Weeds of Athens he doth wear.
This is he my master said
Despisèd the Athenian maid—
80 And here the maiden, sleeping sound
On the dank and dirty ground.
Pretty soul, she durst not lie
Near this lack-love, this kill-courtesy.
Churl,° upon thy eyes I throw   Rude fellow
85 All the power this charm doth owe.°   own
          [*He drops the juice on Lysander's eyelids*]
When thou wak'st, let love forbid
Sleep his seat on thy eyelid.[8]
So, awake when I am gone.
For I must now to Oberon.   *Exit*
          Enter DEMETRIUS *and* HELENA, *running*
90 HELENA   Stay, though thou kill me, sweet Demetrius.
DEMETRIUS   I charge thee hence, and do not haunt me thus.
HELENA   O, wilt thou darkling° leave me? Do not so.   in darkness
DEMETRIUS   Stay, on thy peril;[9] I alone will go.   *Exit*
HELENA   O, I am out of breath in this fond° chase.   foolish
95 The more my prayer, the lesser is my grace.°   reward
Happy is Hermia, wheresoe'er she lies;
For she hath blessèd and attractive° eyes.   magnetic
How came her eyes so bright? Not with salt tears—
If so, my eyes are oft'ner washed than hers.
100 No, no; I am as ugly as a bear,
For beasts that meet me run away for fear.
Therefore no marvel though Demetrius
Do, as° a monster, fly my presence thus.   as if I were
What wicked and dissembling glass of mine
105 Made me compare° with Hermia's sphery eyne!°   compete / starry eyes
But who is here? Lysander, on the ground?
Dead, or asleep? I see no blood, no wound.
Lysander, if you live, good sir, awake.
LYSANDER [*awaking*]   And run through fire I will for thy sweet sake.
110 Transparent[1] Helena, nature shows art°   skill; magic power

---

7. May sleep's rest be shared between us. *pressed:*
closed in sleep.
8. *forbid . . . eyelid:* prevent you from sleeping.

9. Stay here or risk peril (if you follow me).
1. Radiant; capable of being seen through.

That through thy bosom makes me see thy heart.
Where is Demetrius? O, how fit a word
Is that vile name to perish on my sword!
HELENA   Do not say so, Lysander; say not so.
115   What though he love your Hermia? Lord, what though?
Yet Hermia still loves you; then be content.
LYSANDER   Content with Hermia? No, I do repent
The tedious minutes I with her have spent.
Not Hermia but Helena I love.
120   Who will not change a raven for a dove?
The will of man is by his reason swayed,[2]
And reason says you are the worthier maid.
Things growing are not ripe until their season,
So I, being young, till now ripe not to reason.
125   And, touching now the point of human skill,[3]
Reason becomes the marshal[4] to my will,
And leads me to your eyes, where I o'erlook°   *look over; read*
Love's stories written in love's richest book.
HELENA   Wherefore was I to this keen° mockery born?   *sharp*
130   When at your hands did I deserve this scorn?
Is't not enough, is't not enough, young man,
That I did never—no, nor never can—
Deserve a sweet look from Demetrius' eye,
But you must flout my insufficiency?[5]
135   Good troth,° you do me wrong; good sooth,° you do,   *Truly / indeed*
In such disdainful manner me to woo.
But fare you well. Perforce I must confess
I thought you lord of more true gentleness.°   *courtesy; breeding*
O, that a lady of one man refused
140   Should of ° another therefore be abused!   *Exit*   *by*
LYSANDER   She sees not Hermia. Hermia, sleep thou there,
And never mayst thou come Lysander near;
For as a surfeit of the sweetest things
The deepest loathing to the stomach brings,
145   Or as the heresies that men do leave
Are hated most of those they did deceive,[6]
So thou, my surfeit and my heresy,
Of all be hated, but the most of me;
And all my powers, address° your love and might   *direct; apply*
150   To honour Helen, and to be her knight.   *Exit*
HERMIA [*awaking*]   Help me, Lysander, help me! Do thy best
To pluck this crawling serpent from my breast!
Ay me, for pity. What a dream was here?
Lysander, look how I do quake with fear.
155   Methought a serpent ate my heart away,
And you sat smiling at his cruel prey.°   *act of preying*
Lysander—what, removed? Lysander, lord—
What, out of hearing, gone? No sound, no word?
Alack, where are you? Speak an if ° you hear,   *an if = if*
160   Speak, of ° all loves. I swoon almost with fear.   *for the sake of*

---

2. Renaissance psychology considered the will (that is, the passions) to be in constant conflict with, and ideally subject to, the faculty of reason.
3. Reaching (only) now the highest point of human judgment.

4. Officer who led guests to their appointed places.
5. *flout my insufficiency:* mock my shortcomings by pretending they are wonderful qualities.
6. *as the heresies . . . deceive:* as men most hate the false opinions they once held.

No? Then I well perceive you are not nigh.
Either death or you I'll find immediately.　　　　　*Exit*

3.1

Enter the clowns:° [QUINCE, SNUG, BOTTOM, FLUTE,　　　*rustics*
SNOUT, *and* STARVELING]

BOTTOM　Are we all met?

QUINCE　Pat,° pat; and here's a marvellous convenient place for　　*On the dot*
our rehearsal. This green plot shall be our stage, this hawthorn
brake° our tiring-house,° and we will do it in action as we will　　*thicket / dressing room*
5　do it before the Duke.

BOTTOM　Peter Quince?

QUINCE　What sayst thou, bully° Bottom?　　　　*good fellow; jolly*

BOTTOM　There are things in this comedy of Pyramus and
Thisbe that will never please. First, Pyramus must draw a sword
10　to kill himself, which the ladies cannot abide. How answer you
that?

SNOUT　By'r la'kin,[1] a parlous° fear.　　　　　*perilous*

STARVELING　I believe we must leave the killing out, when all is
done.[2]

15　BOTTOM　Not a whit. I have a device to make all well. Write me
a prologue, and let the prologue seem to say we will do no
harm with our swords, and that Pyramus is not killed indeed;
and for the more better assurance, tell them that I, Pyramus,
am not Pyramus, but Bottom the weaver. This will put them
20　out of fear.

QUINCE　Well, we will have such a prologue; and it shall be written in eight and six.[3]

BOTTOM　No, make it two more: let it be written in eight and
eight.

25　SNOUT　Will not the ladies be afeard of the lion?

STARVELING　I fear it, I promise you.

BOTTOM　Masters, you ought to consider with yourself, to bring
in—God shield us—a lion among ladies is a most dreadful
thing;[4] for there is not a more fearful° wild fowl than your lion　　*frightening*
30　living, and we ought to look to't.

SNOUT　Therefore another prologue must tell he is not a lion.

BOTTOM　Nay, you must name his name, and half his face must
be seen through the lion's neck, and he himself must speak
through, saying thus or to the same defect:° 'ladies', or 'fair　　*(for "effect")*
35　ladies, I would wish you' or 'I would request you' or 'I would
entreat you not to fear, not to tremble. My life for yours.[5] If you
think I come hither as a lion, it were pity of ° my life. No, I am　　*a threat to*
no such thing. I am a man, as other men are'—and there,
indeed, let him name his name, and tell them plainly he is
40　Snug the joiner.

QUINCE　Well, it shall be so; but there is two hard things: that is,
to bring the moonlight into a chamber—for you know Pyramus
and Thisbe meet by moonlight.

3.1 Location: Remains the same, although F introduces an act break.
1. By our ladykin (Virgin Mary): a mild oath.
2. When all is said and done.
3. Alternate lines of eight and six syllables (a common
ballad measure).

4. In 1594, at a feast in honor of the christening of
King James's son, a tame lion that was supposed to draw
a chariot was replaced by a black African in order to
avoid frightening the audience.
5. I pledge my life to defend yours.

SNOUT[6]   Doth the moon shine that night we play our play?

45   BOTTOM   A calendar, a calendar—look in the almanac, find out
moonshine, find out moonshine.

Enter [ROBIN GOODFELLOW[7] *the*] *puck* [*invisible*]

QUINCE [*with a book*][8]   Yes, it doth shine that night.

BOTTOM   Why, then may you leave a casement of the great
chamber window where we play open, and the moon may
50   shine in at the casement.

QUINCE   Ay, or else one must come in with a bush of thorns and
a lantern and say he comes to disfigure,[9] or to present,° the   *represent*
person of Moonshine. Then there is another thing: we must
have a wall in the great chamber; for Pyramus and Thisbe, says
55   the story, did talk through the chink of a wall.

SNOUT   You can never bring in a wall. What say you, Bottom?

BOTTOM   Some man or other must present Wall; and let him
have some plaster, or some loam, or some rough-cast[1] about
him, to signify 'wall'; and let him hold his fingers thus, and
60   through that cranny shall Pyramus and Thisbe whisper.

QUINCE   If that may be, then all is well. Come, sit down every
mother's son, and rehearse your parts. Pyramus, you begin.
When you have spoken your speech, enter into that brake; and
so everyone according to his cue.

65   ROBIN [*aside*]   What hempen homespuns[2] have we swagg'ring
here
So near the cradle of the Fairy Queen?
What, a play toward?° I'll be an auditor—   *in preparation*
An actor, too, perhaps, if I see cause.

QUINCE   Speak, Pyramus. Thisbe, stand forth.

70   BOTTOM [*as Pyramus*]   Thisbe, the flowers of odious° savours   *(for "odorous")*
sweet.

QUINCE   Odours, odours.

BOTTOM [*as Pyramus*]   Odours savours sweet.
So hath thy breath, my dearest Thisbe dear.
But hark, a voice. Stay thou but here a while,
75   And by and by I will to thee appear.   *Exit*

ROBIN[3] [*aside*]   A stranger Pyramus than e'er played here. [*Exit*]

FLUTE   Must I speak now?

QUINCE   Ay, marry must you. For you must understand he goes
but to see a noise that he heard, and is to come again.

80   FLUTE [*as Thisbe*]   Most radiant Pyramus, most lily-white of hue,
Of colour like the red rose on triumphant brier;
Most bristly juvenile,° and eke° most lovely Jew,[4]   *lively youth / also*
As true as truest horse that yet would never tire:
I'll meet thee, Pyramus, at Ninny's° tomb.   *fool's*

85   QUINCE   Ninus'[5] tomb, man!—Why, you must not speak that
yet. That you answer to Pyramus. You speak all your part at

---

6. Or Snug: Q2, F abbreviate as "Sn."
7. Robin's entrance here (in F only) is also noted (in both F and Q) at line 65.
8. The book, perhaps comically supplied by Robin, is an editorial conjecture.
9. Blunder for "figure," represent. *bush of thorns:* bundle of thornbush kindling (like the lantern, a traditional accessory of the man in the moon).
1. Mixture of lime and gravel used to plaster outside walls.

2. Peasants, country bumpkins, dressed in coarse homespun fabric made from hemp.
3. Q gives this line to Quince.
4. Not often considered "lovely" by Elizabethan Christians; usually a term of abuse (here echoing the first syllable of "juvenile").
5. Mythical founder of Nineveh, whose wife, Semiramis, was believed to have founded Babylon, the setting for the story of Pyramus and Thisbe.

once, cues and all.—Pyramus, enter: your cue is past; it is
'never tire'.

FLUTE   O.

90   [*As Thisbe*] As true as truest horse that yet would never tire.
        [*Enter* ROBIN *leading* BOTTOM *with the ass-head*]

BOTTOM [*as Pyramus*] If I were fair,° Thisbe, I were° only thine.   handsome / would be

QUINCE   O monstrous! O strange! We are haunted. Pray, mas-
ters; fly, masters: help!   *The clowns all exeunt*

ROBIN   I'll follow you, I'll lead you about a round,°   in circles

95   Through bog, through bush, through brake, through brier.
Sometime a horse I'll be, sometime a hound,
A hog, a headless bear, sometime a fire,°   will-o'-the-wisp
And neigh, and bark, and grunt, and roar, and burn,
Like horse, hound, hog, bear, fire, at every turn.   *Exit*
        *Enter [*BOTTOM[6] *again,] with the ass-head*

100 BOTTOM   Why do they run away? This is a knavery of them to
make me afeard.
        Enter SNOUT

SNOUT   O Bottom, thou art changed. What do I see on thee?

BOTTOM   What do you see? You see an ass-head of your own,[7]
do you?   [*Exit* SNOUT]
        Enter QUINCE

105 QUINCE   Bless thee, Bottom, bless thee. Thou art translated.°   transformed
                                                             Exit

BOTTOM   I see their knavery. This is to make an ass of me, to
fright me, if they could; but I will not stir from this place, do
what they can. I will walk up and down here, and I will sing,
that they shall hear I am not afraid.

110   [*Sings*]   The ousel cock° so black of hue,   male blackbird
                With orange-tawny bill;
                The throstle° with his note so true,   song thrush
                The wren with little quill.°   reed pipe

TITANIA [*awaking*]   What angel wakes me from my flow'ry bed?

115 BOTTOM [*sings*]   The finch, the sparrow, and the lark,
                The plainsong[8] cuckoo grey,
                Whose note full many a man doth mark,
                And dares not answer 'Nay'[9]—

for indeed, who would set his wit to° so foolish a bird? Who   pay heed to

120 would give a bird the lie,[1] though he cry 'Cuckoo' never so?°   ever so much

TITANIA   I pray thee, gentle mortal, sing again.
Mine ear is much enamoured of thy note;
So is mine eye enthrallèd to thy shape;
And thy fair virtue's force[2] perforce doth move me

125 On the first view to say, to swear, I love thee.

BOTTOM   Methinks, mistress, you should have little reason for
that. And yet, to say the truth, reason and love keep little company together nowadays—the more the pity that some honest
neighbours will not make them friends. Nay, I can gleek° upon   make jokes

130 occasion.

TITANIA   Thou art as wise as thou art beautiful.

---

6. He might have remained onstage when the others
left. Entrance noted in F only.
7. You see a figment of your own asinine imagination.
8. A melody sung without adornment; the repeated

"cuckoo" (associated with cuckoldry).
9. Deny (that he is a cuckold).
1. Who would call a bird a liar.
2. Your patience; power of your good qualities.

BOTTOM   Not so, neither; but if I had wit enough to get out of
this wood, I have enough to serve mine own turn.°   *purpose*

TITANIA   Out of this wood do not desire to go.
135   Thou shalt remain here, whether thou wilt or no.
I am a spirit of no common rate:°   *rank*
The summer still° doth tend upon my state;[3]   *always; continually*
And I do love thee. Therefore go with me.
I'll give thee fairies to attend on thee,
140   And they shall fetch thee jewels from the deep,
And sing while thou on pressèd flowers dost sleep;
And I will purge thy mortal grossness° so   *fleshly being*
That thou shalt like an airy spirit go.
Peaseblossom, Cobweb, Mote, and Mustardseed!

Enter four fairies: PEASEBLOSSOM, COBWEB, MOTE,[4] *and*
MUSTARDSEED

A FAIRY   Ready.
ANOTHER   And I.
ANOTHER   And I.
ANOTHER   And I.
145   ALL FOUR   Where shall we go?
TITANIA   Be kind and courteous to this gentleman.
Hop in his walks, and gambol in his eyes.
Feed him with apricots and dewberries,
With purple grapes, green figs, and mulberries;
150   The honeybags steal from the humble-bees,°   *bumblebees*
And for night tapers crop their waxen thighs
And light them at the fiery glow-worms' eyes
To have° my love to bed, and to arise;   *lead*
And pluck the wings from painted butterflies
155   To fan the moonbeams from his sleeping eyes.
Nod to him, elves, and do him courtesies.
A FAIRY   Hail, mortal.
ANOTHER   Hail.
ANOTHER   Hail.
160   ANOTHER   Hail.
BOTTOM   I cry your worships mercy,[5] heartily.—I beseech your
worship's name.
COBWEB   Cobweb.
BOTTOM   I shall desire you of more acquaintance, good Master
165   Cobweb. If I cut my finger,[6] I shall make bold with you.—Your
name, honest gentleman?
PEASEBLOSSOM   Peaseblossom.
BOTTOM   I pray you commend me to Mistress Squash, your
mother, and to Master Peascod,[7] your father. Good Master
170   Peaseblossom, I shall desire you of more acquaintance, too.—
Your name, I beseech you, sir?
MUSTARDSEED   Mustardseed.
BOTTOM   Good Master Mustardseed, I know your patience[8] well.
That same cowardly giantlike ox-beef[9] hath devoured many a
175   gentleman of your house. I promise you your kindred hath

---

3. Serves me, as part of my royal retinue.
4. Speck. "Mote" and "moth" were pronounced alike.
5. I beg pardon of your honors.
6. Cobwebs were used to stop bleeding.

7. Ripe pea pod (called "your father" because it suggests "codpiece"). *Squash:* unripe pea pod.
8. What you have suffered with fortitude.
9. Because beef is often eaten with mustard.

made my eyes water ere now. I desire you of more acquaintance, good Master Mustardseed.
TITANIA [*to the fairies*]   Come, wait upon him, lead him to my bower.
    The moon, methinks, looks with a wat'ry eye,
180   And when she weeps, weeps every little flower,[1]
      Lamenting some enforcèd° chastity.   *violated; involuntary*
    Tie up my love's tongue;[2] bring him silently.   *Exeunt*

3.2

    Enter [OBERON,] *King of Fairies*
OBERON   I wonder if Titania be awaked,
    Then what it was that next came in her eye,
    Which she must dote on in extremity.
      Enter [ROBIN GOODFELLOW *the*] *puck*
    Here comes my messenger. How now, mad spirit?
5   What nightrule° now about this haunted grove?   *night revels; sports*
ROBIN   My mistress with a monster is in love.
    Near to her close° and consecrated bower   *private*
    While she was in her dull° and sleeping hour   *drowsy*
    A crew of patches,° rude mechanicals°   *fools / rough workmen*
10   That work for bread upon Athenian stalls,°   *market stands*
    Were met together to rehearse a play
    Intended for great Theseus' nuptial day.
    The shallowest thickskin of that barren sort,°   *witless lot*
    Who Pyramus presented,° in their sport   *acted*
15   Forsook his scene° and entered in a brake,   *stage*
    When I did him at this advantage take.
    An ass's nole° I fixèd on his head.   *noddle; head*
    Anon his Thisbe must be answerèd,
    And forth my mimic° comes. When they him spy—   *burlesque actor*
20   As wild geese that the creeping fowler° eye,   *hunter of birds*
    Or russet-pated choughs, many in sort,[1]
    Rising and cawing at the gun's report,
    Sever° themselves and madly sweep the sky—   *Scatter*
    So, at his sight, away his fellows fly,
25   And at our stamp[2] here o'er and o'er one falls.
    He° 'Murder' cries, and help from Athens calls.   *One (workman)*
    Their sense thus weak, lost with their fears thus strong,
    Made senseless things begin to do them wrong.
    For briers and thorns at their apparel snatch;
30   Some sleeves, some hats—from yielders all things catch.[3]
    I led them on in this distracted fear,
    And left sweet Pyramus translated there;
    When in that moment, so it came to pass,
    Titania waked and straightway loved an ass.
35 OBERON   This falls out better than I could devise.
    But hast thou yet latched° the Athenian's eyes   *anointed*
    With the love juice, as I did bid thee do?
ROBIN   I took him sleeping; that is finished, too;
    And the Athenian woman by his side,

---

1. Dew was thought to originate on the moon.
2. Bottom is perhaps making involuntary asinine noises.
3.2 Location: The wood.
1. Together, in a flock. *russet-pated choughs:* gray-

headed jackdaws.
2. Editors have wondered how a fairy's presumably
tiny foot could cause the human to fall.
3. Everything robs the timid.

40	That° when he waked of force° she must be eyed.	*So that / necessity*
	Enter DEMETRIUS *and* HERMIA	
	OBERON Stand close. This is the same Athenian.	
	ROBIN This is the woman, but not this the man.	
	[*They stand apart*]	
	DEMETRIUS O, why rebuke you him that loves you so?	
	Lay breath so bitter on your bitter foe.	
45	HERMIA Now I but chide, but I should use thee worse;	
	For thou, I fear, hast given me cause to curse.	
	If thou hast slain Lysander in his sleep,	
	Being o'er shoes° in blood, plunge in the deep,	*Having waded so far*
	And kill me too.	
50	The sun was not so true unto the day	
	As he to me. Would he have stolen away	
	From sleeping Hermia? I'll believe as soon	
	This whole° earth may be bored, and that the moon	*solid*
	May through the centre creep, and so displease	
55	Her brother's noontide with th'Antipodes.[4]	
	It cannot be but thou hast murdered him.	
	So should a murderer look—so dead,° so grim.	*deathly pale*
	DEMETRIUS So should the murdered look, and so should I,	
	Pierced through the heart with your stern cruelty.	
60	Yet you, the murderer, look as bright, as clear	
	As yonder Venus in her glimmering sphere.°	*orbit*
	HERMIA What's this to my Lysander? Where is he?	
	Ah, good Demetrius, wilt thou give him me?	
	DEMETRIUS I had rather give his carcass to my hounds.	
65	HERMIA Out, dog; out, cur. Thou driv'st me past the bounds	
	Of maiden's patience. Hast thou slain him then?	
	Henceforth be never numbered among men.	
	O, once tell true; tell true, even for my sake.	
	Durst thou have looked upon him being awake,	
70	And hast thou killed him sleeping? O brave touch!°	*noble stroke*
	Could not a worm,° an adder do so much?—	*serpent*
	An adder did it, for with doubler[5] tongue	
	Than thine, thou serpent, never adder stung.	
	DEMETRIUS You spend your passion on a misprised mood.°	*in misconceived anger*
75	I am not guilty of Lysander's blood,	
	Nor is he dead, for aught that I can tell.	
	HERMIA I pray thee, tell me then that he is well.	
	DEMETRIUS And if I could, what should I get therefor?°	*for that*
	HERMIA A privilege never to see me more;	
80	And from thy hated presence part I so.	
	See me no more, whether he be dead or no. *Exit*	
	DEMETRIUS There is no following her in this fierce vein.	
	Here therefore for a while I will remain.	
	So sorrow's heaviness[6] doth heavier grow	
85	For debt that bankrupt sleep doth sorrow owe,[7]	
	Which now in some slight measure it will pay,	

---

4. *that . . . Antipodes:* that the moon could creep through a hole bored through the earth's center and emerge on the other side, the Antipodes, displeasing the inhabitants by displacing the noontime sun with the darkness of night. (Apollo, the sun god, was the brother of Diana, the moon goddess.)

5. More forked (of the adder); more duplicitous (of Demetrius).
6. Sadness (punning on "heavy": drowsy).
7. *For . . . owe:* Because of the sleeplessness sorrow causes.

If for his tender here I make some stay.[8]
    [He lies] down [and sleeps]
OBERON *[to* ROBIN*]*   What hast thou done? Thou hast mistaken quite,
   And laid the love juice on some true love's sight.
90   Of thy misprision° must perforce ensue   *mistake*
   Some true love turned, and not a false turned true.
ROBIN   Then fate o'errules, that, one man holding troth,°   *faith*
   A million fail, confounding oath on oath.[9]
OBERON   About the wood go swifter than the wind,
95   And Helena of Athens look° thou find.   *be sure*
   All fancy-sick° she is, and pale of cheer°   *lovesick / face*
   With sighs of love that costs the fresh blood dear.[1]
   By some illusion see thou bring her here.
   I'll charm his eyes against° she do appear.   *in readiness for when*
100 ROBIN   I go, I go—look how I go,
   Swifter than arrow from the Tartar's bow.[2]   *Exit*
OBERON   Flower of this purple dye,
                Hit with Cupid's archery,
                Sink in apple° of his eye.   *pupil*
    [He drops the juice on Demetrius' eyelids]
105   When his love he doth espy,
                Let her shine as gloriously
                As the Venus of the sky.
                When thou wak'st, if she be by,
                Beg of her for remedy.
    *Enter [*ROBIN GOODFELLOW *the] puck*
110 ROBIN   Captain of our fairy band,
                Helena is here at hand,
                And the youth mistook by me,
                Pleading for a lover's fee.°   *reward*
                Shall we their fond° pageant see?   *foolish*
115   Lord, what fools these mortals be!
OBERON   Stand aside. The noise they make
                Will cause Demetrius to awake.
ROBIN   Then will two at once woo one.
                That must needs be sport alone;°   *unique*
120   And those things do best please me
                That befall prepost'rously.°   *ass backward*
    [They stand apart.]
    Enter HELENA, LYSANDER *[following her]*
LYSANDER   Why should you think that I should woo in scorn?
   Scorn and derision never come in tears.
   Look when I vow, I weep; and vows so born,
125   In their nativity all truth appears.[3]
   How can these things in me seem scorn to you,
   Bearing the badge of faith[4] to prove them true?
HELENA   You do advance° your cunning more and more,   *increase; display*
   When truth kills truth[5]—O devilish holy fray!
130   These vows are Hermia's. Will you give her o'er?

---

8. *Which . . . stay:* I will rest here awhile to give sleep
the opportunity to pay off some of its debt to sorrow.
9. Among the millions of faithless men, the one true
man's oath has been subverted by fate.
1. Sighs were thought to cause loss of blood.
2. Tartars, a dark-skinned, supposedly savage people in

Asia Minor, were famed for their archery.
3. *Look . . . appears:* The fact that I am weeping
authenticates my vow's sincerity.
4. Insignia, such as worn on a servant's livery (here, his
tears).
5. When one vow nullifies another.

Weigh oath with oath, and you will nothing weigh.[6]
Your vows to her and me put in two scales
Will even weigh, and both as light as tales.°   *lies; fiction*
LYSANDER   I had no judgement when to her I swore.
135   HELENA   Nor none, in my mind, now you give her o'er.
LYSANDER   Demetrius loves her, and he loves not you.
HELENA[7]   [   ]
DEMETRIUS [*awaking*]   O Helen, goddess, nymph, perfect, divine!
To what, my love, shall I compare thine eyne?
140   Crystal is muddy. O, how ripe in show°   *appearance*
Thy lips, those kissing cherries, tempting grow!
That pure congealèd white—high Taurus'[8] snow,
Fanned with the eastern wind—turns to a crow[9]
When thou hold'st up thy hand. O, let me kiss
145   This princess of pure white, this seal° of bliss!   *pledge*
HELENA   O spite! O hell! I see you all are bent
To set against me for your merriment.
If you were civil, and knew courtesy,
You would not do me thus much injury.
150   Can you not hate me—as I know you do—
But you must join in souls to mock me too?
If you were men, as men you are in show,
You would not use a gentle° lady so,   *well-born; mild*
To vow and swear and superpraise my parts°   *overpraise my qualities*
155   When I am sure you hate me with your hearts.
You both are rivals and love Hermia,
And now both rivals to mock Helena.
A trim° exploit, a manly enterprise—   *fine*
To conjure tears up in a poor maid's eyes
160   With your derision. None of noble sort°   *rank; nature*
Would so offend a virgin, and extort°   *torture*
A poor soul's patience, all to make you sport.
LYSANDER   You are unkind, Demetrius. Be not so.
For you love Hermia; this you know I know.
165   And here with all good will, with all my heart,
In Hermia's love I yield you up my part;
And yours of Helena to me bequeath,
Whom I do love, and will do till my death.
HELENA   Never did mockers waste more idle breath.
170   DEMETRIUS   Lysander, keep thy Hermia. I will none.[1]
If e'er I loved her, all that love is gone.
My heart to her but as guestwise° sojourned   *as a guest*
And now to Helen is it home returned,
There to remain.
LYSANDER   Helen, it is not so.
175   DEMETRIUS   Disparage not the faith thou dost not know,
Lest to thy peril thou aby it dear.°   *pay for it dearly*
       Enter HERMIA
Look where thy love comes; yonder is thy dear.
HERMIA   Dark night, that from the eye his° function takes,   *its*
The ear more quick of apprehension makes.

---

6. *you . . . weigh*: you will find that neither oath has
any substance; you, Lysander, will be found to have no
substance.

7. Helena's retort, awakening Demetrius, may have

been inadvertently omitted by the Q and F texts.
8. Range of high mountains in Asia Minor.
9. *turns to a crow*: appears black by contrast.
1. I will have nothing to do with her.

180   Wherein it doth impair the seeing sense,
     It pays the hearing double recompense.
     Thou art not by mine eye, Lysander, found;
     Mine ear, I thank it, brought me to thy sound.
     But why unkindly didst thou leave me so?
185 LYSANDER   Why should he stay whom love doth press to go?
    HERMIA   What love could press Lysander from my side?
    LYSANDER   Lysander's love, that would not let him bide:
     Fair Helena, who more engilds the night
     Than all yon fiery O's and eyes of light.[2]
190   Why seek'st thou me? Could not this make thee know
     The hate I bare thee made me leave thee so?
    HERMIA   You speak not as you think. It cannot be.
    HELENA [*aside*]   Lo, she is one of this confederacy.
     Now I perceive they have conjoined all three
195   To fashion this false sport in spite of° me.—   *to spite*
     Injurious Hermia, most ungrateful maid,
     Have you conspired, have you with these contrived
     To bait[3] me with this foul derision?
     Is all the counsel° that we two have shared—   *confidences*
200   The sisters' vows, the hours that we have spent
     When we have chid the hasty-footed time
     For parting us—O, is all quite forgot?
     All schooldays' friendship, childhood innocence?
     We, Hermia, like two artificial gods
205   Have with our needles created both one flower,
     Both on one sampler, sitting on one cushion,
     Both warbling of one song, both in one key,
     As if our hands, our sides, voices, and minds
     Had been incorporate. So we grew together,   *of one body*
210   Like to a double cherry: seeming parted,
     But yet an union in partition,
     Two lovely berries moulded on one stem.
     So, with two seeming bodies but one heart,
     Two of the first[4]—like coats in heraldry,
215   Due but to one and crownèd with one crest.
     And will you rend our ancient love asunder,
     To join with men in scorning your poor friend?
     It is not friendly, 'tis not maidenly.
     Our sex as well as I may chide you for it,
220   Though I alone do feel the injury.
    HERMIA   I am amazèd at your passionate words.
     I scorn you not. It seems that you scorn me.
    HELENA   Have you not set Lysander, as in scorn,
     To follow me, and praise my eyes and face?
225   And made your other love, Demetrius—
     Who even but now° did spurn me with his foot—   *just now*
     To call me goddess, nymph, divine, and rare,
     Precious, celestial? Wherefore speaks he this
     To her he hates? And wherefore doth Lysander
230   Deny your love so rich within his soul,

2. Stars (punning on the vowels and on lovers' exclamatory "oh"s and "ay"s). An "o" was a spangle.
3. To torment (as Elizabethans set dogs to bait a bear).
4. A technical phrase in heraldry, referring to the first quartering in a coat of arms, which may be repeated. The friends then have two bodies but a single, over-arching identity.

And tender° me, forsooth, affection,   *offer*
But by your setting on, by your consent?
What though I be not so in grace° as you,   *favor*
So hung upon with love, so fortunate,
235   But miserable most, to love unloved—
This you should pity rather than despise.

HERMIA   I understand not what you mean by this.

HELENA   Ay, do. Persever, counterfeit sad° looks,   *serious*
Make mouths upon° me when I turn my back,   *Make faces at*
240   Wink each at other, hold the sweet jest up.°   *keep up the joke*
This sport well carried shall be chronicled.
If you have any pity, grace, or manners,
You would not make me such an argument.°   *a subject of merriment*
But fare ye well. 'Tis partly my own fault,
245   Which death or absence soon shall remedy.

LYSANDER   Stay, gentle Helena, hear my excuse,
My love, my life, my soul, fair Helena.

HELENA   O excellent!

HERMIA [*to* LYSANDER]   Sweet, do not scorn her so.

DEMETRIUS [*to* LYSANDER]   If she cannot entreat I can compel.[5]

250   LYSANDER   Thou canst compel no more than she entreat.
Thy threats have no more strength than her weak prayers.—
Helen, I love thee; by my life I do.
I swear by that which I will lose for thee
To prove him false that says I love thee not.

255   DEMETRIUS [*to* HELENA]   I say I love thee more than he can do.

LYSANDER   If thou say so, withdraw,[6] and prove it too.

DEMETRIUS   Quick, come.

HERMIA   Lysander, whereto tends all this?
[*She takes him by the arm*]

LYSANDER   Away, you Ethiope.[7]

DEMETRIUS   No, no, sir, yield.°   *(to Hermia)*
Seem to break loose, take on as° you would follow,   *pretend*
260   But yet come not. You are a tame man; go.

LYSANDER [*to* HERMIA]   Hang off,° thou cat, thou burr; vile thing, let loose,   *Let go*
Or I will shake thee from me like a serpent.

HERMIA   Why are you grown so rude? What change is this,
Sweet love?

LYSANDER   Thy love? Out, tawny Tartar, out;
265   Out, loathèd med'cine;[8] O hated potion, hence.

HERMIA   Do you not jest?

HELENA   Yes, sooth,° and so do you.   *truly*

LYSANDER   Demetrius, I will keep my word with thee.

DEMETRIUS   I would I had your bond, for I perceive
A weak bond[9] holds you. I'll not trust your word.

270   LYSANDER   What, should I hurt her, strike her, kill her dead?
Although I hate her, I'll not harm her so.

HERMIA   What, can you do me greater harm than hate?
Hate me—wherefore? O me, what news,° my love?   *what has happened*
Am not I Hermia? Are not you Lysander?

---

5. If Hermia cannot entreat you to stop, I can make you do it.
6. Come with me ("step outside").
7. Allusion to Hermia's dark hair and complexion. Elizabethans generally regarded light complexions as more

beautiful than dark and often stigmatized dark-skinned peoples (such as Ethiopians or Tartars) as ugly.
8. Any drug (including poison).
9. Hermia's weak grasp (with a pun on "bond": oath, in the previous line).

275 I am as fair now as I was erewhile.°   *a while ago*
     Since night you loved me, yet since night you left me.
     Why then, you left me—O, the gods forbid—
     In earnest, shall I say?
     LYSANDER   Ay, by my life,
     And never did desire to see thee more.
280 Therefore be out of hope, of question, doubt.
     Be certain, nothing truer; 'tis no jest
     That I do hate thee and love Helena.
     HERMIA [*to* HELENA] O me, you juggler,° you canker blossom,[1]   *trickster*
     You thief of love—what, have you come by night
     And stol'n my love's heart from him?
285 HELENA   Fine, i'faith.
     Have you no modesty, no maiden shame,
     No touch of bashfulness? What, will you tear
     Impatient answers from my gentle tongue?
     Fie, fie, you counterfeit, you puppet,[2] you!
290 HERMIA Puppet? Why, so! Ay, that way goes the game.
     Now I perceive that she hath made compare
     Between our statures; she hath urged her height,
     And with her personage, her tall personage,
     Her height, forsooth, she hath prevailed with him—
295 And are you grown so high in his esteem
     Because I am so dwarfish and so low?
     How low am I, thou painted maypole?[3] Speak,
     How low am I? I am not yet so low
     But that my nails can reach unto thine eyes.
     HELENA [*to* DEMETRIUS *and* LYSANDER] I pray you, though you
300   mock me, gentlemen,
     Let her not hurt me. I was never curst.°   *quarrelsome*
     I have no gift at all in shrewishness.
     I am a right° maid for my cowardice.   *proper*
     Let her not strike me. You perhaps may think
305 Because she is something° lower than myself   *somewhat*
     That I can match her—
     HERMIA   Lower? Hark again.
     HELENA Good Hermia, do not be so bitter with me.
     I evermore did love you, Hermia,
     Did ever keep your counsels, never wronged you—
310 Save that in love unto Demetrius
     I told him of your stealth° unto this wood.   *stealing away*
     He followed you; for love I followed him.
     But he hath chid me hence, and threatened me
     To strike me, spurn me, nay, to kill me too.
315 And now, so° you will let me quiet go,   *if only*
     To Athens will I bear my folly back,
     And follow you no further. Let me go.
     You see how simple and how fond° I am.   *foolish*
     HERMIA Why, get you gone. Who is't that hinders you?
320 HELENA A foolish heart that I leave here behind.
     HERMIA What, with Lysander?

---

1. Worm that devours blossoms (of love).   3. Proverbial for someone tall and skinny. *painted:*
2. Fraudulent imitation; but Hermia interprets "pup-   insulting allusion to the use of cosmetics.
pet" as a reference to her height.

HELENA	With Demetrius.	
LYSANDER	Be not afraid; she shall not harm thee, Helena.	
DEMETRIUS	No, sir, she shall not, though you take her part.	
HELENA	O, when she is angry she is keen° and shrewd.°	*sharp / shrewish*

325 She was a vixen when she went to school,
And though she be but little, she is fierce.

HERMIA Little again? Nothing but 'low' and 'little'?—
Why will you suffer her to flout me thus?
Let me come to her.

LYSANDER   Get you gone, you dwarf,
330 You *minimus* of hind'ring knot-grass⁴ made,
You bead, you acorn.

DEMETRIUS   You are too officious
In her behalf that scorns your services.
Let her alone. Speak not of Helena.
Take not her part. For if thou dost intend
335 Never so little° show of love to her,   *Even the smallest*
Thou shalt aby° it.   *pay for*

LYSANDER   Now she holds me not.
Now follow, if thou dar'st, to try whose right,
Of thine or mine, is most in Helena.

DEMETRIUS Follow? Nay, I'll go with thee, cheek by jowl.⁵

        Exeunt LYSANDER *and* DEMETRIUS

340 HERMIA You, mistress, all this coil° is long° of you.   *turmoil / because*
Nay, go not back.

HELENA   I will not trust you, I,
Nor longer stay in your curst company.
Your hands than mine are quicker for a fray;°   *fight*
My legs are longer, though, to run away.   [*Exit*]
345 HERMIA I am amazed, and know not what to say.   *Exit*

        OBERON *and* ROBIN [*come forward*]

OBERON This is thy negligence. Still° thou mistak'st,   *Always*
Or else commit'st thy knaveries wilfully.

ROBIN Believe me, king of shadows,° I mistook.   *fairy spirits*
Did not you tell me I should know the man
350 By the Athenian garments he had on?—
And so far° blameless proves my enterprise   *to this extent*
That I have 'nointed an Athenian's eyes;
And so far am I glad it so did sort°   *turn out*
As° this their jangling° I esteem a sport.   *Since / bickering*
355 OBERON Thou seest these lovers seek a place to fight.
Hie° therefore, Robin, overcast the night;   *Hurry*
The starry welkin° cover thou anon   *sky*
With drooping fog as black as Acheron,°   *river of hell*
And lead these testy rivals so astray
360 As° one come not within another's way.   *So that*
Like to Lysander sometime frame thy tongue,
Then stir Demetrius up with bitter wrong;°   *insults*
And sometime rail thou like Demetrius,
And from each other look thou lead them thus
365 Till o'er their brows death-counterfeiting sleep

---

4. Creeping binding weed (its sap was thought to stunt   5. Proverbial for "side by side."
human growth). *minimus*: diminutive thing (Latin).

With leaden legs and batty° wings doth creep.   *batlike*
Then crush this herb into Lysander's eye—
Whose liquor hath this virtuous° property,   *potent*
To take from thence all error with his might,
370 And make his eyeballs roll with wonted° sight.   *normal*
When they next wake, all this derision
Shall seem a dream and fruitless° vision,   *inconsequential*
And back to Athens shall the lovers wend°   *go*
With league° whose date° till death shall never end.   *covenant / duration*
375 Whiles I in this affair do thee employ,
I'll to my queen and beg her Indian boy;
And then I will her charmèd° eye release   *enchanted*
From monster's view, and all things shall be peace.
ROBIN   My fairy lord, this must be done with haste,
380 For night's swift dragons[6] cut the clouds full fast,
And yonder shines Aurora's harbinger,[7]
At whose approach ghosts, wand'ring here and there,
Troop home to churchyards; damnèd spirits all
That in cross-ways and floods[8] have burial
385 Already to their wormy beds are gone,
For fear lest day should look their shames upon.
They wilfully themselves exiled from light,
And must for aye° consort with black-browed night.   *forever*
OBERON   But we are spirits of another sort.
390 I with the morning's love[9] have oftmade sport,
And like a forester[1] the groves may tread
Even till the eastern gate, all fiery red,
Opening on Neptune° with fair blessèd beams   *the sea*
Turns into yellow gold his salt° green streams.   *salty*
395 But notwithstanding, haste, make no delay;
We may effect this business yet ere day.   *[Exit]*
ROBIN   Up and down, up and down,
I will lead them up and down.
I am feared in field and town.
400 Goblin,° lead them up and down.   *(Puck himself)*
Here comes one.
      Enter LYSANDER
LYSANDER   Where art thou, proud Demetrius? Speak thou now.
ROBIN *[shifting place]*[2]   Here, villain, drawn° and ready. Where   *with sword drawn*
  art thou?
LYSANDER   I will be with thee straight.°   *immediately*
ROBIN *[shifting place]*   Follow me then
  To plainer° ground.   *[Exit* LYSANDER*]*[3]   *clearer*
      Enter DEMETRIUS
405 DEMETRIUS *[shifting place]*   Lysander, speak again.
Thou runaway, thou coward, art thou fled?
Speak! In some bush? Where dost thou hide thy head?

---

6. Imagined as drawing the chariots of the goddess of night.
7. Herald of the goddess of dawn; the morning star.
8. In which the drowned were "buried," without Christian sacrament. *cross-ways:* crossroads (where suicides were buried, also without Christian sacrament). Robin is differentiating here between two types of spirits: those who wandered from their churchyard graves and those who have no proper resting place. These two types, both

ghosts of former humans, are differentiated in turn from the fairy spirits by Oberon in the ensuing lines.
9. The love of Aurora, goddess of dawn (or Cephalus, a brave hunter, Aurora's lover).
1. Keeper of a royal forest or private park.
2. In F, this direction is placed in the margin in the middle of this episode. (In what follows, Robin presumably mimics the voices of Demetrius and Lysander.)
3. He might instead wander about the stage.

ROBIN [*shifting place*]   Thou coward, art thou bragging to the stars,
    Telling the bushes that thou look'st for wars,
410   And wilt not come? Come, recreant;° come, thou child,   *coward; wretch*
    I'll whip thee with a rod. He is defiled
    That draws a sword on thee.[4]
DEMETRIUS [*shifting place*]   Yea, art thou there?
ROBIN [*shifting place*]   Follow my voice; we'll try° no manhood here.   *test*
                                    Exeunt

3.3

[*Enter* LYSANDER]
LYSANDER   He goes before me, and still dares me on;
    When I come where he calls, then he is gone.
    The villain is much lighter heeled than I;
    I followed fast, but faster he did fly,
5   That° fallen am I in dark uneven way,   *With the result that*
    And here will rest me.
        [*He lies*] *down*
                        Come, thou gentle day;
    For if but once thou show me thy grey light,
    I'll find Demetrius, and revenge this spite.   [*He sleeps*]
        Enter ROBIN [GOODFELLOW] *and* DEMETRIUS
ROBIN [*shifting place*]   Ho, ho, ho, coward, why com'st thou not?
10   DEMETRIUS   Abide° me if thou dar'st, for well I wot°   *Wait for / know*
    Thou runn'st before me, shifting every place,
    And dar'st not stand nor look me in the face.
    Where art thou now?
ROBIN [*shifting place*]   Come hither, I am here.
DEMETRIUS   Nay, then thou mock'st me. Thou shalt buy° this   *pay for*
    dear°   *dearly*
15   If ever I thy face by daylight see.
    Now go thy way. Faintness constraineth me
    To measure out my length on this cold bed.
        [*He lies down*]
    By day's approach look to be visited.   [*He sleeps*]
        Enter HELENA
HELENA   O weary night, O long and tedious night,
20   Abate° thy hours; shine comforts from the east   *Shorten*
    That I may back to Athens by daylight
        From these that my poor company detest;
    And sleep, that sometimes shuts up sorrow's eye,
    Steal me a while from mine own company.
        [*She lies down and sleeps*]
25   ROBIN   Yet but three? Come one more,
    Two of both kinds makes up four.
        Enter HERMIA
    Here she comes, curst° and sad.   *angry*
    Cupid is a knavish lad
    Thus to make poor females mad.
30   HERMIA   Never so weary, never so in woe,
    Bedabbled° with the dew, and torn with briers,   *Sprinkled*
    I can no further crawl, no further go.
    My legs can keep no pace with my desires.

---

4. I.e., it would be a disgrace to treat you as an honor-   3.3 Location: Scene continues.
able opponent.

Here will I rest me till the break of day.
[*She lies down*]
35   Heavens shield Lysander, if they mean a fray.
[*She sleeps*]
ROBIN   On the ground sleep sound.
              I'll apply to your eye,
              Gentle lover, remedy.
[*He drops the juice on Lysander's eyelids*]
              When thou wak'st thou tak'st
40   True delight in the sight
              Of thy former lady's eye,
        And the country proverb known,
        That 'every man should take his own',
        In your waking shall be shown.
45   Jack shall have Jill,
                  Naught shall go ill,
the man shall have his mare again, and all shall be well. [*Exit*]

4.1

Enter [TITANIA,] *Queen of Fairies, and* [BOTTOM *the*]
clown [*with the ass-head*], *and fairies:* [PEASEBLOSSOM,
COBWEB, MOTE, *and* MUSTARDSEED]

TITANIA [*to* BOTTOM]   Come, sit thee down upon this flow'ry bed,
      While I thy amiable° cheeks do coy,°   *lovable / caress*
      And stick musk-roses in thy sleek smooth head,
      And kiss thy fair large ears, my gentle joy.
5   BOTTOM   Where's Peaseblossom?
PEASEBLOSSOM   Ready.
BOTTOM   Scratch my head, Peaseblossom. Where's Monsieur
      Cobweb?
COBWEB   Ready.
10   BOTTOM   Monsieur Cobweb, good monsieur, get you your
      weapons in your hand and kill me a red-hipped humble-bee
      on the top of a thistle; and, good monsieur, bring me the hon-
      eybag. Do not fret yourself too much in the action, monsieur;
      and, good monsieur, have a care the honeybag break not. I
15   would be loath to have you overflowen with° a honeybag, signor.   *submerged by*
                                              [*Exit* COBWEB]
      Where's Monsieur Mustardseed?
MUSTARDSEED   Ready.
BOTTOM   Give me your neaf,° Monsieur Mustardseed. Pray you,   *fist*
      leave your courtesy,¹ good monsieur.
20   MUSTARDSEED   What's your will?
BOTTOM   Nothing, good monsieur, but to help Cavaliery² Pease-
      blossom³ to scratch. I must to the barber's, monsieur, for
      methinks I am marvellous hairy about the face; and I am such
      a tender ass, if my hair do but tickle me I must scratch.
25   TITANIA   What, wilt thou hear some music, my sweet love?
BOTTOM   I have a reasonable good ear in music. Let's have the
      tongs and the bones.⁴

4.1 Location: The wood. The original text has no act
break here. F has the four lovers sleep through the
action onstage.
1. *leave your courtesy:* stop bowing, or do not stand
bareheaded.

2. Blunder for "Cavalier," perhaps influenced by the
Italian term *cavaliere*.
3. The early texts have "Cobweb" (Shakespeare's or the
printer's error).
4. Triangle and clappers (rustic musical instruments).

Rural music[5]

TITANIA   Or say, sweet love, what thou desir'st to eat.

BOTTOM   Truly, a peck of provender.° I could munch your good   *fodder*

30   dry oats. Methinks I have a great desire to a bottle° of hay. Good   *bundle*
hay, sweet hay, hath no fellow.°   *equal*

TITANIA   I have a venturous fairy that shall seek
The squirrel's hoard, and fetch thee off new nuts.

BOTTOM   I had rather have a handful or two of dried peas. But I

35   pray you, let none of your people stir me. I have an exposition ~metaphor~
of° sleep come upon me.   *disposition to*

TITANIA   Sleep thou, and I will wind thee in my arms.
Fairies, be gone, and be all ways° away.   [*Exeunt* fairies]   *in every direction*
So° doth the woodbine[6] the sweet honeysuckle   *Thus*

40   Gently entwist; the female ivy so
Enrings the barky fingers of the elm.
O how I love thee, how I dote on thee!
      [*They sleep.*]
      Enter ROBIN GOODFELLOW [*the puck*] *and* OBERON[7]
      [*King of Fairies, meeting*]

OBERON   Welcome, good Robin. Seest thou this sweet sight?
Her dotage now I do begin to pity,

45   For meeting her of late behind the wood,
Seeking sweet favours° for this hateful fool,   *love tokens*
I did upbraid her and fall out with her,
For she his hairy temples then had rounded
With coronet of fresh and fragrant flowers,

50   And that same dew which sometime° on the buds   *formerly*
Was wont° to swell like round and orient[8] pearls   *accustomed*
Stood now within the pretty flow'rets' eyes,
Like tears that did their own disgrace bewail.
When I had at my pleasure taunted her,

55   And she in mild terms begged my patience,
I then did ask of her her changeling child,
Which straight she gave me, and her fairy sent
To bear him to my bower in fairyland.
And now I have the boy, I will undo

60   This hateful imperfection of her eyes.
And, gentle puck, take this transformèd scalp
From off the head of this Athenian swain,
That he, awaking when the other° do,   *others*
May all to Athens back again repair,

65   And think no more of this night's accidents
But as the fierce vexation of a dream.
But first I will release the Fairy Queen.
      [*He drops the juice on Titania's eyelids*]
      Be as thou wast wont to be,
      See as thou wast wont to see.

70   Dian's bud o'er Cupid's flower[9]
      Hath such force and blessèd power.

---

5. Probably background music, which continues during the following dialogue, rather than a separate musical interlude. The direction only occurs in F.
6. Here, "woodbine" cannot mean "honeysuckle," as it did at 2.1.251, and thus must refer to a different plant.
7. In Q, he enters earlier, unseen, with Titania and her train.
8. Lustrous (the best pearls were from the Far East).
9. "Dian's bud," the herb of 2.1.184 and 3.2.367, is perhaps *Agnus castus*, or chaste tree: said to preserve chastity and hence the antidote to "Cupid's flower," or the love-in-idleness of 2.1.166 etc.

Now, my Titania, wake you, my sweet queen.
TITANIA [*awaking*]   My Oberon, what visions have I seen!
  Methought I was enamoured of an ass.
OBERON   There lies your love.
75 TITANIA   How came these things to pass?
  O, how mine eyes do loathe his visage now!
OBERON   Silence a while.—Robin, take off this head.—
  Titania, music call, and strike more dead
  Than common sleep of all these five[1] the sense.
80 TITANIA   Music, ho—music such as charmeth sleep.
           Still° *music*   *Soft*
ROBIN [*taking the ass-head off* BOTTOM]   Now when thou wak'st
  with thine own fool's eyes peep.
OBERON   Sound music.
     [*The music changes*]
                    Come, my queen, take hands with me,
  And rock the ground whereon these sleepers be.
     [OBERON *and* TITANIA *dance*]
  Now thou and I are new in amity,
85 And will tomorrow midnight solemnly
  Dance in Duke Theseus' house, triumphantly,
  And bless it to all fair prosperity.
  There shall the pairs of faithful lovers be
  Wedded with Theseus, all in jollity.
90 ROBIN   Fairy King, attend and mark.
  I do hear the morning lark.
OBERON   Then, my queen, in silence sad
  Trip we after nightës[2] shade.
  We the globe can compass° soon,   *orbit*
95 Swifter than the wand'ring moon.
TITANIA   Come, my lord, and in our flight
  Tell me how it came this night
  That I sleeping here was found
  With these mortals on the ground.
                     Exeunt [OBERON, TITANIA, *and*
                    ROBIN. *The*] *sleepers lie still*
     Wind horns [*within*]. *Enter* THESEUS [*with*] EGEUS, HIP-
     POLYTA, *and all his train*
100 THESEUS   Go, one of you, find out the forester,
  For now our observation[3] is performed;
  And since we have the vanguard° of the day,   *earliest part*
  My love shall hear the music of my hounds.
  Uncouple[4] in the western valley; let them go.
105 Dispatch, I say, and find the forester.   [*Exit one*]
  We will, fair Queen, up to the mountain's top,
  And mark the musical confusion
  Of hounds and echo in conjunction.
HIPPOLYTA   I was with Hercules and Cadmus[5] once
110 When in a wood of Crete they bayed° the bear   *brought to bay*
  With hounds of Sparta.[6] Never did I hear

---

1. The lovers and Bottom.
2. The obsolete genitive inflection.
3. "Observance to a morn of May," as at 1.1.167.
4. Release (the dogs, leashed in pairs).
5. Mythical founder of Thebes. (No source for the anecdote is known.)
6. Famous in antiquity as hunting dogs.

Such gallant chiding;° for besides the groves,   *barking*
The skies, the fountains, every region near
Seemed all one mutual cry. I never heard
115   So musical a discord, such sweet thunder.
    THESEUS   My hounds are bred out of the Spartan kind,
        So flewed,[7] so sanded;° and their heads are hung   *sandy-colored*
        With ears that sweep away the morning dew,
        Crook-kneed, and dewlapped[8] like Thessalian bulls,
120   Slow in pursuit, but matched in mouth like bells,
        Each under each.[9] A cry more tuneable[1]
        Was never holla'd to nor cheered with horn
        In Crete, in Sparta, nor in Thessaly.
        Judge when you hear. But soft:° what nymphs are these?   *stop; look*
125   EGEUS   My lord, this is my daughter here asleep,
        And this Lysander; this Demetrius is;
        This Helena, old Nedar's Helena.
        I wonder of their being here together.
    THESEUS   No doubt they rose up early to observe
130   The rite of May, and, hearing our intent,
        Came here in grace of our solemnity.°   *ceremony*
        But speak, Egeus: is not this the day
        That Hermia should give answer of her choice?
    EGEUS   It is, my lord.
135   THESEUS   Go bid the huntsmen wake them with their horns.
                                        [*Exit one*]
            Shout within: wind horns. [*The lovers*] *all start up*
        Good morrow, friends. Saint Valentine[2] is past.
        Begin these wood-birds but to couple now?
    LYSANDER   Pardon, my lord.
            [*The lovers kneel*]
    THESEUS   I pray you all stand up.
            [*The lovers stand*]
        [*To* DEMETRIUS *and* LYSANDER] I know you two are rival enemies.
140   How comes this gentle concord in the world,
        That hatred is so far from jealousy°   *suspicion*
        To sleep by hate, and fear no enmity?
    LYSANDER   My lord, I shall reply amazèdly,°   *confusedly*
        Half sleep, half waking. But as yet, I swear,
145   I cannot truly say how I came here,
        But as I think—for truly would I speak,
        And, now I do bethink me, so it is—
        I came with Hermia hither. Our intent
        Was to be gone from Athens where° we might,   *wherever*
150   Without° the peril of the Athenian law—   *Outside*
    EGEUS [*to* THESEUS]   Enough, enough, my lord, you have enough.
        I beg the law, the law upon his head.—
        They would have stol'n away, they would, Demetrius,
        Thereby to have defeated° you and me—   *defrauded*
155   You of your wife, and me of my consent,
        Of my consent that she should be your wife.
    DEMETRIUS [*to* THESEUS]   My lord, fair Helen told me of their stealth,

---

7. Flews were large hanging, fleshy chaps.   pitch of their barking, like a set of bells.
8. With hanging folds of skin under the neck (compare   1. A pack of hounds more well tuned.
2.1.50).   2. Birds were said to choose their mates on Valentine's
9. *matched . . . each:* harmoniously matched in the   Day.

　　　　Of this their purpose hither to this wood,
　　　　And I in fury hither followed them,
160　　Fair Helena in fancy° following me.　　　　　　　　　　*love*
　　　　But, my good lord, I wot not by what power—
　　　　But by some power it is—my love to Hermia,
　　　　Melted as the snow, seems to me now
　　　　As the remembrance of an idle gaud°　　　　　　　　*a worthless trinket*
165　　Which in my childhood I did dote upon,
　　　　And all the faith, the virtue of my heart,
　　　　The object and the pleasure of mine eye
　　　　Is only Helena. To her, my lord,
　　　　Was I betrothed ere I saw Hermia.
170　　But like in sickness³ did I loathe this food;
　　　　But, as in health come to my natural taste,
　　　　Now I do wish it, love it, long for it,
　　　　And will for evermore be true to it.
　　THESEUS　　Fair lovers, you are fortunately met.
175　　Of this discourse we more will hear anon.—
　　　　Egeus, I will overbear your will,
　　　　For in the temple by and by with us
　　　　These couples shall eternally be knit.—
　　　　And, for° the morning now is something° worn,　　*since / somewhat*
180　　Our purposed hunting shall be set aside.
　　　　Away with us to Athens. Three and three,
　　　　We'll hold a feast in great solemnity.
　　　　Come, Hippolyta.
　　　　　　　　　Exit Duke [THESEUS *with* HIPPOLYTA, EGEUS,
　　　　　　　　　　　　　　and all his train]
　　DEMETRIUS　　These things seem small and undistinguishable,
185　　Like far-off mountains turnèd into clouds.
　　HERMIA　　Methinks I see these things with parted° eye,　　*improperly focused*
　　　　When everything seems double.
　　HELENA　　　　　　　　　　　So methinks,
　　　　And I have found Demetrius like a jewel,
　　　　Mine own and not mine own.⁴
　　DEMETRIUS　　　　　　　　　It seems to me
190　　That yet we sleep, we dream. Do not you think
　　　　The Duke was here and bid us follow him?
　　HERMIA　　Yea, and my father.
　　HELENA　　　　　　　　　And Hippolyta.
　　LYSANDER　　And he did bid us follow to the temple.
　　DEMETRIUS　　Why then, we are awake. Let's follow him,
195　　And by the way let us recount our dreams.　　*Exeunt lovers*
　　　　　　　BOTTOM *wakes*
　　BOTTOM　　When my cue comes, call me, and I will answer. My
　　　　next is 'most fair Pyramus'. Heigh-ho.° Peter Quince? Flute the　　*(Perhaps a yawn)*
　　　　bellows-mender? Snout the tinker? Starveling? God's my life!°　　*Good Lord*
　　　　Stolen hence, and left me asleep?—I have had a most rare
200　　vision. I have had a dream past the wit of man to say what
　　　　dream it was. Man is but an ass if he go about° t'expound this　　*try*
　　　　dream. Methought I was—there is no man can tell what.
　　　　Methought I was, and methought I had—but man is but a

---

3. Only as a person does when ill or nauseated.
4. Mine on the principle of "finders keepers," but once someone else's.

patched fool[5] if he will offer° to say what methought I had. The   venture
205 eye of man hath not heard, the ear of man hath not seen, man's
hand is not able to taste, his tongue to conceive, nor his heart
to report[6] what my dream was. I will get Peter Quince to write
a ballad of this dream. It shall be called 'Bottom's Dream',
because it hath no bottom,[7] and I will sing it in the latter end
210 of a play, before the Duke. Peradventure,° to take it the more   Perhaps
gracious, I shall sing it at her° death.   Exit   (Thisbe's?)

senses all mixed up

4.2
Enter QUINCE, FLUTE, SNOUT, *and* STARVELING

QUINCE Have you sent to Bottom's house? Is he come home
yet?

STARVELING He cannot be heard of. Out of doubt° he is trans-   Doubtless
ported.[1]

5 FLUTE If he come not, then the play is marred. It goes not forward. Doth it?

QUINCE It is not possible. You have not a man in all Athens able
to discharge° Pyramus but he.   perform

FLUTE No, he hath simply the best wit° of any handicraft-man   intellect
10 in Athens.

QUINCE Yea, and the best person,° too; and he is a very para-   looks
mour for a sweet voice.

FLUTE You must say 'paragon'. A paramour is, God bless us, a
thing of naught.°   something wicked

Enter SNUG *the joiner*

15 SNUG Masters, the Duke is coming from the temple, and there
is two or three lords and ladies more married. If our sport° had   entertainment
gone forward we had all been made men.[2]

FLUTE O sweet bully Bottom! Thus hath he lost sixpence a day[3]
during his life. He could not have scaped sixpence a day. An°   If
20 the Duke had not given him sixpence a day for playing Pyramus, I'll be hanged. He would have deserved it. Sixpence a
day in Pyramus, or nothing.

Enter BOTTOM

BOTTOM Where are these lads? Where are these hearts?°   mates

QUINCE Bottom! O most courageous[4] day! O most happy hour!

25 BOTTOM Masters, I am to discourse wonders; but ask me not
what. For if I tell you, I am no true Athenian. I will tell you
everything right as it fell out.

QUINCE Let us hear, sweet Bottom.

BOTTOM Not a word of° me. All that I will tell you is that the   out of
30 Duke hath dined. Get your apparel together, good strings° to (to attach the beards)
your beards, new ribbons to your pumps. Meet presently° at the   immediately
palace; every man look o'er his part. For the short and the long
is, our play is preferred.° In any case let Thisbe have clean   recommended
linen, and let not him that plays the lion pare his nails, for they
35 shall hang out for the lion's claws. And, most dear actors, eat
no onions nor garlic, for we are to utter sweet breath, and I do

---

5. Jester in a patchwork or motley costume.
6. *The eye . . . report*: burlesque of Scripture: "The eye
hath not seen, and the ear hath not heard, neither have
entered into the heart of man" those things that God
has prepared (1 Corinthians 2:9–10 [Bishops' Bible]).
7. Because it is unfathomable, has no substance (foundation).

4.2 Location: Athens.
1. Carried away (by the fairies); transformed.
2. *we . . . men*: our fortunes would have been made.
3. As a royal pension, considerably more than the average daily wage of an Elizabethan workman.
4. Blunder for "brave," meaning "splendid."

not doubt but to hear them say it is a sweet comedy. No more
words. Away, go, away!   *Exeunt*

5.1

Enter THESEUS, HIPPOLYTA, EGEUS,[1] *and [attendant]*
lords

HIPPOLYTA   'Tis strange, my Theseus, that° these lovers speak of.   *that which*
THESEUS   More strange than true. I never may believe
        These antique[2] fables, nor these fairy toys.°   *trifles*
        Lovers and madmen have such seething brains,
5   Such shaping fantasies,° that apprehend°   *imaginations / conceive*
        More than cool reason ever comprehends.
        The lunatic, the lover, and the poet
        Are of imagination all compact.°   *composed*
        One sees more devils than vast hell can hold:
10   That is the madman. The lover, all as frantic,
        Sees Helen's beauty in a brow of Egypt.[3]
        The poet's eye, in a fine frenzy rolling,
        Doth glance from heaven to earth, from earth to heaven,
        And as imagination bodies forth
15   The forms of things unknown, the poet's pen
        Turns them to shapes, and gives to airy nothing
        A local habitation and a name.
        Such tricks hath strong imagination
        That if it would but apprehend some joy
20   It comprehends some bringer° of that joy;   *source*
        Or in the night, imagining some fear,°   *object to be feared*
        How easy is a bush supposed a bear!
HIPPOLYTA   But all the story of the night told over,
        And all their minds transfigured so together,
25   More witnesseth than fancy's images,[4]
        And grows to something of great constancy;°   *consistency*
        But howsoever,° strange and admirable.°   *in any case / wondrous*
            Enter lovers: LYSANDER, DEMETRIUS, HERMIA, *and*
            HELENA
THESEUS   Here come the lovers, full of joy and mirth.
        Joy, gentle friends—joy and fresh days of love
        Accompany your hearts.
30 LYSANDER   More than to us
        Wait in your royal walks, your board, your bed.[5]
THESEUS   Come now, what masques, what dances shall we have
        To wear away this long age of three hours
        Between our after-supper and bed-time?
35   Where is our usual manager of mirth?
        What revels are in hand? Is there no play
        To ease the anguish of a torturing hour?
        Call Egeus.
EGEUS   Here, mighty Theseus.
THESEUS   Say, what abridgement[6] have you for this evening?

5.1 Location: Athens. Theseus's palace.
1. Q does not call for Egeus, but gives all his speeches
to Philostrate (the character briefly addressed in 1.1).
F's substitution of Egeus here may be a mistake (the
possible result of the same actor playing both parts in
an early performance) or an attempt to incorporate the
angry father into the festive close.

2. Ancient; strange, grotesque (as in "antic").
3. In a gypsy's face. *Helen:* Helen of Troy.
4. *More . . . images:* Testifies to something more than
mere figments of the imagination.
5. *More . . . bed:* May even more joy and love attend
your daily lives.
6. Pastime, something to make the evening seem shorter.

40   What masque, what music? How shall we beguile
        The lazy time if not with some delight?
    EGEUS   There is a brief° how many sports are ripe.   *short list*
        Make choice of which your highness will see first.
    LYSANDER[7] [*reads*]   'The battle with the centaurs,[8] to be sung
45   By an Athenian eunuch to the harp.'
    THESEUS   We'll none of that. That have I told my love
        In glory of my kinsman Hercules.[9]
    LYSANDER [*reads*]   'The riot of the tipsy bacchanals
        Tearing the Thracian singer in their rage.'[1]
50   THESEUS   That is an old device,° and it was played   *show*
        When I from Thebes came last a conqueror.
    LYSANDER [*reads*]   'The thrice-three muses mourning for the death
        Of learning, late deceased in beggary.'[2]
    THESEUS   That is some satire, keen and critical,
55   Not sorting with° a nuptial ceremony.   *befitting*
    LYSANDER [*reads*]   'A tedious brief scene of young Pyramus
        And his love Thisbe: very tragical mirth.'
    THESEUS   'Merry' *and* 'tragical'? 'Tedious' *and* 'brief'?—
        That is, hot ice and wondrous strange black[3] snow.
60   How shall we find the concord of this discord?
    EGEUS   A play there is, my lord, some ten words long,
        Which is as 'brief' as I have known a play;
        But by ten words, my lord, it is too long,
        Which makes it 'tedious'; for in all the play
65   There is not one word apt, one player fitted.°   *appropriately cast*
        And 'tragical', my noble lord, it is,
        For Pyramus therein doth kill himself;
        Which when I saw rehearsed, I must confess,
        Made mine eyes water; but more merry tears
70   The passion of loud laughter never shed.
    THESEUS   What are they that do play it?
    EGEUS   Hard-handed men that work in Athens here,
        Which never laboured in their minds till now,
        And now have toiled° their unbreathed° memories   *taxed / unexercised*
75   With this same play against° your nuptial.   *in preparation for*
    THESEUS   And we will hear it.
    EGEUS   No, my noble lord,
        It is not for you. I have heard it over,
        And it is nothing, nothing in the world,
        Unless you can find sport in their intents
80   Extremely stretched,° and conned° with cruel pain   *strained / memorized*
        To do you service.
    THESEUS   I will hear that play;
        For never anything can be amiss
        When simpleness and duty tender it.
        Go, bring them in; and take your places, ladies. [*Exit* EGEUS]

---

7. In Q, Theseus both reads the list and comments on it himself.
8. Probably the battle that occurred when the Centaurs tried to carry off the bride of Theseus's friend Pirithous.
9. According to Plutarch, Hercules and Theseus were cousins.
1. The murder of the poet Orpheus by drunken women, devotees of Dionysus.

2. Possibly a topical reference: Robert Greene, Christopher Marlowe, and Thomas Kyd, university wits who began writing for the stage in the 1580s, all died in desperate circumstances in 1592–94. But satiric laments on the poverty of scholars and poets were commonplace.
3. "Black" is an editorial conjecture. Q and F omit a word that would make "snow" an oxymoron comparable to "hot ice."

85	HIPPOLYTA I love not to see wretchedness o'ercharged,[4]	
	And duty in his service° perishing.	*its attempt to serve*
	THESEUS Why, gentle sweet, you shall see no such thing.	
	HIPPOLYTA He says they can do nothing in this kind.°	*kind of thing*
	THESEUS The kinder we, to give them thanks for nothing.	
90	Our sport shall be to take what they mistake,	
	And what poor duty cannot do,	
	Noble respect° takes it in might, not merit.[5]	*consideration*
	Where I have come, great clerks° have purposèd	*scholars*
	To greet me with premeditated welcomes,	
95	Where I have seen them shiver and look pale,	
	Make periods in the midst of sentences,	
	Throttle their practised accent[6] in their fears,	
	And in conclusion dumbly have broke off,	
	Not paying me a welcome. Trust me, sweet,	
100	Out of this silence yet I picked a welcome,	
	And in the modesty of fearful° duty	*frightened*
	I read as much as from the rattling tongue	
	Of saucy and audacious eloquence.	
	Love, therefore, and tongue-tied simplicity	
105	In least speak most, to my capacity.°	*in my judgment*

[*Enter* EGEUS]

EGEUS   So please your grace, the Prologue is addressed.[7]

THESEUS   Let him approach.

Flourish trumpets. Enter [QUINCE *as*] *the Prologue*

QUINCE [*as Prologue*]   If we offend, it is with our good will.
That you should think: we come not to offend
But with good will. To show our simple skill,
That is the true beginning of our end.
Consider then we come but in despite.
We do not come as minding° to content you,   *intending*
Our true intent is. All for your delight
We are not here. That you should here repent you
The actors are at hand, and by their show
You shall know all that you are like to know.[8]

THESEUS   This fellow doth not stand upon points.[9]

LYSANDER   He hath rid his prologue like a rough° colt: he knows   *an unbroken*
not the stop.[1] A good moral, my lord: it is not enough to speak,
but to speak true.

HIPPOLYTA   Indeed, he hath played on this prologue like a child
on a recorder[2]—a sound, but not in government.°   *control*

THESEUS   His speech was like a tangled chain—nothing°   *not at all*
impaired, but all disordered. Who is next?

Enter with a trumpeter before them [BOTTOM *as*] *Pyra-*
mus, [FLUTE *as*] *Thisbe,* [SNOUT *as*] *Wall,* [STARVELING
as] *Moonshine, and* [SNUG *as*] *Lion* [*for the dumb*
show][3]

---

4. Overburdened. *wretchedness:* incompetence or weakness; poor people.
5. *in . . . merit:* with respect to the giver's capacity, not the merit of the performance.
6. Rehearsed eloquence; usual manner of speaking.
7. The speaker of the Prologue is ready.
8. The humor of Quince's speech rests in its mispunctuation; repunctuated, it becomes a typical courteous address.

9. Bother about niceties; heed punctuation marks.
1. How to rein the colt to a stop; punctuation mark.
2. A woodwind instrument resembling a flute.
3. Elizabethan plays were often prefaced by a "dumb show" in which the actors silently mimed the main action, occasionally to the accompaniment (as here) of a narrator. The artisans may enact the story as Quince tells it, merely adopt symbolic attitudes, or introduce themselves.

QUINCE [*as Prologue*] Gentles, perchance you wonder at this show,
    But wonder on, till truth make all things plain.
  This man is Pyramus, if you would know;
    This beauteous lady Thisbe is, certain.
130 This man with lime and roughcast doth present
    Wall, that vile wall which did these lovers sunder;
  And through Wall's chink, poor souls, they are content
    To whisper; at the which let no man wonder.
  This man, with lantern, dog, and bush of thorn,
135   Presenteth Moonshine. For if you will know,
  By moonshine did these lovers think no scorn°   (*it*) *no disgrace*
    To meet at Ninus' tomb, there, there to woo.
  This grizzly beast, which 'Lion' hight° by name,   *is called*
    The trusty Thisbe coming first by night
140 Did scare away, or rather did affright;
  And as she fled, her mantle she did fall,°   *drop*
    Which Lion vile with bloody mouth did stain.
  Anon comes Pyramus, sweet youth and tall,°   *brave*
    And finds his trusty Thisbe's mantle slain;
145 Whereat with blade—with bloody, blameful blade—
    He bravely broached° his boiling bloody breast;   *stabbed*
  And Thisbe, tarrying in mulberry shade,
    His dagger drew and died. For all the rest,
  Let Lion, Moonshine, Wall, and lovers twain
150 At large° discourse, while here they do remain.   *length*
              Exeunt all [*the clowns*] *but* [SNOUT *as*] *Wall*
THESEUS   I wonder if the lion be to speak.
DEMETRIUS   No wonder, my lord—one lion may when many
asses do.
SNOUT [*as Wall*]   In this same interlude° it doth befall   *play*
155 That I, one Snout by name, present a wall;
  And such a wall as I would have you think
  That had in it a crannied hole or chink,
  Through which the lovers Pyramus and Thisbe
  Did whisper often, very secretly.
160 This loam, this roughcast, and this stone doth show
  That I am that same wall; the truth is so.
  And this the cranny is, right and sinister,⁴
  Through which the fearful lovers are to whisper.
THESEUS   Would you desire lime and hair to speak better?
165 DEMETRIUS   It is the wittiest partition⁵ that ever I heard dis-
course, my lord.
              Enter [BOTTOM *as*] *Pyramus*
THESEUS   Pyramus draws near the wall. Silence.
BOTTOM [*as Pyramus*]   O grim-looked° night, O night with hue   *grim-looking*
    so black,
  O night which ever art when day is not;
170 O night, O night, alack, alack, alack,
    I fear my Thisbe's promise is forgot.
  And thou, O wall, O sweet O lovely wall,
    That stand'st between her father's ground and mine,
  Thou wall, O wall, O sweet and lovely wall,

---

4. Left; running horizontally. Or on the one side   5. Wall; formal term for part of an oration.
(Pyramus's) and the other (Thisbe's).

175   Show me thy chink, to blink through with mine eyne.
             [*Wall shows his chink*]
         Thanks, courteous wall. Jove shield thee well for this.
         But what see I? No Thisbe do I see.
         O wicked wall, through whom I see no bliss,
         Cursed be thy stones[6] for thus deceiving me.
180 THESEUS The wall methinks, being sensible,° should curse   *capable of feeling*
         again.°   *back*
     BOTTOM [*to* THESEUS] No, in truth, sir, he should not. 'Deceiv-
         ing me' is Thisbe's cue. She is to enter now, and I am to spy
         her through the wall. You shall see, it will fall pat° as I told you.   *precisely*
             Enter [FLUTE *as*] Thisbe
185   Yonder she comes.
     FLUTE [*as Thisbe*] O wall, full often hast thou heard my moans
         For parting my fair Pyramus and me.
         My cherry lips have often kissed thy stones,
         Thy stones with lime and hair knit up in thee.
190 BOTTOM [*as Pyramus*] I see a voice. Now will I to the chink
         To spy an° I can hear my Thisbe's face.   *if*
         Thisbe?
     FLUTE [*as Thisbe*] My love—thou art my love, I think.
     BOTTOM [*as Pyramus*] Think what thou wilt, I am thy lover's
         grace°   *gracious lover*
         And like Lemander[7] am I trusty still.
195 FLUTE [*as Thisbe*] And I like Helen,[8] till the fates me kill.
     BOTTOM [*as Pyramus*] Not Shaphalus to Procrus[9] was so true.
     FLUTE [*as Thisbe*] As Shaphalus to Procrus, I to you.
     BOTTOM [*as Pyramus*] O kiss me through the hole of this vile wall.
     FLUTE [*as Thisbe*] I kiss the wall's hole, not your lips at all.
     BOTTOM [*as Pyramus*] Wilt thou at Ninny's tomb meet me
200   straightway?
     FLUTE [*as Thisbe*] Tide° life, tide death, I come without delay.   *Betide; come*
             [*Exeunt* BOTTOM *and* FLUTE *severally*]
     SNOUT [*as Wall*] Thus have I, Wall, my part dischargèd so;
         And being done, thus Wall away doth go.   **Exit**
     THESEUS Now is the wall down between the two neighbours.
205 DEMETRIUS No remedy, my lord, when walls are so wilful to°   *as to*
         hear without warning.[1]
     HIPPOLYTA This is the silliest stuff that ever I heard.
     THESEUS The best in this kind are but shadows,[2] and the worst
         are no worse if imagination amend them.
210 HIPPOLYTA It must be your imagination, then, and not theirs.
     THESEUS If we imagine no worse of them than they of them-
         selves, they may pass for excellent men. Here come two noble
         beasts in: a man and a lion.
             Enter [SNUG *as*] Lion, [*and* STARVELING *as*] Moonshine
             [*with a lantern, thorn bush, and dog*]
     SNUG [*as Lion*] You, ladies, you whose gentle hearts do fear

---

6. Punning on "testicles."
7. Blunder for "Leander," who drowned while swimming across the Hellespont to meet his lover, Hero.
8. Helen of Troy was notoriously untrustworthy; a
blunder for "Hero."
9. Blunder for "Cephalus" and "Procris." Procris was in
fact seduced by her husband in disguise as another
man; he later accidentally killed her.
1. Informing the parents. *hear*: proverbially, "walls
have ears."
2. Mere likenesses without substance. *kind*: profession
(that is, actors)

215   The smallest monstrous mouse that creeps on floor,
        May now perchance both quake and tremble here
            When lion rough in wildest rage doth roar.
        Then know that I as Snug the joiner am
        A lion fell,³ nor else no lion's dam.
220   For if I should as Lion come in strife
        Into this place, 'twere pity on my life.

THESEUS   A very gentle beast, and of a good conscience.

DEMETRIUS   The very best at a beast, my lord, that e'er I saw.

LYSANDER   This lion is a very fox⁴ for his valour.

225 THESEUS   True, and a goose⁵ for his discretion.

DEMETRIUS   Not so, my lord, for his valour cannot carry his discretion, and the fox carries the goose.

THESEUS   His discretion, I am sure, cannot carry his valour, for
the goose carries not the fox. It is well. Leave it to his discretion,
230 and let us listen to the moon.

STARVELING [*as Moonshine*]   This lantern doth the hornèd°   *crescent*
      moon present.

DEMETRIUS   He should have worn the horns on his head.⁶

THESEUS   He is no crescent,° and his horns are invisible within   *waxing moon*
the circumference.

235 STARVELING [*as Moonshine*]   This lantern doth the hornèd moon present.
      Myself the man i'th' moon do seem to be.

THESEUS   This is the greatest error of all the rest—the man
should be put into the lantern. How is it else the man i'th'
moon?

240 DEMETRIUS   He dares not come there for° the candle; for you see   *for fear of*
it is already in snuff.⁷

HIPPOLYTA   I am aweary of this moon. Would he would change.

THESEUS   It appears by his small light of discretion that he is in
the wane; but yet in courtesy, in all reason, we must stay the
245 time.

LYSANDER   Proceed, Moon.

STARVELING   All that I have to say is to tell you that the lantern
is the moon, I the man i'th' moon, this thorn bush my thorn
bush, and this dog my dog.

250 DEMETRIUS   Why, all these should be in the lantern, for all these
are in the moon. But silence; here comes Thisbe.

        *Enter [*FLUTE *as*] *Thisbe*

FLUTE [*as Thisbe*]   This is old Ninny's tomb. Where is my love?

SNUG [*as Lion*]   O.

        *Lion roars. Thisbe [*drops her mantle and*] runs off*

DEMETRIUS   Well roared, Lion.

255 THESEUS   Well run, Thisbe.

HIPPOLYTA   Well shone, Moon.—Truly, the moon shines with a
good grace.

        [*Lion worries Thisbe's mantle*]

THESEUS   Well moused,⁸ Lion.

DEMETRIUS   And then came Pyramus.

        *Enter [*BOTTOM *as*] *Pyramus*

260 LYSANDER   And so the lion vanished.   [*Exit Lion*]

---

3. Fierce; or skin (punning on the costume to which
Snug reassuringly calls attention).
4. Symbolic of low cunning, rather than courage.
5. Symbolic of foolishness.

6. The symbol of a cuckold.
7. In need of snuffing; angry.
8. The mantle is like a mouse in the mouth of a cat.

BOTTOM [*as Pyramus*]   Sweet moon, I thank thee for thy sunny beams.
   I thank thee, moon, for shining now so bright;
   For by thy gracious, golden, glittering gleams
   I trust to take of truest Thisbe sight.
265   But stay, O spite!
      But mark, poor knight,
   What dreadful dole° is here?   grief
      Eyes, do you see?
      How can it be?
270   O dainty duck, O dear!
      Thy mantle good,
      What, stained with blood?
   Approach, ye furies fell.
      O fates,⁹ come, come,
275   Cut thread and thrum,¹
   Quail,° crush, conclude, and quell.°   Overpower / kill
THESEUS   This passion—and² the death of a dear friend—would
   go near to make a man look sad.
HIPPOLYTA   Beshrew my heart, but I pity the man.
280 BOTTOM [*as Pyramus*]   O wherefore, nature, didst thou lions frame,
   Since lion vile hath here deflowered³ my dear?—
   Which is—no, no, which *was*—the fairest dame
   That lived, that loved, that liked, that looked, with cheer.
      Come tears, confound;
285   Out sword, and wound
   The pap° of Pyramus.   breast
      Ay, that left pap, **nipple**
   Where heart doth hop.
   Thus die I: thus, thus, thus.
      [*He stabs himself*]
290   Now am I dead,
      Now am I fled,
   My soul is in the sky.
      Tongue, lose thy light;
      Moon, take thy flight.   [*Exit Moonshine*]
295   Now die, die, die, die, die.   [*He dies*]
DEMETRIUS   No die but an ace for him; for he is but one.⁴
LYSANDER   Less than an ace, man; for he is dead; he is nothing.
THESEUS   With the help of a surgeon he might yet recover and
   prove an ass.
300 HIPPOLYTA   How chance Moonshine is gone before Thisbe
   comes back and finds her lover.
THESEUS   She will find him by starlight.
      Enter [FLUTE *as*] *Thisbe*
   Here she comes, and her passion° ends the play.   passionate speech
HIPPOLYTA   Methinks she should not use a long one for such a
305   Pyramus. I hope she will be brief.
DEMETRIUS   A mote° will turn the balance which Pyramus,   speck

---

9. The three Fates in Greek mythology spun and cut
the thread of a person's life.
1. A technical term from Bottom's occupation: the
tufted end of a weaver's warp, or set of yarns placed
lengthwise in a loom when the woven fabric is cut.
2. Only if combined with. *passion*: suffering; extravagant

speech.
3. Ruined (but commonly suggesting "deprived of her
virginity"); his error for "devoured."
4. Pun on "die" as one of a pair of dice. *one*: the ace, or
lowest throw.

which[5] Thisbe, is the better—he for a man, God warrant us;
she for a woman, God bless us.

LYSANDER She hath spied him already with those sweet eyes.

310 DEMETRIUS And thus she means, videlicet:[6]

FLUTE [*as Thisbe*] Asleep, my love?
    What, dead, my dove?
    O Pyramus, arise.
    Speak, speak. Quite dumb?
315   Dead, dead? A tomb
  Must cover thy sweet eyes.
    These lily lips,
    This cherry nose,
  These yellow cowslip cheeks
320   Are gone, are gone.
    Lovers, make moan.
  His eyes were green as leeks.
    O sisters three,°   *the Fates*
    Come, come to me
325 With hands as pale as milk.
    Lay them in gore,
    Since you have shore°   *shorn*
  With shears his thread of silk.
    Tongue, not a word.
330   Come, trusty sword,
  Come, blade, my breast imbrue.°   *stain with blood*
    [*She stabs herself*]
  And farewell friends,
    Thus Thisbe ends.
  Adieu, adieu, adieu.   [*She dies*]

335 THESEUS Moonshine and Lion are left to bury the dead.

DEMETRIUS Ay, and Wall too.

BOTTOM[7] No, I assure you, the wall is down that parted their
  fathers. Will it please you to see the epilogue or to hear a bergamask dance[8] between two of our company?

340 THESEUS No epilogue, I pray you; for your play needs no excuse.
  Never excuse; for when the players are all dead there need
  none to be blamed. Marry, if he that writ it had played Pyramus
  and hanged himself in Thisbe's garter it would have been a
  fine tragedy; and so it is, truly, and very notably discharged. But
345 come, your bergamask. Let your epilogue alone.
      [BOTTOM *and* FLUTE[9] *dance a bergamask, then exeunt*]
  The iron tongue of midnight hath told° twelve.   *counted; tolled*
  Lovers, to bed; 'tis almost fairy time.
  I fear we shall outsleep the coming morn
350 As much as we this night have overwatched.°   *stayed awake too late*
  This palpable-gross° play hath well beguiled   *palpably crude*
  The heavy° gait of night. Sweet friends, to bed.   *drowsy; slow*
  A fortnight hold we this solemnity
  In nightly revels and new jollity.   *Exeunt*

Poem here - blazon of beauties

---

5. *which . . . which:* whether . . . or.
6. As follows. *means:* moans; lodges a formal legal
complaint.
7. Spoken by Snug, the Lion, in Q.

8. A dance named after Bergamo, in Italy (commonly
ridiculed for its rusticity).
9. The only "two of our company" onstage at the end of
the play.

5.2

Enter Puck [ROBIN GOODFELLOW, with a broom]

ROBIN   Now the hungry lion roars,
      And the wolf behowls the moon,
    whilst the heavy° ploughman snores,   *weary*
      All with weary task fordone.°   *"done in"; exhausted*
5   Now the wasted brands° do glow   *burned-out logs*
      Whilst the screech-owl, screeching loud,
    Puts the wretch that lies in woe
      In remembrance of a shroud.
    Now it is the time of night
10   That the graves, all gaping wide,
    Every one lets forth his sprite[1]
      In the churchway paths to glide;
    And we fairies that do run
      By the triple Hecate's[2] team
15   From the presence of the sun,
      Following darkness like a dream,
    Now are frolic.° Not a mouse   *merry*
    Shall disturb this hallowed house.
    I am sent with broom[3] before
20   To sweep the dust behind° the door.   *from behind*

Enter [OBERON and TITANIA,] King and Queen of
Fairies, with all their train

OBERON   Through the house give glimmering light.
      By the dead and drowsy fire
    Every elf and fairy sprite
      Hop as light as bird from brier,
25   And this ditty after me
    Sing, and dance it trippingly.
TITANIA   First rehearse your song by rote,
    To each word a warbling note.
    Hand in hand with fairy grace
30   Will we sing and bless this place.

The song.[4] [The fairies dance]

OBERON   Now until the break of day
    Through this house each fairy stray.
    To the best bride bed will we,[5]
    Which by us shall blessèd be,
35   And the issue there create°   *created; conceived*
    Ever shall be fortunate.
    So shall all the couples three
    Ever true in loving be,
    And the blots of nature's hand
40   Shall not in their issue stand.
    Never mole, harelip, nor scar,
    Nor mark prodigious° such as are   *ominous birthmark*
    Despisèd in nativity
    Shall upon their children be.

5.2 Location: Theseus's palace.
1. Each grave lets forth its ghost.
2. Hecate was goddess of the moon and night, and had three realms: heaven (as Cynthia), earth (as Diana), and hell (as Proserpine).
3. One of his traditional emblems; he helped good housekeepers and punished lazy ones.
4. F does not assign lines 31–52 to Oberon. They are indented and printed in italics as "The Song."
5. Oberon and Titania will bless the bed of Theseus and Hippolyta.

45 With this field-dew consecrate[6]
Every fairy take his gait°   *way*
And each several° chamber bless   *separate*
Through this palace with sweet peace;
And the owner of it blessed
50 Ever shall in safety rest.
Trip away, make no stay,
Meet me all by break of day.
Exeunt [all but ROBIN]

across

Epilogue

ROBIN   If we shadows have offended,
Think but this, and all is mended:
That you have but slumbered here,
While these visions did appear;
5 And this weak and idle theme,
No more yielding but° a dream,   *than*
Gentles, do not reprehend.
If you pardon, we will mend.
And as I am an honest puck,
10 If we have unearnèd luck
Now to 'scape the serpent's tongue,[1]
We will make amends ere long,
Else the puck a liar call.
So, good night unto you all.
15 Give me your hands,° if we be friends,   *applause*
And Robin shall restore amends.

Additional Passage

An unusual quantity and kind of mislineation in Q1 has persuaded most scholars that
the text at the beginning of 5.1 was revised, with new material written in the margins.
The Oxford editors here offer a reconstruction of the passage as originally drafted, which
can be compared with 5.1.1–86 of the edited text.

5.1

Enter THESEUS, HIPPOLYTA, *and* PHILOSTRATE
HIPPOLYTA   'Tis strange, my Theseus, that these lovers speak of.
THESEUS   More strange than true. I never may believe
These antique fables, nor these fairy toys.
Lovers and mad men have such seething brains.
5 One sees more devils than vast hell can hold:
That is the madman. The lover, all as frantic,
Sees Helen's beauty in a brow of Egypt.
Such tricks hath strong imagination
That if it would but apprehend some joy
10 It comprehends some bringer of that joy;
Or in the night, imagining some fear,
How easy is a bush supposed a bear!
HIPPOLYTA   But all the story of the night told over,
And all their minds transfigured so together,

---

6. Consecrated, blessed. Playfully alludes to traditional
Catholic custom of blessing the bride bed with holy
water.

Epilogue
1. Hissing from the audience.

15 More witnesseth than fancy's images,
    And grows to something of great constancy;
    But howsoever, strange and admirable.
            Enter the lovers: LYSANDER, DEMETRIUS, HERMIA, *and*
            HELENA
    THESEUS   Here come the lovers, full of joy and mirth.
    Come now, what masques, what dances shall we have
20 To ease the anguish of a torturing hour?
    Call Philostrate.
    PHILOSTRATE   Here mighty Theseus.
    THESEUS   Say, what abridgement have you for this evening?
    What masque, what music? How shall we beguile
    The lazy time if not with some delight?
25 PHILOSTRATE   There is a brief how many sports are ripe.
    Make choice of which your highness will see first.
    THESEUS   'The battle with the centaurs to be sung
    By an Athenian eunuch to the harp.'
    We'll none of that. That have I told my love
30 In glory of my kinsman Hercules.
    'The riot of the tipsy Bacchanals
    Tearing the Thracian singer in their rage.'
    That is an old device, and it was played
    When I from Thebes came last a conquerer.
35 'The thrice-three Muses mourning for the death
    Of learning, late deceased in beggary.'
    That is some satire, keen and critical,
    Not sorting with a nuptial ceremony.
    'A tedious brief scene of young Pyramus
40 And his love Thisby.' 'Tedious' *and* 'brief'?
    PHILOSTRATE   A play there is, my lord, some ten words long,
    Which is as 'brief' as I have known a play;
    But by ten words, my lord, it is too long,
    Which makes it 'tedious'; for in all the play
45 There is not one word apt, one player fitted.
    THESEUS   What are they that do play it?
    PHILOSTRATE   Hard-handed men that work in Athens here,
    Which never laboured in their minds till now,
    And now have toiled their unbreathed memories
50 With this same play against your nuptial.
    THESEUS   Go, bring them in; and take your places, ladies.
                                    Exit PHILOSTRATE
    HIPPOLYTA   I love not to see wretchedness o'ercharged
    And duty in his service perishing.

The Merchant of Venice

Jew. Jew. Jew. The word echoes through *The Merchant of Venice.* The play has generated controversy for centuries. Is it anti-Semitic? Does it criticize anti-Semitism? Does it merely represent anti-Semitism without either endorsement or condemnation? Are the Christians right to call Shylock, the Jewish moneylender, a "devil," an "inexorable dog"; or is he merely the understandably resentful victim of their bigotry? Does Portia, Shylock's antagonist in the courtroom, exemplify the best in womanly virtue, or is she a manipulative virago? These questions about character suggest others that might be phrased more generally. What are the obligations of majority cultures to minorities in their midst? Do universally shared human characteristics outweigh racial and religious differences, or are such differences decisive?

Perhaps these issues seem more pressing nowadays than they did for Shakespeare. He could hardly could have predicted Nazi genocide or other modern forms of "ethnic cleansing." Nor could he have foreseen the opportunities and problems faced by multiracial societies centuries after his death. Nevertheless, by Shakespeare's time, the legacy of Jew hating in western Europe was already long and bitter. Depictions of fiendish Jews were routine in medieval and Renaissance drama; the villainous protagonist of Christopher Marlowe's *Jew of Malta,* a popular success in the early 1590s, was only the latest precedent. In 1594, shortly before Shakespeare wrote *The Merchant of Venice,* an outpouring of anti-Semitic outrage was triggered by the case of Roderigo Lopez, a Portuguese Jewish convert to Christianity accused of attempting to murder Queen Elizabeth.

Of course, the existence of anti-Semitism in sixteenth-century England says little about Shakespeare's own attitudes. He could have written *The Merchant of Venice* either to capitalize on or to criticize the prejudices of his society. Interestingly, Shakespeare had probably never encountered practicing Jews, since they had been forcibly expelled from England in the Middle Ages. And England was not alone in its intolerance. In 1492, Spain banished all non-Christians. Christians fought among themselves as well: during the sixteenth century, northern Europe saw decades of bloody conflict between Catholics and Protestants, while much of southern Europe was in the grip of the Inquisition. The impulse behind these persecutions was the conviction that a stable society required a shared belief system. A community based on consensus can indeed be impressively cohesive. Its homogeneity, however, makes it impatient of those who do not share its assumptions. Moreover, by the 1590s, when Shakespeare wrote *The Merchant of Venice,* bloody religious conflict all over Europe was making such consensus seem increasingly elusive—something obtainable, if at all, only at appalling human cost.

Possibly Venice seemed to Shakespeare to offer an alternative social prototype. Although it had no natural resources to speak of, it was the richest city in Renaissance Europe, located where the products of Asia could most conveniently be exchanged with those of western Europe. As a town of traders, Venice was full of foreigners: Turks, Jews, Arabs, Africans, Christians of various nationalities and denominations. By sixteenth-century standards, the city was unusually tolerant of diversity. This relative toleration was intimately linked with the city's wealth: its legal guarantees of fair treatment for all were designed to keep its markets running smoothly. Antonio tells Solanio:

> The Duke cannot deny the course of law,
> For the commodity that strangers have

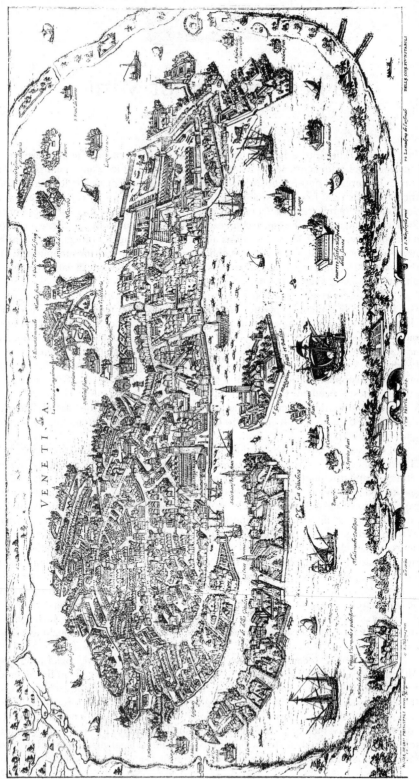

Prospect of Venice. From George Braun and Franz Hogenberg, *Civitates Orbis Terrarum* (1593).

> With us in Venice, if it be denied,
> Will much impeach the justice of the state,
> Since that the trade and profit of the city
> Consisteth of all nations.
>
> (3.3.26–31)

Shakespeare stresses, even exaggerates, this evenhanded cosmopolitanism. Historically, for instance, Venetian Jews were confined to a ghetto, gated and locked at night, but Shakespeare either did not know this fact or chose to ignore it. Venice thus provided Shakespeare with an example—perhaps the only example in sixteenth-century Europe—of a place where people with little in common culturally might coexist peacefully solely because it was materially expedient to do so. The laws of the marketplace seemed to have little to do with religion or nationality.

In *The Merchant of Venice,* Shakespeare juxtaposes social relations based on similarity with social relations based on economic self-interest. The Christian gentlemen who populate the opening scenes comprise a community with a common value system. Acutely aware of what they have in common, these individuals are openhanded to others in their group. When Bassanio asks Antonio for a loan, Antonio rushes to supply him even though he does not have the money at hand. When Graziano asks a favor of Bassanio, Bassanio grants it before he even hears what it is. Later in the play, when Portia finds out that Antonio's life is forfeit because of 3,000 ducats, she instantly offers to pay twelve times that sum to redeem him. Not entirely surprisingly, Bassanio is an amiable spendthrift whose plan to recoup his monetary losses involves considerable risk:

> In my schooldays, when I had lost one shaft,
> I shot his fellow of the selfsame flight
> The selfsame way, with more advisèd watch,
> To find the other forth; and by adventuring both,
> I oft found both.
>
> (1.1.140–44)

"Oft" is not "always." Sometimes, presumably, Bassanio lost both arrows. His temperamental similarity to his friend Antonio, the merchant-adventurer, is an optimism about gambling at long odds.

Such prodigal panache is undeniably attractive, especially in comedy, where generic conventions typically ensure that characters beat long odds. It generates, moreover, some of the most gorgeous poetry of the play, a language of risky munificence, in which phenomenal wealth is accumulated only to be splendidly dispersed. Salerio, for instance, describes a shipwreck as a beautiful squandering of luxury goods:

> dangerous rocks,
> Which, touching but my gentle vessel's side,
> Would scatter all her spices on the stream,
> Enrobe the roaring waters with my silks.
>
> (1.1.31–34)

Likewise, Portia tells Bassanio:

> for myself alone
> I would not be ambitious in my wish
> To wish myself much better, yet for you
> I would be trebled twenty times myself,
> A thousand times more fair, ten thousand times more rich,
> That only to stand high in your account
> I might in virtues, beauties, livings, friends,
> Exceed account.
>
> (3.2.150–57)

Unfortunately, it soon becomes obvious that the Christians' generosity, grace, and self-assurance have a disconcerting racist tinge. The magnanimous, depressive Antonio proudly acknowledges kicking and spitting on Shylock. The charming Portia rejoices in the failure of her black suitor to choose the correct casket: "Let all of his complexion choose me so" (2.7.79). These people find it hard to deal with those different from themselves: their society is based as much on the exclusion of the alien as on the inclusion of the similar. The moral ambiguity of the Christians' outlook is captured in their fondness for the loaded word "kind," which in Renaissance English meant not only "compassionate" but "similar," or "akin." People act benevolently toward those who are of the same *kind* as themselves.

Shylock's relation to the Venetian Christians exemplifies a different social mechanism. Unable to trust to love and generosity, Shylock relies instead on contractually enforceable promises and networks of mutual material need. Shylock's emphasis on purely economic factors means that he does not think about money the way Antonio and Bassanio do. He tends not to spend but to conserve, not to expand but to defend, not to seek risk but to minimize it. When he imagines disaster, he envisions not a spectacular swirl of silk and spices, but a sordid scenario of thievery and nibbling rats.

Although Shylock identifies strongly with his "sacred nation," his "tribe," and although he apparently relies on fellow Jews like Tubal, the play gives little sense of Jewish community. The play represents Shylock as an isolated figure, shunned by his daughter, abandoned by his servant. His calculating, loveless existence seems to result from the way he manages his property. Or perhaps isolation has made him cautious and selfish. Shylock has little motive to be generous with the Christians who despise him, and every reason to believe that he cannot depend on others to rescue him from misfortune.

The psychological and social contrasts between the Christians and Shylock reflect both class and religious differences. The Christians' magnificent improvidence is, in Shakespeare's time, a distinctively aristocratic trait. A true gentleman refuses to be too obviously concerned with monetary expenditure, especially where friends are concerned. He also feels socially obliged to display himself properly. Bassanio spends huge sums of borrowed money equipping himself for his trip to Belmont, even though all he technically need do is arrive alone and select the correct casket. Coming to Portia unattended or in shabby clothes is unthinkable even though (or perhaps because) "all the wealth I had," as Bassanio freely admits, "ran in my veins" (3.2.253–54). By contrast Shylock, despite his evident wealth, is obviously no gentleman. He locks up his possessions, regrets how much his servant eats, fumes over the money he spends searching for his missing daughter.

At the same time, the opposition between the Christians and Shylock seems rooted in religious disparities. Judaism in the play is presented not in its actual complexity but as a sixteenth-century Christian like Shakespeare would have construed it, as a set of dramatically vivid contrasts with Christian norms. The law of Moses, as set down in Deuteronomy and Leviticus, specifies

"Jews." From Jost Amman, *The Panoplia* (1568).

numerous aspects of the observant Jew's life—what to eat and wear, how to worship, how to conduct business, how to punish crimes. The Mosaic code places a high value upon justice and emphasizes the importance of adhering to the letter of the law. Shylock's Judaism reveals itself not merely in his distinctive dress and his avoidance of pork, but in his trust of literal meanings, his respect for observable facts, his expectation that contracts will be rigorously enforced.

The typical Christian outlook is different. Christians obtain divine approval not by wearing certain garments, avoiding particular foods, or circumcising their boys, but by believing in Christ's power to save them. The central virtues in this religious system are not justice and scrupulous compliance with the law but charity, mercy, and a willingness to believe what seems incredible. In the terms Shakespeare provides in *The Merchant of Venice*, the Christian demeanor is entrepreneurial, even reckless, the spiritual equivalent of what Antonio does with his ships or Bassanio does with the money he borrows from his friend. "Give up everything you have and follow me," Jesus tells his would-

Young man in Venice. From Cesare Vecellio, *De gli habiti antichi et moderni* (1590).

be follower, advice echoed in the inscription on the lead casket: "Who chooseth me must give and hazard all he hath." Like the word "kind," the similarly complex word "gentle" is used repeatedly in the play to describe this distinctive set of traits: the word simultaneously refers to considerate behavior, to aristocratic family background, and to "gentile," or Christian, religious convictions.

The differences between Christian and Jew become starkly apparent over the issue of usury. Antonio thinks he ought to lend money to friends as an act of charity, properly performed as freely as God Himself dispenses grace. "For when did friendship take / A breed for barren metal of his friend?" (1.3.128–29). The charging of interest seems improperly to generate money from money alone: wealth loses its purely instrumental quality and acquires an uncanny capacity to "breed," or reproduce, like a live organism. Usury, blurring the distinction between the domain of the spirit and the merely material realm, threatens to collapse friendship, a spiritual relationship, into a mere economic transaction.

Shylock, by contrast, refuses to distinguish between human relations and money relations. His "pound of flesh" proposal, baldly insisting that flesh is convertible to ducats, demands that the Christians violate their own taboo against confusing categories of spirit and matter, flesh and money, live and dead. Thus Bassanio initially finds the bargain absolutely unacceptable. At the same time, the very existence of the taboo encourages the Christians to accept Shylock's characterization of the contract as a "merry sport": they simply cannot believe he is serious. Antonio mistakenly binds himself under the gross but entirely typical misapprehension that Shylock has mysteriously become "kind."

As the play proceeds, it modifies somewhat these initially vivid contrasts between Christian and Jew. Shylock pretends that he thinks of people in purely material, economic terms; but he becomes a moving character precisely at those moments when he admits another kind of value. After Jessica's flight, Solanio claims that Shylock has been seen running through the streets crying, "O, my ducats! O, my daughter! . . . My ducats and my daughter!" (2.8.15ff.). It is impossible to know how accurate this rumor might be: the equation of ducats and daughter is exactly what Christians expect of Shylock. But when Shylock finally appears onstage, he says nothing of the kind. When Tubal tells him that Jessica has exchanged a turquoise ring for a monkey, Shylock replies: "Out upon her! Thou torturest me, Tubal. It was my turquoise. I had it of Leah when I was a bachelor. I would not have given it for a wilderness of monkeys" (3.1.100–02). Insisting upon the sentimental value of the turquoise ring, Shylock seems directly to deny the convertibility of human into monetary relations. His grief over his daughter's defection, and her insensitivity to his relation with her dead mother, exceeds his financial loss. Likewise in the courtroom, Shylock is remarkable not for his calculating prudence but for his refusal to be swayed by monetary appeals. There is something in the quality of his oppression that he refuses to convert into a payoff.

The Christians are also more complicated than they profess to be. Although human values, in their view, transcend marketplace values, and they are commanded to love not only neighbors but even enemies, only some persons elicit a humane response. Others are disregarded or treated as nonhuman. When Salerio and Solanio ridicule Shylock, he protests: "Hath not a Jew eyes? Hath not a Jew hands, organs, dimensions, senses, affections, passions; fed with the same food, hurt with the same weapons, subject to the same diseases, healed by the same means, warmed and cooled by the same winter and summer as a Christian is?" (3.1.49–54). Shylock asserts that a common human experience of embodiment ought to override considerations of religious or racial difference. These lines are among the most memorable in the play, but the argument does not follow from the position Shylock has taken earlier. Rather, it is effective because it exposes Christian hypocrisy. Similarly, in the trial scene, Shylock points out that the Christian practice of slavery plainly sets a monetary value upon human beings. The Christians' creed mandates universal love, but they fail to behave in accord with their precepts.

These inconsistencies haunt the play's friendships and marriages. Marriage is a hybrid social relation: obviously associated with love and with the reproduction of living organisms, it is simultaneously a property relation, involving the economic alliance of individuals and families. Bassanio's courtship of Portia is doubly motivated: he loves her, and he needs her money. The language of his attraction, even at its most generous and disinterested, is full of the metaphors of commerce and exchange. And although Antonio protests against thinking of friendship as an economic transaction, it is not difficult to construe his generosity as an attempt to buy Bassanio's love. So although the Christians attempt to differentiate spiritual values from economic ones, those values continually turn out to be intimately intertwined.

The casket test directly confronts this problem. The failures of Morocco and Aragon demonstrate that it is possible to find a plausible reason for choosing any one of the three caskets. But when Bassanio makes his choice, we see how the test works: it can be solved only by one who views its puzzles from the correct point of view. Bassanio must abstract from his particular relation with Portia to a general distinction between "ornament" and "truth":

> Look on beauty
> And you shall see 'tis purchased by the weight,
> Which therein works a miracle in nature,
> Making them lightest that wear most of it.
> (3.2.88–91)

Surely Bassanio does not believe that because Portia is lovely, she must be unchaste. Instead, his upbringing as a Christian gentleman has acquainted him with a particular frame of mind that prefers invisible over visible things, spirit over body, metaphor over literal meaning. The same cultural background makes him willing to take chances: to "hazard all he hath" on the unprepossessing lead casket. Because every suitor gets the same chance, the casket test seems to be fair; in fact, it is rather like those "objective" intelligence tests that, in subtle or not-so-subtle ways, reward the belief systems of dominant groups while stigmatizing outsiders. In this case, the person best fitted to be Portia's husband is one who, by Christian standards, knows the limitations and right use of wealth. This knowledge enables him to value characteristics in his wife—virtue, intelligence, and beauty—that make her precious in more than monetary ways.

One of the surprises of the casket test is that it takes place at all. Portia's obedience to her dead father's apparently irrational plans for her is remarkable in comedy, for comic heroines more often, like Jessica, defy their fathers than conscientiously follow their orders. Perhaps Portia could be seen as synthesizing the best of Jewish and Christian characteristics; obeying the letter of a wise Father's law, even while cultivating the spiritual virtues of love and generosity. Perhaps, then, Jewish and Christian outlooks are not *necessarily* in conflict (any more than there is a necessary conflict in being, as Portia is, both rich and beautiful). Certainly Portia's respect for the letter of the law, combined with her willingness to go beyond that letter, makes her the only character who can effectively confront Shylock in the trial scene.

When she disguises herself as a young lawyer, Portia becomes one of many Shakespearean comic heroines to assume male attire. The power that she achieves by her transvestism signals an interesting development in Shakespeare's treatment of the relations between men and women. Earlier plays often differentiate sharply between the sexes: between the male political domain and the female domestic domain in *Richard II*, between the male street and the female bedchamber in *Romeo and Juliet*. In *The Merchant of Venice* and the comedies Shakespeare wrote immediately thereafter, women seem to possess a new liberty of action. Their freedom coincides with another new development in Shakespearean comedy, the presence of a scapegoat character—someone like Shylock, who cannot be assimilated into the comic society at the end of the play. Perhaps when the most serious social threats seem to be posed by outsiders, there is more freedom for women within the "in" group: the crucial bifurcation is no longer between male and female but between "us" and "them."

Portia's legal strategy is complex, and thus the trial has several stages. At first, she both offers and recommends generosity:

> Therefore, Jew,
> Though justice be thy plea, consider this:
> That in the course of justice none of us
> Should see salvation. We do pray for mercy,
> And that same prayer doth teach us all to render
> The deeds of mercy.
>
> (4.1.192–97)

Not surprisingly, Shylock is deaf to this eloquence. Portia's argument is based on the distinctively Christian premise that salvation is an undeserved gift. She derives her authority from the Lord's Prayer: "forgive us our trespasses as we forgive those who trespass against us." But Shylock doesn't accept, or even perhaps know the existence of, a prayer that supposedly "teaches us all." Portia's plea for tolerance and compassion might seem to rest on universal premises, but in fact Portia's "we" who "pray for mercy" neatly excludes the Jew.

The judgment upon Shylock at the end of the trial has disturbed many critics and audiences. After the Christians win the case—not only saving Antonio's life but also keeping the 3,000 ducats Shylock had lent Bassanio—Portia seems to take exactly the revenge she has up to now deplored. Her legal ground is provided by a previously unmentioned law against any alien who plots the death of a Venetian citizen. The law in which Shylock trusted, because it seemed to provide a refuge from prejudice, turns out to have prejudice inscribed within it from the start. In this respect, it resembles the casket test—everybody seems to get the same chance, but in fact the test blatantly favors the insider.

Portia and the Duke apparently regard the dismissal of Shylock as merciful; his *life* is preserved, although half or all of his mere money is taken away. Portia's sentence forces Shylock to behave as a Christian citizen and father should: to worship in a Christian church, to grant money to his daughter, to recognize the difference between spiritual and economic well-being. Eschewing lethal force, the Duke demands that Shylock acquiesce in his punishment: "I am content," he says at last. But what else can he say? The coercive inclusion of Shylock in the Christian community seems all the more violent because it professes to renounce coercion, dropping "as the gentle rain from heaven." If designating people outcasts is bad, compelling them to participate in a society they find intolerable may be even worse.

The Merchant of Venice thus hovers on the edge of tragedy. Shylock's ferocious negativity is poised against, and arguably elicited by, the Christians' hypocritical refusal to admit the way their spiritual lives depend on material prosperity. The presence of the scapegoated Jew lays bare the mechanisms by which Venetian society works. Shylock can be reviled and dismissed, but the possibilities that he represents do not simply vanish when he flees the courtroom. Thus the moral disquiet the play raises among directors, readers, and audiences: Christian and Jewish perspectives seem mutually invalidating, and both finally inadequate.

Shakespeare suggests the stubbornness of the problems broached by the play in the way he structures the last act. Most Shakespeare comedies return to the city or the court at the end, or at least look forward to that return; but in *The Merchant of Venice*, the play ends at Belmont, the nostalgically depicted, magically copious "green world." It is as if the formal demand for comic closure conflicts with Shakespeare's awareness that no neat resolution of Venice's problems is forthcoming.

Indeed, some muted version of those problems pursues the Christians even to Portia's estate. The act begins with the banter between the newlyweds Jessica and Lorenzo, who have stayed behind at Belmont in Portia's absence. It is a bit ominous that all the love stories they recall are unhappy ones. Still, the couple's affectionate banter makes the scene a welcome change from what has immediately preceded it. Showing Jessica and Lorenzo in married bliss minutes after the brutal expulsion of Shylock seems an attempt to confine the punitive energies of the play to the usurer alone. The scene offers an alternative vision of interaction between racial groups, one that involves love rather than hatred. Jessica's marriage to a Christian has exempted her from Shylock's fate. Of course, this is a vision not of mutual tolerance but of assimilation: majority cultures do not need to exterminate people unlike themselves if they can merely exterminate their differences. Lorenzo describes to his wife the "music of the spheres"—a perfect heavenly harmony made inaudible by the corruption of this life. Perhaps, analogously, the Christians' failure lies not in the nature of their ideals, but in the imperfect realization of those ideals in the everyday world. The inevitable dissonance between the mundane and the ideal world does not necessarily, however, simply drain the ideal of its meaning.

The moral dilemmas posed by high but perhaps unrealizable ideals come under scrutiny yet again in the ring tricks with which the play ends. After Antonio's trial, Portia-as-Balthazar asks Bassanio for his wedding ring as payment for legal services. This request poses Bassanio a harder problem than Shylock had. Bassanio can imagine breaking a written contract, but not denying the request of an ally to whom he's indebted. By giving the ring to Balthazar, Bassanio demonstrates both that his loyalty to Antonio still outweighs his allegiance to Portia and that he has trouble governing his generous impulses. Portia's trick teaches Bassanio and Antonio that the marital relationship involves unique responsibilities and that those responsibilities impose a limit on munificence.

Again and again in *The Merchant of Venice* oppositions between potentially tragic alternatives miraculously dissolve—between being rich and being virtuous, marrying for money and marrying for love, following paternal orders and making one's own choice, enforcing the letter of the law and enforcing its spirit, remaining faithful to one's wife and loving one's male friend. Balthazar turns out to have been Portia, Bassanio has given his ring to its original owner, and all seems to be well. But by setting the play's last act in a magical world of trust and abundance, Shakespeare stresses the artifice involved in his resolution. Even as this beautiful, troubling play comes to a close, it pointedly emphasizes the distance between the final act's charmed fictional world and the intransigent real one.

KATHARINE EISAMAN MAUS

TEXTUAL NOTE

The textual history of *The Merchant of Venice* is not as complicated as that of some other Shakespeare plays. Two quarto editions exist, both dated 1600 on the title page. One, printed "by I. R. for Thomas Heys," is now called Q1; nineteen copies of this text have survived. Another Quarto (Q2), printed "by I. Roberts," is a falsely dated text actually produced in 1619 by William Jaggard (the same man who printed the First Folio four years later). Yet another version of *The Merchant of Venice* appears in the 1623 First Folio (F).

Q1 seems to have been prepared either directly from Shakespeare's own manuscript or from an accurate transcript of that manuscript. Internal evidence indicates that both Q2 and F were based on copies of Q1. F has some additions, chiefly stage directions, which suggests that a text marked up for stage production was likely to have been consulted at some point in preparing this text. Q1 is not divided into acts or scenes; F adds act divisions. Scene divisions were not added until the eighteenth century.

Q1, therefore, with the exception of some stage directions, is the most reliable authority for a modern text of *The Merchant of Venice*. The Oxford text follows Q1 closely, adopting from F and later editors the traditional divisions into acts and scenes, and accepting many of the Folio stage directions as representing the performance practice of Shakespeare's company.

The title *The Jew of Venice* does not appear in any printed text of the play. It was used, however, when the play was entered on the Stationers' Register in 1598. Since the theatrical company, not a bookseller, was responsible for the entry, the Oxford editors believe that members of Shakespeare's company considered *The Jew of Venice* an acceptable alternative title.

SELECTED BIBLIOGRAPHY

Barber, C. L. "The Merchants and the Jew of Venice: Wealth's Communion and an Intruder." *Shakespeare's Festive Comedy: A Study of Dramatic Form and Its Relation to Social Custom.* Princeton: Princeton University Press, 1959. The Christian's opulent festivity challenged by Shylock's fiercely reductive attitude toward money.

Burckhardt, Sigurd. "*The Merchant of Venice*: The Gentle Bond." *Shakespearean Meanings.* Princeton: Princeton University Press, 1968. 206–89. The importance of various kinds of bonds in *The Merchant of Venice*.

Cohen, Walter. "*The Merchant of Venice* and the Possibilities of Historical Criticism." *English Literary History* 49 (1982): 765–89. The play's theatrical artifice as reflecting economic conflicts in early modern Europe.

Danson, Lawrence. *The Harmonies of "The Merchant of Venice."* New Haven: Yale University Press, 1978. Describes the play's conflicts in detail, and argues for their satisfactory resolution.

Engle, Lars. "Money and Moral Luck in *The Merchant of Venice*." *Shakespearean Pragmatism: Market of His Time.* Chicago: University of Chicago Press, 1993. 77–106. Emotional and financial balance sheets, and their ethical consequences: *The Merchant of Venice* read through the lens of late twentieth-century ethical philosophy.

Gross, Kenneth. *Shylock Is Shakespeare*. Chicago: University of Chicago Press, 2006. Shakespeare's personal connection to Shylock.

Lewalski, Barbara. "Biblical Allusion and Allegory in *The Merchant of Venice*." *Shakespeare Quarterly* 13 (1962): 327–43. Shakespeare's use of biblical typology.

Lupton, Julia Reinhard. "Merchants of Venice, Circles of Citizenship." *Citizen-Saints: Shakespeare and Political Theology*. Chicago: University of Chicago Press, 2005. 75–101. Judaism and citizenship in early modern Venice.

Newman, Karen. "Portia's Ring: Unruly Women and the Structure of Exchange in *The Merchant of Venice*." *Shakespeare Quarterly* 38 (1987): 19–33. Portia, as gift-giver, occupies a position of power usually coded as masculine.

Shapiro, James. *Shakespeare and the Jews*. New York: Columbia University Press, 1996. Anti-Semitism in Shakespeare's time.

Shell, Marc. "'The Wether and the Ewe': Verbal Usury in *The Merchant of Venice*." *Kenyon Review* 1.4 (1979): 65–92. A close analysis of exchange and redemption in *Merchant of Venice*, focusing particularly on Shylock's story of Laban and Jacob.

Wilson, Luke. "Drama and Marine Insurance in Shakespeare's London." *The Law in Shakespeare*. Ed. Constance Jordan and Karen Cunningham. London: Palgrave Macmillan, 2007. 127–42.

FILMS

The Merchant of Venice. 1973. Dir. John Sichel. UK. 131 min. Laurence Olivier as Shylock.

The Merchant of Venice. 1980. Dir. Jack Gold. UK. 157 min. Textually faithful but stilted. Gemma Jones is a chilly, calculating Portia.

The Merchant of Venice. 2001. Dir. Trevor Nunn. UK. 141 min. A film version of an acclaimed Royal National Theatre production, set in Europe between the world wars. Vividly acted, with many interesting directorial choices. Henry Goodman's Shylock is especially memorable.

The Merchant of Venice. 2004. Dir. Michael Radford. UK. 131 min. Al Pacino as Shylock, Lynn Collins as Portia. Sumptuous period costumes and sets. This production emphasizes the disquieting aspects of the play, not only the Venetians' anti-Semitism but the struggle between Portia and Antonio over Bassanio's allegiance.

The Comical History of the Merchant of Venice, or Otherwise Called the Jew of Venice

THE PERSONS OF THE PLAY

ANTONIO, a merchant of Venice
BASSANIO, his friend and Portia's suitor
LEONARDO, Bassanio's servant
LORENZO ⎫
GRAZIANO ⎪
SALERIO ⎬ friends of Antonio and Bassanio
SOLANIO ⎭
SHYLOCK, a Jew
JESSICA, his daughter
TUBAL, a Jew
LANCELOT, a clown, first Shylock's servant and then Bassanio's
GOBBO, his father
PORTIA, an heiress
NERISSA, her waiting-gentlewoman
BALTHASAR ⎱ Portia's servants
STEFANO ⎰
Prince of MOROCCO ⎱ Portia's suitors
Prince of ARAGON ⎰
DUKE of Venice
Magnificoes of Venice
A jailer, attendants, and servants

1.1

Enter ANTONIO, SALERIO, *and* SOLANIO

ANTONIO In sooth,° I know not why I am so sad.　　　　　*truth*
　It wearies me, you say it wearies you,
　But how I caught it, found it, or came by it,
　What stuff 'tis made of, whereof it is born,
5　I am to learn;°　　　　　　　　　　*have yet to discover*
　And such a want-wit° sadness makes of me　　　*dullard*
　That I have much ado to know myself.
SALERIO Your mind is tossing on the ocean,
　There where your argosies° with portly° sail,　*merchant ships / stately*
10　Like signors° and rich burghers on the flood—　　　*lords*
　Or as it were the pageants¹ of the sea—
　Do overpeer° the petty traffickers　　　　　*tower over*
　That curtsy² to them, do them reverence,
　As they fly by them with their woven wings.

1.1 Location: Venice.
1. Movable stages used by itinerant actors or in parades.

2. By bobbing on the waves or by lowering their flags in salute.

SOLANIO [to ANTONIO]   Believe me, sir, had I such venture°   *a risky undertaking*
15   forth
          The better part of my affections would
          Be with my hopes abroad. I should be still°   *always*
          Plucking the grass to know where sits the wind,
          Peering in maps for ports and piers and roads,°   *open harbors*
20   And every object that might make me fear
          Misfortune to my ventures out of doubt
          Would make me sad.
SALERIO   My wind cooling my broth
          Would blow me to an ague° when I thought   *make me shiver*
          What harm a wind too great might do at sea.
25   I should not see the sandy hour-glass run
          But I should think of shallows and of flats,°   *shoals*
          And see my wealthy Andrew,[3] decks in sand,
          Vailing her hightop° lower than her ribs   *Lowering her topmast*
          To kiss her burial.° Should I go to church   *burial place*
30   And see the holy edifice of stone
          And not bethink me straight° of dangerous rocks   *immediately think*
          Which, touching but my gentle vessel's side,
          Would scatter all her spices on the stream,
          Enrobe the roaring waters with my silks,
35   And, in a word, but even now° worth this,°   *moments ago / so much*
          And now worth nothing? Shall I have the thought
          To think on this, and shall I lack the thought
          That such a thing bechanced° would make me sad?   *having occurred*
          But tell not me. I know Antonio
40   Is sad to think upon his merchandise.
ANTONIO   Believe me, no. I thank my fortune for it,
          My ventures are not in one bottom° trusted,   *ship*
          Nor to one place;° nor is my whole estate   *destination*
          Upon the fortune of this present year.
45   Therefore my merchandise makes me not sad.
SOLANIO   Why then, you are in love.
ANTONIO   Fie, fie.
SOLANIO   Not in love neither? Then let us say you are sad
          Because you are not merry, and 'twere as easy
          For you to laugh, and leap, and say you are merry
50   Because you are not sad. Now, by two-headed Janus,[4]
          Nature hath framed strange fellows in her time:
          Some that will evermore peep through their eyes[5]
          And laugh like parrots° at a bagpiper,[6]   *(screeching loudly)*
          And other of such vinegar aspect°   *sour looks*
55   That they'll not show their teeth in way of smile
          Though Nestor[7] swear the jest be laughable.
                    Enter BASSANIO, LORENZO, *and* GRAZIANO
          Here comes Bassanio, your most noble kinsman,
          Graziano, and Lorenzo. Fare ye well.
          We leave you now with better company.
60   SALERIO   I would have stayed till I had made you merry
          If worthier friends had not prevented me.

---

3. Name of a Spanish galleon captured by the English
at Cádiz in 1596.
4. Roman god with faces looking both forward and
backward.

5. Eyes almost shut by violent laughter.
6. Whose music was considered woeful.
7. Sober, elderly Greek hero in *The Iliad*.

ANTONIO Your worth is very dear in my regard.
I take it your own business calls on you,
And you embrace th'occasion to depart.
65 SALERIO Good morrow, my good lords.
BASSANIO Good signors both, when shall we laugh?° Say, when?   *make merry together*
You grow exceeding strange.° Must it be so?   *reserved*
SALERIO We'll make our leisures to attend on° yours.   *suit*

Exeunt SALERIO *and* SOLANIO

LORENZO My lord Bassanio, since you have found Antonio,
70 We two will leave you; but at dinner-time
I pray you have in mind where we must meet.
BASSANIO I will not fail you.
GRAZIANO You look not well, Signor Antonio.
You have too much respect upon the world.°   *anxiety about business*
75 They lose it that do buy it with much care.
Believe me, you are marvellously changed.
ANTONIO I hold the world but as the world, Graziano—
A stage where every man must play a part,
And mine a sad one.
GRAZIANO   Let me play the fool.
80 With mirth and laughter let old⁸ wrinkles come,
And let my liver⁹ rather heat with wine
Than my heart cool with mortifying¹ groans.
Why should a man whose blood is warm within
Sit like his grandsire cut in alabaster,²
85 Sleep when he wakes, and creep into the jaundice³
By being peevish? I tell thee what, Antonio—
I love thee, and 'tis my love that speaks—
There are a sort of men whose visages
Do cream and mantle⁴ like a standing° pond,   *stagnant*
90 And do a wilful stillness entertain
With purpose to be dressed in an opinion°   *a reputation*
Of wisdom, gravity, profound conceit,°   *judgment*
As who should say 'I am Sir Oracle,
And when I ope my lips, let no dog bark.'
95 O my Antonio, I do know of these
That therefore only are reputed wise
For saying nothing, when I am very sure,
If they should speak, would almost damn those ears
Which, hearing them, would call their brothers fools.⁵
100 I'll tell thee more of this another time.
But fish not with this melancholy bait
For this fool gudgeon,° this opinion.—   *tiny, easily caught fish*
Come, good Lorenzo.—Fare ye well a while.
I'll end my exhortation after dinner.
LORENZO [*to* ANTONIO *and* BASSANIO] Well, we will leave you
105   then till dinner-time.
I must be one of these same dumb° wise men,   *mute*
For Graziano never lets me speak.

8. Accompanying old age; abundant.
9. The liver was considered the seat of passion.
1. Deadly (groans were believed to drain blood from the heart).
2. Stone from which tomb effigies were carved.
3. Thought to result from too much yellow bile, a bodily substance associated with irritability.
4. *cream and mantle*: grow a scum; that is, assume a fixed countenance.
5. *would . . . fools*: alluding to Matthew 5:22: "And whosoever shall say to his brother . . . , fool, shall be in danger of hell fire."

GRAZIANO   Well, keep me company but two years more
Thou shalt not know the sound of thine own tongue.
110   ANTONIO   Fare you well. I'll grow a talker for this gear.[6]
GRAZIANO   Thanks, i'faith, for silence is only commendable
In a neat's° tongue dried and a maid not vendible.[7]   an ox's

Exeunt [GRAZIANO *and* LORENZO]

ANTONIO   Yet is that anything now?
BASSANIO   Graziano speaks an infinite deal of nothing, more
115   than any man in all Venice. His reasons° are as two grains of   sensible remarks
wheat hid in two bushels of chaff: you shall seek all day ere
you find them, and when you have them they are not worth
the search.
ANTONIO   Well, tell me now what lady is the same
120   To whom you swore a secret pilgrimage,
That you today promised to tell me of.
BASSANIO   'Tis not unknown to you, Antonio,
How much I have disabled mine estate
By something showing a more swelling port°   extravagant lifestyle
125   Than my faint means would grant continuance,°   allow to continue
Nor do I now make moan to be abridged°   reduced
From such a noble rate;° but my chief care   style
Is to come fairly off from the great debts
Wherein my time, something too prodigal,
130   Hath left me gaged.° To you, Antonio,   pledged
I owe the most in money and in love,
And from your love I have a warranty°   sanction
To unburden all my plots and purposes
How to get clear of all the debts I owe.
135   ANTONIO   I pray you, good Bassanio, let me know it,
And if it stand as you yourself still do,
Within the eye of honour, be assured
My purse, my person, my extremest means
Lie all unlocked to your occasions.°   requirements
140   BASSANIO   In my schooldays, when I had lost one shaft,
I shot his° fellow of the selfsame flight°   its / size and weight
The selfsame way, with more advisèd° watch,   careful
To find the other forth; and by adventuring° both,   hazarding
I oft found both. I urge this childhood proof
145   Because what follows is pure innocence.
I owe you much, and, like a wilful youth,
That which I owe is lost; but if you please
To shoot another arrow that self° way   same
Which you did shoot the first, I do not doubt,
150   As I will watch the aim, or° to find both   either
Or bring your latter hazard° back again,   risk
And thankfully rest debtor for the first.
ANTONIO   You know me well, and herein spend but° time   only lose
To wind about my love with circumstance;°   circumlocution
155   And out of doubt you do me now more wrong
In making question of my uttermost[8]
Than if you had made waste of all I have.
Then do but say to me what I should do

---

6. *for this gear*: as a result of your talk.
7. Sellable—that is, marriageable.
8. In doubting that I would do my utmost to help you.

That in your knowledge may by me be done,
160 And I am pressed unto° it. Therefore speak.   *obliged to do*
BASSANIO   In Belmont is a lady richly left,°   *left a fortune*
And she is fair, and, fairer than that word,
Of wondrous virtues. Sometimes° from her eyes   *At times*
I did receive fair speechless messages.
165 Her name is Portia, nothing undervalued
To⁹ Cato's daughter, Brutus' Portia;¹
Nor is the wide world ignorant of her worth,
For the four winds blow in from every coast
Renownèd suitors, and her sunny locks
170 Hang on her temples like a golden fleece,
Which makes her seat of Belmont Colchis' strand,²
And many Jasons come in quest of her.
O my Antonio, had I but the means
To hold a rival place with one of them,
175 I have a mind presages me such thrift°   *prosperity*
That I should questionless be fortunate.
ANTONIO   Thou know'st that all my fortunes are at sea,
Neither have I money nor commodity°   *goods*
To raise a present sum. Therefore go forth—
180 Try what my credit can in Venice do;
That shall be racked° even to the uttermost   *stretched*
To furnish thee to Belmont, to fair Portia.
Go presently enquire, and so will I,
Where money is; and I no question make
185 To have it of my trust or for my sake.³   *Exeunt [severally]°*   *separately*

1.2

Enter PORTIA *with her waiting-woman,* NERISSA

PORTIA   By my troth,° Nerissa, my little body is aweary of this   *faith*
great world.
NERISSA   You would be,¹ sweet madam, if your miseries were in
the same abundance as your good fortunes are; and yet, for
5   aught I see, they are as sick that surfeit with too much as they
that starve with nothing. It is no mean° happiness, therefore,   *slight*
to be seated in the mean.° Superfluity comes sooner by° white   *middle / sooner gets*
hairs, but competency° lives longer.   *moderate estate*
PORTIA   Good sentences,° and well pronounced.   *aphorisms*
10 NERISSA   They would be better if well followed.
PORTIA   If to do were as easy as to know what were good to do,
chapels had been churches, and poor men's cottages princes'
palaces. It is a good divine° that follows his own instructions. *clergyman*
I can easier teach twenty what were good to be done than to
15 be one of the twenty to follow mine own teaching. The brain
may devise laws for the blood,° but a hot temper² leaps o'er a   *passion*
cold decree. Such a hare is madness, the youth, to skip o'er
the meshes° of good counsel, the cripple.³ But this reasoning   *snares*
is not in the fashion° to choose me a husband. O me, the word   *of a kind*

9. *nothing . . . / To:* no less worthy than.
1. Roman matron famous for heroic fidelity to her husband; a character in *Julius Caesar.*
2. Coast of Colchis, where in classical mythology Jason
won the Golden Fleece.
3. *of . . . sake:* because of my creditworthiness or as a
personal favor.
1.2 Location: Belmont.
1. You would have reason to be weary.
2. An impetuous disposition.
3. Because wisdom is imagined as elderly.

20 'choose'! I may neither choose who I would nor refuse who I
    dislike; so is the will° of a living daughter curbed by the will°   *wish / testament*
    of a dead father. Is it not hard, Nerissa, that I cannot choose
    one nor refuse none?

NERISSA   Your father was ever virtuous, and holy men at their
25 death have good inspirations; therefore the lottery that he
    hath devised in these three chests of gold, silver, and lead,
    whereof who chooses his meaning chooses you, will no doubt
    never be chosen by any rightly but one who you shall rightly
    love. But what warmth is there in your affection towards any
30 of these princely suitors that are already come?

PORTIA   I pray thee overname them, and as thou namest them
    I will describe them; and according to my description, level°   *guess*
    at my affection.

NERISSA   First there is the Neapolitan prince.

35 PORTIA   Ay, that's a colt[4] indeed, for he doth nothing but talk of
    his horse, and he makes it a great appropriation° to his own   *augmentation*
    good parts° that he can shoe him himself. I am much afeard   *own abilities*
    my lady his mother played false with a smith.

NERISSA   Then is there the County Palatine.[5]

40 PORTIA   He doth nothing but frown, as who should say 'An° you   *If*
    will not have me, choose'.° He hears merry tales and smiles   *do as you wish*
    not. I fear he will prove the weeping philosopher[6] when he
    grows old, being so full of unmannerly° sadness in his youth.   *immoderate*
    I had rather be married to a death's-head with a bone in his
45 mouth than to either of these. God defend me from these two!

NERISSA   How say you by the French lord, Monsieur le Bon?

PORTIA   God made him, and therefore let him pass for a man. In
    truth, I know it is a sin to be a mocker, but he—why, he hath
    a horse better than the Neapolitan's, a better bad habit of
50 frowning than the Count Palatine. He is every man in no man.
    If a throstle° sing, he falls straight° a-cap'ring. He will fence   *thrush / immediately*
    with his own shadow. If I should marry him, I should marry
    twenty husbands. If he would despise me, I would forgive him,
    for if he love me to madness, I shall never requite him.

55 NERISSA   What say you then to Falconbridge, the young baron
    of England?

PORTIA   You know I say nothing to him, for he understands not
    me, nor I him. He hath neither Latin, French, nor Italian, and
    you will come into the court and swear that I have a poor pen-
60 nyworth in the English. He is a proper° man's picture, but   *handsome*
    alas, who can converse with a dumb show?° How oddly he is   *pantomime*
    suited! I think he bought his doublet° in Italy, his round hose[7]   *upper garment*
    in France, his bonnet° in Germany, and his behaviour every-   *hat*
    where.

65 NERISSA   What think you of the Scottish lord, his neighbour?

PORTIA   That he hath a neighbourly charity in him, for he bor-
    rowed a box of the ear of the Englishman and swore he would
    pay him again when he was able. I think the Frenchman
    became his surety, and sealed under for another.[8]

4. Foolish young man. Neapolitans were excellent
horsemen.
5. Count possessing royal powers.
6. Heracleitus, a melancholy Greek philosopher.
7. Puffed breeches.

8. The Frenchman vouched for the Scot's payment (of
a box on the ear) and promised to add another himself
(referring to France's frequent promises to help the
Scots against the English).

70 NERISSA   How like you the young German, the Duke of Saxony's
nephew?

PORTIA   Very vilely in the morning when he is sober, and most
vilely in the afternoon when he is drunk. When he is best he
is a little worse than a man, and when he is worst he is little
75 better than a beast. An the worst fall that ever fell, I hope I
shall make shift° to go without him.   *manage*

NERISSA   If he should offer° to choose, and choose the right   *endeavor*
casket, you should refuse to perform your father's will if you
should refuse to accept him.

80 PORTIA   Therefore, for fear of the worst, I pray thee set a deep
glass of Rhenish wine° on the contrary casket; for if the devil   *white German wine*
be within and that temptation without, I know he will choose
it. I will do anything, Nerissa, ere I will be married to a sponge.

NERISSA   You need not fear, lady, the having any of these lords.
85 They have acquainted me with their determinations, which is
indeed to return to their home and to trouble you with no
more suit unless you may be won by some other sort° than   *way*
your father's imposition° depending on the caskets.   *conditions*

PORTIA   If I live to be as old as Sibylla⁹ I will die as chaste as
90 Diana unless I be obtained by the manner of my father's will.
I am glad this parcel of wooers are so reasonable, for there is
not one among them but I dote on his very absence; and I pray
God grant them a fair departure.

NERISSA   Do you not remember, lady, in your father's time, a
95 Venetian, a scholar and a soldier, that came hither in company
of the Marquis of Montferrat?

PORTIA   Yes, yes, it was Bassanio—as I think, so was he called.

NERISSA   True, madam. He of all the men that ever my foolish
eyes looked upon was the best deserving a fair lady.

100 PORTIA   I remember him well, and I remember him worthy of
thy praise.

Enter a SERVINGMAN

How now, what news?

SERVINGMAN   The four strangers seek for you, madam, to take
their leave, and there is a forerunner come from a fifth, the
105 Prince of Morocco, who brings word the Prince his master
will be here tonight.

PORTIA   If I could bid the fifth welcome with so good heart as I
can bid the other four farewell, I should be glad of his
approach. If he have the condition° of a saint and the complex-   *character*
110 ion of a devil,¹ I had rather he should shrive me° than wive me.   *absolve me of my sins*
Come, Nerissa. [*To the* SERVINGMAN] Sirrah, go before.
Whiles we shut the gate upon one wooer,
Another knocks at the door.   *Exeunt*

1.3

Enter BASSANIO *with* SHYLOCK *the Jew*

SHYLOCK   Three thousand ducats.¹ Well.

BASSANIO   Ay, sir, for three months.

SHYLOCK   For three months. Well.

---

9. In classical mythology, the Cumaean Sibyl asked
Apollo for as many years of life as the grains of sand she
held in her hand; she forgot to ask for eternal youth.

1. Devils were imagined as black.
1.3 Location: Street in Venice.
1. Gold coins. The sum is very large.

BASSANIO   For the which, as I told you, Antonio shall be bound.°   *contractually responsible*

5   SHYLOCK   Antonio shall become bound. Well.

BASSANIO   May you stead° me? Will you pleasure me? Shall I   *accommodate*
know your answer?

SHYLOCK   Three thousand ducats for three months, and Antonio
bound.

10   BASSANIO   Your answer to that.

SHYLOCK   Antonio is a good man.

BASSANIO   Have you heard any imputation to the contrary?

SHYLOCK   Ho, no, no, no, no! My meaning in saying he is a good
man is to have you understand me that he is sufficient.° Yet   *of adequate wealth*

15   his means are in supposition.° He hath an argosy bound to   *doubt*
Tripolis, another to the Indies. I understand moreover upon
the Rialto² he hath a third at Mexico, a fourth for England,
and other ventures he hath squandered abroad. But ships are
but boards, sailors but men. There be land rats and water rats,

20   water thieves and land thieves—I mean pirates—and then
there is the peril of waters, winds, and rocks. The man is,
notwithstanding, sufficient. Three thousand ducats. I think I
may take his bond.

BASSANIO   Be assured you may.

25   SHYLOCK   I will be assured³ I may, and that I may be assured,
I will bethink me. May I speak with Antonio?

BASSANIO   If it please you to dine with us.

SHYLOCK   Yes, to smell pork, to eat of the habitation which your
prophet the Nazarite⁴ conjured the devil into! I will buy with

30   you, sell with you, talk with you, walk with you, and so following, but I will not eat with you, drink with you, nor pray
with you.

Enter ANTONIO

[*To* ANTONIO] What news on the Rialto? [*To* BASSANIO] Who is
he comes here?

35   BASSANIO   This is Signor Antonio.

[BASSANIO *and* ANTONIO *speak silently to one another*]

SHYLOCK [*aside*]   How like a fawning publican⁵ he looks.
I hate him for he is a Christian;
But more, for that in low simplicity⁶
He lends out money gratis,° and brings down   *free*

40   The rate of usance° here with us in Venice.   *interest*
If I can catch him once upon the hip⁷
I will feed fat the ancient grudge I bear him.
He hates our sacred nation,° and he rails,   *(the Jews)*
Even there where merchants most do congregate,

45   On me, my bargains, and my well-won thrift°—   *profit*
Which he calls interest. Cursèd be my tribe
If I forgive him.

BASSANIO   Shylock, do you hear?

SHYLOCK   I am debating of my present store,°   *supply of money*
And by the near guess of my memory

2. Merchants' exchange in Venice.
3. Sure (but Shylock uses the word to mean "given financial guarantees").
4. Jesus, who cast devils into a herd of swine.
5. Tax collector; he robs me, but now, like the publican

in Luke 18:10–14 who prays to Jesus for mercy, tries to
ingratiate himself because he wants a favor.
6. In meek honesty; in base folly.
7. *upon the hip*: at a disadvantage (wrestling terminology).

50 I cannot instantly raise up the gross°   *total*
    Of full three thousand ducats. What of that?
    Tubal, a wealthy Hebrew of my tribe,
    Will furnish me. But soft°—how many months   *wait*
    Do you desire? [*To* ANTONIO] Rest you fair, good signor.
55 Your worship was the last man in our mouths.[8]
    ANTONIO Shylock, albeit I neither lend nor borrow
    By taking nor by giving of excess,
    Yet to supply the ripe° wants of my friend   *urgent*
    I'll break a custom. [*To* BASSANIO] Is he yet possessed°   *informed*
60 How much ye would?
    SHYLOCK Ay, ay, three thousand ducats.
    ANTONIO And for three months.
    SHYLOCK I had forgot—three months. [*To* BASSANIO] You told me so.—
    Well then, your bond; and let me see—but hear you,
65 Methoughts you said you neither lend nor borrow
    Upon advantage.°   *interest*
    ANTONIO   I do never use it.
    SHYLOCK When Jacob grazed his uncle Laban's sheep—
    This Jacob from our holy Abram was,
    As his wise mother wrought in his behalf,
70 The third possessor; ay, he was the third[9]—
    ANTONIO And what of him? Did he take interest?
    SHYLOCK No, not take interest, not, as you would say,
    Directly int'rest. Mark what Jacob did:
    When Laban and himself were compromised°   *agreed*
75 That all the eanlings° which were streaked and pied°   *lambs / spotted*
    Should fall as Jacob's hire, the ewes, being rank,°   *in heat*
    In end of autumn turnèd to the rams,
    And when the work of generation° was   *mating*
    Between these woolly breeders in the act,
80 The skilful shepherd peeled me certain wands,[1]
    And in the doing of the deed of kind°   *nature*
    He stuck them up before the fulsome ewes
    Who, then conceiving, did in eaning° time   *lambing*
    Fall° parti-coloured lambs; and those were Jacob's.   *Deliver*
85 This was a way to thrive; and he was blest;
    And thrift is blessing, if men steal it not.
    ANTONIO This was a venture, sir, that Jacob served for[2]—
    A thing not in his power to bring to pass,
    But swayed and fashioned by the hand of heaven.
90 Was this inserted to make interest good,[3]
    Or is your gold and silver ewes and rams?
    SHYLOCK I cannot tell. I make it breed as fast.
    But note me, signor—
    ANTONIO   Mark you this, Bassanio?
    The devil can cite Scripture for his purpose.
95 An evil soul producing holy witness
    Is like a villain with a smiling cheek,

---

8. We were just mentioning you.
9. After Abraham and Isaac; his mother, Rebecca, helped him cheat his brother Esau of his birthright. The story of Laban's sheep is told in Genesis 30:25–43.

1. Stripped part of the bark off some sticks ("me" is colloquial).
2. This was a speculative enterprise on which Jacob staked his wages as a servant.
3. Was this brought up to defend taking interest.

A goodly apple rotten at the heart.
O, what a goodly outside falsehood hath!

SHYLOCK Three thousand ducats. 'Tis a good round sum.
100 Three months from twelve—then let me see the rate.

ANTONIO Well, Shylock, shall we be beholden to you?

SHYLOCK Signor Antonio, many a time and oft
In the Rialto you have rated° me   *berated*
About my moneys and my usances.
105 Still° have I borne it with a patient shrug,   *Always*
For suff'rance is the badge[4] of all our tribe.
You call me misbeliever, cut-throat, dog,
And spit upon my Jewish gaberdine,°   *long coat*
And all for use of that which is mine own.
110 Well then, it now appears you need my help.
Go to, then. You come to me, and you say
'Shylock, we would have moneys'—you say so,
You, that did void your rheum° upon my beard,   *spit*
And foot me as you spurn° a stranger cur   *contemptuously kick*
115 Over your threshold. Moneys is your suit.
What should I say to you? Should I not say
'Hath a dog money? Is it possible
A cur can lend three thousand ducats?' Or
Shall I bend low, and in a bondman's° key,   *slave's*
120 With bated breath and whisp'ring humbleness
Say this: 'Fair sir, you spat on me on Wednesday last;
You spurned me such a day; another time
You called me dog; and for these courtesies
I'll lend you thus much moneys'?

125 ANTONIO I am as like to call thee so again,
To spit on thee again, to spurn thee too.
If thou wilt lend this money, lend it not
As to thy friends; for when did friendship take
A breed[5] for barren metal of his friend?
130 But lend it rather to thine enemy,
Who if he break,° thou mayst with better face   *fail to repay*
Exact the penalty.

SHYLOCK   Why, look you, how you storm!
I would be friends with you, and have your love,
Forget the shames that you have stained me with,
135 Supply your present wants, and take no doit°   *small coin*
Of usance for my moneys; and you'll not hear me.
This is kind[6] I offer.

BASSANIO This were° kindness.   *would be*

SHYLOCK This kindness will I show.
140 Go with me to a notary, seal me there
Your single bond,[7] and, in a merry sport,
If you repay me not on such a day,
In such a place, such sum or sums as are
Expressed in the condition, let the forfeit°   *penalty*
145 Be nominated for an equal° pound   *Be stipulated as an exact*

---

4. For enduring insult is the characteristic.
5. Offspring (interest); alluding to an ancient argument that it was unnatural to use money to "breed," or make, more money.

6. Benevolent; natural (but perhaps with the covert suggestion "in kind").
7. Bond signed by the debtor alone (Antonio) without additional guarantors.

Of your fair flesh to be cut off and taken
In what part of your body pleaseth me.
ANTONIO   Content, in faith. I'll seal to such a bond,
And say there is much kindness in the Jew.
150 BASSANIO   You shall not seal to such a bond for me.
I'll rather dwell in my necessity.°   *remain in need*
ANTONIO   Why, fear not, man; I will not forfeit it.
Within these two months—that's a month before
This bond expires—I do expect return
155 Of thrice three times the value of this bond.
SHYLOCK   O father Abram, what these Christians are,
Whose own hard dealings teaches them suspect
The thoughts of others! [*To* BASSANIO] Pray you tell me this:
If he should break his day, what should I gain
160 By the exaction of the forfeiture?
A pound of man's flesh taken from a man
Is not so estimable,° profitable neither,   *valuable*
As flesh of muttons, beeves, or goats. I say,
To buy his favour I extend this friendship.
165 If he will take it, so. If not, adieu,
And, for my love, I pray you wrong me not.
ANTONIO   Yes, Shylock, I will seal unto this bond.
SHYLOCK   Then meet me forthwith at the notary's.
Give him direction for this merry bond,
170 And I will go and purse the ducats straight,
See to my house—left in the fearful° guard   *doubtful*
Of an unthrifty knave—and presently
I'll be with you.
ANTONIO   Hie thee,° gentle Jew.   *Exit* [SHYLOCK]   *Hurry*
The Hebrew will turn Christian; he grows kind.
175 BASSANIO   I like not fair terms and a villain's mind.
ANTONIO   Come on. In this there can be no dismay.
My ships come home a month before the day.   *Exeunt*

2.1
[*Flourish of cornets.*] *Enter* [*the Prince of*] MOROCCO,
a tawny Moor all in white, and three or four followers
accordingly,[1] *with* PORTIA, NERISSA, *and their train*
MOROCCO [*to* PORTIA]   Mislike me not for my complexion,
The shadowed livery° of the burnished sun,   *servant's uniform*
To whom I am a neighbour and near bred.°   *close kin*
Bring me the fairest creature northward born,
5 Where Phoebus'° fire scarce thaws the icicles,   *the sun god*
And let us make incision for your love
To prove whose blood is reddest,[2] his or mine.
I tell thee, lady, this aspect° of mine   *countenance*
Hath feared° the valiant. By my love I swear,   *frightened*
10 The best regarded virgins of our clime
Have loved it too. I would not change this hue
Except to steal your thoughts, my gentle queen.
PORTIA   In terms of choice I am not solely led
By nice direction° of a maiden's eyes.   *fastidious guidance*

2.1 Location: Belmont.   2. Red blood was considered a sign of valor.
1. Of similar complexion and dress.

15 Besides, the lott'ry of my destiny
Bars me the right of voluntary choosing.
But if my father had not scanted° me,   *limited*
And hedged° me by his wit° to yield myself   *restricted / wisdom*
His wife who wins me by that means I told you,
20 Yourself, renownèd Prince, then stood as fair[3]
As any comer I have looked on yet
For my affection.
MOROCCO   Even for that I thank you.
Therefore I pray you lead me to the caskets
To try my fortune. By this scimitar,
25 That slew the Sophy° and a Persian prince   *Shah of Persia*
That won three fields of Sultan Suleiman,°   *Turkish ruler*
I would o'erstare the sternest eyes that look,
Outbrave the heart most daring on the earth,
Pluck the young sucking cubs from the she-bear,
30 Yea, mock the lion when a° roars for prey,   *he*
To win the lady. But alas the while,
If Hercules and Lichas° play at dice   *Hercules' servant*
Which is the better man, the greater throw
May turn by fortune from the weaker hand.
35 So is Alcides° beaten by his rage,[4]   *Hercules*
And so may I, blind Fortune leading me,
Miss that which one unworthier may attain,
And die with grieving.
PORTIA   You must take your chance,
And either not attempt to choose at all,
40 Or swear before you choose, if you choose wrong
Never to speak to lady afterward
In way of marriage. Therefore be advised.°   *careful*
MOROCCO   Nor will not. Come, bring me unto my chance.
PORTIA   First, forward to the temple. After dinner
Your hazard shall be made.
45 MOROCCO   Good fortune then,
To make me blest or cursèd'st among men.
                          [*Flourish of*] *cornets. Exeunt*

2.2

Enter [LANCELOT] *the clown*
LANCELOT   Certainly my conscience will serve° me to run from   *allow*
this Jew my master. The fiend is at mine elbow and tempts me,
saying to me 'Gobbo, Lancelot Gobbo, good Lancelot,' or
'good Gobbo,' or 'good Lancelot Gobbo—use your legs, take the
5 start,° run away.' My conscience says 'No, take heed, honest   *begone*
Lancelot, take heed, honest Gobbo,' or, as aforesaid, 'honest
Lancelot Gobbo—do not run, scorn running with thy heels.'°   *indignantly (with pun)*
Well, the most courageous fiend bids me pack. '*Via!*'° says the   *Away*
fiend; 'Away!' says the fiend. 'For the heavens, rouse up a brave
10 mind,' says the fiend, 'and run.' Well, my conscience hanging
about the neck of my heart says very wisely to me, 'My honest
friend Lancelot'—being an honest man's son, or rather an honest woman's son, for indeed my father did something smack,

---

3. Seemed as attractive; stood as good a chance.   2.2 Location: Venice.
4. Often amended to "page."

something grow to; he had a kind of taste[1]—well, my con-
15 science says, 'Lancelot, budge not'; 'Budge!' says the fiend;
'Budge not', says my conscience. 'Conscience,' say I, 'you
counsel well'; 'Fiend,' say I, 'you counsel well.' To be ruled by
my conscience I should stay with the Jew my master who, God
bless the mark,[2] is a kind of devil; and to run away from the
20 Jew I should be ruled by the fiend who, saving your reverence,
is the devil himself. Certainly the Jew is the very devil incar-
nation;° and in my conscience, my conscience is but a kind of   *(for "incarnate")*
hard conscience to offer to counsel me to stay with the Jew.
The fiend gives the more friendly counsel. I will run, fiend.
25 My heels are at your commandment. I will run.
        Enter old GOBBO, [*blind,*] *with a basket*
    GOBBO Master young man, you, I pray you, which is the way to
        Master Jew's?
    LANCELOT [*aside*] O heavens, this is my true-begotten father
        who, being more than sand-blind—high-gravel-blind[3]—
30   knows me not. I will try confusions[4] with him.
    GOBBO Master young gentleman, I pray you which is the way
        to Master Jew's?
    LANCELOT Turn up on your right hand at the next turning, but
        at the next turning of all on your left, marry at the very next
35   turning, turn of no hand but turn down indirectly to the Jew's
        house.
    GOBBO By God's sonties,° 'twill be a hard way to hit. Can you   *saints*
        tell me whether one Lancelot that dwells with him dwell with
        him or no?
40 LANCELOT Talk you of young Master[5] Lancelot? [*Aside*] Mark
        me now, now will I raise the waters.[6] [*To* GOBBO] Talk you of
        young Master Lancelot?
    GOBBO No master, sir, but a poor man's son. His father, though
        I say't, is an honest exceeding poor man, and, God be thanked,
45   well to live.[7]
    LANCELOT Well, let his father be what a° will, we talk of young   *he*
        Master Lancelot.
    GOBBO Your worship's friend, and Lancelot, sir.
    LANCELOT But I pray you, *ergo*° old man, *ergo* I beseech you,   *therefore*
50   talk you of young Master Lancelot?
    GOBBO Of Lancelot, an't° please your mastership.   *if it*
    LANCELOT *Ergo* Master Lancelot. Talk not of Master Lancelot,
        father,[8] for the young gentleman, according to fates and destin-
        ies and such odd sayings—the sisters three° and such branches   *the Fates*
55   of learning—is indeed deceased; or, as you would say in plain
        terms, gone to heaven.
    GOBBO Marry, God forbid! The boy was the very staff of my age,
        my very prop.
    LANCELOT [*aside*] Do I look like a cudgel or a hovel-post,° a   *shed post*
60   staff or a prop? [*To* GOBBO] Do you know me, father?

---

1. *my father . . . taste:* that is, my father was licentious.
2. Conventional apology before a rude remark, like
"saving your reverence."
3. Lancelot's coinage for a degree of blindness between
sand-blind (partly blind) and stone-blind.

4. Lancelot's version of "try conclusions" (experiment).
5. "Master" was only applied to gentlemen's sons.
6. Start something; bring on tears.
7. Well-to-do (contradicts the previous line).
8. Customary address to an old man.

GOBBO Alack the day, I know you not, young gentleman. But I
pray you tell me, is my boy—God rest his soul—alive or dead?

LANCELOT Do you not know me, father?

GOBBO Alack, sir, I am sand-blind. I know you not.

65 LANCELOT Nay, indeed, if you had your eyes you might fail of
the knowing me. It is a wise father that knows his own child.⁹
Well, old man, I will tell you news of your son. [*Kneeling*]
Give me your blessing. Truth will come to light; murder cannot be hid long—a man's son may, but in the end truth will

70 out.

GOBBO Pray you, sir, stand up. I am sure you are not Lancelot,
my boy.

LANCELOT Pray you, let's have no more fooling about it, but give
me your blessing. I am Lancelot, your boy that was, your son

75 that is, your child that shall be.

GOBBO I cannot think you are my son.

LANCELOT I know not what I shall think of that, but I am
Lancelot the Jew's man, and I am sure Margery your wife is
my mother.

80 GOBBO Her name is Margery indeed. I'll be sworn, if thou be
Lancelot thou art mine own flesh and blood.
[*He feels Lancelot's head*]
Lord worshipped might he be, what a beard hast thou got!¹
Thou hast got more hair on thy chin than Dobbin my fill-
horse° has on his tail.   *cart horse*

85 LANCELOT It should seem then that Dobbin's tail grows back-
ward.² I am sure he had more hair of his tail than I have of my
face when I last saw him.

GOBBO Lord, how art thou changed! How dost thou and thy
master agree?° I have brought him a present. How 'gree you   *get along*

90 now?

LANCELOT Well, well; but for mine own part, as I have set up
my rest³ to run away, so I will not rest till I have run some
ground. My master's a very Jew.⁴ Give him a present?—give
him a halter!° I am famished in his service. You may tell° every   *noose / count*

95 finger I have with my ribs. Father, I am glad you are come.
Give me° your present to one Master Bassanio, who indeed   *Give*
gives rare new liveries.° If I serve not him, I will run as far as   *servants' uniforms*
God has any ground.
        Enter BASSANIO *with* [LEONARDO *and*] *follower[s]*
O rare fortune! Here comes the man. To him, father, for I am

100 a Jew if I serve the Jew any longer.

BASSANIO [*to one of his men*] You may do so, but let it be so
hasted° that supper be ready at the farthest° by five of the   *hurried / latest*
clock. See these letters delivered, put the liveries to making,
and desire° Graziano to come anon° to my lodging. [*Exit one*] *tell / at once*

105 LANCELOT [*to* GOBBO] To him, father.

GOBBO [*to* BASSANIO] God bless your worship.

BASSANIO Gramercy.° Wouldst thou aught° with me?   *Many thanks / anything*

GOBBO Here's my son, sir, a poor boy—

---

9. Transposing the proverb "A wise child knows his own father."
1. Gobbo mistakes Lancelot's hair for a beard.
2. Gets shorter; grows from the wrong end.

3. As I have definitely determined (phrase in the card game primero meaning "risk everything").
4. Cruel, grasping person; Hebrew. *a very*: an absolute.

LANCELOT [*to* BASSANIO]   Not a poor boy, sir, but the rich Jew's
110   man that would, sir, as my father shall specify.
GOBBO [*to* BASSANIO]   He hath a great infection,° sir, as one   (for "affection"; wish)
      would say, to serve—
LANCELOT   Indeed, the short and the long is, I serve the Jew,
      and have a desire as my father shall specify.
115   GOBBO [*to* BASSANIO]   His master and he, saving your worship's
      reverence, are scarce cater-cousins.°   close friends
LANCELOT [*to* BASSANIO]   To be brief, the very truth is that the
      Jew, having done me wrong, doth cause me, as my father—
      being, I hope, an old man—shall frutify° unto you.   (for "certify")
120   GOBBO [*to* BASSANIO]   I have here a dish of doves that I would
      bestow upon your worship, and my suit is—
LANCELOT [*to* BASSANIO]   In very brief, the suit is impertinent°   (for "pertinent")
      to myself, as your worship shall know by this honest old man;
      and though I say it, though old man, yet, poor man, my father.
125   BASSANIO   One speak for both. What would you?
LANCELOT   Serve you, sir.
GOBBO [*to* BASSANIO]   That is the very defect° of the matter, sir.   (for "effect")
BASSANIO [*to* LANCELOT]   I know thee well. Thou hast obtained
      thy suit.
130   Shylock thy master spoke with me this day,
      And hath preferred thee, if it be preferment[5]
      To leave a rich Jew's service to become
      The follower of so poor a gentleman.
LANCELOT   The old proverb[6] is very well parted between my
135   master Shylock and you, sir: you have the grace of God, sir,
      and he hath enough.
BASSANIO   Thou speak'st it well. [*To* GOBBO]   Go, father, with thy son.
      [*To* LANCELOT]   Take leave of thy old master and enquire
      My lodging out. [*To one of his men*]   Give him a livery
140   More guarded° than his fellows'. See it done.   decorated
LANCELOT [*to* GOBBO]   Father, in. I cannot get a service, no, I
      have ne'er a tongue in my head—well!
          [*He looks at his palm*]
      If any man in Italy have a fairer table[7] which doth offer to swear
      upon a book,[8] I shall have good fortune. Go to, here's a simple°   unremarkable (ironic)
145   line of life, here's a small trifle of wives—alas, fifteen wives is
      nothing. Eleven widows and nine maids is a simple coming-in[9]
      for one man, and then to scape drowning thrice, and to be in
      peril of my life with the edge of a featherbed[1]—here are simple
      scapes. Well, if Fortune be a woman, she's a good wench for
150   this gear.° Father, come. I'll take my leave of the Jew in the   matter
      twinkling.   *Exit* [*with old* GOBBO]
BASSANIO   I pray thee, good Leonardo, think on this.
      These things being bought and orderly bestowed,°   stowed on ship
      Return in haste, for I do feast tonight
155   My best-esteemed acquaintance. Hie thee. Go.
LEONARDO   My best endeavours shall be done herein.
          [*He begins to leave.*] *Enter* GRAZIANO

---

5. And has recommended you, if it be advancement.
6. "The grace of God is gear enough."
7. Palm (Lancelot reads the lines of his palm to predict
the future).
8. To tell the truth (referring to the practice of taking
an oath with the palm on the Bible).
9. A scanty income; an easy sexual entrance.
1. Alluding to a sexual adventure.

GRAZIANO [*to* LEONARDO]   Where's your master?
LEONARDO   Yonder, sir, he walks.
                                                                    Exit
GRAZIANO   Signor Bassanio.
BASSANIO   Graziano.
GRAZIANO   I have a suit to you.
BASSANIO   You have obtained it.
160 GRAZIANO   You must not deny me. I must go with you to Belmont.
BASSANIO   Why then, you must. But hear thee, Graziano,
       Thou art too wild, too rude and bold of voice—
       Parts° that become thee happily enough,   *Attributes*
       And in such eyes as ours appear not faults;
165 But where thou art not known, why, there they show
       Something too liberal.° Pray thee, take pain   *unrestrained*
       To allay with some cold drops of modesty
       Thy skipping spirit, lest through thy wild behaviour
       I be misconstered° in the place I go to,   *misconstrued*
       And lose my hopes.
170 GRAZIANO   Signor Bassanio, hear me.
       If I do not put on a sober habit,°   *behavior; clothing*
       Talk with respect, and swear but now and then,
       Wear prayer books in my pocket, look demurely—
       Nay more, while grace is saying hood mine eyes
175 Thus with my hat,² and sigh, and say 'Amen',
       Use all the observance of civility,
       Like one well studied in a sad ostent°   *solemn appearance*
       To please his grandam,° never trust me more.°   *grandmother / again*
BASSANIO   Well, we shall see your bearing.
180 GRAZIANO   Nay, but I bar tonight. You shall not gauge me
       By what we do tonight.
BASSANIO   No, that were pity.
       I would entreat you rather to put on
       Your boldest suit of mirth, for we have friends
       That purpose merriment. But fare you well.
185 I have some business.
GRAZIANO   And I must to Lorenzo and the rest.
       But we will visit you at supper-time.   *Exeunt* [*severally*]

2.3
Enter JESSICA *and* [LANCELOT] *the clown*
JESSICA   I am sorry thou wilt leave my father so.
       Our house is hell, and thou, a merry devil,
       Didst rob it of some taste of tediousness.
       But fare thee well. There is a ducat for thee.
5   And, Lancelot, soon at supper shalt thou see
       Lorenzo, who is thy new master's guest.
       Give him this letter, do it secretly;
       And so farewell. I would not have my father
       See me in talk with thee.
10 LANCELOT   Adieu. Tears exhibit° my tongue, most beautiful   (*for "inhibit"*)
       pagan; most sweet Jew; if a Christian do not play the knave and
       get thee, I am much deceived. But adieu. These foolish drops
       do something drown my manly spirit. Adieu.

2. Hats were worn at meals but taken off for grace.   **2.3** Location: Shylock's house in Venice.

JESSICA	Farewell, good Lancelot.	*Exit* [LANCELOT]

15 Alack, what heinous sin is it in me
To be ashamed to be my father's child!
But though I am a daughter to his blood,
I am not to his manners.° O Lorenzo,   *behavior*
If thou keep promise I shall end this strife,
20 Become a Christian and thy loving wife.   *Exit*

2.4

Enter GRAZIANO, LORENZO, SALERIO, *and* SOLANIO
LORENZO   Nay, we will slink away in° supper-time,   *during*
Disguise us at my lodging, and return
All in an hour.
GRAZIANO   We have not made good preparation.
5 SALERIO   We have not spoke as yet of ° torchbearers.   *not yet arranged for*
SOLANIO   'Tis vile, unless it may be quaintly ordered,°   *cleverly managed*
And better in my mind not undertook.
LORENZO   'Tis now but four o'clock. We have two hours
To furnish us.
        Enter LANCELOT *with a letter*
        Friend Lancelot, what's the news?
10 LANCELOT [*presenting the letter*]   An° it shall please you to break   *If*
up° this, it shall seem to signify.   *open*
LORENZO [*taking the letter*]   I know the hand. In faith, 'tis a fair
            hand,
And whiter than the paper it writ on
Is the fair hand that writ.
GRAZIANO   Love-news, in faith.
15 LANCELOT [*to* LORENZO]   By your leave, sir.
LORENZO   Whither goest thou?
LANCELOT   Marry, sir, to bid my old master the Jew to sup tonight
with my new master the Christian.
LORENZO   Hold,° here, take this. [*Giving money*] Tell gentle Jessica   *Wait*
20 I will not fail her. Speak it privately.
Go.   *Exit* [LANCELOT *the*] *clown*
        Gentlemen,
Will you prepare you for this masque tonight?
I am provided of a torchbearer.
SALERIO   Ay, marry, I'll be gone about it straight.°   *immediately*
SOLANIO   And so will I.
25 LORENZO   Meet me and Graziano
At Graziano's lodging some hour hence.
SALERIO   'Tis good we do so.   *Exit* [*with* SOLANIO]
GRAZIANO   Was not that letter from fair Jessica?
LORENZO   I must needs tell thee all. She hath directed
30 How I shall take her from her father's house,
What gold and jewels she is furnished with,
What page's suit she hath in readiness.
If e'er the Jew her father come to heaven
It will be for his gentle daughter's sake;
35 And never dare misfortune cross her foot
Unless she° do it under this excuse: *(misfortune)*

2.4 Location: Street in Venice.

That she° is issue° to a faithless Jew.   *(Jessica) / offspring*
Come, go with me. Peruse this as thou goest.
   [*He gives* GRAZIANO *the letter*]
Fair Jessica shall be my torchbearer.   *Exeunt*

2.5

Enter [SHYLOCK *the*] *Jew and his man that was,°*   *former servant*
[LANCELOT] *the clown*

SHYLOCK   Well, thou shalt see, thy eyes shall be thy judge,
The difference of old Shylock and Bassanio.
[*Calling*] What, Jessica! [*To* LANCELOT] Thou shalt not gormandize°   *overeat*
As thou hast done with me. [*Calling*] What, Jessica!
5   [*To* LANCELOT] And sleep and snore and rend apparel out.°   *wear out clothes*
[*Calling*] Why, Jessica, I say!
LANCELOT [*calling*]   Why, Jessica!
SHYLOCK   Who bids thee call? I do not bid thee call.
LANCELOT   Your worship was wont to tell me I could do nothing
without bidding.
        Enter JESSICA
10   JESSICA [*to* SHYLOCK]   Call you? What is your will?
SHYLOCK   I am bid forth to supper, Jessica.
There are my keys. But wherefore° should I go?   *why*
I am not bid for love. They flatter me,
But yet I'll go in hate, to feed upon
15   The prodigal Christian. Jessica, my girl,
Look to my house. I am right loath° to go.   *very unwilling*
There is some ill a-brewing towards my rest,
For I did dream of money-bags tonight.°   *last night*
LANCELOT   I beseech you, sir, go. My young master doth expect
20   your reproach.°   *(for "approach")*
SHYLOCK   So do I his.
LANCELOT   And they have conspired together. I will not say you
shall see a masque, but if you do, then it was not for nothing
that my nose fell a-bleeding on Black Monday° last at six   *Easter Monday*
25   o'clock i'th' morning, falling out that year on Ash Wednesday
was four year in th'afternoon.[1]
SHYLOCK   What, are there masques? Hear you me, Jessica,
Lock up my doors; and when you hear the drum
And the vile squealing of the wry-necked[2] fife,
30   Clamber not you up to the casements then,
Nor thrust your head into the public street
To gaze on Christian fools with varnished° faces,   *painted; masked*
But stop my house's ears—I mean my casements.
Let not the sound of shallow fopp'ry° enter   *frivolity*
35   My sober house. By Jacob's staff[3] I swear
I have no mind of feasting forth° tonight.   *away from home*
But I will go. [*To* LANCELOT] Go you before me, sirrah.
Say I will come.
LANCELOT   I will go before, sir.
        [*Aside to* JESSICA]
Mistress, look out at window for all this.[4]

2.5 Location: Outside Shylock's house.   3. See Genesis 32:10 and Hebrews 11:21.
1. Lancelot mocks Shylock's superstition.   4. *for all this*: despite Shylock's instructions.
2. Fifes were played with the head turned sideways.

40   There will come a Christian by
          Will be worth a Jewës eye.   *[Exit]*

SHYLOCK [*to* JESSICA] What says that fool of Hagar's offspring,[5] ha?
JESSICA His words were 'Farewell, mistress'; nothing else.
SHYLOCK The patch° is kind enough, but a huge feeder,   *fool*
45   Snail-slow in profit,° and he sleeps by day   *proficiency*
          More than the wildcat. Drones hive not with me;
          Therefore I part with him, and part with him
          To one that I would have him help to waste
          His borrowed purse. Well, Jessica, go in.
50   Perhaps I will return immediately.
          Do as I bid you. Shut doors after you.
          Fast bind, fast find[6]—
          A proverb never stale in thrifty mind.   *Exit [at one door]*
JESSICA Farewell; and if my fortune be not crossed,
55   I have a father, you a daughter lost.   *Exit [at another door]*

2.6

Enter the masquers, GRAZIANO *and* SALERIO *[with
      torchbearers]*
GRAZIANO This is the penthouse[1] under which Lorenzo
          Desired us to make stand.
SALERIO   His hour is almost past.
GRAZIANO And it is marvel he outdwells his hour,
          For lovers ever run before the clock.
5   SALERIO O, ten times faster Venus' pigeons[2] fly
          To seal love's bonds new made than they are wont
          To keep obligèd° faith unforfeited.°   *pledged / unbroken*
GRAZIANO That ever holds.° Who riseth from a feast   *remains true*
          With that keen appetite that he sits down?
10   Where is the horse that doth untread° again   *retrace*
          His tedious measures with the unbated fire
          That he did pace them first? All things that are
          Are with more spirit chasèd than enjoyed.
          How like a younker or a prodigal[3]
15   The scarfèd barque° puts from her native bay, *streamer-bedecked ship*
          Hugged and embracèd by the strumpet wind!
          How like the prodigal doth she return,
          With over-weathered ribs° and raggèd sails, *weatherbeaten timbers*
          Lean, rent,° and beggared by the strumpet wind!   *torn*
          Enter LORENZO *[with a torch]*
20   SALERIO Here comes Lorenzo. More of this hereafter.
LORENZO Sweet friends, your patience for my long abode.°   *delay*
          Not I but my affairs have made you wait.
          When you shall please to play the thieves for wives
          I'll watch° as long for you therein. Approach.   *wait*
25   Here dwells my father° Jew. [*Calling*] Ho, who's within? *father-in-law*
          [Enter] JESSICA *above [in boy's apparel]*
JESSICA Who are you? Tell me for more certainty,

---

5. That despicable gentile. Hagar, Abraham's gentile
servant, bore him a son, Ishmael; she and her child
were cast out after the birth of Abraham's legitimate
son, Isaac.
6. Something firmly secured will remain fastened.

2.6 Location: Scene continues.
1. Projecting roof of an upper story.
2. Doves that drew the love goddess's chariot.
3. See Luke 15:11–31. *younker:* fashionable youth;
junior seaman.

Albeit I'll swear that I do know your tongue.
LORENZO   Lorenzo, and thy love.
JESSICA   Lorenzo, certain, and my love indeed,
30   For who love I so much? And now who knows
But you, Lorenzo, whether I am yours?
LORENZO   Heaven and thy thoughts are witness that thou art.
JESSICA   Here, catch this casket. It is worth the pains.
I am glad 'tis night, you do not look on me,
35   For I am much ashamed of my exchange;°   change of clothes
But love is blind, and lovers cannot see
The pretty° follies that themselves commit;   ingenious
For if they could, Cupid himself would blush
To see me thus transformèd to a boy.
40   LORENZO   Descend, for you must be my torchbearer.
JESSICA   What, must I hold a candle to my shames?
They in themselves, good sooth,° are too too light.°   in truth / clear; wanton
Why, 'tis an office of discovery,⁴ love,
And I should be obscured.
LORENZO   So are you, sweet,
45   Even in the lovely garnish° of a boy.   dress
But come at once,
For the close° night doth play the runaway,°   secret / steals away
And we are stayed° for at Bassanio's feast.   waited
JESSICA   I will make fast the doors, and gild myself
50   With some more ducats, and be with you straight.
                                                      [Exit above]
GRAZIANO   Now, by my hood, a gentile, and no Jew.
LORENZO   Beshrew° me but I love her heartily,   Evil befall
For she is wise, if I can judge of her;
And fair she is, if that mine eyes be true;
55   And true she is, as she hath proved herself;
And therefore like herself, wise, fair, and true,
Shall she be placèd in my constant soul.
              Enter JESSICA [below]
What, art thou come? On, gentlemen, away.
Our masquing mates by this time for us stay.
                   Exit [with JESSICA and SALERIO]
              Enter ANTONIO
ANTONIO   Who's there?
60   GRAZIANO   Signor Antonio?
ANTONIO   Fie, fie, Graziano, where are all the rest?
'Tis nine o'clock. Our friends all stay for you.
No masque tonight. The wind is come about.
Bassanio presently° will go aboard.   immediately
65   I have sent twenty out to seek for you.
GRAZIANO   I am glad on't. I desire no more delight
Than to be under sail and gone tonight.   Exeunt

2.7

[Flourish of cornets.] Enter PORTIA with MOROCCO and
both their trains
PORTIA   Go, draw aside the curtains, and discover°   reveal
The several caskets to this noble prince.

---

4. (Torchbearing) is a task of disclosure.   2.7 Location: Belmont.

[*The curtains are drawn aside, revealing three caskets*]
[*To* MOROCCO] Now make your choice.
MOROCCO This first of gold, who° this inscription bears: | *which*
5 'Who chooseth me shall gain what many men desire.'
The second silver, which this promise carries:
'Who chooseth me shall get as much as he deserves.'
This third dull lead, with warning all as blunt:[1]
'Who chooseth me must give and hazard all he hath.'
10 How shall I know if I do choose the right?
PORTIA The one of them contains my picture, Prince.
If you choose that, then I am yours withal.° | *with it*
MOROCCO Some god direct my judgement! Let me see.
I will survey th'inscriptions back again.
15 What says this leaden casket?
'Who chooseth me must give and hazard all he hath.'
Must give, for what? For lead? Hazard for lead?
This casket threatens. Men that hazard all
Do it in hope of fair advantages.
20 A golden mind stoops not to shows of dross.° | *rubbish*
I'll then nor° give nor hazard aught for lead. | *neither*
What says the silver with her virgin hue?
'Who chooseth me shall get as much as he deserves.'
'As much as he deserves': pause there, Morocco,
25 And weigh thy value with an even° hand. | *impartial*
If thou beest rated by thy estimation
Thou dost deserve enough, and yet 'enough'
May not extend so far as to the lady.
And yet to be afeard of my deserving
30 Were but a weak disabling° of myself. | *disparagement*
As much as I deserve—why, that's the lady!
I do in birth deserve her, and in fortunes,
In graces, and in qualities of breeding;
But more than these, in love I do deserve.
35 What if I strayed no farther, but chose here?
Let's see once more this saying graved in gold:
'Who chooseth me shall gain what many men desire.'
Why, that's the lady! All the world desires her.
From the four corners of the earth they come
40 To kiss this shrine, this mortal breathing saint.
The Hyrcanian deserts[2] and the vasty° wilds | *vast*
Of wide Arabia are as throughfares° now | *main roads*
For princes to come view fair Portia.
The watery kingdom, whose ambitious head° | *(of a storm)*
45 Spits in the face of heaven, is no bar
To stop the foreign spirits, but they come
As o'er a brook to see fair Portia.
One of these three contains her heavenly picture.
Is't like° that lead contains her? 'Twere damnation | *probable*
50 To think so base a thought. It° were too gross | *(lead)*
To rib her cerecloth[3] in the obscure grave.
Or shall I think in silver she's immured,° | *enclosed*
Being ten times undervalued to tried° gold? | *purified*

1. Plainly spoken; not sharp (with play on "dull lead").
2. Wild region south of the Caspian Sea.
3. To enclose her shroud (normally covered with a layer of lead).

O sinful thought! Never so rich a gem
55   Was set in worse than gold. They have in England
    A coin that bears the figure of an angel⁴
    Stamped in gold, but that's insculped° upon;   *engraved*
    But here an angel in a golden bed
    Lies all within. Deliver me the key.
60   Here do I choose, and thrive as I may.
          [*He is given a key*]
PORTIA   There, take it, Prince; and if my form° lie there,   *image*
    Then I am yours.
         [MOROCCO *opens the golden casket*]
MOROCCO   O hell! What have we here?
    A carrion death,° within whose empty eye   *A skull*
    There is a written scroll. I'll read the writing.
65   'All that glisters is not gold;
    Often have you heard that told.
    Many a man his life hath sold
    But my outside⁵ to behold.
    Gilded tombs do worms infold.°   *enclose*
70   Had you been as wise as bold,
    Young in limbs, in judgement old,
    Your answer had not been enscrolled.
    Fare you well; your suit is cold.'
    Cold indeed, and labour lost.
75   Then farewell heat, and welcome frost.
    Portia, adieu. I have too grieved a heart
    To take a tedious leave. Thus losers part.
          Exit [*with his train*]. *Flourish* [*of*] *cornets*
PORTIA   A gentle riddance. Draw the curtains, go.
    Let all of his complexion choose me so.
         [*The curtains are drawn.*] *Exeunt*

2.8

Enter SALERIO *and* SOLANIO

SALERIO   Why, man, I saw Bassanio under sail.
    With him is Graziano gone along,
    And in their ship I am sure Lorenzo is not.
SOLANIO   The villain Jew with outcries raised° the Duke,   *roused*
5   Who went with him to search Bassanio's ship.
SALERIO   He came too late. The ship was under sail.
    But there the Duke was given to understand
    That in a gondola were seen together
    Lorenzo and his amorous Jessica.
10   Besides, Antonio certified the Duke
    They were not with Bassanio in his ship.
SOLANIO   I never heard a passion° so confused,   *an outburst*
    So strange, outrageous, and so variable
    As the dog Jew did utter in the streets.
15   'My daughter! O, my ducats! O, my daughter!
    Fled with a Christian! O, my Christian ducats!
    Justice! The law! My ducats and my daughter!
    A sealèd bag, two sealèd bags of ducats,

---

4. The gold coin called angel had the figure of St. Michael on its face.   5. Gold; face that once covered the skull.
2.8 Location: Venice.

	Of double ducats, stol'n from me by my daughter!	
20	And jewels, two stones, two rich and precious stones,[1]	
	Stol'n by my daughter! Justice! Find the girl!	
	She hath the stones upon her, and the ducats!'	

SALERIO   Why, all the boys in Venice follow him,
Crying, 'His stones, his daughter, and his ducats!'

25 SOLANIO   Let good Antonio look he keep his day,°   *repay his debt on time*
Or he shall pay for this.

SALERIO   Marry, well remembered.
I reasoned° with a Frenchman yesterday,   *conversed*
Who told me in the narrow seas° that part   *(English Channel)*
The French and English there miscarried°   *wrecked*
30 A vessel of our country, richly fraught.°   *laden*
I thought upon Antonio when he told me,
And wished in silence that it were not his.

SOLANIO   You were best to tell Antonio what you hear—
Yet do not suddenly, for it may grieve him.

35 SALERIO   A kinder gentleman treads not the earth.
I saw Bassanio and Antonio part.
Bassanio told him he would make some speed
Of his return. He answered, 'Do not so.
Slubber° not business for my sake, Bassanio,   *Hastily perform*
40 But stay the very riping of the time;
And for the Jew's bond which he hath of me,
Let it not enter in your mind° of love.   *interrupt your thoughts*
Be merry, and employ your chiefest thoughts
To courtship and such fair ostents° of love   *displays*
45 As shall conveniently° become you there.'   *properly*
And even there, his eye being big with tears,
Turning his face, he put his hand behind him
And, with affection wondrous sensible,°   *obvious; heartfelt*
He wrung Bassanio's hand; and so they parted.

50 SOLANIO   I think he only loves the world for him.
I pray thee let us go and find him out,
And quicken his embracèd heaviness[2]
With some delight or other.

SALERIO   Do we so.   *Exeunt*

2.9

Enter NERISSA *and a servitor*

NERISSA   Quick, quick, I pray thee, draw the curtain straight.°   *immediately*
The Prince of Aragon hath ta'en his oath,
And comes to his election presently.°   *his choice at once*
[*The servitor draws aside the curtain, revealing the three
caskets. Flourish of cornets.*] *Enter* ARAGON, *his train,
and* PORTIA

PORTIA   Behold, there stand the caskets, noble Prince.
5 If you choose that wherein I am contained,
Straight shall our nuptial rites be solemnized.
But if you fail, without more speech, my lord,
You must be gone from hence immediately.

---

1. With the suggestion "testicles," taken up by the
mocking boys in line 24.

2. And lighten the grief he embraces.
2.9 Location: Belmont.

ARAGON I am enjoined by oath to observe three things:
10   First, never to unfold to anyone
   Which casket 'twas I chose. Next, if I fail
   Of the right casket, never in my life
   To woo a maid in way of marriage.
   Lastly, if I do fail in fortune of my choice,
15   Immediately to leave you and be gone.
PORTIA To these injunctions everyone doth swear
   That comes to hazard° for my worthless self.   *gamble*
ARAGON And so have I addressed° me. Fortune now   *prepared*
   To my heart's hope! Gold, silver, and base lead.
   [*He reads the leaden casket*]
20   'Who chooseth me must give and hazard all he hath.'
   You shall look fairer ere I give or hazard.
   What says the golden chest? Ha, let me see.
   'Who chooseth me shall gain what many men desire.'
   'What many men desire'—that 'many' may be meant
25   By° the fool multitude, that choose by show,   *For*
   Not learning more than the fond° eye doth teach,   *foolish*
   Which pries not to th'interior but, like the martlet,° *swallow*
   Builds in the weather° on the outward wall   *open air*
   Even in the force and road of casualty.°   *mishap*
30   I will not choose what many men desire,
   Because I will not jump° with common spirits   *agree*
   And rank me with the barbarous multitudes.
   Why then, to thee, thou silver treasure-house.
   Tell me once more what title thou dost bear.
35   'Who chooseth me shall get as much as he deserves'—
   And well said too, for who shall go about
   To cozen° fortune, and be honourable   *cheat*
   Without the stamp° of merit? Let none presume *official seal*
   To wear an undeservèd dignity.
40   O, that estates, degrees,° and offices   *social ranks*
   Were not derived° corruptly, and that clear honour *gained*
   Were purchased° by the merit of the wearer!   *acquired*
   How many then should cover that stand bare,[1]
   How many be commanded that command?
45   How much low peasantry would then be gleaned° *separated*
   From the true seed of honour, and how much honour
   Picked from the chaff and ruin of the times
   To be new varnished?° Well; but to my choice. *regain its luster*
   'Who chooseth me shall get as much as he deserves.'
50   I will assume° desert. Give me a key for this,   *claim*
   And instantly unlock my fortunes here.
   [*He is given a key, and opens the silver casket*]
PORTIA Too long a pause for that which you find there.
ARAGON What's here? The portrait of a blinking idiot
   Presenting me a schedule.° I will read it.   *document*
55   How much unlike art thou to Portia!
   How much unlike my hopes and my deservings!
   'Who chooseth me shall have as much as he deserves.'

---

1. Should wear hats who now stand bareheaded (before their social superiors).

Did I deserve no more than a fool's head?
Is that my prize? Are my deserts no better?
60 PORTIA   To offend and judge are distinct offices,[2]
And of opposèd natures.
ARAGON   What is here?
   [*He reads the schedule*]
'The fire seven times tried° this;   *purified*
Seven times tried that judgement is
That did never choose amiss.
65   Some there be that shadows kiss;[3]
Such have but a shadow's bliss.
There be fools alive, iwis,°   *in truth*
Silvered[4] o'er; and so was this.
Take what wife you will to bed,
70   I° will ever be your head.   *(the blinking idiot)*
So be gone; you are sped.'°   *finished*
Still more fool I shall appear
By the time I linger here.
With one fool's head I came to woo,
75   But I go away with two.
Sweet, adieu. I'll keep my oath
Patiently to bear my wroth.°   *grief*
   [*Flourish of cornets. Exit with his train*]
PORTIA   Thus hath the candle singed the moth.
O, these deliberate° fools! When they do choose   *careful*
80   They have the wisdom by their wit to lose.
NERISSA   The ancient saying is no heresy:
Hanging and wiving goes by destiny.
PORTIA   Come, draw the curtain, Nerissa.
   [NERISSA *draws the curtain*]
   Enter MESSENGER
MESSENGER   Where is my lady?
PORTIA   Here. What would my lord?
85 MESSENGER   Madam, there is alighted at your gate
A young Venetian, one that comes before
To signify th'approaching of his lord,
From whom he bringeth sensible regreets,°   *tangible greetings*
To wit, besides commends and courteous breath,
90   Gifts of rich value. Yet° I have not seen   *Until now*
So likely° an ambassador of love.   *suitable*
A day in April never came so sweet
To show how costly° summer was at hand   *lavish*
As this fore-spurrer comes before his lord.
95 PORTIA   No more, I pray thee, I am half afeard
Thou wilt say anon° he is some kin to thee,   *soon*
Thou spend'st such high-day[5] wit in praising him.
Come, come, Nerissa, for I long to see
Quick Cupid's post° that comes so mannerly.   *messenger*
100 NERISSA   Bassanio, Lord Love,° if thy will it be!   *Exeunt*   *Cupid*

---

2. To err and to judge are different functions.
3. Like Narcissus in classical mythology, a youth who
fell in love with his own reflection.
4. Silver-haired (thus apparently wise).
5. Holiday (fit for special occasions).

3.1

Enter SOLANIO *and* SALERIO

SOLANIO   Now, what news on the Rialto?

SALERIO   Why, yet it lives there unchecked[1] that Antonio hath
a ship of rich lading wrecked on the narrow seas—the Good-
wins[2] I think they call the place—a very dangerous flat, and
5   fatal, where the carcasses of many a tall ship lie buried, as they
say, if my gossip Report° be an honest woman of her word.   *Dame Rumor*

SOLANIO   I would she were as lying a gossip in that as ever
knapped° ginger or made her neighbours believe she wept for   *nibbled*
the death of a third husband. But it is true, without any slips
10   of prolixity° or crossing the plain highway of talk, that the   *any wordy lies*
good Antonio, the honest Antonio—O that I had a title good
enough to keep his name company—

SALERIO   Come, the full stop.°   *period*

SOLANIO   Ha, what sayst thou? Why, the end is he hath lost a
15   ship.

SALERIO   I would it might prove the end of his losses.

SOLANIO   Let me say amen betimes, lest the devil cross° my   *thwart*
prayer—

Enter SHYLOCK

for here he comes in the likeness of a Jew. How now, Shylock,
20   what news among the merchants?

SHYLOCK   You knew, none so well, none so well as you, of my
daughter's flight.

SALERIO   That's certain. I for my part knew the tailor that made
the wings[3] she flew withal.

25   SOLANIO   And Shylock for his own part knew the bird was
fledge,° and then it is the complexion° of them all to leave the   *feathered/disposition*
dam.°   *mother (here, parent)*

SHYLOCK   She is damned for it.

SALERIO   That's certain, if the devil may be her judge.

30   SHYLOCK   My own flesh and blood to rebel![4]

SOLANIO   Out upon it, old carrion, rebels it at these years?

SHYLOCK   I say my daughter is my flesh and my blood.

SALERIO   There is more difference between thy flesh and hers
than between jet° and ivory; more between your bloods than   *black mineral*
35   there is between red wine and Rhenish.° But tell us, do you   *white wine*
hear whether Antonio have had any loss at sea or no?

SHYLOCK   There I have another bad match.° A bankrupt, a   *bad deal*
prodigal, who dare scarce show his head on the Rialto; a beggar, that was used to come so smug upon the mart. Let him look
40   to his bond. He was wont to call me usurer: let him look to his
bond. He was wont to lend money for a° Christian courtesy: let   *out of*
him look to his bond.

SALERIO   Why, I am sure if he forfeit thou wilt not take his
flesh. What's that good for?

45   SHYLOCK   To bait fish withal.° If it will feed nothing else it will   *with*
feed my revenge. He hath disgraced me, and hindered me half
a million; laughed at my losses, mocked at my gains, scorned

3.1 Location: Venice.
1. It circulates there without denial.
2. Goodwin Sands, where the Thames joins the sea.
"Goodwin" means "friend."

3. Playing on "wing," a decorative flap on the upper
sleeve.
4. Shylock means "my own offspring"; Solanio pretends
he means "carnal appetite."

my nation, thwarted my bargains, cooled my friends, heated
mine enemies, and what's his reason?—I am a Jew. Hath not a
50 Jew eyes? Hath not a Jew hands, organs, dimensions,° senses,   *bodily form*
affections, passions; fed with the same food, hurt with the
same weapons, subject to the same diseases, healed by the
same means, warmed and cooled by the same winter and
summer as a Christian is? If you prick us do we not bleed? If
55 you tickle us do we not laugh? If you poison us do we not die?
And if you wrong us shall we not revenge? If we are like you
in the rest, we will resemble you in that. If a Jew wrong a
Christian, what is his° humility? Revenge. If a Christian   *(the Christian's)*
wrong a Jew, what should his sufferance° be by Christian   *patience*
60 example? Why, revenge. The villainy you teach me I will execute, and it shall go hard but I will better the instruction.
    Enter a MAN *from Antonio*
MAN [*to* SOLANIO *and* SALERIO] Gentlemen, my master Antonio
is at his house and desires to speak with you both.
SALERIO We have been up and down to seek him.
    Enter TUBAL
65 SOLANIO Here comes another of the tribe. A third cannot be
matched° unless the devil himself turn Jew.   *found to match*
    Exeunt [SOLANIO *and* SALERIO, *with Antonio's* MAN]
SHYLOCK How now, Tubal? What news from Genoa? Hast thou
found my daughter?
TUBAL I often came where I did hear of her, but cannot find
70 her.
SHYLOCK Why, there, there, there, there. A diamond gone cost
me two thousand ducats in Frankfurt.[5] The curse never fell
upon our nation till now—I never felt it till now. Two thousand
ducats in that and other precious, precious jewels. I would my
75 daughter were dead at my foot and the jewels in her ear! Would
she were hearsed° at my foot and the ducats in her coffin! No   *coffined*
news of them? Why, so. And I know not what's spent in the
search. Why thou, loss upon loss: the thief gone with so
much, and so much to find the thief, and no satisfaction, no
80 revenge, nor no ill luck stirring but what lights o' my shoulders,
no sighs but o' my breathing, no tears but o' my shedding.
TUBAL Yes, other men have ill luck too. Antonio, as I heard in
Genoa—
SHYLOCK What, what, what? Ill luck, ill luck?
85 TUBAL Hath an argosy cast away coming from Tripolis.
SHYLOCK I thank God, I thank God! Is it true, is it true?
TUBAL I spoke with some of the sailors that escaped the wreck.
SHYLOCK I thank thee, good Tubal. Good news, good news! Ha,
ha—heard in Genoa?
90 TUBAL Your daughter spent in Genoa, as I heard, one night
fourscore ducats.
SHYLOCK Thou stick'st a dagger in me. I shall never see my gold
again. Fourscore ducats at a sitting? Fourscore ducats?
TUBAL There came divers of Antonio's creditors in my company
95 to Venice that swear he cannot choose but break.°   *go bankrupt*
SHYLOCK I am very glad of it. I'll plague him, I'll torture him.
I am glad of it.

---

5. Site of a jewel market.

TUBAL One of them showed me a ring that he had of your
daughter for a monkey.

100 SHYLOCK Out upon her! Thou torturest me, Tubal. It was my
turquoise. I had it of Leah when I was a bachelor. I would not
have given it for a wilderness of monkeys.

TUBAL But Antonio is certainly undone.

SHYLOCK Nay, that's true, that's very true. Go, Tubal, fee° me   *hire*
105 an officer. Bespeak him a fortnight before. I will have the heart
of him if he forfeit, for were he out of Venice I can make what
merchandise° I will. Go, Tubal, and meet me at our synagogue.   *drive what bargains*
Go, good Tubal; at our synagogue, Tubal.

                                   Exeunt [severally]

3.2

Enter BASSANIO, PORTIA, NERISSA, GRAZIANO, *and all
their trains. [The curtains are drawn aside, revealing the
three caskets]*

PORTIA [*to* BASSANIO] I pray you tarry. Pause a day or two
Before you hazard, for in choosing° wrong   *if you choose*
I lose your company. Therefore forbear a while.
There's something tells me—but it is not love—
5 I would not lose you; and you know yourself
Hate counsels not in such a quality.°   *way*
But lest you should not understand me well—
And yet a maiden hath no tongue but thought—
I would detain you here some month or two
10 Before you venture for me. I could teach you
How to choose right, but then I am forsworn.
So° will I never be; so may you miss me.[1]   *(forsworn)*
But if you do, you'll make me wish a sin,
That I had been forsworn. Beshrew your eyes,
15 They have o'erlooked° me and divided me.   *bewitched*
One half of me is yours, the other half yours—
Mine own, I would say, but if mine, then yours,
And so all yours. O, these naughty° times   *evil*
Puts bars between the owners and their rights;
20 And so, though yours, not yours. Prove it so,
Let fortune go to hell for it, not I.[2]
I speak too long, but tis to piece° the time,   *extend*
To eke° it, and to draw it out in length   *augment*
To stay° you from election.°   *delay / choosing*

BASSANIO   Let me choose,
25 For as I am, I live upon the rack.[3]

PORTIA Upon the rack, Bassanio? Then confess
What treason there is mingled with your love.

BASSANIO None but that ugly treason of mistrust°   *uncertainty*
Which makes me fear° th'enjoying of my love.   *doubt*
30 There may as well be amity and life
'Tween snow and fire as treason and my love.

PORTIA Ay, but I fear you speak upon the rack,
Where men enforcèd do speak anything.

3.2 Location: Belmont.
1. Fail to attain me.
2. *Prove . . . I:* If it turns out thus, let it be fortune's
fault, not mine (for breaking my oath).
3. Instrument of torture used on traitors.

BASSANIO Promise me life and I'll confess the truth.
PORTIA Well then, confess and live.
35 BASSANIO 'Confess and love'
Had been the very sum of my confession.
O happy torment, when my torturer
Doth teach me answers for deliverance!°   *release*
But let me to my fortune and the caskets.
40 PORTIA Away then. I am locked in one of them.
If you do love me, you will find me out.
Nerissa and the rest, stand all aloof.
Let music sound while he doth make his choice.
Then if he lose he makes a swanlike end,⁴
45 Fading in music. That the comparison
May stand more proper, my eye shall be the stream
And wat'ry deathbed for him. He may win,
And what is music then? Then music is
Even as the flourish° when true subjects bow   *fanfare*
50 To a new-crownèd monarch. Such it is
As are those dulcet sounds in break of day
That creep into the dreaming bridegroom's ear
And summon him to marriage.⁵ Now he goes,
With no less presence° but with much more love   *dignity*
55 Than young Alcides when he did redeem
The virgin tribute paid by howling Troy
To the sea-monster.⁶ I stand for sacrifice.
The rest aloof are the Dardanian° wives,   *Trojan*
With blearèd° visages come forth to view   *weepy*
60 The issue° of th'exploit. Go, Hercules.   *outcome*
Live thou,° I live. With much much more dismay   *If you live*
I view the fight than thou that mak'st the fray.
          Here music. A song the whilst BASSANIO *comments on*
          the caskets to himself
[ONE FROM PORTIA'S TRAIN]
          Tell me where is fancy° bred,   *love; infatuation*
          Or° in the heart, or in the head?   *Whether*
65   How begot, how nourishèd?
[ALL]   Reply, reply.
[ONE FROM PORTIA'S TRAIN]
          It is engendered in the eyes,⁷
          With gazing fed; and fancy dies
          In the cradle⁸ where it lies.
70   Let us all ring fancy's knell.
          I'll begin it: ding, dong, bell.
ALL   Ding, dong, bell.
BASSANIO [*aside*] So may the outward shows be least themselves.⁹
The world is still° deceived with ornament.   *continually*
75 In law, what plea so tainted and corrupt
But, being seasoned with a gracious voice,
Obscures the show of evil? In religion,

---

4. The swan was thought to sing only once, just before its death.
5. It was customary to play music under a bridegroom's window on the morning of his wedding.
6. Alcides (Hercules) saved the Trojan princess Hesione when she was to be sacrificed to a sea monster, not because he loved her but to win two horses her father offered as a reward.
7. Love was imagined to enter through the eyes.
8. In infancy, in the eyes (?)
9. Least express the truth.

What damnèd error but some sober brow
Will bless it and approve° it with a text,   prove
80　Hiding the grossness with fair ornament?
There is no vice so simple° but assumes   unalloyed; stupid
Some mark of virtue on his° outward parts.   its
How many cowards whose hearts are all as false
As stairs of sand, wear yet upon their chins
85　The beards of Hercules and frowning Mars,
Who, inward searched,° have livers white as milk?[1]   examined
And these assume but valour's excrement[2]
To render them redoubted.° Look on beauty   feared
And you shall see 'tis purchased by the weight,°   (like cosmetics)
90　Which therein works a miracle in nature,
Making them lightest° that wear most of it.   most licentious
So are those crispèd,° snaky, golden locks   curled
Which makes such wanton gambols with the wind
Upon supposèd fairness,° often known   beauty
95　To be the dowry° of a second head,   endowment (in a wig)
The skull that bred them in the sepulchre.
Thus ornament is but the guilèd° shore   beguiling
To a most dangerous sea, the beauteous scarf
Veiling an Indian° beauty; in a word,   a swarthy (pejorative)
100　The seeming truth which cunning times put on
To entrap the wisest. [Aloud] Therefore, thou gaudy gold,
Hard food for Midas,[3] I will none of thee.
[To the silver casket] Nor none of thee, thou pale and com-
　　　　mon drudge°   laborer (in coins)
'Tween man and man. But thou, thou meagre lead,
105　Which rather threaten'st than dost promise aught,
Thy paleness moves me more than eloquence,
And here choose I. Joy be the consequence!
Portia [aside]　How all the other passions fleet to air,
As° doubtful thoughts, and rash-embraced despair,   Such as
110　And shudd'ring fear, and green-eyed jealousy.
O love, be moderate! Allay thy ecstasy.
In measure rain thy joy; scant° this excess.[4]   lessen
I feel too much thy blessing: make it less,
For fear I surfeit.
　　　　[BASSANIO opens the leaden casket]
BASSANIO　　　　　　What find I here?
115　Fair Portia's counterfeit.° What demi-god[5]   likeness
Hath come so near creation? Move these eyes?
Or whether, riding on the balls of mine,°   my eyes
Seem they in motion? Here are severed lips
Parted with sugar breath. So sweet a bar
120　Should sunder such sweet friends. Here in her hairs
The painter plays the spider, and hath woven
A golden mesh t'untrap° the hearts of men   entrap (phonetic?)
Faster than gnats in cobwebs. But her eyes—
How could he see to do them? Having made one,

---

1. Lily-livered (the liver was considered the seat of
courage).
2. External attribute; hair (the beard).
3. Everything King Midas touched, including his food,
turned to gold.
4. Synonym for "interest" or "usury."
5. Supernaturally gifted painter.

125 Methinks it should have power to steal both his
And leave itself unfurnished.° Yet look how far   *unaccompanied*
The substance of my praise doth wrong this shadow°   *portrait*
In underprizing° it, so far this shadow   *understating*
Doth limp behind the substance.° Here's the scroll,   *real thing (Portia)*
130 The continent° and summary of my fortune.   *container*
  'You that choose not by the view
  Chance as fair° and choose as true.   *Gamble as luckily*
  Since this fortune falls to you,
  Be content, and seek no new.
135   If you be well pleased with this,
  And hold your fortune for your bliss,
  Turn you where your lady is,
  And claim her with a loving kiss.'
A gentle scroll. Fair lady, by your leave,
140 I come by note to give[6] and to receive,
Like one of two contending in a prize,°   *contest*
That thinks he hath done well in people's eyes,
Hearing applause and universal shout,
Giddy in spirit, still gazing in a doubt
145 Whether those peals of praise be his° or no.   *for him*
So, thrice-fair lady, stand I even so,
As doubtful whether what I see be true
Until confirmed, signed, ratified by you.
 PORTIA You see me, Lord Bassanio, where I stand,
150 Such as I am. Though for myself alone
I would not be ambitious in my wish
To wish myself much better, yet for you
I would be trebled twenty times myself,
A thousand times more fair, ten thousand times more rich,
155 That only to stand high in your account°   *estimation*
I might in virtues, beauties, livings,° friends,   *possessions*
Exceed account. But the full sum of me
Is sum of something which, to term in gross,°   *to describe fully*
Is an unlessoned girl, unschooled, unpractisèd,
160 Happy° in this, she is not yet so old   *Fortunate*
But she may learn; happier than this,
She is not bred so dull but she can learn;
Happiest of all is that her gentle spirit
Commits itself to yours to be directed
165 As from her lord, her governor, her king.
Myself and what is mine to you and yours
Is now converted.° But° now I was the lord   *transferred / Just*
Of this fair mansion, master of my servants,
Queen o'er myself; and even now, but now,
170 This house, these servants, and this same myself
Are yours, my lord's. I give them with this ring,
Which when you part from, lose, or give away,
Let it presage the ruin of your love,
And be my vantage to exclaim on you.[7]
175 BASSANIO Madam, you have bereft me of all words.
Only my blood speaks to you in my veins,

---

6. I come by written authorization to give a kiss; to give   7. And be my opportunity to reproach you.
myself.

And there is such confusion in my powers°   *faculties*
As after some oration fairly spoke
By a belovèd prince there doth appear
180   Among the buzzing pleasèd multitude,
Where every something being blent° together   *blended*
Turns to a wild° of nothing save of joy,   *chaos*
Expressed and not expressed. But when this ring
Parts from this finger, then parts life from hence.
185   O, then be bold to say° Bassanio's dead.   *say confidently*

NERISSA   My lord and lady, it is now our time
That have stood by and seen our wishes prosper
To cry 'Good joy, good joy, my lord and lady!'

GRAZIANO   My lord Bassanio, and my gentle lady,
190   I wish you all the joy that you can wish,
For I am sure you can wish none from me.[8]
And when your honours mean to solemnize
The bargain of your faith, I do beseech you
Even at that time I may be married too.

195   BASSANIO   With all my heart, so° thou canst get a wife.   *if*

GRAZIANO   I thank your lordship, you have got me one.
My eyes, my lord, can look as swift as yours.
You saw the mistress, I beheld the maid.
You loved, I loved; for intermission°   *delay*
200   No more pertains to me, my lord, than you.
Your fortune stood upon the caskets there,
And so did mine too, as the matter falls;
For wooing here until I sweat again,°   *repeatedly*
And swearing till my very roof° was dry   *(of his mouth)*
205   With oaths of love, at last—if promise[9] last—
I got a promise of this fair one here
To have her love, provided that your fortune
Achieved her mistress.

PORTIA   Is this true, Nerissa?

NERISSA   Madam, it is, so you stand pleased withal.
210   BASSANIO   And do you, Graziano, mean good faith?

GRAZIANO   Yes, faith, my lord.

BASSANIO   Our feast shall be much honoured in your marriage.

GRAZIANO [*to* NERISSA]   We'll play° with them the first boy for a   *wager*
    thousand ducats.
215   NERISSA   What, and stake down?[1]

GRAZIANO   No, we shall ne'er win at that sport and stake down.

          Enter LORENZO, JESSICA, *and* SALERIO, *a messenger from*
          Venice

But who comes here? Lorenzo and his infidel!
What, and my old Venetian friend Salerio!

BASSANIO   Lorenzo and Salerio, welcome hither,
220   If that the youth of my new int'rest° here   *position*
Have power° to bid you welcome. [*To* PORTIA] By your leave,   *Gives me the right*
I bid my very° friends and countrymen,   *true*
Sweet Portia, welcome.

PORTIA   So do I, my lord. They are entirely welcome.
225   LORENZO   I thank your honour. For my part, my lord,

---

8. You do not need my good wishes.
9. Nerissa's, to wed Graziano.

1. Put the money down now (Graziano follows with a
bawdy joke on "flaccid penis").

My purpose was not to have seen you here,
But meeting with Salerio by the way
He did entreat me past all saying nay
To come with him along.

SALERIO   I did, my lord,
230   And I have reason for it. Signor Antonio
Commends him° to you.   *Sends greeting*
           [He gives BASSANIO *a letter]*

BASSANIO   Ere I ope his letter
I pray you tell me how my good friend doth.

SALERIO   Not sick, my lord, unless it be in mind;
Nor well, unless in mind. His letter there
235   Will show you his estate.°   *situation*
           *[*BASSANIO*] opens the letter [and reads]*

GRAZIANO   Nerissa, *[indicating* JESSICA*]* cheer yon stranger. Bid
    her welcome.
Your hand, Salerio. What's the news from Venice?
How doth that royal° merchant good Antonio?   *princely*
I know he will be glad of our success.
240   We are the Jasons; we have won the fleece.

SALERIO   I would you had won the fleece° that he hath lost. *(punning on "fleets")*

PORTIA   There are some shrewd° contents in yon same paper   *evil*
That steals the colour from Bassanio's cheek.
Some dear friend dead, else nothing in the world
245   Could turn° so much the constitution   *change*
Of any constant° man. What, worse and worse?   *resolute*
With leave, Bassanio, I am half yourself,
And I must freely have the half of anything
That this same paper brings you.

BASSANIO   O sweet Portia,
250   Here are a few of the unpleasant'st words
That ever blotted paper. Gentle lady,
When I did first impart my love to you
I freely told you all the wealth I had
Ran in my veins: I was a gentleman;
255   And then I told you true; and yet, dear lady,
Rating myself at nothing, you shall see
How much I was a braggart. When I told you
My state° was nothing, I should then have told you   *wealth*
That I was worse than nothing, for indeed
260   I have engaged° myself to a dear friend,   *pledged*
Engaged my friend to his mere° enemy,   *utter*
To feed my means. Here is a letter, lady,
The paper° as the body of my friend,   *(ripped open)*
And every word in it a gaping wound
265   Issuing life-blood. But is it true, Salerio?
Hath all his ventures failed? What, not one hit?°   *success*
From Tripolis, from Mexico, and England,
From Lisbon, Barbary, and India,
And not one vessel scape the dreadful touch
270   Of merchant-marring rocks?

SALERIO   Not one, my lord.
Besides, it should appear that if he had
The present° money to discharge° the Jew   *ready / pay*
He° would not take it. Never did I know   *(Shylock)*

A creature that did bear the shape of man
275 So keen° and greedy to confound° a man.   *eager / destroy*
He plies the Duke at morning and at night,
And doth impeach the freedom of the state²
If they deny him justice. Twenty merchants,
The Duke himself, and the magnificoes°   *Venetian magnates*
280 Of greatest port,° have all persuaded° with him,   *dignity / argued*
But none can drive him from the envious° plea   *malicious*
Of forfeiture, of justice, and his bond.
JESSICA   When I was with him I have heard him swear
To Tubal and to Cush, his countrymen,
285 That he would rather have Antonio's flesh
Than twenty times the value of the sum
That he did owe him; and I know, my lord,
If law, authority, and power deny not,
It will go hard with poor Antonio.
290 PORTIA [*to* BASSANIO]   Is it your dear friend that is thus in trouble?
BASSANIO   The dearest friend to me, the kindest man,
The best-conditioned° and unwearied spirit   *best-natured*
In doing courtesies, and one in whom
The ancient Roman honour more appears
295 Than any that draws breath in Italy.
PORTIA   What sum owes he the Jew?
BASSANIO   For me, three thousand ducats.
PORTIA   What, no more?
Pay him six thousand and deface° the bond.   *destroy*
Double six thousand, and then treble that,
300 Before a friend of this description
Shall lose a hair thorough Bassanio's fault.
First go with me to church and call me wife,
And then away to Venice to your friend;
For never shall you lie by Portia's side
305 With an unquiet soul. You shall have gold
To pay the petty debt twenty times over.
When it is paid, bring your true friend along.
My maid Nerissa and myself meantime
Will live as maids and widows. Come, away,
310 For you shall hence upon your wedding day.
Bid your friends welcome, show a merry cheer.°   *countenance*
Since you are dear° bought, I will love you dear.°   *expensively / dearly*
But let me hear the letter of your friend.
BASSANIO [*reads*]   'Sweet Bassanio, my ships have all miscarried,
315 my creditors grow cruel, my estate is very low, my bond to the
Jew is forfeit, and since in paying it, it is impossible I should
live, all debts are cleared between you and I if I might but see
you at my death. Notwithstanding, use your pleasure.° If your   *follow your wishes*
love do not persuade you to come, let not my letter.'
320 PORTIA   O, love! Dispatch all business, and be gone.
BASSANIO   Since I have your good leave to go away
I will make haste, but till I come again
No bed shall e'er be guilty of my stay
Nor rest be interposer 'twixt us twain.   *Exeunt*

2. Accuse the state of not preserving commercial liberty.

3.3

Enter [SHYLOCK] *the Jew,* SOLANIO, ANTONIO, *and the jailer*

SHYLOCK Jailer, look to him. Tell not me of mercy.
This is the fool that lent out money gratis.
Jailer, look to him.

ANTONIO   Hear me yet, good Shylock.

SHYLOCK I'll have my bond. Speak not against my bond.
5 I have sworn an oath that I will have my bond.
Thou called'st me dog before thou hadst a cause,
But since I am a dog, beware my fangs.
The Duke shall grant me justice. I do wonder,
Thou naughty° jailer, that thou art so fond°   *wicked/foolish*
10 To come abroad° with him at his request.   *outside*

ANTONIO I pray thee hear me speak.

SHYLOCK I'll have my bond. I will not hear thee speak.
I'll have my bond, and therefore speak no more.
I'll not be made a soft and dull-eyed° fool   *gullible*
15 To shake the head, relent, and sigh, and yield
To Christian intercessors. Follow not.
I'll have no speaking. I will have my bond.   *Exit*

SOLANIO It is the most impenetrable cur
That ever kept° with men.   *lived*

ANTONIO   Let him alone.
20 I'll follow him no more with bootless° prayers.   *fruitless*
He seeks my life. His reason well I know:
I oft delivered° from his forfeitures   *saved*
Many that have at times made moan to me.
Therefore he hates me.

SOLANIO   I am sure the Duke
25 Will never grant this forfeiture to hold.

ANTONIO The Duke cannot deny° the course of law,   *prevent*
For the commodity that strangers[1] have
With us in Venice, if it be denied,
Will much impeach the justice of the state,
30 Since that the trade and profit of the city
Consisteth of all nations. Therefore go.
These griefs and losses have so bated° me   *diminished*
That I shall hardly spare a pound of flesh
Tomorrow to my bloody creditor.
35 Well, jailer, on. Pray God Bassanio come
To see me pay his debt, and then I care not.   *Exeunt*

3.4

Enter PORTIA, NERISSA, LORENZO, JESSICA, *and*
[BALTHASAR,] *a man of Portia's*

LORENZO [*to* PORTIA] Madam, although I speak it in your presence,
You have a noble and a true conceit°   *conception*
Of godlike amity, which appears most strongly
In bearing thus the absence of your lord.
5 But if you knew to whom you show this honour,

3.3 Location: Street in Venice.
1. For the trading privileges that foreigners (including
Jews).
3.4 Location: Belmont.

How true a gentleman you send relief,
How dear a lover° of my lord your husband,   *friend*
I know you would be prouder of the work
Than customary bounty can enforce you.[1]
10 PORTIA   I never did repent for doing good,
Nor shall not now; for in companions
That do converse and waste° the time together,   *spend (not pejorative)*
Whose souls do bear an equal yoke of love,
There must be needs a like proportion
15 Of lineaments, of manners, and of spirit,
Which makes me think that this Antonio,
Being the bosom lover of my lord,
Must needs be like my lord. If it be so,
How little is the cost I have bestowed
20 In purchasing the semblance of my soul[2]
From out the state of hellish cruelty.
This comes too near the praising of myself,
Therefore no more of it. Hear other things:
Lorenzo, I commit into your hands
25 The husbandry° and manage of my house   *care*
Until my lord's return. For mine own part,
I have toward heaven breathed a secret vow
To live in prayer and contemplation,
Only attended by Nerissa here,
30 Until her husband and my lord's return.
There is a monastery two miles off,
And there we will abide. I do desire you
Not to deny this imposition,°   *decline this charge*
The which my love and some necessity
Now lays upon you.
35 LORENZO   Madam, with all my heart,
I shall obey you in all fair commands.
PORTIA   My people do already know my mind,
And will acknowledge you and Jessica
In place of Lord Bassanio and myself.
40 So fare you well till we shall meet again.
LORENZO   Fair thoughts and happy hours attend on you!
JESSICA   I wish your ladyship all heart's content.
PORTIA   I thank you for your wish, and am well pleased
To wish it back on you. Fare you well, Jessica.
                        Exeunt [LORENZO *and* JESSICA]
45 Now, Balthasar,
As I have ever found thee honest-true,
So let me find thee still. Take this same letter,
And use thou all th'endeavour of a man
In speed to Padua. See thou render this
50 Into my cousin's hands, Doctor Bellario,
And look what notes and garments he doth give thee,
Bring them, I pray thee, with imagined° speed   *all imaginable*
Unto the traject,° to the common° ferry   *ferry / public*
Which trades° to Venice. Waste no time in words,   *goes back and forth*
55 But get thee gone. I shall be there before thee.
BALTHASAR   Madam, I go with all convenient° speed.   [*Exit*]   *due*

---

1. Than ordinary generosity permits you.   2. In redeeming the likeness of my Bassanio (Antonio).

PORTIA   Come on, Nerissa. I have work in hand
   That you yet know not of. We'll see our husbands
   Before they think of us.
NERISSA   Shall they see us?
60 PORTIA   They shall, Nerissa, but in such a habit°   *garb*
   That they shall think we are accomplishèd°   *equipped*
   With that we lack.° I'll hold thee any wager,   *(i.e., penises)*
   When we are both accoutered like young men
   I'll prove the prettier fellow of the two,
65 And wear my dagger with the braver grace,
   And speak between the change of man and boy
   With a reed° voice, and turn two mincing steps   *piping*
   Into a manly stride, and speak of frays
   Like a fine bragging youth, and tell quaint° lies   *elaborate*
70 How honourable ladies sought my love,
   Which I denying, they fell sick and died.
   I could not do withal.° Then I'll repent,   *help it*
   And wish for all that that I had not killed them;
   And twenty of these puny lies I'll tell,
75 That men shall swear I have discontinued° school   *been out of*
   Above° a twelvemonth. I have within my mind   *At least*
   A thousand raw tricks of these bragging Jacks°   *fellows*
   Which I will practise.
NERISSA   Why, shall we turn to³ men?
80 PORTIA   Fie, what a question's that
   If thou wert near a lewd interpreter!
   But come, I'll tell thee all my whole device°   *plan*
   When I am in my coach, which stays for us
   At the park gate; and therefore haste away,
85 For we must measure twenty miles today.   *Exeunt*

3.5
Enter [LANCELOT] the clown, and JESSICA
LANCELOT   Yes, truly; for look you, the sins of the father are to
   be laid upon the children, therefore I promise you I fear° you.   *fear for*
   I was always plain with you, and so now I speak my agitation°   *(for "cogitation")*
   of the matter, therefore be o' good cheer, for truly I think you
5 are damned. There is but one hope in it that can do you any
   good, and that is but a kind of bastard hope, neither.
JESSICA   And what hope is that, I pray thee?
LANCELOT   Marry, you may partly hope that your father got you
   not, that you are not the Jew's daughter.
10 JESSICA   That were a kind of bastard hope indeed. So the sins
   of my mother should be visited upon me.
LANCELOT   Truly then, I fear you are damned both by father and
   mother. Thus, when I shun Scylla your father, I fall into
   Charybdis your mother.¹ Well, you are gone° both ways.   *doomed*
15 JESSICA   I shall be saved by my husband.² He hath made me a
   Christian.
LANCELOT   Truly, the more to blame he! We were Christians

---

3. Turn into (with bawdy suggestion).
3.5 Location: Portia's garden in Belmont.
1. Scylla was a mythological sea monster, Charybdis a
whirlpool in the Strait of Messina. Mariners had to avoid

both, a proverbially difficult task.
2. "The unbelieving wife is sanctified by the husband"
(1 Corinthians 7:14).

enough before, e'en as many as could well live one by another.[3]
This making of Christians will raise the price of hogs. If we
20 grow all to be pork-eaters we shall not shortly have a rasher° on   *bacon strip*
the coals for money.°   *any price*

Enter LORENZO

JESSICA   I'll tell my husband, Lancelot, what you say. Here he
comes.

LORENZO   I shall grow jealous of you shortly, Lancelot, if you
25 thus get my wife into corners.

JESSICA   Nay, you need not fear us, Lorenzo. Lancelot and I are
out.° He tells me flatly there's no mercy for me in heaven   *quarreling*
because I am a Jew's daughter, and he says you are no good
member of the commonwealth, for in converting Jews to Chris-
30 tians you raise the price of pork.

LORENZO [*to* LANCELOT]   I shall answer° that better to the com-   *explain*
monwealth than you can the getting up of the Negro's belly.
The Moor[4] is with child by you, Lancelot.

LANCELOT   It is much that the Moor should be more than rea-
35 son,[5] but if she be less than an honest° woman, she is indeed   *a chaste*
more than I took her for.

LORENZO   How every fool can play upon the word! I think the
best grace of wit will shortly turn into silence, and discourse
grow commendable in none only but parrots. Go in, sirrah, bid
40 them prepare for dinner.

LANCELOT   That is done, sir. They have all stomachs.°   *appetites*

LORENZO   Goodly Lord, what a wit-snapper are you! Then bid
them prepare dinner.

LANCELOT   That is done too, sir; only 'cover'[6] is the word.

45 LORENZO   Will you cover then, sir?

LANCELOT   Not so, sir, neither. I know my duty.

LORENZO   Yet more quarrelling with occasion![7] Wilt thou show
the whole wealth of thy wit in an instant? I pray thee understand a plain man in his plain meaning. Go to thy fellows; bid
50 them cover the table, serve in the meat, and we will come in
to dinner.

LANCELOT   For the table,° sir, it shall be served in. For the meat,   *meal*
sir, it shall be covered.[8] For your coming in to dinner, sir, why,
let it be as humours and conceits° shall govern.   *Exit*   *whims and notions*

55 LORENZO   O dear discretion, how his words are suited![9]
The fool hath planted in his memory
An army of good words, and I do know
A many fools that stand in better place,
Garnished° like him, that for a tricksy word   *Provided (with words)*
60 Defy the matter.° How cheer'st thou,[1] Jessica?   *Refuse to talk sense*
And now, good sweet, say thy opinion:
How dost thou like the Lord Bassanio's wife?

JESSICA   Past all expressing. It is very meet°   *proper*
The Lord Bassanio live an upright life,
65 For, having such a blessing in his lady,

---

3. *well . . . another:* reside next door to one another;
earn a living off one another.
4. Apparently an African woman of Portia's household.
5. Should be bigger than is reasonable (punning on
"more/ Moor").
6. Set the table; but Lancelot puns on "cover" as meaning "put on the hat."

7. Playing on words whenever possible.
8. Served in covered dishes (playfully or unconsciously
reversing Lorenzo's instructions).
9. Adapted to the occasion. *dear discretion:* precious
discrimination (ironic).
1. How are you.

He finds the joys of heaven here on earth,
And if on earth he do not merit it,
In reason he should never come to heaven.
Why, if two gods should play some heavenly match
70 And on the wager lay two earthly women,
And Portia one, there must be something else
Pawned° with the other; for the poor rude world   *Wagered*
Hath not her fellow.
LORENZO   Even such a husband
Hast thou of me as she is for a wife.
75 JESSICA Nay, but ask my opinion too of that!
LORENZO I will anon.° First let us go to dinner.   *soon*
JESSICA Nay, let me praise you while I have a stomach.° *an appetite; desire*
LORENZO No, pray thee, let it serve for table-talk.
Then, howsome'er° thou speak'st, 'mong other things *however*
I shall digest° it.   *ingest; analyze*
80 JESSICA   Well, I'll set you forth.[2]   *Exeunt*

4.1

Enter the DUKE, *the magnificoes,* ANTONIO, BASSANIO,
GRAZIANO, *and* [SALERIO]
DUKE What, is Antonio here?
ANTONIO   Ready, so please your grace.
DUKE I am sorry for thee. Thou art come to answer
A stony adversary, an inhuman wretch
Uncapable of pity, void and empty
From any dram° of mercy.   *trace*
5 ANTONIO   I have heard
Your grace hath ta'en great pains to qualify°   *alleviate*
His rigorous course, but since he stands obdurate,
And that no lawful means can carry me
Out of his envy's° reach, I do oppose   *malice's*
10 My patience to his fury, and am armed°   *prepared*
To suffer with a quietness of spirit
The very tyranny° and rage of his.   *cruelty*
DUKE Go one, and call the Jew into the court.
SALERIO He is ready at the door. He comes, my lord.
Enter SHYLOCK
15 DUKE Make room, and let him stand before our° face. *(the royal "we")*
Shylock, the world thinks—and I think so too—
That thou but lead'st this fashion° of thy malice *sustain the pretense*
To the last hour of act,° and then 'tis thought *brink of performance*
Thou'lt show thy mercy and remorse° more strange° *compassion / extraordinary*
20 Than is thy strange apparent cruelty,
And where thou now exacts the penalty—
Which is a pound of this poor merchant's flesh—
Thou wilt not only loose° the forfeiture,   *waive*
But, touched with human gentleness and love,
25 Forgive a moiety° of the principal,   *part*
Glancing an eye of pity on his losses,
That have of late so huddled° on his back   *piled*
Enough to press a royal merchant down

2. I'll serve you up (like a dinner); I'll extol you. **4.1** Location: The Venetian court.

And pluck commiseration of his state
30 From brassy° bosoms and rough hearts of flint,   *unfeeling*
From stubborn Turks and Tartars never trained
To offices° of tender courtesy.   *acts*
We all expect a gentle answer, Jew.
SHYLOCK   I have possessed° your grace of what I purpose,   *informed*
35 And by our holy Sabbath have I sworn
To have the due and forfeit of my bond.
If you deny it, let the danger° light   *damage*
Upon your charter and your city's freedom.
You'll ask me why I rather choose to have
40 A weight of carrion flesh than to receive
Three thousand ducats. I'll not answer that,
But say it is my humour.° Is it answered?   *caprice*
What if my house be troubled with a rat,
And I be pleased to give ten thousand ducats
45 To have it baned?° What, are you answered yet?   *poisoned*
Some men there are love not a gaping pig,[1]
Some that are mad if they behold a cat,
And others when the bagpipe sings i'th' nose
Cannot contain their urine; for affection,°   *impulse*
50 Mistress of passion, sways it to the mood
Of what it likes or loathes. Now for your answer:
As there is no firm reason to be rendered
Why he° cannot abide a gaping pig,   *one man*
Why he° a harmless necessary cat,   *another*
55 Why he° a woollen bagpipe, but of force°   *yet another / necessarily*
Must yield to such inevitable shame
As to offend himself being offended,
So can I give no reason, nor I will not,
More than a lodged° hate and a certain loathing   *settled*
60 I bear Antonio, that I follow thus
A losing° suit against him. Are you answered?   *An unprofitable*
BASSANIO   This is no answer, thou unfeeling man,
To excuse the current of thy cruelty.
SHYLOCK   I am not bound to please thee with my answers.
65 BASSANIO   Do all men kill the things they do not love?
SHYLOCK   Hates any man the thing he would not kill?
BASSANIO   Every offence is not a hate at first.
SHYLOCK   What, wouldst thou have a serpent sting thee twice?
ANTONIO   I pray you think you question° with the Jew.   *dispute*
70 You may as well go stand upon the beach
And bid the main flood bate his° usual height;   *high tide reduce its*
You may as well use question with the wolf
Why he hath made the ewe bleat for the lamb;
You may as well forbid the mountain pines
75 To wag their high tops and to make no noise
When they are fretten° with the gusts of heaven,   *fretted; agitated*
You may as well do anything most hard
As seek to soften that—than which what's harder?—
His Jewish heart. Therefore, I do beseech you,
80 Make no more offers, use no farther means,

---

1. Roasted pig with its mouth propped open.

But with all brief and plain conveniency°   *suitability*
Let me have judgement and the Jew his will.
BASSANIO [*to* SHYLOCK]   For thy three thousand ducats here is six.
SHYLOCK   If every ducat in six thousand ducats
85   Were in six parts, and every part a ducat,
I would not draw° them. I would have my bond.   *take*
DUKE   How shalt thou hope for mercy, rend'ring none?
SHYLOCK   What judgement shall I dread, doing no wrong?
You have among you many a purchased slave
90   Which, like your asses and your dogs and mules,
You use in abject and in slavish parts°   *roles*
Because you bought them. Shall I say to you
'Let them be free, marry them to your heirs.
Why sweat they under burdens? Let their beds
95   Be made as soft as yours, and let their palates
Be seasoned with such viands.'° You will answer   *food*
'The slaves are ours.' So do I answer you.
The pound of flesh which I demand of him
Is dearly bought. 'Tis mine, and I will have it.
100   If you deny me, fie upon your law:
There is no force in the decrees of Venice.
I stand for judgement. Answer: shall I have it?
DUKE   Upon° my power I may dismiss this court   *In accordance with*
Unless Bellario, a learnèd doctor
105   Whom I have sent for to determine° this,   *resolve*
Come here today.
SALERIO   My lord, here stays without°   *waits outside*
A messenger with letters from the doctor,
New come from Padua.
DUKE   Bring us the letters. Call the messenger. [*Exit* SALERIO]
110   BASSANIO   Good cheer, Antonio. What, man, courage yet!
The Jew shall have my flesh, blood, bones, and all
Ere thou shalt lose for me one drop of blood.
ANTONIO   I am a tainted wether° of the flock,   *castrated ram*
Meetest for death.° The weakest kind of fruit   *Most fit for slaughter*
115   Drops earliest to the ground; and so let me.
You cannot better be employed, Bassanio,
Than to live still and write mine epitaph.
         Enter [SALERIO, *with*] NERISSA [*apparelled as a judge's*
         clerk]
DUKE   Came you from Padua, from Bellario?
NERISSA   From both, my lord. Bellario greets your grace.
       [*She gives a letter to the* DUKE.
       SHYLOCK *whets his knife on his shoe*]
120   BASSANIO [*to* SHYLOCK]   Why dost thou whet thy knife so earnestly?
SHYLOCK   To cut the forfeit from that bankrupt there.
GRAZIANO   Not on thy sole but on thy soul, harsh Jew,
Thou mak'st thy knife keen. But no metal can,
No, not the hangman's° axe, bear° half the keenness   *executioner's / have*
125   Of thy sharp envy.° Can no prayers pierce thee?   *malice*
SHYLOCK   No, none that thou hast wit enough to make.
GRAZIANO   O, be thou damned, inexorable dog,
And for thy life° let justice be accused!   *for allowing you to live*
Thou almost mak'st me waver in my faith

130	To hold opinion with Pythagoras[2]	
That souls of animals infuse themselves	
Into the trunks of men. Thy currish spirit	
Governed a wolf who, hanged for human slaughter,[3]	
Even from the gallows did his fell soul fleet,°	*his cruel soul flit*
135	And, whilst thou lay'st in thy unhallowed dam,	
Infused itself in thee; for thy desires	
Are wolvish, bloody, starved, and ravenous.	

SHYLOCK   Till thou canst rail the seal from off my bond
Thou but offend'st° thy lungs to speak so loud.   *hurt*

Repair thy wit, good youth, or it will fall
To cureless° ruin. I stand here for law.   *incurable*

DUKE   This letter from Bellario doth commend
A young and learnèd doctor to our court.
Where is he?

NERISSA   He attendeth here hard by
To know your answer, whether you'll admit him.

DUKE   With all my heart. Some three or four of you
Go give him courteous conduct° to this place.   *escort*

[Exeunt three or four]

Meantime the court shall hear Bellario's letter.
[*Reads*] 'Your grace shall understand that at the receipt of your
letter I am very sick, but in the instant that your messenger
came, in loving visitation was with me a young doctor of Rome;
his name is Balthasar. I acquainted him with the cause in controversy between the Jew and Antonio, the merchant. We
turned o'er many books together. He is furnished with my opinion which, bettered with his own learning—the greatness
whereof I cannot enough commend—comes with him at my
importunity to fill up° your grace's request in my stead. I   *answer*
beseech you let his lack of years be no impediment to let him
lack° a reverend estimation, for I never knew so young a body   *keep him from having*
with so old a head. I leave him to your gracious acceptance,
whose trial shall better publish his commendation.'[4]

Enter [three or four with] PORTIA [*as Balthasar*]

You hear the learn'd Bellario, what he writes;
And here, I take it, is the doctor come.
[*To* PORTIA   Give me your hand. Come you from old Bellario?

PORTIA   I did, my lord.

DUKE   You are welcome. Take your place.
Are you acquainted with the difference°   *dispute*
That holds this present question[5] in the court?

PORTIA   I am informèd throughly° of the cause.°   *thoroughly / case*
Which is the merchant here, and which the Jew?

DUKE   Antonio and old Shylock, both stand forth.
[ANTONIO *and* SHYLOCK *stand forth*]

PORTIA   Is your name Shylock?

SHYLOCK   Shylock is my name.

PORTIA   Of a strange nature is the suit you follow,
Yet in such rule° that the Venetian law   *order*

2. Greek philosopher who believed in the transmigration of souls.
3. In Elizabethan times, animals were tried and hanged
for wrongdoing; possibly an allusion to the 1594 execution of the Jewish physician Lopez (Latin *lupus*, "wolf").
4. Whose performance ("trial") shall better make
known his worth.
5. That is now being tried.

Cannot impugn you as you do proceed.

175   [*To* ANTONIO] You stand within his danger,° do you not?   *power to harm*

ANTONIO   Ay, so he says.

PORTIA   Do you confess the bond?

ANTONIO   I do.

PORTIA   Then must the Jew be merciful.

SHYLOCK   On what compulsion must I? Tell me that.

PORTIA   The quality of mercy is not strained.°   *compelled*

180   It droppeth as the gentle rain from heaven

Upon the place beneath. It is twice blest:

It blesseth him that gives, and him that takes.

'Tis mightiest in the mightiest. It becomes

The thronèd monarch better than his crown.

185   His sceptre shows the force of temporal power,

The attribute to° awe and majesty,   *of*

Wherein doth sit the dread and fear of kings;

But mercy is above this sceptred sway.

It is enthronèd in the hearts of kings;

190   It is an attribute to God himself,

And earthly power doth then show likest° God's   *most like*

When mercy seasons° justice. Therefore, Jew,   *moderates*

Though justice be thy plea, consider this:

That in the course of justice none of us

195   Should see salvation. We do pray for mercy,

And that same prayer° doth teach us all to render   *(the Lord's Prayer)*

The deeds of mercy. I have spoke thus much

To mitigate the justice of thy plea,°   *your demand for justice*

Which if thou follow, this strict court of Venice

200   Must needs give sentence 'gainst the merchant there.

SHYLOCK   My deeds upon my head!⁶ I crave the law,

The penalty and forfeit of my bond.

PORTIA   Is he not able to discharge the money?

BASSANIO   Yes, here I tender it for him in the court,

205   Yea, twice the sum. If that will not suffice

I will be bound to pay it ten times o'er

On forfeit of my hands, my head, my heart.

If this will not suffice, it must appear

That malice bears down° truth. And, I beseech you,   *overwhelms*

210   Wrest once° the law to your authority.   *For once twist*

To do a great right, do a little wrong,

And curb this cruel devil of his will.

PORTIA   It must not be. There is no power in Venice

Can alter a decree establishèd.

215   'Twill be recorded for a precedent,

And many an error by the same example

Will rush into the state. It cannot be.

SHYLOCK   A Daniel come to judgement, yea, a Daniel!⁷

O wise young judge, how I do honour thee!

220   PORTIA   I pray you let me look upon the bond.

SHYLOCK   Here 'tis, most reverend doctor, here it is.

PORTIA   Shylock, there's thrice thy money offered thee.

---

6. The Jewish crowd at Jesus' trial cried, "His blood be on us, and on our children" (Matthew 27:25).
7. In the Apocrypha, the youth Daniel judges the case of Susanna, accused of inchastity by the Elders; he rescues her and convicts them.

SHYLOCK An oath, an oath! I have an oath in heaven.
Shall I lay perjury upon my soul?
No, not for Venice.
225 PORTIA   Why, this bond is forfeit,
And lawfully by this the Jew may claim
A pound of flesh, to be by him cut off
Nearest the merchant's heart. [*To* SHYLOCK] Be merciful.
Take thrice thy money. Bid me tear the bond.
230 SHYLOCK When it is paid according to the tenor.°   *condition*
It doth appear you are a worthy judge.
You know the law. Your exposition
Hath been most sound. I charge you, by the law
Whereof you are a well-deserving pillar,
235 Proceed to judgement. By my soul I swear
There is no power in the tongue of man
To alter me. I stay° here on my bond.   *insist*
ANTONIO Most heartily I do beseech the court
To give the judgement.
PORTIA   Why, then thus it is:
240 You must prepare your bosom for his knife—
SHYLOCK O noble judge, O excellent young man!
PORTIA For the intent and purpose of the law
Hath full relation to⁸ the penalty
Which here appeareth due upon the bond.
245 SHYLOCK 'Tis very true. O wise and upright judge!
How much more elder art thou than thy looks!
PORTIA [*to* ANTONIO] Therefore lay bare your bosom.
SHYLOCK   Ay, his breast.
So says the bond, doth it not, noble judge?
'Nearest his heart'—those are the very words.
250 PORTIA It is so. Are there balance° here to weigh the flesh?   *scales*
SHYLOCK I have them ready.
PORTIA Have by some surgeon, Shylock, on your charge°   *expense*
To stop his wounds, lest he do bleed to death.
SHYLOCK Is it so nominated in the bond?
255 PORTIA It is not so expressed, but what of that?
'Twere good you do so much for charity.
SHYLOCK I cannot find it. 'Tis not in the bond.
PORTIA [*to* ANTONIO] You, merchant, have you anything to say?
ANTONIO But little. I am armed and well prepared.
260 Give me your hand, Bassanio; fare you well.
Grieve not that I am fall'n to this for you,
For herein Fortune shows herself more kind
Than is her custom; it is still her use°   *commonly her habit*
To let the wretched man outlive his wealth
265 To view with hollow eye and wrinkled brow
An age of poverty, from which ling'ring penance
Of such misery doth she cut me off.
Commend me to your honourable wife.
Tell her the process° of Antonio's end.   *tale*
270 Say how I loved you. Speak me fair° in death,   *well of me*
And when the tale is told, bid her be judge
Whether Bassanio had not once a love.

8. Is entirely in agreement with.

Repent but you° that you shall lose your friend,   *Sorrow only*
And he repents not that he pays your debt;
275   For if the Jew do cut but deep enough,
I'll pay it instantly, with all my heart.
BASSANIO   Antonio, I am married to a wife
Which is as dear to me as life itself,
But life itself, my wife, and all the world
280   Are not with me esteemed above thy life.
I would lose all, ay, sacrifice them all
Here to this devil, to deliver you.
PORTIA [*aside*]   Your wife would give you little thanks for that
If she were by to hear you make the offer.
285   GRAZIANO   I have a wife who, I protest, I love.
I would she were in heaven so she could
Entreat some power to change this currish Jew.
NERISSA [*aside*]   'Tis well you offer it behind her back;
The wish would make else an unquiet house.
290   SHYLOCK [*aside*]   These be the Christian husbands. I have a daughter.
Would any of the stock of Barabbas⁹
Had been her husband rather than a Christian.
[*Aloud*] We trifle° time. I pray thee pursue° sentence.   *waste / proceed with*
PORTIA   A pound of that same merchant's flesh is thine.
295   The court awards it, and the law doth give it.
SHYLOCK   Most rightful judge!
PORTIA   And you must cut this flesh from off his breast.
The law allows it, and the court awards it.
SHYLOCK   Most learnèd judge! A sentence: [*to* ANTONIO] come, prepare.
300   PORTIA   Tarry a little. There is something else.
This bond doth give thee here no jot of blood.
The words expressly are 'a pound of flesh'.
Take then thy bond. Take thou thy pound of flesh.
But in the cutting it, if thou dost shed
305   One drop of Christian blood, thy lands and goods
Are by the laws of Venice confiscate
Unto the state of Venice.
GRAZIANO   O upright judge!
Mark, Jew! O learnèd judge!
SHYLOCK   Is that the law?
310   PORTIA   Thyself shalt see the act;
For as thou urgest justice, be assured
Thou shalt have justice more than thou desir'st.
GRAZIANO   O learnèd judge! Mark, Jew! O learnèd judge!
SHYLOCK   I take this offer, then. Pay the bond thrice,
And let the Christian go.
315   BASSANIO   Here is the money.
PORTIA   Soft,° the Jew shall have all justice. Soft, no haste.   *Not so fast*
He shall have nothing but the penalty.
GRAZIANO   O Jew, an upright judge, a learnèd judge!
PORTIA [*to* SHYLOCK]   Therefore prepare thee to cut off the flesh.
320   Shed thou no blood, nor cut thou less nor more
But just° a pound of flesh. If thou tak'st more   *exactly*
Or less than a just pound, be it but so much

9. Thief whom the Jews asked Pilate to set free instead of Jesus (Mark 15:6–15).

	As makes it light or heavy in the substance°	*weight*
	Or the division° of the twentieth part	*fraction*
325	Of one poor scruple°—nay, if the scale do turn	*tiny weight*
	But in the estimation° of a hair,	*amount*
	Thou diest, and all thy goods are confiscate.	

GRAZIANO A second Daniel, a Daniel, Jew!
Now, infidel, I have you on the hip.[1]

330 PORTIA Why doth the Jew pause? Take thy forfeiture.

SHYLOCK Give me my principal, and let me go.

BASSANIO I have it ready for thee. Here it is.

PORTIA He hath refused it in the open court.
He shall have merely justice and his bond.

335 GRAZIANO A Daniel, still say I, a second Daniel!
I thank thee, Jew, for teaching me that word.

SHYLOCK Shall I not have barely° my principal?   *even*

PORTIA Thou shalt have nothing but the forfeiture
To be so taken at thy peril, Jew.

340 SHYLOCK Why then, the devil give him good of it.
I'll stay no longer question.[2]

PORTIA   Tarry, Jew.
The law hath yet another hold on you.
It is enacted in the laws of Venice,
If it be proved against an alien

345 That by direct or indirect attempts
He seek the life of any citizen,
The party 'gainst the which he doth contrive°   *plot*
Shall seize one half his goods; the other half
Comes to the privy coffer° of the state,   *private treasury*

350 And the offender's life lies in° the mercy   *at*
Of the Duke only, 'gainst all other voice—
In which predicament I say thou stand'st,
For it appears by manifest proceeding
That indirectly, and directly too,

355 Thou hast contrived against the very life
Of the defendant, and thou hast incurred
The danger° formerly by me rehearsed.°   *penalty / described*
Down, therefore, and beg mercy of the Duke.

GRAZIANO [*to* SHYLOCK] Beg that thou mayst have leave to hang thyself—

360 And yet, thy wealth being forfeit to the state,
Thou hast not left the value of a cord.
Therefore thou must be hanged at the state's charge.°   *expense*

DUKE [*to* SHYLOCK] That thou shalt see the difference of our spirit,
I pardon thee thy life before thou ask it.

365 For half thy wealth, it is Antonio's.
The other half comes to the general state,
Which humbleness may drive° unto a fine.   *reduce*

PORTIA Ay, for the state, not for Antonio.[3]

SHYLOCK Nay, take my life and all, pardon not that.

370 You take my house when you do take the prop
That doth sustain my house; you take my life
When you do take the means whereby I live.[4]

---

1. At a disadvantage (see 1.3.41).

2. I'll press my case no further.

3. With respect to the state's half, not Antonio's.

4. "He that taketh away his neighbor's living, slayeth him" (Ecclesiasties 34:22).

PORTIA   What mercy can you render him, Antonio?

GRAZIANO   A halter,° gratis. Nothing else, for God's sake.   *hangman's noose*

375   ANTONIO   So please my lord the Duke and all the court
To quit the fine for one half of his goods,
I am content, so he will let me have
The other half in use,[5] to render it
Upon his death unto the gentleman

380   That lately stole his daughter.
Two things provided more: that for this favour
He presently° become a Christian;   *immediately*
The other, that he do record a gift
Here in the court of all he dies possessed

385   Unto his son, Lorenzo, and his daughter.

DUKE   He shall do this, or else I do recant°   *withdraw*
The pardon that I late pronouncèd here.

PORTIA   Art thou contented, Jew? What dost thou say?

SHYLOCK   I am content.

390   PORTIA   [*to* NERISSA]   Clerk, draw a deed of gift.

SHYLOCK   I pray you give me leave to go from hence.
I am not well. Send the deed after me,
And I will sign it.

DUKE   Get thee gone, but do it.

GRAZIANO   [*to* SHYLOCK]   In christ'ning shalt thou have two godfathers.

395   Had I been judge thou shouldst have had ten more,°   *(to constitute a jury)*
To bring thee to the gallows, not the font.   *Exit* [SHYLOCK]

DUKE   [*to* PORTIA]   Sir, I entreat you home with me to dinner.

PORTIA   I humbly do desire your grace of pardon.
I must away this night toward Padua,

400   And it is meet° I presently set forth.   *proper*

DUKE   I am sorry that your leisure serves you not.°   *you haven't the time*
Antonio, gratify° this gentleman,   *reward*
For in my mind you are much bound to him.

Exit DUKE *and his train*

BASSANIO   [*to* PORTIA]   Most worthy gentleman, I and my friend

405   Have by your wisdom been this day acquitted
Of grievous penalties, in lieu whereof
Three thousand ducats due unto the Jew
We freely cope° your courteous pains withal.   *repay*

ANTONIO   And stand indebted over and above

410   In love and service to you evermore.

PORTIA   He is well paid that is well satisfied,
And I, delivering you, am satisfied,
And therein do account myself well paid.
My mind was never yet more mercenary.

415   I pray you know me when we meet again.
I wish you well; and so I take my leave.

BASSANIO   Dear sir, of force° I must attempt you further.   *necessity*
Take some remembrance of us as a tribute,
Not as fee. Grant me two things, I pray you:

420   Not to deny me, and to pardon me.°   *excuse my urging*

---

5. Antonio's conditions are unclear, because "quit" in line 376 (requite) could mean "pardon" or "make him pay," and "in use" (line 378) could mean either "in trust" or "for my own purposes." But the arrangements for Shylock's property later in the scene suggest that Antonio succeeds in getting Shylock's penalty reduced: Shylock retains half of his wealth, and Antonio holds the other half in trust for Jessica and Lorenzo until Shylock dies, at which point they inherit the whole estate.

PORTIA   You press me far, and therefore I will yield.
[*To* ANTONIO] Give me your gloves. I'll wear them for your sake.
[*To* BASSANIO] And for your love I'll take this ring from you.
Do not draw back your hand. I'll take no more,
425   And you in love shall not deny me this.
BASSANIO   This ring, good sir? Alas, it is a trifle.
I will not shame myself to give you this.
PORTIA   I will have nothing else, but only this;
And now, methinks, I have a mind to it.
430   BASSANIO   There's more depends on this° than on the value.   involved here
The dearest ring in Venice will I give you,
And find it out by proclamation.
Only for this, I pray you pardon me.
PORTIA   I see, sir, you are liberal in offers.
435   You taught me first to beg, and now methinks
You teach me how a beggar should be answered.
BASSANIO   Good sir, this ring was given me by my wife,
And when she put it on she made me vow
That I should neither sell, nor give, nor lose it.
440   PORTIA   That 'scuse serves many men to save their gifts.
An if° your wife be not a madwoman,   An if = If
And know how well I have deserved this ring,
She would not hold out enemy for ever
For giving it to me. Well, peace be with you.
            Exeunt [PORTIA *and* NERISSA]
445   ANTONIO   My lord Bassanio, let him have the ring.
Let his deservings and my love withal
Be valued 'gainst your wife's commandëment.
BASSANIO   Go, Graziano, run and overtake him.
Give him the ring, and bring him, if thou canst,
450   Unto Antonio's house. Away, make haste.   *Exit* GRAZIANO
Come, you and I will thither presently,
And in the morning early will we both
Fly toward Belmont. Come, Antonio.   *Exeunt*

4.2

Enter PORTIA *and* NERISSA [*still disguised*]
PORTIA   Enquire the Jew's house out, give him this deed,[1]
And let him sign it. We'll away tonight,
And be a day before our husbands home.
This deed will be well welcome to Lorenzo.
            Enter GRAZIANO
5   GRAZIANO   Fair sir, you are well o'erta'en.
My lord Bassanio upon more advice°   further thought
Hath sent you here this ring, and doth entreat
Your company at dinner.
PORTIA   That cannot be.
His ring I do accept most thankfully,
10   And so I pray you tell him. Furthermore,
I pray you show my youth old Shylock's house.
GRAZIANO   That will I do.
NERISSA   Sir, I would speak with you.
[*Aside to* PORTIA] I'll see if I can get my husband's ring

4.2 Location: Street in Venice.   1. Mentioned in 4.1.390.

Which I did make him swear to keep for ever.

15 PORTIA [*aside to* NERISSA]   Thou mayst; I warrant we shall have
      old° swearing   *lots of*
  That they did give the rings away to men.
  But we'll outface them, and outswear them too.
  Away, make haste. Thou know'st where I will tarry.
                                      [*Exit at one door*]
NERISSA [*to* GRAZIANO]   Come, good sir, will you show me to this house?
                                  Exeunt [*at another door*]

5.1

Enter LORENZO *and* JESSICA

LORENZO   The moon shines bright. In such a night as this,
  When the sweet wind did gently kiss the trees
  And they did make no noise—in such a night
  Troilus, methinks, mounted the Trojan walls,
5   And sighed his soul toward the Grecian tents
  Where Cressid lay that night.[1]
JESSICA   In such a night
  Did Thisbe fearfully o'ertrip the dew
  And saw the lion's shadow ere himself,
  And ran dismayed away.[2]
LORENZO   In such a night
10   Stood Dido with a willow in her hand
  Upon the wild sea banks, and waft her love
  To come again to Carthage.[3]
JESSICA   In such a night
  Medea gathered the enchanted herbs
  That did renew old Aeson.[4]
LORENZO   In such a night
15   Did Jessica steal° from the wealthy Jew,   *escape; rob*
  And with an unthrift° love did run from Venice   *a spendthrift*
  As far as Belmont.
JESSICA   In such a night
  Did young Lorenzo swear he loved her well,
  Stealing her soul with many vows of faith,
  And ne'er a true one.
20 LORENZO   In such a night
  Did pretty Jessica, like a little shrew,
  Slander her love, and he forgave it her.
JESSICA   I would outnight you, did nobody come.
  But hark, I hear the footing° of a man.   *footsteps*
         Enter [STEFANO,] *a messenger*
25 LORENZO   Who comes so fast in silence of the night?
STEFANO   A friend.
LORENZO   A friend—what friend? Your name, I pray you, friend?
STEFANO   Stefano is my name, and I bring word

5.1 Location: Belmont.
1. Troilus was a Trojan Prince whose lover, Cressida, forsook him for the Greek Diomedes after she was sent from Troy to the Greek camp. See *Troilus and Cressida*.
2. Thisbe, going at night to meet her lover, Pyramus, was frightened by a lion and fled. Pyramus, assuming she was dead, killed himself; when she found his body, Thisbe committed suicide too. The story is dramatized

by "the rude mechanicals" in *A Midsummer Night's Dream*.
3. Dido, Queen of Carthage, was abandoned by her lover, the Trojan hero Aeneas. *willow*: emblem of forsaken love. *waft*: waved to.
4. Medea was a sorceress who loved Jason and helped him win the Golden Fleece; she magically restored Aeson, Jason's father, to youth.

My mistress will before the break of day

30 Be here at Belmont. She doth stray about

By holy crosses,° where she kneels and prays   *roadside shrines*

For happy wedlock hours.

LORENZO   Who comes with her?

STEFANO   None but a holy hermit and her maid.

I pray you, is my master yet returned?

35 LORENZO   He is not, nor we have not heard from him.

But go we in, I pray thee, Jessica,

And ceremoniously let us prepare

Some welcome for the mistress of the house.

      Enter [LANCELOT] *the clown*

LANCELOT [*calling*]   Sola, sola! Wo, ha, ho! Sola, sola!⁵

40 LORENZO   Who calls?

LANCELOT [*calling*]   Sola!—Did you see Master Lorenzo? [*Call-*

ing] Master Lorenzo! Sola, sola!

LORENZO   Leave hollering, man: here.

LANCELOT [*calling*]   Sola!—Where, where?

45 LORENZO   Here.

LANCELOT   Tell him there's a post° come from my master with his   *messenger*

horn full of good news. My master will be here ere morning.

                                     [*Exit*]

LORENZO [*to* JESSICA]   Sweet soul, let's in, and there expect°   *await*

      their coming.

And yet no matter. Why should we go in?

50 My friend Stefano, signify,° I pray you,   *announce*

Within the house your mistress is at hand,

And bring your music forth into the air.   *Exit* STEFANO

How sweet the moonlight sleeps upon this bank!

Here will we sit, and let the sounds of music

55 Creep in our ears. Soft stillness and the night

Become the touches⁶ of sweet harmony.

Sit, Jessica.

      [*They sit*]

        Look how the floor of heaven

Is thick inlaid with patens° of bright gold.   *disks*

There's not the smallest orb which thou behold'st

60 But in his motion like an angel sings,

Still° choiring to the young-eyed⁷ cherubins.   *Continually*

Such harmony⁸ is in immortal souls,

But whilst this muddy vesture of decay°   *this mortal body*

Doth grossly close it° in, we cannot hear it.°   *(the soul) / (the music)*

      [*Enter Musicians*]

65 [*To the Musicians*] Come, ho, and wake Diana⁹ with a hymn.

With sweetest touches pierce your mistress'° ear,   *(Portia's)*

And draw her home with music.

      [*The Musicians*] *play*

JESSICA   I am never merry when I hear sweet music.

LORENZO   The reason is your spirits are attentive,

70 For do but note a wild and wanton herd

Or race° of youthful and unhandled colts,   *group*

---

5. Imitating a messenger's horn.   7. Keen-sighted.
6. Suit the notes (literally, the fingering of a stringed   8. The music of the spheres.
instrument).   9. Goddess of the moon and of chastity.

Fetching mad bounds, bellowing and neighing loud,
Which is the hot condition of their blood,
If they but hear perchance a trumpet sound,
75 Or any air of music touch their ears,
You shall perceive them make a mutual° stand,   *simultaneous*
Their savage eyes turned to a modest gaze
By the sweet power of music. Therefore the poet[1]
Did feign that Orpheus drew° trees, stones, and floods,   *allured*
80 Since naught so stockish,° hard, and full of rage   *stolid*
But music for the time doth change his nature.
The man that hath no music in himself,
Nor is not moved with concord of sweet sounds,
Is fit for treasons, stratagems,° and spoils.°   *plots / plunder*
85 The motions of his spirit are dull as night,
And his affections° dark as Erebus.°   *inclinations / hell*
Let no such man be trusted. Mark the music.
        Enter PORTIA *and* NERISSA [*as themselves*]
PORTIA   That light we see is burning in my hall.
How far that little candle throws his beams—
90 So shines a good deed in a naughty° world.   *an evil*
NERISSA   When the moon shone we did not see the candle.
PORTIA   So doth the greater glory dim the less.
A substitute° shines brightly as a king   *deputy*
Until a king be by, and then his state
95 Empties itself as doth an inland brook
Into the main of waters.° Music, hark.   *the ocean*
NERISSA   It is your music, madam, of the house.
PORTIA   Nothing is good, I see, without respect.°   *reference to context*
Methinks it sounds much sweeter than by day.
100 NERISSA   Silence bestows that virtue on it, madam.
PORTIA   The crow doth sing as sweetly as the lark
When neither is attended,[2] and I think
The nightingale, if she should sing by day,
When every goose is cackling, would be thought
105 No better a musician than the wren.
How many things by season seasoned are[3]
To their right praise and true perfection!
        [*She sees* LORENZO *and* JESSICA]
Peace, ho!
        [*Music ceases*]
        The moon sleeps with Endymion,[4]
And would not be awaked.
LORENZO [*rising*]   That is the voice,
110 Or I am much deceived, of Portia.
PORTIA   He knows me as the blind man knows the cuckoo—
By the bad voice.
LORENZO   Dear lady, welcome home.
PORTIA   We have been praying for our husbands' welfare,
Which speed° we hope the better for our words.   *Who prosper*
Are they returned?
115 LORENZO   Madam, they are not yet,

---

1. Ovid, in *Metamorphoses* 10, tells the story of Orpheus, 3. *by season . . . are:* by proper time are adapted.
a legendary musician.   4. In classical mythology, a shepherd beloved of the
2. Is listened to; is accompanied.   moon goddess, who caused him to sleep forever.

But there is come a messenger before
To signify their coming.
PORTIA   Go in, Nerissa.
Give order to my servants that they take
No note at all of our being absent hence;
120   Nor you, Lorenzo; Jessica, nor you.
               A tucket° sounds   *trumpet flourish*
LORENZO   Your husband is at hand. I hear his trumpet.
We are no tell-tales, madam. Fear you not.
PORTIA   This night, methinks, is but the daylight sick.
It looks a little paler. 'Tis a day
125   Such as the day is when the sun is hid.
        Enter BASSANIO, ANTONIO, GRAZIANO, *and their follow-*
        ers. [GRAZIANO *and* NERISSA *speak silently to one*
        another]
BASSANIO   We should hold day with the Antipodes
If you would walk in absence of the sun.⁵
PORTIA   Let me give light, but let me not be light;°   *unfaithful*
For a light wife doth make a heavy° husband,   *sad*
130   And never be Bassanio so for me.
But God sort° all. You are welcome home, my lord.   *decide*
BASSANIO   I thank you, madam. Give welcome to my friend.
This is the man, this is Antonio,
To whom I am so infinitely bound.
135 PORTIA   You should in all° sense be much bound to him,   *every*
For as I hear he was much bound for you.
ANTONIO   No more than I am well acquitted° of.   *freed*
PORTIA   Sir, you are very welcome to our house.
It must appear in other ways than words,
140 Therefore I scant this breathing courtesy.⁶
GRAZIANO [*to* NERISSA]   By yonder moon I swear you do me wrong.
In faith, I gave it to the judge's clerk.
Would he were gelt° that had it for my part,   *gelded; castrated*
Since you do take it, love, so much at heart.
145 PORTIA   A quarrel, ho, already! What's the matter?
GRAZIANO   About a hoop of gold, a paltry ring
That she did give me, whose posy° was   *motto*
For all the world like cutlers' poetry
Upon a knife—'Love me and leave me not'.
150 NERISSA   What talk you of the posy or the value?
You swore to me when I did give it you
That you would wear it till your hour of death,
And that it should lie with you in your grave.
Though not for me, yet for your vehement oaths
155 You should have been respective° and have kept it.   *careful*
Gave it a judge's clerk?—no, God's my judge,
The clerk will ne'er wear hair on's face that had it.
GRAZIANO   He will an if he live to be a man.
NERISSA   Ay, if a woman live to be a man.
160 GRAZIANO   Now by this hand, I gave it to a youth,
A kind of boy, a little scrubbèd° boy   *stunted*

---

5. *We . . . sun:* We would share daylight with the other side of the world (Antipodes) if you habitually walked when the sun was gone (implying "such is your radiance").
6. I make brief this verbal welcome.

No higher than thyself, the judge's clerk,
A prating° boy that begged it as a fee.   *chattering*
I could not for my heart deny it him.

165 PORTIA You were to blame, I must be plain with you,
To part so slightly with your wife's first gift,
A thing stuck on with oaths upon your finger,
And so riveted with faith unto your flesh.
I gave my love a ring, and made him swear

170 Never to part with it; and here he stands.
I dare be sworn for him he would not leave° it,   *part with*
Nor pluck it from his finger for the wealth
That the world masters.° Now, in faith, Graziano,   *possesses*
You give your wife too unkind a cause of grief.

175 An 'twere to me, I should be mad at it.
BASSANIO [*aside*] Why, I were best to cut my left hand off
And swear I lost the ring defending it.
GRAZIANO [*to* PORTIA] My lord Bassanio gave his ring away
Unto the judge that begged it, and indeed

180 Deserved it, too, and then the boy his clerk,
That took some pains in writing, he begged mine,
And neither man nor master would take aught
But the two rings.
PORTIA [*to* BASSANIO] What ring gave you, my lord?
Not that, I hope, which you received of me.

185 BASSANIO If I could add a lie unto a fault
I would deny it; but you see my finger
Hath not the ring upon it. It is gone.
PORTIA Even so void is your false heart of truth.
By heaven, I will ne'er come in your bed
Until I see the ring.

190 NERISSA [*to* GRAZIANO] Nor I in yours
Till I again see mine.
BASSANIO   Sweet Portia,
If you did know to whom I gave the ring,
If you did know for whom I gave the ring,
And would conceive for what I gave the ring,

195 And how unwillingly I left the ring
When naught would be accepted but the ring,
You would abate the strength of your displeasure.
PORTIA If you had known the virtue° of the ring,   *power*
Or half her worthiness that gave the ring,

200 Or your own honour to contain° the ring,   *retain*
You would not then have parted with the ring.
What man is there so much unreasonable,
If you had pleased to have defended it
With any terms of zeal, wanted° the modesty°   *would lack / moderation*

205 To urge° the thing held as a ceremony?°   *insist on / sacred symbol*
Nerissa teaches me what to believe.
I'll die for't but some woman had the ring.
BASSANIO No, by my honour, madam, by my soul,
No woman had it, but a civil doctor°   *doctor of civil law*

210 Which did refuse three thousand ducats of me,
And begged the ring, the which I did deny him,
And suffered° him to go displeased away,   *permitted*
Even he that had held up the very life

Of my dear friend. What should I say, sweet lady?
215 I was enforced to send it after him.
I was beset with shame and courtesy.
My honour would not let ingratitude
So much besmear it. Pardon me, good lady,
For by these blessèd candles of the night,
220 Had you been there I think you would have begged
The ring of me to give the worthy doctor.
PORTIA   Let not that doctor e'er come near my house.
Since he hath got the jewel that I loved,
And that which you did swear to keep for me,
225 I will become as liberal° as you.   *generous; licentious*
I'll not deny him anything I have,
No, not my body nor my husband's bed.
Know° him I shall, I am well sure of it.   **(with sexual suggestion)**
Lie not a night from home. Watch me like Argus.[7]
230 If you do not, if I be left alone,
Now by mine honour, which is yet mine own,
I'll have that doctor for my bedfellow.
NERISSA [*to* GRAZIANO]   And I his clerk, therefore be well advised
How you do leave me to mine own protection.
235 GRAZIANO   Well, do you so. Let not me take him then,
For if I do, I'll mar the young clerk's pen.°   **(with sexual suggestion)**
ANTONIO   I am th'unhappy subject of these quarrels.
PORTIA   Sir, grieve not you. You are welcome notwithstanding.
BASSANIO   Portia, forgive me this enforcèd wrong,
240 And in the hearing of these many friends
I swear to thee, even by thine own fair eyes,
Wherein I see myself—
PORTIA   Mark you but that?
In both my eyes he doubly sees himself,
In each eye one. Swear by your double° self,   *twofold; deceitful*
And there's an oath of credit.[8]
245 BASSANIO   Nay, but hear me.
Pardon this fault, and by my soul I swear
I never more will break an oath with thee.
ANTONIO [*to* PORTIA]   I once did lend my body for his wealth
Which, but for him that had your husband's ring,
250 Had quite miscarried. I dare be bound again,
My soul upon the forfeit, that your lord
Will never more break faith advisedly.°   *intentionally*
PORTIA   Then you shall be his surety.° Give him this,   *guarantor of a loan*
And bid him keep it better than the other.
255 ANTONIO   Here, Lord Bassanio, swear to keep this ring.
BASSANIO   By heaven, it is the same I gave the doctor!
PORTIA   I had it of him. Pardon me, Bassanio,
For by this ring, the doctor lay with me.
NERISSA   And pardon me, my gentle Graziano,
260 For that same scrubbèd boy, the doctor's clerk,
In lieu of° this last night did lie with me.   *In exchange for*
GRAZIANO   Why, this is like the mending of highways
In summer where the ways are fair enough![9]

---

7. Mythical many-eyed monster.
8. An oath to be believed (ironic).

9. *where . . . enough:* when repair is not required.

What, are we cuckolds ere we have deserved it?

265 PORTIA   Speak not so grossly. You are all amazed.°   *confused*
Here is a letter. Read it at your leisure.
It comes from Padua, from Bellario.
There you shall find that Portia was the doctor,
Nerissa there her clerk. Lorenzo here
270 Shall witness I set forth as soon as you,
And even but now returned. I have not yet
Entered my house. Antonio, you are welcome,
And I have better news in store for you
Than you expect. Unseal this letter soon.
275 There you shall find three of your argosies
Are richly come to harbour suddenly.
You shall not know by what strange accident
I chancèd on this letter.

ANTONIO   I am dumb!°   *dumbstruck*

BASSANIO [*to* PORTIA]   Were you the doctor and I knew you not?

280 GRAZIANO [*to* NERISSA]   Were you the clerk that is to make me cuckold?

NERISSA   Ay, but the clerk that never means to do it
Unless he live until he be a man.

BASSANIO [*to* PORTIA]   Sweet doctor, you shall be my bedfellow.
When I am absent, then lie with my wife.

285 ANTONIO [*to* PORTIA]   Sweet lady, you have given me life and
living,°   *possessions*
For here I read for certain that my ships
Are safely come to road.°   *harbor*

PORTIA   How now, Lorenzo?
My clerk hath some good comforts, too, for you.

NERISSA   Ay, and I'll give them him without a fee.
290 There do I give to you and Jessica
From the rich Jew a special deed of gift,
After his death, of all he dies possessed of.

LORENZO   Fair ladies, you drop manna in the way
Of starvèd people.

PORTIA   It is almost morning,
295 And yet I am sure you are not satisfied
Of these events at full. Let us go in,
And charge us there upon inter'gatories,[1]
And we will answer all things faithfully.

GRAZIANO   Let it be so. The first inter'gatory
300 That my Nerissa shall be sworn on is
Whether till the next night she had rather stay,
Or go to bed now, being two hours to day.
But were the day come, I should wish it dark
Till I were couching° with the doctor's clerk.   *lying*
305 Well, while I live I'll fear no other thing
So sore as keeping safe Nerissa's ring.°   *Exeunt*   (*with sexual suggestion*)

---

1. And question us under oath.

The Merry Wives of Windsor

"The first act of the *Merry Wives* alone contains more life and reality than all German literature." So wrote Friedrich Engels to Karl Marx, his fellow German revolutionary and coauthor with Engels of the *Manifesto of the Communist Party*. Perhaps what he admired in *The Merry Wives of Windsor* (1597–98) is the dramatization of the middle class as it is being formed out of social tensions and verbal distinctions, out of disparate and often contradictory elements. Probably Engels also shared the enthusiasm of four centuries of theater audiences for the play's elaborate intrigues and comic stage business. Certainly this is Shakespeare's most middle-class play in its subject matter, setting, and outlook. It is also his most farcical, more so than even such early works as *The Comedy of Errors* and *The Taming of the Shrew*. Farce and intrigue establish the comic tone that informs the play's ultimate spirit of good-humored reconciliation. They also provide the plot mechanisms through which the characters' parochial self-interest is forged into a capacious social unity where hierarchy, though not permanently eliminated, is temporarily suspended. The particular fusion of these two elements—the theatrical and the social—produces the play's distinctiveness.

The Merry Wives celebrates the playful but chaste behavior of the titular characters, Mistress Page and Mistress Ford, each married to a prosperous burgher. The overt message is delivered by Mistress Page: "Wives may be merry, and yet honest, too" (4.2.89), where "honest" means being sexually faithful to their mates. Page's easy and—from a sexual point of view—justified trust of his wife's fidelity provides a norm from which Ford's irrational jealousy of his wife deviates. The two women's plot against the sexually and economically predatory Sir John Falstaff, their would-be seducer, is also designed to dupe and ultimately cure Ford. In the subplot, the concluding love marriage between Fenton, the impoverished gentleman, and the Pages' daughter Anne, who is beneath him socially but above him financially, affirms romantic love in a way that arguably is also assimilable to citizen values.

The play's time and place reinforce this sense of middle-class community. Together they create the impression of life in an English provincial town as it is being lived at the moment of the play's first performance—a rare phenomenon in Renaissance drama. Although such works as *The Comedy of Errors* and *The Merchant of Venice* depict prosperous citizens of a rank below the aristocracy, those characters live either abroad, or in the past, or both. By contrast, *The Merry Wives* retains a contemporary, domestic, and nonaristocratic feel unique in Shakespearean drama. To be sure, this feel is not uniform; the play refers back to the early fifteenth century. Moreover, not all of the materials from which it is constructed are indigenous: the closest analogue and most likely source for the main plot is found in *Il Pecorone* (1558), by the Italian writer Ser Giovanni Fiorentino. This plot and the primary subplot also draw on ancient Roman comedy, medieval farce, and Renaissance Italian drama. Finally, the play liberally includes characters from both above and below the middle class. Yet the historical allusions do not conjure up a bygone era, the foreign literary and theatrical traditions are reworked into English dramatic and cultural stereotypes, and the upper- and lower-class figures ultimately function to underscore the assimilating power of the middle class.

The play takes a jaundiced view of nearly every character with a claim to social standing. Slender's pretensions to gentility are mocked from beginning to end. His uncle, Justice Shallow, does not fare much better. In the opening scene, Shallow, whose authority is based not in the town but in the county and ultimately in the

Cuckold, his unfaithful wife, and the seducer. From *Roxburghe Ballads* (seventeenth century).

monarchy, acts not to preserve the peace but to undermine it. Similarly ineffectual are the peacemaking efforts of the parson, Sir Hugh Evans, whose honorary title and position as parson indicate that he, too, derives authority from the outside (in this case, from the national church). Evans is also foreign (Welsh), and he seeks to fight a duel with another foreigner (the French Doctor Caius), who is well-to-do and has connections at court.

A different kind of conflict pits the wealthy citizens against their social, but not economic, superiors. Page rejects the love suit of Fenton, and Falstaff is subjected to repeated abuse, in Act 5 functioning as a scapegoat against whom the townspeople can unite. This antagonism between citizen and gentleman is given a financial twist appropriate to the dominant ethos of the play. Page believes that Fenton is motivated by money rather than love, a charge that Fenton admits to Anne was originally true, although he insists that the balance has now shifted:

> I found thee of more value
> Than stamps in gold or sums in sealèd bags;
> And 'tis the very riches of thyself
> That now I aim at.
>
> (3.4.15–18)

Falstaff has no romantic concerns at all, attempting his seductions in the interest perhaps of lust and certainly of profit, metaphorically figured as the fruits of mercantile imperialism. Of Mistress Page he exclaims: "She bears the purse too. She is a region in Guiana, all gold and bounty. I will be cheaters to them both, and they shall be exchequers to me. They shall be my East and West Indies, and I will trade to them both. . . . Sail like my pinnace to these golden shores" (1.3.58–62, 70).

Yet the conclusion tells a different story. Page and his wife, although at cross purposes with each other, have each been trying to marry Anne off to an absurdly unsuitable partner. But when they realize there is no alternative, both husband and wife accept their daughter's marriage with good humor. This stance incorporates Fenton, of course, but is immediately extended by Mistress Page to include Falstaff as well. This act reveals not the servility but the capaciousness, generosity, and adaptability of the citizens' world. The marriage of Fenton to Anne—the main accomplishment of the play, with the exception of the simultaneous duping of Falstaff and curing of

Ford—implicitly marks the reconciliation of the middle class with their social betters. Both plots raise the fear of mercenary, sexually threatening aristocratic interlopers only to emphasize the emptiness of that concern—in one instance because of the comic incompetence of the predator and in the other because of the falseness of the suspicion. Even though the language of the play highlights Fenton's lofty rank—he is the sole character to speak primarily in blank verse—in the end he becomes part of the community. Similarly, the tricking of Falstaff in the final scene draws on the royal and aristocratic heritage of the court masque. But this theatrical form, in which the courtiers become the actors, is here recast in a popular, festive mode.

The concluding scene also includes a compliment to the Order of the Garter uttered in blank verse—to reflect the elevated subject matter—by Mistress Quickly disguised as the Queen of the Fairies (5.5.53–70). The Order of the Garter was an aristocratic fraternity under the patronage of the Queen that inducted new members at Windsor Castle. This passage has the effect of placing the town of Windsor under the protection of the castle of Windsor, just as the town's Garter Inn evokes the castle's more elevated Order of the Garter. These references also seem to be a clue to the play's first performance—probably in April 1597 before Elizabeth in London at the Garter Feast, where candidates were elected to the order for induction the following month. One of those to be elected was the new patron of Shakespeare's acting company, and he may well have commissioned the play for the occasion. There also seems to be a comic reference to a German aristocrat elected at the same time (4.5.61–64). But writing in 1702, and hence with uncertain authority, John Dennis records a different tradition. He claims it was the Queen who, after seeing *1 Henry IV*, ordered Shakespeare to write another play about Falstaff, showing him in love, and to complete it within fourteen days.

It is possible that Shakespeare temporarily put aside the composition of *2 Henry IV*, with which *The Merry Wives* has close verbal affinities, to comply either with his patron or with his Queen—indeed, perhaps rather hurriedly. *The Merry Wives* shares at least the names of a number of characters with the two parts of *Henry IV* and with *Henry V*—Falstaff, of course, but also Mistress Quickly, Shallow, Pistol, Bardolph, and Nim. Fenton supposedly "kept company with the wild Prince and Poins" (3.2.61), an allusion to the future Henry V and one of his companions in the *Henry IV* plays. But even though the names are the same, the characters are not. To take only the most prominent example: the easily duped Falstaff of Windsor lacks the indomitable comic resourcefulness that he repeatedly demonstrates in the history plays. Still, the web of political associations lends a national and monarchical aspect to the more circumscribed events of *The Merry Wives*. The effect is ambiguous, even contradictory: on the one hand, royal power is asserted in its absence; on the other, the middling sort who inhabit the town come to stand for all of England.

The play's generalizing force is further enhanced by a degree of indebtedness to popular culture unusual even for Shakespeare. In keeping with its social milieu, *The Merry Wives* has a far higher percentage of prose than does any other Shakespearean work. Much of it satirically reproduces the language of proverb and cliché; Master Slender and Mistress Quickly in particular depend on clichés that verge on the meaningless. Slender's words to Page convey little more than vague good will along with silly ineptitude: "Master Page, I am glad to see you. Much good do it your good heart! . . . And I thank you always with my heart, la, with my heart. . . . Sir, I thank you. By yea and no, I do" (1.1.65–70). Similarly, Quickly can unleash a barrage of only weakly communicative language that somehow enables her to connect with almost all the other characters: "nobody but has his fault," "the very yea and the no," "that's neither here nor there," "what the goodyear," "thereby hangs a tale," "an honest maid as ever broke bread," "Out upon't" (1.4.12, 82, 93, 106, 130, 131–32, 145).

This unintentionally humorous rhetoric is hardly the only evidence of popular culture in the play. *The Merry Wives* also brings on stage a considerable number of lower-class characters. These are not the clowns and fools of the more aristocratic romantic comedies, but servants: John and Robert, who work for the Fords; Peter Simple, who

Elizabeth I and the Knights of the Garter. Engraved by Michael Gheeraerts the Elder (1576).

waits on Slender; John Rugby and Mistress Quickly, who belong to Caius's household; and, set apart from all of these, Falstaff's hangers-on—Bardolph, Pistol, and Nim. Moreover, in the final scene, when the children of Windsor dress up as fairies to punish Falstaff, they mobilize a popular rural belief, evidently shared by their victim, in mischievous immortal spirits who prey upon the local inhabitants. The insults and injuries Falstaff sustains—suffocation, a dunking in the river, a beating, and pinching— belong to the popular tradition of knockabout physical stage action characteristic of both farce and shaming rituals of the time.

Windsor's sense of community also depends on a cheerfully casual ethnocentrism. Hostility to foreigners is part of the throwaway language of the play (especially the Host's): "base Hungarian wight," "Base Phrygian Turk," "Flemish drunkard," "Cathayan," "Ethiopian," "Francisco," "Castalian King Urinal," "Anthropophaginian" (cannibal), "Bohemian Tartar" (1.3.18, 78; 2.1.20–21, 127; 2.3.24, 29; 4.5.8, 16). One of Ford's jealous fits trades in similar stereotypes: "I will rather trust a Fleming with my butter, Parson Hugh the Welshman with my cheese, an Irishman with my aqua-vitae bottle, or a thief to walk my ambling gelding, than my wife with herself" (2.2.265–68). The same effect is produced by the fragmentary, obscure satirical treatment of Germans generally and of a particular German Duke, who is accused of horse stealing in what there is of the third plot of the play, Caius and Evans's revenge on the Host (4.3, 4.5.51–75).

But clearly it is in the fractured English of the French Caius and Welsh Evans themselves, and the good-humored ridicule it evokes, that the English chauvinism of *The Merry Wives* appears most prominently. Evans "makes fritters of English" (5.5.136); he and Caius "hack our English" (3.1.67). Their marked accents, as well as Caius's frequent reversion to French, call attention to their foreignness. Their silly decision to fight a duel is thwarted by the Host out of affection for the two men and perhaps out of hostility to this aristocratic means of settling disputes. Both the intention and the inability to carry it out intensify the other characters' sense of the superiority of

the English middle class. This sense, communicated to the audience as well, is clear enough in the First Folio (1623)—which the present edition follows—despite the likelihood that Shakespeare composed the text that lies behind it for an aristocratic event. But it is even more consistently emphasized in the First Quarto (1602), which seems to be based on a revision of the original version for popular performance. (See the Textual Note.)

As the title of the play reveals, however, its conflicts are fought primarily in terms of gender. But the meaning of these conflicts, despite their unambiguous outcomes, is unclear. Is the wives' triumph over Falstaff's sexual adventuring and Ford's fantasy of his wife's infidelity a victory for *middle-class* women (as suggested earlier), for middle-class *women,* or for both? The play celebrates the wives' freedom and autonomy, in short their merriness, but that merriness serves primarily to protect their husbands' wealth. Primarily, but not entirely. Though Page proudly contrasts his liberal attitude toward his wife with Ford's misogynist anxiety, Mistress Page's scheming against her husband's plans for their daughter's marriage reveals that female self-assertion does not necessarily dovetail with male desire. In this different sense, Ford's fears are justified, Page's confidence undermined. As it turns out, neither parent prevails, although a woman does: Anne replicates the companionate marriage of her mother and father, but she does so against their will, by insisting on her right to choose her own husband.

A view of gender relations and sexuality less obviously tied to emerging middle-class norms is produced by Mistress Quickly's language. Although the obsessive sexual innuendo of that language often escapes the speaker herself, she is not alone in her heedless punning. Evans in particular evinces a comparable obliviousness to the sexual implications of his own speech, an obliviousness that Quickly's comic misunderstandings during the seemingly extraneous Latin lesson (4.1) are instrumental in revealing. Evans, who doubles as Windsor's schoolmaster, quizzes young William Page on the fundamentals of Latin grammar as they were taught in the first years of school, specifically asking his pupil to recite the possessive plural form (or "genitive case") of the word for "this" ("of these"). Mistress Quickly looks on and comments uncomprehendingly:

what she overlooks in her own speech she detects in a language she cannot understand.

> WILLIAM   Genitive case?
> EVANS   Ay.
> WILLIAM   *Genitivo: 'horum, harum, horum'.*
> MISTRESS QUICKLY   Vengeance of Jenny's case! Fie on her!
>   Never name her, child, if she be a whore.
>
> (4.1.50–54)

Here, "genitive" may suggest "generative" or even "genital" as well as the female name "Jenny"; "case" is slang for "vagina"; and *"horum,"* a genitive plural, evokes the more obvious "whore." The scene turns on conflicts between Latin and English, literacy and illiteracy, middle class and lower, man and woman. This is not an isolated moment. Earlier in the play, the language of grammar, allied to translation as in this scene, acquires a sexual charge as Falstaff boasts of his intention to seduce Mistress Ford:

> FALSTAFF . . . I can construe the action of her familiar style; and
>   the hardest voice of her behaviour, to be Englished rightly, is 'I
>   am Sir John Falstaff's'.
> PISTOL   He hath studied her well, and translated her will: out of
>   honesty, into English.
>
> (1.3.39–43)

A different pattern of sexual allusion emerges when Falstaff finds himself trapped in Ford's house on his second assignation with Mistress Ford, and the wives prevail upon him to escape disguised as the "Aunt of Brentford." Although Ford does not see through the costume, he does spew out a torrent of hostile rhetoric—"A witch, a quean, an old cozening quean!" he begins (4.2.149)—before beating up someone whom he believes, however erroneously, to be an old woman (albeit a disreputable one). But of course the woman he attacks is really Falstaff, whose transvestite outfit anticipates the final moments of *The Merry Wives.* Although neither the Folio nor the Quarto is sufficiently consistent about the colors the various characters wear at the end of the play to make possible an exact reconstruction of how Fenton manages to fool the other suitors and elope with Anne, the central trick is unambiguous. "I came yonder at Eton to marry Mistress Anne Page, and she's a great lubberly boy," Slender laments. "If I had been married to him, for all he was in woman's apparel, I would not have had him" (5.5.169–70, 176–77). Caius finds himself even more deeply entangled in the deception. "Ver is Mistress Page? By Gar, I am cozened! I ha' married *un garçon,* a boy, *un paysan,* by Gar. A boy!" (5.5.186–87). This is not the first such sexual tease. Earlier, Ford comments disapprovingly on the intimacy between the merry wives: "I think if your husbands were dead you two would marry." The charge of what we would now call homosexuality is quickly rejected. "Be sure of that—two other husbands," Mistress Page immediately replies (3.2.11–13). Similarly, the ending entertains the option of man-boy sexual relations only to punish Anne's foolish suitors. Like adultery and financially motivated arranged marriages, these are deviations from the elaborately constructed romantic and sexual norm, whose literal issue is emphasized by the unusual prominence of children in the play.

Yet this is not the whole story. The cross-dressing conclusion points self-referentially beyond the fictional action to the actors who have produced the fiction. Shakespeare wrote for a transvestite theater in which female parts were performed by boys. Members of the audience might well note the distance between the fairy queen—a flattering allusion to Queen Elizabeth—Mistress Quickly, and the fictional character who plays the doubly fictional part. They might also register the real boy actor impersonating these two fictional figures. And at the very end, Slender and Caius are not alone in their predicament: Fenton, too, goes off with a boy dressed as a girl. This conclusion simultaneously celebrates and subverts the theatrical illusion. Renaissance accounts

A "skimmington," a public rite of humiliation for domestic disorder.

praise the lifelike persuasiveness of the best boy actors who impersonated women. Here, the boy gets the girl just as the audience would wish, at the very moment Shakespeare reminds them that they have willingly believed in precisely the falsehood accepted by some of the play's more foolish characters.

This resolution, like *The Merry Wives* as a whole, is at once socially suggestive and visually funny. Much of the pleasure of the play arises from the physical comedy of plot and counterplot—Caius discovering Simple in his closet, Ford in disguise urging Falstaff to seduce his wife, Caius and Evans unknowingly preparing for solo duels, Falstaff repeatedly escaping Ford only to suffer still greater humiliation, the deluded would-be bridegrooms stealing off with the wrong fairies. This effective stage business helps explain the work's success both in the theater and in operatic adaptation (especially Verdi's *Falstaff*, 1893).

Particularly at the end, however, stage business also serves to work out the subplot in a way that unravels the logic of the main plot. By the final scene, the revenge on Falstaff has brought together a socially and verbally heterogeneous and often antagonistic group—not just the merry wives and their servants but also their husbands, Evans, Mistress Quickly, and the children of Windsor. Yet the result is not the expected expulsion of the predatory courtier by a unified town but the undoing of nearly all positions of superiority. The central mechanism for this antiscapegoating outcome is the decision by the Fords and Pages to subject Falstaff to one more round of abuse. Even though they are confident that he no longer poses a threat, perhaps they believe he needs to make amends to the whole town. Thus the main plot, in which Falstaff and Ford are fooled by the wives, is balanced by the subplot, in which the fun at the expense of Caius and Slender is perhaps less important than the thwarting of the Pages, who have plotted against each other and must endure the humiliating reversal of having Ford and Falstaff lecture them. As Falstaff says: "I am glad, though you have ta'en a special stand to strike at me, that your arrow hath glanced" (5.5.211–12). Even Anne acknowledges fault: "Pardon, good father. Good my mother, pardon" (line 194). In the fragmentary third plot, the Host fools Evans and Caius, only to have these two rivals team up to exact revenge from him.

The pattern is that of the duper duped. In the end, the renunciation of plotting and hostility by a compromised group of characters produces a moral leveling. The hierarchies and conflicts that separate man from woman, parent from child, sexual normality from sexual deviancy, town from crown, Englishman from foreigner, upper class from middle class, and middle class from lower are resolved—or, more accurately, evaded—through the good-natured, universal inclusiveness of the conclusion. The middle class at the end of the play is a different, more encompassing category than at the beginning. Its strength lies in its cheerful capacity to absorb all comers despite the conscious efforts of most of the leading characters, its ability to fashion a unity that is felt to be more profound than the multiple conflicts dividing the town. And when Mistress Page invites the other characters to "laugh this sport o'er by a country fire" (5.5.219), she is incorporating within the play an experience that the play itself has sought to provide its audience.

WALTER COHEN

TEXTUAL NOTE

The Merry Wives of Windsor, probably composed and first performed in 1597, survives in two important early printed versions—the First Quarto (Q, 1602) and the First Folio (F, 1623). (The Second Quarto, from 1619, simply reprints the First.) This early publication history partly obscures the likely chronology of composition, however. The version in F is printed from a manuscript prepared by a professional scribe named Ralph Crane, who did a fair amount of editing as he copied. His manuscript is in turn based on either a playhouse promptbook or an authorial manuscript. In either case, the Folio text has a close connection with the first performance of the play. Although a date as late as 1601 remains a possibility, most scholars believe that that performance took place in 1597 in a royal and aristocratic setting—for reasons given in the Introduction.

The First Quarto is almost certainly a reported or recollected text (also known as a "memorial reconstruction"): an account of the play in performance prepared largely from memory by the actors who had the parts of the Host (probably) and Falstaff (possibly). Borrowings from *Henry V* mean that it must have been composed between 1598, the earliest year in which *Henry V* could plausibly have been written, and 1602, when the Quarto of *The Merry Wives* was published. Little over half the length of the Folio *Merry Wives,* it seems to be an attempt to recall a version of the play that had already been adapted and cut. Because the First Quarto derives from the memory of a performance rather than from a manuscript that is directly or indirectly Shakespearean, it lacks textual authority.

Accordingly, all modern editions, including the present one, are based on F, in this respect continuing an unbroken tradition tacitly begun with the Third Quarto (1630), which is based not on the first two Quartos but on F. But from 1602 to 1623, the First Quarto was the only written version of the play publicly available. In addition, various problems with the Folio *Merry Wives* make the First Quarto—as truncated, unreliable, and even garbled as it sometimes is—a crucial resource. Thus, where F gives Ford the pseudonym "Broome," Q offers "Brooke." This is surely the original choice, as the wordplay in Falstaff's expression of gratitude for a gift of wine from the character makes clear: "Such Brookes are welcome to me, that o'erflows such liquor" (2.2.135–36). The name was censored at some point from 1597 on, perhaps because "Brooke" was the family name of the patron of Shakespeare's acting company. F's relatively weak and infrequent oaths again suggest censorship, in this instance probably in response to a law of 1606 prohibiting references to God in the theater. Especially in what look like poorly remembered passages, Q's oaths also seem to lack strict textual fidelity to an authorial or theatrical original. But they are fuller and in that sense more accurate. In addition, Q preserves one or more passages that either are omitted from F or are clearly superior to the comparable phrases included there. And because Ralph Crane's editing of the manuscript for F included placing all stage entrances at the very beginning of each scene regardless of where they actually belonged, the stage directions of Q can be quite helpful.

Still other verbal discrepancies between the two versions point to more general thematic differences. Q omits F's Latin lesson (4.1) as well as its allusion in 5.5 to the Order of the Garter ceremony. At least the second of these cuts, both of which seem to indicate a text designed for a more popular audience than the courtly spectators aimed at by F, may well have been made by Shakespeare's company when it put on *The Merry Wives* in the public, commercial theater. References to rural life in Windsor and to the presence of the court are more frequent in F than in Q, which sometimes has urban allusions instead and which simply omits some elite or courtly material. Only in Q are courtiers mocked by name (Brooke, Mömpelgard), and in general F has the more appreciative view of the court.

Many questions remain about both Q and F. At least one intriguing possibility is worth pondering. F may be based on an authorial manuscript that was used for the initial court performance. Q may be based on the memory of stage performances of a promptbook that incorporates revisions of the authorial manuscript for the public theater. If both hypotheses are correct, F accurately preserves a unique, anomalous first performance; Q inaccurately preserves the different version used for the overwhelming majority of the performances in Shakespeare's lifetime. On this interpretation, the textual situation is paradoxical: Q has more value than is usually assumed, despite its inaccuracy. Because it derives from the memory of performance, its language is less authentically Shakespearean than F's. But because those performances reflect revisions that include Shakespeare's own changes as well as other changes made by his company that he accepted, Q may be more authentically Shakespearean than F in presenting the playwright's final treatment of his material, a treatment that accords greater relative weight to popular material both by excluding high-cultural scenes and by including satirical references and additional allusions to everyday life.

SELECTED BIBLIOGRAPHY

Brown, Pamela Allen. *Better a Shrew Than a Sheep: Women, Drama, and the Culture of Jest in Early Modern England.* Ithaca, N.Y.: Cornell University Press, 2003. 33–55. *The Merry Wives* as a play appealing to women. This study focuses on—and differentiates between—the two wives in the context of communal women's culture, female chastity, and neighborhood gender relations.

Buccola, Regina M. "Shakespeare's Fairy Dance with Religio-Political Controversy in *The Merry Wives of Windsor.*" *Shakespeare and the Culture of Christianity in Early Modern England.* Ed. Dennis Taylor and David Beauregard. New York: Fordham University Press, 2003. 159–79. Connections among fairies, Catholicism, the Welsh, and women in the play and society alike seen in *The Merry Wives* as potentially subversive but ultimately incorporated into an orthodox order.

Erickson, Peter. "The Order of the Garter, the Cult of Elizabeth, and Class-Gender Tension in *The Merry Wives of Windsor.*" *Shakespeare Reproduced: The Text in History and Ideology.* Ed. Jean E. Howard and Marion F. O'Connor. New York: Methuen, 1987. 116–42. Tension between a conservative class hierarchy, emblematized by the Order of the Garter, and a less traditional affirmation of female authority, productive of male anxiety and represented by the wives and their linkage to Elizabeth.

Hall, Jonathan. "The Evacuations of Falstaff (*The Merry Wives of Windsor*)." *Shakespeare and Carnival: After Bakhtin.* Ed. Ronald Knowles. New York: St. Martin's, 1998. 123–51. The domestication of the grotesque, carnivalesque body of Falstaff by a stable bourgeois world.

Helgerson, Richard. "Language Lessons: Linguistic Colonialism, Linguistic Postcolonialism, and the Early Modern English Nation." *Yale Journal of Criticism* 11 (1998): 289–99. Latin versus English versus marginal dialects as colonizing and colonized languages.

Kegl, Rosemary. "'The Adoption of Abominable Terms': Middle Classes, Merry Wives, and the Insults That Shape Windsor." *The Rhetoric of Concealment: Figuring Gender and Class in Renaissance Literature.* Ithaca, N.Y.: Cornell University Press, 1994. 77–125. The language of class and gender hierarchy, with attention to issues of ethnocentrism.

Marcus, Leah. "Levelling Shakespeare: Local Customs and Local Texts." *Shakespeare Quarterly* 42 (1991): 168–78. Contrast of the rural, aristocratic Folio version of the play with the urban, middle-class quarto text.

Melchiori, Giorgio, ed. *The Merry Wives of Windsor*. Walton-on-Thames, Surrey: Thomas Nelson, 2000. Outstanding scholarly edition with a lengthy critical introduction.

Parker, Patricia. "*The Merry Wives of Windsor* and Shakespearean Translation." *Modern Language Quarterly* 52 (1991): 225–61. The scene of Latin instruction (4.1) as integral to the play, revealing links between language and sexuality.

Pittenger, Elizabeth. "Dispatch Quickly: The Mechanical Reproduction of Pages." *Shakespeare Quarterly* 42 (1991): 389–408. Connections among printing, pedagogy, language, and gender hierarchy, also with special attention to 4.1.

Salingar, Leo. "The Englishness of the *The Merry Wives of Windsor*." *Cahiers élisabéthains* 59 (2001): 9–25. General reading of the play covering geographical setting, social structure, farce, and especially nationalist linguistic patterns.

Film

The Merry Wives of Windsor. 1982. Dir. David Hugh Jones. UK. 168 min. BBC production with Ben Kingsley as Ford and Judy Davis as Mistress Ford.

The Merry Wives of Windsor

THE PERSONS OF THE PLAY

MISTRESS Margaret PAGE
Master George PAGE, her husband
ANNE Page, their daughter
WILLIAM Page, their son ⎫ citizens of Windsor
MISTRESS Alice FORD
Master Frank FORD, her husband
JOHN ⎫
ROBERT ⎰ their servants
Sir John FALSTAFF
BARDOLPH ⎫
PISTOL ⎬ Sir John Falstaff's
NIM ⎭ followers
ROBIN, Sir John Falstaff's page
The HOST of the Garter Inn
Sir Hugh EVANS, a Welsh parson
Doctor CAIUS, a French physician
MISTRESS QUICKLY, his housekeeper
John RUGBY, his servant
Master FENTON, a young gentleman, in love with Anne Page
Master Abraham SLENDER
Robert SHALLOW, his uncle, a Justice
Peter SIMPLE, Slender's servant
Children of Windsor, appearing as fairies

1.1

Enter Justice SHALLOW, *[Master]* SLENDER, *and Sir*[1]
Hugh EVANS

SHALLOW   Sir Hugh, persuade me not. I will make a Star Cham-
ber° matter of it. If he were twenty Sir John Falstaffs, he shall
not abuse Robert Shallow, Esquire.°
SLENDER   In the county of Gloucester, Justice of Peace and
5   Coram.[2]
SHALLOW   Ay, cousin° Slender, and Custalorum.
SLENDER   Ay, and Ratolorum[3] too; and a gentleman born, Master Parson, who writes himself 'Armigero'° in any bill, war
rant,quittance,° or obligation: 'Armigero'.
10   SHALLOW   Ay, that I do, and have done any time these three hundred years.
SLENDER   All his successors gone before him hath done't, and all

high court
(just below a knight)

kinsman (here, nephew)

esquire; arms bearer
discharge from debt

1.1 Location: A street, later moving to the entrance to
Page's house.
1. *Justice:* justice of the peace (line 4), a local judge.
Master: regularly used of Slender (beginning at line 47),
a respectful prefix to a name that is similar in meaning to
the modern "Mr.," which derives from it. Sir: clergyman's
honorary title, not indicating knighthood, as it does with
Falstaff (line 2).
2. Blunder for "quorum," designating justices who could

try a felon if a sufficient number of them (two or more)
were present. Literally, *coram* is Latin for "in the presence
of"; to "bring under coram" was to subject someone to
discipline: hence, Slender comically provides an unwittingly accurate account of Shallow's office.
3. "Custalorum" (line 6) and "Ratolorum" are blunders
for *custos rotulorum* (keeper of the rolls), the principal
justice in a county; perhaps a play on "rat."

his ancestors that come after him may. They may give the
dozen white luces° in their coat.°   *pike/coat of arms*

15 SHALLOW It is an old coat.

EVANS The dozen white louses do become an old coad[4] well. It
agrees well passant:[5] it is a familiar° beast to man, and signifies   *familial; too intimate*
love.

SHALLOW The luce is the fresh fish; the salt fish is an old cod.[6]

20 SLENDER I may quarter,[7] coz.°   *kinsman*

SHALLOW You may, by marrying.

EVANS It is marring indeed if he quarter it.

SHALLOW Not a whit.

EVANS Yes, py'r Lady.° If he has a quarter of your coat, there is   *by our Lady (Mary)*
25 but three skirts° for yourself, in my simple conjectures. But that   *coattails*
is all one. If Sir John Falstaff have committed disparagements
unto you, I am of the Church, and will be glad to do my benevolence to make atonements and compromises between you.

SHALLOW The Council[8] shall hear it; it is a riot.

30 EVANS It is not meet° the Council hear a riot. There is no fear   *fitting*
of Got in a riot. The Council, look you, shall desire to hear the
fear of Got, and not to hear a riot. Take your 'visaments in
that.[9]

SHALLOW Ha! O' my life, if I were young again, the sword
35 should end it.

EVANS It is petter that friends is the sword and end it.[1] And there
is also another device in my prain, which peradventure prings
goot discretions with it. There is Anne Page which is daughter
to Master George Page, which is pretty virginity.

40 SLENDER Mistress Anne Page? She has brown hair, and speaks
small° like a woman?   *in a soprano voice*

EVANS It is that fery person for all the 'orld, as just as you will
desire. And seven hundred pounds of moneys, and gold and
silver, is° her grandsire upon his death's-bed—Got deliver to a   *did*
45 joyful resurrections—give, when she is able to overtake seventeen years old. It were a goot motion° if we leave our pribbles   *plan*
and prabbles,° and desire a marriage between Master Abraham   *squabbles*
and Mistress Anne Page.

SLENDER Did her grandsire leave her seven hundred pound?

50 EVANS Ay, and her father is make her a petter penny.°   *will give much more*

SHALLOW I know the young gentlewoman. She has good gifts.°   *qualities*

EVANS Seven hundred pounds and possibilities° is goot gifts.   *financial prospects*

SHALLOW Well, let us see honest Master Page. Is Falstaff there?

EVANS Shall I tell you a lie? I do despise a liar as I do despise
55 one that is false, or as I despise one that is not true. The knight
Sir John is there, and I beseech you be ruled by your well-

---

4. Coat; cod; scrotum. Evans, in what is meant to be a
stereotypical Welsh accent, often pronounces "t" for "d,"
"p" for "b," and "f" for "v" and omits initial "w." "Louses"
is Evans's comic error for "luces" (line 14), a term from
heraldry, the branch of knowledge concerned with the
right to bear arms, with family pedigrees, and with coats
of arms. (See also "Armigero" and "coat," lines 8, 14.)
The error is set up by the two meanings of "old coat"
(noble lineage, worn-out clothing, line 15), and Evans's
pronunciation then provokes further uncomprehending
wordplay by Shallow (line 19).
5. Walking, looking to the right with the right paw raised
(heraldic); surpassingly. The heraldic image is absurd for
a fish, only slightly less so for a louse.

6. Meaning unclear—perhaps a joke involving Evans's
pronunciation ("louses/luces"; "coad/coat/cod"). *fresh:*
freshwater, unpreserved. *salt:* saltwater, salt-cured,
obscene.
7. I may add another (family's) coat to one of the four
parts of my heraldic arms (for instance, through marriage); but in Evans's reply, cut up in quarters. The
humor of this passage (lines 7–25) results from the deflation of social pretentiousness by unintentionally punning
incomprehension.
8. Star Chamber (lines 1–2); but Evans understands it as
"church council."
9. *Take . . . that:* Be advised.
1. The intervention of friends should end the dispute.

willers.° I will peat the door for Master Page.   *well-wishers*
    [*He knocks on the door*]
  What ho! Got pless your house here!
PAGE [*within*]   Who's there?

60 EVANS   Here is Got's plessing and your friend, and Justice Shallow, and here young Master Slender, that peradventures shall
tell you another tale° if matters grow to your likings.   *(a marriage proposal)*
    Enter Master PAGE
PAGE   I am glad to see your worships well. I thank you for my
venison, Master Shallow.

65 SHALLOW   Master Page, I am glad to see you. Much good do it
your good heart! I wished your venison better; it was ill°   *unlawfully (by Falstaff?)*
killed.—How doth good Mistress Page?—And I thank you
always with my heart, la,° with my heart.   *indeed*
PAGE   Sir, I thank you.

70 SHALLOW   Sir, I thank you. By yea and no,° I do.   *(almost meaningless)*
PAGE   I am glad to see you, good Master Slender.
SLENDER   How does your fallow° greyhound, sir? I heard say he   *light-brown*
was outrun on Cotswold.°   *the Cotswold hills*
PAGE   It could not be judged, sir.

75 SLENDER   You'll not confess, you'll not confess.°   *(that the dog lost)*
SHALLOW   That he will not. 'Tis your fault,° 'tis your fault.   *You're in the wrong*
    [*To* PAGE] 'Tis a good dog.
PAGE   A cur, sir.
SHALLOW   Sir, he's a good dog and a fair dog. Can there be more
80 said? He is good and fair. Is Sir John Falstaff here?
PAGE   Sir, he is within; and I would I could do a good office
between you.
EVANS   It is spoke as a Christians ought to speak.
SHALLOW   He hath wronged me, Master Page.

85 PAGE   Sir, he doth in some sort confess it.
SHALLOW   If it be confessed, it is not redressed. Is not that so,
Master Page? He hath wronged me; indeed he hath; at a word,°   *in short*
he hath. Believe me, Robert Shallow, Esquire, saith he is
wronged.
    Enter Sir John FALSTAFF, BARDOLPH, NIM, *and* PISTOL

90 PAGE   Here comes Sir John.
FALSTAFF   Now, Master Shallow, you'll complain of me to the
King?
SHALLOW   Knight, you have beaten my men, killed my deer, and
broke open my lodge.°   *keeper's house*

95 FALSTAFF   But not kissed your keeper's daughter?
SHALLOW   Tut, a pin.° This shall be answered.   *trifling comment*
FALSTAFF   I will answer it straight: I have done all this. That is
now answered.
SHALLOW   The Council shall know this.

100 FALSTAFF   'Twere better for you if it were known in counsel.°   *kept secret*
You'll be laughed at.
EVANS   *Pauca verba,*° Sir John, good worts.   *Few words*
FALSTAFF   Good worts?° Good cabbage!—Slender, I broke your   *words; cabbage*
head. What matter° have you against me?   *complaint*

105 SLENDER   Marry, sir, I have matter in my head against you, and
against your cony-catching° rascals, Bardolph, Nim, and Pistol.   *swindling*
BARDOLPH   You Banbury cheese!°   *thin (like Slender)*
SLENDER   Ay, it is no matter.

PISTOL   How now, Mephistopheles?[2]
110 SLENDER   Ay, it is no matter.
NIM   Slice, I say *pauca, pauca*. Slice, that's my humour.[3]
SLENDER [*to* SHALLOW]   Where's Simple, my man? Can you tell,
     cousin?
EVANS   Peace, I pray you. Now let us understand. There is three
115 umpires in this matter, as I understand: that is, Master Page,
     fidelicet° Master Page; and there is myself, fidelicet myself; and   *namely*
     the three party is, lastly and finally, mine Host of the Garter.°   *(a Windsor inn)*
PAGE   We three to hear it, and end it between them.
EVANS   Fery goot. I will make a prief of it in my notebook, and
120 we will afterwards 'ork upon the cause with as great discreetly
     as we can.
FALSTAFF   Pistol.
PISTOL   He hears with ears.
EVANS   The tevil and his tam!° What phrase is this? 'He hears   *dam (mother)*
125 with ear'! Why, it is affectations.
FALSTAFF   Pistol, did you pick Master Slender's purse?
SLENDER   Ay, by these gloves did he—or I would I might never
     come in mine own great chamber° again else—of seven groats   *hall; bedroom*
     in mill-sixpences, and two Edward shovel-boards[4] that cost me
130 two shilling and twopence apiece of Ed Miller. By these gloves.
FALSTAFF   Is this true, Pistol?
EVANS   No, it is false, if it° is a pickpurse.   *he*
PISTOL   Ha, thou mountain-foreigner!° Sir John and master mine,   *Welshman*
     I combat challenge of this latten bilbo.[5]—
135 Word of denial in thy *labras*° here,   *lips*
     Word of denial: froth and scum, thou liest.
SLENDER [*pointing to* NIM]   By these gloves, then, 'twas he.
NIM   Be advised, sir, and pass good humours.° I will say 'marry,   *behave properly*
     trap with you'[6] if you run the nuthook's humour on me.[7] That
140 is the very note° of it.   *fact*
SLENDER   By this hat, then, he in the red face° had it. For though   *(Bardolph)*
     I cannot remember what I did when you made me drunk, yet
     I am not altogether an ass.
FALSTAFF [*to* BARDOLPH]   What say you, Scarlet and John?[8]
145 BARDOLPH   Why, sir, for my part I say the gentleman had drunk
     himself out of his five sentences.
EVANS   It is 'his five senses'. Fie, what the ignorance is!
BARDOLPH   And being fap,° sir, was, as they say, cashiered.° And   *drunk / kicked out*
     so conclusions passed the careers.[9]
150 SLENDER   Ay, you spake in Latin[1] then, too. But 'tis no matter.
     I'll ne'er be drunk, whilst I live, again, but in honest, civil,
     godly company, for° this trick. If I be drunk, I'll be drunk with   *on account of*
     those that have the fear of God, and not with drunken knaves.
EVANS   So Got 'udge me,° that is a virtuous mind.   *judge*

---

2. The devil in Christopher Marlowe's *Dr. Faustus*,
perhaps played as a thin, gaunt character.
3. "Slice" takes up the Banbury cheese insult (line 107)
and may command Slender to cut off his remarks, to stick
to few words ("*pauca*"). Nim's temperament ("humour")
is to slice Slender with his sword.
4. *groat*: four-penny coin. *mill-sixpences*: new coins that
may have been worth more than their face value. *Edward
shovel-boards*: old shillings. Shallow has paid over twice
their face value because of their use in the game of
shovel board.

5. A sword (from Bilbao, Spain, where fine swords known
for their elasticity were made) made of brass or a brasslike,
yellow mixed metal; probably alluding to Slender's
cowardice and thinness.
6. Get lost; go play a children's game; you'll be caught (?).
7. If you act like a constable in accusing me.
8. Robin Hood's accomplices, Will Scarlet and Little
John; alluding to Bardolph's complexion.
9. Things got out of hand; he misinterpreted things.
1. Slender can't understand Bardolph's slang and so
assumes it must be Latin.

155 FALSTAFF   You hear all these matters denied, gentlemen, you
hear it.
     Enter ANNE *Page* [*with wine*]
PAGE   Nay, daughter, carry the wine in; we'll drink within.
     [*Exit* ANNE]
SLENDER   O heaven, this is Mistress Anne Page!
     Enter [*at another door*] MISTRESS FORD *and* MISTRESS
     PAGE
PAGE   How now, Mistress Ford?
160 FALSTAFF   Mistress Ford, by my troth, you are very well met. By
your leave, good mistress.
     Sir John FALSTAFF *kisses her*
PAGE   Wife, bid these gentlemen welcome.—Come, we have a
hot venison pasty to° dinner. Come, gentlemen, I hope we shall   *pie for*
drink down all unkindness.   *Exeunt all but* SLENDER
165 SLENDER   I had rather than forty shillings I had my book of songs
and sonnets here.[2]
     Enter SIMPLE
How now, Simple, where have you been? I must wait on
myself, must I? You have not the book of riddles about you,
have you?
170 SIMPLE   Book of riddles? Why, did you not lend it to Alice Short-
cake upon Allhallowmas last, a fortnight afore Michaelmas?[3]
     [*Enter* SHALLOW *and* EVANS]
SHALLOW [*to* SLENDER]   Come, coz; come, coz; we stay° for you.   *wait*
[*Aside to him*] A word with you, coz.
     [*He draws* SLENDER *aside*]
Marry, this, coz: there is, as 'twere, a tender,° a kind of tender,   *(marriage) proposal*
175 made afar off ° by Sir Hugh here. Do you understand me?   *indirectly*
SLENDER   Ay, sir, you shall find me reasonable.° If it be so, I shall   *(with Falstaff)*
do that that is reason.
SHALLOW   Nay, but understand me.
SLENDER   So I do, sir.
180 EVANS   Give ear to his motions.° Master Slender, I will descrip-   *proposals*
tion the matter to you, if you be capacity of it.
SLENDER   Nay, I will do as my cousin Shallow says. I pray you
pardon me. He's a Justice of Peace in his country,° simple°   *district / humble; foolish*
though I stand here.
185 EVANS   But that is not the question. The question is concerning
your marriage.
SHALLOW   Ay, there's the point, sir.
EVANS   Marry, is it, the very point of it—to Mistress Anne Page.
SLENDER   Why, if it be so, I will marry her upon any reasonable
190 demands.°   *requests*
EVANS   But can you affection the 'oman? Let us command to
know that of your mouth, or of your lips—for divers philoso-
phers hold that the lips is parcel° of the mouth. Therefore,   *part and parcel*
precisely, can you carry your good will to the maid?
195 SHALLOW   Cousin Abraham Slender, can you love her?
SLENDER   I hope, sir, I will do as it shall become one that would
do reason.

---

2. Probably Richard Tottel's *Miscellany* (1557), an out-
of-date collection of love poetry on whose quotable
quotes Slender wishes to draw in wooing Anne Page.

3. Allhallowmas, or All Saints' Day (November 1), is
actually over a month after Michaelmas, September 29.

EVANS   Nay, Got's lords and his ladies, you must speak positable°   *positively*
    if you can carry her your desires towards her.
200 SHALLOW   That you must. Will you, upon good dowry, marry
    her?
SLENDER   I will do a greater thing than that upon your request,
    cousin, in° any reason.   *within*
SHALLOW   Nay, conceive° me, conceive me, sweet coz. What I   *understand*
205   do is to pleasure you, coz. Can you love the maid?
SLENDER   I will marry her, sir, at your request. But if there be no
    great love in the beginning, yet heaven may decrease° it upon   *(for "increase")*
    better acquaintance, when we are married and have more occa-
    sion to know one another. I hope upon familiarity will grow
210   more contempt.° But if you say 'marry her', I will marry her.   *(for "content")*
    That I am freely dissolved,° and dissolutely.   *(for "resolved")*
EVANS   It is a fery discretion answer, save the faul'° is in the 'ord   *fault*
    'dissolutely'. The 'ort is, according to our meaning, 'resolutely'.
    His meaning is good.
215 SHALLOW   Ay, I think my cousin meant well.
SLENDER   Ay, or else I would I might be hanged, la.
        [*Enter* ANNE *Page*]
SHALLOW   Here comes fair Mistress Anne.—Would I were young
    for your sake, Mistress Anne.
ANNE   The dinner is on the table. My father desires your wor-
220   ships' company.
SHALLOW   I will wait on him, fair Mistress Anne.
EVANS   'Od's° plessed will, I will not be absence at the grace.   *God's*
                [*Exeunt* SHALLOW *and* EVANS]
ANNE [*to* SLENDER]   Will't please your worship to come in, sir?
SLENDER   No, I thank you, forsooth, heartily; I am very well.
225 ANNE   The dinner attends° you, sir.   *awaits*
SLENDER   I am not a-hungry, I thank you, forsooth. [*To* SIMPLE]
    Go, sirrah; for all you are my man, go wait upon my cousin
    Shallow.   [*Exit* SIMPLE]
    A Justice of Peace sometime may be beholden to his friend for
230   a man. I keep but three men and a boy yet, till my mother be
    dead. But what though?° Yet I live like a poor gentleman born.   *what of it*
ANNE   I may not go in without your worship. They will not sit
    till you come.
SLENDER   I'faith, I'll eat nothing. I thank you as much as though
235   I did.
ANNE   I pray you, sir, walk in.
        [*Dogs bark within*]
SLENDER   I had rather walk here, I thank you. I bruised my shin
    th'other day, with playing at sword and dagger with a master of
    fence°—three veneys° for a dish of stewed prunes[4]—and, by   *fencing / bouts*
240   my troth, I cannot abide the smell of hot meat° since. Why do   *food; prostitutes*
    your dogs bark so? Be there bears i'th' town?
ANNE   I think there are, sir. I heard them talked of.
SLENDER   I love the sport° well—but I shall as soon quarrel at[5] it   *bearbaiting*
    as any man in England. You are afraid if you see the bear loose,
245   are you not?
ANNE   Ay, indeed, sir.
SLENDER   That's meat and drink° to me, now. I have seen Sack-   *everyday fare*

---

4. Prostitutes.   5. Object to (?); brawl at (?).

erson[6] loose twenty times, and have taken him by the chain.
But I warrant you, the women have so cried and shrieked at it
250 that it passed.° But women, indeed, cannot abide 'em. They   *surpassed description*
are very ill-favoured,° rough things.   *ugly*
      Enter PAGE
PAGE   Come, gentle Master Slender, come. We stay for you.
SLENDER   I'll eat nothing, I thank you, sir.
PAGE   By cock and pie,° you shall not choose,° sir. Come, come.   *(mild oath) / you must*
255 SLENDER   Nay, pray you lead the way.
PAGE   Come on, sir.
SLENDER   Mistress Anne, yourself shall go first.
ANNE   Not I, sir. Pray you keep on.°   *go on*
SLENDER   Truly, I will not go first, truly, la. I will not do you that
260 wrong.
ANNE   I pray you, sir.
SLENDER   I'll rather be unmannerly than troublesome. You do
yourself wrong, indeed, la.
      Exeunt [SLENDER *first, the others following*]

1.2

Enter Sir Hugh EVANS *and* SIMPLE, *from dinner*
EVANS   Go your ways, and ask of ° Doctor Caius' house which   *concerning*
is the way. And there dwells one Mistress Quickly, which is in
the manner of his 'oman, or his dry-nurse,° or his cook, or his   *housekeeper*
laundry, his washer, and his wringer.
5 SIMPLE   Well, sir.
EVANS   Nay, it is petter yet. Give her this letter, for it is a 'oman
that altogethers acquaintance° with Mistress Anne Page. And   *is well acquainted*
the letter is to desire and require her to solicit your master's
desires to Mistress Anne Page. I pray you be gone.
      [*Exit* SIMPLE]
10 I will make an end of my dinner; there's pippins° and cheese   *apples*
to come.   *Exit*

1.3

Enter Sir John FALSTAFF, BARDOLPH, NIM, PISTOL, *and*
[ROBIN] *the boy*
FALSTAFF   Mine Host of the Garter!
      Enter [*the*] HOST *of the Garter*
HOST   What says my bully rook?° Speak scholarly and wisely.   *fine fellow*
FALSTAFF   Truly, mine Host, I must turn away some of my fol-
lowers.
5 HOST   Discard, bully Hercules, cashier.° Let them wag.° Trot,   *dismiss / go their ways*
trot.
FALSTAFF   I sit° at ten pounds a week.   *lodge*
HOST   Thou'rt an emperor: Caesar, kaiser, and pheezer.[1] I will
entertain° Bardolph. He shall draw, he shall tap.° Said I well,   *employ / tend bar*
10 bully Hector?[2]
FALSTAFF   Do so, good mine Host.

---

6. Famous bear used in bearbaiting.
1.2 Location: Scene continues.
1.3 Location: The Garter Inn.
1. Literally, "one who drives others away"; but the Host
evidently means "vizier" (Turkish viceroy). *Caesar:* the

name of Julius Caesar became a title, "emperor."
2. Greatest of the Trojans who fought in the Trojan War.
Similarly, Hercules (line 5) was the most famous hero of
classical mythology.

HOST   I have spoke; let him follow. [*To* BARDOLPH] Let me see
thee froth and lime.[3] I am at a word:° follow.   *Exit*   I mean what I say

FALSTAFF   Bardolph, follow him. A tapster is a good trade. An
old cloak makes a new jerkin;° a withered servingman a fresh   jacket
tapster. Go; adieu.

BARDOLPH   It is a life that I have desired. I will thrive.   *Exit*

PISTOL   O base Hungarian wight,° wilt thou the spigot wield?   hungry, hidebound man

NIM   He was gotten in drink;[4] his mind is not heroic. Is not the
humour conceited?°   idea witty

FALSTAFF   I am glad I am so acquit of this tinderbox.[5] His thefts
were too open. His filching was like an unskilful singer: he kept
not time.

NIM   The good humour° is to steal at a minute's rest.°   trick / within a minute

PISTOL   'Convey' the wise it call. 'Steal'? Foh, a fico[6] for the
phrase!

FALSTAFF   Well, sirs, I am almost out at heels.°   destitute

PISTOL   Why then, let kibes° ensue.   sore heels

FALSTAFF   There is no remedy: I must cony-catch,° I must shift.°   swindle / live by my wits

PISTOL   Young ravens must have food.

FALSTAFF   Which of you know Ford of this town?

PISTOL   I ken the wight.° He is of substance good.°   know the man / well-off

FALSTAFF   My honest lads, I will tell you what I am about.°   up to; in girth

PISTOL   Two yards and more.

FALSTAFF   No quips now, Pistol. Indeed, I am in the waist two
yards about. But I am now about no waste; I am about thrift.
Briefly, I do mean to make love to Ford's wife. I spy entertainment[7] in her. She discourses, she carves,[8] she gives the leer of
invitation. I can construe[9] the action of her familiar style; and
the hardest voice of her behaviour, to be Englished rightly, is 'I
am Sir John Falstaff's'.

PISTOL   He hath studied her well, and translated her will:[1] out of
honesty,° into English.   chastity

NIM   The anchor is deep.[2] Will that humour pass?°   phrase pass muster

FALSTAFF   Now, the report° goes, she has all the rule of her hus-   rumor
band's purse; he hath a legion of angels.°   gold coins

PISTOL   As many devils entertain, and 'To her, boy!'° say I.   (hunting cry)

NIM   The humour rises; it is good. Humour me the angels![3]

FALSTAFF [*showing letters*]   I have writ me here a letter to her—
and here another to Page's wife, who even now gave me good
eyes too, examined my parts[4] with most judicious oeillades;°   amorous glances
sometimes the beam of her view gilded my foot, sometimes my
portly belly.

PISTOL   Then did the sun on dunghill shine.

NIM   I thank thee for that humour.

3. *froth and lime*: both are ways of cheating the customer—by putting a good head on the beer (to give short measure) and by adulterating wine with lime (to remove acidity and make it sparkle).
4. Begotten when his parents were drunk (thought to make one cowardly).
5. Alluding to Bardolph's red complexion and irascible temper. *acquit*: rid.
6. An abusive insult usually accompanied by the gesture of showing the thumb pushed between index and middle fingers: historically, "fig" (Spanish); allusively, "female genitals."
7. Provision of food, drink, and lodging; ability to give sexual pleasure.

8. Perhaps: acts courteously; gestures broadly with her hands; shows pleasing skill in carving meat—hence, somewhere between ordinary friendliness and sexual enticement.
9. Interpret (beginning a grammatical pun that includes "style," "voice," "Englished," and "translated," lines 39, 40, 42).
1. Intention; sexual desires; legal document (thought of as written in Latin).
2. That's a deep plot; you're out of your depth (?).
3. Perhaps: the plot develops; it's good. Get the money. (Here, as elsewhere in Nim's speech, "humour" means whatever the context demands.)
4. My (sexual) capacities.

FALSTAFF   O, she did so course o'er my exteriors, with such a
greedy intention, that the appetite of her eye did seem to scorch
me up like a burning-glass![5] Here's another letter to her. She
bears the purse too. She is a region in Guiana,[6] all gold and
60   bounty. I will be cheaters[7] to them both, and they shall be
exchequers to me. They shall be my East and West Indies, and
I will trade to them both. [*Giving a letter to* PISTOL] Go bear
thou this letter to Mistress Page, [*giving a letter to* NIM] and
thou this to Mistress Ford. We will thrive, lads, we will thrive.
65   PISTOL [*returning the letter*]   Shall I Sir Pandarus of Troy[8] become,
And by my side wear steel?° Then Lucifer take all.   *And remain a soldier*
NIM [*returning the letter*]   I will run no base humour. Here, take
the humour-letter. I will keep the haviour of reputation.[9]
FALSTAFF [*to* ROBIN]   Hold,° sirrah. Bear you these letters tightly.°   *Take these / safely*
70   Sail like my pinnace° to these golden shores.   *small, fast boat*
[*He gives* ROBIN *the letters*]
Rogues, hence, avaunt!° Vanish like hailstones! Go!   *be gone*
Trudge, plod, away o'th' hoof, seek shelter, pack!°   *be off*
Falstaff will learn the humour of the age:
French thrift, you rogues—myself and skirted page.[1]
Exeunt FALSTAFF *and* [ROBIN] *the boy*
75   PISTOL   Let vultures gripe° thy guts!—for gourd and fullam[2]   *seize*
holds,°   *are profitable*
And high and low beguiles the rich and poor.
Tester° I'll have in pouch° when thou shalt lack,   *Sixpence/purse*
Base Phrygian Turk![3]
NIM   I have operations° which be humours of revenge.   *plans*
PISTOL   Wilt thou revenge?
80   NIM   By welkin° and her stars!   *the sky (poetic)*
PISTOL   With wit or steel?
NIM   With both the humours, I.
I will discuss° the humour of this love to Ford.   *disclose*
PISTOL   And I to Page shall eke° unfold   *also (archaic)*
How Falstaff, varlet vile,
85   His dove will prove,° his gold will hold,   *test; sample*
And his soft couch defile.
NIM   My humour shall not cool. I will incense Ford to deal with
poison; I will possess him with yellowness;[4] for this revolt of
mine° is dangerous. That is my true humour.   *(against Falstaff)*
90   PISTOL   Thou art the Mars of malcontents.[5]
I second thee. Troop on.   *Exeunt*

5. Glass lens used to concentrate the sun's rays and so start a fire.
6. South American country famed for its unexploited wealth and fertility, as were the East and West Indies (line 61).
7. Escheaters, officers of the Exchequer (or Treasury, line 61) responsible for estates that fell forfeit and so came to the crown; deceivers, robbers.
8. Pandarus is the aristocrat who, as Troy is besieged by the Greeks, serves as go-between (or pander) in the affair between Troilus and Cressida, Pandarus's niece. Shakespeare's play on the subject is several years later than *The Merry Wives*.
9. I will behave respectfully.
1. Suggesting that French gentlemen were thought to retain few, though well-dressed, followers. *skirted:* wearing a coat with full tails.
2. *gourd and fullam:* false dice and loaded dice—loaded "high" to produce a four, five, or six, or "low" to produce one, two, or three. See line 76.
3. Terms of abuse. The Turks, Europe's main military foe, were Muslims and hence considered infidels. The Phrygians, early inhabitants of what is now Turkey, were conquered by Europeans; to the classical Greeks, "Phrygian" was equivalent to "slave."
4. Fill him with jealousy. (An inconsistency: in 2.1, Nim goes to Page and Pistol to Ford, who is possessed with yellowness.)
5. Most warlike rebel (Mars was the Roman god of war).

1.4

Enter MISTRESS QUICKLY *and* SIMPLE

MISTRESS QUICKLY What,° John Rugby!   *(a summoning call)*

Enter John RUGBY

I pray thee, go to the casement and see if you can see my master, Master Doctor Caius, coming. If he do, i'faith, and find
anybody in the house, here will be an old° abusing of God's   *will be lots of*
5   patience and the King's English.

RUGBY I'll go watch.

MISTRESS QUICKLY Go; and we'll have a posset¹ for't soon at
night,° in faith, at the latter end of a seacoal² fire.   *toward nightfall*

[*Exit* RUGBY]

An honest, willing, kind fellow as ever servant shall come in
10   house withal;° and, I warrant you, no telltale, nor no   *with*
breedbate.° His worst fault is that he is given to prayer; he is   *troublemaker*
something peevish° that way—but nobody but has his fault. But   *foolish*
let that pass. Peter Simple you say your name is?

SIMPLE Ay, for fault° of a better.   *lack*

15   MISTRESS QUICKLY And Master Slender's your master?

SIMPLE Ay, forsooth.

MISTRESS QUICKLY Does he not wear a great round beard, like
a glover's paring-knife?

SIMPLE No, forsooth; he hath but a little whey face, with a little
20   yellow beard, a Cain-coloured° beard.   *yellow or reddish*

MISTRESS QUICKLY A softly spirited° man, is he not?   *meek-spirited*

SIMPLE Ay, forsooth; but he is as tall a man of his hands as any
is between this and his head.³ He hath fought with a warrener.°   *gamekeeper*

MISTRESS QUICKLY How say you?—O, I should remember him:
25   does he not hold up his head, as it were, and strut in his gait?

SIMPLE Yes, indeed does he.

MISTRESS QUICKLY Well, heaven send Anne Page no worse fortune! Tell Master Parson Evans I will do what I can for your
master. Anne is a good girl, and I wish—

[*Enter* RUGBY]

30   RUGBY Out, alas, here comes my master!   [*Exit*]

MISTRESS QUICKLY We shall all be shent.° Run in here, good   *scolded*
young man; for God's sake, go into this closet. He will not stay
long.

[SIMPLE] *steps into the* [*closet*]

What, John Rugby! John! What, John, I say!

[*Enter* RUGBY]

35   [*Speaking loudly*] Go, John, go enquire for my master. I doubt°   *suspect*
he be not well, that he comes not home.   [*Exit* RUGBY]

[*Singing*] 'And down, down, adown-a' (*etc.*)

Enter Doctor CAIUS

CAIUS Vat is you sing? I do not like dese toys.° Pray you go and   *frivolous tunes*
vetch me in my closet *un boîtier vert*—a box, a green-a box. Do
40   intend° vat I speak? A green-a box.   *Do you hear*

MISTRESS QUICKLY Ay, forsooth, I'll fetch it you. [*Aside*] I am
glad he went not in himself. If he had found the young man,
he would have been horn-mad.°   *mad as a bull*

[*She goes to fetch the box*]

1.4 Location: Dr. Caius's house.   2. Superior coal brought by sea.
1. Restorative drink of hot milk curdled with wine or ale.   3. But he is as brave a man as any is around here.

CAIUS *Fe, fe, fe, fe! Ma foi, il fait fort chaud! Je m'en vais à la*
45   *cour. La grande affaire.*[4]

MISTRESS QUICKLY Is it this, sir?

CAIUS *Oui. Mets-le à ma pochette.*[5] *Dépêche*, quickly! Vere is
       dat knave Rugby?

MISTRESS QUICKLY What, John Rugby! John!

        Enter John [RUGBY]

50 RUGBY Here, sir.

CAIUS You are John Rugby, and you are Jack° Rugby. Come,   *(connotes knavery)*
       take-a your rapier, and come after my heel to the court.

RUGBY 'Tis ready, sir, here in the porch.

        [*He fetches the rapier*]

CAIUS By my trot,° I tarry too long. 'Od's me,° *qu'ai-j' oublié?*[6]   *troth / God save me*
55   Dere is some simples[7] in my closet dat I vill not for the varld I
       shall leave behind.

MISTRESS QUICKLY [*aside*] Ay me, he'll find the young man there,
       and be mad.

CAIUS [*discovering* SIMPLE] O *diable,*° *diable!* Vat is in my   *devil*
60   closet? Villainy, *larron!*° Rugby, my rapier!   *thief*

        [*He takes the rapier*]

MISTRESS QUICKLY Good master, be content.

CAIUS Wherefore shall I be content-a?

MISTRESS QUICKLY The young man is an honest man.

CAIUS What shall de honest man do in my closet? Dere is no
65   honest man dat shall come in my closet.

MISTRESS QUICKLY I beseech you, be not so phlegmatic.[8] Hear
       the truth of it. He came of an errand to me from Parson Hugh.

CAIUS Vell.

SIMPLE Ay, forsooth, to desire her to—

70 MISTRESS QUICKLY Peace, I pray you.

CAIUS Peace-a your tongue. [*To* SIMPLE] Speak-a your tale.

SIMPLE To desire this honest gentlewoman, your maid, to speak
       a good word to Mistress Anne Page for my master in the way of
       marriage.

75 MISTRESS QUICKLY This is all, indeed, la; but I'll ne'er put my
       finger in the fire an need not.[9]

CAIUS Sir Hugh send-a you?—Rugby, *baile*° me some paper.   *bring*

        [RUGBY *brings paper*]

       [*To* SIMPLE] Tarry you a little-a while.

        Doctor [CAIUS] *writes*

MISTRESS QUICKLY [*aside to* SIMPLE] I am glad he is so quiet. If
80   he had been throughly moved,° you should have heard him so   *really angered*
       loud and so melancholy.° But notwithstanding, man, I'll do   *(for "choleric"?)*
       your master what good I can. And the very yea and the no is,
       the French doctor, my master—I may call him my master, look
       you, for I keep his house, and I wash, wring, brew, bake, scour,
85   dress meat° and drink, make the beds, and do all myself—   *prepare food*

SIMPLE [*aside to* MISTRESS QUICKLY] 'Tis a great charge° to come   *burden; (sexual)*
       under one body's hand.

MISTRESS QUICKLY [*aside to* SIMPLE] Are you advised o' that?°   *You're telling me*
       You shall find it a great charge—and to be up early, and down

---

4. French: By my faith, it is very hot. I am going to
court—important business. (The French in this scene
is translated only when Caius fails to do so himself.)
5. Yes, put it in my pocket.
6. What have I forgotten?
7. Medicines composed of one herb or constituent;

unknown to Caius, also the character's name.
8. Cold and dull (Quickly's mistake for the opposite
temperament—choleric, or angry).
9. I'll never put myself in danger by getting involved if
I don't have to.

90 late. But notwithstanding, to tell you in your ear—I would have
    no words of it—my master himself is in love with Mistress
    Anne Page. But notwithstanding that, I know Anne's mind:
    that's neither here nor there.

    CAIUS [*giving the letter to* SIMPLE] You, jack'nape,° give-a this   idiot
95 letter to Sir Hugh. By Gar,° it is a shallenge. I will cut his troat   God
    in de Park, and I will teach a scurvy jackanape priest to meddle
    or make.° You may be gone. It is not good you tarry here. By   interfere
    Gar, I will cut all his two stones.° By Gar, he shall not have a   testicles
    stone to throw at his dog.   [*Exit* SIMPLE]
100 MISTRESS QUICKLY Alas, he speaks but for his friend.
    CAIUS It is no matter-a ver° dat. Do not you tell-a me dat I shall   for
    have Anne Page for myself ? By Gar, I vill kill de jack-priest.°   knave-priest
    And I have appointed mine Host of de Jarteer° to measure our   garter
    weapon.° By Gar, I will myself have Anne Page.   to referee
105 MISTRESS QUICKLY Sir, the maid loves you, and all shall be well.
    We must give folks leave to prate, what the goodyear!°   what the devil
    CAIUS Rugby, come to the court with me. [*To* MISTRESS
    QUICKLY] By Gar, if I have not Anne Page, I shall turn your
    head out of my door. Follow my heels, Rugby.
110 MISTRESS QUICKLY You shall have Anne°—   Anne; an
                         Exeunt Doctor [CAIUS *and* RUGBY]
    —ass-head of your own. No, I know Anne's mind for that.
    Never a woman in Windsor knows more of Anne's mind than
    I do, nor can do more than I do with her, I thank heaven.
    FENTON [*within*] Who's within there, ho!
115 MISTRESS QUICKLY Who's there, I trow?°—Come near° the   wonder / Enter
    house, I pray you.
                         Enter [*Master*] FENTON
    FENTON How now, good woman, how dost thou?
    MISTRESS QUICKLY The better that it pleases your good worship
    to ask.
120 FENTON What news? How does pretty Mistress Anne?
    MISTRESS QUICKLY In truth, sir, and she is pretty, and honest,°   chaste
    and gentle,° and one that is your friend. I can tell you that by   well-bred
    the way, I praise heaven for it.
    FENTON Shall I do any good,° thinkest thou? Shall I not lose my   make any progress
125 suit?
    MISTRESS QUICKLY Troth, sir, all is in His hands above. But not-
    withstanding, Master Fenton, I'll be sworn on a book° she loves   a Bible
    you. Have not your worship a wart above your eye?
    FENTON Yes, marry, have I. What of that?
130 MISTRESS QUICKLY Well, thereby hangs a tale. Good faith, it is
    such another Nan!¹—But I detest,° an honest maid as ever   (for "protest")
    broke bread.°—We had an hour's talk of that wart. I shall never   ate (proverbial)
    laugh but in that maid's company.—But indeed she is given
    too much to allicholy° and musing.—But for you—well—go   (for "melancholy")
135 to!°   come, come
    FENTON Well, I shall see her today. Hold, there's money for
    thee. Let me have thy voice in my behalf. If thou seest her
    before me, commend me.
    MISTRESS QUICKLY Will I? I'faith, that I will. And I will tell your
140 worship more of the wart the next time we have confidence,°   confide
    and of other wooers.

---

1. Nan (Anne) is such an extraordinary (or lively) one.

FENTON   Well, farewell. I am in great haste now.
MISTRESS QUICKLY   Farewell to your worship.   [*Exit* FENTON]
Truly, an honest gentleman; but Anne loves him not, for I
145 know Anne's mind as well as another° does.—Out upon't,[2]   *anyone else*
what have I forgot?   *Exit*

2.1

Enter MISTRESS PAGE, [*with*] *a letter*
MISTRESS PAGE   What, have I scaped love-letters in the holiday
time° of my beauty, and am I now a subject for them? Let me   *heyday*
see.
[*She reads*]
'Ask me no reason why I love you, for though Love use Reason
5 for his precision, he admits him not for his counsellor.[1] You
are not young; no more am I. Go to, then, there's sympathy.°   *agreement*
You are merry; so am I. Ha, ha, then, there's more sympathy.
You love sack,° and so do I. Would you desire better sympathy?   *Spanish wine*
Let it suffice thee, Mistress Page, at the least if the love of sol-
10 dier can suffice, that I love thee. I will not say "pity me"—'tis
not a soldier-like phrase—but I say "love me".
By me, thine own true knight,
By day or night
Or any kind of light,
15 With all his might
For thee to fight,
John Falstaff.'
What a Herod of Jewry° is this! O, wicked, wicked world! One   *bragging stage villain*
that is well-nigh worn to pieces with age, to show himself a
20 young gallant! What an unweighed° behaviour hath this Flem-   *unbalanced*
ish° drunkard picked, i'th' devil's name, out of my conversa-   *(proverbially drunk)*
tion,° that he dares in this manner assay° me? Why, he hath   *conduct / proposition*
not been thrice in my company. What should I say° to him? I   *can I have said*
was then frugal of my mirth, heaven forgive me. Why, I'll
25 exhibit° a bill in the Parliament for the putting down[2] of men.   *introduce*
O God, that I knew how to be revenged on him! For revenged
I will be, as sure as his guts are made of puddings.°   *gut-encased sausages*
Enter MISTRESS FORD
MISTRESS FORD   Mistress Page! By my faith, I was going to your
house.
30 MISTRESS PAGE   And by my faith, I was coming to you. You look
very ill.
MISTRESS FORD   Nay, I'll ne'er believe that: I have° to show to   *have something*
the contrary.
MISTRESS PAGE   Faith, but you do, in my mind.
35 MISTRESS FORD   Well, I do, then. Yet I say I could show you to
the contrary. O Mistress Page, give me some counsel.
MISTRESS PAGE   What's the matter, woman?
MISTRESS FORD   O woman, if it were not for one trifling respect,°   *consideration*
I could come to such honour!°   *rank*
40 MISTRESS PAGE   Hang the trifle, woman; take the honour. What
is it? Dispense with trifles. What is it?

2. Expression of dismay.
2.1 Location: Outside Page's house.
1. That is, Love employs Reason to make strong arguments, or preach, on Love's behalf (a "precision" was a

Puritan), but Love will not accept Reason's advice.
2. *putting down*: suppression; perhaps also an unconscious sexual suggestion that men are to be put down
for the purpose of intercourse.

MISTRESS FORD   If I would but go to hell for an eternal moment
or so, I could be knighted.[3]

MISTRESS PAGE   What? Thou liest! Sir Alice Ford? These knights
45 will hack,° and so thou shouldst not alter the article of thy   (military); (sexual?)
gentry.°   terms of your station

MISTRESS FORD   We burn daylight.° Here: read, read.   waste time
[*She gives* MISTRESS PAGE *a letter*]
Perceive how I might be knighted.
[MISTRESS PAGE *reads*]
I shall think the worse of fat men as long as I have an eye to
50 make difference of° men's liking.° And yet he would not swear,   judge among / looks
praised women's modesty, and gave such orderly and well-
behaved reproof to all uncomeliness° that I would have sworn   improper behavior
his disposition would have gone to° the truth of his words. But   accorded with
they do no more adhere and keep place together than the hun-
55 dred and fifty psalms to the tune of 'Greensleeves'.° What tem-   (popular love song)
pest, I trow, threw this whale, with so many tuns° of oil in his   casks
belly, ashore at Windsor? How shall I be revenged on him? I
think the best way were to entertain him with hope, till the
wicked fire of lust have melted him in his own grease. Did you
60 ever hear the like?

MISTRESS PAGE   Letter for letter, but that the name of Page and
Ford differs.
[*She gives* MISTRESS FORD *her letter*]
To thy great comfort in this mystery of ill opinions,[4] here's the
twin brother of thy letter. But let thine inherit first, for I protest
65 mine never shall. I warrant he hath a thousand of these letters,
writ with blank space for different names—sure, more, and
these are of the second edition. He will print them, out of
doubt°—for he cares not what he puts into the press[5] when he   undoubtedly
would put us two. I had rather be a giantess, and lie under
70 Mount Pelion.[6] Well, I will find you twenty lascivious turtles[7]
ere one chaste man.

MISTRESS FORD   Why, this is the very same: the very hand, the
very words. What doth he think of us?

MISTRESS PAGE   Nay, I know not. It makes me almost ready to
75 wrangle° with mine own honesty.° I'll entertain° myself like   argue / chastity / treat
one that I am not acquainted withal;° for, sure, unless he know   with
some strain in me that I know not myself, he would never have
boarded[8] me in this fury.

MISTRESS FORD   'Boarding' call you it? I'll be sure to keep him
80 above deck.

MISTRESS PAGE   So will I. If he come under my hatches, I'll
never to sea again. Let's be revenged on him. Let's appoint him
a meeting, give him a show of comfort° in his suit, and lead   encouragement
him on with a fine baited° delay till he hath pawned his horses   temptingly alluring
to mine Host of the Garter.[9]

MISTRESS FORD   Nay, I will consent to act any villainy against
him that may not sully the chariness° of our honesty. O that   scrupulous integrity

---

3. Sexually provided with a knight; dubbed a knight.
4. Falstaff's unfounded and hence mysterious belief that
the wives are promiscuous.
5. Printing press; what he presses sexually.
6. The giants were the Titans, who in Greek mythology
rebelled against the Olympian gods and were punished
by being buried under Mt. Pelion.

7. Turtledoves (proverbially true to their mates).
8. Nautical metaphor: accosted; sexually entered.
9. See note to 4.3.11. The plot does not develop in
exactly the way anticipated: "Brooke" supplies Sir John
with funds, so at first he doesn't have to pawn his
horses to raise money for his courting.

my husband saw this letter! It would give eternal food to his
jealousy.

Enter Master FORD [*with*] PISTOL, *and Master* PAGE
[*with*] NIM

90 MISTRESS PAGE   Why, look where he comes, and my goodman°   *husband*
too. He's as far from jealousy as I am from giving him cause;
and that, I hope, is an unmeasurable distance.

MISTRESS FORD   You are the happier woman.

MISTRESS PAGE   Let's consult together against this greasy knight.
95   Come hither.

[*They withdraw*]

FORD   Well, I hope it be not so.

PISTOL   Hope is a curtal° dog in some affairs.   *an unreliable*
Sir John affects° thy wife.   *loves; aims at*

FORD   Why, sir, my wife is not young.

100 PISTOL   He woos both high and low, both rich and poor,
Both young and old, one with another,° Ford.   *indiscriminately*
He loves the gallimaufry,° Ford. Perpend.°   *mixture / Consider*

FORD   Love my wife?

PISTOL   With liver° burning hot. Prevent,   *(seat of the passions)*
105   Or go thou like Sir Actaeon,[1] he,
With Ringwood[2] at thy heels.
O, odious is the name!

FORD   What name, sir?

PISTOL   The horn,° I say. Farewell.   *(of a cuckold)*
110   Take heed; have open eye; for thieves do foot° by night.   *walk; (sexual)*
Take heed ere summer comes, or cuckoo-birds[3] do sing.—
Away, Sir Corporal Nim!—Believe it, Page; he speaks sense.

Exit

FORD [*aside*]   I will be patient. I will find out° this.   *investigate*

NIM [*to* PAGE]   And this is true. I like not the humour of lying.
115   He hath wronged me in some humours. I should° have borne   *was supposed to*
the humoured letter to her; but I have a sword, and it shall bite
upon my necessity.° He loves your wife. There's the short and   *when I need it to*
the long.
My name is Corporal Nim. I speak and I avouch 'tis true.
120   My name is Nim, and Falstaff loves your wife. Adieu.
I love not the humour of bread and cheese.[4] Adieu.   *Exit*

PAGE [*aside*]   The humour of it, quoth a?° Here's a fellow frights   *he*
English out of his° wits.   *its*

FORD [*aside*]   I will seek out Falstaff.

125 PAGE [*aside*]   I never heard such a drawling, affecting° rogue. *affectedly speaking*

FORD [*aside*]   If I do find° it—well.   *ascertain*

PAGE [*aside*]   I will not believe such a Cathayan° though the   *Chinese; scoundrel*
priest o'th' town commended him for° a true man.   *as*

FORD [*aside*]   'Twas a good, sensible fellow. Well.

[MISTRESS PAGE *and* MISTRESS FORD *come forward*]

130 PAGE   How now, Meg?

MISTRESS PAGE   Whither go you, George? Hark you.

---

1. In Greek mythology, Actaeon was turned into a stag
and consequently hunted and killed by his own dogs. The
stag, in particular its horns, was considered an emblem of
the cuckold, the man whose wife was unfaithful to him.
2. Supposed name of one of Actaeon's dogs.
3. The cuckoo's habit of leaving its eggs to be hatched by
others made it the emblem of cuckolders and made the
sound of its call a taunt to cuckolds. Its song is prevalent
in late spring, after the mating season.
4. Nim's meager fare as Falstaff's retainer, or as now
unemployed; a popular name for wood sorrel, an edible
plant also known as cuckoo-bread or cuckoo-cheese—
hence an allusion to cuckolding.

[*They talk apart*]

MISTRESS FORD   How now, sweet Frank? Why art thou melan-
    choly?

FORD   I melancholy? I am not melancholy. Get you home, go.

135   MISTRESS FORD   Faith, thou hast some crotchets° in thy head   *strange notions*
    now. Will you go, Mistress Page?

MISTRESS PAGE   Have with you.°—You'll come to dinner, George?   *I'm coming*

        Enter MISTRESS QUICKLY

    [*Aside to* MISTRESS FORD] Look who comes yonder. She shall
    be our messenger to this paltry knight.

140   MISTRESS FORD [*aside to* MISTRESS PAGE]   Trust me, I thought on
    her. She'll fit it.°   *fit the part*

MISTRESS PAGE [*to* MISTRESS QUICKLY]   You are come to see my
    daughter Anne?

MISTRESS QUICKLY   Ay, forsooth; and I pray how does good Mis-

145   tress Anne?

MISTRESS PAGE   Go in with us and see. We have an hour's talk
    with you.

        Exeunt MISTRESS PAGE, MISTRESS FORD, *and*
                        [MISTRESS] QUICKLY

PAGE   How now, Master Ford?

FORD   You heard what this knave told me, did you not?

150   PAGE   Yes, and you heard what the other told me?

FORD   Do you think there is truth in them?

PAGE   Hang 'em, slaves! I do not think the knight would offer°   *attempt*
    it. But these that accuse him in his intent towards our wives are
    a yoke° of his discarded men—very rogues, now they be out of   *pair*

155   service.

FORD   Were they his men?

PAGE   Marry, were they.

FORD   I like it never the better for that. Does he lie° at the   *lodge*
    Garter?

160   PAGE   Ay, marry, does he. If he should intend this voyage toward
    my wife, I would turn her loose to him; and what he gets more
    of her than sharp words, let it lie on my head.[5]

FORD   I do not misdoubt° my wife, but I would be loath to turn   *mistrust*
    them together. A man may be too confident. I would have

165   nothing lie on my head. I cannot be thus satisfied.

        Enter [*the*] HOST [*of the Garter*]

PAGE   Look where my ranting Host of the Garter comes. There
    is either liquor in his pate or money in his purse when he looks
    so merrily.—How now, mine Host?

HOST   God bless you, bully rook,° God bless you! Thou'rt a gen-   *fine fellow*

170   tleman.

        Enter SHALLOW

    Cavaliero Justice,° I say!   *Gallant knight (comic)*

SHALLOW   I follow, mine Host, I follow.—Good even° and   *afternoon*
    twenty,° good Master Page. Master Page, will you go with us?   *twenty times over*
    We have sport in hand.

175   HOST   Tell him, Cavaliero Justice, tell him, bully rook.

SHALLOW   Sir, there is a fray to be fought between Sir Hugh,
    the Welsh priest, and Caius, the French doctor.

FORD   Good mine Host o'th' Garter, a word with you.

---

5. Let it be my responsibility (but Ford hears an allusion to the cuckold's horns).

HOST   What sayst thou, my bully rook?
          FORD *and the* HOST *talk* [*apart*]
180 SHALLOW [*to* PAGE]   Will you go with us to behold it? My merry
          Host hath had the measuring of their weapons,[6] and, I think,
          hath appointed them contrary° places. For, believe me, I hear   *different*
          the parson is no jester. Hark, I will tell you what our sport shall
          be.
              [*They talk apart*]
185 HOST [*to* FORD]   Hast thou° no suit against my knight, my guest   *Are you sure you have*
          cavaliero?
     FORD   None, I protest. But I'll give you a pottle of burnt° sack to   *two quarts of heated*
          give me recourse° to him and tell him my name is Brooke[7]—   *access*
          only for a jest.
190 HOST   My hand, bully. Thou shalt have egress and regress—said
          I well?—and thy name shall be Brooke. It is a merry knight.
          [*To* SHALLOW *and* PAGE] Will you go, mijn'heers?°   *gentlemen (Dutch)*
     SHALLOW   Have with you, mine Host.
     PAGE   I have heard the Frenchman hath good skill in his rapier.
195 SHALLOW   Tut, sir, I could have told you more. In these times
          you stand on distance—your passes, stoccados,[8] and I know not
          what. 'Tis the heart, Master Page; [*showing his rapier-passes*]
          'tis here,° 'tis here. I have seen the time with my long sword[9] I   *like this?*
          would have made you four tall° fellows skip like rats.   *valiant*
200 HOST   Here, boys; here, here! Shall we wag?°   *go*
     PAGE   Have with you. I had rather hear them scold than fight.
              Exeunt HOST, SHALLOW [*and* PAGE]
     FORD   Though Page be a secure° fool and stands so firmly on his   *an overconfident*
          wife's frailty, yet I cannot put off my opinion so easily. She was
          in his company at Page's house, and what they made° there I   *got up to*
205   know not. Well, I will look further into't; and I have a disguise
          to sound[1] Falstaff. If I find her honest, I lose° not my labour. If   *waste*
          she be otherwise, 'tis labour well bestowed.   *Exit*

2.2

Enter Sir John FALSTAFF *and* PISTOL
     FALSTAFF   I will not lend thee a penny.
     PISTOL   I will retort° the sum in equipage.°   *repay / equipment?*
     FALSTAFF   Not a penny.
     PISTOL [*drawing his sword*]   Why then, the world's mine oyster,
5   which I with sword will open.
     FALSTAFF   Not a penny. I have been content, sir, you should lay
          my countenance to pawn.[1] I have grated upon° my good friends   *harassed*
          for three reprieves for you and your coach-fellow° Nim, or else   *companion*
          you had looked through the grate° like a gemini° of baboons. I   *prison bars / pair*
10   am damned in hell for swearing to gentlemen my friends you
          were good soldiers and tall fellows. And when Mistress Bridget
          lost the handle of her fan,[2] I took't° upon mine honour thou   *swore*
          hadst it not.

6. Has been appointed referee.
7. Q: Brooke; F: Broome. "Brooke" was the family name
of Lord Cobham, who had objected to the characterization of his ancestor Oldcastle in *1 Henry IV.* The name
was changed to "Falstaff." Presumably, another such
objection led to the shift from "Brooke" to "Broome."
8. *In . . . stoccados*: Today, people rely on the distance
between duelists—lunges, thrusts.

9. Obsolete, heavy weapon.
1. To plumb the depths of.
2.2 Location: The Garter Inn.
1. Exploit my reputation (as surety for borrowing money,
etc.).
2. Fans were often made with handles of precious metal
or ivory.

PISTOL   Didst not thou share? Hadst thou not fifteen pence?

15   FALSTAFF   Reason,° you rogue, reason. Thinkest thou I'll endan-
ger my soul gratis?° At a word, hang no more about me. I am
no gibbet° for you. Go, a short knife and a throng, to your
manor of Pickt-hatch, go.³ You'll not bear a letter for me, you
rogue? You stand upon your honour? Why, thou unconfinable
20   baseness, it is as much as I can do to keep the terms of my
honour precise.° Ay, ay, I myself sometimes, leaving the fear of
God on the left hand,⁴ and hiding mine honour in my necessity, am fain to shuffle, to hedge, and to lurch;⁵ and yet you,
you rogue, will ensconce° your rags, your cat-a-mountain°
25   looks, your red-lattice° phrases, and your bold beating° oaths,
under the shelter of your honour! You will not do it, you?

PISTOL   [sheathing his sword]   I do relent. What wouldst thou
more of man?

          Enter ROBIN

ROBIN   Sir, here's a woman would speak with you.

30   FALSTAFF   Let her approach.

          Enter MISTRESS QUICKLY

MISTRESS QUICKLY   Give your worship good morrow.

FALSTAFF   Good morrow, goodwife.

MISTRESS QUICKLY   Not so, an't please your worship.

FALSTAFF   Good maid, then.

35   MISTRESS QUICKLY   I'll be sworn: as my mother was the first hour
I was born.

FALSTAFF   I do believe the swearer.⁶ What° with me?

MISTRESS QUICKLY   Shall I vouchsafe⁷ your worship a word or
two?

40   FALSTAFF   Two thousand, fair woman, and I'll vouchsafe thee
the hearing.

MISTRESS QUICKLY   There is one Mistress Ford, sir—I pray come
a little nearer this ways.

          [She draws FALSTAFF aside]

I myself dwell with Master Doctor Caius—

45   FALSTAFF   Well, on. Mistress Ford, you say.

MISTRESS QUICKLY   Your worship says very true. I pray your worship come a little nearer this ways.

FALSTAFF   I warrant thee nobody hears. Mine own people,° mine
own people.

50   MISTRESS QUICKLY   Are they so? God bless them and make them
His servants!

FALSTAFF   Well, Mistress Ford: what of her?

MISTRESS QUICKLY   Why, sir, she's a good creature. Lord, Lord,
your worship's a wanton! Well, heaven forgive you, and all of
55   us, I pray—

FALSTAFF   Mistress Ford; come, Mistress Ford.

MISTRESS QUICKLY   Marry, this is the short and the long of it. You
have brought her into such a canaries° as 'tis wonderful. The
best courtier of them all, when the court lay° at Windsor, could

---

Glosses (right margin):

15 With good reason
16 for free
17 gallows

21 pure

24 hide / wildcat
25 alehouse / battering?

37 What do you want

48 (Pistol and Robin)

57 (for "quandaries")
58 resided

---

3. Pickpockets used a short knife to cut purse strings in
a crowd. Pickt-hatch was an area of London infamous for
its thieves and prostitutes—hence an unlikely locale for
a "manor" (with a possible pun on "manner," or habits).
4. Disregarding the fear of God.
5. Am obliged to cheat, to be devious, and to steal.

6. Quickly thinks she is asserting her virginity, but by
confusing the proverbs "as good a maid as her mother"
and "as innocent as a newborn babe," she actually claims
the opposite. Falstaff expresses his belief in what she has
literally, but unintentionally, said.
7. Grant (error for "be vouchsafed, or granted, by").

60 never have brought her to such a canary. Yet there has been
knights, and lords, and gentlemen, with their coaches; I warrant you, coach after coach, letter after letter, gift after gift,
smelling so sweetly, all musk; and so rustling, I warrant you, in
silk and gold, and in such aligant° terms, and in such wine and   *(for "elegant")*
65 sugar° of the best and the fairest, that would have won any   *flattery*
woman's heart; and, I warrant you, they could never get an eye-
wink of her. I had myself twenty angels° given me this morn-   *coins (as a bribe)*
ing—but I defy° all angels, in any such sort, as they say, but in   *despise*
the way of honesty. And, I warrant you, they could never get
70 her so much as sip on a cup with the proudest of them all. And
yet there has been earls, nay, which is more, pensioners.⁸ But,
I warrant you, all is one with her.

FALSTAFF   But what says she to me? Be brief, my good she-
Mercury.°   *female messenger*

75 MISTRESS QUICKLY   Marry, she hath received your letter, for the
which she thanks you a thousand times, and she gives you to
notify° that her husband will be absence from his house   *note*
between ten and eleven.

FALSTAFF   Ten and eleven.

80 MISTRESS QUICKLY   Ay, forsooth, and then you may come and
see the picture, she says, that you wot° of. Master Ford, her   *know*
husband, will be from home. Alas, the sweet woman leads an
ill life with him. He's a very jealousy man. She leads a very
frampold° life with him, good heart.   *disagreeable*

85 FALSTAFF   Ten and eleven. Woman, commend me to her. I will
not fail her.

MISTRESS QUICKLY   Why, you say well. But I have another mes-
senger° to your worship. Mistress Page hath her hearty com-   *(for "message")*
mendations to you too; and, let me tell you in your ear, she's
90 as fartuous° a civil modest wife, and one, I tell you, that will   *(for "virtuous")*
not miss you° morning nor evening prayer, as any is in Wind-   *miss*
sor, whoe'er be the other; and she bade me tell your worship
that her husband is seldom from home, but she hopes there
will come a time. I never knew a woman so dote upon a man.
95 Surely I think you have charms,° la; yes, in truth.   *magic powers*

FALSTAFF   Not I, I assure thee. Setting the attraction of my good
parts° aside, I have no other charms.   *(sexual capacities)*

MISTRESS QUICKLY   Blessing on your heart for't!

FALSTAFF   But I pray thee tell me this: has Ford's wife and Page's
100 wife acquainted each other how they love me?

MISTRESS QUICKLY   O God no, sir; that were a jest indeed! They
have not so little grace, I hope. That were a trick indeed! But
Mistress Page would desire you to send her your little page of
all loves.° Her husband has a marvellous infection to⁹ the little   *for love's sake*
105 page; and, truly, Master Page is an honest man. Never a wife
in Windsor leads a better life than she does. Do what she will;
say what she will; take all, pay all; go to bed when she list; rise
when she list;° all is as she will. And, truly, she deserves it, for   *wants*
if there be a kind woman in Windsor, she is one. You must
110 send her your page, no remedy.

FALSTAFF   Why, I will.

MISTRESS QUICKLY   Nay, but do so, then; and, look you, he may

---

8. Gentlemen of the royal bodyguard.   9. For "affection for."

come and go between you both. And in any case have a nay-
word,° that you may know one another's mind, and the boy   *password*
115   never need to understand anything—for 'tis not good that
children should know any wickedness. Old folks, you know,
have discretion, as they say, and know the world.

FALSTAFF   Fare thee well. Commend me to them both. There's
my purse; I am yet thy debtor.—Boy, go along with this
120   woman.   *Exeunt* MISTRESS QUICKLY [*and* ROBIN]
[*Aside*] This news distracts° me.   *bewilders (with joy)*

PISTOL [*aside*]   This punk° is one of Cupid's carriers.°   *whore / messengers*
Clap on° more sails! Pursue! Up with your fights!°   *Set / fighting screens*
Give fire! She is my prize,° or ocean whelm° them all! [*Exit*] *booty/overwhelm*

125   FALSTAFF   Sayst thou so, old Jack?° Go thy ways! I'll make more *(addressing himself)*
of thy old body than I have done. Will they yet look after° thee?   *desire*
Wilt thou, after the expense of so much money, be now a
gainer? Good body, I thank thee. Let them say 'tis grossly°   *crudely*
done; so it be fairly° done, no matter.   *successfully*

                    Enter BARDOLPH [*with sack*]
130   BARDOLPH   Sir John, there's one Master Brooke below would
fain° speak with you and be acquainted with you, and hath sent   *be pleased to*
your worship a morning's draught of sack.

FALSTAFF   Brooke is his name?

BARDOLPH   Ay, sir.

135   FALSTAFF   Call him in. [*Drinking sack*] Such Brookes are welcome to me, that o'erflows such liquor.[1] [*Exit* BARDOLPH]
Aha, Mistress Ford and Mistress Page, have I encompassed°   *outwitted*
you? [*Drinking*] Go to. Via!°   *On with it*

              Enter [BARDOLPH, *and Master*] FORD *disguised like*
                    Brooke

FORD   God bless you, sir.

140   FALSTAFF   And you, sir. Would you speak with me?

FORD   I make bold to press with so little preparation° upon you. *prior notice*

FALSTAFF   You're welcome. What's your will? [*To* BARDOLPH]
Give us leave, drawer.°   [*Exit* BARDOLPH]   *Leave us, bartender*

FORD   Sir, I am a gentleman that have spent much. My name is
145   Brooke.

FALSTAFF   Good Master Brooke, I desire more acquaintance of
you.

FORD   Good Sir John, I sue for yours—not to charge you,° for I   *(with an expense)*
must let you understand I think myself in better plight for a
150   lender than you are;[2] the which hath something° emboldened   *somewhat*
me to this unseasoned° intrusion; for they say if money go   *ill-timed*
before, all ways do lie open.

FALSTAFF   Money is a good soldier, sir, and will on.

FORD   Troth, and I have a bag of money here troubles me. If you
155   will help to bear it, Sir John, take half, or all, for easing me of
the carriage.°   *burden of carrying it*

FALSTAFF   Sir, I know not how I may deserve to be your porter.

FORD   I will tell you, sir, if you will give me the hearing.

FALSTAFF   Speak, good Master Brooke. I shall be glad to be your
160   servant.

FORD   Sir, I hear you are a scholar—I will be brief with you—
and you have been a man long known to me, though I had

---

1. See the Textual Note for the significance of this   2. I am more able to undertake a risk, an obligation, or
wordplay.   a pledge ("plight") as a lender than you are.

never so good means as desire to make myself acquainted with
you. I shall discover° a thing to you wherein I must very much   *reveal*
165 lay open mine own imperfection; but, good Sir John, as you
have one eye upon my follies, as you hear them unfolded, turn
another into the register° of your own, that I may pass with a   *catalog*
reproof the easier, sith° you yourself know how easy it is to be   *since*
such an offender.
170 FALSTAFF Very well, sir, proceed.
FORD There is a gentlewoman in this town; her husband's name
is Ford.
FALSTAFF Well, sir.
FORD I have long loved her, and, I protest° to you, bestowed   *declare*
175 much on her, followed her with a doting observance,°   *attentiveness*
engrossed° opportunities to meet her, fee'd° every slight occa-   *collected / purchased*
sion that could but niggardly give me sight of her; not only
bought many presents to give her, but have given largely° to   *bountifully*
many to know what she would have given.° Briefly, I have pur-   *would like to be given*
180 sued her as love hath pursued me, which hath been on the
wing of all occasions. But, whatsoever I have merited, either in
my mind or in my means, meed° I am sure I have received   *recompense*
none, unless experience be a jewel. That I have purchased at
an infinite rate,° and that hath taught me to say this: *cost*
185 'Love like a shadow flies when substance love pursues,
Pursuing that that flies, and flying what pursues.'³
FALSTAFF Have you received no promise of satisfaction at her
hands?
FORD Never.
190 FALSTAFF Have you importuned her to such a purpose?
FORD Never.
FALSTAFF Of what quality was your love then?
FORD Like a fair house built on another man's ground, so that I
have lost my edifice by mistaking the place where I erected it.
195 FALSTAFF To what purpose have you unfolded this to me?
FORD When I have told you that, I have told you all. Some say
that though she appear honest° to me, yet in other places she   *chaste*
enlargeth° her mirth so far that there is shrewd° construction   *gives rein to / malicious*
made of her. Now, Sir John, here is the heart of my purpose.
200 You are a gentleman of excellent breeding, admirable dis-
course, of great admittance,⁴ authentic in your place° and per-   *of respectable rank*
son, generally allowed° for your many warlike, court-like, and   *universally approved*
learned preparations.°   *accomplishments*
FALSTAFF O sir!
205 FORD Believe it, for you know it. There is money.
     [*He offers money*]
Spend it, spend it; spend more; spend all I have; only give me
so much of your time in exchange of it as to lay an amiable°   *amorous*
siege to the honesty of this Ford's wife. Use your art of wooing,
win her to consent to you. If any man may, you may as soon as
210 any.
FALSTAFF Would it apply well to the vehemency of your
affection that I should win what you would enjoy? Methinks
you prescribe to yourself very preposterously.
FORD O, understand my drift. She dwells so securely° on the   *relies so confidently*

3. *Love . . . what pursues:* Like a shadow, love pursues a   4. Having qualities ensuring ready admittance into
physical object ("substance")/person/money that flees,   high society.
and flees a physical object/person/money that pursues.

215 excellency of her honour that the folly of my soul dares not
present itself. She is too bright to be looked against.° Now,   at
could I come to her with any detection° in my hand, my desires   accusation
had instance° and argument to commend themselves. I could   precedent
drive her then from the ward° of her purity, her reputation, her   defense
220 marriage vow, and a thousand other her° defences which now   of her
are too too strongly embattled against me. What say you to't,
Sir John?

FALSTAFF   Master Brooke, I will first make bold with your money.
[*He takes the money*]
Next, give me your hand.
[*He takes his hand*]
225 And last, as I am a gentleman, you shall, if you will, enjoy
Ford's wife.

FORD   O, good sir!

FALSTAFF   I say you shall.

FORD   Want° no money, Sir John, you shall want none.   Lack

230 FALSTAFF   Want no Mistress Ford, Master Brooke, you shall
want none. I shall be with her, I may tell you, by her own
appointment. Even as you came in to me, her spokesmate, or
go-between, parted from me. I say I shall be with her between
ten and eleven, for at that time the jealous rascally knave her
235 husband will be forth.° Come you to me at night; you shall   away
know how I speed.°   do

FORD   I am blessed in your acquaintance. Do you know Ford,
sir?

FALSTAFF   Hang him, poor cuckoldly knave, I know him not. Yet
240 I wrong him to call him poor. They say the jealous wittolly[5]
knave hath masses of money, for the° which his wife seems to   on account of
me well favoured.° I will use her as the key of the cuckoldly   good-looking
rogue's coffer, and there's my harvest-home.°   profitable harvest

FORD   I would you knew Ford, sir, that you might avoid him if
245 you saw him.

FALSTAFF   Hang him, mechanical salt-butter[6] rogue! I will stare
him out of his wits. I will awe him with my cudgel; it shall
hang like a meteor° o'er the cuckold's horns. Master Brooke,   an (ill-omened) comet
thou shalt know I will predominate over the peasant, and thou
250 shalt lie with his wife. Come to me soon at night. Ford's a
knave, and I will aggravate his style:[7] thou, Master Brooke, shalt
know him for knave and cuckold. Come to me soon at night.
                                                                          Exit

FORD   What a damned epicurean° rascal is this! My heart is   sensual
ready to crack with impatience. Who says this is improvident°   baseless
255 jealousy? My wife hath sent to him, the hour is fixed, the match
is made. Would any man have thought this? See the hell of
having a false woman! My bed shall be abused, my coffers ran-
sacked, my reputation gnawn at, and I shall not only receive
this villainous wrong, but stand under the adoption of abomi-
260 nable terms, and by him that does me this wrong. Terms!
Names! 'Amaimon' sounds well, 'Lucifer' well, 'Barbason' well;
yet they are devils' additions,° the names of fiends. But 'cuck-   names
old', 'wittol'! 'Cuckold'—the devil himself hath not such a

---

5. Willingly cuckolded.
6. *mechanical salt-butter*: lower-class cheap-living;
Flemish salt butter was less expensive than domestic

butter.
7. Increase (irritate) his titles (by adding the title of
"cuckold" to Ford's name).

name. Page is an ass, a secure ass. He will trust his wife, he will
265   not be jealous. I will rather trust a Fleming with my butter,
Parson Hugh the Welshman with my cheese, an Irishman with
my aqua-vitae° bottle, or a thief to walk my ambling gelding,   *whiskey*
than my wife with herself. Then she plots, then she ruminates,
then she devises; and what they think in their hearts they may
270   effect, they will break their hearts but they will effect. God be
praised for my jealousy! Eleven o'clock the hour. I will prevent
this, detect my wife, be revenged on Falstaff, and laugh at Page.
I will about it. Better three hours too soon than a minute too
late. God's my life: cuckold, cuckold, cuckold!   *Exit*

2.3

Enter Doctor CAIUS *and his man [John]* RUGBY [*with rapiers*]

CAIUS   Jack Rugby!
RUGBY   Sir.
CAIUS   Vat is the clock, Jack?
RUGBY   'Tis past the hour, sir, that Sir Hugh promised to meet.
5 CAIUS   By Gar, he has save his soul dat he is no come; he has
pray his Pible well dat he is no come. By Gar, Jack Rugby, he
is dead already if he be come.
RUGBY   He is wise, sir, he knew your worship would kill him if
he came.
10 CAIUS[*drawing his rapier*]   By Gar, de herring is no dead so¹ as
I vill kill him. Take your rapier, Jack. I vill tell you how I vill kill
him.
RUGBY   Alas, sir, I cannot fence.
CAIUS   Villainy,° take your rapier.   (*for "Villain"*)
15 RUGBY   Forbear: here's company.
        [CAIUS *sheathes his rapier.*]
        Enter [the] HOST [*of the Garter, Justice*] SHALLOW, [*Master*] PAGE, *and [Master]* SLENDER
HOST   God bless thee, bully Doctor.
SHALLOW   God save you, Master Doctor Caius.
PAGE   Now, good Master Doctor.
SLENDER   Give you good morrow, sir.
20 CAIUS   Vat be all you, one, two, tree, four, come for?
HOST   To see thee fight, to see thee foin,° to see thee traverse,²   *thrust*
to see thee here, to see thee there; to see thee pass thy punto,
thy stock, thy reverse, thy distance, thy montant.³ Is he dead,
my Ethiopian?⁴ Is he dead, my Francisco?° Ha, bully? What   *Frenchman*
25 says my Aesculapius, my Galen, my heart of elder,⁵ ha? Is he
dead, bully stale?⁶ Is he dead?
CAIUS   By Gar, he is de coward jack-priest° of de vorld. He is not   *knave-priest*
show his face.
HOST   Thou art a Castalian King Urinal,⁷ Hector of Greece, my
30 boy.

2.3 Location: Windsor Park (east of Windsor).
1. Not so dead (from the proverbial simile "dead as a her-ring").
2. Move backward and forward.
3. *pass . . . montant:* use your thrust with the sword point, your thrust, your backhand sword blow, your skill in keeping at the right distance, your upward thrust.
4. Dark-skinned person.
5. Replacing "heart of oak"; as the elder is a soft, low-

growing tree, this is an insult disguised as a compliment. Aesculapius was the classical god of medicine. Galen was a physician of ancient Greece.
6. Decoy or dupe; wine or urine (often used for medical diagnosis).
7. Urine bottle. *Castalian:* of the spring Castalia, which was sacred to the Muses; "cast-stale-ian" (one who diagnoses by inspecting urine; Castilian (Spanish).

CAIUS I pray you bear witness that me have stay six or seven, two, tree hours for him, and he is no come.

SHALLOW He is the wiser man, Master Doctor. He is a curer of souls, and you a curer of bodies. If you should fight you go
35 against the hair° of your professions. Is it not true, Master Page?   *grain*

PAGE Master Shallow, you have yourself been a great fighter, though now a man of peace.

SHALLOW Bodykins,° Master Page, though I now be old and of   *By God's dear body*
the peace, if I see a sword out my finger itches to make one.°   *join in*
40 Though we are justices and doctors and churchmen, Master Page, we have some salt° of our youth in us. We are the sons of   *vigor*
women, Master Page.

PAGE 'Tis true, Master Shallow.

SHALLOW It will be found so, Master Page.—Master Doctor
45 Caius, I am come to fetch you home. I am sworn of the peace. You have showed yourself a wise physician, and Sir Hugh hath shown himself a wise and patient churchman. You must go with me, Master Doctor.

HOST Pardon, guest° Justice. [*To* CAIUS] A word, Monsieur   *(at the Host's inn)*
50 Mockwater.⁸

CAIUS Mockvater? Vat is dat?

HOST Mockwater, in our English tongue, is valour, bully.

CAIUS By Gar, then I have as much mockvater as de Englishman. Scurvy jack-dog° priest! By Gar, me vill cut his   *mongrel*
55 ears.

HOST He will clapper-claw thee tightly,° bully.   *maul thee soundly*

CAIUS Clapper-de-claw? Vat is dat?

HOST That is, he will make thee amends.

CAIUS By Gar, me do look° he shall clapper-de-claw me, for, by   *anticipate*
60 Gar, me vill have it.

HOST And I will provoke him to't, or let him wag.°   *run away*

CAIUS Me tank you for dat.

HOST And moreover, bully—[*Aside to the others*] But first, master guest and Master Page, and eke° Cavaliero Slender, go   *also*
65 you through the town to Frogmore.°   *village near Windsor*

PAGE Sir Hugh is there, is he?

HOST He is there. See what humour he is in, and I will bring the Doctor about by the fields. Will it do well?

SHALLOW We will do it.

70 PAGE, SHALLOW, *and* SLENDER Adieu, good Master Doctor.

Exeunt [PAGE, SHALLOW, *and* SLENDER]

CAIUS[*drawing his rapier*] By Gar, me vill kill de priest, for he speak for a jackanape° to Anne Page.   *on behalf of an idiot*

HOST Let him die. Sheathe thy impatience; throw cold water on thy choler. Go about the fields with me through Frogmore. I
75 will bring thee where Mistress Anne Page is, at a farmhouse a-feasting; and thou shalt woo her. Cried game?⁹ Said I well?

CAIUS [*sheathing his rapier*] By Gar, me dank you vor dat. By Gar, I love you, and I shall procure-a you de good guest: de earl, de knight, de lords, de gentlemen, my patiences.°   *(for "patients")*

80 HOST For the which I will be thy adversary¹ toward Anne Page. Said I well?

8. Implying that Caius's diagnoses from urine are quackery, or that Caius is sterile (water being semen) and so lacking in valor.

9. (Did I say) the chase is on?
1. The Host again makes a joke at the expense of Caius, who understands "adversary" as "advocate."

CAIUS   By Gar, 'tis good. Vell said.
HOST   Let us wag, then.
CAIUS   Come at my heels, Jack Rugby.   *Exeunt*

3.1

Enter Sir Hugh EVANS [*with a rapier, and bearing a
book*] *and* SIMPLE [*bearing Evans's gown*]

EVANS   I pray you now, good Master Slender's servingman, and
friend Simple by your name, which way have you looked for
Master Caius, that calls himself Doctor of Physic?°   *medicine*
SIMPLE   Marry, sir, the Petty Ward, the Park Ward,[1] every way;
5   old Windsor way,[2] and every way but the town way.
EVANS   I most fehemently desire you you will also look that way.
SIMPLE   I will, sir.   [*Exit*]
EVANS [*opening the book*]°   Jeshu pless me, how full of cholers°   *(a Bible?)* / *anger*
I am, and trempling of mind! I shall be glad if he have deceived
10   me. How melancholies I am! I will knog° his urinals about his   *knock*
knave's costard° when I have good opportunities for the 'ork.°   *head* / *work*
Pless my soul!—
[*Singing*]
          To shallow rivers, to whose falls
          Melodious birds sings madrigals.
15   There will we make our peds of roses,
          And a thousand fragrant posies.[3]
          To shallow—
Mercy on me! I have a great dispositions to cry.—
[*Singing*]
          Melodious birds sing madrigals.—
20   When as I sat in Pabylon[4]—
          And a thousand vagram° posies.   *vagrant*
          To shallow *(etc.)*
          [*Enter* SIMPLE]
SIMPLE   Yonder he° is coming. This way, Sir Hugh.   *(Caius)*
EVANS   He's welcome.
25   [*Singing*] 'To shallow rivers to whose falls—' God prosper the
right! What weapons is° he?   *has*
SIMPLE   No weapons, sir. There comes my master, Master Shallow, and another gentleman, from Frogmore, over the stile this
way.
30   EVANS   Pray you give me my gown—or else keep it in your arms.
          [*He reads.*]
          Enter [*Justice*] SHALLOW, [*Master*] SLENDER, *and* [*Mas-
          ter*] PAGE
SHALLOW   How now, Master Parson? Good morrow, good Sir
Hugh. Keep a gamester from the dice and a good student from
his book, and it is wonderful.
SLENDER [*aside*]   Ah, sweet Anne Page!
35   PAGE   God save you, good Sir Hugh.
EVANS   God pless you from° his mercy sake, all of you.   *for*

3.1 Location: In fields near Frogmore.
1. Toward the Little Park and the Great Park.
2. Toward Old Windsor (a village near Shakespeare's
Windsor).
3. Somewhat misrecalled lines from "Come live with me

and be my love," a song by Christopher Marlowe.
4. Evans inserts the first line of a metrical version of
Psalm 137 (with "I" for "we"), which describes the weeping of the exiled Israelites.

SHALLOW   What, the sword and the Word?° Do you study them
both, Master Parson?   the Bible

PAGE   And youthful still: in your doublet and hose⁵ this raw,
40   rheumatic day!

EVANS   There is reasons and causes for it.

PAGE   We are come to you to do a good office, Master Parson.

EVANS   Fery well. What is it?

PAGE   Yonder is a most reverend gentleman, who, belike° having   probably
45   received wrong by some person, is at most odds with his own
gravity and patience that ever you saw.

SHALLOW   I have lived fourscore years and upward; I never heard
a man of his place, gravity, and learning so wide of his own
respect.⁶

50   EVANS   What is he?

PAGE   I think you know him: Master Doctor Caius, the
renowned French physician.

EVANS   Got's will and his passion of my heart! I had as lief° you   I had rather
would tell me of a mess of pottage.°   thick soup

55   PAGE   Why?

EVANS   He has no more knowledge in Hibbocrates⁷ and Galen,
and he is a knave besides—a cowardly knave as you would
desires to be acquainted withal.

PAGE [to SHALLOW]   I warrant you, he's the man should fight
60   with him.

SLENDER [aside]   O sweet Anne Page!

SHALLOW   It appears so by his weapons.

>   Enter the HOST [of the Garter], Doctor CAIUS, and John
>   RUGBY

Keep them asunder—here comes Doctor Caius.

>   [EVANS and CAIUS draw and] offer to fight

PAGE   Nay, good Master Parson, keep in your weapon.

65   SHALLOW   So do you, good Master Doctor.

HOST   Disarm them and let them question.° Let them keep their   debate
limbs whole, and hack our English.

>   [SHALLOW and PAGE take Caius's and Evans's rapiers]

CAIUS [to EVANS]   I pray you let-a me speak a word with your ear.
Wherefore vill you not meet-a me?

70   EVANS [aside to CAIUS]   Pray you use your patience. [Aloud] In
good time!

CAIUS   By Gar, you are de coward, de jack-dog, john-ape.

EVANS [aside to CAIUS]   Pray you let us not be laughing-stocks to
other men's humours. I desire you in friendship, and I will one
75   way or other make you amends. [Aloud] By Jeshu, I will knog
your urinal about your knave's cogscomb.°   coxcomb; head

CAIUS   Diable!° Jack Rugby, mine Host de Jarteer, have I not stay   Devil
for him to kill him? Have I not, at de place I did appoint?

EVANS   As I am a Christians soul, now look you, this is the place
80   appointed. I'll be judgement° by mine Host of the Garter.   judged

HOST   Peace, I say, Gallia and Gaul,° French and Welsh, soul-   Wales and France
curer and body-curer.

CAIUS   Ay, dat is very good, excellent.

HOST   Peace, I say. Hear mine Host of the Garter. Am I politic?°   devious

---

5. Close-fitting jacket and tights—that is, without a
cloak.

6. Indifferent to his own good reputation.

7. Hippocrates (ancient Greek physician).

85 Am I subtle?° Am I a Machiavel?[8] Shall I lose my doctor? No,   *crafty*
he gives me the potions and the motions. Shall I lose my par-
son, my priest, my Sir Hugh? No, he gives me the Proverbs and
the No-verbs.[9] [*To* CAIUS] Give me thy hand terrestrial°—so.   *(as bodily curer)*
[*To* EVANS] Give me thy hand celestial—so. Boys of art,° I have   *learning*
90 deceived you both, I have directed you to wrong places. Your
hearts are mighty, your skins are whole, and let burnt sack be
the issue.° [*To* SHALLOW *and* PAGE] Come, lay their swords to   *outcome*
pawn.[1] [*To* CAIUS *and* EVANS] Follow me, lads of peace, follow,
follow, follow.   *Exit*
95 SHALLOW   Afore God, a mad host! Follow, gentlemen, follow.
                      [*Exeunt* SHALLOW *and* PAGE]
SLENDER [*aside*]   O sweet Anne Page!   [*Exit*]
CAIUS   Ha, do I perceive dat? Have you make-a de sot° of us, ha,   *fool*
ha?
EVANS   This is well: he has made us his vlouting-stog.[2] I desire
100 you that we may be friends, and let us knog our prains together
to be revenge on this same scall,° scurvy, cogging companion,°   *scabby / cheating rogue*
the Host of the Garter.
CAIUS   By Gar, with all my heart. He promise to bring me where
is Anne Page. By Gar, he deceive me too.
105 EVANS   Well, I will smite his noddles.° Pray you follow.   *Exeunt*   *head*

3.2

[*Enter*] ROBIN, [*followed by*] MISTRESS PAGE
MISTRESS PAGE   Nay, keep your way,° little gallant. You were   *go on*
wont° to be a follower,° but now you are a leader. Whether had   *accustomed / servant*
you rather,° lead mine eyes, or eye your master's heels?   *Which would you prefer*
ROBIN   I had rather, forsooth, go before you like a man than fol-
·5 low him° like a dwarf.   *(Falstaff)*
MISTRESS PAGE   O, you are a flattering boy! Now I see you'll be
a courtier.
          Enter Master FORD
FORD   Well met, Mistress Page. Whither go you?
MISTRESS PAGE   Truly, sir, to see your wife. Is she at home?
10 FORD   Ay, and as idle as she may hang together, for want[1] of
company. I think if your husbands were dead you two would
marry.
MISTRESS PAGE   Be sure of that—two other husbands.
FORD   Where had you this pretty weathercock?°   *(Robin)*
15 MISTRESS PAGE   I cannot tell what the dickens his name is my
husband had him of.°—What do you call your knight's name,   *got him from*
sirrah?
ROBIN   Sir John Falstaff.
FORD   Sir John Falstaff?
20 MISTRESS PAGE   He, he; I can never hit on's name. There is such
a league° between my goodman° and he! Is your wife at home   *friendship / husband*
indeed?
FORD   Indeed she is.

8. Follower of Niccolò Machiavelli, Italian political theorist reviled by the Elizabethans, who was held to epito-
mize the "politic" and "subtle."
9. Prohibitions; verbal errors (the Welshman's misuse of
standard English).

1. As a pledge; because they are not needed.
2. Flouting-stock (laughingstock).
3.2 Location: A street in Windsor.
1. And as bored as she can stand to be without falling
apart, for lack.

MISTRESS PAGE   By your leave, sir, I am sick till I see her.

[*Exeunt* ROBIN *and* MISTRESS PAGE]

25   FORD   Has Page any brains? Hath he any eyes? Hath he any
thinking? Sure they sleep; he hath no use of them. Why, this
boy will carry a letter twenty mile, as easy as a cannon will
shoot point-blank twelve score.[2] He pieces out° his wife's incli-   increases
nation; he gives her folly motion and advantage.[3] And now
30   she's going to my wife, and Falstaff's boy with her. A man may
hear this shower sing in the wind.° And Falstaff's boy with her.   hear trouble brewing
Good plots—they are laid; and our revolted° wives share dam-   disloyal
nation together. Well, I will take him;° then torture my wife,   catch him by surprise
pluck the borrowed veil of modesty from the so-seeming Mis-
35   tress Page, divulge° Page himself for a secure° and wilful reveal / an overconfident
Actaeon,° and to these violent proceedings all my neighbours   cuckold
shall cry aim.°   shall applaud

[*Clock strikes*]

The clock gives me my cue, and my assurance bids me search.
There I shall find Falstaff. I shall be rather praised for this than
40   mocked, for it is as positive as the earth is firm that Falstaff is
there. I will go.

Enter Master PAGE, [*Justice*] SHALLOW, [*Master*] SLEN-
DER, [*the*] HOST [*of the Garter*], *Sir Hugh* EVANS, *Doctor*
CAIUS, *and* [*John* RUGBY]

SHALLOW, PAGE, etc.   Well met, Master Ford.

FORD [*aside*]   By my faith, a good knot!° [*To them*] I have good   group (ironic?)
cheer° at home, and I pray you all go with me.   food and drink

45   SHALLOW   I must excuse myself, Master Ford.

SLENDER   And so must I, sir. We have appointed to dine with
Mistress Anne, and I would not break with° her for more   break my word to
money than I'll speak of.

SHALLOW   We have lingered about° a match between Anne Page   delayed in concluding
50   and my cousin Slender, and this day we shall have our answer.

SLENDER   I hope I have your good will, father Page.

PAGE   You have, Master Slender: I stand wholly for you. [*To*
CAIUS] But my wife, Master Doctor, is for you altogether.

CAIUS   Ay, be Gar, and de maid is love-a me. My nursh-a°   housekeeper
55   Quickly tell me so mush.

HOST [*to* PAGE]   What say you to young Master Fenton? He
capers,° he dances, he has eyes of youth; he writes verses, he   leaps in dancing
speaks holiday,° he smells April and May. He will carry't,° he   gaily / succeed
will carry't; 'tis in his buttons° he will carry't.   youth

60   PAGE   Not by my consent, I promise you. The gentleman is of
no having.° He kept company with the wild Prince[4] and Poins.   property
He is of too high a region;° he knows too much. No, he shall   rank
not knit a knot in° his fortunes with the finger of my substance.° strengthen / wealth
If he take her, let him take her simply:° the wealth I have waits   without dowry
65   on my consent, and my consent goes not that way.

FORD   I beseech you heartily, some of you go home with me to
dinner. Besides your cheer, you shall have sport: I will show
you a monster.° Master Doctor, you shall go. So shall you, Mas-   (Falstaff)
ter Page, and you, Sir Hugh.

---

2. Will shoot straight 240 yards.
3. He gives her lust ("folly") prompting and opportunity.
4. Prince Hal (the future Henry V) and Poins (line 61)

in *1* and *2 Henry IV*—actually Falstaff's, rather than Fenton's, companions.

70 SHALLOW Well, God be with you! [*Aside to* SLENDER] We shall
have the freer wooing at Master Page's.

Exeunt SHALLOW *and* SLENDER

CAIUS Go home, John Rugby; I come anon. [*Exit* RUGBY]

HOST Farewell, my hearts. I will to my honest knight Falstaff,
and drink canary° with him. *Exit*   *wine*

75 FORD [*aside*] I think I shall drink in pipe-wine first with him: I'll
make him dance.⁵ [*To* PAGE, CAIUS, *and* EVANS] Will you go,
gentles?°   *gentlemen*

PAGE, CAIUS, *and* EVANS Have with you° to see this monster.   *We are coming*

Exeunt

3.3

Enter MISTRESS FORD *and* MISTRESS PAGE

MISTRESS FORD What, John! What, Robert!

MISTRESS PAGE Quickly, quickly! Is the buck-basket°—   *laundry basket*

MISTRESS FORD I warrant.°—What, Robert, I say!   *I'm sure it is*

MISTRESS PAGE Come, come, come!

Enter [JOHN *and* ROBERT,] *with a buck-basket*

5 MISTRESS FORD Here, set it down.

MISTRESS PAGE Give your men the charge.° We must be brief.   *instructions*

MISTRESS FORD Marry, as I told you before, John and Robert, be
ready here hard by in the brew-house; and when I suddenly
call you, come forth, and without any pause or staggering take
10 this basket on your shoulders. That done, trudge with it in all
haste, and carry it among the whitsters° in Datchet Mead,¹ and   *linen bleachers*
there empty it in the muddy ditch close by the Thames' side.

MISTRESS PAGE [*to* JOHN *and* ROBERT] You will do it?

MISTRESS FORD I ha' told them over and over; they lack no direc-
15 tion.°—Be gone, and come when you are called.   *instructions*

Exeunt [JOHN *and* ROBERT]

Enter ROBIN

MISTRESS PAGE Here comes little Robin.

MISTRESS FORD How now, my eyas-musket,° what news with   *young sparrow hawk*
you?

ROBIN My master Sir John is come in at your back door, Mis-
20 tress Ford, and requests your company.

MISTRESS PAGE You little Jack-a-Lent,° have you been true to us?   *Lenten puppet*

ROBIN Ay, I'll be sworn. My master knows not of your being
here, and hath threatened to put me into everlasting liberty if I
tell you of it;° for he swears he'll turn me away.²   *(Falstaff's visit)*

25 MISTRESS PAGE Thou'rt a good boy. This secrecy of thine shall
be a tailor to thee, and shall make thee a new doublet and
hose.—I'll go hide me.

MISTRESS FORD Do so. [*To* ROBIN] Go tell thy master I am
alone. [*Exit* ROBIN]

30 Mistress Page, remember you your cue.

MISTRESS PAGE I warrant thee. If I do not act it, hiss me.

MISTRESS FORD Go to, then. [*Exit* MISTRESS PAGE]

---

5. *drink . . . dance:* make it uncomfortable for Falstaff.
Pipe wine is wine from the cask, with a pun on "the
whine of musical pipes," which are played for a dance.
Ford also puns on "canary" (line 74), which is also a
dance. Drinking becomes a metaphor for Ford's intention

to make Falstaff dance to his tune.
3.3 Location: Ford's house.
1. Meadow situated between Windsor Little Park and the
Thames.
2. He'll dismiss me.

We'll use this unwholesome humidity,° this gross watery pump-   *body fluids*
kin. We'll teach him to know turtles from jays.[3]

    Enter Sir John FALSTAFF

35 FALSTAFF   Have I caught thee, my heavenly jewel? Why, now let
me die, for I have lived long enough. This is the period° of my   *goal*
ambition. O, this blessed hour!

MISTRESS FORD   O sweet Sir John!

FALSTAFF   Mistress Ford, I cannot cog;° I cannot prate, Mistress   *lie*
40 Ford. Now shall I sin in my wish: I would thy husband were
dead. I'll speak it before the best lord. I would make thee my
lady.

MISTRESS FORD   I your lady, Sir John? Alas, I should be a pitiful
lady.

45 FALSTAFF   Let the court of France show me such another. I see
how thine eye would emulate the diamond. Thou hast the
right arched beauty of the brow that becomes the ship-tire, the
tire-valiant, or any tire of Venetian admittance.[4]

MISTRESS FORD   A plain kerchief, Sir John—my brows become
50 nothing else, nor that well neither.

FALSTAFF   By the Lord, thou art a tyrant° to say so. Thou wouldst   *(punning on "tire")*
make an absolute° courtier, and the firm fixture of thy foot   *a perfect*
would give an excellent motion to thy gait in a semicircled
farthingale.[5] I see what thou wert° if fortune, thy foe, were, with   *would be*
55 nature, thy friend. Come, thou canst not hide it.

MISTRESS FORD   Believe me, there's no such thing in me.

FALSTAFF   What made me love thee? Let that persuade thee
there's something extraordinary in thee. Come, I cannot cog
and say thou art this and that, like a-many of these lisping
60 hawthorn-buds° that come like women in men's apparel and   *young perfumed wooers*
smell like Bucklersbury[6] in simple time;[7] I cannot. But I love
thee, none but thee; and thou deservest it.

MISTRESS FORD   Do not betray° me, sir. I fear you love Mistress   *deceive*
Page.

65 FALSTAFF   Thou mightst as well say I love to walk by the Counter
gate,° which is as hateful to me as the reek of a lime-kiln.   *debtors' prison*

MISTRESS FORD   Well, heaven knows how I love you; and you
shall one day find it.

FALSTAFF   Keep in that mind. I'll deserve it.

70 MISTRESS FORD   Nay, I must tell you, so you do; or else I could
not be in that mind.

    [*Enter* ROBIN]

ROBIN   Mistress Ford, Mistress Ford! Here's Mistress Page at the
door, sweating and blowing,° and looking wildly, and would   *puffing*
needs speak with you presently.°   *immediately*

75 FALSTAFF   She shall not see me. I will ensconce me behind the
arras.°   *wall curtain*

MISTRESS FORD   Pray you do so; she's a very tattling woman.

    FALSTAFF *stands behind the arras.*

    Enter MISTRESS PAGE

What's the matter? How now?

---

3. Gaudy birds, hence flirtatious women. *turtles*: turtledoves, proverbially faithful.
4. Fancifully extravagant headdresses ("tires"), the "ship-
tire" in the form of a ship, that were acceptable in Venice.
"Tire" is from "attire."

5. Skirt shaped with covered hoops at the back.
6. London street where herbs were sold.
7. Summer (when medicinal herbs, or "simples," were
available).

MISTRESS PAGE O Mistress Ford, what have you done? You're
80   shamed, you're overthrown, you're undone for ever.
MISTRESS FORD What's the matter, good Mistress Page?
MISTRESS PAGE O well-a-day,° Mistress Ford! Having an honest   *alas*
    man to° your husband, to give him such cause of suspicion!   *as*
MISTRESS FORD What cause of suspicion?
85 MISTRESS PAGE What cause of suspicion? Out upon you!° How   *(a reproach)*
    am I mistook in you!
MISTRESS FORD Why, alas, what's the matter?
MISTRESS PAGE Your husband's coming hither, woman, with all
    the officers in Windsor, to search for a gentleman that he says
90   is here now in the house, by your consent, to take an ill advan-
    tage of his absence. You are undone.
MISTRESS FORD 'Tis not so, I hope.
MISTRESS PAGE Pray heaven it be not so that you have such a
    man here! But 'tis most certain your husband's coming, with
95   half Windsor at his heels, to search for such a one. I come
    before to tell you. If you know yourself clear,° why, I am glad   *innocent*
    of it; but if you have a friend° here, convey, convey him out.   *lover*
    Be not amazed.° Call all your senses to you. Defend your repu-   *bewildered*
    tation, or bid farewell to your good° life for ever.   *respectable*
100 MISTRESS FORD What shall I do? There is a gentleman, my dear
    friend; and I fear not mine own shame so much as his peril. I
    had rather than a thousand pound he were out of the house.
MISTRESS PAGE For shame, never stand° 'you had rather' and   *waste time over*
    'you had rather'. Your husband's here at hand. Bethink you of
105   some conveyance:° in the house you cannot hide him. O, how *trick; transport*
    have you deceived me! Look, here is a basket. If he be of any
    reasonable stature, he may creep in here; and throw foul linen
    upon him as if it were going to bucking.° Or—it is whiting° *washing / bleaching*
    time—send him by your two men to Datchet Mead.
110 MISTRESS FORD He's too big to go in there. What shall I do?
FALSTAFF [*coming forward*] Let me see't, let me see't, O let me
    see't! I'll in, I'll in. Follow your friend's counsel; I'll in.
MISTRESS PAGE What, Sir John Falstaff! [*Aside to him*] Are these
    your letters, knight?
115 FALSTAFF [*aside to* MISTRESS PAGE] I love thee. Help me away.
    Let me creep in here.
        FALSTAFF *goes into the basket*
    I'll never—
        [MISTRESS PAGE *and* MISTRESS FORD] *put* [*foul*] *clothes*
        over him
MISTRESS PAGE [*to* ROBIN] Help to cover your master, boy.—
    Call your men, Mistress Ford. [*Aside to* FALSTAFF] You dis-
120   sembling knight!
MISTRESS FORD What, John! Robert, John!
        [*Enter* JOHN *and* ROBERT]
    Go take up these clothes here quickly. Where's the cowl-staff?° *pole to carry basket*
        [JOHN *and* ROBERT *fit the cowl-staff*]
    Look how you drumble!° Carry them to the laundress in Dat- *dawdle*
    chet Mead. Quickly, come!
        [*They lift the basket and start to leave.*]
        [*Enter Master*] FORD, [*Master*] PAGE, *Doctor* CAIUS, *and*
        [*Sir Hugh*] EVANS
125 FORD [*to* PAGE, CAIUS, *and* EVANS] Pray you come near. If I sus-

pect without cause, why then, make sport at me; then let me
be your jest—I deserve it. [*To* JOHN *and* ROBERT] How now?
Whither bear you this?

JOHN   To the laundress, forsooth.

130 MISTRESS FORD   Why, what have you to do° whither they bear it?   *to do with*
You were best° meddle with buck-washing!⁸   *(sarcastic)*

FORD   Buck? I would I could wash myself of the buck! Buck,
buck, buck? Ay, buck, I warrant you, buck. And of the season
too, it shall appear.

          [*Exeunt* JOHN *and* ROBERT, *with the basket*]

135 Gentlemen, I have dreamt tonight.° I'll tell you my dream.   *last night*
Here, here, here be my keys. Ascend° my chambers, search,   *Go up to*
seek, find out. I'll warrant we'll unkennel° the fox. Let me stop   *dislodge*
this way° first.   *passage*

       [*He locks the door*]

So, now, uncoop.

140 PAGE   Good Master Ford, be contented. You wrong yourself too
much.

FORD   True, Master Page.—Up, gentlemen! You shall see sport
anon. Follow me, gentlemen.   [*Exit*]

EVANS   This is fery fantastical humours and jealousies.

145 CAIUS   By Gar, 'tis no the fashion of France; it is not jealous in
France.

PAGE   Nay, follow him, gentlemen. See the issue of his search.

          Exeunt [CAIUS, EVANS, *and* PAGE]

MISTRESS PAGE   Is there not a double excellency in this?

MISTRESS FORD   I know not which pleases me better: that my
150 husband is deceived, or Sir John.

MISTRESS PAGE   What a taking° was he in when your husband   *panic*
asked what was in the basket!

MISTRESS FORD   I am half afraid he will have need of washing,⁹
so throwing him into the water will do him a benefit.

155 MISTRESS PAGE   Hang him, dishonest rascal! I would all of the
same strain were in the same distress.

MISTRESS FORD   I think my husband hath some special suspicion
of Falstaff's being here, for I never saw him so gross in his
jealousy till now.

160 MISTRESS PAGE   I will lay a plot to try° that, and we will yet have   *test*
more tricks with Falstaff. His dissolute disease will scarce obey°   *be cured by*
this medicine.

MISTRESS FORD   Shall we send that foolish carrion° Mistress   *rotten flesh*
Quickly to him, and excuse his throwing into the water, and
165 give him another hope, to betray him to another punishment?

MISTRESS PAGE   We will do it. Let him be sent for tomorrow
eight o'clock, to have amends.

       Enter [FORD, PAGE, CAIUS, *and* EVANS]

FORD   I cannot find him. Maybe the knave bragged of that he
could not compass.°   *accomplish*

170 MISTRESS PAGE [*aside to* MISTRESS FORD]   Heard you that?

MISTRESS FORD   You use me well, Master Ford, do you?

FORD   Ay, I do so.

MISTRESS FORD   Heaven make me better than your thoughts!

---

8. Washing that needs bleaching (but Ford thinks of
"buck" as "stag," the horned cuckold, and "to copulate").

9. Fear will have made him urinate.

FORD Amen.

175 MISTRESS PAGE You do yourself mighty wrong, Master Ford.

FORD Ay, ay, I must bear it.

EVANS If there be anypody in the house, and in the chambers, and in the coffers, and in the presses,° heaven forgive my sins at the day of judgement!   *cupboards*

180 CAIUS Be Gar, nor I too. There is nobodies.

PAGE Fie, fie, Master Ford, are you not ashamed? What spirit, what devil suggests this imagination? I would not ha' your dis- temper in this kind for the wealth of Windsor Castle.

FORD 'Tis my fault, Master Page. I suffer for it.

185 EVANS You suffer for a pad conscience. Your wife is as honest a 'omans as I will desires among five thousand, and five hundred too.

CAIUS By Gar, I see 'tis an honest woman.

FORD Well, I promised you a dinner. Come, come, walk in the

190 park. I pray you pardon me. I will hereafter make known to you why I have done this.—Come, wife; come, Mistress Page. I pray you pardon me. Pray heartily pardon me.

PAGE [*to* CAIUS *and* EVANS] Let's go in, gentlemen. [*Aside to them*] But trust me, we'll mock him. [*To* FORD, CAIUS, *and*

195 EVANS] I do invite you tomorrow morning to my house to break- fast. After, we'll a-birding° together. I have a fine hawk for[1] the   *bird hunting* bush. Shall it be so?

FORD Anything.

EVANS If there is one, I shall make two in the company.

200 CAIUS If there be one or two, I shall make-a the turd.

FORD Pray you go, Master Page.

Exeunt [*all but* EVANS *and* CAIUS]

EVANS I pray you now, remembrance tomorrow on the lousy knave mine Host.[2]

CAIUS Dat is good, by Gar; with all my heart.

205 EVANS A lousy knave, to have his gibes and his mockeries.

Exeunt

3.4

Enter Master FENTON *and* ANNE *Page*

FENTON I see I cannot get thy father's love;
Therefore no more turn me to him, sweet Nan.

ANNE Alas, how then?

FENTON   Why, thou must be thyself.°   *in charge of yourself*
He doth object I am too great of birth,

5 And that, my state being galled with° my expense,   *estate being hurt by*
I seek to heal it only by his wealth.
Besides these, other bars he lays before me—
My riots past, my wild societies;°   *companionships*
And tells me 'tis a thing impossible

10 I should love thee but as a property.

ANNE Maybe he tells you true.

FENTON No, heaven so speed° me in my time to come!   *as heaven may prosper*
Albeit I will confess thy father's wealth
Was the first motive that I wooed thee, Anne,

1. For driving birds into.
2. A cryptic reference to the "revenge" proposal at   3.1.101.
    3.4 Location: Outside Page's house.

15 Yet, wooing thee, I found thee of more value
    Than stamps in gold° or sums in sealèd bags;   *stamped gold coins*
    And 'tis the very riches of thyself
    That now I aim at.
ANNE   Gentle Master Fenton,
    Yet seek my father's love, still seek it, sir.
20 If opportunity and humblest suit
    Cannot attain it, why then—
                Enter [Justice] SHALLOW, *[Master]* SLENDER *[richly
                dressed], and* MISTRESS QUICKLY
                             Hark you hither.
                [They talk apart]
SHALLOW Break their talk, Mistress Quickly. My kinsman shall
    speak for himself.
SLENDER I'll make a shaft or a bolt on't.¹ 'Slid,° 'tis but ven-   *By God's eyelid*
25 turing.
SHALLOW Be not dismayed.
SLENDER   No, she shall not dismay me.
    I care not for that, but that I am afeard.
MISTRESS QUICKLY *[to* ANNE*]* Hark ye, Master Slender would
    speak a word with you.
30 ANNE I come to him. *[To* FENTON*]* This is my father's choice.
    O, what a world of vile ill-favoured° faults   *ugly*
    Looks handsome in three hundred pounds a year!°   *(moderate wealth)*
MISTRESS QUICKLY And how does good Master Fenton? Pray
    you, a word with you.
                [She draws FENTON *aside]*
35 SHALLOW She's coming. To her, coz! O boy, thou hadst a
    father!°   *be manly; you're manly*
SLENDER I had a father, Mistress Anne; my uncle can tell you
    good jests of him.—Pray you, uncle, tell Mistress Anne the jest
    how my father stole two geese out of a pen, good uncle.
40 SHALLOW Mistress Anne, my cousin loves you.
SLENDER Ay, that I do, as well as I love any woman in Glouces-
    tershire.
SHALLOW He will maintain you like a gentlewoman.
SLENDER Ay, by God, that I will, come cut and long-tail,° under   *no matter what*
45 the degree° of a squire.   *in the rank*
SHALLOW He will make you a hundred and fifty pounds join-
    ture.°   *widowhood settlement*
ANNE Good Master Shallow, let him woo for himself.
SHALLOW Marry, I thank you for it, I thank you for that good
50 comfort.—She calls you, coz. I'll leave you.
                [He stands aside]
ANNE Now, Master Slender.
SLENDER Now, good Mistress Anne.
ANNE What is your will?
SLENDER My will? 'Od's heartlings,° that's a pretty jest indeed! I   *By God's little hearts*
55 ne'er made my will yet, I thank God; I am not such a sickly
    creature, I give God praise.
ANNE I mean, Master Slender, what would you with me?
SLENDER Truly, for mine own part, I would little or nothing

---

1. I'll do it one way or another (with possible sexual connotation).

with you. Your father and my uncle hath made motions.° If it   *proposals*
60   be my luck, so. If not, happy man be his dole.[2] They can tell
you how things go better than I can.
                Enter Master PAGE [*and*] MISTRESS PAGE
You may ask your father: here he comes.
PAGE   Now, Master Slender.—Love him, daughter Anne.—
Why, how now? What does Master Fenton here?
65   You wrong me, sir, thus still to haunt my house.
I told you, sir, my daughter is disposed of.
FENTON   Nay, Master Page, be not impatient.
MISTRESS PAGE   Good Master Fenton, come not to my child.
PAGE   She is no match for you.
70 FENTON   Sir, will you hear me?
PAGE   No, good Master Fenton.—
Come, Master Shallow; come, son Slender, in.—
Knowing my mind, you wrong me, Master Fenton.
              Exeunt PAGE[, SHALLOW, *and* SLENDER]
MISTRESS QUICKLY [*to* FENTON]   Speak to Mistress Page.
75 FENTON   Good Mistress Page, for that° I love your daughter   *because*
In such a righteous fashion as I do,
Perforce against all checks,° rebukes, and manners   *reproofs*
I must advance the colours° of my love,   *military banners*
And not retire. Let me have your good will.
80 ANNE   Good mother, do not marry me to yon fool.
MISTRESS PAGE   I mean it not; I seek you a better husband.
MISTRESS QUICKLY [*aside to* ANNE]   That's my master, Master
Doctor.
ANNE   Alas, I had rather be set quick i'th' earth°   *half-buried alive*
85   And bowled to death with turnips.
MISTRESS PAGE   Come, trouble not yourself, good Master Fenton.
I will not be your friend nor enemy.
My daughter will I question how she loves you,
And as I find her, so am I affected.°   *inclined*
90 Till then, farewell, sir. She must needs go in.
Her father will be angry.
FENTON   Farewell, gentle mistress.—Farewell, Nan.
            Exeunt [MISTRESS PAGE *and* ANNE]
MISTRESS QUICKLY   This is my doing now. 'Nay', said I, 'will you
cast away your child on a fool and a physician? Look on Master
95   Fenton.' This is my doing.
FENTON   I thank thee, [*giving her a ring*] and I pray thee, once°   *at some time*
tonight
Give my sweet Nan this ring. [*Giving money*] There's for thy
pains.
MISTRESS QUICKLY   Now heaven send thee good fortune!
              Exit FENTON
A kind heart he hath. A woman would run through fire and
100   water for such a kind heart. But yet I would my master had
Mistress Anne; or I would Master Slender had her; or, in sooth,
I would Master Fenton had her. I will do what I can for them
all three, for so I have promised, and I'll be as good as my
word—but speciously° for Master Fenton. Well, I must of°   *(for "specially") / run*

2. Good luck to the successful suitor.

105   another errand to Sir John Falstaff from my two mistresses.
What a beast am I to slack° it!   *Exit*   *to be remiss in*

3.5

Enter Sir John FALSTAFF
FALSTAFF   Bardolph, I say!
    Enter BARDOLPH
BARDOLPH   Here, sir.
FALSTAFF   Go fetch me a quart of sack; put a toast° in't.   *piece of hot toast*
                          [*Exit* BARDOLPH]
    Have I lived to be carried in a basket like a barrow° of butcher's   *wheelbarrow*
5   offal, and to be thrown in the Thames? Well, if I be served
such another trick, I'll have my brains ta'en out and buttered,[1]
and give them to a dog for a New Year's gift. 'Sblood, the rogues
slighted° me into the river with as little remorse as they would   *slid; scorned*
have drowned a blind bitch's° puppies, fifteen i'th' litter! And   *bitch's blind*
10   you may know by my size that I have a kind of alacrity in sinking. If the bottom were as deep as hell, I should down.° I had   *reach the bottom*
been drowned, but that the shore was shelvy° and shallow—a   *made of sandbanks*
death that I abhor, for the water swells a man, and what a thing
should I have been when I had been swelled? By the Lord, a
15   mountain of mummy!°   *dead flesh*
        [*Enter* BARDOLPH, *with two large cups of sack*]
BARDOLPH   Here's Mistress Quickly, sir, to speak with you.
FALSTAFF   Come, let me pour in some sack to the Thames'
water, for my belly's as cold as if I had swallowed snowballs for
pills to cool the reins.°   *kidneys*
        [*He drinks*]
20   Call her in.
BARDOLPH   Come in, woman!
    Enter MISTRESS QUICKLY
MISTRESS QUICKLY [*to* FALSTAFF]   By your leave; I cry you
mercy.[2] Give your worship good morrow!
FALSTAFF [*drinking, then speaking to* BARDOLPH]   Take away
25   these chalices. Go brew° me a pottle° of sack, finely.   *prepare / two quarts*
BARDOLPH   With eggs, sir?
FALSTAFF   Simple of itself.° I'll no pullet-sperms in my brewage.   *Pure*
        [*Exit* BARDOLPH, *with cups*]
    How now?
MISTRESS QUICKLY   Marry, sir, I come to your worship from Mis-
30   tress Ford.
FALSTAFF   Mistress Ford? I have had ford enough: I was thrown
into the ford, I have my belly full of ford.
MISTRESS QUICKLY   Alas the day, good heart, that was not her
fault. She does so take on with her men; they mistook their
35   erection.[3]
FALSTAFF   So did I mine, to build upon a foolish woman's
promise.
MISTRESS QUICKLY   Well, she laments, sir, for it, that it would
yearn° your heart to see it. Her husband goes this morning a-   *grieve*
40   birding. She desires you once more to come to her, between

---

3.5 Location: The Garter Inn.
1. "Buttered" brains may have meant "foolish."
2. *I cry you mercy*: excuse me.

3. Quickly means that Mistress Ford "does take on"
(scold) her servants, who misunderstood her direction,
but there's an obvious, unintentional sexual pun.

eight and nine. I must carry her word° quickly. She'll make *your reply*
you amends, I warrant you.
FALSTAFF Well, I will visit her. Tell her so, and bid her think
what a man is; let her consider his frailty, and then judge of my
45 merit.
MISTRESS QUICKLY I will tell her.
FALSTAFF Do so. Between nine and ten, sayst thou?
MISTRESS QUICKLY Eight and nine, sir.
FALSTAFF Well, be gone. I will not miss° her. *fail*
50 MISTRESS QUICKLY Peace be with you, sir. *Exit*
FALSTAFF I marvel I hear not of Master Brooke; he sent me
word to stay° within. I like his money well. *wait for him*
Enter [Master] FORD, *[disguised as] Brooke*
By the mass, here he comes.
FORD God bless you, sir.
55 FALSTAFF Now, Master Brooke, you come to know what hath
passed between me and Ford's wife.
FORD That indeed, Sir John, is my business.
FALSTAFF Master Brooke, I will not lie to you. I was at her house
the hour she appointed me.
60 FORD And sped you,° sir? *did you succeed*
FALSTAFF Very ill-favouredly,° Master Brooke. *badly*
FORD How so, sir? Did she change her determination?
FALSTAFF No, Master Brooke, but the peaking cornuto° her hus- *sneaking cuckold*
band, Master Brooke, dwelling in a continual 'larum° of jeal- *alarm*
65 ousy, comes me° in the instant of our encounter—after we had *comes*
embraced, kissed, protested, and, as it were, spoke the prologue
of our comedy—and at his heels a rabble of his companions,
thither provoked and instigated by his distemper, and, forsooth,
to search his house for his wife's love.
70 FORD What, while you were there?
FALSTAFF While I was there.
FORD And did he search for you, and could not find you?
FALSTAFF You shall hear. As God would have it, comes in one
Mistress Page, gives intelligence of Ford's approach, and, by
75 her invention and Ford's wife's distraction, they conveyed me
into a buck-basket—
FORD A buck-basket?
FALSTAFF By the Lord, a buck-basket!—rammed me in with foul
shirts and smocks, socks, foul stockings, greasy napkins, that,° *so that*
80 Master Brooke, there was the rankest compound of villainous
smell that ever offended nostril.
FORD And how long lay you there?
FALSTAFF Nay, you shall hear, Master Brooke, what I have suffered to bring this woman to evil, for your good. Being thus
85 crammed in the basket, a couple of Ford's knaves, his hinds,° *servants (pejorative)*
were called forth by their mistress, to carry me, in the name of
foul clothes, to Datchet Lane. They took me on their shoulders, met the jealous knave their master in the door, who asked
them once or twice what they had in their basket. I quaked for
90 fear lest the lunatic knave would have searched it, but fate,
ordaining he should be a cuckold, held° his hand. Well, on *held back*
went he for a search, and away went I for foul clothes. But mark
the sequel, Master Brooke. I suffered the pangs of three several° *different*
deaths. First, an intolerable fright, to be detected with° a jeal- *by*

95 ous rotten bell-wether.⁴ Next, to be compassed like a good
bilbo in the circumference of a peck,⁵ hilt to point, heel to
head. And then, to be stopped° in, like a strong distillation,°   *stoppered / liquid*
with stinking clothes that fretted° in their own grease. Think of   *fermented*
that—a man of my kidney°—think of that—that am as subject   *constitution*
100 to heat as butter, a man of continual dissolution° and thaw. It   *melting*
was a miracle to scape suffocation. And in the height of this
bath, when I was more than half stewed in grease like a Dutch
dish, to be thrown into the Thames and cooled, glowing-hot,
in that surge, like a horseshoe. Think of that—hissing hot—
105 think of that, Master Brooke!

FORD   In good sadness,° sir, I am sorry that for my sake you have   *seriousness*
suffered all this. My suit then is desperate. You'll undertake
her no more?

FALSTAFF   Master Brooke, I will be thrown into Etna° as I have   *Sicilian volcano*
110 been into Thames ere I will leave her thus. Her husband is
this morning gone a-birding. I have received from her another
embassy° of meeting. 'Twixt eight and nine is the hour, Master   *message*
Brooke.

FORD   'Tis past eight already, sir.

115 FALSTAFF   Is it? I will then address me to my appointment.
Come to me at your convenient leisure, and you shall know
how I speed; and the conclusion shall be crowned with your
enjoying her. Adieu. You shall have her, Master Brooke; Master
Brooke, you shall cuckold Ford.   *Exit*

120 FORD   Hum! Ha! Is this a vision? Is this a dream? Do I sleep?
Master Ford, awake! Awake, Master Ford! There's a hole made
in your best coat,⁶ Master Ford. This 'tis to be married! This
'tis to have linen and buck-baskets! Well, I will proclaim myself
what I am. I will now take° the lecher. He is at my house. He   *catch*
125 cannot scape me; 'tis impossible he should. He cannot creep
into a halfpenny purse, nor into a pepperbox. But lest the devil
that guides him should aid him, I will search impossible places.
Though what I am I cannot avoid, yet to be what I would not
shall not make me tame. If I have horns to make one mad, let
130 the proverb go with me: I'll be horn-mad.⁷   *Exit*

4.1

Enter MISTRESS PAGE, [MISTRESS] QUICKLY, [*and*] WIL-
LIAM *Page*

MISTRESS PAGE   Is he at Mistress Ford's already, thinkest thou?

MISTRESS QUICKLY   Sure he is by this,° or will be presently.° But   *now / immediately*
truly he is very courageous°-mad about his throwing into the   *(for "ragingly")*
water. Mistress Ford desires you to come suddenly.°   *at once*

5 MISTRESS PAGE   I'll be with her by and by.° I'll but bring my   *right away*
young man here to school.

Enter [Sir Hugh] EVANS

Look where his master comes. 'Tis a playing day, I see.—How
now, Sir Hugh, no school today?

---

4. Castrated ram, leader of the flock, with a bell round its
neck and a horn like a cuckold's on its head.
5. To be bent double (encompassed) like a flexible sword
(from Bilbao, Spain, where fine swords known for their
elasticity were made) in the cramped space of a laundry
basket (in a receptacle holding a peck, or a quarter of a

bushel).
6. Proverbial for "Your reputation is spoiled."
7. I'll be as furious as a horned animal in breeding season; furious to be a cuckold.
4.1 Location: Outdoors.

EVANS   No, Master Slender is let° the boys leave° to play.   *asked that / be allowed*

10 MISTRESS QUICKLY   Blessing of his heart!

MISTRESS PAGE   Sir Hugh, my husband says my son profits nothing in the world[1] at his book. I pray you ask him some questions
in his accidence.°   *Latin grammar*

EVANS   Come hither, William. Hold up your head. Come.

15 MISTRESS PAGE   Come on, sirrah. Hold up your head. Answer
your master; be not afraid.

EVANS   William, how many numbers is in nouns?

WILLIAM   Two.°   *(singular and plural)*

MISTRESS QUICKLY   Truly, I thought there had been one number

20 more, because they say ''Od's nouns'.[2]

EVANS   Peace your tattlings!—What is 'fair', William?

WILLIAM   *'Pulcher'.*

MISTRESS QUICKLY   Polecats?° There are fairer things than pole-   *Smelly animals; whores*
cats, sure.

25 EVANS   You are a very simplicity 'oman. I pray you peace.—
What is *'lapis'*, William?

WILLIAM   A stone.

EVANS   And what is 'a stone', William?

WILLIAM   A pebble.

30 EVANS   No, it is *'lapis'*. I pray you remember in your prain.

WILLIAM   *'Lapis'.*

EVANS   That is a good William. What is he, William, that does
lend articles?

WILLIAM   Articles are borrowed of the pronoun, and be thus

35 declined. *Singulariter nominativo: 'hic, haec, hoc'.*[3]

EVANS   *Nominativo: 'hig, hag, hog'.*[4] Pray you mark: *genitivo:*°   *genitive*
'huius'. Well, what is your accusative case?

WILLIAM   *Accusativo: 'hinc'*°—   *(for "hunc")*

EVANS   I pray you have your remembrance, child. *Accusativo:*

40 *'hing, hang, hog'.*

MISTRESS QUICKLY   'Hang-hog'[5] is Latin for bacon, I warrant you.

EVANS   Leave your prabbles, 'oman!—What is the focative° case,   *vocative; (obscene)*
William?

WILLIAM   O—*vocativo*, O—

45 EVANS   Remember, William, focative is *caret*.[6]

MISTRESS QUICKLY   And that's a good root.

EVANS   'Oman, forbear.

MISTRESS PAGE [*to* MISTRESS QUICKLY]   Peace.

EVANS   What is your genitive case plural, William?

50 WILLIAM   Genitive case?

EVANS   Ay.

WILLIAM   *Genitivo: 'horum, harum, horum'.*

MISTRESS QUICKLY   Vengeance of° Jenny's case! Fie on her!   *A plague on*
Never name her, child, if she be a whore.[7]

55 EVANS   For shame, 'oman!

MISTRESS QUICKLY   You do ill to teach the child such words. He

---

1. My son fails to improve.
2. God's wounds; three is an odd ("Od's") number.
3. William recites by memory from his textbook. *"Singulariter nominativo"* is "in the nominative singular" (in
which William gives the masculine, feminine, and neuter
of the pronoun "this").
4. The pronunciation in Evans's accent.
5. Alluding to the saying "Hog is not bacon until it be

hanged."
6. Missing. Quickly understands "carrot," whose slang
sense "penis" is supported by a suggestion of "fuck" in
"focative."
7. *Genitive case . . . whore:* "Genitive" is perhaps misun-
derstandable as Latin for "generative" or even "genital"—
as well as "Jenny"; "case" is understood by Quickly to
mean "situation" and also the slang term for "vagina."

teaches him to hick and to hack,° which they'll do fast enough   *drink and copulate?*
of themselves, and to call 'whorum'. Fie upon you!

EVANS   'Oman, art thou lunatics? Hast thou no understandings
60   for thy cases, and the numbers of the genders? Thou art as
foolish Christian creatures as I would desires.

MISTRESS PAGE [*to* MISTRESS QUICKLY]   Prithee, hold thy peace.

EVANS   Show me now, William, some declensions of your pronouns.

65 WILLIAM   Forsooth, I have forgot.

EVANS   It is '*qui, que, quod*'. If you forget your '*qui's*, your '*que's*,
and your '*quod's*,[8] you must be preeches.° Go your ways and   *flogged*
play; go.

MISTRESS PAGE   He is a better scholar than I thought he was.

70 EVANS   He is a good sprag° memory. Farewell, Mistress Page.   *sprack (lively)*

MISTRESS PAGE   Adieu, good Sir Hugh.   [*Exit* EVANS]
Get you home, boy.   [*Exit* WILLIAM]
[*To* MISTRESS QUICKLY] Come, we stay too long.   *Exeunt*

4.2

Enter Sir John FALSTAFF *and* MISTRESS FORD

FALSTAFF   Mistress Ford, your sorrow hath eaten up my sufferance.[1] I see you are obsequious° in your love, and I profess   *devoted*
requital to a hair's breadth:° not only, Mistress Ford, in the   *in full*
simple office of love, but in all the accoutrement, complement,
5   and ceremony of it. But are you sure of your husband now?

MISTRESS FORD   He's a-birding, sweet Sir John.

MISTRESS PAGE [*within*]   What ho, gossip° Ford, what ho!   *friend*

MISTRESS FORD   Step into th' chamber, Sir John.
                  He steps [*into the chamber*]

Enter MISTRESS PAGE

MISTRESS PAGE   How now, sweetheart, who's at home besides
10   yourself?

MISTRESS FORD   Why, none but mine own people.°   *servants*

MISTRESS PAGE   Indeed?

MISTRESS FORD   No, certainly. [*Aside to her*] Speak louder.

MISTRESS PAGE   Truly, I am so glad you have nobody here.

15 MISTRESS FORD   Why?

MISTRESS PAGE   Why, woman, your husband is in his old lines°   *role*
again. He so takes on° yonder with my husband, so rails against   *raves*
all married mankind, so curses all Eve's daughters° of what   *women*
complexion° soever, and so buffets himself on the forehead,   *temperament*
20   crying 'Peer out,[2] peer out!', that any madness I ever yet beheld
seemed but tameness, civility, and patience to this his distemper he is in now. I am glad the fat knight is not here.

MISTRESS FORD   Why, does he talk of him?

MISTRESS PAGE   Of none but him; and swears he was carried out,
25   the last time he searched for him, in a basket, protests to my
husband he is now here, and hath drawn him and the rest of
their company from their sport to make another experiment° of   *trial*
his suspicion. But I am glad the knight is not here. Now he
shall see his own foolery.

---

8. Possibly pronounced as "keys, case, cods," with "keys"
a euphemism for "penis," "case" a term for "vagina," and
"cods" slang for "testicles."
4.2 Location: Ford's house.

1. Your sorrow has made the memory of my suffering disappear.
2. Emerge (addressed to imagined cuckold's horns).

30   MISTRESS FORD   How near is he, Mistress Page?

MISTRESS PAGE   Hard by at street end. He will be here anon.

MISTRESS FORD   I am undone: the knight is here.

MISTRESS PAGE   Why then, you are utterly shamed, and he's but a dead man. What a woman are you! Away with him, away
35   with him! Better shame than murder.

MISTRESS FORD   Which way should he go? How should I bestow°   *dispose of*
him? Shall I put him into the basket again?

[FALSTAFF *comes forth from the chamber*]

FALSTAFF   No, I'll come no more i'th' basket. May I not go out ere he come?

40   MISTRESS PAGE   Alas, three of Master Ford's brothers watch the door with pistols, that none shall issue out. Otherwise you might slip away ere he came. But what make you° here?   *are you doing*

FALSTAFF   What shall I do? I'll creep up into the chimney.

MISTRESS FORD   There they always use to discharge their birding-
45   pieces.°   *bird guns*

MISTRESS PAGE   Creep into the kiln-hole.°   *oven*

FALSTAFF   Where is it?

MISTRESS FORD   He will seek there, on my word. Neither press,°   *cupboard*
coffer, chest, trunk, well, vault, but he hath an abstract° for the   *a list*
50   remembrance of such places, and goes to them by his note. There is no hiding you in the house.

FALSTAFF   I'll go out, then.

MISTRESS PAGE   If you go out in your own semblance, you die, Sir John—unless you go out disguised.

55   MISTRESS FORD   How might we disguise him?

MISTRESS PAGE   Alas the day, I know not. There is no woman's gown big enough for him; otherwise he might put on a hat, a muffler,° and a kerchief, and so escape.   *face scarf*

FALSTAFF   Good hearts, devise something. Any extremity° rather   *extravagance*
60   than a mischief.°   *calamity*

MISTRESS FORD   My maid's aunt, the fat woman of Brentford,³ has a gown above.

MISTRESS PAGE   On my word, it will serve him; she's as big as he is; and there's her thrummed° hat, and her muffler too.—Run   *fringed*
65   up, Sir John.

MISTRESS FORD   Go, go, sweet Sir John. Mistress Page and I will look° some linen for your head.   *look for*

MISTRESS PAGE   Quick, quick! We'll come dress you straight. Put on the gown the while.   *Exit Sir John* [FALSTAFF]

70   MISTRESS FORD   I would my husband would meet him in this shape. He cannot abide the old woman of Brentford. He swears she's a witch, forbade her my house, and hath threatened to beat her.

MISTRESS PAGE   Heaven guide him to thy husband's cudgel, and
75   the devil guide his cudgel afterwards!

MISTRESS FORD   But is my husband coming?

MISTRESS PAGE   Ay, in good sadness° is he, and talks of the basket   *in all seriousness*
too, howsoever⁴ he hath had intelligence.°   *information*

MISTRESS FORD   We'll try° that, for I'll appoint my men to carry   *test*

---

3. Gillian of Brentford, a scurrilous comic figure, per-   friends." Brentford was a village halfway between Wind-
haps historically based, best known for her will, in which   sor and London.
she supposedly "bequeathed a score of farts amongst her   4. By whatever means.

80   the basket again, to meet him at the door with it as they did
last time.

MISTRESS PAGE   Nay, but he'll be here presently. Let's go dress
him like the witch of Brentford.

MISTRESS FORD   I'll first direct my men what they shall do with

85   the basket. Go up; I'll bring linen for him straight.°   *immediately*

MISTRESS PAGE   Hang him, dishonest° varlet! We cannot misuse   *lewd*
him enough.   [*Exit* MISTRESS FORD]
We'll leave a proof by that which we will do,
Wives may be merry, and yet honest,° too.   *chaste*

90   We do not act that° often jest and laugh.   *misbehave who*
'Tis old but true: 'Still swine eats all the draff'.⁵   *Exit*
          Enter MISTRESS FORD [*with* JOHN *and* ROBERT]

MISTRESS FORD   Go, sirs, take the basket again on your shoulders.
Your master is hard at° door. If he bid you set it down, obey   *close to the*
him. Quickly, dispatch!   [*Exit*]

95 JOHN   Come, come, take it up.

ROBERT   Pray heaven it be not full of knight again.

JOHN   I hope not; I had as lief ° bear so much lead.   *I would rather*
       [*They lift*] *the basket*.
       Enter [*Master*] FORD, [*Master*] PAGE, [*Doctor*] CAIUS,
       [*Sir Hugh*] EVANS, *and* [*Justice*] SHALLOW

FORD   Ay, but if it prove true, Master Page, have you any way
then to unfool me again?⁶ [*To* JOHN *and* ROBERT] Set down

100   the basket, villains.
       [JOHN *and* ROBERT *set down the basket*]
Somebody call my wife. Youth in a basket!° O, you panderly   *Fortunate lover?*
rascals! There's a knot,° a gang, a pack, a conspiracy against   *group*
me. Now shall the devil be shamed.°—What, wife, I say!   *truth be known*
Come, come forth! Behold what honest clothes you send forth

105   to bleaching.

PAGE   Why, this passes,° Master Ford. You are not to go loose   *goes beyond all bounds*
any longer; you must be pinioned.

EVANS   Why, this is lunatics; this is mad as a mad dog.

SHALLOW   Indeed, Master Ford, this is not well, indeed.

110 FORD   So say I too, sir.
       [*Enter* MISTRESS FORD]
Come hither, Mistress Ford! Mistress Ford, the honest woman,
the modest wife, the virtuous creature, that hath the jealous
fool to° her husband! I suspect without cause, mistress, do I?   *for*

MISTRESS FORD   God be my witness you do, if you suspect me in

115   any dishonesty.

FORD   Well said, brazen-face; hold it out.°   *keep it up*
       [*He opens the basket and starts to take out clothes*]
Come forth, sirrah!

PAGE   This passes.

MISTRESS FORD [*to* FORD]   Are you not ashamed? Let the clothes

120   alone.

FORD   I shall find you anon.

EVANS   'Tis unreasonable: will you take up your wife's clothes?
Come, away.

---

5. Proverbial: "The quiet swine eats all the hog's wash."   6. Page has evidently accused Ford of making a fool of
In other words, quietness conceals sexual immorality   himself.
(whereas playfulness is innocent; see line 90).

FORD [*to* JOHN *and* ROBERT]   Empty the basket, I say.

125 PAGE   Why, man, why?

FORD   Master Page, as I am a man, there was one conveyed out
of my house yesterday in this basket. Why may not he be there
again? In my house I am sure he is. My intelligence° is true,   *information*
my jealousy is reasonable. [*To* JOHN *and* ROBERT] Pluck me

130 out all the linen.

  [*He takes out clothes*]

MISTRESS FORD   If you find a man there, he shall die a flea's
death.[7]

PAGE   Here's no man.

SHALLOW   By my fidelity, this is not well, Master Ford. This

135 wrongs you.°   *You shame yourself*

EVANS   Master Ford, you must pray, and not follow the imaginations of your own heart. This is jealousies.

FORD   Well, he's not here I seek for.

PAGE   No, nor nowhere else but in your brain.

140 FORD   Help to search my house this one time. If I find not what
I seek, show no colour° for my extremity;° let me for ever be   *excuse / excesses*
your table-sport;° let them say of me, 'As jealous as Ford, that   *laughingstock*
searched a hollow walnut for his wife's leman'.° Satisfy me   *lover*
once more; once more search with me.

  [*Exeunt* JOHN *and* ROBERT *with the basket*]

145 MISTRESS FORD   What ho, Mistress Page! Come you and the old
woman down. My husband will come into the chamber.

FORD   Old woman? What old woman's that?

MISTRESS FORD   Why, it is my maid's Aunt of Brentford.

FORD   A witch, a quean, an old, cozening quean!° Have I not   *cheating hussy*

150 forbid her my house? She comes of errands, does she? We are
simple men; we do not know what's brought to pass under the
profession° of fortune-telling. She works by charms, by spells,   *claim*
by th' figure,[8] and such daubery° as this is, beyond our ele-   *trickery*
ment.° We know nothing.—Come down, you witch, you hag,   *knowledge*

155 you! Come down, I say!

  Enter MISTRESS PAGE, *and* FALSTAFF, *disguised like an*
  old woman.

  [FORD *makes towards them*]

MISTRESS FORD   Nay, good sweet husband!—Good gentlemen,
let him not strike the old woman.

MISTRESS PAGE [*to* FALSTAFF]   Come, Mother Prat.° Come, give   *Buttocks*
me your hand.

160 FORD   I'll prat° her!   *beat; trick*

  FORD *beats* [FALSTAFF]

Out of my door, you witch, you rag, you baggage, you polecat,
you runnion!° Out, out! I'll conjure you, I'll fortune-tell you!   *contemptible woman*

  [*Exit* FALSTAFF]

MISTRESS PAGE   Are you not ashamed? I think you have killed
the poor woman.

165 MISTRESS FORD   Nay, he will do it.—'Tis a goodly credit for you!

FORD   Hang her, witch!

EVANS   By Jeshu, I think the 'oman is a witch indeed. I like not

---

7. Anyone hiding there must be insignificantly small
and used to living in clothes.

8. Astrological or magical diagrams, or wax effigies used
by witches.

when a 'oman has a great peard. I spy a great peard under his
muffler.
170 FORD Will you follow, gentlemen? I beseech you, follow. See
but the issue° of my jealousy. If I cry out° thus upon no trail,   *outcome / bark*
never trust me when I open° again.   *start barking*
PAGE Let's obey his humour° a little further. Come, gentlemen.   *indulge him*
             Exeunt [the men]
MISTRESS PAGE By my troth, he beat him most pitifully.
175 MISTRESS FORD Nay, by th' mass, that he did not—he beat him
most unpitifully, methought.
MISTRESS PAGE I'll have the cudgel hallowed and hung o'er the
altar. It hath done meritorious service.
MISTRESS FORD What think you—may we, with the warrant of
180 womanhood and the witness of a good conscience, pursue
him with any further revenge?
MISTRESS PAGE The spirit of wantonness is sure scared out of
him. If the devil have him not in fee-simple, with fine and
recovery, he will never, I think, in the way of waste attempt us
185 again.[9]
MISTRESS FORD Shall we tell our husbands how we have served
him?
MISTRESS PAGE Yes, by all means, if it be but to scrape the fig-
ures° out of your husband's brains. If they can find in their   *fantasies*
190 hearts the poor, unvirtuous, fat knight shall be any further
afflicted, we two will still be the ministers.
MISTRESS FORD I'll warrant they'll have him publicly shamed,
and methinks there would be no period° to the jest should he   *conclusion*
not be publicly shamed.
195 MISTRESS PAGE Come, to the forge with it, then shape it. I would
not have things cool.   *Exeunt*

4.3

Enter [the] HOST *[of the Garter] and* BARDOLPH
BARDOLPH Sir, the Germans desire to have three of your horses.
The Duke himself will be tomorrow at court, and they° are   *(the Germans)*
going to meet him.
HOST What duke should that be comes° so secretly? I hear not   *who comes*
5 of him in the court. Let me speak with the gentlemen. They
speak English?
BARDOLPH Ay, sir. I'll call them to you.
HOST They shall have my horses, but I'll make them pay; I'll
sauce them.° They have had my house a week at command;[1]   *make them pay dearly*
10 I have turned away my other guests. They must come off:° I'll   *pay up*
sauce them. Come.[2]   *Exeunt*

---

9. Legal terms: If the devil doesn't absolutely own him,
he won't try to despoil us again.
4.3 Location: The Garter Inn.
1. They have had my inn at their disposal for a week.
2. The German Duke is fiction, part of a plot whereby
Caius and Evans revenge themselves on the Host. The
exact details are obscure. A scene or more may have been
censored in which Caius and Evans, or some other characters, disguised themselves as Germans and duped the
Host. Evidently Sir John also parts with his horses: see
5.5.110–11 and 2.1.84–85.

4.4

Enter [Master] PAGE, *[Master]* FORD, MISTRESS PAGE,
MISTRESS FORD, *and Sir Hugh* EVANS

EVANS   'Tis one of the best discretions of a 'oman¹ as ever I did
look upon.

PAGE   And did he send you both these letters at an instant?°   *at the same time*

MISTRESS PAGE   Within a quarter of an hour.

5   FORD   Pardon me, wife. Henceforth do what thou wilt.
I rather will suspect the sun with° cold   *of*
Than thee with wantonness. Now doth thy honour stand,
In him that was of late an heretic,
As firm as faith.

PAGE   'Tis well, 'tis well; no more.

10   Be not as extreme in submission
As in offence.
But let our plot go forward. Let our wives
Yet once again, to make us public sport,
Appoint a meeting with this old fat fellow,

15   Where we may take him and disgrace him for it.

FORD   There is no better way than that they spoke of.

PAGE   How, to send him word they'll meet him in the Park
At midnight? Fie, fie, he'll never come.

EVANS   You say he has been thrown in the rivers, and has been

20   grievously peaten as an old 'oman. Methinks there should be
terrors in him, that he should not come. Methinks his flesh is
punished; he shall have no desires.

PAGE   So think I too.

MISTRESS FORD   Devise but how you'll use° him when he comes,   *treat*

25   And let us two devise to bring him thither.

MISTRESS PAGE   There is an old tale goes that Herne the hunter,
Sometime° a keeper here in Windsor Forest,   *Once*
Doth all the winter time at still midnight
Walk round about an oak with great ragg'd° horns;   *jagged*

30   And there he blasts° the trees, and takes° the cattle,   *blights / bewitches*
And makes milch-kine° yield blood, and shakes a chain   *dairy cattle*
In a most hideous and dreadful manner.
You have heard of such a spirit, and well you know
The superstitious idle-headed eld°   *people of olden times*

35   Received, and did deliver to our age,
This tale of Herne the hunter for a truth.

PAGE   Why, yet there want not° many that do fear   *are*
In deep of night to walk by this Herne's Oak.
But what of this?

MISTRESS FORD   Marry, this is our device:

40   That Falstaff at that oak shall meet with us,
Disguised like Herne, with huge horns on his head.

PAGE   Well, let it not be doubted but he'll come,
And in this shape. When you have brought him thither
What shall be done with him? What is your plot?

45   MISTRESS PAGE   That likewise have we thought upon, and thus.
Nan Page my daughter, and my little son,
And three or four more of their growth,° we'll dress   *size*
Like urchins,° oafs,° and fairies, green and white,   *goblins / elf children*

4.4 Location: Ford's house.   1. Mistress Page is one of the most discreet women.

With rounds of waxen tapers° on their heads,   crowns of candles
50 And rattles in their hands. Upon a sudden,
As Falstaff, she, and I are newly met,
Let them from forth a saw-pit² rush at once,
With some diffusèd° song. Upon their sight   disordered
We two in great amazèdness will fly.
55 Then let them all encircle him about,
And, fairy-like, to pinch the unclean knight,
And ask him why, that hour of fairy revel,
In their so sacred paths he dares to tread
In shape profane.
MISTRESS FORD   And till he tell the truth,
60 Let the supposèd fairies pinch him sound,°   soundly
And burn him with their tapers.
MISTRESS PAGE   The truth being known,
We'll all present ourselves, dis-horn the spirit,
And mock him home to Windsor.
FORD   The children must
Be practised well to this, or they'll ne'er do't.
65 EVANS I will teach the children their behaviours, and I will be
like a jackanapes° also, to burn the knight with my taber.   monkey; evil spirit
FORD That will be excellent. I'll go buy them vizors.°   masks
MISTRESS PAGE My Nan shall be the Queen of all the Fairies,
Finely attirèd in a robe of white.
70 PAGE That silk³ will I go buy—[aside] and in that tire°   attire
Shall Master Slender steal my Nan away,
And marry her at Eton.⁴ [To MISTRESS PAGE] Go send to Fal-
staff straight.
FORD Nay, I'll to him again in name of Brooke.
He'll tell me all his purpose. Sure he'll come.
75 MISTRESS PAGE Fear not you that. [To PAGE, FORD, and EVANS]
Go get us properties°   props
And tricking° for our fairies.   costumes
EVANS Let us about it. It is admirable pleasures, and fery honest
knaveries.   [Exeunt FORD, PAGE, and EVANS]
MISTRESS PAGE Go, Mistress Ford,
80 Send quickly to Sir John, to know his mind.
[Exit MISTRESS FORD]
I'll to the Doctor. He hath my good will,
And none but he, to marry with Nan Page.
That Slender, though well landed,° is an idiot;   owning much land
And he° my husband best of all affects.°   him / likes most
85 The Doctor is well moneyed, and his friends
Potent at court. He, none but he, shall have her,
Though twenty thousand worthier come to crave her.   Exit

4.5

Enter [the] HOST [of the Garter] and SIMPLE
HOST What wouldst thou have, boor? What, thick-skin?° Speak,   dullard
breathe, discuss. Brief, short, quick, snap.
SIMPLE Marry, sir, I come to speak with Sir John Falstaff, from
Master Slender.

---

2. A pit over which wood was sawed.
3. A sign of Page's financial means.

4. Across the Thames from Windsor.
4.5 Location: The Garter Inn.

5 HOST   There's his chamber, his house, his castle, his standing-
bed and truckle-bed.[1] 'Tis[2] painted about with the story of the
Prodigal,° fresh and new. Go knock and call. He'll speak like   *prodigal son (Luke 15)*
an Anthropophaginian° unto thee. Knock, I say.   *cannibal*

SIMPLE   There's an old woman, a fat woman, gone up into his
10 chamber. I'll be so bold as stay, sir, till she come down. I come
to speak with her, indeed.

HOST   Ha, a fat woman? The knight may be robbed. I'll call.—
Bully knight, bully Sir John! Speak from thy lungs military! Art
thou there? It is thine Host, thine Ephesian,° calls.   *mate*

15 FALSTAFF [*within*]   How now, mine Host?

HOST   Here's a Bohemian Tartar tarries° the coming down of thy   *Here a savage awaits*
fat woman. Let her descend, bully, let her descend. My cham-
bers are honourable. Fie, privacy!° Fie!   *secret goings-on*
    Enter Sir John FALSTAFF

FALSTAFF   There was, mine Host, an old fat woman even now
20 with me; but she's gone.

SIMPLE   Pray you, sir, was't not the wise woman° of Brentford?   *woman skilled in magic*

FALSTAFF   Ay, marry was it, mussel-shell.° What would you with   *empty head? gaper?*
her?

SIMPLE   My master, sir, my master Slender, sent to her, seeing
25 her go through the streets, to know, sir, whether one Nim, sir,
that beguiled° him of a chain, had the chain or no.   *cheated*

FALSTAFF   I spake with the old woman about it.

SIMPLE   And what says she, I pray, sir?

FALSTAFF   Marry, she says that the very same man that beguiled
30 Master Slender of his chain cozened° him of it.   *tricked*

SIMPLE   I would I could have spoken with the woman herself. I
had other things to have spoken with her, too, from him.

FALSTAFF   What are they? Let us know.

HOST   Ay, come, quick.

35 SIMPLE   I may not conceal° them, sir.   *(for "reveal")*

HOST   Conceal them, or thou diest.

SIMPLE   Why, sir, they were nothing but about Mistress Anne
Page, to know if it were my master's fortune to have her or no.

FALSTAFF   'Tis, 'tis his fortune.

40 SIMPLE   What, sir?

FALSTAFF   To have her or no. Go say the woman told me so.

SIMPLE   May I be bold to say so, sir?

FALSTAFF   Ay, Sir Tike;° who more bold?   *cur*

SIMPLE   I thank your worship. I shall make my master glad with
45 these tidings.   [*Exit*]

HOST   Thou art clerkly,° thou art clerkly, Sir John. Was there a   *learned*
wise woman with thee?

FALSTAFF   Ay, that there was, mine Host, one that hath taught
me more wit than ever I learned before in my life. And I paid
50 nothing for it, neither, but was paid° for my learning.   *thrashed*
    Enter BARDOLPH [muddy]

BARDOLPH   O Lord, sir, cozenage, mere° cozenage!   *utter*

HOST   Where be my horses? Speak well of them, varletto.°   *varlet*

BARDOLPH   Run away with the cozeners. For so soon as I came
beyond Eton, they threw me off from behind one of them, in a

---

1. Trundle bed, which could be stored under the larger   2. The "it" in "'Tis" refers to either the wall hanging or
standing bed.   the bed hanging.

55   slough of mire, and set spurs and away, like three German
        devils, three Doctor Faustuses.[3]

      HOST   They are gone but to meet the Duke, villain. Do not say
        they be fled. Germans are honest men.

              Enter Sir Hugh EVANS

      EVANS   Where is mine Host?

60   HOST   What is the matter, sir?

      EVANS   Have a care of your entertainments.° There is a friend   *guests*
        of mine come to town tells me there is three cozen° Garmom-   *related; cheating*
        bles[4] that has cozened all the hosts of Reading, of Maidenhead,
        of Colnbrook,° of horses and money. I tell you for good will,   *nearby villages*
65   look you. You are wise, and full of gibes and vlouting-stocks,°   *laughingstocks*
        and 'tis not convenient° you should be cozened. Fare you well.   *appropriate*

                                               Exit

              Enter Doctor CAIUS

      CAIUS   Vere is mine Host de Jarteer?

      HOST   Here, Master Doctor, in perplexity and doubtful dilemma.

      CAIUS   I cannot tell vat is dat, but it is tell-a me dat you make
70   grand preparation for a duke de Jamany.° By my trot,° der is no   *Germany/troth*
        duke that the court is know to come. I tell you for good will.
        Adieu.   *Exit*

      HOST [*to* BARDOLPH]   Hue and cry,° villain, go! [*To* FALSTAFF]   *Raise the alarm*
        Assist me, knight. I am undone. [*To* BARDOLPH] Fly, run, hue
75   and cry, villain. I am undone.

              Exeunt HOST *and* BARDOLPH [*severally*]°   *separately*

      FALSTAFF   I would all the world might be cozened, for I have
        been cozened, and beaten too. If it should come to the ear of
        the court how I have been transformed, and how my transfor-
        mation hath been washed and cudgelled, they would melt me
80   out of my fat, drop by drop, and liquor° fishermen's boots with   *grease*
        me. I warrant they would whip me with their fine wits till I
        were as crestfallen° as a dried pear. I never prospered since I   *shriveled*
        forswore myself at primero.° Well, if my wind were but long   *cards*
        enough,° I would repent.   *(to list all my sins)*

              Enter MISTRESS QUICKLY

85   Now; whence come you?

      MISTRESS QUICKLY   From the two parties, forsooth.

      FALSTAFF   The devil take one party, and his dam° the other, and   *mother*
        so they shall be both bestowed. I have suffered more for their
        sakes, more than the villainous inconstancy of man's disposi-
90   tion is able to bear.

      MISTRESS QUICKLY   O Lord, sir, and have not they suffered? Yes,
        I warrant, speciously° one of them. Mistress Ford, good heart,   *(for "specially")*
        is beaten black and blue, that you cannot see a white spot about
        her.

95   FALSTAFF   What tellest thou me of black and blue? I was beaten
        myself into all the colours of the rainbow, and I was like to be
        apprehended for the witch of Brentford. But that my admirable
        dexterity of wit, my counterfeiting the action of an old woman,

---

3. Bardolph alludes to Marlowe's *Doctor Faustus,* whose titular hero makes a pact with the devil. In one scene, three devils are conjured to "horse" Benvolio, Frederick, and Martino on their backs and throw them in "some lake of mud and dirt" (13.79–85). In the following scene, the three appear muddy and, anticipating Falstaff's punishment, with horns on their heads.

4. Probably an anagram of "Mömpelgard," the name of a German count who aspired to—and was elected to—the Order of the Garter and whom Shakespeare here satirizes.

delivered me, the knave constable had set me i'th' stocks, i'th'
100 common stocks, for a witch.
MISTRESS QUICKLY   Sir, let me speak with you in your chamber.
You shall hear how things go, and, I warrant, to your content.
Here is a letter will say somewhat. Good hearts, what ado here
is to bring you together! Sure one of you does not serve heaven
105 well, that you are so crossed.°   *thwarted*
FALSTAFF   Come up into my chamber.   *Exeunt*

4.6

Enter [Master] FENTON *and [the]* HOST *[of the Garter]*
HOST   Master Fenton, talk not to me. My mind is heavy. I will
give over° all.   *give up*
FENTON   Yet hear me speak. Assist me in my purpose,
And, as I am a gentleman, I'll give thee
5   A hundred pound in gold more than your loss.
HOST   I will hear you, Master Fenton, and I will at the least keep
your counsel.°   *secret*
FENTON   From time to time I have acquainted you
With the dear love I bear to fair Anne Page,
10   Who mutually hath answered my affection,
So far forth as herself might be her chooser,[1]
Even to my wish. I have a letter from her
Of such contents as you will wonder at,
The mirth whereof so larded with my matter°   *mixed with my concern*
15   That neither singly can be manifested
Without the show of both. Fat Falstaff
Hath a great scene. The image° of the jest   *idea*
I'll show you here at large. Hark, good mine Host.
Tonight at Herne's Oak, just 'twixt twelve and one,
20   Must my sweet Nan present° the Fairy Queen—   *play the part of*
[*Showing the letter*]
The purpose why is here—in which disguise,
While other jests are something rank on foot,°   *somewhat thick afoot*
Her father hath commanded her to slip
Away with Slender, and with him at Eton
25   Immediately to marry. She hath consented.
Now, sir, her mother, ever strong against that match
And firm for Doctor Caius, hath appointed
That he shall likewise shuffle her away,
While other sports are tasking of° their minds,   *engaging*
30   And at the dean'ry,[2] where a priest attends,
Straight marry her. To this her mother's plot
She, seemingly obedient, likewise hath
Made promise to the Doctor. Now, thus it rests.°   *things stand thus*
Her father means she shall be all in white;
35   And in that habit,° when Slender sees his time   *dress*
To take her by the hand and bid her go,
She shall go with him. Her mother hath intended,
The better to denote her to the Doctor—
For they must all be masked and visorèd—
40   That quaint° in green she shall be loose enrobed,   *elegantly*

4.6 Location: Scene continues.
1. Insofar as she might choose her own husband.
2. Residence of the dean (the head of the clergy on the
staff of certain churches); (loosely) a parsonage. Here
Fenton refers to the deanery attached to St. George's
Chapel on the property of Windsor Castle.

With ribbons pendant flaring° 'bout her head; *waving down*
And when the Doctor spies his vantage ripe,
To pinch her by the hand, and on that token
The maid hath given consent to go with him.
45 HOST Which means she to deceive, father or mother?
FENTON Both, my good Host, to go along with me.
And here it rests: that you'll procure the vicar
To stay for me at church 'twixt twelve and one,
And, in the lawful name of ° *name of lawful*
50 To give our hearts united ceremony.
HOST Well, husband° your device. I'll to the vicar. *manage well; (pun)*
Bring you the maid, you shall not lack a priest.
FENTON So shall I evermore be bound to thee.
Besides, I'll make a present° recompense. *Exeunt [severally]* *immediate*

5.1

Enter FALSTAFF *and* [MISTRESS] QUICKLY

FALSTAFF Prithee, no more prattling; go; I'll hold.° This is the *keep the appointment*
third time; I hope good luck lies in odd numbers. Away, go!
They say there is divinity° in odd numbers, either in nativity, *divine power*
chance, or death. Away!
5 MISTRESS QUICKLY I'll provide you a chain, and I'll do what I
can to get you a pair of horns.
FALSTAFF Away, I say! Time wears.° Hold up your head, and *passes*
mince.°   *[Exit* MISTRESS QUICKLY] *walk affectedly*
Enter [Master] FORD *[disguised as Brooke]*
How now, Master Brooke? Master Brooke, the matter will be
10 known tonight or never. Be you in the Park about midnight at
Herne's Oak, and you shall see wonders.
FORD Went you not to her yesterday, sir, as you told me you had
appointed?
FALSTAFF I went to her, Master Brooke, as you see,° like a poor *as I am now*
15 old man; but I came from her, Master Brooke, like a poor old
woman. That same knave Ford, her husband, hath the finest
mad devil of jealousy in him, Master Brooke, that ever governed frenzy. I will tell you, he beat me grievously in the shape
of a woman—for in the shape of man, Master Brooke, I fear
20 not Goliath with a weaver's beam,[1] because I know also life is
a shuttle.[2] I am in haste. Go along with me; I'll tell you all,
Master Brooke. Since I plucked geese,° played truant, and *(child's prank)*
whipped top,° I knew not what 'twas to be beaten till lately. *spun a top*
Follow me. I'll tell you strange things of this knave Ford, on
25 whom tonight I will be revenged, and I will deliver his wife
into your hand. Follow. Strange things in hand, Master Brooke.
Follow.   *Exeunt*

5.2

Enter [Master] PAGE, *[Justice]* SHALLOW, *[and Master]*
SLENDER

PAGE Come, come, we'll couch° i'th' Castle ditch till we see the *lie*
light of our fairies. Remember, son Slender, my daughter.
SLENDER Ay, forsooth. I have spoke with her, and we have a nay-

---

5.1 Location: The Garter Inn.
1. The biblical simile for Goliath's spear handle (1 Samuel 17:7).
2. From Job 7:6: "My days are swifter than a weaver's
shuttle."
5.2 Location: An approach to Windsor Park.

word° how to know one another. I come to her in white and   *password*
5   cry 'mum'; she cries 'budget';° and by that we know one   *mumbudget (silence)*
another.

SHALLOW   That's good, too. But what needs either your 'mum'
or her 'budget'? The white will decipher her well enough. [*To*
PAGE] It hath struck ten o'clock.

10 PAGE   The night is dark; lights and spirits will become it well.
God prosper our sport! No man means evil but the devil, and
we shall know him by his horns. Let's away. Follow me.

                                            Exeunt

5.3

Enter MISTRESS PAGE, MISTRESS FORD, [*and Doctor*]
    CAIUS

MISTRESS PAGE   Master Doctor, my daughter is in green. When
you see your time, take her by the hand, away with her to the
deanery, and dispatch it quickly. Go before into the Park. We
two must go together.

5 CAIUS   I know vat I have to do. Adieu.

MISTRESS PAGE   Fare you well, sir.   [*Exit* CAIUS]
My husband will not rejoice so much at the abuse of Falstaff
as he will chafe at the doctor's marrying my daughter. But 'tis
no matter. Better a little chiding than a great deal of heartbreak.

10 MISTRESS FORD   Where is Nan now, and her troop of fairies, and
the Welsh devil Hugh?

MISTRESS PAGE   They are all couched in a pit hard by Herne's
Oak, with obscured lights, which, at the very instant of Falstaff's and our meeting, they will at once display to the night.

15 MISTRESS FORD   That cannot choose but amaze° him.   *That is bound to frighten*

MISTRESS PAGE   If he be not amazed, he will be mocked. If he
be amazed, he will every way be mocked.

MISTRESS FORD   We'll betray him finely.

MISTRESS PAGE   Against such lewdsters and their lechery
20 Those that betray them do no treachery.

MISTRESS FORD   The hour draws on. To the Oak, to the Oak!

                                            Exeunt

5.4

Enter Sir Hugh EVANS [*disguised as a satyr*] *and* [WIL-
LIAM *Page and other children, disguised as*] *fairies*

EVANS   Trib,° trib, fairies! Come! And remember your parts. Be   *Trip*
pold, I pray you. Follow me into the pit, and when I give the
watch'ords, do as I pid you. Come, come; trib, trib!   *Exeunt*

5.5

Enter Sir John FALSTAFF [*disguised as Herne, with horns
on his head, and bearing a chain*]

FALSTAFF   The Windsor bell hath struck twelve; the minute
draws on. Now the hot-blooded gods assist me! Remember,
Jove, thou wast a bull for thy Europa;[1] love set on thy horns. O
powerful love, that in some respects makes a beast a man; in
5 some other, a man a beast! You were also, Jupiter, a swan, for

---

5.3 Location: Scene continues.
5.4 Location: Scene continues.
5.5 Location: Windsor Park.

1. In classical mythology, Jupiter turned himself into a
bull and abducted Europa by swimming across the sea
with her on his back.

the love of Leda.[2] O omnipotent love! How near the god drew
to the complexion of a goose! A fault done first in the form of
a beast—O Jove, a beastly fault!—and then another fault in the
semblance of a fowl—think on't, Jove, a foul fault! When gods
10 have hot° backs, what shall poor men do? For me, I am here a   *lustful*
Windsor stag, and the fattest, I think, i'th' forest. Send me a
cool rut-time,° Jove, or who can blame me to piss my tallow?[3]   *mating season*

Enter MISTRESS FORD [*followed by*] MISTRESS PAGE

Who comes here? My doe!

MISTRESS FORD   Sir John! Art thou there, my deer,° my male   *(pun on "dear")*
15 deer?

FALSTAFF   My doe with the black scut!° Let the sky rain potatoes,   *tail; pubic hair*
let it thunder to the tune of 'Greensleeves',° hail kissing-   *popular love song*
comfits, and snow eringoes;[4] let there come a tempest of provo-
cation,° I will shelter me here.   *sexual incitement*

[*He embraces her*]

20 MISTRESS FORD   Mistress Page is come with me, sweetheart.

FALSTAFF   Divide me like a bribed° buck, each a haunch. I will   *stolen*
keep my sides to myself, my shoulders for the fellow° of this   *keeper*
walk,° and my horns° I bequeath your husbands. Am I a wood-   *forest / (of a cuckold)*
man,° ha? Speak I like Herne the hunter? Why, now is Cupid   *hunter; womanizer*
25 a child of conscience; he makes restitution.° As I am a true   *repays my suffering*
spirit, welcome!

A noise [*within*]

MISTRESS PAGE   Alas, what noise?

MISTRESS FORD   God forgive our sins!

FALSTAFF   What should this be?

30 MISTRESS FORD *and* MISTRESS PAGE   Away, away!

[*Exeunt* MISTRESS FORD *and* MISTRESS PAGE, *running*]

FALSTAFF   I think the devil will not have me damned, lest the oil
that's in me should set hell on fire. He would never else cross
me thus.

Enter Sir Hugh EVANS, [WILLIAM *Page, and children, dis-*
guised as fairies with tapers;] MISTRESS QUICKLY, [*dis-*
guised] *as the Fairy Queen;* ANNE *Page* [*disguised as a*
fairy; and one disguised as Hobgoblin][5]

MISTRESS QUICKLY   Fairies black, grey, green, and white,
35 You moonshine revellers, and shades° of night,   *spirits*
You orphan heirs of fixèd destiny,[6]
Attend° your office° and your quality.°—   *Perform/duty/calling*
Crier° hobgoblin, make the fairy oyes.°   *Town crier/hear ye*

HOBGOBLIN   Elves, list° your names. Silence, you airy toys.°   *listen for/trifles*
40 Cricket,° to Windsor chimneys shalt thou leap.   *(elf's name)*
Where fires thou find'st unraked° and hearths unswept,   *(hence, likely to die)*
There pinch the maids as blue as bilberry.°   *blueberry*
Our radiant Queen hates sluts and sluttery.°   *dirtiness*

FALSTAFF [*aside*]   They are fairies. He that speaks to them shall die.
45 I'll wink° and couch;° no man their works must eye.   *shut my eyes/lie down*

2. Jupiter turned himself into a swan in order to rape
Leda.
3. If I urinate or sweat away my fat (as stags were
thought to do at rutting time).
4. Candied roots of sea holly that, like sweet "potatoes"
(line 16), were considered an aphrodisiac. *kissing-*
comfits: breath sweeteners ("comfits" are candies).
5. Anne, who was assigned the part of the Fairy Queen

at 4.4.68, is here replaced by Quickly, either as part of
the marital scheming or simply as an indication that the
boy actor who played Quickly also is to play this role.
Similarly, Hobgoblin may have been played by Pistol or
simply by the actor who played Pistol.
6. You parentless inheritors of fixed duties (?). (Fairies
were supposed to be parentless.)

[*He lies down, and hides his face*]

EVANS Where's Bead? Go you, and, where you find a maid
    That ere she sleep has thrice her prayers said,
    Raise up° the organs of her fantasy,°   *Stimulate / imagination*
    Sleep she⁷ as sound as careless° infancy.   *carefree*
50   But those as° sleep and think not on their sins,   *who*
    Pinch them, arms, legs, backs, shoulders, sides, and shins.
MISTRESS QUICKLY About,° about!   *To work*
    Search Windsor Castle, elves, within and out.
    Strew good luck, oafs,° on every sacred room,   *elves*
55   That it may stand till the perpetual doom°   *Judgment Day*
    In state° as wholesome as in state° 'tis fit,   *condition / dignity*
    Worthy° the owner, and the owner it.   *Worthy of*
    The several chairs of order⁸ look you scour
    With juice of balm and every precious flower.
60   Each fair instalment,° coat,° and sev'ral crest⁹   *seat / coat of arms*
    With loyal blazon¹ evermore be blessed;
    And nightly, meadow-fairies, look you sing,
    Like to the Garter's compass,° in a ring.   *circle*
    Th'expressure° that it bears, green let it be,   *image*
65   More fertile-fresh than all the field to see;
    And '*Honi soit qui mal y pense*'² write
    In em'rald tufts, flowers purple, blue, and white,
    Like sapphire, pearl, and rich embroidery,
    Buckled below fair knighthood's bending knee—
70   Fairies use flowers for their charactery.°   *lettering*
    Away, disperse!—But till 'tis one o'clock
    Our dance of custom,° round about the oak   *customary dance*
    Of Herne the hunter, let us not forget.
EVANS Pray you, lock hand in hand; yourselves in order set;
75   And twenty glow-worms shall our lanterns be
    To guide our measure° round about the tree.—   *dance*
    But stay; I smell a man of middle earth.°   *a mortal*
FALSTAFF [*aside*] God defend me from that Welsh fairy,
    Lest he transform me to a piece of cheese!
80 HOBGOBLIN [*to* FALSTAFF] Vile worm, thou wast o'erlooked° even   *destined to evil*
    in thy birth.
MISTRESS QUICKLY [*to fairies*] With trial-fire, touch me° his finger-end.   *touch*
    If he be chaste, the flame will back descend,
    And turn him to no pain; but if he start,
    It is the flesh of a corrupted heart.
HOBGOBLIN A trial, come!
85 EVANS   Come, will this wood° take fire?   *(Falstaff's fingers)*
    They [*burn* FALSTAFF *with*] *tapers*
FALSTAFF O, O, O!
MISTRESS QUICKLY Corrupt, corrupt, and tainted in desire.
    About him, fairies; sing a scornful rhyme;
    And, as you trip, still° pinch him to your time.   *continually*
    They [*dance around* FALSTAFF,] *pinch*[*ing*] *him and*
    sing[*ing*]:

---

7. Though she is sleeping; may she sleep.
8. The various stalls assigned, in St. George's Chapel, Windsor, to members of the Order of the Garter (a high dignity that the monarch conferred, marked by a garter worn below the knee).
9. Heraldic device on top of the helmet.
1. Together with the coat of arms on a banner.
2. Shame to him who thinks evil of it (the motto of the Order of the Garter).

FAIRIES

90   Fie on sinful fantasy!
          Fie on lust and luxury!°   *lechery*
          Lust is but a bloody fire,°   *fire of the blood*
          Kindled with unchaste desire,
          Fed in heart, whose flames aspire,°   *rise up*
95   As thoughts do blow them, higher and higher.
          Pinch him, fairies, mutually.°   *all together*
          Pinch him for his villainy.
      Pinch him, and burn him, and turn him about,
    Till candles and starlight and moonshine be out.
      [*During the song*] *Doctor* CAIUS *comes one way and*
      steals away a boy in [*green*]; [*enter*] SLENDER *another*
      way; he takes a boy in [*white*]; *and* FENTON *steals* ANNE.
      [*After the song*] *a noise of hunting within.* [MISTRESS
      QUICKLY, EVANS, HOBGOBLIN, *and*] *fairies run away.* FAL-
      STAFF *rises* [*and starts to run away*]. *Enter Master* PAGE,
      Master FORD, *and their wives*

100 PAGE   Nay, do not fly. I think we have watched you° now.   *caught you in the act*
     Will none but Herne the hunter serve your turn?
   MISTRESS PAGE   I pray you, come, hold up° the jest no higher.°   *prolong / further*
     Now, good Sir John, how like you Windsor wives?
       [*Pointing to Falstaff's horns*]
     See you these, husband? Do not these fair yokes°   *horns*
105   Become the forest better than the town?
   FORD [*to* FALSTAFF]   Now, sir, who's a cuckold now? Master
     Brooke, Falstaff's a knave, a cuckoldly knave. Here are his
     horns, Master Brooke. And, Master Brooke, he hath enjoyed
     nothing of Ford's but his buck-basket, his cudgel, and twenty
110   pounds of money which must be paid to Master Brooke; his
     horses are arrested° for it,[3] Master Brooke.   *seized as security*
   MISTRESS FORD   Sir John, we have had ill luck. We could never
     mate. I will never take you for my love again, but I will always
     count you my deer.
115 FALSTAFF   I do begin to perceive that I am made an ass.
       [*He takes off the horns*]
   FORD   Ay, and an ox, too. Both the proofs are extant.[4]
   FALSTAFF   And these are not fairies? By the Lord, I was three or
     four times in the thought they were not fairies, and yet the
     guiltiness of my mind, the sudden surprise of my powers,°   *mind*
120   drove the grossness of the foppery° into a received belief—in   *deceit*
     despite of the teeth of° all rhyme and reason—that they were   *against*
     fairies. See now how wit may be made a Jack-a-Lent° when 'tis   *butt*
     upon ill employment!
   EVANS   Sir John Falstaff, serve Got and leave your desires, and
125   fairies will not pinse you.
   FORD   Well said, Fairy Hugh.
   EVANS   And leave you your jealousies too, I pray you.
   FORD   I will never mistrust my wife again till thou art able to
     woo her in good English.
130 FALSTAFF   Have I laid my brain in the sun and dried it, that it
     wants° matter to prevent so gross o'er-reaching as this? Am I   *lacks*

---

3. See note to 4.3.11.   The "proofs" are either the horns, which are "extant"
4. "Ox" (fool, cuckold) is inspired by "yokes" (line 104).   (existing), or the "ass" and the "ox."

ridden with° a Welsh goat too? Shall I have a coxcomb° of	harassed by / jester's cap
frieze? 'Tis time I were choked with a piece of toasted cheese.⁵	

EVANS   Seese is not good to give putter; your belly is all putter.

135 FALSTAFF   'Seese' and 'putter'? Have I lived to stand at the taunt
of one that makes fritters of English? This is enough to be the
decay of lust and late walking° through the realm.   *(for sexual purposes)*

MISTRESS PAGE   Why, Sir John, do you think, though° we would   *even if*
have thrust virtue out of our hearts by the head and shoulders,
140 and have given ourselves without scruple to hell, that ever the
devil could have made you our delight?

FORD   What, a hodge-pudding,° a bag of flax?   *sausage*

MISTRESS PAGE   A puffed° man?   *inflated*

PAGE   Old, cold, withered, and of intolerable entrails?

145 FORD   And one that is as slanderous as Satan?

PAGE   And as poor as Job?

FORD   And as wicked as his wife?⁶

EVANS   And given to fornications, and to taverns, and sack, and
wine, and metheglins;° and to drinkings, and swearings, and   *Welsh spiced drink*
150 starings, pribbles and prabbles?°   *raving and squabbles*

FALSTAFF Well, I am your theme; you have the start° of me. I	advantage
am dejected.° I am not able to answer the Welsh flannel. Igno-	humbled

rance itself is a plummet o'er me.⁷ Use me as you will.

FORD Marry, sir, we'll bring you to Windsor, to one Master	
155 Brooke, that you have cozened of money, to whom you should	
have been° a pander. Over and above that° you have suffered,	intended to be / what

I think to repay that money will be a biting affliction.

PAGE   Yet be cheerful, knight. Thou shalt eat a posset⁸ tonight
at my house, where I will desire thee to laugh at my wife that
160 now laughs at thee. Tell her Master Slender hath married her
daughter.

MISTRESS PAGE [aside] Doctors doubt that!° If Anne Page be my	(expresses disbelief)
daughter, she is, by this,° Doctor Caius's wife.	now

Enter [Master] SLENDER

SLENDER   Whoa, ho, ho, father Page!

165 PAGE   Son, how now? How now, son? Have you dispatched?°   *settled the business*

SLENDER Dispatched? I'll make the best in Gloucestershire	
know on't;° would I were hanged, la, else.°	of it / otherwise

PAGE   Of what, son?

SLENDER I came yonder at Eton to marry Mistress Anne Page,	
170 and she's a great lubberly° boy. If it had not been i'th' church,	loutish
I would have swinged° him, or he should have swinged me. If	beaten; screwed
I did not think it had been Anne Page, would I might never	
stir; and 'tis a postmaster's boy.°	stableboy

PAGE   Upon my life, then, you took the wrong.

175 SLENDER What need you tell me that? I think so, when I took a	
boy for a girl. If I had been married to him, for all° he was in	even though

woman's apparel, I would not have had him.

---

5. "Welsh goat" (line 132) refers to the large number of
goats in Wales, "frieze" (line 133) to a coarse wool made
there, and "toasted cheese" to what was supposedly a
favorite Welsh food.
6. Satan slanders Job (Job 1:9–11, 2:4–5); Job's wife
tempts him to curse God (2:9).
7. A "plummet" is a "plumb line," used for measuring
depths, with a pun on "plumbet," a woolen fabric and,

hence, connected with "Welsh flannel," one of Falstaff's names here for Evans (along with "Ignorance").
The ignorant Evans, the "Welsh flannel," is a woolen
fabric over Falstaff, by which Falstaff means that even
the ignorant Evans can plumb Flastaff's depths, can see
his true motives.
8. Take a restorative drink of hot milk curdled with
wine or ale.

PAGE   Why, this is your own folly. Did not I tell you how you
should know my daughter by her garments?

180   SLENDER   I went to her in white and cried 'mum', and she cried
'budget', as Anne and I had appointed; and yet it was not Anne,
but a postmaster's boy.

MISTRESS PAGE   Good George, be not angry. I knew of your purpose, turned my daughter into green, and indeed she is now

185   with the Doctor at the deanery, and there married.

        Enter Doctor [CAIUS]

CAIUS   Ver is Mistress Page? By Gar, I am cozened! I ha' married
un garçon, a boy, *un paysan*,° by Gar. A boy! It is not Anne   *a peasant*
Page, by Gar. I am cozened.

PAGE   Why, did you take her in green?

190   CAIUS   Ay, be Gar, and 'tis a boy. Be Gar, I'll raise all Windsor.

FORD   This is strange. Who hath got the right Anne?

        Enter [*Master*] FENTON *and* ANNE

PAGE   My heart misgives me: here comes Master Fenton.—
How now, Master Fenton?

ANNE   Pardon, good father. Good my mother, pardon.

195   PAGE   Now, mistress, how chance you went not with Master Slender?

MISTRESS PAGE   Why went you not with Master Doctor, maid?

FENTON   You do amaze° her. Hear the truth of it.   *confuse*
You would have married her, most shamefully,
Where there was no proportion° held in love.   *balance*

200   The truth is, she and I, long since contracted,°   *betrothed*
Are now so sure° that nothing can dissolve° us.   *united / separate*
Th'offence is holy that she hath committed,
And this deceit loses the name of craft,
Of disobedience, or unduteous title,°   *undutifulness*

205   Since therein she doth evitate° and shun   *avoid*
A thousand irreligious cursèd hours
Which forcèd marriage would have brought upon her.

FORD [*to* PAGE *and* MISTRESS PAGE]   Stand not amazed. Here is no remedy.
In love the heavens themselves do guide the state;

210   Money buys lands, and wives are sold by fate.

FALSTAFF   I am glad, though you have ta'en a special stand° to   *hunter's station*
strike at me, that your arrow hath glanced.°   *missed*

PAGE   Well, what remedy? Fenton, heaven give thee joy!
What cannot be eschewed must be embraced.

215   FALSTAFF   When night-dogs run, all sorts of deer are chased.⁹

MISTRESS PAGE   Well, I will muse° no further. Master Fenton,   *complain*
Heaven give you many, many merry days!
Good husband, let us every one go home,
And laugh this sport o'er by a country fire,
Sir John and all.

220   FORD   Let it be so, Sir John.
To Master Brooke you yet shall hold your word,
For he tonight shall lie with Mistress Ford.   *Exeunt*

---

9. When "dogs" (the failed suitors) run out of control
at night, they may catch "all sorts of deer" (the disguised boys, rather than Anne). In other words, you
can't control nocturnal intrigue.

Much Ado About Nothing

Much Ado About Nothing, first published in 1600 and probably written in 1598, weaves together two stories: the benevolent luring of Beatrice and Benedick into mutual declarations of love and the villainous luring of Claudio into the mistaken belief that Hero is unchaste. For the former plot, there seems to be no specific source, though Shakespeare would have encountered stories of scorners of love who fall in love (including Chaucer's *Troilus and Criseyde*). For the story of the virtuous lady falsely accused, sources abound, including Ludovico Ariosto's wonderful version in Canto V of *Orlando Furioso* (1516, translated into English by Sir John Harington in 1591) and Matteo Bandello's twenty-second *Novella* (1554, translated into French by François de Belleforest in 1574). Shakespeare probably knew these and other versions, both dramatic and nondramatic, among them a tragic retelling by Edmund Spenser in Book II of *The Faerie Queene* (1590). By deftly intertwining the two plots, *Much Ado About Nothing* mingles lightheartedness with a certain haunting sadness.

This sadness is a recurrent note in Shakespeare's earlier comedies: *The Comedy of Errors* opens with a condemned man's lament, *The Merchant of Venice* is darkened by Antonio's melancholy and Shylock's bitter rage, and *Love's Labour's Lost* (which features in Biron and Rosaline a pair of sparring lovers who strikingly anticipate Benedick and Beatrice) ends with a death. In several later comedies, most notably *Measure for Measure*, the darkness is so intensified as to make the term "comedy" seem a problem. But in *Much Ado About Nothing*, Shakespeare creates a balance of laughter, longing, and pain that he equals only in two other great romantic comedies from the same period, *As You Like It* and *Twelfth Night, or What You Will*. The titles of all three plays convey an impression of easy, festive wit, a magical effortlessness that is in fact the product of an extraordinary discipline and skill.

This cunning use of effort to produce the effect of effortlessness can be understood in the light of Baldassare Castiglione's famous courtesy manual *The Book of the Courtier* (1528). Castiglione's remarkable book, published in an English translation in 1561, depicts a witty and sophisticated group of men and women who, in several extended conversations, discuss the qualities that must be possessed by the ideal courtier. The courtier, as they envisage him, must be equally adept at making war and at making love. He must be able to assist the Prince and to dance elegantly, to grasp the subtleties of diplomacy and to sing in a pleasant, unaffected voice, to engage in philosophical speculation and to tell amusing after-dinner stories. In similar fashion, court ladies must be at once modest and spirited, chaste and slyly knowing, unspoiled and elegant. These are, in less idealized and rarefied form, the social roles that Benedick and Beatrice are called upon to play. They are roles that demand exceptionally versatile actors.

Such courtly performances, Castiglione's conversationalists acknowledge, risk seeming stilted and artificial; will be successful only if they appear entirely spontaneous and natural. However carefully they prepare their parts, courtiers should hide all signs of study and rehearsal. To achieve grace, they must practice what Castiglione calls *sprezzatura*, a cultivated nonchalance. *Sprezzatura* is a technique for the manipulation of appearance, for masking the hard work that underlies successful performances. This masking is an open secret: others know that you are masking, but they must keep this knowledge suspended in the belief that it is a breach of decorum to acknowledge their own knowledge.

The society of *The Book of the Courtier* lives with other open secrets. Dark forces lie just outside the charmed circle of delightful lords and ladies: war, arbitrary power, the high risk of betrayal and double-dealing, the commodification of women, the grinding labor to which the great mass of human beings are condemned. The courtier's artful refusal to acknowledge any of these forces could be a mode of escapism, but Castiglione is alert to reality's harsh demands. For him, fashioning the self is a means not of withdrawing from a treacherous world, but of operating successfully within it.

Like Castiglione's *Courtier, Much Ado About Nothing* (whose title suggests the playwright's own mastery of *sprezzatura*) is pervasively concerned with social performance that seems at once spontaneous and calculated. Beatrice and Benedick, at the play's center, are both exquisitely self-conscious, but their self-consciousness takes the paradoxical form of a jaunty indifference to conventional niceties, an almost reckless exuberance that masks a heightened sensitivity to the social currents in which they swim.

By contrast, Don John, the bastard brother, characterizes himself from the start as a radically antisocial creature: "I had rather be a canker in a hedge than a rose in his grace, and it better fits my blood to be disdained of all than to fashion a carriage to rob love from any" (1.3.21–23). These are the sentiments of the outsider, one who, like the bastard Edmund in *King Lear,* is not properly part of the family and kinship network, and they are sufficient, in this play, to account for Don John's relentless, curiously disinterested villainy. He is a man who refuses to "fashion a carriage"—to observe the appropriate code of manners—and this refusal is itself a sign of rebellion. For manners are the lived texture of social life in *Much Ado*, not in the sense of a compulsory set of rules but rather in the sense of an evolving awareness of mutual obligation and interconnectedness.

There is, to be sure, something like compulsion in the obligations and pressures within which the men and women of *Much Ado* live, but the play frustrates any attempt to strip away the fabric of graciousness, apparent choice, and pretended spontaneity with which the compulsions are dressed. An exchange in the comedy's opening moments exemplifies the perfect balance between obligation and will that governs the play's vision of social life. Leonato, the Governor of Messina, is informed by letter of the imminent arrival of Don Pedro of Aragon. Entertainment must be provided at once, and Don Pedro's first words call attention to the pressure of compulsory courtesy: "Good Signor Leonato, are you come to meet your trouble? The fashion of the world is to avoid cost, and you encounter it." It is obviously the fashion of the world to apologize in just this way for imposition, and such an apology calls for an equally conventional denial that any trouble is involved. Leonato duly produces such a denial, a particularly gracious and well-turned one: "Never came trouble to my house in the likeness of your grace; for trouble being gone, comfort should remain, but when you depart from me, sorrow abides and happiness takes his leave." Don Pedro responds to this exquisite compliment with an elegantly modified renewal of his first words and then a polite turn toward Leonato's daughter, Hero: "You embrace your charge too willingly. I think this is your daughter" (1.1.77–85).

In a strict calculation of power politics, these words are meaningless: they posture emptily above the "real" social exchange, which involves the obligation of the civilian authority toward the military authority (as it happens, a foreign military) at the close of a successful campaign. But such a view neglects the importance of graceful social performance, performance whose ease signals the elite status of the speakers and tacitly acknowledges the possibility of failure or refusal. With a ceremonial greeting such as this, the possibility may seem merely theoretical, but in fact it comes to hover over the entire play (whose main plot is in effect formally initiated by Don Pedro's polite notice of Leonato's daughter). By the fifth act, after Don Pedro's officer Claudio has publicly humiliated and repudiated his intended bride, all courtesy has withered away, and only bitterness and recrimination exist between the gracious host and his princely guest.

Dogberry's zany sleuthing resolves the crisis, but the crucial point is that there is nothing absolute and automatic about the code of manners. Social rituals are vulnerable to disruption and misunderstanding, and this vulnerability underscores the importance of consciously keeping up appearances, patrolling social perimeters, and fabricating civility.

In Castiglione's world, there is a high premium placed on the concealment of the labor expended in this fabrication, but Shakespeare's comedy gives us glimpses in the frequent references to the support staff and attentiveness involved in entertainment: "Where is my cousin, your son? Hath he provided this music?" (1.2.1–2); "Being entertained for a perfumer, as I was smoking a musty room . . ." (1.3.46–47); "The revellers are entering, brother. Make good room" (2.1.70). Social labor is still more visible in the diverse kinds of discourse in which the characters participate or to which they refer: greeting, entertainment, embassy, formal letter, conjuration, courtship, epigraph, sonneteering, gossip, legal deposition, aggressive wit, formal denunciation, ritualized apology.

Each of these forms of speech requires a display of skill and hence confers a measure of the honor or shame to which the characters of *Much Ado About Nothing* are intensely attuned. Honor and shame are particularly social emotions, the emotions of those who exist in a world of watching and being watched. "Nothing" in Shakespeare's time was pronounced "noting": this is a play obsessed with characters noting other characters. Hence the special force of *masking,* where the serious business of watching is playfully disrupted by disguise, and hence too the crucial significance of those scenes in which Beatrice and Benedick think they are noting others and are in reality being noted (and tricked). Sensitivity to the possibility of being shamed—which includes being laughed at, rejected, insulted, dishonored, humiliated, and so forth—is never very far from the characters of *Much Ado.* It extends from Leonato, who thinks that death is the fairest cover for his daughter's public humiliation, to Benedick, whose intellectual and sexual endurance is ridiculed by Beatrice when he ducks out of their first exchange with "a jade's trick" (1.1.118), to Dogberry, who longs to be writ down an ass. At its core is intense male anxiety about female infidelity, manifested in the constant nervous jokes about cuckoldry and played on viciously by Don John. "If I see anything tonight why I should not marry her, tomorrow," Claudio tells Don John, "in the congregation where I should wed, there will I shame her." Don Pedro promises to join with his friend "to disgrace her" (3.2.103–07).

Honor and shame, as the play develops them, are closely bound up with linguistic performance. Language is society's way of being intimately present in the individual; the characters may adjust to that social presence, may like Beatrice and Benedick playfully resist it, may like Dogberry distort it unintentionally, but the shared codes of language are more powerful than any individual.

Close attention to the language of *Much Ado About Nothing* begins with the observation that the comedy is written largely, though not entirely, in prose, a medium far more familiar to modern audiences than the blank verse that dominates many of Shakespeare's plays. This prose, however, is of a kind to which we are no longer accustomed. Modern prose tends by design to be rather plain and colorless; Elizabethan prose is often playful, rhetorically inventive, and richly metaphorical. *Much Ado About Nothing* at once plays elaborate prose games and pokes fun at them, as when Benedick complains that lovesick Claudio "was wont to speak plain and to the purpose, like an honest man and a soldier, and now is he turned orthography. His words are a very fantastical banquet, just so many strange dishes" (2.3.16–19). Shakespeare was certainly capable of writing what we would regard as clear, uncluttered prose: "I learn in this letter that Don Pedro of Aragon comes this night to Messina" (1.1.1–2). But he could also produce astonishing rhetorical effects:

> She told me—not thinking I had been myself—that I was the Prince's jester, that I was duller than a great thaw, huddling jest upon jest with such impossible conveyance upon me that I stood like a man at a mark, with a whole army shooting at me. She speaks poniards, and every word stabs. If her breath were as terrible as her terminations, there were no living near her, she would infect to the North Star. I would not marry her though she were endowed with all that Adam had left him before he transgressed. She would have made Hercules have turned spit, yea, and have cleft his club to make the fire, too. (2.1.212–21)

A night watchman. From Thomas Dekker, *The Belman of London* (1608).

The wonderful improvisational piling up of images, each at once subtly linked to the preceding one and yet swerving in a new direction, captures the movement of Benedick's mind: the rush of genuine anger and hurt feelings mingled with the impulse to turn his pain into a comically misogynistic performance to entertain Don Pedro (a performance that, ironically, confirms the charge—that he is the Prince's jester—that originally stung him).

Linguistic performance is the social equivalent of the performance in warfare that is both alluded to and conspicuously excluded from the play's action. Language is violence, and language is the alternative to violence: the play entertains both hypotheses and plays them off against each other. "There is a kind of merry war betwixt Signor Benedick and her," says Leonato of his niece. "They never meet but there's a skirmish of wit between them" (1.1.49–51). If words are the agents of civility, they are also dangerous weapons: "Thy slander hath gone through and through her heart, / And she lies buried with her ancestors"; "God knows, I loved my niece, / And she is dead, slandered to death by villains" (5.1.68–69, 87–88). What we glimpse in the symbolic murder of Hero is not only the maligning power of slander, but also the aggressive potential of even polite or playful speech. The "merry war" between Beatrice and Benedick leaves scars.

The more one attends to the language of *Much Ado About Nothing*, the more it seems saturated with violence. In the lighthearted opening scene alone, there are almost constant comic references to war, plague, betrayal, heresy, burning at the stake, blinding, hanging, spying, poisoning. To be sure, the horrors are not themselves realized dramatically in the play; they are present as mere jokes. Nonetheless, they are present, recalled again and again by the constant threat of disaster, by symbolic death, by public shaming. Even in the tidal rush of the comic resolution, amid the marriages, the music, and the dance, Benedick's final words, indeed the final words of the play, deliberately call attention to the violence that the language has continually, if obliquely, registered. Informed of Don John's capture, Benedick declares, "Think not on him till tomorrow, I'll devise thee brave punishments for him. Strike up, pipers." *Dance* (5.4.121–22).

Viewed in the light of the close, with its conspicuous deferral of torture, but only until tomorrow, the play does not simply transform human misery and violence into wit, but rather addresses itself to the ways in which society manages to endure, to reproduce, to avoid immersion in its own destructive element, to dance. It does so by conscious and unconscious deferral, by the manipulation of appearances, by the deployment of illusions that are known by at least some of its members (the worst and the best) to be illusions.

Illusions are tricks and deceptions, but they are also the social fictions men and women live by. Claudio and Hero exist in the play almost entirely in and as such fictions: their emotions seem less something they possess inwardly than something constructed for them out of the appropriate conventions and rituals. A more complex manifestation in the play of the primacy of illusion is the relation between Beatrice and Benedick. The plot to trick the celebrated skirmishers into marriage originates with Don Pedro, who promises, if Leonato, Hero, and Claudio cooperate with him, to "fash-

Lovers sparring with torches. From George Wither, *A Collection of Emblemes* (1635).

ion" the match. The key to his success is his ability to mobilize the social code of shame and honor to which Beatrice and Benedick are bound and to use this code as a means to discipline—to shape into a plot that will culminate in marriage—the powerful chafing between them. For both Beatrice and Benedick, the force that pushes them toward declarations of love and hence toward marriage vows is as much hearing themselves criticized by their friends as hearing that the other is desperately in love. "Can this be true?" asks Beatrice, her ears burning. "Stand I condemned for pride and scorn so much?" (3.1.108–09). "I hear how I am censured," Benedick declares, resolving that he "must not seem proud" (2.3.199–200, 202–03).

The conspiratorial fabrication of appearances so as to manipulate the code of shame and honor has the odd effect of establishing a link between the socially approved practices of Don Pedro and the wicked practices of Don John, his bastard brother. Shakespeare seems to go out of his way to call attention to this link: moments after Don Pedro undertakes to "fashion" the affection between Beatrice and Benedick, the villainous Borachio declares that he "will so fashion the matter that Hero shall be absent" and hence can be impersonated by Margaret. In effect, the play's term for the social system in which all the characters—evil as well as virtuous—are involved is "fashion." Shakespeare deftly uses the term both as noun and verb—that is, both to designate the images (including the fashionable costumes) that elicit emotions and to describe the process that shapes these images.

Fashion is closely related not only to image but also to verbal style, which in the aesthetics of the period was regarded as a kind of dress. "The body of your discourse," laughs Benedick, "is sometimes guarded with fragments, and the guards are but slightly basted on neither" (1.1.232–34). The pervasiveness of fashion allows the possibility of drastic deception, but it is also society's redemptive principle. The movement of the play is not so much the unmasking of fraud to reveal the true, virtuous essence within as rather the refashioning, after a dangerous illusion, of the proper image and the appropriate words: "Sweet Hero," cries Claudio after his eyes have been opened to the deception, "now thy image doth appear / In the rare semblance that I loved it first" (5.1.235–36).

The fashioning with which the play is concerned complicates any simple opposition between authentic inner feelings and social norms. This is, after all, a plot that features a wooing by masked proxy instead of direct wooing, a theatrical ritual of remorse instead of remorse, a declaration of love based upon a set of illusions and motivated by the fear of shame. Near the play's close, we see Benedick struggling to compose the required sonnet to Beatrice—an entirely conventional exercise performed to fulfill the theatrical role in which he has been cast ("myself in love"). And in the final moments, when the deception is revealed, it is this exercise, rather than any feelings of the heart, that confirms the match. "I'll be sworn upon't that he loves her," declares Claudio:

> For here's a paper written in his hand,
> A halting sonnet of his own pure brain,
> Fashioned to Beatrice.

When a similar sonnet by Beatrice is produced, Benedick cries, "A miracle! Here's our own hands against our hearts" (5.4.85–88, 91).

Many readers of the play, and most performers, have tried to reverse this formulation: Beatrice and Benedick's conversations may be hostile, the interpretation goes, but in their hearts they are, and have long been, deeply in love. Beatrice seems to refer to an earlier time when she had given her heart to Benedick and had evidently been disappointed: "once before he won it of me, with false dice" (2.1.243–44). If they do not declare their love, it is because they are too defensive or, alternatively, too wise to play society's conventional game. In a world of pervasive conventionality and social control, one clever way to insist upon some spontaneity and hence to achieve some authenticity is to quarrel. Perhaps. But what if we do not dismiss their own words? What if we take the conspiracy against them seriously? Beatrice and Benedick would in that case not "love" each other from the start; it would not at all be clear that they love each other, entirely independent of social manipulation, at the close. They are, at least to some extent, tricked into marriage; without the pressure that moves them to professions of love, they would have remained unmarried. Beatrice and Benedick constantly tantalize us with the possibility of an identity quite different from that of Claudio and Hero, an identity deliberately fashioned to resist the constant pressure of society. But that pressure finally prevails. Marriage is a social conspiracy.

If such a view seems ultimately too unsentimental to be tenable in a romantic comedy, it nonetheless makes possible the brilliant scene in which Benedick asks what he can do to prove his love for Beatrice, and Beatrice replies, "Kill Claudio" (4.1.287). Similarly, it helps to account for the laughter provoked by the disillusioned exchange very near the play's close: "Do not you love me?" "Why no, no more than reason" (5.4.74). In both cases, where we might expect tender words, we get the opposite. If we feel nonetheless that romantic love triumphs in the end, we do so in effect because we—audience and readers—participate in the conspiracy to gull the pair into marriage by insisting that they love each other more than reason. In doing so, we confer upon the general restoration of civility at the play's close something more deeply pleasurable.

Benedick and Beatrice have rational arguments, grounded in the gender politics of their world, for remaining single. Benedick knows that a married man must put his honor at risk by entrusting it to a woman, while Beatrice knows that a married woman must put her integrity at risk by submitting herself to a man: "Would it not grieve a woman to be overmastered with a piece of valiant dust?" (2.1.51–52). Even when they are manipulated into declaring their love, they cannot settle into the language of conventional courtship: "Thou and I are too wise," Benedick tells Beatrice, "to woo peaceably" (5.2.61). Their union at the close is a triumph of folly over the "wisdom" of the

A man trapped in the yoke of matrimony. From Henry Peacham. *Minerva Britanna* (1612).

single life, a triumph that recalls Erasmus's *Praise of Folly,* where love is said to be possible only because men and women are induced to put aside their reason and plunge into saving foolishness. Why should they do so? The answer is that it is better to live in illusion than in social isolation and that, as Benedick says, "the world must be peopled" (2.3.213–14).

In most productions of the play, audiences are made to feel that submission to the discipline of love and marriage—"taming my wild heart" (3.1.113), as Beatrice so wonderfully puts it—is a magnificent release of love and energy. Shakespeare had already experimented with comparable themes in *The Taming of the Shrew*, but Petruchio's conquest of Kate seems, at least for many modern viewers, too brutal to accept without a lingering sense of constriction and loss. What keeps the conclusion of *Much Ado About Nothing* from appearing brittle or bitter is a sense that the triumph of illusion is life-affirming, a sense that the friction between Beatrice and Benedick can be turned into mutual pleasure.

If the Claudio/Hero plot and the Beatrice/Benedick plot are two ways in which Shakespeare's comedy shows the saving necessity of illusion, there is a third manifestation: the illusion that evil manifests itself as Don John—that is, in a supremely incompetent and finally impotent form—and that, although it fools clear-eyed and sophisticated observers like Don Pedro, it may be exposed by a bumbling idiot like Dogberry. Some years later, Shakespeare returned to a ruthlessly disillusioned version of the same story, the lover tricked into believing that his beloved has been unfaithful, and called it not *Much Ado About Nothing* but *Othello*.

STEPHEN GREENBLATT

TEXTUAL NOTE

"*Much adoe about Nothing . . . Written by William Shakespeare*" was first published in 1600, in a quarto (Q) printed by Valentine Simmes (or Sims) for Andrew Wise and William Aspley. This is the only version of the play that appeared during Shakespeare's lifetime. The title page states that the play "hath been sundrie times publikely acted by the right honourable, the Lord Chamberlaine his seruants."

Much Ado About Nothing is listed in a Stationers' Register entry of August 4, 1600, along with *As You Like It, Henry V,* and Ben Jonson's *Every Man in His Humour.* All are marked "to be staied"—that is, not published without further permission. It is generally thought that the Lord Chamberlain's Men were attempting to ensure that they would be paid for any printing of these popular plays and that the release of *Much Ado About Nothing* later that same year indicates that the company had resolved whatever dispute had led them to stay publication.

Most scholars, including the Oxford editors, believe that the 1600 Quarto of *Much Ado About Nothing* was set from Shakespeare's "foul papers"—that is, his own manuscript of the play. Evidence includes the omission of several entrances and exits, certain loose ends in the dialogue, and the presence of "ghost" characters. For example, Q's stage directions at the beginning of Acts 1 and 2 list Leonato's wife, Innogen, but Innogen neither speaks nor is spoken to in the course of the play. Evidently she is the ghostly trace of an idea that the playwright abandoned.

Q's speech prefixes are inconsistent, another characteristic feature of foul papers, and in 4.2 they preserve the names of the actors Shakespeare had in mind for two of the comic parts: Will Kemp for Dogberry and Richard Cowley for Verges. Since Kemp left the Lord Chamberlain's Men in 1599, scholars think the play must have been first performed before the date of his departure. And since Francis Meres does not include *Much Ado About Nothing* in a list of Shakespeare's plays he compiled in September 1598 (unless that is what he meant by the play he calls *Loue Labours wonne*), scholars think it probable that the play was first performed after that date. Therefore the likeliest date of the first performance is the winter of 1598–99.

The First Folio (1623) text of the play (F) was based on Q. There are no act or scene divisions in Q; F indicates only act divisions (with the exception of 1.1).

SELECTED BIBLIOGRAPHY

Barish, Jonas A. "Pattern and Purpose in the Prose of *Much Ado About Nothing.*" *Rice University Studies* 60.2 (Spring 1974): 19–30. Variations in the play's mannered rhetorical scheme offer insights into its characters and situations.

Berger, Harry, Jr. "Against the Sink-a-Pace: Sexual and Family Politics in *Much Ado About Nothing.*" *Shakespeare Quarterly* 33 (1982): 302–13. Characterizes Messina's gender conventions in terms of virtue, constancy, reputation, deception, and fashion.

Berry, Ralph. *Shakespeare's Comedies: Explorations in Form.* Princeton: Princeton University Press, 1972. 154–74. Focusing on the difficult reconciliation of sensory experience and judgment, *Much Ado About Nothing* explores the limits of knowledge.

Cook, Carol. " 'The Sign and Semblance of Her Honor': Reading Gender Difference in *Much Ado About Nothing.*" *PMLA* 101.2 (1986): 186–202. The play presents the polysemous threat of woman in a world where men are the manipulators and interpreters of signs.

Everett, Barbara. "*Much Ado About Nothing*: The Unsociable Comedy." *English Comedy.* Ed. Michael Cordner, Peter Holland, and John Kerrigan. New York: Cambridge University Press, 1994. 68–84. Shakespeare's realistic portrait of love in society typically mixes its comic nothings with serious concerns.

Gay, Penny. "*Much Ado About Nothing*: A Kind of Merry War." *As She Likes It: Shakespeare's Unruly Women.* London: Routledge, 1994. 143–77. Performance history since the 1950s, spotlighting representations of Beatrice and Benedick.

Howard, Jean. "Renaissance Antitheatricality and the Politics of Gender and Rank in *Much Ado About Nothing.*" *Shakespeare Reproduced: The Text in History and Ideology.* Ed. Jean E. Howard and Marion F. O'Connor. New York: Methuen, 1987. 163–87. *Much Ado About Nothing* supports Elizabethan ideology, condemning marginal social groups through accusations of illegitimate theatrical practice.

Moisan, Thomas. "Deforming Sources: Literary Antecedants and Their Traces in *Much Ado About Nothing.*" *Shakespeare Studies* 31 (2003): 165–83. The play's furtive and ambivalent relationship to its sources reflects its depiction of character, politics, power, and representation.

Myhill, Nova. "Spectatorship in/of *Much Ado About Nothing.*" *Studies in English Literature* 39.2 (1999): 291–311. Considers how *Much Ado About Nothing*'s unreliable "notings" challenge the theater audience's assumptions of omniscience and invulnerability.

Salingar, Leo. "Borachio's Indiscretion: Some Noting about Much Ado." *The Italian World of English Renaissance Drama: Cultural Exchange and Intertextuality.* Ed. Michele Marrapodi. London: Associated University Presses, 1998. 225–38. *Much Ado About Nothing* as a bittersweet masquerade of social ambiguity and false communications.

Traugott, John. "Creating a Rational Rinaldo: A Study in the Mixture of the Genres of Comedy and Romance in *Much Ado About Nothing.*" *Genre* 15 (1982): 157–81. Shows how comedy and romance contaminate and purify each other, one becoming ennobled and the other cured of cruelty.

FILM

Much Ado About Nothing. 1993. Dir. Kenneth Branagh. UK/USA. 111 min. Festive romp set in sunny, country-house Italy. With Kenneth Branagh and Emma Thompson.

Much Ado About Nothing

The Persons of the Play

DON PEDRO, Prince of Aragon

BENEDICK, of Padua }
CLAUDIO, of Florence } lords, companions of Don Pedro

BALTHASAR, attendant on Don Pedro, a singer

DON JOHN, the bastard brother of Don Pedro

BORACHIO }
CONRAD } followers of Don John

LEONATO, governor of Messina

HERO, his daughter

BEATRICE, an orphan, his niece

ANTONIO, an old man, brother of Leonato

MARGARET }
URSULA } waiting-gentlewomen attendant on Hero

FRIAR FRANCIS

DOGBERRY, the Constable in charge of the Watch

VERGES, the Headborough, Dogberry's partner

A SEXTON

WATCHMEN

A BOY, serving Benedick

Attendants and messengers

1.1

Enter LEONATO, *governor of Messina,* HERO *his*
daughter, and BEATRICE *his niece, with a*
MESSENGER

LEONATO I learn in this letter that Don Pedro of Aragon comes
this night to Messina.

MESSENGER He is very near by this. He was not three leagues off
when I left him.

5 LEONATO How many gentlemen have you lost in this action?°   *campaign*

MESSENGER But few of any sort,° and none of name.°   *rank / distinction*

LEONATO A victory is twice itself when the achiever brings home
full numbers. I find here that Don Pedro hath bestowed much
honour on a young Florentine called Claudio.

10 MESSENGER Much deserved on his part, and equally remem-
bered° by Don Pedro. He hath borne himself beyond the prom-   *rewarded*
ise of his age, doing in the figure of a lamb the feats of a lion.
He hath indeed better bettered° expectation than you must   *exceeded*
expect of me to tell you how.

15 LEONATO He hath an uncle here in Messina will be very much
glad of it.

MESSENGER I have already delivered him letters, and there
appears much joy in him—even so much that joy could not
show itself modest° enough without a badge° of bitterness.°   *moderate / show / grief*

1.1 Location: Messina (a city in Sicily). Before the house of Leonato.

20   LEONATO   Did he break out into tears?

MESSENGER   In great measure.

LEONATO   A kind° overflow of kindness,° there are no faces truer   *natural / tenderness*
than those that are so washed. How much better is it to weep
at joy than to joy at weeping!

25   BEATRICE   I pray you, is Signor Montanto[1] returned from the
wars, or no?

MESSENGER   I know none of that name, lady. There was none
such in the army, of any sort.

LEONATO   What is he that you ask for, niece?

30   HERO   My cousin means Signor Benedick of Padua.[2]

MESSENGER   O, he's returned, and as pleasant° as ever he was.   *entertaining*

BEATRICE   He set up his bills° here in Messina, and challenged   *public notices*
Cupid at the flight;[3] and my uncle's fool,° reading the chal-   *jester*
lenge, subscribed for Cupid and challenged him at the bird-

35   bolt.[4] I pray you, how many hath he killed and eaten in these
wars? But how many hath he killed? For indeed I promised to
eat all of his killing.

LEONATO   Faith, niece, you tax° Signor Benedick too much. But   *abuse*
he'll be meet° with you, I doubt it not.   *even*

40   MESSENGER   He hath done good service, lady, in these wars.

BEATRICE   You had musty victual, and he hath holp° to eat it. He   *helped*
is a very valiant trencherman,° he hath an excellent stomach.   *eater*

MESSENGER   And a good soldier too, lady.

BEATRICE   And a good soldier° to a lady, but what is he to a lord?   *servant; lady-killer*

45   MESSENGER   A lord to a lord, a man to a man, stuffed° with all   *well furnished*
honourable virtues.

BEATRICE   It is so, indeed. He is no less than a stuffed man.° But   *mannequin*
for the stuffing—well, we are all mortal.[5]

LEONATO   You must not, sir, mistake my niece. There is a kind

50   of merry war betwixt Signor Benedick and her. They never
meet but there's a skirmish of wit between them.

BEATRICE   Alas, he gets nothing by that. In our last conflict four
of his five wits[6] went halting° off, and now is the whole man   *limping*
governed with one, so that if he have wit enough to keep him-

55   self warm,[7] let him bear it for a difference[8] between himself
and his horse, for it is all the wealth that he hath left to be
known a reasonable creature. Who is his companion now? He
hath every month a new sworn brother.

MESSENGER   Is't possible?

60   BEATRICE   Very easily possible. He wears his faith° but as the   *loyalty*
fashion of his hat, it ever changes with the next block.[9]

MESSENGER   I see, lady, the gentleman is not in your books.°   *favor*

BEATRICE   No. An° he were, I would burn my study. But I pray   *If*
you, who is his companion? Is there no young squarer° now   *boisterous quarreler*

65   that will make a voyage with him to the devil?

MESSENGER   He is most in the company of the right noble
Claudio.

---

1. In fencing, a montanto is an upright blow or thrust.
2. A city in northern Italy.
3. To an archery match. (He claimed to surpass Cupid
at arousing love.)
4. To a contest using bird bolts, or blunt, short-range
arrows allowed to fools and children (and thus appropriate to young Cupid). *subscribed for*: took up the
challenge on behalf of.

5. But as for what he is made of (his "stuffing"), he is
probably as faulty as the rest of us.
6. *five wits*: mental faculties (memory, imagination,
judgment, fantasy, and common sense).
7. If he have minimal common sense.
8. Let him display the fact in his coat of arms in order
to distinguish himself.
9. Newest mold for a hat; fashion.

BEATRICE O Lord, he will hang upon him like a disease. He is
sooner caught than the pestilence,° and the taker° runs pres-   *plague / victim*
70 ently° mad. God help the noble Claudio. If he have caught the   *immediately*
Benedick, it will cost him a thousand pound ere a° be cured.   *he*

MESSENGER I will hold friends[1] with you, lady.

BEATRICE Do, good friend.

LEONATO You will never run mad,[2] niece.

75 BEATRICE No, not till a hot January.

MESSENGER Don Pedro is approached.

Enter DON PEDRO, CLAUDIO, BENEDICK, BALTHASAR, *and*
[DON] JOHN *the bastard*

DON PEDRO Good Signor Leonato, are you come to meet your
trouble? The fashion° of the world is to avoid cost, and you   *custom*
encounter° it.   *go to meet*

80 LEONATO Never came trouble to my house in the likeness of
your grace; for trouble being gone, comfort should remain, but
when you depart from me, sorrow abides and happiness takes
his leave.

DON PEDRO You embrace your charge° too willingly. I think this   *duty*
85 is your daughter.

LEONATO Her mother hath many times told me so.

BENEDICK Were you in doubt, sir, that you asked her?

LEONATO Signor Benedick, no, for then were you a child.

DON PEDRO You have it full,[3] Benedick. We may guess by this
90 what you are, being a man. Truly, the lady fathers herself.[4] Be
happy, lady, for you are like an honourable father.

BENEDICK If Signor Leonato be her father, she would not have
his head;[5] on her shoulders for all Messina, as like him as she
is.

95 BEATRICE[6] I wonder that you will still° be talking, Signor Bene-   *always*
dick. Nobody marks you.

BENEDICK What, my dear Lady Disdain! Are you yet living?

BEATRICE Is it possible disdain should die while she hath such
meet° food to feed it as Signor Benedick? Courtesy itself must   *suitable*
100 convert° to disdain if you come in her presence.   *turn*

BENEDICK Then is courtesy a turncoat. But it is certain I am
loved of° all ladies, only you excepted. And I would I could   *by*
find in my heart that I had not a hard heart, for truly I love
none.

105 BEATRICE A dear happiness to women. They would else have
been troubled with a pernicious suitor. I thank God and my
cold blood I am of your humour° for that. I had rather hear my   *disposition*
dog bark at a crow than a man swear he loves me.

BENEDICK God keep your ladyship still in that mind. So some
110 gentleman or other shall scape a predestinate° scratched face.   *escape an inevitable*

BEATRICE Scratching could not make it worse an 'twere such a
face as yours were.

BENEDICK Well, you are a rare parrot-teacher.[7]

BEATRICE A bird of my tongue is better than a beast of yours.[8]

---

1. I will stay on good terms (so as not to provoke your
sarcasm).
2. "Catch the Benedick."
3. Your sarcasm is fully repaid.
4. She shows by her looks who her father is.
5. The head of an old man.

6. During Beatrice and Benedick's conversation, Don
Pedro talks with Leonato (see line 119).
7. Chatterer (repetitive, like one who teaches a parrot
to speak).
8. A bird with my powers of speech is better than a
dumb beast who, like you, has none.

115 BENEDICK   I would my horse had the speed of your tongue,
and so good a continuer.⁹ But keep your way,° i' God's name. I   *carry on*
have done.

BEATRICE   You always end with a jade's trick.¹ I know you of old.

DON PEDRO   That is the sum of all, Leonato. Signor Claudio and
120   Signor Benedick, my dear friend Leonato hath invited you all.
I tell him we shall stay here at the least a month, and he heartily prays some occasion may detain us longer. I dare swear he
is no hypocrite, but prays from his heart.

LEONATO   If you swear, my lord, you shall not be forsworn. [*To*
125   DON JOHN] Let me bid you welcome, my lord. Being° recon-   *Since you are*
ciled to the Prince your brother, I owe you all duty.

DON JOHN   I thank you. I am not of many words, but I thank you.

LEONATO [*to* DON PEDRO]   Please it your grace lead on?

DON PEDRO   Your hand, Leonato. We will go together.²

Exeunt. Manent° BENEDICK *and* CLAUDIO   *Remain*

130 CLAUDIO   Benedick, didst thou note the daughter of Signor Leonato?

BENEDICK   I noted her not,³ but I looked on her.

CLAUDIO   Is she not a modest young lady?

BENEDICK   Do you question me as an honest man should do, for
135   my simple true judgement, or would you have me speak after
my custom, as being a professed tyrant° to their sex?   *pitiless critic*

CLAUDIO   No, I pray thee speak in sober judgement.

BENEDICK   Why, i'faith, methinks she's too low° for a high   *short*
praise, too brown for a fair praise, and too little for a great
140   praise. Only this commendation I can afford her, that were she
other than she is she were unhandsome, and being no other
but as she is, I do not like her.

CLAUDIO   Thou thinkest I am in sport.° I pray thee tell me truly   *jest*
how thou likest her.

145 BENEDICK   Would you buy her, that you enquire after her?

CLAUDIO   Can the world buy such a jewel?

BENEDICK   Yea, and a case to put it into. But speak you this with
a sad° brow, or do you play the flouting jack, to tell us Cupid   *serious*
is a good hare-finder and Vulcan a rare carpenter?⁴ Come, in
150   what key shall a man take° you to go° in the song?   *understand / join*

CLAUDIO   In mine eye she is the sweetest lady that ever I looked
on.

BENEDICK   I can see yet without spectacles, and I see no such
matter. There's her cousin, an she were not possessed with a
155   fury, exceeds her as much in beauty as the first of May doth the
last of December. But I hope you have no intent to turn husband, have you?

CLAUDIO   I would scarce trust myself though I had sworn the
contrary, if Hero would be my wife.

160 BENEDICK   Is't come to this? In faith, hath not the world one
man but he will wear his cap with suspicion?⁵ Shall I never see

---

9. And had your staying power ("continuer," in horsemanship, means "stayer").
1. A trick worthy of a badly trained horse (here, dropping out of a race).
2. We will walk out hand in hand (and thus avoid taking precedence).
3. I paid her no special attention.
4. *play . . . carpenter:* spout praises contrary to fact and

intended satirically. Blind Cupid is poorly suited to the
sharp-sighted sport of hunting hares, while Vulcan, the
god of fire, was an excellent ("rare") blacksmith, not a
carpenter. *flouting jack:* mocking rogue.
5. *but . . . suspicion:* who will not be suspected of wearing his cap in order to hide a cuckold's horns (conventional sign of a wife's infidelity).

a bachelor of three-score again? Go to,° i'faith, an thou wilt
needs thrust thy neck into a yoke, wear the print of it, and sigh
away Sundays.[6] Look, Don Pedro is returned to seek you.

Enter DON PEDRO

Go on

165 DON PEDRO   What secret hath held you here that you followed
not to Leonato's?

BENEDICK   I would your grace would constrain me to tell.

DON PEDRO   I charge thee on thy allegiance.

BENEDICK   You hear, Count Claudio? I can be secret as a dumb
170 man, I would have you think so. But on my allegiance, mark
you this, on my allegiance! He is in love. With who? Now that
is your grace's part. Mark how short his answer is: with Hero,
Leonato's short daughter.

CLAUDIO   If this were so, so were it uttered.[7]

175 BENEDICK   Like the old tale, my lord—it is not so, nor 'twas not
so, but indeed, God forbid it should be so.[8]

CLAUDIO   If my passion change not shortly, God forbid it should
be otherwise.

DON PEDRO   Amen, if you love her, for the lady is very well
180 worthy.

CLAUDIO   You speak this to fetch me in,° my lord.

to trick me

DON PEDRO   By my troth, I speak my thought.

CLAUDIO   And in faith, my lord, I spoke mine.

BENEDICK   And by my two faiths and troths,[9] my lord, I spoke
185 mine.

CLAUDIO   That I love her, I feel.

DON PEDRO   That she is worthy, I know.

BENEDICK   That I neither feel how she should be loved nor know
how she should be worthy is the opinion that fire cannot melt
190 out of me. I will die in it at the stake.

DON PEDRO   Thou wast ever an obstinate heretic in the despite°

contempt

of beauty.

CLAUDIO   And never could maintain his part° but in the force of

argument

his will.[1]

195 BENEDICK   That a woman conceived me, I thank her. That she
brought me up, I likewise give her most humble thanks. But
that I will have a recheat winded in my forehead, or hang my
bugle in an invisible baldric,[2] all women shall pardon me.
Because I will not do them the wrong to mistrust any,[3] I will
200 do myself the right to trust none. And the fine° is—for the

conclusion

which I may go the finer[4]—I will live a bachelor.

DON PEDRO   I shall see thee ere I die look pale with love.

BENEDICK   With anger, with sickness, or with hunger, my lord;
not with love. Prove° that ever I lose more blood with love than

If you prove

205 I will get again with drinking,[5] pick out mine eyes with a bal-

6. thrust . . . Sundays: take on the burdens and tedium
of marriage, when you might be enjoying yourself as a
bachelor.
7. so . . . uttered: this is how Benedick would tell it.
8. In an English fairy tale (a variant on the Bluebeard
story), a man suspected by his bride-to-be of having
killed his former wives denies his guilt with the refrain
Benedick quotes.
9. His loyalty to both Don Pedro and Claudio, and jok-
ingly, his duplicity.
1. But through prideful obstinacy rather than reason.
2. But . . . baldric: But that I should wear a cuckold's

horns. A recheat was a call sounded ("winded") on a
horn to recall the hounds. A baldric was a belt to hold
a horn ("bugle"); it was invisible, a sign of the cuckold's
ignorance.
3. Because I do not wish to wrong women by suspect-
ing any of infidelity.
4. I may dress better (because he will have more money
to spare).
5. lose . . . drinking: alluding to the belief that sighing
like a lover caused the blood to evaporate, and drinking
wine renewed it.

lad-maker's[6] pen and hang me up at the door of a brothel house
for the sign of blind Cupid.[7]

DON PEDRO Well, if ever thou dost fall from this faith thou wilt
prove a notable argument.°   *subject of talk*

210 BENEDICK If I do, hang me in a bottle like a cat, and shoot at
me,[8] and he that hits me, let him be clapped on the shoulder
and called Adam.[9]

DON PEDRO Well, as time shall try.° 'In time the savage bull doth   *prove*
bear the yoke.'[1]

215 BENEDICK The savage bull may, but if ever the sensible° Bene-   *rational*
dick bear it, pluck off the bull's horns and set them in my forehead, and let me be vilely painted, and in such great letters as
they write 'Here is good horse to hire' let them signify under
my sign 'Here you may see Benedick, the married man'.

220 CLAUDIO If this should ever happen thou wouldst be horn-mad.[2]

DON PEDRO Nay, if Cupid have not spent all his quiver in Venice[3] thou wilt quake for this shortly.

BENEDICK I look for an earthquake[4] too, then.

DON PEDRO Well, you will temporize with the hours.[5] In the
225 mean time, good Signor Benedick, repair° to Leonato's, com-   *go*
mend me to him, and tell him I will not fail him at supper, for
indeed he hath made great preparation.

BENEDICK I have almost matter° enough in me for such an   *intelligence*
embassage.° And so I commit you—   *errand*

230 CLAUDIO To the tuition[6] of God, from my house if I had it—

DON PEDRO The sixth of July,
>
> Your loving friend,
>
> Benedick.

BENEDICK Nay, mock not, mock not. The body of your discourse is sometime guarded with fragments,[7] and the guards
are but slightly basted on[8] neither. Ere you flout° old ends° any   *mock / clichés*
235 further, examine your conscience. And so I leave you.   *Exit*

CLAUDIO My liege, your highness now may do me good.

DON PEDRO My love is thine to teach. Teach it but how
And thou shalt see how apt it is to learn
Any hard lesson that may do thee good.

240 CLAUDIO Hath Leonato any son, my lord?

DON PEDRO No child but Hero. She's his only heir.
Dost thou affect° her, Claudio?   *love*

CLAUDIO   O my lord,
When you went onward on this ended action°   *campaign*
I looked upon her with a soldier's eye,
245 That liked, but had a rougher task in hand
Than to drive liking to the name of love.
But now I am returned, and that° war-thoughts   *now that*

---

6. Popular love poet or satirist.
7. A painted sign, such as might hang before a brothel.
8. *hang . . . me*: cats in baskets ("bottles") were common Elizabethan targets for recreational archery.
9. Perhaps Adam Bell, a celebrated archer.
1. Proverbial; here, apparently a variation on a line
from Thomas Kyd's *Spanish Tragedy* (c. 1587): "In time
the savage bull sustains the yoke" (2.1.3).
2. Furious, raving like a wild beast (referring to the
rage of a cuckolded husband).
3. Venice was famous in Shakespeare's time for its beautiful courtesans. *spent all his quiver*: used all his arrows.

4. An earthquake would be as unlikely as my quaking
with love.
5. You will soften as time passes; with perhaps a bawdy
pun on "hours," "whores" (pronounced similarly).
6. Protection (Claudio and Don Pedro parody a conventional formula for ending a letter).
7. *The body . . . fragments*: The substance (also punning on the dressmaker's "bodice") of what you say is
sometimes ornamented ("guarded") with odds and ends
("fragments") such as you are mocking me for using.
8. And the decorative phrases are barely relevant.

Have left their places vacant, in their rooms
Come thronging soft and delicate desires,
250 All prompting me how fair young Hero is,
Saying I liked her ere I went to wars.
DON PEDRO Thou wilt be like a lover presently,
And tire the hearer with a book of words.°   *lover's set speeches*
If thou dost love fair Hero, cherish it,
255 And I will break° with her, and with her father,   *speak*
And thou shalt have her. Was't not to this end
That thou began'st to twist° so fine a story?   *spin*
CLAUDIO How sweetly you do minister to love,
That know love's grief by his complexion!°   *by its appearance*
260 But lest my liking might too sudden seem
I would have salved° it with a longer treatise.   *smoothed*
DON PEDRO What need the bridge much broader than the flood?°   *river*
The fairest grant is the necessity.⁹
Look what° will serve is fit. 'Tis once:° thou lovest,   *Whatever / In brief*
265 And I will fit thee with the remedy.
I know we shall have revelling° tonight.   *festivity; masked ball*
I will assume thy part° in some disguise,   *role*
And tell fair Hero I am Claudio.
And in her bosom I'll unclasp my heart¹
270 And take her hearing prisoner with the force
And strong encounter° of my amorous tale.   *assault*
Then after to her father will I break,
And the conclusion is, she shall be thine.
In practice let us put it presently.°   *Exeunt*   *at once*

1.2

Enter LEONATO *and* [ANTONIO,] *an old man brother to*
Leonato, [*severally*]°   *separately*
LEONATO How now, brother, where is my cousin,° your son?   *kinsman (nephew)*
Hath he provided this music?
ANTONIO He is very busy about it. But brother, I can tell you
strange news that you yet dreamt not of.
5 LEONATO Are they good?
ANTONIO As the event stamps them.¹ But they have a good
cover, they show well outward. The Prince and Count Clau-
dio, walking in a thick-pleached² alley in mine orchard,° were   *garden*
thus much overheard by a man of mine: the Prince discovered°   *revealed*
10 to Claudio that he loved my niece, your daughter, and meant
to acknowledge it this night in a dance, and if he found her
accordant° he meant to take the present time by the top³ and   *consenting*
instantly break° with you of it.   *speak*
LEONATO Hath the fellow any wit° that told you this?   *intelligence*
15 ANTONIO A good sharp fellow. I will send for him, and question
him yourself.
LEONATO No, no. We will hold it as a dream till it appear° itself.   *manifest*
But I will acquaint my daughter withal,° that she may be the   *with it*

---

9. The best gift is something that is truly needed.
1. And I will privately reveal to her my feelings (as if
I were you).
1.2 Location: Leonato's house.
1. As good as the outcome ("event") proves ("stamps")

them. The image is of news bound in a book with a
handsome cover.
2. Enclosed by trees with intertwining boughs.
3. He meant to seize the opportunity. (Time is proverbially bald except for the "top," or forelock.)

better prepared for an answer if peradventure° this be true. Go **by chance**
20 you and tell her of it.

    [*Enter Attendants*][4]

Cousins, you know what you have to do. O, I cry you mercy,[5]
friend. Go you with me and I will use your skill.—Good
cousin, have a care this busy time.   *Exeunt*

1.3

Enter [DON] JOHN *the bastard and* CONRAD, *his companion*

CONRAD   What the goodyear, my lord, why are you thus out of
measure[1] sad?

DON JOHN   There is no measure in the occasion that breeds it,
therefore the sadness is without limit.

5 CONRAD   You should hear reason.

DON JOHN   And when I have heard it, what blessing brings it?

CONRAD   If not a present° remedy, at least a patient sufferance. **an immediate**

DON JOHN   I wonder that thou—being, as thou sayst thou art,
born under Saturn[2]—goest about to apply a moral medicine to

10   a mortifying mischief.° I cannot hide what I am. I must be sad **a deadly sickness**
when I have cause, and smile at no man's jests; eat when I have
stomach,° and wait for no man's leisure; sleep when I am **appetite**
drowsy, and tend on° no man's business; laugh when I am **attend to**
merry, and claw° no man in his humour.° **flatter / mood**

15 CONRAD   Yea, but you must not make the full show of this till
you may do it without controlment.° You have of late stood **restraint**
out° against your brother, and he hath ta'en you newly into his **rebelled**
grace,° where it is impossible you should take true root but by **favor**
the fair weather that you make yourself. It is needful that you

20   frame the season for your own harvest.

DON JOHN   I had rather be a canker° in a hedge than a rose[3] in **wild rose; weed**
his grace, and it better fits my blood° to be disdained of all than **disposition**
to fashion° a carriage° to rob love from any. In this, though I **affect; feign / behavior**
cannot be said to be a flattering honest man, it must not be

25   denied but I am a plain-dealing villain. I am trusted with a
muzzle, and enfranchised with a clog.[4] Therefore I have
decreed° not to sing in my cage. If I had my mouth I would **determined**
bite. If I had my liberty I would do my liking. In the mean
time, let me be that I am, and seek not to alter me.

30 CONRAD   Can you make no use of your discontent?

DON JOHN   I make all use of it, for I use it only. Who comes
here?

    Enter BORACHIO[5]

What news, Borachio?

BORACHIO   I came yonder from a great supper. The Prince your

---

4. The attendants are evidently engaged in preparations for the reveling (2.1). "Cousins" (line 21) may be dependents in Leonato's household.
5. I beg your pardon (perhaps because he has not initially recognized one of the attendants, or because he has bumped into him). Leonato's reference to "skill" suggests that he might be talking to a musician.
1.3 Location: Leonato's house.
1. *What the goodyear:* unexplained exclamation. *out of measure:* disproportionately.

2. Born when Saturn was in the ascendant (therefore "saturnine," melancholy).
3. Cultivated rose.
4. I am trusted by being muzzled (in other words, not trusted at all), and given my freedom with a clog (a heavy block of wood attached to an animal or man as a restraint).
5. The name, from the Spanish for "wine bottle," was used for drunkards.

35 brother is royally entertained by Leonato, and I can give you
    intelligence of an intended marriage.

DON JOHN   Will it serve for any model° to build mischief on?   *ground plan*
    What is he for a fool[6] that betroths himself to unquietness?

BORACHIO   Marry,[7] it is your brother's right hand.

40 DON JOHN   Who, the most exquisite Claudio?

BORACHIO   Even he.

DON JOHN   A proper squire.[8] And who, and who? Which way
    looks he?

BORACHIO   Marry, on Hero, the daughter and heir of Leonato.

45 DON JOHN   A very forward March chick.[9] How came you to this?

BORACHIO   Being entertained for a perfumer,[1] as I was smoking°   *perfuming*
    a musty room comes me the Prince and Claudio hand in hand,
    in sad° conference. I whipped me behind the arras,° and there   *serious / wall hanging*
    heard it agreed upon that the Prince should woo Hero for him-
50 self and, having obtained her, give her to Count Claudio.

DON JOHN   Come, come, let us thither. This may prove food to
    my displeasure.° That young start-up° hath all the glory of my   *hatred / upstart*
    overthrow. If I can cross[2] him any way I bless myself every way.
    You are both sure,° and will assist me?   *reliable*

55 CONRAD   To the death, my lord.

DON JOHN   Let us to the great supper. Their cheer is the greater
    that° I am subdued. Would the cook were o' my mind.[3] Shall   *since*
    we go prove° what's to be done?   *find out*

BORACHIO   We'll wait° upon your lordship.   *Exeunt*   *attend*

2.1

Enter LEONATO, [ANTONIO] *his brother,* HERO *his daugh-*
ter, BEATRICE *his niece[,* MARGARET, *and* URSULA]

LEONATO   Was not Count John here at supper?

ANTONIO   I saw him not.

BEATRICE   How tartly° that gentleman looks. I never can see him   *sour*
    but I am heartburned[1] an hour after.

5 HERO   He is of a very melancholy disposition.

BEATRICE   He were° an excellent man that were made just in the   *would be*
    midway between him and Benedick. The one is too like an
    image° and says nothing, and the other too like my lady's eldest *a statue*
    son,[2] evermore tattling.°   *chattering*

10 LEONATO   Then half Signor Benedick's tongue in Count John's
    mouth, and half Count John's melancholy in Signor Benedick's
    face—

BEATRICE   With a good leg and a good foot, uncle, and money
    enough in his purse—such a man would win any woman in
15 the world, if a° could get her good will.   *he*

LEONATO   By my troth, niece, thou wilt never get thee a husband
    if thou be so shrewd° of thy tongue.   *shrewish*

ANTONIO   In faith, she's too curst.°   *sharp-tongued*

BEATRICE   Too curst is more[3] than curst. I shall lessen God's

---

6. What kind of fool is he.
7. By the Virgin Mary (a mild oath).
8. A fine young lover (ironic).
9. Precocious youngster, like a bird hatched early in
the season.
1. Being hired to burn sweet herbs (to mask unpleasant domestic odors).

2. Thwart (punning on "make the sign of the cross").
3. *o' my mind:* inclined to poison the food.
2.1 Location: Leonato's house.
1. I suffer from heartburn, caused by Don John's tart
looks.
2. That is, a spoiled child.
3. By one, punning on "too/two."

20   sending that way, for it is said God sends a curst cow short
horns,[4] but to a cow too curst he sends none.

LEONATO   So, by being too curst, God will send you no horns.

BEATRICE   Just,° if he send me no husband,[5] for the which bless-   *Just so*
ing I am at him upon my knees every morning and evening.

25   Lord, I could not endure a husband with a beard on his face. I
had rather lie in the woollen.[6]

LEONATO   You may light on a husband that hath no beard.

BEATRICE   What should I do with him—dress him in my apparel
and make him my waiting gentlewoman? He that hath a beard

30   is more than a youth, and he that hath no beard is less than a
man; and he that is more than a youth is not for me, and he
that is less than a man, I am not for him. Therefore I will even
take sixpence in earnest of the bearherd and lead his apes into
hell.[7]

35 LEONATO   Well then, go you into hell?

BEATRICE   No, but° to the gate, and there will the devil meet me   *only*
like an old cuckold with horns on his head, and say, 'Get you
to heaven, Beatrice, get you to heaven. Here's no place for you
maids.' So deliver I up my apes and away to Saint Peter fore

40   the heavens.[8] He shows me where the bachelors[9] sit, and there
live we as merry as the day is long.

ANTONIO [to HERO]   Well, niece, I trust you will be ruled by your
father.

BEATRICE   Yes, faith, it is my cousin's duty to make curtsy and

45   say, 'Father, as it please you.' But yet for all that, cousin, let
him be a handsome fellow, or else make another curtsy and
say, 'Father, as it please me.'

LEONATO   Well, niece, I hope to see you one day fitted with a
husband.

50 BEATRICE   Not till God make men of some other mettle° than   *substance*
earth. Would it not grieve a woman to be overmastered with° a   *by*
piece of valiant dust?—to make an account of her life to a clod
of wayward marl?° No, uncle, I'll none. Adam's sons are my   *clay*
brethren, and truly I hold it a sin to match in my kindred.[1]

55 LEONATO [to HERO]   Daughter, remember what I told you. If the
Prince do solicit you in that kind,[2] you know your answer.

BEATRICE   The fault will be in the music, cousin, if you be not
wooed in good time. If the Prince be too important,° tell him   *importunate*
there is measure[3] in everything, and so dance out the answer.

60   For hear me, Hero, wooing, wedding, and repenting is as a
Scotch jig, a measure, and a cinquepace.[4] The first suit° is hot   *courtship*
and hasty, like a Scotch jig—and full as fantastical; the wed-
ding mannerly° modest, as a measure, full of state and   *graciously*
ancientry.° And then comes repentance, and with his bad legs   *old-fashioned decorum*

---

4. Proverbial: God makes sure that the vicious ("curst")
have little power to do harm.
5. That is, if God sent her a husband, she would cuckold him.
6. Sleep between rough blankets (without sheets).
7. *take . . . hell:* take advance payment from the bear
keeper (who trained bears for the popular sport of bearbaiting and who usually had charge of other animals);
leading apes into hell was the proverbial fate of old
maids.

8. Peter is gatekeeper of heaven. Q prints "Peter: for
the heavens"; it is possible that Beatrice means "as far
as heaven is concerned."
9. Unwed men or women.
1. *to . . . kindred:* to marry incestuously.
2. *in that kind:* that is, to marry him.
3. Moderation (punning on the name of a slow, stately
dance [line 63] and continuing the link between dancing and wooing "in good time" [line 58]).
4. A lively five-step dance.

65   falls into the cinquepace faster and faster till he sink into his
        grave.

LEONATO   Cousin, you apprehend passing° shrewdly.   *understand more than*

BEATRICE   I have a good eye, uncle. I can see a church by day-
        light.[5]

70 LEONATO   The revellers are entering, brother. Make good room.

> *Enter* [DON] PEDRO [*the*] *Prince,* CLAUDIO, BENEDICK,
> *and* BALTHASAR, DON JOHN, [*and* BORACHIO, *as*] *Mask-*
> *ers, with a drum*

DON PEDRO [*to* HERO]   Lady, will you walk a bout with your
        friend?[6]

HERO   So you walk softly, and look sweetly, and say nothing, I
        am yours for the walk; and especially when I walk away.

75 DON PEDRO   With me in your company?

HERO   I may say so when I please.

DON PEDRO   And when please you to say so?

HERO   When I like your favour;° for God defend the lute should   *face*
        be like the case.[7]

80 DON PEDRO   My visor° is Philemon's roof. Within the house is   *mask*
        Jove.[8]

HERO   Why, then, your visor should be thatched.[9]

DON PEDRO   Speak low if
        you speak love.

> [*They move aside*]

BALTHASAR [*to* MARGARET]   Well, I would you did like me.

MARGARET   So would not I, for your own sake, for I have many

85   ill° qualities.   *bad*

BALTHASAR   Which is one?

MARGARET   I say my prayers aloud.

BALTHASAR   I love you the better—the hearers may cry amen.

MARGARET   God match me with a good dancer.

90 BALTHASAR   Amen.

MARGARET   And God keep him out of my sight when the dance
        is done. Answer, clerk.[1]

BALTHASAR   No more words. The clerk is answered.

> [*They move aside*]

URSULA [*to* ANTONIO]   I know you well enough, you are Signor
95   Antonio.

ANTONIO   At a word,° I am not.   *In short*

URSULA   I know you by the waggling of your head.

ANTONIO   To tell you true, I counterfeit him.

URSULA   You could never do him so ill-well[2] unless you were the
100   very man. Here's his dry hand up and down.[3] You are he, you
        are he.

ANTONIO   At a word, I am not.

URSULA   Come, come, do you think I do not know you by your

---

5. That is, see what's in front of me.

6. Often used to mean "lover." *walk a bout:* take a turn (apparently a term in dancing).

7. God forbid your face should be as unappealing as your mask.

8. The peasant Philemon and his wife, Baucis, entertained Jove, disguised, in their humble cottage (Ovid, *Metamorphoses* 8). This and the following line are in "fourteeners," a verse form old-fashioned in Shake-

speare's time but used by Arthur Golding in his 1567 translation of the *Metamorphoses*.

9. According to Golding, Philemon's roof was "thatched all with straw"; Hero means that the mask should be fitted with false hair or beard.

1. That is, say "Amen" again. The parish clerk led the responses in church services.

2. *do him so ill-well:* mime his imperfections so ably.

3. His wrinkled hand exactly.

excellent wit? Can virtue° hide itself ? Go to, mum,° you are   *excellence / be quiet*
105   he. Graces will appear, and there's an end.[4]
         [*They move aside*]
   BEATRICE [*to* BENEDICK]   Will you not tell me who told you so?
   BENEDICK   No, you shall pardon me.
   BEATRICE   Nor will you not tell me who you are?
   BENEDICK   Not now.
110   BEATRICE   That I was disdainful, and that I had my good wit out
       of the Hundred Merry Tales[5]—well, this was Signor Benedick
       that said so.
   BENEDICK   What's he?
   BEATRICE   I am sure you know him well enough.
115   BENEDICK   Not I, believe me.
   BEATRICE   Did he never make you laugh?
   BENEDICK   I pray you, what is he?
   BEATRICE   Why, he is the Prince's jester, a very dull fool. Only
       his° gift is in devising impossible° slanders. None but libertines   *His only / unbelievable*
120   delight in him, and the commendation is not in his wit but in
       his villainy,° for he both pleases men and angers them, and   *rudeness*
       then they laugh at him, and beat him. I am sure he is in the
       fleet.° I would he had boarded me.[6]   *company (of dancers)*
   BENEDICK   When I know the gentleman, I'll tell him what you
125   say.
   BEATRICE   Do, do. He'll but break a comparison[7] or two on me,
       which peradventure° not marked, or not laughed at, strikes him   *perhaps*
       into melancholy, and then there's a partridge wing saved, for
       the fool will eat no supper that night.
         Music
130   We must follow the leaders.°   *leaders in the dance*
   BENEDICK   In every good thing.
   BEATRICE   Nay, if they lead to any ill I will leave them at the
       next turning.
         Dance. Exeunt [*all but* DON JOHN, BORACHIO, *and*
         CLAUDIO]
   DON JOHN [*aside to* BORACHIO]   Sure my brother is amorous on
135   Hero, and hath withdrawn her father to break with him about
       it. The ladies follow her, and but one visor° remains.   *(man wearing a) mask*
   BORACHIO [*aside to* DON JOHN]   And that is Claudio. I know him
       by his bearing.
   DON JOHN   Are not you Signor Benedick?
140   CLAUDIO   You know me well. I am he.
   DON JOHN   Signor, you are very near my brother in his love.° He   *favor*
       is enamoured on Hero. I pray you dissuade him from her. She
       is no equal for his birth. You may do the part of an honest man
       in it.
145   CLAUDIO   How know you he loves her?
   DON JOHN   I heard him swear his affection.
   BORACHIO   So did I, too, and he swore he would marry her
       tonight.
   DON JOHN   Come, let us to the banquet.°   *after-dinner sweets*
             Exeunt. Manet° CLAUDIO   *Remains*

---

4. And that is all there is to be said.   7. He'll only try out, or "crack," a satirical comparison
5. A famously bad joke-book, first published in 1526.   (as one "breaks" a lance).
6. Assaulted me like a ship.

150	CLAUDIO Thus answer I in name of Benedick,	
	But hear these ill news with the ears of Claudio.	
	'Tis certain° so, the Prince woos for himself.	*certainly*
	Friendship is constant in all other things	
	Save in the office° and affairs of love.	*business*
155	Therefore all° hearts in love use their own tongues.	*let all*
	Let every eye negotiate for itself,	
	And trust no agent; for beauty is a witch	
	Against whose charms faith° melteth into blood.°	*loyalty / passion*
	This is an accident of hourly proof,[8]	
160	Which I mistrusted° not. Farewell, therefore, Hero.	*suspected*

     Enter BENEDICK

BENEDICK   Count Claudio?

CLAUDIO   Yea, the same.

BENEDICK   Come, will you go with me?

CLAUDIO   Whither?

165	BENEDICK Even to the next willow,[9] about your own business,	
	County.° What fashion will you wear the garland° of? About	*Count / (of willow)*
	your neck, like an usurer's chain?[1] Or under your arm, like a	
	lieutenant's scarf?[2] You must wear it one° way, for the Prince	*some*
	hath got your Hero.	
170	CLAUDIO I wish him joy of her.	
	BENEDICK Why, that's spoken like an honest drover;° so they sell	*cattle dealer*
	bullocks. But did you think the Prince would have served you	
	thus?	
	CLAUDIO I pray you leave me.	
175	BENEDICK Ho, now you strike like the blind man—'twas the boy	
	that stole your meat, and you'll beat the post.[3]	
	CLAUDIO If it° will not be, I'll leave you. *Exit*	*(your departure)*
	BENEDICK Alas, poor hurt fowl, now will he creep into sedges.[4]	
	But that my Lady Beatrice should know me, and not know me!	
180	The Prince's fool! Ha, it may be I go under that title because I	
	am merry. Yea, but so I am apt to do myself wrong. I am not so	
	reputed. It is the base, though bitter, disposition of Beatrice	
	that puts the world into her person, and so gives me out.[5] Well,	
	I'll be revenged as I may.	

     Enter [DON PEDRO *the*] *Prince*

185	DON PEDRO Now, signor, where's the Count? Did you see him?	
	BENEDICK Troth, my lord, I have played the part of Lady Fame.°	*Lady Rumor*
	I found him here as melancholy as a lodge in a warren.[6] I told	
	him—and I think I told him true—that your grace had got the	
	good will of this young lady, and I offered him my company to	
190	a willow tree, either to make him a garland, as being forsaken,	
	or to bind him up a rod,° as being worthy to be whipped.	*bundle of sticks*
	DON PEDRO To be whipped—what's his fault?	
	BENEDICK The flat° transgression of a schoolboy who, being	*stupid*
	overjoyed with finding a bird's nest, shows it his companion,	
195	and he steals it.	

---

8. This is an occurrence demonstrated every hour, common event.
9. Symbol of unrequited love.
1. A gold chain worn by a moneylender.
2. A sash across the chest.
3. Probably alluding to a folktale, which existed in various forms, of a boy who robbed and played a trick on his blind master. *post:* pillar (with play on Benedick as

the "post," or messenger, who bears bad news).
4. *creep into sedges:* hide to nurse his wounds, as an injured bird crawls into the tall grass along a riverbank.
5. It is Beatrice's low but sarcastic disposition that makes her believe the whole world is of her opinion and represents me accordingly.
6. As a burrow in a rabbit warren. (The rabbit was a traditional symbol of melancholy.)

DON PEDRO   Wilt thou make a trust a transgression? The transgression is in the stealer.

BENEDICK   Yet it had not been amiss the rod had been made,
and the garland too, for the garland he might have worn him-
200 self, and the rod he might have bestowed on you, who, as I take
it, have stolen his bird's nest.

DON PEDRO   I will but teach them° to sing, and restore them to   *(the chicks)*
the owner.

BENEDICK   If their singing answer your saying, by my faith you
205 say honestly.⁷

DON PEDRO   The Lady Beatrice hath a quarrel to° you. The gen-   *with*
tleman that danced with her told her she is much wronged by
you.

BENEDICK   O, she misused° me past the endurance of a block.   *abused*
210 An oak but with one green leaf on it⁸ would have answered
her. My very visor began to assume life and scold with her.
She told me—not thinking I had been myself—that I was the
Prince's jester, that I was duller than a great thaw,⁹ huddling
jest upon jest with such impossible conveyance° upon me that   *speed*
215 I stood like a man at a mark,° with a whole army shooting at   *target*
me. She speaks poniards,° and every word stabs. If her breath   *daggers*
were as terrible as her terminations,° there were no living near   *expressions*
her, she would infect to the North Star.¹ I would not marry her
though she were endowed with all that Adam had left him
220 before he transgressed. She would have made Hercules have
turned spit, yea, and have cleft his club to make the fire, too.²
Come, talk not of her. You shall find her the infernal Ate° in   *goddess of discord*
good apparel. I would to God some scholar would conjure³
her, for certainly, while she is here a man may live as quiet in
225 hell as in a sanctuary, and people sin upon purpose because
they would go thither, so indeed all disquiet, horror, and per-
turbation follows° her.   *attends upon*

Enter CLAUDIO *and* BEATRICE, [*and*] LEONATO [*with*]
HERO

DON PEDRO   Look, here she comes.

BENEDICK   Will your grace command me any service to the
230 world's end? I will go on the slightest errand now to the Antipodes that you can devise to send me on. I will fetch you a tooth-
picker° now from the furthest inch of Asia, bring you the length   *toothpick*
of Prester John's foot, fetch you a hair off the Great Cham's
beard, do you any embassage to the pigmies,⁴ rather than hold
235 three words' conference with this harpy.⁵ You have no employment for me?

DON PEDRO   None but to desire your good company.

BENEDICK   O God, sir, here's a dish I love not. I cannot endure
my Lady Tongue.   *Exit*

7. If they sing as you say they will—if you have wooed
Hero for Claudio—then you are talking honorably.
8. An oak with barely any life remaining in it.
9. When the muddy roads kept everyone at home.
1. Thought to be the remotest star.
2. The Amazon Omphale made Hercules wear her
clothes and spin; Benedick imagines an even greater
humiliation and more menial duty—turning the spit.
3. Conjure the evil spirits out of, or supernaturally

consign to hell. *scholar:* learned person (who could
speak Latin, the language of exorcism).
4. *Prester John's . . . pigmies:* all distant, fantastic figures. In legend, Prester John ruled in Ethiopia, while
the Great Cham (Kublai Khan) reigned in Mongolia,
and a race of dwarfs was said to inhabit the mountains
of India.
5. Mythical creature with the face and body of a
woman and the wings and claws of a bird of prey.

240 DON PEDRO   Come, lady, come, you have lost the heart of Signor
        Benedick.
    BEATRICE   Indeed, my lord, he lent it me a while, and I gave
        him use° for it, a double heart for his single one. Marry, once   *interest*
        before he won it of ° me, with false dice. Therefore your grace   *from*
245   may well say I have lost it.
    DON PEDRO   You have put him down, lady, you have put him
        down.[6]
    BEATRICE   So I would not he should do me, my lord, lest I
        should prove the mother of fools. I have brought Count Clau-
250   dio, whom you sent me to seek.
    DON PEDRO   Why, how now, Count, wherefore are you sad?
    CLAUDIO   Not sad, my lord.
    DON PEDRO   How then? Sick?
    CLAUDIO   Neither, my lord.
255 BEATRICE   The Count is neither sad, nor sick, nor merry, nor
        well, but civil° count, civil[7] as an orange, and something° of   *serious / somewhat*
        that jealous complexion.[8]
    DON PEDRO   I'faith, lady, I think your blazon° to be true, though   *formal description*
        I'll be sworn, if he be so, his conceit° is false. Here, Claudio, I   *imagined idea*
260   have wooed in thy name, and fair Hero is won. I have broke°   *spoken*
        with her father and his good will obtained. Name the day of
        marriage, and God give thee joy.
    LEONATO   Count, take of me my daughter, and with her my for-
        tunes. His grace hath made the match, and all grace say amen
265   to it.[9]
    BEATRICE   Speak, Count, 'tis your cue.
    CLAUDIO   Silence is the perfectest herald of joy. I were but little
        happy if I could say how much. [*To* HERO] Lady, as you are
        mine, I am yours. I give away myself for you, and dote upon
270   the exchange.
    BEATRICE [*to* HERO]   Speak, cousin. Or, if you cannot, stop his
        mouth with a kiss, and let not him speak, neither.
    DON PEDRO   In faith, lady, you have a merry heart.
    BEATRICE   Yea, my lord, I thank it. Poor fool, it keeps on the
275   windy° side of care.—My cousin tells him in his ear that he is   *windward; safe*
        in her heart.
    CLAUDIO   And so she doth, cousin.
    BEATRICE   Good Lord, for alliance![1] Thus goes everyone to the
        world but I, and I am sunburnt.[2] I may sit in a corner and cry
280   'Heigh-ho for a husband'.[3]
    DON PEDRO   Lady Beatrice, I will get you one.
    BEATRICE   I would rather have one of your father's getting.° Hath   *begetting*
        your grace ne'er a° brother like you? Your father got excellent   *no*
        husbands if a maid could come by them.
285 DON PEDRO   Will you have me, lady?
    BEATRICE   No, my lord, unless I might have another for working

---

6. Humiliated him. (Beatrice, in reply, puns on the
physical sense.)
7. Punning on "Seville," famous for its bitter oranges.
8. Yellow (the traditional color of jealousy).
9. And may God, the source of all grace, confirm it.
1. Kinship through marriage. (Claudio has just

addressed Beatrice as one of the family.)
2. Unattractive, and therefore unlikely to marry.
(Suntans, like dark complexions, were unfashionable.)
goes . . . to the world: gets married.
3. Title of a ballad; probably a catchphrase in Shakespeare's time.

days. Your grace is too costly to wear every day. But I beseech
your grace, pardon me. I was born to speak all mirth and no
matter.°   *substance*

290   DON PEDRO   Your silence most offends me, and to be merry best
becomes you; for out o' question, you were born in a merry
hour.

BEATRICE   No, sure, my lord, my mother cried. But then there
was a star danced, and under that was I born. [*To* HERO *and*
295   CLAUDIO] Cousins, God give you joy.

LEONATO   Niece, will you look to those things I told you of?

BEATRICE   I cry you mercy,° uncle. [*To* DON PEDRO] By your   *I beg your pardon*
grace's pardon.   *Exit* BEATRICE

DON PEDRO   By my troth, a pleasant-spirited lady.

300   LEONATO   There's little of the melancholy element in her, my
lord. She is never sad° but when she sleeps, and not ever° sad   *serious / not always*
then; for I have heard my daughter say she hath often dreamt
of unhappiness and waked herself with laughing.

DON PEDRO   She cannot endure to hear tell of a husband.

305   LEONATO   O, by no means. She mocks all her wooers out of suit.°   *wooing (her)*

DON PEDRO   She were an excellent wife for Benedick.

LEONATO   O Lord, my lord, if they were but a week married they
would talk themselves mad.

DON PEDRO   County Claudio, when mean you to go to church?

310   CLAUDIO   Tomorrow, my lord. Time goes on crutches till love
have all his rites.

LEONATO   Not till Monday, my dear son, which is hence a just
sevennight, and a time too brief, too, to have all things answer°   *match*
my mind.°   *wishes*

315   DON PEDRO   Come, you shake the head at so long a breathing,°   *an interval*
but I warrant° thee, Claudio, the time shall not go dully by us.   *assure*
I will in the interim undertake one of Hercules' labours, which
is to bring Signor Benedick and the Lady Beatrice into a mountain of affection th'one with th'other. I would fain° have it a   *gladly*
320   match, and I doubt not but to fashion it, if you three will but
minister such assistance as I shall give you direction.

LEONATO   My lord, I am for you, though it cost me ten nights'
watchings.°   *staying awake*

CLAUDIO   And I, my lord.

325   DON PEDRO   And you too, gentle Hero?

HERO   I will do any modest office,° my lord, to help my cousin   *task*
to a good husband.

DON PEDRO   And Benedick is not the unhopefullest° husband   *least promising*
that I know. Thus far can I praise him: he is of a noble strain,°   *descent*
330   of approved° valour and confirmed honesty.° I will teach you   *proven / honor*
how to humour your cousin that she shall fall in love with
Benedick, and I, with your two helps, will so practise on°   *so trick*
Benedick that, in despite of his quick wit and his queasy stom-
ach,° he shall fall in love with Beatrice. If we can do this,   *qualms (about love)*
335   Cupid is no longer an archer; his glory shall be ours, for we are
the only love-gods. Go in with me, and I will tell you my drift.°   *scheme*
                                        Exeunt

2.2

Enter [DON] JOHN *and* BORACHIO

DON JOHN   It is so. The Count Claudio shall marry the daughter
of Leonato.

BORACHIO   Yea, my lord, but I can cross° it.   *thwart*

DON JOHN   Any bar, any cross, any impediment will be medi-
5   cinable° to me. I am sick in displeasure to him, and whatsoever   *medicinal*
comes athwart his affection ranges evenly with mine.[1] How
canst thou cross this marriage?

BORACHIO   Not honestly, my lord, but so covertly that no dishonesty shall appear in me.

10   DON JOHN   Show me briefly how.

BORACHIO   I think I told your lordship a year since how much
I am in the favour of Margaret, the waiting gentlewoman to
Hero.

DON JOHN   I remember.

15   BORACHIO   I can at any unseasonable instant of the night
appoint° her to look out at her lady's chamber window.   *arrange with*

DON JOHN   What life is in that to be the death of this marriage?

BORACHIO   The poison of that lies in you to temper.° Go you to   *concoct*
the Prince your brother. Spare not to tell him that he hath
20   wronged his honour in marrying the renowned Claudio—
whose estimation° do you mightily hold up°—to a contami-   *reputation / esteem*
nated stale,° such a one as Hero.   *prostitute*

DON JOHN   What proof shall I make of that?

BORACHIO   Proof enough to misuse° the Prince, to vex° Claudio,   *deceive / torment*
25   to undo Hero, and kill Leonato. Look you for any other issue?°   *result*

DON JOHN   Only to despite° them I will endeavour anything.   *Merely to spite*

BORACHIO   Go then. Find me a meet hour to draw Don Pedro
and the Count Claudio alone. Tell them that you know that
Hero loves me. Intend° a kind of zeal both to the Prince and   *Pretend*
30   Claudio as in° love of your brother's honour who hath made   *as if for*
this match, and his friend's reputation who is thus like to be
cozened with the semblance of a maid,[2] that you have discovered thus. They will scarcely believe this without trial. Offer
them instances, which shall bear no less likelihood than to see
35   me at her chamber window, hear me call Margaret Hero, hear
Margaret term me Claudio.[3] And bring them to see this the
very night before the intended wedding, for in the mean time
I will so fashion the matter that Hero shall be absent, and there
shall appear such seeming truth of Hero's disloyalty that jeal-
40   ousy shall be called assurance,[4] and all the preparation° over-   *wedding preparation*
thrown.

DON JOHN   Grow this° to what adverse issue it can, I will put it   *Let this lead*
in practice. Be cunning in the working this,° and thy fee is a   *of this*
thousand ducats.°   *gold coins*

45   BORACHIO   Be you constant in the accusation, and my cunning
shall not shame me.

DON JOHN   I will presently go learn their day of marriage.

Exeunt

2.2 Location: Leonato's house.
1. And whatever frustrates his wishes conforms with
mine.
2. To be cheated with the mere appearance of a virgin.

3. Most editors assume an error here and emend to
"Borachio."
4. That suspicion shall be called certainty.

2.3

Enter BENEDICK

BENEDICK   Boy!

[*Enter* BOY]

BOY   Signor?

BENEDICK   In my chamber window lies a book. Bring it hither to
me in the orchard.

5 BOY   I am here already,¹ sir.

BENEDICK   I know that, but I would have thee hence and here
again.   *Exit* [BOY]
I do much wonder that one man, seeing how much another
man is a fool when he dedicates his behaviours to love, will,
10 after he hath laughed at such shallow follies in others, become
the argument° of his own scorn by falling in love. And such a   subject
man is Claudio. I have known when there was no music with
him but the drum and the fife, and now had he rather hear the
tabor and the pipe.² I have known when he would have walked
15 ten mile afoot to see a good armour, and now will he lie ten
nights awake carving° the fashion of a new doublet.° He was   designing / jacket
wont° to speak plain and to the purpose, like an honest man   accustomed
and a soldier, and now is he turned orthography.³ His words
are a very fantastical° banquet, just so many strange dishes. May   poetic
20 I be so converted, and see° with these eyes? I cannot tell. I   still see
think not. I will not be sworn but love may transform me to an
oyster, but I'll take my oath on it, till he have made an oyster
of me he shall never make me such a fool. One woman is fair,
yet I am well. Another is wise, yet I am well. Another virtuous,
25 yet I am well. But till all graces be in one woman, one woman
shall not come in my grace.° Rich she shall be, that's certain.   favor
Wise, or I'll none.⁴ Virtuous, or I'll never cheapen° her. Fair,   bargain for
or I'll never look on her. Mild, or come not near me. Noble, or
not I for an angel.⁵ Of good discourse, an excellent musician,
30 and her hair shall be of what colour it please God. Ha! The
Prince and Monsieur Love. I will hide me in the arbour.

[*He hides.*]

Enter [DON PEDRO *the*] *Prince,* LEONATO, *and* CLAUDIO⁶

DON PEDRO   Come, shall we hear this music?

CLAUDIO   Yea, my good lord. How still the evening is,
As° hushed on purpose to grace harmony.   As if

35 DON PEDRO   [*aside*] See you where Benedick hath hid himself?

CLAUDIO   [*aside*] O, very well, my lord. The music ended,
We'll fit the hid-fox with a pennyworth.⁷

Enter BALTHASAR *with music*

DON PEDRO   Come, Balthasar, we'll hear that song again.

BALTHASAR   O good my lord, tax° not so bad a voice   task
40 To slander music any more than once.

DON PEDRO   It is the witness still° of excellency   the mark always

---

2.3 Location: Leonato's garden.
1. That is, it's as good as done. (Benedick takes him literally.)
2. The drum and fife were used by the military; the tabor (a small drum) and pipe were used in social festivities.
3. Become overelaborate in his speech.
4. Or I'll have none (of her).
5. Not I, though she be an angel (punning on coins: an

angel was worth 10 shillings, and a noble 6 shillings 8 pence).
6. Q's stage direction includes "Music," which seems premature as the singer, Balthasar, enters at line 38.
7. We'll give our sly eavesdropper more than he bargained for. *hid-fox:* apparently refers to the game of hide-and-seek (compare *Hamlet* 4.2.28: "Hide, fox, and all after").

To put a strange face on[8] his own perfection.
I pray thee sing, and let me woo° no more.   *cajole*
BALTHASAR   Because you talk of wooing[9] I will sing,
45   Since many a wooer doth commence his suit
To her he thinks not worthy, yet he woos,
Yet will he swear he loves.
DON PEDRO   Nay pray thee, come;
Or if thou wilt hold longer argument,
Do it in notes.°   *music*
BALTHASAR   Note this before my notes:
50   There's not a note of mine that's worth the noting.
DON PEDRO   Why, these are very crotchets[1] that he speaks—
Note notes, forsooth, and nothing![2]
       [*The accompaniment begins*]
BENEDICK   Now, divine air! Now is his soul ravished. Is it not
strange that sheep's guts[3] should hale° souls out of men's bod-   *drag*
55   ies? Well, a horn[4] for my money, when all's done.
BALTHASAR [*sings*]
             Sigh no more, ladies, sigh no more.
                  Men were deceivers ever,
             One foot in sea, and one on shore,
                  To one thing constant never.
60   Then sigh not so, but let them go,
                  And be you blithe and bonny,°   *beautiful*
             Converting all your sounds of woe
                  Into hey nonny, nonny.

             Sing no more ditties, sing no more
65   Of dumps[5] so dull and heavy.
             The fraud of men was ever so
                  Since summer first was leafy.
             Then sigh not so, but let them go,
                  And be you blithe and bonny,
70   Converting all your sounds of woe
                  Into hey nonny, nonny.

DON PEDRO   By my troth, a good song.
BALTHASAR   And an ill singer, my lord.
DON PEDRO   Ha, no, no, faith. Thou singest well enough for a
75   shift.°   *to make do*
BENEDICK [*aside*]   An° he had been a dog that should have   *If*
howled thus, they would have hanged him; and I pray God his
bad voice bode no mischief. I had as lief° have heard the night-   *as gladly*
raven,° come what plague could have come after it.   *bird of ill omen*
80   DON PEDRO   Yea, marry,[6] dost thou hear, Balthasar? I pray thee
get us some excellent music, for tomorrow night we would
have it at the Lady Hero's chamber window.

---

8. *To put . . . on:* Not to admit.
9. Because you put it in terms of wooing (and so are likely to continue to flatter me insincerely).
1. Whimsies; quarter notes (in music).
2. *Note . . . nothing:* Get on with your singing, and nothing else. ("Nothing" and "noting" sounded the same in Elizabethan pronunciation. Compare the same play on words in the title.)
3. Used to string musical instruments.
4. Military or hunting horn.
5. Melancholy tunes or moods.
6. A mild oath. (Don Pedro is continuing the speech interrupted by Benedick's aside.)

BALTHASAR   The best I can, my lord.   *Exit*

DON PEDRO   Do so. Farewell. Come hither, Leonato. What was
85   it you told me of today, that your niece Beatrice was in love
     with Signor Benedick?

CLAUDIO [*aside*]   O, ay, stalk on, stalk on. The fowl sits.⁷—I did
     never think that lady would have loved any man.

LEONATO   No, nor I neither. But most wonderful° that she   *astounding*
90   should so dote on Signor Benedick, whom she hath in all out-
     ward behaviours seemed ever to abhor.

BENEDICK [*aside*]   Is't possible? Sits the wind in that corner?

LEONATO   By my troth, my lord, I cannot tell what to think of it.
     But that she loves him with an enraged° affection, it is past the   *a frenzied*
95   infinite° of thought.   *furthest bounds*

DON PEDRO   Maybe she doth but counterfeit.

CLAUDIO   Faith, like° enough.   *likely*

LEONATO   O God! Counterfeit? There was never counterfeit of
     passion came so near the life of passion as she discovers° it.   *exhibits*

100 DON PEDRO   Why, what effects of passion shows she?

CLAUDIO [*aside*]   Bait the hook well. This fish will bite.

LEONATO   What effects, my lord? She will sit you⁸—you heard
     my daughter tell you how.

CLAUDIO   She did indeed.

105 DON PEDRO   How, how, I pray you? You amaze me. I would have
     thought her spirit had been invincible against all assaults of
     affection.

LEONATO   I would have sworn it had, my lord, especially against
     Benedick.

110 BENEDICK [*aside*]   I should think this a gull,° but that the white-   *trick*
     bearded fellow speaks it. Knavery cannot, sure, hide himself in
     such reverence.

CLAUDIO   [*aside*]   He hath ta'en th'infection. Hold° it up.   *Keep*

DON PEDRO   Hath she made her affection known to Benedick?

115 LEONATO   No, and swears she never will. That's her torment.

CLAUDIO   'Tis true, indeed, so your daughter says. 'Shall I,' says
     she, 'that have so oft encountered him with scorn, write to him
     that I love him?'

LEONATO   This says she now when she is beginning to write to
120 him, for she'll be up twenty times a night, and there will she sit
     in her smock° till she have writ a sheet of paper. My daughter   *slip*
     tells us all.

CLAUDIO   Now you talk of a sheet of paper, I remember a pretty
     jest your daughter told us of.

125 LEONATO   O, when she had writ it and was reading it over, she
     found Benedick and Beatrice between the sheet.

CLAUDIO   That.

LEONATO   O, she tore the letter into a thousand halfpence,°   *small pieces*
     railed at herself that she should be so immodest to write to one
130 that she knew would flout° her. 'I measure him,' says she, 'by   *jeer at*
     my own spirit, for I should flout him if he writ to me, yea,
     though I love him I should.'

CLAUDIO   Then down upon her knees she falls, weeps, sobs,
     beats her heart, tears her hair, prays, curses, 'O sweet Benedick,
135 God give me patience.'

---

7. *stalk . . . sits:* go on quietly. Our prey has alighted.   8. She will sit down (i.e., weak with lovesickness).

LEONATO   She doth indeed, my daughter says so, and the ecstasy° — *passion*
hath so much overborne her that my daughter is sometime
afeard she will do a desperate outrage° to herself. It is very true. — *injury*

140 DON PEDRO   It were good that Benedick knew of it by some
other, if she will not discover° it. — *reveal*

CLAUDIO   To what end? He would make but a sport of it and
torment the poor lady worse.

DON PEDRO   An he should, it were an alms° to hang him. She's — *a charitable deed*
an excellent sweet lady, and, out of all suspicion,° she is vir- — *doubt*

145 tuous.

CLAUDIO   And she is exceeding wise.

DON PEDRO   In everything but in loving Benedick.

LEONATO   O my lord, wisdom and blood° combating in so tender — *passion*
a body, we have ten proofs to one that blood hath the victory. I

150 am sorry for her, as I have just cause, being her uncle and her
guardian.

DON PEDRO   I would she had bestowed this dotage° on me. I — *infatuation*
would have doffed⁹ all other respects° and made her half — *considerations*
myself. I pray you tell Benedick of it, and hear what a° will say. — *he*

155 LEONATO   Were it good, think you?

CLAUDIO   Hero thinks surely she will die, for she says she will die
if he love her not, and she will die ere she make her love
known, and she will die if he woo her, rather than she will
bate° one breath of her accustomed crossness.° — *abate / contrariness*

160 DON PEDRO   She doth well. If she should make tender° of her — *make an offer*
love 'tis very possible he'll scorn it, for the man, as you know
all, hath a contemptible° spirit. — *contemptuous*

CLAUDIO   He is a very proper° man. — *handsome*

DON PEDRO   He hath indeed a good outward happiness.¹

165 CLAUDIO   Before God; and in my mind, very wise.

DON PEDRO   He doth indeed show some sparks that are like wit.

CLAUDIO   And I take him to be valiant.

DON PEDRO   As Hector,² I assure you; and in the managing of
quarrels you may say he is wise, for either he avoids them with

170 great discretion or undertakes them with a most Christianlike
fear.

LEONATO   If he do fear God, a must necessarily keep peace. If
he break the peace, he ought to enter into a quarrel with fear
and trembling.

175 DON PEDRO   And so will he do, for the man doth fear God, howsoever it seems not in him by some large° jests he will make. — *broad*
Well, I am sorry for your niece. Shall we go seek Benedick and
tell him of her love?

CLAUDIO   Never tell him, my lord. Let her wear it out with good

180 counsel.° — *advice*

LEONATO   Nay, that's impossible. She may wear her heart out
first.

DON PEDRO   Well, we will hear further of it by° your daughter. — *from*
Let it cool the while. I love Benedick well, and I could wish he

185 would modestly examine himself to see how much he is unworthy so good a lady.

---

9. Set aside or cast off.   2. The noblest and bravest Trojan warrior.
1. He is well endowed with looks and bearing.

LEONATO   My lord, will you walk? Dinner is ready.
CLAUDIO [*aside*]   If he do not dote on her upon this, I will never
   trust my expectation.°   *predictions*
190   DON PEDRO [*aside*]   Let there be the same net spread for her,
   and that must your daughter and her gentlewomen carry.° The   *manage*
   sport will be when they hold one an opinion of another's dotage, and no such matter.³ That's the scene that I would see,
   which will be merely a dumb show.⁴ Let us send her to call
195   him in to dinner.
                 Exeunt [DON PEDRO, CLAUDIO, *and* LEONATO]
BENEDICK [*coming forward*]   This can be no trick. The confer-
   ence was sadly borne.° They have the truth of this from Hero.   *seriously conducted*
   They seem to pity the lady. It seems her affections have their
   full bent.⁵ Love me! Why, it must be requited. I hear how I am
200   censured. They say I will bear myself proudly if I perceive the
   love come from her. They say too that she will rather die than
   give any sign of affection. I did never think to marry. I must not
   seem proud. Happy are they that hear their detractions and can
   put them to mending.° They say the lady is fair. 'Tis a truth, I   *amending*
205   can bear them witness. And virtuous—'tis so, I cannot reprove°   *contradict*
   it. And wise, but for loving me. By my troth, it is no addition to
   her wit⁶—nor no great argument of her folly, for I will be horribly in love with her. I may chance have some odd quirks° and   *quips*
   remnants of wit broken on° me because I have railed so long   *cracked against*
210   against marriage; but doth not the appetite alter? A man loves
   the meat in his youth that he cannot endure in his age. Shall
   quips and sentences° and these paper bullets of the brain awe   *epigrams*
   a man from the career° of his humour?° No. The world must   *swift course / liking*
   be peopled. When I said I would die a bachelor, I did not think
215   I should live till I were married. Here comes Beatrice.
        Enter BEATRICE
   By this day, she's a fair lady. I do spy some marks of love in her.
BEATRICE   Against my will I am sent to bid you come in to
   dinner.
BENEDICK   Fair Beatrice, I thank you for your pains.
220   BEATRICE   I took no more pains for those thanks than you take
   pains to thank me. If it had been painful I would not have
   come.
BENEDICK   You take pleasure, then, in the message?
BEATRICE   Yea, just so much as you may take upon a knife's
225   point and choke a daw withal.° You have no stomach,° signor?   *jackdaw with / appetite*
   Fare you well.   *Exit*
BENEDICK   Ha! 'Against my will I am sent to bid you come in to
   dinner.' There's a double meaning in that. 'I took no more
   pains for those thanks than you took pains to thank me.' That's
230   as much as to say 'Any pains that I take for you is as easy as
   thanks.'—If I do not take pity of her I am a villain. If I do not
   love her I am a Jew.⁷ I will go get her picture.⁸   *Exit*

3. *when . . . matter:* when each believes that the other
is madly in love, without any basis in fact.
4. A pantomime (because words for once will fail
them).
5. Are stretched to the limit (like a bent bow).

6. No additional proof of her intelligence.
7. That is, lacking in Christian charity (an anti-Semitic
stereotype).
8. *get her picture:* have her portrait painted (for a love
locket) or sketch it himself.

3.1

Enter HERO *and two gentlewomen,* MARGARET *and*
            URSULA

HERO   Good Margaret, run thee to the parlour.
            There shalt thou find my cousin Beatrice
            Proposing° with the Prince and Claudio.   *Talking*
            Whisper her ear, and tell her I and Ursula
5   Walk in the orchard, and our whole discourse
            Is all of her. Say that thou overheard'st us,
            And bid her steal into the pleachèd¹ bower
            Where honeysuckles, ripened by the sun,
            Forbid the sun to enter—like favourites
10   Made proud by princes, that advance their pride
            Against that power that bred it.² There will she hide her
            To listen° our propose.° This is thy office.   *hear / conversation*
            Bear thee well in it, and leave us alone.
MARGARET   I'll make her come, I warrant you, presently. [*Exit*]
15   HERO   Now, Ursula, when Beatrice doth come,
            As we do trace° this alley up and down   *pace*
            Our talk must only be of Benedick.
            When I do name him, let it be thy part
            To praise him more than ever man did merit.
20   My talk to thee must be how Benedick
            Is sick in love with Beatrice. Of this matter
            Is little Cupid's crafty arrow made,
            That only wounds by hearsay.³
                        Enter BEATRICE
                                                Now begin,
            For look where Beatrice like a lapwing⁴ runs
25   Close by the ground to hear our conference.
URSULA   The pleasant'st angling is to see the fish
            Cut with her golden oars the silver stream
            And greedily devour the treacherous bait.
            So angle we for Beatrice, who even now
30   Is couchèd° in the woodbine coverture.⁵   *hidden*
            Fear you not my part of the dialogue.
HERO   Then go we near her, that her ear lose nothing
            Of the false-sweet bait that we lay for it.—
                        [*They approach Beatrice's hiding-place*]
            No, truly, Ursula, she is too disdainful.
35   I know her spirits are as coy° and wild   *disdainful; shy*
            As haggards° of the rock.   *wild female hawks*
URSULA   But are you sure
            That Benedick loves Beatrice so entirely?
HERO   So says the Prince and my new trothèd lord.
URSULA   And did they bid you tell her of it, madam?
40   HERO   They did entreat me to acquaint her of it,
            But I persuaded them, if they loved Benedick,
            To wish him wrestle with affection
            And never to let Beatrice know of it.
URSULA   Why did you so? Doth not the gentleman

3.1 Location: Leonato's garden.
1. Screened by intertwining branches.
2. *that advance . . . it:* who presumptuously oppose the
power that created them.

3. Wounds by rumor or gossip.
4. A peewit, a bird that scuttles along the ground.
5. In the honeysuckle arbor.

45   Deserve as full° as fortunate a bed   *fully*
     As ever Beatrice shall couch upon?
     HERO   O god of love! I know he doth deserve
     As much as may be yielded to a man.
     But nature never framed a woman's heart
50   Of prouder stuff than that of Beatrice.
     Disdain and scorn ride sparkling in her eyes,
     Misprising° what they look on, and her wit   *Despising*
     Values itself so highly that to her
     All matter else seems° weak. She cannot love,   *other matters seem*
55   Nor take no shape nor project of affection,[6]
     She is so self-endearèd.
     URSULA   Sure, I think so.
     And therefore certainly it were not good
     She knew his love, lest she'll make sport at it.
     HERO   Why, you speak truth. I never yet saw man,
60   How° wise, how noble, young, how rarely° featured,   *However / finely*
     But she would spell him backward.[7] If fair-faced,
     She would swear the gentleman should be her sister.
     If black,° why nature, drawing of an antic,°   *dark / a buffoon*
     Made a foul blot.° If tall, a lance ill headed;   *error*
65   If low, an agate[8] very vilely cut;
     If speaking, why, a vane blown with all winds;
     If silent, why, a block movèd with° none.   *by*
     So turns she every man the wrong side out,
     And never gives to truth and virtue that
70   Which simpleness° and merit purchaseth.°   *integrity / deserve*
     URSULA   Sure, sure, such carping is not commendable.
     HERO   No, not to be so odd and from all fashions[9]
     As Beatrice is cannot be commendable.
     But who dare tell her so? If I should speak
75   She would mock me into air, O, she would laugh me
     Out of myself, press me to death[1] with wit.
     Therefore let Benedick, like covered fire,
     Consume away in sighs,[2] waste inwardly.
     It were a better death than die with mocks,
80   Which is as bad as die with tickling.
     URSULA   Yet tell her of it, hear what she will say.
     HERO   No. Rather I will go to Benedick
     And counsel him to fight against his passion.
     And truly, I'll devise some honest° slanders   *harmless*
85   To stain my cousin with. One doth not know
     How much an ill word may empoison liking.
     URSULA   O, do not do your cousin such a wrong.
     She cannot be so much without true judgement,
     Having so swift and excellent a wit
90   As she is prized° to have, as to refuse   *esteemed*
     So rare a gentleman as Signor Benedick.

---

6. *Nor take . . . affection:* Nor form the image or even the concept of love.
7. She would speak of his virtues as faults.
8. Tiny figures were carved in agates and used as seals or in rings.
9. *from all fashions:* contrary to normal behavior.

1. Crushing weights were loaded upon accused criminals who refused to enter a plea; Hero suggests that she will be silenced with mockery and then mocked for her silence.
2. Each sigh was said to draw a drop of blood from the heart.

HERO   He is the only man of Italy,
    Always excepted my dear Claudio.
URSULA   I pray you be not angry with me, madam,
95   Speaking my fancy. Signor Benedick,
    For shape, for bearing, argument,[3] and valour
    Goes foremost in report through Italy.
HERO   Indeed, he hath an excellent good name.
URSULA   His excellence did earn it ere he had it.
100   When are you married, madam?
HERO   Why, every day, tomorrow.[4] Come, go in.
    I'll show thee some attires and have thy counsel
    Which is the best to furnish me tomorrow.
URSULA [aside]   She's limed,[5] I warrant you. We have caught
105   her, madam.
HERO [aside]   If it prove so, then loving goes by haps.°   chance
    Some Cupid kills with arrows, some with traps.
                                    Exeunt [HERO *and* URSULA]
BEATRICE [coming forward]   What fire is in mine ears?[6] Can this be true?
    Stand I condemned for pride and scorn so much?
110   Contempt, farewell; and maiden pride, adieu.
    No glory lives behind the back of such.[7]
    And, Benedick, love on. I will requite thee,
    Taming my wild heart to thy loving hand.[8]
    If thou dost love, my kindness shall incite thee
115   To bind our loves up in a holy band.
    For others say thou dost deserve, and I
    Believe it better than reportingly.°   *Exit*   *than as mere rumor*

3.2

Enter [DON PEDRO *the*] *Prince,* CLAUDIO, BENEDICK,
    and LEONATO

DON PEDRO   I do but stay till your marriage be consummate, and
    then go I toward Aragon.
CLAUDIO   I'll bring° you thither, my lord, if you'll vouchsafe° me.   *accompany / allow*
5 DON PEDRO   Nay, that would be as great a soil in the new gloss
    of your marriage as to show a child his new coat and forbid
    him to wear it. I will only be bold with° Benedick for his com-   *only ask*
    pany, for from the crown of his head to the sole of his foot he
    is all mirth. He hath twice or thrice cut Cupid's bow-string,
10   and the little hangman° dare not shoot at him. He hath a heart   *rogue; executioner*
    as sound as a bell, and his tongue is the clapper, for what his
    heart thinks his tongue speaks.
BENEDICK   Gallants, I am not as I have been.
LEONATO   So say I. Methinks you are sadder.°   *more serious*
15 CLAUDIO   I hope he be in love.
DON PEDRO   Hang him, truant! There's no true drop of blood
    in him to be truly touched with love. If he be sad, he wants°   *lacks*
    money.

---

3. Intellect and rhetorical skill.
4. From tomorrow on, I shall be a married woman
every day.
5. Snared with birdlime, a glue spread on branches to
catch birds.
6. Proverbially, if others were talking about you else-

where, your ears would burn.
7. No one praises such people behind their backs.
8. In falconry, the bird is tamed by the hand of the falconer.
3.2 Location: Leonato's house.

BENEDICK   I have the toothache.[1]
DON PEDRO   Draw° it.   *Extract*
20 BENEDICK   Hang it.
CLAUDIO   You must hang it first and draw it afterwards.[2]
DON PEDRO   What? Sigh for the toothache?
LEONATO   Where is but a humour[3] or a worm.
BENEDICK   Well, everyone can master a grief but he that has it.
25 CLAUDIO   Yet say I he is in love.
DON PEDRO   There is no appearance of fancy° in him, unless it   *love*
      be a fancy that he hath to strange disguises, as to be a Dutch-
      man today, a Frenchman tomorrow, or in the shape of two
      countries at once, as a German from the waist downward, all
30   slops,° and a Spaniard from the hip upward, no doublet.[4]   *baggy breeches*
      Unless he have a fancy to this foolery, as it appears he hath, he
      is no fool for fancy, as you would have it appear he is.
CLAUDIO   If he be not in love with some woman there is no
      believing old° signs. A° brushes his hat o' mornings, what should   *time-honored / He*
35   that bode?
DON PEDRO   Hath any man seen him at the barber's?
CLAUDIO   No, but the barber's man hath been seen with him,
      and the old ornament of his cheek hath already stuffed ten-
      nis balls.[5]
40 LEONATO   Indeed, he looks younger than he did by the loss of a
      beard.
DON PEDRO   Nay, a rubs himself with civet.° Can you smell him   *perfume*
      out[6] by that?
CLAUDIO   That's as much as to say the sweet youth's in love.
45 DON PEDRO   The greatest note of it is his melancholy.
CLAUDIO   And when was he wont to wash[7] his face?
DON PEDRO   Yea, or to paint himself?—for the which I hear what
      they say of him.
CLAUDIO   Nay, but his jesting spirit, which is now crept into a
50   lute-string, and now governed by stops.[8]
DON PEDRO   Indeed, that tells a heavy tale for him. Conclude,
      conclude, he is in love.
CLAUDIO   Nay, but I know who loves him.
DON PEDRO   That would I know, too. I warrant, one that knows
55   him not.
CLAUDIO   Yes, and his ill conditions,° and in despite of all, dies   *qualities*
      for him.
DON PEDRO   She shall be buried with her face upwards.[9]
BENEDICK   Yet is this no charm for the toothache. Old signor,
60   walk aside with me. I have studied eight or nine wise words to
      speak to you which these hobby-horses° must not hear.   *clowns*
                    [*Exeunt* BENEDICK *and* LEONATO]
DON PEDRO   For° my life, to break° with him about Beatrice.   *Upon / speak*

1. Toothaches supposedly plagued lovers.
2. *hang it:* a mild expletive (like "darn it"). Claudio
plays on the notion of hanging criminals, who were
then cut down and "drawn" (disemboweled).
3. Poisonous fluid in the body (which, along with
worms, was thought to be the cause of toothache).
4. His doublet is covered with a Spanish cloak.
5. Benedick has shaved off his beard. Tennis balls were
stuffed with hair.
6. Detect his secret (with play on literal "smell").

7. When was he accustomed to use cosmetics on (compare "paint" in following line).
8. Frets on a lute's fingerboard; restraints. (Lutes were
associated with lovers' serenades.)
9. That is, in Benedick's arms, where she will die (Elizabethan slang for "orgasm") in the act of love; perhaps a
joking reversal of the idea that as one responsible for
her own fate, she should be buried, like a suicide, with
her face downward.

CLAUDIO　'Tis even so. Hero and Margaret[1] have by this° played _now_
　　their parts with Beatrice, and then the two bears will not bite
65　　one another when they meet.
　　　　　　　Enter [DON] JOHN _the bastard_
　DON JOHN　My lord, and brother, God save you.
　DON PEDRO　Good-e'en,° brother. _Good evening_
　DON JOHN　If your leisure served I would speak with you.
　DON PEDRO　In private?
70　DON JOHN　If it please you. Yet Count Claudio may hear, for
　　what I would speak of concerns him.
　DON PEDRO　What's the matter?
　DON JOHN　[_to_ CLAUDIO]　Means your lordship to be married
　　tomorrow?
75　DON PEDRO　You know he does.
　DON JOHN　I know not that when he knows what I know.
　CLAUDIO　If there be any impediment, I pray you discover° it. _reveal_
　DON JOHN　You may think I love you not. Let that appear here-
　　after, and aim better at° me by that I now will manifest. For my _think better of_
80　　brother, I think he holds you well° and in dearness° of heart _in high respect / affection_
　　hath holp° to effect your ensuing marriage—surely suit ill _helped_
　　spent, and labour ill bestowed.
　DON PEDRO　Why, what's the matter?
　DON JOHN　I came hither to tell you, and, circumstances short-
85　　ened°—for she has been too long a-talking of[2]—the lady is _put simply_
　　disloyal.° _unfaithful_
　CLAUDIO　Who, Hero?
　DON JOHN　Even she. Leonato's Hero, your Hero, every man's
　　Hero.
90　CLAUDIO　Disloyal?
　DON JOHN　The word is too good to paint out° her wickedness. I _fully describe_
　　could say she were worse. Think you of a worse title, and I will
　　fit her to it. Wonder not till further warrant.° Go but with me _evidence_
　　tonight, you shall see her chamber window entered, even the
95　　night before her wedding day. If you love her then, tomorrow
　　wed her. But it would better fit your honour to change your
　　mind.
　CLAUDIO　May this be so?
　DON PEDRO　I will not think it.
100　DON JOHN　If you dare not trust that you see, confess not that you
　　know.[3] If you will follow me I will show you enough, and when
　　you have seen more and heard more, proceed accordingly.
　CLAUDIO　If I see anything tonight why I should not marry her,
　　tomorrow, in the congregation where I should wed, there will
105　　I shame her.
　DON PEDRO　And as I wooed for thee to obtain her, I will join
　　with thee to disgrace her.
　DON JOHN　I will disparage her no farther till you are my wit-
　　nesses. Bear it coldly° but till midnight, and let the issue show _calmly_
110　　itself.
　DON PEDRO　O day untowardly turned!° _miserably changed_
　CLAUDIO　O mischief strangely thwarting!

---

1. Ursula and Hero played the trick on Beatrice with
help from Margaret.
2. For we have already talked about her too much.

3. If you won't risk seeing for yourself, don't claim to
know.

DON JOHN   O plague right well prevented!—So will you say
when you have seen the sequel.   *Exeunt*

3.3

Enter DOGBERRY *and his compartner* [VERGES], *with the*
WATCH[1]

DOGBERRY   Are you good men and true?

VERGES   Yea, or else it were pity but they should suffer salvation,[2]
body and soul.

DOGBERRY   Nay, that were a punishment too good for them if
5   they should have any allegiance° in them, being chosen for the   *(for "disloyalty")*
Prince's watch.

VERGES   Well, give them their charge,° neighbour Dogberry.   *instructions*

DOGBERRY   First, who think you the most desertless° man to be   *(for "deserving")*
constable?[3]

10   SECOND WATCHMAN   Hugh Oatcake, sir, or George Seacoal, for
they can write and read.

DOGBERRY   Come hither, neighbour Seacoal, God hath blest
you with a good name.[4] To be a well-favoured° man is the gift   *good-looking*
of fortune, but to write and read comes by nature.

15   FIRST WATCHMAN   Both which, Master Constable—

DOGBERRY   You have. I knew it would be your answer. Well, for
your favour,° sir, why, give God thanks, and make no boast of   *looks*
it. And for your writing and reading, let that appear when there
is no need of such vanity. You are thought here to be the most
20   senseless° and fit man for the constable of the watch, therefore   *(for "sensible")*
bear you the lantern. This is your charge: you shall compre-
hend all vagrom[5] men. You are to bid any man stand,° in the   *stop*
Prince's name.

FIRST WATCHMAN   How if a will not stand?

25   DOGBERRY   Why then take no note of him, but let him go, and
presently° call the rest of the watch together, and thank God   *immediately*
you are rid of a knave.

VERGES   If he will not stand when he is bidden he is none of the
Prince's subjects.

30   DOGBERRY   True, and they are to meddle with none but the
Prince's subjects.—You shall also make no noise in the streets,
for for the watch to babble and to talk is most tolerable° and   *(for "intolerable")*
not to be endured.

A WATCHMAN   We will rather sleep than talk. We know what
35   belongs° to a watch.   *is appropriate*

DOGBERRY   Why, you speak like an ancient° and most quiet   *experienced*
watchman, for I cannot see how sleeping should offend. Only
have a care that your bills[6] be not stolen. Well, you are to call
at all the alehouses and bid those that are drunk get them to
40   bed.

A WATCHMAN   How if they will not?

DOGBERRY   Why then, let them alone till they are sober. If they

3.3 Location: A street.
1. Watchmen who patrolled the streets, proclaiming the hour and performing police duties. "Verges" probably alludes to a "verge," or wand of office, carried by officials.
2. For "damnation." (Verges and Dogberry repeatedly say the opposite of what they mean.)
3. The leader of the Watch. (Dogberry himself is the parish constable.) Q's speech prefixes are confusing in this scene, making it difficult to identify the leader of the Watch; some of them have been rearranged.
4. Sea coal from Newcastle was known for its high quality (thus the "good name").
5. For "vagrant." *comprehend:* for "apprehend."
6. Weapons (long shafts with blades or ax heads).

make you not then the better answer, you may say they are not
the men you took them for.

45 A WATCHMAN   Well, sir.

DOGBERRY   If you meet a thief you may suspect him, by virtue of
your office, to be no true° man; and for such kind of men, the   honest
less you meddle or make° with them why, the more is° for your   have to do / better it is
honesty.

50 A WATCHMAN   If we know him to be a thief, shall we not lay
hands on him?

DOGBERRY   Truly, by your office you may, but I think they that
touch pitch will be defiled.[7] The most peaceable way for you if
you do take a thief is to let him show himself what he is, and

55 steal out of your company.

VERGES   You have been always called a merciful man, partner.

DOGBERRY   Truly, I would not hang a dog by my will, much
more° a man who hath any honesty in him.   (for "less")

VERGES   If you hear a child cry in the night you must call to the

60 nurse and bid her still° it.   calm

A WATCHMAN   How if the nurse be asleep and will not hear us?

DOGBERRY   Why then, depart in peace and let the child wake
her with crying, for the ewe that will not hear her lamb when
it baes will never answer a calf° when he bleats.   blockhead

65 VERGES   'Tis very true.

DOGBERRY   This is the end of the charge. You, constable, are to
present° the Prince's own person.[8] If you meet the Prince in the   represent
night you may stay° him.   stop

VERGES   Nay, by'r Lady, that I think a cannot.

70 DOGBERRY   Five shillings to one on't with any man that knows
the statutes he may stay him. Marry, not without° the Prince   unless
be willing, for indeed the watch ought to offend no man, and
it is an offence to stay a man against his will.

VERGES   By'r Lady, I think it be so.

75 DOGBERRY   Ha ha ha! Well, masters, good night. An there be
any matter of weight chances,° call up me. Keep your fellows'   that occurs
counsels, and your own, and good night. Come, neighbour.

FIRST WATCHMAN   Well, masters, we hear our charge. Let us go
sit here upon the church bench till two, and then all to bed.

80 DOGBERRY   One word more, honest neighbours. I pray you
watch about Signor Leonato's door, for the wedding being
there tomorrow, there is a great coil° tonight. Adieu. Be vigi-   to-do, bustle
tant,° I beseech you.   (for "vigilant")

Exeunt [DOGBERRY *and* VERGES. *The* WATCH *sit*]
Enter BORACHIO *and* CONRAD

BORACHIO   What, Conrad!

85 FIRST WATCHMAN [*aside*]   Peace; stir not.

BORACHIO   Conrad, I say.

CONRAD   Here, man, I am at thy elbow.

BORACHIO   Mass,° an my elbow itched,[9] I thought there would a   By the mass
scab[1] follow.

---

7. A proverbial saying, derived from the Apocryphal
book of Ecclesiasticus (13:1).
8. Dogberry presents a parodic version of the notion
that the monarch's authority was in theory separable
from his person (others could represent that authority

when he was physically absent).
9. Proverbially, itching elbows alerted you against
shady company.
1. Contemptible person; punning on a literal "scab."

90   CONRAD   I will owe thee an answer for that. And now, forward
with thy tale.

     BORACHIO   Stand thee close, then, under this penthouse,° for it   *overhanging structure*
drizzles rain, and I will, like a true drunkard, utter² all to thee.

     A WATCHMAN [*aside*]   Some treason, masters. Yet stand close.°   *keep hidden*

95   BORACHIO   Therefore, know I have earned of Don John a thousand ducats.

     CONRAD   Is it possible that any villainy should be so dear?°   *valuable*

     BORACHIO   Thou shouldst rather ask if it were possible any vil-
lainy should be so rich. For when rich villains have need of

100   poor ones, poor ones may make what price they will.

     CONRAD   I wonder at it.

     BORACHIO   That shows thou art unconfirmed.° Thou knowest   *inexperienced*
that the fashion of a doublet, or a hat, or a cloak is nothing to³
a man.

105   CONRAD   Yes, it is apparel.

     BORACHIO   I mean the fashion.

     CONRAD   Yes, the fashion is the fashion.

     BORACHIO   Tush, I may as well say the fool's the fool. But seest
thou not what a deformed° thief⁴ this fashion is?   *deforming*

110   A WATCHMAN [*aside*]   I know that Deformed. A° has been a vile   *He*
thief this seven year. A goes up and down° like a gentleman. I   *struts here and there*
remember his name.

     BORACHIO   Didst thou not hear somebody?

     CONRAD   No, 'twas the vane on the house.

115   BORACHIO   Seest thou not, I say, what a deformed thief this fashion is, how giddily a turns about all the hot-bloods° between   *dandies*
fourteen and five-and-thirty, sometimes fashioning them like
Pharaoh's soldiers in the reechy° painting,⁵ sometime like god   *grimy*
Bel's⁶ priests in the old church window, sometime like the

120   shaven Hercules⁷ in the smirched, worm-eaten tapestry, where
his codpiece⁸ seems as massy as his club?

     CONRAD   All this I see, and I see that the fashion wears out more
apparel than the man.⁹ But art not thou thyself giddy with the
fashion, too, that thou hast shifted¹ out of thy tale into telling

125   me of the fashion?

     BORACHIO   Not so, neither. But know that I have tonight wooed
Margaret, the Lady Hero's gentlewoman, by the name of Hero.
She leans me° out at her mistress' chamber window, bids me a   *leans*
thousand times good night—I tell this tale vilely, I should first

130   tell thee how the Prince, Claudio, and my master, planted and
placed and possessed² by my master, Don John, saw afar off in
the orchard this amiable° encounter.   *loving*

     CONRAD   And thought they Margaret was Hero?

     BORACHIO   Two of them did, the Prince and Claudio, but the

135   devil my master knew she was Margaret, and partly by his oaths,

---

2. The drunken Borachio, whose name means "drunkard," alludes to the Latin tag *in vino veritas*.
3. Tells us nothing about (but Conrad takes him to
mean "means nothing to").
4. Used here to mean "rogue"—but also that keeping
up with fashion robs men of their money.
5. Perhaps refers to a painting of the fleeing Israelites
pursued by Pharaoh's army.
6. Bel (Baal) was a Babylonian god who had seventy
priests. His story, told in the biblical Apocrypha, is

sometimes depicted in stained-glass windows.
7. Probably referring to the story of Omphale (compare
2.1.220), or perhaps confusing Hercules with Samson.
8. Pouch, often stuffed and ornamented, worn over a
man's breeches, covering the genitals.
9. *fashion . . . man*: fashions change before clothes
wear out.
1. Punning on "changed clothes."
2. Informed; but, perhaps also, controlled (as by the
devil).

which first possessed them, partly by the dark night, which did
deceive them, but chiefly by my villainy, which did confirm
any slander that Don John had made, away went Claudio
enraged, swore he would meet her as he was appointed next
140   morning at the temple,° and there, before the whole congrega-   church
tion, shame her with what he saw o'ernight, and send her home
again without a husband.
FIRST WATCHMAN [coming forward] We charge you in the
Prince's name. Stand.
145   A WATCHMAN   Call up the right³ Master Constable. We have here
recovered the most dangerous piece of lechery⁴ that ever was
known in the commonwealth.
FIRST WATCHMAN   And one Deformed is one of them. I know
him—a wears a lock.⁵
150   CONRAD   Masters, masters!
A WATCHMAN   You'll be made bring Deformed forth, I warrant
you.
CONRAD   Masters—
A WATCHMAN   Never speak. We charge you. Let us obey° you to   (for "compel")
155   go with us.
BORACHIO [to CONRAD]   We are like to prove a goodly° commod-   fine (ironic)
ity, being taken up of these men's bills.⁶
CONRAD   A commodity in question,⁷ I warrant you. Come, we'll
obey you.   Exeunt

3.4

Enter HERO, MARGARET, *and* URSULA

HERO   Good Ursula, wake my cousin Beatrice, and desire her to
rise.
URSULA   I will, lady.
HERO   And bid her come hither.
5   URSULA   Well.°   [Exit]   Very well
MARGARET   Troth, I think your other rebato° were better.   stiffly wired ruff
HERO   No, pray thee, good Meg, I'll wear this.
MARGARET   By my troth, 's° not so good, and I warrant° your   it's / I am sure
cousin will say so.
10   HERO   My cousin's a fool, and thou art another: I'll wear none
but this.
MARGARET   I like the new tire° within excellently, if the hair were   headdress with wig
a thought browner. And your gown's a most rare fashion, i'faith.
I saw the Duchess of Milan's gown that they praise so.
15   HERO   O, that exceeds,° they say.   surpasses all
MARGARET   By my troth, 's but a night-gown° in respect of yours—   dressing gown
cloth o' gold, and cuts, and laced with silver, set with pearls,
down sleeves, side sleeves, and skirts round underborne with a
bluish tinsel.¹ But for a fine, quaint,° graceful, and excellent   elegant
20   fashion, yours is worth ten on't.

---

3. Respectfully, as in "right worshipful."
4. For "treachery." *recovered:* for "discovered."
5. A "lovelock," or curl of hair, worn by courtiers.
6. *being . . . bills:* a multiple pun: after we have been
hoisted on their halberds (weapons); been arrested on
their warrants; been obtained on credit ("taken up") in
exchange for their bonds ("bills").
7. Of doubtful value; about to be judicially interrogated.

3.4 Location: Leonato's house.
1. *cloth . . . tinsel:* made of silk or woolen cloth interwoven with gold thread, with ornamental slashes
("cuts") showing the fabric beneath, and decorated
with silver embroidery or lace and with pearls; with fitted ("down") sleeves and another pair that hung open
from the shoulder; trimmed at the hem or fully lined
("underborne") with another kind of metallic fabric.

HERO   God give me joy to wear it, for my heart is exceeding
heavy.

MARGARET   'Twill be heavier soon by the weight of a man.

HERO   Fie upon thee, art not ashamed?

25 MARGARET   Of what, lady? Of speaking honourably? Is not marriage honourable in° a beggar? Is not your lord honourable   *even in*
without marriage? I think you would have me say 'saving your
reverence,² a husband'. An° bad thinking do not wrest° true   *If / pervert*
speaking, I'll offend nobody. Is there any harm in 'the heavier
30 for a husband'? None, I think, an it be the right husband and
the right wife—otherwise 'tis light° and not heavy. Ask my Lady   *licentious*
Beatrice else. Here she comes.

          Enter BEATRICE

HERO   Good morrow, coz.

BEATRICE   Good morrow, sweet Hero.

35 HERO   Why, how now? Do you speak in the sick tune?

BEATRICE   I am out of all other tune, methinks.

MARGARET   Clap 's° into 'Light o' love'. That goes without a bur-   *Let us shift*
den.³ Do you sing it, and I'll dance it.

BEATRICE   Ye light o' love with your heels.⁴ Then if your hus-
40 band have stables enough, you'll see he shall lack no barns.⁵

MARGARET   O illegitimate construction!⁶ I scorn that with my
heels.⁷

BEATRICE   [*to* HERO]   'Tis almost five o'clock, cousin. 'Tis time
you were ready. By my troth, I am exceeding ill. Heigh-ho!

45 MARGARET   For a hawk, a horse,⁸ or a husband?

BEATRICE   For the letter that begins them all—h.⁹

MARGARET   Well, an you be not turned Turk,¹ there's no more
sailing by the star.²

BEATRICE   What means the fool, trow?°   *I wonder*

50 MARGARET   Nothing, I. But God send everyone their heart's
desire.

HERO   These gloves the Count sent me, they are an excellent
perfume.³

BEATRICE   I am stuffed,⁴ cousin. I cannot smell.

55 MARGARET   A maid, and stuffed! There's goodly catching of cold.

BEATRICE   O, God help me, God help me. How long have you
professed apprehension?°   *claimed to be witty*

MARGARET   Ever since you left it. Doth not my wit become me
rarely?°   *excellently*

60 BEATRICE   It is not seen enough. You should wear it in your cap.⁵
By my troth, I am sick.

MARGARET   Get you some of this distilled *carduus benedictus*,⁶
and lay it to your heart. It is the only thing for a qualm.°   *sudden faintness*

HERO   There thou prickest her with a thistle.

---

2. A polite expression of apology (as if "husband" were
an offensive term).
3. Bass part (for a man's voice), with play on heavy
"weight of a man." "Light o' Love" was a popular tune.
4. *Ye . . . heels:* Your dancing toys with love ("light-
heeled" was slang for "promiscuous").
5. Punning on "bairns," children.
6. A multiple pun: forced interpretation; making of
bastards; illegal building (of stables and barns).
7. I kick that away (reject it).
8. Responding to Beatrice's ostentatious sigh as a
hunting cry.

9. Punningly: "ache" was pronounced in the same way.
1. If you have not reneged (on your vows against marriage). "To turn Turk" is, in the Christian proverb, to
become a renegade (by going over to the enemy, the
Muslim Turks).
2. No more navigating by the polestar. (No truths can
be trusted from now on.)
3. Perfumed gloves were fashionable.
4. In the nose; Margaret follows with an obscene pun.
5. Like the coxcomb of a professional fool.
6. Holy thistle, or blessed thistle (a medicinal herb
good for the heart).

65 BEATRICE   Benedictus—why Benedictus? You have some moral[7]
in this Benedictus.

MARGARET   Moral? No, by my troth, I have no moral meaning. I
meant plain holy-thistle. You may think perchance° that I think   *perhaps*
you are in love. Nay, by'r Lady, I am not such a fool to think
70 what I list,° nor I list not to think what I can, nor indeed I   *please*
cannot think, if I would think my heart out of thinking, that
you are in love, or that you will be in love, or that you can be in
love. Yet Benedick was such another,[8] and now is he become a
man. He swore he would never marry, and yet now in despite
75 of his heart he eats his meat without grudging.[9] And how you
may be converted I know not, but methinks you look with your
eyes, as other women do.

BEATRICE   What pace is this that thy tongue keeps?

MARGARET   Not a false gallop.[1]

Enter URSULA

80 URSULA [*to* HERO]   Madam, withdraw. The Prince, the Count,
Signor Benedick, Don John, and all the gallants of the town
are come to fetch you to church.

HERO   Help to dress me, good coz, good Meg, good Ursula.

Exeunt

3.5

Enter LEONATO, *and* [DOGBERRY] *the constable, and*
[VERGES] *the headborough*°   *local constable*

LEONATO   What would you with me, honest neighbour?

DOGBERRY   Marry, sir, I would have some confidence° with you   *(for "conference")*
that decerns° you nearly.   *(for "concerns")*

LEONATO   Brief° I pray you, for you see it is a busy time with me.   *Be brief*

5 DOGBERRY   Marry, this it is, sir.

VERGES   Yes, in truth it is, sir.

LEONATO   What is it, my good friends?

DOGBERRY   Goodman° Verges, sir, speaks a little off the mat-   *(commoner's title)*
ter°—an old man, sir, and his wits are not so blunt° as, God   *subject / (for "sharp")*
10 help, I would desire they were. But in faith, honest as the skin
between his brows.

VERGES   Yes, I thank God, I am as honest as any man living that
is an old man and no honester than I.

DOGBERRY   Comparisons are odorous.° Palabras,[1] neighbour   *(for "odious")*
15 Verges.

LEONATO   Neighbours, you are tedious.[2]

DOGBERRY   It pleases your worship to say so, but we are the poor
Duke's° officers. But truly, for mine own part, if I were as   *the Duke's poor*
tedious as a king I could find in my heart to bestow it all of
20 your worship.

LEONATO   All thy tediousness on me, ah?

DOGBERRY   Yea, an 'twere a thousand pound more than 'tis, for I
hear as good exclamation[3] on your worship as of any man in
the city, and though I be but a poor man, I am glad to hear it.

25 VERGES   And so am I.

---

7. Hidden meaning (with ensuing pun on "no moral"
as "immoral").
8. Benedick was once an enemy of love.
9. Nonetheless, he has a perfectly good appetite.
1. Not a canter. (I am not speaking at a false pace.)
3.5 Location: Leonato's house.

1. Be brief (from a Spanish expression, *pocas palabras*:
"few words").
2. Dogberry takes it to mean "rich."
3. Properly, "accusation"; but Dogberry probably
intends "acclamation."

LEONATO   I would fain° know what you have to say.   *gladly*

VERGES   Marry, sir, our watch tonight, excepting your worship's
presence,[4] ha' ta'en a couple of as arrant knaves as any in Messina.

30 DOGBERRY   A good old man, sir. He will be talking. As they say,
when the age is in, the wit is out.[5] God help us, it is a world to
see.[6] Well said, i'faith, neighbour Verges. Well, God's a good
man. An° two men ride of a horse, one must ride behind. An   *If*
honest soul, i'faith, sir, by my troth he is, as ever broke bread.[7]

35 But, God is to be worshipped, all men are not alike, alas, good
neighbour.

LEONATO   Indeed, neighbour, he comes too short of you.

DOGBERRY   Gifts that God gives!

LEONATO   I must leave you.

40 DOGBERRY   One word, sir. Our watch, sir, have indeed comprehended two auspicious[8] persons, and we would have them this
morning examined before your worship.

LEONATO   Take their examination yourself, and bring it me. I am
now in great haste, as it may appear unto you.

45 DOGBERRY   It shall be suffigance.°   *(for "sufficient")*

LEONATO   Drink some wine ere you go. Fare you well.
        [*Enter a* MESSENGER]

MESSENGER   My lord, they stay° for you to give your daughter to   *wait*
her husband.

LEONATO   I'll wait upon them, I am ready.
        [*Exeunt* LEONATO *and* MESSENGER]

50 DOGBERRY   Go, good partner, go get you to Francis Seacoal,[9]
bid him bring his pen and inkhorn to the jail. We are now to
examination° these men.   *(for "examine")*

VERGES   And we must do it wisely.

DOGBERRY   We will spare for no wit, I warrant you. Here's that°   *that which*
55 shall drive some of them to a non-com.[1] Only get the learned
writer to set down our excommunication,° and meet me at the   *(for "examination")*
jail.   *Exeunt*

4.1

Enter [DON PEDRO *the*] *Prince,* [DON JOHN *the*] *bastard,*
LEONATO, FRIAR [FRANCIS], CLAUDIO, BENEDICK,
HERO, *and* BEATRICE

LEONATO   Come, Friar Francis, be brief. Only to the plain form
of marriage, and you shall recount their particular duties
afterwards.

FRIAR [*to* CLAUDIO]   You come hither, my lord, to marry this
5 lady?

CLAUDIO   No.

LEONATO   To be married to her. Friar, you come to marry her.

FRIAR [*to* HERO]   Lady, you come hither to be married to this
count?

---

4. For "respecting your worship's presence": an apology
for speaking what might displease.
5. Dogberry's version of the proverb "When the wine is
in, the wit is out."
6. Dogberry seems to mean "a strange world"; the
expression normally meant "wonderful to behold."
7. Dogberry strings together three proverbial sentences,

all of which are remembered correctly but irrelevantly.
8. For "suspicious." *comprehended*: for "apprehended."
9. Refers to the Sexton in 4.2, not the George Seacoal
of the Watch in 3.3.
1. For "nonplus" (bewilderment); perhaps confused by
Dogberry with *non compos mentis* (insane).
4.1 Location: A church.

10 HERO I do.

FRIAR If either of you know any inward° impediment why you   secret
should not be conjoined, I charge you on your souls to utter it.

CLAUDIO Know you any, Hero?

HERO None, my lord.

15 FRIAR Know you any, Count?

LEONATO I dare make his answer—none.

CLAUDIO O, what men dare do! What men may do! What men
daily do, not knowing what they do!

BENEDICK How now! Interjections? Why then, some be of
20 laughing, as 'ah, ha, he!'[1]

CLAUDIO Stand thee by, Friar. Father, by your leave,
Will you with free and unconstrainèd soul
Give me this maid, your daughter?

LEONATO As freely, son, as God did give her me.

25 CLAUDIO And what have I to give you back whose worth
May counterpoise° this rich and precious gift?   equal

DON PEDRO Nothing, unless you render her again.

CLAUDIO Sweet Prince, you learn° me noble thankfulness.   teach
There, Leonato, take her back again.

30 Give not this rotten orange to your friend.
She's but the sign° and semblance of her honour.   mere appearance
Behold how like a maid she blushes here!
O, what authority and show of truth
Can cunning sin cover itself withal!

35 Comes not that blood° as modest evidence   blush
To witness° simple virtue? Would you not swear,   testify to
All you that see her, that she were a maid,
By these exterior shows? But she is none.
She knows the heat of a luxurious° bed.   lustful

40 Her blush is guiltiness, not modesty.

LEONATO What do you mean, my lord?

CLAUDIO   Not to be married,
Not to knit my soul to an approvèd° wanton.   a proven

LEONATO Dear my lord, if you in your own proof°   testing (of her)
Have vanquished the resistance of her youth
45 And made defeat of her virginity—

CLAUDIO I know what you would say. If I have known her,
You will say she did embrace me as a husband,
And so extenuate the forehand sin.[2]

No, Leonato,
50 I never tempted her with word too large,°   immodest
But as a brother to his sister showed
Bashful sincerity and comely love.

HERO And seemed I ever otherwise to you?

CLAUDIO Out on thee,[3] seeming! I will write against it.
55 You seem to me as Dian in her orb,[4]
As chaste as is the bud ere it be blown.°   blossom
But you are more intemperate in your blood°   passion

---

1. Benedick alludes to a passage in William Lily's Latin
grammar, used in all Elizabethan schools: "Some [inter-
jections] are of laughing; as Ha ha he" (1567 edition).
2. And so sin only in anticipation of marriage.
3. A curse; "thee" could refer to Hero or "seeming"
(putting on a false show).
4. Diana (Roman goddess of chastity and of the moon)
in her orbit, or sphere of activity.

       Than Venus or those pampered animals
       That rage in savage sensuality.
60 HERO   Is my lord well that he doth speak so wide?°   *wildly*
    LEONATO   Sweet Prince, why speak not you?
    DON PEDRO   What should I speak?
       I stand dishonoured, that have gone about°   *have tried*
       To link my dear friend to a common stale.°   *prostitute*
    LEONATO   Are these things spoken, or do I but dream?
65 DON JOHN   Sir, they are spoken, and these things are true.
    BENEDICK   This looks not like a nuptial.
    HERO   'True'! O God!
    CLAUDIO   Leonato, stand I here?
       Is this the Prince? Is this the Prince's brother?
70   Is this face Hero's? Are our eyes our own?
    LEONATO   All this is so. But what of this, my lord?
    CLAUDIO   Let me but move° one question to your daughter,   *put*
       And by that fatherly and kindly° power   *natural*
       That you have in her, bid her answer truly.
75 LEONATO [*to* HERO]   I charge thee do so, as thou art my child.
    HERO   O God defend me, how am I beset!
       What kind of catechizing[5] call you this?
    CLAUDIO   To make you answer truly to your name.[6]
    HERO   Is it not Hero? Who can blot that name
       With any just reproach?
80 CLAUDIO   Marry, that can Hero.
       Hero itself[7] can blot out Hero's virtue.
       What man was he talked with you yesternight
       Out at your window betwixt twelve and one?
       Now if you are a maid, answer to this.
85 HERO   I talked with no man at that hour, my lord.
    DON PEDRO   Why, then are you no maiden. Leonato,
       I am sorry you must hear. Upon mine honour,
       Myself, my brother, and this grievèd° Count   *wronged*
       Did see her, hear her, at that hour last night
90   Talk with a ruffian at her chamber window,
       Who hath indeed, most like a liberal° villain,   *loose-tongued*
       Confessed the vile encounters they have had
       A thousand times in secret.
    DON JOHN   Fie, fie, they are
       Not to be named, my lord, not to be spoke of.
95   There is not chastity enough in language
       Without offence to utter them. Thus, pretty lady,
       I am sorry for thy much misgovernment.°   *ample misconduct*
    CLAUDIO   O Hero! What a Hero hadst thou been
       If half thy outward graces had been placed
100   About thy thoughts and counsels of thy heart!
       But fare thee well, most foul, most fair, farewell
       Thou pure impiety and impious purity.
       For° thee I'll lock up all the gates of love,   *Because of*
       And on my eyelids shall conjecture° hang   *suspicion*

---

5. A catechism was a set of formal questions and
answers used to teach church doctrine.
6. To make you admit that you are what you have been
called.
7. The name (or reputation) of Hero.

105   To turn all beauty into thoughts of harm,
     And never shall it more be gracious.°   *attractive*
  LEONATO   Hath no man's dagger here a point for me?
          [HERO *falls to the ground*]
  BEATRICE   Why, how now, cousin, wherefore sink you down?
  DON JOHN   Come. Let us go. These things come thus to light
110   Smother her spirits° up.   *vital forces*
           [*Exeunt* DON PEDRO, DON JOHN, *and* CLAUDIO]
  BENEDICK   How doth the lady?
  BEATRICE   Dead, I think. Help, uncle.
     Hero, why Hero! Uncle, Signor Benedick, Friar—
  LEONATO   O fate, take not away thy heavy hand.
     Death is the fairest cover for her shame
     That may be wished for.
115 BEATRICE   How now, cousin Hero?
  FRIAR [*to* HERO]   Have comfort, lady.
  LEONATO [*to* HERO]   Dost thou look up?
  FRIAR   Yea, wherefore should she not?
  LEONATO   Wherefore? Why, doth not every earthly thing
120   Cry shame upon her? Could she here deny
     The story that is printed in her blood?°   *blush*
     Do not live, Hero, do not ope thine eyes,
     For did I think thou wouldst not quickly die,
     Thought I thy spirits were stronger than thy shames,
125   Myself would on the rearward° of reproaches   *in the wake*
     Strike at thy life. Grieved I I had but one?
     Chid I for that at frugal nature's frame?°   *plan*
     O one too much by thee! Why had I one?
     Why ever wast thou lovely in my eyes?
130   Why had I not with charitable hand
     Took up a beggar's issue at my gates,
     Who smirchèd thus° and mired with infamy,   *(as you are)*
     I might have said 'No part of it is mine,
     This shame derives itself from unknown loins.'
135   But mine, and mine I loved, and mine I praised,
     And mine that I was proud on,° mine so much   *of*
     That I myself was to myself not mine,[8]
     Valuing of her—why she, O she is fallen
     Into a pit of ink, that the wide sea
140   Hath drops too few to wash her clean again,
     And salt too little which may season[9] give
     To her foul tainted flesh.
  BENEDICK   Sir, sir, be patient.
     For my part, I am so attired in wonder
     I know not what to say.
145 BEATRICE   O, on my soul, my cousin is belied.°   *slandered*
  BENEDICK   Lady, were you her bedfellow last night?
  BEATRICE   No, truly not, although until last night
     I have this twelvemonth been her bedfellow.
  LEONATO   Confirmed, confirmed. O, that is stronger made
150   Which was before° barred up with ribs of iron.   *already*
     Would the two princes lie? And Claudio lie,

---

8. That I cared nothing for myself in comparison.   9. Give renewal. (Salt is a preservative for meat.)

Who loved her so that, speaking of her foulness,
Washed it with tears? Hence from her, let her die.
FRIAR   Hear me a little,
155 For I have only been silent so long
And given way unto this course of fortune[1]
By noting of the lady.[2] I have marked
A thousand blushing apparitions
To start into her face, a thousand innocent shames
160 In angel whiteness beat away those blushes,
And in her eye there hath appeared a fire
To burn the errors° that these princes hold   *(like heretics)*
Against her maiden truth. Call me a fool,
Trust not my reading nor my observations,
165 Which with experimental seal doth warrant
The tenor of my book.[3] Trust not my age,
My reverence, calling, nor divinity,
If this sweet lady lie not guiltless here
Under some biting error.
LEONATO   Friar, it cannot be.
170 Thou seest that all the grace that she hath left
Is that she will not add to her damnation
A sin of perjury. She not denies it.
Why seek'st thou then to cover with excuse
That which appears in proper° nakedness?   *true*
175 FRIAR [*to* HERO]   Lady, what man is he you are accused of?
HERO   They know that do accuse me. I know none.
If I know more of any man alive
Than that which maiden modesty doth warrant,
Let all my sins lack mercy. O my father,
180 Prove you that any man with me conversed
At hours unmeet,° or that I yesternight   *improper*
Maintained the change° of words with any creature,   *exchange*
Refuse° me, hate me, torture me to death.   *Disown*
FRIAR   There is some strange misprision° in the princes. *misunderstanding*
185 BENEDICK   Two of them have the very bent of° honour, *are wholly devoted to*
And if their wisdoms be misled in this
The practice° of it lives in John the bastard,   *trickery*
Whose spirits toil in frame of° villainies.   *in plotting*
LEONATO   I know not. If they speak but truth of her
190 These hands shall tear her. If they wrong her honour
The proudest of them shall well hear of it.
Time hath not yet so dried this blood of mine,
Nor age so eat up my invention,°   *cleverness*
Nor fortune made such havoc of my means,°   *wealth*
195 Nor my bad life reft me so much of friends,
But they shall find awaked in such a kind°   *manner*
Both strength of limb and policy° of mind,   *cunning*
Ability in means, and choice of friends,
To quit me of[4] them throughly.°   *thoroughly*
FRIAR   Pause awhile,

---

1. Q erroneously sets the beginning of the speech in cramped prose; some words seem to have been lost in the compression.
2. *By . . . lady:* So I could observe, or because I was observing, Hero.
3. *Which . . . book:* Which guarantees, with the confirmation of experience, the truth of the conclusions I have drawn from my study.
4. To be avenged upon.

200	And let my counsel sway you in this case.
	Your daughter here the princes left for dead,
	Let her a while be secretly kept in,
	And publish° it that she is dead indeed.	announce
	Maintain a mourning ostentation,°	formal display
205	And on your family's old monument°	burial vault
	Hang mournful epitaphs, and do all rites
	That appertain unto a burial.

LEONATO   What shall become of this? What will this do?

FRIAR   Marry, this, well carried,° shall on her behalf   *managed*

210 Change slander to remorse.° That is some good.   *pity*
But not for that dream I on this strange course,
But on° this travail look for greater birth.[5]   *from*
She—dying, as it must be so maintained,
Upon the instant that she was accused—

215 Shall be lamented, pitied, and excused
Of° every hearer. For it so falls out   *By*
That what we have, we prize not to the worth°   *full value*
Whiles we enjoy it, but, being lacked and lost,
Why then we rack[6] the value, then we find

220 The virtue that possession would not show us
Whiles it was ours. So will it fare with Claudio.
When he shall hear she died upon° his words,   *as a result of*
Th'idea° of her life shall sweetly creep   *The image*
Into his study of imagination,°   *reverie*

225 And every lovely organ° of her life   *aspect*
Shall come apparelled in more precious habit,
More moving-delicate, and full of life,
Into the eye and prospect° of his soul   *vision*
Than when she lived indeed. Then shall he mourn,

230 If ever love had interest in his liver,[7]
And wish he had not so accusèd her,
No, though he thought his accusation true.
Let this be so, and doubt not but success°   *what follows*
Will fashion the event° in better shape   *result*

235 Than I can lay it down in likelihood.
But if all aim but this be levelled false,[8]
The supposition of the lady's death
Will quench the wonder of her infamy.
And if it sort° not well, you may conceal her,   *turn out*

240 As best befits her wounded reputation,
In some reclusive° and religious life,   *cloistered*
Out of all eyes, tongues, minds, and injuries.°   *calumny*

BENEDICK   Signor Leonato, let the Friar advise you.
And though you know my inwardness° and love   *intimacy*

245 Is very much unto the Prince and Claudio,
Yet, by mine honour, I will deal in this
As secretly and justly as your soul
Should with your body.

LEONATO   Being that I flow in° grief,   *Since I am flooded by*

250 The smallest twine may lead me.

---

5. Look for a more important consequence (with pun on "travail" as "labor pains" as well as "effort").
6. Stretch (as on a rack, an instrument of torture).
7. Thought of as the seat of passions, including love.
8. But if we miss our aim in all but this.

FRIAR 'Tis well consented. Presently away,
For to strange sores strangely they strain the cure.[9]
[*To* HERO] Come, lady, die to live. This wedding day
Perhaps is but prolonged.° Have patience, and endure.   *postponed*
Exeunt [*all but* BEATRICE *and* BENEDICK]

255 BENEDICK Lady Beatrice, have you wept all this while?
BEATRICE Yea, and I will weep a while longer.
BENEDICK I will not desire that.
BEATRICE You have no reason, I do it freely.
BENEDICK Surely I do believe your fair cousin is wronged.
260 BEATRICE Ah, how much might the man deserve of me that
would right her!
BENEDICK Is there any way to show such friendship?
BEATRICE A very even° way, but no such friend.   *clear*
BENEDICK May a man do it?
265 BEATRICE It is a man's office, but not yours.
BENEDICK I do love nothing in the world so well as you. Is not
that strange?
BEATRICE As strange as the thing I know not. It were as possible
for me to say I loved nothing so well as you, but believe me
270 not, and yet I lie not. I confess nothing nor I deny nothing. I
am sorry for my cousin.
BENEDICK By my sword, Beatrice, thou lovest me.
BEATRICE Do not swear and eat it.[1]
BENEDICK I will swear by it that you love me, and I will make
275 him eat it that says I love not you.
BEATRICE Will you not eat your word?
BENEDICK With no sauce that can be devised to it. I protest° I   *affirm*
love thee.
BEATRICE Why then, God forgive me.
280 BENEDICK What offence, sweet Beatrice?
BEATRICE You have stayed me in a happy hour.[2] I was about to
protest I loved you.
BENEDICK And do it with all thy heart.
BEATRICE I love you with so much of my heart that none is left
285 to protest.
BENEDICK Come, bid me do anything for thee.
BEATRICE Kill Claudio.
BENEDICK Ha! Not for the wide world.
BEATRICE You kill me to deny° it. Farewell.   *by refusing*
290 BENEDICK Tarry, sweet Beatrice.
BEATRICE I am gone though I am here. There is no love in
you.—Nay, I pray you, let me go.
BENEDICK Beatrice.
BEATRICE In faith, I will go.
295 BENEDICK We'll be friends first.
BEATRICE You dare easier be friends with me than fight with
mine enemy.
BENEDICK Is Claudio thine enemy?
BEATRICE Is a not approved in the height[3] a villain, that hath
300 slandered, scorned, dishonoured my kinswoman? O that I were

---

9. Compare the proverb "A desperate disease must
have a desperate cure."
1. Eat your words, go back on your oath. Benedick takes

it to mean his sword (as does F: "swear by it and eat it").
2. You have stopped me at a fortunate moment.
3. Is he not proved in the highest degree.

a man! What, bear her in hand[4] until they come to take hands, and then with public accusation, uncovered° slander, unmitigated rancour—O God that I were a man! I would eat his heart in the market place.   *barefaced*

305   BENEDICK   Hear me, Beatrice.

    BEATRICE   Talk with a man out at a window—a proper saying!°   *a likely story*

    BENEDICK   Nay, but Beatrice.

    BEATRICE   Sweet Hero, she is wronged, she is slandered, she is undone.

310   BENEDICK   Beat—

    BEATRICE   Princes and counties! Surely a princely testimony, a goodly count,[5] Count Comfit,° a sweet gallant, surely. O that I   *Sugarplum* were a man for his sake! Or that I had any friend would be a man for my sake! But manhood is melted into courtesies,

315   valour into compliment, and men are only turned into tongue, and trim° ones, too. He is now as valiant as Hercules that° only   *fine (ironic) / who* tells a lie and swears it. I cannot be a man with° wishing, there   *by* fore I will die a woman with grieving.

    BENEDICK   Tarry, good Beatrice. By this hand, I love thee.

320   BEATRICE   Use it for my love some other way than swearing by it.

    BENEDICK   Think you in your soul the Count Claudio hath wronged Hero?

    BEATRICE   Yea, as sure as I have a thought or a soul.

325   BENEDICK   Enough, I am engaged,° I will challenge him. I will   *pledged* kiss your hand, and so I leave you. By this hand, Claudio shall render me a dear account.° As you hear of me, so think of me.   *pay me dearly* Go comfort your cousin. I must say she is dead. And so, farewell.   *[Exeunt]*

4.2

Enter [DOGBERRY and VERGES] the constables, and the Town Clerk [the SEXTON], in gowns,[1] [and the WATCH, with] BORACHIO [and CONRAD]

  DOGBERRY   Is our whole dissembly° appeared?   *(for "assembly")*

  VERGES   O, a stool and a cushion for the Sexton.

  SEXTON *[sits]*   Which be the malefactors?[2]

  DOGBERRY   Marry, that am I, and my partner.

5   VERGES   Nay, that's certain, we have the exhibition° to examine.   *(for "commission")*

  SEXTON   But which are the offenders that are to be examined? Let them come before Master Constable.

  DOGBERRY   Yea, marry, let them come before me. What is your name, friend?

10   BORACHIO   Borachio.

  DOGBERRY *[to the SEXTON]*   Pray write down 'Borachio'. *[To CON RAD]* Yours, sirrah?[3]

  CONRAD   I am a gentleman, sir, and my name is Conrad.

  DOGBERRY   Write down 'Master Gentleman Conrad'.—Masters,

15   do you serve God?

---

4. *bear her in hand:* lead her on with false hopes.
5. Story, tale (with plays on "count" as a legal indictment and as Claudio's title).
4.2 Location: A prison or hearing room in Messina.
1. Constables wore black gowns. The Sexton is presumably Francis Seacoal (3.5.50). Q's direction calls him the town clerk, an office more appropriate to his

function in the scene than sexton, with which, however, it seems often to have been combined.
2. Dogberry seems to mistake "malefactors" for "factors," or agents.
3. Contemptuous, since "sirrah" is used to address inferiors, provoking Conrad's claim to be a gentleman.

CONRAD *and* BORACHIO   Yea, sir, we hope.

DOGBERRY   Write down that they hope they serve God. And
write 'God' first, for God defend° but God should go before[4]   *forbid*
such villains. Masters, it is proved already that you are little
20 better than false knaves, and it will go near to be thought so
shortly. How answer you for yourselves?

CONRAD   Marry, sir, we say we are none.

DOGBERRY   A marvellous witty° fellow, I assure you, but I will go   *clever*
about with° him. Come you hither, sirrah. A word in your ear,   *will outwit*
25 sir. I say to you it is thought you are false knaves.

BORACHIO   Sir, I say to you we are none.

DOGBERRY   Well, stand aside. Fore God, they are both in a tale.°   *telling the same story*
Have you writ down that they are none?

SEXTON   Master Constable, you go not the way to examine. You
30 must call forth the watch that are their accusers.

DOGBERRY   Yea, marry, that's the eftest° way. Let the watch come   *(for "aptest")*
forth. Masters, I charge you in the Prince's name accuse these
men.

FIRST WATCHMAN   This man said, sir, that Don John, the Prince's
35 brother, was a villain.

DOGBERRY   Write down Prince John a villain. Why, this is flat
perjury,[5] to call a prince's brother villain.

BORACHIO   Master Constable.

DOGBERRY   Pray thee, fellow, peace. I do not like thy look, I
40 promise thee.

SEXTON   What heard you him say else?

SECOND WATCHMAN   Marry, that he had received a thousand
ducats of Don John for accusing the Lady Hero wrongfully.

DOGBERRY   Flat burglary, as ever was committed.

45 VERGES   Yea, by mass,[6] that it is.

SEXTON   What else, fellow?

FIRST WATCHMAN   And that Count Claudio did mean upon° his   *with*
words to disgrace Hero before the whole assembly, and not
marry her.

50 DOGBERRY   O villain! Thou wilt be condemned into everlasting
redemption° for this.   *(for "damnation")*

SEXTON   What else?

WATCH   This is all.

SEXTON   And this is more, masters, than you can deny. Prince
55 John is this morning secretly stolen away. Hero was in this manner accused, in this very manner refused, and upon the grief of
this suddenly died. Master Constable, let these men be bound
and brought to Leonato's. I will go before and show him their
examination.   [*Exit*]

60 DOGBERRY   Come, let them be opinioned.°   *(for "pinioned")*

VERGES   Let them be, in the hands—

CONRAD   Off, coxcomb![7]

DOGBERRY   God's° my life, where's the Sexton? Let him write   *God save*
down the Prince's officer coxcomb. Come, bind them. Thou
65 naughty varlet!°   *wicked knave*

CONRAD   Away, you are an ass, you are an ass.

---

4. (Punningly) take precedence over.
5. Perhaps a mistake for "treason" or "slander."
6. "By the mass," a common oath.

7. This is an emendation of a corrupt passage, given in
Q as part of the previous speech. These words could be
spoken by Borachio.

DOGBERRY Dost thou not suspect° my place? Dost thou not sus- *(for "respect")*
pect my years? O that he were here to write me down an ass!
But masters, remember that I am an ass. Though it be not
70 written down, yet forget not that I am an ass. No, thou villain,
thou art full of piety,° as shall be proved upon thee by good *(for "impiety")*
witness. I am a wise fellow, and which is more, an officer, and
which is more, a householder, and which is more, as pretty a
piece of flesh[8] as any is in Messina, and one that knows the
75 law, go to, and a rich fellow enough, go to, and a fellow that
hath had losses,[9] and one that hath two gowns, and everything
handsome about him. Bring him away. O that I had been writ
down an ass! *Exeunt*

5.1

Enter LEONATO *and* [ANTONIO] *his brother*

ANTONIO If you go on thus, you will kill yourself,
And 'tis not wisdom thus to second° grief *assist*
Against yourself.
LEONATO I pray thee cease thy counsel,
Which falls into mine ears as profitless
5 As water in a sieve. Give not me counsel,
Nor let no comforter delight mine ear
But such a one whose wrongs do suit° with mine. *match*
Bring me a father that so loved his child,
Whose joy of° her is overwhelmed like mine, *in*
10 And bid him speak of patience.
Measure his woe the length and breadth of mine,
And let it answer every strain° for strain, *strong feeling*
As thus for thus, and such a grief for such,
In every lineament, branch, shape, and form.
15 If such a one will smile and stroke his beard,
Bid sorrow wag,° cry 'hem'[1] when he should groan, *be off*
Patch° grief with proverbs, make misfortune drunk° *Mend / insensible*
With candle-wasters,[2] bring him yet to me,
And I of him will gather patience.
20 But there is no such man, for, brother, men
Can counsel and speak comfort to that grief
Which they themselves not feel, but tasting it
Their counsel turns to passion, which before
Would give preceptial° medicine to rage, *precepts as*
25 Fetter strong madness in a silken thread,
Charm ache with air° and agony with words. *breath*
No, no, 'tis all men's office° to speak patience *business*
To those that wring° under the load of sorrow, *writhe*
But no man's virtue nor sufficiency° *ability*
30 To be so moral° when he shall endure *moralizing*
The like himself. Therefore give me no counsel.
My griefs cry louder than advertisement.° *advice*
ANTONIO Therein do men from children nothing differ.
LEONATO I pray thee peace, I will be flesh and blood,
35 For there was never yet philosopher

---

8. *as pretty . . . flesh:* as fine (or gallant) a mortal man.
9. *hath had losses:* was once richer.
5.1 Location: Near Leonato's house.

1. Clear his throat (as if about to make a speech).
2. Philosophers, burners of midnight oil (and their works).

That could endure the toothache patiently,
However they have writ the style of gods,
And made a pish at chance and sufferance.[3]
ANTONIO   Yet bend° not all the harm upon yourself. | *direct*
40 Make those that do offend you suffer, too.
LEONATO   There thou speak'st reason, nay I will do so.
My soul doth tell me Hero is belied,
And that shall Claudio know, so shall the Prince,
And all of them that thus dishonour her.

       Enter [DON PEDRO *the*] *Prince and* CLAUDIO

45 ANTONIO   Here comes the Prince and Claudio hastily.
DON PEDRO   Good e'en,° good e'en. | *evening*
CLAUDIO   Good day to both of you.
LEONATO   Hear you, my lords?
DON PEDRO   We have some haste, Leonato.
LEONATO   Some haste, my lord! Well, fare you well, my lord.
Are you so hasty now? Well, all is one.° | *no matter*
50 DON PEDRO   Nay, do not quarrel with us, good old man.
ANTONIO   If he could right himself with quarrelling,
Some of us° would lie low. | *(Don Pedro and Claudio)*
CLAUDIO   Who wrongs him?
LEONATO   Marry, thou dost wrong me, thou dissembler, thou.[4]
Nay, never lay thy hand upon thy sword,
I fear thee not.
55 CLAUDIO   Marry, beshrew° my hand | *curse*
If it should give your age such cause of fear.
In faith, my hand meant nothing to[5] my sword.
LEONATO   Tush, tush, man, never fleer° and jest at me. | *sneer; mock*
I speak not like a dotard nor a fool,
60 As under privilege of age to brag
What I have done being young, or what would do
Were I not old. Know Claudio to thy head,° | *face*
Thou hast so wronged mine innocent child and me
That I am forced to lay my reverence by
65 And with grey hairs and bruise of many days
Do challenge thee to trial of a man.° | *of manhood*
I say thou hast belied mine innocent child.
Thy slander hath gone through and through her heart,
And she lies buried with her ancestors,
70 O, in a tomb where never scandal slept
Save this of hers, framed° by thy villainy. | *created*
CLAUDIO   My villainy?
LEONATO   Thine, Claudio, thine I say.
DON PEDRO   You say not right, old man.
LEONATO   My lord, my lord,
I'll prove it on his body if he dare,
75 Despite his nice fence[6] and his active practice,
His May of youth and bloom of lustihood.° | *virility*
CLAUDIO   Away, I will not have to do with you.
LEONATO   Canst thou so doff me?° Thou hast killed my child. | *brush me off*
If thou kill'st me, boy, thou shalt kill a man.

---

3. *writ . . . sufferance:* written as if they transcended
human passion, and expressed themselves scornfully
about (said "pish" to) bad luck and suffering.

4. "Thou" is used contemptuously here.
5. My hand had no designs upon.
6. His nimble fencing (said contemptuously).

80 ANTONIO He shall kill two of us, and men indeed.
  But that's no matter, let him kill one first.
  Win me and wear me.[7] Let him answer me.°   *(in a duel)*
  Come follow me boy, come sir boy, come follow me,
  Sir boy, I'll whip you from your foining fence.[8]
85 Nay, as I am a gentleman, I will.
  LEONATO Brother.
  ANTONIO Content yourself.° God knows, I loved my niece,   *Don't interfere*
  And she is dead, slandered to death by villains
  That dare as well answer a man indeed
90 As I dare take a serpent by the tongue.
  Boys, apes,° braggarts, jacks,° milksops!   *fools / knaves*
  LEONATO Brother Antony—
  ANTONIO Hold you content. What, man, I know them, yea
  And what they weigh, even to the utmost scruple.°   *¹⁄₂₄ ounce*
95 Scambling, outfacing, fashion-monging boys,[9]
  That lie, and cog,° and flout,° deprave,° and slander,   *cheat / mock / defame*
  Go anticly,° and show an outward hideousness,[1]   *outlandishly dressed*
  And speak off half a dozen dangerous words,
  How they might hurt their enemies, if they durst,
100 And this is all.
  LEONATO But brother Antony—
  ANTONIO Come, 'tis no matter,
  Do not you meddle, let me deal in this.
  DON PEDRO Gentlemen both, we will not wake° your patience.   *test*
105 My heart is sorry for your daughter's death,
  But on my honour she was charged with nothing
  But what was true and very full of proof.
  LEONATO My lord, my lord—
  DON PEDRO   I will not hear you.
  LEONATO No? Come brother, away. I will be heard.
110 ANTONIO And shall, or some of us will smart for it.
                Exeunt [LEONATO *and* ANTONIO]
      Enter BENEDICK
  DON PEDRO See, see, here comes the man we went to seek.
  CLAUDIO Now signor, what news?
  BENEDICK [*to* DON PEDRO] Good day, my lord.
  DON PEDRO Welcome, signor. You are almost come to part
115 almost a fray.
  CLAUDIO We had liked to have had° our two noses snapped off   *We nearly had*
  with° two old men without teeth.   *by*
  DON PEDRO Leonato and his brother. What thinkest thou? Had
  we fought, I doubt° we should have been too young for them.   *suspect*
120 BENEDICK In a false quarrel there is no true valour. I came to
  seek you both.
  CLAUDIO We have been up and down to seek thee, for we are
  high-proof° melancholy and would fain have it beaten away.   *to a high degree*
  Wilt thou use thy wit?
125 BENEDICK It is in my scabbard. Shall I draw it?
  DON PEDRO Dost thou wear thy wit by thy side?

---

7. A form of challenge: let him beat me and only then boast of it.
8. Thrusting position in fencing (Antonio probably means that he will compel Claudio to close with him in the duel, or that he will literally take a whip to him).
9. *Scambling . . . boys*: Quarrelsome, insolent, faddish boys.
1. A fearsome exterior.

CLAUDIO   Never any did so, though very many have been beside
their wit.° I will bid thee draw as we do the minstrels,[2] draw to   *out of their minds*
pleasure us.

130   DON PEDRO   As I am an honest man he looks pale. Art thou sick,
or angry?

CLAUDIO   What, courage, man. What though care killed a cat,
thou hast mettle° enough in thee to kill care.   *spirit; courage*

BENEDICK   Sir, I shall meet your wit in the career° an you   *at full gallop*
135   charge° it against me. I pray you choose another subject.   *aim*

CLAUDIO   Nay then, give him another staff.° This last was broke   *lance*
cross.[3]

DON PEDRO   By this light, he changes° more and more. I think   *changes color*
he be angry indeed.

140   CLAUDIO   If he be, he knows how to turn his girdle.[4]

BENEDICK   [*aside to* CLAUDIO]   Shall I speak a word in your ear?

CLAUDIO   God bless° me from a challenge.   *protect*

BENEDICK   You are a villain. I jest not. I will make it good how
you dare, with what° you dare, and when you dare. Do me   *whatever weapon*
145   right,[5] or I will protest° your cowardice. You have killed a sweet   *proclaim*
lady, and her death shall fall heavy on you. Let me hear from
you.

CLAUDIO   Well, I will meet you, so I may have good cheer.

DON PEDRO   What, a feast, a feast?

150   CLAUDIO   I'faith, I thank him, he hath bid me to a calf's head
and a capon, the which if I do not carve most curiously,° say   *daintily*
my knife's naught.° Shall I not find a woodcock[6] too?   *useless*

BENEDICK   Sir, your wit ambles[7] well, it goes easily.

DON PEDRO   I'll tell thee how Beatrice praised thy wit the other
155   day. I said thou hadst a fine wit. 'True,' said she, 'a fine little
one.' 'No,' said I, 'a great wit.' 'Right,' says she, 'a great gross
one.' 'Nay,' said I, 'a good wit.' 'Just,' said she, 'it hurts nobody.'
'Nay,' said I, 'the gentleman is wise.' 'Certain,' said she, 'a wise
gentleman.'[8] 'Nay,' said I, 'he hath the tongues.'°   *knows several languages*
160   believe,' said she, 'for he swore a thing to me on Monday night
which he forswore on Tuesday morning. There's a double
tongue, there's two tongues.' Thus did she an hour together
trans-shape° thy particular virtues, yet at last she concluded   *distort*
with a sigh thou wast the properest° man in Italy.   *handsomest*

165   CLAUDIO   For the which she wept heartily and said she cared
not.

DON PEDRO   Yea, that she did. But yet for all that, an if° she did   *an if = if*
not hate him deadly she would love him dearly. The old man's
daughter told us all.

170   CLAUDIO   All, all. And moreover, God saw him when he was hid
in the garden.[9]

DON PEDRO   But when shall we set the savage bull's horns on the
sensible Benedick's head?

---

2. *draw . . . minstrels:* draw a sword, the way a minstrel
is bidden to draw a bow across his musical instrument.
3. Was snapped in the middle, like a badly handled
lance. (Claudio is mocking Benedick's attempt at wit.)
4. A colloquialism of uncertain derivation, possibly
meaning "let him get on with it" or "that's his problem."
5. Give me satisfaction.
6. The calf's head, capon, and woodcock were varieties

of food that also symbolize stupidity.
7. Moves slowly (in other words, it does not gallop as a
quick wit would).
8. A phrase often used ironically to mean "an old fool."
9. Allusion to Genesis 3:8 (Adam attempting to hide
from God in the Garden of Eden); contains a half-
hidden reference to the trick played on Benedick in the
garden.

CLAUDIO   Yea, and text underneath, 'Here dwells Benedick the
175   married man'.[1]
BENEDICK   Fare you well, boy, you know my mind. I will leave
you now to your gossip-like° humour. You break° jests as brag-   old-womanish / crack
garts do their blades[2] which, God be thanked, hurt not. [*To*
DON PEDRO] My lord, for your many courtesies I thank you.
180   I must discontinue your company. Your brother the bastard is
fled from Messina. You have among you killed a sweet and
innocent lady. For my lord Lackbeard there, he and I shall
meet, and till then, peace be with him.   *Exit*
DON PEDRO   He is in earnest.
185   CLAUDIO   In most profound earnest, and, I'll warrant you, for the
love of Beatrice.
DON PEDRO   And hath challenged thee.
CLAUDIO   Most sincerely.
DON PEDRO   What a pretty thing man is when he goes in his
190   doublet and hose and leaves off his wit![3]
        Enter [DOGBERRY *and* VERGES] *the constables,* [*the*
        WATCH,] CONRAD, *and* BORACHIO
CLAUDIO   He is then a giant to an ape. But then is an ape a
doctor to such a man.[4]
DON PEDRO   But soft you,° let me be. Pluck up,° my heart, and   wait / Collect yourself
be sad. Did he not say my brother was fled?
195   DOGBERRY   Come you sir, if justice cannot tame you, she shall
ne'er weigh more reasons[5] in her balance.° Nay, an you be a   scales
cursing hypocrite once,° you must be looked to.   even once
DON PEDRO   How now, two of my brother's men bound? Borachio one.
200   CLAUDIO   Hearken after° their offence, my lord.   Inquire into
DON PEDRO   Officers, what offence have these men done?
DOGBERRY   Marry, sir, they have committed false report, more-
over they have spoken untruths, secondarily they are slanders,°   (for "slanderers")
sixth and lastly they have belied a lady, thirdly they have veri-
205   fied° unjust things, and to conclude, they are lying knaves.   affirmed as true
DON PEDRO   First I ask thee what they have done, thirdly I ask
thee what's their offence, sixth and lastly why they are committed,° and to conclude, what you lay to their charge.   held on arrest
CLAUDIO   Rightly reasoned, and in his own division.° And by my   logical organization
210   troth there's one meaning well suited.[6]
DON PEDRO   [*to* CONRAD *and* BORACHIO]   Who have you offended, masters, that you are thus bound to your answer?[7] This
learned constable is too cunning to be understood. What's your
offence?
215   BORACHIO   Sweet Prince, let me go no farther to mine answer.°   trial; account
Do you hear me, and let this Count kill me. I have deceived
even your very eyes. What your wisdoms could not discover,
these shallow fools have brought to light, who in the night overheard me confessing to this man how Don John your brother

---

1. Claudio and Don Pedro recall that Benedick joked
that if he ever fell in love, his friends could set horns in
his forehead, have his picture painted, and title it
"Benedick, the married man" (1.1.215–19).
2. Braggarts secretly dent their swords to make it
appear that they have been dealing fierce blows.
3. When he puts on fine clothes but forgets to wear his
brain.

4. Such a man is much bigger than an ape, but an ape
is a learned man ("doctor") compared with him.
5. Legal cases. Also, "reason" was pronounced like
"raisin," producing a comic image here.
6. Dressed in several different costumes (with play on
legal "suit").
7. Required to respond (punning on "bound over for
trial" and "bound with ropes").

220 incensed° me to slander the Lady Hero, how you were brought   *incited*
into the orchard and saw me court Margaret in Hero's gar-
ments, how you disgraced her when you should marry her. My
villainy they have upon record, which I had rather seal° with   *confirm; end*
my death than repeat over to my shame. The lady is dead upon
225 mine and my master's false accusation, and briefly, I desire
nothing but the reward of a villain.

DON PEDRO [*to* CLAUDIO] Runs not this speech like iron through
your blood?

CLAUDIO I have drunk poison whiles he uttered it.

230 DON PEDRO [*to* BORACHIO] But did my brother set thee on to
this?

BORACHIO Yea, and paid me richly for the practice° of it.   *execution*

DON PEDRO He is composed and framed° of treachery,   *made up*
And fled he is upon this villainy.

235 CLAUDIO Sweet Hero, now thy image doth appear
In the rare semblance° that I loved it first.   *likeness*

DOGBERRY Come, bring away the plaintiffs.° By this time our   (*for "defendants"*)
Sexton hath reformed° Signor Leonato of the matter. And mas-   (*for "informed"*)
ters, do not forget to specify, when time and place shall serve,
240 that I am an ass.

VERGES Here, here comes Master Signor Leonato, and the Sexton, too.

          Enter LEONATO, [ANTONIO *his*] *brother, and the* SEXTON

LEONATO Which is the villain? Let me see his eyes,
That when I note another man like him
245 I may avoid him. Which of these is he?

BORACHIO If you would know your wronger, look on me.

LEONATO Art thou the slave that with thy breath hast killed
Mine innocent child?

BORACHIO   Yea, even I alone.

LEONATO No, not so, villain, thou beliest thyself.
250 Here stand a pair of honourable men.°   *men of rank*
A third is fled that had a hand in it.
I thank you, Princes, for my daughter's death.
Record it with your high and worthy deeds.
'Twas bravely done, if you bethink you of it.

255 CLAUDIO I know not how to pray your patience,
Yet I must speak. Choose your revenge yourself,
Impose° me to what penance your invention   *Subject*
Can lay upon my sin. Yet sinned I not
But in mistaking.

DON PEDRO   By my soul, nor I,
260 And yet to satisfy this good old man
I would bend under any heavy weight
That he'll enjoin me to.

LEONATO I cannot bid you bid my daughter live—
That were impossible—but I pray you both
265 Possess° the people in Messina here   *Inform*
How innocent she died, and if your love
Can labour aught in sad invention,[8]
Hang her an epitaph upon her tomb
And sing it to her bones, sing it tonight.

8. Can create any fruit from your sad imagination.

270   Tomorrow morning come you to my house,
    And since you could not be my son-in-law,
    Be yet my nephew. My brother hath a daughter,
    Almost the copy of my child that's dead,
    And she alone is heir to both of us.[9]
275   Give her the right you should have giv'n her cousin,
    And so dies my revenge.
CLAUDIO   O noble sir!
    Your overkindness doth wring tears from me.
    I do embrace your offer; and dispose
    For henceforth° of poor Claudio.   *For the future*
280 LEONATO   Tomorrow then I will expect your coming.
    Tonight I take my leave. This naughty° man   *evil*
    Shall face to face be brought to Margaret,
    Who I believe was packed° in all this wrong,   *confederate*
    Hired to it by your brother.
BORACHIO   No, by my soul, she was not,
285   Nor knew not what she did when she spoke to me,
    But always hath been just and virtuous
    In anything that I do know by° her.   *of*
DOGBERRY [*to* LEONATO]   Moreover, sir, which indeed is not
    under white and black, this plaintiff[1] here, the offender, did
290   call me ass. I beseech you let it be remembered in his punish-
    ment. And also the watch heard them talk of one Deformed.
    They say he wears a key in his ear and a lock hanging by it,[2]
    and borrows money in God's name, the which he hath used°   *done habitually*
    so long and never paid that now men grow hard-hearted and
295   will lend nothing for God's sake.[3] Pray you examine him upon
    that point.
LEONATO   I thank thee for thy care and honest pains.
DOGBERRY   Your worship speaks like a most thankful and rever-
    end youth, and I praise God for you.
300 LEONATO [*giving him money*]   There's for thy pains.
DOGBERRY   God save the foundation.[4]
LEONATO   Go. I discharge thee of thy prisoner, and I thank thee.
DOGBERRY   I leave an arrant knave with your worship, which I
    beseech your worship to correct yourself,[5] for the example of
305   others. God keep your worship, I wish your worship well. God
    restore you to health. I humbly give you leave to depart, and
    if a merry meeting may be wished, God prohibit° it. Come,   *(for "permit")*
    neighbour.   *Exeunt* [DOGBERRY *and* VERGES]
LEONATO   Until tomorrow morning, lords, farewell.
310 ANTONIO   Farewell, my lords. We look for you tomorrow.
DON PEDRO   We will not fail.
CLAUDIO   Tonight I'll mourn with Hero.
LEONATO [*to the* WATCH] Bring you these fellows on.—We'll talk
    with Margaret
    How her acquaintance grew with this lewd° fellow.   *Exeunt*   *worthless*

---

9. Shakespeare (or Leonato) has apparently forgotten
Antonio's son mentioned at 1.2.1.
1. For "defendant." *under white and black:* in writing.
2. Dogberry's garbled recollection of the lovelock mentioned at 3.3.149.
3. "In God's name" and "for God's sake" were phrases

used by beggars.
4. A conventional response to alms from a charitable
foundation.
5. Dogberry wishes Leonato himself to punish ("correct") Borachio but accidentally says that Leonato
should be punished.

5.2

Enter BENEDICK *and* MARGARET

BENEDICK   Pray thee, sweet Mistress Margaret, deserve well at
my hands by helping me to the speech of Beatrice.

MARGARET   Will you then write me a sonnet in praise of my
beauty?

5   BENEDICK   In so high a style, Margaret, that no man living shall
come over¹ it, for in most comely truth, thou deservest it.

MARGARET   To have no man come over me—why, shall I always
keep below stairs?²

BENEDICK   Thy wit is as quick as the greyhound's mouth, it

10   catches.

MARGARET   And yours as blunt as the fencer's foils,³ which hit
but hurt not.

BENEDICK   A most manly wit, Margaret, it will not hurt a
woman. And so I pray thee call Beatrice. I give thee the buck-

15   lers.⁴

MARGARET   Give us the swords. We have bucklers of our own.

BENEDICK   If you use them, Margaret, you must put in the pikes
with a vice°—and they are dangerous weapons for maids.   *screw*

MARGARET   Well, I will call Beatrice to you, who I think hath

20   legs.   *Exit*

BENEDICK   And therefore will come.⁵

　　　　　[*Sings*]   The god love
　　　　　　　　　　That sits above,
　　　　　　　　　　And knows me, and knows me,

25　　　　　　　　　　How pitiful I deserve—⁶
I mean in singing; but in loving, Leander the good swimmer,
Troilus the first employer of panders,⁷ and a whole book full
of these quondam carpet-mongers⁸ whose names yet run
smoothly in the even road of a blank verse, why they were never

30   so truly turned over and over° as my poor self in love. Marry, I   *head over heels*
cannot show it in rhyme. I have tried. I can find out no rhyme
to 'lady' but 'baby', an innocent° rhyme; for 'scorn' 'horn', a   *a childish*
hard⁹ rhyme; for 'school' 'fool', a babbling rhyme. Very omi-
nous endings. No, I was not born under a rhyming planet,¹ nor

35   I cannot woo in festival terms.°   *in fancy rhetoric*
　　　　　Enter BEATRICE
Sweet Beatrice, wouldst thou come when I called thee?

BEATRICE   Yea, signor, and depart when you bid me.

BENEDICK   O, stay but till then.

BEATRICE   'Then' is spoken. Fare you well now. And yet ere I go,

---

5.2 Location: Near Leonato's house or in his garden.
1. Surpass; climb over (punning on "stile": stairs over
a fence). Margaret humorously takes "come over" in a
sexual sense.
2. In the servants' quarters (and therefore never as a
"mistress").
3. Practice rapiers, capped at the tip.
4. Benedick offers to surrender by giving up the bucklers: shields with spikes ("pikes") in the center. Margaret bawdily interprets this as the female sexual organ.
5. A popular question and answer of the time was
"How came you hither?" "On my legs."
6. How greatly I deserve pity (but Benedick takes it as

"How pitifully small my deserts are"). These four lines
are the beginning of a popular sentimental ballad.
7. Troilus, loving Cressida, employed her uncle Pandarus as go-between. Leander swam the Hellespont
nightly to be with his love, Hero.
8. Knights of long ago ("quondam") who avoided military service and spent their time in ladies' carpeted
boudoirs.
9. Disagreeable, because horns were associated with
cuckoldry.
1. At a time when the stars would influence me to
become a poet.

40 　　　let me go with that° I came for, which is with knowing what *what*
　　　hath passed between you and Claudio.
　　BENEDICK　Only foul words, and thereupon I will kiss thee.
　　BEATRICE　Foul words is but foul wind, and foul wind is but foul
　　　breath, and foul breath is noisome,° therefore I will depart *nauseating*
45 　　unkissed.
　　BENEDICK　Thou hast frighted the word out of his° right sense,° *its / meaning; wits*
　　　so forcible is thy wit. But I must tell thee plainly, Claudio
　　　undergoes° my challenge, and either I must shortly hear from *is subject to*
　　　him or I will subscribe° him a coward. And I pray thee now tell *proclaim*
50 　　me, for which of my bad parts didst thou first fall in love with
　　　me?
　　BEATRICE　For them all together, which maintain so politic° a *cunningly governed*
　　　state of evil that they will not admit any good part to intermin-
　　　gle with them. But for which of my good parts did you first
55 　　suffer° love for me? *feel*
　　BENEDICK　Suffer love—a good epithet.° I do suffer° love indeed, *expression / suffer from*
　　　for I love thee against my will.
　　BEATRICE　In spite of your heart, I think. Alas, poor heart. If you
　　　spite it for my sake I will spite it for yours, for I will never love
60 　　that which my friend hates.
　　BENEDICK　Thou and I are too wise to woo peaceably.
　　BEATRICE　It appears not in this confession.[2] There's not one
　　　wise man among twenty that will praise himself.
　　BENEDICK　An old, an old instance,° Beatrice, that lived in the *proverb*
65 　　time of good neighbours.[3] If a man do not erect in this age his
　　　own tomb ere he dies, he shall live no longer in monument° *remembrance*
　　　than the bell rings and the widow weeps.
　　BEATRICE　And how long is that, think you?
　　BENEDICK　Question[4]—why, an hour in clamour° and a quarter *ringing*
70 　　in rheum.° Therefore is it most expedient for the wise, if Don *tears*
　　　Worm—his conscience[5]—find no impediment to the contrary,
　　　to be the trumpet of his own virtues, as I am to myself. So
　　　much for praising myself who, I myself will bear witness, is
　　　praiseworthy. And now tell me, how doth your cousin?
75 　BEATRICE　Very ill.
　　BENEDICK　And how do you?
　　BEATRICE　Very ill too.
　　BENEDICK　Serve God, love me, and mend.° There will I leave *recover*
　　　you too, for here comes one in haste.
　　　　　Enter URSULA
80 　URSULA　Madam, you must come to your uncle. Yonder's old
　　　coil° at home. It is proved my lady Hero hath been falsely *great disturbance*
　　　accused, the Prince and Claudio mightily abused,° and Don *deceived*
　　　John is the author of all, who is fled and gone. Will you come
　　　presently?
85 　BEATRICE　Will you go hear this news, signor?
　　BENEDICK　I will live in thy heart, die[6] in thy lap, and be buried
　　　in thy eyes. And moreover, I will go with thee to thy uncle's.
　　　　　　　　　　　　　　　　　　　　　　　　Exeunt

---

2. Since it is not wise to claim to be wise.　　　　5. Facetious way of referring to the proverbial gnawing
3. In the good old days, when neighbors praised each　"worm of conscience."
other.　　　　　　　　　　　　　　　　　　　6. With the common Elizabethan connotation of
4. That is the question.　　　　　　　　　　　　orgasm.

5.3

Enter CLAUDIO, [DON PEDRO *the*] *Prince, and three or
four with tapers*][1] *all in black*

CLAUDIO   Is this the monument of Leonato?

A LORD   It is, my lord.

CLAUDIO[2]   [*reading from a scroll*]

        Done to death by slanderous tongues
        Was the Hero that here lies.

5   Death in guerdon° of her wrongs   *recompense*
        Gives her fame which never dies.
        So the life that died with° shame   *from*
        Lives in death with glorious fame.

[*He hangs the*] *epitaph* [*on the tomb*]

        Hang thou there upon the tomb,
10   Praising her when I am dumb.

Now music sound, and sing your solemn hymn.

Song

        Pardon, goddess of the night,[3]
        Those that slew thy virgin knight,[4]
        For the which with songs of woe
15   Round about her tomb they go.
        Midnight, assist our moan,
        Help us to sigh and groan,
          Heavily, heavily.
        Graves yawn, and yield your dead
20   Till death be uttered,°   *fully lamented*
          Heavily, heavily.

CLAUDIO   Now, unto thy bones good night.
    Yearly will I do this rite.

DON PEDRO   Good morrow, masters, put your torches out.
25   The wolves have preyed,[5] and look, the gentle day
    Before the wheels of Phoebus[6] round about
      Dapples the drowsy east with spots of grey.
    Thanks to you all, and leave us. Fare you well.

CLAUDIO   Good morrow, masters. Each his several° way.   *separate*

30 DON PEDRO   Come, let us hence, and put on other weeds,°   *garments*
    And then to Leonato's we will go.

CLAUDIO   And Hymen now with luckier issue speed 's[7]
    Than this° for whom we rendered up this woe.   *Exeunt*   *this woman*

5.4

Enter LEONATO, [ANTONIO,] BENEDICK, BEATRICE, MAR-
GARET, URSULA, FRIAR [FRANCIS], *and* HERO

FRIAR   Did I not tell you she was innocent?

LEONATO   So are the Prince and Claudio who accused her
    Upon° the error that you heard debated.   *Because of*

5.3 Location: A churchyard.
1. Candles or torches carried in token of penitence.
2. In Q, the poem is headed "Epitaph" and is not
ascribed to a particular speaker.
3. Diana, Roman goddess of the moon and patroness
of virgins.

4. Hero (imagined as a knight, or follower, of Diana).
5. Have finished preying (for the night has passed).
6. The sun god's chariot wheels.
7. And may Hymen (Greek god of marriage) grant us
more favorable results.
5.4 Location: Leonato's house.

But Margaret was in some fault for this,
5   Although against her will° as it appears   *unintentionally*
      In the true course of all the question.°   *investigation*
ANTONIO   Well, I am glad that all things sorts° so well.   *turn out*
BENEDICK   And so am I, being else by faith° enforced   *my pledge*
      To call young Claudio to a reckoning for it.
10   LEONATO   Well, daughter, and you gentlewomen all,
      Withdraw into a chamber by yourselves,
      And when I send for you come hither masked.
                    Exeunt [BEATRICE, HERO, MARGARET, *and* URSULA]
      The Prince and Claudio promised by this hour
      To visit me. You know your office,° brother,   *task*
15   You must be father to your brother's daughter,
      And give her to young Claudio.
ANTONIO   Which I will do with confirmed° countenance.   *serious*
BENEDICK   Friar, I must entreat your pains, I think.
FRIAR   To do what, signor?
20   BENEDICK   To bind me or undo° me, one of them.   *ruin; unbind*
      Signor Leonato, truth it is, good signor,
      Your niece regards me with an eye of favour.
LEONATO   That eye my daughter lent her, 'tis most true.
BENEDICK   And I do with an eye of love requite her.
25   LEONATO   The sight whereof I think you had from me,
      From Claudio and the Prince. But what's your will?
BENEDICK   Your answer, sir, is enigmatical.
      But for my will, my will is° your good will   *is that*
      May stand with ours this day to be conjoined
30   In the state of honourable marriage,
      In which, good Friar, I shall desire your help.
LEONATO   My heart is with your liking.
FRIAR   And my help.
      Here comes the Prince and Claudio.
                    Enter [DON PEDRO *the*] *Prince and* CLAUDIO *with attendants*
DON PEDRO   Good morrow to this fair assembly.
35   LEONATO   Good morrow, Prince. Good morrow, Claudio.
      We here attend you. Are you yet° determined   *still*
      Today to marry with my brother's daughter?
CLAUDIO   I'll hold my mind,° were she an Ethiope.[1]   *intention*
LEONATO   Call her forth, brother, here's the Friar ready.
                                         [*Exit* ANTONIO]
40   DON PEDRO   Good morrow, Benedick. Why, what's the matter
      That you have such a February face,
      So full of frost, of storm and cloudiness?
CLAUDIO   I think he thinks upon the savage bull.[2]
      Tush, fear not, man, we'll tip thy horns with gold,
45   And all Europa° shall rejoice at thee   *Europe*
      As once Europa did at lusty Jove
      When he would play the noble beast in love.[3]
BENEDICK   Bull Jove, sir, had an amiable° low,   *amorous*
      And some such strange bull leapt your father's cow

1. In other words, black and therefore, according to the Elizabethan racist stereotype, ugly.
2. Continuing the teasing of 5.1.172.
3. In Greek mythology, Jove took the form of a bull to carry off the princess Europa, with whom he was in love.

50 And got a calf° in that same noble feat   *begot a blockhead*
    Much like to you, for you have just his bleat.

        Enter [ANTONIO *with*] HERO, BEATRICE, MARGARET, *and*
        URSULA [*masked*]

CLAUDIO For this I owe you.[4] Here comes other reck'nings.°   *accounts to settle*
    Which is the lady I must seize upon?

ANTONIO This same is she, and I do give you her.

55 CLAUDIO Why then, she's mine. Sweet, let me see your face.

LEONATO No, that you shall not till you take her hand
    Before this Friar and swear to marry her.

CLAUDIO [*to* HERO] Give me your hand before this holy friar.
    I am your husband if you like of me.°   *like me*

60 HERO [*unmasking*] And when I lived I was your other wife;
    And when you loved, you were my other husband.

CLAUDIO Another Hero!

HERO   Nothing certainer.
    One Hero died defiled,° but I do live,   *slandered*
    And surely as I live, I am a maid.

65 DON PEDRO The former Hero, Hero that is dead!

LEONATO She died, my lord, but whiles her slander lived.

FRIAR All this amazement can I qualify°   *lessen*
    When after that the holy rites are ended
    I'll tell you largely° of fair Hero's death.   *in full*

70   Meantime, let wonder° seem familiar,°   *marvels / commonplace*
    And to the chapel let us presently.

BENEDICK Soft and fair,° Friar, which is Beatrice?   *Wait a minute*

BEATRICE [*unmasking*] I answer to that name, what is your will?

BENEDICK Do not you love me?

BEATRICE   Why no, no more than reason.

75 BENEDICK Why then, your uncle and the Prince and Claudio
    Have been deceived. They swore you did.

BEATRICE Do not you love me?

BENEDICK   Troth no, no more than reason.

BEATRICE Why then, my cousin, Margaret, and Ursula
    Are much deceived, for they did swear you did.

80 BENEDICK They swore that you were almost sick for me.

BEATRICE They swore that you were wellnigh dead for me.

BENEDICK 'Tis no such matter. Then you do not love me?

BEATRICE No, truly, but in friendly recompense.

LEONATO Come, cousin, I am sure you love the gentleman.

85 CLAUDIO And I'll be sworn upon't that he loves her,
    For here's a paper written in his hand,
    A halting sonnet of his own pure brain,
    Fashioned° to Beatrice.   *Addressed*

HERO   And here's another,
    Writ in my cousin's hand, stol'n from her pocket,

90   Containing her affection unto Benedick.

BENEDICK A miracle! Here's our own hands against our hearts.[5]
    Come, I will have thee, but by this light, I take thee for pity.

BEATRICE I would not deny you, but by this good day, I yield
    upon great persuasion, and partly to save your life, for I was

95   told you were in a consumption.°   *wasting away ill*

---

4. I will pay you back later (for the insults).

5. Our own handwritten testimony contradicts the indifference we claim to feel in our hearts (or proves our hearts to be guilty of loving).

BENEDICK [*kissing her*]   Peace, I will stop your mouth.

DON PEDRO   How dost thou, Benedick the married man?

BENEDICK   I'll tell thee what, Prince: a college of wit-crackers
cannot flout° me out of my humour. Dost thou think I care for   *jeer*
100   a satire or an epigram? No, if a man will be beaten with brains,
a° shall wear nothing handsome about him.[6] In brief, since I   *he*
do purpose° to marry, I will think nothing to any purpose that   *intend*
the world can say against it, and therefore never flout at me for
what I have said against it. For man is a giddy thing, and this is
105   my conclusion. For thy part, Claudio, I did think to have
beaten thee, but in that thou art like° to be my kinsman, live   *likely*
unbruised, and love my cousin.

CLAUDIO   I had well hoped thou wouldst have denied Beatrice,
that I might have cudgelled thee out of thy single life to make
110   thee a double dealer,° which out of question thou wilt be, if   *married man; adulterer*
my cousin do not look exceeding narrowly° to thee.   *closely*

BENEDICK   Come, come, we are friends, let's have a dance ere
we are married, that we may lighten our own hearts and our
wives' heels.

115   LEONATO   We'll have dancing afterward.

BENEDICK   First, of my word. Therefore play, music. [*To* DON
PEDRO] Prince, thou art sad, get thee a wife, get thee a wife.
There is no staff more reverend than one tipped with horn.[7]

       Enter MESSENGER

MESSENGER   My lord, your brother John is ta'en in flight,
120   And brought with armèd men back to Messina.

BENEDICK   Think not on him till tomorrow, I'll devise thee
brave° punishments for him. Strike up, pipers.   *fine*

       Dance [*and exeunt*]

---

6. No, if a man is easily injured by ridicule, he will
never even dare to dress well (since that would provoke

attention).
7. A final allusion to the cuckold's horns.

As You Like It

Much of *As You Like It* takes place in a forest, where characters in flight from treachery at court and injustice in the family take refuge. The play thus participates in the rich tradition of Renaissance pastoral literature in which the rustic world of forest and field offers an alternative to and a sanctuary from the urban or courtly milieu to which it is contrasted. The pastoral mode had its origins in ancient Greece, where the poet Theocritus used rural settings and rustic shepherds to explore the sorrows of love and the harsh injustices of daily life. The Roman poet Virgil expanded this tradition, elaborating in particular the opposition between city and country life that in the Renaissance was often transmuted into an opposition between court and country. In England, many of Shakespeare's contemporaries worked in pastoral forms, particularly Edmund Spenser, whose *Shepheardes Calendar* (1579) was modeled on Virgil's *Eclogues,* and Sir Philip Sidney, whose vast prose romance *The Countess of Pembrokes Arcadia* was first published in revised form in 1590.

As a literary mode, pastoral can take many forms. There can be pastoral lyrics, dialogues, prose romances, and dramas. Certain topics and situations, however, are common features of many kinds of pastoral. Often, for example, exiles from urban or courtly life temporarily take up residence in the country where they live and converse with shepherds, often disguising *themselves* as shepherds before an eventual return to the life from which they had fled. In their rural retreat, they hold singing contests and discuss the relative merits of country and court life, whether nature is improved or spoiled by art, and whether "gentleness" (meaning both "nobility" and "a virtuous nature") is a condition one can achieve or to which one must be born.

Fundamental to pastoral debates is a concern about the relationship of what is "natural" to what is "artificial," that is, about whether what human beings have made—cities, gardens, or systems of social hierarchy—is preferable to the simplicity and lack of artifice supposedly found in rural settings and communities. This preoccupation makes pastoral particularly suited to social criticism. Pastoral figures often dissect the evils of various ways of life—the cruelty of hard-hearted mistresses, the greed of landlords, the deceit of courtiers, and the venality of the clergy. But while pastoral frequently celebrates simplicity, it does so in a highly artful manner, drawing on conventions that have been part of the Western literary tradition for at least two thousand years. Pastoral is therefore not so much a spontaneous expression of "natural" simplicity as the artful imitation of such simplicity by characters exiled from more sophisticated realms who for a time assume the guise of shepherds and play an elaborate game of "Let's pretend." Hence the many disguises found in pastoral, where courtiers pose as rustic shepherds, men as women, women as men, and dukes as forest outlaws. To minds of a stolidly serious cast, pastoral can appear to be a silly, escapist genre. To those less dismissive of the world of "Let's pretend," it offers an opportunity to see more clearly—and perhaps then to change—the world in which one ordinarily lives by entering for a time the playful, meditative, and artificial realm of imaginary shepherds.

In *As You Like It,* Shakespeare gave himself over to the pleasures and the seriousness of pastoral without seeming to find them antithetical. In the main action, a good ruler, Duke Senior, has been ousted from his throne by a usurping younger brother, Duke Frederick. The banished Duke takes refuge in the Forest of Ardenne, where he lives like Robin Hood with a band of loyal followers. When his daughter, Rosalind, companion to Frederick's daughter, Celia, is likewise banished, she disguises herself as a

First page of the *Gest of Robin Hood*, one of the most important sixteenth-century renditions of the Robin Hood legend.

young man named Ganymede and also journeys to Ardenne. Celia, posing as a lowborn woman named Aliena, goes with her, as does Touchstone the clown. A second line of action concerns two other brothers: Orlando, the youngest son, and Oliver, the oldest son of Sir Rowland de Bois. The inheritor of his father's estate, Oliver treats Orlando cruelly, denying him the education befitting a gentleman. In danger both from Duke Frederick and from his brother, Orlando also flees to the forest, accompanied by Adam, his dead father's eighty-year-old servant. By Act 2, all of these refugees from court life find themselves in a natural world, which, in spite of its considerable hardships, they prefer to the treachery of court. Ardenne is not Edenic. There are lions and snakes in this pastoral retreat and real shepherds like Corin who speak matter-of-factly about the hard and dirty labor that tending real sheep entails. But in Ardenne, there is also room for courtship games, for brotherly kindness, and for music. In fact, this play contains more songs than any other Shakespearean drama. In their song-filled green world, the characters hunt deer, tend sheep, and converse endlessly about love, exile, and the relative merits of court and country. Eventually, their chief troubles resolved, most return to court, leaving the forest once more to its native inhabitants and to those few courtiers who permanently embrace it.

The broad outlines of this story are taken from Thomas Lodge's enormously popular prose romance *Rosalynde*, written in 1586–87 and published in 1590, although Shakespeare changes many details and points of emphasis. In Lodge, for example, the Duke Senior and Duke Frederick characters are not brothers, but in both the ducal and the Orlando-Oliver plots, Shakespeare makes the enmity of brothers the principal sign of the corruption of "civilized" life. In Lodge, moreover, the father in the Orlando-Oliver plot does not follow the English custom of primogeniture, by which all property is settled on the oldest son; instead, he divides his property among his male offspring according to their merits. By having Oliver inherit almost everything, Shakespeare evokes an English social practice that caused great hardship to many younger brothers. The court women are handled differently as well by Shakespeare: he reduces the Celia character's centrality and instead emphasizes Rosalind and her love affair with Orlando. Shakespeare also tempers the violence of Lodge's resolution and adds to his cast of characters. In *Rosalynde*, the exiled Duke defeats the usurper in battle, but Shakespeare's Frederick has a religious conversion and voluntarily relinquishes the dukedom. Oliver Martext, William, Audrey, Touchstone the clown, and Jaques the melancholy satirist are all Shakespeare's creations. Jaques, in particular, adds a touch of caustic salt and Touchstone a dash of earthy realism to the play's exploration of competing value systems.

In fact, *As You Like It* is poised carefully on the razor's edge separating fantasy from harsh reality. Shakespeare's use of place is a case in point. Lodge's romance is set in the Forest of Ardenne, an ancient woodland comprising part of what is now France, Belgium, and Luxembourg. Shakespeare also uses a French setting, and this edition emphasizes that fact by giving the French spelling, "Ardenne," to the forest. But in the First Folio (1623), this woodland is called the Forest of Arden, an anglicized spelling that also happens to be the name of an English forest near Shakespeare's birthplace in Warwickshire. This fortuitous overlapping of French and English place-names is indicative of the play's double vision. Overtly set in a fantastical foreign kingdom, *As You Like It* nonetheless alludes to places (such as the Forest of Arden), people (such as Robin Hood), and practices (such as primogeniture) native to Shakespeare's own England. Through the distancing artifice of pastoral, the play deals with problems close to home.

Lodge's prose romance is not the only source for *As You Like It*. The play also draws upon *The Tale of Gamelyn*, a violent Middle English narrative in which a younger brother seeks revenge upon an older brother who mistreats him, and which explicitly evokes the name of Robin Hood, the popular English hero whose deeds were celebrated in countless ballads and stories. In the opening scene of *As You Like It*, Charles the wrestler reports that the banished Duke is "already in the forest of Ardenne, and a many merry men with him; and there they live like the old Robin Hood of England. They say many young gentlemen flock to him every day, and fleet the time carelessly, as they did in the golden world" (1.1.99–103). Shakespeare could count on his audience to know the story of Robin Hood, and its evocation carried certain associations. The legendary figure and his band of men stood not only for the community and brotherhood characteristic of the Golden Age and absent in modern life, but also for resistance to tyranny. The great forests of England were the King's own preserves. To kill the deer in those forests was a crime against the monarch. Yet Robin Hood lived in the forest, dined on the King's deer, and opposed King John's unjust reign. In the 1590s, many of those resisting the enclosure of farmland for sheep grazing took refuge in forest areas, and poaching the King's deer had long been one way the poor defied the law to feed themselves when food was short, as it often was because of bad food harvests in the late 1590s.

As You Like It only obliquely alludes to this immediate social context, but Act 1 depicts a world of injustice and social disorder that both motivates the flight to Ardenne and evokes the tradition of opposition to injustice associated with Robin Hood. Orlando's situation speaks to the peculiarly English plight of younger brothers who, under the system of primogeniture, inherited little from their fathers and were often at the mercy of elder siblings. Oliver is a nightmare version of an eldest son: he deprives Orlando of a gentleman's education, connives with the Duke's professional wrestler to have his brother injured, and throws his father's old servant, Adam, out of the house. His cruelty is echoed by the tyranny of Duke Frederick. The play's opening thus clearly underscores the existence of inhumanity and tyrannical willfulness in the court and in the household of old Sir Rowland's eldest son. Less clear is whether this corruption stems from human institutions, particularly the system of primogeniture, or from the "naturally" evil natures of Frederick and Oliver. The play does not answer this or other thorny questions directly. In fact, it seems organized to provoke thought rather than urge conclusions, and the ending does not so much lay out a plan for social reform as indulge the fantasy that all desires, however contradictory, can be fulfilled through marriage and the renewal of brotherly affection. The play's most sustained examination of human folly focuses on the behavior of those who succumb to Cupid's arrows. There are many lovers in Ardenne, and for almost none does the course of love run smooth. Lovesickness was a recognized malady in early modern culture, a condition that so disordered those who endured it that it could cause paleness, sighing, tears, fainting, melancholy, palpitations, and a host of other symptoms. The play represents all lovers as slightly mad and approaches their tribulations with a mixture of sympathy, detached amusement, and analytical curiosity. In part, Shakespeare draws on the critical capacities of pastoral to explore the causes of lovers' unhappiness and to probe the surprisingly complex issue of what is natural in matters of love and sexual desire. In this regard, the play takes little for granted—neither the stability of gender difference nor the naturalness of heterosexuality nor the invariant nature of being in love.

Rosalind and Orlando are the play's most prominent lovers, and through their courtship the play begins its exploration of the problems of loving well. Orlando, for example, loves by the book—that is, in imitation of the conventions employed by the fourteenth-century Italian poet Petrarch, whose love poems to a woman named Laura established one of the paradigmatic love rhetorics of Renaissance culture. Conventionally, the Petrarchan lover worships and idealizes a woman who is inaccessible to him, either because of her rank or because of her cold heart. He burns with passion; he wastes from despair; she does not respond. Orlando, rushing through the forest pinning bad love poems on trees, is a sendup of a Petrarchan lover. Touchstone makes fun of his verses; Rosalind, dressed as a man but pretending to be "Rosalind" in order to cure Orlando of his lovesickness, delights in showing how exaggerated and unrealistic are the Petrarchan lover's claims for the perfection of his mistress and the vastness of his suffering. As she caustically says to him, when he protests that he will die for his passion: "Men have died from time to time, and worms have eaten them, but not for love" (4.1.91–92). She is equally hard on the idealization of women, insisting that real women can be fickle and bad-tempered as easily as they can be goddesses. One way to interpret Orlando and Rosalind's interactions is to see her slowly educating him in a more realistic and egalitarian approach to the relationship of man to woman than that offered by the Petrarchan tradition. Yet the self-mockery, realism, and genuine regard for the other that come to characterize their relationship are hardly in themselves natural behaviors, but ones in which Orlando must be tutored.

Rosalind and Orlando, however, are not the only lovers in the forest. There is also the mooning shepherd, Silvius, who believes no one has ever loved with his intensity, and his proud mistress, Phoebe, who thinks much too well of her own limited charms and throws herself quite inappropriately into the part of the disdainful Petrarchan mistress. As Rosalind informs her: "I must tell you friendly in your ear, / Sell when you can. You are not for all markets" (3.5.60–61). Even Touchstone, ever ready to puncture the romantic ravings of Orlando and Rosalind, Silvius and Phoebe, cannot escape love's call. Functioning as the clown figure often does, to provide a detached commentary on the action around him, Touchstone is nonetheless a participant as well as an observer. His "love" is about as natural—in the sense of urgently physical—and as far removed from Petrarchan idealizations as can be imagined. His intended, Audrey, does not know what "poetical" means, and Touchstone laments that she has such a rudimentary command of language that she often cannot understand what he says to her. And yet, as he confides to Jaques, "As the ox hath his bow, sir, the horse his curb, and the falcon her bells, so man hath his desires" (3.3.65–66)—that is, as each creature has some restraint placed on his movement, so a man's sexual desires constrain him to accommodate himself to a woman, even one like Audrey, and to the marriage yoke. If Orlando and Silvius live too much in the thrall of poetic idealizations, Touchstone and Audrey starkly reveal what love looks like when it is reduced to a matter of pure desire, and all artfulness, all poetry, and all sweet amorous delay are eschewed.

The figure who instigates much of the play's talk about love is Rosalind, one of Shakespeare's liveliest heroines. Her attractiveness stems partly from the fact that she is at once an observer and critic of others and herself a full participant in the whirligig of love. In this, she resembles Touchstone and differs from the melancholy Jaques, who persistently catalogs the follies of others but holds back from full participation in the life around him. (Fittingly, Jaques remains in the forest at the end of the play, when most of the others return to their lives outside the pastoral retreat.) Rosalind is at the center of nearly everything that happens in As You Like It, and the complexity of her role is enhanced by the fact that for much of four acts she dresses like a man and successfully passes for one. In the 1590s, Shakespeare wrote a number of other comedies (Two Gentlemen of Verona, The Merchant of Venice, Twelfth Night) in which women dress as men to protect themselves from danger, to pursue a lover, or temporarily to acquire the prerogatives of the socially dominant gender. Rosalind's is arguably the most complicated of these cases of cross-dressing because she not only passes as a man, but while in her male disguise plays the role of Rosalind in her forest encounters with Orlando. A woman disguised as a man thus makes her own identity into a fiction she performs!

Rosalind's complex cross-dressing has many consequences. For one thing, it makes problematic how natural are the gender distinctions that supposedly separate man from woman. In a literal sense, clothes here make the man—or woman. A doublet and hose and a swaggering demeanor effectively create the illusion of masculinity, and Rosalind uses her disguise to try on the privileges of the supposedly superior sex. Far from a passive object of Petrarchan adoration, she takes charge of her escape from Frederick's court and her encounters with Orlando in the forest. Typically, Renaissance women remained under the control of their fathers and mothers until marriage bequeathed them to the care of a husband. Rosalind's special circumstances—a father banished, an uncle who wants her gone from court—put her in an unusual situation. Her decision to cross-dress further sets her apart. Mobile, loquacious, and bossy, Rosalind confutes the idea that women are by nature passive, silent, and in need of masculine supervision. At the same time, she exhibits certain stereotypically "female" behavior: to Celia she confesses how much she is in love with Orlando, and when he is wounded, she faints when she sees his blood on a cloth. Perhaps the point is that the figure of the cross-dressed Rosalind keeps open the question of what a woman (or a man) "really" is.

To the question of how men and women differ, Renaissance anatomical theory gave some answers dissimilar to those we now take for granted. According to Galen, an ancient Greek anatomist whose work on the body was widely influential in the early modern period, men and woman had the same anatomical structures; women were simply less perfect than men, there having been less heat present when they were conceived. This meant, among other things, that women's genitalia were just like a man's—with the vagina and ovaries corresponding to the penis and scrotum—except that they had not been pushed outside the body as a man's had been. Because by this account male-female difference was less grounded in ideas of absolute bodily difference than is typical today, much emphasis was placed on behavioral differences and on distinctions of dress. Preachers enjoined women to be chaste, silent, and obedient, and forbade them to wear the clothes of the opposite sex. In such a context, female cross-dressing, however playfully undertaken, always threatened to expose the artifice of gender distinctions by showing how easily one sex could assume the clothes and ape the behavior of the other.

The particularities of Rosalind's disguise, moreover, complicate her representation

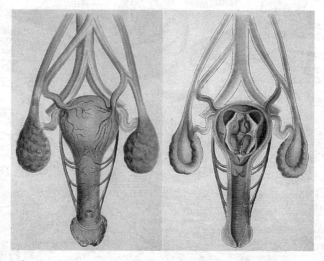

Typical sixteenth-century anatomy-book illustration of the female organs of generation. *Left:* the vagina and uterus are almost indistinguishable from the male penis and scrotum. *Right:* they have been cut open to reveal a tiny fetus in the uterus. From Fritz Weindler, *Geschichte der Gynäkologisch-anatomischen Abbildung* (1908). (Originally appeared in George Bartisch, *Kunstbuch*, 1575.)

even further. In disguise, Rosalind calls herself Ganymede, a name that had long-standing and unmistakable associations with homoerotic love. In Greek mythology, Ganymede was a beautiful boy whom Jove desired and whom he seized and carried to Mount Olympus to be cupbearer to the gods. A number of early modern paintings, woodcuts, and engravings depict the moment when Jove, in the form of an eagle, sweeps the boy away from earth and into the heavens. In Shakespeare's day, the word "Ganymede" commonly signified a young boy who was the lover of another (usually older) man. Shakespeare could hardly have been unaware of these associations when he had Rosalind choose this name as her alias. Consequently, when the cross-dressed heroine commands Orlando to woo his "Rosalind," he woos a figure who is dressed like a man and who bears a name signifying his status as a homoerotic love object. In performance, what the audience *sees* is one "man" flirting with another, even while the audience *knows* that one of these "men" is a woman. Provocatively, Shakespeare uses Orlando and Rosalind's encounters to overlay a story of male-female desire with traces of another tale of a man's love for a boy.

Long before *As You Like It* was penned, pastoral had been used to depict the beauty of both male friendship and homoerotic love. Edmund Spenser, in the January Eclogue of *The Shepheardes Calendar*, describes the passion of Hobbinol for Colin Cloute, who in turn loves an unresponsive woman named Rosalind. Commenting on this passage, E. K., the anonymous annotator of *The Shepheardes Calendar*, drew on classical precedent to defend pederastic love (love of an older man for a younger boy) as less dangerous than gynerastic love (love of man for woman). Since women were generally considered men's intellectual and moral inferiors, love for a woman was—so the argument went—less likely to be a rational passion than was love for a boy or a man. In the 1580s, Richard Barnfield wrote a pastoral work called *The Affectionate Shepherd*, in which the male speaker celebrates his love for a beautiful young man named Ganymede.

Ganymede being abducted by Jupiter in the form of an eagle. Woodcut by Virgil Solis. From *Metamorphosis Ovidii* . . . (1563).

Shakespeare is therefore not unique in introducing a Ganymede figure into the pastoral landscape, though he does so with a difference. In *As You Like It,* Ganymede is a disguise, a persona assumed and eventually discarded by Rosalind. As with much else in this play, Shakespeare thus has things at least two ways at once. For several acts, Orlando seems to pursue in one person both a boy and a woman, but in the final scene Rosalind reassumes her female clothes and Ganymede disappears, thus ending the play with an emphasis on the culmination of male-female love in marriage. But even this is not quite the whole story. On the Renaissance stage, women's parts were played by boy actors. In the Epilogue, which she speaks, Rosalind calls attention to this fact, making it clear that if Orlando has finally won his Rosalind, the two players who enact this union are a young boy and a man.

In *As You Like It,* the erotic possibilities never seem to stop. The friendship between Rosalind and Celia, for example, is remarkably close. Charles the wrestler says, "Never two ladies loved as they do" (1.1.97). Celia readily gives up her father, her fortune, and her position at the court to follow Rosalind to Ardenne, where the two women in effect set up household together. Although they are yoked in love like Juno's swans, from the beginning Celia is afraid that Rosalind does not love her as much as she loves Rosalind (1.2.6–11). Quite quickly, Rosalind's primary interest does become her pursuit of Orlando. Yet in the midst of her love games with him, Rosalind also dallies with the ambitious and amorous Phoebe, who has taken the disguised Rosalind for a man. Overtly, Rosalind scorns Phoebe and directs her to love Silvius, but she also takes care to tell Phoebe where she lives (3.5.75–76) and encourages her attentions even as she denies them. As with other relationships in the play, it is not altogether clear whom Phoebe really desires: is it the man she thinks she sees or the woman beneath? Though the play eventually deposits Rosalind, Celia, and Phoebe all within Hymen's circle, it does so only after raising the possibility of other erotic conjunctions, including woman's love for woman.

In part, *As You Like It* can play so freely with various erotic possibilities because in the early modern period people were not assumed, as they often are today, to have a fixed sexual identity, to *be,* that is, a lesbian or a heterosexual. Often, one could engage in a range of sexual practices without contradiction. Depending on life stage and social circumstance, a man might have sex with a dependent man, such as a servant, and with a woman, such as his wife. The point is that performing a specific sexual act did not presume—or guarantee—a particular sexual identity. And yet Shakespeare's comedy, like many others, also acknowledges the social weight that the early modern period placed on marriage, the institution through which political alliances were forged, property passed, and lineage established. *As You Like It* both celebrates and pokes fun at the social inevitability of marriage by having Hymen, god of marriage, appear onstage in the last act to preside over a veritable spate of betrothals—four, to be exact. As Jaques suggests (5.4.35–36), it is indeed as if the beasts were proceeding, two by two, into Noah's ark.

Besides yoking individual man to individual woman, marriage in this play also helps to resolve seemingly intractable social problems. For example, Orlando's situation as younger brother is miraculously ameliorated through his marriage to Rosalind. As her husband, he becomes Duke Senior's heir, thus achieving a fortune equal to his gentle nature. Again, the play has things two ways at once. Duke Senior is restored to his dukedom, which confirms the prerogatives of older brothers, but Orlando does not have to suffer permanently the disadvantages of being a younger son. Primogeniture is simultaneously affirmed and circumvented. Moreover, when Oliver reforms, that reformation is sealed by his marriage to Celia, an indication that he now takes part in the communal life of his culture without the willful displays of indifference and selfishness that marked his earlier behavior.

Yet as this comedy celebrates marriage, it also registers a certain resistance to it and persistently maps alternative routings of desire. Rosalind registers that resistance when she complains of how avidly men court women before marriage and how indifferently they treat them afterward: "Men are April when they woo, December when they wed" (4.1.124–25). Marriage, she implies, can dull a man's desire and lessen a woman's emotional power over him. It also, of course, made women legally subject to their husbands. When Rosalind doffs her man's disguise to become a wife, she relinquishes many kinds of freedom. But the play also records *men's* resistance to marriage, partly through its many cuckold jokes. These jokes acknowledge that marriage may not fully circumscribe or satisfy a woman's sexual desires, that a man's control of his wife's sexuality may be more fiction than fact, leaving him vulnerable to public mockery. As the Duke's men sing as they bring home a slaughtered deer:

> Take thou no scorn to wear the horn;
> It was a crest ere thou wast born.
>   Thy father's father wore it,
>   And thy father bore it.
>   (4.2.14–17)

The song transforms cuckold anxiety into entertainment, but it cannot erase that anxiety.

Consider, as well, the strange moment when Orlando comes across his brother Oliver lying asleep under an old oak. As Oliver sleeps, a female snake approaches his open mouth, threatening his life. Though the snake is frightened off, it is immediately replaced in this fantastic, dreamlike scenario by a hungry female lion with whom Orlando fights in order to save his brother's life (4.3.97–131). Twice, danger is represented in female form, and the reconciliation of the two brothers occurs only when Orlando spills his blood to beat back these threats. In *As You Like It*, as marriage is both desired and feared, so the feminine is represented as both an attraction and a source of danger.

In pastoral, little is immune from critique; the world men and women have made is an imperfect world. Yet the remarkable thing about *As You Like It* is that critique does not cancel affirmation. The play anatomizes court life and exposes its treachery, but many leave Ardenne to journey back to the court when Frederick has repented and the benevolent Duke Senior has returned to power. The play likewise dissects the problems of marriage, yet many marry at the end. Pastoral has a utopian as well as a critical dimension. The green world of shepherds holds traces of the simplicity of a lost Golden Age, and a sojourn in that world can prompt transformations in the everyday world to which the sojourners return. *As You Like It* is to a remarkable degree open to the infinite malleability of human beings and their social practices. A duke can become a forest outlaw and embrace the change; a tyrannical usurper can be touched by the words of a holy man, relinquish his power, and retire from the world. What men and women have marred, they may also mend.

It is with the heroine, however, that *As You Like It* offers its richest dramatization of a figure who plays endlessly with the limits and possibilities of her circumstances. This is true even in the Epilogue, when Rosalind, now in woman's clothing, steps forward to address the audience and solicit their applause. The persona of Ganymede cast aside, the heroine appears as the woman she "really is." But it is precisely at this moment of closure that she breaks the dramatic frame to remind the audience of *another* reality: that "she" is played by a "he." Dressed like a woman but declaring she is not, this unpredictable figure, this he/she, continues to the end to defy the fixed identities and the exclusionary choices of the everyday world, offering instead a world of multiple possibilities and transformable identities, a world as perhaps we might come to like it.

JEAN E. HOWARD

TEXTUAL NOTE

As You Like It was probably written between 1598 and 1600. It was entered in the Stationers' Register on August 4, 1600, but no edition followed this entry. Francis Meres, one of Shakespeare's contemporaries, in September of 1598 published a list of the Shakespeare plays known to him. It did not include *As You Like It*, suggesting that the play was performed sometime after that date but prior to its entry in the Stationers' Register. Two topical references suggest 1599 as the likely time of composition. At one point, Jaques, the play's cynical satirist, opines, "All the world's a stage" (2.7.138), perhaps an allusion to the motto *Totus mundus agit histrionem* (All the world plays the actor), of the Globe Theater, to which Shakespeare's company moved in the summer of 1599. Elsewhere, Touchstone, the play's clown, refers to the time "since the little wit that fools have was silenced" (1.2.74–75), a possible reference to the banning and burning of satirical books in June of 1599 by order of the Bishop of London.

The play was first published in the First Folio of 1623 (F) either from a promptbook or, less probably, from a literary transcript of either the promptbook or Shakespeare's foul papers. The present edition follows the act and scene divisions of F.

SELECTED BIBLIOGRAPHY

Colie, Rosalie L. "Perspectives on Pastoral: Romance, Comic and Tragic." *Shakespeare's Living Art*. Princeton: Princeton University Press, 1974. 243–83. Analyzes the many pastoral conventions found in *As You Like It* and how they contribute to the play's perspectivism—that is, its juxtaposition of competing viewpoints.

Crane, Mary. "Theatrical Practice and the Ideologies of Status in *As You Like It*." *Shakespeare's Brain: Reading with Cognitive Theory*. Princeton: Princeton University Press, 2001. 67–93. Examines how, through its emphasis on words like *villain* and *clown*, *As You Like It* explores possibilities for upward and downward mobility in the world of the play and in the social world at large, including the theatrical community of which Shakespeare was a part.

Elam, Keir. "As They Did in the Golden World: Romantic Rapture and Semantic Rapture in *As You Like It*." *Reading the Renaissance: Culture, Poetics, and Drama*. Ed. Jonathan Hart. New York: Garland, 1996. 163–76. Focuses on the way Shakespeare rewrites pastoral in *As You Like It* to banish nostalgia and linguistic earnestness in favor of the magical, forward-looking affirmations of romance.

Erickson, Peter. "Sexual Politics and Social Structure in *As You Like It*." *Patriarchal Structures in Shakespeare's Drama*. Berkeley: University of California Press, 1985. 15–38. Argues that the play advocates a benevolent patriarchy that ultimately subordinates women to men while allowing men to assume nurturing functions.

Howard, Jean E. "Power and Eros: Crossdressing in Dramatic Representation and Theatrical Practice." *The Stage and Social Struggle in Early Modern England*. London: Routledge, 1994. 93–128. Examines cross-dressing as a convention through which *As You Like It* and other comedies explore the politics of early modern gender relations and the fluidity of sexual desire.

Marshall, Cynthia. "The Doubled Jaques and Constructions of Negation in *As You Like It*." *Shakespeare Quarterly* 49 (1998): 375–92. Argues that in *As You Like It* the repression of melancholia, registered as a trace in the figure of Jaques, allows for the release of the high spirits and verbal fireworks proper to comedy.

Montrose, Louis. " 'The Place of a Brother' in *As You Like It*: Social Process and Comic Form." *Shakespeare Quarterly* 32 (1981): 28–54. Argues that in *As You Like It* the process of comedy repairs the negative consequences of primogeniture for younger sons as Orlando finds a surrogate father in Duke Senior and a fortune through marriage.

Neely, Carol Thomas. "Destabilizing Lovesickness, Gender, and Sexuality: *Twelfth Night* and *As You Like It*." *Distracted Subjects: Madness and Gender in Shakespeare and Early Modern Culture.* Ithaca, N.Y.: Cornell University Press, 2004. 99–135. Details the increasingly strong link between lovesickness and women in the Renaissance and compares its representation in *Twelfth Night* and *As You Like It.*

Traub, Valerie. "The Homoerotics of Shakespearean Comedy." *Desire and Anxiety: Circulations of Sexuality in Shakespearean Drama.* London: Routledge, 1992. 117–44. Explores the role of the boy actor in the production and circulation of homoerotic desire and argues that *As You Like It* playfully refuses the binary distinction between the heteroerotic and the homoerotic.

Wilson, Richard. "Like the Old Robin Hood: *As You Like It* and the Enclosure Riots." *Will Power: Essays on Shakespearean Authority.* London: Harvester Wheatsheaf, 1993. 63–82. Connects *As You Like It* to the social disturbances and food shortages of the 1590s but argues that the play pulls back from lodging a radical critique of social injustice.

FILMS

As You Like It. 1936. Dir. Paul Czinner. UK. 96 min. This black-and-white film features Laurence Olivier, in his first Shakespeare performance on film, as the dashing but moody Orlando with Elisabeth Bergner as an insipid Rosalind. Charming woodland scenes in a significantly cut production.

As You Like It. 1978. Dir. Basil Coleman. UK. 150 min. Traditional BBC-TV production with lively performances by Helen Mirren as Rosalind, Angharad Rees as Celia, and Victoria Plucknett as Phoebe. Playing Jaques, Richard Pasco brings poignant understatement to the famous "seven ages of man" speech.

As You Like It. 2006. Dir. Kenneth Branagh. UK. 127 min. In this gorgeous production, the action is relocated from medieval France to nineteenth-century Japan. With Bryce Dallas Howard (Rosalind), David Oyelowo (Orlando), Rowola Garai (Celia), Brian Blessed (Duke Senior and Duke Frederick), and Alfred Molina (Touchstone).

As You Like It

THE PERSONS OF THE PLAY

DUKE SENIOR, living in banishment
ROSALIND, his daughter, later disguised as Ganymede
AMIENS
JAQUES } Lords attending on him
TWO PAGES
DUKE FREDERICK
CELIA, his daughter, later disguised as Aliena
LE BEAU, a courtier attending on him
CHARLES, Duke Frederick's wrestler
TOUCHSTONE, a clown
OLIVER, eldest son of Sir Rowland de Bois
JAQUES
ORLANDO } his younger brothers
ADAM, a former servant of Sir Rowland
DENIS, Oliver's servant
SIR OLIVER MARTEXT, a country clergyman
CORIN, an old shepherd
SILVIUS, a young shepherd, in love with Phoebe
PHOEBE, a shepherdess
WILLIAM, a countryman, in love with Audrey
AUDREY, a goatherd, betrothed to Touchstone
HYMEN, god of marriage
Lords, pages, and other attendants

1.1

Enter ORLANDO *and* ADAM

ORLANDO As I remember, Adam, it was upon this fashion
bequeathed me by will but poor° a thousand crowns,[1] and, as   *only*
thou sayst, charged° my brother on his blessing[2] to breed me   *he (my father) charged*
well—and there begins my sadness. My brother Jaques he
5   keeps at school,° and report speaks goldenly of his profit. For   *university*
my part, he keeps me rustically at home—or, to speak more
properly, stays° me here at home unkept;° for call you that   *detains / uncared for*
keeping for a gentleman of my birth, that differs not from the
stalling of an ox? His horses are bred better, for besides that
10   they are fair with° their feeding, they are taught their manège,[3]   *handsome because of*
and to that end riders dearly° hired. But I, his brother, gain   *expensively*
nothing under him but growth, for the which his animals on
his dunghills are as much bound to him as I. Besides this nothing that he so plentifully gives me, the something that nature
15   gave me his countenance° seems to take from me. He lets me   *conduct*
feed with his hinds,° bars me[4] the place of a brother, and as   *farmworkers*
much as in him lies, mines my gentility with my education.[5]

1.1 Location: The orchard of Oliver's house, in the
vicinity of Duke Frederick's court in France.
1. Equivalent to about 250 English pounds. Orlando's
inheritance is worth twice as much as Adam's life sav-
ings (see 2.3.39).

2. On pain of losing his blessing.
3. Paces and actions of a trained horse.
4. Excludes me from.
5. Undermines my gentility by my (poor) education.

This is it, Adam, that grieves me; and the spirit of my father,
which I think is within me, begins to mutiny against this servi-
20 tude. I will no longer endure it, though yet I know no wise
remedy how to avoid it.

    Enter OLIVER

ADAM Yonder comes my master, your brother.

ORLANDO Go apart, Adam, and thou shalt hear how he will
shake me up.°   *insult me*

    [ADAM *stands aside*]

25 OLIVER Now, sir, what make you° here?   *are you doing*

ORLANDO Nothing. I am not taught to make anything.

OLIVER What mar you then, sir?

ORLANDO Marry,[6] sir, I am helping you to mar that which God
made, a poor unworthy brother of yours, with idleness.

30 OLIVER Marry, sir, be better employed, and be nought° awhile.   *get lost*

ORLANDO Shall I keep your hogs, and eat husks with them?
What prodigal portion have I spent, that I should come to such
penury?[7]

OLIVER Know you where you are, sir?

35 ORLANDO O sir, very well; here in your orchard.

OLIVER Know you before whom, sir?

ORLANDO Ay, better than him I am before knows me. I know
you are my eldest brother, and in the gentle condition of blood
you should so know me.[8] The courtesy of nations[9] allows you
40 my better, in that you are the first-born; but the same tradition
takes not away my blood, were there twenty brothers betwixt
us. I have as much of my father in me as you, albeit I confess
your coming before me is nearer to his reverence.[1]

OLIVER [*assailing him*] What, boy!

45 ORLANDO [*seizing him by the throat*] Come, come, elder
brother, you are too young° in this.   *inexperienced*

OLIVER Wilt thou lay hands on me, villain?°   *PUN*   *lowborn man; scoundrel*

ORLANDO I am no villein.° I am the youngest son of Sir Rowland   *serf (pun on "villain")*
de Bois. He was my father, and he is thrice a villain that says
50 such a father begot villeins. Wert thou not my brother, I would
not take this hand from thy throat till this other had pulled out
thy tongue for saying so. Thou hast railed on° thyself.   *abused*

ADAM [*coming forward*] Sweet masters, be patient. For your
father's remembrance, be at accord.

55 OLIVER [*to* ORLANDO] Let me go, I say.

ORLANDO I will not till I please. You shall hear me. My father
charged you in his will to give me good education. You have
trained me like a peasant, obscuring and hiding from me all
gentleman-like qualities.° The spirit of my father grows strong   *accomplishments*
60 in me, and I will no longer endure it. Therefore allow me such
exercises° as may become a gentleman, or give me the poor   *pursuits*
allottery° my father left me by testament. With that I will go   *portion*
buy my fortunes.

OLIVER And what wilt thou do—beg when that is spent? Well,

---

6. An oath, derived from the name of the Virgin Mary.
7. Alluding to the biblical parable of the prodigal son (Luke 15:11–32), who after squandering his share of his father's fortune envied the swine he tended and wished to eat their fodder.
8. And because of the noble blood that we share, you

should acknowledge me as a brother.
9. Customs of civil society. Referring to the English system of primogeniture, which allowed for the transmission of all property to the eldest son.
1. Your being older than I makes you more worthy of the respect that he commanded.

65   sir, get you in. I will not long be troubled with you. You shall
     have some part of your will. I pray you, leave me.
ORLANDO   I will no further offend you than becomes me for my
     good.
OLIVER [*to* ADAM]   Get you with him, you old dog.
70   ADAM   Is 'old dog' my reward? Most true, I have lost my teeth in
     your service. God be with my old master, he would not have
     spoke such a word.   *Exeunt* ORLANDO [*and*] ADAM
OLIVER   Is it even so? Begin you to grow upon me?[2] I will physic°   *give medicine to*
     your rankness,[3] and yet give no thousand crowns neither.
75   Holla, Denis!
               Enter DENIS
DENIS   Calls your worship?
OLIVER   Was not Charles, the Duke's wrestler, here to speak with
     me?
DENIS   So please you, he is here at the door, and importunes
80   access to you.
OLIVER   Call him in.   [*Exit* DENIS]
     'Twill be a good way. And tomorrow the wrestling is.
               Enter CHARLES
CHARLES   Good morrow to your worship.
OLIVER   Good Monsieur Charles—what's the new news at the
85   new court?
CHARLES   There's no news at the court, sir, but the old news: that
     is, the old Duke is banished by his younger brother, the new
     Duke, and three or four loving lords have put themselves into
     voluntary exile with him, whose lands and revenues enrich the
90   new Duke; therefore he gives them good leave° to wander.   *full permission*
OLIVER   Can you tell if Rosalind, the Duke's daughter, be ban-
     ished with her father?
CHARLES   O no; for the Duke's daughter her cousin so loves her,
     being ever from their cradles bred° together, that she would   *brought up*
95   have followed her exile, or have died to stay behind her. She is
     at the court, and no less beloved of her uncle than his own
     daughter; and never two ladies loved as they do.
OLIVER   Where will the old Duke live?
CHARLES   They say he is already in the forest of Ardenne,[4] and a
100 many merry men with him; and there they live like the old
     Robin Hood[5] of England. They say many young gentlemen
     flock to him every day, and fleet° the time carelessly,° as they   *pass / without worries*
     did in the golden world.[6]
OLIVER   What, you wrestle tomorrow before the new Duke?
105 CHARLES   Marry do I, sir, and I came to acquaint you with a
     matter. I am given, sir, secretly to understand that your younger
     brother, Orlando, hath a disposition to come in disguised
     against me to try a fall.° Tomorrow, sir, I wrestle for my credit,°   *bout / reputation*
     and he that escapes me without some broken limb, shall acquit
110 him well. Your brother is but young and tender, and for your
     love I would be loath to foil° him, as I must for my own honour   *defeat*

2. To grow so big you crowd upon me.
3. Overgrown vegetation; diseased blood.
4. The name of an ancient forest encompassing parts
of France, Belgium, and Luxembourg. F uses the anglicized spelling "Arden," evoking the English forest of
Arden near Shakespeare's birthplace in Warwickshire.
5. A legendary English outlaw, associated with

Nottingham's Sherwood Forest, who robbed from the
rich and gave his plunder to the poor.
6. Alluding to the classical myth of an earlier world of
perpetual spring, abundance, and ease from which
humankind had degenerated (Ovid, *Metamorphoses* 1).
This golden world was often identified with a pastoral life.

if he come in. Therefore out of my love to you I came hither to acquaint you withal,° that either you might stay° him from his intendment,° or brook° such disgrace well as he shall run
115 into, in that it is a thing of his own search,° and altogether against my will.

OLIVER Charles, I thank thee for thy love to me, which thou shalt find I will most kindly requite. I had myself notice of my brother's purpose herein, and have by underhand° means
120 laboured to dissuade him from it; but he is resolute. I'll tell thee, Charles, it is the stubbornest young fellow of France, full of ambition, an envious emulator of every man's good parts,° a secret and villainous contriver against me his natural brother. Therefore use thy discretion. I had as lief° thou didst break his
125 neck as his finger. And thou wert best look to't; for if thou dost him any slight disgrace, or if he do not mightily grace° himself on thee, he will practise° against thee by poison, entrap thee by some treacherous device, and never leave thee till he hath ta'en thy life by some indirect means or other. For I assure thee—
130 and almost with tears I speak it—there is not one so young and so villainous this day living. I speak but brotherly[7] of him, but should I anatomize° him to thee as he is, I must blush and weep, and thou must look pale and wonder.

CHARLES I am heartily glad I came hither to you. If he come
135 tomorrow I'll give him his payment. If ever he go alone° again, I'll never wrestle for prize more. And so God keep your worship.

OLIVER Farewell, good Charles.   *Exit* [CHARLES]
Now will I stir this gamester.° I hope I shall see an end of him,
140 for my soul—yet I know not why—hates nothing more than he. Yet he's gentle;° never schooled, and yet learned; full of noble device;° of all sorts enchantingly beloved;[8] and, indeed, so much in the heart of the world, and especially of my own people, who best know him, that I am altogether misprized.°
145 But it shall not be so long. This wrestler shall clear all.° Nothing remains but that I kindle° the boy thither,° which now I'll go about.   *Exit*

	with this / keep
	intent / endure
	seeking
	subtle
	qualities
	willingly
	win credit for
	plot
	dissect; fully open
	walk without aid
	(Orlando)
	of noble character
	purposes
	despised
	fix everything
	urge / (to the court)

1.2

Enter ROSALIND *and* CELIA

CELIA I pray thee Rosalind, sweet my coz,° be merry.   cousin

ROSALIND Dear Celia, I show more mirth than I am mistress of; and would you yet I were merrier? Unless you could teach me to forget a banished father you must not learn° me how to
5 remember any extraordinary pleasure.   teach

CELIA Herein I see thou lovest me not with the full weight that I love thee. If my uncle, thy banished father, had banished thy uncle, the Duke my father, so° thou hadst been still with me I could have taught my love to take thy father for mine. So
10 wouldst thou, if the truth of thy love to me were so righteously tempered° as mine is to thee.   provided / properly constituted / circumstances

ROSALIND Well, I will forget the condition of my estate° to rejoice in yours.

7. In a manner proper to a brother.
8. Beloved of all ranks as if by enchantment.

1.2 Location: The grounds of Duke Frederick's court.

15 CELIA   You know my father hath no child but I, nor none is like
to have. And truly, when he dies thou shalt be his heir; for what
he hath taken away from thy father perforce,° I will render thee   *by force*
again in affection. By mine honour I will, and when I break
that oath, let me turn monster. Therefore, my sweet Rose, my
dear Rose, be merry.

20 ROSALIND   From henceforth I will, coz, and devise sports.° Let   *entertainments*
me see, what think you of falling in love?

CELIA   Marry, I prithee do, to make sport withal;° but love no   *to provide amusement*
man in good earnest, nor no further in sport neither than with
safety of a pure blush thou mayst in honour come off again.[1]

25 ROSALIND   What shall be our sport, then?

CELIA   Let us sit and mock the good housewife Fortune[2] from
her wheel, that her gifts may henceforth be bestowed equally.

ROSALIND   I would we could do so, for her benefits are mightily
misplaced; and the bountiful blind woman° doth most mistake   *(Fortune)*
30 in her gifts to women.

CELIA   'Tis true; for those that she makes fair she scarce makes
honest,° and those that she makes honest she makes very ill-   *chaste*
favouredly.°   *ugly*

ROSALIND   Nay, now thou goest from Fortune's office° to   *function*
35 Nature's. Fortune reigns in° gifts of the world, not in the linea-   *presides over*
ments of nature.°   *one's natural features*

Enter [TOUCHSTONE[3] *the*] *clown*

CELIA   No. When Nature hath made a fair creature, may she not
by Fortune fall into the fire? Though Nature hath given us wit
to flout at Fortune, hath not Fortune sent in this fool to cut off
40 the argument?

ROSALIND   Indeed, there is Fortune too hard for Nature, when
Fortune makes Nature's natural° the cutter-off of Nature's wit.   *fool*

CELIA   Peradventure° this is not Fortune's work, neither, but   *Perhaps*
Nature's, who perceiveth our natural wits too dull to reason of
45 such goddesses, and hath sent this natural for our whetstone;°   *stone to sharpen tools*
for always the dullness of the fool is the whetstone of the wits.
How now, wit: whither wander you?[4]

TOUCHSTONE   Mistress, you must come away to your father.

CELIA   Were you made the messenger?

50 TOUCHSTONE   No, by mine honour, but I was bid to come for
you.

ROSALIND   Where learned you that oath, fool?

TOUCHSTONE   Of a certain knight that swore 'by his honour' they
were good pancakes, and swore 'by his honour' the mustard
55 was naught.° Now I'll stand to it° the pancakes were naught and   *worthless / affirm*
the mustard was good, and yet was not the knight forsworn.°   *perjured*

CELIA   How prove you that in the great heap of your knowledge?

ROSALIND   Ay, marry, now unmuzzle your wisdom.

TOUCHSTONE   Stand you both forth now. Stroke your chins, and
60 swear by your beards that I am a knave.

CELIA   By our beards—if we had them—thou art.

---

1. Than, with the protection afforded by your innocence ("pure blush"), you may honorably escape
("come off again").
2. Referring to the blind goddess of classical mythology
who directed human destiny with the movements of her
wheel, here likened to the mistress of a household with

a spinning wheel.
3. A touchstone was a black mineral used to test the
purity of gold and silver. Touchstone, the fool, tests the
wit of those he encounters.
4. Alluding to the catchphrase "wandering wits."

TOUCHSTONE   By my knavery—if I had it—then I were; but if
you swear by that that is not, you are not forsworn. No more
was this knight, swearing by his honour, for he never had any;
65   or if he had, he had sworn it away before ever he saw those
pancakes or that mustard.

CELIA   Prithee, who is't that thou meanest?

TOUCHSTONE   One that old Frederick, your father, loves.

CELIA[5]   My father's love is enough to honour him. Enough,
70   speak no more of him; you'll be whipped for taxation° one of   *slander*
these days.

TOUCHSTONE   The more pity that fools may not speak wisely
what wise men do foolishly.

CELIA   By my troth, thou sayst true; for since the little wit that
75   fools have was silenced,[6] the little foolery that wise men have
makes a great show. Here comes Monsieur Le Beau.

            Enter LE BEAU

ROSALIND   With his mouth full of news.

CELIA   Which he will put on° us as pigeons feed their young.   *force upon*

ROSALIND   Then shall we be news-crammed.[7]

80   CELIA   All the better: we shall be the more marketable. *Bonjour,*°   *Good day*
Monsieur Le Beau, what's the news?

LE BEAU   Fair princess, you have lost much good sport.

CELIA   Sport? Of what colour?°   *kind*

LE BEAU   What colour, madam? How shall I answer you?

85   ROSALIND   As wit and fortune will.°   *desire*

TOUCHSTONE   Or as the destinies decrees.

CELIA   Well said. That was laid on with a trowel.[8]

TOUCHSTONE   Nay, if I keep not my rank[9]—

ROSALIND   Thou losest thy old smell.

90   LE BEAU   You amaze° me, ladies. I would have told you of good   *confuse*
wrestling, which you have lost the sight of.

ROSALIND   Yet tell us the manner of the wrestling.

LE BEAU   I will tell you the beginning, and if it please your lady-
ships you may see the end, for the best is yet to do,° and here,   *to come*
95   where you are, they are coming to perform it.

CELIA   Well, the beginning that is dead and buried.

LE BEAU   There comes an old man and his three sons—

CELIA   I could match this beginning with an old tale.[1]

LE BEAU   Three proper° young men, of excellent growth and   *handsome*
100   presence.

ROSALIND   With bills° on their necks: 'Be it known unto all men   *proclamations*
by these presents'[2]—

LE BEAU   The eldest of the three wrestled with Charles, the
Duke's wrestler, which Charles in a moment threw him, and
105   broke three of his ribs, that there is little hope of life in him.
So he served the second, and so the third. Yonder they lie, the

---

5. F attributes this speech to Rosalind, but most editors
assign it to Celia on the grounds that she asked the
question to which Touchstone has just responded. It is
unlikely that Rosalind would insert herself here or insist
on the preeminence of her father's love over Frederick's.
6. This is a possible allusion to the Bishop of London's
order for the burning of satirical books in June 1599.
7. Forced to digest news, with a pun on "mews" as
meaning the cages in which pigeons were kept before
being fattened, or "crammed," for the table.

8. Bluntly; excessively. With a reference to a builder's
heavy application of mortar.
9. My status (as a jester). Rosalind then puns on the
meaning of "rank" as "foul smelling."
1. *Old tale:* Celia suggests that the motif of a father and
his three sons is the starting point for many familiar
folktales.
2. That is, by these legal documents. A legal phrase
that appears at the start of formal documents, with a
pun on "presence."

poor old man their father making such pitiful dole° over them   *mourning*
that all the beholders take his part with weeping.

ROSALIND　Alas!

110　TOUCHSTONE　But what is the sport, monsieur, that the ladies
have lost?

LE BEAU　Why, this that I speak of.

TOUCHSTONE　Thus men may grow wiser every day. It is the first
time that ever I heard breaking of ribs was sport for ladies.

115　CELIA　Or I, I promise thee.

ROSALIND　But is there any else° longs to see this broken music³   *anyone else who*
in his sides? Is there yet another dotes upon rib-breaking? Shall
we see this wrestling, cousin?

LE BEAU　You must if you stay here, for here is the place
120　appointed for the wrestling, and they are ready to perform it.

CELIA　Yonder sure they are coming. Let us now stay and see it.

Flourish.⁴ Enter DUKE [FREDERICK], *Lords,* ORLANDO,
CHARLES, *and attendants*

DUKE FREDERICK　Come on. Since the youth will not be
entreated,° his own peril on his forwardness.⁵   *persuaded (to desist)*

ROSALIND　Is yonder the man?

125　LE BEAU　Even he, madam.

CELIA　Alas, he is too young. Yet he looks successfully.°   *as if he would do well*

DUKE FREDERICK　How now, daughter and cousin;⁶ are you
crept hither to see the wrestling?

ROSALIND　Ay, my liege, so please you give us leave.

130　DUKE FREDERICK　You will take little delight in it, I can tell you,
there is such odds° in the man. In pity of the challenger's youth   *superiority*
I would fain° dissuade him, but he will not be entreated. Speak   *willingly*
to him, ladies; see if you can move him.

CELIA　Call him hither, good Monsieur Le Beau.

135　DUKE FREDERICK　Do so. I'll not be by.

[*He stands aside*]

LE BEAU　[*to* ORLANDO]　Monsieur the challenger, the Princess
calls for you.

ORLANDO　I attend them with all respect and duty.

ROSALIND　Young man, have you challenged Charles the wres-
140　tler?

ORLANDO　No, fair Princess. He is the general challenger; I come
but in as others do, to try with him the strength of my youth.

CELIA　Young gentleman, your spirits are too bold for your years.
You have seen cruel proof of this man's strength. If you saw
145　yourself with your eyes, or knew yourself with your judgement,⁷
the fear° of your adventure would counsel you to a more equal   *danger*
enterprise. We pray you for your own sake to embrace your
own safety and give over this attempt.

ROSALIND　Do, young sir. Your reputation shall not therefore be
150　misprized.° We will make it our suit to the Duke that the wres-   *undervalued*
tling might not go forward.

ORLANDO　I beseech you, punish me not with your hard
thoughts,° wherein I confess me much guilty to deny so fair   *displeasure*

---

3. Literally, a musical composition for a variety of
instruments; here referring to the labored breathing
caused by the broken ribs.
4. The sounding of horns or trumpets to signal the
arrival of an important person.

5. *his own . . . forwardness:* let the danger he encounters be blamed on his own rashness.
6. *cousin:* a term used to signify many kinship relations.
7. If you used your discernment and judgment upon
yourself.

and excellent ladies anything. But let your fair eyes and gentle
wishes go with me to my trial, wherein if I be foiled,° there is   defeated
but one shamed that was never gracious,° if killed, but one   in favor
dead that is willing to be so. I shall do my friends no wrong, for
I have none to lament me; the world no injury, for in it I have
nothing. Only in the world I fill up a place which may be better
supplied when I have made it empty.
ROSALIND   The little strength that I have, I would it were with
you.
CELIA   And mine, to eke out hers.
ROSALIND   Fare you well. Pray heaven I be deceived in you.
CELIA   Your heart's desires be with you.
CHARLES   Come, where is this young gallant that is so desirous
to lie with his mother earth?[8]
ORLANDO   Ready, sir; but his will° hath in it a more modest   (sexual) desire
working.°   undertaking
DUKE FREDERICK   You shall try but one fall.
CHARLES   No, I warrant your grace you shall not entreat him to
a second that have so mightily persuaded him from a first.
ORLANDO   You mean to mock me after; you should not have
mocked me before. But come your ways.°   let's begin
ROSALIND [to ORLANDO]   Now Hercules be thy speed,[9] young
man!
CELIA   I would I were invisible, to catch the strong fellow by the
leg.
          [CHARLES and ORLANDO] wrestle
ROSALIND   O excellent young man!
CELIA   If I had a thunderbolt in mine eye, I can tell who should
down.
          [ORLANDO throws CHARLES.] Shout
DUKE FREDERICK   No more, no more.
ORLANDO   Yes, I beseech your grace.
I am not yet well breathed.°   exercised
DUKE FREDERICK   How dost thou, Charles?
LE BEAU   He cannot speak, my lord.
DUKE FREDERICK   Bear him away.
          [Attendants carry CHARLES off]
What is thy name, young man?
ORLANDO   Orlando, my liege, the youngest son of Sir Rowland
de Bois.
DUKE FREDERICK   I would thou hadst been son to some man else.
The world esteemed thy father honourable,
But I did find him still° mine enemy.   always
Thou shouldst have better pleased me with this deed
Hadst thou descended from another house.
But fare thee well, thou art a gallant youth.
I would thou hadst told me of another father.
          Exeunt DUKE [FREDERICK, LE BEAU, TOUCHSTONE,[1]
                         Lords, and attendants]
CELIA [to ROSALIND]   Were I my father, coz, would I do this?

8. To fall to the ground. Echoing biblical descriptions
of the body's return to earth at death and punning on
"lie with" as slang for "have sexual relations with."
9. May Hercules bring you luck. Alluding to a mythological wrestling match in which Hercules, whose name was
synonymous with physical strength, vanquished Antaeus.
1. Although F does not indicate an exit for Touchstone,
many editors assume that he leaves the stage with the
Duke's party and does not reappear until 2.4.

ORLANDO   I am more proud to be Sir Rowland's son,
    His youngest son, and would not change that calling°   *title*
200   To be adopted heir to Frederick.
ROSALIND   My father loved Sir Rowland as his soul,
    And all the world was of my father's mind.
    Had I before known this young man his son
    I should have given him tears unto° entreaties   *as well as*
    Ere he should thus have ventured.
205 CELIA   Gentle° cousin,   *Noble; kind*
    Let us go thank him, and encourage him.
    My father's rough and envious° disposition   *spiteful*
    Sticks° me at heart.—Sir, you have well deserved.   *Stabs*
    If you do keep your promises in love
210   But justly,° as you have exceeded all promise,   *to the same degree*
    Your mistress shall be happy.
ROSALIND [*giving him a chain from her neck*]   Gentleman,
    Wear this for me—one out of suits° with fortune,   *favor*
    That could° give more but that her hand lacks means.   *would*
    Shall we go, coz?
CELIA   Ay. Fare you well, fair gentleman.
    [ROSALIND *and* CELIA *turn to go*]
215 ORLANDO [*aside*]   Can I not say 'I thank you'? My better parts
    Are all thrown down, and that which here stands up
    Is but a quintain,[2] a mere lifeless block.
ROSALIND [*to* CELIA]   He calls us back. My pride fell with my fortunes,
    I'll ask him what he would.—Did you call, sir?
220   Sir, you have wrestled well, and overthrown
    More than your enemies.
CELIA   Will you go, coz?
ROSALIND   Have with you.° [*To* ORLANDO] Fare you well.   *I'll go with you*
                Exeunt [ROSALIND *and* CELIA][3]
ORLANDO   What passion hangs these weights upon my tongue?
225   I cannot speak to her, yet she urged conference.°   *conversation*
    Enter LE BEAU
    O poor Orlando! Thou art overthrown.
    Or° Charles or something weaker masters thee.   *Either*
LE BEAU   Good sir, I do in friendship counsel you
    To leave this place. Albeit you have deserved
230   High commendation, true applause, and love,
    Yet such is now the Duke's condition°   *state of mind*
    That he misconsters° all that you have done.   *misconstrues*
    The Duke is humorous.[4] What he is indeed
    More suits you to conceive than I to speak of.
235 ORLANDO   I thank you, sir. And pray you tell me this,
    Which of the two was daughter of the Duke
    That here was at the wrestling?
LE BEAU   Neither his daughter, if we judge by manners—
    But yet indeed the shorter[5] is his daughter.

---

2. A wooden post used as a target in jousts and other aristocratic sports. Orlando suggests that his reason and speech (his "better parts") have been "thrown down," or defeated, in his encounter with Rosalind, leaving him standing speechless, like a post.
3. F marks only a single exit for Rosalind here, but Celia almost certainly accompanies her offstage.
4. Moody. The term derives from Renaissance medical theory, which held that good mental and physical health depended on the proper balance of four bodily fluids, or humors.
5. F reads "taller," but see 1.3.109, where Rosalind declares that she is "more than common tall" and will therefore disguise herself as a man. Shakespeare may not have been consistent in determining who was to be the taller woman.

240 The other is daughter to the banished Duke,
And here detained by her usurping uncle
To keep his daughter company, whose loves
Are dearer than the natural bond of sisters.
But I can tell you that of late this Duke
245 Hath ta'en displeasure 'gainst his gentle niece,
Grounded upon no other argument°   *reason*
But that the people praise her for her virtues
And pity her for her good father's sake.
And, on my life, his malice 'gainst the lady
250 Will suddenly break forth. Sir, fare you well.
Hereafter, in a better world than this,
I shall desire more love and knowledge of you.
ORLANDO   I rest much bounden° to you. Fare you well.   *obliged*
                    [*Exit* LE BEAU]
Thus must I from the smoke into the smother,[6]
255 From tyrant Duke unto a tyrant brother.—
But heavenly Rosalind!   *Exit*

1.3

Enter CELIA *and* ROSALIND

CELIA   Why cousin, why Rosalind—Cupid have mercy,[1] not a
word?

ROSALIND   Not one to throw at a dog.

CELIA   No, thy words are too precious to be cast away upon curs.
5   Throw some of them at me. Come, lame me with reasons.[2]

ROSALIND   Then there were two cousins laid up, when the one
should be lamed with reasons and the other mad without any.

CELIA   But is all this for your father?

ROSALIND   No, some of it is for my child's father.[3] O how full of
10   briers is this working-day world!

CELIA   They are but burs, cousin, thrown upon thee in holiday
foolery. If we walk not in the trodden paths our very petticoats
will catch them.

ROSALIND   I could shake them off my coat. These burs are in my
15   heart.

CELIA   Hem[4] them away.

ROSALIND   I would try, if I could cry 'hem' and have him.

CELIA   Come, come, wrestle with thy affections.

ROSALIND   O, they take the part of a better wrestler than myself.

20   CELIA   O, a good wish upon you!° You will try in time, in despite   *good luck to you*
of a fall.[5] But turning these jests out of service,° let us talk in   *dismissing these jokes*
good earnest. Is it possible on such a sudden you should fall
into so strong a liking with old Sir Rowland's youngest son?

ROSALIND   The Duke my father loved his father dearly.

25   CELIA   Doth it therefore ensue that you should love his son
dearly? By this kind of chase° I should hate him, for my father   *logic*
hated his father dearly; yet I hate not Orlando.

ROSALIND   No, faith, hate him not, for my sake.

6. Out of the frying pan into the fire. *smother:* thick,
suffocating smoke.
1.3 Location: Duke Frederick's court.
1. May Cupid (god of love) be compassionate.
2. Throw so many reasons (for your silence) at me that
if they were stones, I would be made lame.

3. That is, for one who will be father to my child.
4. Cough, with a pun on "bur" (line 14) as meaning
"something that sticks in your throat."
5. You are destined to wrestle with him eventually even
though it will cause you to fall, with a pun on "fall" as
"lapse from chastity."

CELIA   Why should I not? Doth he not deserve well?
   Enter DUKE [FREDERICK], *with Lords*
30   ROSALIND   Let me love him for that, and do you love him
  because I do. Look, here comes the Duke.
CELIA   With his eyes full of anger.
DUKE FREDERICK [*to* ROSALIND]   Mistress, dispatch you with your safest haste,⁶
  And get you from our court.
35   ROSALIND   Me, uncle?
DUKE FREDERICK   You, cousin.
  Within these ten days if that thou beest found
  So near our public court as twenty miles,
  Thou diest for it.
ROSALIND   I do beseech your grace
40   Let me the knowledge of my fault bear with me.
  If with myself I hold intelligence,°   *I communicate*
  Or have acquaintance with mine own desires,
  If that I do not dream, or be not frantic°—   *insane*
  As I do trust I am not—then, dear uncle,
45   Never so much as in a thought unborn
  Did I offend your highness.
DUKE FREDERICK   Thus do all traitors.
  If their purgation° did consist in words   *exoneration*
  They are as innocent as grace itself.
  Let it suffice thee that I trust thee not.
50   ROSALIND   Yet your mistrust cannot make me a traitor.
  Tell me whereon the likelihood depends?
DUKE FREDERICK   Thou art thy father's daughter—there's enough.
ROSALIND   So was I when your highness took his dukedom;
  So was I when your highness banished him.
55   Treason is not inherited, my lord,
  Or if we did derive it from our friends,°   *relatives*
  What's that to me? My father was no traitor.
  Then, good my liege, mistake me not so much
  To think my poverty is treacherous.
60   CELIA   Dear sovereign, hear me speak.
DUKE FREDERICK   Ay, Celia, we stayed° her for your sake,   *detained*
  Else had she with her father ranged° along.   *roamed*
CELIA   I did not then entreat to have her stay.
  It was your pleasure, and your own remorse.°   *pity; sense of guilt*
65   I was too young that time to value her,
  But now I know her. If she be a traitor,
  Why, so am I. We still° have slept together,   *always*
  Rose at an instant,° learned, played, eat together, *at the same moment*
  And wheresoe'er we went, like Juno's swans
70   Still we went coupled and inseparable.⁷
DUKE FREDERICK   She is too subtle° for thee, and her smoothness, *cunning*
  Her very silence, and her patience
  Speak to the people, and they pity her.
  Thou art a fool. She robs thee of thy name,°   *reputation*
75   And thou wilt show more bright and seem more virtuous
  When she is gone. Then open not thy lips.

---

6. Leave quickly, which is your best safety.
7. That is, yoked together inseparably like the swans that draw the chariot of Juno (queen of the gods).

According to Ovid, swans were associated with Venus (goddess of love), not with Juno.

Firm and irrevocable is my doom°   *judgment*
Which I have passed upon her. She is banished.
CELIA   Pronounce that sentence then on me, my liege.
80   I cannot live out of her company.
DUKE FREDERICK   You are a fool.—You, niece, provide yourself.°   *make preparation*
If you outstay the time, upon mine honour
And in the greatness of my word,[8] you die.
                                    Exit DUKE [FREDERICK, *with Lords*]
CELIA   O my poor Rosalind, whither wilt thou go?
85   Wilt thou change° fathers? I will give thee mine.   *exchange*
I charge thee, be not thou more grieved than I am.
ROSALIND   I have more cause.
CELIA   Thou hast not, cousin.
Prithee, be cheerful. Know'st thou not the Duke
Hath banished me, his daughter?
ROSALIND   That he hath not.
90   CELIA   No, hath not? Rosalind, lack'st thou then the love
Which teacheth thee that thou and I am one?
Shall we be sundered? Shall we part, sweet girl?
No. Let my father seek another heir.
Therefore devise with me how we may fly,
95   Whither to go, and what to bear with us,
And do not seek to take your change upon you,[9]
To bear your griefs yourself, and leave me out.
For by this heaven, now at our sorrows pale,
Say what thou canst, I'll go along with thee.
100 ROSALIND   Why, whither shall we go?
CELIA   To seek my uncle in the forest of Ardenne.
ROSALIND   Alas, what danger will it be to us,
Maids as we are, to travel forth so far!
Beauty provoketh thieves sooner than gold.
105 CELIA   I'll put myself in poor and mean° attire,   *lowly*
And with a kind of umber[1] smirch my face.
The like do you, so shall we pass along
And never stir° assailants.   *provoke*
ROSALIND   Were it not better,
Because that I am more than common tall,
110   That I did suit° me all points° like a man,   *dress / ways*
A gallant curtal-axe° upon my thigh,   *short sword*
A boar-spear[2] in my hand, and in my heart,
Lie there what hidden woman's fear there will.
We'll have a swashing° and a martial outside,   *swaggering*
115   As many other mannish cowards have,
That do outface it with their semblances.[3]
CELIA   What shall I call thee when thou art a man?
ROSALIND   I'll have no worse a name than Jove's own page,
And therefore look you call me Ganymede.[4]
120   But what will you be called?

---

8. And in accordance with the power of my decree as Duke.
9. To bear alone the burden of your change of fortunes.
1. Brown pigment. By rubbing it on their faces, Rosalind and Celia take on the dark or sunburned complexion that in Elizabethan society marked the low social status of those who labored outside. Ladies wore masks to keep their complexions white.

2. A long-bladed spear used to impale boar.
3. Who brazenly defy the world with the mere appearance of bravery.
4. The name of a beautiful young man who, according to classical mythology, was so beloved by Jove (king of the gods) that Jove carried him off to heaven and made him his cupbearer. Also a slang term for a young man who sold his sexual services to or was kept by an older man.

CELIA   Something that hath a reference to my state.
   No longer Celia, but Aliena.°   *"the estranged one"*
ROSALIND   But cousin, what if we essayed° to steal   *tried*
   The clownish fool out of your father's court.
125   Would he not be a comfort to our travel?
CELIA   He'll go along o'er the wide world with me.
   Leave me alone to woo him. Let's away,
   And get our jewels and our wealth together,
   Devise the fittest time and safest way
130   To hide us from pursuit that will be made
   After my flight. Now go we in content,
   To liberty, and not to banishment.   *Exeunt*

2.1

Enter DUKE SENIOR, AMIENS,[1] *and two or three* LORDS
like° foresters   *dressed as*
DUKE SENIOR   Now, my co-mates and brothers in exile,
   Hath not old custom° made this life more sweet   *long acquaintance*
   Than that of painted pomp?° Are not these woods   *artificial splendor*
   More free from peril than the envious court?
5   Here feel we not the penalty of Adam,[2]
   The seasons' difference,° as° the icy fang   *change / such as*
   And churlish° chiding of the winter's wind,   *rough*
   Which when it bites and blows upon my body
   Even till I shrink with cold, I smile, and say
10   'This is no flattery. These are counsellors
   That feelingly° persuade me what I am.'   *through my senses*
   Sweet are the uses° of adversity   *benefits*
   Which, like the toad, ugly and venomous,
   Wears yet a precious jewel in his head;[3]
15   And this our life, exempt from public haunt,°   *free from crowds*
   Finds tongues in trees, books in the running brooks,
   Sermons in stones, and good in everything.
AMIENS   I would not change it. Happy is your grace
   That can translate the stubbornness of fortune
20   Into so quiet and so sweet a style.
DUKE SENIOR   Come, shall we go and kill us venison?
   And yet it irks me the poor dappled fools,°   *innocent creatures*
   Being native burghers° of this desert° city,   *citizens / unpeopled*
   Should in their own confines with forkèd heads°   *two-pronged arrows*
   Have their round haunches gored.
25   FIRST LORD   Indeed, my lord,
   The melancholy Jaques[4] grieves at that,
   And in that kind° swears you do more usurp   *vein*
   Than doth your brother that hath banished you.
   Today my lord of Amiens and myself
30   Did steal behind him as he lay along°   *stretched out*
   Under an oak, whose antic° root peeps out   *old; oddly shaped*
   Upon the brook that brawls° along this wood,   *loudly flows*

2.1 Location: The Forest of Ardenne.
1. The name of a town in northern France with which this character is perhaps associated.
2. In Genesis 3, Adam's punishment for disobeying God involved expulsion from Eden and the laying of a curse upon the earth. This was frequently interpreted as the end of the temperate climate associated with paradise.

3. The toad was popularly believed to be poisonous and to have in its head a jewel, the toadstone.
4. Jaques's name, usually pronounced with two syllables, puns on "jakes," the word for "privy" (toilet). He is a stock figure of the melancholic man prone to solitude and black thoughts because of an excess of black bile, one of the four humors.

To the which place a poor sequestered° stag   *cut off from the herd*
That from the hunter's aim had ta'en a hurt
35 Did come to languish. And indeed, my lord,
The wretched animal heaved forth such groans
That their discharge did stretch his leathern coat
Almost to bursting, and the big round tears
Coursed° one another down his innocent nose   *Pursued*
40 In piteous chase. And thus the hairy fool,
Much markèd of° the melancholy Jaques,   *observed by*
Stood on th'extremest verge° of the swift brook,   *farthest edge*
Augmenting it with tears.
DUKE SENIOR   But what said Jaques?
Did he not moralize° this spectacle?   *draw a moral from*
45 FIRST LORD   O yes, into a thousand similes.
First, for his weeping into the needless° stream;   *needing no more water*
'Poor deer,' quoth he, 'thou mak'st a testament
As worldlings do, giving thy sum of more°   *your supplement*
To that which had too much.' Then being there alone,
50 Left and abandoned of° his velvet friend,[5]   *by*
'Tis right,' quoth he, 'thus misery doth part°   *separate from*
The flux° of company.' Anon a careless[6] herd   *flow*
Full of the pasture° jumps along by him   *Full from grazing*
And never stays to greet him. 'Ay,' quoth Jaques,
55 'Sweep on, you fat and greasy citizens,
'Tis just the fashion. Wherefore should you look
Upon that poor and broken bankrupt there?'
Thus most invectively he pierceth through
The body of the country, city, court,
60 Yea, and of this our life, swearing that we
Are mere usurpers, tyrants, and what's worse,°   *whatever is worse*
To fright the animals and to kill them up°   *off*
In their assigned and native dwelling place.
DUKE SENIOR   And did you leave him in this contemplation?
65 SECOND LORD   We did, my lord, weeping and commenting
Upon the sobbing deer.
DUKE SENIOR   Show me the place.
I love to cope° him in these sullen fits,   *contend with*
For then he's full of matter.°   *material for thought; pus*
FIRST LORD   I'll bring you to him straight.°   *immediately*
                              Exeunt

2.2

Enter DUKE [FREDERICK], *with* LORDS

DUKE FREDERICK   Can it be possible that no man saw them?
It cannot be. Some villains of my court
Are of consent and sufferance in this.[1]
FIRST LORD   I cannot hear of any that did see her.
5 The ladies her attendants of her chamber
Saw her abed, and in the morning early
They found the bed untreasured of their mistress.
SECOND LORD   My lord, the roynish° clown at whom so oft   *vulgar*

---

5. Smooth-coated companion. Alluding both to the velvet covering the male deer's antlers and to an expensive fabric worn by the prosperous.

6. Just then a carefree.
2.2 Location: Duke Frederick's court.
1. Have agreed to and tolerated this.

Your grace was wont° to laugh is also missing.   *accustomed*
10   Hisperia, the Princess' gentlewoman,
      Confesses that she secretly o'erheard
      Your daughter and her cousin much commend
      The parts° and graces of the wrestler   *qualities*
      That did but lately foil the sinewy Charles,
15   And she believes wherever they are gone
      That youth is surely in their company.
DUKE FREDERICK   Send to his brother;° fetch that gallant hither.   *(Oliver)*
      If he° be absent, bring his brother to me,   *(Orlando)*
      I'll make him find him. Do this suddenly,
20   And let not search and inquisition quail°   *fail*
      To bring again° these foolish runaways.   *Exeunt [severally]°*   *back / separately*

2.3

Enter ORLANDO *and* ADAM *[meeting]*
ORLANDO   Who's there?
ADAM   What, my young master, O my gentle master,
      O my sweet master, O you memory
      Of old Sir Rowland, why, what make you° here!   *what are you doing*
5   Why are you virtuous? Why do people love you?
      And wherefore° are you gentle, strong, and valiant?   *why*
      Why would you be so fond° to overcome   *foolish*
      The bonny prizer° of the humorous° Duke?   *robust champion / moody*
      Your praise is come too swiftly home before you.
10   Know you not, master, to some kind of men
      Their graces° serve them but as enemies?   *virtues*
      No more° do yours. Your virtues, gentle master,   *No better*
      Are sanctified and holy traitors to you.
      O, what a world is this, when what is comely
15   Envenoms° him that bears it!   *Poisons*
ORLANDO   Why, what's the matter?
ADAM   O, unhappy youth,
      Come not within these doors. Within this roof
      The enemy of all your graces lives,
20   Your brother—no, no brother—yet the son—
      Yet not the son, I will not call him son—
      Of him I was about to call his father,
      Hath heard your praises, and this night he means
      To burn the lodging where you use° to lie,   *are accustomed*
25   And you within it. If he fail of that,
      He will have other means to cut you off.
      I overheard him and his practices.°   *plots*
      This is no place,° this house is but a butchery.°   *home / slaughterhouse*
      Abhor it, fear it, do not enter it.
30   ORLANDO   Why, whither, Adam, wouldst thou have me go?
ADAM   No matter whither, so you come not here.
ORLANDO   What, wouldst thou have me go and beg my food,
      Or with a base and boisterous° sword enforce   *violent*
      A thievish living on the common road?
35   This I must do, or know not what to do.
      Yet this I will not do, do how I can.

2.3 Location: Oliver's house.

I rather will subject me to the malice
Of a diverted blood[1] and bloody° brother.   *murderous*

ADAM   But do not so. I have five hundred crowns,[2]
40   The thrifty hire I saved[3] under your father,
        Which I did store to be my foster-nurse[4]
        When service should in my old limbs lie lame,°   *be lamely performed*
        And unregarded age in corners thrown.°   *be thrown*
        Take that, and he that doth the ravens feed,
45   Yea providently caters for the sparrow,[5]
        Be comfort to my age. Here is the gold.
        All this I give you. Let me be your servant.
        Though I look old, yet I am strong and lusty,°   *robust*
        For in my youth I never did apply
50   Hot and rebellious° liquors in my blood,   *unhealthful*
        Nor did not with unbashful forehead° woo   *bold countenance*
        The means of weakness and debility.
        Therefore my age is as a lusty winter,
        Frosty but kindly.° Let me go with you,   *pleasant; natural*
55   I'll do the service of a younger man
        In all your business and necessities.

ORLANDO   O good old man, how well in thee appears
        The constant° service of the antique world,   *faithful*
        When service sweat° for duty, not for meed!°   *labored / reward*
60   Thou art not for the fashion of these times,
        Where none will sweat but for promotion,
        And having that do choke their service up°   *cease service*
        Even with the having. It is not so with thee.
        But, poor old man, thou prun'st a rotten tree,
65   That cannot so much as a blossom yield
        In lieu of° all thy pains and husbandry.°   *return for / gardening*
        But come thy ways. We'll go along together,
        And ere we have thy youthful wages spent,
        We'll light upon some settled low content.°   *humble contentment*
70 ADAM   Master, go on, and I will follow thee
        To the last gasp with truth and loyalty.
        From seventeen years till now almost fourscore
        Here lived I, but now live here no more.
        At seventeen years, many their fortunes seek,
75   But at fourscore, it is too late a week.°   *a time*
        Yet fortune cannot recompense me better
        Than to die well, and not my master's debtor.   *Exeunt*

2.4

Enter ROSALIND [*in man's clothes*] *for*° *Ganymede;*   *as*
CELIA *for Aliena,* [*a shepherdess;*] *and* TOUCHSTONE
[*the*] *clown*

ROSALIND   O Jupiter,[1] how weary are my spirits!
TOUCHSTONE   I care not for my spirits, if my legs were not weary.
ROSALIND   I could find in my heart to disgrace my man's apparel

---

1. Of a kinship diverted from its natural course.
2. Approximately 125 English pounds.
3. The wages I thriftily saved.
4. Caretaker. A foster nurse was a woman hired to breast-feed and care for other people's children.
5. Alluding to various biblical passages (especially

Luke 12:6 and 22–24 and Psalm 147:9) that characterize God as the caretaker of all creatures.
2.4 Location: The remainder of Act 2 takes place in the Forest of Ardenne.
1. Another name for Jove, king of the gods in classical mythology and Ganymede's master.

and to cry like a woman. But I must comfort the weaker vessel,°   *woman*

5   as doublet and hose² ought to show itself courageous to petti-
    coat; therefore, courage, good Aliena!

CELIA   I pray you, bear with me. I cannot go no further.

TOUCHSTONE   For my part, I had rather bear with you than bear
    you. Yet I should bear no cross³ if I did bear you, for I think

10   you have no money in your purse.

ROSALIND   Well, this is the forest of Ardenne.

TOUCHSTONE   Ay, now am I in Ardenne; the more fool I. When
    I was at home I was in a better place; but travellers must be
    content.

        Enter CORIN *and* SILVIUS

15   ROSALIND   Ay, be so, good Touchstone. Look you, who comes
    here—a young man and an old in solemn talk.

CORIN [*to* SILVIUS]   That is the way to make her scorn you still.

SILVIUS   O Corin, that thou knew'st how I do love her!

CORIN   I partly guess; for I have loved ere now.

20   SILVIUS   No, Corin, being old thou canst not guess,
    Though in thy youth thou wast as true a lover
    As ever sighed upon a midnight pillow.
    But if thy love were ever like to mine—
    As sure I think did never man love so—

25   How many actions most ridiculous
    Hast thou been drawn to by thy fantasy?°   *imagination*

CORIN   Into a thousand that I have forgotten.

SILVIUS   O, thou didst then never love so heartily.
    If thou rememberest not the slightest folly

30   That ever love did make thee run into,
    Thou hast not loved.
    Or if thou hast not sat as I do now,
    Wearing° thy hearer in thy mistress' praise,   *Wearying*
    Thou hast not loved.

35   Or if thou hast not broke from company
    Abruptly, as my passion now makes me,
    Thou hast not loved.
    O, Phoebe, Phoebe, Phoebe!   *Exit*

ROSALIND   Alas, poor shepherd, searching of° thy wound,   *probing*

40   I have by hard adventure° found mine own.   *unlucky chance*

TOUCHSTONE   And I mine. I remember when I was in love I
    broke my sword upon a stone and bid him take that for coming
    a-night to Jane Smile,⁴ and I remember the kissing of her bat-
    let,⁵ and the cow's dugs° that her pretty chapped hands had   *udder*

45   milked; and I remember the wooing of a peascod instead of
    her, from whom I took two cods, and giving her them again,
    said with weeping tears, 'Wear these for my sake.'⁶ We that are
    true lovers run into strange capers. But as all is mortal in
    nature, so is all nature in love mortal in folly.⁷

---

2. That is, as manhood (signified by male attire, close-fitting jacket and breeches).
3. Trouble; money, specifically Elizabethan coins stamped with the image of a cross.
4. *I broke . . . Smile:* I struck a stone as though it were a rival to me in my nocturnal visits to Jane Smile.
5. A wooden bat for beating clothes while washing them.

6. *wooing . . . sake':* referring to English country courtship rituals in which a pea pod ("peascod") and its husks ("cods") were considered lucky gifts. "Peascod" and "cods" were also slang terms for "male genitalia," suggesting the implicit sexual import of these gifts.
7. So all lovers show their humanity in their foolishness.

50   ROSALIND   Thou speak'st wiser than thou art ware° of.   *aware*
      TOUCHSTONE   Nay, I shall ne'er be ware° of mine own wit till I   *wary*
      break my shins against it.
      ROSALIND   Jove, Jove, this shepherd's passion
      Is much upon my fashion.°   *of my sort*
55   TOUCHSTONE   And mine, but it grows something° stale with me.   *somewhat*
      CELIA   I pray you, one of you question yon man
      If he for gold will give us any food.
      I faint almost to death.
      TOUCHSTONE [*to* CORIN]   Holla, you clown!°   *peasant; yokel*
60   ROSALIND   Peace, fool, he's not thy kinsman.
      CORIN   Who calls?
      TOUCHSTONE   Your betters, sir.
      CORIN   Else are they very wretched.
      ROSALIND [*to* TOUCHSTONE]   Peace, I say. [*To* CORIN]   Good
            even° to you, friend.   *evening*
65   CORIN   And to you, gentle sir, and to you all.
      ROSALIND   I prithee, shepherd, if that love or gold
      Can in this desert place buy entertainment,°   *accommodation*
      Bring us where we may rest ourselves, and feed.
      Here's a young maid with travel much oppressed,
      And faints for succour.°   *for lack of aid (food)*
70   CORIN   Fair sir, I pity her,
      And wish, for her sake more than for mine own,
      My fortunes were more able to relieve her.
      But I am shepherd to another man,
      And do not shear the fleeces that I graze.
75   My master is of churlish° disposition,   *miserly*
      And little recks° to find the way to heaven   *thinks*
      By doing deeds of hospitality.
      Besides, his cot,° his flocks, and bounds of feed°   *cottage / grazing rights*
      Are now on sale, and at our sheepcote° now   *cottage*
80   By reason of his absence there is nothing
      That you will feed on. But what is, come see,
      And in my voice⁸ most welcome shall you be.
      ROSALIND   What° is he that shall buy his flock and pasture?   *Who*
      CORIN   That young swain that you saw here but erewhile,°   *just now*
85   That little cares for buying anything.
      ROSALIND   I pray thee, if it stand with honesty,
      Buy thou the cottage, pasture, and the flock,
      And thou shalt have to pay° for it of us.   *the money to pay*
      CELIA   And we will mend° thy wages. I like this place,   *improve*
90   And willingly could waste° my time in it.   *spend*
      CORIN   Assuredly the thing is to be sold.
      Go with me. If you like upon report
      The soil, the profit, and this kind of life,
      I will your very faithful feeder° be,   *servant*
95   And buy it with your gold right suddenly.   *Exeunt*

8. And insofar as my authority stretches.

2.5

Enter AMIENS, JAQUES, *and other [Lords dressed as foresters]*

AMIENS [*sings*]¹   Under the greenwood tree
         Who loves to lie with me,
         And turn° his merry note   *tune*
         Unto the sweet bird's throat,°   *voice*
5   Come hither, come hither, come hither.
         Here shall he see
         No enemy
         But winter and rough weather.

JAQUES   More, more, I prithee, more.

10 AMIENS   It will make you melancholy, Monsieur Jaques.

JAQUES   I thank it. More, I prithee, more. I can suck melancholy
out of a song as a weasel sucks eggs. More, I prithee, more.

AMIENS   My voice is ragged,° I know I cannot please you.   *harsh*

JAQUES   I do not desire you to please me, I do desire you to sing.

15   Come, more; another stanza. Call you 'em stanzas?²

AMIENS   What you will, Monsieur Jaques.

JAQUES   Nay, I care not for their names,³ they owe me nothing.
Will you sing?

AMIENS   More at your request than to please myself.

20 JAQUES   Well then, if ever I thank any man, I'll thank you. But
that° they call compliment is like th'encounter of two dog-   *what*
apes,° and when a man thanks me heartily methinks I have   *dog-faced baboons*
given him a penny and he renders me the beggarly thanks.⁴
Come, sing; and you that will not, hold your tongues.

25 AMIENS   Well, I'll end the song.—Sirs, cover the while.⁵
       [*Lords prepare food and drink*]
The Duke will drink under this tree. [*To* JAQUES] He hath been
all this day to look° you.   *searching for*

JAQUES   And I have been all this day to avoid him. He is too
disputable° for my company. I think of as many matters as he,   *argumentative*
30   but I give heaven thanks, and make no boast of them. Come,
warble, come.

ALL [*sing*]⁶   Who doth ambition shun,
         And loves to live i'th' sun,
         Seeking the food he eats
35   And pleased with what he gets,
         Come hither, come hither, come hither.
         Here shall he see
         No enemy
         But winter and rough weather.

40 JAQUES   I'll give you a verse to this note° that I made yesterday in   *tune*
despite of my invention.⁷

AMIENS   And I'll sing it.

JAQUES   Thus it goes:
         If it do come to pass
45   That any man turn ass,

2.5

1. F does not indicate who sings this song. Traditionally
it has been assigned to Amiens, whose part may have
been played by Robert Armin, a clown who joined
Shakespeare's company in 1599 and who was known
for his fine singing voice.
2. A relatively new, and Italianate, word at the time of
the play's composition.

3. Punning on the legal sense of "names" as "signatures
of borrowers."
4. Excessive thanks, like that given by a beggar.
5. Set the table in the meantime.
6. F's direction before this song reads: "Song. Altogether here."
7. Even though I have little power of creativity.

Leaving his wealth and ease
A stubborn will to please,
Ducdame,[8] ducdame, ducdame.
Here shall he see
50   Gross fools as he,
An if° he will come to me.   *If only*

AMIENS What's that 'ducdame'?

JAQUES 'Tis a Greek[9] invocation to call fools into a circle. I'll go
sleep if I can. If I cannot, I'll rail against all the firstborn of
55 Egypt.[1]

AMIENS And I'll go seek the Duke; his banquet[2] is prepared.
                                                Exeunt

2.6

Enter ORLANDO *and* ADAM

ADAM Dear master, I can go no further. O, I die for food. Here
lie I down and measure out my grave. Farewell, kind master.

ORLANDO Why, how now, Adam? No greater heart in thee? Live
a little, comfort° a little, cheer thyself a little. If this uncouth°   *be comforted / wild*
5 forest yield anything savage I will either be food for it or bring it
for food to thee. Thy conceit° is nearer death than thy powers.   *imagination*
For my sake be comfortable. Hold death awhile at the arm's
end. I will here be with thee presently,° and if I bring thee not   *soon*
something to eat, I will give thee leave to die. But if thou diest
10 before I come, thou art a mocker of my labour. Well said. Thou
lookest cheerly,° and I'll be with thee quickly. Yet thou liest in   *cheerfully*
the bleak air. Come, I will bear thee to some shelter, and thou
shalt not die for lack of a dinner if there live anything in this
desert.° Cheerly, good Adam.   [ORLANDO *carries* ADAM *off*]   *uninhabited place*

2.7

Enter DUKE SENIOR *and* LORD[S] *like*° *outlaws*   *dressed as*

DUKE SENIOR I think he be transformed into a beast,
For I can nowhere find him like° a man.   *in the shape of*

FIRST LORD My lord, he is but even now gone hence.
Here was he merry, hearing of a song.

5 DUKE SENIOR If he, compact of jars,° grow musical   *made up of discords*
We shall have shortly discord in the spheres.[1]
Go seek him. Tell him I would speak with him.

Enter JAQUES

FIRST LORD He saves my labour by his own approach.

DUKE SENIOR Why, how now, monsieur, what a life is this,
10 That your poor friends must woo your company!
What, you look merrily.

JAQUES A fool, a fool, I met a fool i'th' forest,
A motley fool[2]—a miserable world!—
As I do live by food, I met a fool,

---

8. A word of unknown meaning. Possibly a variation on
a Welsh phrase meaning "Come hither" or on a Gypsy
phrase meaning "I foretell."
9. "Greek" was used to signify anything unintelligible.
1. According to Exodus 11 and 12, the Hebrew God
caused the deaths of all firstborn Egyptian children
after Pharaoh would not let the Israelites leave his
country. Jaques may be vowing to denounce all firstborn
sons, which would include Duke Senior.

2. A light meal of sweetmeats and wine.
2.7
1. Alluding to the Pythagorean belief that the earth
was the center of eight concentric spheres whose movements created a heavenly harmony (the music of the
spheres) inaudible to humans.
2. Someone wearing "motley," the multicolored costume conventionally associated with fools and jesters.

15 Who laid him down and basked him in the sun,
    And railed on Lady Fortune in good terms,
    In good set° terms, and yet a motley fool.   *outspoken; rhetorical*
    'Good morrow, fool,' quoth I. 'No, sir,' quoth he,
    'Call me not fool till heaven hath sent me fortune.'³
20 And then he drew a dial⁴ from his poke,°   *pocket; pouch*
    And looking on it with lack-lustre eye
    Says very wisely 'It is ten o'clock.'
    'Thus we may see', quoth he, 'how the world wags.°   *moves on*
    'Tis but an hour ago since it was nine,
25 And after one hour more 'twill be eleven.
    And so from hour to hour we ripe and ripe,
    And then from hour to hour we rot and rot;
    And thereby hangs a tale.'⁵ When I did hear
    The motley fool thus moral on the time
30 My lungs began to crow like chanticleer,°   *a rooster*
    That fools should be so deep°-contemplative,   *profoundly*
    And I did laugh sans° intermission   *without*
    An hour by his dial. O noble fool,
    A worthy fool—motley's the only wear.°   *garb worth wearing*
35 DUKE SENIOR   What fool is this?
    JAQUES   O worthy fool!—One that hath been a courtier,
    And says 'If ladies be but young and fair
    They have the gift to know it.' And in his brain,
    Which is as dry⁶ as the remainder° biscuit   *last*
40 After a voyage, he hath strange places° crammed   *sites; commonplaces*
    With observation, the which he vents
    In mangled forms. O that I were a fool,
    I am ambitious for a motley coat.
    DUKE SENIOR   Thou shalt have one.
    JAQUES   It is my only suit,°   *request; costume*
45 Provided that you weed your better judgements
    Of all opinion that grows rank° in them   *wild*
    That I am wise. I must have liberty
    Withal, as large a charter° as the wind,   *license*
    To blow on whom I please, for so fools have;
50 And they that are most gallèd° with my folly,   *vexed*
    They most must laugh. And why, sir, must they so?
    The why is plain as way to parish church:
    He that a fool doth very wisely hit
    Doth very foolishly, although he smart,
55 Seem aught but senseless of the bob.° If not,   *unaware of the taunt*
    The wise man's folly is anatomized°   *dissected; laid open*
    Even by the squandering glances° of the fool.   *random hits*
    Invest me in my motley. Give me leave
    To speak my mind, and I will through and through
60 Cleanse the foul body of th'infected world,
    If they will patiently receive my medicine.
    DUKE SENIOR   Fie on thee, I can tell what thou wouldst do.

3. Referring to the proverbial notion that fortune favored fools.
4. Probably a portable sundial about the size of a napkin ring.
5. *'Tis . . . tale*: the puns and sexual wordplay in these lines suggest a story of male sexual activity leading to debility: "hour" puns on "whore" (they were pronounced similarly); "ripe" means "to come of age sexually"; "rot" puns on "rut," which means "to have sex in an animal-like state of excitement"; and "tale" puns on "tail," slang for "penis." "And thereby hangs a tale" was an Elizabethan commonplace.
6. According to Renaissance medical theory, dry brains signified slow wits and strong memories.

JAQUES	What, for a counter,[7] would I do but good?	
DUKE SENIOR	Most mischievous foul sin, in chiding sin;	
65	For thou thyself hast been a libertine,	
	As sensual as the brutish sting° itself,	*lust*
	And all th'embossèd sores and headed evils[8]	
	That thou with licence of free foot° hast caught	*travel*
	Wouldst thou disgorge° into the general world.	*vomit*
70 JAQUES	Why, who cries out on pride°	*extravagance*
	That can therein tax° any private party?	*blame*
	Doth it not flow as hugely as the sea,	
	Till that the weary very means° do ebb?	*source itself*
	What woman in the city do I name	
75	When that I say the city-woman bears	
	The cost° of princes on unworthy shoulders?	*costly attire*
	Who can come in and say that I mean her	
	When such a one as she, such is her neighbour?	
	Or what is he of basest function,°	*lowliest social status*
80	That says his bravery° is not on° my cost,	*fine attire / at*
	Thinking that I mean him, but therein suits	
	His folly to the mettle° of my speech?	*spirit*
	There then, how then, what then, let me see wherein	
	My tongue hath wronged him. If it do him right,°	*describe him justly*
85	Then he hath wronged himself. If he be free,°	*virtuous*
	Why then my taxing° like a wild goose flies,	*reproof*
	Unclaimed of any man. But who comes here?	

Enter ORLANDO [*with sword drawn*]

ORLANDO	Forbear, and eat no more!	
JAQUES	Why, I have eat° none yet.	*eaten*
ORLANDO	Nor shalt not till necessity be served.	
90 JAQUES	Of what kind° should this cock come of?	*lineage; stock*
DUKE SENIOR	Art thou thus boldened, man, by thy distress?	
	Or else a rude despiser of good manners,	
	That in civility thou seem'st so empty?	
ORLANDO	You touched my vein° at first. The thorny point	*assessed my condition*
95	Of bare distress hath ta'en from me the show	
	Of smooth civility. Yet am I inland bred,[9]	
	And know some nurture. But forbear, I say.	
	He dies that touches any of this fruit	
	Till I and my affairs are answerèd.°	*satisfied*
100 JAQUES	An° you will not be answered with reason, I must die.	*If*
DUKE SENIOR	What would you have? Your gentleness° shall force	*gentility; kindness*
	More than your force move us to gentleness.	
ORLANDO	I almost die for food; and let me have it.	
DUKE SENIOR	Sit down and feed, and welcome to our table.	
105 ORLANDO	Speak you so gently? Pardon me, I pray you.	
	I thought that all things had been savage here,	
	And therefore put I on the countenance	
	Of stern commandment. But whate'er you are	
	That in this desert inaccessible,	
110	Under the shade of melancholy boughs,	

7. In return for a coin of no value (normally used for reckoning sums).
8. Swollen sores and boils that have come to a head. Both were symptoms of venereal disease.

9. Brought up in a civilized way—that is, raised in the country's interior regions rather than near its supposedly savage borders.

Lose and neglect the creeping hours of time,
If ever you have looked on better days,
If ever been where bells have knolled° to church,   *summoned*
If ever sat at any good man's feast,
115   If ever from your eyelids wiped a tear,
And know what 'tis to pity, and be pitied,
Let gentleness my strong enforcement be,[1]
In the which hope I blush, and hide my sword.
DUKE SENIOR   True is it that we have seen better days,
120   And have with holy bell been knolled to church,
And sat at good men's feasts, and wiped our eyes
Of drops that sacred pity hath engendered.
And therefore sit you down in gentleness,
And take upon command° what help we have   *at your will*
125   That to your wanting may be ministered.
ORLANDO   Then but forbear your food a little while
Whiles, like a doe, I go to find my fawn
And give it food. There is an old poor man
Who after me hath many a weary step
130   Limped in pure love. Till he be first sufficed,°   *satisfied*
Oppressed with two weak° evils, age and hunger,   *enfeebling*
I will not touch a bit.
DUKE SENIOR   Go find him out,
And we will nothing waste° till you return.   *consume*
ORLANDO   I thank ye; and be blessed for your good comfort!
                             [Exit]
135   DUKE SENIOR   Thou seest we are not all alone unhappy.
This wide and universal theatre
Presents more woeful pageants° than the scene   *spectacles*
Wherein we play in.
JAQUES   All the world's a stage,
And all the men and women merely players.
140   They have their exits and their entrances,
And one man in his time plays many parts,
His acts being seven ages. At first the infant,
Mewling° and puking in the nurse's arms.   *Crying*
Then the whining schoolboy with his satchel
145   And shining morning face, creeping like snail
Unwillingly to school. And then the lover,
Sighing like furnace,[2] with a woeful ballad
Made to his mistress' eyebrow. Then, a soldier,
Full of strange oaths, and bearded like the pard,[3]
150   Jealous in honour,[4] sudden, and quick in quarrel,
Seeking the bubble reputation
Even in the cannon's mouth. And then the justice,
In fair round belly with good capon[5] lined,°   *filled; stuffed*
With eyes severe and beard of formal cut,
155   Full of wise saws° and modern° instances;   *sayings / trite*
And so he plays his part. The sixth age shifts

---

1. Let natural kindness or gentility be what compels your compassion.
2. Emitting sighs as a furnace emits smoke.
3. Leopard. The soldier's bristling mustache is being compared to the leopard's whiskers.
4. Vigilant in matters of honor.
5. A cock, castrated and fattened as a delicacy (proverbially, a bribe for magistrates).

Into the lean and slippered pantaloon,[6]
With spectacles on nose and pouch on side,
His youthful hose, well saved, a world too wide
160 For his shrunk shank,° and his big, manly voice,　　　　　　*calf*
Turning again toward childish treble, pipes
And whistles in his° sound. Last scene of all,　　　　　　　　*its*
That ends this strange, eventful history,
Is second childishness and mere° oblivion,　　　　　　　　*complete*
165 Sans° teeth, sans eyes, sans taste, sans everything.　　　　*Without*
　　　　Enter ORLANDO [*bearing*] ADAM
DUKE SENIOR　Welcome. Set down your venerable burden
　　And let him feed.
ORLANDO　I thank you most for him.
ADAM　So had you need;
170 I scarce can speak to thank you for myself.
DUKE SENIOR　Welcome. Fall to. I will not trouble you
　　As yet to question you about your fortunes.
　　Give us some music, and, good cousin, sing.
AMIENS [*sings*][7]　　　Blow, blow, thou winter wind,
175 　　　　　　Thou art not so unkind
　　　　　　　　As man's ingratitude.
　　　　　　Thy tooth is not so keen,
　　　　　　Because thou art not seen,
　　　　　　　　Although thy breath be rude.°　　　　*rough*
180 　　　　Hey-ho, sing hey-ho, unto the green holly.[8]
　　　　Most friendship is feigning, most loving, mere folly.
　　　　　　Then hey-ho, the holly;
　　　　　　This life is most jolly.

　　　　　　Freeze, freeze, thou bitter sky,
185 　　　　　　That dost not bite so nigh°　　　　　　*closely*
　　　　　　　　As benefits forgot.
　　　　　　Though thou the waters warp,°　　*cause to contract; freeze*
　　　　　　Thy sting is not so sharp
　　　　　　　　As friend remembered not.
190 　　　　Hey-ho, sing hey-ho, unto the green holly.
　　　　Most friendship is feigning, most loving, mere folly.
　　　　　　Then hey-ho, the holly;
　　　　　　This life is most jolly.
DUKE SENIOR [*to* ORLANDO]　If that you were the good Sir Rowland's son,
195 As you have whispered faithfully you were,
And as mine eye doth his effigies° witness　　　　　　　*likeness*
Most truly limned° and living in your face,　　　　　*portrayed*
Be truly welcome hither. I am the Duke
That loved your father. The residue of your fortune,
200 Go to my cave and tell me. [*To* ADAM] Good old man,
Thou art right welcome, as thy master is.—
[*To* LORDS] Support him by the arm. [*To* ORLANDO] Give me your hand,
And let me all your fortunes understand.　　　　*Exeunt*

---

6. A foolish old man named after a figure in *commedia dell'arte*, Italian popular comedy.
7. Again, F does not indicate who sings this song. It is usually assigned to Amiens.
8. The evergreen associated with English holiday festivities.

3.1

Enter DUKE [FREDERICK], *Lords, and* OLIVER

DUKE FREDERICK   Not see him since? Sir, sir, that cannot be.
But were I not the better part made° mercy,   composed of
I should not seek an absent argument°   subject
Of my revenge, thou present. But look to it:
5   Find out thy brother wheresoe'er he is.
Seek him with candle.° Bring him, dead or living,   diligently
Within this twelvemonth, or turn° thou no more   return
To seek a living in our territory.
Thy lands, and all things that thou dost call thine
10 Worth seizure, do we seize into our hands
Till thou canst quit° thee by thy brother's mouth   acquit
Of what we think against thee.
OLIVER   O that your highness knew my heart in this.
I never loved my brother in my life.
DUKE FREDERICK   More villain thou. [*To Lords*] Well, push
15   him out of doors,
And let my officers of such a nature°   whose job it is
Make an extent° upon his house and lands.   a writ of seizure
Do this expediently,° and turn° him going. *Exeunt [severally]*   quickly / set

3.2

Enter ORLANDO [with a paper]

ORLANDO   Hang there, my verse, in witness of my love;
And thou thrice-crownèd queen of night,[1] survey
With thy chaste eye, from thy pale sphere above,
Thy huntress' name° that my full life doth sway.°   (Rosalind) / rule
5   O Rosalind, these trees shall be my books,
And in their barks my thoughts I'll character°   inscribe
That every eye which in this forest looks
Shall see thy virtue witnessed everywhere.
Run, run, Orlando; carve on every tree
10 The fair, the chaste, and unexpressive° she.   *Exit*[2]   inexpressible
Enter CORIN *and* [TOUCHSTONE *the*] *clown*
CORIN   And how like you this shepherd's life, Master Touchstone?
TOUCHSTONE   Truly, shepherd, in respect of° itself, it is a good   with regard to
life; but in respect that it is a shepherd's life, it is naught.° In   worthless
respect that it is solitary, I like it very well; but in respect that it
15 is private, it is a very vile life. Now in respect it is in the fields,
it pleaseth me well; but in respect it is not in the court, it is
tedious. As it is a spare° life, look you, it fits my humour° well;   frugal / temperament
but as there is no more plenty in it, it goes much against my
stomach.° Hast any philosophy in thee, shepherd?   inclination
20 CORIN   No more but that I know the more one sickens, the worse
at ease he is, and that he that wants° money, means, and con-   lacks
tent is without three good friends; that the property of rain is to

---

3.1   Location: Duke Frederick's court.
3.2   Location: The remaining scenes of the play take place in the Forest of Ardenne.
1.   The goddess who ruled on earth as Diana, patron of chastity and of the hunt; in the heavens as Cynthia, Phoebe, or Luna, goddess of the moon; and in the underworld as Hecate.

2. Orlando's appearance at lines 1–10 is self-contained and could form a separate scene. However, the ensuing conversation between Corin and Touchstone appears to take place on the same spot where Orlando has just stood, making the action continuous. This edition, like F, makes Orlando's lines part of the longer scene involving Corin, Touchstone, and eventually Rosalind and others.

wet, and fire to burn; that good pasture makes fat sheep; and
that a great cause of the night is lack of the sun; that he that
25 hath learned no wit by nature nor art may complain° of good   *lament his lack*
breeding or comes of a very dull kindred.
TOUCHSTONE   Such a one is a natural philosopher.[3] Wast ever in
court, shepherd?
CORIN   No, truly.
30 TOUCHSTONE   Then thou art damned.
CORIN   Nay, I hope.
TOUCHSTONE   Truly thou art damned, like an ill-roasted egg, all
on one side.
CORIN   For not being at court? Your reason?
35 TOUCHSTONE   Why, if thou never wast at court thou never sawest
good manners.° If thou never sawest good manners, then thy   *etiquette; morals*
manners must be wicked, and wickedness is sin, and sin is dam-
nation. Thou art in a parlous° state, shepherd.   *perilous*
CORIN   Not a whit, Touchstone. Those that are good manners at
40 the court are as ridiculous in the country as the behaviour of
the country is most mockable at the court. You told me you
salute not at the court but° you kiss your hands. That courtesy   *unless*
would be uncleanly if courtiers were shepherds.
TOUCHSTONE   Instance,° briefly; come, instance.   *An example*
45 CORIN   Why, we are still° handling our ewes, and their fells,° you   *constantly / skins*
know, are greasy.
TOUCHSTONE   Why, do not your courtier's hands sweat? And is
not the grease of a mutton as wholesome as the sweat of a man?
Shallow, shallow. A better instance, I say. Come.
50 CORIN   Besides, our hands are hard.
TOUCHSTONE   Your lips will feel them the sooner. Shallow again.
A more sounder instance. Come.
CORIN   And they are often tarred over with the surgery of our
sheep;[4] and would you have us kiss tar? The courtier's hands
55 are perfumed with civet.[5]
TOUCHSTONE   Most shallow, man. Thou worms' meat in respect
of° a good piece of flesh indeed, learn of the wise, and per-   *in comparison with*
pend:° civet is of a baser birth than tar, the very uncleanly flux°   *consider / discharge*
of a cat. Mend° the instance, shepherd.   *Improve*
60 CORIN   You have too courtly a wit for me. I'll rest.
TOUCHSTONE   Wilt thou rest damned? God help thee, shallow
man. God make incision in thee, thou art raw.[6]
CORIN   Sir, I am a true labourer. I earn that° I eat, get° that I   *what / make*
wear; owe no man hate, envy no man's happiness; glad of other
65 men's good, content with my harm;° and the greatest of my   *misfortune*
pride is to see my ewes graze and my lambs suck.
TOUCHSTONE   That is another simple° sin in you, to bring the   *simpleminded*
ewes and the rams together, and to offer° to get your living by   *undertake*
the copulation of cattle; to be bawd to a bell-wether,[7] and to
70 betray a she-lamb of a twelve-month to a crooked-pated old

---

3. A born philosopher; a philosopher who studies natural phenomena; a fool.
4. Referring to the practice of treating sheep wounds
with tar.
5. A musk-scented substance obtained from the anal
glands of certain cats.

6. Make a cut to let blood (and thus cure you of your
"raw"ness, or inexperience); make a cut to score you, as
raw meat was scored in preparation for cooking.
7. The leading sheep of a flock, who usually wore a
bell.

cuckoldly ram,[8] out of all reasonable match. If thou beest not damned for this, the devil himself will have no shepherds.[9] I cannot see else how thou shouldst scape.

CORIN Here comes young Master Ganymede, my new mistress's
75 brother.

Enter ROSALIND [*as Ganymede*]

ROSALIND [*reads*] 'From the east to western Ind°   *Indies*
    No jewel is like Rosalind.
    Her worth being mounted on the wind
    Through all the world bears Rosalind.
80   All the pictures fairest lined°   *drawn*
    Are but black to° Rosalind.   *compared to*
    Let no face be kept in mind
    But the fair of Rosalind.'

TOUCHSTONE I'll rhyme you so eight years together, dinners, and
85 suppers, and sleeping-hours excepted. It is the right butter-
women's rank to market.[1]

ROSALIND Out, fool.

TOUCHSTONE For a taste:
    If a hart° do lack a hind,°   *male deer / female deer*
90   Let him seek out Rosalind.
    If the cat will after kind,°   *act naturally; mate*
    So, be sure, will Rosalind.
    Wintered garments must be lined,[2]
    So must slender Rosalind.
95   They that reap must sheaf and bind,
    Then to cart[3] with Rosalind.
    'Sweetest nut hath sourest rind',
    Such a nut is Rosalind.
    He that sweetest rose will find
100   Must find love's prick,° and Rosalind.   *thorn; penis*
This is the very false gallop of verses.° Why do you infect your-   *way verses canter on*
self with them?

ROSALIND Peace, you dull fool, I found them on a tree.

TOUCHSTONE Truly, the tree yields bad fruit.

105 ROSALIND I'll graft it with you,° and then I shall graft it with a   *(punning on "yew")*
medlar;[4] then it will be the earliest fruit i'th' country, for you'll
be rotten ere you be half-ripe, and that's the right° virtue of the   *true*
medlar.

TOUCHSTONE You have said; but whether wisely or no, let the
110 forest judge.

Enter CELIA [*as Aliena*], *with a writing*

ROSALIND Peace, here comes my sister, reading. Stand aside.

CELIA [*reads*] 'Why should this a desert be?
    For it is unpeopled? No.
    Tongues I'll hang on every tree,
115   That shall civil° sayings show.   *civilized*

8. Cuckolds, men whose wives were sexually unfaithful, supposedly wore horns to signify their shame. The
ram may *make* cuckolds—that is, be lecherous.
crooked-pated: with crooked horns.
9. It will be because the devil refuses to admit shepherds into hell.
1. *It . . . market:* The rhymes are truly like a stream of
dairywomen going to market at the same time. Such
women were proverbially talkative.

2. Clothes worn in winter must be stuffed with material, with a pun on "lined" as meaning "mated," used
especially of female animals.
3. A cart on which harvests were transported to the
market; a cart on which women accused of prostitution
or other forms of disorderly conduct were transported
and exposed to public abuse.
4. A tree whose fruit was not ripe until it was so soft as
to be rotten, with a pun on "meddler," one who meddles.

Some, how brief the life of man
    Runs his erring° pilgrimage,   *wandering*
That the stretching of a span
    Buckles in his sum of age.[5]
120   Some of violated vows
    'Twixt the souls of friend and friend.
But upon the fairest boughs,
    Or at every sentence end,
Will I 'Rosalinda' write,
125   Teaching all that read to know
The quintessence of every sprite°   *spirit; soul*
    Heaven would in little show.[6]
Therefore heaven nature charged
    That one body should be filled
130   With all graces wide-enlarged.[7]
    Nature presently° distilled   *at once*
Helen's cheek, but not her heart,[8]
    Cleopatra's[9] majesty,
Atalanta's better part,[1]
135   Sad Lucretia's modesty.[2]
Thus Rosalind of many parts
    By heavenly synod° was devised   *assembly*
Of many faces, eyes, and hearts
    To have the touches° dearest prized.   *traits*
140   Heaven would that she these gifts should have
And I to live and die her slave.'

ROSALIND O most gentle Jupiter! What tedious homily of love
have you wearied your parishioners withal, and never cried
'Have patience, good people.'

145 CELIA How now, back, friends. Shepherd, go off a little. Go with
him, sirrah.

TOUCHSTONE Come, shepherd, let us make an honourable
retreat, though not with bag and baggage, yet with scrip and
scrippage.[3]   *Exit [with* CORIN]

150 CELIA Didst thou hear these verses?

ROSALIND O yes, I heard them all, and more, too, for some of
them had in them more feet° than the verses would bear.   *metrical units*

CELIA That's no matter; the feet might bear° the verses.   *carry*

ROSALIND Ay, but the feet were lame, and could not bear them-
155 selves without° the verse, and therefore stood lamely in the   *out of*
verse.

CELIA But didst thou hear without wondering how thy name
should be° hanged and carved upon these trees?   *came to be*

---

5. *the stretching . . . age:* the width of an open hand (a "span") encompasses an entire lifetime. A comparison derived from verses appearing in Elizabethan prayer books.
6. Which heaven would portray in miniature, or through one individual (Rosalind).
7. Graces that otherwise have been widely distributed.
8. The features, but not the false heart, of Helen of Troy. Supposedly Helen's abduction by Paris from her husband, Menelaus, was the event that precipitated the Trojan War. In some accounts, Helen is blamed for her abduction and so could be said to have a false heart.
9. Queen of Egypt and the tragic heroine of Shake-

speare's *Antony and Cleopatra.*
1. In Greek myth, Atalanta was a fleet-footed and chaste hunter who challenged her suitors to a race. She was only defeated when one of them dropped three golden apples, which she stopped to pick up. The reference here is possibly to her beauty or her speed, rather than her greed.
2. Lucretia killed herself to save her honor after being raped by Tarquin (a story told by Shakespeare in *The Rape of Lucrece*).
3. Though not with the belongings retained by an army in retreat, yet with a shepherd's pouch and its contents.

ROSALIND I was seven of the nine days out of the wonder[4] before
160 you came; for look here what I found on a palm-tree; [*showing
CELIA the verses*] I was never so berhymed since Pythagoras'
time that I was an Irish rat,[5] which I can hardly remember.

CELIA Trow you° who hath done this?   *Can you imagine*

ROSALIND Is it a man?

165 CELIA And a chain that you once wore about his neck. Change
you colour?

ROSALIND I prithee, who?

CELIA O Lord, Lord, it is a hard matter for friends to meet. But
mountains may be removed with° earthquakes, and so   *moved by*
170 encounter.

ROSALIND Nay, but who is it?

CELIA Is it possible?

ROSALIND Nay, I prithee now with most petitionary vehemence,
tell me who it is.

175 CELIA O wonderful, wonderful, and most wonderful-wonderful,
and yet again wonderful, and after that out of all whooping![6]

ROSALIND Good my complexion![7] Dost thou think, though I am
caparisoned° like a man, I have a doublet and hose in my dispo-   *dressed*
sition? One inch of delay more is a South Sea of discovery.[8] I
180 prithee tell me who is it quickly, and speak apace.° I would   *at once*
thou couldst stammer, that thou mightst pour this concealed
man out of thy mouth as wine comes out of a narrow-mouthed
bottle—either too much at once, or none at all. I prithee, take
the cork out of thy mouth, that I may drink thy tidings.

185 CELIA So you may put a man in your belly.°   *stomach; womb*

ROSALIND Is he of God's making? What manner of man? Is his
head worth a hat? Or his chin worth a beard?

CELIA Nay, he hath but a little beard.

ROSALIND Why, God will send more, if the man will be thank-
190 ful. Let me stay° the growth of his beard, if thou delay me not   *wait for*
the knowledge of his chin.

CELIA It is young Orlando, that tripped up the wrestler's heels
and your heart both in an instant.

ROSALIND Nay, but the devil take mocking. Speak sad brow and
195 true maid.[9]

CELIA I'faith, coz, 'tis he.

ROSALIND Orlando?

CELIA Orlando.

ROSALIND Alas the day, what shall I do with my doublet and
200 hose! What did he when thou sawest him? What said he? How
looked he? Wherein went he?° What makes he here? Did he   *What was he wearing*
ask for me? Where remains he? How parted he with thee? And
when shalt thou see him again? Answer me in one word.

CELIA You must borrow me Gargantua's[1] mouth first, 'tis a word

---

4. Referring to the proverbial "nine days' wonder," a
novelty that caused amazement.
5. I was never so overwhelmed with rhyme since the
days of the ancient Greeks, when I was an Irish rat.
Alluding to Pythagoras's doctrine of the transmigration
of souls and to the popular belief in England that Irish
bards were capable of rhyming rats to death.
6. After that, beyond what all shouts of astonishment
can express.
7. An expression of impatience. "Complexion" means

"temperament," believed to be caused by the particular
mixture of the four humors in one's body. Her meaning
seems to be: Pay attention to my womanly temperament
(which is impatient)!
8. More delay will seem as infinite as a voyage of discovery to the South Seas.
9. Speak seriously and as a virtuous woman or on your
honor as a virgin.
1. A voracious giant famous in French folklore and
from the writings of Rabelais.

205   too great for any mouth of this age's size. To say ay and no to
these particulars is more than to answer in a catechism.[2]

ROSALIND   But doth he know that I am in this forest, and in
man's apparel? Looks he as freshly as he did the day he wrestled?

210   CELIA   It is as easy to count atomies° as to resolve the proposi-   *specks (of dust)*
tions° of a lover; but take a taste of my finding him, and relish   *answer the questions*
it with good observance.[3] I found him under a tree, like a
dropped acorn—

ROSALIND   It may well be called Jove's tree[4] when it drops forth
215   such fruit.

CELIA   Give me audience, good madam.

ROSALIND   Proceed.

CELIA   There lay he, stretched along like a wounded knight—

ROSALIND   Though it be pity to see such a sight, it well becomes
220   the ground.

CELIA   Cry 'holla'° to thy tongue, I prithee: it curvets° unseason-   *hold / leaps about*
ably.—He was furnished° like a hunter—   *dressed*

ROSALIND   O ominous—he comes to kill my heart.

CELIA   I would sing my song without a burden;° thou bringest   *refrain*
225   me out of tune.

ROSALIND   Do you not know I am a woman? When I think, I
must speak.—Sweet, say on.

               Enter ORLANDO *and* JAQUES

CELIA   You bring me out.° Soft, comes he not here?   *make me lose the tune*

ROSALIND   'Tis he. Slink by, and note him.

230   [ROSALIND *and* CELIA *stand aside*]

JAQUES [*to* ORLANDO] I thank you for your company, but, good
faith, I had as lief° have been myself alone.   *as willingly*

ORLANDO   And so had I. But yet for fashion' sake, I thank you too
for your society.

JAQUES   God b'wi'you;° let's meet as little as we can.   *Good-bye*

235   ORLANDO   I do desire we may be better strangers.

JAQUES   I pray you mar no more trees with writing love-songs in
their barks.

ORLANDO   I pray you mar no more of my verses with reading
them ill-favouredly.°   *unsympathetically*

240   JAQUES   Rosalind is your love's name?

ORLANDO   Yes, just.

JAQUES   I do not like her name.

ORLANDO   There was no thought of pleasing you when she was
christened.

245   JAQUES   What stature is she of?

ORLANDO   Just as high as my heart.

JAQUES   You are full of pretty answers. Have you not been
acquainted with goldsmiths' wives, and conned them out of
rings?[5]

250   ORLANDO   Not so; but I answer you right painted cloth,[6] from
whence you have studied your questions.

---

2. A summary, in question-and-answer form, of basic
tenets of religious doctrine. In Shakespeare's time, all
members of the Church of England learned to recite
such a catechism.
3. And enhance its flavor by paying careful attention.
4. The oak was traditionally viewed as sacred to Jove, the
god of thunder, and was said therefore to be often struck

by lightning.
5. Romantic verses were often inscribed on rings sold
in shops managed by the wives of goldsmiths; with a
pun on "rings" as a slang term for "vaginas."
6. I answer you in the style of the pithy sayings issuing
from the mouths of figures in painted wall hangings (a
popular and inexpensive form of interior decoration).

JAQUES   You have a nimble wit; I think 'twas made of Atalanta's
heels.[7] Will you sit down with me, and we two will rail against
our mistress the world, and all our misery?

255   ORLANDO   I will chide no breather° in the world but myself,   *person*
against whom I know most faults.

JAQUES   The worst fault you have is to be in love.

ORLANDO   'Tis a fault I will not change for your best virtue. I am
weary of you.

260   JAQUES   By my troth, I was seeking for a fool when I found you.

ORLANDO   He is drowned in the brook. Look but in, and you
shall see him.

JAQUES   There I shall see mine own figure.

ORLANDO   Which I take to be either a fool or a cipher.[8]

265   JAQUES   I'll tarry no longer with you. Farewell, good Signor
Love.

ORLANDO   I am glad of your departure. Adieu, good Monsieur
Melancholy.   [*Exit* JAQUES][9]

ROSALIND [*to* CELIA]   I will speak to him like a saucy lackey, and

270   under that habit° play the knave with him. [*To* ORLANDO] Do   *guise; disguise*
you hear, forester?

ORLANDO   Very well. What would you?

ROSALIND   I pray you, what is't o'clock?

ORLANDO   You should ask me what time o' day. There's no clock

275   in the forest.

ROSALIND   Then there is no true lover in the forest, else sighing
every minute and groaning every hour would detect° the lazy   *reveal*
foot of time as well as a clock.

ORLANDO   And why not the swift foot of time? Had not that been

280   as proper?

ROSALIND   By no means, sir. Time travels in divers paces with
divers persons. I'll tell you who time ambles withal,° who time   *with*
trots withal, who time gallops withal, and who he stands still
withal.

285   ORLANDO   I prithee, who doth he trot withal?

ROSALIND   Marry, he trots hard° with a young maid between the   *uncomfortably*
contract of her marriage and the day it is solemnized. If the
interim be but a se'nnight,° time's pace is so hard that it seems   *week*
the length of seven year.

290   ORLANDO   Who ambles time withal?

ROSALIND   With a priest that lacks Latin, and a rich man that
hath not the gout; for the one sleeps easily because he cannot
study, and the other lives merrily because he feels no pain, the
one lacking the burden of lean and wasteful° learning, the   *weakening*

295   other knowing no burden of heavy tedious penury.° These time   *poverty*
ambles withal.

ORLANDO   Who doth he gallop withal?

ROSALIND   With a thief to the gallows; for though he go as softly°   *slowly*
as foot can fall, he thinks himself too soon there.

300   ORLANDO   Who stays it still withal?

---

7. See note to 3.2.134.
8. A zero; punning on "figure" (line 263) as meaning
"numeral."
9. Editors usually give Jaques an exit here, although
none is indicated in F. It would not be out of character,
however, for Jaques to remain onstage in the background
during Orlando and Rosalind's exchange (as he does during Touchstone's courting of Audrey in 3.3) and to exit
with them at the end of the scene.

ROSALIND With lawyers in the vacation; for they sleep between
term[1] and term, and then they perceive not how time moves.

ORLANDO Where dwell you, pretty youth?

ROSALIND With this shepherdess, my sister, here in the skirts° of   *edges*
305 the forest, like fringe upon a petticoat.

ORLANDO Are you native of this place?

ROSALIND As the coney° that you see dwell where she is kin-   *rabbit*
dled.°   *born*

ORLANDO Your accent is something finer than you could pur-
310 chase° in so removed° a dwelling.   *acquire / remote*

ROSALIND I have been told so of many; but indeed an old religious uncle of mine taught me to speak, who was in his youth
an inland man; one that knew courtship° too well, for there he   *court life; wooing*
fell in love. I have heard him read many lectures against it, and
315 I thank God I am not a woman, to be touched with so many
giddy offences as he hath generally taxed their whole sex
withal.

ORLANDO Can you remember any of the principal evils that he
laid to the charge of women?

320 ROSALIND There were none principal; they were all like one
another as halfpence are, every one fault seeming monstrous
till his fellow-fault came to match it.

ORLANDO I prithee, recount some of them.

ROSALIND No. I will not cast away my physic but° on those that   *my medicine except*
325 are sick. There is a man haunts the forest that abuses our young
plants with carving Rosalind on their barks; hangs odes upon
hawthorns and elegies on brambles; all, forsooth, deifying the
name of Rosalind. If I could meet that fancy-monger,° I would   *dealer in love*
give him some good counsel, for he seems to have the quotid-
330 ian[2] of love upon him.

ORLANDO I am he that is so love-shaked. I pray you, tell me your
remedy.

ROSALIND There is none of my uncle's marks upon you. He
taught me how to know a man in love, in which cage of rushes[3]
335 I am sure you are not prisoner.

ORLANDO What were his marks?

ROSALIND A lean cheek, which you have not; a blue eye[4] and
sunken, which you have not; an unquestionable° spirit, which   *a taciturn*
you have not; a beard neglected, which you have not—but I
340 pardon you for that, for simply your having in beard° is a   *such beard as you have*
younger brother's revenue.[5] Then your hose should be ungar-
tered, your bonnet unbanded,° your sleeve unbuttoned, your   *lacking a band*
shoe untied, and everything about you demonstrating a careless
desolation. But you are no such man. You are rather point-
345 device° in your accoutrements, as loving yourself than seeming   *extremely precise*
the lover of any other.

ORLANDO Fair youth, I would I could make thee believe I love.

ROSALIND Me believe it? You may as soon make her that you love
believe it, which I warrant she is apter to do than to confess
350 she does. That is one of the points in the which women still°   *always*

---

1. *terms:* limited periods of time in which the courts
were in session and when lawyers were therefore busy.
Vacation came between terms.
2. Daily recurring fever said to be a sign of love.
3. A prison easy to escape from.

4. An eye ringed with dark circles (suggesting insom-
nia).
5. Younger brothers traditionally received small inher-
itances, here suggesting that Orlando's beard is likewise
thin or small.

give the lie to their consciences. But in good sooth,° are you   *truth*
he that hangs the verses on the trees wherein Rosalind is so
admired?

ORLANDO   I swear to thee, youth, by the white hand of Rosalind,
355   I am that he, that unfortunate he.

ROSALIND   But are you so much in love as your rhymes speak?

ORLANDO   Neither rhyme nor reason can express how much.

ROSALIND   Love is merely a madness, and I tell you, deserves as
well a dark house and a whip as madmen do;[6] and the rea-
360   son why they° are not so punished and cured is that the lunacy   *(lovers)*
is so ordinary that the whippers are in love too. Yet I profess
curing it by counsel.

ORLANDO   Did you ever cure any so?

ROSALIND   Yes, one; and in this manner. He was to imagine me
365   his love, his mistress; and I set him every day to woo me. At
which time would I, being but a moonish° youth, grieve, be   *changeable*
effeminate,[7] changeable, longing and liking, proud, fantasti-
cal,° apish,° shallow, inconstant, full of tears, full of smiles; for   *capricious / affected*
every passion something, and for no passion truly anything, as
370   boys and women are for the most part cattle of this colour—
would now like him, now loathe him; then entertain him,°   *treat him kindly*
then forswear him; now weep for him, then spit at him, that I
drave° my suitor from his mad humour of love to a living   *drove*
humour° of madness, which was to forswear the full stream of   *an actual condition*
375   the world and to live in a nook merely monastic.° And thus I   *as a hermit*
cured him, and this way will I take upon me to wash your liver[8]
as clean as a sound sheep's heart, that there shall not be one
spot of love in't.

ORLANDO   I would not be cured, youth.

380   ROSALIND   I would cure you if you would but call me Rosalind
and come every day to my cot,° and woo me.   *cottage*

ORLANDO   Now by the faith of my love, I will. Tell me where it
is.

ROSALIND   Go with me to it, and I'll show it you. And by the way
385   you shall tell me where in the forest you live. Will you go?

ORLANDO   With all my heart, good youth.

ROSALIND   Nay, you must call me Rosalind.—Come, sister. Will
you go?   *Exeunt*

3.3

Enter [TOUCHSTONE *the*] *clown and* AUDREY, [*followed
by*] JAQUES

TOUCHSTONE   Come apace, good Audrey. I will fetch up your
goats, Audrey. And how, Audrey, am I the man yet? Doth my
simple feature° content you?   *appearance*

AUDREY   Your features, Lord warrant° us—what features?   *defend*

5   TOUCHSTONE   I am here with thee and thy goats as the most
capricious° poet honest Ovid was among the Goths.[1]   *witty; lascivious*

---

6. Confinement in a dark room and whipping, common
treatments for insanity, were believed to rid the insane
of the devils that possessed them.

7. Like a woman; sensual or self-indulgent; a term
often used to deride men perceived as excessive in their
sexual interest in women.

8. In Renaissance medical theory, the seat of the passions.

3.3

1. Punning on "goats / Goths," which were similarly
pronounced, and referring to the Roman poet's exile
among the Goths.

JAQUES [*aside*]   O knowledge ill-inhabited; worse than Jove in a
thatched house.[2]

TOUCHSTONE   When a man's verses cannot be understood, nor a
10   man's good wit seconded with° the forward child, understand-   *supported by*
ing, it strikes a man more dead than a great reckoning° in a   *tavern bill*
little room.[3] Truly, I would the gods had made thee poetical.

AUDREY   I do not know what 'poetical' is. Is it honest in deed
and word? Is it a true thing?

15   TOUCHSTONE   No, truly; for the truest poetry is the most
feigning,° and lovers are given to poetry; and what they swear   *imaginative; false*
in poetry it may be said, as lovers, they do feign.

AUDREY   Do you wish, then, that the gods had made me poetical?

TOUCHSTONE   I do, truly; for thou swearest to me thou art hon-
20   est.° Now if thou wert a poet, I might have some hope thou   *chaste*
didst feign.

AUDREY   Would you not have me honest?

TOUCHSTONE   No, truly, unless thou wert hard-favoured;° for   *ugly*
honesty coupled to beauty is to have honey a sauce to sugar.

25   JAQUES [*aside*]   A material° fool.   *full of matter or sense*

AUDREY   Well, I am not fair, and therefore I pray the gods make
me honest.

TOUCHSTONE   Truly, and to cast away honesty upon a foul slut
were to put good meat into an unclean dish.

30   AUDREY   I am not a slut, though I thank the gods I am foul.[4]

TOUCHSTONE   Well, praised be the gods for thy foulness. Slut-
tishness may come hereafter. But be it as it may be, I will marry
thee; and to that end I have been with Sir Oliver Martext, the
vicar of the next village, who hath promised to meet me in this
35   place of the forest, and to couple us.

JAQUES [*aside*]   I would fain° see this meeting.   *gladly*

AUDREY   Well, the gods give us joy.

TOUCHSTONE   Amen.—A man may, if he were of a fearful heart,
stagger° in this attempt; for here we have no temple but the   *hesitate*
40   wood, no assembly but horn-beasts.[5] But what though? Courage. As horns are odious, they are necessary. It is said many a
man knows no end of his goods.[6] Right: many a man has good
horns, and knows no end of them. Well, that is the dowry of
his wife, 'tis none of his own getting.[7] Horns? Even so. Poor
45   men alone? No, no; the noblest deer hath them as huge as the
rascal.° Is the single man therefore blessed? No. As a walled   *young or lean deer*
town is more worthier than a village, so is the forehead of a
married man more honourable than the bare brow of a bache-
lor. And by how much defence° is better than no skill, by so   *skill in self-defense*
50   much is a horn more precious than to want.°   *to lack (one)*

Enter SIR OLIVER MARTEXT

Here comes Sir Oliver.—Sir Oliver Martext, you are well met.
Will you dispatch us here under this tree, or shall we go with
you to your chapel?

---

2. In *Metamorphoses* 8, Ovid tells how the king of the
gods was given shelter for a time in the humble
dwelling of Philemon and Baucis.
3. These lines have been taken to refer to the death in
1593 of Christopher Marlowe, a contemporary playwright, in a quarrel in a tavern over a bill.
4. Ugly. Audrey apparently takes "foul" as a term of
praise.

5. Horned beasts such as deer, goats, and the like that
inhabited the forest, with an allusion to the horns of the
cuckolded husband.
6. A proverbial expression suggesting a man so wealthy
he can't count all his money.
7. 'tis . . . *getting*: he is not responsible for the horns;
he is not responsible for conceiving his children (since
his wife has been sexually unfaithful).

SIR OLIVER MARTEXT   Is there none here to give the woman?
55   TOUCHSTONE   I will not take her on gift of any man.
SIR OLIVER MARTEXT   Truly she must be given, or the marriage
is not lawful.
JAQUES   [*coming forward*]   Proceed, proceed. I'll give her.
TOUCHSTONE   Good even, good Monsieur What-ye-call't. How
60   do you, sir? You are very well met. God'ield you for your last
company.[8] I am very glad to see you. Even a toy° in hand here,   *trifling matter*
sir.
       [JAQUES *removes his hat*]
Nay, pray be covered.°   *replace your hat*
JAQUES   Will you be married, motley?
65   TOUCHSTONE   As the ox hath his bow,° sir, the horse his curb,[9]   *yoke*
and the falcon her bells,[1] so man hath his desires; and as
pigeons bill,° so wedlock would be nibbling.   *rub bill to bill*
JAQUES   And will you, being a man of your breeding, be married
under a bush, like a beggar? Get you to church, and have a
70   good priest that can tell you what marriage is. This fellow will
but join you together as they join wainscot;° then one of you   *wood paneling*
will prove a shrunk panel and, like green timber, warp,° warp.   *go wrong; shrink*
TOUCHSTONE   I am not in the mind but° I were better to be mar-   *not sure but that*
ried of° him than of another, for he is not like to marry me   *by*
75   well, and not being well married, it will be a good excuse for
me hereafter to leave my wife.
JAQUES   Go thou with me, and let me counsel thee.
TOUCHSTONE   Come, sweet Audrey.
We must be married,° or we must live in bawdry.°   *(properly wed) / in sin*
80   Farewell, good Master Oliver. Not
                 O, sweet Oliver,
                 O, brave Oliver,
                 Leave me not behind thee[2]
       but
85   Wind° away,   *Go*
                 Begone, I say,
                 I will not to wedding with thee.
SIR OLIVER MARTEXT [*aside*]   'Tis no matter. Ne'er a fantastical
knave of them all shall flout me out of my calling.
                                          Exeunt

3.4
Enter ROSALIND [*as Ganymede*] *and* CELIA [*as Aliena*]
ROSALIND   Never talk to me. I will weep.
CELIA   Do, I prithee, but yet have the grace to consider that tears
do not become a man.
ROSALIND   But have I not cause to weep?
5   CELIA   As good cause as one would desire; therefore weep.
ROSALIND   His very hair is of the dissembling colour.[1]
CELIA   Something° browner than Judas's. Marry, his kisses are   *Somewhat*
Judas's own children.
ROSALIND   I'faith, his hair is of a good colour.

---

8. God yield you (a salutation meaning "May God
reward you") for your recent companionship.
9. A bit placed in the horse's mouth to control its
movements.
1. Bells attached to a falcon's legs before releasing it for

the hunt so that it might be easily reclaimed afterward.
2. Lines from a popular Elizabethan ballad.
3.4
1. Alluding to the tradition that Judas, the disciple who
betrayed Jesus, had red hair.

10 CELIA   An excellent colour. Your chestnut was ever the only
colour.

ROSALIND   And his kissing is as full of sanctity as the touch of
holy bread.[2]

CELIA   He hath bought a pair of cast° lips of Diana.[3] A nun of   *cast-off; sculpted*
15 winter's sisterhood° kisses not more religiously. The very ice of   *devoted to coldness*
chastity is in them.

ROSALIND   But why did he swear he would come this morning,
and comes not?

CELIA   Nay, certainly, there is no truth in him.

20 ROSALIND   Do you think so?

CELIA   Yes. I think he is not a pick-purse, nor a horse-stealer; but
for his verity° in love, I do think him as concave° as a covered   *truthfulness / hollow*
goblet, or a worm-eaten nut.

ROSALIND   Not true in love?

25 CELIA   Yes, when he is in. But I think he is not in.

ROSALIND   You have heard him swear downright he was.

CELIA   'Was' is not 'is'. Besides, the oath of a lover is no stronger
than the word of a tapster. They are both the confirmer of false
reckonings. He attends° here in the forest on the Duke your   *waits*
30 father.

ROSALIND   I met the Duke yesterday, and had much question°   *conversation*
with him. He asked me of what parentage I was. I told him, of
as good as he, so he laughed and let me go. But what talk we
of fathers when there is such a man as Orlando?

35 CELIA   O that's a brave° man. He writes brave verses, speaks   *splendid*
brave words, swears brave oaths, and breaks them bravely, quite
traverse,[4] athwart the heart of his lover, as a puny° tilter that   *an unskilled*
spurs his horse but° on one side breaks his staff, like a noble   *only*
goose.° But all's brave that youth mounts, and folly guides.   *fool*
40 Who comes here?

Enter CORIN

CORIN   Mistress and master, you have oft enquired
After the shepherd that complained of love
Who you saw sitting by me on the turf,
Praising the proud disdainful shepherdess
That was his mistress.

45 CELIA   Well, and what of him?

CORIN   If you will see a pageant truly played
Between the pale complexion of true love
And the red glow of scorn and proud disdain,[5]
Go hence a little, and I shall conduct you,
If you will mark° it.   *observe*

50 ROSALIND [*to* CELIA]   O come, let us remove.
The sight of lovers feedeth those in love.
[*To* CORIN] Bring us to this sight, and you shall say
I'll prove a busy actor in their play.   *Exeunt*

---

2. Referring to bread blessed after the Eucharist during Christian religious services and distributed to those
who did not take Communion.
3. The goddess of chastity. See note to 3.2.2.
4. Crossways. A term from jousting used to designate

the dishonorable practice of breaking one's lance
across, rather than directly against, an opponent's
shield.
5. Referring to the paleness of Silvius, the true lover,
and the red cheeks of the disdainful Phoebe.

3.5

Enter SILVIUS *and* PHOEBE

SILVIUS   Sweet Phoebe, do not scorn me, do not, Phoebe.
Say that you love me not, but say not so
In bitterness. The common executioner,
Whose heart th'accustomed sight of death makes hard,
5   Falls not° the axe upon the humbled neck   *Does not let fall*
But first begs° pardon. Will you sterner be   *Without first begging*
Than he that dies and lives by bloody drops?
         Enter ROSALIND [*as Ganymede*], CELIA [*as Aliena*], *and*
         CORIN [*and stand aside*]
PHOEBE [*to* SILVIUS]   I would not be thy executioner.
I fly thee for I would not injure thee.
10   Thou tell'st me there is murder in mine eye.
'Tis pretty, sure, and very probable
That eyes, that are the frail'st and softest things,
Who shut their coward gates on atomies,°   *dust motes*
Should be called tyrants, butchers, murderers.
15   Now I do frown on thee with all my heart,
And if mine eyes can wound, now let them kill thee.
Now counterfeit to swoon, why now fall down;
Or if thou canst not, O, for shame, for shame,
Lie not, to say mine eyes are murderers.
20   Now show the wound mine eye hath made in thee.
Scratch thee but with a pin, and there remains
Some scar of it. Lean upon a rush,
The cicatrice and capable impressure[1]
Thy palm some moment keeps. But now mine eyes,
25   Which I have darted at thee, hurt thee not;
Nor I am sure there is no force in eyes
That can do hurt.
SILVIUS   O dear Phoebe,
If ever—as that ever may be near—
30   You meet in some fresh cheek the power of fancy,°   *love*
Then shall you know the wounds invisible
That love's keen arrows make.
PHOEBE   But till that time
Come not thou near me. And when that time comes,
Afflict me with thy mocks, pity me not,
35   As till that time I shall not pity thee.
ROSALIND [*coming forward*]   And why, I pray you? Who might
                be your mother,
That you insult, exult, and all at once,°   *all in one breath*
Over the wretched? What though you have no beauty—
As, by my faith, I see no more in you
40   Than without candle may go dark to bed[2]—
Must you be therefore proud and pitiless?
Why, what means this? Why do you look on me?
I see no more in you than in the ordinary°   *common run*
Of nature's sale-work.°—'Od's my little life,[3]   *ready-made goods*
45   I think she means to tangle° my eyes, too.   *entrap*
No, faith, proud mistress, hope not after it.

3.5
1. The scarlike mark and the impression that the skin
receives.

2. *I see . . . bed:* I see you have not enough beauty to
light your way to bed without a candle.
3. An abbreviated version of the oath "God save my life."

'Tis not your inky brows, your black silk hair,
Your bugle° eyeballs, nor your cheek of cream,   *like black glass beads*
That can entame my spirits to your worship.°   *the worship of you*
50 [*To* SILVIUS] You, foolish shepherd, wherefore do you follow her
Like foggy south,° puffing with wind and rain?[4]   *south wind*
You are a thousand times a properer° man   *more attractive*
Than she a woman. 'Tis such fools as you
That makes the world full of ill-favoured° children.   *ugly*
55 'Tis not her glass° but you that flatters her,   *mirror*
And out of you° she sees herself more proper   *from you (as mirror)*
Than any of her lineaments can show her.
[*To* PHOEBE] But, mistress, know yourself; down on your knees
And thank heaven, fasting, for a good man's love;
60 For I must tell you friendly in your ear,
Sell when you can. You are not for all markets.
Cry the man mercy,° love him, take his offer;   *Beg his pardon*
Foul is most foul, being foul to be a scoffer.[5]—
So, take her to thee, shepherd. Fare you well.
65 PHOEBE Sweet youth, I pray you chide a year together.°   *without interruption*
I had rather hear you chide than this man woo.
ROSALIND [*to* PHOEBE] He's fallen in love with your foulness, [*to*
SILVIUS] and she'll fall in love with my anger. If it be so, as fast
as she answers thee with frowning looks, I'll sauce° her   *sharply rebuke*
70 with bitter words.
[*To* PHOEBE] Why look you so upon me?
PHOEBE For no ill will I bear you.
ROSALIND I pray you do not fall in love with me,
For I am falser than vows made in wine.°   *when drinking*
75 Besides, I like you not. If you will know my house,
'Tis at the tuft of olives,° here hard by.   *olive trees*
[*To* CELIA] Will you go, sister? [*To* SILVIUS] Shepherd, ply her
    hard.°—   *assail her vigorously*
Come, sister. [*To* PHOEBE] Shepherdess, look on him better,
And be not proud. Though all the world could see,
80 None could be so abused in sight as he.—
Come, to our flock.   *Exeunt* [ROSALIND, CELIA, *and* CORIN][6]
PHOEBE [*aside*] Dead shepherd,[7] now I find thy saw of might:°   *your saying powerful*
'Who ever loved that loved not at first sight?'
SILVIUS Sweet Phoebe—
PHOEBE   Ha, what sayst thou, Silvius?
85 SILVIUS Sweet Phoebe, pity me.
PHOEBE Why, I am sorry for thee, gentle Silvius.
SILVIUS Wherever sorrow is, relief would be.
If you do sorrow at my grief in love,
By giving love your sorrow and my grief
90 Were both extermined.°   *Would both be ended*
PHOEBE Thou hast my love, is not that neighbourly?[8]
SILVIUS I would have you.
PHOEBE   Why, that were covetousness.[9]

---

4. That is, with sighs and tears.
5. The ugly seem most ugly when they are abusive.
6. F marks a single exit for Rosalind here, but it is unlikely that Celia and Corin remain.
7. Referring to Christopher Marlowe, poet and playwright who died in 1593. Line 83 is taken from his poem *Hero and Leander*.

8. With a reference to Romans 13:9: "Thou shalt love thy neighbour as thyself."
9. With a reference to Exodus 20:17: "Thou shalt not covet thy neighbour's house, thou shalt not covet thy neighbour's wife, nor his manservant, nor his maidservant, nor his ox, nor his ass, nor any thing that is thy neighbour's."

Silvius, the time was that I hated thee;
And yet it is not° that I bear thee love.   *it has not yet happened*
95   But since that thou canst talk of love so well,
Thy company, which erst° was irksome to me,   *formerly*
I will endure; and I'll employ thee, too.
But do not look for further recompense
Than thine own gladness that thou art employed.
100 SILVIUS   So holy and so perfect is my love,
And I in such a poverty of grace,[1]
That I shall think it a most plenteous crop
To glean the broken ears° after the man   *(of corn)*
That the main harvest reaps. Loose now and then
105 A scattered° smile, and that I'll live upon.   *stray*
PHOEBE   Know'st thou the youth that spoke to me erewhile?
SILVIUS   Not very well, but I have met him oft,
And he hath bought the cottage and the bounds°   *pastures*
That the old Carlot once was master of.
110 PHOEBE   Think not I love him, though I ask for him.
'Tis but a peevish boy. Yet he talks well.
But what care I for words? Yet words do well
When he that speaks them pleases those that hear.
It is a pretty youth—not very pretty—
115 But sure he's proud; and yet his pride becomes him.
He'll make a proper° man. The best thing in him   *handsome*
Is his complexion; and faster than his tongue
Did make offence, his eye did heal it up.
He is not very tall; yet for his years he's tall.
120 His leg is but so-so; and yet 'tis well.
There was a pretty redness in his lip,
A little riper and more lusty-red
Than that mixed in his cheek. 'Twas just the difference
Betwixt the constant red and mingled damask.[2]
125 There be some women, Silvius, had they marked him
In parcels° as I did, would have gone near   *Item by item*
To fall in love with him; but for my part,
I love him not, nor hate him not. And yet
Have I more cause to hate him than to love him,
130 For what had he to do to chide at me?
He said mine eyes were black, and my hair black,
And now I am remembered, scorned at me.
I marvel why I answered not again.
But that's all one. Omittance is no quittance.[3]
135 I'll write to him a very taunting letter,
And thou shalt bear it. Wilt thou, Silvius?
SILVIUS   Phoebe, with all my heart.
PHOEBE   I'll write it straight.°   *immediately*
The matter's in my head and in my heart.
I will be bitter with him, and passing° short.   *extremely*
140 Go with me, Silvius.   *Exeunt*

---

1. And I so lacking in (your) favor.
2. *constant . . . damask:* uniform red and a mixture of
red and white characteristic of certain kinds of roses.

3. A proverbial expression meaning that a debt is not
canceled simply because one fails ("omits") to exact it.

4.1

Enter ROSALIND [*as Ganymede*], CELIA [*as Aliena*], *and*
JAQUES

JAQUES   I prithee, pretty youth, let me be better acquainted with
thee.

ROSALIND   They say you are a melancholy fellow.

JAQUES   I am so. I do love it better than laughing.

5   ROSALIND   Those that are in extremity of either are abominable
fellows, and betray themselves to every modern censure worse
than drunkards.

JAQUES   Why, 'tis good to be sad° and say nothing.   *serious*

ROSALIND   Why then, 'tis good to be a post.

10 JAQUES   I have neither the scholar's melancholy, which is emula-
tion,° nor the musician's, which is fantastical,° nor the court-   *envy / overly fanciful*
ier's, which is proud, nor the soldier's, which is ambitious, nor
the lawyer's, which is politic, nor the lady's, which is nice,° nor   *fastidious*
the lover's, which is all these; but it is a melancholy of mine

15 own, compounded of many simples,° extracted from many   *ingredients*
objects,° and indeed the sundry contemplation of my travels,[1]   *sights*
in° which my often° rumination wraps me in a most humor-   *upon / frequent*
ous° sadness.   *moody*

ROSALIND   A traveller! By my faith, you have great reason to be

20 sad. I fear you have sold your own lands to see other men's.
Then to have seen much and to have nothing is to have rich
eyes and poor hands.

JAQUES   Yes, I have gained my experience.

Enter ORLANDO

ROSALIND   And your experience makes you sad. I had rather have

25 a fool to make me merry than experience to make me sad—
and to travel for it too!

ORLANDO   Good day and happiness, dear Rosalind.

JAQUES   Nay then, God b'wi'you an° you talk in blank verse.   *if*

ROSALIND   Farewell, Monsieur Traveller. Look you lisp,[2] and

30 wear strange° suits; disable° all the benefits of your own coun-   *foreign / disparage*
try; be out of love with your nativity,° and almost chide God for   *birthplace*
making you that countenance you are, or I will scarce think
you have swam in a gondola.[3]   [*Exit* JAQUES][4]
Why, how now, Orlando? Where have you been all this while?

35 You a lover? An you serve me such another trick, never come
in my sight more.

ORLANDO   My fair Rosalind, I come within an hour of my
promise.

ROSALIND   Break an hour's promise in love! He that will divide a

40 minute into a thousand parts and break but a part of the thousand part of a minute in the affairs of love, it may be said of
him that Cupid hath clapped him o'th' shoulder, but I'll warrant him heartwhole.[5]

ORLANDO   Pardon me, dear Rosalind.

4.1
1. The various thoughts arising during my travels, with
a pun on "travails," meaning "labors."
2. Speak with an affected (foreign) accent.
3. Ridden in a gondola—that is, seen Venice, a popular destination for English travelers.

4. F marks no exit for Jaques here, but he and Rosalind
have formally parted, and Jaques enters with a new
group of characters at the beginning of 4.2.
5. Cupid has tapped him (as in an arrest) or wounded
him (with his arrow), but I'll guarantee he left his heart
intact.

45 ROSALIND Nay, an you be so tardy, come no more in my sight.
I had as lief be wooed of a snail.

ORLANDO Of a snail?

ROSALIND Ay, of a snail; for though he comes slowly, he carries
his house on his head—a better jointure,° I think, than you   *marriage settlement*
50 make a woman. Besides, he brings his destiny with him.

ORLANDO What's that?

ROSALIND Why, horns, which such as you are fain to be
beholden to your wives for.[6] But he comes armed in his fortune,[7] and prevents the slander of his wife.

55 ORLANDO Virtue is no hornmaker, and my Rosalind is virtuous.

ROSALIND And I am your Rosalind.

CELIA It pleases him to call you so; but he hath a Rosalind of a
better leer° than you.   *more attractive*

ROSALIND Come, woo me, woo me, for now I am in a holiday
60 humour, and like enough to consent. What would you say to
me now an I were your very, very Rosalind?

ORLANDO I would kiss before I spoke.

ROSALIND Nay, you were better speak first, and when you were
gravelled° for lack of matter you might take occasion to kiss.   *at a loss*
65 Very good orators, when they are out,° they will spit; and for   *speechless*
lovers, lacking—God warr'nt° us— matter, the cleanliest shift°   *defend / cleverest device*
is to kiss.

ORLANDO How if the kiss be denied?

ROSALIND Then she puts you to entreaty, and there begins new
70 matter.

ORLANDO Who could be out, being before his beloved mistress?

ROSALIND Marry, that should you if I were your mistress, or I
should think my honesty ranker than my wit.[8]

ORLANDO What, of my suit?[9]

75 ROSALIND Not out of your apparel, and yet out of your suit. Am
not I your Rosalind?

ORLANDO I take some joy to say you are because I would be
talking of her.

ROSALIND Well, in her person I say I will not have you.

80 ORLANDO Then in mine own person I die.

ROSALIND No, faith; die by attorney.° The poor world is almost   *proxy*
six thousand years old,[1] and in all this time there was not any
man died in his own person, videlicet,° in a love-cause. Troi-   *namely*
lus[2] had his brains dashed out with a Grecian club, yet he did
85 what he could to die before, and he is one of the patterns of
love. Leander,[3] he would have lived many a fair year though
Hero had turned nun if it had not been for a hot midsummer
night, for, good youth, he went but forth to wash him in the
Hellespont and, being taken with the cramp, was drowned; and
90 the foolish chroniclers of that age found° it was Hero of Sestos.   *claimed*
But these are all lies. Men have died from time to time, and
worms have eaten them, but not for love.

---

6. An allusion to the cuckold's horns.
7. Equipped with the insignia of his destined future.
8. I would think my chastity was fouler than my intelligence; with a pun on "out" (lines 65, 71) as meaning
"not permitted sexual entrance."
9. My petition. Orlando asks if he will be at a loss for
words ("out") in furthering his courtship ("suit"). Ros-

alind puns on "suit" as meaning "clothing."
1. Elizabethan divines generally dated the world's creation somewhere around 4000 B.C.E.
2. The forsaken Trojan lover of Cressida, killed by the
Greek warrior Achilles.
3. In Greek mythology, the lover of Hero; he swam the
Hellespont nightly to visit her and was drowned.

ORLANDO   I would not have my right° Rosalind of this mind, for   *true*
I protest her frown might kill me.

95 ROSALIND   By this hand, it will not kill a fly. But come, now I
will be your Rosalind in a more coming-on° disposition; and   *agreeable*
ask me what you will, I will grant it.

ORLANDO   Then love me, Rosalind.

ROSALIND   Yes, faith, will I, Fridays and Saturdays and all.

100 ORLANDO   And wilt thou have me?

ROSALIND   Ay, and twenty such.

ORLANDO   What sayst thou?

ROSALIND   Are you not good?

ORLANDO   I hope so.

105 ROSALIND   Why then, can one desire too much of a good thing?
[*To* CELIA] Come, sister, you shall be the priest and marry us.—
Give me your hand, Orlando.—What do you say, sister?

ORLANDO [*to* CELIA]   Pray thee, marry us.

CELIA   I cannot say the words.

110 ROSALIND   You must begin, 'Will you, Orlando'—

CELIA   Go to.[4] Will you, Orlando, have to wife this Rosalind?

ORLANDO   I will.

ROSALIND   Ay, but when?

ORLANDO   Why now, as fast as she can marry us.

115 ROSALIND   Then you must say, 'I take thee, Rosalind, for wife.'

ORLANDO   I take thee, Rosalind, for wife.

ROSALIND   I might ask you for your commission;° but I do take   *authority*
thee, Orlando, for my husband. There's a girl goes before° the   *who anticipates*
priest; and certainly a woman's thought runs before her actions.

120 ORLANDO   So do all thoughts; they are winged.

ROSALIND   Now tell me how long you would have her after you
have possessed her?

ORLANDO   For ever and a day.

ROSALIND   Say a day without the ever. No, no, Orlando; men are

125 April when they woo, December when they wed. Maids are
May when they are maids, but the sky changes when they are
wives. I will be more jealous of thee than a Barbary cock-
pigeon[5] over his hen, more clamorous than a parrot against°   *in expectation of*
rain, more new-fangled° than an ape, more giddy in my desires   *in love with novelty*

130 than a monkey. I will weep for nothing, like Diana in the fountain,[6] and I will do that when you are disposed to be merry. I
will laugh like a hyena, and that when thou art inclined to
sleep.

ORLANDO   But will my Rosalind do so?

135 ROSALIND   By my life, she will do as I do.

ORLANDO   O, but she is wise.

ROSALIND   Or else she could not have the wit to do this. The
wiser, the waywarder. Make° the doors upon a woman's wit,   *Close*
and it will out at the casement. Shut that, and 'twill out at the

140 key-hole. Stop that, 'twill fly with the smoke out at the
chimney.

---

4. An expression of mild impatience.
5. An ornamental bird, traditionally an emblem of
jealousy. It was introduced into Europe from Asia by
Turks, whom Elizabethans associated with North
Africa's Barbary Coast. Turkish husbands were imag-

ined by the English to be excessively vigilant about the
sexual fidelity of their wives.
6. Referring to the figures of the goddess Diana used as
centerpieces for ornamental fountains in London and
elsewhere.

ORLANDO   A man that had a wife with such a wit, he might say
'Wit, whither wilt?'[7]

ROSALIND   Nay, you might keep that check° for it till you met   *rebuke*
145   your wife's wit going to your neighbour's bed.

ORLANDO   And what wit could wit have to excuse that?

ROSALIND   Marry, to say she came to seek you there. You shall
never take her without her answer unless you take her without
her tongue. O, that woman that cannot make her fault her
150   husband's occasion,[8] let her never nurse her child herself, for
she will breed it like a fool.

ORLANDO   For these two hours, Rosalind, I will leave thee.

ROSALIND   Alas, dear love, I cannot lack thee two hours.

ORLANDO   I must attend the Duke at dinner. By two o'clock I
155   will be with thee again.

ROSALIND   Ay, go your ways, go your ways. I knew what you
would prove;° my friends told me as much, and I thought no   *turn out to be*
less. That flattering tongue of yours won me. 'Tis but one cast
away,° and so, come, death! Two o'clock is your hour?   *one lover jilted*

160   ORLANDO   Ay, sweet Rosalind.

ROSALIND   By my troth, and in good earnest, and so God mend
me, and by all pretty oaths that are not dangerous, if you break
one jot of your promise or come one minute behind your hour,
I will think you the most pathetical° break-promise, and the   *pathetic*
165   most hollow lover, and the most unworthy of her you call Rosalind that may be chosen out of the gross° band of the unfaith-   *entire*
ful. Therefore beware my censure, and keep your promise.

ORLANDO   With no less religion° than if thou wert indeed my   *faith*
Rosalind. So, adieu.

170   ROSALIND   Well, Time is the old justice that examines all such
offenders; and let Time try.° Adieu.   *Exit* [ORLANDO]   *determine*

CELIA   You have simply misused° our sex in your love-prate. We   *completely slandered*
must have your doublet and hose plucked over your head, and
show the world what the bird hath done to her own nest.

175   ROSALIND   O coz, coz, coz, my pretty little coz, that thou didst
know how many fathom deep I am in love. But it cannot be
sounded. My affection hath an unknown bottom, like the Bay
of Portugal.

CELIA   Or rather bottomless, that° as fast as you pour affection   *so that*
180   in, it runs out.

ROSALIND   No, that same wicked bastard of Venus,[9] that was
begot of thought, conceived of spleen,° and born of madness,   *caprice*
that blind rascally boy that abuses° everyone's eyes because his   *deceives*
own are out, let him be judge how deep I am in love. I'll tell
185   thee, Aliena, I cannot be out of the sight of Orlando. I'll go
find a shadow° and sigh till he come.   *shady place*

CELIA   And I'll sleep.   *Exeunt*

---

7. Wit, where would you go? A catchphrase addressed
to one who talks too much.
8. Who cannot make her error a means of putting her

husband in the wrong.
9. Cupid, the son of Venus by her lover Mercury, not by
her husband, Vulcan.

4.2

Enter JAQUES *and* LORDS [*dressed as*] *foresters*[1]

JAQUES Which is he that killed the deer?

FIRST LORD Sir, it was I.

JAQUES [*to the others*] Let's present him to the Duke like a
Roman conqueror. And it would do well to set the deer's horns
5 upon his head for a branch° of victory. Have you no song, for- *wreath*
ester, for this purpose?

SECOND LORD Yes, sir.

JAQUES Sing it. 'Tis no matter how it be in tune, so it make
noise enough.

10 LORDS [*sing*][2] What shall he have that killed the deer?
   His leather skin and horns to wear.
   Then sing him home; the rest shall bear° *carry; sing*
    This burden.° *(the deer); refrain*
   Take thou no scorn° to wear the horn; *Do not disdain*
15   It was a crest[3] ere thou wast born.
    Thy father's father wore it,
    And thy father bore it.
   The horn, the horn, the lusty horn
   Is not a thing to laugh to scorn. *Exeunt*

4.3

Enter ROSALIND [*as Ganymede*] *and* CELIA [*as Aliena*]

ROSALIND How say you now? Is it not past two o'clock? And
here much Orlando.

CELIA I warrant you, with pure love and troubled brain he hath
ta'en his bow and arrows and is gone forth to sleep.

Enter SILVIUS

5 Look who comes here.

SILVIUS [*to* ROSALIND] My errand is to you, fair youth.
My gentle Phoebe did bid me give you this.
  [*He offers* ROSALIND *a letter, which she takes and reads*]
I know not the contents, but as I guess
By the stern brow and waspish action
10 Which she did use as she was writing of it,
It bears an angry tenor. Pardon me;
I am but as a guiltless messenger.

ROSALIND Patience herself would startle at this letter,
And play the swaggerer. Bear this, bear all.
15 She says I am not fair, that I lack manners;
She calls me proud, and that she could not love me
Were man as rare as Phoenix.[1] 'Od's° my will, *God's*
Her love is not the hare that I do hunt.
Why writes she so to me? Well, shepherd, well,
20 This is a letter of your own device.

SILVIUS No, I protest; I know not the contents.
Phoebe did write it.

ROSALIND   Come, come, you are a fool,

4.2
1. F's stage direction—"Enter Jaques and Lords,
Foresters"—leaves ambiguous whether Jaques and the
lords are dressed as foresters or are accompanied by
them.
2. F does not assign this song to anyone. The stage

direction reads: "Music, Song."
3. Coat of arms; head ornament.
4.3
1. A legendary bird of Arabia, supposedly unique,
which lived five hundred years, died in flames, and was
reborn from its own ashes.

	And turned° into the extremity of love.	*brought*
	I saw her hand. She has a leathern hand,	
25	A free-stone° coloured hand. I verily did think	*yellow-brown limestone*
	That her old gloves were on; but 'twas her hands.	
	She has a housewife's hand—but that's no matter.	
	I say she never did invent this letter.	
	This is a man's invention, and his hand.	
30	SILVIUS Sure, it is hers.	
	ROSALIND Why, 'tis a boisterous and a cruel style,	
	A style for challengers. Why, she defies me,	
	Like Turk to Christian.² Women's gentle brain	
	Could not drop forth such giant-rude invention,	
35	Such Ethiop³ words, blacker in their effect	
	Than in their countenance. Will you hear the letter?	
	SILVIUS So please you, for I never heard it yet,	
	Yet heard too much of Phoebe's cruelty.	
	ROSALIND She Phoebes me.⁴ Mark how the tyrant writes:	
40	Read[s] 'Art thou god to shepherd turned,	
	That a maiden's heart hath burned?'	
	Can a woman rail thus?	
	SILVIUS Call you this railing?	
	ROSALIND read[s] 'Why, thy godhead laid apart,°	*set aside*
45	Warr'st thou with a woman's heart?'	
	Did you ever hear such railing?	
	'Whiles the eye of man did woo me	
	That could do no vengeance° to me.'—	*harm*
	Meaning me a beast.	
50	'If the scorn of your bright eyne°	*eyes*
	Have power to raise such love in mine,	
	Alack, in me what strange effect	
	Would they work in mild aspect?°	*if they looked kindly*
	Whiles you chid me I did love;	
55	How then might your prayers move?	
	He that brings this love to thee	
	Little knows this love in me,	
	And by him seal up thy mind⁵	
	Whether that thy youth and kind°	*nature*
60	Will the faithful offer take	
	Of me, and all that I can make,°	*offer you*
	Or else by him my love deny,	
	And then I'll study how to die.'	
	SILVIUS Call you this chiding?	
65	CELIA Alas, poor shepherd.	
	ROSALIND Do you pity him? No, he deserves no pity. [*To* SIL-	
	VIUS] Wilt thou love such a woman? What, to make thee an	
	instrument,⁶ and play false strains upon thee?—not to be	
	endured. Well, go your way to her—for I see love hath made	
70	thee a tame snake—and say this to her: that if she love me, I	

---

2. Alluding to medieval plays in which Turks and Christians appeared as bitter enemies or to a common Elizabethan perception of the Turk as an enemy to the Christian countries of western Europe.
3. Ethiopian. In Elizabethan racial discourse, the term signified blackness and evil.
4. Addresses me as Phoebe would—that is, in a disdainful manner.
5. And by means of him (Silvius), send your thoughts to me (in a letter).
6. Tool; musical instrument.

charge her to love thee. If she will not, I will never have her
unless thou entreat for her. If you be a true lover, hence, and
not a word; for here comes more company.   *Exit* SILVIUS
    Enter OLIVER
OLIVER   Good morrow, fair ones. Pray you, if you know,
75 Where in the purlieus° of this forest stands   *outskirts*
    A sheepcote fenced about with olive trees?
CELIA   West of this place, down in the neighbour bottom.°   *next valley*
    The rank of osiers° by the murmuring stream   *row of willows*
    Left on your right hand brings you to the place.
80 But at this hour the house doth keep itself.
    There's none within.
OLIVER   If that an eye may profit by a tongue,
    Then should I know you by description.
    Such garments, and such years. 'The boy is fair,
85 Of female favour,° and bestows° himself   *appearance / behaves*
    Like a ripe° sister. The woman low°   *mature / short*
    And browner than her brother.' Are not you
    The owner of the house I did enquire for?
CELIA   It is no boast, being asked, to say we are.
90 OLIVER   Orlando doth commend him to you both,
    And to that youth he calls his Rosalind
    He sends this bloody napkin.° Are you he?   *handkerchief*
ROSALIND   I am. What must we understand by this?
OLIVER   Some of my shame, if you will know of me
95 What man I am, and how, and why, and where
    This handkerchief was stained.
CELIA   I pray you tell it.
OLIVER   When last the young Orlando parted from you,
    He left a promise to return again
    Within an hour, and pacing through the forest,
100 Chewing the food of sweet and bitter fancy,
    Lo what befell. He threw his eye aside,
    And mark what object° did present itself.   *what a spectacle*
    Under an old oak, whose boughs were mossed with age
    And high top bald with dry antiquity,
105 A wretched, ragged man, o'ergrown with hair,
    Lay sleeping on his back. About his neck
    A green and gilded snake had wreathed itself,
    Who with her head, nimble in threats, approached
    The opening of his mouth. But suddenly
110 Seeing Orlando, it unlinked° itself,   *uncoiled*
    And with indented° glides did slip away   *undulating*
    Into a bush, under which bush's shade
    A lioness, with udders all drawn dry,[7]
    Lay couching, head on ground, with catlike watch
115 When that° the sleeping man should stir. For 'tis   *In readiness for when*
    The royal disposition of that beast
    To prey on nothing that doth seem as dead.
    This seen, Orlando did approach the man
    And found it was his brother, his elder brother.
120 CELIA   O, I have heard him speak of that same brother,
    And he did render him the most unnatural

---

7. Having been nursed dry, the lion would be ferociously hungry.

That lived amongst men.
OLIVER   And well he might so do,
For well I know he was unnatural.
ROSALIND   But to Orlando. Did he leave him there,
125   Food to the sucked and hungry lioness?
OLIVER   Twice did he turn his back, and purposed so.
But kindness, nobler ever than revenge,
And nature, stronger than his just occasion,°   *fair opportunity*
Made him give battle to the lioness,
130   Who quickly fell before him; in which hurtling°   *conflict*
From miserable slumber I awaked.
CELIA   Are you his brother?
ROSALIND   Was't you he rescued?
CELIA   Was't you that did so oft contrive° to kill him?   *plot*
OLIVER   'Twas I, but 'tis not I. I do not shame
135   To tell you what I was, since my conversion
So sweetly tastes, being the thing I am.
ROSALIND   But for° the bloody napkin?   *What about*
OLIVER   By and by.
When from the first to last betwixt us two
Tears our recountments° had most kindly bathed—   *narratives*
140   As how I came into that desert place—
I' brief, he led me to the gentle Duke,
Who gave me fresh array, and entertainment,°   *hospitality*
Committing me unto my brother's love,
Who led me instantly unto his cave,
145   There stripped himself, and here upon his arm
The lioness had torn some flesh away,
Which all this while had bled. And now he fainted,
And cried in fainting upon Rosalind.
Brief, I recovered° him, bound up his wound,   *revived*
150   And after some small space, being strong at heart,
He sent me hither, stranger as I am,
To tell this story, that you might excuse
His broken promise, and to give this napkin,
Dyed in his blood, unto the shepherd youth
155   That he in sport doth call his Rosalind.
          [ROSALIND *faints*]
CELIA   Why, how now, Ganymede, sweet Ganymede!
OLIVER   Many will swoon when they do look on blood.
CELIA   There is more in it. Cousin Ganymede!
OLIVER   Look, he recovers.
160   ROSALIND   I would I were at home.
CELIA   We'll lead you thither.
          [*To* OLIVER] I pray you, will you take him by the arm?
OLIVER   Be of good cheer, youth. You a man? You lack a man's
heart.
165   ROSALIND   I do so, I confess it. Ah, sirrah, a body would think
this was well counterfeited. I pray you, tell your brother how
well I counterfeited. Heigh-ho!
OLIVER   This was not counterfeit. There is too great testimony in
your complexion that it was a passion of earnest.°   *a genuine fit*
170   ROSALIND   Counterfeit, I assure you.
OLIVER   Well then, take a good heart, and counterfeit to be a
man.

ROSALIND   So I do; but, i'faith, I should have been a woman by
right.

175   CELIA   Come, you look paler and paler. Pray you, draw home-
wards. Good sir, go with us.

OLIVER   That will I, for I must bear answer back
How you excuse my brother, Rosalind.

ROSALIND   I shall devise something. But I pray you commend
180   my counterfeiting to him. Will you go?   *Exeunt*

5.1

Enter [TOUCHSTONE *the*] *clown and* AUDREY

TOUCHSTONE   We shall find a time, Audrey. Patience, gentle
Audrey.

AUDREY   Faith, the priest was good enough, for all the old gentleman's° saying.   *(Jaques's)*

5   TOUCHSTONE   A most wicked Sir Oliver, Audrey, a most vile
Martext. But, Audrey, there is a youth here in the forest lays
claim to you.

AUDREY   Ay, I know who 'tis. He hath no interest in me° in the   *no right to me*
world. Here comes the man you mean.

Enter WILLIAM

10   TOUCHSTONE   It is meat and drink to me to see a clown.° By my   *peasant; yokel*
troth, we that have good wits have much to answer for. We
shall be flouting; we cannot hold.°   *refrain*

WILLIAM   Good ev'n, Audrey.

AUDREY   God ye° good ev'n, William.   *God give you*

15   WILLIAM [*to* TOUCHSTONE]   And good ev'n to you, sir.

TOUCHSTONE   Good ev'n, gentle friend. Cover thy head,[1] cover
thy head. Nay, prithee, be covered. How old are you, friend?

WILLIAM   Five-and-twenty, sir.

TOUCHSTONE   A ripe age. Is thy name William?

20   WILLIAM   William, sir.

TOUCHSTONE   A fair name. Wast born i'th' forest here?

WILLIAM   Ay, sir, I thank God.

TOUCHSTONE   Thank God—a good answer. Art rich?

WILLIAM   Faith, sir, so-so.

25   TOUCHSTONE   So-so is good, very good, very excellent good. And
yet it is not, it is but so-so. Art thou wise?

WILLIAM   Ay, sir, I have a pretty wit.

TOUCHSTONE   Why, thou sayst well. I do now remember a saying: 'The fool doth think he is wise, but the wise man knows
30   himself to be a fool.' The heathen philosopher, when he had a
desire to eat a grape, would open his lips when he put it into
his mouth, meaning thereby that grapes were made to eat, and
lips to open.[2] You do love this maid?

WILLIAM   I do, sir.

35   TOUCHSTONE   Give me your hand. Art thou learned?

WILLIAM   No, sir.

TOUCHSTONE   Then learn this of me: to have is to have. For it is
a figure in rhetoric° that drink, being poured out of a cup into   *rhetorical commonplace*
a glass, by filling the one doth empty the other. For all your

---

5.1
1. Evidently William has taken off his hat in a gesture
of deference.

2. Touchstone's speech may be a response to William's
gaping mouth.

40   writers do consent that *ipse* is he.[3] Now you are not *ipse*, for I
     am he.
     WILLIAM   Which he, sir?
     TOUCHSTONE   He, sir, that must marry this woman. Therefore,
     you clown, abandon—which is in the vulgar, leave—the soci-
45   ety—which in the boorish is company—of this female—which
     in the common is woman; which together is, abandon the soci-
     ety of this female, or, clown, thou perishest; or, to thy better
     understanding, diest; or, to wit, I kill thee, make thee away,
     translate thy life into death, thy liberty into bondage. I will deal
50   in poison with thee, or in bastinado,° or in steel. I will bandy   *beating with a club*
     with thee in faction, I will o'errun thee with policy.[4] I will kill
     thee a hundred and fifty ways. Therefore tremble, and depart.
     AUDREY   Do, good William.
     WILLIAM   God rest you merry, sir.   *Exit*
              Enter CORIN
55   CORIN   Our master and mistress seeks you. Come, away, away.
     TOUCHSTONE   Trip, Audrey, trip, Audrey. [*To* CORIN] I attend, I
     attend.   *Exeunt*

5.2

             Enter ORLANDO *and* OLIVER
     ORLANDO   Is't possible that on so little acquaintance you should
     like her? That but seeing, you should love her? And loving,
     woo? And wooing, she should grant? And will you persevere to
     enjoy her?
5   OLIVER   Neither call the giddiness° of it in question, the poverty   *foolish haste*
     of her, the small acquaintance, my sudden wooing, nor her
     sudden consenting; but say with me, 'I love Aliena'; say with
     her, that she loves me; consent with both that we may enjoy
     each other. It shall be to your good, for my father's house and
10   all the revenue that was old Sir Rowland's will I estate° upon   *settle*
     you, and here live and die a shepherd.
             Enter ROSALIND [*as Ganymede*]
     ORLANDO   You have my consent. Let your wedding be tomorrow.
     Thither will I invite the Duke and all's contented followers. Go
     you, and prepare Aliena; for look you, here comes my Rosalind.
15   ROSALIND   God save you, brother.
     OLIVER   And you, fair sister.   [*Exit*]
     ROSALIND   O, my dear Orlando, how it grieves me to see thee
     wear thy heart in a scarf.°   *sling*
     ORLANDO   It is my arm.
20   ROSALIND   I thought thy heart had been wounded with the claws
     of a lion.
     ORLANDO   Wounded it is, but with the eyes of a lady.
     ROSALIND   Did your brother tell you how I counterfeited to
     swoon when he showed me your handkerchief?
25   ORLANDO   Ay, and greater wonders than that.
     ROSALIND   O, I know where you are. Nay, 'tis true. There was
     never anything so sudden but the fight of two rams, and Cae-

---

3. For all authorities agree that *ipse* is translated as "he himself." The Latin word was proverbially applied to successful lovers.

4. I will contend ("bandy") with you in argument, I will overwhelm you with craftiness.
5.2

sar's thrasonical° brag of 'I came, saw, and overcame',[1] for your   *boastful*
brother and my sister no sooner met but they looked; no sooner
30 looked but they loved; no sooner loved but they sighed; no
sooner sighed but they asked one another the reason; no sooner
knew the reason but they sought the remedy; and in these
degrees have they made a pair° of stairs to marriage, which they   *flight*
will climb incontinent,° or else be incontinent[2] before mar-   *hastily*
35 riage. They are in the very wrath of love,° and they will together.   *heat of passion*
Clubs cannot part them.

ORLANDO   They shall be married tomorrow, and I will bid the
Duke to the nuptial. But O, how bitter a thing it is to look into
happiness through another man's eyes. By so much the more
40 shall I tomorrow be at the height of heart-heaviness by how
much I shall think my brother happy in having what he wishes
for.

ROSALIND   Why, then, tomorrow I cannot serve your turn[3] for
Rosalind?

45 ORLANDO   I can live no longer by thinking.

ROSALIND   I will weary you then no longer with idle talking.
Know of me then—for now I speak to some purpose—that I
know you are a gentleman of good conceit.° I speak not this   *understanding*
that you should bear a good opinion of my knowledge, inso-
50 much° I say I know you are; neither do I labour for a greater   *inasmuch as*
esteem than may in some little measure draw a belief from you
to do yourself good,[4] and not to grace me. Believe then, if you
please, that I can do strange things. I have since I was three
year old conversed° with a magician, most profound in his art,   *associated*
55 and yet not damnable.[5] If you do love Rosalind so near the
heart as your gesture° cries it out, when your brother marries   *behavior*
Aliena shall you marry her. I know into what straits of fortune
she is driven, and it is not impossible to me, if it appear not
inconvenient to you, to set her before your eyes tomorrow,
60 human as she is, and without any danger.

ORLANDO   Speakest thou in sober meanings?

ROSALIND   By my life, I do, which I tender° dearly, though I say   *value*
I am a magician. Therefore put you in your best array, bid°   *invite*
your friends: for if you will be married tomorrow, you shall;
65 and to Rosalind if you will.

Enter SILVIUS *and* PHOEBE

Look, here comes a lover of mine and a lover of hers.

PHOEBE [*to* ROSALIND]   Youth, you have done me much ungentleness,°   *discourtesy*
To show the letter that I writ to you.

ROSALIND   I care not if I have. It is my study
70 To seem despiteful° and ungentle to you.   *contemptuous*
You are there followed by a faithful shepherd.
Look upon him; love him. He worships you.

PHOEBE [*to* SILVIUS]   Good shepherd, tell this youth what 'tis to love.

SILVIUS   It is to be all made of sighs and tears,
75 And so am I for Phoebe.

---

1. Caesar's well-known announcement of military victory, quoted as it appears in Thomas North's translation of Plutarch's *Lives* (1579).
2. Be sexually unrestrained.
3. Substitute for Rosalind; satisfy you sexually in Rosalind's place.

4. *neither . . . good:* nor am I attempting to enhance my reputation more than is necessary to persuade you to do yourself some good.
5. That is, not meriting execution for heresy. Elizabethan statutes made certain forms of witchcraft and black magic punishable by death.

PHOEBE   And I for Ganymede.

ORLANDO   And I for Rosalind.

ROSALIND   And I for no woman.

SILVIUS   It is to be all made of faith and service,

80   And so am I for Phoebe.

PHOEBE   And I for Ganymede.

ORLANDO   And I for Rosalind.

ROSALIND   And I for no woman.

SILVIUS   It is to be all made of fantasy,

85   All made of passion, and all made of wishes,

All adoration, duty, and observance,°   *devotion*

All humbleness, all patience and impatience,

All purity, all trial, all obedience,

And so am I for Phoebe.

90   PHOEBE   And so am I for Ganymede.

ORLANDO   And so am I for Rosalind.

ROSALIND   And so am I for no woman.

PHOEBE [*to* ROSALIND]   If this be so, why blame you me to love
you?

95   SILVIUS [*to* PHOEBE]   If this be so, why blame you me to love
you?

ORLANDO   If this be so, why blame you me to love you?

ROSALIND   Why do you speak too, 'Why blame you me to love
you?'

100   ORLANDO   To her that is not here nor doth not hear.

ROSALIND   Pray you, no more of this, 'tis like the howling of Irish
wolves against the moon.[6]   [*To* SILVIUS] I will help you if I can.
[*To* PHOEBE] I would love you if I could.—Tomorrow meet
me all together. [*To* PHOEBE] I will marry you if ever I

105   marry woman, and I'll be married tomorrow. [*To* ORLANDO] I
will satisfy you if ever I satisfy man, and you shall be married
tomorrow. [*To* SILVIUS] I will content you if what pleases you
contents you, and you shall be married tomorrow. [*To*
ORLANDO] As you love Rosalind, meet. [*To* SILVIUS] As you

110   love Phoebe, meet. And as I love no woman, I'll meet. So fare
you well. I have left you commands.

SILVIUS   I'll not fail, if I live.

PHOEBE   Nor I.

ORLANDO   Nor I.   *Exeunt* [*severally*]

5.3

Enter [TOUCHSTONE *the*] *clown and* AUDREY

TOUCHSTONE   Tomorrow is the joyful day, Audrey, tomorrow
will we be married.

AUDREY   I do desire it with all my heart; and I hope it is no
dishonest° desire to desire to be a woman of the world.° Here   *unchaste / married*

5   come two of the banished Duke's pages.

Enter two PAGES

FIRST PAGE   Well met, honest gentleman.

TOUCHSTONE   By my troth, well met. Come, sit, sit, and a song.

---

6. That is, it is barbaric. The howling of wolves at the
moon was a proverbial way of referring to an irrational or
futile course of action. Irish wolves might be perceived as
especially disorderly, for Ireland's abundance of wolves
was for many Elizabethan writers a mark of that country's lack of civility.
5.3

SECOND PAGE   We are for you.° Sit i'th' middle.   *That suits us*

FIRST PAGE   Shall we clap into't roundly, without hawking[1], or
10   spitting, or saying we are hoarse, which are the only° prologues   *proper*
to a bad voice?

SECOND PAGE   I'faith, i'faith, and both in a tune,° like two gipsies   *in unison*
on a horse.

BOTH PAGES [*sing*][2]   It was a lover and his lass,
15   With a hey, and a ho, and a hey-nonny-no,
That o'er the green cornfield° did pass   *field of wheat*
In spring-time, the only pretty ring-time,°   *time for weddings*
When birds do sing, hey ding-a-ding ding,
Sweet lovers love the spring.

20   Between the acres of the rye,
With a hey, and a ho, and a hey-nonny-no,
These pretty country folks would lie,
In spring-time, the only pretty ring-time,
When birds do sing, hey ding-a-ding ding,
25   Sweet lovers love the spring.

This carol they began that hour,
With a hey, and a ho, and a hey-nonny-no,
How that a life was but a flower,
In spring-time, the only pretty ring-time,
30   When birds do sing, hey ding-a-ding ding,
Sweet lovers love the spring.

And therefore take° the present time,   *seize*
With a hey, and a ho, and a hey-nonny-no,
For love is crownèd with the prime,°   *spring; perfection*
35   In spring time, the only pretty ring-time,
When birds do sing, hey ding-a-ding ding,
Sweet lovers love the spring.

TOUCHSTONE   Truly, young gentlemen, though there was no
great matter° in the ditty, yet the note[3] was very untunable.   *sense*
40   FIRST PAGE   You are deceived, sir, we kept time, we lost not our
time.

TOUCHSTONE   By my troth, yes, I count it but time lost to hear
such a foolish song. God b'wi'you, and God mend your voices.
Come, Audrey.   *Exeunt* [*severally*]

5.4

Enter DUKE SENIOR, AMIENS, JAQUES, ORLANDO, OLIVER,
[*and*] CELIA [*as Aliena*]

DUKE SENIOR   Dost thou believe, Orlando, that the boy
Can do all this that he hath promisèd?

ORLANDO   I sometimes do believe, and sometimes do not,
As those that fear they hope,[1] and know they fear.

Enter ROSALIND [*as Ganymede*], [*with*] SILVIUS *and*
PHOEBE

---

1. Shall we begin energetically and at once, without clearing our throats?
2. F does not include this speech prefix, simply the world "song." This is one of the few Shakespeare songs for which contemporary music survives. It is set for a single voice with lute accompaniment in Thomas Morley's *First Booke of Ayres* (1600).
3. Yet the music was disagreeable.
5.4
1. Fear that their hope will not be fulfilled.

5 ROSALIND Patience once more, whiles our compact is urged.°   *declared*
[*To the* DUKE] You say if I bring in your Rosalind
You will bestow her on Orlando here?
DUKE SENIOR That would I, had I° kingdoms to give with her.   *even if I had*
ROSALIND [*to* ORLANDO] And you say you will have her when I
bring her?
10 ORLANDO That would I, were I of all kingdoms king.
ROSALIND [*to* PHOEBE] You say you'll marry me if I be willing?
PHOEBE That will I, should I die the hour after.
ROSALIND But if you do refuse to marry me
You'll give yourself to this most faithful shepherd?
15 PHOEBE So is the bargain.
ROSALIND [*to* SILVIUS] You say that you'll have Phoebe if she will.
SILVIUS Though to have her and death were both one thing.
ROSALIND I have promised to make all this matter even.°   *smooth*
Keep you your word, O Duke, to give your daughter.
20 You yours, Orlando, to receive his daughter.
Keep your word, Phoebe, that you'll marry me,
Or else refusing me to wed this shepherd.
Keep your word, Silvius, that you'll marry her
If she refuse me; and from hence I go
25 To make these doubts all even. *Exeunt* ROSALIND *and* CELIA
DUKE SENIOR I do remember in this shepherd boy
Some lively° touches of my daughter's favour.°   *vivid / appearance*
ORLANDO My lord, the first time that I ever saw him,
Methought he was a brother to your daughter.
30 But, my good lord, this boy is forest-born,
And hath been tutored in the rudiments
Of many desperate° studies by his uncle,   *dangerous*
Whom he reports to be a great magician
Obscurèd in the circle of this forest.[2]
Enter [TOUCHSTONE *the*] *clown and* AUDREY
35 JAQUES There is sure another flood toward,° and these couples   *at hand*
are coming to the ark.[3] Here comes a pair of very strange
beasts, which in all tongues are called fools.
TOUCHSTONE Salutation and greeting to you all.
JAQUES [*to the* DUKE] Good my lord, bid him welcome. This is
40 the motley-minded° gentleman that I have so often met in the   *foolish-brained*
forest. He hath been a courtier, he swears.
TOUCHSTONE If any man doubt that, let him put me to my purgation.[4] I have trod a measure,° I have flattered a lady, I have   *danced*
been politic with my friend, smooth with mine enemy, I have
45 undone° three tailors, I have had four quarrels, and like to have   *made bankrupt*
fought° one.   *came close to fighting*
JAQUES And how was that ta'en up?°   *settled*
TOUCHSTONE Faith, we met, and found the quarrel was upon
the seventh cause.
50 JAQUES How, seventh cause?—Good my lord, like this fellow.
DUKE SENIOR I like him very well.
TOUCHSTONE God'ield you, sir, I desire you of the like. I press

---

2. Concealed within the boundaries of this forest. Perhaps a reference to the magic circle within which magi-
cians were supposed to be able to practice their art safely.
3. Alluding to a biblical account in Genesis 7:2 in
which pairs of male and female animals shelter on
Noah's ark to escape the flood that covers the earth.
4. Let me be put to trial to clear myself (of the charge
of lying).

in here, sir, amongst the rest of the country copulatives,[5] to
swear, and to forswear, according as marriage binds and blood
breaks.° A poor virgin, sir, an ill-favoured thing, sir, but mine   *passion rebels*
own. A poor humour° of mine, sir, to take that that no man else   *whim*
will. Rich honesty° dwells like a miser, sir, in a poor house, as   *chastity*
your pearl in your foul oyster.

DUKE SENIOR By my faith, he is very swift and sententious.°   *witty and wise*

TOUCHSTONE According to the fool's bolt,[6] sir, and such dulcet
diseases.°   *sweet afflictions*

JAQUES But for the seventh cause. How did you find the quarrel on the seventh cause?

TOUCHSTONE Upon a lie seven times removed.—Bear your body
more seeming,° Audrey.—As thus, sir: I did dislike[7] the cut of   *becomingly*
a certain courtier's beard. He sent me word if I said his beard
was not cut well, he was in the mind it was. This is called the
Retort Courteous. If I sent him word again it was not well cut,
he would send me word he cut it to please himself. This is
called the Quip Modest. If again it was not well cut, he disa-
bled° my judgement. This is called the Reply Churlish. If again   *disparaged*
it was not well cut, he would answer I spake not true. This is
called the Reproof Valiant. If again it was not well cut, he
would say I lie. This is called the Countercheck° Quarrelsome.   *rebuff*
And so to the Lie Circumstantial,° and the Lie Direct.   *indirect*

JAQUES And how oft did you say his beard was not well cut?

TOUCHSTONE I durst go no further than the Lie Circumstantial,
nor he durst not give me the Lie Direct; and so we measured
swords,[8] and parted.

JAQUES Can you nominate° in order now the degrees of the lie?   *name*

TOUCHSTONE O sir, we quarrel in print, by the book,[9] as you
have books for good manners.[1] I will name you the degrees.
The first, the Retort Courteous; the second, the Quip Modest;
the third, the Reply Churlish; the fourth, the Reproof Valiant;
the fifth, the Countercheck Quarrelsome; the sixth, the Lie
with Circumstance; the seventh, the Lie Direct. All these you
may avoid but the Lie Direct; and you may avoid that, too, with
an 'if'. I knew when seven justices could not take up° a quarrel,   *settle*
but when the parties were met themselves, one of them
thought but of an 'if', as 'If you said so, then I said so', and they
shook hands and swore brothers.° Your 'if' is the only peace   *became sworn brothers*
maker; much virtue in 'if'.

JAQUES [*to the* DUKE] Is not this a rare fellow, my lord? He's as
good at anything, and yet a fool.

DUKE SENIOR He uses his folly like a stalking-horse,[2] and under
the presentation° of that he shoots his wit.   *appearance*

Still° *music. Enter* HYMEN[3] [*with*] ROSALIND *and* CELIA   *Soft*
[*as themselves*]

HYMEN Then is there mirth in heaven

---

5. People about to copulate.
6. And his wittiness quickly disappears. Alluding to the
proverb "A fool's bolt (or arrow) is soon shot."
7. Show my dislike of.
8. Checked that our swords were of the same length
(as was usual prior to a duel).
9. According to the rules as set down in books on the
etiquette of dueling. Touchstone's speech exposes the
absurd aspects of the elaborate codes of behavior set

forth in such books.
1. Elizabethan England witnessed an outpouring of
courtesy literature aimed at both social aspirants and
established courtiers.
2. A real or imitation horse used as a means of camou-
flage in hunting.
3. The god of marriage in classical mythology, conventionally depicted as a young man who carried a veil and
a bridal torch.

When earthly things made even°	*set right*
Atone° together.	*Are at one; unite*

100 Good Duke, receive thy daughter;
    Hymen from heaven brought her,
      Yea, brought her hither,
    That thou mightst join her hand with his
    Whose heart within his bosom is.

105 ROSALIND [*to the* DUKE]   To you I give myself, for I am yours.
    [*To* ORLANDO] To you I give myself, for I am yours.
    DUKE SENIOR   If there be truth in sight, you are my daughter.
    ORLANDO   If there be truth in sight, you are my Rosalind.
    PHOEBE   If sight and shape be true,
110   Why then, my love adieu!
    ROSALIND [*to the* DUKE]   I'll have no father if you be not he.
    [*To* ORLANDO]   I'll have no husband if you be not he,
    [*To* PHOEBE]   Nor ne'er wed woman if you be not she.

HYMEN Peace, ho, I bar° confusion.	*forbid*

115   'Tis I must make conclusion
      Of these most strange events.
    Here's eight that must take hands

To join in Hymen's bands,°	*bonds of marriage*

      If truth holds true contents.[4]
    [*To* ORLANDO *and* ROSALIND]

120 You and you no cross° shall part.	*adversity*

    [*To* OLIVER *and* CELIA]
    You and you are heart in heart.
    [*To* PHOEBE]

You to his love must accord,°	*consent*
Or have a woman to° your lord.	*as*

    [*To* TOUCHSTONE *and* AUDREY]

You and you are sure together°	*tightly bound*

125   As the winter to foul weather.—
    Whiles a wedlock hymn we sing,

Feed° yourselves with questioning,	*Satisfy*

    That reason wonder may diminish
    How thus we met, and these things finish.

Song

130 Wedding is great Juno's° crown,	*goddess of marriage*

      O blessèd bond of board and bed.
    'Tis Hymen peoples every town.

High° wedlock then be honourèd.	*Solemn*

    Honour, high honour and renown
135   To Hymen, god of every town.
    DUKE SENIOR [*to* CELIA]   O my dear niece, welcome thou art to me,
    Even daughter; welcome in no less degree.[5]
    PHOEBE [*to* SILVIUS]   I will not eat my word. Now thou art mine,

Thy faith my fancy° to thee doth combine.	*love*

    Enter [JAQUES DE BOIS, *the*] *second brother*
140 JAQUES DE BOIS   Let me have audience for a word or two.
    I am the second son of old Sir Rowland,

---

4. If truth is true; if truth please you.   5. You are no less welcome than a daughter.

That bring these tidings to this fair assembly.
Duke Frederick, hearing how that every day
Men of great worth resorted to this forest,
145 Addressed a mighty power,° which were on foot,   *army*
In his own conduct,° purposely to take   *Under his command*
His brother here, and put him to the sword.
And to the skirts° of this wild wood he came   *outskirts*
Where, meeting with an old religious man,
150 After some question° with him was converted   *conversation*
Both from his enterprise and from the world,
His crown bequeathing to his banished brother,
And all their lands restored to them again
That were with him exiled. This to be true
I do engage° my life.   *pledge*
155 DUKE SENIOR   Welcome, young man.
Thou offer'st fairly° to thy brothers' wedding: *You bring fine gifts*
To one° his lands withheld, and to the other°   *(Oliver) / (Orlando)*
A land itself at large,⁶ a potent° dukedom.   *powerful*
First, in this forest let us do° those ends   *accomplish*
160 That here were well begun, and well begot.°   *conceived*
And after, every° of this happy number   *every one*
That have endured shrewd° days and nights with us   *evil*
Shall share the good of our returnèd fortune
According to the measure of their states.°   *ranks*
165 Meantime, forget this new-fallen° dignity   *newly acquired*
And fall into our rustic revelry.
Play, music, and you brides and bridegrooms all,
With measure heaped in joy to th' measures fall.⁷
JAQUES   Sir, by your patience.° [*To* JAQUES DE BOIS] If I heard   *with your permission*
        you rightly
170 The Duke hath put on a religious life
And thrown into neglect the pompous° court.   *ceremonious*
JAQUES DE BOIS   He hath.
JAQUES   To him will I. Out of these convertites°   *converts*
There is much matter to be heard and learned.
[*To the* DUKE]
175 You to your former honour I bequeath;
Your patience and your virtue well deserves it.
[*To* ORLANDO]
You to a love that your true faith doth merit;
[*To* OLIVER]
You to your land, and love, and great allies;°   *relatives*
[*To* SILVIUS]
You to a long and well-deservèd bed;
[*To* TOUCHSTONE]
180 And you to wrangling, for thy loving voyage
Is but for two months victualled.°—So, to your pleasures;   *supplied with food*
I am for other than for dancing measures.
DUKE SENIOR   Stay, Jaques, stay.
JAQUES   To see no pastime, I. What you would have°   *like (from me)*
185 I'll stay to know at your abandoned cave.   *Exit*

---

6. An entire country. As Rosalind's husband, Orlando
is heir to the dukedom returned to Duke Senior.

7. With a measure of overflowing joy, begin your
dances ("measures").

DUKE SENIOR   Proceed, proceed. We'll so begin these rites
    As we do trust they'll end, in true delights.
        [*They dance; then*] *exeunt* [*all but* ROSALIND][8]

[Epilogue]

ROSALIND [*to the audience*]   It is not the fashion to see the lady
the epilogue;[1] but it is no more unhandsome than to see the
lord the prologue. If it be true that good wine needs no bush,[2]
'tis true that a good play needs no epilogue. Yet to good wine
they do use good bushes, and good plays prove the better by
the help of good epilogues. What a case° am I in then, that am   *plight; costume*
neither a good epilogue nor cannot insinuate° with you in the   *ingratiate myself*
behalf of a good play! I am not furnished like a beggar, there-
fore to beg will not become me. My way is to conjure° you;   *charge; bewitch*
and I'll begin with the women. I charge you, O women, for the
love you bear to men, to like as much of this play as please you.
And I charge you, O men, for the love you bear to women—as
I perceive by your simpering none of you hates them—that
between you and the women the play° may please. If I were a   *drama; love play*
woman[3] I would kiss as many of you as had beards that pleased
me, complexions that liked° me, and breaths that I defied° not.   *pleased / disdained*
And I am sure, as many as have good beards, or good faces, or
sweet breaths will for my kind offer, when I make curtsy, bid
me farewell.°   *Exit*   *(with applause)*

8. F indicates only a single exit for Duke Senior, but most editors assume that Rosalind remains alone onstage to deliver the Epilogue.
Epilogue
1. In the vast majority of Elizabethan plays, the Epilogue is spoken by a male character.

2. Advertisement. A proverb derived from the practice of hanging a branch of ivy in tavern windows to indicate that wine was for sale.
3. A pointed reference to the fact that women's roles in the Elizabethan theater were played by boys.

Twelfth Night

Shakespeare's contemporary Thomas Coryat wrote that he witnessed something quite remarkable when he went to the theater in Venice: "I saw women act, a thing that I never saw before." That an Englishman had to travel abroad to see women actors for the first time is not surprising. All the great women's roles in Elizabethan and Jacobean plays were written to be performed by trained adolescent boys, and boys played the female parts as well in all grammar school and university productions. But what struck Coryat in Venice was neither the gratifying naturalness of finally seeing women play women's parts nor the comparative inadequacy of English boy actors. Rather, he was impressed that the women actors managed to hold their own in representing the female sex: "They performed it," he writes, "with as good a grace, as ever I saw any masculine Actor."

Recent scholars have observed that there were in fact occasions in which audiences in England could have seen women performing: troupes from abroad, including women actors, occasionally toured England, and English women performed in the theatrical spectacles known as masques and in other entertainments. But in England, women did not perform on the public stage (the word "actress" had not yet entered the English language), and the remarks of Coryat and others suggest that their absence was rarely if ever lamented. The boy actors were evidently extraordinarily skillful, and the audiences were sufficiently immersed in the conventions both of theater and of social life in general to accept gesture, makeup, and above all dress as a convincing representation of femininity.

Twelfth Night, or What You Will, written for Shakespeare's all-male company, plays brilliantly with these conventions. The comedy depends on an actor's ability to transform himself, through costume, voice, and gesture, into a young noblewoman, Viola, who transforms herself, through costume, voice, and gesture, into a young man, Cesario. The play's delicious complications follow from the emotional crosscurrents that Viola's transformation engenders. Shipwrecked on a strange coast and bereft of her twin brother, the disguised Viola finds a place in the service of the powerful Duke Orsino, with whom she promptly falls in love. Orsino is in love with Lady Olivia, a wealthy aristocrat whose household includes, among its servants and dependents, a steward or house manager, a waiting-gentlewoman, a professional entertainer, and a down-at-the-heels, perpetually drunken uncle. When Orsino sends Cesario to help him woo the proud Olivia, Olivia not only rejects the Duke's suit but falls in love with his messenger. Discomfited to learn that she is the object of Olivia's love, Viola reflects on the plot's impassioned triangle:

> My master loves her dearly,
> And I, poor monster, fond as much on him,
> And she, mistaken, seems to dote on me.
> What will become of this?
>
> (2.2.31–34)

"Poor monster": in *Twelfth Night,* clothes do not simply reveal or disguise identity; they partly constitute identity—or so Viola playfully imagines—making her a strange, hybrid creature. To be sure, she understands perfectly well the narrow biological definition of her sex (though in the characteristically male-centered language of Shakespeare's culture, she phrases that definition in terms of what she "lacks" [3.4.269]). Yet there is something almost magical in this play about costume, so that even at the close, when identities have been sorted out and the couples happily matched, Orsino cannot bring himself to call his bride-to-be by her rightful name or to address her as a woman:

> Cesario, come—
> For so you shall be while you are a man;
> But when in other habits you are seen,
> Orsino's mistress, and his fancy's queen.
> (5.1.372–75)

It would have been simple for Shakespeare to devise a concluding scene in which Viola appears in women's "habits," but he goes out of his way to leave her in men's clothes and hence to disrupt with a delicate comic touch the return to the "normal." The transforming power of costume unsettles fixed categories of gender and social class, and allows characters to explore emotional territory that a culture officially hostile to same-sex desire and cross-class marriage would ordinarily have ruled out of bounds. In *Twelfth Night,* conventional expectations repeatedly give way to a different way of perceiving the world.

Shakespeare wrote *Twelfth Night* around 1601. He had already written such comedies as *A Midsummer Night's Dream, Much Ado About Nothing,* and *As You Like It,* with their playful, subtly ironic investigations of the ways in which heterosexual couples are produced out of the murkier crosscurrents of male and female friendships; as interesting, perhaps, he had probably just recently completed *Hamlet,* with its unprecedented exploration of mourning, betrayal, antic humor, and tragic isolation. *Twelfth Night* would prove to be, in the view of many critics, both the most perfect and in some sense the last of the great festive comedies. Shakespeare returned to comedy later in his career, but always with more insistent overtones of bitterness, loss, and grief. There are dark notes in *Twelfth Night* as well: Olivia is in mourning for her brother, Viola thinks that her brother, too, is dead, Antonio believes that he has been betrayed by the man he loves, Orsino threatens to kill Cesario. Desire is repeatedly linked to frustration and loss. But these notes are swept up in the current of sweet music that pervades the play, and the characters are all drawn into a giddy, carnivalesque dance of illusion, disguise, folly, and clowning.

The play's subtitle, *What You Will,* underscores the celebratory spirit associated with Twelfth Night, the Feast of the Epiphany (January 6), which in Elizabethan England marked the culminating night of the traditional Christmas revels. On Twelfth Night 1601, the queen's guest of honor was a twenty-eight-year-old Italian nobleman, Don Virginio Orsino, Duke of Bracciano. Orsino wrote to his wife that he was entertained that night with "a mingled comedy, with pieces of music and dances." Since the company that performed was the Lord Chamberlain's Men—Shakespeare's company—it has been argued that the comedy was *Twelfth Night,* but there is no scholarly consensus on this hypothesis. The title, in any case, would for Shakespeare's contemporaries have conjured up a whole series of time-honored festivities associated with the midwinter season. A rigidly hierarchical social order that ordinarily demanded deference, sobriety, and strict obedience to authority temporarily gave way to raucous rituals of inversion: young boys were crowned for a day as bishops and carried through the streets in mock religious processions; abstemiousness was toppled by bouts of heavy drinking and feasting; the spirit of parody, folly, and misrule reigned briefly in places normally reserved for stern-faced moralists and sober judges.

The fact that these festivities were associated with Christian holidays—the Epiphany marked the visit of the Three Kings to Bethlehem to worship the Christ child—did not altogether obscure the continuities with pagan winter rituals such as the Roman Saturnalia, with its comparably explosive release from everyday discipline into a disorderly realm of belly laughter and belly cheer. Puritans emphasized these continuities in launching a fierce attack on the Elizabethan festive calendar and its whole ethos, just as they attacked the theater for what they saw as its links with paganism, idleness, and sexual license. Elizabethan and Jacobean authorities in the church and the state had their own concerns about idleness and subversion, but they generally protected and patronized both festive ritual and theater on the grounds that these provided a valuable release from tensions that might otherwise prove dangerous. Sobriety, piety, and discipline were no doubt admirable virtues, but most human beings were not saints. "Dost thou think because thou art virtuous," the drunken Sir Toby asks the censorious steward Malvolio, "there shall be no more cakes and ale?" (2.3.103–04).

Fittingly, the earliest firm record of a performance of *Twelfth Night*, as noted in the diary of John Manningham, was "at our feast" in the Middle Temple (one of London's law schools) in February 1602. Manningham wrote observantly that the play was "much like the *Comedy of Errors*, or *Menaechmi* in Plautus, but most like and near to that in Italian called *Inganni*." That is, *Twelfth Night* resembles Shakespeare's own earlier play on identical twins (along with that play's Roman source) and still more resembles a series of sixteenth-century Italian comedies built around the intertwining themes of love, fraud (*inganno*), and mistaken identity. Several of these comedies feature the plot device of a female twin who takes service as a page with the man she loves. Closest of these to Shakespeare's comedy is *Gl'Ingannati* (The Deceived), written for performance at Carnival time in Siena in 1531 and translated into French in 1543. It seems likely that Shakespeare knew this play or one that derived from it, and may have picked up several details in addition to the overall plot line. But the tone of *Gl'Ingannati*, with its bawdy jokes about nuns and old men, its sly, sardonic servants, and its farcical intrigues, is far from *Twelfth Night*'s mingled melancholy and delight, its bittersweet play of divided and contradictory desires. Tellingly, in the Italian comedy, the heroine is all along plotting to win the love of the man she serves; she has disguised herself in order to dissuade him from wooing elsewhere. Viola's predicament—her attempt to serve Orsino even at the cost of her own deepest longings—represents a wholly different emotional register.

That predicament is not Shakespeare's invention; he found it, with many other elements of his plot, in an English story, Barnabe Riche's tale "Apollonius and Silla" in *Riche His Farewell to Militarie Profession* (1581), which was in turn based on French and Italian sources. Riche is too addicted to moralizing to explore his heroine's character with much subtlety, but he does underscore how painful it is for her to hide her feelings while acting as go-between, and hence he anticipates, if only woodenly, the mood that Shakespeare exquisitely captures in Viola's lines about one who "sat like patience on a monument, / Smiling at grief" (2.4.113–14). There is less precedent, in Riche or in any of the known sources, for the aspect of *Twelfth Night* that Manningham

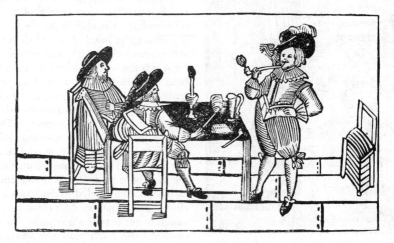

Gentlemen drinking and smoking. From Phillip Stubbes, *The Anatomie of Abuses* (1583).

found particularly memorable and that has continued to delight audiences: the gulling of Malvolio.

Malvolio (*mal volio*, "ill will") is explicitly linked to those among Shakespeare's contemporaries most hostile to the theater and to such holidays as Twelfth Night: "Sometimes," says Lady Olivia's waiting-gentlewoman Maria, "he is a kind of puritan" (2.3.125). When we first see Malvolio, he is harshly critical of Feste the clown, who is attempting to win back Olivia's favor. "Unless you laugh and minister occasion to him," Malvolio sourly observes, "he is gagged" (1.5.74–75). Though ungenerous, the observation is canny, for comedy does seem to depend on a collaborative spirit from which Malvolio conspicuously excludes himself. He is a man without friends. More dangerously, he is a man in a socially dependent position with a gift for acquiring enemies, as he does when he tries to silence the noisy revelry of that classic carnivalesque threesome a drunkard, a blockhead, and a professional fool: Olivia's uncle Sir Toby, his boon companion Sir Andrew Aguecheek, and Feste.

Olivia remarks to Malvolio that he is "sick of self-love" (1.5.77), and it is this narcissism that his enemies exploit to undo him. When Malvolio finds Maria's forged letter, he is in the midst of a deliciously self-gratifying fantasy that he has married Olivia, a fantasy less of erotic bliss than of social domination. The dream of rising above his station fuels his credulous eagerness to interpret the letter according to his fondest wishes and to comply with its absurd suggestions for his festive dress and demeanor. This compliance, by making it seem to Olivia that he has gone mad, renders Malvolio vulnerable to a further humiliation. In a parody of the age's brutal "therapy" for insanity, he is clapped into a dark room and subjected to a mock exorcism. Finally, he suffers what is perhaps the cruelest punishment for someone who dreams that greatness will be thrust upon him: he is simply forgotten. When in the play's final moments he is released, Malvolio is in no mood to join in the general air of communal wonder and rejoicing. More alone than ever, he introduces into the comedy's resolution an extraordinary note of vindictive bitterness: "I'll be revenged on the whole pack of you!" (5.1.365). Shakespeare does not hide the cruelty of the treatment to which Malvolio has been subjected—"He hath been most notoriously abused" (5.1.366), says Olivia— nor does he shrink from showing the audience other disagreeable qualities in Sir Toby and his companions. But while the close of the comedy seems to embrace these failings in a tolerant, bemused, aristocratic recognition of human folly, it can find no place for Malvolio's blend of puritanism and social climbing.

Malvolio is scapegoated for indulging in a fantasy that colors several of the key relationships in *Twelfth Night*: the fantasy of winning the hand of one of the noble and enormously wealthy aristocrats who reign over the social world of the play. The beautiful heiress Olivia, mistress of a great house, is a glittering prize that lures not only Malvolio but also the foolish Sir Andrew and the elegant, imperious Duke Orsino. In falling in love with the Duke's graceful messenger (and, as she thinks she has done, in marrying him), Olivia seems to have made precisely the kind of match that had fueled Malvolio's social-climbing imagination. As it turns out, the match is not between unequals: "Be not amazed," the Duke tells her when she realizes that she has married someone she

Lutenist. By Jost Amman.

scarcely knows. "Right noble is his blood" (5.1.257). The social order, then, has not been overturned: as in a carnival, when the disguises are removed, the revelers resume their "proper," socially and sexually approved positions.

Yet there is something decidedly improper about the perverse erotic excitement that the play discovers in disguise, displacement, indirection, and deferral and something irreducibly strange about the marriages with which *Twelfth Night* ends. Sir Toby has married Maria as a reward for devising the plot against Malvolio. Olivia has entered into a "contract of eternal bond of love" (5.1.152) with someone whose actual identity is only revealed to her after the marriage ceremony. (In Riche's version of the story, she is pregnant and her marriage saves her from social disgrace, but Shakespeare omits this plot twist, thereby raising the tone but heightening the irrationality of the finale.) The strangeness of the bond between virtual strangers is matched by the strangeness of Orsino's instantaneous decision to marry Cesario—as soon as "he" can become Viola by changing into women's clothes. Only a few minutes earlier, in a fit of jealous rage at Olivia's love for Cesario, Orsino had threatened to kill "the lamb that I do love" (5.1.126); now he will wed that lamb.

The sudden transformation is prepared for in part by Orsino's passionate insistence that he loves the boy he intends to kill and in part by the earlier signs of intimacy between them: "I have," he tells Cesario, "unclasped / To thee the book even of my secret soul" (1.4.12–13). But this intimacy has been formed around Orsino's grand passion for Olivia, a passion that is reiterated through virtually the entire play. The revelation at the play's climax—"One face, one voice, one habit, and two persons" (5.1.208)—forces a realignment of all the relationships. With Sebastian married to Olivia, Viola becomes Olivia's "sister" (or, as we would say, sister-in-law); and by marrying Viola, Orsino likewise makes Olivia his "sweet sister" (5.1.371). Orsino then will continue in a sense to "love" Olivia but only through the bond of kinship formed by the linked twins: a strangely appropriate fate for someone who tried to woo by proxy!

That this solution does not seem entirely zany—that it seems a fit ending for a romantic comedy—depends on several key features in *Twelfth Night*'s emotional landscape. It is significant that Orsino's love for Olivia, though poetically intense, is detached from any direct personal encounter. Not only does her vow of a seven-year seclusion compel Orsino to delegate his passion to a messenger, this passion seems largely self-regarding and self-indulgent. His famous opening lines on the paradoxes of love—its close intertwining of fulfillment and decline, stealing and giving, freshness and decay—revolve around the contemplation less of the lady than of his own solitary, self-gratifying imagination: "So full of shapes is fancy / That it alone is high fantastical" (1.1.14–15). The play does not ridicule Orsino's aristocratic reveries, although they seem at moments like elegant versions of what is cruelly mocked in Malvolio, but it does invite the audience to treat them with a certain ironic detachment.

Orsino's love seems to circle all too readily back upon himself: he is fascinated by his role as melancholy lover. That self-absorption is not the only shape of passion is made clear by several contrasting figures of whom the most selfless is the sea captain Antonio, consumed with desire for his friend Sebastian. In a play full of coy allusions to same-sex desire, Antonio's "willing love" (3.3.11) is the most explicit representation of passion as absolute devotion, a willingness to sacrifice everything in the service of the beloved. The mistaken belief that this devotion has been callously betrayed is one of the play's most poignant moments, a moment perhaps only partially redeemed by the manifest relief and joy with which the newly wed Sebastian greets his friend in the last act.

Intense, intimate bonding between men is a recurrent theme in Shakespeare's culture. (A comparable interest in female friendship is reflected in the love between Hermia and Helena in *A Midsummer Night's Dream* and Rosalind and Celia in *As You Like It*.) Shakespeare explores the pleasures and perils of male friendship in such plays as *The Two Gentlemen of Verona, The Merchant of Venice,* and *Much Ado About Nothing* and, most famously, in the sonnets to the fair young man whom he calls "the master-mistress of my passion" (sonnet 20). Orsino expresses doubt that a woman can love with an intensity equal to a man's:

> There is no woman's sides
> Can bide the beating of so strong a passion
> As love doth give my heart; no woman's heart
> So big, to hold so much. They lack retention.
> (2.4.91–94)

It is perhaps this belief (which the play proves to be utterly wrong) that conditions the only authentic emotional bond that we see Orsino forge, the bond with his devoted young servant Cesario. In conversation with Cesario, the haughty Duke manages for a few moments at least to escape from his languid self-absorption and express interest in someone else's thoughts and feelings: "What dost thou know?"; "And what's her history?"; "But died thy sister of her love, my boy?" (2.4.103, 108, 118). These simple questions, modest in themselves, are sufficiently distinct from Orsino's usual manner of speech to signal both a curiosity and a responsiveness that he does not manifest with anyone else. Part of the quirky delight of the play's resolution is to give to the union between Orsino and Viola something of the intimacy that had only seemed possible between men.

This resolution depends principally on the remarkable qualities of the play's central character, Viola. Like Antonio, Viola is prepared to sacrifice herself for her beloved: "And I most jocund, apt, and willingly," she tells Orsino, "to do you rest a thousand deaths would die" (5.1.128–29). But where Antonio experiences passion as tragic compulsion—he speaks of Sebastian's beauty as "witchcraft" drawing him into danger—Viola's spirit, as her word "jocund" suggests, is extraordinarily resilient. No sooner does she sadly observe that her brother must have perished in the shipwreck than she remarks, "Perchance he is not drowned" (1.2.4); no sooner does she find herself isolated and unprotected than she determines to serve Lady Olivia, and then, learning that this route is blocked, she at once resolves to disguise herself as a man and serve Orsino instead. Here and throughout the play, Viola seems to draw on an inward principle of hope. That principle, along with an improvisational boldness, an eloquent tongue, and a keen wit, enables her to keep afloat in an increasingly mad swirl of misunderstandings and cross-purposes.

Those misunderstandings, of course, are largely her creation in the sense that they mainly derive from a disguise that confounds the distinction between male and female. "They shall yet belie thy happy years / That say thou art a man," Orsino says to Cesario (1.4.29–30). The description that follows seems to imagine that boys begin almost as girls and only subsequently become males:

> Diana's lip
> Is not more smooth and rubious; thy small pipe
> Is as the maiden's organ, shrill and sound,
> And all is semblative a woman's part.
> (1.4.30–33)

This perception of ambiguity, rooted in early modern ideas about sexuality and gender, is one of the elements that enabled a boy actor in this period convincingly to mime "a woman's part." According to an ancient anatomical tradition, still highly influential in Shakespeare's time, sexual difference is not absolute: males and females share a single physiological structure whose differentiation only occurs over time. Such a theory implies a prolonged period of indistinction upon which *Twelfth Night* continually plays, and that helps to account for the emotional tangle that the cross-dressed Viola inspires.

Having, in her role as intermediary, aroused Olivia's love, Viola does not see how to disabuse the enamored Countess without abandoning the disguise. For all her lively resolution, she is passive in the face of the complexities she has engendered, counting on time and chance to sort out what she cannot: "O time, thou must untangle this, not

I. / It is too hard a knot for me t'untie" (2.2.38–39). Perhaps this passivity, or more accurately this trust in time, is a form of wisdom in a world where everything seems topsy-turvy. If so, it is a wisdom that links Viola to the fool Feste, who exults at the play's close in what he calls "the whirligig of time" (5.1.364).

Feste does not have a major part in the comedy's plot, but he shares with Viola a place at its imaginative center. A few years before the creation of *Twelfth Night,* the famous, boisterous clown Will Kempe quit Shakespeare's company in a huff and was replaced by Robert Armin, a comic actor of unusual sensitivity and subtlety. In paying handsome tribute to Feste's intelligence, Viola seems to acknowledge Armin's special gift: "This fellow is wise enough to play the fool, / And to do that well craves a kind of wit" (3.1.53–54). His wit often takes the form of a perverse literalism that slyly calls attention to the play's repeated confounding of such simple binaries as male and female, outside and inside, role and reality. The paradox of the wise fool, celebrated by Erasmus in his famous *Praise of Folly* (1509), is one that fascinated Shakespeare, who returned to it in plays as diverse as *As You Like It* and *King Lear.* In *Twelfth Night,* Feste is irresponsible, vulnerable, and dependent, but he also understands, as he teasingly shows Olivia, that it is foolish to bewail forever a loss that cannot be recovered. And he understands that it is important to take such pleasures as life offers and not to wait: "In delay there lies no plenty," he sings. "Then come kiss me, sweet and twenty. / Youth's a stuff will not endure" (2.3.46–48). There is in this wonderful song, as in all of his jests, a current of sadness. Feste knows, as the refrain of the last of his songs puts it, that "the rain it raineth every day" (5.1.379). His counsel is for "present mirth" and "present laughter" (2.3.44). This is, of course, the advice of a fool. But do the Malvolios of the world have anything wiser to suggest?

STEPHEN GREENBLATT

TEXTUAL NOTE

The text of *Twelfth Night* is mercifully straightforward: the play first appeared in the 1623 First Folio (F), and the text is unusually clean, including careful act and scene divisions. Contemporary or near-contemporary musical settings survive for several of the songs in the play. For example, "O mistress mine" (2.3.35ff.) appears in three early versions, including Thomas Morley's *First Book of Consort Lessons* (1599). "Hold thy peace" (2.3.59) appears in a manuscript book of rounds collected by Thomas Lant (1580), as well as a version printed in 1609. The well-known setting for Feste's epilogue, "When that I was and a little tiny boy" (5.1.376), was first printed in Joseph Vernon's 1772 volume *The New Songs in the Pantomime of the Witches: The Celebrated Epilogue in the Comedy of Twelfth Night . . . Sung by Mr. Vernon at Vaux Hall, Composed by J. Vernon.* It is not entirely clear whether this setting was composed by Vernon (as the title page seems to suggest) or arranged from a traditional tune.

SELECTED BIBLIOGRAPHY

Auden, W. H. "Music in Shakespeare." *The Dyer's Hand, and Other Essays.* New York: Random House, 1948. Analyzing songs from the plays, Auden reflects on music as a social exercise, dramatic convention, and supernatural signifier.

Bloom, Harold, ed. *William Shakespeare's "Twelfth Night."* Modern Critical Interpretation series. New York: Chelsea House, 1987. Essays written since the 1960s, treating the representation of character, music, class ideology, gender, and role-playing.

Booth, Stephen. *"Twelfth Night* 1.1: The Audience as Malvolio." *Shakespeare's "Rough Magic": Essays in Honor of C. L. Barber.* Ed. Peter Erickson and Coppélia Kahn.

Newark: University of Delaware Press, 1985. 149–67. An otherwise nonsensical play makes sense only when audiences ignore the textual evidence in favor of contextual probability.

Callaghan, Dympna. "'And all is semblative a woman's part': Body Politics and *Twelfth Night*." *Shakespeare Without Women: Representing Gender and Race on the Renaissance Stage*. New York: Routledge, 2000. 26–48. The misogynistic ridicule of Olivia's genitals in the Malvolio letter is an assertion of male control over the female body.

Gay, Penny. "*Twelfth Night*: Desire and Its Discontents." *As She Likes It: Shakespeare's Unruly Women*. London: Routledge, 1994. 17–47. Describes key postwar English stage productions.

Greenblatt, Stephen. "Fiction and Friction." *Shakespearean Negotiations: The Circulation of Social Energy in Renaissance England*. Berkeley: University of California Press, 1988. 66–93. In light of contemporary anatomical theories, relates sexual chafing to verbal sparring and the generation of identity.

Hollander, John. "*Twelfth Night* and the Morality of Indulgence." *Sewanee Review* 67 (1959): 220–38. In *Twelfth Night*'s intense moral vision, the surfeit of appetite through indulgence leads to the rebirth of the unencumbered self.

Neely, Carol Thomas. *Distracted Subjects: Madness and Gender in Shakespeare and Early Modern Culture*. Ithaca: Cornell University Press, 2004. *Twelfth Night*'s displaced erotic choices cohere with changing medical discourse about pathological female lovesickness.

Orgel, Stephen. *Impersonations: The Performance of Gender in Shakespeare's England*. Cambridge, Mass.: Cambridge University Press, 1996. Approaches paradoxes in English playacting practice through contemporary notions of gender construction and sexual desire.

Wells, Stanley, ed. "*Twelfth Night*": *Critical Essays*. New York: Garland, 1986. Twenty essays from the nineteenth century onward, treating mainly formal and structural aspects and early twentieth-century productions.

FILM

Twelfth Night. 1996. Dir. Trevor Nunn. UK. 134 min. Romantic Celtic coastlines combine with a poignant musical score, a stuffy Malvolio, and a gravely wise Feste. With Ben Kingsley, Helena Bonham Carter, and Nigel Hawthorne.

Twelfth Night, or What You Will

The Persons of the Play

ORSINO, Duke of Illyria
VALENTINE ⎱ attending on Orsino
CURIO ⎰
FIRST OFFICER
SECOND OFFICER
VIOLA, a lady, later disguised as Cesario
A CAPTAIN
SEBASTIAN, her twin brother
ANTONIO, another sea-captain
OLIVIA, a Countess
MARIA, her waiting-gentlewoman
SIR TOBY Belch, Olivia's kinsman
SIR ANDREW Aguecheek, companion of Sir Toby
MALVOLIO, Olivia's steward
FABIAN, a member of Olivia's household
FESTE the clown, her jester
A PRIEST
A SERVANT of Olivia
Musicians, sailors, lords, attendants

1.1

Music. Enter ORSINO *Duke of Illyria,* CURIO, *and other lords*

ORSINO If music be the food of love, play on,
Give me excess of it that, surfeiting,
The appetite may sicken and so die.
That strain again, it had a dying fall.°   *cadence*
5 O, it came o'er my ear like the sweet sound
That breathes upon a bank of violets,
Stealing and giving odour. Enough, no more,
'Tis not so sweet now as it was before.
　　　　[Music ceases]
O spirit of love, how quick and fresh° art thou   *lively and eager*
10 That, notwithstanding thy capacity
Receiveth as the sea,° naught enters there,   *Receives without limit*
Of what validity° and pitch° so e'er,   *value / height; excellence*
But falls into abatement° and low price   *lesser value*
Even in a minute! So full of shapes is fancy°   *love; desire*
15 That it alone is high fantastical.°   *uniquely imaginative*
CURIO Will you go hunt, my lord?
ORSINO　　　　　　　　　　What, Curio?
CURIO　　　　　　　　　　　　　　The hart.
ORSINO Why so I do, the noblest that I have.[1]
O, when mine eyes did see Olivia first
Methought she purged the air of pestilence;[2]

1.1 Location: Illyria, Greek and Roman name for the
eastern Adriatic coast; probably not suggesting a real
country to Shakespeare's audience.

1. Orsino plays on "hart/heart."
2. Plague and other illnesses were thought to be caused
by bad air.

20   That instant was I turned into a hart,
    And my desires, like fell° and cruel hounds,   *savage*
    E'er since pursue me.³

        Enter VALENTINE

              How now, what news from her?

VALENTINE   So please my lord, I might not be admitted,
    But from her handmaid do return this answer:
25   The element itself till seven years' heat⁴
    Shall not behold her face at ample° view,   *full*
    But like a cloistress° she will veilèd walk   *nun*
    And water once a day her chamber round
    With eye-offending brine°—all this to season   *stinging tears*
30   A brother's dead love,⁵ which she would keep fresh
    And lasting in her sad remembrance.

ORSINO   O, she that hath a heart of that fine° frame   *exquisitely made*
    To pay this debt of love but to a brother,
    How will she love when the rich golden shaft⁶
35   Hath killed the flock of all affections else°   *other emotions*
    That live in her—when liver, brain, and heart,⁷
    These sovereign thrones, are all supplied, and filled
    Her sweet perfections⁸ with one self° king!   *one and the same*
    Away before me to sweet beds of flowers.
40   Love-thoughts lie rich when canopied with bowers.

                      Exeunt

1.2

      Enter VIOLA, *a* CAPTAIN, *and sailors*

VIOLA¹   What country, friends, is this?

CAPTAIN   This is Illyria, lady.

VIOLA   And what should I do in Illyria?
    My brother, he is in Elysium.²
    Perchance° he is not drowned. What think you sailors?   *Perhaps*
5 CAPTAIN   It is perchance° that you yourself were saved.   *by chance*

VIOLA   O my poor brother!—and so perchance may he be.

CAPTAIN   True, madam, and to comfort you with chance,³
    Assure yourself, after our ship did split,
    When you and those poor number savèd with you
10   Hung on our driving boat,⁴ I saw your brother,
    Most provident in peril, bind himself—
    Courage and hope both teaching him the practice—
    To a strong mast that lived° upon the sea,   *remained afloat*
    Where, like Arion⁵ on the dolphin's back,
15   I saw him hold acquaintance with the waves
    So long as I could see.

VIOLA *[giving money]*   For saying so, there's gold.

---

3. Alluding to the classical legend of Actaeon, who was turned into a stag and hunted by his own hounds for having seen Artemis naked.
4. The sky itself / for seven hot summers.
5. *all . . . love:* all this to preserve (by the salt of the tears) the love of a dead brother.
6. Of Cupid's golden-tipped arrow, which caused desire.
7. In Elizabethan psychology, these were the seats of passion, intellect, and feeling.
8. *and filled . . . perfections:* and all her flawless qualities

are governed by.
1.2 Location: The coast of Illyria.
1. Viola is not named in the dialogue until 5.1.237.
2. The heaven of classical mythology.
3. With what may have happened.
4. The ship's boat. *driving:* being driven by the wind.
5. A legendary Greek musician who, in order to save himself from being murdered on a voyage, jumped overboard and was carried to land by a dolphin.

Mine own escape unfoldeth to° my hope,   *encourages*
Whereto thy speech serves for authority,°   *support*
The like of him.⁶ Know'st thou this country?

20 CAPTAIN Ay, madam, well, for I was bred and born
Not three hours' travel from this very place.
VIOLA Who governs here?
CAPTAIN   A noble duke, in nature
As in name.
VIOLA   What is his name?
CAPTAIN   Orsino.
VIOLA Orsino. I have heard my father name him.
25 He was a bachelor then.
CAPTAIN And so is now, or was so very late,°   *lately*
For but a month ago I went from hence,
And then 'twas fresh in murmur°—as, you know,   *newly rumored*
What great ones do the less will prattle of—
30 That he did seek the love of fair Olivia.
VIOLA What's she?
CAPTAIN A virtuous maid, the daughter of a count
That died some twelvemonth since, then leaving her
In the protection of his son, her brother,
35 Who shortly also died, for whose dear love,
They say, she hath abjured the sight
And company of men.
VIOLA   O that I served that lady,
And might not be delivered° to the world   *revealed*
Till I had made mine own occasion mellow,°   *ripe (to be revealed)*
What my estate° is.   *social rank*
40 CAPTAIN   That were hard to compass,°   *achieve*
Because she will admit no kind of suit,°   *petition*
No, not the Duke's.
VIOLA There is a fair behaviour⁷ in thee, captain,
And though that nature with a beauteous wall
45 Doth oft close in pollution, yet of thee
I will believe thou hast a mind that suits
With this thy fair and outward character.⁸
I pray thee—and I'll pay thee bounteously—
Conceal me what I am, and be my aid
50 For such disguise as haply shall become
The form of my intent.⁹ I'll serve this duke.
Thou shalt present me as an eunuch¹ to him.
It may be worth thy pains, for I can sing,
And speak to him in many sorts of music
55 That will allow° me very worth his service.   *prove*
What else may hap, to time I will commit.
Only shape thou thy silence to my wit.°   *imagination; plan*
CAPTAIN Be you his eunuch, and your mute² I'll be.
When my tongue blabs, then let mine eyes not see.
60 VIOLA I thank thee. Lead me on.   *Exeunt*

---

6. That he too has survived.
7. Outward appearance; conduct.
8. Appearance (suggesting moral qualities).
9. *as . . . intent:* that perhaps may be fitting to my purpose. *form:* shape.
1. Castrati (hence, "eunuchs") were prized as male sopranos; the disguise would have explained Viola's

feminine voice. Viola (or perhaps Shakespeare) seems to have changed plans: she presents herself instead as a young page.
2. In Turkish harems, eunuchs served as guards and were assisted by "mutes" (usually servants whose tongues had been cut out).

1.3

Enter SIR TOBY [*Belch*] *and* MARIA

SIR TOBY What a plague means my niece to take the death of
her brother thus? I am sure care's an enemy to life.

MARIA By my troth, Sir Toby, you must come in earlier o' nights.
Your cousin,[1] my lady, takes great exceptions to your ill hours.

5 SIR TOBY Why, let her except, before excepted.[2]

MARIA Ay, but you must confine yourself within the modest°   moderate
limits of order.

SIR TOBY Confine? I'll confine myself no finer[3] than I am. These
clothes are good enough to drink in, and so be these boots too;

10 an° they be not, let them hang themselves in their own straps.   if

MARIA That quaffing and drinking will undo you. I heard my
lady talk of it yesterday, and of a foolish knight that you brought
in one night here to be her wooer.

SIR TOBY Who, Sir Andrew Aguecheek?

15 MARIA Ay, he.

SIR TOBY He's as tall a man as any's[4] in Illyria.

MARIA What's that to th' purpose?

SIR TOBY Why, he has three thousand ducats a year.

MARIA Ay, but he'll have but a year in all these ducats.[5] He's a

20 very° fool, and a prodigal.   an absolute

SIR TOBY Fie that you'll say so! He plays o'th' viol-de-gamboys,[6]
and speaks three or four languages word for word without
book,° and hath all the good gifts of nature.   from memory

MARIA He hath indeed, almost natural,[7] for besides that he's a

25 fool, he's a great quarreller, and but that he hath the gift° of a   talent; present
coward to allay the gust° he hath in quarrelling, 'tis thought   gusto
among the prudent he would quickly have the gift of a grave.

SIR TOBY By this hand, they are scoundrels and substractors[8] that
say so of him. Who are they?

30 MARIA They that add, moreover, he's drunk nightly in your
company.

SIR TOBY With drinking healths to my niece. I'll drink to her as
long as there is a passage in my throat and drink in Illyria. He's
a coward and a coistrel° that will not drink to my niece till his   horse groom; lout

35 brains turn o'th' toe, like a parish top. What wench, *Castiliano,*
vulgo,[9] for here comes Sir Andrew Agueface.

Enter SIR ANDREW [*Aguecheek*]

SIR ANDREW Sir Toby Belch! How now, Sir Toby Belch?

SIR TOBY Sweet Sir Andrew.

SIR ANDREW [*to* MARIA] Bless you, fair shrew.[1]

40 MARIA And you too, sir.

SIR TOBY Accost, Sir Andrew, accost.[2]

SIR ANDREW What's that?

1.3 Location: The Countess Olivia's house.
1. Term used generally of kinsfolk.
2. Playing on the legal jargon *exceptis excipiendis,* "with
the previously stated exceptions." Sir Toby refuses to take
Olivia's displeasure seriously.
3. Suggesting both "a refined manner of dress" and
"narrowly" (referring to his girth).
4. Any (man) who is. *tall:* brave; worthy. (Maria takes it
in the modern sense of height.)
5. He'll spend his fortune in a year.
6. A facetious corruption of "viola da gamba," a bass viol
held between the knees.

7. Idiots and fools were called "naturals."
8. Corruption of "detractors." (In reply, Maria puns on
"substract" as "subtract.")
9. Variously interpreted, but may mean "Speak of the
devil," since Castilians were considered devilish, and
vulgo refers to the common tongue (?). *parish top:* parishes kept large tops that were spun by whipping them,
for the parishioners' amusement and exercise.
1. Andrew possibly confuses "shrew" (ill-tempered
woman) with "mouse," an endearment.
2. Address (her); originally a naval term meaning "go
alongside; greet."

SIR TOBY   My niece's chambermaid.[3]

SIR ANDREW   Good Mistress Accost, I desire better acquaintance.

45   MARIA   My name is Mary, sir.

SIR ANDREW   Good Mistress Mary Accost.

SIR TOBY   You mistake, knight. 'Accost' is front° her, board her,   *confront*
    woo her, assail[4] her.

SIR ANDREW   By my troth, I would not undertake[5] her in this
50   company.° Is that the meaning of 'accost'?   *the audience*

MARIA   Fare you well, gentlemen.

SIR TOBY   An thou let part so,[6] Sir Andrew, would thou mightst
    never draw sword again.

SIR ANDREW   An you part so, mistress, I would I might never draw
55   sword again. Fair lady, do you think you have fools in hand?°   *to deal with*

MARIA   Sir, I have not you by th' hand.

SIR ANDREW   Marry, but you shall have, and here's my hand.

MARIA [*taking his hand*]   Now sir, thought is free.[7] I pray you,
    bring your hand to th' buttery-bar,[8] and let it drink.

60   SIR ANDREW   Wherefore, sweetheart? What's your metaphor?

MARIA   It's dry,[9] sir.

SIR ANDREW   Why, I think so. I am not such an ass but I can
    keep my hand dry.[1] But what's your jest?

MARIA   A dry jest,[2] sir.

65   SIR ANDREW   Are you full of them?

MARIA   Ay, sir, I have them at my fingers' ends.[3] Marry, now I let
    go your hand I am barren.°   *Exit*   *empty of jokes*

SIR TOBY   O knight, thou lackest a cup of canary.[4] When did I
    see thee so put down?[5]

70   SIR ANDREW   Never in your life, I think, unless you see canary
    put me down. Methinks sometimes I have no more wit than a
    Christian° or an ordinary man has; but I am a great eater of   *an average man*
    beef,[6] and I believe that does harm to my wit.

SIR TOBY   No question.

75   SIR ANDREW   An I thought that, I'd forswear it. I'll ride home
    tomorrow, Sir Toby.

SIR TOBY   *Pourquoi*,° my dear knight?   *Why*

SIR ANDREW   What is 'Pourquoi'? Do, or not do? I would I had
    bestowed that time in the tongues[7] that I have in fencing, danc-
80   ing, and bear-baiting. O, had I but followed the arts!

SIR TOBY   Then hadst thou had an excellent head of hair.

SIR ANDREW   Why, would that have mended° my hair?   *improved*

SIR TOBY   Past question, for thou seest it will not curl by nature.[8]

SIR ANDREW   But it becomes me well enough, does't not?

85   SIR TOBY   Excellent, it hangs like flax on a distaff,[9] and I hope to
    see a housewife[1] take thee between her legs and spin it off.[2]

---

3. Lady-in-waiting; not a menial servant, but a gentle-woman in attendance on a great lady.
4. *board*: speak to; tackle. *assail*: greet (also nautical).
5. Take her on (with sexual implication).
6. If you let her go without protest or without bidding her farewell.
7. The customary retort to "Do you think I am a fool?"
8. Ledge on the half door to a buttery or a wine cellar on which drinks were served.
9. Thirsty; but also thought to be a sign of impotence.
1. Alluding to the proverb "Even fools have enough wit to come in out of the rain."
2. A stupid joke (referring to Andrew's stupidity); an ironic quip; a joke about dryness.

3. Always ready; or "by th' hand" (1ine 56).
4. A sweet wine, like sherry, originally from the Canary Islands.
5. Defeated in repartee; "put down" with drink.
6. Contemporary medicine held that beef dulled the intellect.
7. Foreign languages; Toby takes him to mean "curling tongs."
8. To contrast with Andrew's "arts" (line 80).
9. In spinning, flax would hang in long, thin, yellowish strings on the "distaff," a pole held between the knees.
1. Housewives spun flax; the pronunciation, "huswife," also suggests the meaning "prostitute."
2. Make him bald (as a result of venereal disease).

SIR ANDREW   Faith, I'll home tomorrow, Sir Toby. Your niece
will not be seen, or if she be, it's four to one she'll none of me.
The Count himself here hard by woos her.

90   SIR TOBY   She'll none o'th' Count. She'll not match above her
degree,° neither in estate,[3] years, nor wit, I have heard her   *social rank*
swear't. Tut, there's life in't,[4] man.

SIR ANDREW   I'll stay a month longer. I am a fellow o'th' strangest
mind i'th' world. I delight in masques and revels sometimes
95   altogether.

SIR TOBY   Art thou good at these kickshawses,[5] knight?

SIR ANDREW   As any man in Illyria, whatsoever he be, under the
degree of my betters; and yet I will not compare with an old
man.[6]

100   SIR TOBY   What is thy excellence in a galliard,[7] knight?

SIR ANDREW   Faith, I can cut a caper.[8]

SIR TOBY   And I can cut the mutton to't.

SIR ANDREW   And I think I have the back-trick[9] simply as strong
as any man in Illyria.

105   SIR TOBY   Wherefore are these things hid? Wherefore have these
gifts a curtain[1] before 'em? Are they like to take dust, like Mistress Mall's[2] picture? Why dost thou not go to church in a galliard, and come home in a coranto?[3] My very walk should be a
jig. I would not so much as make water but in a cinquepace.[4]
110   What dost thou mean? Is it a world to hide virtues in? I did
think by the excellent constitution of thy leg it was formed
under the star of a galliard.[5]

SIR ANDREW   Ay, 'tis strong, and it does indifferent° well in a   *moderately*
divers-coloured stock.° Shall we set about some revels?   *stocking*

115   SIR TOBY   What shall we do else—were we not born under
Taurus?[6]

SIR ANDREW   Taurus? That's sides and heart.

SIR TOBY   No, sir, it is legs and thighs: let me see thee caper.
[SIR ANDREW *capers*]
Ha, higher! Ha ha, excellent.   *Exeunt*

1.4

Enter VALENTINE, *and* VIOLA [*as Cesario*] *in man's attire*

VALENTINE   If the Duke continue these favours towards you,
Cesario, you are like to be much advanced. He hath known
you but three days, and already you are no stranger.

VIOLA   You either fear his humour° or my negligence, that you   *moodiness*
5   call in question the continuance of his love. Is he inconstant,
sir, in his favours?

VALENTINE   No, believe me.

Enter DUKE, CURIO, *and attendants*

3. Status; possession.
4. Proverbial: "While there's life, there's hope."
5. Trifles; trivialities (from the French *quelque chose*).
6. Expert (perhaps a backhanded compliment).
7. A lively, complex dance, including the caper.
8. Leap. (Toby puns on the pickled flower buds used in
a sauce of mutton.)
9. Probably a dance movement, a kick of the foot behind
the body (also suggesting sexual prowess, with later reference to "mutton" as "prostitute").

1. Used to protect paintings from dust.
2. Like "Moll[y]," "Mall" was a nickname for "Mary."
3. An even more rapid dance than the galliard.
4. Galliard, or, more properly, the steps joining the figures of the dance; punning on "sink," as in "sewer."
5. Astrological influences favorable to dancing.
6. The astrological sign of the bull was usually thought
to govern the neck and throat (appropriate to heavy
drinkers).
1.4 Location: Orsino's palace.

VIOLA I thank you. Here comes the Count.

ORSINO Who saw Cesario, ho?

10 VIOLA On your attendance,° my lord, here. *Waiting at your service*

ORSINO [*to* CURIO *and attendants*] Stand you a while aloof.° [*To* *aside*
    VIOLA] Cesario,
    Thou know'st no less but all.° I have unclasped *than everything*
    To thee the book even of my secret soul.
    Therefore, good youth, address thy gait° unto her, *go*
15   Be not denied access, stand at her doors,
    And tell them there thy fixèd foot shall grow° *take root*
    Till thou have audience.

VIOLA   Sure, my noble lord,
  If she be so abandoned to her sorrow
  As it is spoke, she never will admit me.

20 ORSINO Be clamorous, and leap all civil bounds,[1]
    Rather than make unprofited° return. *unsuccessful*

VIOLA Say I do speak with her, my lord, what then?

ORSINO O then unfold the passion of my love,
    Surprise[2] her with discourse of my dear° faith. *heartfelt*
25   It shall become thee well to act my woes—
    She will attend it better in thy youth
    Than in a nuncio's° of more grave aspect.° *messenger's / appearance*

VIOLA I think not so, my lord.

ORSINO   Dear lad, believe it;
    For they shall yet belie thy happy years
30   That say thou art a man. Diana's lip
    Is not more smooth and rubious;° thy small pipe° *ruby red / voice*
    Is as the maiden's organ, shrill and sound,[3]
    And all is semblative° a woman's part. *like*
    I know thy constellation[4] is right apt
35   For this affair. [*To* CURIO *and attendants*] Some four or five attend him.
    All if you will, for I myself am best
    When least in company. [*To* VIOLA] Prosper well in this
    And thou shalt live as freely as thy lord,
    To call his fortunes thine.

VIOLA   I'll do my best
40   To woo your lady—[*aside*] yet a barful strife[5]—
  Whoe'er I woo, myself would be his wife. *Exeunt*

1.5

Enter MARIA, *and* [FESTE,[1] *the*] *clown*

MARIA Nay, either tell me where thou hast been or I will not
  open my lips so wide as a bristle may enter in° way of thy *by*
  excuse. My lady will hang thee for thy absence.

FESTE Let her hang me. He that is well hanged in this world
5   needs to fear no colours.[2]

MARIA Make that good.° *Explain that*

FESTE He shall see none to fear.

---

1. All constraints of polite behavior.
2. Capture by unexpected attack (of military origin).
3. High-pitched and uncracked.
4. Nature and abilities (as supposedly determined by the stars).

5. An undertaking full of impediments.
1.5 Location: Olivia's house.
1. The name is used only once, at 2.4.11.
2. Proverbial for "fear nothing." *colours:* worldly deceptions, with a pun on "collars" as "hangman's noose."

MARIA A good lenten³ answer. I can tell thee where that saying
was born, of 'I fear no colours'.

10 FESTE Where, good Mistress Mary?

MARIA In the wars,⁴ and that may you be bold to say in your
foolery.

FESTE Well, God give them wisdom that have it; and those that
are fools, let them use their talents.⁵

15 MARIA Yet you will be hanged for being so long absent, or to be
turned away⁶—is not that as good as a hanging to you?

FESTE Many a good hanging prevents a bad marriage;⁷ and for
turning away, let summer bear it out.°   make it endurable

MARIA You are resolute then?

20 FESTE Not so neither, but I am resolved on two points.°   matters; laces

MARIA That if one break, the other will hold; or if both break,
your gaskins° fall.   wide breeches

FESTE Apt, in good faith, very apt. Well, go thy way. If Sir Toby
would leave drinking thou wert as witty a piece of Eve's flesh⁸

25 as any in Illyria.

MARIA Peace, you rogue, no more o' that. Here comes my lady.
Make your excuse wisely, you were best.°   [Exit]   you had better

    Enter Lady OLIVIA, *with* MALVOLIO° [*and attendants*]   "ill will"

FESTE [*aside*] Wit,⁹ an't° be thy will, put me into good fooling!   if it
Those wits that think they have thee do very oft prove fools,

30 and I that am sure I lack thee may pass for a wise man. For
what says Quinapalus?¹—'Better a witty fool than a foolish wit.'
[*To* OLIVIA] God bless thee, lady.

OLIVIA [*to attendants*] Take the fool away.

FESTE Do you not hear, fellows? Take away the lady.

35 OLIVIA Go to, you're a dry² fool. I'll no more of you. Besides,
you grow dishonest.°   unreliable

FESTE Two faults, madonna,° that drink and good counsel will   my lady
amend, for give the dry fool drink, then is the fool not dry; bid
the dishonest man mend° himself : if he mend, he is no longer   reform

40 dishonest; if he cannot, let the botcher° mend him. Anything   tailor; cobbler
that's mended is but patched. Virtue that transgresses is but
patched with sin, and sin that amends is but patched with virtue. If that this simple syllogism will serve, so. If it will not, what
remedy? As there is no true cuckold but calamity, so beauty's a

45 flower.³ The lady bade take away the fool, therefore I say again,
take her away.

OLIVIA Sir, I bade them take away you.

FESTE Misprision⁴ in the highest degree! Lady, 'Cucullus non
facit monachum'⁵—that's as much to say as I wear not motley⁶

50 in my brain. Good madonna, give me leave to prove you a fool.

---

3. Thin or meager (like Lenten fare).
4. *In the wars*: "colours" in line 9 refers to military flags.
5. Alluding to the parable of the talents, Matthew 25.
The comic implication is that a fool should strive to
increase his measure of folly. Since "fool" and "fowl" had
similar pronunciations, there may also be a play on
"talents/talons."
6. Dismissed; also, perhaps, turned off or hanged.
7. *Many . . . marriage*: Proverbial. *hanging*: execution;
sexual prowess.
8. Woman. Feste may imply both that Maria and Toby
would make a good match and that Maria is as witty as

Toby is sober.
9. Intelligence, which is often contrasted with will.
1. Feste frequently invents his own authorities.
2. Dull, but Feste interprets as "thirsty." *Go to*: an
expression of impatience.
3. *As . . . flower*: In taking her vow (1.2.36–37), Olivia
has wedded herself to calamity but must be unfaithful,
or let pass her moment of beauty.
4. Misapprehension; wrongful arrest.
5. The cowl does not make the monk (a Latin proverb).
6. The multicolored costume of a fool.

OLIVIA   Can you do it?

FESTE   Dexteriously,° good madonna.   *Dexterously*

OLIVIA   Make your proof.

FESTE   I must catechize[7] you for it, madonna. Good my mouse

55   of virtue,° answer me.   *My good virtuous mouse*

OLIVIA   Well, sir, for want of other idleness° I'll bide° your proof.   *pastime / await*

FESTE   Good madonna, why mournest thou?

OLIVIA   Good fool, for my brother's death.

FESTE   I think his soul is in hell, madonna.

60   OLIVIA   I know his soul is in heaven, fool.

FESTE   The more fool, madonna, to mourn for your brother's
soul, being in heaven. Take away the fool, gentlemen.

OLIVIA   What think you of this fool, Malvolio? Doth he not
mend?[8]

65   MALVOLIO   Yes, and shall do till the pangs of death shake him.
Infirmity,° that decays the wise, doth ever make the better fool.[9]   *(Old) age*

FESTE   God send you, sir, a speedy infirmity for the better
increasing your folly. Sir Toby will be sworn that I am no fox,
but he will not pass his word for twopence that you are no fool.

70   OLIVIA   How say you to that, Malvolio?

MALVOLIO   I marvel your ladyship takes delight in such a barren
rascal. I saw him put down° the other day with an ordinary fool   *defeated in repartee*
that has no more brain than a stone. Look you now, he's out of
his guard° already. Unless you laugh and minister occasion[1] to   *defenseless*

75   him, he is gagged. I protest I take these wise men that crow so
at these set° kind of fools no better than the fools' zanies.°   *artificial / "straight men"*

OLIVIA   O, you are sick of self-love, Malvolio, and taste with a
distempered[2] appetite. To be generous, guiltless, and of free°   *magnanimous*
disposition is to take those things for birdbolts[3] that you deem

80   cannon bullets. There is no slander in an allowed fool, though
he do nothing but rail; nor no railing in a known discreet man,
though he do nothing but reprove.

FESTE   Now Mercury indue thee with leasing,[4] for thou speakest
well of fools.

Enter MARIA

85   MARIA   Madam, there is at the gate a young gentleman much
desires to speak with you.

OLIVIA   From the Count Orsino, is it?

MARIA   I know not, madam. 'Tis a fair young man, and well
attended.

90   OLIVIA   Who of my people hold him in delay?

MARIA   Sir Toby, madam, your kinsman.

OLIVIA   Fetch him off, I pray you, he speaks nothing but mad-
man.° Fie on him. Go you, Malvolio. If it be a suit from the   *madman's talk*
Count, I am sick, or not at home—what you will to dismiss it.

Exit MALVOLIO

95   Now you see, sir, how your fooling grows old,° and people dis-   *stale*
like it.

FESTE   Thou hast spoke for us, madonna, as if thy eldest son

---

7. Question (as in catechism, which tests the orthodoxy of belief).
8. Improve, but Malvolio takes "mend" to mean "grow
more foolish."
9. Make the fool more foolish.

1. And give opportunity.
2. An unbalanced; a sick.
3. Blunt arrows for shooting birds.
4. May Mercury, the god of deception, endow you with
the talent of tactful lying.

should be a fool, whose skull Jove cram with brains, for—here
he comes—
    Enter SIR TOBY
100 one of thy kin has a most weak *pia mater*.[5]
OLIVIA By mine honour, half-drunk. What is he at the gate,
    cousin?°   *kinsman*
SIR TOBY A gentleman.
OLIVIA A gentleman? What gentleman?
105 SIR TOBY 'Tis a gentleman here. [*He belches*] A plague o' these
    pickle herring! [*To* FESTE] How now, sot?°   *fool; drunkard*
FESTE Good Sir Toby.
OLIVIA Cousin, cousin, how have you come so early by this
    lethargy?
110 SIR TOBY Lechery? I defy lechery. There's one° at the gate.   *someone*
OLIVIA Ay, marry, what is he?
SIR TOBY Let him be the devil an° he will, I care not. Give me   *if*
    faith,[6] say I. Well, it's all one.°   *Exit*   *it doesn't matter*
OLIVIA What's a drunken man like, fool?
115 FESTE Like a drowned man, a fool, and a madman—one
    draught above heat[7] makes him a fool, the second mads him,
    and a third drowns him.
OLIVIA Go thou and seek the coroner, and let him sit o'° my   *hold an inquest for*
    coz,° for he's in the third degree of drink, he's drowned. Go   *cousin; uncle*
120 look after him.
FESTE He is but mad yet, madonna, and the fool shall look to
    the madman.   [*Exit*]
    Enter MALVOLIO
MALVOLIO Madam, yon young fellow swears he will speak with
    you. I told him you were sick—he takes on him to understand
125 so much, and therefore° comes to speak with you. I told him   *for that very reason*
    you were asleep—he seems to have a foreknowledge of that
    too, and therefore comes to speak with you. What is to be said
    to him, lady? He's fortified against any denial.
OLIVIA Tell him he shall not speak with me.
130 MALVOLIO He's been told so, and he says he'll stand at your door
    like a sheriff's post,[8] and be the supporter to a bench, but he'll
    speak with you.
OLIVIA What kind o' man is he?
MALVOLIO Why, of mankind.°   *like any other*
135 OLIVIA What manner of man?
MALVOLIO Of very ill manner: he'll speak with you, will you or
    no.
OLIVIA Of what personage° and years is he?   *appearance*
MALVOLIO Not yet old enough for a man, nor young enough for
140 a boy; as a squash[9] is before 'tis a peascod, or a codling° when   *an unripe apple*
    'tis almost an apple. 'Tis with him in standing water° between   *at the turn of the tide*
    boy and man. He is very well-favoured,° and he speaks very   *handsome*
    shrewishly.° One would think his mother's milk were scarce   *sharply*
    out of him.
145 OLIVIA Let him approach. Call in my gentlewoman.
MALVOLIO Gentlewoman, my lady calls.   *Exit*

---

5. Brain; or literally, the membrane enclosing it.
6. To defy the devil by faith alone.
7. One drink ("draught")/beyond the quantity necessary
to warm him.

8. A decorative post set before a sheriff's door, as a sign
of authority.
9. An undeveloped pea pod.

Enter MARIA

OLIVIA   Give me my veil. Come, throw it o'er my face.
We'll once more hear Orsino's embassy.

Enter VIOLA [*as Cesario*]

VIOLA   The honourable lady of the house, which is she?

150   OLIVIA   Speak to me, I shall answer for her. Your will.

VIOLA   Most radiant, exquisite, and unmatchable beauty.—I pray
you, tell me if this be the lady of the house, for I never saw
her. I would be loath to cast away° my speech, for besides that   *waste*
it is excellently well penned, I have taken great pains to

155   con° it. Good beauties, let me sustain° no scorn; I am very   *memorize / suffer*
'countable,° even to the least sinister usage.[1]   *sensitive*

OLIVIA   Whence came you, sir?

VIOLA   I can say little more than I have studied,[2] and that question's out of my part. Good gentle one, give me modest° assur-   *adequate*

160   ance if you be the lady of the house, that I may proceed in my
speech.

OLIVIA   Are you a comedian?°   *an actor*

VIOLA   No, my profound heart;[3] and yet—by the very fangs of
malice I swear—I am not that I play. Are you the lady of the

165   house?

OLIVIA   If I do not usurp[4] myself, I am.

VIOLA   Most certain if you are she you do usurp yourself, for what
is yours to bestow is not yours to reserve. But this is from my
commission.° I will on with my speech in your praise, and then   *beyond my instructions*

170   show you the heart of my message.

OLIVIA   Come to what is important in't, I forgive you° the praise.   *excuse you from*

VIOLA   Alas, I took great pains to study it, and 'tis poetical.

OLIVIA   It is the more like to be feigned, I pray you keep it in. I
heard you were saucy° at my gates, and allowed your approach   *impertinent*

175   rather to wonder at you than to hear you. If you be not mad,°   *utterly mad*
be gone. If you have reason,° be brief. 'Tis not that time of   *any sanity*
moon with me to make one in so skipping a dialogue.[5]

MARIA   Will you hoist sail, sir? Here lies your way.

VIOLA   No, good swabber, I am to hull[6] here a little longer.

180   [*To* OLIVIA] Some mollification for your giant,[7] sweet lady. Tell
me your mind, I am a messenger.[8]

OLIVIA   Sure, you have some hideous matter to deliver when the
courtesy° of it is so fearful. Speak your office.°   *introduction / business*
   declaration

VIOLA   It alone concerns your ear. I bring no overture° of war,

185   no taxation of homage.[9] I hold the olive[1] in my hand. My words
are as full of peace as matter.°   *meaning*

OLIVIA   Yet you began rudely. What are you? What would you?

VIOLA   The rudeness that hath appeared in me have I learned
from my entertainment.° What I am and what I would are as   *reception*

190   secret as maidenhead;° to your ears, divinity; to any others',   *virginity*
profanation.

---

1. To the slightest discourteous treatment.
2. Learned by heart (a theatrical term).
3. My most wise lady; upon my soul.
4. Counterfeit; misappropriate.
5. *'Tis . . . dialogue:* I am not lunatic enough to take part
in so flighty a conversation. (Lunacy was thought to be
influenced by the phases of the moon.)
6. To lie unanchored with lowered sails. *swabber:* a

cleaner of boat decks.
7. Mythical giants guarded ladies; here, also mocking
Maria's diminutive size. *Some . . . for:* Please pacify.
8. From Orsino; Olivia pretends she understands her to
mean a king's messenger, or a messenger-at-arms,
employed on important state affairs.
9. Demand for dues paid to a superior.
1. Olive branch (as a symbol of peace).

OLIVIA [to MARIA and attendants]   Give us the place alone, we
    will hear this divinity.°   [Exeunt MARIA and attendants]   religious discourse
    Now sir, what is your text?²
195 VIOLA   Most sweet lady—
    OLIVIA   A comfortable° doctrine, and much may be said of it.   comforting
    Where lies your text?
    VIOLA   In Orsino's bosom.
    OLIVIA   In his bosom? In what chapter of his bosom?
200 VIOLA   To answer by the method,° in the first of his heart.   in the same style
    OLIVIA   O, I have read it. It is heresy. Have you no more to say?
    VIOLA   Good madam, let me see your face.
    OLIVIA   Have you any commission from your lord to negotiate
    with my face? You are now out of° your text. But we will draw   straying from
205   the curtain and show you the picture.
        [She unveils]
    Look you, sir, such a one I was this present.³ Is't not well done?
    VIOLA   Excellently done, if God did all.⁴
    OLIVIA   'Tis in grain,° sir, 'twill endure wind and weather.   The dye is fast
    VIOLA   'Tis beauty truly blent,⁵ whose red and white
210   Nature's own sweet and cunning° hand laid on.   skillful
    Lady, you are the cruell'st she° alive   woman
    If you will lead these graces to the grave
    And leave the world no copy.⁶
    OLIVIA   O sir, I will not be so hard-hearted. I will give out divers
215   schedules° of my beauty. It shall be inventoried and every parti-   various inventories
    cle and utensil labelled⁷ to my will, as, item, two lips, indiffer-
    ent° red; item, two grey eyes, with lids⁸ to them; item, one neck,   moderate
    one chin, and so forth. Were you sent hither to praise° me?   appraise; flatter
    VIOLA   I see you what you are, you are too proud,
220   But if° you were the devil, you are fair.   Even if
    My lord and master loves you. O, such love
    Could be but recompensed though⁹ you were crowned
    The nonpareil of beauty.°   An unequaled beauty
    OLIVIA   How does he love me?
    VIOLA   With adorations, fertile° tears,   ever-flowing
225   With groans that thunder love, with sighs of fire.
    OLIVIA   Your lord does know my mind, I cannot love him.
    Yet I suppose him virtuous, know him noble,
    Of great estate, of fresh and stainless youth,
    In voices well divulged,° free,° learned, and valiant,   spoken of / generous
230   And in dimension and the shape of nature¹
    A gracious person; but yet I cannot love him.
    He might have took his answer long ago.
    VIOLA   If I did love you in° my master's flame,°   with / passion
    With such a suff'ring, such a deadly° life,   deathlike
235   In your denial I would find no sense,
    I would not understand it.

---

2. Quotation (as a theme of a sermon, in keeping with
"divinity," "doctrine," "heresy," etc.).
3. Portraits usually gave the year of painting. "This
present" was a term used to date letters.
4. If it is natural (without the use of cosmetics).
5. Blended, or mixed (of paints). Shakespeare uses the
same metaphor in sonnet 20, lines 1–2, and Viola's next
lines recall sonnet 11, lines 13–14. As Cesario, Viola is
playing with established conventions of poetic courtship.

6. Viola means "child"; Olivia takes her to mean "list" or
"inventory."
7. Every single part and article added as a codicil (parodying the legal language of a last will and testament).
8. Eyelids, but also punning on "pot lids" (punning on
"utensil" as a household implement).
9. Could . . . though: Would have to be requited even if.
1. dimension . . . shape of nature: the two terms are
synonymous, meaning "bodily form."

OLIVIA   Why, what would you?
VIOLA   Make me a willow² cabin at your gate
         And call upon my soul° within the house,   *(Olivia)*
         Write loyal cantons of contemnèd° love,   *songs of rejected*
240   And sing them loud even in the dead of night;
         Halloo³ your name to the reverberate° hills,   *echoing*
         And make the babbling gossip of the air⁴
         Cry out 'Olivia!' O, you should not rest
         Between the elements of air and earth
245   But you should pity me.
OLIVIA   You might do much.
         What is your parentage?
VIOLA   Above my fortunes, yet my state° is well.   *social status*
         I am a gentleman.
OLIVIA   Get you to your lord.
250   I cannot love him. Let him send no more,
         Unless, perchance, you come to me again
         To tell me how he takes it. Fare you well.
         I thank you for your pains. [*Offering a purse*] Spend this for me.
VIOLA   I am no fee'd post,° lady. Keep your purse.   *hired messenger*
255   My master, not myself, lacks recompense.
         Love make his heart of flint that you shall love,⁵
         And let your fervour, like my master's, be
         Placed in contempt. Farewell, fair cruelty.   *Exit*
OLIVIA   'What is your parentage?'
260   'Above my fortunes, yet my state is well.
         I am a gentleman.' I'll be sworn thou art.
         Thy tongue, thy face, thy limbs, actions, and spirit
         Do give thee five-fold blazon.⁶ Not too fast. Soft,° soft—   *Wait*
         Unless the master were the man.⁷ How now?
265   Even so quickly may one catch the plague?
         Methinks I feel this youth's perfections
         With an invisible and subtle stealth
         To creep in at mine eyes. Well, let it be.
         What ho, Malvolio.
                    Enter MALVOLIO
MALVOLIO   Here, madam, at your service.
270 OLIVIA   Run after that same peevish messenger
         The County's° man. He left this ring behind him,   *Count's*
         Would I° or not. Tell him I'll none of it.   *Whether I wished it*
         Desire him not to flatter with° his lord,   *encourage*
         Nor hold him up with hopes. I am not for him.
275   If that the youth will come this way tomorrow,
         I'll give him reasons for't. Hie thee,° Malvolio.   *Hurry*
MALVOLIO Madam, I will.   *Exit* [*at one door*]
OLIVIA   I do I know not what, and fear to find
         Mine eye too great a flatterer for my mind.⁸

---

2. Traditional symbol of rejected love.
3. Shout; or perhaps "hallow," as in "bless."
4. For the love of Narcissus, the nymph Echo wasted
away to a mere voice, only able to repeat whatever she
heard spoken.
5. *Love . . . love:* May love make the heart of the man you

love as hard as flint.
6. Formal description of a gentleman's coat of arms.
7. If Orsino were Cesario (*man:* servant).
8. My eye (through which love has entered my heart) has
seduced my reason.

280 Fate, show thy force. Ourselves we do not owe.°   *own*
What is decreed must be; and be this so.

                                    [Exit at another door]

2.1

Enter ANTONIO *and* SEBASTIAN

ANTONIO   Will you stay no longer, nor will° you not that I go   *wish*
    with you?

SEBASTIAN   By your patience, no. My stars shine darkly over me.
    The malignancy of my fate[1] might perhaps distemper° yours,   *infect*
5   therefore I shall crave of you your leave that I may bear my
    evils alone. It were a bad recompense for your love to lay any
    of them on you.

ANTONIO   Let me yet know of you whither you are bound.

SEBASTIAN   No, sooth,° sir. My determinate° voyage is mere   *truly / destined*
10   extravagancy.° But I perceive in you so excellent a touch of   *idle wandering*
    modesty° that you will not extort from me what I am willing to   *politeness*
    keep in. Therefore it charges me in manners[2] the rather to
    express° myself. You must know of me then, Antonio, my name   *reveal*
    is Sebastian, which I called Roderigo. My father was that Sebas-
15   tian of Messaline[3] whom I know you have heard of. He left
    behind him myself and a sister, both born in an° hour. If the   *within the same*
    heavens had been pleased, would we had so ended. But you,
    sir, altered that, for some hour before you took me from the
    breach° of the sea was my sister drowned.   *surf*

20 ANTONIO   Alas the day!

SEBASTIAN   A lady, sir, though it was said she much resembled
    me, was yet of many accounted beautiful. But though I could
    not with such estimable° wonder over-far believe that, yet   *appreciative*
    thus far I will boldly publish° her: she bore a mind that   *proclaim*
25   envy° could not but call fair. She is drowned already, sir, with   *malice*
    salt water, though I seem to drown her remembrance again
    with more.

ANTONIO   Pardon me, sir, your bad entertainment.[4]

SEBASTIAN   O good Antonio, forgive me your trouble.

30 ANTONIO   If you will not murder me[5] for my love, let me be your
    servant.

SEBASTIAN   If you will not undo what you have done—that is,
    kill him whom you have recovered°—desire it not. Fare ye well   *rescued*
    at once. My bosom is full of kindness,° and I am yet° so near   *tender emotion / still*
35   the manners of my mother[6] that upon the least occasion more
    mine eyes will tell tales of me.° I am bound to the Count   *betray my feelings*
    Orsino's court. Farewell.   *Exit*

ANTONIO   The gentleness° of all the gods go with thee!   *favor*
    I have many enemies in Orsino's court,
40   Else would I very shortly see thee there.
    But come what may, I do adore thee so
    That danger shall seem sport, and I will go.   *Exit*

2.1 Location: Near the coast of Illyria.
1. Evil influence of the stars; "malignancy" also signifies
a deadly disease.
2. Therefore courtesy requires.
3. Possibly Messina, Sicily.
4. Your poor reception; your inhospitality.
5. Murder him by insisting that they part.
6. So near woman's readiness to weep.

2.2

Enter VIOLA *as Cesario, and* MALVOLIO, *at several° doors*   *separate*

MALVOLIO Were not you ev'n° now with the Countess Olivia?   *just*

VIOLA Even now, sir, on° a moderate pace, I have since arrived   *at*
but hither.°   *come only this far*

MALVOLIO [*offering a ring*] She returns this ring to you, sir.

5 You might have saved me my pains to have taken° it away your- *by taking*
self. She adds, moreover, that you should put your lord into a
desperate assurance° she will none of him. And one thing *hopeless certainty*
more: that you be never so hardy° to come again in his affairs, *bold*
unless it be to report your lord's taking of this.[1] Receive it so.

10 VIOLA She took the ring of me.[2] I'll none of it.

MALVOLIO Come, sir, you peevishly threw it to her, and her will
is it should be so returned.
    [*He throws the ring down*]
It if be worth stooping for, there it lies, in your eye;° if not, be *sight*
it his that finds it.   *Exit*

15 VIOLA [*picking up the ring*] I left no ring with her. What means this lady?
Fortune forbid my outside° have not charmed her.   *appearance*
She made good view of° me, indeed so much   *looked carefully at*
That straight methought her eyes had lost° her tongue,   *made her lose*
For she did speak in starts, distractedly.

20 She loves me, sure. The cunning of her passion
Invites me in° this churlish messenger.   *by means of*
None of my lord's ring! Why, he sent her none.
I am the man.[3] If it be so—as 'tis—
Poor lady, she were better love a dream!

25 Disguise, I see thou art a wickedness
Wherein the pregnant enemy[4] does much.
How easy is it for the proper false[5]
In women's waxen hearts to set their forms![6]
Alas, our frailty is the cause, not we,

30 For such as we are made of, such we be.[7]
How will this fadge?° My master loves her dearly,   *turn out*
And I, poor monster,[8] fond° as much on him,   *dote*
And she, mistaken, seems to dote on me.
What will become of this? As I am man,

35 My state is desperate° for my master's love.   *hopeless*
As I am woman, now, alas the day,
What thriftless° sighs shall poor Olivia breathe!   *unprofitable*
O time, thou must untangle this, not I.
It is too hard a knot for me t'untie.   [*Exit*]

2.3

Enter SIR TOBY *and* SIR ANDREW

SIR TOBY Approach, Sir Andrew. Not to be abed after midnight
is to be up betimes,° and *diliculo surgere,*[1] thou knowest.   *early*

2.2 Location: Between Olivia's house and Orsino's
palace.
1. Reception of this rejection.
2. Viola pretends to believe Olivia's story. *of:* from.
3. The man with whom she has fallen in love.
4. The devil, who is always quick and ready (to deceive).
5. Handsome, but deceitful (men).

6. *In . . . forms:* To impress their images on women's
affections (as a seal stamps its image in wax).
7. For being made of frail flesh, we are frail.
8. Since she is both man and woman.
2.3 Location: Olivia's house.
1. Part of a Latin proverb, meaning "to rise at dawn (is
most healthy)."

SIR ANDREW   Nay, by my troth,° I know not; but I know to be up   *faith*
late is to be up late.

5   SIR TOBY   A false conclusion. I hate it as an unfilled can.° To be   *tankard*
up after midnight and to go to bed then is early; so that to go
to bed after midnight is to go to bed betimes. Does not our lives
consist of the four elements?[2]

SIR ANDREW   Faith, so they say, but I think it rather consists of
10   eating and drinking.

SIR TOBY   Thou'rt a scholar; let us therefore eat and drink. Marian, I say, a stoup° of wine.   *two-pint tankard*
        Enter [FESTE, the] clown

SIR ANDREW   Here comes the fool, i'faith.

FESTE   How now, my hearts. Did you never see the picture of
15   'we three'?[3]

SIR TOBY   Welcome, ass. Now let's have a catch.[4]

SIR ANDREW   By my troth, the fool has an excellent breast.° I had   *singing voice*
rather than forty shillings I had such a leg,° and so sweet a   *(for dancing)*
breath to sing, as the fool has. In sooth, thou wast in very gra-
20   cious fooling last night, when thou spokest of Pigrogromitus, of
the Vapians passing the equinoctial of Queubus.[5] 'Twas very
good, i'faith. I sent thee sixpence for thy leman.° Hadst it?   *sweetheart*

FESTE   I did impeticos thy gratility;[6] for Malvolio's nose is no
whipstock. My lady has a white hand, and the Myrmidons are
25   no bottle-ale houses.[7]

SIR ANDREW   Excellent! Why, this is the best fooling, when all is
done. Now a song.

SIR TOBY   [*to* FESTE]   Come on, there is sixpence for you. Let's
have a song.

30   SIR ANDREW   [*to* FESTE]   There's a testril[8] of me, too. If one knight
give a—[9]

FESTE   Would you have a love-song, or a song of good life?

SIR TOBY   A love song, a love-song.

SIR ANDREW   Ay, ay. I care not for good life.

FESTE   (*sings*)
35   O mistress mine, where are you roaming?
            O stay and hear, your true love's coming,
                That can sing both high and low.
            Trip° no further, pretty sweeting.   *Go*
            Journeys end in lovers meeting,
40   Every wise man's son doth know.[1]

SIR ANDREW   Excellent good, i'faith.

SIR TOBY   Good, good.

FESTE   What is love? 'Tis not hereafter,
            Present mirth hath present laughter.
45   What's to come is still° unsure.   *always*
            In delay there lies no plenty,

---

2. The four elements, thought to make up all matter,
were earth, air, fire, and water.
3. A trick picture portraying two fools' or asses' heads, the
third being the viewer.
4. Round: a simple song for several voices.
5. *Pigrogromitus . . . Queubus:* Feste's mock learning.
equinoctial: equator of the astronomical heavens.
6. Comic jargon for "impocket (or impetticoat) your gra-
tuity."
7. *for . . . houses:* perhaps it is the sheer inscrutability of
Feste's foolery that so impresses Sir Andrew (line 26).

whipstock: handle of a whip. *bottle-ale houses:* cheap
taverns.
8. Sir Andrew's version of "tester" (sixpence).
9. In F, "give a" appears at the end of a justified line; an
omission is possible.
1. *O mistress . . . know:* the words are not certainly
Shakespeare's; they fit the tune of an instrumental piece
printed in Thomas Morley's *First Book of Consort Lessons* (1599). *wise man's son:* wise men were thought to
have foolish sons.

Then come kiss me, sweet and twenty.°   *twenty times sweet*
Youth's a stuff will not endure.

SIR ANDREW   A mellifluous voice, as I am true knight.

50   SIR TOBY   A contagious breath.[2]

SIR ANDREW   Very sweet and contagious, i'faith.

SIR TOBY   To hear by the nose, it is dulcet in contagion.[3] But
shall we make the welkin° dance indeed? Shall we rouse the   *sky*
night-owl in a catch that will draw three souls out of one

55   weaver?[4] Shall we do that?

SIR ANDREW   An° you love me, let's do't. I am dog° at a catch.   *If / clever*

FESTE   By'r Lady, sir, and some dogs will catch well.

SIR ANDREW   Most certain. Let our catch be 'Thou knave'.

FESTE   'Hold thy peace, thou knave',[5] knight. I shall be con-

60   strained in't to call thee knave, knight.

SIR ANDREW   'Tis not the first time I have constrained one to call
me knave. Begin, fool. It begins 'Hold thy peace'.

FESTE   I shall never begin if I hold my peace.

SIR ANDREW   Good, i'faith. Come, begin.

[*They sing the*] catch.

Enter MARIA

65   MARIA   What a caterwauling do you keep here! If my lady have
not called up her steward Malvolio and bid him turn you out
of doors, never trust me.

SIR TOBY   My lady's a Cathayan,[6] we are politicians,° Malvolio's   *schemers*
a Peg-o'-Ramsey,[7] and 'Three merry men be we'. Am not I con-

70   sanguineous?[8] Am I not of her blood? Tilly-vally°—'lady'!   *Fiddlesticks*
'There dwelt a man in Babylon, lady, lady.'[9]

FESTE   Beshrew° me, the knight's in admirable fooling.   *Curse*

SIR ANDREW   Ay, he does well enough if he be disposed, and so
do I, too. He does it with a better grace, but I do it more

75   natural.[1]

SIR TOBY   'O' the twelfth day of December'[2]—

MARIA   For the love o' God, peace.

Enter MALVOLIO

MALVOLIO   My masters, are you mad? Or what are you? Have
you no wit,° manners, nor honesty,° but to gabble like tinkers   *sense / decency*

80   at this time of night? Do ye make an alehouse of my lady's
house, that ye squeak out your coziers' catches without any
mitigation or remorse[3] of voice? Is there no respect of place,
persons, nor time in you?

SIR TOBY   We did keep time, sir, in our catches. Sneck up!°   *Go hang yourself*

85   MALVOLIO   Sir Toby, I must be round° with you. My lady bade   *plainspoken*
me tell you that though she harbours you as her kinsman she's
nothing allied to your disorders. If you can separate yourself
and your misdemeanours you are welcome to the house. If not,

2. Catchy voice; with a play on "disease-causing air."
3. If one could hear through the nose, the sound would
be sweetly ("dulcet") infectious.
4. Weavers were traditionally addicted to psalm singing,
so to move them with popular catches would be a great
triumph. Music was said to be able to draw the soul from
the body.
5. The words of the catch are "Hold thy peace, I prithee
hold thy peace, thou knave" (see Textual Note). Each
singer repeatedly calls the others knaves and tells them
to stop singing.
6. Chinese; but also ethnocentric slang for "trickster" or

"cheat."
7. Name of a dance and popular song; here, used
contemptuously.
8. A blood relative of Olivia's. '*Three . . . we*': a refrain
from a popular song.
9. The opening and refrain of a popular song called
"Constant Susanna."
1. Effortlessly; but unconsciously playing on "fool" or
"idiot."
2. Snatch of a ballad; or possibly a drunken version of
"twelfth day of Christmas"—that is, Twelfth Night.
3. Without any abating or softening.

90   an it would please you to take leave of her she is very willing to
bid you farewell.

SIR TOBY   'Farewell, dear heart, since I must needs be gone.'[4]

MARIA   Nay, good Sir Toby.

FESTE   'His eyes do show his days are almost done.'

MALVOLIO   Is't even so?

95 SIR TOBY   'But I will never die.'

FESTE   'Sir Toby, there you lie.'

MALVOLIO   This is much credit to you.

SIR TOBY   'Shall I bid him go?'

FESTE   'What an if° you do?'   *an if=if*

100 SIR TOBY   'Shall I bid him go, and spare not?'

FESTE   'O no, no, no, no, you dare not.'

SIR TOBY   Out o' tune, sir, ye lie. [*To* MALVOLIO] Art any more
than a steward? Dost thou think because thou art virtuous there
shall be no more cakes and ale?[5]

105 FESTE   Yes, by Saint Anne, and ginger[6] shall be hot i'th' mouth,
too.

SIR TOBY   Thou'rt i'th' right. [*To* MALVOLIO] Go, sir, rub your
chain with crumbs.[7] [*To* MARIA] A stoup of wine, Maria.

MALVOLIO   Mistress Mary, if you prized my lady's favour at any-

110 thing more than contempt you would not give means° for this   *drink*
uncivil rule.° She shall know of it, by this hand.   *Exit*[8]   *behavior*

MARIA   Go shake your ears.°   *(like an ass)*

SIR ANDREW   'Twere as good a deed as to drink when a man's a-
hungry to challenge him the field° and then to break promise   *to a duel*

115 with him, and make a fool of him.

SIR TOBY   Do't, knight. I'll write thee a challenge, or I'll deliver
thy indignation to him by word of mouth.

MARIA   Sweet Sir Toby, be patient for tonight. Since the youth
of the Count's was today with my lady she is much out of quiet.

120 For Monsieur Malvolio, let me alone with him. If I do not gull
him into a nayword[9] and make him a common recreation,° do   *sport; jest*
not think I have wit enough to lie straight in my bed. I know I
can do it.

SIR TOBY   Possess° us, possess us, tell us something of him.   *Inform*

125 MARIA   Marry, sir, sometimes he is a kind of puritan.[1]

SIR ANDREW   O, if I thought that I'd beat him like a dog.

SIR TOBY   What, for being a puritan? Thy exquisite° reason, dear   *ingenious*
knight.

SIR ANDREW   I have no exquisite reason for't, but I have reason

130 good enough.

MARIA   The dev'l a puritan that he is, or anything constantly but
a time-pleaser,° an affectioned° ass that cons state without book   *boot licker / affected*
and utters it by great swathes;[2] the best persuaded of himself,[3]
so crammed, as he thinks, with excellencies, that it is his

4. Part of another song that Sir Toby and Feste adapt for
the occasion.

5. *cakes and ale*: traditionally associated with church
festivals, and therefore disliked by Puritans.

6. Used to spice ale. *Saint Anne*: mother of the Virgin;
the oath would be offensive to Puritans who attacked her
cult.

7. Clean your steward's chain; mind your own business.

8. Feste plays no further part in this scene, and he seems
not to be present by line 153. This is the suggested exit

for him.

9. If I do not trick ("gull") him into a byword (for
"dupe").

1. Could mean "morally strict and censorious," as well as
"a follower of the Puritan religious faith."

2. *cons . . . swathes*: memorizes dignified and high-flown
language and utters it in great sweeps (like hay falling
under a scythe).

3. Having the highest opinion of himself.

135 grounds of faith° that all that look on him love him; and on   *his creed*
that vice in him will my revenge find notable cause to work.
SIR TOBY What wilt thou do?
MARIA I will drop in his way some obscure epistles of love,
wherein by the colour of his beard, the shape of his leg, the
140 manner of his gait, the expressure° of his eye, forehead, and   *expression*
complexion, he shall find himself most feelingly personated.° I   *represented*
can write very like my lady your niece; on a forgotten° matter   *bygone*
we can hardly make distinction of our hands.°   *handwriting*
SIR TOBY Excellent, I smell a device.
145 SIR ANDREW I have't in my nose too.
SIR TOBY He shall think by the letters that thou wilt drop that
they come from my niece, and that she's in love with him.
MARIA My purpose is indeed a horse of that colour.
SIR ANDREW And your horse now would make him an ass.
150 MARIA Ass° I doubt not.   *(punning on "as")*
SIR ANDREW O, 'twill be admirable.
MARIA Sport royal, I warrant you. I know my physic° will work   *medicine*
with him. I will plant you two—and let the fool make a third—
where he shall find the letter. Observe his construction° of it.   *interpretation*
155 For this night, to bed, and dream on the event.° Farewell.   *outcome*

                                        Exit

SIR TOBY Good night, Penthesilea.[4]
SIR ANDREW Before me,[5] she's a good wench.
SIR TOBY She's a beagle true bred, and one that adores me. What
o' that?
160 SIR ANDREW I was adored once, too.
SIR TOBY Let's to bed, knight. Thou hadst need send for more
money.
SIR ANDREW If I cannot recover° your niece, I am a foul way   *win*
out.°   *out of money*
165 SIR TOBY Send for money, knight. If thou hast her not i'th' end,
call me cut.[6]
SIR ANDREW If I do not, never trust me, take it how you will.
SIR TOBY Come, come, I'll go burn some sack,[7] 'tis too late to
go to bed now. Come knight, come knight.   *Exeunt*

2.4

Enter Duke, VIOLA [*as Cesario*], CURIO, *and others*

ORSINO Give me some music. Now good morrow,° friends.   *morning*
Now good Cesario, but° that piece of song,   *just*
That old and antic° song we heard last night.   *quaint*
Methought it did relieve my passion° much,   *suffering*
5 More than light airs and recollected° terms   *studied; artificial*
Of these most brisk and giddy-pacèd times.
Come, but one verse.
CURIO He is not here, so please your lordship, that should sing
it.
10 ORSINO Who was it?

---

4. Queen of the Amazons (a joke about Maria's small   "female genitals."
size).   7. I'll go warm and spice some Spanish wine.
5. On my soul (a mild oath).   2.4 Location: Orsino's palace.
6. A dock-tailed horse; also, slang for "gelding" or for

CURIO   Feste the jester, my lord, a fool that the lady Olivia's
    father took much delight in. He is about the house.
ORSINO   Seek him out, and play the tune the while.

                                            [*Exit* CURIO]
    Music plays
    [*To* VIOLA] Come hither, boy. If ever thou shalt love,

15   In the sweet pangs of it remember me;
    For such as I am, all true lovers are,
    Unstaid° and skittish in all motions° else   *Unstable / emotions*
    Save in the constant image of the creature
    That is beloved. How dost thou like this tune?

20 VIOLA   It gives a very echo to the seat
    Where love is throned.[1]
ORSINO   Thou dost speak masterly.°   *expertly*
    My life upon't, young though thou art thine eye
    Hath stayed upon some favour° that it loves.   *face*
    Hath it not, boy?
VIOLA   A little, by your favour.°   *leave; face*
ORSINO   What kind of woman is't?

25 VIOLA   Of your complexion.
ORSINO   She is not worth thee then. What years, i'faith?
VIOLA   About your years, my lord.
ORSINO   Too old, by heaven. Let still° the woman take   *always*
    An elder than herself. So wears° she to him;   *adapts*
30   So sways she level[2] in her husband's heart.
    For, boy, however we do praise ourselves,
    Our fancies° are more giddy and unfirm,   *affections*
    More longing, wavering, sooner lost and worn,°   *exhausted*
    Than women's are.
VIOLA   I think° it well, my lord.   *believe*
35 ORSINO   Then let thy love be younger than thyself,
    Or thy affection cannot hold the bent;[3]
    For women are as roses, whose fair flower
    Being once displayed,° doth fall that very hour.   *opened*
VIOLA   And so they are. Alas that they are so:
40   To die even° when they to perfection grow.   *just*
    Enter CURIO *and* [FESTE, *the*] *clown*
ORSINO [*to* FESTE]   O fellow, come, the song we had last night.
    Mark it, Cesario, it is old and plain.
    The spinsters,° and the knitters in the sun,   *spinners*
    And the free° maids that weave their thread with bones,[4]   *carefree*
45   Do use to chant it. It is silly sooth,°   *simple truth*
    And dallies with° the innocence of love,   *lingers lovingly on*
    Like the old° age.   *golden*
FESTE   Are you ready, sir?
ORSINO   I prithee, sing.
    Music
50 FESTE [*sings*]   Come away,° come away death,   *Come hither*
              And in sad cypress[5] let me be laid.
              Fie away, fie away breath,
              I am slain by a fair cruel maid.

---

1. *It . . . throned:* It reflects back to the heart.
2. So does she balance influence and affection.
3. Cannot remain at full stretch (like the tautness of a bowstring).

4. Spools made from bone on which lace (called "bone lace") was woven.
5. Cypress-wood coffin. Like yews, cypresses were emblematic of mourning.

My shroud of white, stuck all with yew,° yew sprigs
55   O prepare it.
My part of death no one so true
      Did share it.[6]
Not a flower, not a flower sweet

      On my black coffin let there be strewn.
60 Not a friend, not a friend greet
      My poor corpse, where my bones shall be thrown.
A thousand thousand sighs to save,
      Lay me O where
Sad true lover never find my grave,
65   To weep there.

ORSINO [*giving money*]   There's for thy pains.
FESTE   No pains, sir. I take pleasure in singing, sir.
ORSINO   I'll pay thy pleasure then.
FESTE   Truly, sir, and pleasure will be paid,° one time or   *paid for*
70 another.
ORSINO   Give me now leave° to leave° thee.   *permission / dismiss*
FESTE   Now the melancholy god[7] protect thee, and the tailor
make thy doublet of changeable taffeta,[8] for thy mind is a very
opal.[9] I would have men of such constancy put to sea, that their
75 business might be everything, and their intent° everywhere, for   *destination*
that's it that always makes a good voyage of nothing.[1] Farewell.
                                              Exit

ORSINO   Let all the rest give place:°   [*Exeunt* CURIO *and others*]   *withdraw*
                     Once more, Cesario,
Get thee to yon same sovereign cruelty.
Tell her my love, more noble than the world,
80 Prizes not quantity of dirty lands.
The parts° that fortune hath bestowed upon her   *possessions*
Tell her I hold as giddily[2] as fortune;
But 'tis that miracle and queen of gems
That nature pranks° her in attracts my soul.   *adorns*
85 VIOLA   But if she cannot love you, sir?
ORSINO   I cannot be so answered.
VIOLA   Sooth,° but you must.   *In truth*
Say that some lady, as perhaps there is,
Hath for your love as great a pang of heart
As you have for Olivia. You cannot love her.
90 You tell her so. Must she not then be answered?
ORSINO   There is no woman's sides
Can bide° the beating of so strong a passion   *withstand*
As love doth give my heart; no woman's heart
So big, to hold so much. They lack retention.°   *constancy*
95 Alas, their love may be called appetite,
No motion of the liver, but the palate,[3]
That suffer surfeit, cloyment,° and revolt.°   *satiety / revulsion*
But mine is all as hungry as the sea,

---

6. *My part . . . it:* No one has died so true to love as I.
7. Saturn (thought to control the melancholic).
8. Shot silk, whose color changes with the angle of vision. *doublet:* close-fitting jacket.
9. An iridescent gemstone that changes color depending on the angle from which it is seen.
1. *that's . . . nothing:* this fickle lack of direction can

make a voyage in the notoriously changeful sea carefree and consonant with one's desires.
2. Lightly (fortune being fickle).
3. *appetite . . . palate:* appetite, like the palate, is easily sated, and thus lacks the emotional depth and complexity of real love, whose seat is the liver. *motion:* impulse.

And can digest as much. Make no compare
100 Between that love a woman can bear me
And that I owe° Olivia. *have for*
VIOLA Ay, but I know—
ORSINO What dost thou know?
VIOLA Too well what love women to men may owe.
105 In faith, they are as true of heart as we.
My father had a daughter loved a man
As it might be, perhaps, were I a woman
I should your lordship.
ORSINO And what's her history?
VIOLA A blank, my lord. She never told her love,
110 But let concealment, like a worm i'th' bud,
Feed on her damask⁴ cheek. She pined in thought,
And with a green and yellow° melancholy *pale and sallow*
She sat like patience on a monument,⁵
Smiling at grief. Was not this love indeed?
115 We men may say more, swear more, but indeed
Our shows are more than will;⁶ for still° we prove *always*
Much in our vows, but little in our love.
ORSINO But died thy sister of her love, my boy?
VIOLA I am all the daughters of my father's house,
120 And all the brothers too; and yet I know not.
Sir, shall I to this lady?
ORSINO Ay, that's the theme,
To her in haste. Give her this jewel. Say
My love can give no place, bide no denay.⁷ *Exeunt [severally]*

2.5

Enter SIR TOBY, SIR ANDREW, *and* FABIAN
SIR TOBY Come thy ways,° Signor Fabian. *Come along*
FABIAN Nay, I'll come. If I lose a scruple° of this sport let me be *miss a scrap*
boiled to death with melancholy.¹
SIR TOBY Wouldst thou not be glad to have the niggardly rascally
5 sheep-biter² come by some notable shame?
FABIAN I would exult, man. You know he brought me out o'
favour with my lady about a bear-baiting³ here.
SIR TOBY To anger him we'll have the bear again, and we will
fool° him black and blue, shall we not, Sir Andrew? *mock*
10 SIR ANDREW An° we do not, it is pity of our lives. *If*
Enter MARIA [*with a letter*]
SIR TOBY Here comes the little villain. How now, my metal of
India?⁴
MARIA Get ye all three into the box-tree.° Malvolio's coming *hedge of boxwood*
down this walk. He has been yonder i' the sun practising behav-
15 iour to his own shadow this half-hour. Observe him, for the
love of mockery, for I know this letter will make a contempla-
tive° idiot of him. Close,° in the name of jesting! *vacuous / Keep close; hide*

---

4. Pink and white, like a damask rose.
5. A memorial statue symbolizing patience.
6. Our displays of love are greater than our actual feelings.
7. My love cannot be bated, nor tolerate refusal.
2.5 Location: Olivia's garden.

1. Melancholy was a cold humor; "boiled" puns on "bile," the surplus of which produced melancholy.
2. Literally, a dog that attacks sheep; here, a malicious sneak.
3. Puritans disapproved of blood sports like bearbaiting.
4. A woman worth her weight in gold.

[*The men hide.* MARIA *places the letter*]

Lie thou there, for here comes the trout that must be caught
with tickling.⁵   *Exit*

Enter MALVOLIO

20 MALVOLIO 'Tis but fortune, all is fortune. Maria once told me
she° did affect° me, and I have heard herself come thus near,   *(Olivia) / care for*
that should she fancy° it should be one of my complexion.   *fall in love*
Besides, she uses me with a more exalted respect than anyone
else that follows her. What should I think on't?

25 SIR TOBY Here's an overweening rogue.

FABIAN O, peace! Contemplation makes a rare turkeycock⁶ of
him—how he jets° under his advanced° plumes!   *struts / raised*

SIR ANDREW 'Slight,⁷ I could so beat the rogue.

SIR TOBY Peace, I say.

30 MALVOLIO To be Count Malvolio!

SIR TOBY Ah, rogue.

SIR ANDREW Pistol him, pistol him.

SIR TOBY Peace, peace.

MALVOLIO There is example° for't: the Lady of the Strachey mar-   *precedent*
35 ried the yeoman of the wardrobe.⁸

SIR ANDREW Fie on him, Jezebel.⁹

FABIAN O peace, now he's deeply in. Look how imagination
blows him.°   *puffs him up*

MALVOLIO Having been three months married to her, sitting in
40 my state°—   *chair of state*

SIR TOBY O for a stone-bow¹ to hit him in the eye!

MALVOLIO Calling my officers° about me, in my branched² vel-   *household attendants*
vet gown, having come from a day-bed° where I have left Olivia   *couch*
sleeping—

45 SIR TOBY Fire and brimstone!

FABIAN O peace, peace.

MALVOLIO And then to have the humour of state³ and—after a
demure travel of regard,⁴ telling them I know my place, as I
would they should do theirs—to ask for my kinsman Toby.

50 SIR TOBY Bolts and shackles!

FABIAN O peace, peace, peace, now, now.

MALVOLIO Seven of my people with an obedient start make° out   *go*
for him. I frown the while, and perchance wind up my watch,
or play with my—[*touching his chain*]⁵ some rich jewel. Toby
55 approaches; curtsies° there to me.   *bows*

SIR TOBY Shall this fellow live?

FABIAN Though our silence be drawn from us with cars,⁶ yet
peace.

MALVOLIO I extend my hand to him thus, quenching my famil-
60 iar smile with an austere regard of control—

SIR TOBY And does not Toby take° you a blow o' the lips, then?   *give*

---

5. Flattery; trout can be caught by stroking them under
the gills.
6. Proverbially proud; they display their feathers like
peacocks.
7. By God's light (an oath).
8. Perhaps an allusion to a noblewoman who had married her manservant, but there is no certain identification. *yeoman of the wardrobe*: keeper of clothes and linen.
9. Biblical allusion to the proud wife of Ahab, King of
Israel.

1. Catapult, or crossbow for stones.
2. Embroidered with branch patterns.
3. To adopt the grand air of exalted greatness.
4. After casting my eyes gravely about the room.
5. Malvolio momentarily forgets that he will have abandoned his steward's chain; watches were an expensive
luxury at this time.
6. A prisoner might be tied to two carts or chariots
("cars") and pulled by horses in opposite directions to
extort information.

MALVOLIO Saying 'Cousin Toby, my fortunes, having cast me
on your niece, give me this prerogative of speech'—
SIR TOBY What, what!
65 MALVOLIO 'You must amend your drunkenness.'
SIR TOBY Out, scab.
FABIAN Nay, patience, or we break the sinews of our plot.
MALVOLIO 'Besides, you waste the treasure of your time with a
foolish knight'—
70 SIR ANDREW That's me, I warrant you.
MALVOLIO 'One Sir Andrew.'
SIR ANDREW I knew 'twas I, for many do call me fool.
MALVOLIO [*seeing the letter*] What employment° have we here?   *business*
FABIAN Now is the woodcock near the gin.[7]
75 SIR TOBY O peace, and the spirit of humours intimate[8] reading
aloud to him.
MALVOLIO [*taking up the letter*] By my life, this is my lady's
hand. These be her very c's, her u's, and her t's,[9] and thus
makes she her great P's. It is in contempt of° question her   *beyond*
80 hand.
SIR ANDREW Her c's, her u's, and her t's? Why that?
MALVOLIO [*reads*] 'To the unknown beloved, this, and my good
wishes.' Her very phrases! [*Opening the letter*] By your leave,
wax[1]—soft,° and the impressure her Lucrece,[2] with which she   *wait*
85 uses to seal° —'tis my lady. To whom should this be?   *habitually seals*
FABIAN This wins him, liver and all.
MALVOLIO   'Jove knows I love,
                But who?
           Lips do not move,
90   No man must know.'
    'No man must know.' What follows? The numbers altered.°   *meter changed*
    'No man must know.' If this should be thee, Malvolio?
SIR TOBY Marry, hang thee, brock.[3]
MALVOLIO 'I may command where I adore,
95   But silence like a Lucrece knife
        With bloodless stroke my heart doth gore.
        M.O.A.I. doth sway my life.'
FABIAN A fustian° riddle.   *bombastic*
SIR TOBY Excellent wench, say I.
100 MALVOLIO 'M.O.A.I. doth sway my life.' Nay, but first let me
see, let me see, let me see.
FABIAN What dish o' poison has she dressed° him!   *prepared*
SIR TOBY And with what wing the staniel checks at it![4]
MALVOLIO 'I may command where I adore.' Why, she may com-
105 mand me. I serve her, she is my lady. Why, this is evident to
any formal capacity.° There is no obstruction in this. And the   *normal intelligence*
end—what should that alphabetical position° portend? If I   *arrangement*
could make that resemble something in me. Softly—'M.O.A.I.'
SIR TOBY O ay,[5] make up that, he is now at a cold scent.

---

7. Snare. *woodcock*: a proverbially foolish bird.
8. And may a capricious impulse suggest.
9. Malvolio unwittingly spells out "cut," slang for "female
genitals"; the meaning is compounded by "great P's." In
fact, these letters do not appear on the outside of the
letter.

1. *By . . . wax*: addressed to the sealing wax.
2. The figure of Lucrece, Roman model of chastity, is the
device ("impressure") imprinted on the seal.
3. Badger (proverbially stinking).
4. And with what alacrity the sparrow hawk goes after it.
5. *O, ay*: playing on "O.I."

110 FABIAN Sowter will cry upon't for all this, though it be as rank
as a fox.[6]

MALVOLIO 'M.' Malvolio—'M'—why, that begins my name.

FABIAN Did not I say he would work it out? The cur is excellent
at faults.[7]

115 MALVOLIO 'M.' But then there is no consonancy in the sequel.[8]
That suffers under probation.[9] 'A' should follow, but 'O' does.

FABIAN And 'O'[1] shall end, I hope.

SIR TOBY Ay, or I'll cudgel him, and make him cry 'O!'

MALVOLIO And then 'I' comes behind.

120 FABIAN Ay, an you had any eye behind you you might see more
detraction° at your heels than fortunes before you.   *defamation*

MALVOLIO 'M.O.A.I.' This simulation° is not as the former; and   *disguise; riddle*
yet to crush° this a little, it would bow° to me, for every one of   *force / yield; point*
these letters are in my name. Soft, here follows prose: 'If this

125 fall into thy hand, revolve.° In my stars° I am above thee, but   *consider / fortunes*
be not afraid of greatness. Some are born great, some achieve
greatness, and some have greatness thrust upon 'em. Thy fates
open their hands,° let thy blood and spirit embrace them, and   *bestow gifts*
to inure° thyself to what thou art like° to be, cast thy humble   *accustom / likely*

130 slough,[2] and appear fresh. Be opposite° with a kinsman, surly   *contrary*
with servants. Let thy tongue tang arguments of state;[3] put thy-
self into the trick of singularity.° She thus advises thee that sighs   *cultivate eccentricity*
for thee. Remember who commended thy yellow stockings,
and wished to see thee ever cross-gartered.[4] I say remember, go

135 to,[5] thou art made if thou desirest to be so; if not, let me see
thee a steward still, the fellow of servants, and not worthy to
touch Fortune's fingers. Farewell. She that would alter services[6] with thee,

                     The Fortunate-Unhappy.'

140 Daylight and champaign discovers[7] not more. This is open.° I   *clear*
will be proud, I will read politic° authors, I will baffle[8] Sir   *political*
Toby, I will wash off gross acquaintance, I will be point-device
the very man.[9] I do not now fool myself, to let imagination
jade° me; for every reason excites to this, that my lady loves me.   *trick*

145 She did commend my yellow stockings of late, she did praise
my leg, being cross-gartered, and in this she manifests herself
to my love, and with a kind of injunction drives me to these
habits° of her liking. I thank my stars, I am happy. I will be   *clothes*
strange,° stout,° in yellow stockings, and cross-gartered, even   *aloof / proud*

150 with the swiftness of putting on. Jove and my stars be praised.
Here is yet a postscript. 'Thou canst not choose but know who
I am. If thou entertainest° my love, let it appear in thy smiling,   *accept*
thy smiles become thee well. Therefore in my presence still°   *constantly*
smile, dear my sweet, I prithee.' Jove, I thank thee. I will smile,

155 I will do everything that thou wilt have me.   *Exit*

6. "Sowter" (the name of a hound), having lost the scent, will start to bay loudly as he picks up the new, rank (stinking) smell of the fox. *though:* as though.

7. At picking up a scent after it is momentarily lost. A "fault" is a "cold scent" (line 109).

8. There is no consistency in what follows.

9. That weakens upon being put to the test.

1. As in the hangman's noose; the last letter of Malvolio's name; or "O" as a lamentation.

2. A snake's old skin, which peels away.

3. Let your tongue ring out arguments of statecraft or politics.

4. An antiquated way of adjusting a garter—going once below the knee, crossing behind it, and knotting above the knee at the side.

5. An emphatic expression, like "I tell you."

6. Change places (of servant and mistress or master).

7. *champaign discovers:* open countryside reveals.

8. Term used to describe the formal unmaking of a knight; hence, "disgrace."

9. I will be in every detail the identical man (described in the letter).

[SIR TOBY, SIR ANDREW, *and* FABIAN *come from hiding*]

FABIAN I will not give my part of this sport for a pension of
thousands to be paid from the Sophy.°   *Shah of Persia*

SIR TOBY I could marry this wench for this device.

SIR ANDREW So could I, too.

160 SIR TOBY And ask no other dowry with her but such another jest.

Enter MARIA

SIR ANDREW Nor I neither.

FABIAN Here comes my noble gull-catcher.°   *trickster*

SIR TOBY [*to* MARIA] Wilt thou set thy foot o' my neck?

SIR ANDREW [*to* MARIA] Or o' mine either?

165 SIR TOBY [*to* MARIA] Shall I play my freedom at tray-trip,[1] and
become thy bondslave?

SIR ANDREW [*to* MARIA] I'faith, or I either?

SIR TOBY [*to* MARIA] Why, thou hast put him in such a dream
that when the image of it leaves him, he must run mad.

170 MARIA Nay, but say true, does it work upon him?

SIR TOBY Like aqua vitae° with a midwife.   *spirits; liquor*

MARIA If you will then see the fruits of the sport, mark his first
approach before my lady. He will come to her in yellow stockings, and 'tis a colour she abhors, and cross-gartered, a fashion

175 she detests; and he will smile upon her, which will now be so
unsuitable to her disposition, being addicted to a melancholy
as she is, that it cannot but turn him into a notable contempt.[2]
If you will see it, follow me.

SIR TOBY To the gates of Tartar,° thou most excellent devil of   *hell*

180 wit.

SIR ANDREW I'll make one,° too.   *Exeunt*   *go along*

3.1

Enter VIOLA [*as Cesario*] *and* [FESTE, *the*] *clown* [*with
pipe and tabor*][1]

VIOLA Save° thee, friend, and thy music. Dost thou live by thy   *God save*
tabor?

FESTE No, sir, I live by° the church.   *near*

VIOLA Art thou a churchman?

5 FESTE No such matter, sir. I do live by[2] the church for I do live
at my house, and my house doth stand by the church.

VIOLA So thou mayst say the king lies by[3] a beggar if a beggar
dwell near him, or the church stands° by thy tabor if thy tabor   *is maintained*
stand by the church.

10 FESTE You have said, sir. To see this age!—A sentence° is but a   *saying*
cheverel° glove to a good wit, how quickly the wrong side may   *kidskin*
be turned outward.

VIOLA Nay, that's certain. They that dally nicely° with words   *play subtly*
may quickly make them wanton.[4]

15 FESTE I would therefore my sister had had no name, sir.

VIOLA Why, man?

FESTE Why, sir, her name's a word, and to dally with that word

---

1. A game of dice in which the winner throws a three
("tray" is from the Spanish *tres*). *play*: wager.
2. A notorious object of contempt.
3.1 Location: Olivia's garden.
1. The dialogue demands only a tabor, but jesters com-

monly played a pipe with one hand while tapping a tabor
(small drum, hanging from the neck) with the other.
2. I do earn my keep with.
3. Lives near; punning on "goes to bed with."
4. Equivocal; Feste puns on the sense "unchaste."

might make my sister wanton. But indeed, words are very rascals since bonds disgraced them.[5]

20 VIOLA Thy reason, man?

FESTE Troth, sir, I can yield you none without words, and words
are grown so false I am loath to prove reason with them.

VIOLA I warrant thou art a merry fellow, and carest for nothing.

FESTE Not so, sir, I do care for something; but in my con-
25 science, sir, I do not care for you. If that be to care for nothing,
sir, I would it would make you invisible.

VIOLA Art not thou the Lady Olivia's fool?

FESTE No indeed, sir, the Lady Olivia has no folly, she will keep
no fool, sir, till she be married, and fools are as like husbands
30 as pilchards[6] are to herrings—the husband's the bigger. I am
indeed not her fool, but her corrupter of words.

VIOLA I saw thee late° at the Count Orsino's.   *lately*

FESTE Foolery, sir, does walk about the orb[7] like the sun, it
shines everywhere. I would be sorry, sir, but the fool should be
35 as oft with your master as with my mistress.[8] I think I saw your
wisdom[9] there.

VIOLA Nay, an thou pass upon[1] me, I'll no more with thee. [*Giving money*] Hold, there's expenses for thee.

FESTE Now Jove in his next commodity° of hair send thee a   *shipment*
40 beard.

VIOLA By my troth I'll tell thee, I am almost sick for one,[2]
though I would not have it grow on *my* chin. Is thy lady within?

FESTE Would not a pair of these have bred,[3] sir?

VIOLA Yes, being kept together and put to use.[4]

45 FESTE I would play Lord Pandarus[5] of Phrygia, sir, to bring a
Cressida to this Troilus.

VIOLA [*giving money*]   I understand you, sir, 'tis well begged.

FESTE The matter I hope is not great, sir; begging but a beggar—Cressida was a beggar.[6] My lady is within, sir. I will con-
50 ster° to them whence you come. Who you are and what you   *explain*
would are out of my welkin—I might say 'element', but the
word is over-worn.[7]   *Exit*

VIOLA This fellow is wise enough to play the fool,
And to do that well craves a kind of wit.°   *intelligence*
55 He must observe their mood on whom he jests,
The quality of persons, and the time,
And, like the haggard, check at every feather
That comes before his eye.[8] This is a practice°   *skill*
As full of labour as a wise man's art,
60 For folly that he wisely shows is fit,[9]

---

5. Since legal contracts replaced a man's word of honor.
("Bonds" plays on "sworn statements" and "fetters," beto-
kening criminality.)
6. Small fish similar to herring.
7. World; the sun was still believed to circle the earth.
8. I, Feste, should visit master and mistress alike;
Orsino should be called "fool" as often as Olivia.
9. *your wisdom:* a mocking title for Cesario.
1. If you express an opinion of; if you joke about.
2. Almost eager for a beard; almost pining for a man
(Orsino).
3. Would not a pair of coins such as these have multi-
plied (with possible pun on "be enough to buy bread").

4. *put to use:* invested to produce interest.
5. Go-between, or "pander," since Feste needs a "mate"
for his coin(s). Shakespeare dramatizes the story in
Troilus and Cressida.
6. In asking for the "mate" to his Troilus coin, Feste
draws on a version of the story of Troilus and Cressida in
which Cressida became a beggar.
7. "Welkin" (sky or air) is synonymous with one meaning
of "element," used in what Feste regards as the overworn
phrase "out of my element."
8. *And . . . eye:* As a wild hawk ("haggard") must be sensitive to its prey's disposition.
9. For folly that he skillfully displays is proper.

But wise men, folly-fall'n, quite taint[1] their wit.
Enter SIR TOBY *and* [SIR] ANDREW

SIR TOBY   Save you, gentleman.

VIOLA   And you, sir.

SIR ANDREW   *Dieu vous garde,*[2] *monsieur.*

65   VIOLA   *Et vous aussi, votre serviteur.*[3]

SIR ANDREW   I hope, sir, you are, and I am yours.

SIR TOBY   Will you encounter[4] the house? My niece is desirous
you should enter if your trade be to her.

VIOLA   I am bound to° your niece, sir: I mean she is the list° of   *for / destination*
70   my voyage.

SIR TOBY   Taste° your legs, sir, put them to motion.   *Try*

VIOLA   My legs do better understand° me, sir, than I understand   *stand under*
what you mean by bidding me taste my legs.

SIR TOBY   I mean to go, sir, to enter.

75   VIOLA   I will answer you with gait and entrance.
Enter OLIVIA, *and* [MARIA, *her*] *gentlewoman*
But we are prevented.°   [*To* OLIVIA] Most excellent accom-   *anticipated*
plished lady, the heavens rain odours on you.

SIR ANDREW [*to* SIR TOBY]   That youth's a rare° courtier; 'rain   *an excellent*
odours'—well.°   *well put*

80   VIOLA   My matter hath no voice,° lady, but to your own most   *must not be spoken*
pregnant° and vouchsafed° ear.   *receptive / proffered*

SIR ANDREW [*to* SIR TOBY]   'Odours', 'pregnant', and 'vouchsafed'—I'll get 'em all three all ready.[5]

OLIVIA   Let the garden door be shut, and leave me to my
85   hearing.   [*Exeunt* SIR TOBY, SIR ANDREW, *and* MARIA]
Give me your hand, sir.

VIOLA   My duty, madam, and most humble service.

OLIVIA   What is your name?

VIOLA   Cesario is your servant's name, fair princess.

90   OLIVIA   My servant, sir? 'Twas never merry world[6]
Since lowly feigning° was called compliment.   *pretended humility*
You're servant to the Count Orsino, youth.

VIOLA   And he is yours, and his must needs be yours.
Your servant's servant is *your* servant, madam.

95   OLIVIA   For° him, I think not on him. For his thoughts,   *As for*
Would they were blanks rather than filled with me.

VIOLA   Madam, I come to whet your gentle thoughts
On his behalf.

OLIVIA   O by your leave,[7] I pray you.
I bade you never speak again of him;
100   But would you undertake another suit,
I had rather hear you to solicit that
Than music from the spheres.[8]

VIOLA   Dear lady—

OLIVIA   Give me leave, beseech you. I did send,
After the last enchantment you did here,
105   A ring in chase of you. So did I abuse°   *deceive; dishonor*

---

1. Discredit; spoil. *folly-fall'n:* fallen into folly.
2. God protect you (French).
3. And you also, (I am) your servant. (Sir Andrew's awkward reply demonstrates that his French is limited.)
4. Pedantry for "enter" (Toby mocks Viola's courtly language).

5. *I'll . . . ready:* to commit to memory for later use.
6. *'Twas . . . world:* the proverbial "Things have never
been the same."
7. Permit me to interrupt (polite expression).
8. Exquisite music thought to be made by the planets as
they moved, but inaudible to mortal ears.

Myself, my servant, and I fear me you.°   *and, as I fear, you*
Under your hard construction[9] must I sit,
To force° that on you in a shameful cunning   *For forcing*
Which you knew none of yours. What might you think?
110 Have you not set mine honour at the stake
And baited it with all th'unmuzzled thoughts[1]
That tyrannous heart can think? To one of your receiving°   *perception*
Enough is shown. A cypress,[2] not a bosom,
Hides my heart. So let me hear you speak.
     VIOLA   I pity you.
115 OLIVIA   That's a degree to° love.   *toward*
     VIOLA   No, not a grece,° for 'tis a vulgar proof°   *step / common experience*
That very oft we pity enemies.
     OLIVIA   Why then, methinks 'tis time to smile again.[3]
O world, how apt° the poor are to be proud!   *ready*
120 If one should be a prey, how much the better
To fall before the lion than the wolf![4]
        Clock strikes
The clock upbraids me with the waste of time.
Be not afraid, good youth, I will not have you;
And yet when wit and youth is come to harvest
125 Your wife is like to reap a proper° man.   *handsome; worthy*
There lies your way, due west.
     VIOLA   Then westward ho![5]
Grace and good disposition° attend your ladyship.   *peace of mind*
You'll nothing, madam, to my lord by me?
     OLIVIA   Stay. I prithee tell me what thou[6] think'st of me.
130 VIOLA   That you do think you are not what you are.[7]
     OLIVIA   If I think so, I think the same of you.[8]
     VIOLA   Then think you right, I am not what I am.
     OLIVIA   I would you were as I would have you be.
     VIOLA   Would it be better, madam, than I am?
135 I wish it might, for now I am your fool.[9]
     OLIVIA [*aside*]   O, what a deal of scorn looks beautiful
In the contempt and anger of his lip!
A murd'rous guilt shows not itself more soon
Than love that would seem hid. Love's night is noon.[1]
140 [*To* VIOLA] Cesario, by the roses of the spring,
By maidhood, honour, truth, and everything,
I love thee so that, maugre° all thy pride,   *despite*
Nor° wit nor reason can my passion hide.   *Neither*
Do not extort thy reasons from this clause,[2]
145 For that° I woo, thou therefore hast no cause.   *That because*
But rather reason thus with reason fetter:[3]
Love sought is good, but given unsought, is better.

---

9. Your unfavorable interpretation (of my behavior).
1. *set . . . thoughts:* as bears that were tied up at the stake and baited with dogs.
2. Veil of transparent silken gauze; the cypress tree was also emblematic of mourning.
3. Time to discard love's melancholy.
4. *If . . . wolf:* If I had to fall prey to love, it would have been better to succumb to the noble Orsino than to the hardhearted Cesario.
5. Thames watermen's cry to attract passengers for the court at Westminster from London.
6. Olivia changes from "you" to the familiar "thou."

7. That you think you are in love with a man, but you are mistaken.
8. Olivia may think that Cesario has suggested that she is mad; or she may imply that she thinks that Cesario, despite his subordinate position, is noble.
9. You have made a fool of me.
1. Love, though attempting secrecy, still shines out as bright as day.
2. Do not take the position that just because I woo you, you are under no obligation to reciprocate.
3. But instead constrain your reasoning with this argument.

VIOLA   By innocence I swear, and by my youth,
   I have one heart, one bosom, and one truth,
150 And that no woman has, nor never none
   Shall mistress be of it save I alone.
   And so adieu, good madam. Never more
   Will I my master's tears to you deplore.°   *lament*
OLIVIA   Yet come again, for thou perhaps mayst move
155 That heart which now abhors, to like his love.

                              Exeunt [severally]

3.2

         Enter SIR TOBY, SIR ANDREW, *and* FABIAN
SIR ANDREW   No, faith, I'll not stay a jot longer.
SIR TOBY   Thy reason, dear venom,° give thy reason.   *venomous one*
FABIAN   You must needs yield your reason, Sir Andrew.
SIR ANDREW   Marry, I saw your niece do more favours to the
5   Count's servingman than ever she bestowed upon me. I saw't
   i'th' orchard.°   *garden*
SIR TOBY   Did she see thee the while, old boy? Tell me that.
SIR ANDREW   As plain as I see you now.
FABIAN   This was a great argument° of love in her toward you.   *proof*
10 SIR ANDREW   'Slight,° will you make an ass o' me?   *By God's light*
FABIAN   I will prove it legitimate, sir, upon the oaths of judgement and reason.
SIR TOBY   And they have been grand-jurymen[1] since before
   Noah was a sailor.
15 FABIAN   She did show favour to the youth in your sight only to
   exasperate you, to awake your dormouse° valour, to put fire in   *meek; timid*
   your heart and brimstone in your liver. You should then have
   accosted her, and with some excellent jests, fire-new from the
   mint,° you should have banged the youth into dumbness. This   *newly minted*
20 was looked for at your hand, and this was balked.° The double   *neglected*
   gilt[2] of this opportunity you let time wash off, and you are now
   sailed into the north of my lady's opinion,[3] where you will hang
   like an icicle on a Dutchman's[4] beard unless you do redeem it
   by some laudable attempt either of valour or policy.°   *cunning*
25 SIR ANDREW   An't° be any way, it must be with valour, for policy   *If it*
   I hate. I had as lief° be a Brownist as a politician.[5]   *as soon*
SIR TOBY   Why then, build me thy fortunes upon the basis of
   valour. Challenge me° the Count's youth to fight with him,   *for me*
   hurt him in eleven places. My niece shall take note of it; and
30 assure thyself, there is no love-broker in the world can more
   prevail in man's commendation with woman than report of
   valour.
FABIAN   There is no way but this, Sir Andrew.
SIR ANDREW   Will either of you bear me a challenge to him?
35 SIR TOBY   Go, write it in a martial hand, be curst° and brief. It is   *sharp*
   no matter how witty so it be eloquent and full of invention.°   *imagination; untruth*

3.2 Location: Olivia's house.
1. Grand jurymen were supposed to be good judges of evidence.
2. Twice gilded, and as such, Sir Andrew's "golden opportunity" to prove both love and valor.
3. Into Olivia's cold disfavor.
4. Perhaps an allusion to navigator Willem Barents, who led an expedition to the Arctic in 1596–97.
5. Schemer. A Brownist was a member of the Puritan sect founded in 1581 by Robert Browne.

Taunt him with the licence of ink.[6] If thou 'thou'st'[7] him some
thrice, it shall not be amiss, and as many lies° as will lie in thy   *accusations of lying*
sheet of paper, although the sheet were big enough for the bed
40   of Ware,[8] in England, set 'em down, go about it. Let there be
gall[9] enough in thy ink; though thou write with a goose-pen,[1]
no matter. About it.

SIR ANDREW   Where shall I find you?

SIR TOBY   We'll call thee at the cubiculo.° Go.   *little chamber*

Exit SIR ANDREW

45 FABIAN   This is a dear manikin° to you, Sir Toby.   *puppet*

SIR TOBY   I have been dear° to him, lad, some two thousand   *costly*
strong or so.

FABIAN   We shall have a rare letter from him; but you'll not
deliver't.

50 SIR TOBY   Never trust me then; and by all means stir on the youth
to an answer. I think oxen and wain-ropes[2] cannot hale° them   *drag*
together. For Andrew, if he were opened and you find so much
blood in his liver[3] as will clog° the foot of a flea, I'll eat the rest   *weigh down*
of th'anatomy.°   *cadaver*

55 FABIAN   And his opposite,° the youth, bears in his visage no great   *adversary*
presage of cruelty.

Enter MARIA

SIR TOBY   Look where the youngest wren of nine[4] comes.

MARIA   If you desire the spleen,° and will laugh yourselves into   *a laughing fit*
stitches, follow me. Yon gull° Malvolio is turned heathen, a   *fool*
60 very renegado,[5] for there is no Christian that means to be saved
by believing rightly can ever believe such impossible passages
of grossness.[6] He's in yellow stockings.

SIR TOBY   And cross-gartered?

MARIA   Most villainously,° like a pedant° that keeps a school i'th'   *abominably / teacher*
65 church.[7] I have dogged him like his murderer. He does obey
every point of the letter that I dropped to betray him. He does
smile his face into more lines than is in the new map with the
augmentation of the Indies.[8] You have not seen such a thing as
'tis. I can hardly forbear hurling things at him. I know my lady
70 will strike him. If she do, he'll smile, and take't for a great
favour.

SIR TOBY   Come bring us, bring us where he is.   *Exeunt*

3.3

Enter SEBASTIAN *and* ANTONIO

SEBASTIAN   I would not by my will have troubled you,
But since you make your pleasure of your pains
I will no further chide you.

ANTONIO   I could not stay behind you. My desire,

---

6. *licence of ink:* freedom taken in writing, but not risked
in conversation.
7. Call him "thou" (an insult to a stranger).
8. Famous Elizabethan bedstead, nearly eleven feet
square, now in the Victoria and Albert Museum, London.
9. Oak gall, an ingredient in ink; bitterness or rancor.
1. Quill made of a goose feather. (The goose was proverbially cowardly and foolish.)
2. Wagon ropes pulled by oxen.
3. Supposed to be the source of blood, which engendered courage.

4. The smallest of small birds; the smallest wren in a
family of nine.
5. Renegade (Spanish); a Christian converted to Islam.
6. Such patent absurdities (in the letter).
7. Because no schoolroom is available in a small rustic
community.
8. Possibly refers to a map published in 1599 showing
the East Indies more fully than in earlier maps and
crisscrossed by many rhumb lines.
3.3 Location: A street scene.

5   More sharp than filèd steel, did spur me forth,
And not all° love to see you—though so much   *only*
As might have drawn one to a longer voyage—
But jealousy° what might befall your travel,   *apprehension*
Being skilless in° these parts, which to a stranger,   *unfamiliar to*
10   Unguided and unfriended, often prove
Rough and unhospitable. My willing love
The rather° by these arguments of fear   *more willingly*
Set forth in your pursuit.

SEBASTIAN   My kind Antonio,
I can no other answer make but thanks,
15   And thanks; and ever oft° good turns   *very often*
Are shuffled off° with such uncurrent[1] pay.   *shrugged off*
But were my worth as is my conscience° firm,   *sense of indebtedness*
You should find better dealing. What's to do?
Shall we go see the relics° of this town?   *sights*
20 ANTONIO   Tomorrow, sir. Best first go see your lodging.

SEBASTIAN   I am not weary, and 'tis long to night.
I pray you let us satisfy our eyes
With the memorials and the things of fame
That do renown this city.

ANTONIO   Would you'd pardon me.
25 I do not without danger walk these streets.
Once in a sea-fight 'gainst the Count his° galleys   *(the Count's)*
I did some service, of such note indeed
That were I ta'en° here it would scarce be answered.[2]   *captured*

SEBASTIAN   Belike° you slew great number of his people.   *Perhaps*
30 ANTONIO   Th'offence is not of such a bloody nature,
Albeit the quality° of the time and quarrel   *circumstances*
Might well have given us bloody argument.°   *cause for bloodshed*
It might have since been answered in repaying
What we took from them, which for traffic's° sake   *trade's*
35 Most of our city did. Only myself stood out,
For which if I be latchèd° in this place   *caught*
I shall pay dear.

SEBASTIAN   Do not then walk too open.

ANTONIO   It doth not fit me. Hold, sir, here's my purse.
In the south suburbs at the Elephant°   *name of an inn*
40 Is best to lodge. I will bespeak our diet°   *order our meals*
Whiles you beguile° the time and feed your knowledge   *pass*
With viewing of the town. There shall you have me.

SEBASTIAN   Why I your purse?

ANTONIO   Haply° your eye shall light upon some toy°   *Perhaps / trifle*
45 You have desire to purchase; and your store°   *resources*
I think is not for idle markets,[3] sir.

SEBASTIAN   I'll be your purse-bearer, and leave you
For an hour.

ANTONIO   To th' Elephant.

SEBASTIAN   I do remember.

Exeunt [*severally*]

---

1. Out of currency; worthless.
2. It would be difficult for me to make reparation (and
thus my life would be in danger).
3. Not large enough to spend on luxuries.

3.4

Enter OLIVIA *and* MARIA

OLIVIA [*aside*]   I have sent after him, he says he'll come.
　　How shall I feast him? What bestow of° him?　　　　　　　　　　*on*
　　For youth is bought more oft than begged or borrowed.[1]
　　I speak too loud.
5　　[*To* MARIA] Where's Malvolio? He is sad° and civil,°　　　*sober / respectful*
　　And suits well for a servant with my fortunes.
　　Where is Malvolio?

MARIA   He's coming, madam, but in very strange manner. He is
　　sure possessed,° madam.　　　　　　　　　　　　　*(by the devil); insane*

10　OLIVIA   Why, what's the matter? Does he rave?

MARIA   No, madam, he does nothing but smile. Your ladyship
　　were best to have some guard about you if he come, for sure
　　the man is tainted in's wits.

OLIVIA   Go call him hither.　　　　　　　　　　　　[*Exit* MARIA]
　　　　　　　　　　　　　　　　　　　　　I am as mad as he,
15　If sad and merry madness equal be.

Enter MALVOLIO [*cross-gartered and wearing yellow*
　　stockings, with MARIA]

　　How now, Malvolio?

MALVOLIO   Sweet lady, ho, ho!

OLIVIA   Smil'st thou? I sent for thee upon a sad occasion.°　　*about a serious matter*

MALVOLIO   Sad, lady? I could be sad. This does make some
20　obstruction in the blood, this cross-gartering, but what of that?
　　If it please the eye of one, it is with me as the very true sonnet°　　*song*
　　is, 'Please one, and please all'.[2]

OLIVIA   Why, how dost thou, man? What is the matter with thee?

MALVOLIO   Not black in my mind, though yellow[3] in my legs. It
25　did come to his hands, and commands shall be executed. I
　　think we do know the sweet roman hand.°　　　　　　*italic calligraphy*

OLIVIA   Wilt thou go to bed,[4] Malvolio?

MALVOLIO [*kissing his hand*]   To bed? 'Ay, sweetheart, and I'll
　　come to thee.'[5]

30　OLIVIA   God comfort thee. Why dost thou smile so, and kiss thy
　　hand so oft?

MARIA   How do you, Malvolio?

MALVOLIO   At your request?—yes, nightingales answer daws.[6]

MARIA   Why appear you with this ridiculous boldness before my
35　lady?

MALVOLIO   'Be not afraid of greatness'—'twas well writ.

OLIVIA   What meanest thou by that, Malvolio?

MALVOLIO   'Some are born great'—

OLIVIA   Ha?

40　MALVOLIO   'Some achieve greatness'—

OLIVIA   What sayst thou?

MALVOLIO   'And some have greatness thrust upon them.'

OLIVIA   Heaven restore thee.

3.4 Location: The garden of Olivia's house.
1. "Better to buy than to beg or borrow" was proverbial.
2. If I please one, I please all I care to please (words of a popular bawdy ballad).
3. Black and yellow biles indicated choleric and melancholic dispositions, respectively. "Black and yellow" was

the name of a popular song; to "wear yellow hose" was to be jealous.
4. In order to cure his madness with sleep.
5. A line from a popular song.
6. Shall I deign to reply to you? Yes, since even the nightingale sings in response to the crowing of the jackdaw.

MALVOLIO 'Remember who commended thy yellow
45   stockings'—
OLIVIA 'Thy yellow stockings'?
MALVOLIO 'And wished to see thee cross-gartered.'
OLIVIA 'Cross-gartered'?
MALVOLIO 'Go to, thou art made, if thou desirest to be so.'
50   OLIVIA Am I made?
MALVOLIO 'If not, let me see thee a servant still.'
OLIVIA Why, this is very midsummer madness.
        Enter a SERVANT
SERVANT Madam, the young gentleman of the Count Orsino's
        is returned. I could hardly entreat him back. He attends your
55   ladyship's pleasure.
OLIVIA I'll come to him.   [*Exit* SERVANT]
        Good Maria, let this fellow be looked to. Where's my cousin
        Toby? Let some of my people have a special care of him, I
        would not have him miscarry° for the half of my dowry.   come to harm
        Exeunt [OLIVIA *and* MARIA, *severally*]
60   MALVOLIO O ho, do you come near° me now? No worse man   appreciate
        than Sir Toby to look to me. This concurs directly with the
        letter, she sends him on purpose, that I may appear stubborn to
        him, for she incites me to that in the letter. 'Cast thy humble
        slough,' says she, 'be opposite with a kinsman, surly with ser-
65   vants, let thy tongue tang arguments of state, put thyself into
        the trick of singularity', and consequently° sets down the man-   subsequently
        ner how, as a sad face, a reverend carriage, a slow tongue, in
        the habit of some sir of note,° and so forth. I have limed[7] her,   gentleman
        but it is Jove's doing, and Jove make me thankful. And when
70   she went away now, 'let this fellow be looked to'. Fellow![8]—not
        'Malvolio', nor after my degree, but 'fellow'. Why, everything
        adheres together that no dram of a scruple, no scruple of a
        scruple,[9] no obstacle, no incredulous or unsafe circumstance—
        what can be said?—nothing that can be can come between me
75   and the full prospect of my hopes. Well, Jove, not I, is the doer
        of this, and he is to be thanked.
        Enter [SIR] TOBY, FABIAN, *and* MARIA
SIR TOBY Which way is he, in the name of sanctity? If all the
        devils of hell be drawn in little,[1] and Legion[2] himself possessed
        him, yet I'll speak to him.
80   FABIAN Here he is, here he is. [*To* MALVOLIO] How is't with you,
        sir? How is't with you, man?
MALVOLIO Go off, I discard you. Let me enjoy my private.° Go   privacy
        off.
MARIA Lo, how hollow° the fiend speaks within him. Did not I   resonantly
85   tell you? Sir Toby, my lady prays you to have a care of him.
MALVOLIO Aha, does she so?
SIR TOBY Go to, go to. Peace, peace, we must deal gently with
        him. Let me alone.° How do you, Malvolio? How is't with you?   Leave him to me

---

7. Birds were caught by smearing sticky birdlime on
branches.
8. Malvolio takes the word to mean "companion."
9. *no dram . . . scruple:* both phrases mean "no scrap of
a doubt." *dram:* one-eighth of a fluid ounce. *scruple:* one-
third of a dram.
1. Be contracted into a small space (punning on

"painted in miniature").
2. Alluding to a scene of exorcism in Mark 5:8–9: "For
he [Jesus] said unto him, Come out of the man, thou
unclean spirit. And he asked him, What is thy name? And
he answered saying, My name is Legion: for we are
many."

What, man, defy the devil. Consider, he's an enemy to man-
90   kind.

MALVOLIO   Do you know what you say?

MARIA   La° you, an you speak ill of the devil, how he takes it at   *Look*
    heart. Pray God he be not bewitched.

FABIAN   Carry his water to th' wise woman.³

95 MARIA   Marry, and it shall be done tomorrow morning, if I live.
    My lady would not lose him for more than I'll say.

MALVOLIO   How now, mistress?

MARIA   O Lord!

SIR TOBY   Prithee hold thy peace, this is not the way. Do you not
100   see you move° him? Let me alone with him.   *anger*

FABIAN   No way but gentleness, gently, gently. The fiend is
    rough,° and will not be roughly used.   *violent*

SIR TOBY   Why how now, my bawcock?⁴ How dost thou, chuck?

MALVOLIO   Sir!

105 SIR TOBY   Ay, biddy,° come with me. What man, 'tis not for grav-   *hen*
    ity° to play at cherry-pit⁵ with Satan. Hang him, foul collier.⁶   *for a man of dignity*

MARIA   Get him to say his prayers. Good Sir Toby, get him to
    pray.

MALVOLIO   My prayers, minx?°   *impertinent girl*

110 MARIA   No, I warrant you, he will not hear of godliness.

MALVOLIO   Go hang yourselves, all. You are idle° shallow things,   *foolish*
    I am not of your element.° You shall know more hereafter.   *social sphere*

                                                    Exit

SIR TOBY   Is't possible?

FABIAN   If this were played upon a stage, now, I could condemn
115   it as an improbable fiction.

SIR TOBY   His very genius° hath taken the infection of the   *spirit*
    device,° man.   *trick*

MARIA   Nay, pursue him now, lest the device take air and taint.⁷

FABIAN   Why, we shall make him mad indeed.

120 MARIA   The house will be the quieter.

SIR TOBY   Come, we'll have him in a dark room and bound.⁸ My
    niece is already in the belief that he's mad. We may carry it
    thus° for our pleasure and his penance till our very pastime,   *continue the pretense*
    tired out of breath, prompt us to have mercy on him, at which
125   time we will bring the device to the bar⁹ and crown thee for a
    finder of madmen.¹ But see, but see.

           Enter SIR ANDREW [*with a paper*]

FABIAN   More matter for a May morning.²

SIR ANDREW   Here's the challenge, read it. I warrant there's vine-
    gar and pepper in't.

130 FABIAN   Is't so saucy?

SIR ANDREW   Ay—is't? I warrant him. Do but read.

SIR TOBY   Give me.

    [*Reads*] 'Youth, whatsoever thou art, thou art but a scurvy
    fellow.'

---

3. *water:* urine (for medical diagnosis). *wise woman:* local
healer, "good witch."
4. Fine fellow (from the French *beau coq,* "fine bird").
5. A children's game in which cherrystones were thrown
into a hole.
6. Dirty coal man (the devil was supposed to be black).
7. Spoil (like leftover food) by exposure to air; become

known (and thus ruined).
8. Customary treatments for madness.
9. Into the open court (to be judged).
1. *finder of madmen:* one of a jury "finding," or declaring,
a man to be mad.
2. More pastime fit for a holiday.

135 FABIAN Good, and valiant.

SIR TOBY 'Wonder not, nor admire° not in thy mind why I do   *marvel*
call thee so, for I will show thee no reason for't.'

FABIAN A good note, that keeps you from the blow of the law.[3]

SIR TOBY 'Thou comest to the Lady Olivia, and in my sight she
140 uses thee kindly; but thou liest in thy throat,° that is not the   *deeply*
matter I challenge thee for.'

FABIAN Very brief, and to exceeding good sense [*aside*] -less.[4]

SIR TOBY 'I will waylay thee going home, where if it be thy
chance to kill me'—

145 FABIAN Good.

SIR TOBY 'Thou killest me like a rogue and a villain.'

FABIAN Still you keep o'th' windy side[5] of the law—good.

SIR TOBY 'Fare thee well, and God have mercy upon one of our
souls. He may have mercy upon mine, but my hope is better,[6]
150 and so look to thyself.
Thy friend as thou usest him, and thy sworn enemy,
                              Andrew Aguecheek.'
If this letter move° him not, his legs cannot. I'll give't him.   *provoke*

MARIA You may have very fit occasion for't. He is now in some
155 commerce° with my lady, and will by and by depart.   *conversation*

SIR TOBY Go, Sir Andrew. Scout me° for him at the corner of   *Look out*
the orchard like a bum-baily.[7] So soon as ever thou seest him,
draw, and as thou drawest, swear horrible, for it comes to pass
oft that a terrible oath, with a swaggering accent sharply
160 twanged off, gives manhood more approbation° than ever   *credit*
proof° itself would have earned him. Away.   *trial*

SIR ANDREW Nay, let me alone for swearing.[8]   *Exit*

SIR TOBY Now will not I deliver his letter, for the behaviour of
the young gentleman gives him out to be of good capacity° and   *ability*
165 breeding. His employment between his lord and my niece
confirms no less. Therefore this letter, being so excellently
ignorant, will breed no terror in the youth. He will find it
comes from a clodpoll.° But, sir, I will deliver his challenge by   *blockhead*
word of mouth, set upon Aguecheek a notable report of valour,
170 and drive the gentleman—as I know his youth will aptly receive
it[9]—into a most hideous opinion of his rage, skill, fury, and
impetuosity. This will so fright them both that they will kill one
another by the look, like cockatrices.[1]

Enter OLIVIA, *and* VIOLA [*as Cesario*]

FABIAN Here he comes with your niece. Give them way° till he   *Stand aside*
175 take leave, and presently after him.

SIR TOBY I will meditate the while upon some horrid message
for a challenge.   [*Exeunt* SIR TOBY, FABIAN, *and* MARIA]

OLIVIA I have said too much unto a heart of stone,
And laid mine honour too unchary° out.   *carelessly*
180 There's something in me that reproves my fault,
But such a headstrong potent fault it is
That it but mocks reproof.

---

3. That protects you from a charge of a breach of peace.
4. F's "sence-lesse" appears to use the hyphen to signal an aside.
5. To windward (and therefore safe, not exposed to the law's blasts).
6. *my hope is better*: Andrew means he expects to survive, but he ineptly implies that he expects to be damned.

7. Petty sheriff's officer employed to arrest debtors.
8. Have no doubts as to my swearing ability.
9. As I know his inexperience will readily believe the report.
1. Basilisks; mythical creatures supposed to kill at a glance.

VIOLA   With the same 'haviour
    That your passion bears[2] goes on my master's griefs.

OLIVIA [*giving a jewel*]   Here, wear this jewel[3] for me, 'tis my picture—

185   Refuse it not, it hath no tongue to vex you—
    And I beseech you come again tomorrow.
    What shall you ask of me that I'll deny,
    That honour, saved, may upon asking give?[4]

VIOLA   Nothing but this: your true love for my master.

190 OLIVIA   How with mine honour may I give him that
    Which I have given to you?

VIOLA   I will acquit you.[5]

OLIVIA   Well, come again tomorrow. Fare thee well.
    A fiend like thee might bear my soul to hell.   *Exit*

      Enter [SIR] TOBY *and* FABIAN

SIR TOBY   Gentleman, God save thee.

195 VIOLA   And you, sir.

SIR TOBY   That defence thou hast, betake thee to't. Of what
nature the wrongs are thou hast done him, I know not, but thy
intercepter, full of despite,° bloody as the hunter, attends° thee   *defiance / awaits*
at the orchard end. Dismount thy tuck,[6] be yare° in thy prepara-   *prompt*

200   tion, for thy assailant is quick, skilful, and deadly.

VIOLA   You mistake, sir, I am sure no man hath any quarrel to
me. My remembrance° is very free and clear from any image   *memory*
of offence done to any man.

SIR TOBY   You'll find it otherwise, I assure you. Therefore, if you

205   hold your life at any price, betake you to your guard, for your
opposite° hath in him what youth, strength, skill, and wrath can   *opponent*
furnish man withal.

VIOLA   I pray you, sir, what is he?

SIR TOBY   He is knight dubbed with unhatched[7] rapier and on

210   carpet consideration,[8] but he is a devil in private brawl. Souls
and bodies hath he divorced three, and his incensement at this
moment is so implacable that satisfaction can be none but by
pangs of death and sepulchre. Hob nob[9] is his word,° give't or   *motto*
take't.

215 VIOLA   I will return again into the house and desire some con-
duct° of the lady. I am no fighter. I have heard of some kind of   *escort*
men that put quarrels purposely on others, to taste° their   *test*
valour. Belike this is a man of that quirk.

SIR TOBY   Sir, no. His indignation derives itself out of a very com-

220   petent° injury, therefore get you on, and give him his desire.   *sufficient*
Back you shall not to the house unless you undertake that° with   *(a duel)*
me which with as much safety you might answer him. There-
fore on, or strip your sword stark naked, for meddle° you must,   *engage in a duel*
that's certain, or forswear to wear iron about you.[1]

225 VIOLA   This is as uncivil as strange. I beseech you do me this
courteous office, as to know of° the knight what my offence   *ascertain from*
to him is. It is something of my negligence, nothing of my
purpose.

---

2. *'haviour . . . bears:* behavior that characterizes your
lovesickness.
3. Jeweled ornament, here a brooch or a locket with
Olivia's picture.
4. That honor may grant without compromising itself.
5. I will release you from your promise.

6. Draw your rapier.
7. Unhacked, or undented; never used in battle.
8. A "carpet knight" obtained his title through connections at court rather than valor on the battlefield.
9. Have or have not ("all or nothing").
1. Or forfeit your right to wear a sword.

SIR TOBY   I will do so. Signor Fabian, stay you by this gentleman
230　till my return.   *Exit*

VIOLA   Pray you, sir, do you know of this matter?

FABIAN   I know the knight is incensed against you even to a mor-
tal arbitrement,° but nothing of the circumstance more.   *deadly duel*

VIOLA   I beseech you, what manner of man is he?

235　FABIAN   Nothing of that wonderful promise to read him by his
form² as you are like to find him in the proof of his valour. He
is indeed, sir, the most skilful, bloody, and fatal opposite that
you could possibly have found in any part of Illyria. Will you°   *If you will*
walk towards him, I will make your peace with him if I can.

240　VIOLA   I shall be much bound to you for't. I am one that had
rather go with Sir Priest³ than Sir Knight—I care not who
knows so much of my mettle.°   *Exeunt*   *disposition*
Enter [SIR] TOBY *and* [SIR] ANDREW

SIR TOBY   Why, man, he's a very devil, I have not seen such a
virago.⁴ I had a pass° with him, rapier, scabbard, and all, and   *fencing bout*
245　he gives me the stuck-in⁵ with such a mortal motion that it is
inevitable, and on the answer,° he pays you as surely as your   *return hit*
feet hits the ground they step on. They say he has been fencer
to the Sophy.°   *Shah of Persia*

SIR ANDREW   Pox on't, I'll not meddle with him.

250　SIR TOBY   Ay, but he will not now be pacified, Fabian can scarce
hold him yonder.

SIR ANDREW   Plague on't, an° I thought he had been valiant and   *if*
so cunning in fence I'd have seen him damned ere I'd have
challenged him. Let him let the matter slip and I'll give him
255　my horse, grey Capulet.

SIR TOBY   I'll make the motion.° Stand here, make a good show   *offer*
on't—this shall end without the perdition of souls.°   *loss of lives*
[*Aside*] Marry, I'll ride your horse as well as I ride you.
Enter FABIAN, *and* VIOLA [*as Cesario*]
[*Aside to* FABIAN] I have his horse to take up° the quarrel, I have   *settle*
260　persuaded him the youth's a devil.

FABIAN [*aside to* SIR TOBY]   He is as horribly conceited⁶ of him,
and pants and looks pale as if a bear were at his heels.

SIR TOBY [*to* VIOLA]   There's no remedy, sir, he will fight with
you for's oath' sake. Marry, he hath better bethought him of his
265　quarrel, and he finds that now scarce to be worth talking of.
Therefore draw for the supportance of his vow, he protests he
will not hurt you.

VIOLA [*aside*]   Pray God defend me. A little thing would make
me tell them how much I lack of a man.

270　FABIAN [*to* SIR ANDREW]   Give ground if you see him furious.

SIR TOBY   Come, Sir Andrew, there's no remedy, the gentleman
will for his honour's sake have one bout with you, he cannot
by the duello° avoid it, but he has promised me, as he is a   *code of dueling*
gentleman and a soldier, he will not hurt you. Come on, to't.

275　SIR ANDREW   Pray God he keep his oath.
Enter ANTONIO

---

2. *Nothing . . . form:* From his outward appearance,
you cannot perceive him to be as remarkable.
3. Priests were often addressed as "sir."
4. Woman warrior (suggesting great ferocity with a

feminine appearance).
5. Thrust (from the Italian *stoccata*).
6. He has as terrifying an idea.

VIOLA   I do assure you 'tis against my will.
[SIR ANDREW *and* VIOLA *draw their swords*]
ANTONIO [*drawing his sword, to* SIR ANDREW]   Put up your sword.
If this young gentleman
Have done offence, I take the fault on me.
If you offend him, I for him defy you.

280   SIR TOBY   You, sir? Why, what are you?
ANTONIO   One, sir, that for his love dares yet do more
Than you have heard him brag to you he will.
SIR TOBY [*drawing his sword*]   Nay, if you be an undertaker,[7] I
am for you.
Enter OFFICERS

285   FABIAN   O, good Sir Toby, hold. Here come the officers.
SIR TOBY [*to* ANTONIO]   I'll be with you anon.
VIOLA [*to* SIR ANDREW]   Pray, sir, put your sword up if you please.
SIR ANDREW   Marry will I, sir, and for that° I promised you I'll be   *as for that*
as good as my word. He will bear you easily, and reins well.
[SIR ANDREW *and* VIOLA *put up their swords*]

290   FIRST OFFICER   This is the man, do thy office.
SECOND OFFICER   Antonio, I arrest thee at the suit of Count
Orsino.
ANTONIO   You do mistake me, sir.
FIRST OFFICER   No, sir, no jot. I know your favour° well,   *face*
295   Though now you have no seacap on your head.
[*To* SECOND OFFICER] Take him away, he knows I know him well.
ANTONIO   I must obey. [*To* VIOLA] This comes with seeking you.
But there's no remedy, I shall answer° it.   *answer for*
What will you do now my necessity
300   Makes me to ask you for my purse? It grieves me
Much more for what I cannot do for you
Than what befalls myself. You stand amazed,
But be of comfort.
SECOND OFFICER   Come, sir, away.
ANTONIO [*to* VIOLA]   I must entreat of you some of that money.
305   VIOLA   What money, sir?
For the fair kindness you have showed me here,
And part° being prompted by your present trouble,   *in part*
Out of my lean and low ability
I'll lend you something. My having is not much.
310   I'll make division of my present° with you.   *ready money*
Hold, [*offering money*] there's half my coffer.
ANTONIO   Will you deny me now?
Is't possible that my deserts to you
Can lack persuasion?[8] Do not tempt my misery,
Lest that it make me so unsound° a man   *morally weak*
315   As to upbraid you with those kindnesses
That I have done for you.
VIOLA   I know of none,
Nor know I you by voice, or any feature.
I hate ingratitude more in a man
Than lying, vainness, babbling drunkenness,

---

7. One who would take upon himself a task (here, a challenge).

8. *Is't . . . persuasion:* Is it possible my past kindness can fail to persuade you?

320   Or any taint of vice whose strong corruption
     Inhabits our frail blood.
     ANTONIO   O heavens themselves!
     SECOND OFFICER   Come, sir, I pray you go.
     ANTONIO   Let me speak a little. This youth that you see here
     I snatched one half out of the jaws of death,
325   Relieved him with such sanctity° of love,   *great devotion*
     And to his image,[9] which methought did promise
     Most venerable worth,[1] did I devotion.
     FIRST OFFICER   What's that to us? The time goes by, away.
     ANTONIO   But O, how vile an idol proves this god!
330   Thou hast, Sebastian, done good feature° shame.   *physical beauty*
     In nature there's no blemish but the mind.
     None can be called deformed but the unkind.
     Virtue is beauty, but the beauteous evil
     Are empty trunks o'er-flourished[2] by the devil.
335   FIRST OFFICER   The man grows mad, away with him. Come, come, sir.
     ANTONIO   Lead me on.   *Exit* [*with* OFFICERS]
     VIOLA [*aside*]   Methinks his words do from such passion fly
     That he believes himself. So do not I.[3]
     Prove true, imagination, O prove true,
340   That I, dear brother, be now ta'en for you!
     SIR TOBY   Come hither, knight. Come hither, Fabian. We'll
     whisper o'er a couplet or two of most sage saws.°   *sayings; maxims*
          [*They stand aside*]
     VIOLA   He named Sebastian. I my brother know
     Yet living in my glass.° Even such and so   *mirror*
345   In favour° was my brother, and he went   *appearance*
     Still° in this fashion, colour, ornament,   *Always*
     For him I imitate. O, if it prove,
     Tempests are kind, and salt waves fresh in love!   *Exit*
     SIR TOBY [*to* SIR ANDREW]   A very dishonest,° paltry boy, and   *dishonorable*
350   more a coward than a hare. His dishonesty appears in leaving
     his friend here in necessity, and denying him; and for his cow-
     ardship, ask Fabian.
     FABIAN   A coward, a most devout coward, religious in it.
     SIR ANDREW   'Slid,° I'll after him again, and beat him.   *By God's eyelid*
355   SIR TOBY   Do, cuff him soundly, but never draw thy sword.
     SIR ANDREW   An I do not—   [*Exit*]
     FABIAN   Come, let's see the event.°   *outcome*
     SIR TOBY   I dare lay any money 'twill be nothing yet.°   *Exeunt*   *after all*

4.1
Enter SEBASTIAN *and* [FESTE, *the*] *clown*

     FESTE   Will you° make me believe that I am not sent for you?   *Are you trying to*
     SEBASTIAN   Go to, go to, thou art a foolish fellow,
     Let me be clear° of thee.   *rid*
     FESTE   Well held out,° i'faith! No, I do not know you, nor I am   *kept up*
5   not sent to you by my lady to bid you come speak with her, nor

---

9. Appearance (with a play on "religious icon").
1. *did . . . worth*: was worthy of veneration.
2. Chests decorated with carving or painting; beautified
bodies.

3. *So do not I*: I do not entirely believe the passionate
hope (for my brother's rescue) that is arising in me.
4.1 Location: Near Olivia's house.

your name is not Master Cesario, nor this is not my nose, neither. Nothing that is so, is so.

SEBASTIAN I prithee vent° thy folly somewhere else,   *utter; excrete*
Thou know'st not me.

10 FESTE Vent my folly! He has heard that word of some great
man, and now applies it to a fool. Vent my folly—I am afraid
this great lubber° the world will prove a cockney.° I prithee   *lout / sissy*
now ungird thy strangeness,¹ and tell me what I shall 'vent' to
my lady? Shall I 'vent' to her that thou art coming?

15 SEBASTIAN I prithee, foolish Greek,° depart from me.   *buffoon*
There's money for thee. If you tarry longer
I shall give worse payment.

FESTE By my troth, thou hast an open hand. These wise men
that give fools money get themselves a good report,° after four-   *reputation*
20 teen years' purchase.²

　　　　　Enter [SIR] ANDREW, [SIR] TOBY, *and* FABIAN

SIR ANDREW [*to* SEBASTIAN] Now, sir, have I met you again?
[*Striking him*] There's for you.

SEBASTIAN [*striking* SIR ANDREW *with his dagger*] Why, there's
for thee, and there, and there.
Are all the people mad?

25 SIR TOBY [*to* SEBASTIAN, *holding him back*] Hold, sir, or I'll throw
your dagger o'er the house.

FESTE This will I tell my lady straight,° I would not be in some   *straightaway*
of your coats for twopence.   [*Exit*]

SIR TOBY Come on, sir, hold.

30 SIR ANDREW Nay, let him alone, I'll go another way to work with
him. I'll have an action of battery° against him if there be any   *a lawsuit for assault*
law in Illyria. Though I struck him first, yet it's no matter for
that.

SEBASTIAN Let go thy hand.

35 SIR TOBY Come, sir, I will not let you go. Come, my young soldier, put up your iron. You are well fleshed.³ Come on.

SEBASTIAN [*freeing himself*] I will be free from thee. What wouldst thou now?
If thou dar'st tempt me further, draw thy sword.

SIR TOBY What, what? Nay then, I must have an ounce or two
40 of this malapert° blood from you.   *impudent*

　　　　　[SIR TOBY *and* SEBASTIAN *draw their swords.*]
　　　　　Enter OLIVIA

OLIVIA Hold, Toby, on thy life I charge thee hold.

SIR TOBY Madam.

OLIVIA Will it be ever thus? Ungracious wretch,
Fit for the mountains and the barbarous caves,
45 Where manners ne'er were preached—out of my sight!
Be not offended, dear Cesario.
[*To* SIR TOBY] Rudesby,° be gone.   *Ruffian*

　　　　　[*Exeunt* SIR TOBY, SIR ANDREW, *and* FABIAN]
　　　　　　　　　　I prithee, gentle friend,
Let thy fair wisdom, not thy passion sway
In this uncivil and unjust extent°   *assault*

---

1. *I . . . strangeness:* Stop pretending not to know me.
(Feste mocks Sebastian's affected language.)
2. *after . . . purchase:* at a high price. The purchase price

of land was normally twelve times its annual rent.
3. Experienced in combat. Hunting hounds were said to
be "fleshed" after being fed part of their first kill.

50 Against thy peace. Go with me to my house,
And hear thou there how many fruitless pranks
This ruffian hath botched up,° that thou thereby   *clumsily contrived*
Mayst smile at this. Thou shalt not choose but go.
Do not deny. Beshrew° his soul for me,   *Curse*
55 He started one poor heart of mine in thee.⁴
SEBASTIAN   What relish° is in this? How runs the stream?   *task; meaning*
Or° I am mad, or else this is a dream.   *Either*
Let fancy° still my sense in Lethe⁵ steep.   *imagination*
If it be thus to dream, still let me sleep.
60 OLIVIA   Nay, come, I prithee, would thou'dst be ruled by me.
SEBASTIAN   Madam, I will.
OLIVIA   O, say so, and so be.   *Exeunt*

4.2

Enter MARIA [*carrying a gown and false beard, and*
FESTE, *the*] *clown*
MARIA   Nay, I prithee put on this gown and this beard, make
him believe thou art Sir Topas¹ the curate. Do it quickly. I'll
call Sir Toby the whilst.°   *Exit*   *in the meantime*
FESTE   Well, I'll put it on, and I will dissemble² myself in't, and
5   I would I were the first that ever dissembled in such a gown.
[*He disguises himself*]
I am not tall enough to become the function well,³ nor lean
enough to be thought a good student,° but to be said° 'an hon-   *(of divinity) / reputed*
est man and a good housekeeper'° goes as fairly as⁴ to say 'a   *host*
careful man and a great scholar'. The competitors° enter.   *associates*
Enter [SIR] TOBY [*and* MARIA]
10 SIR TOBY   Jove bless thee, Master Parson.
FESTE   *Bonos dies*,⁵ Sir Toby, for, as the old hermit of Prague,⁶
that never saw pen and ink, very wittily° said to a niece of King   *intelligently*
Gorboduc,° 'That that is, is.' So I, being Master Parson, am   *legendary British king*
Master Parson; for what is 'that' but 'that', and 'is' but 'is'?
15 SIR TOBY   To him, Sir Topas.
FESTE   What ho, I say, peace in this prison.
SIR TOBY   The knave counterfeits well—a good knave.
        MALVOLIO *within*
MALVOLIO   Who calls there?
FESTE   Sir Topas the curate, who comes to visit Malvolio the
20 lunatic.
MALVOLIO   Sir Topas, Sir Topas, good Sir Topas, go to my lady.
FESTE   Out, hyperbolical fiend,⁷ how vexest thou this man! Talk-
est thou nothing but of ladies?
SIR TOBY   Well said, Master Parson.
25 MALVOLIO   Sir Topas, never was man thus wronged. Good Sir

---

4. *He . . . thee:* By attacking Sebastian, Sir Toby frightened Olivia, who has exchanged hearts with Sebastian.
started: an allusion to hunting, creating a pun on "hart /
heart."
5. The mythical river of oblivion.
4.2 Location: Olivia's house, where Malvolio will be
found (offstage) "in a dark room and bound" (3.4.121).
1. The comical hero of Chaucer's *Rime of Sir Topas*.
Also alluding to the mineral topaz, which was thought to

have special curative qualities for insanity.
2. Disguise; with subsequent play on "lie."
3. Grace the priestly office. *tall:* stout, rather than of
great height.
4. *goes as fairly as:* sounds as well as.
5. Good day (false Latin).
6. Probably an invented authority.
7. Feste treats Malvolio as a man possessed by vehement
("hyperbolical") evil spirits.

Topas, do not think I am mad. They have laid me here in hideous darkness.

FESTE   Fie, thou dishonest Satan—I call thee by the most mod-
est° terms, for I am one of those gentle ones that will use the
30   devil himself with courtesy. Sayst thou that house° is dark?

MALVOLIO   As hell, Sir Topas.

FESTE   Why, it hath bay windows transparent as barricadoes, and
the clerestories[8] toward the south-north are as lustrous as
ebony,[9] and yet complainest thou of obstruction?

35   MALVOLIO   I am not mad, Sir Topas; I say to you this house is
dark.

FESTE   Madman, thou errest. I say there is no darkness but ignorance, in which thou art more puzzled than the Egyptians in
their fog.[1]

40   MALVOLIO   I say this house is as dark as ignorance, though ignorance were as dark as hell; and I say there was never man thus
abused. I am no more mad than you are. Make the trial of it in
any constant question.°

FESTE   What is the opinion of Pythagoras[2] concerning wildfowl?

45   MALVOLIO   That the soul of our grandam might haply° inhabit a
bird.

FESTE   What thinkest thou of his opinion?

MALVOLIO   I think nobly of the soul, and no way approve his
opinion.

50   FESTE   Fare thee well. Remain thou still in darkness. Thou shalt
hold th'opinion of Pythagoras ere I will allow of thy wits,° and
fear to kill a woodcock[3] lest thou dispossess the soul of thy grandam. Fare thee well.

MALVOLIO   Sir Topas, Sir Topas!

55   SIR TOBY   My most exquisite Sir Topas.

FESTE   Nay, I am for all waters.[4]

MARIA   Thou mightst have done this without thy beard and
gown, he sees thee not.

SIR TOBY [to FESTE]   To him in thine own voice, and bring me
60   word how thou findest him. I would we were well rid of this
knavery. If he may be conveniently delivered, I would he were,
for I am now so far in offence with my niece that I cannot
pursue with any safety this sport to the upshot. [To MARIA]
Come by and by to my chamber.   Exit [with MARIA]

65   FESTE [sings][5]   'Hey Robin, jolly Robin,
                              Tell me how thy lady does.'

MALVOLIO   Fool!

FESTE   'My lady is unkind, pardie.'[6]

MALVOLIO   Fool!

70   FESTE   'Alas, why is she so?'

MALVOLIO   Fool, I say!

FESTE   'She loves another.'
                 Who calls, ha?

mildest

room

logical discussion

perhaps

certify your sanity

8. Upper windows, usually in a church or great hall. *bar-ricadoes:* barricades (subsequent paradoxes are equiva-lent to "as clear as mud").
9. A dense and naturally dull black wood.
1. One of the plagues of Egypt was a "black darkness" lasting for three days (Exodus 10:21–23).
2. An ancient Greek philosopher who held that the same

soul could successively inhabit different creatures.
3. A traditionally stupid bird.
4. I am able to turn my hand to anything.
5. Feste's song, which makes Malvolio aware of his pres-ence, is traditional. There is a version by Sir Thomas Wyatt.
6. A corruption of the French *pardieu,* "by God."

MALVOLIO   Good fool, as ever thou wilt deserve well at my hand,
help me to a candle and pen, ink, and paper. As I am a gentleman, I will live to be thankful to thee for't.

FESTE   Master Malvolio?

MALVOLIO   Ay, good fool.

FESTE   Alas, sir, how fell you besides° your five wits?[7]   *out of*

MALVOLIO   Fool, there was never man so notoriously° abused. I   *outrageously*
am as well in my wits, fool, as thou art.

FESTE   But as well? Then you are mad indeed, if you be no better in your wits than a fool.

MALVOLIO   They have here propertied me,[8] keep me in darkness,
send ministers to me, asses, and do all they can to face me[9] out
of my wits.

FESTE   Advise you° what you say, the minister is here.   *Be careful*
[*As Sir Topas*] Malvolio, Malvolio, thy wits the heavens restore.
Endeavour thyself to sleep, and leave thy vain bibble-babble.

MALVOLIO   Sir Topas.

FESTE [*as Sir Topas*]   Maintain no words with him, good fellow.
[*As himself*] Who I, sir? Not I, sir. God b'wi' you,° good Sir   *God be with you*
Topas. [*As Sir Topas*] Marry, amen. [*As himself*] I will, sir, I
will.

MALVOLIO   Fool, fool, fool, I say.

FESTE   Alas, sir, be patient. What say you, sir? I am shent° for   *scolded*
speaking to you.

MALVOLIO   Good fool, help me to some light and some paper. I
tell thee I am as well in my wits as any man in Illyria.

FESTE   Well-a-day° that you were, sir.   *Alas*

MALVOLIO   By this hand, I am. Good fool, some ink, paper, and
light, and convey what I will set down to my lady. It shall advantage thee more than ever the bearing of letter did.

FESTE   I will help you to't. But tell me true, are you not mad
indeed, or do you but counterfeit?

MALVOLIO   Believe me, I am not, I tell thee true.

FESTE   Nay, I'll ne'er believe a madman till I see his brains. I
will fetch you light, and paper, and ink.

MALVOLIO   Fool, I'll requite it in the highest degree. I prithee,
be gone.

FESTE   I am gone, sir,
               And anon, sir,
                  I'll be with you again,
               In a trice,
               Like to the old Vice,[1]
                  Your need to sustain,
               Who with dagger of lath
               In his rage and his wrath
                  Cries 'Aha,' to the devil,
               Like a mad lad,
               'Pare thy nails, dad,
                  Adieu, goodman[2] devil.'   *Exit*

---

7. Usually regarded as common sense, fantasy, memory, judgment, and imagination.
8. Treated me as a piece of property.
9. *face me:* brazenly construe me as.

1. A stock comic figure in the old morality plays; the Vice often carried a wooden dagger.
2. Yeoman; a title given to one not of gentle birth, hence a parting insult to Malvolio.

4.3

Enter SEBASTIAN

SEBASTIAN   This is the air, that is the glorious sun.
This pearl she gave me, I do feel't and see't,
And though 'tis wonder that enwraps me thus,
Yet 'tis not madness. Where's Antonio then?
5 I could not find him at the Elephant,
Yet there he was,° and there I found this credit,°   *had been / report*
That he did range the town to seek me out.
His counsel now might do me golden service,
For though my soul disputes well with my sense[1]
10 That this may be some error but no madness,
Yet doth this accident and flood of fortune
So far exceed all instance,° all discourse,°   *precedent / reasoning*
That I am ready to distrust mine eyes
And wrangle with my reason that persuades me
15 To any other trust° but that I am mad,   *belief*
Or else the lady's mad. Yet if 'twere so
She could not sway° her house, command her followers,   *rule*
Take and give back affairs and their dispatch[2]
With such a smooth, discreet, and stable bearing
20 As I perceive she does. There's something in't
That is deceivable.° But here the lady comes.   *deceptive*

Enter OLIVIA *and* PRIEST

OLIVIA   Blame not this haste of mine. If you mean well
Now go with me, and with this holy man,
Into the chantry by.° There before him,   *nearby chapel*
25 And underneath that consecrated roof,
Plight me the full assurance of your faith,[3]
That my most jealous° and too doubtful soul   *anxious*
May live at peace. He shall conceal it
Whiles° you are willing it shall come to note,   *Until*
30 What° time we will our celebration keep   *At which*
According to my birth.° What do you say?   *rank*
SEBASTIAN   I'll follow this good man, and go with you,
And having sworn truth, ever will be true.
OLIVIA   Then lead the way, good father, and heavens so shine
35 That they may fairly note° this act of mine.   *Exeunt*   *look favorably upon*

5.1

Enter [FESTE, *the*] *clown and* FABIAN

FABIAN   Now, as thou lovest me, let me see his letter.
FESTE   Good Master Fabian, grant me another request.
FABIAN   Anything.
FESTE   Do not desire to see this letter.
5 FABIAN   This is to give a dog, and in recompense desire my dog
again.[1]

Enter Duke, VIOLA [*as Cesario*], CURIO, *and lords*

ORSINO   Belong you to the Lady Olivia, friends?

4.3 Location: Near Olivia's house.
1. For though my reason and my sense both concur.
2. Undertake business, and ensure that it is carried
out.
3. Enter into the solemn contract of betrothal.
5.1 Location: Before Olivia's house.

1. Perhaps a reference to an anecdote, recorded in
John Manningham's diary, in which Queen Elizabeth
requested a dog, and the donor, when granted a wish in
return, asked for the dog back.

FESTE   Ay, sir, we are some of her trappings.°   *ornaments*
ORSINO   I know thee well. How dost thou, my good fellow?
10   FESTE   Truly, sir, the better for my foes and the worse for my
friends.
ORSINO   Just the contrary—the better for thy friends.
FESTE   No, sir, the worse.
ORSINO   How can that be?
15   FESTE   Marry, sir, they praise me, and make an ass of me. Now
my foes tell me plainly I am an ass, so that by my foes, sir, I
profit in the knowledge of myself, and by my friends I am
abused;° so that, conclusions to be as kisses, if your four nega-   *deceived*
tives make your two affirmatives,² why then the worse for my
20   friends and the better for my foes.
ORSINO   Why, this is excellent.
FESTE   By my troth, sir, no, though it please you to be one of my
friends.
ORSINO   [*giving money*]   Thou shalt not be the worse for me.
25   There's gold.
FESTE   But° that it would be double-dealing,³ sir, I would you   *Except for the fact*
could make it another.
ORSINO   O, you give me ill counsel.
FESTE   Put your grace in your pocket,⁴ sir, for this once, and let
30   your flesh and blood obey it.⁵
ORSINO   Well, I will be so much a sinner to° be a double-dealer.   *as to*
[*Giving money*] There's another.
FESTE   *Primo, secundo, tertio*⁶ is a good play,° and the old saying   *game*
is 'The third pays for all'.⁷ The triplex,° sir, is a good tripping   *triple time in music*
35   measure, or the bells of Saint Bennet,⁸ sir, may put you in
mind—'one, two, three'.
ORSINO   You can fool no more money out of me at this throw.°   *throw of the dice*
If you will let your lady know I am here to speak with her, and
bring her along with you, it may awake my bounty further.
40   FESTE   Marry, sir, lullaby to your bounty till I come again. I go,
sir, but I would not have you to think that my desire of having
is the sin of covetousness. But as you say, sir, let your bounty
take a nap, I will awake it anon.   *Exit*
          Enter ANTONIO *and* OFFICERS
VIOLA   Here comes the man, sir, that did rescue me.
45   ORSINO   That face of his I do remember well,
Yet when I saw it last it was besmeared
As black as Vulcan⁹ in the smoke of war.
A baubling° vessel was he captain of,   *trifling*
For shallow draught and bulk unprizable,¹
50   With which such scatheful° grapple did he make   *destructive*
With the most noble bottom° of our fleet   *ship*

2. *conclusions . . affirmatives:* as in grammar, a double
negative can make an affirmative (and therefore four neg-
atives can make two affirmatives); so when a coy girl is
asked for a kiss, her four refusals can be construed as
"yes, yes."
3. A duplicity; a double donation.
4. Set aside (pocket up) your virtue; also (with a play on
the customary form of address for a duke, "your grace"),
reach into your pocket and grace me with another coin.
5. Let your normal human instincts (as opposed to

grace) follow the "ill counsel" (line 28).
6. First, second, third (Latin); perhaps an allusion to a
dice throw or a child's game.
7. Third time lucky (proverbial).
8. A London church, across the Thames from the Globe,
was known as St. Bennet Hithe.
9. Blacksmith of the Roman gods.
1. Of no value because of its small size. *draught:* water
displaced by a vessel.

That very envy° and the tongue of loss°   *even enmity / the losers*
Cried fame and honour on him. What's the matter?
FIRST OFFICER Orsino, this is that Antonio
55 That took the Phoenix and her freight from Candy,[2]
And this is he that did the *Tiger* board
When your young nephew Titus lost his leg.
Here in the streets, desperate of shame and state,[3]
In private brabble° did we apprehend him.   *brawl*
60 **VIOLA** He did me kindness, sir, drew on my side,[4]
But in conclusion put strange speech upon° me. *spoke strangely to*
I know not what 'twas but distraction.°   *if not insanity*
ORSINO [*to* ANTONIO] Notable° pirate, thou salt-water thief, *Notorious*
What foolish boldness brought thee to their mercies
65 Whom thou in terms so bloody and so dear°   *dire*
Hast made thine enemies?
ANTONIO   Orsino, noble sir,
Be pleased that I shake off these names you give me.
Antonio never yet was thief or pirate,
Though, I confess, on base° and ground enough *foundation*
70 Orsino's enemy. A witchcraft drew me hither.
That most ingrateful boy there by your side
From the rude sea's enragèd and foamy mouth
Did I redeem. A wreck past hope he was.
His life I gave him, and did thereto add
75 My love without retention° or restraint,   *reservation*
All his in dedication. For his sake
Did I expose myself, pure° for his love,   *only*
Into the danger of this adverse° town,   *hostile*
Drew to defend him when he was beset,
80 Where being apprehended, his false cunning—
Not meaning to partake with me in danger—
Taught him to face me out of his acquaintance,[5]
And grew a twenty years' removèd thing
While one would wink,[6] denied me mine own purse,
85 Which I had recommended° to his use   *consigned*
Not half an hour before.
VIOLA How can this be?
ORSINO When came he to this town?
ANTONIO Today, my lord, and for three months before,
90 No int'rim, not a minute's vacancy,°   *interval*
Both day and night did we keep company.
   Enter OLIVIA *and attendants*
ORSINO Here comes the Countess. Now heaven walks on earth.
But for thee, fellow—fellow, thy words are madness.
Three months this youth hath tended upon me.
95 But more of that anon. Take him aside.
OLIVIA What would my lord, but that he may not have,[7]
Wherein Olivia may seem serviceable?
Cesario, you do not keep promise with me.
VIOLA Madam—

---

2. Candia, capital of Crete.
3. *desperate . . . state:* recklessly oblivious of the danger to his honor and his position (as a free man and public enemy).
4. Drew his sword in my defense.

5. To brazenly deny my acquaintance.
6. *And . . . wink:* In the wink of an eye, pretended we had been estranged for twenty years.
7. Except that which he may not have (my love).

100 ORSINO Gracious Olivia—
OLIVIA What do you say, Cesario? Good my lord—
VIOLA My lord would speak, my duty hushes me.
OLIVIA If it be aught° to the old tune, my lord,   *anything*
It is as fat and fulsome° to mine ear   *gross and offensive*
105 As howling after music.
ORSINO Still so cruel?
OLIVIA Still so constant, lord.
ORSINO What, to perverseness? You uncivil lady,
To whose ingrate and unauspicious° altars   *unfavorable*
110 My soul the faithfull'st off 'rings hath breathed out
That e'er devotion tendered—what shall I do?
OLIVIA Even what it please my lord that shall become° him.   *be fitting for*
ORSINO Why should I not, had I the heart to do it,
Like to th' Egyptian thief, at point of death
115 Kill what I love[8]—a savage jealousy
That sometime savours nobly.° But hear me this: *of nobility*
Since you to non-regardance° cast my faith,   *oblivion*
And that I partly know the instrument
That screws° me from my true place in your favour,   *wrenches*
120 Live you the marble-breasted tyrant still.
But this your minion,° whom I know you love,   *darling*
And whom, by heaven I swear, I tender° dearly,   *regard*
Him will I tear out of that cruel eye
Where he sits crownèd in his master's spite.[9]
125 [*To* VIOLA] Come, boy, with me. My thoughts are ripe in mischief.
I'll sacrifice the lamb that I do love
To spite a raven's heart within a dove.
VIOLA And I most jocund,° apt,° and willingly   *cheerfully / ready*
To do you rest a thousand deaths would die.
OLIVIA Where goes Cesario?
130 VIOLA   After him I love
More than I love these eyes, more than my life,
More by all mores[1] than e'er I shall love wife.
If I do feign, you witnesses above,
Punish my life for tainting of my love.
135 OLIVIA Ay me detested, how am I beguiled!
VIOLA Who does beguile you? Who does do you wrong?
OLIVIA Hast thou forgot thyself ? Is it so long?
Call forth the holy father.   [*Exit an attendant*]
ORSINO [*to* VIOLA]   Come, away.
OLIVIA Whither, my lord? Cesario, husband, stay.
ORSINO Husband?
140 OLIVIA   Ay, husband. Can he that deny?
ORSINO [*to* VIOLA] Her husband, sirrah?[2]
VIOLA   No, my lord, not I.
OLIVIA Alas, it is the baseness of thy fear
That makes thee strangle thy propriety.[3]
Fear not, Cesario, take thy fortunes up,

---

8. In Heliodorus of Emesa's *Ethiopica*, a Greek prose
romance translated into English in 1569 and popular in
Shakespeare's day, the Egyptian robber chief Thyamis
tries to kill his captive Chariclea, whom he loves, when he
is in danger from a rival band.

9. To the mortification of his master.
1. More beyond all comparison.
2. Contemptuous form of address to an inferior.
3. That makes you deny your identity (as my husband).

145 Be that thou know'st thou art, and then thou art
As great as that° thou fear'st.   *him whom*
        Enter PRIEST
                        O welcome, father.
Father, I charge thee by thy reverence
Here to unfold—though lately we intended
To keep in darkness what occasion° now   *necessity*
150 Reveals before 'tis ripe—what thou dost know
Hath newly passed between this youth and me.
PRIEST   A contract of eternal bond of love,
Confirmed by mutual joinder° of your hands,   *joining*
Attested by the holy close° of lips,   *meeting*
155 Strengthened by interchangement of your rings,
And all the ceremony of this compact
Sealed in my function,[4] by my testimony;
Since when, my watch hath told me, toward my grave
I have travelled but two hours.
160 ORSINO [*to* VIOLA]   O thou dissembling cub, what wilt thou be
When time hath sowed a grizzle on thy case?[5]
Or will not else thy craft° so quickly grow   *craftiness*
That thine own trip shall be thine overthrow?[6]
Farewell, and take her, but direct thy feet
165 Where thou and I henceforth may never meet.
VIOLA   My lord, I do protest.
OLIVIA   O, do not swear!
Hold little° faith, though thou hast too much fear.   *Preserve some*
        Enter SIR ANDREW
SIR ANDREW   For the love of God, a surgeon—send one pres-
ently° to Sir Toby.   *immediately*
170 OLIVIA   What's the matter?
SIR ANDREW   He's broke° my head across, and has given Sir Toby   *cut*
a bloody coxcomb,[7] too. For the love of God, your help! I had
rather than forty pound I were at home.
OLIVIA   Who has done this, Sir Andrew?
175 SIR ANDREW   The Count's gentleman, one Cesario. We took him
for a coward, but he's the very devil incardinate.[8]
ORSINO   My gentleman, Cesario?
SIR ANDREW   'Od's lifelings,° here he is. [*To* VIOLA] You broke   *By God's little lives*
my head for nothing, and that that I did I was set on to do't by
180 Sir Toby.
VIOLA   Why do you speak to me? I never hurt you.
You drew your sword upon me without cause,
But I bespake you fair,[9] and hurt you not.
        Enter [SIR] TOBY *and* [FESTE, *the*] *clown*
SIR ANDREW   If a bloody coxcomb be a hurt you have hurt me. I
185 think you set nothing by° a bloody coxcomb. Here comes Sir   *think nothing of*
Toby, halting.° You shall hear more; but if ° he had not been   *limping / if only*
in drink he would have tickled° you othergates° than he did.   *chastised / in other ways*
ORSINO [*to* SIR TOBY]   How now, gentleman? How is't with you?

---

4. Ratified by priestly authority.
5. A gray hair ("grizzle") on your hide (sustaining the
metaphor of "cub").
6. That your attempt to trip someone else will be the
cause of your downfall.

7. Head; also, a fool's cap, which resembles the crest of
a cock.
8. Sir Andrew's blunder for "incarnate" (in the flesh).
9. But I spoke courteously to you.

	SIR TOBY That's all one,° he's hurt me, and there's th'end on't.	*No matter*
190	[*To* FESTE] Sot,° didst see Dick Surgeon, sot?	*Fool; drunkard*
	FESTE O, he's drunk, Sir Toby, an hour agone. His eyes were	
	set¹ at eight i'th' morning.	
	SIR TOBY Then he's a rogue, and a passy-measures pavan.² I hate	
	a drunken rogue.	
195	OLIVIA Away with him! Who hath made this havoc with them?	
	SIR ANDREW I'll help you, Sir Toby, because we'll be dressed³	
	together.	
	SIR TOBY Will *you* help—an ass-head, and a coxcomb,° and a	*fool*
	knave; a thin-faced knave, a gull?°	*dupe*
200	OLIVIA Get him to bed, and let his hurt be looked to.	

[*Exeunt* SIR TOBY, SIR ANDREW, FESTE, *and* FABIAN]

Enter SEBASTIAN

	SEBASTIAN [*to* OLIVIA] I am sorry, madam, I have hurt your kinsman,	
	But had it been the brother of my blood	
	I must have done no less with wit and safety.⁴	
	You throw a strange regard upon me,° and by that	*regard me strangely*
205	I do perceive it hath offended you.	
	Pardon me, sweet one, even for the vows	
	We made each other but so late ago.	
	ORSINO One face, one voice, one habit, and two persons,	
	A natural perspective,⁵ that is and is not.	
210	SEBASTIAN Antonio! O, my dear Antonio,	
	How have the hours racked and tortured me	
	Since I have lost thee!	
	ANTONIO Sebastian are you?	
	SEBASTIAN Fear'st thou° that, Antonio?	*Do you doubt*
215	ANTONIO How have you made division of yourself?	
	An apple cleft in two is not more twin	
	Than these two creatures. Which is Sebastian?	
	OLIVIA Most wonderful!°	*full of wonder*
	SEBASTIAN [*seeing* VIOLA] Do I stand there? I never had a brother,	
220	Nor can there be that deity° in my nature	*divine power*
	Of here and everywhere.° I had a sister,	*Of omnipresence*
	Whom the blind waves and surges have devoured.	
	Of charity,° what kin are you to me?	*Please*
	What countryman? What name? What parentage?	
225	VIOLA Of Messaline. Sebastian was my father.	
	Such a Sebastian was my brother, too.	
	So went he suited° to his watery tomb.	*in appearance; clad*
	If spirits can assume both form and suit	
	You come to fright us.	
	SEBASTIAN A spirit I am indeed,	
230	But am in that dimension grossly clad	
	Which from the womb I did participate.⁶	
	Were you a woman, as the rest goes even,°	*the rest suggests*
	I should my tears let fall upon your cheek	
	And say 'Thrice welcome, drownèd Viola.'	
235	VIOLA My father had a mole upon his brow.	

---

1. Closed (as the sun sets).
2. A variety of the slow dance known as "pavane" (from the Italian *passamezzo pavana*). Sir Toby may think its swaying movements suggest drunkenness.
3. We'll have our wounds dressed.

4. With any sense of my welfare.
5. An optical illusion produced by nature (rather than by a mirror).
6. *But . . . participate*: I am clad, like all mortals, in the flesh in which I was born.

SEBASTIAN And so had mine.
VIOLA And died that day when Viola from her birth
    Had numbered thirteen years.
SEBASTIAN O, that record is lively[7] in my soul.
240   He finishèd indeed his mortal act
    That day that made my sister thirteen years.
VIOLA If nothing lets° to make us happy both   *hinders*
    But this my masculine usurped attire,
    Do not embrace me till each circumstance
245   Of place, time, fortune do cohere and jump°   *agree*
    That I am Viola, which to confirm
    I'll bring you to a captain in this town
    Where lie my maiden weeds,° by whose gentle help   *clothes*
    I was preserved to serve this noble count.
250   All the occurrence of my fortune since
    Hath been between this lady and this lord.
SEBASTIAN [*to* OLIVIA] So comes it, lady, you have been mistook.
    But nature to her bias drew in that.[8]
    You would have been contracted° to a maid,   *betrothed*
255   Nor are you therein, by my life, deceived.
    You are betrothed both to a maid and man.[9]
ORSINO [*to* OLIVIA] Be not amazed. Right noble is his blood.
    If this be so, as yet the glass seems true,[1]
    I shall have share in this most happy wreck.
260   [*To* VIOLA] Boy, thou hast said to me a thousand times
    Thou never shouldst love woman like to me.
VIOLA And all those sayings will I overswear,°   *swear again*
    And all those swearings keep as true in soul
    As doth that orbèd continent[2] the fire
    That severs day from night.
265 ORSINO   Give me thy hand,
    And let me see thee in thy woman's weeds.
VIOLA The captain that did bring me first on shore
    Hath my maid's garments. He upon some action°   *legal charge*
    Is now in durance,° at Malvolio's suit,   *prison*
270   A gentleman and follower of my lady's.
OLIVIA He shall enlarge° him. Fetch Malvolio hither—   *release*
    And yet, alas, now I remember me,
    They say, poor gentleman, he's much distraught.
        Enter [FESTE, *the*] *clown with a letter, and* FABIAN
    A most extracting° frenzy of mine own   *distracting*
275   From my remembrance clearly banished his.
    How does he, sirrah?
FESTE Truly, madam, he holds Beelzebub at the stave's end[3] as
    well as a man in his case may do. He's here writ a letter to you.
    I should have given't you today morning. But as a madman's
280   epistles are no gospels,[4] so it skills° not much when they are   *matters*
    delivered.
OLIVIA Open't and read it.

---

7. The memory of that is vivid.
8. But nature followed her inclination. (The image is from the game of bowls, which uses a ball with an off-centered weight that causes it to curve away from a straight course.)
9. *maid and man:* a man who is a virgin.
1. *the glass seems true:* the "natural perspective" (line

209) continues to seem real.
2. Referring to either the sun or the sphere within which the sun was thought to be fixed.
3. He holds the devil (who threatens to possess him) at a distance (proverbial).
4. Gospel truths. *epistles:* letters (playing on the sense of apostolic accounts of Christ in the New Testament).

FESTE Look then to be well edified when the fool delivers° the   *speaks the words of*
madman. [*Reads*] 'By the Lord, madam'—
285 OLIVIA How now, art thou mad?
FESTE No, madam, I do but read madness. An your ladyship
will have it as it ought to be you must allow *vox*.[5]
OLIVIA Prithee, read i'thy right wits.
FESTE So I do, madonna, but to read his right wits[6] is to read
290 thus. Therefore perpend,° my princess, and give ear.   *pay attention*
OLIVIA [*to* FABIAN] Read it you, sirrah.
                    [FESTE *gives the letter to* FABIAN]
FABIAN (*reads*) 'By the Lord, madam, you wrong me, and the
world shall know it. Though you have put me into darkness
and given your drunken cousin rule over me, yet have I the
295 benefit of my senses as well as your ladyship. I have your own
letter that induced me to the semblance I put on, with the
which I doubt not but to do myself much right or you much
shame. Think of me as you please. I leave my duty a little
unthought of, and speak out of my injury.[7]
300   The madly-used Malvolio.
OLIVIA Did he write this?
FESTE Ay, madam.
ORSINO This savours not much of distraction.°   *insanity*
OLIVIA See him delivered,° Fabian, bring him hither.   *released*
305 My lord, so please you—these things further thought on—
To think me as well a sister as a wife,[8]
One day shall crown th'alliance[9] on't, so please you,
Here at my house and at my proper cost.°   *own expense*
ORSINO Madam, I am most apt° t'embrace your offer.   *ready*
310 [*To* VIOLA] Your master quits° you, and for your service done him   *releases*
So much against the mettle° of your sex,   *disposition*
So far beneath your soft and tender breeding,
And since you called me master for so long,
Here is my hand. You shall from this time be
Your master's mistress.
315 OLIVIA [*to* VIOLA]   A sister, you are she.
                    Enter MALVOLIO
ORSINO Is this the madman?
OLIVIA   Ay, my lord, this same.
How now, Malvolio?
MALVOLIO   Madam, you have done me wrong,
Notorious wrong.
OLIVIA   Have I, Malvolio? No.
MALVOLIO [*showing a letter*] Lady, you have. Pray you peruse that letter.
320 You must not now deny it is your hand.°   *handwriting*
Write from° it if you can, in hand or phrase,   *differently from*
Or say 'tis not your seal, not your invention.°   *composition*
You can say none of this. Well, grant it then,
And tell me in the modesty of honour[1]
325 Why you have given me such clear lights° of favour,   *signs*

5. The appropriate voice (Latin).
6. To accurately represent his mental state.
7. I neglect the formality I owe you as your servant and
speak as an injured person.
8. To think as well of me as of a sister-in-law as you would

have thought of me as a wife.
9. The impending double-marriage ceremony.
1. Tell me with the propriety that becomes a noblewoman.

Bade me come smiling and cross-gartered to you,
To put on yellow stockings, and to frown
Upon Sir Toby and the lighter° people,   *lesser*
And acting° this in an obedient hope,   *Upon doing*
330 Why have you suffered me to be imprisoned,
Kept in a dark house, visited by the priest,
And made the most notorious geck° and gull   *fool*
That e'er invention° played on? Tell me why?   *trickery*
OLIVIA Alas, Malvolio, this is not my writing,
335 Though I confess much like the character,°   *handwriting*
But out of question, 'tis Maria's hand.
And now I do bethink me, it was she
First told me thou wast mad; then cam'st° in smiling,   *you came*
And in such forms which here were presupposed° *previously suggested*
340 Upon thee in the letter. Prithee be content;
This practice hath most shrewdly passed² upon thee,
But when we know the grounds and authors of it
Thou shalt be both the plaintiff and the judge
Of thine own cause.
   FABIAN   Good madam, hear me speak,
345 And let no quarrel nor no brawl to come
Taint the condition of this present hour,
Which I have wondered° at. In hope it shall not,   *marveled*
Most freely I confess myself and Toby
Set this device against Malvolio here
350 Upon° some stubborn and uncourteous parts° *Because / behavior*
We had conceived against him.³ Maria writ
The letter, at Sir Toby's great importance,°   *importunity*
In recompense whereof he hath married her.
How with a sportful malice it was followed°   *followed through*
355 May rather pluck on° laughter than revenge   *incite*
If that the injuries be justly weighed
That have on both sides passed.
OLIVIA [*to* MALVOLIO] Alas, poor fool, how have they baffled° thee! *disgraced*
FESTE Why, 'Some are born great, some achieve greatness, and
360 some have greatness thrown upon them.' I was one, sir, in this
interlude,° one Sir Topas, sir; but that's all one. 'By the Lord, *comedy*
fool, I am not mad'—but do you remember, 'Madam, why
laugh you at such a barren rascal, an you smile not, he's
gagged'—and thus the whirligig° of time brings in his revenges. *spinning top*
365 MALVOLIO I'll be revenged on the whole pack of you. [*Exit*]
OLIVIA He hath been most notoriously abused.
ORSINO Pursue him, and entreat him to a peace.
He hath not told us of the captain yet. [*Exit one or more*]
When that is known, and golden time convents,° *summons; is convenient*
370 A solemn combination shall be made
Of our dear souls. Meantime, sweet sister,
We will not part from hence.° Cesario, come— *(Olivia's house)*
For so you shall be while you are a man;
But when in other habits you are seen,
375 Orsino's mistress, and his fancy's° queen. *love's; imagination's*
         Exeunt [*all but* FESTE]

---

2. This trick has most mischievously played.   3. *We . . . him:* To which we took exception.

FESTE (*sings*) When that I was and a little tiny boy,
   With hey, ho, the wind and the rain,
  A foolish thing was but a toy,
   For the rain it raineth every day.

380   But when I came to man's estate,
   With hey, ho, the wind and the rain,
  'Gainst knaves and thieves men shut their gate,
   For the rain it raineth every day.

  But when I came, alas, to wive,
385   With hey, ho, the wind and the rain,
  By swaggering° could I never thrive,   *bullying*
   For the rain it raineth every day.

  But when I came unto my beds,
   With hey, ho, the wind and the rain,
390   With tosspots° still had drunken heads,   *drunkards*
   For the rain it raineth every day.

  A great while ago the world begun,
   With hey, ho, the wind and the rain,
  But that's all one, our play is done,
395   And we'll strive to please you every day. *Exit*

Troilus and Cressida

Audiences or readers who come to *Troilus and Cressida* (1601–02) from the *Iliad* are in for a shock. Where Homer sings of heroic conflict culminating in the epic battle between Hector and Achilles, Shakespeare gives center stage to a love story that, like the events of the Trojan War itself, he treats in skeptical, arguably cynical, fashion. Where Homer finds tragic grandeur in the events he portrays, Shakespeare finds only carnage, a carnage not relieved by a romantic plot that ends in disillusionment. This unfamiliar recasting of traditional material produces a darkly ironic view of sexuality and politics that feels radically modern.

Shakespeare knew Homer through George Chapman's *Seaven Bookes of the Iliades of Homer* (1598) and perhaps through earlier English and French translations. (The frontispiece from Chapman's *Homer* suggests the standard view of the Trojan War at the time.) More generally, the English monarchy had long traced its lineage back to Troy. For the titular figures—and, hence, for his core narrative—Shakespeare almost certainly drew on Geoffrey Chaucer's *Troilus and Criseyde* (1380s), which views the central relationship through the code of courtly love and produces an aristocratic medieval tragedy from the failure of that love. Shakespeare was also indebted to a range of other texts: classical (Virgil's *Aeneid*, Ovid's *Metamorphoses*, perhaps several plays of Euripides), medieval (John Lydgate's *Troy Book*, early fifteenth century), and Renaissance (probably including Robert Greene's *Euphues His Censure to Philautus*, 1587). In *Doctor Faustus* (1592), a tragedy that broadly influenced Shakespeare, Christopher Marlowe's titular figure lovingly apostrophizes Helen of Troy: "Was this the face that launched a thousand ships, / And burned the topless towers of Ilium?" And in 1599, a London theatrical company apparently performed Thomas Dekker and Henry Chettle's *Troyelles and Cresseda*, but only a fragmentary list of little more than stage entrances and exits survives today. The lost drama may have covered the same territory as *Troilus and Cressida* from an epic, didactic, and sentimental perspective to which Shakespeare and his company, perceiving the commercial opportunities of a rival work on the topic, stingingly replied.

Less speculative is the ironic effect *Troilus and Cressida* achieves by self-consciously retelling a familiar story. The lovers swear oaths of fidelity that, as the audience but not the characters realize, anticipate their quite different literary reputations. Cressida's uncle, the go-between Pandarus, provides a summary: "If ever you prove false one to another, . . . let all pitiful goers-between be called to the world's end after my name: call them all panders. Let all constant men be Troiluses, all false women Cressids, and all brokers-between panders" (3.2.185–90). Here Pandarus's initial neutrality ("If ever you prove false one to another") reverts to the traditional sexual double standard, a shift predictive of the outcome and already voiced in the lovers' immediately preceding speeches, where only Cressida's faithfulness is open to question. Similarly, the military plot calls attention to the very different Homeric version of its tale. Achilles is outfought by Hector and must avail himself of the Trojan's chivalric generosity: "Pause, if thou wilt" (5.6.14). Achilles then treacherously employs his soldiers, the Myrmidons, to ambush and kill Hector:

> HECTOR I am unarmed. Forgo this vantage, Greek.
> ACHILLES Strike, fellows, strike! This is the man I seek.
> . . . .
> On, Myrmidons, and cry you all amain,
> 'Achilles hath the mighty Hector slain!'
> (5.9.9–14)

In addition to deflating the epic account, the passage explains how that false account arose in the first place. Such literary self-consciousness reconciles conflicting interpretations while helping to produce a movement toward increasing bitterness.

The play breaks in equally startling fashion with the drama Shakespeare composed in the first half of his career. The romantic comedies from *Two Gentlemen of Verona* (1590–91) to *Twelfth Night* (1601) generally focus on romantic attachment and conclude in marriage. By contrast, *Troilus and Cressida* moves from extramarital sex to infidelity, recriminations, deception, self-deception, venereal disease, and despair. The English history plays from *The First Part of the Contention of the Two Famous Houses of York and Lancaster* (*2 Henry VI*; 1591) to *Henry V* (1599) usually turn on martial action

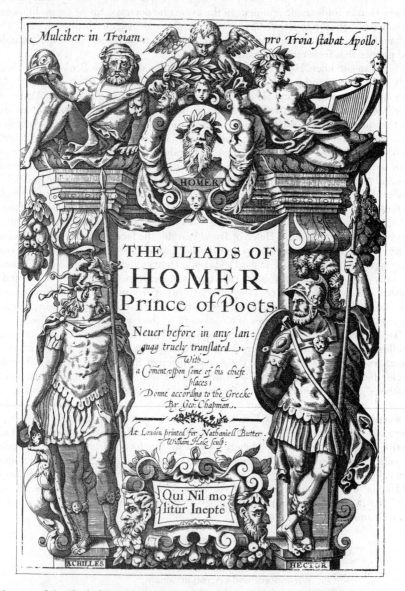

Title page of the *Iliad* of Homer in George Chapman's translation (1611?). Shakespeare probably used the less complete 1598 edition.

in defense of the state. Again in contrast, *Troilus and Cressida* casts doubt on the moral legitimacy of war, increasingly seen as an arena of mindless brutality.

Nonetheless, the play hardly emerges from nowhere. First, its negativity is partly anticipated in the sources, beginning with the *Iliad*. That poem's nostalgic admiration for warrior culture is tinged with an awareness of human suffering. Robert Henryson's *Testament of Cresseid* (late fifteenth century) moralistically punishes Cressida's infidelity by the infliction of leprosy, and William Caxton's *Recuyell of the Historyes of Troye* (the first English printed book, about 1474) has a jaundiced view of the Trojan War. Similarly, Shakespeare's earlier comedies and histories hint at the dyspeptic vision of *Troilus and Cressida*. More important, London stage practice of the period provides a suggestive context. The children's theaters that reopened in 1599 popularized misogynistic dramatic satire, to which *Troilus and Cressida* responds. The play arguably participates in the battle of rival playwrights at the turn of the century, known as the Poets' War. The ridiculous figure of Ajax may satirize Ben Jonson, whose own drama had criticized Shakespeare's works. And the railing Thersites perhaps points to John Marston, the most vituperative of the satiric playwrights. Within Shakespeare's own oeuvre, *Troilus and Cressida*'s tone anticipates the so-called problem plays, *Measure for Measure* and *All's Well That Ends Well*. Further, beginning in 1599 with *Julius Caesar*, Shakespeare initiated a decade-long appropriation of classical history in which—to oversimplify—Rome is the subject of tragedy and Greece of satire. But a satiric streak and especially a loathing of women, sexuality, and the diseased body are major strands within Shakespeare's tragic period as a whole (1599–1608), appearing at least as early as *Hamlet* (1600), with which *Troilus and Cressida* has much in common.

Finally, because the play is hardly homogeneous in tone, it sometimes connects with less bitter motifs in Shakespeare's earlier work. Troilus's initial state echoes the comically extravagant romantic excess in which Duke Orsino begins *Twelfth Night*. When asked by an attendant whether he will hunt the "hart" (deer, with a pun on "heart," line 16), the Duke explains that when he first saw Olivia, he was

> . . . turned into a hart,
> And my desires, like fell and cruel hounds,
> E'er since pursue me.
>
> (1.1.20–22)

Lovesick Troilus also renounces the hunt:

> Why should I war without the walls of Troy
> That find such cruel battle here within?
> Each Trojan that is master of his heart,
> Let him to field—Troilus, alas, hath none.
>
> (1.1.2–5)

This opening succeeds the military exposition of the Prologue and is followed by scenes of sexual comedy, cynical politics, satiric abuse, and perverse idealism. By the time any of these perspectives is repeated, one-third of the play is over. *Troilus and Cressida* thus entertains a dizzying multiplicity of views: one of its salient features is its generic hybridity.

Hence, even though ironic disillusionment becomes increasingly pervasive, it does not subsume all other perspectives. As a result, the nature of the work has always provoked disagreement. Early seventeenth-century references label it variously a history, a comedy, and a tragedy. By adding satire to the list, twentieth-century critics intensified the uncertainty of their predecessors. Although Shakespeare's entire career is marked by the mixing of genres and by the consequent violation of neoclassical norms that separated comedy sharply from tragedy, *Troilus and Cressida* represents an extreme. The play never adopts a consistent outlook in its dismantling of the leading aristocratic narrative forms—medieval chivalric romance and classical epic.

This disorientation is also produced within particular scenes. Even with the general darkening of tone, the play eschews a homogenized outlook. In Act 5, Scene 2, one of Shakespeare's most celebrated forays into eavesdropping, Diomedes and Cressida have an assignation, Troilus and Ulysses secretly watch them, Thersites covertly observes both pairs of figures, and the audience sees all five characters. Cressida's behavior elicits judgments from Diomedes and especially from Cressida herself; it also produces the following commentary.

ULYSSES   . . . Cressid was here but now.
TROILUS   Let it not be believed, for womanhood.

A neuer writer, to an euer reader. Newes.

ETernall reader, you haue heere a new play, neuer stal'd with the Stage, neuer clapper-clawd with the palmes of the vulger, and yet passing full of the palme comicall; for it is a birth of your braine, that neuer vnder-tooke any thing commicall, vainely: And were but the vaine names of commedies changde for the titles of Commodities, or of Playes for Pleas; you should see all those grand censors, that now stile them such vanities, flock to them for the maine grace of their grauities: especially this authors Commedies, that are so fram'd to the life, that they serue for the most common Commentaries, of all the actions of our liues shewing such a dexteritie, and power of witte, that the most displeased with Playes, are pleasd with his Commedies. And all such dull and heauy-witted worldlings, as were neuer capable of the witte of a Commedie, comming by report of them to his representations, haue found that witte there, that they neuer found in them-selues, and haue parted better wittied then they came: feeling an edge of witte set vpon them, more then euer they dreamd they had braine to grinde it on. So much and such sauored salt of witte is in his Commedies, that they seeme (for their height of pleasure) to be borne in that sea that brought forth Venus. Amongst all there is none more witty then this: And had I time I would comment vpon it, though I know it needs not, (for so

¶ 2   much

This prefatory epistle (continued on the facing page) was added to the second state of the 1609 Quarto of *Troilus and Cressida* (Qb). It is not found in the first state (Qa) or in the First Folio (F) and is not included in the present edition. See the Textual Note.

Think: we had mothers. Do not give advantage
To stubborn critics, apt without a theme
For depravation to square the general sex
By Cressid's rule. Rather, think this not Cressid.
ULYSSES   What hath she done, Prince, that can soil our mothers?
TROILUS   Nothing at all, unless that this were she.
THERSITES [aside]   Will a swagger himself out on's own eyes?

(5.2.128–36)

Troilus oscillates between misogynistic generalization and idealistic denial of Cressida's infidelity, Ulysses rejects extrapolation from individual to gender, and Thersites ridicules Troilus's willful blindness. This pattern suggests that the play's view is broader than Thersites'. What that view is, however, is another matter. Although the audience apparently

THE EPISTLE.

much as will make you thinke your testerne well be-
stowd) but for so much worth, as euen poore I know to be
stuft in it. It deserues such a labour, as well as the best
Commedy in Terence or Plautus. And beleeue this,
that when hee is gone, and his Commedies out of sale,
you will scramble for them, and set vp a new English
Inquisition. Take this for a warning, and at the perrill
of your pleasures losse, and Iudgements, refuse not, nor
like this the lesse, for not being sullied, with the smoaky
breath of the multitude; but thanke fortune for the
scape it hath made amongst you. Since by the grand
possessors wills I beleeue you should haue prayd for them
rather then beene prayd. And so I leaue all such to bee
prayd for (for the states of their wits healths)
that will not praise it.
Vale.

occupies a privileged position, it must synthesize incompatible perspectives and recognize that its privilege cannot guarantee comprehensive judgment. Rather, multiple eavesdropping onstage opens up an infinite regress that extends to the spectators, thereby undermining interpretive certainty. This uncertainty holds throughout *Troilus and Cressida*.

The play's urge to provide philosophical rationales for even the most trivial actions intensifies this effect. The characters disagree with each other and with themselves in the sense that their words bear little relation to their deeds. If this discrepancy had a casual feel to it, it might be easy to overlook. But the linkage of policy questions to foundational principles highlights the practical irrelevance of those principles. Further, since the military story remains almost devoid of combat until Act 5, the play sustains interest by relying on talk and on decisions about how—or even whether—to prosecute the war. In the meeting of the Greek leaders (1.3), Ulysses considers Achilles' defection from the war an illustration of the disruption of "degree" (1.3.82)—of a hierarchically ordered world—by mere power. His is the most famous speech in the play, and it is often read as Shakespeare's own orthodox credo. The dramatic context undermines this judgment, however. Ulysses' humanely conservative political vision sits oddly with the manipulative scheme that he immediately proposes in the same scene to return Achilles to the fray. Similarly, Ulysses complains that Patroclus amuses Achilles by satirically impersonating the other Greek leaders. To illustrate, he reproduces Patroclus's performances, in the process ridiculing Agamemnon and Nestor. And his own satiric voice is repeatedly heard, most often on the subject of Ajax.

A similar slippage from lofty precept to dubious behavior marks the corresponding Trojan council (2.2), hence establishing a parallel between the contending camps. In debating with Troilus the merits of fighting for Helen, Hector asserts, "Every tithe-soul, 'mongst many thousand dimes [souls], / Hath been as dear as Helen" (2.2.18–19). He continues:

> HECTOR   Brother, she [Helen] is not worth what she doth cost
>   The holding.
> TROILUS   What's aught but as 'tis valued?
> HECTOR   But value dwells not in particular will.
>   It holds his estimate and dignity
>   As well wherein 'tis precious of itself
>   As in the prizer.
>
> (2.2.50–55)

In response to Troilus's subjective view, then, Hector offers an objective standard that, he insists, must carry equal weight.

Undeterred, Troilus argues against returning Helen to end the war by appealing to constancy of purpose.

> I take today a wife, and my election
> Is led on in the conduct of my will;
> . . . .
> . . . How may I avoid—
> Although my will distaste what it elected—
> The wife I chose? There can be no evasion
> To blench from this and to stand firm by honour.
>
> (2.2.60–67)

Troilus's defense of marital commitment unwittingly militates against his own position, however. Helen is Menelaus's wife, not Paris's, and Troilus himself gives no thought to marrying Cressida. Even Hector, the noblest character in the play, cannot make good on his words. Claiming that to keep Helen is both self-destructive and immoral, he wins the debate with Troilus (and Paris). But partly inspired by the desire for chivalric glory, he collapses intellectually, agreeing to continue fighting for the Trojans' "dignities," the very aristocratic honor he had just seen through.

The friendly chivalric combat between two noble kinsmen, Hector and Ajax. From Geffrey Whitney, *A Choice of Emblemes* (1586).

The Trojan council of war is echoed at least twice. Hector's disabused view of Helen is more bitterly refracted when Paris asks who deserves her more, "myself or Menelaus" (4.1.56). Diomedes replies,

> He merits well to have her that doth seek her,
> Not making any scruple of her soilure,
> With such a hell of pain and world of charge;
> And you as well to keep her that defend her,
> Not palating the taste of her dishonour,
> With such a costly loss of wealth and friends.
> (4.1.57–62)

In addition, Helen is branded a "whore" by both Thersites and Diomedes (2.3.65, 4.1.68) before that term comes to be attached to Cressida. Misogyny thus informs anti-war sentiment—the play's dominant position. Second, however, when the Greek leaders earlier snub Achilles to get him to fight, Ulysses tells the shaken warrior that value consists not in merit but in reputation—almost the opposite of Hector's position. And the play provides no resolution to this argument.

The romantic plot also holds contradictory outlooks in tension. Reacting against earlier twentieth-century criticism that identified with Troilus, recent discussions have looked skeptically at the male lover and sympathetically at the woman who apparently betrays him. Troilus has a mundane goal: "Her bed is India; there she lies, a pearl" (1.1.96). This sensual motivation turns Cressida into an object of exchange. The idealized image of love he articulates elsewhere is not simply ironized by this jarring juxtaposition: the metaphor parallels the businesslike enterprise of seduction in which Pandarus is so instrumental. When Troilus calls himself as "skilless as unpractised infancy" and "simpler than the infancy of truth" (1.1.12, 3.2.157), he continues his self-regarding rhetoric in a different vein, distances himself from his own sexually aggressive behavior, and arguably imagines sexual intercourse between adults as the relationship between infant and mother. Troilus also fears a subsequent letdown: he worries "that the will is infinite and the execution confined; that the desire is boundless and the act a slave to limit" (3.2.76–77).

Disappointment is Cressida's anxiety as well, although her concern is male inconstancy: "Yet hold I off. Women are angels, wooing; / Things won are done. Joy's soul lies in the doing" (1.2.264–65). Cressida's ambivalence turns on the conviction, deeply embedded in gender inequality, that female sexual surrender cools male ardor. She seems to act out of multiple motives—love and sexual desire, vulnerability, fear of betrayal, the possibility of the self-betrayal of her feelings out of the need to protect herself, and the tendency to understand herself as others define her. The play validates this ambivalence. She has been abandoned by her father, and her remaining relative seeks only to send her to bed with Troilus. Following their first and only night together, the lovers' common fear is realized. Troilus cheerfully gets up to leave, over Cressida's objections. The news that she will be swapped for Antenor—will literally become an object of exchange—elicits passionate refusal from her but immediate resignation from him. Although her reference to "the merry Greeks" (4.5.55) arouses Troilus's jealousy, Cressida interprets his renewed passion as further devaluation of her. Upon her arrival in the enemy camp, she is kissed by the Greek leaders in a scene that has been taken to reveal everything from her wantonness to a near gang rape. Reunited with a father who delivers her to Diomedes, she acts with characteristic ambiguity, perhaps combining ambivalence, a sense of entrapment, desperation, weakness, desire, and manipulation.

But one should not simply reverse Troilus's self-understanding, seeing him as victimizer and Cressida as victim. The play provides the material for competing interpretations without privileging any of them. In a way, this uncertainty does not matter. Troilus and Cressida's relationship is a zero-sum game in that however one explains their behavior, the effect is to undermine ideals that prove to have been overrated all along. Ambiguity and degradation also mark the military climax, in which Hector compounds his failure in the Trojan council by disastrous chivalric generosity. Driven by honor, he insists on fighting, although he is warned not to, and the fate of Troy hangs on his health. Ulysses, Ajax, and Troilus all remark on his habit of sparing a defeated foe. This habit is accompanied by the assumption, despite clear evidence to the contrary, that others operate similarly. Thus, when Hector disarms before Achilles comes upon him, he becomes an easy target. With this implicit judgment of Hector, the play universalizes its critique. The result is a near moral vacuum. Although aristocratic norms retain a vestige of their former appeal, the struggle to live—and die—by them is scarcely worth the effort. The play may thus gesture toward the political crisis at the end of Elizabeth's reign, highlighted by the execution of the Earl of Essex, whose ambitious factionalism (perhaps echoed in Achilles) and chivalric competitiveness (perhaps exemplified by Hector) more generally marked the behavior of competing groups of courtiers who had long sought the queen's favor.

The systematic ambiguity of *Troilus and Cressida,* though perhaps not its movement toward disillusionment, is intensified by the early publishing history of the play. (See the Textual Note.) The First Quarto emphasizes Troilus, Cressida, and Pandarus on the title page and is prefaced by an anonymous prose epistle that defines the work as a comedy. (See the facsimile reproduction of the epistle on pages 754–55.) The version in the First Folio (1623) is called a tragedy and lacks the epistle, instead introducing the play by a verse Prologue that says nothing of the lovers while focusing on the Trojan War itself, which it treats in heroic terms. In other words, the two texts set up antithetical expectations for their readers. The Quarto closes much as it opens—with Pandarus's lewd and satiric identification with the audience. (See the indented text after 5.11.31.) Although the Folio provides the same conclusion, perhaps it was meant to end with Troilus's despairing, vengeful response to Hector's death. That hypothesis governs the present edition, which views the Folio as the revised and, hence, more authoritative text. Although beginnings and endings cannot determine the meaning of a play, they have disproportionate weight. The modified Folio printed here, like the Quarto, provides a consistent frame around the play, with the difference that the frame is heroic rather than satiric. But the present text does not convert satire into tragedy; in any version, there is satire as well as tragedy. The present text, then, slightly reduces the likelihood that tragic elements will be drowned in a sea of bitter irony.

The Quarto's satiric thrust and the claim in its epistle that the work was never performed in a public theater have given rise to the theory that it was composed for, or even limited to, elite private performance—possibly at one of the Inns of Court (law schools) or at Cambridge. This view, often supported by emphasis on the play's Latinate language, legal references, and penchant for philosophical argument, is contradicted by contemporary documents and is certainly at odds with Shakespeare's normal practice. Possibly, however, *Troilus and Cressida* was relatively unsuccessful at the Globe; probably, it was influenced by the Inns of Court; possibly it was performed there, at Cambridge, or in both locales. Whatever the truth, the debate about the nature and location of the early audience reproduces the ambivalence about the genre of *Troilus and Cressida*: coterie performance implies satire; the public stage, tragedy.

This uncertainty did not sit well with neoclassical writers. In 1679, John Dryden removed "that heap of rubbish" which prevented the play from being a proper tragedy. He has Cressida remain true to Troilus but commit suicide, and he uses Achilles to kill off Troilus. Dryden's radical adaptation was occasionally staged between 1679 and 1734. Thereafter, *Troilus and Cressida* went unperformed until 1898, perhaps because of its grim outlook. Especially in the last fifty years, however, its unsettling proliferation of incompatible meanings and bitter view of love and war have made it extremely popular. Just as Shakespeare's history plays were mobilized to support patriotic sentiment, *Troilus and Cressida* has given expression to antiwar views—on the eve of both world wars, repeatedly during the Vietnam War in the 1960s and 1970s, and recently with reference to the Balkans. Consequently, Thersites sometimes becomes the central spokesman of the play; Ulysses, advocate of traditional hierarchy, accordingly is ironized. Similarly, increased sympathy for Cressida inspired by feminism has led to a complementary depreciation of Troilus.

But does the play offer an alternative system of positive values, even if those values cannot be openly articulated? In this explicitly sexual work, the best place to look may be moments with only an implicitly sexual undertone. The ceremonial exchanges between the leaders of the rival armies suggest the lure of homosocial coupling, which simultaneously excludes women and drives the men back to battle. Performances since the 1960s have frequently been sensitive to this motif. Hector challenges "the fair'st of Greece," by which he means not a woman but a man, and indeed a man who will "dare avow her [his mistress's] beauty and her worth / In other arms than hers" (1.3.262, 268–69). Ulysses resorts to similar wordplay when trying to persuade Achilles to overcome the scruples of heterosexual love: "Better would it fit Achilles much / To throw down Hector than Polyxena" (3.3.200–01).

But one cannot consistently link either misogyny to antiwar views or same-sex bonding to a warrior ethos. Everything has a flip side. An ambivalent imagistic pattern connecting women, effeminacy, and sexual deviation comes closest to providing a countervision to the heroic ethos. Cassandra interrupts the Trojan council with prophecies of doom, a tactic she repeats with equal lack of success in seconding Andromache's efforts to prevent Hector from entering battle near the end of the play. Priam sums up the primarily female forces urging inaction when he tells Hector, "Go back. / Thy wife hath dreamt, thy mother hath had visions, / Cassandra doth foresee" (5.3.64–66). Paris reports, "I would fain have armed today, but my Nell [Helen] would not have it so" (3.1.127–28). And Achilles' not-so-secret love for Polyxena keeps him out of the war entirely: "Fall, Greeks; fail, fame; honour, or go or stay. / My major vow lies here; this I'll obey" (5.1.38–39). More strikingly, the warriors internalize the female perspective. Achilles has "a woman's longing, / . . . To see great Hector in his weeds of peace" (3.3.230–32). Troilus cannot fight because his love for Cressida makes him "weaker than a woman's tear, / . . . Less valiant than the virgin in the night" (1.1.9–11). Hector echoes the sentiment in opening his attack on the war: "There is no lady . . . / More ready to cry out, 'Who knows what follows?' / Than Hector is" (2.2.10–13). Ajax calls the play's leading satirist "Mistress Thersites" (2.1.34), and when faced with "a bastard son of Priam's" (5.8.7) on the battlefield, Thersites makes an illogical, if life-saving, argument: "I am a bastard, too. I love bastards. . . . Take heed: the quarrel's most ominous to us. If the son of a whore fight for a whore, he tempts judgement" (5.8.8–13). Here, Thersites' cowardice conjures up a brotherhood of sexual illegitimacy opposed to meaningless slaughter. Finally, Patroclus complains to Achilles that their enforced leisure makes him loathed as "an effeminate man" (3.3.211):

> . . . I stand condemned for this.
> They think my little stomach to the war
> And your great love to me restrains you thus.
> (3.3.212–14)

What "they think" may be true. Thersites calls Patroclus "Achilles' brach" (bitch hound, 2.1.109), later describing him as "Achilles' male varlet . . . his masculine whore" (5.1.14–16). The death of "my sweet Patroclus" (5.1.32) causes Achilles to break his vow and seek revenge, just as the loss of Cressida turns Troilus toward savagery. In a play about the most famous war in Western literature, opposition to battle brings disgrace. But in such moments—moments of sexual, romantic, or familial intimacy rooted in female or homoerotic experience—an alternative to both aristocratic values and their ironic deflation can be glimpsed.

WALTER COHEN

TEXTUAL NOTE

The textual history of *Troilus and Cressida* (1601–02) poses complex problems of potential interpretive significance. In early 1603, "The booke of Troilus and Cresseda as yt is acted by my lo: Chamberlens Men" was listed in the Stationers' Register—a necessary prelude to authorized publication. In fact, the play was not published; a second entry in the Stationers' Register, this one from 1609, now refers to "THE history of Troylus and Cressida," but with no mention of theatrical performance. The First Quarto (Q) appeared the same year in two distinct states. The earlier version, like the 1609 Stationers' Register, calls it "THE Historie of Troylus and Cresseida" but echoes the 1603 Stationers' Register in evoking stage history—"*As it was acted by the Kings Maiesties seruants at the Globe.*" (Shakespeare's acting company, the Lord Chamberlain's Men, became the King's Men after James succeeded Elizabeth on the throne in 1603.) The second version's title page announces "THE Famous Historie of Troylus *and* Cresseid," goes on to emphasize their love and Pandarus's role, and omits any mention of performance. That omission is developed in a new prefatory epistle, which calls the play a comedy, appeals to elite literary taste by saying that it was never acted in the public theater, and implies—correctly, it seems—that publication is unauthorized.

Moreover, when the First Folio (F) was being prepared for publication in 1623, *Troilus and Cressida* was originally intended to follow *Romeo and Juliet* in the tragedy section. But after only three pages of it were set, printing was discontinued. The play was finally incorporated at the last minute, too late to be mentioned in the Catalogue (table of contents). It excluded the epistle but included a new Prologue, a reset version of its Folio first page, the remaining two pages of the original and incomplete Folio printing, and newly set type for the remainder of the play. It was placed between *All Is True (Henry VIII)*, the last of the histories, and *Coriolanus*, which was meant to be the first of the tragedies. In this intermediate zone, the work in effect became the initial tragedy of the volume, bearing the title "THE TRAGEDIE OF Troylus and Cressida."

Beyond revealing an uncertainty about genre that has continued to the present day, this twenty-year sequence leaves a number of issues obscure. Why was the play not published in 1603: lack of authorization, fear of political reprisals, or, most likely, no real intention to publish? Was it performed at the Globe (probably) or just for an elite audience at the law schools known as the Inns of Court or Cambridge (perhaps in addition to, less likely instead of, the Globe)? Why did the printer of Q change the title page and insert the prefatory epistle in midstream: access to new information, discovery of the epistle at the end of the play manuscript, desire to distance the work from the King's Men, or, most likely, hope of selling more copies? When was the epistle written: 1603 or, more likely, 1609? None of these questions admits of a definitive answer. The delay in printing the Folio version, however, is perhaps less mysterious: it may have been necessitated by copyright troubles that were subsequently resolved.

Equally contentious are the questions about Q and F—their nature, the texts that stand behind them, their relationship to each other. Both, scholars agree, are authoritative in the sense of ultimately deriving from authorial manuscripts. After that, there is less agreement. Q appears to derive from a copy of Shakespeare's draft that has been revised, probably—but not certainly—by Shakespeare. The three pages of the false start in printing the F version are based exclusively on Q, and presumably the initial intention was to follow this procedure throughout the play. But most of the actual F text relies on a substantively different manuscript of *Troilus and Cressida* that usually, but not always, seems to represent an earlier Shakespearean version than the one behind Q. This version has been annotated for performance and hence is a promptbook. In addition, after the first three pages F intermittently relies on Q. It is likely, then, that the F *Troilus* derives from both the manuscript and Q. (Alternatively, it may depend solely on the promptbook manuscript after the first three pages, but that manuscript then would have been influenced by Q.) Accordingly, neither Q nor F has clear priority. The Oxford editors, however, believe that only F incorporates Shakespeare's revisions. Thus, except in a few long passages (1.1.0–1.2.215, 2.2.103–209, 3.3.1–95, and 4.6.0–64), this edition tends to follow F.

For the most part, the consequences of this decision are modest. Both Q and F end with an epilogue spoken by Pandarus, introduced by a three-line exchange between him and Troilus in which Troilus angrily dismisses him. Only F, however, includes almost the identical three lines at the end of Act 5, Scene 3. Both locations cannot be correct. But since this earlier placement occurs only in F and hence is viewed by the Oxford editors as Shakespeare's final judgment on the matter, it is retained in the present edition while Pandarus's epilogue is cut and printed as an indented passage. This excision, the exclusion of the epistle as well as other (very brief) passages found in Q but not F, and the inclusion of the Prologue as well as other (somewhat longer) passages found in F but not Q all point in the same direction. They slightly reduce the satiric elements in the portrayal of Troilus, Cressida, and Pandarus and, more important, downplay the central love affair and shift the focus to the Trojan War itself. These thematic matters are treated in greater detail in the Introduction.

Neither Q nor F has act or scene divisions, with the exception of the first scene in F, which is labeled "*Actus Primus. Scœna Prima.*" Editors have supplied these divisions since the early eighteenth century. This edition, unlike most of its predecessors, begins a new scene each time the stage is cleared. Accordingly, Act 4 includes a new Scene 3 after 4.2.75 and a new Scene 7 after 4.6.119, for a total of seven scenes rather than the conventional five. Similarly, Act 5 has a new Scene 8 after 5.7.8, for a total of eleven rather than ten scenes. These changes are discussed in the footnotes.

SELECTED BIBLIOGRAPHY

Bednarz, James P. *Shakespeare and the Poets' War*. New York: Columbia University Press, 2001. 32–52, 257–64. Links the play to the satirical Poets' War of about 1599–1602, with Ajax representing Ben Jonson and Thersites John Marston.

Bredbeck, Gregory W. *Sodomy and Interpretation: Marlowe to Milton*. Ithaca, N.Y.: Cornell University Press, 1991. 33–47. Satire and statecraft joined in the (unjustified) charge of sodomy against Patroclus, a strategy that serves Greek political ends in a chaotic world.

Charnes, Linda. "'So Unsecret to Ourselves': Notorious Identity and the Material Subject in Shakespeare's *Troilus and Cressida*." *Shakespeare Quarterly* 40 (1989): 413–40. The characters' literary reputation as fixed identities against which they struggle in the effort to assert their own subjectivity.

Girard, René. "The Politics of Desire in *Troilus and Cressida*." *Shakespeare and the Question of Theory*. Ed. Patricia Parker and Geoffrey Hartman. New York: Methuen, 1985. 188–209. The love plot and the war plot as instances of mimetic desire (desire inspired by emulous rivalry); generally sympathetic to Cressida and unsympathetic to Troilus.

Grady, Hugh. *Shakespeare's Universal Wolf: Studies in Early Modern Reification*. Oxford: Clarendon, 1996. 58–94. Argues that, philosophically, the play negates all value, seeing a world, from which it dissents, dominated by desire, power, capital, and instrumental reason unlinked to ethics.

James, Heather. *Shakespeare's Troy: Drama, Politics, and the Translation of Empire*. New York: Cambridge University Press, 1997. 85–118. Shakespeare's refusal to choose among alternative versions of the Troy legend, some of which trace a direct lineage from the Trojan to the English monarchy, the result being a conflicted play rooted in the late Elizabethan crisis.

Mallin, Eric S. "Emulous Factions and the Collapse of Chivalry: *Troilus and Cressida*." *Representations* 29 (1990): 145–79. Links the play to the nostalgic chivalry of the Essex faction at court, in tension with the actual reality of self-interested greed.

Martin, Priscilla, ed. *Shakespeare, "Troilus and Cressida": A Casebook*. London: Macmillan, 1976. Three hundred years of criticism beginning in 1679, concentrating on 1945–1975.

Shirley, Frances A., ed. *Troilus and Cressida*. New York: Cambridge University Press, 2005. Performance history, followed by a text of the play with notes on staging from various productions.

Yachnin, Paul. "The Perfection of Ten": Populuxe Art and Artisanal Value in *Troilus and Cressida*." *Shakespeare Quarterly* 56 (2005): 306–28. *Troilus and Cressida* as an upscale, deluxe satire performed by a popular, artisan acting company whose need to win audience approval informs the play's debates about value and reputation.

FILM

Troilus & Cressida. 1981. Dir. Jonathan Miller. UK. 190 min. Relatively conservative BBC production that steers clear of homoeroticism but that offers a spirited, rather than a debased, Cressida and makes use of TV's resources by utilizing both broad background shots and intimate close-ups.

Troilus and Cressida

The Persons of the Play

PROLOGUE

Trojans

PRIAM, King of Troy
HECTOR
DEIPHOBUS
HELENUS, a priest
PARIS } his sons
TROILUS
MARGARETON, a bastard
CASSANDRA, Priam's daughter, a prophetess
ANDROMACHE, wife of Hector
AENEAS
ANTENOR } commanders
PANDARUS, a lord
CRESSIDA, his niece
CALCHAS, her father, who has joined the Greeks
HELEN, wife of Menelaus, now living with Paris
ALEXANDER, servant of Cressida
Servants of Troilus, musicians, soldiers, attendants

Greeks

AGAMEMNON, Commander-in-Chief
MENELAUS, his brother
NESTOR
ULYSSES
ACHILLES
PATROCLUS, his companion
DIOMEDES
AJAX
THERSITES
MYRMIDONS, soldiers of Achilles
Servants of Diomedes, soldiers

Prologue

[*Enter the* PROLOGUE *armed*][1]

PROLOGUE In Troy there lies the scene. From isles of Greece
  The princes orgulous, their high blood chafed,[2]
  Have to the port of Athens sent their ships,
  Fraught° with the ministers and instruments   *Weighted down*
5 Of cruel war. Sixty-and-nine, that wore

Prologue
1. In armor (see line 23); perhaps referring to Ben Jonson's prologue to *Poetaster* (1601), in which an armed figure appears to defend Jonson's embattled reputation among playwrights. *Troilus and Cressida*'s Ajax is sometimes seen as a further jab at Jonson's warlike posturing. The Prologue first appeared in F. Modern editions tend

to include an epistle to the reader either before the opening list of characters, in the notes, or in an appendix. The epistle prefaced the second state of Q and was probably not written by Shakespeare. It is excluded here, but a photograph of it as it appeared in Q is provided. See the Textual Note and Introduction.
2. The princes proud, their noble blood heated.

Their crownets° regal, from th'Athenian bay   *coronets*
Put forth toward Phrygia,[3] and their vow is made
To ransack Troy, within whose strong immures°   *fortifications*
The ravished° Helen, Menelaus' queen,   *kidnapped (sexual)*
10 With wanton Paris sleeps—and that's the quarrel.
To Tenedos° they come,   *island near Troy*
And the deep-drawing barques[4] do there disgorge
Their warlike freightage; now on Dardan[5] plains
The fresh and yet unbruisèd Greeks do pitch
15 Their brave pavilions.° Priam's six-gated city—   *finely arrayed tents*
Dardan and Timbria, Helias, Chetas, Troien,
And Antenorides—with massy staples°   *bolt holes*
And corresponsive and full-filling bolts
Spar up the sons of Troy.[6]
20 Now expectation, tickling skittish° spirits   *excitable*
On one and other side, Trojan and Greek,
Sets all on hazard.° And hither am I come,   *at stake*
A Prologue armed—but not in confidence
Of author's pen or actor's voice,[7] but suited
25 In like conditions as our argument[8]—
To tell you, fair beholders, that our play
Leaps o'er the vaunt° and firstlings of those broils,   *preliminaries*
Beginning in the middle,[9] starting thence away
To what may be digested in a play.
30 Like or find fault; do as your pleasures are;
Now, good or bad, 'tis but the chance of war.   [*Exit*]

1.1

Enter PANDARUS, *and* TROILUS [*armed*]

TROILUS   Call here my varlet.° I'll unarm again.   *page (of genteel birth)*
Why should I war without° the walls of Troy   *outside*
That° find such cruel battle here within?°   *Who / in myself*
Each Trojan that is master of his heart,
5 Let him to field—Troilus, alas, hath none.[1]
PANDARUS   Will this gear° ne'er be mended?   *affair*
TROILUS   The Greeks are strong, and skilful to their strength,[2]
Fierce to their skill, and to their fierceness valiant.
But I am weaker than a woman's tear,
10 Tamer than sleep, fonder° than ignorance,   *sillier*
Less valiant than the virgin in the night,
And skilless as unpractised infancy.
PANDARUS   Well, I have told you enough of this. For my part, I'll

---

3. The region around Troy (now northwestern Turkey).
4. Boats riding deeply in the water (because they are heavily laden).
5. Trojan. Dardanus was the mythical founder of the city.
6. The sons of Troy shut up the six-gated city. (But the inverted syntax also suggests that the city, whose six gates the Prologue has just named, shuts in "the sons of Troy.")
7. *not . . . voice:* not confident of success at writing or acting.
8. *suited . . . argument:* dressed appropriately for our subject (unlike Jonson's).
9. On the model of epic poetry in the Homeric tradition and as recommended by the ancient Latin poet Horace

in his *Art of Poetry.* Despite the play's classical subject matter, the double plot and generic hybridity deviate from what Renaissance critics understood to be classical dramatic norms. But the play comes close to observing two of the three supposedly Aristotelian unities (of time, place, and action) by compressing events after Act 1, Scene 2, into little more than forty-eight hours and by restricting the scene to Troy and its immediate surroundings.
1.1 Location: Troy.
1. Has no heart for battle (having lost his heart to Cressida).
2. And as skilled as they are strong.

not meddle nor make° no farther. He that will have a cake out   *be involved (proverbial)*
15   of the wheat must tarry° the grinding.   *wait for*

TROILUS   Have I not tarried?

PANDARUS   Ay, the grinding; but you must tarry the boulting.°   *sifting*

TROILUS   Have I not tarried?

PANDARUS   Ay, the boulting; but you must tarry the leavening.

20 TROILUS   Still have I tarried.

PANDARUS   Ay, to the leavening; but here's yet in the word 'here-
    after' the kneading, the making of the cake, the heating the
    oven, and the baking—nay, you must stay the cooling too, or
    ye may chance burn your lips.

25 TROILUS   Patience herself, what goddess e'er she be,
      Doth lesser blench at suff'rance[3] than I do.
      At Priam's royal table do I sit
      And when fair Cressid comes into my thoughts—
      So, traitor![4] 'When she comes'? When is she thence?

30 PANDARUS   Well, she looked yesternight fairer than ever I saw
    her look, or any woman else.

TROILUS   I was about to tell thee: when my heart,
      As wedged° with a sigh, would rive° in twain,   *divided / tear apart*
      Lest Hector or my father should perceive me
35   I have, as when the sun doth light askance,°   *obliquely*
      Buried this sigh in wrinkle of a smile.
      But sorrow that is couched° in seeming gladness   *concealed*
      Is like that mirth fate turns to sudden sadness.

PANDARUS   An° her hair were not somewhat darker than Hel-   *If*
40   en's[5]—well, go to,° there were no more comparison between   *say no more*
    the women. But, for my part, she is my kinswoman; I would
    not, as they term it, 'praise'° her. But I would somebody had   *compliment; appraise*
    heard her talk yesterday, as I did. I will not dispraise your sister
    Cassandra's wit, but—

45 TROILUS   O Pandarus! I tell thee, Pandarus,
      When I do tell thee 'There my hopes lie drowned',
      Reply not in how many fathoms deep
      They lie endrenched. I tell thee I am mad
      In Cressid's love; thou answer'st 'She is fair',
50   Pourest in the open ulcer of my heart
      Her eyes, her hair, her cheek, her gait, her voice;
      Handlest in thy discourse, O, that her hand,[6]
      In whose comparison all whites are ink
      Writing their own reproach, to° whose soft seizure°   *compared to / grasp*
55   The cygnet's down is harsh, and spirit of sense[7]
      Hard as the palm of ploughman. This thou tell'st me—
      As true thou tell'st me—when I say I love her.
      But saying thus, instead of oil and balm
      Thou lay'st in every gash that love hath given me
60   The knife that made it.

PANDARUS   I speak no more than truth.

---

3. Shies away less from suffering. (Shakespeare presumably means more, not "lesser.")

4. Troilus considers himself a "traitor" to Cressida for ever forgetting her.

5. Pandarus shows the standard Elizabethan hostility to dark hair or a dark complexion.

6. *Handlest . . . hand:* You treat in your discussion, O, that hand of hers. (Troilus's use of "handlest" reminds him of Cressida's hand.)

7. The quintessential medium of feeling or touch that conveyed sense impressions from body to mind.

TROILUS   Thou dost not speak so much.
PANDARUS   Faith, I'll not meddle in it. Let her be as she is. If she
    be fair, 'tis the better for her; an she be not, she has the mends°   cure (cosmetics)
65   in her own hands.
TROILUS   Good Pandarus, how now, Pandarus!
PANDARUS   I have had my labour for my travail.° Ill thought on   my pains as payment
    of her and ill thought on of you. Gone between and between,
    but small thanks for my labour.
70   TROILUS   What, art thou angry, Pandarus? What, with me?
PANDARUS   Because she's kin to me, therefore she's not so fair as
    Helen. An she were not kin to me, she would be as fair o'
    Friday as Helen is on Sunday.[8] But what care I? I care not an
    she were a blackamoor. 'Tis all one to me.
75   TROILUS   Say I she is not fair?
PANDARUS   I do not care whether you do or no. She's a fool to
    stay behind her father.[9] Let her to the Greeks—and so I'll tell
    her the next time I see her. For my part, I'll meddle nor make
    no more i'th' matter.
80   TROILUS   Pandarus—
PANDARUS   Not I.
TROILUS   Sweet Pandarus—
PANDARUS   Pray you, speak no more to me. I will leave all as I
    found it. And there an end.   Exit
        Alarum°   Trumpet call to arms
85   TROILUS   Peace, you ungracious clamours! Peace, rude sounds!
    Fools on both sides. Helen must needs be fair
    When with your blood you daily paint° her thus.   daub (as with rouge)
    I cannot fight upon this argument.°   on these grounds
    It is too starved a subject° for my sword.   too weak a reason
90   But Pandarus—O gods, how do you plague me!
    I cannot come to Cressid but by Pandar,
    And he's as tetchy to be° wooed to woo   touchy about being
    As she is stubborn-chaste against all suit.
    Tell me, Apollo, for thy Daphne's love,[1]
95   What Cressid is, what Pandar, and what we?
    Her bed is India;[2] there she lies, a pearl.
    Between our Ilium° and where she resides   Priam's palace
    Let it be called the wild and wand'ring flood,
    Ourself the merchant, and this sailing Pandar
100   Our doubtful° hope, our convoy,° and our barque.   uncertain / escort
        Alarum. Enter AENEAS
AENEAS   How now, Prince Troilus? Wherefore not afield?
TROILUS   Because not there. This woman's answer sorts,°   is fitting
    For womanish it is to be from thence.
    What news, Aeneas, from the field today?
105   AENEAS   That Paris is returnèd home, and hurt.
TROILUS   By whom, Aeneas?
AENEAS   Troilus, by Menelaus.

---

8. An . . . Sunday: If she weren't my kinswoman (with the
result that my praise seems biased), she'd be as beautiful
in everyday dress as Helen is in her finest clothes.
9. She's a fool not to leave with her father, Calchas, a
prophet who deserted to the Greeks, having foreseen
their victory.

1. For your love of Daphne. Daphne was a nymph who
prayed (successfully) to be turned into a bay tree to escape
the advances of Apollo, god of poetry.
2. Source of jewels, precious metals, exotic spices, and
rich fabrics.

TROILUS   Let Paris bleed, 'tis but a scar to scorn:
    Paris is gored with Menelaus' horn.[3]
        Alarum
AENEAS   Hark what good sport is out of town° today.   *outside Troy*
110 TROILUS   Better at home, if 'would I might' were 'may'.
    But to the sport abroad—are you bound thither?
AENEAS   In all swift haste.
TROILUS   Come, go we then together.   *Exeunt*

1.2

Enter [above] CRESSIDA *and her [servant* ALEXANDER]
CRESSIDA   Who were those went by?
ALEXANDER   Queen Hecuba and Helen.
CRESSIDA   And whither go they?
ALEXANDER   Up to the eastern tower,
    Whose height commands as subject all the vale,°   *valley*
    To see the battle. Hector, whose patience
5   Is as a virtue fixed,° today was moved.°   *unwavering / angry*
    He chid Andromache and struck his armourer
    And, like as there were husbandry in war,
    Before the sun rose[1] he was harnessed light,°   *in lightweight armor*
    And to the field goes he, where every flower
10   Did as a prophet weep° what it foresaw   *Was wet with dew at*
    In Hector's wrath.
CRESSIDA   What was his cause of anger?
ALEXANDER   The noise° goes this: there is among the Greeks   *rumor*
    A lord of Trojan blood, nephew° to Hector;   *relation*
    They call him Ajax.
CRESSIDA   Good,° and what of him?   *Well*
15 ALEXANDER   They say he is a very man *per se,*°   *unique man*
    And stands alone.°   *is preeminent*
CRESSIDA   So do all men
    Unless they are drunk, sick, or have no legs.
ALEXANDER   This man, lady, hath robbed many beasts of their
    particular additions:° he is as valiant as the lion, churlish as the   *characteristics*
20   bear, slow as the elephant—a man into whom nature hath so
    crowded humours[2] that his valour is crushed into folly, his folly
    farced° with discretion. There is no man hath a virtue that he   *stuffed*
    hath not a glimpse° of, nor any man an attaint° but he carries   *hint / flaw*
    some stain of it. He is melancholy without cause and merry
25   against the hair;° he hath the joints of everything, but every-   *against the grain*
    thing so out of joint that he is a gouty Briareus, many hands
    and no use, or purblind Argus, all eyes and no sight.[3]
CRESSIDA   But how should this man that makes me smile make
    Hector angry?
30 ALEXANDER   They say he yesterday coped° Hector in the battle   *engaged*
    and struck him down, the disdain° and shame whereof hath   *indignation*
    ever since kept Hector fasting and waking.

---

3. *'tis . . . horn:* it's just a trivial wound (or a wound given
in return for Paris's scorn of Menelaus): Paris is wounded
by the emblem of the cuckold (having seduced Helen,
Menelaus's wife).
1.2 Location: Troy.
1. *Like . . . rose:* as if there were prudent management in
war as in agriculture, where the conscientious laborer

gets up before dawn. The comparison continues with
"field" and "flower" (line 9).
2. Peculiarities. Humors were the four main bodily fluids
and were believed to determine a person's temperament.
3. He is a giant (Briareus), whose hundred hands are
ruined by gout, or totally blind Argus, whose hundred eyes
Juno deprived of sight because he fell asleep guarding Io.

CRESSIDA Who comes here?

ALEXANDER Madam, your uncle Pandarus.

        Enter PANDARUS [*above*]

35 CRESSIDA Hector's a gallant man.

ALEXANDER As may be in the world, lady.

PANDARUS What's that? What's that?

CRESSIDA Good morrow, uncle Pandarus.

PANDARUS Good morrow, cousin° Cressid. What do you talk   *relation*

40   of?— Good morrow, Alexander.—How do you, cousin? When

were you at Ilium?

CRESSIDA This morning, uncle.

PANDARUS What were you talking of when I came? Was Hector

armed and gone ere ye came to Ilium? Helen was not up, was

45 she?

CRESSIDA Hector was gone but Helen was not up?

PANDARUS E'en so. Hector was stirring early.

CRESSIDA That were we talking of, and of his anger.

PANDARUS Was he angry?

50 CRESSIDA So he° says here.   *Alexander*

PANDARUS True, he was so. I know the cause too. He'll lay about

him today, I can tell them that. And there's Troilus will not

come far behind him. Let them take heed of Troilus, I can tell

them that too.

55 CRESSIDA What, is he angry too?

PANDARUS Who, Troilus? Troilus is the better man of the two.

CRESSIDA O Jupiter! There's no comparison.

PANDARUS What, not between Troilus and Hector? Do you

know a man if you see him?

60 CRESSIDA Ay, if I ever saw him before and knew him.[4]

PANDARUS Well, I say Troilus is Troilus.°   *(that special man)*

CRESSIDA Then you say as I say, for I am sure

He is not Hector.

PANDARUS No, nor Hector is not Troilus, in some degrees.°   *respects*

65 CRESSIDA 'Tis just to each of them: he is himself.

PANDARUS Himself? Alas, poor Troilus, I would he were.

CRESSIDA So he is.

PANDARUS Condition I had gone barefoot to India.[5]

CRESSIDA He is not Hector.

70 PANDARUS Himself? No, he's not himself. Would a° were him-   *he*

self! Well, the gods are above, time must friend or end.° Well,   *befriend or kill him*

Troilus, well, I would my heart were in her body. No, Hector

is not a better man than Troilus.

CRESSIDA Excuse me.[6]

75 PANDARUS He is elder.

CRESSIDA Pardon me, pardon me.

PANDARUS Th'other's not come to't.° You shall tell me another   *his prime; intercourse*

tale when th'other's come to't. Hector shall not have his will[7]

this year.

80 CRESSIDA He shall not need it if he have his own.

PANDARUS Nor his qualities.

---

4. Here and in the following lines, Cressida obstinately takes Pandarus's figurative language literally. Recognized him; met an ideal man; saw him from the front ("before") and had sexual intercourse with ("knew") him.

5. If I'd gone barefoot (on pilgrimage) to India—an impossibility.

6. Cressida disagrees, as in line 76.

7. Troilus's resolve; Troilus's sexual desire.

CRESSIDA   No matter.

PANDARUS   Nor his beauty.

CRESSIDA   'Twould not become him; his own's better.

85   PANDARUS   You have no judgement, niece. Helen herself swore
th'other day that Troilus for a brown favour,[8] for so 'tis, I must
confess—not brown neither—

CRESSIDA   No, but brown.

PANDARUS   Faith, to say truth, brown and not brown.

90   CRESSIDA   To say the truth, true and not true.

PANDARUS   She praised his complexion above Paris'.

CRESSIDA   Why, Paris hath colour enough.

PANDARUS   So he has.

CRESSIDA   Then Troilus should° have too much. If she praised   *must therefore*
95   him above, his° complexion is higher than his;° he having col-   *Troilus's / Paris's*
our enough, and the other higher, is too flaming a praise for
a good complexion. I had as lief Helen's golden tongue had
commended Troilus for a copper nose.[9]

PANDARUS   I swear to you, I think Helen loves him better than
100   Paris.

CRESSIDA   Then she's a merry Greek[1] indeed.

PANDARUS   Nay, I am sure she does. She came to him th'other
day into the compassed° window, and you know he has not past   *bay*
three or four hairs on his chin—

105   CRESSIDA   Indeed, a tapster's° arithmetic may soon bring his par-   *the simplest*
ticulars therein to a total.

PANDARUS   Why, he is very young—and yet will he within three
pound lift as much as his brother Hector.

CRESSIDA   Is he so young a man and so old a lifter?°   *so practiced a thief*

110   PANDARUS   But to prove to you that Helen loves him: she came
and puts me° her white hand to his cloven chin.   *puts me = puts*

CRESSIDA   Juno have mercy! How came it cloven?

PANDARUS   Why, you know, 'tis dimpled. I think his smiling
becomes him better than any man in all Phrygia.

115   CRESSIDA   O he smiles valiantly.

PANDARUS   Does he not?

CRESSIDA   O yes, an't were a cloud in autumn.[2]

PANDARUS   Why, go to then. But to prove to you that Helen loves
Troilus—

120   CRESSIDA   Troilus will stand to the proof[3] if you'll prove it so.

PANDARUS   Troilus? Why, he esteems her no more than I esteem
an addle° egg.   *rotten*

CRESSIDA   If you love an addle egg as well as you love an idle
head you would eat chickens i'th' shell.[4]

125   PANDARUS   I cannot choose but laugh to think how she tickled
his chin. Indeed, she has a marvellous white hand, I must
needs confess—

CRESSIDA   Without the rack.°   *being tortured*

PANDARUS   And she takes upon her to spy a white hair on his
130   chin.

---

8. Notwithstanding his (unfashionably) dark or tanned
face.
9. Red nose, caused by drinking; perhaps also an artificial
nose, made necessary by syphilis.
1. Slang for a reveler or wanton, implying good
fellowship and superficiality; here, appropriately applied

to Helen and more generally to the Greeks, at least as
they treat Cressida.
2. As if he were a rain cloud.
3. Will uphold the proof; will have an erection.
4. An addled egg often resulted from the chick dying
during hatching.

CRESSIDA Alas, poor chin! Many a wart is richer.°   (in hairs)
PANDARUS But there was such laughing! Queen Hecuba laughed
    that° her eyes ran o'er.   so much that
CRESSIDA With millstones.[5]
135 PANDARUS And Cassandra laughed.
CRESSIDA But there was a more temperate fire under the pot of
    her eyes[6]—or did her eyes run o'er too?
PANDARUS And Hector laughed.
CRESSIDA At what was all this laughing?
140 PANDARUS Marry,[7] at the white hair that Helen spied on Troilus'
    chin.
CRESSIDA An't had been a green hair I should have laughed too.
PANDARUS They laughed not so much at the hair as at his pretty°   witty
    answer.
145 CRESSIDA What was his answer?
PANDARUS Quoth she, 'Here's but two-and-fifty hairs on your
    chin, and one of them is white.'
CRESSIDA This is her question.
PANDARUS That's true, make no question of that. 'Two-and-fifty
150 hairs,' quoth he, 'and one white? That white hair is my father,
    and all the rest are his sons.'[8] 'Jupiter!' quoth she, 'which of
    these hairs° is Paris my husband?' 'The forked[9] one,' quoth he,   pun on "heirs"
    'pluck't out and give it him.' But there was such laughing, and
    Helen so blushed and Paris so chafed° and all the rest so   (was) so irritated
155 laughed, that it passed.°   surpassed description
CRESSIDA So let it now, for it has been a great while going by.
PANDARUS Well, cousin, I told you a thing yesterday. Think on't.
CRESSIDA So I do.
PANDARUS I'll be sworn 'tis true. He will weep you an't° were a   for you as if he
160 man born in April.°   month of showers
CRESSIDA And I'll spring up in his tears an't° were a nettle   as if I
    against° May.   in anticipation of
          A retreat [is] sound[ed]
PANDARUS Hark, they are coming from the field. Shall we stand
    up here and see them as they pass toward Ilium? Good niece,
165 do, sweet niece Cressida.
CRESSIDA At your pleasure.
PANDARUS Here, here, here's an excellent place, here we may
    see most bravely.° I'll tell you them all by their names as they   very finely
    pass by, but mark Troilus above the rest.
          Enter AENEAS [*passing by below*]
170 CRESSIDA Speak not so loud.
PANDARUS That's Aeneas. Is not that a brave° man? He's one of   splendid; courageous
    the flowers° of Troy, I can tell you. But mark Troilus; you shall   finest men
    see anon.
          Enter ANTENOR [*passing by below*]
CRESSIDA Who's that?
175 PANDARUS That's Antenor. He has a shrewd wit, I can tell you,

---

5. A hard-hearted person was proverbially said to weep
millstones rather than tears. Cressida doesn't think the
story is particularly funny.
6. Cassandra's tears are "more temperate" because she
was associated with mournful, doom-laden prophecy.
Cressida imagines tears of laughter as a pot boiling over.

7. An oath based on the name of the Virgin Mary, here
meaning "Why," elsewhere "Indeed."
8. Priam reputedly had fifty sons. The "forked" hair (line
152) apparently counts as two.
9. Like a cuckold's horns, thereby suggesting Helen's
unfaithfulness to Paris.

and he's a man good enough. He's° one o'th' soundest judge-   *He has*
ments in Troy whosoever,° and a proper man of person.¹ When   *of any man*
comes Troilus? I'll show you Troilus anon. If he see me you
shall see him nod at me.

180   CRESSIDA Will he give you the nod?

     PANDARUS You shall see.

     CRESSIDA If he do, the rich shall have more.²

       Enter HECTOR [*passing by below*]

     PANDARUS That's Hector, that, that, look you, that. There's a
fellow!— Go thy way, Hector!—There's a brave man, niece. O

185   brave Hector! Look how he looks. There's a countenance. Is't
not a brave man?

     CRESSIDA O a brave man.

     PANDARUS Is a° not? It does a man's heart good. Look you what   *he*
hacks are on his helmet. Look you yonder, do you see? Look

190   you there. There's no jesting. There's laying on, take't off who
will,³ as they say. There be hacks.

     CRESSIDA Be those with swords?

       Enter PARIS [*passing by below*]

     PANDARUS Swords, anything, he cares not. An the devil come to
him it's all one.° By God's lid° it does one's heart good. Yonder   *the same / eyelid*

195   comes Paris, yonder comes Paris. Look ye yonder, niece. Is't
not a gallant° man too? Is't not? Why, this is brave now. Who   *fine*
said he came hurt home today? He's not hurt. Why, this will
do Helen's heart good now, ha! Would I could see Troilus now.
You shall see Troilus anon.

       Enter HELENUS [*passing by below*]

200   CRESSIDA Who's that?

     PANDARUS That's Helenus. I marvel where Troilus is. That's
Helenus. I think he went not forth today. That's Helenus.

     CRESSIDA Can Helenus fight, uncle?

     PANDARUS Helenus? No—yes, he'll fight indifferent° well. I mar-   *fairly*

205   vel where Troilus is.

       [*A Shout*]

  Hark, do you not hear the people cry 'Troilus'? Helenus is a
priest.

       Enter TROILUS [*passing by below*]

     CRESSIDA What sneaking fellow comes yonder?

     PANDARUS Where? Yonder? That's Deiphobus.—'Tis Troilus!

210   There's a man, niece, h'm? Brave Troilus, the prince of chivalry!

     CRESSIDA Peace, for shame, peace.

     PANDARUS Mark him, note him. O brave Troilus! Look well
upon him, niece. Look you how his sword is bloodied and

215   his helm more hacked than Hector's, and how he looks and
how he goes.° O admirable youth! He ne'er saw three-and-   *walks*
twenty. —Go thy way, Troilus, go thy way!—Had I a sister were
a grace,⁴ or a daughter a goddess, he should take his choice. O
admirable man! Paris? Paris is dirt to him, and I warrant Helen

220   to change° would give an eye to boot.   *exchange*

       Enter common soldiers [*passing by below*]

---

1. Good-looking man.
2. If Troilus acknowledges Pandarus with a nod, this will make Pandarus even more of a noddy, a fool.
3. There's hard fighting, denials notwithstanding (with wordplay: "laying on" versus "take't off").
4. The three Graces were goddesses of beauty and charm.

CRESSIDA Here comes more.

PANDARUS Asses, fools, dolts. Chaff and bran, chaff and bran.
Porridge° after meat. I could live and die i'th' eyes of Troilus.   *Soup*
Ne'er look, ne'er look, the eagles are gone. Crows and daws,°   *jackdaws; fools*
225 crows and daws. I had rather be such a man as Troilus than
Agamemnon and all Greece.

CRESSIDA There is among the Greeks Achilles, a better man
than Troilus.

PANDARUS Achilles? A drayman,° a porter, a very camel.   *cart driver*
230 CRESSIDA Well, well.

PANDARUS Well, well? Why, have you any discretion? Have you
any eyes? Do you know what a man is? Is not birth,° beauty,   *lineage*
good shape, discourse,° manhood, learning, gentleness,° virtue,   *eloquence / gentility*
youth, liberality, and so forth, the spice and salt that season a
235 man?

CRESSIDA Ay, a minced⁵ man—and then to be baked with no
date in the pie, for then the man's date is out.⁶

PANDARUS You are such another woman!° One knows not at   *like other women*
what ward you lie.⁷

240 CRESSIDA Upon my back to defend my belly,⁸ upon my wit to
defend my wiles, upon my secrecy° to defend mine honesty,⁹   *privacy; genitals*
my mask to defend my beauty,° and you to defend all these—   *(from sun)*
and at all these wards I lie at a thousand watches.¹

PANDARUS Say one of your watches.

245 CRESSIDA 'Nay, I'll watch you for that'—and that's one of the
chiefest of them too.² If I cannot ward what I would not have
hit,° I can watch you for° telling how I took the blow— unless   *(sexually) / from*
it swell past hiding,° and then it's past watching.   *(from pregnancy)*

PANDARUS You are such another!

Enter BOY

250 BOY Sir, my lord would instantly speak with you.

PANDARUS Where?

BOY At your own house.

PANDARUS Good boy, tell him I come.   [*Exit* BOY]
I doubt° he be hurt. Fare ye well, good niece.   *fear*

255 CRESSIDA Adieu, uncle.

PANDARUS I'll be with you, niece, by and by.

CRESSIDA To bring, uncle?

PANDARUS Ay, a token from Troilus.

CRESSIDA By the same token, you are a bawd.°   *pander; pimp*

Exeunt PANDARUS [*and* ALEXANDER]

260 Words, vows, gifts, tears, and love's full sacrifice
He offers in another's enterprise;
But more in Troilus thousandfold I see
Than in the glass° of Pandar's praise may be.   *mirror*
Yet hold I off. Women are angels, wooing;³

---

5. Affected (punning on "mincemeat" to suggest the multiple ingredients of Troilus and thus beginning to develop Pandarus's "spice and salt" metaphor).
6. The man is flavorless; out of date; not in female genitalia.
7. A man doesn't know what position of defense in fencing ("ward") you adopt. (A man doesn't know how to deal with you.)
8. Vagina. Lying on one's back is not, of course, the obvious way to defend one's virginity.

9. Reputation.
1. Ways of guarding; hours of the night; the duties of a watchman (playing on "watch" and "ward," line 243); devotional exercises (line 244). "Watch" as a verb is also implied: observe (line 245); prevent (line 246); worry (line 247).
2. Presumably the immediately preceding phrase is one of her chief devotional exercises.
3. Men call women angels only while wooing them.

265 Things won are done. Joy's soul lies in the doing.
That she beloved knows naught that knows not this:
Men price the thing ungained more than it is.°   °is worth
That she was never yet that ever knew
Love got so sweet as when desire did sue.[4]
270 Therefore this maxim out of° love I teach: °taken from
Achievement is command; ungained, beseech.[5]
Then though my heart's contents[6] firm love doth bear,
Nothing of that shall from mine eyes appear.   *Exit*

1.3

Sennet.° Enter AGAMEMNON, NESTOR, ULYSSES, DIO-   *Fanfare*
MEDES, [*and*] MENELAUS, *with others*
AGAMEMNON   Princes, what grief hath set the jaundice° on your cheeks?   °sickliness
The ample proposition that hope makes
In all designs begun on earth below
Fails in the promised largeness. Checks° and disasters   °Obstacles
5 Grow in the veins[1] of actions highest reared,
As knots, by the conflux° of meeting sap,   °confluence
Infects the sound pine and diverts his° grain   °its
Tortive° and errant° from his course of growth.   °Contorted / °straying
Nor, princes, is it matter new to us
10 That we come short of our suppose° so far   °intention
That after seven years' siege yet Troy walls stand,
Sith° every action that hath gone before,   °Since
Whereof we have record, trial did draw
Bias and thwart,[2] not answering° the aim   °living up to
15 And that unbodied figure° of the thought   °theoretical design
That gave't surmisèd shape. Why then, you princes,
Do you with cheeks abashed behold our works,
And think them shames, which are indeed naught else
But the protractive trials of great Jove
20 To find persistive constancy in men?
The fineness of which mettle° is not found   °temperament; metal
In fortune's love—for then the bold and coward,
The wise and fool, the artist° and unread,   °learned
The hard and soft, seem all affined° and kin.   °related
25 But in the wind and tempest of her frown
Distinction with a loud and powerful fan,
Puffing at all, winnows the light away,[3]
And what hath mass or matter by itself
Lies rich in virtue and unminglèd.
30 NESTOR   With due observance of° thy godly seat,°   °respect to / °throne
Great Agamemnon, Nestor shall apply°   °gloss
Thy latest words. In the reproof of° chance   °rebuff by; rebuttal of
Lies the true proof of men. The sea being smooth,
How many shallow bauble°-boats dare sail   °toy
35 Upon her patient breast, making their way

---

4. *That . . . sue:* No woman has ever known making love
with a man to be as sweet as when it is still desired for the
first time.
5. Once a woman yields, the man controls her; what the
man doesn't have he must plead for.
6. *contents':* happiness; *con'tents:* substance.
1.3 Location: The Greek camp outside Troy.

1. It is assumed that trees have veins through which sap
flows.
2. *trial . . . thwart:* attempting the deed ("action") called
it into being crookedly and in a manner at odds with the
purpose.
3. The comparison is to light, dry chaff blown away from
grain.

With those of nobler bulk!
But let the ruffian Boreas° once enrage   *North wind*
The gentle Thetis,[4] and anon behold
The strong-ribbed barque through liquid mountains cut,
40 Bounding between the two moist elements°   *(water and air)*
Like Perseus' horse.° Where's then the saucy° boat   *(winged Pegasus) / bold*
Whose weak untimbered sides but even° now   *just*
Co-rivalled greatness? Either to harbour fled,
Or made a toast for Neptune.[5] Even so
45 Doth valour's show and valour's worth divide
In storms of fortune. For in her° ray and brightness   *(fortune's)*
The herd hath more annoyance by the breese°   *gadfly*
Than by the tiger; but when the splitting wind
Makes flexible the knees° of knotted° oaks   *tough timber / gnarled*
50 And flies flee under shade, why then the thing of courage,°   *brave person*
As roused with rage, with rage doth sympathize,[6]
And with an accent tuned in selfsame key
Retorts to chiding fortune.
ULYSSES   Agamemnon,
Thou great commander, nerve° and bone of Greece,   *sinew*
55 Heart of our numbers,° soul and only spirit   *troops*
In whom the tempers and the minds of all
Should be shut up,° hear what Ulysses speaks.   *encapsulated*
Besides th'applause° and approbation   *approval*
The which, [*to* AGAMEMNON] most mighty for thy place and
        sway,°   *position and power*
60 And thou, [*to* NESTOR] most reverend for thy stretched-out life,
I give to both your speeches—which were such
As, Agamemnon, every hand of Greece
Should hold up high in brass,° and such again   *record permanently*
As, venerable Nestor, hatched[7] in silver,
65 Should with a bond of air, strong as the axle-tree[8]
On which the heavens ride, knit all Greeks' ears
To his experienced tongue—yet let it please both,
Thou [*to* AGAMEMNON] great, and [*to* NESTOR] wise, to hear Ulysses speak.
AGAMEMNON   Speak, Prince of Ithaca, and be't of less expect°   *likelihood*
70 That matter needless, of importless burden,°   *irrelevant meaning*
Divide thy lips, than we are confident
When rank° Thersites opes his mastic° jaws   *rancid / abusive*
We shall hear music, wit, and oracle.
ULYSSES   Troy, yet upon his basis,° had been down   *still standing*
75 And the great Hector's sword had lacked a master
But for these instances:°   *causes*
The specialty° of rule hath been neglected.   *rights and duties*
And look how many° Grecian tents do stand   *however many*
Hollow° upon this plain: so many hollow° factions.   *Empty / false*
80 When that the general is not like the hive
To whom the foragers° shall all repair,   *food collectors*
What honey is expected? Degree° being vizarded,°   *Rank / concealed*

---

4. Sea goddess (mother of Achilles), here standing for the sea.
5. Morsel of toasted bread, floated in wine, for the god of the sea.
6. Himself enraged, behaves like the raging storm.
7. Etched with parallel lines, as if inlaid with precious

metal (alluding to Nestor's white hair and beard, or his wrinkled face).
8. *bond of air:* persuasive rhetoric. *axle-tree:* the axis on which the universe was imagined to revolve, earth being at the center.

Th'unworthiest shows as fairly in the masque
[   ].[9]
85   The heavens themselves, the planets, and this centre°   (the earth)
     Observe degree, priority, and place,
     Infixture,° course, proportion, season, form,   Fixity
     Office° and custom, in all line of order.   Function
     And therefore is the glorious planet Sol[1]
90   In noble eminence enthroned and sphered°   placed in orbit
     Amidst the other,° whose med'cinable[2] eye   rest
     Corrects the ill aspects° of planets evil   astrological influence
     And posts° like the commandment of a king,   hastens
     Sans° check, to good and bad. But when the planets   Without
95   In evil mixture to disorder wander,[3]
     What plagues and what portents, what mutiny?
     What raging of the sea, shaking of earth?
     Commotion in the winds, frights, changes,° horrors   political strife
     Divert and crack, rend and deracinate°   uproot
100 The unity and married calm of states
     Quite from their fixture. O when degree is shaked,
     Which is the ladder to all high designs,
     The enterprise is sick. How could communities,
     Degrees in schools,° and brotherhoods° in cities,   Academic rank / guilds
105 Peaceful commerce from dividable° shores,   isolated
     The primogenity° and due of birth,   primogeniture
     Prerogative of age, crowns, sceptres, laurels,
     But by degree stand in authentic place?
     Take but degree away, untune that string,
110 And hark what discord follows. Each thing meets
     In mere oppugnancy.° The bounded waters   total antagonism
     Should lift their bosoms higher than the shores
     And make a sop° of all this solid globe;   lump of soaked bread
     Strength should be lord of imbecility,°   weakness
115 And the rude son should strike his father dead.
     Force should be right—or rather, right and wrong,
     Between whose endless jar justice resides,[4]
     Should lose their names, and so should justice too.
     Then everything includes itself in° power,   comes down to
120 Power into will,° will into appetite;   egotism; lust
     And appetite, an universal wolf,
     So doubly seconded with will and power,
     Must make perforce an universal prey,°   seizing
     And last eat up himself. Great Agamemnon,
125 This chaos, when degree is suffocate,
     Follows the choking.
     And this neglection of degree it is
     That by a pace goes backward in a purpose
     It hath to climb.[5] The general's disdained
130 By him one step below; he, by the next;
     That next, by him beneath. So every step,

9. A line providing the contrast to "Th'unworthiest" may
be lost.
1. In the Ptolemaic system, the sun was thought to be a
planet revolving round the earth.
2. Curative. The eyes were thought to see by emitting
rays—like the sun. Kings sometimes claimed a similar
ability to cure.

3. The word "planets" means "wanderers," referring to
their apparently erratic course, as seen from earth. *evil
mixture:* wicked coupling.
4. Justice stands between the clashing ("jar") of the
opposing contenders.
5. *That . . . climb:* That drops back step by step when it
intends to climb.

Exampled by the first pace that is sick
Of his superior, grows to an envious fever
Of pale and bloodless emulation.°   *sick rivalry*
135 And 'tis this fever that keeps Troy on foot,°   *standing*
Not her own sinews. To end a tale of length:
Troy in our weakness lives, not in her strength.
   NESTOR   Most wisely hath Ulysses here discovered°   *revealed*
The fever whereof all our power is sick.
140   AGAMEMNON   The nature of the sickness found, Ulysses,
What is the remedy?
   ULYSSES   The great Achilles, whom opinion° crowns   *consensus*
The sinew and the forehand° of our host,°   *strongest / army*
Having his ear full of his airy° fame   *lofty; insubstantial*
145 Grows dainty of° his worth, and in his tent   *too conscious of*
Lies mocking our designs. With him Patroclus
Upon a lazy bed the livelong day
Breaks scurrile° jests   *scurrilous*
And, with ridiculous and awkward action°   *gesture*
150 Which, slanderer, he 'imitation' calls,
He pageants° us. Sometime, great Agamemnon,   *mimics*
Thy topless deputation° he puts on,   *supreme rank*
And like a strutting player, whose conceit
Lies in his hamstring[6] and doth think it rich
155 To hear the wooden dialogue and sound
'Twixt his stretched footing and the scaffoldage,[7]
Such to-be-pitied and o'er-wrested seeming°   *pitiful imitation*
He acts thy greatness in. And when he speaks
'Tis like a chime a-mending, with terms unsquared[8]
160 Which from the tongue of roaring Typhon[9] dropped
Would seem hyperboles. At this fusty° stuff   *stale; bombastic*
The large Achilles on his pressed[1] bed lolling
From his deep chest laughs out a loud applause,
Cries 'Excellent! 'Tis Agamemnon just.°   *exactly*
165 Now play me Nestor, hem° and stroke thy beard,   *(as in "ahem")*
As he being dressed to° some oration.'   *preparing for*
That's done as near as the extremest ends
Of parallels, as like as Vulcan and his wife.[2]
Yet god° Achilles still cries, 'Excellent!   *semidivine (ironic)*
170 'Tis Nestor right. Now play him me, Patroclus,
Arming to answer in° a night alarm'.   *respond to*
And then forsooth the faint° defects of age   *weak*
Must be the scene of mirth: to cough and spit,
And with a palsy, fumbling on his gorget,°   *throat armor*
175 Shake in and out the rivet.° And at this sport   *fastening bolt*
Sir Valour dies,° cries, 'O enough, Patroclus!   *(laughing)*
Or give me ribs of steel. I shall split all
In pleasure of my spleen.'° And in this fashion   *(seat of mirth)*
All our abilities, gifts, natures, shapes,

6. *whose . . . hamstring*: whose brains are in his thighs.
7. *To hear . . . scaffoldage*: To hear the sound of his long, powerful strides (and dull speech?) on the platform stage.
8. Like bells being repaired (or tuned?), with ill-fitting expressions.
9. Monster with a hundred heads, each uttering the cry of a different beast; eventually buried by Jupiter under (and so associated with) a volcano.

1. Weighed down (by Achilles).
2. *as near . . . wife*: as closely as the ends of parallel lines (which, since they are equidistant, never meet), and as the ugly, limping god Vulcan, the smith, resembles his beautiful wife Venus. Ulysses is stressing how bad the acting is, while at the same time covertly belittling Agamemnon and Nestor.

180 Severals and generals of grace exact,[3]
Achievements, plots, orders, preventions,°   *precautions*
Excitements° to the field or speech for truce,   *Urgings*
Success or loss, what is or is not, serves
As stuff for these two to make paradoxes.°   *absurdities*
185 NESTOR   And in the imitation of these twain
Who, as Ulysses says, opinion crowns
With an imperial voice, many are infect.°   *infected*
Ajax is grown self-willed and bears his head
In such a rein,° in full as proud a place   *So high*
190 As broad Achilles, and keeps° his tent like him,   *stays within*
Makes factious feasts, rails on° our state of war   *complains about*
Bold as an oracle, and sets Thersites,
A slave whose gall° coins slanders like a mint,   *rancor*
To match us in comparisons with dirt,
195 To weaken and discredit our exposure,°   *exposed position*
How rank° so ever rounded in with° danger.   *densely / hemmed in by*
ULYSSES   They tax° our policy and call it cowardice,   *criticize*
Count wisdom as no member of the war,
Forestall prescience° and esteem no act   *advance planning*
200 But that of hand. The still and mental parts
That do contrive how many hands shall strike
When fitness° calls them on, and know by measure   *the right moment*
Of their observant toil the enemy's weight,°   *power*
Why, this hath not a finger's dignity.
205 They call this 'bed-work', 'mapp'ry',° 'closet war'.   *mere mapping; planning*
So that the ram that batters down the wall,
For the great swinge and rudeness of his poise[4]
They place before° his hand that made the engine,°   *exalt above / (the ram)*
Or those that with the finesse° of their souls   *subtlety*
210 By reason guide his execution.°   *the ram's use*
NESTOR   Let this be granted, and Achilles' horse
Makes many Thetis' sons.[5]
       Tucket°   *Trumpet call*
AGAMEMNON   What trumpet?
Look, Menelaus.
MENELAUS   From Troy.
       Enter AENEAS *[and a trumpeter]*
AGAMEMNON   What would you fore° our tent?   *before*
215 AENEAS   Is this great Agamemnon's tent I pray you?
AGAMEMNON   Even this.
AENEAS   May one that is a herald and a prince
Do a fair message to his kingly ears?
AGAMEMNON   With surety° stronger than Achilles' arm,   *security*
220 Fore all the Greekish heads, which with one voice
Call Agamemnon heart and general.
AENEAS   Fair leave and large° security. How may   *generous*
A stranger to those most imperial looks
Know them from eyes of other mortals?
AGAMEMNON   How?
225 AENEAS   Ay, I ask that I might waken reverence

---

3. Supreme merits, possessed individually and in common.
4. Because of the impetus and violence of its impact.

5. *Let . . . sons:* If this is true, then Achilles' horse is worth many Achilleses. Thetis was the mother of Achilles.

And on the cheek be ready with a blush
Modest as morning when she coldly eyes
The youthful Phoebus.[6]
Which is that god in office, guiding men?
230 Which is the high and mighty Agamemnon?
AGAMEMNON [*to the Greeks*]   This Trojan scorns us, or the men of Troy
Are ceremonious courtiers.
AENEAS   Courtiers as free,° as debonair,° unarmed,   *generous / gracious*
As bending° angels—that's their fame in peace.   *ministering*
235 But when they would seem soldiers they have galls,[7]
Good arms, strong joints, true swords—and great Jove's acorn[8]
Nothing so full of heart.° But peace, Aeneas,   *courage; nutmeat*
Peace, Trojan; lay thy finger on thy lips.
The worthiness of praise distains° his worth,   *stains*
240 If that the praised himself bring the praise forth.
But what, repining,° the enemy commends,   *grudging(ly)*
That breath fame blows; that praise, sole pure, transcends.
AGAMEMNON   Sir, you of Troy, call you yourself Aeneas?
AENEAS   Ay, Greek,° that is my name.   *cheater (slang)*
AGAMEMNON   What's your affair, I pray you?
245 AENEAS   Sir, pardon, 'tis for Agamemnon's ears.
AGAMEMNON   He hears naught privately that comes from Troy.
AENEAS   Nor I from Troy come not to whisper him.
I bring a trumpet to awake his ear,
To set his sense on the attentive bent,
And then to speak.
250 AGAMEMNON   Speak frankly° as the wind.   *freely*
It is not Agamemnon's sleeping hour.
That thou shalt know, Trojan, he is awake,
He tells thee so himself.
AENEAS   Trumpet,° blow loud.   *Trumpeter*
Send thy brass voice through all these lazy tents,
255 And every Greek of mettle let him know
What Troy means fairly shall be spoke aloud.
      The trumpet sound[s]
We have, great Agamemnon, here in Troy
A prince called Hector—Priam is his father—
Who in this dull and long-continued truce
260 Is resty° grown. He bade me take a trumpet   *lazy*
And to this purpose speak: 'Kings, princes, lords,
If there be one among the fair'st of Greece
That holds his honour higher than his ease,
That seeks his praise more than he fears his peril,
265 That knows his valour and knows not his fear,
That loves his mistress more than in confession
With truant vows to her own lips he loves,[9]
And dare avow her beauty and her worth
In other arms than hers°—to him this challenge.   *armor; Hector's arms*
270 Hector in view of Trojans and of Greeks
Shall make it good, or do his best to do it:
He hath a lady wiser, fairer, truer,
Than ever Greek did compass° in his arms,   *hold*

---

6. *Modest . . . Phoebus:* Modest as Aurora, the blushing
dawn personified, when she coldly eyes Apollo, the sun
god ("youthful" because it is early morning).
7. But when it is time for them to be warriors, their courageous tempers do not tolerate mistreatment.
8. The oak was Jupiter's tree.
9. *That . . . loves:* Who will declare his love with stronger
proof (deeds) than unreliable, private promises.

And will tomorrow with his trumpet call
275 Midway between your tents and walls of Troy
To rouse a Grecian that is true in love.
If any come, Hector shall honour him.
If none, he'll say in Troy when he retires
The Grecian dames are sunburnt° and not worth   *not fair*
280 The splinter° of a lance.' Even so much.   *breaking; fragment*
AGAMEMNON   This shall be told our lovers, Lord Aeneas.
If none of them have soul in such a kind,
We left them all at home. But we are soldiers,
And may that soldier a mere recreant prove
285 That means not, hath not,[1] or is not in love.
If then one is, or hath, or means to be,
That one meets Hector. If none else, I'll be he.
NESTOR [*to* AENEAS]   Tell him of Nestor, one that was a man
When Hector's grandsire sucked. He is old now,
290 But if there be not in our Grecian mould°   *character; model*
One noble man that hath one spark of fire
To answer for his love, tell him from me
I'll hide my silver beard in a gold beaver°   *helmet's face guard*
And in my vambrace° put this withered brawn,°   *forearm armor / arm*
295 And meeting him will tell him that my lady
Was fairer than his grandam, and as chaste
As may be in the world. His youth in flood,°   *Despite his youth*
I'll prove this truth with my three drops of blood.
AENEAS   Now heavens forbid such scarcity of youth.
300 ULYSSES   Amen.
AGAMEMNON   Fair Lord Aeneas, let me touch° your hand.   *shake*
To our pavilion shall I lead you first.
Achilles shall have word of this intent;
So shall each lord of Greece, from tent to tent.
305 Yourself shall feast with us before you go,
And find the welcome of a noble foe.
                Exeunt. Manent° ULYSSES *and* NESTOR   *Remain*
ULYSSES   Nestor!
NESTOR   What says Ulysses?
ULYSSES   I have a young
Conception in my brain; be you my time[2]
To bring it to some shape.
NESTOR   What is't?
ULYSSES   This 'tis:
310 Blunt wedges rive° hard knots. The seeded pride   *split*
That hath to this maturity blown° up   *swelled*
In rank° Achilles must or° now be cropped   *overgrown / either*
Or, shedding,° breed a nursery of like evil   *dropping its seed*
To overbulk° us all.   *overrun*
NESTOR   Well, and how?
315 ULYSSES   This challenge that the gallant Hector sends,
However it is spread in general name,
Relates in purpose only to Achilles.
NESTOR   The purpose is perspicuous,° even as substance°   *easy to see / wealth*
Whose grossness little characters sum up.[3]

---

1. Who does not aim (to be), has never been.
2. *Conception . . . time:* The primary meaning (unfolding of a plan) metaphorically extended to pregnancy's onset and gestation period, the latter associated with the male

and aged Nestor, who is oddly associated with this female and ordinarily youthful activity, presumably because he embodies the passage of time.
3. Whose size is reckoned by small figures (on paper).

320 And, in the publication, make no strain[4]
But that Achilles, were his brain as barren
As banks of Libya°—though, Apollo knows,   *the Sahara desert*
'Tis dry° enough—will with great speed of judgement,   *infertile; empty*
Ay with celerity, find Hector's purpose
325 Pointing on him.°   *himself*
ULYSSES   And wake him to the answer, think you?
NESTOR   Yes, 'tis most meet.° Who may you else oppose,   *fitting*
That can from Hector bring his honour off,
If not Achilles? Though't be a sportful combat,
330 Yet in this trial much opinion° dwells,   *reputation*
For here the Trojans taste our dear'st repute
With their fin'st palate. And trust to me, Ulysses,
Our imputation° shall be oddly poised[5]   *reputation*
In this wild° action: for the success,   *uncontrollable*
335 Although particular, shall give a scantling
Of good or bad unto the general[6]—
And in such indices,° although small pricks   *tables of contents*
To° their subsequent volumes, there is seen   *Compared to*
The baby figure of the giant mass
340 Of things to come at large. It is supposed
He that meets Hector issues from our choice,
And choice, being mutual act of all our souls,
Makes merit her election,° and doth boil,   *grounds of choice*
As 'twere, from forth us all a man distilled
345 Out of our virtues—who miscarrying,°   *should he lose*
What heart from hence receives the conqu'ring part
To steel a strong opinion to themselves?[7]
Which entertained, limbs are e'en his instruments,
In no less working than are swords and bows
350 Directive by the limbs.[8]
ULYSSES   Give pardon to my speech:
Therefore 'tis meet° Achilles meet not Hector.   *appropriate*
Let us like merchants show our foulest wares
And think perchance they'll sell. If not,
The lustre of the better yet to show°   *not yet shown*
355 Shall show the better. Do not consent
That ever Hector and Achilles meet,
For both our honour and our shame in this
Are dogged with two strange followers.°   *surprising results*
NESTOR   I see them not with my old eyes. What are they?
360 ULYSSES   What glory our Achilles shares° from Hector,   *gains*
Were he not proud we all should wear° with him.   *share*
But he already is too insolent,
And we were better parch in Afric sun
Than in the pride and salt° scorn of his eyes,   *bitter*
365 Should he scape Hector fair. If he were foiled,
Why then we did our main opinion° crush   *common reputation*
In taint of° our best man. No, make a lott'ry,   *In the dishonor of*

4. And, with the announcement, do not doubt.
5. Disproportionately judged.
6. *the success . . . general*: the outcome, although relating only to one person, shall serve as an example of the whole army's abilities.
7. *What . . . themselves*: What (Greek) warriors could possibly get a sense of victory from this that would make them feel more confident?; what motivation will the Trojans get from this to make them feel more confident?
8. *Which . . . limbs*: Assuming that this confidence ("strong opinion") is received from the victory, the soldiers' limbs become the mechanisms ("instruments") of that confidence in the same way that swords and bows are subject to direction by the limbs themselves.

	And by device let blockish° Ajax draw	*blockheaded*
	The sort° to fight with Hector. Among ourselves	*lot*
370	Give him allowance° as the worthier man—	*acknowledgment*
	For that will physic the great Myrmidon,[9]	
	Who broils in° loud applause, and make him fall°	*is excited by / lower*
	His crest, that prouder than blue Iris[1] bends.	
	If the dull brainless Ajax come safe off,	
375	We'll dress him up in voices;° if he fail,	*sing his praises*
	Yet go we under our opinion still	
	That we have better men. But hit or miss,	
	Our project's life° this shape of sense° assumes:	*success / rationale*
	Ajax employed plucks down Achilles' plumes.	
380	NESTOR Now, Ulysses, I begin to relish thy advice,	
	And I will give a taste of it forthwith	
	To Agamemnon. Go we to him straight.°	*immediately*
	Two curs shall tame each other; pride alone	
	Must tarre the mastiffs on,[2] as 'twere° their bone. *Exeunt*	*if it were*

2.1

Enter AJAX *and* THERSITES

AJAX Thersites.

THERSITES Agamemnon—how if he had boils, full,° all over, generally?   *(of pus)*

AJAX Thersites.

5 THERSITES And those boils did run? Say so, did not the General run then? Were not that a botchy core?°   *ulcerous center*

AJAX Dog.

THERSITES Then there would come some matter° from him. I see none now.   *pus; sense*

10 AJAX Thou bitch-wolf's son, canst thou not hear? Feel then.
     [*He*] *strikes* [THERSITES]

THERSITES The plague of Greece upon thee, thou mongrel[1] beef-witted° lord!   *dumb as an ox*

AJAX Speak then, thou unsifted leaven,° speak! I will beat[2] thee into handsomeness.°   *dough / decency; good looks*

15 THERSITES I shall sooner rail thee into wit and holiness. But I think thy horse will sooner con° an oration than thou learn a prayer without book.°   *memorize / by heart*
     [AJAX *strikes him*]
Thou canst strike, canst thou? A red murrain° o' thy jade's[3] tricks.   *bloody plague*

20 AJAX Toad's stool![4]
     [*He strikes* THERSITES]
Learn me° the proclamation.   *Instruct me (about)*

THERSITES Dost thou think I have no sense,° thou strikest me thus?   *feeling*

AJAX The proclamation.

25 THERSITES Thou art proclaimed a fool, I think.

AJAX Do not, porcupine,[5] do not. My fingers itch.°   *(to hit you)*

---

9. Will give medicine to (purge) Achilles, who led the Myrmidons.
1. Goddess of the rainbow; blue flower.
2. Must incite these large, aggressive dogs.
2.1 Location: The Greek camp.
1. Ajax's mother was Trojan; hence, he was of mixed

breed, "mongrel."
2. Punning on the pounding of bread dough.
3. Temperamental horse's.
4. Toadstools were once thought to be a toad's poisonous excrement (stool).

THERSITES I would thou didst itch from head to foot. An° I had   *If*
the scratching of thee, I would make thee the loathsomest
scab in Greece.

30   AJAX I say, the proclamation.

THERSITES Thou grumblest and railest every hour on Achilles,
and thou art as full of envy at his greatness as Cerberus is at
Proserpina's[6] beauty, ay, that thou barkest at him.

AJAX Mistress[7] Thersites.

35   THERSITES Thou shouldst strike him.

AJAX Cobloaf.°   *Small crusty loaf*

THERSITES He would pun° thee into shivers° with his fist, as a   *pound / pieces*
sailor breaks a biscuit.

AJAX You whoreson cur.
      [He strikes THERSITES*]*

40   THERSITES Do! Do!°   *Go on*

AJAX Thou stool° for a witch.   *privy*
      [He strikes THERSITES*]*

THERSITES Ay, do, do! Thou sodden-witted° lord, thou hast in   *boiled-brained*
thy skull no more brain than I have in mine elbows. An *asnico*°   *little ass*
may tutor thee. Thou scurvy valiant ass, thou art here but to

45   thrash Trojans, and thou art bought and sold[8] among those of
any wit like a barbarian slave. If thou use° to beat me, I will   *continue*
begin at thy heel and tell what thou art by inches, thou thing
of no bowels,° thou.   *with no pity*

AJAX You dog.

50   THERSITES You scurvy lord.

AJAX You cur.
      [He strikes THERSITES*]*

THERSITES Mars his idiot!° Do, rudeness! Do, camel, do, do!   *God of war's jester*
      Enter ACHILLES *and* PATROCLUS

ACHILLES Why, how now, Ajax? Wherefore do ye thus?
How now, Thersites? What's the matter, man?

55   THERSITES You see him there? Do you?

ACHILLES Ay. What's the matter?

THERSITES Nay, look upon him.

ACHILLES So I do. What's the matter?

THERSITES Nay, but regard him well.

60   ACHILLES 'Well'? Why, I do so.

THERSITES But yet you look not well upon him.[9] For whoso-
mever you take him to be, he is Ajax.°   *a jakes = toilet*

ACHILLES I know that, fool.

THERSITES Ay, but 'that fool' knows not himself.[1]

65   AJAX Therefore I beat thee.[2]

THERSITES Lo,° lo, lo, lo, what modicums of wit he utters. His   *Behold (sarcastic)*
evasions have ears thus long.[3] I have bobbed° his brain more   *thumped*

---

5. The porcupine's sharp quills were emblematic of the
satirist (here, Thersites).
6. Cerberus was the monstrous three-headed dog who
guarded the gate of Hades. Proserpina was Queen of
Hades and wife of Pluto, god of the underworld.
7. Because a woman's only weapon was thought to be her
tongue, because Thersites is a coward, or because he is
believed to be homosexual.
8. You are traded like goods—hence, treated as an object,
treated contemptuously.
9. Thersites is probably feigning amazement that Achil-

les can look at Ajax and yet not see what a fool he is; but
he may also mean that Achilles does not do well to favor
("look . . . upon") him.
1. Thersites deliberately understands Achilles' line without the intended comma: "I know that fool" (Ajax), rather
than "I know that [fact], fool."
2. Ajax thinks Thersites is calling himself (rather than
Ajax) a "fool" who does not know himself.
3. His efforts to dodge witty rejoinders are like an
ass's—hence asinine.

than he has beat my bones. I will° buy nine sparrows for a   can
penny, and his *pia mater*° is not worth the ninth part of a spar-   brain
70   row. This lord, Achilles—Ajax, who wears his wit in his belly
and his guts in his head—I'll tell you what I say of him.
ACHILLES   What?
THERSITES   I say, this Ajax—
    [AJAX *threatens to strike him*]
ACHILLES   Nay, good Ajax.
75   THERSITES   Has not so much wit—
    [AJAX *threatens to strike him*]
ACHILLES [*to* AJAX]   Nay, I must hold° you.   restrain
THERSITES   As will stop the eye of Helen's needle,[4] for whom he
comes to fight.
ACHILLES   Peace, fool.
80   THERSITES   I would have peace and quietness, but the fool° will   Ajax
not. He, there, that he, look you there.
AJAX   O thou damned cur I shall—
ACHILLES [*to* AJAX]   Will you set your wit to° a fool's?   against
THERSITES   No, I warrant you, for a fool's will shame it.
85   PATROCLUS   Good words,° Thersites.   Speak with restraint
ACHILLES [to AJAX]   What's the quarrel?
AJAX   I bade the vile owl[5] go learn me the tenor of the proclamation, and he rails upon me.
THERSITES   I serve thee not.
90   AJAX   Well, go to, go to.
THERSITES   I serve here voluntary.°   as a volunteer
ACHILLES   Your last service was sufferance. 'Twas not voluntary:
no man is beaten voluntary. Ajax was here the voluntary, and
you as under an impress.[6]
95   THERSITES   E'en so. A great deal of your wit, too, lies in your
sinews, or else there be liars. Hector shall have a great catch an
a° knock out either of your brains. A were as good° crack a   if he / might as well
fusty° nut with no kernel.   rotten
ACHILLES   What, with me too, Thersites?
100   THERSITES   There's Ulysses and old Nestor, whose wit was
mouldy ere your grandsires had nails on their toes, yoke you
like draught oxen and make you plough up the war.°   (*pun on ware = crops*)
ACHILLES   What? What?
THERSITES   Yes, good sooth. To° Achilles! To, Ajax, to—   (*urging on the oxen*)
105   AJAX   I shall cut out your tongue.
THERSITES   'Tis no matter. I shall speak as much wit as thou
afterwards.
PATROCLUS   No more words, Thersites, peace.
THERSITES   I will hold my peace when Achilles' brach° bids me,   bitch
110   shall I?
ACHILLES   There's for you, Patroclus.
THERSITES   I will see you hanged like clodpolls° ere I come any   blockheads
more to your tents. I will keep where there is wit stirring, and
leave the faction of fools.   *Exit*
115   PATROCLUS   A good riddance.

4. "Eye" perhaps alludes to "vagina"; "needle" is also   6. As a conscript; being hit as though with a stamp (by
obscene. *stop*: fill.   Ajax).
5. The owl is associated with evil portent.

ACHILLES [*to* AJAX] Marry, this, sir, is proclaimed through all our host:
  That Hector, by the fifth hour° of the sun,   *11 A.M.*
  Will with a trumpet 'twixt our tents and Troy
  Tomorrow morning call some knight to arms
120 That hath a stomach,° and such a one that dare   *appetite for combat*
  Maintain—I know not what. 'Tis trash. Farewell.
AJAX Farewell. Who shall answer him?
ACHILLES I know not. 'Tis put to lott'ry. Otherwise,
  He knew his man.   [*Exeunt* ACHILLES *and* PATROCLUS]
125 AJAX O, meaning you? I will go learn more of it.   *Exit*

2.2

[*Sennet.*] Enter [*King*] PRIAM, HECTOR, TROILUS, PARIS,
  and HELENUS
PRIAM After so many hours, lives, speeches spent,
  Thus once again says Nestor from the Greeks:
  'Deliver Helen, and all damage else—
  As honour, loss of time, travail,° expense,   *hard labor*
5 Wounds, friends, and what else dear° that is consumed   *beloved; costly*
  In hot digestion of this cormorant° war—   *rapacious*
  Shall be struck off.'° Hector, what say you to't?   *expunged*
HECTOR Though no man lesser fears the Greeks than I,
  As far as toucheth my particular,° yet, dread Priam,   *own concerns*
10 There is no lady of more softer bowels,°   *compassion*
  More spongy to suck in° the sense of fear,   *able to absorb*
  More ready to cry out, 'Who knows what follows?'
  Than Hector is. The wound of peace is surety,[1]
  Surety secure; but modest doubt is called
15 The beacon° of the wise, the tent[2] that searches   *lighthouse*
  To th' bottom of the worst. Let Helen go.
  Since the first sword was drawn about this question,
  Every tithe-soul, 'mongst many thousand dimes,
  Hath been as dear as Helen[3]—I mean, of ours.
20 If we have lost so many tenths of ours
  To guard a thing not ours—nor worth to us,
  Had it our name, the value of one ten[4]—
  What merit's in that reason which denies
  The yielding of her up?
TROILUS   Fie, fie, my brother!
25 Weigh you the worth and honour of a king
  So great as our dread father in a scale
  Of common ounces? Will you with counters° sum   *worthless chips*
  The past-proportion of his infinite,[5]
  And buckle in a waist most fathomless[6]
30 With spans° and inches so diminutive   *nine inches*
  As fears and reasons?° Fie, for godly shame!   *(pun on "raisins")*
HELENUS No marvel though you bite so sharp at reasons,

2.2 Location: The palace in Troy.
1. (Overconfident) sense of security.
2. Surgeon's probe.
3. *Every . . . Helen:* Every soul taken to pay the tithe (a tenth of one's goods, paid as a tax), among many thousand "dimes" (tenths; tithes paid, through soldiers' deaths), has been as valuable as Helen.
4. Even if Helen were Trojan, the value of one-tenth (one

of the men lost).
5. Add up the infinitude of his measurelessness.
6. Most immeasurable even in fathoms (6 foot lengths, used in calculating sea depths). "Waist" puns on "waste" as uninhabited expanse, especially the ocean, and as the squandering of resources (the second unintended by Troilus).

<table>
<tr><td>35</td><td>You are so empty of them. Should not our father
Bear the great sway of his affairs with reason
Because your speech hath none that tells him so?</td><td></td></tr>
</table>

You are so empty of them. Should not our father
Bear the great sway of his affairs with reason
35 Because your speech hath none that tells him so?
TROILUS   You are for dreams and slumbers, brother priest.
You fur your gloves with 'reason'.[7] Here are your reasons:
You know an enemy intends you harm,
You know a sword employed is perilous,
40 And reason flies the object of all harm.°   *any sight of danger*
Who marvels then, when Helenus beholds
A Grecian and his sword, if he do set
The very wings of reason to his heels
And fly like chidden Mercury[8] from Jove,
45 Or like a star disorbed?° Nay, if we talk of reason,   *a shooting star*
Let's shut our gates and sleep. Manhood and honour
Should have hare° hearts, would they but fat their thoughts   *timid*
With this crammed° reason. Reason and respect°   *fattened / deliberation*
Make livers° pale and lustihood° deject.   *courage / energy*
50 HECTOR   Brother, she is not worth what she doth cost
The holding.°   *To keep*
TROILUS   What's aught but as 'tis valued?[9]
HECTOR   But value dwells not in particular will.°   *individual desire*
It holds his° estimate and dignity   *its*
As well wherein 'tis precious of itself
55 As in the prizer. 'Tis mad idolatry
To make the service° greater than the god;   *the devotion paid*
And the will dotes that is inclinable
To what infectiously itself affects
Without some image of th'affected merit.[1]
60 TROILUS   I take today a wife, and my election°   *choice*
Is led on in the conduct° of my will;   *under the guidance*
My will enkindled by mine eyes and ears,
Two traded° pilots 'twixt the dangerous shores   *experienced*
Of will and judgement. How may I avoid—
65 Although my will distaste what it elected—
The wife I chose? There can be no evasion
To blench° from this and to stand firm by honour.   *shy away*
We turn not back° the silks upon° the merchant   *don't return / to*
When we have spoiled them; nor the remainder viands°   *uneaten food*
70 We do not throw in unrespective° sewer   *undiscriminating*
Because we now are full. It was thought meet°   *appropriate that*
Paris should do some vengeance on the Greeks.
Your breath of full consent bellied° his sails;   *swelled*
The seas and winds, old wranglers,° took a truce   *opponents*
75 And did him service. He touched the ports desired,
And for an old aunt whom the Greeks held captive[2]
He brought a Grecian queen,° whose youth and freshness   *pun on quean = whore?*

---

7. You rationalize your desire for comfort.
8. Messenger of the gods, usually pictured with wings on his heels. Mercury was once arraigned before Jove for stealing cattle and was ordered to go and return them.
9. That is, no absolute measure of value exists; there is only the esteem granted to an object by particular individuals.
1. *the will . . . merit:* the will is foolishly obsessed that is committed to what it likes in a sick way (having caught this desire like a disease), without some conception of that object's real value. The point is related to Jesus' attack on the scribes and Pharisees in Matthew 23, for instance verse 19: "whether is greater, the offering, or the altar which sanctifieth the offering?"
2. Hesione, Priam's sister, kidnapped by the Greeks; "aunt" is also slang for "whore." The "vengeance" (line 72) is for the kidnapping.

Wrinkles Apollo's and makes stale the morning.[3]
Why keep we her? The Grecians keep our aunt.
80   Is she worth keeping? Why, she is a pearl
Whose price hath launched above a thousand ships[4]
And turned crowned kings to merchants.
If you'll avouch 'twas wisdom Paris went—
As you must needs, for you all cried, 'Go, go!';
85   If you'll confess he brought home noble prize—
As you must needs, for you all clapped your hands
And cried, 'Inestimable!'—why do you now
The issue° of your proper° wisdoms rate,°   result / own / berate
And do a deed that never fortune did:[5]
90   Beggar the estimation[6] which you prized
Richer than sea and land? O theft most base,
That we have stol'n what we do fear to keep!
But thieves unworthy of a thing so stol'n,
That in their country did them that disgrace
95   We fear to warrant in our native place.[7]
CASSANDRA [within]
Cry, Trojans, cry!
PRIAM   What noise? What shriek is this?
TROILUS   'Tis our mad sister. I do know her voice.
CASSANDRA [within]   Cry, Trojans!
HECTOR   It is Cassandra.

Enter CASSANDRA[8] *raving, with her hair about her ears*

100   CASSANDRA   Cry, Trojans, cry! Lend me ten thousand eyes
And I will fill them with prophetic tears.
HECTOR   Peace, sister, peace.
CASSANDRA   Virgins and boys, mid-age, and wrinkled old,°   old people
Soft infancy that nothing canst° but cry,   can do
105   Add to my clamours. Let us pay betimes°   in advance
A moiety° of that mass° of moan to come.   portion / sum
Cry, Trojans, cry! Practise your eyes with tears.°   Learn to weep
Troy must not be, nor goodly Ilium stand.
Our firebrand[9] brother, Paris, burns us all.
110   Cry, Trojans, cry! Ah Helen, and ah woe!
Cry, cry 'Troy burns!'—or else let Helen go.   *Exit*
HECTOR   Now, youthful Troilus, do not these high strains
Of divination in our sister work
Some touches of remorse? Or is your blood
115   So madly hot that no discourse of reason,
Nor fear of bad success° in a bad cause,   outcome
Can qualify° the same?   moderate
TROILUS   Why, brother Hector,
We may not think the justness of each act
Such and no other than the event doth form it,[1]

---

3. Helen's "youth and freshness" by comparison make Apollo's (hence also the sun's) "youth and freshness" seem old and rosy dawn seem dried out (but also, unintentionally on Troilus's part, sluttish).
4. A well-worn phrase even when Marlowe used it in *Doctor Faustus:* "Was this the face that launched a thousand ships?" Here given a mercantile turn.
5. And act more erratically than fortune.
6. Deem worthless the valued object.
7. *That . . . place:* (We Trojans) who in Greece dishon-

ored the Greeks but back home are afraid to stand up for what we did.
8. Apollo gave Cassandra the gift of prophecy to win her love, but because she rejected his wooing, he cursed her by causing her prophecies to be disregarded.
9. When pregnant with Paris, Hecuba dreamed of giving birth to a firebrand.
1. *We . . . it:* We must not judge the "justness" of our cause only by the results.

120 Nor once deject° the courage of our minds	*reduce*
Because Cassandra's mad. Her brainsick raptures	
Cannot distaste° the goodness of a quarrel	*make distasteful*
Which hath our several honours all engaged	
To make it gracious.° For my private part,	*righteous; successful*
125 I am no more touched° than all Priam's sons.	*implicated*

And Jove forbid there should be done amongst us
Such things as might offend the weakest spleen
To fight for and maintain.[2]

PARIS   Else might the world convince° of levity   *convict*
130   As well my undertakings as your counsels.
         But I attest° the gods, your full consent   *call to witness*
         Gave wings to my propension° and cut off   *leaning*
         All fears attending on so dire a project.
         For what, alas, can these my single arms?°   *can my arms do alone*
135   What propugnation° is in one man's valour   *defense*
         To stand the push° and enmity of those   *thrust*
         This quarrel would excite?° Yet I protest,   *incite to battle*
         Were I alone to pass° the difficulties   *endure*
         And had as ample power as I have will,
140   Paris should ne'er retract what he hath done
         Nor faint in the pursuit.

PRIAM   Paris, you speak
         Like one besotted° on your sweet delights.   *drunk*
         You have the honey still, but these the gall.
         So° to be valiant is no praise at all.   *In such circumstances*
145 PARIS   Sir, I propose not merely to myself°   *for my own benefit*
         The pleasures such a beauty brings with it,
         But I would have the soil of her fair rape[3]
         Wiped off in honourable keeping her.
         What treason were it to the ransacked° queen,   *carried off as plunder*
150   Disgrace to your great worths, and shame to me,
         Now to deliver her possession up
         On terms of base compulsion? Can it be
         That so degenerate a strain° as this   *impulse*
         Should once set footing in your generous° bosoms?   *noble*
155   There's not the meanest spirit on our party
         Without a heart to dare or sword to draw
         When Helen is defended; nor none so noble
         Whose life were ill bestowed or death unfamed
         Where Helen is the subject. Then I say:
160   Well may we fight for her whom we know well
         The world's large spaces cannot parallel.

HECTOR   Paris and Troilus, you have both said well,
         But on the cause and question now in hand
         Have glossed° but superficially—not much   *commented*
165   Unlike young men, whom Aristotle thought
         Unfit to hear moral philosophy.[4]
         The reasons you allege do more conduce
         To the hot passion of distempered blood
         Than to make up a free determination

---

2. *And Jove . . . maintain:* We ("Priam's sons") shouldn't undertake something unless even the least courageous of us is willing to fight to defend it.
3. The defilement (of Helen or Paris, or both) resulting from her proper (also, beautiful) abduction (also, sexual violation).
4. Political philosophy. This is an anachronistic reference to Aristotle's *Nicomachean Ethics* 1.3.

170 'Twixt right and wrong; for pleasure and revenge
Have ears more deaf than adders⁵ to the voice
Of any true decision. Nature craves
All dues be rendered to their owners. Now,
What nearer debt in all humanity
175 Than wife is to the husband? If this law
Of nature be corrupted through affection,°   lust
And that great minds, of partial° indulgence   though prejudiced
To their benumbèd° wills, resist the same,   dulled
There is a law in each well-ordered nation
180 To curb those raging appetites that are
Most disobedient and refractory.°   stubborn
If Helen then be wife to Sparta's king,
As it is known she is, these moral laws
Of nature and of nations speak aloud
185 To have her back returned. Thus to persist
In doing wrong extenuates not wrong,
But makes it much more heavy. Hector's opinion
Is this in way of° truth—yet ne'ertheless,   with respect to
My sprightly° brethren, I propend° to you   spirited / incline
190 In resolution to keep Helen still;
For 'tis a cause that hath no mean dependence
Upon our joint and several° dignities.   separate
TROILUS   Why, there you touched the life of our design.
Were it not glory that we more affected°   desired
195 Than the performance of our heaving spleens,°   acting on our anger
I would not wish a drop of Trojan blood
Spent more in her defence. But, worthy Hector,
She is a theme of honour and renown,
A spur to valiant and magnanimous° deeds,   noble
200 Whose present courage may beat down our foes,
And fame in time to come canonize° us—   glorify
For I presume brave Hector would not lose
So rich advantage of a promised glory
As smiles upon the forehead° of this action   countenance
For the wide world's revenue.
205 HECTOR   I am yours,
You valiant offspring of great Priamus.
I have a roisting° challenge sent amongst   boisterous
The dull and factious nobles of the Greeks
Will shriek amazement to their drowsy spirits.
210 I was advertised their great general⁶ slept
Whilst emulation° in the army crept;   jealous rivalry
This I presume will wake him.   [Flourish.] Exeunt

2.3

Enter THERSITES
THERSITES   How now, Thersites? What, lost in the labyrinth of
thy fury? Shall the elephant Ajax carry it° thus? He beats me   get away with it
and I rail at him. O worthy satisfaction! Would it were other-

---

5. Adders were proverbially deaf. See Psalms 58:4–5:
"like the deaf adder that stoppeth his ear. Which heareth
not the voice of the enchanter, though he be most expert

in charming."
6. I was told that Achilles (Agamemnon?) slept.
2.3 Location: The Greek camp, outside Achilles' tent.

wise: that I could beat him whilst he railed at me. 'Sfoot,° I'll
5 learn to conjure and raise devils but I'll see some issue of my
spiteful execrations.¹ Then there's Achilles: a rare engineer.² If
Troy be not taken till these two undermine it, the walls will
stand till they fall of themselves. O thou great thunder-darter of
Olympus, forget that thou art Jove, the king of gods; and Mer-
10 cury, lose all the serpentine craft of thy caduceus,³ if ye take
not that little, little, less than little wit from them that they
have—which short-armed ignorance⁴ itself knows is so abundant—scarce it will not in circumvention° deliver a fly from a
spider without drawing their massy irons° and cutting the web.
15 After this, the vengeance on the whole camp—or rather, the
Neapolitan bone-ache,° for that methinks is the curse depen-
dent° on those that war for a placket.⁵ I have said my prayers,
and devil Envy say 'Amen'.—What ho! My lord Achilles!

Enter PATROCLUS [*at the door to the tent*]

PATROCLUS Who's there? Thersites? Good Thersites, come in
20 and rail.   [*Exit*]
THERSITES If I could ha' remembered a gilt counterfeit, thou
wouldst not have slipped out of my contemplation;⁶ but it is no
matter. Thyself upon thyself!⁷ The common curse of mankind,
folly and ignorance, be thine in great revenue!° Heaven bless°
25 thee from a tutor, and discipline come not near thee! Let thy
blood° be thy direction° till thy death! Then if she that lays thee
out says thou art a fair corpse, I'll be sworn and sworn upon't
she never shrouded any but lazars.°

[*Enter* PATROCLUS]

Amen.—Where's Achilles?
30 PATROCLUS What, art thou devout? Wast thou in prayer?
THERSITES Ay. The heavens hear me!
PATROCLUS Amen.

Enter ACHILLES

ACHILLES Who's there?
PATROCLUS Thersites, my lord.
35 ACHILLES Where? Where? O where?—Art thou come? Why,
my cheese,° my digestion, why hast thou not served thyself
into my table so many meals? Come: what's Agamemnon?
THERSITES Thy commander, Achilles.—Then tell me, Patroclus, what's Achilles?
40 PATROCLUS Thy lord, Thersites. Then tell me, I pray thee,
what's Thersites?
THERSITES Thy knower, Patroclus. Then tell me, Patroclus,
what art thou?
PATROCLUS Thou mayst tell, that knowest.
45 ACHILLES O tell, tell.
THERSITES I'll decline the whole question.⁸ Agamemnon com-

Right margin glosses:
God's foot
craftiness
swords
syphilis
impending
amounts / save
lust / guide
lepers; sick bodies
digestive aid

---

1. *but I'll . . . execrations:* if I must, in order to get tangible results from my contemptuous curses. "Spiteful"
keeps its unintended sense of "malicious."
2. Constructor of military earthworks and machines.
3. Mercury's emblem, a rod entwined by snakes.
Known for "craft," Mercury was the patron of thieves.
4. Ignorance is "short-armed" because most things are
beyond its grasp.
5. Petticoat; woman; woman's genitalia (obscene).

6. If I could have remembered a fake gold coin (worthless
Patroclus), you wouldn't have been forgotten (punning on
"slip," a counterfeit coin) in my devout meditation (which
focused on Ajax and Achilles, but only to curse them).
7. To be Patroclus is the worst possible fate—hence,
Thersites' curse on him is to be himself.
8. I'll recite in order the entire subject under investigation. "Decline," "Derive" (line 55), and "positive" (line
58) are all grammatical terms.

mands Achilles, Achilles is my lord, I am Patroclus' knower,
and Patroclus is a fool.

PATROCLUS You rascal.

50 THERSITES Peace, fool, I have not done.

ACHILLES [to PATROCLUS] He is a privileged man.[9]—Proceed,
Thersites.

THERSITES Agamemnon is a fool, Achilles is a fool, Thersites is
a fool, and as aforesaid Patroclus is a fool.

55 ACHILLES Derive this.° Come.   *Show your reasoning*

THERSITES Agamemnon is a fool to offer to command Achilles;
Achilles is a fool to be commanded of Agamemnon; Thersites
is a fool to serve such a fool; and Patroclus is a fool positive.°   *absolute*

PATROCLUS Why am I a fool?

60 THERSITES Make that demand to the Creator. It suffices me
thou art. Look you, who comes here?

  Enter AGAMEMNON, ULYSSES, NESTOR, DIOMEDES, AJAX,
    and CALCHAS

ACHILLES Patroclus, I'll speak with nobody.—Come in with me,
Thersites.   *Exit*

THERSITES Here is such patchery,° such juggling° and such   *foolery / deception*
65 knavery. All the argument is a whore and a cuckold. A good
quarrel to draw[1] emulous° factions and bleed to death upon.   *envious*
Now the dry serpigo° on the subject, and war and lechery con-   *skin disease*
found all.   [*Exit*]

AGAMEMNON [to PATROCLUS] Where is Achilles?

70 PATROCLUS Within his tent; but ill-disposed,° my lord.   *unwell; bad-tempered*

AGAMEMNON Let it be known to him that we are here.
He faced° our messengers, and we lay by   *bullied*
Our appertainments,° visiting of him.   *rights of rank*
Let him be told so, lest perchance he think

75 We dare not move the question of our place,°   *assert our authority*
Or know not what we are.

PATROCLUS   I shall so say to him.   [*Exit*]

ULYSSES We saw him at the opening of his tent.
He is not sick.

AJAX Yes, lion-sick:° sick of proud heart. You may call it 'melan-   *sick with pride*
80 choly'[2] if you will favour the man, but by my head 'tis pride.
But why? Why? Let him show us the cause. [*To* AGAMEMNON]
A word, my lord.

    [AJAX *and* AGAMEMNON *talk apart*]

NESTOR What moves Ajax thus to bay at him?

ULYSSES Achilles hath inveigled° his fool from him.   *enticed away*

85 NESTOR Who? Thersites?

ULYSSES He.

NESTOR Then will Ajax lack matter,[3] if he have lost his argument.°   *subject matter*

ULYSSES No, you see, he *is* his argument that *has* his argument:[4]
90 Achilles.

NESTOR All the better—their fraction° is more our wish than   *division*

---

9. An acknowledged fool could speak with impunity.
1. Attract to itself, like a magnet; extract, like a sword;
tear to pieces; drag to execution.
2. A fashionable philosophical malady.
3. Something to say; sense; pus.

4. Achilles is the person who is Ajax's argument. Since
Achilles has taken Thersites (who used to be Ajax's object
of derision) as the object of his derision, Ajax has transferred his scorn from Thersites to Achilles.

their faction.° But it was a strong council that a fool could dis-   *union in rebellion*
unite.°   *(ironic)*

ULYSSES   The amity that wisdom knits not, folly may easily untie.
    Enter PATROCLUS

95   Here comes Patroclus.

NESTOR   No Achilles with him.

ULYSSES   The elephant hath joints, but none for courtesy:[5] his
legs are legs for necessity, not for flexure.°   *bending*

PATROCLUS [*to* AGAMEMNON]   Achilles bids me say he is much sorry

100   If anything more than your sport and pleasure
Did move your greatness and this noble state°   *company*
To call upon him. He hopes it is no other
But for your health and your digestion's sake:
An after-dinner's breath.°   *exercise*

AGAMEMNON   Hear you, Patroclus.

105   We are too well acquainted with these answers.
But his evasion, winged thus swift with scorn,
Cannot outfly° our apprehensions.°   *escape / understanding*
Much attribute° he hath, and much the reason   *reputation*
Why we ascribe it to him. Yet all his virtues,

110   Not virtuously on his own part beheld,
Do in our eyes begin to lose their gloss,
Yea, and like fair fruit in an unwholesome dish
Are like to rot untasted. Go and tell him
We come to speak with him—and you shall not sin

115   If you do say we think him over-proud
And under-honest, in self-assumption° greater   *his own opinion*
Than in the note of judgement. And worthier than himself
Here tend° the savage strangeness° he puts on,   *wait on / aloofness*
Disguise the holy strength of their command,

120   And underwrite in an observing kind°   *submit compliantly to*
His humorous predominance[6]—yea, watch
His pettish lunes,[7] his ebbs, his flows, as if
The passage and whole carriage° of this action   *means and ends*
Rode on his tide. Go tell him this, and add

125   That if he overhold° his price so much   *overestimate*
We'll none of him, but let him, like an engine
Not portable, lie under this report:
'Bring action hither, this cannot go to war.'
A stirring° dwarf we do allowance give   *bustling*

130   Before a sleeping giant. Tell him so.

PATROCLUS   I shall, and bring his answer presently.°   *immediately*

AGAMEMNON   In second voice° we'll not be satisfied;   *By proxy (Patroclus)*
We come to speak with him.—Ulysses, enter you.
    Exit ULYSSES [*with* PATROCLUS]

AJAX   What is he more than another?

135 AGAMEMNON   No more than what he thinks he is.[8]

AJAX   Is he so much? Do you not think he thinks himself a better
man than I am?

AGAMEMNON   No question.

---

5. The elephant's supposed lack of knee joints made it resemble a proud, unbowing man.
6. His idiosyncratic assumption of superiority; the domination of one particular "humor" (temperament)—pride.
7. His fits of madness (caused by the moon's changing

phases; as the moon also produces sea tides, hence "ebbs," "flows," and "tide," lines 122, 124). "Lunes" is an editorial emendation of F's "lines."
8. He's the only one with a high opinion of him; he's worth as much as he thinks he is.

AJAX   Will you subscribe his thought, and say he is?

140 AGAMEMNON   No, noble Ajax. You are as strong, as valiant, as
wise, no less noble, much more gentle, and altogether more
tractable.

AJAX   Why should a man be proud? How doth pride grow? I
know not what it is.

145 AGAMEMNON   Your mind is the clearer, Ajax, and your virtues
the fairer. He that is proud eats up himself. Pride is his own
glass,° his own trumpet, his own chronicle—and whatever   *its own mirror*
praises itself but in the deed devours the deed in the praise.[9]

Enter ULYSSES

AJAX   I do hate a proud man as I hate the engendering° of toads.   *mating*

150 NESTOR [*aside*]   Yet he loves himself. Is't not strange?

ULYSSES   Achilles will not to the field tomorrow.

AGAMEMNON   What's his excuse?

ULYSSES   He doth rely on none,
But carries on the stream of his dispose°   *disposition*
Without observance or respect of any,

155 In will peculiar and in self-admission.[1]

AGAMEMNON   Why, will he not, upon our fair request,
Untent his person and share the air with us?

ULYSSES   Things small as nothing, for request's sake only,[2]
He makes important. Possessed° he is with greatness,   *Bewitched*

160 And speaks not to himself but with a pride
That quarrels at self-breath.[3] Imagined worth
Holds in his blood such swoll'n and hot discourse
That 'twixt his mental and his active parts
Kingdomed Achilles[4] in commotion° rages   *insurrection*

165 And batters 'gainst himself. What should I say?
He is so plaguy proud that the death tokens of it[5]
Cry 'No recovery'.

AGAMEMNON   Let Ajax go to him.
[*To* AJAX] Dear lord, go you and greet him in his tent.
'Tis said he holds you well and will be led,

170 At your request, a little from himself.°   *from his self-conceit*

ULYSSES   O Agamemnon, let it not be so.
We'll consecrate the steps that Ajax makes
When they go from Achilles. Shall the proud lord
That bastes his arrogance with his own seam[6]

175 And never suffers matter° of the world   *the affairs*
Enter his thoughts, save° such as do revolve   *except*
And ruminate° himself—shall he be worshipped   *turn on*
Of that° we hold an idol more than he?   *By one who*
No, this thrice-worthy and right valiant lord

180 Must not so stale his palm,° nobly acquired,   *sully his honor*
Nor by my will assubjugate° his merit,   *reduce to subjection*
As amply titled as Achilles' is,
By going to Achilles—
That were to enlard his fat-already pride

---

9. Whatever self-praise arises except from silently performing the noble deed itself destroys the deed by the act
of praising it.
1. In self-will and in acknowledgment of only his own
authority.
2. Merely because they are asked for.
3. *And . . . self-breath:* Achilles is not even satisfied with

what he himself has to say in praise of his merits; he is too
proud to talk even to himself.
4. Achilles' body is imagined as a state at civil war.
5. He is so annoyingly (diseasedly) proud that the fatal
signs of plague.
6. Fat; appearance. Achilles is accused of feeding self-
flattery to his already inflated arrogance.

185 And add more coals to Cancer[7] when he burns
With entertaining great Hyperion.° *the sun*
This lord go to him? Jupiter forbid,
And say in thunder 'Achilles, go to him'.
NESTOR [*aside to* DIOMEDES] O this is well. He rubs the vein of him.° *stirs up Ajax*
190 DIOMEDES [*aside to* NESTOR] And how his silence drinks up this applause.
AJAX If I go to him, with my armèd fist
I'll pash° him o'er the face. *smash*
AGAMEMNON   O no, you shall not go.
AJAX An a° be proud with me, I'll feeze° his pride. *If he / take care of*
Let me go to him.
195 ULYSSES Not for the worth that hangs upon our quarrel.° *(with Troy)*
AJAX A paltry insolent fellow.
NESTOR [*aside*] How he describes himself!
AJAX Can he not be sociable?
ULYSSES [*aside*] The raven chides blackness.
200 AJAX I'll let his humour's blood.[8]
AGAMEMNON [*aside*] He will be the physician that should be the
patient.
AJAX An all men were o' my mind—
ULYSSES [*aside*] Wit would be out of fashion.
205 AJAX A should not bear it so. A should eat swords[9] first. Shall
pride carry it?
NESTOR [*aside*] An't would, you'd carry half.
AJAX A would have ten shares.[1]
ULYSSES [*aside*] I will knead him; I'll make him supple.° He's *compliant*
210 not yet through warm.[2]
NESTOR [*aside*] Farce° him with praises. Pour in, pour in! His *Stuff; sauce*
ambition is dry.° *thirsty*
ULYSSES [*to* AGAMEMNON] My lord, you feed too much on this dislike.
NESTOR [*to* AGAMEMNON] Our noble general, do not do so.
215 DIOMEDES [*to* AGAMEMNON] You must prepare to fight without Achilles.
ULYSSES Why, 'tis this naming of him° does him harm. *(as our sole hope)*
Here is a man°—but 'tis before his face. *Ajax*
I will be silent.
NESTOR   Wherefore should you so?
He is not emulous,° as Achilles is. *hungry for praise*
220 ULYSSES Know the whole world he is as valiant—
AJAX A whoreson dog, that shall palter° thus with us—would he *deal evasively*
were a Trojan!
NESTOR What a vice were it in Ajax now—
ULYSSES If he were proud—
DIOMEDES   Or covetous of praise—
ULYSSES Ay, or surly borne—
225 DIOMEDES   Or strange,° or self-affected.° *aloof / egotistical*
ULYSSES [*to* AJAX] Thank the heavens, lord, thou art of sweet
composure.° *temperament*

7. And add fuel to the fire. Cancer is the sign of the Zodiac that begins on June 21—hence, a symbol of summer heat.
8. I'll cure his illness (pride) by bloodletting, as a doctor would to get rid of surplus humors.
9. He wouldn't carry on so. He would be defeated in combat (eat his words).
1. Probably alluding to the ten shares into which the Lord Chamberlain's Men's assets were divided—hence,

everything.
2. Warm all through. In F, the speech prefixes for lines 208–09 are reversed. In the arrangement printed here, Ajax's line refers to Achilles and Ulysses' to Ajax, whom Ulysses says he plans to manipulate further. In F's version, Ulysses gets the first line, which refers to Ajax, who in the next two lines describes what he'll do to Achilles. Q has still another approach, and additional variations are found in modern editions.

Praise him that got thee, she that gave thee suck.
Famed be thy tutor, and thy parts of nature°   *natural attributes*
Thrice famed beyond, beyond all erudition.[3]
230   But he that disciplined thine arms to fight—
And give him half. And for thy vigour,
Let Mars divide eternity in twain,
Bull-bearing Milo[4] his addition° yield   *reputation*
To sinewy Ajax. I will not praise thy wisdom,
235   Which like a bourn, a pale, a shore confines[5]
Thy spacious and dilated° parts. Here's Nestor,   *ample; famous*
Instructed by the antiquary° times: *ancient*
He must, he is, he cannot but be, wise.
But pardon, father Nestor: were your days
240   As green[6] as Ajax', and your brain so tempered,°   *composed*
You should not have the eminence of° him,   *be superior to*
But be as° Ajax.   *equal to*
AJAX   Shall I call you father?°   *guide*
ULYSSES   Ay, my good son.
DIOMEDES   Be ruled by him, Lord Ajax.
ULYSSES [*to* AGAMEMNON]   There is no tarrying here: the hart Achilles
245   Keeps thicket.° Please it our great general°   *stays home / Agamemnon*
To call together all his state° of war.   *council*
Fresh kings° are come today to Troy; tomorrow   *Reinforcements*
We must with all our main of power° stand fast.   *utmost strength*
And here's a lord, come knights from east to west°   *the whole world*
250   And cull their flower,[7] Ajax shall cope° the best.   *match*
AGAMEMNON   Go we to counsel. Let Achilles sleep.
Light boats sail swift, though greater hulks draw deep.[8] *Exeunt*

3.1

Music sounds within. Enter PANDARUS [*at one door*] *and*
a SERVANT [*at another door*]

PANDARUS   Friend? You. Pray you, a word. Do not you follow the
young Lord Paris?
SERVANT   Ay, sir, when he goes before me.
PANDARUS   You depend upon him,° I mean.   *serve him*
5   SERVANT   Sir, I do depend upon the Lord.°   *God; Paris*
PANDARUS   You depend upon a notable gentleman; I must needs
praise him.
SERVANT   The Lord be praised!
PANDARUS   You know me—do you not?
10   SERVANT   Faith, sir, superficially.
PANDARUS   Friend, know me better. I am the Lord Pandarus.
SERVANT   I hope I shall know your honour better.[1]
PANDARUS   I do desire it.

---

3. Ajax's glory exceeds anything scholars might say about it. Also ironic: learning constitutes no part of it.
4. Famous Greek athlete who bore a four-year-old bull on his shoulders.
5. Which like a boundary, a fence, a shore limits the uses of (probably ironic).
6. Young, fresh; immature; gullible.
7. And choose their best men.
8. We will progress more swiftly without Achilles (perhaps alluding to the famous success of "light" English ships against the "greater hulks" of the Spanish Armada). This line is doubly ironic: on the one hand, Ajax can hardly be called a "light boat"; on the other, the Greeks as a whole have already been associated with "deep-drawing" boats in the Prologue (line 12).
3.1 Location: Troy's palace.
1. I hope to get to know you better. I hope to learn of an improvement in your spiritual health. The double meaning here is typical of the servant's playful mockery of Pandarus, which partly contrasts Pandarus' secular concerns with more important, albeit anachronistic, Christian ones.

SERVANT   You are in the state of grace?[2]

15   PANDARUS   Grace? Not so, friend. 'Honour' and 'lordship' are my
titles. What music is this?

SERVANT   I do but partly know, sir. It is music in parts.

PANDARUS   Know you the musicians?

SERVANT   Wholly, sir.

20   PANDARUS   Who play they to?

SERVANT   To the hearers, sir.

PANDARUS   At whose pleasure, friend?

SERVANT   At mine, sir, and theirs that love music.

PANDARUS   'Command' I mean, friend.

25   SERVANT   Who shall I command, sir?

PANDARUS   Friend, we understand not one another. I am too
courtly and thou too cunning. At whose request do these men
play?

SERVANT   That's to't° indeed, sir. Marry, sir, at the request of   *to the point*

30   Paris my lord, who's there in person; with him, the mortal°   *living; fatal*
Venus, the heart-blood of beauty, love's visible soul°—   *love incarnate*

PANDARUS   Who, my cousin Cressida?

SERVANT   No, sir, Helen. Could not you find out that by her
attributes?

35   PANDARUS   It should seem, fellow, that thou hast not seen the
Lady Cressid. I come to speak with Paris from the Prince Troilus. I will make a complimental° assault upon him, for my busi-   *courteous*
ness seethes.°   *boils; is pressing*

SERVANT   Sodden business! There's a stewed[3] phrase, indeed.

Enter PARIS *and* HELEN *[attended by musicians]*

40   PANDARUS   Fair be to you, my lord, and to all this fair company.
Fair desires in all fair measure fairly guide them—especially
to you, fair Queen. Fair thoughts be your fair pillow.

HELEN   Dear lord, you are full of fair words.

PANDARUS   You speak your fair pleasure, sweet Queen. [*To* PARIS]

45   Fair prince, here is good broken music.[4]

PARIS   You have broke° it, cousin,[5] and by my life you shall make   *interrupted*
it whole again. You shall piece it out° with a piece of your   *repair it*
performance.° —Nell, he is full of harmony.   *performed by you*

PANDARUS   Truly, lady, no.

50   HELEN   O sir.

[*She tickles him*]

PANDARUS   Rude,° in sooth, in good sooth very rude.   *Unskilled; unmusical*

PARIS   Well said, my lord. Will you say so in fits?[6]

PANDARUS   I have business to my lord, dear Queen.—My lord,
will you vouchsafe me a word?

55   HELEN   Nay, this shall not hedge° us out. We'll hear you sing,   *keep*
certainly.

PANDARUS   Well, sweet Queen, you are pleasant with° me.—But   *teasing*
marry, thus, my lord: my dear lord and most esteemed friend,
your brother Troilus—

2. Theologically (deliberately misunderstanding Pandarus's "desire" in line 13 as a wish for moral improvement rather than social acquaintance). Pandarus
proceeds to misunderstand "grace" as the status of
being called "your grace" (a Duke's title).
3. "Stewed" (overdone, literally and metaphorically;
associated with stews, or brothels) puns on "sodden,"
which means "boiled" (picking up on "seethes," line 38);

is stupid; is drunk; is being treated for venereal disease.
4. Music for instruments of different kinds—for
example, strings and woodwind.
5. Kinsman (used especially by sovereigns to noblemen, whether or not related).
6. Would you please say (do you insist on saying) so in
sections of songs or music (fits and starts; spasms of
laughter)?

60 HELEN   My lord Pandarus, honey-sweet lord.

PANDARUS   Go to, sweet Queen, go to!—commends himself
most affectionately to you.

HELEN   You shall not bob° us out of our melody. If you do, our   *swindle*
melancholy⁷ upon your head.

65 PANDARUS   Sweet Queen, sweet Queen, that's a sweet Queen.
Ay, faith—

HELEN   And to make a sweet lady sad is a sour offence.

PANDARUS   Nay, that shall not serve your turn; that shall it not,
in truth, la. Nay, I care not for such words. No, no.—And, my
70 lord, he desires you that, if the King call for him at supper, you
will make his excuse.

HELEN   My lord Pandarus.

PANDARUS   What says my sweet Queen, my very very sweet
Queen?

75 PARIS   What exploit's in hand? Where sups he tonight?

HELEN   Nay, but my lord—

PANDARUS   What says my sweet Queen? My cousin will fall out
with you.⁸

HELEN [*to* PARIS]   You must not° know where he sups.   *are not supposed to*

80 PARIS   I'll lay my life, with my dispenser⁹ Cressida.

PANDARUS   No, no! No such matter. You are wide.° Come, your   *way off target*
dispenser is sick.

PARIS   Well, I'll make 's° excuse.   *his*

PANDARUS   Ay, good my lord. Why should you say Cressida? No,
85 your poor dispenser's sick.

PARIS   'I spy.'¹

PANDARUS   You spy? What do you spy?—[*To a musician*] Come,
give me an instrument.—Now, sweet Queen.

HELEN   Why, this is kindly done!

90 PANDARUS   My niece is horrible° in love with a thing you have,   *horribly*
sweet Queen.

HELEN   She shall have it, my lord—if it be not my lord Paris.

PANDARUS   He? No, she'll none of him. They two are twain.°   *estranged*

HELEN   Falling in,² after falling out,° may make them three.   *arguing*

95 PANDARUS   Come, come, I'll hear no more of this. I'll sing you a
song now.

HELEN   Ay, ay, prithee. Now by my troth, sweet lord, thou hast a
fine forehead.³

[*She strokes his forehead*]

PANDARUS   Ay, you may, you may.°   *(go on)*

100 HELEN   Let thy song be love. 'This love will undo us all.' O
Cupid, Cupid, Cupid!

PANDARUS   Love? Ay, that it shall,° i'faith.   *(be); (undo us)*

PARIS   Ay, good now,° 'Love, love, nothing but love'.   *please*

PANDARUS   In good truth, it° begins so.   *the song; love*

7. May our "melancholy" mood (supposedly cured by
music) be.
8. *What . . . you:* If you (Helen) keep interrupting, my
"cousin" Paris (as in line 46) will be angry with you; if
you keep inquiring about private affairs, my "cousin"
Cressida will be angry with you.
9. Excuser (of Troilus's failure to attend dinner); pro-
visioner (again, of dinner); bestower of (sexual) favors;
dispenser of cures (with "sick," lines 82, 85, a remedy

for Troilus's lovesickness). Here and in lines 82 and 85,
"dispenser" is an editorial emendation for "disposer," of
uncertain meaning but perhaps suggesting that Cressida can do what she likes with Troilus and Paris.
1. I understand (alluding to a child's game).
2. "Falling in" sexually, so as to produce a child.
3. Impudence; modesty; sign of male beauty; hint of
cuckoldry.

105 [*Sings*] Love, love, nothing but love, still° love, still more!   *always*
　　　For O love's bow
　　　Shoots buck and doe.°   *male and female*
　　　The shaft° confounds   *arrow; penis*
　　　Not that it wounds
110 But tickles still the sore.⁴
　　　　These lovers cry 'O! O!', they die.°   *perish; have an orgasm*
　　　　Yet that which seems the wound to kill°   *mortal wound*
　　　　Doth turn 'O! O!' to 'ha ha he!'⁵
　　　　So dying love lives still.
115 　　　'O! O!' a while, but 'ha ha ha!'
　　　　'O! O!' groans out for 'ha ha ha!'—

　　Heigh-ho.
　　HELEN　In love—ay, faith, to the very tip of the nose.
　　PARIS　He eats nothing but doves,° love, and that breeds hot   *emblem of true love*
120 　blood, and hot blood begets hot thoughts, and hot thoughts
　　beget hot deeds, and hot deeds is love.
　　PANDARUS　Is this the generation° of love: hot blood, hot thoughts,   *genealogy*
　　and hot deeds? Why, they are vipers. Is love a generation of
　　vipers?⁶
　　　　[*Alarum*]
125 　Sweet lord, who's afield today?
　　PARIS　Hector, Deiphobus, Helenus, Antenor, and all the gal-
　　lantry of Troy. I would fain have° armed today, but my Nell   *like to have*
　　would not have it so. How chance my brother Troilus went
　　not?
130 HELEN　He hangs the lip° at something. You know all, Lord Pan-   *looks despondent*
　　darus.
　　PANDARUS　Not I, honey-sweet Queen. I long to hear how they
　　sped today.— You'll remember your brother's excuse?
　　PARIS　To a hair.°   *Exactly*
135 PANDARUS　Farewell, sweet Queen.
　　HELEN　Commend me to your niece.
　　PANDARUS　I will, sweet Queen.   [*Exit*]
　　　　Sound a retreat
　　PARIS　They're come from field. Let us to Priam's hall
　　To greet the warriors. Sweet Helen, I must woo you
140 To help unarm our Hector. His stubborn buckles,
　　With these your white enchanting fingers touched,
　　Shall more obey than to the edge of steel°   *sword blade*
　　Or force of Greekish sinews. You shall do more
　　Than all the island kings:° disarm great Hector.   *Greek lords*
145 HELEN　'Twill make us proud to be his servant, Paris;
　　Yea, what he shall receive of us in duty
　　Gives us more palm in° beauty than we have—   *fame for*
　　Yea, overshines ourself.
　　PARIS　　　　　　　　　Sweet above thought, I love thee!
　　　　　　　　　　　　　　Exeunt

---

4. Wound; four-year-old buck.　　　　　　　　　　　to a biblical phrase—for instance, the "generation of
5. Turns pain to joy; turns ecstasy to derision.　　　vipers" in Matthew 23:33, promising damnation.
6. Anachronistic allusion, not intended by Pandarus,

3.2

Enter PANDARUS *[at one door] and Troilus'* MAN *[at another door]*

PANDARUS How now, where's thy master? At my cousin
Cressida's?

MAN No, sir, he stays for you to conduct him thither.

Enter TROILUS

PANDARUS O here he comes.—How now, how now?

5 TROILUS Sirrah, walk off.   [*Exit* MAN]

PANDARUS Have you seen my cousin?

TROILUS No, Pandarus, I stalk about her door
Like a strange° soul upon the Stygian banks   newly arrived
Staying for waftage.¹ O be thou my Charon,

10 And give me swift transportance to those fields²
Where I may wallow° in the lily beds   roll around
Proposed for° the deserver. O gentle Pandar,³   Promised to
From Cupid's shoulder pluck his painted° wings   brightly colored
And fly with me to Cressid.

15 PANDARUS Walk here i'th' orchard.° I'll bring her straight. *Exit*   garden

TROILUS I am giddy. Expectation whirls me round.
Th'imaginary relish° is so sweet   pleasant anticipation
That it enchants my sense. What will it be
When that the wat'ry° palates taste indeed   watering

20 Love's thrice-repurèd nectar?⁴ Death, I fear me,
Swooning destruction, or some joy too fine,°   exquisite
Too subtle-potent, tuned too sharp in sweetness°   (musically)
For the capacity of my ruder powers.
I fear it much, and I do fear besides

25 That I shall lose distinction° in my joys,   power to discriminate
As doth a battle° when they charge on heaps   army
The enemy flying.

Enter PANDARUS

PANDARUS She's making her ready. She'll come straight.° You   immediately
must be witty now. She does so blush, and fetches her wind° so   breath

30 short as if she were frayed with a spirit.⁵ I'll fetch her. It is the
prettiest villain!° She fetches her breath as short as a new-ta'en⁶   (affectionate)
sparrow.   *Exit*

TROILUS Even such a passion doth embrace my bosom.
My heart beats thicker° than a feverous pulse,   faster

35 And all my powers do their bestowing° lose,   function
Like vassalage at unawares° encount'ring   vassals unexpectedly
The eye of majesty.

Enter PANDARUS, *[with]* CRESSIDA *[veiled]*

PANDARUS [*to* CRESSIDA] Come, come, what need you blush?
Shame's a baby. [*To* TROILUS] Here she is now. Swear the oaths

40 now to her that you have sworn to me. [*To* CRESSIDA] What,
are you gone again? You must be watched ere you be made
tame,⁷ must you? Come your ways, come your ways. An you
draw backward, we'll put you i'th' thills.⁸ [*To* TROILUS] Why do

---

3.2 Location: Cressida's garden.
1. Waiting to be ferried across. The dead were carried across the river Styx into the underworld by the ferryman Charon.
2. The Elysian Fields, which were reserved for the blessed dead ("the deserver" line 12).
3. The shortened form of the name here helps define

Pandarus as a pander.
4. Thrice-purified drink of the gods (giving immortality).
5. Frightened by a ghost.
6. Just captured.
7. Hawks were kept awake at night to tame them.
8. If you back away, we'll back you, like a horse, into the shafts of a cart.

you not speak to her? [*To* CRESSIDA] Come, draw this curtain,
45 and let's see your picture.[9] [*He unveils her*] Alas the day! How
loath you are to offend daylight! An't were dark, you'd close° *agree; unite*
sooner. So, so. [*To* TROILUS] Rub on, and kiss the mistress.[1]
[*They kiss*] How now, a kiss in fee farm!° Build there, carpenter, *perpetual land tenure*
the air° is sweet. Nay, you shall fight your hearts out ere I part *her breath*
50 you. The falcon as the tercel,[2] for° all the ducks i'th' river. Go *I'd bet*
to, go to.
TROILUS You have bereft me of all words, lady.
PANDARUS Words pay no debts; give her deeds. But she'll
bereave you o'th' deeds° too, if she call your activity° in ques- *wear you out / virility*
55 tion. [*They kiss*] What, billing° again? Here's 'in witness *kissing*
whereof the parties interchangeably'.[3] Come in, come in. I'll
go get a fire.°   [*Exit*] *(for the bedroom)*
CRESSIDA Will you walk in, my lord?
TROILUS O Cressida, how often have I wished me thus.
60 CRESSIDA Wished, my lord? The gods grant—O, my lord!
TROILUS What should they grant? What makes this pretty abrup-
tion?° What too-curious dreg° espies my sweet lady in the foun- *pause / speck of dirt*
tain of our love?
CRESSIDA More dregs than water, if my fears have eyes.
65 TROILUS Fears make devils of cherubims;° they never see truly. *predict the worst*
CRESSIDA Blind fear, that seeing° reason leads, finds safer foot- *clear-sighted*
ing than blind reason, stumbling without fear. To fear the worst
oft cures the worse.
TROILUS O let my lady apprehend no fear. In all Cupid's pag-
70 eant there is presented no monster.
CRESSIDA Nor nothing monstrous neither?
TROILUS Nothing but our undertakings,° when we vow to weep *promises*
seas, live in fire, eat rocks, tame tigers, thinking it harder for
our mistress to devise imposition enough° than for us to *a big enough challenge*
75 undergo any difficulty imposed. This is the monstruosity in
love, lady—that the will is infinite and the execution confined;
that the desire is boundless and the act° a slave to limit. *(sex) act*
CRESSIDA They say all lovers swear more performance than they
are able, and yet reserve an ability that they never perform:
80 vowing more than the perfection of ten,° and discharging less *(lovers)*
than the tenth part of one. They that have the voice of lions
and the act of hares, are they not monsters?
TROILUS Are there such? Such are not we. Praise us as we are
tasted;° allow° us as we prove. Our head shall go bare till merit *tested / praise*
85 crown it. No perfection in reversion[4] shall have a praise in
present. We will not name desert° before his° birth, and being *mention merit / its*
born his addition° shall be humble. Few words to fair faith.[5] *title*
Troilus shall be such to Cressid as what envy can say worst
shall be a mock for his truth;[6] and what truth can speak truest,
90 not truer[7] than Troilus.
CRESSIDA Will you walk in, my lord?

9. Cressida's face is veiled. Pictures were curtained for
protection against light and dust.
1. Metaphor from the game of bowls: keep on course,
and touch gently the master ball (a small ball at which
bowls were aimed).
2. The female hawk as (eagerly as) the male.
3. A garbled version of a betrothal; also a contractual
legal formula completed by the words "have set their

hands and seals."
4. No perfection by right of eventual succession (like
lands or title)—hence, in the future.
5. Brevity goes with honesty (proverbial).
6. *as . . . truth:* that envy's most malicious comment on
Troilus can only be to mock him for constancy.
7. *not truer:* could not be more reliable.

Enter PANDARUS

PANDARUS   What, blushing still? Have you not done talking yet?

CRESSIDA   Well, uncle, what folly° I commit I dedicate to you.   *whatever indiscretion*

PANDARUS   I thank you for that. If my lord get a boy of you, you'll

95   give him me. Be true to my lord. If he flinch,° chide me for it.   *(sexually)*

TROILUS [*to* CRESSIDA]   You know now your hostages:° your uncle's   *pledges*
  word and my firm faith.

PANDARUS   Nay, I'll give my word for her too. Our kindred,
  though they be long ere they are wooed, they are constant

100   being won. They are burrs, I can tell you: they'll stick where
  they are thrown.°   *laid (sexual)*

CRESSIDA   Boldness comes to me now, and brings me heart.
  Prince Troilus, I have loved you night and day
  For many weary months.

105   TROILUS   Why was my Cressid then so hard to win?

CRESSIDA   Hard to seem won; but I was won, my lord,
  With the first glance that ever—pardon me:
  If I confess much, you will play the tyrant.
  I love you now, but till now not so much

110   But I might master it. In faith, I lie:
  My thoughts were like unbridled children, grown
  Too headstrong for their mother. See, we fools!
  Why have I blabbed? Who shall be true to us,°   *women*
  When we are so unsecret to ourselves?°   *betray ourselves*

115   But though I loved you well, I wooed you not—
  And yet, good faith, I wished myself a man,
  Or that we women had men's privilege
  Of speaking first. Sweet, bid me hold my tongue,
  For in this rapture I shall surely speak

120   The thing I shall repent. See, see, your silence,
  Cunning in dumbness, in my weakness draws
  My soul of counsel° from me. Stop my mouth.   *most secret thoughts*

TROILUS   And shall, albeit sweet music issues thence.
  [*He kisses her*]

PANDARUS   Pretty, i' faith.

125   CRESSIDA [*to* TROILUS]   My lord, I do beseech you pardon me.
  'Twas not my purpose thus to beg a kiss.
  I am ashamed. O heavens, what have I done?
  For this time will I take my leave, my lord.

TROILUS   Your leave, sweet Cressid?

130   PANDARUS   Leave? An you take leave till tomorrow morning—

CRESSIDA   Pray you, content you.°   *be quiet*

TROILUS   What offends you, lady?

CRESSIDA   Sir, mine own company.

TROILUS   You cannot shun yourself.

CRESSIDA   Let me go and try.

135   I have a kind of self resides with you—
  But an unkind° self, that itself will leave   *unnatural*
  To be another's fool. Where is my wit?
  I would be gone. I speak I know not what.

TROILUS   Well know they what they speak that speak so wisely.

140   CRESSIDA   Perchance, my lord, I show more craft° than love,   *cunning*
  And fell so roundly° to a large° confession   *openly / full*
  To angle for° your thoughts. But you are wise,   *fish for*

Or else you love not[8]—for to be wise and love
Exceeds man's might: that dwells with gods above.
145 TROILUS   O that I thought it could be in a woman—
As, if it can, I will presume in° you—   *it to be in*
To feed for aye° her lamp and flames of love,   *forever*
To keep her constancy in plight° and youth,   *health*
Outliving beauty's outward,° with a mind   *exterior*
150 That doth renew swifter than blood° decays;   *passion*
Or that persuasion could but thus convince me
That my integrity and truth to you
Might be affronted° with the match and weight°   *met / same amount*
Of such a winnowed[9] purity in love.
155 How were I then uplifted! But alas,
I am as true as truth's simplicity,°   *truth itself*
And simpler° than the infancy of truth.   *more naive*
CRESSIDA   In that I'll war° with you.   *compete*
TROILUS   O virtuous fight,
When right with right wars who shall be most right.
160 True swains in love shall in the world to come
Approve° their truth by Troilus. When their rhymes,   *Attest*
Full of protest,° of oath and big compare,[1]   *protestation*
Wants° similes, truth tired with iteration°—   *Lack / repetition*
'As true as steel, as plantage to the moon,[2]
165 As sun to day, as turtle° to her mate,   *turtledove*
As iron to adamant,° as earth to th' centre'[3]—   *a magnet*
Yet, after all comparisons of truth,
As truth's authentic author to be cited,
'As true as Troilus' shall crown up the verse
And sanctify the numbers.°   *verses*
170 CRESSIDA   Prophet may you be!
If I be false, or swerve a hair from truth,
When time is old and hath forgot itself,
When water drops have worn the stones of Troy
And blind oblivion swallowed cities up,
175 And mighty states characterless are grated[4]
To dusty nothing, yet let memory
From false° to false among false maids in love   *falsehood*
Upbraid my falsehood. When they've said, 'as false
As air, as water, wind or sandy earth,
180 As fox to lamb, or wolf to heifer's calf,
Pard° to the hind, or stepdame to her son',   *Panther; leopard*
Yea, let them say, to stick the heart° of falsehood,   *hit the bullseye*
'As false as Cressid'.
PANDARUS   Go to, a bargain made. Seal it, seal it. I'll be the wit-
185 ness. Here I hold your hand; here, my cousin's.[5] If ever you
prove false one to another, since I have taken such pain to
bring you together, let all pitiful goers-between be called to the
world's end after my name: call them all panders. Let all con-

---

8. Alternative explanations for why he has made no "large confession" (line 141).
9. Grain is "winnowed" (separated from worthless light chaff).
1. Exaggerated comparisons.
2. Plants were supposed to be affected in growth by the moon.
3. The earth's surface to the earth's center, or axis.
4. Are ground up unrecorded.
5. Taking hands before a witness could be regarded as a (civil) marriage.

stant men be Troiluses, all false women Cressids, and all
190 brokers-between° panders. Say 'Amen'.   *pimps*
TROILUS   Amen.
CRESSIDA   Amen.
PANDARUS   Amen. Whereupon I will show you a chamber with
a bed—which bed, because it shall not speak of your pretty
195 encounters, press it to death.[6] Away!
                              Exeunt [TROILUS *and* CRESSIDA]
And Cupid grant all tongue-tied maidens° here   *male or female virgins*
Bed, chamber, pander to provide this gear.°   *Exit*   *equipment*

3.3

Flourish. Enter ULYSSES, DIOMEDES, NESTOR, AGAMEM-
NON, MENELAUS, [AJAX,] *and* CALCHAS[1]

CALCHAS   Now, princes, for the service I have done you,
Th'advantage° of the time prompts me aloud   *opportunity*
To call for recompense. Appear° it to your mind   *Let it appear*
That through the sight I bear in things to come
5 I have abandoned Troy, left my profession,°   *priestly role*
Incurred a traitor's name, exposed myself
From certain and possessed conveniences
To doubtful fortunes, sequest'ring° from me all   *divorcing*
That time, acquaintance, custom, and condition°   *position*
10 Made tame° and most familiar to my nature,   *accustomed*
And here to do you service am become
As new into the world, strange, unacquainted.
I do beseech you, as in way of taste,°   *a foretaste*
To give me now a little benefit
15 Out of those many registered in promise°   *many promised things*
Which you say live to come° in my behalf.   *wait to be fulfilled*
AGAMEMNON   What wouldst thou of us, Trojan? Make demand.
CALCHAS   You have a Trojan prisoner called Antenor,
Yesterday took. Troy holds him very dear.
20 Oft have you—often have you thanks therefor°—   *for it*
Desired my Cressid in right great exchange,[2]
Whom Troy hath still denied. But this Antenor
I know is such a wrest[3] in their affairs
That their negotiations° all must slack,   *affairs of state*
25 Wanting his manage,° and they will almost   *guidance*
Give us a prince of blood,° a son of Priam,   *a royal prince*
In change of° him. Let him be sent, great princes,   *exchange for*
And he shall buy my daughter, and her presence
Shall quite strike off° all service I have done   *annul*
In most accepted° pain.   *willingly undertaken*
30 AGAMEMNON   Let Diomedes bear him,
And bring us Cressid hither; Calchas shall have
What he requests of us. Good Diomed,
Furnish you fairly° for this interchange;   *completely ready yourself*
Withal° bring word if Hector will tomorrow   *At the same time*
35 Be answered in his challenge. Ajax is ready.

---

6. Customary punishment for an accused person who
remained silent and would not plead.
3.3 Location: The Greek camp.
1. Calchas is Cressida's father, a Trojan priest siding
with the Greeks.

2. In return for someone important.
3. Tuning key for a stringed instrument (hence probably related to "slack," line 24); peg for tightening a sur-
gical ligature.

DIOMEDES   This shall I undertake, and 'tis a burden
Which I am proud to bear.   *Exit [with* CALCHAS]
        Enter ACHILLES *and* PATROCLUS *in their tent*
ULYSSES   Achilles stands i'th' entrance of his tent.
Please it our general pass strangely° by him,   *aloofly*
40 As if he were forgot; and, princes all,
Lay negligent and loose° regard upon him.   *casual*
I will come last. 'Tis like he'll question me
Why such unplausive° eyes are bent, why turned on him.   *unapproving*
If so, I have derision medicinable°   *health-giving scorn*
45 To use° between your strangeness and his pride,   *act as intermediary*
Which his own will shall have desire to drink.
It may do good. Pride hath no other glass
To show itself but pride;⁴ for supple knees°   *bowing and scraping*
Feed arrogance and are the proud man's fees.°   *expected reward*
50 AGAMEMNON   We'll execute your purpose and put on
A form° of strangeness as we pass along.   *appearance*
So do each lord, and either greet him not
Or else disdainfully, which shall shake him more
Than if not looked on. I will lead the way.
        [*They pass by the tent, in turn*]
55 ACHILLES   What, comes the general to speak with me?
You know my mind: I'll fight no more 'gainst Troy.
AGAMEMNON [*to* NESTOR]   What says Achilles? Would he aught with us?
NESTOR [*to* ACHILLES]   Would you, my lord, aught with the general?
ACHILLES   No.
NESTOR [*to* AGAMEMNON]   Nothing, my lord.
AGAMEMNON   The better.
        [*Exeunt* AGAMEMNON *and* NESTOR]
ACHILLES [*to* MENELAUS]   Good day, good day.
60 MENELAUS   How do you? How do you?   [*Exit*]
ACHILLES [*to* PATROCLUS]
What, does the cuckold scorn me?
AJAX   How now, Patroclus?
ACHILLES   Good morrow, Ajax.
AJAX   Ha?
ACHILLES   Good morrow.
AJAX   Ay, and good next day too.   *Exit*
ACHILLES [*to* PATROCLUS]   What mean these fellows? Know they
        not Achilles?
65 PATROCLUS   They pass by strangely. They were used to bend,
To send their smiles before them to Achilles,
To come as humbly as they use° to creep   *are accustomed*
To holy altars.
ACHILLES   What, am I poor° of late?   *insignificant*
'Tis certain, greatness once fall'n out with fortune
70 Must fall out with men too. What the declined is
He shall as soon read in the eyes of others
As feel in his own fall; for men, like butterflies,
Show not their mealy° wings but to the summer,   *powdery*
And not a man, for being simply man,
75 Hath any honour, but° honour for those honours   *but instead has*
That are without° him—as place, riches, and favour: *external to*

---

4. *Pride . . . pride:* A proud person recognizes excessive pride only when shown it in others.

	Prizes of accident° as oft as merit;	*that come by chance*
	Which, when they fall, as being slippery standers° —	*on an uncertain base*
	The love that leaned on them, as slippery too—	
80	Doth one° pluck down another, and together	*The one doth*
	Die in the fall. But 'tis not so with me.	
	Fortune and I are friends. I do enjoy	
	At ample point° all that I did possess,	*Fully*
	Save° these men's looks—who do methinks find out	*Except*
85	Something not worth in me such rich beholding°	*attention*
	As they have often given. Here is Ulysses;	
	I'll interrupt his reading. How now, Ulysses?	

ULYSSES Now, great Thetis' son.

ACHILLES What are you reading?

90 ULYSSES A strange fellow here

	Writes me that man, how dearly ever parted,°	*however valuably endowed*
	How much in having, or without or in,[5]	
	Cannot make boast to have that which he hath,	
	Nor feels not what he owes,° but by reflection—	*owns*
95	As when his virtues, shining upon others,	
	Heat them, and they retort° that heat again	*cast back*
	To the first givers.	

ACHILLES   This is not strange, Ulysses.

	The beauty that is borne here in the face	
	The bearer knows not, but commends itself	
100	To others' eyes. Nor doth the eye itself,	
	That most pure spirit of sense,° behold itself,	*of the five senses*
	Not going from itself; but eye to eye opposed	
	Salutes each other with each other's form.[6]	
	For speculation° turns not to itself	*sight*
105	Till it hath travelled and is mirrored there	
	Where it may see itself. This is not strange at all.	

	ULYSSES I do not strain at° the position° —	*question / thesis*
	It is familiar—but at the author's drift;	
	Who in his circumstance expressly° proves	*in detail explicitly*
110	That no man is the lord of anything,	
	Though in and of him there be much consisting,°	*value*
	Till he communicate his parts° to others.	*qualities*
	Nor doth he of himself know them for aught°	*as valuable*
	Till he behold them formèd in th'applause	
115	Where they're extended—who,° like an arch,° reverb'rate	*(the applauders) / vault*
	The voice again; or, like a gate of steel	
	Fronting° the sun, receives and renders back	*Facing*
	His figure° and his heat. I was much rapt in this,	*Its appearance*
	And apprehended here immediately	
120	The unknown Ajax.	
	Heavens, what a man is there! A very horse,	
	That has he knows not what.° Nature, what things there are,	*doesn't know himself*
	Most abject in regard and dear in use.°	*Despised but useful*
	What things again, most dear in the esteem	
125	And poor in worth. Now shall we see tomorrow	
	An act that very° chance doth throw upon him.	*pure*

5. However much he possesses, either externally or
internally.
6. *Not going . . . form*: Being unable to leave itself; but
two eyes (in two people), looking at each other, can
show both people their images.

Ajax renowned? O heavens, what some men do,
While some men leave to do.°   *leave undone*
How some men creep in skittish Fortune's hall
130 Whiles others play the idiots in her eyes;[7]
How one man eats into another's pride
While pride is fasting in his wantonness.[8]
To see these Grecian lords! Why, even already
They clap the lubber° Ajax on the shoulder,   *lout*
135 As if his foot were on brave Hector's breast
And great Troy shrinking.°   *cowering; declining*
ACHILLES   I do believe it,
For they passed by me as misers do by beggars,
Neither gave to me good word nor look.
What, are my deeds forgot?
  ULYSSES   Time hath, my lord,
140 A wallet° at his back, wherein he puts   *satchel*
Alms for oblivion, a great-sized monster[9]
Of ingratitudes. Those scraps are good deeds past,
Which are devoured as fast as they are made,
Forgot as soon as done. Perseverance, dear my lord,
145 Keeps honour bright. To have done° is to hang   *rely on past deeds*
Quite out of fashion, like a rusty mail°   *coat of armor*
In monumental mock'ry.° Take the instant way,   *a useless monument*
For honour travels in a strait so narrow,
Where one but goes abreast.° Keep then the path,   *must go single file*
150 For emulation hath a thousand sons
That one by one pursue: if you give way,
Or hedge aside from the direct forthright,°   *straightforward path*
Like to an entered tide they all rush by
And leave you hindmost;
155 Or, like a gallant horse fall'n in first rank,
Lie there for pavement to the abject rear,°   *worthless rearguard*
O'errun and trampled on. Then what they do in present,
Though less than yours in past, must o'ertop yours.
For Time is like a fashionable host,
160 That slightly shakes his parting guest by th' hand
And, with his arms outstretched as he would° fly,   *as if he wanted to*
Grasps in the comer. Welcome ever smiles,
And Farewell goes out sighing. O let not virtue seek
Remuneration for the thing it was;
165 For beauty, wit,
High birth, vigour of bone,° desert in service,°   *strength / worthiness*
Love, friendship, charity, are subjects all
To envious and calumniating time.
One touch of nature° makes the whole world kin°—   *natural fault / similar*
170 That all with one consent praise new-born gauds,°   *toys*
Though they are made and moulded of things past,
And give to dust that is a little gilt°   *gilded*
More laud than gilt o'er-dusted.°   *older treasures*
The present eye praises the present object.
175 Then marvel not, thou great and complete man,

---

7. While others act like fools to get Fortune's attention; do nothing to get Fortune's attention.
8. While the second man in effect starves his pride, and hence his reputation, through his odd behavior.

9. *Alms for oblivion:* Feats that won't be remembered. Traditionally, if you wore your satchel behind you, it contained your vices, which you in this way forgot. *monster:* time or, more likely, oblivion.

That all the Greeks begin to worship Ajax,
Since things in motion sooner catch the eye
Than what not stirs. The cry° went once on thee,   *approval*
And still it might, and yet it may again,
180   If thou wouldst not entomb thyself alive
And case° thy reputation in thy tent,   *shut up*
Whose glorious deeds but in these fields of late
Made emulous missions 'mongst the gods themselves,[1]
And drove great Mars to faction.°   *to take sides*
ACHILLES   Of this my privacy
I have strong reasons.
185   ULYSSES   But 'gainst your privacy
The reasons are more potent and heroical.
'Tis known, Achilles, that you are in love
With one of Priam's daughters.°   *Polyxena*
ACHILLES   Ha? Known?
ULYSSES   Is that a wonder?
The providence that's in a watchful state[2]
190   Knows almost every grain of Pluto's[3] gold,
Finds bottom in th'uncomprehensive° deeps,   *unimaginable*
Keeps place with aught,[4] and almost like the gods
Do infant thoughts unveil in their dumb cradles.[5]
There is a mystery, with whom relation°   *report*
195   Durst never meddle, in the soul of state,
Which hath an operation more divine
Than breath or pen can give expressure° to.   *expression*
All the commerce° that you have had with Troy   *dealings*
As perfectly is ours as yours,[6] my lord;
200   And better would it fit Achilles much
To throw down° Hector than Polyxena.   *(in war); (in love)*
But it must grieve young Pyrrhus° now at home,   *Achilles' son*
When fame shall in his island sound her trump
And all the Greekish girls shall tripping sing,
205   'Great Hector's sister did Achilles win,
But our great Ajax bravely beat down *him*'.°   *(Hector)*
Farewell, my lord. I as your lover° speak.   *good friend*
The fool slides o'er the ice that you should break.[7]   *[Exit]*
PATROCLUS   To this effect, Achilles, have I moved you.
210   A woman impudent° and mannish grown   *immodest*
Is not more loathed than an effeminate° man   *cowardly*
In time of action. I stand condemned for this.
They think my little stomach to° the war   *appetite for*
And your great love to me restrains you thus.
215   Sweet, rouse yourself, and the weak wanton Cupid
Shall from your neck unloose his amorous fold°   *embrace*
And like a dew-drop from the lion's mane
Be shook to air.
ACHILLES   Shall Ajax fight with Hector?
PATROCLUS   Ay, and perhaps receive much honour by him.

---

1. Caused the gods to join the fight on both sides in an effort to match Achilles.
2. Government foresight is compared to divine "providence"—perhaps ironically.
3. God of the underworld (regularly identified with Plutus, god of wealth).
4. Stays abreast of everything.

5. *Do . . . cradles:* Discovers thoughts before they are spoken.
6. Is as well known to us (the other Greek leaders) as to you.
7. Perhaps: Ajax (the fool) is engaged in superficial action, whereas only you can initiate real combat.

220	ACHILLES I see my reputation is at stake.	
	My fame is shrewdly gored.°	*severely wounded*
	PATROCLUS O then beware:	

ACHILLES   I see my reputation is at stake.
My fame is shrewdly gored.°   *severely wounded*
PATROCLUS   O then beware:
Those wounds heal ill that men do give themselves.
Omission to do what is necessary
Seals a commission to a blank of danger,[8]
225   And danger like an ague subtly taints
Even then when we sit idly in the sun.[9]
ACHILLES   Go call Thersites hither, sweet Patroclus.
I'll send the fool to Ajax, and desire him
T'invite the Trojan lords after the combat
230   To see us here unarmed. I have a woman's longing,
An appetite that I am sick withal,°   *with*
To see great Hector in his weeds° of peace,   *garments*
      Enter THERSITES
To talk with him and to behold his visage
Even to my full of view.°—A labour saved.   *in full view*
235   THERSITES   A wonder!
ACHILLES   What?
THERSITES   Ajax goes up and down the field, as° asking for him-   *as if*
self.[1]
ACHILLES   How so?
240   THERSITES   He must° fight singly tomorrow with Hector, and is   *is to*
so prophetically proud of an heroical cudgelling° that he raves   *(by Hector)*
in saying nothing.
ACHILLES   How can that be?
THERSITES   Why, a° stalks up and down like a peacock—a stride   *he*
245   and a stand; ruminates like an hostess that hath no arithmetic
but her brain to set down her reckoning;[2] bites his lip with a
politic regard,° as who should say 'There were wit in this head,   *judicious expression*
an't would out'°—and so there is; but it lies as coldly in him as   *if it would come out*
fire in a flint, which will not show without knocking.° The   *striking (into flame)*
250   man's undone for ever, for if Hector break not his neck i'th'
combat he'll break't himself in vainglory. He knows not me. I
said, 'Good morrow, Ajax', and he replies, 'Thanks, Agamemnon'. What think you of this man that takes me for the Gen-
eral? He's grown a very land-fish,° languageless, a monster. A   *unnatural creature*
255   plague of opinion! A man may wear it on both sides like a
leather jerkin.[3]
ACHILLES   Thou must be my ambassador to him, Thersites.
THERSITES   Who, I? Why, he'll answer nobody. He professes not
answering.° Speaking is for beggars. He wears his tongue in's   *refuses to respond*
260   arms. I will put on° his presence. Let Patroclus make demands   *imitate*
to me. You shall see the pageant of Ajax.
ACHILLES   To him, Patroclus. Tell him I humbly desire the valiant Ajax to invite the most valorous Hector to come unarmed
to my tent, and to procure safe-conduct for his person of the
265   magnanimous and most illustrious six-or-seven-times-honoured
captain-general of the Grecian army, Agamemnon; et cetera.
Do this.

8. Gives danger free rein (literally, provides danger with a blank warrant to fill in as it pleases).
9. *danger . . . sun:* danger, like a fever, insidiously weakens (causes shivering) even when one is sitting in the sun.
1. Punning on "Ajax" and "a jakes" (a toilet), the point presumably being that Ajax is so terrified by battle, he

cannot help relieving himself.
2. Like the hostess at an inn whose mathematical ineptitude makes it hard for her to work out the bill.
3. A plague on conceit (or reputation)! One can wear it either way (conceit or reputation) like a reversible jacket (but it's still the same pride).

PATROCLUS [*to* THERSITES]   Jove bless great Ajax!

THERSITES   H'm.

270 PATROCLUS   I come from the worthy Achilles—

THERSITES   Ha?

PATROCLUS   Who most humbly desires you to invite Hector to his tent—

THERSITES   H'm!

275 PATROCLUS   And to procure safe-conduct from Agamemnon.

THERSITES   Agamemnon?

PATROCLUS   Ay, my lord.

THERSITES   Ha!

PATROCLUS   What say you to't?

280 THERSITES   God b'wi' you,° with all my heart.   (*dismissive*)

PATROCLUS   Your answer, sir?

THERSITES   If tomorrow be a fair day, by eleven o'clock it will go
one way or other. Howsoever, he shall pay for me ere° he has   *pay dearly before*
me.

285 PATROCLUS   Your answer, sir?

THERSITES   Fare ye well, with all my heart.

ACHILLES   Why, but he is not in this tune,° is he?   *mood*

THERSITES   No, but he's out o' tune thus. What music will be in
him when Hector has knocked out his brains, I know not. But

290 I am feared° none, unless the fiddler Apollo get his sinews to   *afraid*
make catlings⁴ on.

ACHILLES   Come, thou shalt bear a letter to him straight.

THERSITES   Let me carry another to his horse, for that's the more
capable° creature.   *intelligent*

295 ACHILLES   My mind is troubled like a fountain stirred,
And I myself see not the bottom of it.   [*Exit with* PATROCLUS]

THERSITES   Would the fountain of your mind were clear again,
that I might water an ass at it. I had rather be a tick in a sheep
than such a valiant ignorance.°   *Exit*   *puffed-up fool*

4.1

Enter at one door AENEAS *with a torch; at another* PARIS,
DEIPHOBUS, ANTENOR, [*and*] DIOMEDES *the Grecian,*
with torch[-*bearers*]

PARIS   See, ho! Who is that there?

DEIPHOBUS   It is the Lord Aeneas.

AENEAS   Is the Prince there in person?
Had I so good occasion to lie long

5 As you, Prince Paris, nothing but heavenly business
Should rob my bed-mate of my company.

DIOMEDES   That's my mind too. Good morrow, Lord Aeneas.

PARIS   A valiant Greek, Aeneas, take his hand.
Witness the process of your speech,¹ wherein

10 You told how Diomed e'en a whole week by days°   *every day*
Did haunt you in the field.

AENEAS [*to* DIOMEDES]   Health to you, valiant sir,
During all question of° the gentle truce.   *conversations during*
But when I meet you armed, as black defiance

---

4. Instrument strings made of catgut.
4.1 Location: A street in Troy.

1. *Witness . . . speech:* As the thrust of your narrative
made clear (that he is valiant).

As heart can think or courage execute.
15 DIOMEDES The one and other Diomed embraces.
Our bloods are now in calm; and so long, health.
But when contention and occasion meet,°   *it's time to fight*
By Jove I'll play the hunter for thy life
With all my force, pursuit, and policy.°   *cunning*
20 AENEAS And thou shalt hunt a lion that will fly
With his face backward.² In humane gentleness,
Welcome to Troy. Now by Anchises' life,
Welcome indeed! By Venus'³ hand I swear
No man alive can love in such a sort°   *to such an extent*
25 The thing he means to kill more excellently.
DIOMEDES We sympathize.° Jove, let Aeneas live—   *feel the same*
If to my sword his fate be not the glory—
A thousand complete courses of the sun;
But, in mine emulous honour,⁴ let him die
30 With every joint a wound—and that, tomorrow.
AENEAS We know each other well.
DIOMEDES We do, and long to know each other worse.
PARIS This is the most despitefull'st gentle greeting,
The noblest hateful love, that e'er I heard of.
35 What business, lord, so early?
AENEAS I was sent for to the King; but why, I know not.
PARIS His purpose meets you:° 'twas to bring this Greek   *I'll tell you why*
To Calchas' house, and there to render him,
For the enfreed Antenor, the fair Cressid.
40 Let's have your company, or if you please
Haste there before us. [*Aside*] I constantly° do think—   *firmly*
Or rather, call my thought a certain knowledge—
My brother Troilus lodges there tonight.
Rouse him and give him note of our approach,
45 With the whole quality° wherefore. I fear   *cause*
We shall be much unwelcome.
AENEAS [*aside*]   That I assure you.
Troilus had rather Troy were borne to Greece
Than Cressid borne from Troy.
PARIS [*aside*]   There is no help.
The bitter disposition of the time
50 Will have it so.
[*Aloud*] On, lord, we'll follow you.
AENEAS Good morrow all.   *Exit*
PARIS And tell me, noble Diomed—faith, tell me true,
Even in the soul of sound good-fellowship—
55 Who in your thoughts merits fair Helen most,
Myself or Menelaus?
DIOMEDES   Both alike.
He merits well to have her that doth seek her,
Not making any scruple of her soilure,°   *issue of her dishonor*
With such a hell of pain and world of charge;°   *expense*
60 And you as well to keep her that defend her,
Not palating the taste of° her dishonour,   *Not even tasting*

---

2. In the imagery of heraldry for chivalric combat, a lion walking and looking back over his shoulder; also, Aeneas will still fight even as he retreats.

3. Anchises and Venus, the goddess of love, were Aeneas's parents.
4. If his death will increase my honor.

With such a costly loss of wealth and friends.
He like a puling° cuckold would drink up   *whining*
The lees and dregs of a flat 'tamèd piece;⁵
65 You like a lecher out of whorish loins
Are pleased to breed out your inheritors.
Both merits poised,° each weighs nor less nor more,   *weighed in the scales*
But he as he: which heavier for a whore?⁶
PARIS You are too bitter to your countrywoman.
70 DIOMEDES She's bitter to her country. Hear me, Paris.
For every false drop in her bawdy veins
A Grecian's life hath sunk; for every scruple°   *tiny unit of weight*
Of her contaminated carrion° weight   *putrid*
A Trojan hath been slain. Since she could speak
75 She hath not given so many good words breath
As, for her, Greeks and Trojans suffered death.
PARIS Fair Diomed, you do as chapmen° do: *merchants*
Dispraise the thing that you desire to buy.
But we in silence hold this virtue well:°   *act similarly*
80 We'll but commend what we intend to sell.⁷—
Here lies our way.   *Exeunt*

4.2

Enter TROILUS *and* CRESSIDA
TROILUS Dear, trouble not yourself. The morn is cold.
CRESSIDA Then, sweet my lord, I'll call mine uncle down.
He shall unbolt the gates.
TROILUS   Trouble him not.
To bed, to bed! Sleep lull those pretty eyes
5   And give as soft attachment° to thy senses   *imprisonment*
As to infants empty of all thought.
CRESSIDA Good morrow, then.
TROILUS I prithee now, to bed.
CRESSIDA Are you aweary of me?
10 TROILUS O Cressida! But that the busy day,
Waked by the lark, hath roused the ribald° crows,   *offensively noisy*
And dreaming night will hide our joys no longer,
I would not from thee.
CRESSIDA   Night hath been too brief.
TROILUS Beshrew the witch! With venomous wights¹ she stays
15 As hideously as hell, but flies° the grasps of love   *flees*
With wings more momentary-swift than thought.
You will catch cold and curse me.
CRESSIDA Prithee, tarry. You men will never tarry.
O foolish Cressid! I might have still held off,
20 And then you would have tarried.—Hark, there's one up.
[*She veils herself*]
PANDARUS [*within*] What's° all the doors open here?   *Why are*
TROILUS It is your uncle.
CRESSIDA A pestilence on him! Now will he be mocking.
I shall have such a life.

---

5. Of a stale insipid (penetrated) cask of wine (woman).
6. But one the same as the other: which more deserves (is made sadder by) the whore?
7. We'll praise only what we're trying to sell. (But we

don't intend to bargain for Helen and so won't praise her.)
4.2 Location: Cressida's house.
1. Curse the night! With evil people (who are hateful to each other).

Enter PANDARUS

25 PANDARUS   How now, how now, how go° maidenheads?   *what's the price of*
   [*To* CRESSIDA] Here, you, maid! Where's my cousin Cressid?²
   CRESSIDA [*unveiling*]   Go hang yourself. You naughty, mocking uncle!
     You bring me to do°—and then you flout me too.   *have sex*
   PANDARUS   To do what? To do what?—Let her say what.— What
30 have I brought you to do?
   CRESSIDA   Come, come, beshrew° your heart. You'll ne'er be good,   *curses on*
     Nor suffer others.°   *let others be good*
   PANDARUS   Ha ha! Alas, poor wretch. Ah, poor *capocchia*,° hast   *simpleton; foreskin*
     not slept tonight? Would he not—a naughty man—let it sleep?
35 A bugbear° take him.   *goblin*
   CRESSIDA [*to* TROILUS]   Did not I tell you? Would he were
     knocked i'th' head.°   *killed*
           One knocks [*within*]
     Who's that at door?—Good uncle, go and see.—
     My lord, come you again into my chamber.
     You smile and mock me, as if I meant naughtily.
40 TROILUS   Ha ha!
   CRESSIDA   Come, you are deceived, I think of no such thing.
           [*One*] *knock*[*s within*]
     How earnestly they knock! Pray you come in.
     I would not for half Troy have you seen here.
                       Exeunt [TROILUS *and* CRESSIDA]
   PANDARUS   Who's there? What's the matter? Will you beat down
45 the door?
           [*He opens the door. Enter* AENEAS]
     How now, what's the matter?
   AENEAS   Good morrow, lord, good morrow.
   PANDARUS   Who's there? My Lord Aeneas? By my troth,
     I knew you not. What news with you so early?
   AENEAS   Is not Prince Troilus here?
50 PANDARUS   Here? What should he do here?
   AENEAS   Come, he is here, my lord. Do not deny him.
     It doth import° him much to speak with me.   *concern*
   PANDARUS   Is he here, say you? It's more than I know, I'll be
     sworn. For my own part, I came in late. What should he do
55 here?
   AENEAS   Whoa! Nay, then. Come, come, you'll do him wrong
     Ere you are ware.° You'll be so true to him   *aware*
     To be false to him.° Do not you know of him,   *As to harm him*
     But yet go fetch him hither. Go.
                           [*Exit* PANDARUS]³
     Enter TROILUS
60 TROILUS   How now, what's the matter?
   AENEAS   My lord, I scarce have leisure to salute you,
     My matter is so rash.° There is at hand   *urgent*
     Paris your brother and Deiphobus,
     The Grecian Diomed, and our Antenor

---

2. Pandarus pretends not to recognize Cressida, now
that she is no longer a virgin. It is possible that he
addresses her as "maid" (line 26) because she is wearing
a veil, which suggests a modesty appropriate to virgins.
3. Editors usually keep him on and have Cressida enter
alone at what is the beginning of 4.3 in this edition.

65 Delivered to us—and for him° forthwith, (Antenor)
Ere the first sacrifice, within this hour,
We must give up to Diomedes' hand
The Lady Cressida.
TROILUS   Is it so concluded?
AENEAS   By Priam and the general state° of Troy. council
70 They are at hand, and ready to effect it.
TROILUS   How my achievements mock me.
I will go meet them—and, my Lord Aeneas,
We° met by chance: you did not find me here. (Pretend that) we
AENEAS   Good, good, my lord: the untold secrecies° of nature untold secrets
75 Have not more gift in taciturnity. Exeunt

4.3

Enter PANDARUS *and* CRESSIDA[1]

PANDARUS   Is't possible? No sooner got but lost. The devil take
Antenor! The young prince will go mad. A plague upon Ante-
nor! I would they had broke 's neck.
CRESSIDA   How now? What's the matter? Who was here?
5 PANDARUS   Ah, ah!
CRESSIDA   Why sigh you so profoundly? Where's my lord?
Gone? Tell me, sweet uncle, what's the matter?
PANDARUS   Would I were as deep under the earth as I am above.
CRESSIDA   O the gods! What's the matter?
10 PANDARUS   Pray thee, get thee in. Would thou hadst ne'er been
born. I knew thou wouldst be his death. O poor gentleman! A
plague upon Antenor!
CRESSIDA   Good uncle, I beseech you on my knees; I beseech
you, what's the matter?
15 PANDARUS   Thou must be gone, wench, thou must be gone.
Thou art changed° for Antenor. Thou must to thy father, and exchanged
be gone from Troilus. 'Twill be his death. 'Twill be his bane.
He cannot bear it.
CRESSIDA   O you immortal gods! I will not go.
20 PANDARUS   Thou must.
CRESSIDA   I will not, uncle. I have forgot my father.
I know no touch of consanguinity,
No kin, no love, no blood, no soul, so near me
As the sweet Troilus. O you gods divine,
25 Make Cressid's name the very crown° of falsehood height
If ever she leave Troilus. Time, force, and death
Do to this body what extremity you can,
But the strong base and building of my love
Is as the very centre of the earth,
30 Drawing all things to it. I'll go in and weep—
PANDARUS   Do, do.
CRESSIDA   Tear my bright hair, and scratch my praisèd cheeks,
Crack my clear voice with sobs, and break my heart
With sounding 'Troilus'. I will not go from Troy. Exeunt

4.3 Location: Scene continues.
1. Most modern editions do not mark a scene break here;
this affects the numbering of the following lines and
scenes. See note to 4.2.59 and Textual Note.

4.4

Enter PARIS, TROILUS, AENEAS, DEIPHOBUS, ANTENOR,
and DIOMEDES

PARIS   It is great morning,° and the hour prefixed°   *daylight / arranged*
Of her delivery to this valiant Greek
Comes fast upon us. Good my brother Troilus,
Tell you the lady what she is to do,
And haste her to the purpose.

5   TROILUS   Walk into her house.
I'll bring her to the Grecian presently°—   *immediately*
And to his hand when I deliver her,
Think it an altar, and thy brother Troilus
A priest, there off'ring to it his own heart.

10   PARIS   I know what 'tis to love,
And would,° as I shall pity, I could help.—   *wish*
Please you walk in, my lords?   *Exeunt*

4.5

Enter PANDARUS *and* CRESSIDA

PANDARUS   Be moderate, be moderate.
CRESSIDA   Why tell you me of moderation?
The grief is fine,° full, perfect that I taste,   *undiluted*
And violenteth° in a sense° as strong   *rages / manner*
5   As that which causeth it.° How can I moderate it?   *(her love)*
If I could temporize with° my affection   *adjust to*
Or brew° it to a weak and colder palate,°   *dilute / taste*
The like allayment° could I give my grief.   *dilution*
My love admits no qualifying dross;°   *modifying impurity*
10   No more° my grief, in such a precious loss.   *Any more than does*
Enter TROILUS
PANDARUS   Here, here, here he comes. Ah, sweet ducks!
CRESSIDA [*embracing him*]   O Troilus, Troilus!
PANDARUS   What a pair of spectacles° is here! Let me embrace   *sights*
you too. 'O heart', as the goodly saying is,
15   'O heart, heavy heart,
            Why sigh'st thou without breaking?'
where he answers again
            'Because thou canst not ease thy smart
            By friendship nor by speaking.'
20   There was never a truer rhyme. Let us cast away nothing, for
we may live to have need of such a verse. We see it, we see it.
How now, lambs?
TROILUS   Cressid, I love thee in so strained° a purity   *refined*
That the blest gods, as° angry with my fancy°—   *as if / love*
25   More bright in zeal than the devotion which
Cold lips blow to their deities—take thee from me.
CRESSIDA   Have the gods envy?
PANDARUS   Ay, ay, ay, ay, 'tis too plain a case.
CRESSIDA   And is it true that I must go from Troy?
TROILUS   A hateful truth.
30   CRESSIDA   What, and from Troilus too?
TROILUS   From Troy and Troilus.

4.4 Location: Outside Cressida's house.   4.5 Location: Inside Cressida's house.

CRESSIDA   Is't possible?
TROILUS   And suddenly°—where injury of° chance   *immediately / injurious*
Puts back° leave-taking, jostles roughly by   *Prevents*
All time of pause, rudely beguiles° our lips   *deprives*
35   Of all rejoindure,° forcibly prevents   *joining again*
Our locked embrasures, strangles our dear vows
Even in the birth of our own labouring breath.°   *(as in childbirth)*
We two, that with so many thousand sighs
Did buy each other, must poorly sell ourselves
40   With the rude brevity and discharge of one.°   *(sigh)*
Injurious Time now with a robber's haste
Crams his rich thiev'ry up, he knows not how.[1]
As many farewells as be stars in heaven,
With distinct breath and consigned° kisses to them,   *ratifying*
45   He fumbles up° into a loose adieu   *clumsily combines*
And scants us with a single famished kiss,
Distasted[2] with the salt of broken° tears.   *interrupted*
        Enter AENEAS
AENEAS   My lord, is the lady ready?
TROILUS [*to* CRESSIDA]   Hark, you are called. Some say the *genius*° so   *guardian spirit*
50   Cries 'Come!' to him that instantly must die.
        [*To* PANDARUS] Bid them have patience. She shall come anon.
PANDARUS   Where are my tears? Rain, to lay this wind,° or my   *allay my sighs*
heart will be blown up by the root.   [*Exit with* AENEAS]
CRESSIDA   I must then to the Grecians.
TROILUS   No remedy.
55   CRESSIDA   A woeful Cressid 'mongst the merry Greeks![3]
When shall we see again?
TROILUS   Hear me, my love: be thou but true of heart—
CRESSIDA   I true? How now! What wicked deem° is this?   *thought*
TROILUS   Nay, we must use expostulation° kindly,   *conversation*
60   For it° is parting from us.   *the opportunity*
I speak not 'Be thou true' as fearing thee—
For I will throw my glove to° Death himself   *challenge*
That there's no maculation° in thy heart—   *stain of infidelity*
But 'Be thou true' say I, to fashion in°   *introduce*
65   My sequent° protestation: 'Be thou true,   *following*
And I will see thee'.
CRESSIDA   O you shall be exposed, my lord, to dangers
As infinite as imminent. But I'll be true.
TROILUS   And I'll grow friend with danger. Wear this sleeve.[4]
70   CRESSIDA   And you this glove. When shall I see you?
TROILUS   I will corrupt the Grecian sentinels
To° give thee nightly visitation.   *In order that I may*
But yet, be true.
CRESSIDA   O heavens! 'Be true' again!
75   TROILUS   Hear why I speak it, love.
The Grecian youths are full of quality,
Their loving well composed, with gifts of nature flowing,
And swelling o'er with arts° and exercise.°   *education / practice*
How novelty may move, and parts with person,°   *talent and good looks*
80   Alas, a kind of godly° jealousy—   *divinely sanctioned*

1. Compresses his stolen goods (farewell kisses) into a   3. Common phrase for licentious revelers, here also
short period, distractedly.   meant literally.
2. Made distasteful.   4. Often detachable in Elizabethan dress.

Which I beseech you call a virtuous sin—
Makes me afeard.

CRESSIDA   O heavens, you love me not!

TROILUS   Die I a villain then!

85   In this I do not call your faith° in question   *fidelity*
So mainly° as my merit.[5] I cannot sing,   *much*
Nor heel the high lavolt, nor sweeten talk,[6]
Nor play at subtle games—fair virtues all,
To which the Grecians are most prompt and pregnant.°   *ready*

90   But I can tell that in each grace of these
There lurks a still and dumb-discoursive° devil   *silently communicating*
That tempts most cunningly. But be not tempted.

CRESSIDA   Do you think I will?

TROILUS   No, but something may be done that we will not,°   *do not will*

95   And sometimes we are devils to ourselves,
When we will tempt the frailty of our powers,
Presuming on their changeful potency.°   *unreliable strength*

AENEAS (*within*)   Nay, good my lord!

TROILUS   Come, kiss, and let us part.

PARIS [*at the door*]   Brother Troilus?

TROILUS   Good brother, come you hither,

100   And bring Aeneas and the Grecian with you. *Exit* [PARIS]

CRESSIDA   My lord, will you be true?

TROILUS   Who, I? Alas, it is my vice, my fault.
Whiles others fish with craft° for great opinion,°   *guile / reputation*
I with great truth catch mere simplicity;[7]

105   Whilst some with cunning gild their copper crowns,°   *coins; heads*
With truth and plainness I do wear° mine bare.   *dress; erode*

          Enter [PARIS, AENEAS, ANTENOR, DEIPHOBUS, *and* DIO-
          MEDES]

Fear not my truth. The moral° of my wit   *maxim*
Is 'plain and true!'; there's all the reach of it.—
Welcome, Sir Diomed. Here is the lady

110   Which for Antenor we deliver you.
At the port,° lord, I'll give her to thy hand,   *gate of the city*
And by the way possess° thee what she is.   *instruct*
Entreat° her fair, and by my soul, fair Greek,   *Treat*
If e'er thou stand at mercy of my sword,

115   Name Cressid, and thy life shall be as safe
As Priam is in Ilium.

DIOMEDES   Fair Lady Cressid,
So please you, save the thanks this prince expects.[8]
The lustre in your eye, heaven in your cheek,
Pleads your fair usage;° and to Diomed   *treatment*

120   You shall be mistress, and command him wholly.

TROILUS   Grecian, thou dost not use me courteously,
To shame the zeal of my petition towards thee
In praising her. I tell thee, lord of Greece,
She is as far high-soaring o'er thy praises

---

5. Deserts; good works, deserving of salvation (picking up the religious language of the preceding lines, especially "faith," line 85).
6. Nor dance the "lavolt" (which involved spectacular jumps), nor flatter.
7. Absolute rusticity (sincerity).
8. *save . . . expects:* you won't need to thank Troilus for the good treatment I will give you.

125   As thou unworthy to be called her servant.⁹
       I charge thee use her well, even for my charge;°   simply at my command
       For, by the dreadful Pluto, if thou dost not,
       Though the great bulk Achilles be thy guard
       I'll cut thy throat.
       DIOMEDES   O be not moved,° Prince Troilus.   angry
130   Let me be privileged by my place and message
       To be a speaker free. When I am hence
       I'll answer to my lust.° And know you, lord,   do as I please
       I'll nothing do on charge.° To her own worth   command
       She shall be prized; but that° you say 'Be't so',   simply because
135   I'll speak it in my spirit and honour 'No!'
       TROILUS   Come, to the port.—I'll tell thee, Diomed,
       This brave° shall oft make thee to hide thy head.—   boast
       Lady, give me your hand, and as we walk
       To our own selves bend we our needful talk.
               [Exeunt TROILUS, CRESSIDA, and DIOMEDES]
               [A] trumpet sound[s]
       PARIS   Hark, Hector's trumpet.
140   AENEAS   How have we spent this morning?
       The Prince must think me tardy and remiss,
       That swore to ride before him in the field.
       PARIS   'Tis Troilus' fault. Come, come to field with him.
       DEIPHOBUS   Let us make ready straight.
145   AENEAS   Yea, with a bridegroom's fresh alacrity
       Let us address° to tend on Hector's heels.   prepare
       The glory of our Troy doth this day lie
       On his fair worth and single chivalry.   Exeunt

                          4.6
           Enter AJAX armed, ACHILLES, PATROCLUS, AGAMEMNON,
           MENELAUS, ULYSSES, NESTOR[, a trumpeter, and others]
       AGAMEMNON   Here art thou in appointment° fresh and fair,   equipment
       Anticipating time¹ with starting° courage.   bounding
       Give with thy trumpet a loud note to Troy,
       Thou dreadful° Ajax, that the appallèd air   causing fear
5   May pierce the head of the great combatant
       And hale° him hither.   draw
       AJAX   Thou trumpet,° there's my purse.   trumpeter
               [He gives him money]
       Now crack thy lungs and split thy brazen pipe.°   trumpet; windpipe
       Blow, villain,° till thy spherèd bias° cheek   servant / puffed-out
       Outswell the colic of puffed Aquilon.²
10   Come, stretch thy chest and let thy eyes spout blood;
       Thou blow'st for Hector.
               [The trumpet sounds]
       ULYSSES   No trumpet answers.
       ACHILLES   'Tis but early days.
       AGAMEMNON   Is not yond Diomed with Calchas' daughter?
15   ULYSSES   'Tis he. I ken° the manner of his gait.   recognize

---

9. Like "mistress" (line 120), a cliché of courtly love.
4.6 Location: Between the Greek camp and Troy.
1. Ajax has not waited for Hector to appear with his
challenge.

2. Outswells the intestinal pain (from bloating) of the
north wind (Aquilon). (Winds on contemporary maps
were represented as human heads blowing.)

He rises on the toe: that spirit of his
In aspiration lifts him from the earth.
  [*Enter* DIOMEDES *and* CRESSIDA]
AGAMEMNON [*to* DIOMEDES]   Is this the Lady Cressid?
DIOMEDES   Even she.
AGAMEMNON   Most dearly welcome to the Greeks, sweet lady.
  [*He kisses her*]
20 NESTOR [*to* CRESSIDA]   Our General doth salute you with a kiss.
ULYSSES   Yet is the kindness but particular;°   *from only one of us*
'Twere better she were kissed in general.
NESTOR   And very courtly counsel. I'll begin.
  [*He kisses her*]
So much for Nestor.
25 ACHILLES   I'll take that winter° from your lips, fair lady.   *Nestor's old age*
  [*He kisses her*]
Achilles bids you welcome.
MENELAUS [*to* CRESSIDA]   I had good argument° for kissing once.   *Helen*
PATROCLUS   But that's no argument for kissing now;
For thus [*stepping between them*] popped° Paris in his   *thrust in*
  hardiment,°   *boldness; hardness*
30 And parted thus you and your argument.
  [*He kisses her*]
ULYSSES [*aside*]   O deadly gall, and theme of all our scorns!
For which we lose our heads to gild his horns.°   *cuckold's horns*
PATROCLUS [*to* CRESSIDA]   The first was Menelaus' kiss; this, mine.
Patroclus kisses you.
  [*He kisses her again*]
MENELAUS   O this is trim.°   *excellent*
35 PATROCLUS [*to* CRESSIDA]   Paris and I kiss evermore° for him.   *always*
MENELAUS   I'll have my kiss, sir.—Lady, by your leave.
CRESSIDA   In kissing do you render or receive?
MENELAUS   Both take and give.
CRESSIDA   I'll make my match to live,°   *bet my life*
The kiss you take is better than you give.
40 Therefore no kiss.
MENELAUS   I'll give you boot:° I'll give you three for one.   *profit*
CRESSIDA   You are an odd³ man: give even or give none.
MENELAUS   An odd man, lady? Every man is odd.
CRESSIDA   No, Paris is not—for you know 'tis true
45 That you are odd, and he is even° with you.   *has gotten even*
MENELAUS   You fillip me o'th' head.⁴
CRESSIDA   No, I'll be sworn.
ULYSSES   It were no match, your nail against his horn.⁵
May I, sweet lady, beg a kiss of you?
CRESSIDA   You may.
ULYSSES   I do desire it.
CRESSIDA   Why, beg too.
50 ULYSSES   Why then, for Venus' sake, give me a kiss,
When Helen is a maid again, and his°—   *Menelaus's*
CRESSIDA   I am your debtor; claim it when 'tis due.

---

3. *odd* (lines 42–45): strange; unique; left out; single
(lacking a partner); opposite of "even" (line 45).
4. You tease me about being a cuckold (literally, flick
your fingernail on my head).
5. No contest, Cressida's fingernail against Menelaus's
cuckold's horn (which is far harder).

ULYSSES   Never's my day,° and then a kiss of you.   *the due date*
DIOMEDES   Lady, a word. I'll bring you to your father.
        [*They talk apart*]
NESTOR   A woman of quick sense.°   *intelligence; sexuality*
55   ULYSSES   Fie, fie upon her!
      There's language in her eye, her cheek, her lip;
      Nay, her foot speaks. Her wanton spirits look out°   *are exposed*
      At every joint and motive° of her body.   *moving limb*
      O these encounterers so glib of tongue,
60   That give accosting° welcome ere it comes,   *an approach*
      And wide unclasp the tables° of their thoughts   *tablets*
      To every ticklish° reader, set them down°   *lustful / mark them*
      For sluttish spoils of opportunity°   *As easy sexual prey*
      And daughters of the game.°   *prostitutes*
                              Exeunt [DIOMEDES *and* CRESSIDA]
        Flourish
65   ALL   The Trojans' trumpet.°   *(Trojan strumpet)*
        Enter all of Troy: HECTOR [*armed*], PARIS, AENEAS, HELE-
          NUS, *and attendants* [*among them* TROILUS]
AGAMEMNON   Yonder comes the troop.
AENEAS [*coming forward*]   Hail, all you state° of Greece! What   *noblemen*
      shall be done°   *rewarded*
      To him that victory commands? Or do you purpose
      A victor shall be known? Will you° the knights   *Do you wish that*
70   Shall to the edge of all extremity°   *the death*
      Pursue each other, or shall they be divided
      By any voice or order of the field?⁶
      Hector bade ask.
AGAMEMNON   Which way would Hector have it?
AENEAS   He cares not; he'll obey conditions.°   *your choice*
75   ACHILLES   'Tis done like Hector—but securely° done,   *too boldly*
      A little proudly, and great deal disprising°   *underestimating*
      The knight opposed.
AENEAS   If not Achilles, sir,
      What is your name?
ACHILLES   If not Achilles, nothing.
AENEAS   Therefore Achilles. But whate'er, know this:
80   In the extremity of great and little,
      Valour and pride excel themselves in Hector,
      The one° almost as infinite as all,   *(valor)*
      The other° blank as nothing. Weigh him well,   *(pride)*
      And that which looks like pride is courtesy.
85   This Ajax is half made of Hector's blood,⁷
      In love whereof half Hector stays at home.
      Half heart, half hand, half Hector comes to seek
      This blended knight, half Trojan and half Greek.
ACHILLES   A maiden° battle, then? O I perceive you.   *bloodless*
        [*Enter* DIOMEDES]
90   AGAMEMNON   Here is Sir Diomed.—Go, gentle knight,
      Stand by our Ajax. As you and Lord Aeneas
      Consent° upon the order° of their fight,   *Decide / terms*

---

6. By any umpire or rules of combat?   7. Ajax was Priam's nephew.

So be it: either to the uttermost
Or else a breath.°   *bout of exercise*
    [Exeunt AJAX, DIOMEDES, HECTOR, *and* AENEAS]*[8]
    The combatants being kin
95 Half stints their strife before their strokes begin.
ULYSSES They are opposed already.
AGAMEMNON What Trojan is that same that looks so heavy?°   *sorrowful*
ULYSSES The youngest son of Priam, a true knight:
    They call him Troilus.
100 Not yet mature, yet matchless-firm of word,
    Speaking in deeds and deedless in his tongue;°   *not boastful*
    Not soon provoked, nor being provoked soon calmed;
    His heart and hand both open and both free.°   *generous*
    For what he has he gives; what thinks, he shows;
105 Yet gives he not till judgement guide his bounty,°   *generosity*
    Nor dignifies an impare° thought with breath.   *unworthy*
    Manly as Hector but more dangerous,
    For Hector in his blaze of wrath subscribes°   *relents*
    To tender objects, but he in heat of action
110 Is more vindicative° than jealous love.   *vindictive*
    They call him Troilus, and on him erect
    A second hope as fairly built as Hector.
    Thus says Aeneas, one that knows the youth
    Even to his inches, and with private soul[9]
115 Did in great Ilium thus translate° him to me.   *describe*
    Alarum
AGAMEMNON They are in action.
NESTOR Now, Ajax, hold thine own!
TROILUS Hector, thou sleep'st! Awake thee!
AGAMEMNON His blows are well disposed. There, Ajax!   *[Exeunt]*

4.7

[Enter HECTOR *and* AJAX *fighting, and* AENEAS *and* DIO-
MEDES *interposing.] Trumpets cease*[1]
DIOMEDES You must no more.
AENEAS   Princes, enough, so please you.
AJAX I am not warm yet. Let us fight again.
DIOMEDES As Hector pleases.
HECTOR   Why then will I no more.—
    Thou art, great lord, my father's sister's son,
5 A cousin-german° to great Priam's seed.   *first cousin*
    The obligation of our blood forbids
    A gory emulation° 'twixt us twain.   *competition*
    Were thy commixtion° Greek and Trojan so°   *blending / such*
    That thou couldst say 'This hand is Grecian all,
10 And this is Trojan; the sinews of this leg
    All Greek, and this all Troy; my mother's blood
    Runs on the dexter° cheek, and this sinister°   *right / left*
    Bounds in my father's,' by Jove multipotent°   *most powerful*
    Thou shouldst not bear from me a Greekish member°   *part of the body*

---

8. The combat might take place onstage.
9. *Even . . . soul:* In utmost detail, and in confidence.
4.7 Location: Scene continues.

1. Most modern editions do not mark a scene break
here; this affects the numbering of the following lines
as well as the following scenes. See Textual Note.

15 Wherein my sword had not impressure made
    Of our rank° feud. But the just gods gainsay°   heated / prohibit
    That any drop thou borrowed'st from thy mother,
    My sacred aunt, should by my mortal sword
    Be drained. Let me embrace thee, Ajax.
20 By him that thunders,° thou hast lusty arms.   Jupiter
    Hector would have them fall upon him thus.°   in an embrace
    Cousin, all honour to thee.
AJAX   I thank thee, Hector.
    Thou art too gentle and too free a man.
    I came to kill thee, cousin, and bear hence
25 A great addition° earnèd in thy death.   title
HECTOR   Not Neoptolemus² so mirable,°   wonderful
    On whose bright crest° Fame with her loud'st oyez°   helmet / hear ye
    Cries 'This is he!', could promise to himself
    A thought of added honour torn from Hector.
30 AENEAS   There is expectance here from both the sides
    What further you will do.
HECTOR   We'll answer it:
    The issue° is embracement.—Ajax, farewell.   conclusion
AJAX   If I might in entreaties find success,
    As seld° I have the chance, I would desire   seldom
35 My famous cousin to our Grecian tents.
DIOMEDES   'Tis Agamemnon's wish—and great Achilles
    Doth long to see unarmed the valiant Hector.
HECTOR   Aeneas, call my brother Troilus to me,
    And signify this loving interview
40 To the expecters of our Trojan part.°   awaiting Trojans
    Desire them home.°   [Exit AENEAS]   to go home
            Give me thy hand, my cousin.
    I will go eat with thee, and see your knights.
            Enter AGAMEMNON and the rest [AENEAS, ULYSSES,
            MENELAUS, NESTOR, ACHILLES, PATROCLUS, TROILUS,
            and others]
AJAX   Great Agamemnon comes to meet us here.
HECTOR [to AENEAS]   The worthiest of them,° tell me name by name. the Greeks
45 But for Achilles, mine own searching eyes
    Shall find him by his large and portly size.
AGAMEMNON [embracing him]   Worthy of arms, as welcome as to° one   as you can be to
    That would be rid of such an enemy.
    But that's no welcome. Understand more clear:
50 What's past and what's to come is strewed with husks
    And formless ruin of oblivion,
    But in this extant° moment faith and troth,   present
    Strained purely from all hollow bias-drawing,³
    Bids thee with most divine integrity
55 From heart of very heart, 'Great Hector, welcome!'
HECTOR   I thank thee, most imperious° Agamemnon.   imperial
AGAMEMNON [to TROILUS]   My well-famed lord of Troy, no less to you.
MENELAUS   Let me confirm my princely brother's greeting.
    You brace° of warlike brothers, welcome hither.   pair
            [He embraces HECTOR and TROILUS]

---

2. Achilles' son Pyrrhus (but Shakespeare may have   3. Freed from all insincerity and indirectness.
thought Neoptolemus was Achilles' surname).

HECTOR [to AENEAS]   Who must we answer?

60 AENEAS   The noble Menelaus.

HECTOR   O, you, my lord! By Mars his° gauntlet, thanks.   *Mars's*
    Mock not that I affect° th'untraded° oath.   *choose / unfamiliar*
    Your quondam° wife swears still by Venus' glove.[4]   *former*
    She's well, but bade me not commend her to you.

65 MENELAUS   Name her not now, sir. She's a deadly theme.

HECTOR   O, pardon. I offend.

NESTOR   I have, thou gallant Trojan, seen thee oft,
    Labouring for destiny,[5] make cruel way
    Through ranks of Greekish youth, and I have seen thee

70 As hot as Perseus° spur thy Phrygian steed,   *(on winged Pegasus)*
    And seen thee scorning forfeits and subduements,[6]
    When thou hast hung° th'advancèd sword i'th' air,   *kept high*
    Not letting it decline° on the declined,°   *fall / fallen*
    That I have said unto my standers-by,

75 'Lo, Jupiter is yonder, dealing life'.[7]
    And I have seen thee pause and take thy breath,
    When that a ring of Greeks have hemmed thee in,
    Like an Olympian,° wrestling. This have I seen;   *a god*
    But this thy countenance, still° locked in steel,   *always*

80 I never saw till now. I knew thy grandsire[8]
    And once fought with him. He was a soldier good,
    But—by great Mars, the captain of us all—
    Never like thee. Let an old man embrace thee;
    And, worthy warrior, welcome to our tents.
        [He embraces HECTOR]

85 AENEAS [to HECTOR]   'Tis the old Nestor.

HECTOR   Let me embrace thee, good old chronicle,°   *record of history*
    That hast so long walked hand in hand with time.
    Most reverend Nestor, I am glad to clasp thee.

NESTOR   I would my arms could match thee in contention°   *in battle*

90 As they contend with thee in courtesy.

HECTOR   I would they could.

NESTOR   Ha! By this white beard I'd fight with thee tomorrow.
    Well, welcome, welcome! I have seen the time.[9]

ULYSSES   I wonder now how yonder city stands

95 When we have here her base and pillar by us?

HECTOR   I know your favour,° Lord Ulysses, well.   *face*
    Ah, sir, there's many a Greek and Trojan dead
    Since first I saw yourself and Diomed
    In Ilium on your Greekish embassy.

100 ULYSSES   Sir, I foretold you then what would ensue.
    My prophecy is but half his journey yet;
    For yonder walls that pertly front your town,
    Yon towers whose wanton° tops do buss° the clouds,   *reckless / kiss*
    Must kiss their own feet.

HECTOR   I must not believe you.

105 There they stand yet, and modestly I think
    The fall of every Phrygian stone will cost

---

4. *Venus' glove*: contrasting with Mars's gauntlet and
alluding to Venus's adultery with Mars; possibly with an
obscene innuendo.
5. Doing the Fates' work for them.
6. Scorning those whose lives might have been forfeit

and (possible) conquests.
7. Giving life being the gods' prerogative.
8. Laomedon, builder of Troy's walls.
9. That is, the time when I could have met you in combat.

A drop of Grecian blood. The end crowns all,
And that old common arbitrator Time
Will one day end it.
ULYSSES   So to him we leave it.
110   Most gentle and most valiant Hector, welcome.
        [*He embraces him*]
    After the General, I beseech you next
    To feast with me and see me at my tent.
ACHILLES   I shall forestall thee, Lord Ulysses. [*To* HECTOR] Thou!°   (*insulting*)
    Now, Hector, I have fed mine eyes on thee.
115   I have with exact view perused° thee, Hector,   *minutely looked over*
    And quoted° joint by joint.   *taken note*
HECTOR   Is this Achilles?
ACHILLES   I am Achilles.
HECTOR   Stand fair,° I pray thee, let me look on thee.   *open to view*
ACHILLES   Behold thy fill.
120   HECTOR   Nay, I have done already.
ACHILLES   Thou art too brief. I will the second time,
    As° I would buy thee, view thee limb by limb.   *As though*
HECTOR   O, like a book of sport° thou'lt read me o'er.   *hunting manual*
    But there's more in me than thou understand'st.
125   Why dost thou so oppress[1] me with thine eye?
ACHILLES   Tell me, you heavens, in which part of his body
    Shall I destroy him—whether there, or there, or there—
    That I may give the local wound a name,
    And make distinct the very breach whereout
130   Hector's great spirit flew? Answer me, heavens.
HECTOR   It would discredit the blest gods, proud man,
    To answer such a question. Stand again.°   *Let me look again*
    Think'st thou to catch my life so pleasantly°   *easily*
    As to prenominate° in nice° conjecture   *name in advance / exact*
    Where thou wilt hit me dead?
135   ACHILLES   I tell thee, yea.
HECTOR   Wert thou the oracle to tell me so,
    I'd not believe thee. Henceforth guard thee well.
    For I'll not kill thee there, nor there, nor there,
    But, by the forge that stithied° Mars his helm,   *forged*
140   I'll kill thee everywhere, yea, o'er and o'er.—
    You wisest Grecians, pardon me this brag:
    His insolence draws folly from my lips.
    But I'll endeavour deeds to match these words,
    Or may I never—
AJAX   Do not chafe thee,° cousin.—   *get angry*
145   And you, Achilles, let these threats alone,
    Till accident or purpose bring you to't.
    You may have every day enough of Hector,
    If you have stomach.° The general state,° I fear,   *appetite / Greek lords*
    Can scarce entreat you to be odd° with him.   *at odds*
150   HECTOR [*to* ACHILLES]   I pray you, let us see you in the field.
    We have had pelting° wars since you refused   *paltry*
    The Grecians' cause.
ACHILLES   Dost thou entreat me, Hector?

---

1. Molest; in heraldry, place a perpendicular or diagonal stripe across an animal (continuing the metaphor of Hector as a hunted animal from "book of sport," line 123).

Tomorrow do I meet thee, fell as death;
Tonight, all friends.

HECTOR   Thy hand upon that match.

155 AGAMEMNON   First, all you peers of Greece, go to my tent.
There in the full convive you.° Afterwards,   *feast together*
As Hector's leisure and your bounties shall
Concur together, severally entreat° him.   *individually invite*
Beat loud the taborins,° let the trumpets blow,   *small drums*
160 That this great soldier may his welcome know.

[*Flourish.*] *Exeunt* [*all but* TROILUS *and* ULYSSES]

TROILUS   My Lord Ulysses, tell me, I beseech you,
In what place of the field doth Calchas keep?°   *reside*

ULYSSES   At Menelaus' tent, most princely Troilus.
There Diomed doth feast with him tonight—
165 Who neither looks on heaven nor on earth,
But gives all gaze and bent° of amorous view   *inclination*
On the fair Cressid.

TROILUS   Shall I, sweet lord, be bound to you so much,
After we part from Agamemnon's tent,
To bring me thither?

170 ULYSSES   You shall command me, sir.
As gentle° tell me, of what honour was   *courteously*
This Cressida in Troy? Had she no lover there
That wails her absence?

TROILUS   O sir, to such as boasting show their scars°   *brag of past wounds*
175 A mock is due. Will you walk on, my lord?
She was beloved, she loved; she is, and doth.
But still sweet love is food for fortune's tooth.   *Exeunt*

5.1

Enter ACHILLES *and* PATROCLUS

ACHILLES   I'll heat his blood with Greekish wine tonight,
Which with my scimitar I'll cool° tomorrow.   *expose to air*
Patroclus, let us feast him to the height.

PATROCLUS   Here comes Thersites.

Enter THERSITES

ACHILLES   How now, thou core° of envy,   *(of an ulcer)*
5 Thou crusty botch[1] of nature, what's the news?

THERSITES   Why, thou picture° of what thou seemest, and idol *mere image*
of idiot-worshippers, here's a letter for thee.

ACHILLES   From whence, fragment?°   *scrap of leftovers*

THERSITES   Why, thou full dish of fool,[2] from Troy.

[ACHILLES *reads the letter*]

10 PATROCLUS   Who keeps the tent now?[3]

THERSITES   The surgeon's box or the patient's wound.

PATROCLUS   Well said, adversity.° And what need these tricks?   *perversity*

THERSITES   Prithee be silent, boy. I profit not by thy talk. Thou
art thought to be Achilles' male varlet.°   *servant; concubine?*

15 PATROCLUS   'Male varlet', you rogue? What's that?

THERSITES   Why, his masculine whore. Now the rotten diseases

---

5.1. Location: The Greek camp, near Achilles' tent.
1. You scab-encrusted (bad-tempered) boil.
2. Punning on the name of a dessert, probably clotted
cream or egg custard.

3. Who stays in the tent now? Thersites can no longer
taunt Achilles for remaining indoors. But Thersites
deliberately mistakes Patroclus to mean the surgeon's
probe or lint used to clean a wound.

of the south, guts-griping, ruptures, catarrhs, loads o' gravel
i'th' back, lethargies, cold palsies, and the like,⁴ take and take
again such preposterous discoveries!°   *revealed perversion*

19.1   THERSITES *Why, his masculine whore. Now the rotten*
diseases of the south, the guts-griping, ruptures, loads
o' gravel in the back, lethargies, cold palsies, raw eyes,
dirt-rotten livers, wheezing lungs, bladders full of
19.5   *impostume,° sciaticas, lime-kilns° i'th' palm, incur-*   *abscess / burning*
able bone-ache, and the rivelled fee-simple of the
tetter,⁵ take and take again such preposterous dis-
coveries.

20   PATROCLUS Why, thou damnable box of envy thou, what
mean'st thou to curse thus?
THERSITES Do I curse thee?
PATROCLUS Why, no, you ruinous butt,° you whoreson indistin-   *leaky tub*
guishable cur,° no.   *formless beast*
25   THERSITES No? Why art thou then exasperate?° Thou idle   *irritated*
immaterial skein of sleave-silk, thou green sarsenet flap⁶ for a
sore eye,⁷ thou tassel of a prodigal's purse, thou! Ah, how the
poor world is pestered with such waterflies!° Diminutives of   *tiny, flashy insects*
nature.
30   PATROCLUS Out, gall!
THERSITES Finch egg!°   *(small, gaudy egg)*
ACHILLES My sweet Patroclus, I am thwarted quite
From my great purpose in tomorrow's battle.
Here is a letter from Queen Hecuba,
35   A token from her daughter, my fair love,
Both taxing° me, and gaging° me to keep   *reproving / binding*
An oath that I have sworn. I will not break it.
Fall, Greeks; fail, fame; honour, or° go or stay.   *either*
My major vow lies here; this I'll obey.—
40   Come, come, Thersites, help to trim° my tent.   *decorate*
This night in banqueting must all be spent.—
Away, Patroclus.   *Exeunt* [ACHILLES *and* PATROCLUS]
THERSITES With too much blood° and too little brain these two   *passion*
may run mad, but if with too much brain and too little blood
45   they do, I'll be a curer of madmen.⁸ Here's° Agamemnon: an   *Take*
honest fellow enough, and one that loves quails,° but he has   *(as food); prostitutes*
not so much brain as ear-wax. And the goodly transformation
of Jupiter there, his brother the bull,⁹ the primitive° statue and   *archetypal*
oblique° memorial of cuckolds, a thrifty shoeing-horn in a   *perverse*
50   chain, hanging at his brother's leg:¹ to what form but that he is
should wit larded with malice and malice farced° with wit turn   *stuffed*
him to? To an ass were nothing: he is both ass and ox. To an
ox were nothing: he is both ox and ass. To be a dog, a mule, a
cat, a fitchew,² a toad, a lizard, an owl, a puttock,° or a herring   *kite*

4. These may be separate diseases, but they can nearly
all be symptoms of venereal disease. *south:* referring to
the arrival of venereal disease in Europe after the Cru-
sades and its association with Italy, particularly Naples.
loads . . . back: kidney stones. *lethargies:* inertia. *palsies:*
paralysis. *and the like:* for the additional diseases listed
in Q's more elaborate version of this speech, see the
indented passage following (lines 19.1–19.8).
5. Incurable syphilis, and the shriveled absolute possession (as of property) of skin disease.
6. *Thou idle . . . flaps:* You insubstantial fine silk

thread, you immature patch of silk fabric.
7. Possible symptom of venereal disease.
8. A paradox and distinct improbability: a fool curing a
madman.
9. Jupiter made himself into a bull to rape Europa; but
Menelaus is bull-like for almost the opposite reason—
he has the horns of a cuckold.
1. A convenient tool (the shoehorn, suggested by the
cuckold's horn, was sometimes worn on "a chain")
available to serve Agamemnon; also, always underfoot.
2. Polecat (proverbially lecherous and stinking).

55 without a roe,° I would not care; but to be Menelaus!—I would   *(of no value)*
conspire against destiny. Ask me not what I would be if I were
not Thersites, for I care not to be° the louse of a lazar, so³ I   *wouldn't mind being*
were not Menelaus.—Hey-day, sprites and fires.⁴

Enter HECTOR, AJAX, AGAMEMNON, ULYSSES, NESTOR,
[MENELAUS, TROILUS,] *and* DIOMEDES, *with lights*

AGAMEMNON   We go wrong, we go wrong.
AJAX   No, yonder 'tis:
There, where we see the light.
60 HECTOR   I trouble you.
AJAX   No, not a whit.

Enter ACHILLES

ULYSSES   Here comes himself° to guide you.   *the man himself*
ACHILLES   Welcome, brave Hector. Welcome, princes all.
AGAMEMNON [*to* HECTOR]   So now, fair prince of Troy, I bid good night.
Ajax commands the guard to tend on you.
65 HECTOR   Thanks and good night to the Greeks' general.
MENELAUS   Good night, my lord.
HECTOR   Good night, sweet Lord Menelaus.
THERSITES [*aside*]   Sweet draught!⁵ 'Sweet', quoth a?° Sweet   *he*
sink,° sweet sewer.   *cesspool*
ACHILLES   Good night and welcome both at once, to those
70 That go or tarry.
AGAMEMNON   Good night.

Exeunt AGAMEMNON [*and*] MENELAUS

ACHILLES   Old Nestor tarries, and you too, Diomed.
Keep Hector company an hour or two.
DIOMEDES   I cannot, lord. I have important business
75 The tide° whereof is now.—Good night, great Hector.   *time*
HECTOR   Give me your hand.
ULYSSES [*aside to* TROILUS]   Follow his torch, he goes to Calchas' tent.
I'll keep you company.
TROILUS [*aside*]   Sweet sir, you honour me.
HECTOR [*to* DIOMEDES]   And so good night.
ACHILLES   Come, come, enter my tent.

Exeunt [DIOMEDES, *followed by* ULYSSES *and* TROILUS,
at one door; and ACHILLES, HECTOR, AJAX, *and* NESTOR
at another door]

80 THERSITES   That same Diomed's a false-hearted rogue, a most
unjust knave. I will no more trust him when he leers° than I   *smiles*
will a serpent when he hisses. He will spend his mouth and
promise like Brabbler the hound, but when he performs astronomers foretell it: that is prodigious, there will come some
85 change.⁶ The sun borrows of the moon⁷ when Diomed keeps
his word. I will rather leave to see Hector than not to dog him.⁸
They say he keeps a Trojan drab,° and uses the traitor Calchas   *whore*
his tent. I'll after.—Nothing but lechery! All incontinent var-
lets!   *Exit*

---

3. The louse of a leper, as long as.
4. The Greeks approach with torches, suggesting night;
Thersites imagines them to be light-bearing spirits.
5. Drink; team of beasts used for pulling wagons;
cesspool, toilet.
6. *He will . . . change:* He will bark and "promise" (that
there is prey) like a hound that is noisy (quarrelsome),
even when off the scent, but when he actually "per-

forms" (acts in good faith, keeps his word), astronomers
make predictions on that basis: it is such a rare event that
they consider it an ominous warning of a cosmic happening (often indicative of massive political upheaval).
7. It was well known that the moon's light was merely
a reflection of the sun's.
8. I'll stop seeing Hector rather than give up tailing
Diomedes.

5.2

Enter DIOMEDES

DIOMEDES   What, are you up here? Ho! Speak!

CALCHAS [*at the door*]   Who calls?

DIOMEDES   Diomed. Calchas, I think. Where's your daughter?

CALCHAS [*at the door*]   She comes to you.

Enter TROILUS *and* ULYSSES [*unseen*]

5   ULYSSES [*aside*]   Stand where the torch may not discover° us.   disclose

TROILUS [*aside*]   Cressid comes forth to him.

Enter CRESSIDA

DIOMEDES   How now, my charge?

CRESSIDA   Now, my sweet guardian. Hark, a word with you.

[*She whispers to him.*]

[*Enter* THERSITES, *unseen*]

TROILUS [*aside*]   Yea, so familiar?

ULYSSES [*aside*]   She will sing any man at first sight.¹

10   THERSITES [*aside*]   And any man may sing her, if he can take her

clef. She's noted.²

DIOMEDES   Will you remember?

CRESSIDA   Remember? Yes.

DIOMEDES   Nay, but do then,

15   And let your mind be coupled with your words.

TROILUS [*aside*]   What should she remember?

ULYSSES [*aside*]   List!°   Listen

CRESSIDA   Sweet honey Greek, tempt me no more to folly.°   promiscuity

THERSITES [*aside*]   Roguery.

20   DIOMEDES   Nay, then!

CRESSIDA   I'll tell you what—

DIOMEDES   Fo, fo! Come, tell a pin.° You are forsworn.   tell me nothing

CRESSIDA   In faith, I cannot.° What would you have me do?   do as I promised

THERSITES [*aside*]   A juggling trick: to be secretly open.³

25   DIOMEDES   What did you swear you would bestow on me?

CRESSIDA   I prithee, do not hold me to mine oath.

Bid me do anything but that, sweet Greek.

DIOMEDES   Good night.

TROILUS [*aside*]   Hold, patience!

ULYSSES [*aside*]   How now, Trojan?

CRESSIDA   Diomed.

30   DIOMEDES   No, no, good night. I'll be your fool no more.

TROILUS [*aside*]   Thy better must.°   (*be Cressida's fool*)

CRESSIDA   Hark, one word in your ear.

[*She whispers to him*]

TROILUS [*aside*]   O plague and madness!

ULYSSES [*aside*]   You are movèd, Prince. Let us depart, I pray you,

35   Lest your displeasure should enlarge itself

To wrathful terms. This place is dangerous,

The time right deadly. I beseech you go.

TROILUS [*aside*]   Behold, I pray you.

ULYSSES [*aside*]   Nay, good my lord, go off.

You flow° to great distraction. Come, my lord.   rise; flood

TROILUS [*aside*]   I prithee, stay.

5.2 Location: Outside Calchas's tent.
1. As in sight reading of music; Cressida does not need
to know the man beforehand to play (upon) him.
2. *if . . . noted*: if he can take her musical key (also, her

cleft, or pudenda). She's like music written down; she's
notorious.
3. *juggling*: often meant sexual dexterity. *open*: public;
available for sexual intercourse.

40 ULYSSES [*aside*]   You have not patience. Come.
TROILUS [*aside*]   I pray you, stay. By hell and all hell's torments,
    I will not speak a word.
DIOMEDES   And so good night.
CRESSIDA   Nay, but you part in anger.
TROILUS [*aside*]   Doth that grieve thee?
    O withered truth!
ULYSSES [*aside*]   Why, how now, lord?
TROILUS [*aside*]   By Jove,
45   I will be patient.
            [DIOMEDES *starts to go*]
CRESSIDA   Guardian! Why, Greek!
DIOMEDES   Fo, fo! Adieu. You palter.°   *equivocate*
CRESSIDA   In faith, I do not. Come hither once again.
ULYSSES [*aside*]   You shake, my lord, at something. Will you go?
    You will break out.
TROILUS [*aside*]   She strokes his cheek.
50 ULYSSES [*aside*]   Come, come.
TROILUS [*aside*]   Nay, stay. By Jove, I will not speak a word.
    There is between my will and all offences°   *any bad deeds*
    A guard° of patience. Stay a little while.   *barrier*
THERSITES [*aside*]   How the devil Luxury° with his fat rump and   *lust*
55   potato⁴ finger tickles these together! Fry, lechery, fry.⁵
DIOMEDES   But will you then?
CRESSIDA   In faith, I will, la. Never trust me else.
DIOMEDES   Give me some token for the surety of it.
CRESSIDA   I'll fetch you one.   *Exit*
60 ULYSSES [*aside*]   You have sworn patience.
TROILUS [*aside*]   Fear me not, sweet lord.
    I will not be myself, nor have cognition°   *awareness*
    Of what I feel. I am all patience.
            Enter CRESSIDA [*with Troilus' sleeve*]
THERSITES [*aside*]   Now the pledge! Now, now, now.
65 CRESSIDA   Here Diomed, keep this sleeve.
TROILUS [*aside*]   O beauty, where is thy faith?
ULYSSES [*aside*]   My lord.
TROILUS [*aside*]   I will be patient; outwardly I will.
CRESSIDA   You look upon that sleeve. Behold it well.
70   He loved me—O false wench!—give't me again.
            [*She takes it back*]
DIOMEDES   Whose was't?
CRESSIDA   It is no matter, now I ha't again.
    I will not meet with you tomorrow night.
    I prithee, Diomed, visit me no more.
75 THERSITES [*aside*]   Now she sharpens.⁶ Well said, whetstone.
DIOMEDES   I shall have it.
CRESSIDA   What, this?
DIOMEDES   Ay, that.
CRESSIDA   O all you gods! O pretty pretty pledge!
80   Thy master now lies thinking on his bed
    Of thee and me, and sighs, and takes my glove
    And gives memorial° dainty kisses to it—   *in remembrance*

---

4. The Spanish, or sweet, potato was thought to be an   5. In the fires of lust and of hell.
aphrodisiac.   6. Becomes harsh; whets his desire.

DIOMEDES   As I kiss thee.
    [*He snatches the sleeve*]
CRESSIDA   Nay, do not snatch it from me.
  He that takes that doth take my heart withal.
85 DIOMEDES   I had your heart before; this follows it.
  TROILUS [*aside*]   I did swear patience.
  CRESSIDA   You shall not have it, Diomed. Faith, you shall not.
  I'll give you something else.
DIOMEDES   I will have this. Whose was it?
CRESSIDA   It is no matter.
DIOMEDES   Come, tell me whose it was?
90 CRESSIDA   'Twas one's that loved me better than you will.
  But now you have it, take it.
DIOMEDES   Whose was it?
CRESSIDA   By all Diana's waiting-women[7] yond,
  And by herself, I will not tell you whose.
DIOMEDES   Tomorrow will I wear it on my helm,
95 And grieve° his spirit that dares not challenge it.   *afflict*
TROILUS [*aside*]   Wert thou the devil and wor'st it on thy horn,
  It should be challenged.
CRESSIDA   Well, well, 'tis done, 'tis past—and yet it is not.
  I will not keep my word.
DIOMEDES   Why then, farewell.
100 Thou never shalt mock Diomed again.
CRESSIDA   You shall not go. One cannot speak a word
  But it straight starts you.°   *makes you run off*
DIOMEDES   I do not like this fooling.
TROILUS [*aside*]   Nor I, by Pluto—but that that likes° not you   *pleases*
  Pleases me best.
DIOMEDES   What, shall I come? The hour—
105 CRESSIDA   Ay, come. O Jove, do come. I shall be plagued.[8]
DIOMEDES   Farewell till then.
CRESSIDA   Good night. I prithee, come.
                                 Exit [DIOMEDES]
  Troilus, farewell. One eye yet looks on thee,
  But with my heart the other eye doth see.
  Ah, poor our° sex! This fault in us I find: *our poor*
110 The error of our eye directs our mind.
  What error° leads must err. O then conclude: *wandering*
  Minds swayed by eyes are full of turpitude.   *Exit*
THERSITES [*aside*]   A proof of strength she could not publish more[9]
  Unless she said, 'My mind is now turned whore'.
ULYSSES   All's done, my lord.
TROILUS   It is.
115 ULYSSES   Why stay we then?
TROILUS   To make a recordation to my soul
  Of every syllable that here was spoke.
  But if I tell how these two did co-act,
  Shall I not lie in publishing a truth?
120 Sith yet there is a credence in my heart,
  An esperance° so obstinately strong,   *hope*

---

7. The stars (Diana being the goddess of the moon and, ironically, of chastity).
8. Vexed; teased (but also alluding to her eventual fate in late medieval narrative, as a leper). See the Introduction.
9. She could not make a strong proof known more clearly.

That doth invert th'attest° of eyes and ears,   *reverse the testimony*
As if those organs had deceptious° functions   *deceptive*
Created only to calumniate.
Was Cressid here?

125 ULYSSES   I cannot conjure,° Trojan.   *produce a ghost*

TROILUS   She was not, sure.

ULYSSES   Most sure, she was.

TROILUS   Why, my negation hath no taste of madness.

ULYSSES   Nor mine, my lord. Cressid was here but now.

TROILUS   Let it not be believed, for° womanhood.   *for the sake of*

130   Think: we had mothers. Do not give advantage
To stubborn critics, apt without a theme
For depravation° to square the general sex   *denigration*
By Cressid's rule.[1] Rather, think this not Cressid.

ULYSSES   What hath she done, Prince, that can soil our mothers?

135 TROILUS   Nothing at all, unless that this were she.

THERSITES *[aside]*   Will a swagger himself out on's own eyes?[2]

TROILUS   This, she? No, this is Diomed's Cressida.
If beauty have a soul, this is not she.
If souls guide vows, if vows be sanctimonies,°   *sacred things*
140   If sanctimony° be the gods' delight,   *sanctity*
If there be rule in unity itself,°   *unity is indivisible*
This is not she. O madness of discourse,°   *reason*
That cause[3] sets up with and against thyself!
Bifold authority, where reason can revolt
145   Without perdition, and loss assume all reason
Without revolt![4] This is and is not Cressid.
Within my soul there doth conduce° a fight   *come together*
Of this strange nature, that a thing inseparate°   *indivisible*
Divides more wider than the sky and earth,
150   And yet the spacious breadth of this division
Admits no orifex° for a point as subtle°   *orifice / fine*
As Ariachne's[5] broken woof° to enter.   *weaving thread*
Instance,° O instance, strong as Pluto's gates: *Evidence*
Cressid is mine, tied with the bonds of heaven.
155   Instance, O instance, strong as heaven itself:
The bonds of heaven are slipped, dissolved, and loosed,
And with another knot, five-finger-tied,[6]
The fractions° of her faith, orts° of her love,   *pieces / leftover scraps*
The fragments, scraps, the bits and greasy relics
160   Of her o'er-eaten° faith, are bound to Diomed.   *eaten-away; surfeited*

ULYSSES   May worthy Troilus e'en be half attached
With that which here his passion doth express?[7]

TROILUS   Ay, Greek, and that shall be divulgèd well

---

1. *to square . . . rule:* to measure all women by the standard of Cressida.
2. Will he bluster himself out of (the evidence of) his own eyes?
3. *Case*; plea (where, here, defendant and plaintiff are one).
4. *Bifold . . . revolt:* The meaning is obscure. Perhaps: Divided authority, where reason (belief in the testimony of the senses) can revolt against itself (by claiming that this is not in fact Cressida) without being accused of loss of reason ("perdition"); and where loss of reason (inability to trust the senses), without rebelling against reason, can lay claim to being the highest form of reason precisely

because the sensual evidence, which ought to be the highest form of reason, lies (because this cannot be Cressida).
5. A conflation of Arachne the weaver, turned into a spider by Athena for overweening pride in her work, and Ariadne, who gave Theseus a ball of thread to mark his way out of the Labyrinth of her father.
6. United by human hands (Cressida's and Diomedes') as opposed to "the bonds of heaven" (line 156); evilly consummated (alluding to the devil's five fingers, symbolizing the steps to lechery).
7. *May . . . express:* Can worthy Troilus be even half as affected as he seems to be?

In characters as red as Mars his° heart | *Mars's*
165 Inflamed with Venus. Never did young man fancy° | *love*
With so eternal and so fixed a soul.
Hark, Greek: as much as I do Cressid love,
So much by weight hate I her Diomed.
That sleeve is mine that he'll bear in his helm.
170 Were it a casque° composed by Vulcan's[8] skill, | *helmet*
My sword should bite it. Not the dreadful spout
Which shipmen do the hurricano° call, | *waterspout*
Constringed° in mass by the almighty sun, | *Drawn together*
Shall dizzy° with more clamour Neptune's ear | *stun*
175 In his descent, than shall my prompted° sword | *eager*
Falling on Diomed.
THERSITES [*aside*]   He'll tickle it for his concupy.[9]
TROILUS   O Cressid, O false Cressid! False, false, false.
Let all untruths stand by° thy stainèd name, | *be compared with*
And they'll seem glorious.
180 ULYSSES   O contain yourself.
Your passion draws ears hither.
          Enter AENEAS
AENEAS [*to* TROILUS]   I have been seeking you this hour, my lord.
Hector by this° is arming him in Troy. | *by this time*
Ajax your guard stays to conduct you home.
185 TROILUS   Have° with you, Prince.—My courteous lord, adieu.— | *I shall come*
Farewell, revolted fair; and Diomed,
Stand fast and wear a castle° on thy head. | *strong defense*
ULYSSES   I'll bring you to the gates.
TROILUS   Accept distracted thanks.
          Exeunt TROILUS, AENEAS, *and* ULYSSES
THERSITES   Would I could meet that rogue Diomed! I would
190 croak like a raven.[1] I would bode,° I would bode. Patroclus will | *foretell evil*
give me anything for the intelligence° of this whore. The parrot | *secret information*
will not do more for an almond[2] than he for a commodious
drab.° Lechery, lechery, still wars and lechery! Nothing else | *willing whore*
holds fashion. A burning devil° take them!   *Exit* | *venereal disease*

5.3

          Enter HECTOR [*armed*] *and* ANDROMACHE
ANDROMACHE   When was my lord so much ungently tempered
To stop his ears against admonishment?
Unarm, unarm, and do not fight today.
HECTOR   You train° me to offend you. Get you in. | *teach*
5 By all the everlasting gods, I'll go.
ANDROMACHE   My dreams will sure prove ominous to the day.° | *true omens of the day*
HECTOR   No more, I say.
          Enter CASSANDRA
CASSANDRA   Where is my brother Hector?
ANDROMACHE   Here, sister, armed and bloody in intent.
Consort° with me in loud and dear° petition, | *Join / earnest*

---

8. Smith of the gods, Vulcan made armor for various classical heroes, most notably Achilles.
9. (Probably) Troilus will "tickle" (beat [ironic]) Diomedes' helmet for his lust (his concubine).

1. Proverbially birds of ill omen.
2. *The parrot . . . almond:* Proverbial for a brainless passion for a trivial delicacy.
5.3 Location: Priam's palace.

10   Pursue we him on knees—for I have dreamed
     Of bloody turbulence, and this whole night
     Hath nothing been but shapes and forms of slaughter.
CASSANDRA   O 'tis true.
HECTOR   Ho! Bid my trumpet sound.
CASSANDRA   No notes of sally, for the heavens, sweet brother.
15 HECTOR   Begone, I say. The gods have heard me swear.
CASSANDRA   The gods are deaf to hot and peevish° vows.   *headstrong*
     They° are polluted off 'rings, more abhorred   *Rash vows*
     Than spotted livers° in the sacrifice.   *ruined offerings*
ANDROMACHE [*to* HECTOR]   O, be persuaded. Do not count it holy
20   To hurt by being just.° It is as lawful,   *true to your vow*
     For we would° give much, to use violent thefts,   *Because we want to*
     And rob in the behalf of charity.
CASSANDRA   It is the purpose that makes strong the vow,
     But vows to every purpose must not° hold.   *do not have to*
     Unarm, sweet Hector.
25 HECTOR   Hold you still,° I say.   *Stop it*
     Mine honour keeps the weather[1] of my fate.
     Life every man holds dear, but the dear° man   *worthy*
     Holds honour far more precious-dear than life.
             Enter TROILUS [*armed*]
     How now, young man, mean'st thou to fight today?
30 ANDROMACHE [*aside*]   Cassandra, call my father° to persuade.   *father-in-law*
                                     Exit CASSANDRA
HECTOR   No, faith, young Troilus. Doff thy harness,° youth.   *Disarm*
     I am today i'th' vein of° chivalry.   *mood for*
     Let grow thy sinews till their knots be strong,
     And tempt not yet the brushes° of the war.   *encounters*
35   Unarm thee, go—and doubt thou not, brave boy,
     I'll stand today for thee and me and Troy.
TROILUS   Brother, you have a vice of mercy in you,
     Which better fits a lion[2] than a man.
HECTOR   What vice is that? Good Troilus, chide me for it.
40 TROILUS   When many times the captive° Grecian falls   *miserable*
     Even in the fan and wind of your fair sword,[3]
     You bid them rise and live.
HECTOR   O 'tis fair play.
TROILUS   Fool's play, by heaven, Hector.
45 HECTOR   How now! How now!
TROILUS   For th' love of all the gods,
     Let's leave the hermit pity with our mother
     And, when we have our armours buckled on,
     The venomed vengeance ride upon our swords,
50   Spur them to ruthful° work, rein them from ruth.°   *woeful / pity*
HECTOR   Fie, savage, fie!
TROILUS   Hector, then 'tis wars.°   *then it's a true war*
HECTOR   Troilus, I would not have you fight today.
TROILUS   Who should withhold me?
     Not fate, obedience, nor the hand of Mars

---

1. My honor stays to windward (in sailing, a ship windward of another takes its wind, and so gets the better of
it).
2. Lions were said not to attack any animal that submitted to them.
3. The rapidly moving sword is like a fan, blowing his
enemies down before he reaches them.

55 Beck'ning with fiery truncheon[4] my retire,
Not Priamus and Hecuba on knees,
Their eyes o'er-gallèd° with recourse° of tears,   *sore / repeated flow*
Nor you, my brother, with your true sword drawn
Opposed to hinder me, should stop my way
60 But by my ruin.

    Enter PRIAM *and* CASSANDRA

CASSANDRA   Lay hold upon him, Priam, hold him fast.
He is thy crutch: now if thou loose thy stay,°   *prop*
Thou on him leaning and all Troy on thee,
Fall all together.
PRIAM   Come, Hector, come. Go back.
65 Thy wife hath dreamt, thy mother hath had visions,
Cassandra doth foresee, and I myself
Am like a prophet suddenly enrapt°   *inspired*
To tell thee that this day is ominous.
Therefore come back.
HECTOR   Aeneas is afield,
70 And I do stand engaged to many Greeks,
Even in the faith of valour,° to appear   *warrior's honor*
This morning to them.
PRIAM   Ay, but thou shalt not go.
HECTOR [*kneeling*]   I must not break my faith.
75 You know me dutiful; therefore, dear sire,
Let me not shame respect,° but give me leave   *duty to a parent*
To take that course, by your consent and voice,
Which you do here forbid me, royal Priam.
CASSANDRA   O Priam, yield not to him.
ANDROMACHE   Do not, dear father.
80 HECTOR   Andromache, I am offended with you.
Upon the love you bear me, get you in.   *Exit* ANDROMACHE
TROILUS   This foolish, dreaming, superstitious girl
Makes all these bodements.°   *warnings*
CASSANDRA   O farewell, dear Hector.
Look how thou diest; look how thy eye turns pale;
85 Look how thy wounds do bleed at many vents.
Hark how Troy roars, how Hecuba cries out,
How poor Andromache shrills her dolours forth.
Behold: distraction, frenzy, and amazement
Like witless antics° one another meet,   *buffoons*
90 And all cry 'Hector, Hector's dead, O Hector!'
TROILUS   Away, away!
CASSANDRA   Farewell. Yet soft:° Hector, I take my leave.   *wait a moment*
Thou dost thyself and all our Troy deceive.   *Exit*
HECTOR [*to* PRIAM]   You are amazed, my liege, at her exclaim.°   *outcry*
95 Go in and cheer the town. We'll forth and fight,
Do deeds of praise, and tell you them at night.
PRIAM   Farewell. The gods with safety stand about thee.
    [*Exeunt* PRIAM *and* HECTOR *severally*.°] *Alarum*   *separately*
TROILUS   They are at it, hark! Proud Diomed, believe
I come to lose my arm or win my sleeve.

    Enter PANDARUS

100 PANDARUS   Do you hear, my lord, do you hear?

---

4. Staff of office (carried by the marshal of a formal combat).

TROILUS What now?

PANDARUS Here's a letter come from yon poor girl.

TROILUS Let me read.

[TROILUS *reads the letter*]

PANDARUS A whoreson phthisic,° a whoreson rascally phthisic so   *consumptive cough*
105   troubles me, and the foolish fortune of this girl, and what one
thing, what another, that I shall leave you one o' these days.
And I have a rheum° in mine eyes too, and such an ache in my   *watery discharge*
bones° that unless a man were cursed I cannot tell what to   *(suggesting syphilis)*
think on't.—What says she there?

TROILUS [*tearing the letter*] Words, words, mere words, no mat-
110   ter from the heart.

Th'effect° doth operate another way.   *Her action*

Go, wind, to wind: there turn and change together.[5]

My love with words and errors° still she feeds,   *lies*

But edifies another with her deeds.

115 PANDARUS Why, but hear you—

TROILUS Hence, broker-lackey!° Ignomy° and shame   *pimp / Ignominy*

Pursue thy life, and live aye with thy name. *Exeunt* [*severally*][6]

5.4

Alarum. Enter THERSITES [*in*] *excursions*°   *advancing troops*

THERSITES Now they are clapper-clawing° one another. I'll go   *thrashing*
look on. That dissembling abominable varlet Diomed has got
that same scurvy doting foolish young knave's sleeve of Troy°   *Trojan knave's sleeve*
there in his helm. I would fain see them meet, that that same
5   young Trojan ass that loves the whore there might send that
Greekish whoremasterly villain with the sleeve back to the dissembling luxurious drab of a sleeveless errand.[1] O'th' t'other
side, the policy° of those crafty swearing rascals—that stale old   *statecraft; scheming*
mouse-eaten dry cheese Nestor and that same dog-fox° Ulys-   *crafty one*
10   ses—is proved not worth a blackberry.° They set me up° in   *proved worthless / set up*
policy that mongrel cur Ajax against that dog of as bad a kind
Achilles. And now is the cur Ajax prouder than the cur Achilles, and will not arm today—whereupon the Grecians began
to proclaim barbarism,[2] and policy grows into an ill opinion.°   *gets a bad reputation*

Enter DIOMEDES, [*followed by*] TROILUS

15 Soft, here comes sleeve and t'other.

TROILUS [*to* DIOMEDES] Fly not, for shouldst thou take the river Styx[3]
I would swim after.

DIOMEDES   Thou dost miscall retire.°   *mistake my retreat*

I do not fly, but advantageous care°   *tactical caution*

Withdrew me from the odds of multitude. Have at thee!

[*They fight*]

20 THERSITES Hold thy whore, Grecian! Now for thy whore, Trojan! Now the sleeve, now the sleeve!

[*Exit* DIOMEDES, *driving in* TROILUS]

Enter HECTOR [*behind*]

---

5. Go, empty words, into the breeze: there, along with
the air, toss about ("turn" was often used of sexual infidelity).
6. The last three lines of this scene are not in Q. A similar exchange occurs at the end of the play in both Q and
F. See indented passage after 5.11.31 and Textual Note.
5.4 Location: The rest of the play takes place on the

battlefield.
1. To the lying, lecherous slut on a pointless errand
(punning on the actual sleeve).
2. Began to set up whim and ignorance in authority
("barbarism" being normally contrasted with "Greek").
3. Even if you should enter the river of the underworld
(as prey hoping to make the hunter lose the scent).

HECTOR   What art thou, Greek? Art thou for Hector's match?
Art thou of blood° and honour?   *nobility*
THERSITES   No, no, I am a rascal, a scurvy railing knave, a very
25   filthy rogue.
HECTOR   I do believe thee: live.[4]
THERSITES   God-a-mercy,° that thou wilt believe me—   *Thank God*
                              [*Exit* HECTOR]
but a plague break thy neck for frighting me. What's become
of the wenching rogues? I think they have swallowed one
30   another. I would laugh at that miracle—yet in a sort lechery
eats itself. I'll seek them.   *Exit*

5.5
Enter DIOMEDES *and* SERVANTS
DIOMEDES   Go, go, my servant, take thou Troilus' horse.
Present the fair steed to my Lady Cressid.
Fellow, commend my service to her beauty.
Tell her I have chastised the amorous Trojan,
And am her knight by proof.°   *(of deeds)*
5   SERVANT   I go, my lord.   [*Exit*]
Enter AGAMEMNON
AGAMEMNON   Renew, renew! The fierce Polydamas
Hath beat down Menon; bastard Margareton
Hath Doreus prisoner,
And stands colossus-wise waving his beam°   *spearshaft*
10   Upon the pashèd° corpses of the kings   *smashed*
Epistropus and Cedius; Polixenes is slain,
Amphimacus and Thoas deadly hurt,
Patroclus ta'en or slain, and Palamedes
Sore hurt and bruised; the dreadful sagittary[1]
15   Appals our numbers.° Haste we, Diomed,   *soldiers*
To reinforcement, or we perish all.
Enter NESTOR [*with Patroclus' body*]
NESTOR   Go, bear Patroclus' body to Achilles,
And bid the snail-paced Ajax arm for shame.
                [*Exit one or more with the body*]
There is a thousand Hectors in the field.
20   Now here he fights on Galathe his horse,
And there lacks work; anon he's there afoot,
And there they fly or die, like scalèd schools[2]
Before the belching° whale. Then is he yonder,   *spouting*
And there the strawy Greeks, ripe for his edge,°   *sword blade*
25   Fall down before him like the mower's swath.
Here, there, and everywhere he leaves and takes,[3]
Dexterity so obeying appetite
That what he will he does, and does so much
That proof° is called impossibility.   *his achievement*
Enter ULYSSES
30   ULYSSES   O courage, courage, princes! Great Achilles
Is arming, weeping, cursing, vowing vengeance.

---

4. Here Hector is at once contemptuous and merciful.   2. Scaly (armor-clad) schools of fish.
5.5   3. He spares and kills; possibly, he "leaves" the dead
1. A legendary centaurlike beast, armed with bow and   and "takes" on the living.
arrows.

Patroclus' wounds have roused his drowsy blood,
Together with his mangled Myrmidons,
That noseless, handless, hacked and chipped come to him
35 Crying on° Hector. Ajax hath lost a friend   *Complaining of*
And foams at mouth, and he is armed and at it,
Roaring for Troilus—who hath done today
Mad and fantastic execution,
Engaging and redeeming of° himself   *Risking and saving*
40 With such a careless force and forceless care°   *effortless diligence*
As if that luck, in very spite of cunning,°   *his foes' skill*
Bade him win all.
   Enter AJAX
AJAX   Troilus, thou coward Troilus!   *Exit*
DIOMEDES   Ay, there, there!   *Exit*
45 NESTOR   So, so, we draw together.°   *join forces*
   Enter ACHILLES
ACHILLES   Where is this Hector?
Come, come, thou brave boy-queller, show thy face.
Know what it is to meet Achilles angry.
Hector! Where's Hector? I will none but Hector.   *Exeunt*

5.6

   Enter AJAX
AJAX   Troilus, thou coward Troilus! Show thy head!
   Enter DIOMEDES
DIOMEDES   Troilus, I say! Where's Troilus?
AJAX   What wouldst thou?
DIOMEDES   I would correct° him.   *chastise*
AJAX   Were I the general, thou shouldst have my office
5   Ere° that correction.—Troilus, I say! What, Troilus!   *Before you should have*
   Enter TROILUS
TROILUS   O traitor Diomed! Turn thy false face, thou traitor,
And pay the life thou ow'st me for my horse.
DIOMEDES   Ha, art thou there?
AJAX   I'll fight with him alone. Stand, Diomed.
10 DIOMEDES   He is my prize; I will not look upon.°   *be a spectator*
TROILUS   Come, both you cogging° Greeks, have at you both!   *cheating*
   [*They fight.*]
   Enter HECTOR
HECTOR   Yea, Troilus? O well fought, my youngest brother!
   Exit TROILUS [*driving* DIOMEDES *and* AJAX *in*]
   Enter ACHILLES [*behind*]
ACHILLES   Now do I see thee.—Ha! Have at thee, Hector.
   [*They fight.* ACHILLES *is bested*]
HECTOR   Pause, if thou wilt.
15 ACHILLES   I do disdain thy courtesy, proud Trojan.
Be happy that my arms are out of use.°   *practice*
My rest and negligence befriends thee now;
But thou anon shalt hear of me again.
Till when, go seek thy fortune.   *Exit*
HECTOR   Fare thee well.
20   I would have been much more a fresher man
Had I expected thee.
   Enter TROILUS [*in haste*]

How now, my brother?
TROILUS Ajax hath ta'en° Aeneas. Shall it be?   *taken captive*
No, by the flame of yonder glorious heaven,
He shall not carry him. I'll be ta'en too,
25 Or bring him off.° Fate, hear me what I say: *rescue Aeneas*
I reck° not though thou end my life today.   *Exit*   *care*
            Enter one in [sumptuous] armour
HECTOR Stand, stand, thou Greek! Thou art a goodly mark.°   *target*
No? Wilt thou not? I like thy armour well.
I'll frush° it and unlock the rivets all,   *smash*
But I'll be master of it.   *[Exit one in armour]*
30   Wilt thou not, beast, abide?
Why then, fly on; I'll hunt thee for thy hide.   *Exit*

5.7
            Enter ACHILLES *with Myrmidons*
ACHILLES Come here about me, you my Myrmidons.
Mark what I say. Attend me where I wheel;°   *range*
Strike not a stroke, but keep yourselves in breath,
And when I have the bloody Hector found,
5 Empale° him with your weapons round about.   *Fence in*
In fellest° manner execute your arms.   *fiercest*
Follow me, sirs, and my proceedings eye.
It is decreed Hector the great must die.   *Exeunt*

5.8
            Enter MENELAUS *and* PARIS, *[fighting, then]* THERSITES[1]
THERSITES The cuckold and the cuckold-maker are at it.—
Now, bull! Now, dog! 'Loo,[2] Paris, 'loo! Now, my double-
horned[3] Spartan! 'Loo, Paris, 'loo! The bull has the game.°   *is winning*
Ware° horns, ho!   *Exit* MENELAUS, *[driving in]* PARIS   *Beware*
            Enter BASTARD *[behind]*
5 BASTARD Turn, slave, and fight.
THERSITES What art thou?
BASTARD A bastard son of Priam's.
THERSITES I am a bastard, too. I love bastards. I am bastard
begot, bastard instructed, bastard in mind, bastard in valour,
10 in everything illegitimate. One bear will not bite another, and
wherefore should one bastard? Take heed: the quarrel's most
ominous to us. If the son of a whore fight for a whore, he tempts
judgement. Farewell, bastard.   *[Exit]*
BASTARD The devil take thee, coward.   *Exit*

5.9
            Enter HECTOR *[dragging the one in sumptuous armour]*
HECTOR *[taking off the helmet]* Most putrefièd core, so fair without,
Thy goodly armour thus hath cost thy life.
Now is my day's work done. I'll take good breath.
Rest, sword: thou hast thy fill of blood and death.

5.8
1. Most modern editions do not mark a scene break
here; this affects the numbering of the following lines
and scenes. See Textual Note.

2. Halloo (shout to encourage dogs chasing game or in
bullbaiting).
3 Two-horned, like a bull; horned because a cuckold.
5.9

[*He disarms.*]
Enter ACHILLES *and his Myrmidons [surrounding*
HECTOR]

5 ACHILLES   Look, Hector, how the sun begins to set,
How ugly night comes breathing at his heels.
Even with the veil[1] and dark'ning of the sun
To close the day up, Hector's life is done.
HECTOR   I am unarmed. Forgo this vantage, Greek.
10 ACHILLES   Strike, fellows, strike! This is the man I seek.
[*The Myrmidons kill* HECTOR]
So, Ilium, fall thou. Now, Troy, sink down.
Here lies thy heart, thy sinews, and thy bone.—
On, Myrmidons, and cry you all amain,°   with full force
'Achilles hath the mighty Hector slain!'
[*A*] *retreat* [*is sounded*]
15 Hark, a retire upon our Grecian part.
[*Another retreat is sounded*]
A MYRMIDON   The Trojan trumpets sound the like, my lord.
ACHILLES   The dragon wing of night o'erspreads the earth
And, stickler°-like, the armies separates.   referee (in combat)
My half-supped° sword, that frankly° would have fed,   half-satisfied / freely
20 Pleased with this dainty bait,° thus goes to bed.   snack
[*He sheathes his sword*]
Come, tie his body to my horse's tail.
Along the field I will the Trojan trail.   *Exeunt* [*dragging the bodies*]

5.10

[*A*] *retreat* [*is*] *sound*[*ed*]. *Enter* AGAMEMNON, AJAX,
MENELAUS, NESTOR, DIOMEDES, *and the rest, marching.*
[*A*] *shout* [*within*]
AGAMEMNON   Hark, hark! What shout is that?
NESTOR   Peace, drums.
MYRMIDONS (*within*)   Achilles!
Achilles! Hector's slain! Achilles!
DIOMEDES   The bruit° is: Hector's slain, and by Achilles.   report
AJAX   If it be so, yet bragless let it be.
5 Great Hector was a man as good as he.
AGAMEMNON   March patiently along. Let one be sent
To pray Achilles see us at our tent.
If in his death the gods have us befriended,
Great Troy is ours, and our sharp° wars are ended.   fierce
Exeunt [*marching*]

5.11

Enter AENEAS, PARIS, ANTENOR, *and* DEIPHOBUS
AENEAS   Stand, ho! Yet are we masters of the field.
Never go home; here starve[1] we out the night.
Enter TROILUS
TROILUS   Hector is slain.
ALL THE OTHERS   Hector? The gods forbid.

---

1. At the same time as the setting.
5.11
1. Wait in discomfort; outlast, kill by starvation (the
night being imagined as a city under siege).

TROILUS   He's dead, and at the murderer's horse's tail
5   In beastly sort° dragged through the shameful field.   *manner*
         Frown on, you heavens; effect your rage with speed;
         Sit, gods, upon your thrones, and smite at Troy.
         I say, at once: let your brief plagues be mercy,[2]
         And linger not our sure destructions on.
10 AENEAS   My lord, you do discomfort all the host.°   *army*
    TROILUS   You understand me not that tell me so.
         I do not speak of flight, of fear of death,
         But dare all imminence that gods and men
         Address their dangers in.[3] Hector is gone.
15   Who shall tell Priam so, or Hecuba?
         Let him that will a screech-owl aye° be called   *voice of doom always*
         Go into Troy and say their Hector's dead.
         There is a word° will Priam turn to stone,   *sentence*
         Make wells and Niobes[4] of the maids and wives,
20   Cold statues of the youth, and in a word
         Scare Troy out of itself. But march away.
         Hector is dead; there is no more to say.
         Stay yet.—You vile abominable tents
         Thus proudly pitched upon our Phrygian plains,
25   Let Titan° rise as early as he dare,   *sun god Hyperion*
         I'll through and through you! And thou great-sized coward,°   *Achilles*
         No space of earth shall sunder our two hates.
         I'll haunt thee like a wicked conscience still,
         That mouldeth goblins swift as frenzy's thoughts.
30   Strike a free march! To Troy with comfort° go: *this one comfort*
         Hope of revenge shall hide our inward woe.   [*Exeunt marching*][5]
                [*Enter* PANDARUS]
1.1 PANDARUS   But hear you, hear you.
     TROILUS   Hence, broker-lackey. [*Strikes him*] *Ignomy and shame*
             Pursue thy like, and live aye with thy name.   Exeunt [*all but* PANDARUS]
     PANDARUS   *A goodly medicine for my aching bones. O*
1.5   *world, world, world!—thus is the poor agent despised.*
             O traitors and bawds, how earnestly are you set a° work,   *to*
             and how ill requited! Why should our endeavour be so
             desired and the performance so loathed? What verse
             for it? What instance° for it? Let me see,   *traditional saying*
1.10   *Full merrily the humble-bee doth sing*
                 Till he hath lost his honey and his sting,
                 And being once subdued in armèd tail,[6]
                 Sweet honey and sweet notes together fail.
             Good traders in the flesh, set this in your painted cloths:[7]
1.15   *As many as be here of Pandar's hall,°*   *guild hall*
                 Your eyes, half out,[8] *weep out at Pandar's fall.*
                 Or if you cannot weep, yet give some groans,
                 Though not for me, yet for your aching bones.°   *(from syphilis)*
                 Brethren and sisters of the hold-door trade,°   *Pimps and bawds*

2. Be mercifully quick in destruction.
3. *But . . . in:* But dare all impending danger that gods
and men prepare for me.
4. Mythical Queen of Thebes, who wept so much at
the murder of her children by the gods that the gods
turned her into a statue that flowed with water.
5. For the extended conclusion with Pandarus's epilogue, see indented passage below (lines 31.1–31.24).

The exit marked here is deferred until line 31.3. For discussion, see the Textual Note and Introduction.
6. And having lost his sting: alluding to impotence
caused by venereal disease.
7. Inexpensive substitutes for tapestries, often including moralistic inscriptions.
8. Half-blinded by venereal disease.

31.20   *Some two months hence my will shall here be made.*[9]
It should be now, but that my fear is this:
Some gallèd goose of Winchester would hiss.[1]
Till then I'll sweat[2] *and seek about for eases,*
And at that time bequeath you my diseases.   *Exit*

---

9. "Here" is possibly a reference to the stage of the Globe and hence the promise of a sequel that never materialized; it has also been taken to refer to an Inn of Court, where young men studied law, a plausible place to make a "will" and thus hypothesized by some scholars to be the location of the first performance. See the Introduction.

1. A prostitute or customer afflicted with venereal disease, from the diocese of Winchester (which had jurisdiction over Southwark, home of both the brothels and the Globe), would disapprove—of the will and/or the play. 2. Usual treatment for venereal disease.

Measure for Measure

A young man is in grave trouble with the law, and his beautiful sister goes to the magistrate to plead for mercy. The magistrate offers to remit the penalty if the sister will sleep with him. It is an old story in more ways than one. Shakespeare knew several sixteenth-century versions: the Italian Giovanbattista Giraldi Cinthio produced both prose and dramatic renderings, and in 1578 the English playwright George Whetstone published *Promos and Cassandra*, the most important source for *Measure for Measure*. Shakespeare took the title of his play from Jesus' Sermon on the Mount: "Judge not, that ye be not judged. For with what judgment ye judge, ye shall be judged: and with what measure ye mete, it shall be measured to you again" (Matthew 7:1–2). Jesus' advice combines threat with promise: a prudent fear of heavenly retaliation persuades believers not to pass judgment themselves, while at the same time, an apparent abdication of equity is folded into an overall scheme of just compensation. As we shall see, the passage in all its complexity complements the intricacies of Shakespeare's treatment of the ancient tale.

 Measure for Measure was performed in 1604 at a pivotal moment in Shakespeare's career. The play is the last in a long series of comedies that explore complex issues of sex, marriage, and personal identity. Its tone, themes, and methods of characterization, however, veer close to tragedy, the genre that largely, though not exclusively, preoccupied Shakespeare in the years immediately following. Many critics, therefore, classify *Measure for Measure* as a "problem" comedy. The designation attests both to the difficult moral issues that the play confronts and to the boldness with which it stretches—some would say shatters—the normal limits of comic form.

 The play's distinctiveness becomes evident almost immediately. In Act 1, Scene 2, Claudio and his pregnant lover, Juliet, appear in the custody of the Provost, being led away to prison. Their crime is premarital sex; the penalty, for Claudio at least, is death. The seriousness of their situation is not in itself unusual: "The course of true love never did run smooth," Lysander remarks in *A Midsummer Night's Dream*, and if it did, it would hardly make an engrossing dramatic subject. Nonetheless, Claudio's initial description of his plight is quite remarkable:

> LUCIO Why, how now, Claudio? Whence comes this restraint?
> CLAUDIO From too much liberty, my Lucio, liberty.
> As surfeit is the father of much fast,
> So every scope, by the immoderate use,
> Turns to restraint. Our natures do pursue,
> Like rats that raven down their proper bane,
> A thirsty evil; and when we drink, we die.
>
> (1.2.104–10)

Claudio likens his passion for his beloved to a rat's craving for poison: compulsive, irrational, and self-destructive. Excessive indulgence, or "surfeit," inevitably brings regret and punishment in its train. Claudio sounds as if he is describing the most arrant kind of lust, although, as he will subsequently explain, he is actually "precontracted" to Juliet, bound by a promise of marriage that many in Renaissance England saw as providing conjugal privileges. (Shakespeare himself may have subscribed to this view, since his wife gave birth to their daughter five months after their wedding. More pertinently, the Duke, in his guise as a friar, affirms that the precontract sanctions Mariana's intimacy with Angelo later in the play.) Interestingly, however, neither Claudio nor Juliet is inclined to argue that their devotion to one another mitigates their guilt. Instead, they admit that they have committed "fornication," a severely condemnatory term that conflates all kinds of sex outside of marriage under the same rubric, recognizing no difference between long-term relationships and sheerest promiscuity.

As the play continues, it becomes clear that Claudio's imagery of suicidal animalism, havoc, and pollution is not merely the consequence of his immediate agitation, but expresses a profound assumption of the society in which he lives. For his sister, Isabella, sexual intercourse is "what I abhor to name" (3.1.100); the Duke deplores Pompey's "filthy vice" and Juliet's "most offenseful act"; the wise Escalus acknowledges Claudio's "error" even as he attempts to alleviate his punishment. Few doubt that human sexuality is an essentially sordid matter, a sign of degradation rather than a means of creativity or love. Occasional glimpses of an alternative vision—Lucio's brief, radiant analogy between Juliet's pregnancy and agricultural fertility, for instance—by their very rarity reinforce the prevailing pessimism.

Such austere views of human sexuality have ancient roots. When the Duke calls Vienna's sex laws "needful bits and curbs to headstrong weeds" (1.3.20), he recalls an image from Plato, who compared the desiring part of the soul to a useful but refractory horse, which the rational part of the soul needs to keep strictly bridled and under firm control. When Isabella refers to erotic desire as a "natural guiltiness" (2.2.142), she draws upon a traditional Christian connection between sexuality and original sin, the disobedience committed by Adam and Eve in the Garden of Eden and passed on to all their offspring as a kind of intrinsic pollution.

To say that a view is traditional, however, is not to say that it is inevitable. What makes sexuality so troublesome in this particular play? In Shakespeare's earlier, more optimistic comedies, the prospect of heterosexual consummation usually seems automatically to entail marriage, so that the weddings with which the plays conclude seem to follow spontaneously from the eroticism that fuels the plot. By marrying and establishing a family, the young couples simultaneously satisfy their mutual yearning for one another, and their community's demand for clear kinship structures and for orderly means of transferring property to "legitimate" members of a new generation. In *Measure for Measure*, however, the link between heterosexual desire and marriage seems to have snapped. Claudio and Juliet defer their wedding day; Angelo abandons Mariana; Lucio refuses to support his child or marry its mother. Prostitution flourishes. Rampant promiscuity makes syphilis a familiar ailment and a standard topic for nervous jokes.

Charioteer with two galloping horses. From Geffrey Whitney, *A Choice of Emblemes* (1586).

Once carnal desire comes unhinged from the institution of marriage, it begins to seem subversive of personal and civic order. And if one believes, rightly or wrongly, that one's sexuality is intrinsically antisocial and depraved, then complete sexual renunciation might seem the wisest course. In *Measure for Measure*, the morally ambitious characters—the Duke, Angelo, and Isabella—initially assume that their virtue is tied up with, perhaps even identical with, their chastity. "Believe not that the dribbling dart of love / Can pierce a complete bosom," the Duke boasts to the Friar (1.3.2–3). Angelo attempts to protect his reputation for austerity even as he hopelessly compromises his scruples in secret. Isabella believes that sleeping with Angelo will defile her forever, even if she does so in order to save her brother's life.

The value of celibacy is endorsed by characters who do not themselves aspire to such high standards of conduct. Lucio is a libertine, but he believes that Isabella's intention to enter a nunnery renders her "a thing enskied and sainted" (1.4.33). Likewise, Pompey admits that his life as a pimp "does stink in some sort, sir" (3.1.283). A few of those who cannot be chaste themselves are, like Claudio, capable of moments of shame or self-loathing; others, like Lucio, shruggingly accept their lack of saintliness. The Vienna of *Measure for Measure* is full of people unlikely to be enlisted for projects of social or spiritual improvement: the moronic Elbow, the impenitent Pompey, the unregenerate Mistress Overdone, the "gravel-hearted" Barnardine, the heedless First and Second Gentlemen, the gullible Froth. These people are part of the commonwealth, subject to the law, and willy-nilly part, too, of a Catholic church that aspires—unlike some of the Protestant sects of Shakespeare's time—to include the entire community. Should the laws of this community reflect its stringent ideals or the actual behavior of most of its members? Throughout the play, those who aspire to belong to a principled moral elite deplore the weaknesses of the reprobate. At the same time, because the rascals in *Measure for Measure* are so vividly memorable, the play also suggests that moral "failure" is often at least as humanly compelling as moral excellence is—at least moral excellence defined in the narrow, self-denying terms that prevail in Vienna.

For the intransigent majority unable or unwilling to control the horses of lust, the "needful bits and curbs" of which the Duke speaks impose an external system of repression. Such a system would not have been unfamiliar to Shakespeare's original audience. Courts administered by the Church of England prosecuted many sexual infractions: among them fathering or giving birth to a bastard, committing adultery or bigamy, deserting a spouse, reneging on a wedding engagement, or groundlessly accusing others of such transgressions. Convicted individuals could be fined, whipped, displayed in the marketplace, or made to announce their sins in church. (Thus Claudio and Juliet are paraded about the streets of Vienna before being taken to prison, to humiliate them and to serve as an example for others.) Repeat offenders were excommunicated, or cast out of the church.

Underlying such proceedings was the assumption, as in *Measure for Measure*, that morality could and should be legislated; that the sexual conduct of individuals was the business of the entire community. Indeed, in the early seventeenth century, when Shakespeare was writing *Measure for Measure,* an increasingly powerful group of Puritans, or "precisians," argued that the church courts' punishments were far too mild. Threats of disgrace and excommunication failed to deter the most egregious offenders, who had no reputation to lose and were unlikely to fret at their exclusion from church. Moreover, shaming punishments worked less well in the increasingly busy, heterogeneous neighborhoods of Jacobean London than they had in the smaller rural communities for which they had originally been designed.

In *Measure for Measure,* the repeated characterization of Angelo as "precise" associates him with the rigorists of Shakespeare's time; and since Viennese justice treats Claudio more strictly than it does professionals in the sex trade, the question of what constitutes adequate severity is certainly at issue. Perhaps, then, the play comprises Shakespeare's reflection on an issue of contemporary concern: what would happen if, as some argued, sexual misconduct could be punished with death? At the same time, Shakespeare carefully distinguishes the world of his play from seventeenth-century England, most obviously by making Vienna a Catholic city peopled with the nuns and friars who had been eliminated from Protestant England over half a century earlier. For despite obvious connections between *Measure for Measure* and some of the issues of its own day, Shakespeare's play hardly constitutes a clear policy recommendation. He is more deeply attentive to general issues about the often-vexed relationship between civic life and human passion, and between religious commitment and the conduct of secular affairs. What happens to individuals and a community when sexuality is viewed as transgressive, when it becomes the subject of public discipline? Is it possible or advisable to regulate sexual behavior through the courts? How do religious convictions affect the experience of sexual desire? These concerns resonate in an era like our own, characterized by a lack of consensus in religion and in sexual mores, by widespread transformations in the institution of marriage, and by debates over the extent to which the state ought to monitor the sexual behavior of citizens.

In *Measure for Measure,* Angelo's disastrous career suggests one possible effect of strict sexual self-denial: that the habits of restraint can themselves provoke sexual excitement. Rigid and self-righteous, Angelo seems not to have experienced the violence of desire until Isabella's first visit on behalf of her brother awakens his appetite:

> What's this? What's this? Is this her fault or mine?
> The tempter or the tempted, who sins most, ha?
> Not she; nor doth she tempt; but it is I
> That, lying by the violet in the sun,
> Do, as the carrion does, not as the flower,
> Corrupt with virtuous season.
>
> (2.2.167–72)

Like Claudio, Angelo thinks of passion in terms of death and decay, but the resemblance between the two men ends there. Angelo imagines himself as tainted meat rotting all the

Jost Amman, Poor Clare nun, from *Cleri totius Romanae ecclesiae subjecti* (1585).

faster under the very sun that gives life to innocent, lovely things. What ought to improve Angelo—his keen appreciation for the presence of virtue—makes him worse.

Angelo is sexually aroused by prohibition. Mariana loves him, and his relationship with her breaches no social norms; he discards her. Isabella is ostentatiously pristine, and her nun's habit marks her as taboo; he finds her irresistible. In order to extract pleasure from the encounter, however, Angelo must force himself to remain aware of the principles he attempts so flagrantly to violate. If he rationalized his behavior or blamed it on Isabella, he would lose the nearly sensual luxury of self-hatred. Therefore, the lucidity with which Angelo analyzes his own motives leads not to penitence but to an increasing moral recklessness. His inclination to categorize all sexual conduct as transgressive actually makes his offense easier to commit. Propositioning Isabella in their second meeting together, he tells her: "I have begun, / And now I give my sensual race the rein" (2.4.159–60). Angelo explains why he cannot govern himself with the same image the Duke used to underscore the necessity of control. Once embarked on the "sensual race," he imagines, there is no alternative to utter abandon.

For Isabella, however, sleeping with Angelo is out of the question. Some modern critics have found her defiance heroic, others chilling or selfish. Doubtless in Shakespeare's time, she elicited a similarly mixed response. Shakespeare alters his source story considerably to expand Isabella's role and specify its implications more exactly. In Whetstone's *Promos and Cassandra*, the sister has no plans to enter a convent, and she eventually goes to bed with the deputy in order to save her brother's life. For Isabella, by contrast, virginity is a principled choice, not an accident of youth. The vow of lifelong, religiously dedicated chastity she plans to take is a matter about which Shakespeare's contemporaries had conflicting feelings. One effect of England's break with the Catholic Church had been a spectacular change in official attitudes toward celibacy. While Catholics honored sexual renunciation and demanded that their clergy remain chaste, Protestants discouraged veneration of the Virgin Mary, abolished convents and monasteries, and urged clergy to marry. Despite these alterations, however, a powerful appreciation for virginity and belief in its semimagical powers persisted in Reformation England, cut loose from its explicitly religious moorings. The effect of Shakespeare's innovations on Whetstone, then, is both to heighten the ambivalence of the story and to focus the moral spotlight on Isabella's convictions and the choices that follow from them.

Isabella believes that she would damn herself by sleeping with Angelo.

> Better it were a brother died at once
> Than that a sister, by redeeming him,
> Should die for ever.
>
> (2.4.107–9)

Is she right? St. Augustine, the most influential Christian writer on sexual morality, insists that since sin is a property of the will, not a physical state, persons who are forced to perform sexual acts are blameless. If chastity is a state of mind, then the fate of Isabella's body is possibly independent of, and irrelevant to, the fate of her soul. Perhaps, in fact, by acquiescing to Angelo, Isabella would perform an act of charity, generously sacrificing her own preferences for Claudio's benefit. On the other hand, female "virtue" has traditionally been defined in physical as well as mental terms, so that chastity, the spiritual attitude, is hard to separate from virginity, the bodily condition. Moreover, Isabella is not exactly a rape victim; she must, as Angelo says, "fit her consent" to his proposal. Does that consent, however reluctant, contaminate her with his sin? Quite possibly. Would it permanently unsuit her for her religious vocation? Quite possibly. Clearly it is reasonable, then, for Isabella to be cautious; and no one, says Augustine, is obliged to put him- or herself in eternal peril merely in order to save the life of another person.

Since, however, Shakespeare characteristically translates sweeping moral questions into scrupulously personal terms, apparently reasonable general maxims do not entirely suffice to explain Isabella's motives. On one hand, her obstinacy seems justified after the fact, when Angelo decides to execute Claudio, because clearly her capitulation would not have saved her brother's life. On the other hand, Isabella's obsession with her own purity seems excessive, especially in 3.1, when it manifests itself in gross insensitivity to her plaintive, terrified brother. Moreover, her fervent yearning for constraint, like Angelo's, seems luridly imbued with sadomasochism.

> were I under the terms of death,
> Th'impression of keen whips I'd wear as rubies,
> And strip myself to death as to a bed
> That longing have been sick for, ere I'd yield
> My body up to shame.
>
> (2.4.100–04)

At such moments, Isabella seems not to be exterminating or transcending her own sexuality, but redirecting it in ways of which she is not entirely conscious. She not only shares Angelo's assumption that the sexual act is a defilement, but like him she finds discipline exciting. With all our disapproval of Angelo's abuse of power and our sympathy with Isabella's indignation, we can still see how their conflict arises as much from their similarities as from their differences.

Isabella's difficulty is hard to resolve because it is unclear how much her chastity is worth. Is it more valuable than her brother's life? Is it more valuable than her own life, which she would throw down for Claudio, she claims, "as frankly as a pin" (3.1.105)? Is it only fair, as Angelo claims, to yield him her body as compensation for overlooking Claudio's offense, or is "lawful mercy . . . nothing kin to foul redemption" (2.4.113–14)? Shakespeare provides no answer to these questions, but the conflict they produce yields the play's most vividly realized interactions. As the title suggests, *Measure for Measure* is obsessed with problems of substitution and commensurability—from the opening scene in which Angelo takes over as the Duke's deputy to Angelo's proposal that Isabella vindicate Claudio by committing his sin herself, to the bed trick that replaces Isabella with Mariana, to the Provost's exchange of Ragusine's head for Claudio's. Even the most apparently trivial comic interchanges persistently echo the concern with equivalence, proportionality, and relative priority: the Gentlemen argue about whether they are cut from lists or velvet; Pompey and Abhorson debate the relative standing of bawd and hangman.

Questions of equivalence seem to underlie the very possibility of justice, even the possibility of any ethical thinking. When a person commits a misdeed, restoring the status quo ante is usually impossible. Thus the wrongdoer ought, we feel, either to make adequate restitution or to suffer in rough proportion to the anguish he or she has caused, rendering, in the biblical phrase, measure for measure. In sexual matters, however, such problems of equivalence are murky, because there is no consensus regarding how apparently straightforward bodily acts ought to be interpreted. Angelo compares Claudio's offense to murder and counterfeiting; Lucio thinks it is trivial, "a game of tick-tack" (1.2.167). What seem to be the same actions can be evaluated in wildly different ways, depending on one's frame of reference: to the abstemious Angelo, Claudio's behavior looks like gross debauchery, while to Mistress Overdone's dissolute patrons, it looks positively restrained. Motives alter what seem to be the same actions, so that we are inclined to regard Claudio more leniently than Lucio, who abandoned his mistress after making her pregnant. So do outcomes: the bed trick means that Angelo, intending to commit an impermissible act, in fact performs a licit one, unknowingly laying the groundwork for his pardon in the final scene.

The commitment of several characters to a Christian religious vocation further complicates the possibility of establishing some kind of commensurability. Isabella, especially, assumes that spiritual goods like honor and purity are infinitely more important than secular, visible possessions. In her system of values, a promise of ardent prayer constitutes the most potent bribe she can offer Angelo, beside which gold is barren and trivial. The counterintuitive otherworldliness of Isabella's concept of commensurability is central to Christianity, a religion founded on the spectacularly lopsided substitution of the blameless Christ for sinful humanity in the system of God's justice. But since such religious convictions are not subject to the verification of the senses, they are open to challenge by those more firmly attached to the things of this world. For Claudio, any fate seems better than death. His hierarchy of priorities is different from Isabella's, and so, therefore, are his conceptions of commensurability.

How are such drastic discrepancies between the various characters' moral and social outlooks to be reconciled? The agent for bringing order and justice is Duke Vincentio, a concealed authority who learns everybody's secrets in the course of the play. Far from providing an authoritative solution to the play's ethical impasse, however, the Duke has elicited almost as much controversy as Isabella. Some critics see him as a version of God, "like power divine," as Angelo declares in the final scene. Some have suggested that the Duke was meant to compliment the diffident King James I, who at the time of the play's first performance had just ascended the English throne, after the death of his extroverted predecessor, Elizabeth I. More skeptical critics see the Duke as a schemer who foists his dirty work onto political subordinates and meddles impudently, even sacrilegiously, with the lives of his subjects.

The Duke's function as clergyman reflects the fact that the problems of *Measure for Measure* can only be solved by someone who can obtain access to the concealed realm of motives and intentions, a privilege usually reserved for a confessor. But merely knowing such information will not bring practical redress of injustice. So at the same time, unlike a clergyman, he must retain the secular ruler's ability to mandate changes in the world in order to bring matters to a satisfactory conclusion. A prince disguised as a friar, the Duke bridges, however unsteadily, the gap between knowledge and power. An actual sovereign with such prerogatives would approach tyranny—for that reason, the functions of priest and lay magistrate were ordinarily separated even in Shakespeare's time, when church and state were far more closely allied than they are today. In the play's fictional Vienna, however, the Duke's sweeping authority conveniently allows him to impose a resolution.

There are limits to Vincentio's power. Not even a Duke can sequester erotic fervor from the cruelty and disorder with which it has proven to be so intimately and insidiously allied. Not even a Duke can make passion tractable. The best he can manage is to introduce his subjects to some socially sanctioned medium between celibacy and abandon. Marriage in *Measure for Measure* is thus patently not a happy aspiration but a stopgap measure imposed on reluctant or noncommittal individuals, for whom the alternative in several cases is death. Indeed, Lucio, forthright as usual, complains that marriage is a worse fate than hanging; the others are distinctly muted in their response to the Duke's nuptial stratagems. Claudio and Juliet are given no lines in which to celebrate their reunion; nor do we hear that Angelo, who claims to "crave death more willingly than mercy" (5.1.470), is grateful to be preserved as Mariana's husband. Isabella remains silent in the face of the Duke's unexpected proposal of marriage, leaving it an open question whether she is overwhelmed with joy or gripped with horror, whether the Duke provides her with a socially and personally satisfying alternative to the cloister or merely recapitulates Angelo's harassment.

The pro forma quality of the coupling with which *Measure for Measure* concludes suggests that marital union is not, finally, the resolution toward which the play most convincingly moves. Most of the last scene is devoted to finding a way out of the difficulties posed by the radical moral incommensurabilities described above. In quick succession, the Duke's trial rehearses the normal outcome of Isabella's complaint—her condemnation and Angelo's exoneration—and then demonstrates that in this instance, almost miraculously, Angelo's secret vice will be made manifest after all. But this disclosure does not end the play, for the Duke's plan demands that Isabella plead for Angelo's life "against all sense," as the Sermon on the Mount commands her to do. The simple asceticism of the flesh with which *Measure for Measure* begins is displaced at last by a more subtle and exacting asceticism of the spirit, as Isabella renounces the hunger for vengeance in favor of a forgiveness that goes very much against the grain. Only this principled willingness to overlook injury and tolerate difference, the play seems to imply, can still the jostling among heterogeneous moral perspectives that endlessly complicate life in Vienna.

KATHARINE EISAMAN MAUS

TEXTUAL NOTE

The First Folio (1623, F) is the only authoritative text for most of *Measure for Measure*, and the *Norton Shakespeare* in general follows F closely. This text has some puzzling features. In F's 1.2, Claudio's imprisonment is first announced by Mistress Overdone, then shortly thereafter described by Pompey to Mistress Overdone, who seems unaware of the situation she has just related. The Oxford editors believe that *Measure for Measure* was adapted by Thomas Middleton for a performance after Shakespeare's death. In this scene, they argue, F reproduces in succession both the adapted text and the passage it was designed to replace. The same theory would explain some curious features of the action at the end of Act 3 and the beginning of Act 4: Mariana's song seems to have been taken from *The Bloody Brother*, a play first performed around 1617, and the Duke's soliloquy during the absence of Mariana and Isabella is irrelevant to its context. The adapter, in the course of rewriting the beginning of Act 4, probably switched this soliloquy with the one at the end of Act 3.

Because the line between adapted and original material is impossible to recover with any certainty, this edition does not attempt to restore a supposedly "Shakespearean" version of the play, but instead reconstructs the version presumably performed by the King's Men a few years before the printing of the Folio. This reconstruction departs from F only in omitting the short, redundant Shakespearean passage. The omitted passage is reproduced as an appendix, as is the soliloquy at the end of Act 3 as the Oxford editors believe Shakespeare originally wrote it (see Additional Passages). Mariana's song at the beginning of Act 4 has been collated with the authoritative manuscript originally belonging to John Wilson, the composer who set the lyric to music; as a result, F's "but" in line 6 has been emended to "though."

SELECTED BIBLIOGRAPHY

Adelman, Janet. "Bed Tricks: On Marriage as the End of Comedy in *All's Well That Ends Well* and *Measure for Measure*." *Shakespeare's Personality*. Ed. Norman H. Holland, Sidney Homan, and Bernard J. Paris. Berkeley: University of California Press, 1989. 151–74. Sexuality as defilement and marriage as punishment in *Measure for Measure*.

Baines, Barbara. "Assaying the Power of Chastity in *Measure for Measure*." *Studies in English Literature* 30 (1990): 248–98. Isabella's chastity as an active virtue in the Vienna of *Measure for Measure*.

Bennett, Josephine Waters. *"Measure for Measure" as Royal Entertainment*. New York: Columbia University Press, 1966. The play as it reflects James I's court, political philosophy, and royal persona.

Bloom, Harold, ed. *William Shakespeare's "Measure for Measure."* New York: Chelsea House, 1987. Anthology of critical essays.

Dollimore, Jonathan. "Transgression and Surveillance in *Measure for Measure*." *Political Shakespeare: New Essays in Cultural Materialism*. Ed. Jonathan Dollimore and Alan Sinfield. Ithaca, N.Y.: Cornell University Press, 1985. 72–87.

Engle, Lars. "*Measure for Measure* and Modernity: The Problem of the Skeptic's Authority." *Shakespeare and Modernity: Early Modern to Millennium*. Ed. Hugh Grady. New York: Routledge, 2000. 85–104. Ethical relativism and difficulties of judgment.

Hawkins, Harriett. *Measure for Measure.* Boston: Twayne, 1987. Chapters on stage history, critical reception, and the play's major interpretive cruxes.

Knight, G. Wilson. *"Measure for Measure* and the Gospels." *The Wheel of Fire: Essays in Interpretation of Shakespeare's Sombre Tragedies.* London: Oxford University Press, 1930. 80–106. Duke Vincentio as godlike: *Measure for Measure* as a Christian play.

Maus, Katharine Eisaman. "Sexual Secrecy in *Measure for Measure." Inwardness and Theater in the English Renaissance.* Chicago: University of Chicago Press, 1995. 157–81. Sexual privacy as a challenge for legal supervision and as the grounds for character in *Measure for Measure.*

Shell, Marc. *The End of Kinship: "Measure for Measure," Incest, and the Ideal of Universal Siblinghood.* Stanford: Stanford University Press, 1988. Proper and improper exchanges in the Christian world of *Measure for Measure,* in which everyone is a brother or sister to everyone else.

Shuger, Debora Kuller. *Political Theologies in Shakespeare's England: The Sacred and the State in "Measure for Measure."* New York: Palgrave, 2001. *Measure for Measure* shows the intimate connection between problems of governance and religion in early modern Europe.

Wheeler, Richard P. *Shakespeare's Development* and *the Problem Comedies: Turn and Counter-Turn.* Berkeley: University of California Press, 1981. 1–33, 92–153. Detailed psychoanalytic interpretation.

FILM

Measure for Measure. 1979. Dir. Desmond Davis. UK. BBC-TV production. Nuanced performances from the entire ensemble, particularly Tim Pigott-Smith (Angelo), Kenneth Colley (Duke), Kate Nelligan (Isabella), and Frank Middlemass (Pompey).

Measure for Measure

THE PERSONS OF THE PLAY

Vincentio, the DUKE of Vienna
ANGELO, appointed his deputy
ESCALUS, an old lord, appointed Angelo's secondary
CLAUDIO, a young gentleman
JULIET, betrothed to Claudio
ISABELLA, Claudio's sister, novice to a sisterhood of nuns
LUCIO, a 'fantastic'
Two other such GENTLEMEN
FROTH, a foolish gentleman
MISTRESS OVERDONE, a bawd
POMPEY, her clownish servant
A PROVOST
ELBOW, a simple constable
A JUSTICE
ABHORSON, an executioner
BARNARDINE, a dissolute condemned prisoner
MARIANA, betrothed to Angelo
A BOY, attendant on Mariana
FRIAR PETER
FRANCESCA, a nun
VARRIUS, a lord, friend to the Duke
Lords, officers, citizens, servants

1.1

Enter DUKE, ESCALUS, [*and other*] *lords*

DUKE Escalus.
ESCALUS My lord.
DUKE Of government the properties to unfold°   explain
  Would seem in me t'affect° speech and discourse,   love; show off
5 Since I am put° to know that your own science°   obliged / knowledge
  Exceeds in that the lists° of all advice   limits
  My strength can give you. Then no more remains
  But this: to° your sufficiency,° as your worth is able, rely on / ability
  And let them[1] work. The nature of our people,
10 Our city's institutions and the terms°   procedures
  For common justice, you're as pregnant° in   expert
  As art° and practice hath enrichèd any   learning
  That we remember.
      [*He gives* ESCALUS *papers*]
          There is our commission,
  From which we would not have you warp.°   deviate
  [*To a lord*]   Call hither,
15 I say bid come before us, Angelo.   [*Exit lord*]

1.1 Location: The play takes place in Vienna. Some scene locations can merely be inferred. This scene may be set in the Duke's palace.

1. The referent of "them" is unclear. Perhaps a line is missing.

[*To* ESCALUS] What figure of us think you he will bear?[2]—
For you must know we have with special soul°   *deliberation*
Elected° him our absence to supply,°   *Chosen / make up for*
Lent him our terror, dressed him with our love,
20 And given his deputation° all the organs°   *deputyship / instruments*
Of our own power. What think you of it?
ESCALUS If any in Vienna be of worth
To undergo° such ample grace° and honour,   *sustain / favor*
It is Lord Angelo.
    Enter ANGELO
DUKE   Look where he comes.
25 ANGELO Always obedient to your grace's will,
I come to know your pleasure.
DUKE   Angelo,
There is a kind of character[3] in thy life
That to th'observer doth thy history°   *life story*
Fully unfold. Thyself and thy belongings°   *endowments*
30 Are not thine own so proper° as to waste   *exclusively*
Thyself upon thy virtues, they on thee.
Heaven doth with us as we with torches do,
Not light them for themselves; for if our virtues
Did not go forth of° us, 'twere all alike   *from*
35 As if we had them not.[4] Spirits are not finely touched
But to fine issues;[5] nor nature never lends
The smallest scruple° of her excellence   *bit*
But, like a thrifty goddess, she determines°   *ordains*
Herself the glory of a creditor,
40 Both thanks and use.° But I do bend° my speech *interest / direct*
To one that can my part in him advertise.°   *make known*
Hold[6] therefore, Angelo.
In our remove be thou at full ourself.
Mortality° and mercy in Vienna   *Power to kill*
45 Live in thy tongue and heart. Old Escalus,
Though first in question, is thy secondary.[7]
Take thy commission.
ANGELO   Now good my lord,
Let there be some more test made of my metal° *(variant of "mettle")*
Before so noble and so great a figure
Be stamped upon it.
50 DUKE   No more evasion.
We have with leavened° and preparèd choice   *fermented (mature)*
Proceeded to you; therefore take your honours.
    [ANGELO *takes his commission*]
Our haste from hence is of so quick condition
That it prefers itself, and leaves unquestioned[8]
55 Matters of needful value. We shall write to you
As time and our concernings° shall importune,°   *affairs / demand*
How it goes with us; and do look° to know   *expect*
What doth befall you here. So fare you well.

---

2. How do you think he will represent me (with the royal
plural)? Angelo is imagined bearing his ruler's image like
a coin; compare "metal" in line 48.
3. Handwriting; engraved pattern.
4. *Heaven . . . not:* similarly, Jesus, in Matthew 5:14–16,
tells his followers not to hide their light under a bushel.

5. *Spirits . . . issues:* Spirits are not made fine except to
do fine deeds.
6. Silence; take (this commission).
7. Though first to be addressed, is your subordinate.
8. That it takes precedence, and leaves unconsidered.

To th' hopeful execution do I leave you
Of your commissions.

60 ANGELO   Yet give leave, my lord,
That we may bring you something° on the way.   *some distance*
DUKE   My haste may not admit° it;   *permit*
Nor need you, on mine honour, have to do
With° any scruple. Your scope is as mine own,
65 So to enforce or qualify° the laws   *mitigate*
As to your soul seems good. Give me your hand.
I'll privily away. I love the people,
But do not like to stage me° to their eyes.   *display myself*
Though it do well,° I do not relish well   *is politically useful*
70 Their loud applause and *aves*° vehement;   *salutations*
Nor do I think the man of safe discretion°   *sound judgment*
That does affect° it. Once more, fare you well.   *desire*
ANGELO   The heavens give safety to your purposes!
ESCALUS   Lead forth and bring you back in happiness!
75 DUKE   I thank you. Fare you well.   *Exit*
ESCALUS   I shall desire you, sir, to give me leave
To have free° speech with you; and it concerns me   *frank*
To look into the bottom of my place.[1]
A power I have, but of what strength and nature
80 I am not yet instructed.°   *informed*
ANGELO   'Tis so with me. Let us withdraw together,
And we may soon our satisfaction have
Touching that point.
ESCALUS   I'll wait upon° your honour.   *Exeunt*   *accompany*

1.2

Enter LUCIO, *and two other* GENTLEMEN

LUCIO   If the Duke with the other dukes come not to composi-
tion° with the King of Hungary, why then, all the dukes fall   *agreement*
upon° the King.   *attack*
FIRST GENTLEMAN   Heaven grant us its peace, but not the King
5   of Hungary's!
SECOND GENTLEMAN   Amen.
LUCIO   Thou concludest like the sanctimonious pirate, that went
to sea with the Ten Commandments, but scraped° one out of   *erased*
the table.°   *tablet*
10 SECOND GENTLEMAN   'Thou shalt not steal'?
LUCIO   Ay, that he razed.
FIRST GENTLEMAN   Why, 'twas a commandment to command
the captain and all the rest from their functions: they put forth
to steal. There's not a soldier of us all that in the thanksgiving
15 before meat° do relish the petition well that prays for peace.   *food*
SECOND GENTLEMAN   I never heard any soldier dislike° it.   *express aversion to*
LUCIO   I believe thee, for I think thou never wast where grace
was said.
SECOND GENTLEMAN   No? A dozen times at least.
20 FIRST GENTLEMAN   What, in metre?
LUCIO   In any proportion,° or in any language.   *meter*

---

9. *have to do* / *With*: worry about.
1. To examine my duties thoroughly.
1.2. Location: A street or public place. In F, as here, the
scene begins with what is evidently an interpolation
introduced after Shakespeare's death. A reconstruction
of the original opening appears at the end of the play as
Additional Passage A.

FIRST GENTLEMAN I think, or in any religion.

LUCIO Ay, why not? Grace is grace despite of all controversy;[1] as
    for example, thou thyself art a wicked villain despite of all
25 grace.

FIRST GENTLEMAN Well, there went but a pair of shears between us.[2]

LUCIO I grant—as there may between the lists° and the velvet.   *selvages*
    Thou art the list.

FIRST GENTLEMAN And thou the velvet. Thou art good velvet,
30 thou'rt a three-piled[3] piece, I warrant thee. I had as lief° be a   *had rather*
    list of an English kersey° as be piled as thou art pilled,[4] for a   *wool cloth*
    French velvet. Do I speak feelingly° now?   *to the point; painfully*

LUCIO I think thou dost, and indeed with most painful feeling°   *conviction*
    of thy speech. I will out of thine own confession learn to begin°   *drink to*
35 thy health, but whilst I live forget to drink after thee.°   *(to avoid infection)*

FIRST GENTLEMAN I think I have done myself wrong,° have I   *laid myself open to that*
    not?

SECOND GENTLEMAN Yes, that thou hast, whether thou art
    tainted or free.°   *sick or well*

    Enter [MISTRESS OVERDONE]

40 LUCIO Behold, behold, where Madam Mitigation° comes! I   *(of sexual desire)*
    have purchased as many diseases under her roof as come to—

SECOND GENTLEMAN To what, I pray?

LUCIO Judge.°   *Guess*

SECOND GENTLEMAN To three thousand dolours° a year?   *pains; dollars*

45 FIRST GENTLEMAN Ay, and more.

LUCIO A French crown° more.   *coin; syphilitic sore*

FIRST GENTLEMAN Thou art always figuring° diseases in me, but   *imagining*
    thou art full of error—I am sound.°   *healthy*

LUCIO Nay not, as one would say, healthy, but so sound° as   *resounding*
50 things that are hollow—thy bones are hollow,[5] impiety° has   *wickedness*
    made a feast of thee.

FIRST GENTLEMAN [*to* MISTRESS OVERDONE] How now, which of
    your hips has the most profound sciatica?[6]

MISTRESS OVERDONE Well, well! There's one yonder arrested
55 and carried to prison was worth five thousand of you all.

SECOND GENTLEMAN Who's that, I pray thee?

MISTRESS OVERDONE Marry° sir, that's Claudio, Signor Claudio.   *By the Virgin Mary*

FIRST GENTLEMAN Claudio to prison? 'Tis not so.

MISTRESS OVERDONE Nay, but I know 'tis so. I saw him arrested,
60 saw him carried away; and, which is more, within these three
    days his head to be chopped off.

LUCIO But after° all this fooling, I would not have it so. Art thou   *despite*
    sure of this?

MISTRESS OVERDONE I am too sure of it, and it is for getting
65 Madame Julietta with child.

LUCIO Believe me, this may be. He promised to meet me two
    hours since and he was ever precise in promise-keeping.

---

1. Referring to the religious controversy over whether human beings are saved by divine grace or by good works. *grace:* divine favor; prayer before a meal.
2. We are cut from the same cloth.
3. Very plush; full of rectal sores (a symptom of syphilis). Lucio accuses the First Gentleman of being a "list," a selvage or edging of inferior cloth; the Gentleman retorts that he'd rather be a plain selvage than an expensively "piled" velvet like Lucio. Lucio then uses the Gentleman's knowledge of "piles" to score a point against him.
4. Ruined; made bald (a sign of syphilis, the "French pox"). Syphilitic sores were covered with velvet patches.
5. Syphilis causes bones to become brittle.
6. Ache in the sciatic vein of the hip, associated with venereal disease.

SECOND GENTLEMAN Besides, you know, it draws° something   *approaches*
    near to the speech we had to such a purpose.
70 FIRST GENTLEMAN But most of all agreeing with the proclamation.
LUCIO Away; let's go learn the truth of it.
                        Exeunt [LUCIO *and* GENTLEMEN]
MISTRESS OVERDONE Thus, what with the war, what with the
    sweat,° what with the gallows, and what with poverty, I am cus-   *plague*
    tom-shrunk.°   *short on customers*
    Enter [POMPEY *the*] *Clown*
75 How now, what's the news with you?
POMPEY You have not heard of the proclamation, have you?
MISTRESS OVERDONE What proclamation, man?
POMPEY All houses in the suburbs[7] of Vienna must be plucked° down.   *torn*
MISTRESS OVERDONE And what shall become of those in the city?
80 POMPEY They shall stand for seed.[8] They had gone down too,
    but that a wise burgher put in° for them.   *citizen interceded*
MISTRESS OVERDONE But shall all our houses of resort in the
    suburbs be pulled down?
POMPEY To the ground, mistress.
85 MISTRESS OVERDONE Why, here's a change indeed in the com-
    monwealth. What shall become of me?
POMPEY Come, fear not you. Good counsellors° lack no clients.   *attorneys*
    Though you change your place, you need not change your
    trade. I'll be your tapster still. Courage, there will be pity taken
90 on you. You that have worn your eyes almost out in the ser-
    vice,[9] you will be considered.°   *recompensed*
    [*A noise within*]
MISTRESS OVERDONE What's to do° here, Thomas Tapster?[1]   *the matter*
    Let's withdraw!
    Enter PROVOST,° CLAUDIO, JULIET,[2] [*and*] *officers;* LUCIO   *jailer*
    and [*the*] *two* GENTLEMEN
POMPEY Here comes Signor Claudio, led by the Provost to
95 prison; and there's Madame Juliet.
               Exeunt [MISTRESS OVERDONE *and* POMPEY]
CLAUDIO [*to the* PROVOST] Fellow, why dost thou show me thus
    to th' world?
    Bear me to prison, where I am committed.
PROVOST I do it not in evil disposition,
    But from Lord Angelo by special charge.
100 CLAUDIO Thus can the demigod Authority
    Make us pay down for our offence, by weight,°   *fully*
    The bonds of ° heaven. On whom it will, it will;[3]   *obligations to*
    On whom it will not, so; yet still 'tis just.
LUCIO Why, how now, Claudio? Whence comes this restraint?
105 CLAUDIO From too much liberty,° my Lucio, liberty.   *looseness*
    As surfeit is the father of much fast,°   *gluttony precedes fasting*
    So every scope,° by the immoderate use,   *freedom*
    Turns to restraint. Our natures do pursue,

---

7. London brothels ("houses") were located outside the city walls, where civic authorities had difficulty controlling them.
8. Grain for the next crop; semen.
9. "Eye" was slang for "female genital"; blindness is another symptom of syphilis.
1. Stock name for a tapster (bartender).

2. Claudio and Juliet are perhaps wearing white sheets of penance; such public humiliations were common punishments for sexual transgressions.
3. Paul has God say in Romans 9:15: "I will have mercy on him, to whom I will show mercy: and will have compassion on him, on whom I will have compassion."

	Like rats that raven° down their proper bane,°	devour / poison
110	A thirsty evil; and when we drink, we die.	

LUCIO If I could speak so wisely under an arrest, I would send
for certain of my creditors.[4] And yet, to say the truth, I had as
lief have the foppery° of freedom as the morality of imprison-   *folly*
ment. What's thy offence, Claudio?

115 CLAUDIO What but to speak of would offend again.

LUCIO What, is't murder?

CLAUDIO   No.

LUCIO   Lechery?

CLAUDIO   Call it so.

PROVOST Away, sir; you must go.

CLAUDIO One word, good friend.

[*The* PROVOST *shows assent*]

Lucio, a word with you.

120 LUCIO A hundred, if they'll do you any good.

[CLAUDIO *and* LUCIO *speak apart*]

Is lechery so looked after?

CLAUDIO Thus stands it with me. Upon a true contract,[5]
I got possession of Julietta's bed.

	You know the lady; she is fast° my wife,	nearly; entirely
125	Save that we do the denunciation° lack	declaration
	Of outward order.° This we came not to	public ceremony
	Only for propagation° of a dower	enlargement
	Remaining in the coffer of her friends,°	relatives
	From whom we thought it meet° to hide our love	appropriate
130	Till time had made them for° us. But it chances	favorably disposed to
	The stealth of our most mutual° entertainment	reciprocal; intimate
	With character too gross° is writ on Juliet.	writing too large

LUCIO With child, perhaps?

CLAUDIO   Unhapp'ly even so.

	And the new deputy now for the Duke—	
135	Whether it be the fault and glimpse° of newness,	glitter
	Or whether that the body public be	
	A horse whereon the governor doth ride,	
	Who, newly in the seat, that it may know	
	He can command, lets it straight° feel the spur—	immediately
140	Whether the tyranny be in his place,°	office
	Or in his eminence that fills it up—	
	I stagger in.° But this new governor	hesitate to say
	Awakes me all the enrollèd° penalties	recorded
	Which have, like unscoured armour, hung by th' wall	
145	So long that fourteen zodiacs° have gone round,	years
	And none of them been worn; and, for a name,°	reputation
	Now puts the drowsy and neglected act	
	Freshly on me. 'Tis surely for a name.	

	LUCIO I warrant° it is; and thy head stands so tickle° on thy	I'm sure / insecurely
150	shoulders that a milkmaid, if she be in love, may sigh it off.[6]	
	Send after the Duke, and appeal to him.	

---

4. Who, Lucio implies, would have him arrested for nonpayment of debts.
5. A secret plighting of troth, as opposed to public nuptials; in seventeenth-century England, such a contract could constitute legal marriage if made in the present tense ("I marry you" rather than "I will marry you") and followed by sexual consummation. The nature of the contract between Claudio and Juliet is unclear.
6. That a milkmaid's lovesick sigh may blow it off (with wordplay on "maidenhead").

CLAUDIO   I have done so, but he's not to be found.
I prithee, Lucio, do me this kind service.
This day my sister should the cloister enter,
155 And there receive her approbation.°   become a novice
Acquaint her with the danger of my state.
Implore her in my voice that she make friends
To the strict deputy. Bid herself assay° him.   try
I have great hope in that, for in her youth
160 There is a prone° and speechless dialect   eager; submissive
Such as move men; beside, she hath prosperous art°   skill
When she will play with reason and discourse,
And well she can persuade.
LUCIO   I pray she may—as well for the encouragement of thy
165 like,° which else would stand under grievous imposition,° as for   those like you / burden
the enjoying of thy life, who I would be sorry should be thus
foolishly lost at a game of tick-tack.[7] I'll to her.
CLAUDIO   I thank you, good friend Lucio.
LUCIO   Within two hours.
170 CLAUDIO   Come, officer; away.
            Exeunt [LUCIO and GENTLEMEN at one door;
            CLAUDIO, JULIET, PROVOST, and officers at another]

                    1.3
            Enter DUKE and [a] FRIAR
DUKE   No, holy father, throw away that thought.
Believe not that the dribbling[1] dart of love
Can pierce a complete° bosom. Why I desire thee   an invulnerable
To give me secret harbour hath a purpose
5 More grave and wrinkled° than the aims and ends   (suggesting aged wisdom)
Of burning youth.
FRIAR   May your grace speak of it?
DUKE   My holy sir, none better knows than you
How I have ever loved the life removed,°   retired
And held in idle price° to haunt assemblies   thought it frivolous
10 Where youth and cost a witless bravery° keeps.   pointless ostentation
I have delivered to Lord Angelo—
A man of stricture° and firm abstinence—   self-restraint
My absolute power and place here in Vienna;
And he supposes me travelled to Poland—
15 For so I have strewed it in the common ear,°   ears of common people
And so it is received.° Now, pious sir,   believed
You will demand of me why I do this.
FRIAR   Gladly, my lord.
DUKE   We have strict statutes and most biting laws,
20 The needful bits and curbs to headstrong weeds,[2]
Which for this fourteen years we have let slip;°   slide
Even like an o'ergrown lion in a cave
That goes not out to prey. Now, as fond° fathers,   doting
Having bound up the threat'ning twigs of birch
25 Only to stick it in their children's sight
For terror, not to use, in time the rod

---

7. A kind of backgammon scored by placing pegs into holes; with sexual innuendo.
1.3 Location: A Friar's cell.
1. Inadequate, like an arrow shot without sufficient force.

2. Since "bits and curbs" are parts of bridles, many editors emend "weeds" to "jades" or "steeds," but the Oxford English Dictionary records several instances of "weed" as a slang term for a worthless horse.

More mocked becomes than feared: so our decrees,
Dead to infliction,° to themselves are dead;   *Never inflicted*
And Liberty plucks Justice by the nose,³
30 The baby beats the nurse, and quite athwart
Goes all decorum.
FRIAR   It rested in° your grace   *remained possible for*
To unloose this tied-up Justice when you pleased,
And it in you more dreadful would have seemed
Than in Lord Angelo.
DUKE   I do fear, too dreadful.
35 Sith° 'twas my fault to give the people scope,   *Since*
'Twould be my tyranny to strike and gall° them   *chafe*
For what I bid them do—for we bid this be done
When evil deeds have their permissive pass,°   *unhindered passage*
And not the punishment. Therefore indeed, my father,
40 I have on Angelo imposed the office,
Who may in th'ambush° of my name strike home,   *under cover*
And yet my nature never in the fight
T'allow in slander.° And to behold his sway,°   *To permit slander / rule*
I will as 'twere a brother of your order
45 Visit both prince° and people. Therefore, I prithee,   *ruler*
Supply me with the habit, and instruct me
How I may formally in person bear°   *behave in character*
Like a true friar. More reasons for this action
At our more leisure shall I render you.
50 Only this one: Lord Angelo is precise,°   *puritanical*
Stands at a guard with envy,° scarce confesses   *on guard against desire*
That his blood flows, or that his appetite
Is more to bread than stone. Hence shall we see
If power change purpose, what our seemers be.   *Exeunt*

1.4

Enter ISABELLA, *and* FRANCESCA, *a nun*
ISABELLA   And have you nuns no farther privileges?
FRANCESCA   Are not these large° enough?   *generous*
ISABELLA   Yes, truly. I speak not as desiring more,
But rather wishing a more strict restraint
5 Upon the sisterhood, the votarists of Saint Clare.
LUCIO (*within*)   Ho, peace be in this place!
ISABELLA [*to* FRANCESCA]   Who's that which calls?
FRANCESCA   It is a man's voice. Gentle Isabella.
Turn you the key, and know° his business of° him.   *find out / from*
You may, I may not; you are yet unsworn.
10 When you have vowed, you must not speak with men
But in the presence of the prioress.
Then if you speak, you must not show your face;
Or if you show your face, you must not speak.
[LUCIO *calls within*]
He calls again. I pray you answer him.
[*She stands aside*]¹
15 ISABELLA   Peace and prosperity! Who is't that calls?
[*She opens the door*]

---

3. Licentiousness insults the administration of law.   austere discipline.
1.4 Location: A convent of St. Clare, an order known for   1. Or Francesca may exit here.

[*Enter* LUCIO]

LUCIO Hail, virgin, if you be—as those cheek-roses°   glowing cheeks
  Proclaim you are no less. Can you so stead° me   help
  As bring me to the sight of Isabella,
  A novice of this place, and the fair sister
20 To her unhappy° brother Claudio?   unfortunate
ISABELLA Why her unhappy brother? Let me ask,
  The rather for I now must make you know
  I am that Isabella, and his sister.
LUCIO Gentle and fair, your brother kindly greets you.
25 Not to be weary° with you, he's in prison.   tedious
ISABELLA Woe me! For what?
LUCIO For that which, if myself might be his judge,
  He should receive his punishment in thanks.
  He hath got his friend° with child.   lover
ISABELLA   Sir, make me not your story.°   don't tell me tales
30 LUCIO 'Tis true. I would not—though 'tis my familiar° sin   habitual
  With maids to seem the lapwing,² and to jest
  Tongue far from heart—play with all virgins so.
  I hold you as a thing enskied° and sainted   placed in heaven
  By your renouncement, an immortal spirit,
35 And to be talked with in sincerity
  As with a saint.
ISABELLA You do blaspheme the good in mocking me.
LUCIO Do not believe it. Fewness° and truth, 'tis thus: In few words
  Your brother and his lover have embraced.
40 As those that feed grow full, as blossoming time
  That from the seedness° the bare fallow° brings   sowing / plowland
  To teeming foison,° even so her plenteous womb   abundance
  Expresseth his full tilth° and husbandry.³   tillage
ISABELLA Someone with child by him? My cousin Juliet?
45 LUCIO Is she your cousin?
ISABELLA Adoptedly,° as schoolmaids change° their names   By choice / exchange
  By vain° though apt affection.   foolish
LUCIO   She it is.
ISABELLA O, let him marry her!
LUCIO   This is the point.
  The Duke is very strangely gone from hence;
50 Bore many gentlemen—myself being one—
  In hand and hope of action;⁴ but we do learn,
  By those that know the very nerves° of state,   sinews (inward secrets)
  His giving out° were of an infinite distance   What he proclaimed
  From his true-meant design. Upon° his place,   In
55 And with full line° of his authority,   extent
  Governs Lord Angelo—a man whose blood
  Is very snow-broth;° one who never feels   melted snow
  The wanton stings and motions° of the sense,   stimulants and impulses
  But doth rebate° and blunt his natural edge   dull
60 With profits of the mind, study, and fast.
  He, to give fear to use° and liberty,   custom
  Which have for long run by the hideous law

2. Bird that cries alarm when far from its nest, a common   4. *Bore . . . action*: Deceived us into hoping for some
figure for deception.   military action.
3. Cultivation (punning on "husband").

As mice by lions, hath picked out an act°   *a statute*
Under whose heavy° sense your brother's life   *oppressive*
65 Falls into forfeit. He arrests him on it,
And follows close the rigour of the statute
To make him an example. All hope is gone,
Unless you have the grace by your fair prayer
To soften Angelo. And that's my pith°   *essence*
70 Of business 'twixt you and your poor brother.
ISABELLA   Doth he so seek his life?
LUCIO   Has censured° him already,   *sentenced*
And, as I hear, the Provost hath a warrant
For's execution.
ISABELLA   Alas, what poor
Ability's in me to do him good?
75 LUCIO   Assay the power you have.
ISABELLA   My power? Alas, I doubt.
LUCIO   Our doubts are traitors,
And makes us lose the good we oft might win,
By fearing to attempt. Go to Lord Angelo;
80 And let him learn to know, when maidens sue,
Men give like gods, but when they weep and kneel,
All their petitions are as freely theirs
As° they themselves would owe° them.   *As if / were to own*
ISABELLA   I'll see what I can do.
LUCIO   But speedily.
ISABELLA   I will about it straight,°   *immediately*
85 No longer staying but to give the Mother°   *Mother Superior*
Notice of my affair.° I humbly thank you.   *business*
Commend me to my brother. Soon at night
I'll send him certain word of my success.°   *fortune (good or bad)*
LUCIO   I take my leave of you.
ISABELLA   Good sir, adieu.
Exeunt [ISABELLA *and* FRANCESCA *at one door,*
LUCIO *at another door*]

2.1

Enter ANGELO, ESCALUS, *and servants;* [a] JUSTICE
ANGELO   We must not make a scarecrow of the law,
Setting it up to fear° the birds of prey,   *frighten*
And let it keep one shape till custom make it
Their perch, and not their terror.
ESCALUS   Ay, but yet
5 Let us be keen, and rather cut a little
Than fall and bruise to death. Alas, this gentleman
Whom I would save had a most noble father.
Let but your honour know—
Whom I believe to be most strait° in virtue—   *rigorous*
10 That in the working of your own affections,°   *passions*
Had time cohered with place, or place with wishing,
Or that the resolute acting of your blood°   *desire*
Could have attained th'effect° of your own purpose—   *fulfillment*
Whether you had not sometime in your life

2.1 Location: The court of justice.

15 Erred in this point which now you censure° him,   condemn in
And pulled the law upon you.
    ANGELO   'Tis one thing to be tempted, Escalus,
Another thing to fall. I not° deny   do not
The jury passing on the prisoner's life
20 May in the sworn twelve have a thief or two
Guiltier than him they try. What knows the law[1]
That thieves do pass on thieves? What's open° made to justice,   evident
That justice seizes. 'Tis very pregnant:°   clear
The jewel that we find, we stoop and take't
25 Because we see it, but what we do not see
We tread upon and never think of it.
You may not so extenuate his offence
For° I have had such faults; but rather tell me,   Because
When I that censure him do so offend,
30 Let mine own judgement pattern out° my death,   give precedent for
And nothing come in partial.° Sir, he must die.   no allowances be made
    ESCALUS   Be it as your wisdom will.
    ANGELO   Where is the Provost?
            Enter PROVOST
    PROVOST   Here, if it like your honour.
    ANGELO   See that Claudio
Be execute by nine tomorrow morning.
35 Bring him his confessor, let him be prepared,
For that's the utmost of his pilgrimage.°   [*Exit* PROVOST]   life's journey
    ESCALUS   Well, heaven forgive him, and forgive us all!
Some rise by sin, and some by virtue fall.
Some run from brakes of vice,[2] and answer none;°   not at all
40 And some condemnèd for a fault alone.°   single imperfection
            Enter ELBOW, FROTH, POMPEY, *and officers*
    ELBOW   Come, bring them away. If these be good people in a
commonweal, that do nothing but use their abuses° in com-   do their bad deeds
mon houses,° I know no law. Bring them away.   brothels
    ANGELO   How now, sir? What's your name? And what's the matter?
45 ELBOW   If it please your honour, I am the poor Duke's constable,
and my name is Elbow. I do lean° upon justice, sir; and do   depend
bring in here before your good honour two notorious benefactors.[3]
    ANGELO   Benefactors? Well! What benefactors are they?
Are they not malefactors?
50 ELBOW   If it please your honour, I know not well what they are;
but precise[4] villains they are, that I am sure of, and void of all
profanation° in the world that good Christians ought to have.   (for "reverence")
    ESCALUS [*to* ANGELO]   This comes off° well; here's a wise officer!   turns out
    ANGELO   Go to, what quality° are they of ? Elbow is your name?   rank
55 Why dost thou not speak, Elbow?
    POMPEY   He cannot, sir; he's out at elbow.[5]
    ANGELO   What are you, sir?
    ELBOW   He, sir? A tapster, sir, parcel bawd;° one that serves a bad   part-time pimp

---

1. What does the law know; who knows what law.
2. F has "brakes of ice," a famous crux; often amended
as here. *brakes:* thickets.
3. Elbow comically misuses words; here he means
"malefactors," criminals.

4. Elbow means "precious"; "precise" (morally scrupulous) is elsewhere applied to Angelo.
5. Ragged; perplexed at the sound of his name. Pompey
loves to play on the double meanings of words.

woman whose house, sir, was, as they say, plucked down in the

60   suburbs; and now she professes a hot-house,° which I think is   *pretends to run a sauna*
a very ill house too.

ESCALUS   How know you that?

ELBOW   My wife, sir, whom I detest° before heaven and your   *(for "protest")*
honour—

65 ESCALUS   How, thy wife?

ELBOW   Ay, sir, whom I thank heaven is an honest woman—

ESCALUS   Dost thou detest her therefor?

ELBOW   I say, sir, I will detest myself also, as well as she, that this
house, if it be not a bawd's house, it is pity of her life,° for it is   *a great pity*

70   a naughty° house.   *wicked*

ESCALUS   How dost thou know that, constable?

ELBOW   Marry, sir, by my wife, who, if she had been a woman
cardinally° given, might have been accused in fornication,   *(for "carnally")*
adultery, and all uncleanliness there.

75 ESCALUS   By the woman's means?

ELBOW   Ay, sir, by Mistress Overdone's means. But as she° spit   *(Elbow's wife)*
in his° face, so she defied him.   *(Pompey's)*

POMPEY [*to* ESCALUS]   Sir, if it please your honour, this is not so.

ELBOW   Prove it before these varlets° here, thou honourable   *villains*

80   man, prove it.

ESCALUS [*to* ANGELO]   Do you hear how he misplaces?°   *confuses his words*

POMPEY   Sir, she came in great with child, and longing—saving
your honour's reverence°—for stewed prunes.[6] Sir, we had but   *excuse the expression*
two in the house, which at that very distant° time stood, as it   *(for "instant")*

85   were, in a fruit dish[7]—a dish of some threepence; your honours
have seen such dishes; they are not china dishes, but very good
dishes.

ESCALUS   Go to, go to, no matter for the dish, sir.

POMPEY   No, indeed, sir, not of° a pin; you are therein in the   *worth*

90   right. But to the point. As I say, this Mistress Elbow, being, as I
say, with child, and being great-bellied, and longing, as I said,
for prunes; and having but two in the dish, as I said, Master
Froth here, this very man, having eaten the rest, as I said, and,
as I say, paying for them very honestly; for, as you know, Master

95   Froth, I could not give you threepence again.°   *in change*

FROTH   No, indeed.

POMPEY   Very well. You being, then, if you be remembered,
cracking the stones of the foresaid prunes—

FROTH   Ay, so I did indeed.

100 POMPEY   Why, very well.—I telling you then, if you be remembered, that such a one and such a one were past cure of the
thing you wot of,[8] unless they kept very good diet, as I told
you—

FROTH   All this is true.

105 POMPEY   Why, very well then—

ESCALUS   Come, you are a tedious fool. To the purpose. What
was done to Elbow's wife that he hath cause to complain of?
Come me° to what was done to her.   *Get*

POMPEY   Sir, your honour cannot come to that yet.[9]

---

6. Commonly served in brothels; also suggesting "testicles" in the series of double entendres that follows.
7. Slang term for "female genital."

8. Euphemism for syphilis. *wot:* know.
9. Taking "done" in the sexual sense, Pompey pretends
shock at Escalus's salaciousness.

110 ESCALUS No, sir, nor I mean it not.°   *I don't mean that*
POMPEY Sir, but you shall come to it, by your honour's leave.
And I beseech you, look into° Master Froth here, sir, a man of   *consider*
fourscore pound a year,[1] whose father died at Hallowmas°—   *Nov. 1, All Saint's Day*
was't not at Hallowmas, Master Froth?
115 FROTH All Hallow Eve.°   *Halloween*
POMPEY Why, very well. I hope here be truths. He, sir, sitting,
as I say, in a lower° chair, sir—'twas in the Bunch of Grapes,[2]   *reclining?*
where indeed you have a delight to sit, have you not?
FROTH I have so, because it is an open room,[3] and good for
120 winter.
POMPEY Why, very well then. I hope here be truths.
ANGELO This will last out a night in Russia,
When nights are longest there. [*To* ESCALUS] I'll take my leave,
And leave you to the hearing of the cause,°   *case*
125 Hoping you'll find good cause to whip them all.
ESCALUS I think no less. Good morrow to your lordship.

                                                   Exit [ANGELO]
Now, sir, come on, what was done to Elbow's wife, once more?
POMPEY Once, sir? There was nothing done to her once.
ELBOW I beseech you, sir, ask him what this man did to my wife.
130 POMPEY I beseech your honour, ask me.
ESCALUS Well, sir, what did this gentleman to her?
POMPEY I beseech you, sir, look in this gentleman's face. Good
Master Froth, look upon his honour. 'Tis for a good purpose.
Doth your honour mark° his face?   *note*
135 ESCALUS Ay, sir, very well.
POMPEY Nay, I beseech you, mark it well.
ESCALUS Well, I do so.
POMPEY Doth your honour see any harm in his face?
ESCALUS Why, no.
140 POMPEY I'll be supposed° upon a book° his face is the worst   *(for "deposed") / Bible*
thing about him. Good, then—if his face be the worst thing
about him, how could Master Froth do the constable's wife any
harm? I would know that of your honour.
ESCALUS He's in the right, constable; what say you to it?
145 ELBOW First, an it like° you, the house is a respected[4] house;   *if it please*
next, this is a respected fellow; and his mistress is a respected
woman.
POMPEY [*to* ESCALUS] By this hand, sir, his wife is a more
respected person than any of us all.
150 ELBOW Varlet, thou liest; thou liest, wicked varlet. The time is
yet to come that she was ever respected with man, woman, or
child.
POMPEY Sir, she was respected with him before he married with her.
ESCALUS Which is the wiser here, justice or iniquity? [*To*
155 ELBOW] Is this true?
ELBOW [*to* POMPEY] O thou caitiff, O thou varlet, O thou wicked
Hannibal![5] I respected with her before I was married to her?
[*To* ESCALUS] If ever I was respected with her, or she with

---

1. Eighty pounds was a low income for a gentleman. The
father's recent death means that Froth has just come into
his inheritance.
2. A room in a tavern.

3. A public room (where fires were kept burning).
4. For "suspected."
5. Blunder for "cannibal"; also, both Hannibal and Pompey were famous generals of ancient times.

me, let not your worship think me the poor Duke's officer. [*To*
160 POMPEY] Prove this, thou wicked Hannibal,[6] or I'll have mine
action of battery° on thee.   *(for "slander")*
                                                        struck
ESCALUS If he took° you a box o'th' ear you might have your
action of slander too.

ELBOW Marry, I thank your good worship for it. What is't your
165 worship's pleasure I shall do with this wicked caitiff?°   *knave*

ESCALUS Truly, officer, because he hath some offences in him
that thou wouldst discover° if thou couldst, let him continue in   *expose*
his courses° till thou knowest what they are.   *conduct*

ELBOW Marry, I thank your worship for it.—Thou seest, thou
170 wicked varlet now, what's come upon thee. Thou art to continue now, thou varlet, thou art to continue.

ESCALUS [*to* FROTH] Where were you born, friend?

FROTH Here in Vienna, sir.

ESCALUS Are you of fourscore pounds a year?

175 FROTH Yes, an't please you, sir.

ESCALUS So. [*To* POMPEY] What trade are you of, sir?

POMPEY A tapster, a poor widow's tapster.

ESCALUS Your mistress's name?

POMPEY Mistress Overdone.

180 ESCALUS Hath she had any more than one husband?

POMPEY Nine, sir—Overdone by the last.[7]

ESCALUS Nine?—Come hither to me, Master Froth. Master
Froth, I would not have you acquainted with tapsters. They will
draw you,[8] Master Froth, and you will hang them.° Get you   *get them hanged*
185 gone, and let me hear no more of you.

FROTH I thank your worship. For mine own part, I never come
into any room in a tap-house but I am drawn in.

ESCALUS Well, no more of it, Master Froth. Farewell.

[*Exit* FROTH]

Come you hither to me, Master Tapster. What's your name,
190 Master Tapster?

POMPEY Pompey.

ESCALUS What else?

POMPEY Bum, sir.

ESCALUS Troth, and your bum is the greatest thing about you;
195 so that, in the beastliest sense, you are Pompey the Great.[9]
Pompey, you are partly a bawd, Pompey, howsoever you colour
it in being a tapster, are you not? Come, tell me true; it shall
be the better for you.

POMPEY Truly, sir, I am a poor fellow that would live.

200 ESCALUS How would you live, Pompey? By being a bawd? What
do you think of the trade, Pompey? Is it a lawful trade?

POMPEY If the law would allow it, sir.

ESCALUS But the law will not allow it, Pompey; nor it shall not°   *nor shall it*
be allowed in Vienna.

205 POMPEY Does your worship mean to geld and spay all the youth
of the city?

ESCALUS No, Pompey.

---

6. Ancient Carthaginian general who waged war
against Rome; possibly Escalus means "cannibal."
7. She takes her name from Overdone, her last husband; her last husband wore her out.

8. Get you beer; steal your substance; convey you to execution.
9. The Roman general Pompey was surnamed "the
Great."

POMPEY Truly, sir, in my poor opinion they will to't then. If your
worship will take order° for the drabs° and the knaves, you need   measures / whores
210   not to fear the bawds.
ESCALUS There is pretty orders beginning, I can tell you. It is
but heading° and hanging.   beheading
POMPEY If you head and hang all that offend that way but for
ten year together, you'll be glad to give out a commission° for   an order
215   more heads. If this law hold° in Vienna ten year, I'll rent the   remain
fairest house in it after threepence a bay.[1] If you live to see this
come to pass, say Pompey told you so.
ESCALUS Thank you, good Pompey; and in requital of° your   return for
prophecy, hark you. I advise you, let me not find you before
220   me again upon any complaint whatsoever; no, not for° dwelling   even for
where you do. If I do, Pompey, I shall beat you to your tent,
and prove a shrewd Caesar to you;[2] in plain dealing, Pompey,
I shall have you whipped. So for this time, Pompey, fare you well.
POMPEY I thank your worship for your good counsel; [aside] but
225   I shall follow it as the flesh and fortune shall better determine.
Whip me? No, no; let carman° whip his jade.°   cart driver / horse
The valiant heart's not whipped out of his trade.   *Exit*
ESCALUS Come hither to me, Master Elbow; come hither, Mas-
ter Constable. How long have you been in this place of con-
230   stable?
ELBOW Seven year and a half, sir.
ESCALUS I thought, by the readiness in the office, you had continued in it some time. You say seven years together?
ELBOW And a half, sir.
235   ESCALUS Alas, it hath been great pains to you. They do you
wrong to put you so oft upon't. Are there not men in your ward
sufficient° to serve it?   fit
ELBOW Faith, sir, few of any wit in such matters. As they are
chosen, they are glad to choose me for them. I do it for some
240   piece of money, and go through with all.
ESCALUS Look° you bring me in the names of some six or seven,   See that
the most sufficient of your parish.
ELBOW To your worship's house, sir?
ESCALUS To my house. Fare you well.
                        [*Exit* ELBOW *with officers*]
245   What's o'clock, think you?
JUSTICE Eleven, sir.
ESCALUS I pray you home to dinner with me.[3]
JUSTICE I humbly thank you.
ESCALUS It grieves me for the death of Claudio,
250   But there's no remedy.
JUSTICE Lord Angelo is severe.
ESCALUS It is but needful.
Mercy is not itself that oft looks so.
Pardon is still° the nurse of second woe.   always
255   But yet, poor Claudio! There is no remedy.
Come, sir.   *Exeunt*

---

1. Townhouse rental was based on the number of front   harsh.
windows ("bays").   3. Dinner was served at midday. *pray:* ask.
2. Julius Caesar defeated Pompey in 48 B.C.E. *shrewd:*

2.2

Enter PROVOST [*and a*] SERVANT

SERVANT   He's hearing of a cause;° he will come straight.°   *case / right away*
    I'll tell him of you.

PROVOST   Pray you do.   [*Exit* SERVANT]
                             I'll know
    His pleasure; maybe he will relent. Alas,
    He° hath but as offended in a dream.   *(Claudio)*
5   All sects,° all ages, smack° of this vice; and he   *kinds of people / partake*
    To die for't!

        Enter ANGELO

ANGELO   Now, what's the matter, Provost?

PROVOST   Is it your will Claudio shall die tomorrow?

ANGELO   Did not I tell thee yea? Hadst thou not order?
    Why dost thou ask again?

PROVOST   Lest I might be too rash.

10   Under your good correction, I have seen
    When after execution judgement hath
    Repented o'er his doom.°   *sentence*

ANGELO   Go to; let that be mine.°   *my concern*
    Do you your office, or give up your place,
    And you shall well be spared.°   *easily be done without*

PROVOST   I crave your honour's pardon.

15   What shall be done, sir, with the groaning Juliet?
    She's very near her hour.°   *(of childbirth)*

ANGELO   Dispose of her
    To some more fitter place, and that with speed.

        [*Enter* SERVANT]

SERVANT   Here is the sister of the man condemned
    Desires access to you.

ANGELO   Hath he a sister?

20 PROVOST   Ay, my good lord; a very virtuous maid,
    And to be shortly of a sisterhood,
    If not already.

ANGELO   Well, let her be admitted.   [*Exit* SERVANT]
    See you the fornicatress be removed.
    Let her have needful but not lavish means.
    There shall be order° for't.   *written direction*

        Enter LUCIO *and* ISABELLA

25 PROVOST   God save your honour.

ANGELO   Stay a little while. [*To* ISABELLA] You're welcome.
    What's your will?

ISABELLA   I am a woeful suitor to your honour.
    Please° but your honour hear me.   *If it please*

ANGELO   Well, what's your suit?

ISABELLA   There is a vice that most I do abhor,
30   And most desire should meet the blow of justice,
    For which I would not plead, but that I must;
    For which I must not plead, but that I am
    At war 'twixt will and will not.

ANGELO   Well, the matter?

ISABELLA   I have a brother is condemned to die.

2.2 Location: A room in the court of justice.

35   I do beseech you, let it be his fault,°   *his fault be condemned*
      And not my brother.
      PROVOST [*aside*]   Heaven give thee moving graces!°   *the gift of persuasion*
      ANGELO   Condemn the fault, and not the actor° of it?   *doer*
      Why, every fault's condemned ere it be done.
      Mine were the very cipher of a function,
40   To fine° the faults whose fine° stands in record,   *condemn / penalty*
      And let go by° the actor.   *leave unpunished*
      ISABELLA   O just but severe law!
      I had a brother, then. Heaven keep your honour.
      LUCIO [*aside to* ISABELLA]   Give't not o'er° so. To him again;   *Don't give up*
          entreat him.
      Kneel down before him; hang upon° his gown.   *cling to*
45   You are too cold. If you should need a pin,
      You could not with more tame a tongue desire it.
      To him, I say!
      ISABELLA [*to* ANGELO]   Must he needs° die?   *necessarily*
      ANGELO   Maiden, no remedy.
50   ISABELLA   Yes, I do think that you might pardon him,
      And neither heaven nor man grieve at the mercy.
      ANGELO   I will not do't.
      ISABELLA   But can you if you would?
      ANGELO   Look what° I will not, that I cannot do.   *Whatever*
      ISABELLA   But might you do't, and do the world no wrong,
55   If so your heart were touched with that remorse°   *pity*
      As mine is to him?
      ANGELO   He's sentenced; 'tis too late.
      LUCIO [*aside to* ISABELLA]   You are too cold.
      ISABELLA   Too late? Why, no; I that do speak a word
60   May call° it again. Well, believe this,   *retract*
      No ceremony° that to great ones 'longs,   *symbolic accessory*
      Not the king's crown, nor the deputed sword,
      The marshal's truncheon, nor the judge's robe,
      Become them with one half so good a grace
65   As mercy does.
      If he had been as you and you as he,
      You would have slipped like him, but he, like you,
      Would not have been so stern.
      ANGELO   Pray you be gone.
      ISABELLA   I would to heaven I had your potency,°   *power*
70   And you were Isabel! Should it then be thus?
      No; I would tell what 'twere to be a judge,
      And what a prisoner.
      LUCIO [*aside to* ISABELLA]   Ay, touch him;[1] there's the vein.°   *that's the style*
      ANGELO   Your brother is a forfeit of the law,
      And you but waste your words.
      ISABELLA   Alas, alas!
75   Why, all the souls that were were forfeit[2] once,
      And He that might the vantage° best have took   *advantage*
      Found out° the remedy.[3] How would you be   *Procured*
      If He which is the top° of judgement should   *highest pattern or source*
      But judge you as you are? O, think on that,

---

1. Influence him; but perhaps Isabella touches Angelo's arm or garment here.

2. Lost (as a result of Adam and Eve's disobedience).

3. By saving all mankind in the person of Christ.

80 And mercy then will breathe within your lips,
　　Like man new made.°　　　　　　　　　　　*renewed by faith*
　　ANGELO　　　　　　　Be you content, fair maid.°　　*(with play on "new made")*
　　It is the law, not I, condemn your brother.
　　Were he my kinsman, brother, or my son,
　　It should be thus with him. He must die tomorrow.
85 ISABELLA　Tomorrow? O, that's sudden! Spare him, spare him!
　　He's not prepared for death. Even for our kitchens
　　We kill the fowl of season.° Shall we serve heaven　　*at the proper time*
　　With less respect than we do minister
　　To our gross selves? Good good my lord, bethink you:
90 Who is it that hath died for this offence?
　　There's many have committed it.
　　LUCIO [*aside*]　　　　　　　　　Ay, well said.
　　ANGELO　The law hath not been dead, though it hath slept.
　　Those many had not dared to do that evil
　　If the first that did th'edict infringe
95 Had answered for his deed. Now 'tis awake,
　　Takes note of what is done, and, like a prophet,
　　Looks in a glass° that shows what future evils,　　*mirror*
　　Either raw,° or by remissness new conceived　　*unripe*
　　And so in progress to be hatched and born,
100 Are now to have no successive degrees,[4]
　　But ere they live, to end.
　　ISABELLA　　　　　　　Yet show some pity.
　　ANGELO　I show it most of all when I show justice,
　　For then I pity those I do not know
　　Which a dismissed° offence would after gall,°　　*Whom a pardoned / hurt*
105 And do him right that, answering° one foul wrong,　　*paying for*
　　Lives not to act another. Be satisfied.
　　Your brother dies tomorrow. Be content.
　　ISABELLA　So you must be the first that gives this sentence,
　　And he that suffers. O, it is excellent
110 To have a giant's strength, but it is tyrannous
　　To use it like a giant.
　　LUCIO [*aside to* ISABELLA]　That's well said.
　　ISABELLA　Could great men thunder
　　As Jove[5] himself does, Jove would never be quiet,
115 For every pelting° petty officer　　*paltry*
　　Would use his heaven for thunder, nothing but thunder.
　　Merciful heaven,
　　Thou rather with thy sharp and sulphurous° bolt　　*fiery*
　　Split'st the unwedgeable and gnarlèd oak
120 Than the soft myrtle. But man, proud man,
　　Dressed in a little brief authority,
　　Most ignorant of what he's most assured,
　　His glassy° essence, like an angry ape[6]　　*fragile; illusory*
　　Plays such fantastic tricks before high heaven
125 As makes the angels weep, who, with our spleens,[7]
　　Would all themselves laugh mortal.

---

4. Future stages of development.
5. King of the Roman gods, whose weapon was the thunderbolt.
6. A figure of grotesque mimicry.
7. Thought to be the seat of laughter.

LUCIO [*aside to* ISABELLA]   O, to him, to him, wench!° He will   girl
    relent.
      He's coming;° I perceive't.   yielding
PROVOST [*aside*]   Pray heaven she win him!
ISABELLA   We cannot weigh our brother with ourself.[8]
130   Great men may jest with saints; 'tis wit in them,
    But in the less,° foul profanation.   ordinary people
LUCIO [*aside to* ISABELLA]   Thou'rt i'th' right, girl. More o' that.
ISABELLA   That in the captain's but a choleric word,
    Which in the soldier is flat blasphemy.
135 LUCIO [*aside to* ISABELLA]   Art advised o' that?° More on't.   So you know about that
ANGELO   Why do you put° these sayings upon me?   impose
ISABELLA   Because authority, though it err like others,
    Hath yet a kind of medicine in itself
    That skins the vice o'th' top.[9] Go to your bosom;
140   Knock there, and ask your heart what it doth know
    That's like my brother's fault. If it confess
    A natural guiltiness, such as is his,
    Let it not sound a thought upon your tongue
    Against my brother's life.
ANGELO [*aside*]   She speaks, and 'tis such sense°   sound advice
145   That my sense breeds° with it. [*To* ISABELLA] Fare you well.   desire increases
ISABELLA   Gentle my° lord, turn back.   My gracious
ANGELO   I will bethink me.° Come again tomorrow.   consider
ISABELLA   Hark how I'll bribe you; good my lord, turn back.
ANGELO   How, bribe me?
150 ISABELLA   Ay, with such gifts that° heaven shall share with° you.   as / apportion to
LUCIO [*aside to* ISABELLA]   You had marred all else.
ISABELLA   Not with fond° shekels of the tested° gold,   foolish / refined
    Or stones,° whose rate° are either rich or poor   jewels / value
    As fancy values them; but with true prayers,
155   That shall be up at heaven and enter there
    Ere sunrise, prayers from preservèd° souls,   protected
    From fasting maids whose minds are dedicate
    To nothing temporal.
ANGELO   Well, come to me tomorrow.
160 LUCIO [*aside to* ISABELLA]   Go to;° 'tis well; away.   Come on
ISABELLA   Heaven keep your honour[1] safe.
ANGELO [*aside*]   Amen;
    For I am that way going to temptation,
    Where prayer is crossed.°   corrupted; frustrated
ISABELLA   At what hour tomorrow
    Shall I attend your lordship?
165 ANGELO   At any time fore noon.
ISABELLA   God save your honour.
ANGELO [*aside*]   From thee; even from thy virtue.
           [*Exeunt* ISABELLA, LUCIO, *and* PROVOST]
    What's this? What's this? Is this her fault or mine?
    The tempter or the tempted, who sins most, ha?
    Not she; nor doth she tempt; but it is I
170   That, lying by the violet in the sun,
    Do, as the carrion does, not as the flower,

---

8. We cannot judge others as we judge ourselves.
9. That causes a skin to grow over the sore.

1. Isabella calls Angelo "your honor" as a term of respect;
   Angelo understands the phrase as referring to his virtue.

Corrupt with virtuous season.° Can it be   *Rot in fine weather*
That modesty may more betray our sense°   *seduce our appetite*
Than woman's lightness?° Having waste ground enough,   *licentiousness*
175 Shall we desire to raze the sanctuary,
And pitch° our evils there? O, fie, fie, fie!   *hurl; set up*
What dost thou, or what art thou, Angelo?
Dost thou desire her foully for those things
That make her good? O, let her brother live!
180 Thieves for their robbery have authority,
When judges steal themselves. What, do I love her,
That I desire to hear her speak again,
And feast upon her eyes? What is't I dream on?
O cunning enemy,° that, to catch a saint,°   *(Satan) / holy person*
185 With saints dost bait thy hook! Most dangerous
Is that temptation that doth goad us on
To sin in loving virtue. Never could the strumpet,
With all her double vigour°—art and nature—   *twofold power*
Once stir my temper;° but this virtuous maid   *excite me*
190 Subdues me quite. Ever till now
When men were fond,° I smiled, and wondered how.   *Exit*   *infatuated*

2.3

Enter [at one door] the DUKE, *[disguised as a friar,] and*
[at another door, the] PROVOST

DUKE   Hail to you, Provost!—so I think you are.
PROVOST   I am the Provost. What's your will, good friar?
DUKE   Bound by my charity and my blest order,
I come to visit the afflicted spirits
5 Here in the prison.[1] Do me the common right°   *right of all clerics*
To let me see them, and to make me know
The nature of their crimes, that I may minister
To them accordingly.
PROVOST   I would do more than that, if more were needful.

Enter JULIET

10 Look, here comes one, a gentlewoman of mine,°   *in my care*
Who, falling in the flaws° of her own youth,   *faults; gusts of passion*
Hath blistered her report.° She is with child,   *reputation*
And he that got° it, sentenced—a young man   *begot*
More fit to do another such offence
15 Than die for this.
DUKE   When must he die?
PROVOST   As I do think, tomorrow.
[*To* JULIET] I have provided for you. Stay a while,
And you shall be conducted.
20 DUKE   Repent you, fair one, of the sin you carry?
JULIET   I do, and bear the shame most patiently.
DUKE   I'll teach you how you shall arraign° your conscience,   *accuse*
And try your penitence if it be sound
Or hollowly put on.
25 JULIET   I'll gladly learn.
DUKE   Love you the man that wronged you?
JULIET   Yes, as I love the woman that wronged him.

2.3 Location: The prison.
1. Echoing 1 Peter 3:19: "He . . . went, and preached unto the spirits that were in prison."

DUKE So then it seems your most offenceful act		
Was mutually committed?		
JULIET Mutually.		
30 DUKE Then was your sin of heavier° kind than his.		*graver*
JULIET I do confess it and repent it, father.		
DUKE 'Tis meet° so, daughter. But lest you do repent		*appropriate*
As that° the sin hath brought you to this shame—		*Because*
Which sorrow is always toward ourselves, not heaven,		
35 Showing we would not spare heaven[2] as we love it,		
But as we stand in fear—		
JULIET I do repent me as it is an evil,		
And take the shame with joy.		
DUKE There rest.°		*remain*
Your partner, as I hear, must die tomorrow,		
40 And I am going with instruction to him.		
Grace go with you. *Benedicite!*° *Exit*		*Bless you*
JULIET Must die tomorrow? O injurious law,		
That respites me a life[3] whose very comfort		
Is still a dying horror!		
PROVOST 'Tis pity of° him. *Exeunt*		*for*

2.4

Enter ANGELO

ANGELO When I would pray and think, I think and pray		
To several° subjects: heaven hath my empty words,		*different*
Whilst my invention,° hearing not my tongue,		*imagination*
Anchors on Isabel; God in my mouth,		
5 As if I did but only chew his name,		
And in my heart the strong and swelling evil		
Of my conception.[1] The state° whereon I studied		*statecraft; dignity*
Is like a good thing, being often read,		
Grown seared° and tedious. Yea, my gravity,		*arid*
10 Wherein—let no man hear me—I take pride,		
Could I with boot° change for an idle plume[2]		*advantage*
Which the air beats in vain. O place,° O form,°		*rank / formality*
How often dost thou with thy case,° thy habit,°		*appearance / dress*
Wrench awe from fools, and tie the wiser souls		
15 To thy false seeming! Blood, thou art blood.[3]		
Let's write 'good angel'[4] on the devil's horn—		
'Tis now the devil's crest.°		*heraldic device*

Enter SERVANT

How now? Who's there?		
SERVANT One Isabel, a sister, desires access to you.		
ANGELO Teach her the way. [*Exit* SERVANT]		
O heavens,		
20 Why does my blood thus muster° to my heart,		*crowd*
Making both it unable° for itself,		*weak*
And dispossessing all my other parts		
Of necessary fitness?		
So play° the foolish throngs with one that swoons—		*act*

2. Relieve heaven from distress.
3. Pregnant women were spared the death penalty, at least until after childbirth.
2.4 Location: A room in the court of justice.
1. *the strong . . . conception:* the wickedness of my idea; original sin, inherited through the parents.

2. A frivolous feather, as worn in the hats of rakish youths.
3. That is, basic passions cannot be eradicated (contrasts with 1.4.56–58).
4. With pun on Angelo's name.

25 Come all to help him, and so stop the air
By which he should revive—and even so
The general subject° to a well-wished king — *common people*
Quit their own part° and, in obsequious fondness,° — *place / foolish love*
Crowd to his presence, where their untaught° love — *ignorant*
Must needs appear offence.

Enter ISABELLA

30 How now, fair maid?

ISABELLA   I am come to know your pleasure.

ANGELO [*aside*]   That you might know⁵ it would much better
please me
Than to demand° what 'tis. [*To* ISABELLA] Your brother cannot live. — *ask*

ISABELLA   Even so.° Heaven keep your honour.⁶ — *So be it*

35 ANGELO   Yet may he live a while, and it may be
As long as you or I. Yet he must die.

ISABELLA   Under your sentence?

ANGELO   Yea.

ISABELLA   When, I beseech you?—that in his reprieve,

40 Longer or shorter, he may be so fitted° — *prepared*
That his soul sicken not.

ANGELO   Ha, fie, these filthy vices! It were as good
To pardon him that hath from nature stolen
A man already made,⁷ as to remit° — *excuse*

45 Their saucy sweetness that do coin God's image
In stamps that are forbid.⁸ 'Tis all as easy
Falsely° to take away a life true° made — *Wrongly / legitimately*
As to put metal⁹ in restrainèd° moulds, — *forbidden*
To make a false one.

50 ISABELLA   'Tis set down so in heaven, but not in earth.

ANGELO   Say you so? Then I shall pose° you quickly. — *ask*
Which had you rather: that the most just law
Now took your brother's life, or, to redeem him,
Give up your body to such sweet uncleanness
As she that he hath stained?

55 ISABELLA   Sir, believe this.
I had rather give my body than my soul.

ANGELO   I talk not of your soul. Our compelled sins
Stand more for number than for account.¹

ISABELLA   How say you?

ANGELO   Nay, I'll not warrant that,² for I can speak

60 Against the thing I say. Answer to this.
I now, the voice of the recorded law,
Pronounce a sentence on your brother's life.
Might there not be a charity in sin
To save this brother's life?

ISABELLA   Please° you to do't, — *If it please*

65 I'll take it as a peril to my soul
It is no sin at all, but charity.

ANGELO   Pleased you to do't at peril of your soul
Were equal poise° of sin and charity. — *balance*

---

5. With pun on "carnal knowledge."
6. A form of farewell.
7. *hath . . . made:* has committed murder.
8. *coin . . . forbid:* counterfeit God's image (by begetting illegitimate children).

9. Variant spelling of "mettle" (spirit). Some thought the child's spirit was conveyed in its father's semen.
1. *Our . . . account:* Sins we are forced to commit fill out the list but are not held against us.
2. I'll not guarantee that to be true.

ISABELLA   That I do beg his life, if it be sin,
70   Heaven let me bear it. You granting° of my suit,   *Supposing you grant*
If that be sin, I'll make it my morn prayer
To have it added to the faults of mine,
And nothing of your answer.
ANGELO   Nay, but hear me.
Your sense pursues not mine.[3] Either you are ignorant,
75   Or seem so craftily, and that's not good.
ISABELLA   Let me be ignorant, and in nothing good
But graciously° to know I am no better.   *by God's grace*
ANGELO   Thus wisdom wishes to appear most bright
When it doth tax° itself: as these black masks[4]   *reprove*
80   Proclaim an enshield° beauty ten times louder   *a shielded*
Than beauty could, displayed. But mark me.
To be receivèd° plain, I'll speak more gross.°   *understood / clearly*
Your brother is to die.
ISABELLA   So.°   *Yes*
85   ANGELO   And his offence is so, as it appears,
Accountant° to the law upon that pain.°   *Accountable / penalty*
ISABELLA   True.
ANGELO   Admit° no other way to save his life—   *Suppose*
As I subscribe not° that nor any other—   *agree to neither*
90   But, in the loss of question,[5] that you his sister,
Finding yourself desired of such a person
Whose credit with the judge, or own great place,°   *rank*
Could fetch your brother from the manacles
Of the all-binding law, and that there were
95   No earthly mean to save him, but that either
You must lay down the treasures of your body
To this supposed,° or else to let him suffer—   *supposed man*
What would you do?
ISABELLA   As much for my poor brother as myself.
100   That is, were I under the terms° of death,   *sentence*
Th'impression of keen whips I'd wear as rubies,
And strip myself to death as to a bed
That longing have been sick for, ere I'd yield
My body up to shame.
105   ANGELO   Then must your brother die.
ISABELLA   And 'twere the cheaper way.
Better it were a brother died at once
Than that a sister, by redeeming him,
Should die for ever.°   *be eternally damned*
110   ANGELO   Were not you then as cruel as the sentence
That you have slandered so?
ISABELLA   Ignominy in ransom and free pardon
Are of two houses;° lawful mercy   *different families*
Is nothing kin to foul redemption.
115   ANGELO   You seemed of late to make the law a tyrant,
And rather proved° the sliding of your brother   *argued*
A merriment than a vice.
ISABELLA   O pardon me, my lord. It oft falls out
To have what we would° have, we speak not what we mean.   *wish to*

---

3. You don't follow my meaning; your desire is not
aroused by mine.

4. Worn at court entertainments.

5. For the sake of discussion.

120 I something° do excuse the thing I hate   *to some extent*
    For his advantage that I dearly love.
ANGELO   We are all frail.[6]
ISABELLA   Else° let my brother die—   *Otherwise*
    If not a federy,° but only he,   *confederate*
    Owe and succeed thy weakness.[7]
ANGELO   Nay, women are frail too.
125 ISABELLA   Ay, as the glasses° where they view themselves,   *mirrors*
    Which are as easy broke as they make forms.
    Women? Help, heaven! Men their creation° mar   *origin*
    In profiting by them. Nay, call us ten times frail,
    For we are soft as our complexions are,
    And credulous to false prints.[8]
130 ANGELO   I think it well,°   *agree completely*
    And from this testimony of your own sex,
    Since I suppose we are made to be no stronger
    Than faults may shake our frames, let me be bold.°   *presumptuous*
    I do arrest° your words. Be that you are;   *seize upon*
135   That is, a woman. If you be more,° you're none.   *(that is, better)*
    If you be one, as you are well expressed°   *shown to be*
    By all external warrants,° show it now,   *evidence*
    By putting on the destined livery.[9]
ISABELLA   I have no tongue° but one. Gentle my lord,   *speech*
140   Let me entreat you speak the former language.
ANGELO   Plainly conceive, I love you.
ISABELLA   My brother did love Juliet,
    And you tell me that he shall die for it.
ANGELO   He shall not, Isabel, if you give me love.
145 ISABELLA   I know your virtue hath a licence[1] in't,
    Which seems a little fouler than it is,
    To pluck on° others.   *test; mislead*
ANGELO   Believe me, on mine honour,
    My words express my purpose.
ISABELLA   Ha, little honour to be much believed,
150   And most pernicious purpose! Seeming, seeming!
    I will proclaim° thee, Angelo; look for't.   *denounce*
    Sign me a present° pardon for my brother,   *an immediate*
    Or with an outstretched throat I'll tell the world aloud
    What man thou art.
ANGELO   Who will believe thee, Isabel?
155   My unsoiled name, th'austereness of my life,
    My vouch° against you, and my place i'th' state,   *attestation*
    Will so your accusation overweigh
    That you shall stifle in your own report,°   *story; reputation*
    And smell of calumny. I have begun,
160   And now I give my sensual race the rein.
    Fit thy consent to my sharp appetite.
    Lay by all nicety and prolixious° blushes   *coyness and excessive*
    That banish what they sue for. Redeem thy brother
    By yielding up thy body to my will,

---

6. Echoing Ecclesiasticus 8:5: "We are all worthy blame."
7. Own and inherit the weakness under discussion, or the weakness that you possess.
8. And receptive to false impressions; referring to Angelo's counterfeiting imagery, lines 45ff.
9. That is, by accepting women's sexual destiny and subjection to men. *livery*: servant's uniform.
1. Liberty to seem licentious.

165 Or else he must not only die the death,
But thy unkindness° shall his death draw out   *unnaturalness*
To ling'ring sufferance.° Answer me tomorrow,   *torment*
Or by the affection° that now guides me most,   *passion*
I'll prove a tyrant to him. As for you,
170 Say what you can, my false o'erweighs your true.   *Exit*

ISABELLA   To whom should I complain? Did I tell this,
Who would believe me? O perilous mouths,
That bear in them one and the selfsame tongue
Either of condemnation or approof,°   *approval*
175 Bidding the law make curtsy° to their will,   *submit*
Hooking both right and wrong to th'appetite,
To follow as it draws! I'll to my brother.
Though he hath fall'n by prompture° of the blood,   *instigation*
Yet hath he in him such a mind of honour
180 That had he twenty heads to tender° down   *pay*
On twenty bloody blocks, he'd yield them up
Before his sister should her body stoop
To such abhorred pollution.
Then Isabel live chaste, and brother die:
185 More than our brother is our chastity.
I'll tell him yet of Angelo's request,
And fit his mind to death, for his soul's rest.   *Exit*

3.1

Enter DUKE [*disguised as a friar*], CLAUDIO, *and* PROVOST

DUKE   So then you hope of pardon from Lord Angelo?
CLAUDIO   The miserable have no other medicine
But only hope.
I've hope to live, and am prepared to die.
5 DUKE   Be absolute° for death. Either death or life   *resolved*
Shall thereby be the sweeter. Reason thus with life.
If I do lose thee, I do lose a thing
That none but fools would keep. A breath thou art,
Servile to all the skyey influences[1]
10 That dost this habitation where thou keep'st°   *live*
Hourly afflict. Merely° thou art death's fool,°   *Utterly / dupe*
For him thou labour'st by thy flight to shun,
And yet runn'st toward him still.° Thou art not noble,   *always*
For all th'accommodations° that thou bear'st   *material comforts*
15 Are nursed by baseness.[2] Thou'rt by no means valiant,
For thou dost fear the soft and tender fork°   *forked tongue*
Of a poor worm.° Thy best of rest is sleep,   *snake*
And that thou oft provok'st,° yet grossly fear'st   *summon*
Thy death, which is no more. Thou art not thyself,°   *self-contained*
20 For thou exist'st on many a thousand grains
That issue out of dust.° Happy thou art not,   *grow from the ground*
For what thou hast not, still thou striv'st to get,
And what thou hast, forget'st. Thou art not certain,°   *stable*
For thy complexion° shifts to strange effects   *temperament*
25 After° the moon. If thou art rich, thou'rt poor,[3]   *Following*

3.1 Location: The prison.
1. Subject to all the influences of the heavenly bodies.
2. Are grown from plants and animals; made by lower-class people.

3. From Revelation 3:17: "For thou sayest, I am rich and increased with goods, and have need of nothing, and knowest not how thou art wretched and miserable, and poor, and blind, and naked."

For like an ass whose back with ingots bows,
Thou bear'st thy heavy riches but a journey,
And death unloads thee. Friend hast thou none,
For thine own bowels,° which do call thee sire,   *offspring*
30   The mere effusion° of thy proper° loins,   *very emission / own*
Do curse the gout, serpigo,° and the rheum,°   *skin disease / congestion*
For ending thee no sooner. Thou hast nor youth nor age,
But as it were an after-dinner's sleep
Dreaming on both; for all thy blessèd youth
35   Becomes as agèd,° and doth beg the alms°   *as if old / for money*
Of palsied eld;° and when thou art old and rich,   *old people*
Thou hast neither heat,° affection, limb,° nor beauty,   *desire / strength*
To make thy riches pleasant. What's in this
That bears the name of life? Yet in this life
40   Lie hid more thousand° deaths; yet death we fear   *a thousand more*
That makes these odds° all even.   *irregularities*
CLAUDIO   I humbly thank you.
To sue° to live, I find I seek to die,   *ask*
And seeking death, find life.⁴ Let it come on.
ISABELLA [*within*]   What ho! Peace here, grace, and good company!
45   PROVOST   Who's there? Come in; the wish deserves a welcome.
DUKE [*to* CLAUDIO]   Dear sir, ere long I'll visit you again.
CLAUDIO   Most holy sir, I thank you.
          Enter ISABELLA
ISABELLA   My business is a word or two with Claudio.
PROVOST   And very welcome. Look, signor, here's your sister.
DUKE   Provost, a word with you.
50   PROVOST   As many as you please.
          [*The* DUKE *and* PROVOST *draw aside*]
DUKE   Bring me to hear them speak where I may be concealed.
          [*They conceal themselves*]
CLAUDIO   Now sister, what's the comfort?
ISABELLA   Why, as all comforts are: most good, most good indeed.
Lord Angelo, having affairs to heaven,
55   Intends you for his swift ambassador,
Where you shall be an everlasting leiger.°   *resident ambassador*
Therefore your best appointment° make with speed.   *preparation*
Tomorrow you set on.°   *forward*
CLAUDIO   Is there no remedy?
ISABELLA   None but such remedy as, to save a head,
60   To cleave a heart in twain.
CLAUDIO   But is there any?
ISABELLA   Yes, brother, you may live.
There is a devilish mercy in the judge,
If you'll implore it, that will free your life,
But fetter you till death.
65   CLAUDIO   Perpetual durance?°   *imprisonment*
ISABELLA   Ay, just,° perpetual durance; a restraint,   *exactly so*
Though all the world's vastidity° you had,   *vastness*
To a determined scope.⁵
CLAUDIO   But in what nature?

---

4. Echoing Matthew 16:25: "For whosoever will save his life, shall lose it: and whosoever shall lose his life for my sake, shall find it."

5. Constricted space (by the awareness of the means by which he had been saved).

ISABELLA   In such a one as you consenting to't
70   Would bark[6] your honour from that trunk° you bear,   *body; tree trunk*
And leave you naked.
CLAUDIO   Let me know the point.
ISABELLA   O, I do fear thee, Claudio, and I quake
Lest thou a feverous° life shouldst entertain,°   *feverish / cherish*
And six or seven winters more respect°   *esteem*
75   Than a perpetual honour. Dar'st thou die?
The sense° of death is most in apprehension,°   *awareness / anticipation*
And the poor beetle that we tread upon
In corporal sufferance° finds a pang as great   *bodily suffering*
As when a giant dies.
CLAUDIO   Why give you me this shame?
80   Think you I can a resolution fetch°   *derive*
From flow'ry° tenderness? If I must die,   *florid*
I will encounter darkness as a bride,
And hug it in mine arms.
ISABELLA   There spake my brother; there my father's grave
85   Did utter forth a voice. Yes, thou must die.
Thou art too noble to conserve a life
In base appliances.° This outward-sainted deputy,   *ignoble means*
Whose settled° visage and deliberate word   *composed*
Nips youth i'th' head[7] and follies doth enew°   *drive into hiding*
90   As falcon doth the fowl, is yet a devil.
His filth within being cast,[8] he would appear
A pond as deep as hell.
CLAUDIO   The precise[9] Angelo?
ISABELLA   O, 'tis the cunning livery of hell
The damnedest body to invest° and cover   *dress*
95   In precise guards!° Dost thou think, Claudio: *trimmings*
If I would yield him my virginity,
Thou might'st be freed!
CLAUDIO   O heavens, it cannot be!
ISABELLA   Yes, he would give't thee, from this rank offence,
So to offend him still.[1] This night's the time
100   That I should do what I abhor to name,
Or else thou diest tomorrow.
CLAUDIO   Thou shalt not do't.
ISABELLA   O, were it but my life,
I'd throw it down for your deliverance
As frankly° as a pin.   *freely*
105   CLAUDIO   Thanks, dear Isabel.
ISABELLA   Be ready, Claudio, for your death tomorrow.
CLAUDIO   Yes. Has he affections in him
That thus can make him bite the law by th' nose°   *flout the law*
When he would force it? Sure it is no sin,
110   Or of the deadly seven[2] it is the least.
ISABELLA   Which is the least?
CLAUDIO   If it were damnable, he being so wise,
Why would he for the momentary trick°   *trifle*

---

6. Strip off, like bark from a tree.
7. As a hawk kills a bird.
8. Cleaned out; measured; vomited.
9. F has "prenzie" here and in line 95; some editors emend (as here) to "precise," others to "princely."

1. *give't thee . . . still:* grant you freedom in return for his foul sin, so that you might continue offending him.
2. Seven deadly sins (pride, lechery, envy, anger, covetousness, gluttony, and sloth).

Be perdurably fined?° O Isabel!   *eternally punished*
115 ISABELLA   What says my brother?
CLAUDIO   Death is a fearful thing.
ISABELLA   And shamèd life a hateful.
CLAUDIO   Ay, but to die, and go we know not where;
To lie in cold obstruction,° and to rot;   *congealment*
120 This sensible warm motion° to become   *conscious warm body*
A kneaded clod, and the dilated° spirit   *expansive; released*
To bath in fiery floods, or to reside
In thrilling° region of thick-ribbèd ice;   *bitterly cold*
To be imprisoned in the viewless° winds,   *unseeing; invisible*
125 And blown with restless violence round about
The pendent° world; or to be worse than worst   *hanging in space*
Of those that lawless and incertain thought³
Imagine howling—'tis too horrible!
The weariest and most loathèd worldly life
130 That age, ache, penury, and imprisonment
Can lay on nature is a paradise
To what we fear of death.
ISABELLA   Alas, alas!
CLAUDIO   Sweet sister, let me live.
135 What sin you do to save a brother's life,
Nature dispenses with° the deed so far   *excuses*
That it becomes a virtue.
ISABELLA   O, you beast!
O faithless coward, O dishonest wretch,
Wilt thou be made a man° out of my vice?   *given life*
140 Is't not a kind of incest to take life
From thine own sister's shame? What should I think?
Heaven shield° my mother played my father fair,   *forbid*
For such a warpèd slip of wilderness°   *shoot of wild stock*
Ne'er issued from his blood. Take my defiance,°   *rejection*
145 Die, perish! Might but my bending down
Reprieve thee from thy fate, it should proceed.
I'll pray a thousand prayers for thy death,
No word to save thee.
CLAUDIO   Nay, hear me, Isabel.
150 ISABELLA   O fie, fie, fie!
Thy sin's not accidental,° but a trade.°   *casual / habit*
Mercy to thee would prove itself a bawd.⁴
'Tis best that thou diest quickly.
        [*She parts from* CLAUDIO]
CLAUDIO   O hear me, Isabella.
DUKE [*coming forward to* ISABELLA]   Vouchsafe a word, young
155   sister, but one word.
ISABELLA   What is your will?
DUKE   Might you dispense with your leisure,° I would by and by   *spare the time*
   have some speech with you. The satisfaction I would require
   is likewise your own benefit.
160 ISABELLA   I have no superfluous leisure; my stay must be stolen
   out of other affairs; but I will attend° you a while.   *await*
DUKE [*standing aside with* CLAUDIO]   Son, I have overheard what
   hath passed between you and your sister. Angelo had never the

---

3. Of those whom unbridled and dubious conjecture.   4. By facilitating sinful behavior.

purpose to corrupt her; only he hath made an assay° of her virtue, to practise his judgement with the disposition of natures. She, having the truth of honour° in her, hath made him that gracious° denial which he is most glad to receive. I am confessor to Angelo, and I know this to be true. Therefore prepare yourself to death. Do not falsify° your resolution with hopes that are fallible. Tomorrow you must die. Go to your knees and make ready.

a trial
chastity
virtuous
corrupt

CLAUDIO Let me ask my sister pardon. I am so out of love with life that I will sue to be rid of it.

DUKE Hold you there.° Farewell.

Remain so resolved

[CLAUDIO *joins* ISABELLA][5]

Provost, a word with you.

PROVOST [*coming forward*] What's your will, father?

DUKE That now you are come, you will be gone. Leave me a while with the maid. My mind° promises with my habit° no loss shall touch her by my company.

intention / friar's gown

PROVOST In good time.° *Exit* [*with* CLAUDIO]

Very well

DUKE The hand that hath made you fair hath made you good. The goodness that is cheap in beauty makes beauty brief in goodness;[6] but grace,° being the soul of your complexion,° shall keep the body of it ever fair. The assault that Angelo hath made to you fortune hath conveyed to my understanding; and but that frailty hath examples° for his falling, I should wonder at Angelo. How will you do to content this substitute,° and to save your brother?

virtue / constitution
precedents
deputy

ISABELLA I am now going to resolve him. I had rather my brother die by the law than my son should be unlawfully born. But O, how much is the good Duke deceived in Angelo! If ever he return and I can speak to him, I will open my lips in vain, or discover° his government.[7]

expose

DUKE That shall not be much amiss. Yet as the matter now stands, he will avoid° your accusation: he made trial of you only. Therefore fasten your ear on my advisings. To the love I have in doing good, a remedy presents itself. I do make myself believe that you may most uprighteously do a poor wronged lady a merited benefit, redeem your brother from the angry law, do no stain to your own gracious person, and much please the absent Duke, if peradventure he shall ever return to have hearing of this business.

quash

ISABELLA Let me hear you speak farther. I have spirit to do anything that appears not foul in the truth of my spirit.

DUKE Virtue is bold, and goodness never fearful. Have you not heard speak of Mariana, the sister of Frederick, the great soldier who miscarried° at sea?

perished

ISABELLA I have heard of the lady, and good words went with her name.

DUKE She should this Angelo have married, was affianced to her oath, and the nuptial appointed;° between which time of the contract and limit° of the solemnity, her brother Frederick was wrecked at sea, having in that perished vessel the dowry of his

wedding day set
date

5. The Duke's conversation with the Provost provides an opportunity for a silent reconciliation.

6. The goodness that is little valued by the beautiful makes beauty short-lived.

7. Conduct; mode of governing.

sister. But mark how heavily this befell to the poor gentlewoman. There she lost a noble and renowned brother, in his
love toward her ever most kind and natural; with him, the portion and sinew° of her fortune, her marriage dowry; with both,   *mainstay*
her combinate° husband, this well-seeming Angelo.   *betrothed*

ISABELLA   Can this be so? Did Angelo so leave her?

DUKE   Left her in her tears, and dried not one of them with his
comfort; swallowed° his vows whole, pretending° in her discov-   *retracted / alleging*
eries of dishonour;° in few, bestowed her on her own lamenta-   *unchastity*
tion, which she yet wears for his sake; and he, a marble° to her   *impervious*
tears, is washed with them, but relents not.

ISABELLA   What a merit were it in death to take this poor maid
from the world! What corruption in this life, that it will let this
man live! But how out of this can she avail?°   *profit*

DUKE   It is a rupture that you may easily heal, and the cure of it
not only saves your brother, but keeps you from dishonour in
doing it.

ISABELLA   Show me how, good father.

DUKE   This forenamed maid hath yet in her the continuance of
her first affection.° His unjust unkindness, that in all reason
should have quenched her love, hath, like an impediment in   *passion*
the current, made it more violent and unruly. Go you to
Angelo, answer his requiring with a plausible obedience, agree
with his demands to the point;° only refer yourself to this advan-   *exactly*
tage: first, that your stay with him may not be long; that the
time may have all shadow° and silence in it; and the place   *darkness*
answer to convenience. This being granted in course, and now
follows all. We shall advise this wronged maid to stead up° your   *fulfill*
appointment, go in your place. If the encounter acknowledge
itself° hereafter, it may compel him to her recompense; and   *becomes known*
hear, by this is your brother saved, your honour untainted, the
poor Mariana advantaged, and the corrupt deputy scaled.[8] The
maid will I frame° and make fit for his attempt. If you think   *prepare*
well to carry this, as you may, the doubleness of the benefit
defends the deceit from reproof. What think you of it?

ISABELLA   The image of it gives me content already, and I trust
it will grow to a most prosperous perfection.°   *completion*

DUKE   It lies much in your holding up. Haste you speedily to
Angelo. If for this night he entreat you to his bed, give him
promise of satisfaction. I will presently to Saint Luke's; there
at the moated grange° resides this dejected[9] Mariana. At that   *country house*
place call upon me; and dispatch° with Angelo, that it may be   *settle*
quickly.

ISABELLA   I thank you for this comfort. Fare you well, good
father.   *Exit*

Enter ELBOW, [POMPEY *the*] *Clown, and officers*[1]

ELBOW   Nay, if there be no remedy for it but that you will needs°   *you must*
buy and sell men and women like beasts, we shall have all the
world drink brown and white bastard.°   *sweet wine (with pun)*

DUKE   O heavens, what stuff is here?

POMPEY   'Twas never merry world since, of two usuries,[2] the

---

8. Overreached; weighed (and found wanting).
9. Depressed; rejected.
1. The rest of the scene takes place on the street. Some

editors begin a new scene here, though the Duke remains
onstage.
2. Lending of money at interest; prostitution.

merriest was put down, and the worser allowed by order of law,[3]
265   a furred gown° to keep him warm—and furred with fox on   *(worn by usurers)*
    lambskins too, to signify that craft,° being richer than inno-   *cunning*
    cency, stands for the facing.[4]

ELBOW Come your way, sir.—Bless you, good father friar.[5]
DUKE And you, good brother father. What offence hath this man
270   made you, sir?
ELBOW Marry, sir, he hath offended the law; and, sir, we take
    him to be a thief, too, sir, for we have found upon him, sir, a
    strange picklock,° which we have sent to the deputy.   *skeleton key*
DUKE [*to* POMPEY] Fie, sirrah, a bawd,° a wicked bawd!   *pimp*
275   The evil that thou causest to be done,
    That is thy means to live. Do thou but think
    What 'tis to cram a maw or clothe a back
    From such a filthy vice. Say to thyself,
    'From their abominable and beastly touches
280   I drink, I eat, array° myself, and live'.   *dress*
    Canst thou believe thy living is a life,
    So stinkingly depending?° Go mend, go mend.   *dependent*
POMPEY Indeed it does stink in some sort, sir. But yet, sir, I
    would prove—
285 DUKE Nay, if the devil have given thee proofs for sin,
    Thou wilt prove° his.—Take him to prison, officer.   *prove to be*
    Correction° and instruction must both work   *Punishment*
    Ere this rude° beast will profit.°   *barbarous / improve*
ELBOW He must before the deputy, sir; he has given him warn-
290   ing. The deputy cannot abide a whoremaster. If he be a whore-
    monger and comes before him, he were as good go a mile on
    his errand.[6]
DUKE That° we were all as some would seem to be—   *Would that*
    Free from our faults, or faults from seeming free.°   *free from seeming*
295 ELBOW His neck will come to° your waist: a cord,[7] sir.   *end up like*
        Enter LUCIO
POMPEY I spy comfort, I cry bail. Here's a gentleman, and a
    friend of mine.
LUCIO How now, noble Pompey? What, at the wheels of Cae-
    sar? Art thou led in triumph?[8] What, is there none of Pygmali-
300   on's images[9] newly made woman to be had now, for putting
    the hand in the pocket and extracting clutched?[1] What reply,
    ha? What sayst thou to this tune, matter, and method?[2] Is't not
    drowned i'th' last rain,[3] ha? What sayst thou, trot?° Is the world   *bawd*
    as it was, man? Which is the way? Is it sad and few words? Or
305   how? The trick° of it?   *style*
DUKE Still° thus and thus; still worse!   *Always*
LUCIO How doth my dear morsel thy mistress? Procures she still, ha?

---

3. A statute of 1570 allowed interest of 10 percent or less.
4. Is used to trim the garment; displays itself to the world.
5. Absurd, since "friar" means "brother"; hence the Duke's reply.
6. *he were . . . errand:* he would be better doing anything rather than that.
7. Encircled by a rope, as the friar's cord encircles his waist.

8. After Roman victories, vanquished generals were paraded behind the chariot wheels of their conquerors.
9. In classical legend, the sculptor Pygmalion fell in love with one of his statues, who was given life by Venus, the goddess of love; with a play on "become a woman" (lose one's virginity).
1. Clenched, with money for bail.
2. This style, topic, and sequence of thought.
3. Overwhelmed with recent misfortune.

POMPEY Troth, sir, she hath eaten up° all her beef,° and she is *worn out / prostitutes*
    herself in the tub.[4]

310 LUCIO Why, 'tis good, it is the right of it, it must be so. Ever
    your fresh whore and your powdered[5] bawd; an unshunned° *unavoidable*
    consequence, it must be so. Art going to prison, Pompey?

POMPEY Yes, faith, sir.

LUCIO Why 'tis not amiss, Pompey. Farewell. Go; say I sent thee
315   thither. For debt, Pompey, or how?

ELBOW For being a bawd, for being a bawd.

LUCIO Well then, imprison him. If imprisonment be the due of
    a bawd, why, 'tis his right. Bawd is he doubtless, and of antiq-
    uity° too—bawd born.° Farewell, good Pompey. Commend me *long standing / at birth*
320   to the prison, Pompey. You will turn good husband° now, Pom- *householder*
    pey; you will keep the house.

POMPEY I hope, sir, your good worship will be my bail?

LUCIO No, indeed, will I not, Pompey; it is not the wear.° I will *fashion*
    pray, Pompey, to increase your bondage. If you take it not
325   patiently, why, your mettle° is the more. Adieu, trusty Pom- *spirit; shackles*
    pey.— Bless you, friar.

DUKE And you.

LUCIO Does Bridget paint° still, Pompey, ha? *use cosmetics*

ELBOW [*to* POMPEY] Come your ways, sir, come.

330 POMPEY [*to* LUCIO] You will not bail me then, sir?

LUCIO Then, Pompey, nor now.—What news abroad,° friar, *in the world*
    what news?

ELBOW [*to* POMPEY] Come your ways, sir, come.

LUCIO Go to kennel, Pompey,[6] go.
                [*Exeunt* ELBOW, POMPEY, *and officers*]
335   What news, friar, of the Duke?

DUKE I know none. Can you tell me of any?

LUCIO Some say he is with the Emperor of Russia; other some,° *some others*
    he is in Rome. But where is he, think you?

DUKE I know not where; but wheresoever, I wish him well.

340 LUCIO It was a mad, fantastical trick° of him to steal from the *eccentric caprice*
    state, and usurp the beggary he was never born to. Lord Angelo
    dukes it° well in his absence; he puts transgression to't.[7] *plays the Duke*

DUKE He does well in't.

LUCIO A little more lenity to lechery would do no harm in him.
345   Something too crabbed° that way, friar. *Somewhat too harsh*

DUKE It is too general a vice, and severity must cure it.

LUCIO Yes, in good sooth, the vice is of a great° kindred, it is *an extensive; powerful*
    well allied.° But it is impossible to extirp° it quite, friar, till *connected / extirpate*
    eating and drinking be put down. They say this Angelo was not
350   made by man and woman, after this downright[8] way of cre-
    ation. Is it true, think you?

DUKE How should he be made, then?

LUCIO Some report a sea-maid° spawned him, some that he was *mermaid*
    begot between two stockfishes.° But it is certain that when he *dried fish*
355   makes water his urine is congealed ice; that I know to be true.
    And he is a motion ungenerative;[9] that's infallible.° *certain*

DUKE You are pleasant,° sir, and speak apace.° *merry / unrestrainedly*

---

4. Pickling tub for preserving ("powdering") beef; sweating tub for curing venereal disease.
5. Pickled; covered with cosmetic powder.
6. "Pompey" was a common dog's name.

7. He prosecutes lawbreaking vigorously.
8. In accordance with this straightforward.
9. An impotent puppet.

LUCIO Why, what a ruthless thing is this in him, for the rebellion of a codpiece¹ to take away the life of a man! Would the
360   Duke that is absent have done this? Ere he would have hanged
a man for the getting° a hundred bastards, he would have paid   *begetting*
for the nursing a thousand. He had some feeling of the sport,
he knew the service,° and that instructed him to mercy.   *(of prostitution)*
DUKE I never heard the absent Duke much detected° for   *accused*
365   women; he was not inclined that way.
LUCIO O sir, you are deceived.
DUKE 'Tis not possible.
LUCIO Who, not the Duke? Yes, your beggar of fifty; and his
use° was to put a ducat in her clack-dish.² The Duke had cro-   *custom*
370   chets° in him. He would be drunk too, that let me inform you.   *odd notions*
DUKE You do him wrong, surely.
LUCIO Sir, I was an inward° of his. A shy fellow was the Duke,   *intimate*
and I believe I know the cause of his withdrawing.
DUKE What, I prithee, might be the cause?
375   LUCIO No, pardon, 'tis a secret must be locked within the teeth
and the lips. But this I can let you understand. The greater file
of the subject° held the Duke to be wise.   *majority of the people*
DUKE Wise? Why, no question but he was.
LUCIO A very superficial, ignorant, unweighing° fellow.   *injudicious*
380   DUKE Either this is envy° in you, folly, or mistaking. The very   *malice*
stream° of his life, and the business he hath helmed,° must,   *course / steered*
upon a warranted need,° give him a better proclamation.° Let   *necessarily / reputation*
him be but testimonied° in his own bringings-forth,° and he   *proven / public actions*
shall appear to the envious a scholar, a statesman, and a soldier.
385   Therefore you speak unskilfully,° or, if your knowledge be   *ignorantly*
more, it is much darkened in your malice.
LUCIO Sir, I know him and I love him.
DUKE Love talks with better knowledge, and knowledge with
dearer love.
390   LUCIO Come, sir, I know what I know.
DUKE I can hardly believe that, since you know not what you
speak. But if ever the Duke return, as our prayers are he may,
let me desire you to make your answer before him. If it be
honest you have spoke, you have courage to maintain it. I am
395   bound to call upon° you; and I pray you, your name?   *accuse*
LUCIO Sir, my name is Lucio, well known to the Duke.
DUKE He shall know you better, sir, if I may live to report you.
LUCIO I fear you not.
DUKE O, you hope the Duke will return no more, or you imag-
400   ine me too unhurtful an opposite.° But indeed I can do you   *adversary*
little harm; you'll forswear this again.°   *at another time*
LUCIO I'll be hanged first. Thou art deceived in me, friar. But
no more of this. Canst thou tell if Claudio die tomorrow or no?
DUKE Why should he die, sir?
405   LUCIO Why? For filling a bottle with a tundish.° I would the   *funnel (with innuendo)*
Duke we talk of were returned again; this ungenitured agent°   *sexless deputy*
will unpeople the province with continency. Sparrows° must   *(proverbially lustful)*
not build in his house-eaves, because they are lecherous. The
Duke yet would have dark deeds darkly answered:° he would   *secretly requited*
410   never bring them to light. Would he were returned. Marry, this

---

1. Padded pouch worn over a man's breeches.   2. Begging bowl (with sexual innuendo).

Claudio is condemned for untrussing.° Farewell, good friar. I   *undoing his leggings*
prithee pray for me. The Duke, I say to thee again, would eat
mutton on Fridays.[3] He's not past it yet, and, I say to thee, he
would mouth° with a beggar, though she smelt° brown bread   *kiss / smelled of*
415 and garlic.[4] Say that I said so. Farewell.   *Exit*

DUKE   No might nor greatness in mortality°   *mortal existence*
Can censure scape;° back-wounding calumny[5]   *escape censure*
The whitest virtue strikes. What king so strong
Can tie the gall° up in the slanderous tongue?   *rancor*
    Enter ESCALUS, PROVOST, *and* [MISTRESS OVERDONE]
But who comes here?

420 ESCALUS [*to the* PROVOST]   Go, away with her to prison.

MISTRESS OVERDONE   Good my lord, be good to me. Your honour is accounted a merciful man, good my lord.

ESCALUS   Double and treble admonition,[6] and still forfeit in the
same kind!° This would make mercy swear[7] and play the tyrant.   *way*

425 PROVOST   A bawd of eleven years' continuance, may it please
your honour.

MISTRESS OVERDONE   My lord, this is one Lucio's information°   *accusation*
against me. Mistress Kate Keepdown was with child by him in
the Duke's time; he promised her marriage. His child is a year
430 and a quarter old come Philip and Jacob.[8] I have kept it myself;
and see how he goes about° to abuse° me.   *out of his way / injure*

ESCALUS   That fellow is a fellow of much licence. Let him be
called before us. Away with her to prison. Go to, no more
words. Provost, my brother° Angelo will not be altered; Claudio   *colleague*
435 must die tomorrow. Let him be furnished with divines, and
have all charitable preparation.[9] If my brother wrought by° my   *acted according to*
pity, it should not be so with him.

PROVOST   So please you, this friar hath been with him and
advised him for th'entertainment° of death.   *acceptance*
    [*Exeunt* PROVOST *and* MISTRESS OVERDONE]

440 ESCALUS   Good even, good father.

DUKE   Bliss and goodness on you.

ESCALUS   Of whence are you?

DUKE   Not of this country, though my chance° is now   *fortune*
To use it for my time.° I am a brother   *dwell here at present*
445 Of gracious order, late come from the See°   *Vatican*
In special business from his Holiness.

ESCALUS   What news abroad i'th' world?

DUKE   None, but that there is so great a fever on goodness that
the dissolution of it must cure it.[1] Novelty is only in request,°   *alone in demand*
450 and it is as dangerous to be aged in° any kind of course as it is   *habituated to*
virtuous to be inconstant in any undertaking. There is scarce
truth° enough alive to make societies secure, but security[2]   *honesty; loyalty*
enough to make fellowships° accursed. Much upon° this riddle   *partnerships/According to*
runs the wisdom of the world. This news is old enough, yet it

---

3. *mutton:* prostitute (slang); it was forbidden to eat meat on Fridays.
4. The food of the poor.
5. *back-wounding calumny:* slander ("calumny") is cowardly because it is not done to the victim's face.
6. Exceeding that recommended by Paul in Titus 3:10: "Reject him that is an heretic, after once or twice admonition."
7. Varying the proverbial "make a saint swear."

8. May 1 was the Feast of St. Philip and St. James (Jacob), but also the time of sexually licentious May Day festivities, when the child was presumably conceived.
9. Spiritual preparation enjoined by Christian charity.
1. *there is . . . it:* that is, goodness is so sick that only death will "cure" it.
2. Financial bonds liable to forfeit; blind trustfulness. *societies:* association with others.

455 is every day's news. I pray you, sir, of what disposition was the Duke?

ESCALUS One that, above all other strifes, contended especially
to know himself.[3]

DUKE What pleasure was he given to?

ESCALUS Rather rejoicing to see another merry than merry at

460 anything which professed° to make him rejoice; a gentleman   *attempted*
of all temperance. But leave we him to his events,° with a   *affairs*
prayer they may prove prosperous, and let me desire to know°   *ask*
how you find Claudio prepared. I am made to understand that
you have lent him visitation.°   *visited him*

465 DUKE He professes to have received no sinister measure° from   *unjust treatment*
his judge, but most willingly humbles himself to the determi-
nation° of justice. Yet had he framed° to himself, by the instruc-   *sentence / imagined*
tion of his frailty, many deceiving promises of life, which I, by
my good leisure,° have discredited to him; and now is he   *gradually*

470 resolved to die.

ESCALUS You have paid the heavens your function, and the prisoner the very debt of your calling.[4] I have laboured for the
poor gentleman to the extremest shore° of my modesty, but my   *utmost limit*
brother-justice have I found so severe that he hath forced me

475 to tell him he is indeed Justice.[5]

DUKE If his own life answer° the straitness° of his proceeding, it   *correspond to / strictness*
shall become him well; wherein if he chance to fail, he hath
sentenced° himself.   *condemned*

ESCALUS I am going to visit the prisoner. Fare you well.

480 DUKE Peace be with you.   [*Exit* ESCALUS][6]

He who the sword of heaven[7] will bear
Should be as holy as severe,
Pattern in himself to know,
Grace to stand, and virtue go,[8]

485 More nor less to others paying
Than by self-offences° weighing.   *his own offenses*
Shame to him whose cruel striking
Kills for faults of his own liking!
Twice treble shame on Angelo,

490 To weed my vice,[9] and let his grow!
O, what may man within him hide,
Though angel on the outward side!
How may likeness made in crimes[1]
Make my practice on the times

495 To draw with idle spiders' strings
Most ponderous and substantial things?[2]
Craft against vice I must apply.
With Angelo tonight shall lie
His old betrothèd but despisèd.

500 So disguise shall, by th' disguisèd,[3]
Pay with falsehood false exacting,
And perform an old contracting.   *Exit*

3. "Know thyself" was proverbial advice.
4. You have repaid the heavens for giving you your vocation, and given the prisoner all he can expect of a friar.
5. Absolute justice personified.
6. For a reconstruction of the following episodes as they
were originally written, see Additional Passage B.
7. The authority of a ruler, conferred by God.
8. When to stand firm, and when to take action (?).

9. The Duke speaks as a representative sinner.
1. How can the similarity between Claudio's and
Angelo's offenses.
2. *To draw . . . things:* the law was proverbially compared
to a spider's web, which caught small insects but which
large insects could break through. *idle:* ineffectual.
3. Mariana, "disguised" as Isabella.

4.1

MARIANA [*discovered with a*] BOY *singing*

BOY Take, O take those lips away
That so sweetly were forsworn,°   *perjured*
And those eyes, the break of day
Lights° that do mislead° the morn;   *Suns / guide falsely*

5   But my kisses bring again, bring again,°   *return*
Seals of love, though sealed in vain, sealed in vain.

Enter DUKE [*disguised as a friar*]

MARIANA   Break off thy song, and haste thee quick away.
Here comes a man of comfort, whose advice
Hath often stilled my brawling° discontent.   [*Exit* BOY]   *clamorous*

10   I cry you mercy,° sir, and well could wish   *beg your pardon*
You had not found me here so musical.
Let me excuse me, and believe me so:°   *in this*
My mirth it much displeased, but pleased my woe.[1]

DUKE   'Tis good; though music oft hath such a charm°   *magic spell*

15   To make bad good,° and good provoke to harm. I pray you tell   *bad appear good*
me, hath anybody enquired for me here today? Much upon°   *at about*
this time have I promised here to meet.

MARIANA   You have not been enquired after; I have sat here all day.

Enter ISABELLA

DUKE   I do constantly° believe you; the time is come even now.   *assuredly*

20   I shall crave your forbearance° a little. Maybe I will call upon   *departure; patience*
you anon, for some advantage to yourself.

MARIANA   I am always bound to you.   *Exit*

DUKE   Very well met, and welcome.
What is the news from this good deputy?

25   ISABELLA   He hath a garden circummured° with brick,   *walled about*
Whose western side is with a vineyard backed;
And to that vineyard is a planckèd° gate,   *made of planks*
That makes his opening with this bigger key.
This other doth command a little door

30   Which from the vineyard to the garden leads.
There have I made my promise
Upon the heavy° middle of the night   *In the gloomy*
To call upon him.

DUKE   But shall you on your knowledge° find this way?   *with this information*

35   ISABELLA   I have ta'en a due and wary note upon't.
With whispering and most guilty diligence,
In action all of precept,° he did show me   *With explanatory gestures*
The way twice o'er.

DUKE   Are there no other tokens°   *signs*
Between you 'greed concerning her observance?[2]

40   ISABELLA   No, none, but only a repair° i'th' dark,   *journey to the place*
And that I have possessed° him my most° stay   *informed / longest*
Can be but brief, for I have made him know
I have a servant comes with me along
That stays upon° me, whose persuasion is   *waits for*
I come about my brother.

45   DUKE   'Tis well borne up.°   *maintained*

4.1 Location: Mariana's house. Probably Mariana and the Boy are "discovered" by drawing back a curtain to reveal the characters within an alcove at the back of the stage.

1. The music drove away mirth but nurtured melancholy.
2. That she (Mariana) must observe.

I have not yet made known to Mariana
A word of this.—What ho, within! Come forth!

     Enter MARIANA

[*To* MARIANA] I pray you be acquainted with this maid.
She comes to do you good.

ISABELLA   I do desire the like.

50 DUKE [*to* MARIANA]   Do you persuade yourself° that I respect you?   *believe*

MARIANA   Good friar, I know you do, and so have found it.

DUKE   Take then this your companion° by the hand,   *partner*
Who hath a story ready for your ear.
I shall attend your leisure;° but make haste,   *wait until you are ready*
The vaporous night approaches.

55 MARIANA [*to* ISABELLA]   Will't please you walk aside?

     Exeunt [MARIANA *and* ISABELLA]

DUKE[3] O place° and greatness, millions of false° eyes   *rank / misjudging*
Are stuck° upon thee; volumes of report°   *fixed / rumors*
Run with their false and most contrarious quest°   *misguided inquiry*
Upon thy doings; thousand escapes° of wit   *sallies*
60 Make thee the father° of their idle dream,°   *subject / fantasy*
And rack[4] thee in their fancies.

     Enter MARIANA *and* ISABELLA

               Welcome. How agreed?

ISABELLA   She'll take the enterprise upon her, father,
If you advise it.

DUKE   It is not my consent,
But my entreaty too.

ISABELLA [*to* MARIANA]   Little have you to say
65 When you depart from him but, soft and low,
'Remember now my brother'.

MARIANA   Fear me not.[5]

DUKE   Nor, gentle daughter, fear you not at all.
He is your husband on a pre-contract.°   *formal betrothal*
To bring you thus together 'tis no sin,
70 Sith that° the justice of your title to him   *Since*
Doth flourish° the deceit. Come, let us go.   *give propriety to*
Our corn's to reap, for yet our tilth's° to sow.   *Exeunt*   *tilled land*

4.2

     Enter PROVOST *and* [POMPEY]

PROVOST   Come hither, sirrah. Can you cut off a man's head?

POMPEY   If the man be a bachelor, sir, I can; but if he be a married man, he's his wife's head,[1] and I can never cut off a woman's head.[2]

5 PROVOST   Come, sir, leave me° your snatches,° and yield me a   *stop / quips*
direct answer. Tomorrow morning are to die Claudio and Bar-
nardine. Here is in our prison a common executioner, who in
his office lacks a helper. If you will take it on you to assist him,
it shall redeem you from your gyves;° if not, you shall have   *fetters*

---

3. The following lines, which seem out of context, may
have originally been part of the Duke's soliloquy at the
end of Act 3.
4. Misrepresent (literally, "torture by stretching").
5. Rely upon me; but the Duke takes "fear" in its modern
sense.

4.2 Location: The prison.
1. Alluding to Paul's doctrine "the husband is the wife's
head," Ephesians 5:23.
2. Playing on "married woman's maidenhead," an
improbability.

10 your full time of imprisonment, and your deliverance with an
unpitied° whipping; for you have been a notorious bawd. *unmerciful*

POMPEY Sir, I have been an unlawful bawd time out of mind,
but yet I will be content to be a lawful hangman. I would be
glad to receive some instruction from my fellow partner.

15 PROVOST What ho, Abhorson! Where's Abhorson there?

Enter ABHORSON

ABHORSON Do you call, sir?

PROVOST Sirrah, here's a fellow will help you tomorrow in your
execution. If you think it meet, compound with him by the
year,³ and let him abide here with you; if not, use him for the
20 present, and dismiss him. He cannot plead his estimation° with *reputation*
you; he hath been a bawd.

ABHORSON A bawd, sir? Fie upon him, he will discredit our mystery.⁴

PROVOST Go to, sir, you weigh equally; a feather will turn the scale.

Exit

POMPEY Pray, sir, by your good favour°—for surely, sir, a good *permission*
25 favour° you have, but that you have a hanging look⁵—do you *face*
call, sir, your occupation a mystery?

ABHORSON Ay, sir, a mystery.

POMPEY Painting,⁶ sir, I have heard say is a mystery; and your
whores, sir, being members of my occupation, using painting,
30 do prove my occupation a mystery. But what mystery there
should be in hanging, if I should be hanged I cannot imagine.

ABHORSON Sir, it is a mystery.

POMPEY Proof.

ABHORSON Every true man's apparel fits your thief⁷—

35 POMPEY If it be too little for your thief, your true man thinks it
big enough.° If it be too big for your thief, your thief thinks it *a big enough loss*
little enough.° So every true man's apparel fits your thief. *a small enough gain*

Enter PROVOST

PROVOST Are you agreed?

POMPEY Sir, I will serve him, for I do find your hangman is
40 a more penitent trade than your bawd—he doth oftener ask
forgiveness.⁸

PROVOST [*to* ABHORSON] You, sirrah, provide your block and
your axe tomorrow, four o'clock.

ABHORSON [*to* POMPEY] Come on, bawd, I will instruct thee in
45 my trade. Follow.

POMPEY I do desire to learn, sir, and I hope, if you have occasion
to use me for your own turn, you shall find me yare.° For truly, *skillful; eager*
sir, for your kindness I owe you a good turn.⁹

PROVOST Call hither Barnardine and Claudio.

Exeunt [ABHORSON *and* POMPEY]

50 Th'one has my pity; not a jot the other,
Being a murderer, though he were my brother.

Enter CLAUDIO

Look, here's the warrant, Claudio, for thy death.
'Tis now dead midnight, and by eight tomorrow
Thou must be made immortal. Where's Barnardine?

---

3. Settle regular terms of employment with him.
4. Profession, requiring specialized skills and training.
5. Downcast expression; hangman's face.
6. Artist's occupation; use of cosmetics.
7. Abhorson implies that the thief assumes the character of an honest man by stealing his clothing; he also
suggests an analogy between the thief and the hangman, who was awarded the clothes of his victims.
8. Executioners customarily asked forgiveness of their
victims before killing them.
9. Favor; turning off the scaffold.

55 CLAUDIO   As fast locked up in sleep as guiltless labour
When it lies starkly° in the travailer's° bones.   *stiffly / worker's*
He will not wake.
PROVOST   Who can do good on him?
Well, go prepare yourself.
    [Knocking within]
                 But hark, what noise?
Heaven give your spirits comfort!   *[Exit* CLAUDIO*]*
    [Knocking again]
                 By and by!
60 I hope it is some pardon or reprieve
For the most gentle Claudio.
    Enter DUKE *[disguised as a friar]*
                 Welcome, father.
DUKE   The best and wholesom'st spirits of the night
Envelop you, good Provost! Who called here of late?
PROVOST   None since the curfew¹ rung.
65 DUKE   Not Isabel?
PROVOST   No.
DUKE   They will then, ere't be long.
PROVOST   What comfort is for Claudio?
DUKE   There's some in hope.
70 PROVOST   It is a bitter° deputy.   *cruel*
DUKE   Not so, not so; his life is paralleled
Even with the stroke and line² of his great justice.
He doth with holy abstinence subdue
That in himself which he spurs on his power
75 To qualify° in others. Were he mealed° with that   *moderate / stained*
Which he corrects, then were he tyrannous;
But this being so, he's just.
    [Knocking within]
                 Now are they come.
    [The PROVOST *goes to a door]*
This is a gentle Provost. Seldom when°   *Rarely*
The steelèd° jailer is the friend of men.   *hard-hearted*
    [Knocking within]
    [To PROVOST*]* How now, what noise? That spirit's possessed
80   with haste
That wounds th'unlisting postern° with these strokes.   *unyielding door*
PROVOST   There he° must stay until the officer   *(the messenger)*
Arise to let him in. He° is called up.   *(the officer)*
DUKE   Have you no countermand for Claudio yet,
But he must die tomorrow?
85 PROVOST   None, sir, none.
DUKE   As near the dawning, Provost, as it is,
You shall hear more ere morning.
PROVOST   Happily°   *Perhaps*
You something know, yet I believe there comes
No countermand. No such example° have we;   *precedent*
90 Besides, upon the very siege° of justice   *seat*
Lord Angelo hath to the public ear
Professed the contrary.

1. Evening bell, rung at 9:00 P.M.
2. Exact course; also suggesting ax blows and hanging ropes.

Enter a MESSENGER

This is his lordship's man.

DUKE   And here comes Claudio's pardon.

95   MESSENGER [*giving a paper to* PROVOST]   My lord hath sent you
this note, and by me this further charge: that you swerve not
from the smallest article of it, neither in time, matter, or other
circumstance. Good morrow; for, as I take it, it is almost day.

PROVOST   I shall obey him.   [*Exit* MESSENGER]

100 DUKE [*aside*]   This is his pardon, purchased by such sin
For which the pardoner himself is in.
Hence hath offence his° quick celerity,   its
When it is borne in high authority.
When vice makes mercy, mercy's so extended

105 That for the fault's love[3] is th'offender friended.°—   befriended
Now sir, what news?

PROVOST   I told you: Lord Angelo, belike thinking me remiss in
mine office, awakens me with this unwonted putting-on;°   urging
methinks strangely, for he hath not used° it before.   practiced

110 DUKE   Pray you let's hear.

PROVOST [*reading the letter*]   'Whatsoever you may hear to the
contrary, let Claudio be executed by four of the clock, and in
the afternoon Barnardine. For my better satisfaction, let me
have Claudio's head sent me by five. Let this be duly per-

115 formed, with a thought that more depends on it than we must
yet deliver.° Thus fail not to do your office, as you will answer   make known
it at your peril.'
What say you to this, sir?

DUKE   What is that Barnardine, who is to be executed in th'afternoon?

120 PROVOST   A Bohemian born, but here nursed up and bred; one
that is a prisoner nine years old.°   nine years a prisoner

DUKE   How came it that the absent Duke had not either delivered him to his liberty or executed him? I have heard it was
ever his manner to do so.

125 PROVOST   His friends still° wrought reprieves for him; and indeed   continually
his fact,° till now in the government of Lord Angelo, came not   crime
to an undoubtful° proof.   a certain

DUKE   It is now apparent?

PROVOST   Most manifest, and not denied by himself.

130 DUKE   Hath he borne himself penitently in prison? How seems
he to be touched?°   affected

PROVOST   A man that apprehends death no more dreadfully but as
a drunken sleep; careless, reckless, and fearless of what's past,
present, or to come; insensible of mortality, and desperately

135 mortal.[4]

DUKE   He wants° advice.   needs

PROVOST   He will hear none. He hath evermore had the liberty
of the prison. Give him leave to escape hence, he would not.
Drunk many times a day, if not many days entirely° drunk. We   continuously

140 have very oft awaked him as if to carry him to execution, and
showed him a seeming warrant for it; it hath not moved him at all.

DUKE   More of him anon. There is written in your brow, Provost,
honesty and constancy. If I read it not truly, my ancient skill

---

3. For love of the fault.   4. Reckless of death, and in a state of mortal sin.

beguiles me. But in the boldness° of my cunning,° I will lay   *confidence / skill*
145   myself in hazard.⁵ Claudio, whom here you have warrant to
    execute, is no greater forfeit to the law than Angelo who hath
    sentenced him. To make you understand this in a manifested
    effect,° I crave but four days' respite, for the which you are to   *clear demonstration*
    do me both a present° and a dangerous courtesy.°   *an immediate / favor*
150 PROVOST   Pray sir, in what?
  DUKE   In the delaying death.
  PROVOST   Alack, how may I do it, having the hour limited, and
    an express command under penalty to deliver his head in the
    view of Angelo? I may make my case as Claudio's to cross° this   *oppose*
155   in the smallest.
  DUKE   By the vow of mine order, I warrant you, if my instructions
    may be your guide, let this Barnardine be this morning exe-
    cuted, and his head borne to Angelo.
  PROVOST   Angelo hath seen them both, and will discover° the   *discern*
160   favour.
  DUKE   O, death's a great disguiser, and you may add to it. Shave
    the head and tie the beard, and say it was the desire of the
    penitent to be so bared before his death; you know the course
    is common. If anything fall to you upon° this more than thanks   *as a result of*
165   and good fortune, by the saint whom I profess,⁶ I will plead
    against it with my life.
  PROVOST   Pardon me, good father, it is against my oath.
  DUKE   Were you sworn to the Duke or to the deputy?
  PROVOST   To him and to his substitutes.
170 DUKE   You will think you have made no offence if the Duke
    avouch° the justice of your dealing?   *vouch for*
  PROVOST   But what likelihood is in that?
  DUKE   Not a resemblance,° but a certainty. Yet since I see you   *likelihood*
    fearful, that neither my coat,° integrity, nor persuasion can with   *religious garb*
175   ease attempt you,° I will go further than I meant, to pluck all   *win you over*
    fears out of you. [*Showing a letter*] Look you, sir, here is the
    hand and seal of the Duke. You know the character,° I doubt   *handwriting*
    not, and the signet is not strange to you?
  PROVOST   I know them both.
180 DUKE   The contents of this is the return of the Duke. You shall
    anon° over-read it at your pleasure, where you shall find within   *right away*
    these two days he will be here. This is a thing that Angelo
    knows not, for he this very day receives letters of strange tenor,
    perchance of the Duke's death, perchance entering into some
185   monastery; but by chance nothing of what is writ.° Look, th'un-   *written here*
    folding star⁷ calls up the shepherd. Put not yourself into amaze-
    ment° how these things should be. All difficulties are but easy   *perplexity*
    when they are known. Call your executioner, and off with Bar-
    nardine's head. I will give him a present shrift,° and advise him   *an immediate confession*
190   for a better place. Yet° you are amazed; but this° shall abso-   *Still / (the letter)*
    lutely resolve you.° Come away, it is almost clear dawn.   *free you from doubt*

                                        Exeunt

---

5. I will bet on it; I will put myself in peril.   7. Morning star (which tells the shepherd he may
6. The patron saint of my order.   safely release the sheep from the fold).

4.3

Enter [POMPEY]

POMPEY I am as well acquainted here as I was in our house of
profession.[1] One would think it were Mistress Overdone's own
house, for here be many of her old customers. First, here's
young Master Rash; he's in for a commodity[2] of brown paper
5   and old ginger, nine score and seventeen pounds, of which he
made five marks ready money.[3] Marry, then ginger[4] was not
much in request, for the old women were all dead.[5] Then is
there here one Master Caper,° at the suit of Master Threepile[6]   *fashionable dance*
the mercer,° for some four suits of peach-coloured satin, which   *cloth dealer*
10   now peaches° him a beggar. Then have we here young Dizzy,   *impeaches; declares*
and young Master Deepvow, and Master Copperspur and Mas-
ter Starve-lackey[7] the rapier and dagger man,[8] and young Drop-
hair[9] that killed lusty Pudding,° and Master Forthright the   *stuffed guts*
tilter,° and brave Master Shoe-tie the great traveller,[1] and wild   *fencer*
15   Half-can that stabbed Pots,[2] and I think forty more, all great
doers in our trade, and are now 'for the Lord's sake'.[3]

Enter ABHORSON

ABHORSON Sirrah, bring Barnardine hither.

POMPEY Master Barnardine! You must rise[4] and be hanged,
Master Barnardine!

20   ABHORSON What ho, Barnardine!

BARNARDINE [*within*] A pox o' your throats! Who makes that
noise there? What are you?

POMPEY Your friends, sir; the hangman. You must be so good,
sir, to rise and be put to death.

25   BARNARDINE Away, you rogue, away! I am sleepy.

ABHORSON Tell him he must awake, and that quickly too.

POMPEY Pray, Master Barnardine, awake till you are executed,
and sleep afterwards.

ABHORSON Go in to him and fetch him out.

30   POMPEY He is coming, sir, he is coming. I hear his straw rustle.

ABHORSON Is the axe upon the block, sirrah?

POMPEY Very ready, sir.

Enter BARNARDINE

BARNARDINE How now, Abhorson, what's the news with you?

ABHORSON Truly, sir, I would desire you to clap into[5] your pray-
35   ers, for, look you, the warrant's come.

BARNARDINE You rogue, I have been drinking all night. I am not
fitted for't.

POMPEY O, the better, sir; for he that drinks all night, and is
hanged betimes° in the morning, may sleep the sounder all the   *early*
40   next day.

Enter DUKE [*disguised as a friar*]

4.3 Location: Scene continues.
1. Religious house ("nunnery" was slang for "brothel").
2. To evade the statutory limit on interest, usurers would
give borrowers part of their loan in practically worthless
"commodities," which they were supposed to sell for
ready money. *he's in for:* he's in for falling into debt over.
3. Rash paid 197 pounds for the "commodity," a very
large sum, and sold it for about 3.3 pounds.
4. Used to make warming tonics.
5. Presumably victims of the 1603 plague, mentioned
earlier by Mistress Overdone.

6. Richest sort of velvet.
7. One who fails to feed his servants.
8. Suggesting a reputation for brawling.
9. Premature baldness was a sign of syphilis.
1. Observer of foreign fashions (probably ironic).
2. Suggesting drinking cups.
3. The cry of prisoners begging from the prison grate.
Prisoners had to pay for their own food and lodging.
4. Get out of bed; mount the scaffold.
5. Immediately begin; join your hands for.

ABHORSON [*to* BARNARDINE]   Look you, sir, here comes your
   ghostly° father. Do we jest now, think you?   *spiritual*
DUKE [*to* BARNARDINE]   Sir, induced by my charity, and hearing
   how hastily you are to depart, I am come to advise you, comfort
45   you, and pray with you.
BARNARDINE   Friar, not I. I have been drinking hard all night,
   and I will have more time to prepare me, or they shall beat out
   my brains with billets.° I will not consent to die this day, that's   *thick sticks*
   certain.
50 DUKE   O sir, you must; and therefore, I beseech you,
   Look forward on the journey you shall go.
BARNARDINE   I swear I will not die today, for any man's persuasion.
DUKE   But hear you—
BARNARDINE   Not a word. If you have anything to say to me,
55   come to my ward,° for thence will not I today.   *Exit*   *cell*
DUKE   Unfit to live or die. O gravel° heart!   *(i.e., hard)*
   After him, fellows; bring him to the block.
                    [*Exeunt* ABHORSON *and* POMPEY]
       Enter PROVOST
PROVOST   Now, sir, how do you find the prisoner?
DUKE   A creature unprepared, unmeet° for death;   *unfit*
60   And to transport° him in the mind he is   *execute (euphemistic)*
   Were damnable.
PROVOST   Here in the prison, father,
   There died this morning of a cruel fever
   One Ragusine, a most notorious pirate,
   A man of Claudio's years, his beard and head
65   Just of his colour. What if we do omit°   *disregard*
   This reprobate till he were well inclined,
   And satisfy the deputy with the visage
   Of Ragusine, more like to Claudio?
DUKE   O, 'tis an accident that heaven provides.
70   Dispatch it presently; the hour draws on
   Prefixed° by Angelo. See this be done,   *Fixed in advance*
   And sent according to command, whiles I
   Persuade this rude° wretch willingly to die.   *uncivilized*
PROVOST   This shall be done, good father, presently.
75   But Barnardine must die this afternoon;
   And how shall we continue° Claudio,   *maintain*
   To save me from the danger that might come
   If he were known alive?
DUKE   Let this be done:
   Put them in secret holds,° both Barnardine and Claudio.   *cells*
80   Ere twice the sun hath made his journal° greeting   *daily*
   To yonder generation,⁶ you shall find
   Your safety manifested.
PROVOST   I am your free dependant.°   *willing servant*
DUKE   Quick, dispatch, and send the head to Angelo.
                          Exit [PROVOST]
   Now will I write letters to Angelo⁷—
85   The Provost, he shall bear them—whose contents
   Shall witness to him I am near at home,

6. That is, the people outside the prison.
7. "Angelo" may be an error for "Varrius," whom the Duke meets outside the city in 4.5.

And that by great injunctions° I am bound   *for compelling reasons*
To enter publicly. Him I'll desire
To meet me at the consecrated fount
90 A league below the city, and from thence,
By cold gradation° and well-balanced form,   *deliberate degrees*
We shall proceed with Angelo.

        Enter PROVOST [*with Ragusine's head*]

PROVOST Here is the head; I'll carry it myself.
DUKE Convenient° is it. Make a swift return,   *Suitable*
95 For I would commune° with you of such things   *confer*
That want no ear but yours.
PROVOST I'll make all speed.   *Exit*
ISABELLA [*within*] Peace, ho, be here!
DUKE The tongue of Isabel. She's come to know
100 If yet her brother's pardon be come hither;
But I will keep her ignorant of her good,
To make her heavenly comforts of° despair   *out of*
When it is least expected.
ISABELLA [*within*]   Ho, by your leave!

        Enter ISABELLA

DUKE Good morning to you, fair and gracious daughter.
105 ISABELLA The better, given me° by so holy a man.   *so greeted*
Hath yet the deputy sent my brother's pardon?
DUKE He hath released him, Isabel, from the world.
His head is off and sent to Angelo.
ISABELLA Nay, but it is not so.
DUKE   It is no other.
110 Show your wisdom, daughter, in your close° patience.   *silent*
ISABELLA O, I will to° him and pluck out his eyes!   *will go to*
DUKE You shall not be admitted to his sight.
ISABELLA [*weeping*] Unhappy Claudio! Wretched Isabel!
Injurious world! Most damnèd Angelo!
115 DUKE This nor° hurts him, nor profits you a jot.   *neither*
Forbear it, therefore; give your cause° to heaven.   *grievance*
Mark what I say, which you shall find
By every syllable a faithful verity.
The Duke comes home tomorrow—nay, dry your eyes—
120 One of our convent, and his confessor,
Gives me this instance.° Already he hath carried   *indication*
Notice to Escalus and Angelo,
Who do prepare to meet him at the gates,
There to give up their power. If you can pace° your wisdom   *train to walk*
125 In that good path that I would wish it go,
And you shall have your bosom° on this wretch,   *desire*
Grace° of the Duke, revenges to your heart,   *Favor*
And general honour.
ISABELLA   I am directed by you.
DUKE This letter, then, to Friar Peter give.
130 'Tis that he sent me of the Duke's return.
Say by this token I desire his company
At Mariana's house tonight. Her cause and yours
I'll perfect° him withal, and he shall bring you   *fully instruct*
Before the Duke, and to the head of° Angelo   *and directly to*
135 Accuse him home and home.° For my poor self,   *to the utmost*
I am combinèd° by a sacred vow,   *bound*

And shall be absent. [*Giving the letter*] Wend you° with this letter.   *Depart*
Command these fretting° waters from your eyes   *agitated; corrosive*
With a light heart. Trust not my holy order
If I pervert° your course.   *lead astray*
          Enter LUCIO
                              Who's here?
140   LUCIO   Good even.°   *evening*
Friar, where's the Provost?
      DUKE   Not within, sir.
      LUCIO   O pretty Isabella, I am pale at mine heart to see thine
      eyes so red. Thou must be patient. I am fain to dine and sup
      with water and bran;[8] I dare not for my head fill my belly; one
145   fruitful° meal would set me to't.[9] But they say the Duke will be   *plentiful*
      here tomorrow. By my troth, Isabel, I loved thy brother. If the
      old fantastical° Duke of dark corners° had been at home, he   *capricious/secret places*
      had lived.   [*Exit* ISABELLA]
      DUKE   Sir, the Duke is marvellous° little beholden to your   *remarkably*
150   reports; but the best is, he lives not° in them.   *is not to be found*
      LUCIO   Friar, thou knowest not the Duke so well as I do. He's a
      better woodman[1] than thou tak'st him for.
      DUKE   Well, you'll answer° this one day. Fare ye well.   *account for*
      LUCIO   Nay, tarry, I'll go along with thee. I can tell thee pretty
155   tales of the Duke.
      DUKE   You have told me too many of him already, sir, if they be
      true; if not true, none were enough.
      LUCIO   I was once before him for getting a wench with child.
      DUKE   Did you such a thing?
160   LUCIO   Yes, marry, did I; but I was fain to forswear it. They would
      else° have married me to the rotten medlar.[2]   *otherwise*
      DUKE   Sir, your company is fairer° than honest. Rest you well.   *more speciously pleasant*
      LUCIO   By my troth, I'll go with thee to the lane's end. If bawdy
      talk offend you, we'll have very little of it. Nay, friar, I am a
165   kind of burr; I shall stick.   *Exeunt*

4.4

          Enter ANGELO *and* ESCALUS
      ESCALUS   Every letter he hath writ hath disvouched other.°   *repudiated the others*
      ANGELO   In most uneven and distracted manner. His actions
      show much like to madness. Pray heaven his wisdom be not
      tainted.° And why meet him at the gates, and redeliver our   *impaired*
5   authorities there?
      ESCALUS   I guess not.
      ANGELO   And why should we proclaim it in an hour before his
      entering, that if any crave redress of injustice, they should
      exhibit° their petitions in the street?   *present*
10   ESCALUS   He shows his reason for that—to have a dispatch° of   *prompt settlement*
      complaints, and to deliver us from devices° hereafter, which   *contrivances*
      shall then have no power to stand against us.
      ANGELO   Well, I beseech you let it be proclaimed.
      Betimes° i'th' morn I'll call you at your house.   *Early*

---

8. Diet thought to suppress lust.   2. Kind of pear eaten when rotten; slang for "prostitute."
9. Would incite me to lechery.   4.4 Location: Vienna.
1. Hunter (literally, of game; here, of women).

15 Give notice to such men of sort and suit°   *rank and retinue*
As are to meet him.
ESCALUS   I shall, sir. Fare you well.
ANGELO   Good night.   *Exit* [ESCALUS]
This deed unshapes° me quite, makes me unpregnant°   *destroys/unready*
20 And dull to all proceedings. A deflowered maid,
And by an eminent body[1] that enforced°   *exerted; raped*
The law against it! But that her tender shame
Will not proclaim against her maiden loss,°   *loss of virginity*
How might she tongue° me! Yet reason dares her no,[2]   *reproach*
25 For my authority bears off a credent bulk,[3]
That no particular° scandal once can touch   *private; single*
But it confounds° the breather. He should have lived,   *confutes; overthrows*
Save that his riotous youth, with dangerous sense,°   *sensibility; sensuality*
Might in the times to come have ta'en revenge
30 By° so receiving a dishonoured life   *Because of*
With ransom of such shame. Would yet he had lived.
Alack, when once our grace we have forgot,
Nothing goes right; we would, and we would not.   *Exit*

4.5

Enter DUKE, [*in his own habit*] *and* FRIAR PETER
DUKE   These letters at fit time deliver me.
The Provost knows our purpose and our plot.
The matter being afoot, keep° your instruction,   *observe*
And hold you ever to our special drift,°   *purpose*
5 Though sometimes you do blench° from this to that   *swerve*
As cause doth minister.° Go call at Flavio's house,   *serve*
And tell him where I stay. Give the like notice
To Valentinus, Rowland, and to Crassus,
And bid them bring the trumpets° to the gate.   *trumpeters*
But send me Flavius first.
10 FRIAR PETER   It shall be speeded well.°   [*Exit*]   *quickly done*
     Enter VARRIUS
DUKE   I thank thee, Varrius; thou hast made good haste.
Come, we will walk.° There's other of our friends   *withdraw*
Will greet us here anon. My gentle° Varrius!   *Exeunt*   *noble*

4.6

     Enter ISABELLA *and* MARIANA
ISABELLA   To speak so indirectly° I am loath—   *evasively*
I would say the truth, but to accuse him so,
That is your part—yet I am advised to do it,
He says, to veil full purpose.
MARIANA   Be ruled by him.
5 ISABELLA   Besides, he tells me that if peradventure
He speak against me on the adverse side,
I should not think it strange, for 'tis a physic°   *medicine*
That's bitter to sweet end.
     Enter [FRIAR] PETER
MARIANA   I would Friar Peter—

---

1. Person (also suggesting the physical body).
2. Makes her dare not.
3. Sustains such massive credibility.

4.5 Location: Outside the city.
4.6 Location: A street near the city gates.

10 ISABELLA O, peace; the friar is come.

FRIAR PETER Come, I have found you out a stand° most fit,   *place*
    Where you may have such vantage° on the Duke   *advantageous position*
    He shall not pass you. Twice have the trumpets sounded.[1]
    The generous° and gravest citizens   *noble*
15 Have hent° the gates, and very near upon   *reached*
    The Duke is ent'ring; therefore hence, away.   *Exeunt*

5.1

Enter [at one door] DUKE, VARRIUS, [*and*] *lords;* [*at
another door*] ANGELO, ESCALUS, LUCIO, *citizens* [*and
officers*]

DUKE [*to* ANGELO] My very worthy cousin,° fairly met.   *fellow nobleman*
    [*To* ESCALUS] Our old and faithful friend, we are glad to see you.

ANGELO *and* ESCALUS Happy return be to your royal grace.

DUKE Many and hearty thankings to you both.
5   We have made enquiry of you, and we hear
    Such goodness of your justice that our soul
    Cannot but yield you forth to public thanks,
    Forerunning more requital.°   *greater reward*

ANGELO   You make my bonds° still greater.   *obligations*

DUKE O, your desert speaks loud, and I should wrong it
10   To lock it in the wards° of covert bosom,   *prison cells*
    When it deserves with characters° of brass   *letters*
    A forted° residence 'gainst the tooth of time   *fortified*
    And razure° of oblivion. Give me your hand,   *erasure*
    And let the subject° see, to make them know   *people*
15 That outward courtesies would fain proclaim
    Favours that keep° within. Come, Escalus,   *dwell*
    You must walk by us on our other hand,
    And good supporters[1] are you.
        [*They walk forward*]
        Enter [FRIAR] PETER *and* ISABELLA

FRIAR PETER Now is your time. Speak loud, and kneel before him.
20 ISABELLA [*kneeling*] Justice, O royal Duke! Vail your regard°   *Look down*
    Upon a wronged—I would fain° have said, a maid.   *like to*
    O worthy prince, dishonour not your eye
    By throwing it on any other object,
    Till you have heard me in my true complaint,
25   And given me justice, justice, justice, justice!

DUKE Relate your wrongs. In what? By whom? Be brief.
    Here is Lord Angelo shall give you justice.
    Reveal yourself° to him.   *(your complaint)*

ISABELLA   O worthy Duke,
    You bid me seek redemption of the devil.
30   Hear me yourself, for that which I must speak
    Must either punish me, not being believed,
    Or wring redress from you. Hear me, O hear me, hear!

ANGELO My lord, her wits, I fear me, are not firm.
    She hath been a suitor to me for her brother,
    Cut off° by course of justice.   *Executed*
35 ISABELLA [*standing*]   By course of justice!

---

1. The third flourish will signal the Duke's arrival.
5.1 Location: The city gates.

1. Attendants; in heraldry, "supporters" are figures
depicted beside a shield, holding it up.

ANGELO   And she will speak most bitterly and strange.

ISABELLA   Most strange, but yet most truly, will I speak.
   That Angelo's forsworn, is it not strange?
   That Angelo's a murderer, is't not strange?
40   That Angelo is an adulterous thief,
   An hypocrite, a virgin-violator,
   Is it not strange, and strange?

DUKE   Nay, it is ten times strange!

ISABELLA   It is not truer he is Angelo
   Than this is all as true as it is strange.
45   Nay, it is ten times true, for truth is truth
   To th'end of reck'ning.[2]

DUKE   Away with her. Poor soul,
   She speaks this in th'infirmity of sense.

ISABELLA   O prince, I conjure° thee, as thou believ'st   *appeal to*
   There is another comfort than this world,
50   That thou neglect me not with that opinion
   That I am touched with madness. Make not impossible
   That which but seems unlike.° 'Tis not impossible   *unlikely*
   But° one, the wicked'st caitiff° on the ground,   *That/villain*
   May seem as shy,° as grave, as just, as absolute,°   *reserved/perfect*
55   As Angelo; even so may Angelo,
   In all his dressings, characts,[3] titles, forms,°   *formalities*
   Be an arch-villain. Believe it, royal prince,
   If he be less, he's nothing; but he's more,
   Had I more name for badness.

DUKE   By mine honesty,
60   If she be mad, as I believe no other,
   Her madness hath the oddest frame° of sense,   *shape*
   Such a dependency° of thing on thing   *connected sequence*
   As e'er I heard in madness.

ISABELLA   O gracious Duke,
   Harp not on that, nor do not banish reason
65   For inequality;[4] but let your reason serve
   To make the truth appear where it seems hid,
   And hide the false seems° true.   *that seems*

DUKE   Many that are not mad
   Have sure more lack of reason. What would you say?

ISABELLA   I am the sister of one Claudio,
70   Condemned upon the act of° fornication   *decree against*
   To lose his head, condemned by Angelo.
   I, in probation of a sisterhood,
   Was sent to by my brother, one Lucio
   As° then the messenger.   *Being*

LUCIO   That's I, an't like your grace.
75   I came to her from Claudio, and desired her
   To try her gracious fortune with Lord Angelo
   For her poor brother's pardon.

ISABELLA   That's he indeed.

DUKE [*to* LUCIO]   You were not bid to speak.

---

2. *for truth . . . reck'ning:* echoing 1 Esdras 4:38: "But
truth doth abide, and is strong forever, and liveth and
reigneth for ever and ever." *reck'ning:* day of reckoning.

3. Signs (of office).

4. Difference in rank (between Isabella and Angelo); discrepancy (between my report and what seems true).

LUCIO   No, my good lord,
    Nor wished to hold my peace.
80 DUKE   I wish you now, then. Pray you take note of it;
    And when you have a business for yourself,
    Pray heaven you then be perfect.
LUCIO   I warrant° your honour.   assure
DUKE   The warrant's⁵ for yourself; take heed to't.
ISABELLA   This gentleman told somewhat of my tale—
85 LUCIO   Right.
DUKE   It may be right, but you are i'the wrong
    To speak before your time. [*To* ISABELLA] Proceed.
ISABELLA   I went
    To this pernicious caitiff deputy—
DUKE   That's somewhat madly spoken.
ISABELLA   Pardon it;
    The phrase is to the matter.°   appropriate
90 DUKE   Mended again.
    The matter; proceed.
ISABELLA   In brief, to set the needless process by,⁶
    How I persuaded, how I prayed and kneeled,
    How he refelled° me, and how I replied—   repelled
95   For this was of much length—the vile conclusion
    I now begin with grief and shame to utter.
    He would not, but by gift of my chaste body
    To his concupiscible° intemperate lust,   desirous
    Release my brother; and after much debatement,
100   My sisterly remorse confutes° mine honour,   overcomes
    And I did yield to him. But the next morn betimes,
    His purpose surfeiting,° he sends a warrant   satisfied
    For my poor brother's head.
DUKE   This is most likely!
ISABELLA   O, that it were as like° as it is true!   probable
105 DUKE   By heaven, fond° wretch, thou knows't not what thou speak'st,   foolish
    Or else thou art suborned against his honour
    In hateful practice.° First, his integrity   conspiracy
    Stands without blemish. Next, it imports no reason°   makes no sense
    That with such vehemency he should pursue
110   Faults proper° to himself. If he had so offended,   belonging
    He would have weighed thy brother by himself,
    And not have cut him off. Someone hath set you on.°   incited you
    Confess the truth, and say by whose advice
    Thou cam'st here to complain.
ISABELLA   And is this all?
115   Then, O you blessèd ministers° above,   angels
    Keep me in patience, and with ripened time
    Unfold the evil which is here wrapped up
    In countenance!⁷ Heaven shield your grace from woe,
    As I, thus wronged, hence unbelievèd go.
120 DUKE   I know you'd fain be gone. An officer!
    To prison with her.
        [*An officer guards* ISABELLA]
        Shall we thus permit

---

5. That is, for arrest, punning on the verb in line 83.   7. In false appearance; in royal favor.
6. To skip unnecessary parts of the story.

A blasting° and a scandalous breath to fall   *blighting*
On him so near us? This needs must be a practice.°   *conspiracy*
Who knew of your intent and coming hither?
125 ISABELLA   One that I would were here, Friar Lodowick.[8]

                                           [*Exit, guarded*]

DUKE   A ghostly father, belike. Who knows that Lodowick?
LUCIO   My lord, I know him. 'Tis a meddling friar;
        I do not like the man. Had he been lay, my lord,
        For certain words he spake against your grace
130   In your retirement, I had swinged° him soundly.   *beat*
DUKE   Words against me? This'° a good friar, belike!   *This is*
        And to set on this wretched woman here
        Against our substitute! Let this friar be found.

                                      [*Exit one or more*]

LUCIO   But yesternight, my lord, she and that friar,
135   I saw them at the prison. A saucy friar,
         A very scurvy fellow.
FRIAR PETER   Blessed be your royal grace!
        I have stood by, my lord, and I have heard
        Your royal ear abused. First hath this woman
        Most wrongfully accused your substitute,
140   Who is as free from touch or soil with her
        As she from one ungot.°   *not yet begotten*
DUKE   We did believe no less.
        Know you that Friar Lodowick that she speaks of?
FRIAR PETER   I know him for a man divine and holy,
        Not scurvy, nor a temporary meddler,[9]
145   As he's reported by this gentleman;
        And, on my trust, a man that never yet
        Did, as he vouches,° misreport your grace.   *asserts*
LUCIO   My lord, most villainously; believe it.
FRIAR PETER   Well, he in time may come to clear himself;
150   But at this instant he is sick, my lord,
        Of a strange fever. Upon his mere° request,   *Solely at his*
        Being come to knowledge that there was complaint
        Intended 'gainst Lord Angelo, came I hither
        To speak, as from his mouth, what he doth know
155   Is true and false, and what he with his oath
        And all probation° will make up full clear   *proof*
        Whensoever he's convented.° First, for this woman: *summoned*
        To justify° this worthy nobleman,   *vindicate*
        So vulgarly and personally accused,
160   Her shall you hear disprovèd to her eyes,
        Till she herself confess it.
DUKE   Good friar, let's hear it.

                                      [*Exit* FRIAR PETER]

        Do you not smile at this, Lord Angelo?
        O heaven, the vanity of wretched fools!
        Give us some seats.
              [*Seats are brought in*]
                            Come, cousin Angelo,

---

8. Evidently the Duke's name when in disguise.   9. Meddler in temporal matters.

165   In this I'll be impartial; be you judge
        Of your own cause.[1]
              [*The* DUKE *and* ANGELO *sit*]
              Enter [FRIAR PETER *and*] MARIANA [*veiled*]
                  Is this the witness, friar?
    First let her show her face, and after speak.
  MARIANA Pardon, my lord, I will not show my face
    Until my husband bid me.
170 DUKE What, are you married?
  MARIANA No, my lord.
  DUKE Are you a maid?°   *unmarried woman; virgin*
  MARIANA No, my lord.
  DUKE A widow then?
175 MARIANA Neither, my lord.
  DUKE Why, you are nothing then; neither maid, widow, nor wife!
  LUCIO My lord, she may be a punk,° for many of them are nei-   *prostitute*
    ther maid, widow, nor wife.
  DUKE Silence that fellow. I would° he had some cause to prattle   *wish*
180   for himself.°   *(in his own defense)*
  LUCIO Well, my lord.
  MARIANA My lord, I do confess I ne'er was married,
    And I confess besides, I am no maid.
    I have known[2] my husband, yet my husband
185   Knows not that ever he knew me.
  LUCIO He was drunk then, my lord, it can be no better.
  DUKE For the benefit of silence, would thou wert so too.
  LUCIO Well, my lord.
  DUKE This is no witness for Lord Angelo.
190 MARIANA Now I come to't, my lord.
    She that accuses him of fornication
    In self-same manner doth accuse my husband,
    And charges him, my lord, with such a time
    When I'll depose° I had him in mine arms   *testify*
    With all th'effect° of love.   *manifestations*
195 ANGELO   Charges she more than me?
  MARIANA Not that I know.
  DUKE   No? You say your husband.
  MARIANA Why just,° my lord, and that is Angelo,   *just so*
    Who thinks he knows that he ne'er knew my body,
    But knows, he thinks, that he knows Isabel's.
200 ANGELO This is a strange abuse.° Let's see thy face.   *imposture*
  MARIANA [*unveiling*] My husband bids me; now I will unmask.
    This is that face, thou cruel Angelo,
    Which once thou swor'st was worth the looking on.
    This is the hand which, with a vowed contract,
205   Was fast belocked in thine. This is the body
    That took away the match° from Isabel,   *assignation*
    And did supply° thee at thy garden-house   *satisfy*
    In her imagined person.
  DUKE [*to* ANGELO] Know you this woman?
210 LUCIO Carnally, she says.
  DUKE Sirrah, no more!

---

1. Ironically recalling the principle that no one ought   2. Had sexual intercourse with.
to judge his or her own cause.

LUCIO Enough, my lord.

ANGELO My lord, I must confess I know this woman;
And five years since there was some speech of marriage
215 Betwixt myself and her, which was broke off,
Partly for that her promisèd proportions°   *dowry*
Came short of composition,° but in chief   *the agreed sum*
For that her reputation was disvalued°   *discredited*
In levity;° since which time of five years   *For wantonness*
220 I never spake with her, saw her, nor heard from her,
Upon my faith and honour.

MARIANA [*kneeling before the* DUKE] Noble prince,
As there comes light from heaven, and words from breath,
As there is sense° in truth, and truth in virtue,   *significance*
I am affianced this man's wife, as strongly
225 As words could make up vows. And, my good lord,
But Tuesday night last gone, in's garden-house,
He knew me as a wife. As this is true,
Let me in safety raise me from my knees,
Or else forever be confixèd° here,   *fixed firmly*
A marble monument.

230 ANGELO   I did but smile till now.
Now, good my lord, give me the scope° of justice.   *extent*
My patience here is touched.° I do perceive   *irritated*
These poor informal° women are no more   *disorderly*
But instruments° of some more mightier member°   *agents/power*
235 That sets them on. Let me have way, my lord,
To find this practice out.

DUKE [*standing*]   Ay, with my heart,
And punish them even to your height of pleasure.—
Thou foolish friar, and thou pernicious woman
Compact with° her that's gone, think'st thou thy oaths,   *In league with*
240 Though they would swear down each particular saint,
Were testimonies against his worth and credit
That's sealed in approbation?° You, Lord Escalus,   *ratified by proof*
Sit with my cousin; lend him your kind pains
To find out this abuse, whence 'tis derived.
245 There is another friar that set them on.
Let him be sent for.
            [ESCALUS *sits*]

FRIAR PETER Would he were here, my lord, for he indeed
Hath set the women on to this complaint.
Your Provost knows the place where he abides,
And he may fetch him.

250 DUKE [*to one or more*] Go, do it instantly. [*Exit one or more*]
[*To* ANGELO] And you, my noble and well-warranted cousin,
Whom it concerns to hear this matter forth,°   *out*
Do with your injuries as seems you best
In any chastisement. I for a while will leave you,
255 But stir not you till you have well determined°   *passed judgment*
Upon these slanderers.

ESCALUS   My lord, we'll do it throughly.°   *thoroughly*
                              Exit [DUKE]

Signor Lucio, did not you say you knew that Friar Lodowick to
be a dishonest person?

LUCIO   *Cucullus non facit monachum:*[3] honest in nothing but in
260   his clothes; and one that hath spoke most villainous speeches
         of the Duke.
ESCALUS   We shall entreat you to abide here till he come, and
         enforce° them against him. We shall find this friar a notable   *urge*
         fellow.
265 LUCIO   As any in Vienna, on my word.
ESCALUS   Call that same Isabel here once again; I would speak
         with her.   [*Exit one or more*]
         [*To* ANGELO] Pray you, my lord, give me leave to question. You
         shall see how I'll handle her.
270 LUCIO   Not better than he, by her own report.
ESCALUS   Say you?
LUCIO   Marry, sir, I think if you handled her privately, she would
         sooner confess; perchance publicly she'll be ashamed.
ESCALUS   I will go darkly° to work with her.   *privately; soberly*
275 LUCIO   That's the way, for women are light[4] at midnight.
              Enter ISABELLA [*guarded*]
ESCALUS [*to* ISABELLA]   Come on, mistress, here's a gentle-
         woman denies all that you have said.
              Enter DUKE [*disguised as a friar, hooded, and*] PROVOST
LUCIO   My lord, here comes the rascal I spoke of, here with the
         Provost.
280 ESCALUS   In very good time. Speak not you to him till we call
         upon you.
LUCIO   Mum.
ESCALUS [*to the* DUKE]   Come, sir, did you set these women on
         to slander Lord Angelo? They have confessed you did.
285 DUKE   'Tis false.
ESCALUS   How! Know you where you are?
DUKE   Respect to your great place, and let the devil
         Be sometime honoured fore his burning throne.[5]
         Where is the Duke? 'Tis he should hear me speak.
290 ESCALUS   The Duke's in° us, and we will hear you speak.   *power is vested in*
         Look you speak justly.°   *accurately*
DUKE   Boldly at least.
         [*To* ISABELLA *and* MARIANA]   But O, poor souls,
         Come you to seek the lamb here of the fox,
         Good night to your redress! Is the Duke gone?
         Then is your cause gone too. The Duke's unjust
295   Thus to retort° your manifest appeal,°   *cast back / accusation*
         And put your trial in the villain's mouth
         Which here you come to accuse.
LUCIO   This is the rascal, this is he I spoke of.
ESCALUS   Why, thou unreverend and unhallowed° friar,   *impious*
300   Is't not enough thou hast suborned these women
         To accuse this worthy man but, in foul mouth,
         And in the witness of his proper° ear,   *own*
         To call him villain, and then to glance° from him   *ricochet*
         To th' Duke himself, to tax° him with injustice?   *reproach*

---

3. The hood does not make the monk (proverbial).   5. *let . . . throne:* that is, the devil, too, seated on his
4. Licentious; exploiting the unintentional sexual sug-   throne in hell, seems a figure of honor. *fore:* before.
gestion of Escalus's "go darkly to work."

305   Take him hence; to th' rack with him. We'll touse° you   *tear*
        Joint by joint—but we will know his⁶ purpose.
        What, 'unjust'?
        DUKE   Be not so hot. The Duke
        Dare no more stretch this finger of mine than he
        Dare rack his own. His subject am I not,
310   Nor here provincial.⁷ My business in this state
        Made me a looker-on here in Vienna,
        Where I have seen corruption boil and bubble
        Till it o'errun the stew;° laws for all faults,   *cauldron; brothel*
        But faults so countenanced that the strong statutes
315   Stand like the forfeits⁸ in a barber's shop,
        As much in mock as mark.
        ESCALUS   Slander to th' state!
        Away with him to prison.
        ANGELO   What can you vouch against him, Signor Lucio?
320   Is this the man that you did tell us of?
        LUCIO   'Tis he, my lord.—Come hither, goodman Bald-pate.⁹
        Do you know me?
        DUKE   I remember you, sir, by the sound of your voice.¹ I met
        you at the prison, in the absence of the Duke.
325   LUCIO   O, did you so? And do you remember what you said of
        the Duke?
        DUKE   Most notedly, sir.
        LUCIO   Do you so, sir? And was the Duke a fleshmonger,° a fool,   *whoremaster*
        and a coward, as you then reported him to be?
330   DUKE   You must, sir, change persons with me ere you make that
        my report. You indeed spoke so of him, and much more, much
        worse.
        LUCIO   O, thou damnable fellow! Did not I pluck thee by the
        nose° for thy speeches?   *(gesture of contempt)*
335   DUKE   I protest I love the Duke as I love myself.
        ANGELO   Hark how the villain would close² now, after his trea-
        sonable abuses.
        ESCALUS   Such a fellow is not to be talked withal. Away with him
        to prison. Where is the Provost? Away with him to prison. Lay
340   bolts° enough upon him. Let him speak no more. Away with   *fetters*
        those giglets° too, and with the other confederate companion.³   *strumpets*
        [MARIANA *is raised to her feet, and is guarded.*
        The PROVOST *makes to seize the* DUKE]
        DUKE   Stay, sir, stay a while.
        ANGELO   What, resists he? Help him, Lucio.
        LUCIO [*to the* DUKE]   Come, sir; come, sir; come, sir! Foh,° sir!   *(expression of disgust)*
345   Why, you bald-pated lying rascal, you must be hooded, must
        you? Show your knave's visage, with a pox to you! Show your
        sheep-biting face,⁴ and be hanged an hour!⁵ Will't not off?
        [*He pulls off the friar's hood, and discovers the* DUKE.
        ANGELO *and* ESCALUS *rise*]

---

6. The friar's; the confusion of pronouns suggests Escalus's fury.

7. Subject to local ecclesiastical authorities.

8. Jocular list of penalties for minor infractions.

9. Mr. Bald-head: "goodman" was a form of address for a man below the rank of gentleman; friars shaved their heads.

1. The friar's hood presumably covers his face so that he cannot see Lucio.

2. Conclude; hide himself; come to a settlement.

3. Fellow (contemptuous).

4. Like the wolf in sheep's clothing.

5. Jocular way of saying "be hanged." Animals were sometimes executed like human beings for destroying life or property.

DUKE   Thou art the first knave that e'er madest a duke.
    First, Provost, let me bail these gentle three.
350   [*To* LUCIO] Sneak not away, sir, for the friar and you
    Must have a word anon. [*To one or more*] Lay hold on him.
LUCIO   This may prove worse than hanging.
DUKE [*to* ESCALUS] What you have spoke, I pardon. Sit you down.
    We'll borrow place° of him.   *seat; office*
    [ESCALUS *sits*]
    [*To* ANGELO]   Sir, by your leave.
    [*He takes Angelo's seat*]
355   Hast thou or° word or wit or impudence   *either*
    That yet can do thee office?° If thou hast,   *service*
    Rely upon it till my tale be heard,
    And hold no longer out.
ANGELO   O my dread lord,
    I should be guiltier than my guiltiness
360   To think I can be undiscernible,
    When I perceive your grace, like power divine,
    Hath looked upon my passes.[6] Then, good prince,
    No longer session° hold upon my shame,   *inquiry*
    But let my trial be mine own confession.
365   Immediate sentence then, and sequent° death,   *thereafter*
    Is all the grace I beg.
DUKE   Come hither, Mariana.
    [*To* ANGELO] Say, wast thou e'er contracted to this woman?
ANGELO   I was, my lord.
DUKE   Go, take her hence and marry her instantly.
370   Do you the office, friar; which consummate,°   *finished*
    Return him here again. Go with him, Provost.
        Exeunt [ANGELO, MARIANA, FRIAR PETER, *and the* PROVOST]
ESCALUS   My lord, I am more amazed at his dishonour
    Than at the strangeness of it.°   *(the situation)*
DUKE   Come hither, Isabel.
    Your friar is now your prince. As I was then
375   Advertising° and holy to your business,   *Attentive*
    Not changing heart with habit I am still
    Attorneyed° at your service.   *Engaged as advocate*
ISABELLA   O, give me pardon,
    That I, your vassal, have employed and pained°   *troubled*
    Your unknown sovereignty.
DUKE   You are pardoned, Isabel.
380   And now, dear maid, be you as free° to us.   *generous*
    Your brother's death I know sits at your heart,
    And you may marvel why I obscured myself,
    Labouring to save his life, and would not rather
    Make rash remonstrance° of my hidden power   *demonstration*
385   Than let him so be lost. O most kind maid,
    It was the swift celerity of his death,
    Which I did think with slower foot came on,
    That brained° my purpose. But peace be with him!   *killed*
    That life is better life, past fearing death,
390   Than that which lives to fear. Make it your comfort,
    So happy is your brother.

---

6. Actions, trespasses; recalling Job 34:21: "For his eyes are upon the ways of man, and he seeth all his goings."

ISABELLA   I do, my lord.

Enter ANGELO, MARIANA, [FRIAR] PETER, [*and*] PROVOST

DUKE   For this new-married man approaching here,
Whose salt° imagination yet hath wronged   *salacious*
Your well-defended honour, you must pardon
395   For Mariana's sake; but as he adjudged° your brother—   *condemned*
Being criminal in double violation
Of sacred chastity and of promise-breach,
Thereon dependent, for your brother's life—
The very mercy° of the law cries out   *Even the merciful aspect*
400   Most audible, even from his proper° tongue,   *its own*
'An Angelo for Claudio, death for death'.
Haste still° pays haste, and leisure° answers leisure;   *always / deliberation*
Like doth quit° like, and measure still for measure.   *requite*
Then, Angelo, thy fault's thus manifested,
405   Which, though° thou wouldst deny, denies thee vantage.°   *even if / (i.e., clemency)*
We do condemn thee to the very block
Where Claudio stooped to death, and with like haste.
Away with him.

MARIANA   O my most gracious lord,
I hope you will not mock me with a husband!
410   DUKE   It is your husband mocked you with a husband.
Consenting to the safeguard of your honour,
I thought your marriage fit; else imputation,°   *censure*
For that he knew you, might reproach your life,
And choke your good to come.° For his possessions,   *ruin your prospects*
415   Although by confiscation they are ours,[7]
We do enstate and widow you° with all,   *give you widow's rights*
To buy you a better husband.

MARIANA   O my dear lord,
I crave no other, nor no better man.

DUKE   Never crave him; we are definitive.°   *resolute*

MARIANA   Gentle my liege—
420   DUKE   You do but lose your labour.—
Away with him to death. [*To* LUCIO] Now, sir, to you.

MARIANA [*kneeling*]   O my good lord!—Sweet Isabel, take my part;
Lend me your knees, and all my life to come
I'll lend you all my life to do you service.

425   DUKE   Against all sense you do importune her.
Should she kneel down in mercy of this fact,°   *crime*
Her brother's ghost his pavèd bed° would break,   *stone-covered grave*
And take her hence in horror.

MARIANA   Isabel,
Sweet Isabel, do yet but kneel by me.
430   Hold up your hands; say nothing; I'll speak all.
They say best men are moulded out of faults,
And, for the most,° become much more the better   *most part*
For being a little bad. So may my husband.
O Isabel, will you not lend a knee?

DUKE   He dies for Claudio's death.

435   ISABELLA [*kneeling*]   Most bounteous sir,
Look, if it please you, on this man condemned
As if my brother lived. I partly think

---

7. Because a felon's property was forfeit to the crown.

A due sincerity governed his deeds,
Till he did look on me. Since it is so,
440 Let him not die. My brother had but justice,
In that he did the thing for which he died.
For Angelo,
His act did not o'ertake his bad intent,
And must be buried° but as an intent   *(i.e., forgotten)*
445 That perished by the way. Thoughts are no subjects,[8]
Intents but merely thoughts.

MARIANA   Merely, my lord.

DUKE   Your suit's unprofitable. Stand up, I say.
    [MARIANA *and* ISABELLA *stand*]
  I have bethought me of another fault.
  Provost, how came it Claudio was beheaded
  At an unusual hour?

450 PROVOST   It was commanded so.

DUKE   Had you a special warrant for the deed?

PROVOST   No, my good lord, it was by private message.

DUKE   For which I do discharge you of your office.
  Give up your keys.

PROVOST   Pardon me, noble lord.
455 I thought it was a fault, but knew it not,
Yet did repent me after more advice;°   *deliberation*
For° testimony whereof one in the prison   *As*
That should by private order else° have died   *otherwise*
I have reserved alive.

460 DUKE   What's he?

PROVOST   His name is Barnardine.

DUKE   I would thou hadst done so by Claudio.
  Go fetch him hither. Let me look upon him.   [*Exit* PROVOST]

ESCALUS   I am sorry one so learned and so wise
465 As you, Lord Angelo, have still° appeared,   *always*
Should slip so grossly, both in the heat of blood
And lack of tempered judgement afterward.

ANGELO   I am sorry that such sorrow I procure,°   *cause*
And so deep sticks it in my penitent heart
470 That I crave death more willingly than mercy.
'Tis my deserving, and I do entreat it.

    Enter BARNARDINE *and* PROVOST; CLAUDIO, [*muffled,*°   *with his face wrapped*
    and] JULIET

DUKE   Which is that Barnardine?

PROVOST   This, my lord.

DUKE   There was a friar told me of this man.
  [*To* BARNARDINE] Sirrah, thou art said to have a stubborn soul
475 That apprehends no further than this world,
And squar'st° thy life according. Thou'rt condemned;   *frames*
But, for those earthly faults,[9] I quit° them all,   *pardon*
And pray thee take this mercy to provide
For better times to come.—Friar, advise him.
480 I leave him to your hand. [*To* PROVOST] What muffled fellow's that?

PROVOST   This is another prisoner that I saved,
Who should have died when Claudio lost his head,
As like almost to Claudio as himself.

---

8. Thoughts are not subject to prosecution.   9. Offenses subject to earthly punishment.

[*He unmuffles* CLAUDIO]
DUKE [*to* ISABELLA]   If he be like your brother, for his sake

485   Is he pardoned; and for your lovely sake
Give me your hand, and say you will be mine.[1]
He is my brother° too. But fitter time for that.   (*as a brother-in-law*)
By this Lord Angelo perceives he's safe.
Methinks I see a quick'ning in his eye.

490   Well, Angelo, your evil quits° you well.   *recompenses*
Look that you love your wife,'her worth worth° yours.   *being equal to*
I find an apt remission° in myself;   *inclination to mercy*
And yet here's one in place° I cannot pardon.   *present*
[*To* LUCIO] You, sirrah, that knew me for a fool, a coward,

495   One all of luxury,° an ass, a madman,   *lasciviousness*
Wherein have I so deserved of you
That you extol me thus?
LUCIO   Faith, my lord, I spoke it but according to the trick.° If   *fashion*
you will hang me for it, you may; but I had rather it would

500   please you I might be whipped.
DUKE   Whipped first, sir, and hanged after.
Proclaim it, Provost, round about the city,
If any woman wronged by this lewd fellow,
As I have heard him swear himself there's one

505   Whom he begot with child, let her appear,
And he shall marry her. The nuptial finished,
Let him be whipped and hanged.
LUCIO   I beseech your highness, do not marry me to a whore.
Your highness said even now I made you a duke; good my lord,

510   do not recompense me in making me a cuckold.
DUKE   Upon mine honour, thou shalt marry her.
Thy slanders I forgive, and therewithal
Remit thy other forfeits.°—Take him to prison,   *punishments*
And see our pleasure herein executed.

515   LUCIO   Marrying a punk, my lord, is pressing to death,[2] whip-
ping, and hanging.
DUKE   Slandering a prince deserves it.   [*Exit* LUCIO *guarded*]
She, Claudio, that you wronged, look you restore.[3]
Joy to you, Mariana. Love her, Angelo.

520   I have confessed her,° and I know her virtue.   *been her confessor*
Thanks, good friend Escalus, for thy much goodness.
There's more behind° that is more gratulate.°   *to come / gratifying*
Thanks, Provost, for thy care and secrecy.
We shall employ thee in a worthier place.

525   Forgive him, Angelo, that brought you home
The head of Ragusine for Claudio's.
Th'offence pardons itself. Dear Isabel,
I have a motion° much imports your good,   *proposal*
Whereto, if you'll a willing ear incline,

530   What's mine is yours, and what is yours is mine.
[*To all*] So bring° us to our palace, where we'll show   *accompany*
What's yet behind that's meet you all should know.   [*Exeunt*]

---

1. It is not clear how Isabella responds to the Duke's pro-   2. Executing by crushing under heavy weights.
posal of marriage.   3. To her good name, by marrying her.

Additional Passages

The text of *Measure for Measure* given in this edition is probably that of an adapted version made for Shakespeare's company after his death. Adaptation seems to have affected two passages, printed below as the Oxford editors believe Shakespeare to have written them.

A. 1.2.0.1–104

The passage begins with seven lines that the adapter (believed to be Thomas Middleton) intended to be replaced by 1.2.52–71 of the play as printed here. The adapter must have contributed all of 1.2.0.1–74, which in the earliest and subsequent printed texts precede the discussion between the clown (Pompey) and the bawd (Mistress Overdone) about Claudio's arrest. Lucio's entry alone at line 36 below, some eleven lines after his reentry with the two Gentlemen and the Provost's party in the adapted text, probably represents Shakespeare's original intention. In his version, Juliet, present but silent in the adapted text both in 1.2 and 5.1, probably did not appear in either scene; accordingly, the words "and there's Madam Juliet" (1.2.95) must also be the reviser's work, and do not appear below.

Enter POMPEY *and* MISTRESS OVERDONE, *meeting*

MISTRESS OVERDONE   How now, what's the news with you?
POMPEY   Yonder man is carried to prison.
MISTRESS OVERDONE   Well! What has he done?
POMPEY   A woman.
5   MISTRESS OVERDONE   But what's his offence?
POMPEY   Groping for trouts[1] in a peculiar° river.   private
MISTRESS OVERDONE   What, is there a maid[2] with child by him?
POMPEY   No, but there's a woman with maid[3] by him: you have
      not heard of the proclamation, have you?
10   MISTRESS OVERDONE   What proclamation, man?
POMPEY   All houses in the suburbs of Vienna must be plucked down.
MISTRESS OVERDONE   And what shall become of those in the city?
POMPEY   They shall stand for seed. They had gone down too, but
      that a wise burgher put in for them.
15   MISTRESS OVERDONE   But shall all our houses of resort in the
      suburbs be pulled down?
POMPEY   To the ground, mistress.
MISTRESS OVERDONE   Why, here's a change indeed in the commonwealth. What shall become of me?
20   POMPEY   Come, fear not you. Good counsellors lack no clients.
      Though you change your place, you need not change your
      trade. I'll be your tapster still. Courage, there will be pity taken
      on you. You that have worn your eyes almost out in the service,
      you will be considered.
      A noise within
25   MISTRESS OVERDONE   What's to do here, Thomas Tapster?
      Let's withdraw!
      Enter the PROVOST *and* CLAUDIO
POMPEY   Here comes Signor Claudio, led by the Provost to
      prison.   *Exeunt* MISTRESS OVERDONE *and* POMPEY
CLAUDIO   Fellow, why dost thou show me thus to th' world?
30   Bear me to prison, where I am committed.
PROVOST   I do it not in evil disposition,

---

1. Literally, a way of catching trout by tickling their bellies.

2. Young woman (but Pompey understands "virgin").
3. Pregnant with a baby girl.

But from Lord Angelo by special charge.
CLAUDIO   Thus can the demigod Authority
Make us pay down for our offence, by weight,
35   The bonds of heaven. On whom it will, it will;
On whom it will not, so; yet still 'tis just.
     Enter LUCIO
LUCIO   Why, how now, Claudio? Whence comes this restraint?

B. 3.1.479–4.1.65

Before revision, there would have been no act break and no song; the lines immediately
following the song would also have been absent. The Duke's soliloquies "He who the
sword of heaven will bear" and "O place and greatness" have evidently been transposed
in revision; in the original, the end of "O place and greatness" would have led straight
on to the Duke's meeting with Isabella and then Mariana.

ESCALUS   I am going to visit the prisoner. Fare you well.
DUKE   Peace be with you.   *Exit* ESCALUS
       O place and greatness, millions of false eyes
       Are stuck upon thee; volumes of report
5   Run with their false and most contrarious quest
       Upon thy doings; thousand escapes of wit
       Make thee the father of their idle dream,
       And rack thee in their fancies.
            Enter ISABELLA
DUKE   Very well met.
       What is the news from this good deputy?
10 ISABELLA   He hath a garden circummured with brick,
       Whose western side is with a vineyard backed;
       And to that vineyard is a planckèd gate,
       That makes his opening with this bigger key.
       This other doth command a little door
15   Which from the vineyard to the garden leads.
       There have I made my promise
       Upon the heavy middle of the night
       To call upon him.
DUKE   But shall you on your knowledge find this way?
20 ISABELLA   I have ta'en a due and wary note upon't.
       With whispering and most guilty diligence,
       In action all of precept, he did show me
       The way twice o'er.
DUKE   Are there no other tokens
       Between you 'greed concerning her observance?
25 ISABELLA   No, none, but only a repair i'th' dark,
       And that I have possessed him my most stay
       Can be but brief, for I have made him know
       I have a servant comes with me along
       That stays upon me, whose persuasion is
       I come about my brother.
30 DUKE   'Tis well borne up.
       I have not yet made known to Mariana
       A word of this.—What ho, within! Come forth!
            Enter MARIANA
       [*To* MARIANA] I pray you be acquainted with this maid.
       She comes to do you good.

ISABELLA   I do desire the like.
35 DUKE [*to* MARIANA] Do you persuade yourself that I respect you?
MARIANA   Good friar, I know you do, and so have found it.
DUKE   Take then this your companion by the hand,
    Who hath a story ready for your ear.
    I shall attend your leisure; but make haste,
    The vaporous night approaches.
40 MARIANA   Will't please you walk aside.

                                   Exeunt MARIANA *and* ISABELLA

DUKE   He who the sword of heaven will bear
    Should be as holy as severe,
    Pattern in himself to know,
    Grace to stand, and virtue go,
45 More nor less to others paying
    Than by self-offences weighing.
    Shame to him whose cruel striking
    Kills for faults of his own liking!
    Twice treble shame on Angelo,
50 To weed my vice, and let his grow!
    O, what may man within him hide,
    Though angel on the outward side!
    How may likeness made in crimes
    Make my practice on the times
55 To draw with idle spiders' strings
    Most ponderous and substantial things?
    Craft against vice I must apply.
    With Angelo tonight shall lie
    His old betrothed but despisèd.
60 So disguise shall, by th' disguisèd,
    Pay with falsehood false exacting,
    And perform an old contracting.

                        Enter MARIANA *and* ISABELLA

    Welcome. How agreed?
ISABELLA   She'll take the enterprise upon her, father,
65   If you advise it.

All's Well That Ends Well

In innumerable old folktales, an unknown or lowborn young man of great courage, intelligence, or expertise addresses himself to a serious peril: a dragon no one can slay, a riddle no one can solve, a wound no one can cure. The grateful recipient of his aid— a king or mighty duke—rewards the youth with marriage to a princess who would ordinarily be far above his station. *All's Well That Ends Well* retells this popular tale of fantastic upward mobility but with the genders reversed: the resourceful young quester is female, the marital prize male. Shakespeare did not invent the reversal; he adapted his plot from a story in Boccaccio's *Decameron* that is itself a retelling of a traditional tale. But *All's Well That Ends Well* considerably heightens the heroine's risk-taking initiative, making Helen's adventures in the first two acts correspond more precisely, in sexually transposed form, to the masculine quest-romance pattern.

Even today, this reversal makes the story seem problematic. In the customary masculine version, no one inquires into the feelings of the noblewoman who is the champion's prize. But in *All's Well*, when a man becomes a reward, he reacts with astonished anger:

> BERTRAM   My wife, my liege? I shall beseech your highness,
> In such a business give me leave to use
> The help of mine own eyes.
> KING   Know'st thou not, Bertram,
> What she has done for me?
> BERTRAM   Yes, my good lord,
> But never hope to know why I should marry her.
>   (2.3.102–6)

After the wedding ceremony, Bertram flees without consummating the union. He leaves behind a letter detailing for Helen two apparently impossible conditions she must satisfy before he will consider her his wife: "When thou canst get the ring upon my finger, which never shall come off, and show me a child begotten of thy body that I am father to, then call me husband" (3.2.55–57).

Folklorists have traced the second part of the play, in which Helen ingeniously fulfills Bertram's stipulations, to yet another old tale, that of the "clever wench" who ultimately wins a reluctant husband's affection by turning his recalcitrance to her own benefit. In Helen's case, however, her "unfeminine" audacity both before and after her wedding has repelled some commentators. Others have expressed doubts about Helen's bed trick, wherein she secretly substitutes herself for another woman and becomes pregnant by the spouse who thinks he loathes her. How, they wonder, could such a maneuver possibly convert anyone, much less Bertram, into a loving husband?

By rewriting the comic plot, then, Shakespeare makes the difference in conventional expectations for men and women vividly clear. His revisions implicitly challenge those conventions, making them seem artificial and restrictive. At the same time, the deviations from comic norms in *All's Well* also might be taken as reflecting badly on the hero and heroine. The generic uneasiness of the play has led some critics to classify it as a "problem comedy," a category that also includes *Measure for Measure* and sometimes *Troilus and Cressida*. Editors conjecture that all three plays were written between 1602 and 1606, a period in which Shakespeare was largely preoccupied with tragedy: *Hamlet, Othello, King Lear, Timon of Athens, Macbeth,* and *Antony and Cleopatra* are roughly contemporaneous compositions. The "problem comedies" often seem closer in theme and tone to these tragedies than to the sunnier romantic comedies Shakespeare wrote in the 1590s.

Nonetheless, *All's Well* has obvious connections to Shakespeare's earlier achievements. In *The Merchant of Venice, As You Like It,* and *Much Ado About Nothing,* Shakespeare had gradually developed the dramatic possibilities of an articulate, assertive, and sympathetic heroine—a kind of character virtually without precedent in the Western tradition. Helen is recognizably one of this company: generally beloved by those around her, premaritally chaste but intensely sexual, tenacious in pursuit of the man she desires. Bertram is likewise a version of a standard Shakespearean type: the immature youth who finds aggressively "masculine" enterprises like hunting or war emotionally easier to negotiate than the complications of heterosexual intimacy. Bertram's predecessors include the unwilling Adonis in *Venus and Adonis,* the naive Claudio in *Much Ado About Nothing,* the edgily unself-conscious Hotspur of *1 Henry IV,* and the narcissistic young man of the sonnets. Both Helen and Bertram, however, "push the envelop" of their generic type. No previous comic heroine finds herself, as Helen does, publicly repudiated by the man she loves, and thus none need show herself as relentless as Helen in seeking a remedy. And Bertram is surely the most perfidious, and the most thoroughly disgraced, of Shakespeare's callow males.

In its portrayal of older characters, too, *All's Well* seems to develop out of Shakespeare's previous romantic plays. In much Greek and Roman comedy, parents or parent surrogates attempt to hinder their children's sexual happiness, and as a young playwright Shakespeare adhered to this ancient convention. In *A Midsummer Night's Dream* and *Romeo and Juliet,* written in the mid-1590s, parents are killjoys who block the glorious passions of youth out of mere peevishness. But in *The Merchant of Venice,* written a year or two later, Shylock's paternal possessiveness contrasts with the wise policy of Portia's father, whose strict constraints upon his daughter's marital options in fact ensure her happiness. In *Much Ado About Nothing* (1598), the sexually anxious young couples seem incapable of forming heterosexual pairs without the intervention of elders and friends. In *All's Well That Ends Well,* the marriage between Helen and Bertram is unthinkable without the support of the Countess and the King; the match is also roundly endorsed by the elderly courtier Lafeu. If the oldsters are culpable, it is for pushing the young people together prematurely, not for keeping them apart.

Arguably this change in perspective is a consequence of Shakespeare's own aging. By the time he wrote *All's Well,* he was the father of two marriageable daughters, and surviving records indicate that he had strong opinions about the men they wed. At any rate, the role of family members in Shakespeare's romantic plays becomes more benign, even essential for the pairing-off with which the comedies conclude; by the time of the late romances, in fact, the primary dramatic emphasis tends to be less on the young couple than on their parents. Seen in such a light, *All's Well* marks an important transition in the generational dynamics of Shakespearean comedy.

At the same time, the expanded role of family and friends in "making a match" seems to reflect an increasing pessimism about sex. In both *All's Well* and *Measure for Measure,* mutual desire fails to flower spontaneously between eligible bachelors and maidens. Moreover, even when desire is somehow kindled, its relationship to the institution of lifelong monogamy seems difficult. In *All's Well,* erotic passion burns hottest not when it is gratified but when its goal is still unattained. Bertram wants Diana only so long as she rebuffs him:

> Madding my eagerness with her restraint,
> As all impediments in fancy's course
> Are motives of more fancy.
>
> (5.3.215–17)

Once he imagines he has deflowered her, he deserts her without compunction. Bertram behaves reprehensibly, and yet Helen's more steadfast love, too, seems at least in part an effect of distance and difficulty. In Act 1, she declares Bertram to be a "bright particular star," fascinating although inaccessible, and perhaps *because* inaccessible. The obstacles Bertram places in the way of their union seem to make him all the more precious in Helen's eyes and to stimulate her extraordinary efforts to win his affections. But the more resolutely she strives to catch him, the more difficult it becomes to imagine her content with him once he is caught.

In sexual matters, apparently, as soon as one gets what one thinks one wants, it no longer seems so intensely appealing. "Success" brings disillusion in its train. In *All's Well*, this unfortunate arrangement is reflected in passages and episodes that oscillate painfully between imagined extremes of distance and intimacy. In Act 2, Helen frets about the social gap that separates her from Bertram: he seems too alien for her. But when the Countess pleads that Helen consider her a "mother," Helen suffers a paroxysm of anxiety on the opposite count: that she and Bertram may be all too closely allied. "God's mercy, maiden!" exclaims the Countess. "Does it curd thy blood / To say I am thy mother?" (1.3.133–34). Helen's hysterical overreaction suggests that she fears being "too close" at the same time she fears being "too remote." Later in *All's Well*, the bed trick rehearses, in another key, a similar paradox of intimacy and distance. Fleeing his home and a spouse closely associated with his upbringing, Bertram lusts after a foreign woman. But this foreigner turns out, unbeknownst to him, to be his own wife.

Thus the fundamental structure of sexual desire seems inimical to a durably happy marriage, but marriage nonetheless remains the only socially approved arena for sexual expression. Caught in this dilemma, lovers simply cannot be trusted to make proper arrangements among themselves. The community therefore assumes a new prominence in initiating and regulating marriages. In *All's Well*, two means of such regulation are central to the plot. The first is the institution of wardship, a remnant of the feudal system. Minors who inherited estates automatically fell into the care of their feudal superiors: the King in Bertram's case, the Countess in Helen's. Once the guardian chose a marriage partner of suitable social rank for the "ward," the ward could not refuse the match except by forfeiting much of his property; thus the tense exchange in 2.3 between Bertram and the King about Helen's qualifications in this respect.

Another form of external pressure is brought to bear upon Bertram at the end of the play, when Helen once again appeals to the King to enforce her claim. The hearing that ensues resembles those of the ecclesiastical courts, judicial bodies that settled complaints of sexual misconduct in early modern England. The conflicting testimony of Diana and Bertram painfully recalls the proceedings of the "bawdy courts," as they were popularly known: interminable prosecutions and counterprosecutions for premarital fornication, breach of promise, adultery, child support, and sexual slander—cases in which, as here, evidence was often hard to come by and truth difficult to unearth.

In the early seventeenth century, both wardship and the judicial regulation of sexual conduct were topics of considerable controversy. Some people fiercely resented any meddling in their domestic and sexual affairs, but others wanted the courts to monitor such behavior even more aggressively. Likewise, some attacked wardship on the grounds that guardians often trampled on the

Drummers before an encampment. From Geffrey Whitney, *A Choice of Emblemes* (1586).

personal inclinations of the ward, while others argued that young heirs and heiresses required supervision to prevent their seduction by unscrupulous gold diggers. In both cases, the point at issue is whether sexual conduct is an essentially personal matter or a matter for public concern. By making both the custom of wardship and the procedures of the bawdy courts crucial to the plot of *All's Well*, Shakespeare seems to endorse the assumption upon which both institutions are premised: that individuals are not competent to manage their own sexual lives, and that stern legal measures are required to coerce the likes of Bertram into matrimony.

A comedy normally depicts the progress of young lovers toward marriage, and in *All's Well*, Bertram's stubborn resistance to his generically mandated fate has important consequences. The protagonists of almost all comedies undergo some kind of suffering in the middle acts of the play, but that suffering is overcome. The happy ending retrospectively makes the hardships that preceded it seem worthwhile; conversely, pain validates and gives an appropriate significance to the concluding felicities. Despite its cheerful once-and-for-all title, *All's Well That Ends Well* does not conform to this time-worn pattern. Instead, the play constantly derails narrative expectations and promises endings that turn out to be mirages. Helen cures the King and weds Bertram, but the story is not yet over. She must then encounter Bertram somehow (whether by accident or design is unclear) and arrange to bed him. Then she must make sure she is pregnant; then she must return to France to beg justice of the King. The action continues past the point where one would expect it to terminate, again and again requiring the expenditure of additional effort and ingenuity on Helen's part: early in Act 5, even the King's court turns out to be surprisingly difficult to locate.

Helen's stamina is not demanded of the other characters, but they, too, persist willy-nilly after one might have expected them to subside, and they resurface after one might have expected them to vanish. The King is preparing for his own death when Helen's arrival returns him to the life he had resigned himself to losing. Later, Bertram believes that by fleeing Italy for France he has left Helen behind; similarly, he forsakes Diana. But the two women decline to evaporate. They reappear together in a scene that begins with the King announcing that "the nature of [Bertram's] great offence is dead" (5.3.23), then revives and exacerbates his offense, then declares it buried once more.

Occasion with her forelock. From Geffrey Whitney, *A Choice of Emblemes* (1586). She must be "taken by the forelock"—that is, at the moment when she presents herself; the back of her head is bald to signify that once she is past, she can no longer be grasped. See *All's Well That Ends Well* 5.3.40.

These aborted endings, continual deferrals, unanticipated reemergences, and surprising persistences inevitably make the actual end of the play seem rather arbitrary. Eventually it becomes hard to credit the permanence of any resolution, any happy ending. When, in the play's final lines, the King blithely promises Diana her choice of husbands from among his stable of remaining wards, *All's Well* may seem not to be drawing to a close, but merely to be forecasting its own reiteration. The play's open-endedness has generated both dismay and appreciation, depending on the temperament of the critic and, often, on his or her convictions about literary form. Those who prefer celebratory and romantic modes often find the play's lack of convincing closure a disturbing flaw. Those who find the happy endings of most comedies wishful and unrealistic tend to applaud Shakespeare's eschewal of easy answers.

Once again, *All's Well's* apparent noncompliance with "normal" comic practice implicitly suggests limitations inherent in the comic forms it forsakes. In 2.4, when Helen asks Lavatch whether the Countess is well, Lavatch replies that "she is not well," despite the fact that "she's very well and wants nothing i'th' world." To the baffled Helen, Lavatch goes on to explain that he does not consider the Countess well because "she's not in heaven, whither God send her quickly" (lines 2ff.). In Lavatch's mind, only the dead are happy, a notion that gives a distinctly uncomical twist to the concept of ending well. Consciously or not, Lavatch echoes a long tradition of classical and Christian thought that emphasizes the misery of this world and defers true happiness until after death. In 4.3, the first Lord Dumaine relates this apparently inevitable misery to the intransigence of human passions, an intransigence imagined in the Christian tradition in terms of original sin. "As we are ourselves, what things are we" (lines 19–20). Only divine grace can remedy the defects of human nature in general and of human sexuality in particular. Only another world can offer the prospect of true, lasting felicity. But comedy is a secular mode, lacking the means to represent heaven or divine intervention, and to that extent its happy endings must be illusory or partial. *All's Well* is not unique among Shakespearean comedies in gesturing beyond the mundane, imperfect world with which plays are necessarily concerned, to an ideal world that cannot be directly represented in the theater. Lorenzo's discussion of the music of the spheres in *The Merchant of Venice* and Isabella's acute conviction of divine mentorship in *Measure for Measure* likewise have the effect of implicitly contrasting the limited bliss of comic endings with an unlimited, indescribable counterpart.

But although absolute fulfillment may be impossible in this world, relative improvements are surely feasible. In *All's Well*, it seems that a community can constructively intervene to correct, at least provisionally, some of the grosser imperfections of individuals. In Act 4, Bertram acknowledges that he has misjudged Paroles and at the end of the play begs pardon for his behavior, finally promising to love his wife "ever ever dearly." These apparent changes of heart are not motivated by an instinctive sense of regret for his past actions or by a spontaneous upwelling of love for Helen. Rather, the vigorous efforts of his mother, his king, his friends, and his wife force him onto the path that seems best for him whether he likes it or not. Those critics who find his apparent reformation at the end of the play unconvincing are often those skeptical of whether this kind of social pressure will suffice to rescue Bertram from himself. If, however, we are to believe that Bertram is salvageable, as the play implies, then we must acknowledge the effectiveness of the community's efforts to rectify him.

Obviously a society can have these beneficial effects on its more wayward members only if its moral intuitions are fundamentally sound, and only if its coercive resources have the potential to induce heartfelt, lasting change. The King can force Bertram to marry Helen and to acknowledge the legitimacy of the child in her womb. But such decrees will ensure Bertram's *love* of Helen only if his inner convictions somehow follow from, or develop out of, his external submission to the King's commands. How actual—not merely apparent—compliance might be achieved is suggested in a speech in which the King warmly remembers Bertram's father, the late Count of Roussillon. The old Count, according to the King, adhered to a traditional aristocratic code: he was careful to speak no more than he was willing to defend with his sword. Thought, word, and deed were thus inextricable. The King characterizes this inextricability as "honor," for honor and its corollary, shame, bridge the gap between external behavior and private states of mind, internalizing social scruples so that the aristocrat behaves well even in the absence of obvious incentives or punishments. At best, honor is thus a "clock to itself," a self-regulating mechanism. Only when that clock fails to function properly— as it fails in Bertram's case—must the same results be compelled by clumsier, more obviously extrinsic means.

In his comments on the old Count, the King claims that the up-and-coming generation has an insufficiently vivid conception of honor and its importance:

> Such a man
> Might be a copy to these younger times,
> Which followed well would demonstrate them now
> But goers-backward.
>
> (1.2.45–48)

The danger of such a regression is embodied in Paroles, whose name means "words." Paroles exhibits all the superficial signs of courtiership—wit, lavish dress, a familiarity with military and courtly jargons—without any of the real skills or virtues those signs are supposed to indicate. Paroles endangers the social processes by which the world of *All's Well* is imagined to operate, estranging externals from inner substance and subversively demonstrating limitations in the courtly code of honor. He is tightly connected to Bertram, not merely through their friendship but by similarities in their circumstances. The staged drum trick on Paroles coincides temporally with the unstageable bed trick on Bertram, and there are clear thematic parallels as well: both victims are blind, morally as well as literally, to plots perpetrated by close acquaintances masquerading as strangers.

Still, Paroles's menace should not be overestimated. Everyone except Bertram sees through him instantly, and Bertram's inability to discern Paroles's pretenses is a telling mark of his immaturity. Once Bertram finally recognizes that Paroles is a "counterfeit module," moreover, he recoils violently from his former friend and adviser. Bertram may be gauche and inattentive, but he recognizes gross cowardice when he sees it, and in that rudimentary recognition of the difference between honorable and dishonorable conduct will lie the possibility of his reform.

Paroles, then, both incarnates Bertram's flaws and diminishes Bertram's culpability. "Your son was misled with a snipped-taffeta fellow there," opines Lafeu indignantly to the Countess, "whose villainous saffron would have made all the unbaked and doughy youth of a nation in his colour" (4.5.1–3). If, in the world of *All's Well,* good associates and benign forms of institutional duress can maneuver Bertram in the right direction, then bad associates and bad customs likewise have the power to exacerbate his worst impulses. On the other hand, unlike a sterner and more principled character, the "unbaked" Bertram retains the capacity to be reformed, like a lump of dough, despite his unpromising shape.

In less obvious ways, Paroles's presence in *All's Well* also deflects criticism from Helen. Helen's marital plans involve, as she herself admits, quite startling social ambi-

Foppish camp follower. Peter Flötner (mid-sixteenth century).

tions. Marrying Bertram will elevate her from the relatively large gentry class to a tiny elite at the pinnacle of the social pyramid. In a hierarchically stratified society where people are supposed to "know their places," such aspirations might well seem disruptive. But Paroles, a cruder and less principled social climber, helps clarify the actually *conservative* nature of Helen's desires. In marked contrast to the craven Paroles, Helen is willing to certify her words with her body as honorable aristocrats are supposed to do, proposing to sacrifice life and reputation if her promises to cure the King prove empty. Helen's conviction that words must suit actions, that her tongue must obey her hand, marks her as "noble" despite her lack of material resources, and gain her the respect of the older members of the nobility, such as the King, the Countess, and Lafeu. Thus marriage to Bertram seems to remedy an unaccountable lapse in the proper social order, rather than to create a breach in that order.

Left deliberately vague is what relationship, if any, merit really has with birth. On the one hand, Helen's excellence seems to belie her humble origins; on the other hand, although both Helen and Diana are poor, it is carefully specified that they are not "base" persons of artisan or peasant stock. Their gentility, however modest, seems to lend their upward mobility a respectability that Paroles's attempts at self-promotion can never possess. Paroles thus draws off criticism that Helen might otherwise attract for violating class boundaries. Similarly, his presence in the play serves partially to allay criticism of Helen's sexual transgressiveness: his boastful inaction is so obviously worse than Helen's vigorous but possibly "unfeminine" enterprise that once again he seems an instructive example that tells in Helen's favor.

Although Paroles functions as a scapegoat of sorts, at the end of the play he does not suffer the scapegoat's usual cruel fate. After his disgrace, his dramatic function as corrupter of Bertram and foil to Helen is evidently complete, and we might imagine that we have seen the last of him. But like so many other characters in *All's Well*, good and bad, Paroles has a surprising durability. "Simply the thing I am," he declares, "shall make me live" (4.3.310–11). Like Helen and Diana, he reappears in the final scenes, reinserting himself, in a reduced capacity, into a world that had scorned him. The partial, incremental improvement promised by the conclusion of *All's Well That Ends Well* may from some points of view seem disappointing. But its pessimism inspires a certain tolerance, a forbearance that allows even the ridiculous or debased to find a home.

KATHARINE EISAMAN MAUS

TEXTUAL NOTE

All's Well That Ends Well was first printed in the Folio of 1623 (F), and all subsequent editions have relied on that text. The presence in F of some stage directions that explain rather than merely indicate the action, as well as variant speech prefixes in different scenes (for instance, "Countess," "Mother," "Old Countess"), suggests that the printed text was prepared directly from Shakespeare's "foul papers," or manuscript draft. Some textual scholars believe that before printing, this manuscript must have been further annotated by the King's Men's bookkeeper, the person who prepared play texts for performance. Unfortunately, perhaps because of difficulties reading the foul papers, the compositors did a poor job of setting up the text, forcing later editors to make an unusual number of conjectural emendations.

The Oxford edition preserves the Folio act divisions and the traditional editorial (that is, non-Shakespearean) scene divisions. For those familiar with other editions of the play, the primary novelty of the Oxford text will be its decision to use "Helen" instead of "Hellena" to designate the heroine. In fact, the latter form occurs only four times in the play and only once in dialogue, so the Oxford editors argue that Shakespeare's preference was clearly for the two-syllable name.

SELECTED BIBLIOGRAPHY

Bradbrook, Muriel. "Virtue Is the True Nobility: A Study of the Structure of *All's Well That Ends Well*." *Review of English Studies* n.s. 1 (1950): 289–301. True nobility of virtue, as exemplified by Helen, versus the false nobility of birth, as exemplified by Bertram.

Calderwood, James L. "Styles of Knowing in *All's Well*." *Modern Language Quarterly* 25 (1964): 272–94. Sexuality and honor for Helen and Bertram.

Donaldson, Ian. "*All's Well That Ends Well*: Shakespeare's Play of Endings." *Essays in Criticism* 27 (1977): 34–55. Discusses the play's preoccupation with endings and its problematic final scene.

Engle, Lars. "Shakespeare Normativity in *All's Well That Ends Well*." *Shakespeare Studies Today*. Ed. Graham Bradshaw, Tom Bishop, and Mark Turner. Shakespeare International Yearbook 4. Burlington, Vt.: Ashgate, 2004. 264–79. The establishment and violation of norms in *All's Well That Ends Well*.

Frye, Northrop. *The Myth of Deliverance: Reflections on Shakespeare's Problem Comedies*. Toronto: University of Toronto Press, 1983. General discussion of patterns of reversal in the problem comedies.

Hodgdon, Barbara. "The Making of Virgins and Mothers: Sexual Signs, Substitute Scenes, and Doubled Presences in *All's Well That Ends Well*." *Philological Quarterly* 66 (1987): 47–72. The character of Helen, as Shakespeare develops it from the source story in Boccaccio's *Decameron*.

Huston, J. Dennis. "'Some Stain of Soldier': The Functions of Paroles in *All's Well That Ends Well*." *Shakespeare Quarterly* 21 (1970): 431–38. Paroles compared with Helen.

Muir, Kenneth, and Stanley Wells, eds. *Aspects of Shakespeare's "Problem Plays": Articles Reprinted from Shakespeare Survey*. New York: Cambridge University Press, 1982. Essays on *Measure for Measure, All's Well That Ends Well*, and *Troilus and Cressida*, with selected reviews of theater productions from 1953 to 1976.

Parker, Patricia. "*All's Well That Ends Well*: Increase and Multiply." *Creative Imitation: New Essays on Renaissance Literature in Honor of Thomas M. Greene*. Ed. David Quint, Margaret Ferguson, G. W. Pigman, and Wayne Rebhorn. Binghamton, N.Y.: Medieval & Renaissance Texts & Studies, 1992. 355–90. Linguistic and sexual deferral and displacement as the key to abundance in *All's Well That Ends Well*.

Traister, Barbara Howard. "'Doctor She': Healing and Sex in *All's Well That Ends Well*." *A Companion to Shakespeare Works, IV: Poems, Problem Comedies, Late Plays*. Blackwell Companions to Literature and Culture 20. Ed. Richard Dutton and Jean E. Howard. Malden, Mass.: Blackwell, 2003. 333–47. Helen as lovesick physician.

Wheeler, Richard P. "Imperial Love and the Dark House: *All's Well That Ends Well*." *Shakespeare's Development and the Problem Comedies: Turn and Counter-Turn*. Berkeley: University of California Press, 1981. 35–91. Detailed psychoanalytic reading.

Zitner, Sheldon P. *All's Well That Ends Well*. Boston: Twayne, 1989. Stage and reception histories as well as critical commentary on the play.

FILM

All's Well That Ends Well. 1981. Dir. Elijah Moshinsky. UK. 142 min. From BBC-TV. An elegant production, with sets and lighting that recall the paintings of Vermeer and Caravaggio. Compelling performances from Angela Down (Helen), Celia Johnson (Countess), Donald Sinden (King), and Ian Charleson (Bertram).

All's Well That Ends Well

THE PERSONS OF THE PLAY

The Dowager COUNTESS of Roussillon
BERTRAM, Count of Roussillon, her son
HELEN, an orphan, attending on the Countess
LAVATCH, a Clown, the Countess's servant
REYNALDO, the Countess's steward
PAROLES, Bertram's companion
The KING of France
LAFEU, an old lord
FIRST LORD DUMAINE ⎫
SECOND LORD DUMAINE ⎭ brothers
INTERPRETER, a French soldier
A GENTLEMAN Austringer
The DUKE of Florence
WIDOW Capilet
DIANA, her daughter
MARIANA, a friend of the Widow
Lords, attendants, soldiers, citizens

1.1

Enter young BERTRAM *Count of Roussillon, his mother*
[*the* COUNTESS], HELEN, [*and*] *Lord* LAFEU, *all in black*

COUNTESS   In delivering my son from me I bury a second husband.[1]

BERTRAM   And I in going, madam, weep o'er my father's death
anew; but I must attend° his majesty's command, to whom I   heed
5   am now in ward,[2] evermore in subjection.

LAFEU   You shall find of the King a husband,° madam; you, sir,   patron
a father. He that so generally° is at all times good must of neces-   universally
sity hold° his virtue to you, whose worthiness would stir it up   uphold
where it wanted° rather than lack it where there is such abun-   was lacking
10   dance.

COUNTESS   What hope is there of his majesty's amendment?°   improvement

LAFEU   He hath abandoned his physicians,[3] madam, under
whose practices he hath persecuted time with hope,[4] and finds
no other advantage in the process but only the losing of hope
15   by time.

COUNTESS   This young gentlewoman had a father—O that 'had':
how sad a passage° 'tis!—whose skill was almost as great as his   expression; passing away
honesty;° had it° stretched so far, would have made nature   integrity / (his skill)
immortal, and death should have play for lack of work. Would
20   for the King's sake he were living. I think it would be the death
of the King's disease.

1.1 Location: Bertram's palace in Roussillon, in south-
west France.
1. Giving up my son grieves me as much as my husband's death (playing on "deliver" as "give birth").
2. Upon the old Count's death, the King becomes guardian of Bertram's estate until he comes of age. A guardian

could arrange his ward's marriage, provided the match
was with a social equal.
3. Playing on the usual "His physicians have abandoned
him" (given up hope of his cure).
4. Afflicted his days by hoping for a cure.

LAFEU How called you the man you speak of, madam?

COUNTESS He was famous, sir, in his profession, and it was his
great right to be so: Gérard de Narbonne.[5]

25 LAFEU He was excellent indeed, madam. The King very lately
spoke of him, admiringly and mourningly. He was skilful
enough to have lived still, if knowledge could be set up against
mortality.

BERTRAM What is it, my good lord, the King languishes of?

30 LAFEU A fistula,° my lord.   abscess (often anal)

BERTRAM I heard not of it before.

LAFEU I would it were not notorious.°—Was this gentlewoman   known to everyone
the daughter of Gérard de Narbonne?

COUNTESS His sole child, my lord, and bequeathed to my over-

35 looking.[6] I have those hopes of her good that her education°   upbringing
promises; her dispositions she inherits, which makes fair gifts°   abilities
fairer—for where an unclean mind carries virtuous qualities,°   acquired skills
there commendations go with pity:° they are virtues and traitors   mingle with regret
too.[7] In her they are the better for their simpleness.° She   purity

40 derives° her honesty and achieves her goodness.   inherits

LAFEU Your commendations, madam, get from her tears.

COUNTESS 'Tis the best brine a maiden can season° her praise   preserve (as with salt)
in. The remembrance of her father never approaches her heart
but the tyranny of her sorrows takes all livelihood° from her   liveliness

45 cheek.—No more of this, Helen. Go to, no more, lest it be
rather thought you affect° a sorrow than to have—   make a show of

HELEN I do affect a sorrow indeed, but I have it too.

LAFEU Moderate lamentation is the right of the dead, excessive
grief the enemy to the living.

50 COUNTESS If the living be not enemy to the grief, the excess
makes it soon mortal.°   fatal

BERTRAM [kneeling] Madam, I desire your holy wishes.°   blessing

LAFEU How understand we that?[8]

COUNTESS Be thou blessed, Bertram, and succeed thy father

55 In manners° as in shape. Thy blood and virtue[9]   behavior
Contend for empire in thee, and thy goodness
Share with thy birthright. Love all, trust a few,
Do wrong to none. Be able° for thine enemy   a match for
Rather in power than use,[1] and keep thy friend

60 Under thy own life's key.[2] Be checked° for silence   criticized
But never taxed for speech.° What heaven more will   rebuked for chatter
That thee may furnish° and my prayers pluck down,   embellish
Fall on thy head. Farewell. [To LAFEU] My lord,
'Tis an unseasoned° courtier. Good my lord,   immature
Advise him.

65 LAFEU   He cannot want the best
That shall attend his love.[3]

COUNTESS Heaven bless him!—Farewell, Bertram.

BERTRAM [rising] The best wishes that can be forged° in your   fashioned
thoughts be servants to you.°   [Exit COUNTESS]   assist you

---

5. Town just north of Roussillon.
6. Guardianship (Helen is the Countess's ward, as
Bertram is the King's).
7. Because the skills are used for evil purposes.
8. Possibly a misplaced line; possibly Lafeu thinks
Bertram's interruption discourteous.

9. (May) your noble birth and acquired goodness.
1. By having power, rather than using it.
2. keep . . . key: safeguard your friend's life as you do
your own.
3. He . . . love: He will not lack the best advice my
affection for him can supply.

70   [*To* HELEN] Be comfortable° to my mother, your mistress, and   *comforting*
make much of her.
    LAFEU   Farewell, pretty lady. You must hold the credit° of your   *uphold the reputation*
father.   *Exeunt* BERTRAM *and* LAFEU
    HELEN   O were that all! I think not on my father,
75   And these great tears grace his remembrance more
Than those I shed for him.[4] What was he like?
I have forgot him. My imagination
Carries no favour° in't but Bertram's.   *face; liking; love token*
I am undone. There is no living, none,
80   If Bertram be away. 'Twere all one
That° I should love a bright particular star   *It is just as if*
And think to wed it, he is so above me.
In his bright radiance and collateral[5] light
Must I be comforted, not in his sphere.
85   Th'ambition in my love thus plagues itself.
The hind° that would be mated by the lion   *doe*
Must die for love. 'Twas pretty, though a plague,
To see him every hour, to sit and draw
His archèd brows, his hawking° eye, his curls,   *sharp*
90   In our heart's table°—heart too capable°   *drawing table / receptive*
Of every line and trick° of his sweet favour.°   *trait / face*
But now he's gone, and my idolatrous fancy°   *love*
Must sanctify his relics.[6] Who comes here?
            Enter PAROLES
One that goes with him. I love him for his sake—
95   And yet I know him a notorious liar,
Think him a great way° fool, solely° a coward.   *mostly a / completely*
Yet these fixed evils sit so fit in him°   *fit him so well*
That they take place[7] when virtue's steely bones°   *rigid severity*
Looks bleak i'th' cold wind. Withal, full oft we see
100   Cold wisdom waiting on superfluous folly.
    PAROLES   Save° you, fair queen.   *God save*
    HELEN   And you, monarch.
    PAROLES   No.
    HELEN   And no.
105   PAROLES   Are you meditating on virginity?
    HELEN   Ay. You have some stain° of soldier in you, let me ask   *tinge*
you a question. Man is enemy to virginity: how may we barri-
cado° it against him?   *barricade*
    PAROLES   Keep him out.
110   HELEN   But he assails, and our virginity, though valiant in the
defence, yet is weak. Unfold to us some warlike resistance.
    PAROLES   There is none. Man, setting down before° you, will   *laying siege to*
undermine you and blow you up.[8]
    HELEN   Bless our poor virginity from underminers and blowers-
115   up. Is there no military policy° how virgins might blow up   *strategy*
men?
    PAROLES   Virginity being blown down, man will quicklier be
blown up.° Marry,[9] in blowing him down again, with the   *have an erection*

---

4. *grace . . . him:* are a better tribute to my father than those (few) tears I actually shed for him.
5. Rotating in a separate orbit (in Ptolomaic astronomy).
6. Must worship what reminds me of him.
7. Take precedence.

8. *undermine you:* dig tunnels under you (to plant explosives). *blow you up:* punning on "inflate," "make you pregnant."
9. By Mary (a mild oath).

breach yourselves made you lose your city. It is not politic° in   *expedient*
120   the commonwealth of nature to preserve virginity. Loss of virginity is rational increase,[1] and there was never virgin got° till   *begotten*
virginity was first lost. That° you were made of is mettle° to   *What / substance*
make virgins. Virginity by being once lost may be ten times
found;° by being ever kept it is ever lost. 'Tis too cold a com-   *reproduced tenfold*
125   panion, away with't.
    HELEN   I will stand for't° a little, though therefore I die a virgin.   *defend it*
    PAROLES   There's little can be said in't.° 'Tis against the rule of   *for it*
nature. To speak on the part of virginity is to accuse your moth-
ers, which is most infallible disobedience. He that hangs him-
130   self is a virgin:[2] virginity murders itself, and should be buried
in highways, out of all sanctified limit,[3] as a desperate
offendress against nature. Virginity breeds mites, much like a
cheese;[4] consumes itself to the very paring, and so dies with
feeding his own stomach.° Besides, virginity is peevish, proud,   *pride*
135   idle, made of self-love—which is the most inhibited° sin in the   *prohibited*
canon.° Keep it not, you cannot choose but lose by't. Out   *scriptures*
with't![5] Within t'one year it will make itself two, which is a
goodly increase, and the principal[6] itself not much the worse.
Away with't.
140   HELEN   How might one do, sir, to lose it to her own liking?
    PAROLES   Let me see. Marry, ill, to like him that ne'er it likes.[7]
'Tis a commodity will lose the gloss with lying:° the longer kept,   *remaining idle*
the less worth. Off with't while 'tis vendible.° Answer the time   *salable*
of request.[8] Virginity like an old courtier wears her cap out of
145   fashion, richly suited° but unsuitable,° just like the brooch and *dressed / inappropriate*
the toothpick, which wear not now.[9] Your date° is better in   *fruit; age*
your pie and your porridge than in your cheek, and your virginity, your old virginity, is like one of our French withered pears:[1]
it looks ill, it eats drily, marry, 'tis a withered pear—it was for-
150   merly better, marry, yet 'tis a withered pear. Will you anything
with it?
    HELEN   Not my virginity, yet . . . [2]
      There° shall your master have a thousand loves,   *(At court)*
      A mother and a mistress and a friend,
155   A phoenix,[3] captain, and an enemy,
      A guide, a goddess, and a sovereign,
      A counsellor, a traitress, and a dear:
      His humble ambition, proud humility,
      His jarring concord and his discord dulcet,[4]
160   His faith, his sweet disaster, with a world
      Of pretty fond adoptious christendoms
      That blinking Cupid gossips.[5] Now shall he—
      I know not what he shall. God send him well.
      The court's a learning place, and he is one—

1. *rational increase:* judicious growth in the human ("rational") population.
2. A suicide, like a virgin, is a self-destroyer.
3. Consecrated ground (in which suicides were denied burial).
4. Cheese was thought to generate spontaneously the mites that fed on it.
5. Get rid of it; put it out at interest.
6. Original investment (the woman's body).
7. To please him who doesn't appreciate virginity.

8. Respond to demand (greatest in youth).
9. Which are no longer in fashion.
1. Dried pears (suggesting aged female genitals).
2. Not with *my* virginity: not my virginity *yet* (but soon).
3. The mythical phoenix was a one-of-a-kind bird; hence, marvelous, unique being.
4. Harmonious (all these oxymorons were typical of courtly love poetry).
5. *pretty . . . gossips:* foolish nicknames given when blind Cupid is godfather at a christening.

165 PAROLES What one, i'faith?
HELEN That I wish well. 'Tis pity.
PAROLES What's pity?
HELEN That wishing well had not a body in't
  Which might be felt,° that we, the poorer born,   *perceived*
170 Whose baser stars do shut us up in wishes,[6]
  Might with effects of them follow our friends
  And show what we alone must° think, which never   *must only*
  Returns us thanks.°   *wins us gratitude*
      Enter [a] PAGE
PAGE Monsieur Paroles, my lord calls for you.   [*Exit*]
175 PAROLES Little Helen, farewell. If I can remember thee I will
  think of thee at court.
HELEN Monsieur Paroles, you were born under a charitable star.
PAROLES Under Mars,[7] I.
HELEN I especially think *under* Mars.
180 PAROLES Why '*under* Mars'?
HELEN The wars hath so kept you under that you must needs be
  born under Mars.
PAROLES When he was predominant.°   *in the ascendant*
HELEN When he was retrograde,[8] I think rather.
185 PAROLES Why think you so?
HELEN You go so much backward when you fight.
PAROLES That's for advantage.°   *tactical gain*
HELEN So is running away, when fear proposes the safety. But
  the composition° that your valour and fear makes in you is a   *truce; mixture*
190 virtue of a good wing,[9] and I like the wear° well.   *habit; fashion*
PAROLES I am so full of businesses I cannot answer thee acutely.
  I will return perfect courtier, in the which my instruction shall
  serve to naturalize° thee, so thou wilt be capable of a courtier's *familiarize*
  counsel and understand what advice shall thrust upon thee;
195 else thou diest in thine unthankfulness, and thine ignorance
  makes thee away.° Farewell. When thou hast leisure say thy   *puts an end to you*
  prayers; when thou hast none remember thy friends.[1] Get thee
  a good husband and use° him as he uses thee. So farewell.   *treat*
                                                        [*Exit*]
HELEN Our remedies oft in ourselves do lie
200 Which we ascribe to heaven. The fated° sky   *destiny-ordaining*
  Gives us free scope, only doth backward pull
  Our slow designs when we ourselves are dull.°   *sluggish*
  What power is it which mounts my love so high,[2]
  That makes me see and cannot feed mine eye?
205 The mightiest space in fortune nature brings
  To join like likes and kiss like native things.[3]
  Impossible be strange° attempts to those   *unusual*
  That weigh their pains in sense[4] and do suppose
  What hath been cannot be. Who ever strove
210 To show her merit that did miss° her love?   *fail to achieve*

6. Whose less elevated destinies confine us merely to
wishing.
7. The planet was identified with the god of war.
8. Retreating (said of a planet's apparent movement relative to the zodiac).
9. *of a good wing:* that is, rapid in flight; also, with large
shoulder flaps. Paroles is foppishly dressed.
1. Unclear: perhaps, Say your prayers when you have the

chance, and when you're too busy, rely on your friends
instead.
2. Which elevates my love to so lofty an object.
3. *The mightiest . . . things:* Natural affect brings persons greatly distant in rank together as if they were similar and conjoins them as if they had a common origin.
4. Who vividly imagine the difficulties.

The King's disease—my project may deceive me,
But my intents are fixed and will not leave me.   *Exit*

1.2

A flourish of cornetts.° *Enter the* KING *of France with let-*   horn fanfare
ters, [*the two* LORDS DUMAINE,] *and divers attendants*

KING   The Florentines and Sienese are by th'ears,°   quarreling
Have fought with equal fortune, and continue
A braving° war.   defiant; gallant
FIRST LORD DUMAINE   So 'tis reported, sir.
KING   Nay, 'tis most credible: we here receive it
5   A certainty vouched from our cousin° Austria,   fellow sovereign
With caution that the Florentine will move° us   entreat
For speedy aid—wherein our dearest friend°   (the Duke of Austria)
Prejudicates° the business, and would seem   Prejudges
To have us make denial.
FIRST LORD DUMAINE   His love and wisdom
10   Approved° so to your majesty may plead   Proven
For amplest credence.
KING   He hath armed° our answer,   hardened
And Florence is denied before he comes.
Yet for our gentlemen that mean to see
The Tuscan service, freely have they leave
To stand on either part.°   fight on either side
15   SECOND LORD DUMAINE   It well may serve
A nursery to¹ our gentry, who are sick°   pining
For breathing° and exploit.   exercise
KING   What's he comes here?
          Enter BERTRAM, LAFEU, *and* PAROLES
FIRST LORD DUMAINE   It is the Count Roussillon, my good lord,
          Young Bertram.
KING [*to* BERTRAM]   Youth, thou bear'st thy father's face.
20   Frank° nature, rather curious° than in haste,   generous / meticulous
Hath well composed thee. Thy father's moral parts°   qualities
Mayst thou inherit, too. Welcome to Paris.
BERTRAM   My thanks and duty are your majesty's.
KING   I would I had that corporal soundness now
25   As when thy father and myself in friendship
First tried our soldiership. He did look far°   see deeply
Into the service° of the time, and was   military service
Discipled of° the bravest. He lasted long,   Followed by; taught by
But on us both did haggish° age steal on,   witchlike; malevolent
30   And wore us out of act.° It much repairs me   action
To talk of your good father. In his youth
He had the wit which I can well observe
Today in our young lords, but they may jest
Till their own scorn return to them unnoted²
35   Ere they can hide their levity in honour.³
So like a courtier,° contempt nor bitterness   paradigm of courtesy
Were in his pride° or sharpness;⁴ if they were   self-esteem

1.2 Location: The King's court at Paris.
1. As a training school for.
2. *they may . . . unnoted:* their ridicule merely rebounds
upon them, ignored by others.

3. Before they can compensate for their frivolity with
noble acts.
4. Keenness of wit.

His equal had awaked them,[5] and his honour—
Clock to itself°—knew the true minute when   *Self-regulating*
40   Exception° bid him speak, and at this time   *Disapproval*
His tongue obeyed his hand.[6] Who were below him
He used as creatures of another place,[7]
And bowed his eminent top° to their low ranks,   *head*
Making them proud of his humility,
45   In their poor praise he humbled.[8] Such a man
Might be a copy° to these younger times,   *model*
Which followed well would demonstrate them now
But goers-backward.°   *backsliders*

BERTRAM   His good remembrance, sir,
Lies richer in your thoughts than on his tomb.
50   So in approof° lives not his epitaph   *confirmation*
As in your royal speech.

KING   Would I were with him! He would always say—
Methinks I hear him now; his plausive° words   *praiseworthy*
He scattered not in ears, but grafted them[9]
55   To grow there and to bear. 'Let me not live'—
This his good melancholy oft began
On the catastrophe° and heel of pastime,   *end*
When it was out°—'Let me not live', quoth he,   *finished*
'After my flame lacks oil, to be the snuff[1]
60   Of younger spirits, whose apprehensive° senses   *quick*
All but new things disdain, whose judgements are
Mere fathers of their garments,[2] whose constancies°   *loyalties*
Expire before their fashions.' This he wished.
I after him do after° him wish too,   *in harmony with*
65   Since I nor wax nor honey can bring home,
I quickly were dissolvèd° from my hive   *removed*
To give some labourers room.

SECOND LORD DUMAINE   You're lovèd, sir.
They that least lend it you° shall lack° you first.   *grant you love / miss*

KING   I fill a place, I know't.—How long is't, Count,
70   Since the physician at your father's died?
He was much famed.

BERTRAM   Some six months since, my lord.

KING   If he were living I would try him yet.—
Lend me an arm.—The rest have worn me out
With several applications.° Nature and sickness   *various treatments*
75   Debate it at their leisure.[3] Welcome, Count.
My son's no dearer.

BERTRAM   Thank your majesty.   [*Flourish.*] *Exeunt*

1.3

Enter the COUNTESS, [REYNALDO *her*] *steward, and*
[*behind,* LAVATCH *her*] *clown*

COUNTESS   I will now hear. What say you of this gentlewoman?

---

5. *if they were . . . them:* if ever he spoke bitterly or contemptuously, it was to a social equal.
6. He said no more than he would back up with action.
7. He treated as people of a higher station.
8. He willingly humbled himself to praise their poor selves.
9. He did not strew (words) superficially among his hearers (like seed), but planted them permanently (as twigs

of fruit trees are grafted to a tree trunk).
1. Burned upper wick, which if not trimmed keeps the lower part from burning properly.
2. *whose judgements . . . garments:* whose mental prowess creates only new clothes.
3. Argue over my condition at length.
1.3 Location: Roussillon.

REYNALDO　Madam, the care I have had to even your content[1] I
wish might be found in the calendar° of my past endeavours,　　　　　*record*
for then we wound our modesty and make foul the clearness of
5　our deservings, when of ourselves we publish° them.　　　　　*advertise*
COUNTESS　What does this knave here? [*To* LAVATCH] Get you
gone, sirrah. The complaints I have heard of you I do not all
believe. 'Tis my slowness that I do not, for I know you lack not
folly to commit them and have ability enough to make such
10　knaveries yours.
LAVATCH　'Tis not unknown to you, madam, I am a poor fellow.
COUNTESS　Well, sir?
LAVATCH　No, madam, 'tis not so well that I am poor, though
many of the rich are damned. But if I may have your ladyship's
15　good will to go to the world,° Isbel the woman° and I will do as　　*marry / maidservant*
we may.[2]
COUNTESS　Wilt thou needs be a beggar?
LAVATCH　I do beg your good will in this case.
COUNTESS　In what case?
20　LAVATCH　In Isbel's case and mine own. Service is no heritage,[3]
and I think I shall never have the blessing of God till I have
issue o' my body, for they say bairns° are blessings.　　　　　*children*
COUNTESS　Tell me thy reason why thou wilt marry.
LAVATCH　My poor body, madam, requires it. I am driven on by
25　the flesh, and he must needs go that the devil drives.
COUNTESS　Is this all your worship's reason?
LAVATCH　Faith, madam, I have other holy reasons,[4] such as they
are.
COUNTESS　May the world know them?
30　LAVATCH　I have been, madam, a wicked creature, as you—and
all flesh and blood—are, and indeed I do marry that I may
repent.[5]
COUNTESS　Thy marriage sooner than thy wickedness.
LAVATCH　I am out o' friends, madam, and I hope to have friends
35　for my wife's sake.
COUNTESS　Such friends are thine enemies, knave.
LAVATCH　You're shallow,° madam—in great friends, for the　　*a superficial judge*
knaves come to do that for me which I am aweary of. He that
ears° my land spares my team, and gives me leave to in° the　　*plows / harvest*
40　crop. If I be his cuckold, he's my drudge. He that comforts my
wife is the cherisher of my flesh and blood; he that cherishes
my flesh and blood loves my flesh and blood; he that loves my
flesh and blood is my friend; *ergo*, he that kisses my wife is my
friend. If men could be contented to be what they are,° there　　*(cuckolds)*
45　were no fear in marriage. For young Chairbonne the puritan
and old Poisson the papist,[6] howsome'er their hearts are severed in religion, their heads are both one:° they may jowl°　　*identical / bump*
horns together like any deer i'th' herd.[7]
COUNTESS　Wilt thou ever be a foul-mouthed and calumnious
50　knave?

---

1. To meet your desires.　　　　　　　　　　alluding to the proverb "Marry in haste and repent at lei-
2. Will do our best (with sexual pun on "do").　sure").
3. A servant has little to leave his children (proverbial;　6. *chair bonne*: good meat (French). *poisson*: fish. Catho-
with sexual pun on "service").　　　　　　lics ate fish on fast days, but Puritans rejected the cus-
4. Other motives sanctified by the marriage ceremony;　tom.
with puns on "holy" ("hole-y") and "reasons" ("raisings").　7. Cuckolds were supposed to have horns in their fore-
5. That I may make my illicit sexual activity lawful (but　heads.

LAVATCH   A prophet? Ay, madam, and I speak the truth the next°   *most direct*
    way.
    [*He sings*]   For I the ballad will repeat,
                Which men full true shall find:
55   Your marriage comes by destiny,
               Your cuckoo sings by kind.[8]
COUNTESS   Get you gone, sir. I'll talk with you more anon.
REYNALDO   May it please you, madam, that he bid Helen come
    to you? Of her I am to speak.
60   COUNTESS [*to* LAVATCH]   Sirrah, tell my gentlewoman I would
    speak with her. Helen, I mean.
LAVATCH [*sings*]
      'Was this fair face the cause', quoth she,[9]
      'Why the Grecians sackèd Troy?
      Fond° done, done fond. Was this[1] King Priam's joy?'   *Foolishly; lovingly*
65   With that she sighèd as she stood,
      With that she sighèd as she stood,
        And gave this sentence° then: *maxim*
      'Among nine bad if one be good,
      Among nine bad if one be good,
70   There's yet one good in ten.'
COUNTESS   What, 'one good in ten'? You corrupt[2] the song,
    sirrah.
LAVATCH   One good *woman* in ten, madam, which is a purifying
    o'th' song. Would God would serve the world so all the year!
75   We'd find no fault with the tithe-woman[3] if I were the parson.
    One in ten, quoth a?° An° we might have a good woman born   *did he say / If*
    but ere every blazing star,° or at an earthquake, 'twould mend   *comet*
    the lottery° well. A man may draw his heart out ere a pluck[4]   *improve the odds*
    one.
80   COUNTESS   You'll be gone, sir knave, and do as I command you.
LAVATCH   That man should be at woman's command, and yet
    no hurt done! Though honesty be no puritan,[5] yet it will do no
    hurt;° it will wear the surplice of humility over the black gown   *harm*
    of a big heart.[6] I am going, forsooth. The business is for Helen
85   to come hither.   *Exit*
COUNTESS   Well now.
REYNALDO   I know, madam, you love your gentlewoman
    entirely.
COUNTESS   Faith, I do. Her father bequeathed her to me, and
90   she herself without other advantage[7] may lawfully make title
    to° as much love as she finds. There is more owing her than is   *claim*
    paid, and more shall be paid her than she'll demand.
REYNALDO   Madam, I was very late° more near her than I think   *recently*
    she wished me. Alone she was, and did communicate to her
95   self, her own words to her own ears; she thought, I dare vow for

---

8. *by kind*: according to its nature (the cuckoo's song was supposed to mock cuckolds).
9. Lavatch is reminded of the "fair face" of Helen of Troy, the most famous cuckold maker. *she*: probably Hecuba, wife of Priam and mother of Paris, Helen's lover.
1. *this*: probably refers to Paris.
2. Debase (the original presumably had "one bad in ten," referring to Paris, Priam's only bad son).
3. One-tenth of the parish produce was tithed to the church.

4. Before he draw (as from a lottery).
5. Though my honest self is not morally strict.
6. *it will wear . . . heart*: that is, Lavatch will conceal his pride under apparent meekness. Some Puritan ministers obeyed English ecclesiastical law by wearing the surplice, or priestly garment, but with a black Calvinist gown underneath.
7. Even without any interest accrued (Helen being regarded as the "principal" bequeathed by her father).

her, they touched not any stranger sense.[8] Her matter° was, she   *subject*
loved your son. Fortune, she said, was no goddess, that had put
such difference betwixt their two estates;° Love no god, that   *social stations*
would not extend his might only where qualities were level;[9]
100   Dian° no queen of virgins, that would suffer her poor knight   *goddess of chastity*
surprised[1] without rescue in the first assault or ransom after-
ward. This she delivered in the most bitter touch° of sorrow that   *strain*
e'er I heard virgin exclaim in; which I held my duty speedily to
acquaint you withal, sithence° in the loss that may happen it   *since*
105   concerns you something to know it.
COUNTESS   You have discharged this honestly. Keep it to yourself. Many likelihoods informed me of this before, which hung
so tott'ring in the balance that I could neither believe nor mis-
doubt.° Pray you, leave me. Stall° this in your bosom, and I   *doubt / Enclose*
110   thank you for your honest care. I will speak with you further
anon.   *Exit steward*
   Enter HELEN
COUNTESS [*aside*]   Even so it was with me when I was young.
   If ever we are nature's, these° are ours: this thorn   *(love pangs)*
   Doth to our rose of youth rightly belong.
115   Our blood° to us, this to our blood is born;   *passions*
   It is the show° and seal of nature's truth,   *sign*
   Where love's strong passion is impressed in youth.
   By our remembrances of days foregone,
   Such were our faults—or° then we thought them none.   *although*
120   Her eye is sick on't.° I observe her now.   *with it*
HELEN   What is your pleasure, madam?
COUNTESS   You know, Helen,
  I am a mother to you.
HELEN   Mine honourable mistress.
COUNTESS   Nay, a mother.
  Why not a mother? When I said 'a mother',
125   Methought you saw a serpent. What's in 'mother'
  That you start at it? I say I am your mother,
  And put you in the catalogue of those
  That were enwombèd mine. 'Tis often seen
  Adoption strives with nature, and choice breeds
130   A native slip to us from foreign seeds.[2]
  You ne'er oppressed me with a mother's groan,°   *(in childbirth)*
  Yet I express to you a mother's care.
  God's mercy, maiden! Does it curd thy blood
  To say I am thy mother? What's the matter,
135   That this distempered° messenger of wet,°   *disturbed / rain; tears*
  The many-coloured Iris,[3] rounds thine eye?
  Why, that you are my daughter?
HELEN   That I am not.
COUNTESS   I say I am your mother.
HELEN   Pardon, madam.
  The Count Roussillon cannot be my brother.
140   I am from humble, he from honoured name;
  No note° upon my parents, his all noble.   *distinction*

8. Any other persons' hearing.
9. Would not exercise his power except where rank was
equal.
1. Would allow her poor devotee to be captured.

2. *choice . . . seeds*: a twig chosen from foreign seed
becomes, once engrafted, part of our plant.
3. Goddess of rainbows (Helen's tear-filled eyes are iridescent).

My master, my dear lord he is, and I
His servant live and will his vassal die.
He must not be my brother.
COUNTESS   Nor I your mother?

145 HELEN   You are my mother, madam. Would you were—
So° that my lord your son were not my brother—   *Provided*
Indeed my mother! Or were you both our mothers°   *mother of us both*
I care no more for than I do for heaven,
So I were not his sister. Can 't no other

150 But, I your daughter, he must be my brother?
COUNTESS   Yes, Helen, you might be my daughter-in-law.
God shield you mean it not! 'Daughter' and 'mother'
So strive upon your pulse. What, pale again?
My fear hath catched your fondness.° Now I see   *love; folly*

155 The myst'ry of your loneliness, and find
Your salt tears' head.° Now to all sense 'tis gross:°   *source / obvious*
You love my son. Invention[4] is ashamed
Against° the proclamation of thy passion   *In the face of*
To say thou dost not. Therefore tell me true,

160 But tell me then 'tis so—for look, thy cheeks
Confess it t'one to th'other, and thine eyes
See it so grossly shown in thy behaviours
That in their kind° they speak it. Only sin   *after their fashion*
And hellish obstinacy tie thy tongue,

165 That truth should be suspected.° Speak, is 't so?   *doubted*
If it be so you have wound a goodly clew;[5]
If it be not, forswear 't.° Howe'er,° I charge thee,   *deny it / In any case*
As heaven shall work in me for thine avail,°   *benefit*
To tell me truly.
HELEN   Good madam, pardon me.
COUNTESS   Do you love my son?

170 HELEN   Your pardon, noble mistress.
COUNTESS   Love you my son?
HELEN   Do not you love him, madam?
COUNTESS   Go not about.[6] My love hath in 't a bond
Whereof the world takes note.° Come, come, disclose   *society recognizes*
The state of your affection, for your passions
Have to the full appeached.°   *informed against you*

175 HELEN   Then I confess,
Here on my knee, before high heaven and you,
That before you° and next unto high heaven   *even more than I love you*
I love your son.
My friends° were poor but honest; so's my love.   *relatives*

180 Be not offended, for it hurts not him
That he is loved of me. I follow him not
By any token° of presumptuous suit,°   *manifestations / wooing*
Nor would I have him till I do deserve him,
Yet never know how that desert should be.

185 I know I love in vain, strive against hope;
Yet in this captious° and intenable° sieve   *receptive / unretentive*
I still° pour in the waters of my love   *continually*
And lack not to lose still.° Thus, Indian-like,   *And keep losing it*

---

4. (Your) capacity to invent excuses.   6. Don't beat around the bush.
5. You have made a fine tangle of thread (mess).

Religious in mine error, I adore
190 The sun that looks upon his worshipper
But knows of him no more. My dearest madam,
Let not your hate encounter with° my love   *oppose*
For loving where you do; but if yourself,
Whose agèd honour cites° a virtuous youth,   *testifies to*
195 Did ever in so true a flame of liking
Wish chastely and love dearly, that your Dian
Was both herself and Love,[7] then give pity
To her whose state is such that cannot choose
But lend and give where she is sure to lose,
200 That seeks to find not that° her search implies,   *what*
But riddle-like[8] lives sweetly where she dies.
COUNTESS   Had you not lately an intent—speak truly—
To go to Paris?
HELEN   Madam, I had.
205 COUNTESS   Wherefore? Tell true.
HELEN   I will tell truth, by grace itself I swear.
You know my father left me some prescriptions
Of rare and proved effects, such as his reading
And manifest° experience had collected   *obvious*
210 For general sovereignty,° and that he willed me   *effectiveness*
In heedfull'st reservation° to bestow them,   *With most sparing care*
As notes whose faculties inclusive were
More than they were in note.[9] Amongst the rest
There is a remedy, approved,° set down,   *tested*
215 To cure the desperate languishings whereof
The King is rendered lost.°   *held to be dying*
COUNTESS   This was your motive
For Paris, was it? Speak.
HELEN   My lord your son made me to think of this,
Else Paris and the medicine and the King
220 Had from the conversation of my thoughts
Haply° been absent then.   *Perhaps*
COUNTESS   But think you, Helen,
If you should tender° your supposèd aid,   *offer*
He would receive it? He and his physicians
Are of a° mind: he, that they cannot help him;   *one*
225 They, that they cannot help. How shall they credit
A poor unlearnèd virgin, when the schools,
Embowelled° of their doctrine, have left off   *Emptied*
The danger to itself?
HELEN   There's something in't
More than my father's skill, which was the great'st
230 Of his profession, that his good receipt°   *prescription*
Shall for my legacy be sanctified
By th' luckiest stars in heaven, and would your honour
But give me leave to try success,° I'd venture   *test the outcome*
The well-lost life of mine on his grace's cure
235 By such a day, an hour.
COUNTESS   Dost thou believe't?

---

7. Venus, goddess of erotic love, is usually the antagonist of Diana, goddess of chastity; Helen's love reconciles them.

8. Paradoxically; retaining her secret.
9. As . . . note: As prescriptions of greater powers than were recognized.

HELEN   Ay, madam, knowingly.[1]
COUNTESS   Why, Helen, thou shalt have my leave and love,
 Means and attendants, and my loving greetings
240 To those of mine in court. I'll stay at home
 And pray God's blessing into thy attempt.
 Be gone tomorrow, and be sure of this:
 What I can help thee to, thou shalt not miss.°   *Exeunt*   *lack*

2.1

Flourish cornetts. Enter the KING [*carried in a chair*],
with [*the two* LORDS DUMAINE,] *divers young lords tak-*
ing leave for the Florentine war, [*and* BERTRAM] *and*
PAROLES

KING   Farewell, young lords. These warlike principles°   *military precepts*
 Do not throw from you. And you, my lords,[1] farewell.
 Share the advice betwixt you; if both gain all,
 The gift doth stretch itself as 'tis received,
 And is enough for both.
5 FIRST LORD DUMAINE 'Tis our hope, sir,
 After well-entered soldiers,[2] to return
 And find your grace in health.
KING   No, no, it cannot be—and yet my heart
 Will not confess he owes° the malady   *it owns*
10 That doth my life besiege. Farewell, young lords.
 Whether I live or die, be you the sons
 Of worthy Frenchmen; let higher° Italy—   *northern*
 Those bated° that inherit but the fall   *dwindled peoples*
 Of the last monarchy[3]—see that you come
15 Not to woo honour but to wed it. When
 The bravest questant° shrinks, find what you seek,   *seeker*
 That fame may cry you loud.° I say farewell.   *acclaim you loudly*
FIRST LORD DUMAINE   Health at your bidding serve your majesty.
KING   Those girls of Italy, take heed of them.
20 They say our French lack language to deny
 If they demand.° Beware of being captives[4]   *request*
 Before you serve.°   *(militarily)*
BOTH LORDS DUMAINE   Our hearts receive your warnings.
KING   Farewell.—Come hither to me.
  [*Some lords stand aside with the* KING]
FIRST LORD DUMAINE [*to* BERTRAM]   O my sweet lord, that you
 will stay behind us.
PAROLES   'Tis not his fault, the spark.°   *spirited person*
25 SECOND LORD DUMAINE   O 'tis brave° wars.   *splendid*
PAROLES   Most admirable! I have seen those wars.
BERTRAM   I am commanded° here, and kept a coil° with   *(to stay) / fussed over*
 'Too young' and 'the next year' and ''tis too early'.
PAROLES   An° thy mind stand to't, boy, steal away bravely.   *If*
30 BERTRAM   I shall stay here the forehorse to a smock,[5]
 Creaking my shoes on the plain masonry,[6]

---

1. Fully aware of what I am doing.
2.1 Location: The King's palace.
1. Presumably leaving to take the opposite side in the war.
2. After we are well initiated as soldiers.
3. Perhaps the Holy Roman Empire, the Medici, or the papacy.
4. Of your mistresses.
5. Lead horse of a team driven by a woman (figuratively, part of a dancing couple).
6. Level stonework (of the palace floors, in contrast to the rough battlefield).

Till honour be bought up,° and no sword worn   *all acquired (by others)*
But one to dance with. By heaven, I'll steal away.
FIRST LORD DUMAINE   There's honour in the theft.
PAROLES   Commit it, Count.
35   SECOND LORD DUMAINE   I am your accessary.° And so, farewell.   *accomplice*
BERTRAM   I grow° to you,   *am deeply attached*
And our parting is a tortured body.
FIRST LORD DUMAINE   Farewell, captain.
SECOND LORD DUMAINE   Sweet Monsieur Paroles.
PAROLES   Noble heroes, my sword and yours are kin. Good
40   sparks and lustrous, a word, good mettles.° You shall find in the   *spirits; sword blades*
regiment of the Spinii one Captain Spurio, with his cicatrice,°   *scar*
an emblem of war, here on his sinister° cheek. It was this very   *left*
sword entrenched it. Say to him I live, and observe his reports°   *note his reply*
for me.
45   FIRST LORD DUMAINE   We shall, noble captain.
PAROLES   Mars dote on you for his novices.
                    [*Exeunt both* LORDS DUMAINE]
[*To* BERTRAM] What will ye do?
BERTRAM   Stay° the King.   *Await*
PAROLES   Use a more spacious ceremony° to the noble lords.   *expansive courtesy*
50   You have restrained yourself within the list° of too cold an   *limit*
adieu. Be more expressive to them, for they wear themselves
in the cap of the time,[7] there do muster true gait;[8] eat, speak,
and move under the influence of the most received° star—and   *fashionable*
though the devil lead the measure,° such are to be followed.   *dance*
55   After them, and take a more dilated° farewell.   *extended*
BERTRAM   And I will do so.
PAROLES   Worthy fellows, and like to prove most sinewy sword-
men.   *Exeunt* [BERTRAM *and* PAROLES]
          Enter LAFEU [*to the* KING]
LAFEU [*kneeling*]   Pardon, my lord, for me and for my tidings.
60   KING   I'll fee[9] thee to stand up.
LAFEU [*rising*]   Then here's a man stands that has bought his pardon.
I would you had kneeled, my lord, to ask me mercy,
And that at my bidding you could so stand up.
KING   I would I had, so I had broke thy pate°   *head*
And asked thee mercy for't.
65   LAFEU   Good faith, across![1]
But my good lord, 'tis thus: will you be cured
Of your infirmity?
KING   No.
LAFEU   O will you eat
No grapes, my royal fox?[2] Yes, but you will,
My noble grapes, an if° my royal fox   *an if=if*
70   Could reach them. I have seen a medicine°   *physician; remedy*
That's able to breathe life into a stone,
Quicken° a rock, and make you dance canary°   *Animate / a lively dance*
With sprightly fire and motion; whose simple° touch   *mere; medicinal herb*
Is powerful to araise King Pépin,[3] nay,

---

7. Are ornaments of fashion.
8. Display grace of movement.
9. Pay (not merely "pardon").
1. A weak jest: in tilting, a blow "across" is a bad hit.

2. In Aesop, a fox pretends not to want a bunch of
grapes he cannot reach.
3. Eighth-century French King.

75	To give great Charlemagne[4] a pen in's hand,	
	And write to her a love-line.	
	KING What 'her' is this?	
	LAFEU Why, Doctor She. My lord, there's one arrived,	
	If you will see her. Now by my faith and honour,	
	If seriously I may convey my thoughts	
80	In this my light deliverance,° I have spoke	*mode of speaking*
	With one that in her sex, her years, profession,°	*claims of skill*
	Wisdom and constancy, hath amazed me more	
	Than I dare blame my weakness.° Will you see her—	*(as an old man)*
	For that is her demand—and know her business?	
	That done, laugh well at me.	
85	KING Now, good Lafeu,	
	Bring in the admiration,° that we with thee	*marvel*
	May spend our wonder too, or take off thine	
	By wond'ring how thou took'st° it.	*came by*
	LAFEU Nay, I'll fit° you,	*satisfy*
	And not be all day neither.	
	[*He goes to the door*]	
90	KING Thus he his special nothing° ever prologues.	*trifles*
	LAFEU [*to* HELEN, *within*] Nay, come your ways.°	*come along*
	Enter HELEN	
	KING This haste hath wings indeed.	
	LAFEU [*to* HELEN] Nay, come your ways.	
	This is his majesty. Say your mind to him.	
95	A traitor[5] you do look like, but such traitors	
	His majesty seldom fears. I am Cressid's uncle,[6]	
	That dare leave two together. Fare you well.	
	Exeunt [*all but the* KING *and* HELEN]	
	KING Now, fair one, does your business follow us?	
	HELEN Ay, my good lord. Gérard de Narbonne was my father;	
	In what he did profess, well found.°	*found to be good*
100	KING I knew him.	
	HELEN The rather will I spare my praises towards him;	
	Knowing him is enough. On's° bed of death	*On his*
	Many receipts he gave me, chiefly one	
	Which, as the dearest issue[7] of his practice,	
105	And of his old experience th'only darling,	
	He bade me store up as a triple° eye	*third*
	Safer than mine own two, more dear. I have so,	
	And hearing your high majesty is touched	
	With that malignant cause wherein the honour	
110	Of my dear father's gift stands chief in power,[8]	
	I come to tender it and my appliance°	*treatment*
	With all bound° humbleness.	*dutiful*
	KING We thank you, maiden,	
	But may not be so credulous of cure,	
	When our most learnèd doctors leave us, and	
115	The congregated College[9] have concluded	
	That labouring art° can never ransom nature	*medical skill*
	From her inaidable estate.° I say we must not	*condition*

---

4. Pépin's son, founder of the Holy Roman Empire.
5. Because she avoids the King's gaze.
6. Pandarus, the go-between for Troilus and Cressida and archetypal pimp.

7. Best product; favorite child.
8. *malignant . . . power:* disease for which my father's honored gift is most effective.
9. Assembled College of Physicians.

So stain our judgement or corrupt our hope,
To prostitute° our past-cure malady   *submit*
120   To empirics,[1] or to dissever so
Our great self and our credit,[2] to esteem
A senseless help,° when help past sense we deem.   *An unbelievable cure*
HELEN   My duty then shall pay me for my pains.
I will no more enforce mine office° on you,   *service*
125   Humbly entreating from your royal thoughts
A modest one[3] to bear me back again.
KING   I cannot give thee less, to be called grateful.
Thou thought'st to help me, and such thanks I give
As one near death to those that wish him live.
130   But what at full I know, thou know'st no part;°   *not at all*
I knowing all my peril, thou no art.
HELEN   What I can do can do no hurt to try,
Since you set up your rest° 'gainst remedy.   *stake everything*
He that of greatest works is finisher
135   Oft does them by the weakest minister.
So holy writ in babes hath judgement shown
When judges have been babes;[4] great floods have flow'n
From simple sources, and great seas have dried.
When miracles have by th' great'st been denied
140   [   ][5]
Oft expectation fails, and most oft there
Where most it promises, and oft it hits°   *succeeds*
Where hope is coldest and despair most fits.
KING   I must not hear thee. Fare thee well, kind maid.
145   Thy pains, not used, must by thyself be paid:
Proffers not took reap thanks° for their reward.   *only thanks*
HELEN   Inspirèd merit so by breath is barred.[6]
It is not so with him that all things knows
As 'tis with us that square our guess by shows;[7]
150   But most it is presumption in us when
The help of heaven we count the act of men.
Dear sir, to my endeavours give consent.
Of heaven, not me, make an experiment.
I am not an impostor, that proclaim
155   Myself against the level of mine aim,[8]
But know I think, and think I know most sure,
My art is not past° power, nor you past cure.   *without*
KING   Art thou so confident? Within what space
Hop'st thou my cure?
HELEN   The great'st grace lending grace,
160   Ere twice the horses of the sun shall bring
Their fiery coacher his diurnal ring,°   *daily round*
Ere twice in murk and occidental damp

---

1. Physicians whose methods were based on experience rather than on medical theory. In early modern Europe, "theoretical" practitioners, like the members of the French College of Physicians, often considered their "empirical" colleagues mere quacks; the "empirics" usually hailed from lower social classes and had less formal education.
2. *to dissever . . . credit:* to open such a gap between my royal station and my gullibility.
3. A favorable thought appropriate to a woman and a subject.
4. *So . . . babes:* "Thou hast hid these things from the wise and men of understanding, and hast opened them unto babes" (Matthew 11:25).
5. The Oxford editors conjecture a lost line here.
6. Divinely inspired virtue is thus denied by human speech.
7. Who base our conjectures on appearances.
8. *proclaim . . . aim:* boast in advance of the accuracy of my aim; declare myself to be different from what I am.

Moist Hesperus° hath quenched her sleepy lamp,   *the evening star*
Or four-and-twenty times the pilot's glass°   *hourglass*
165 Hath told the thievish minutes how they pass,
What is infirm from your sound parts shall fly,
Health shall live free, and sickness freely die.
KING Upon thy certainty and confidence
What dar'st thou venture?°   *risk*
HELEN   Tax° of impudence,   *Accusation*
170 A strumpet's boldness, a divulgèd shame;
Traduced by odious ballads, my maiden's name
Seared[9] otherwise, nay—worse of worst—extended[1]
With vilest torture, let my life be ended.
KING Methinks in thee some blessèd spirit doth speak,
175 His powerful sound within an organ weak;
And what impossibility would slay
In common sense, sense saves another way.[2]
Thy life is dear, for all that life can rate
Worth name of life in thee hath estimate:°   *is present*
180 Youth, beauty, wisdom, courage, all
That happiness and prime[3] can happy call.
Thou this to hazard needs must intimate[4]
Skill infinite, or monstrous desperate.
Sweet practiser,° thy physic I will try,   *practitioner; schemer*
185 That ministers thine own death if I die.
HELEN If I break time, or flinch in property[5]
Of what I spoke, unpitied let me die,
And well deserved. Not helping, death's my fee.
But if I help, what do you promise me?
KING Make thy demand.
190 HELEN   But will you make it even?°   *satisfy it*
KING Ay, by my sceptre and my hopes of heaven.
HELEN Then shalt thou give me with thy kingly hand
What husband in thy power I will command.
Exempted be from me the arrogance
195 To choose from forth the royal blood of France,
My low and humble name to propagate
With any branch or image of thy state;°   *royal place*
But such a one, thy vassal, whom I know
Is free for me to ask, thee to bestow.
200 KING Here is my hand. The premises observed,°   *conditions fulfilled*
Thy will by my performance shall be served.
So make the choice of thy own time, for I,
Thy resolved patient, on thee still° rely.   *always*
More should I question thee, and more I must,
205 Though more to know could not be more to trust:
From whence thou cam'st, how tended on°—but rest   *attended*
Unquestioned[6] welcome, and undoubted blessed.—
Give me some help here, ho! If thou proceed
As high as word, my deed shall match thy deed.
    Flourish. Exeunt [*the* KING, *carried, and* HELEN]

---

9. Branded (like a criminal).
1. Prolonged; stretched on the rack.
2. *sense . . . way:* makes sense in another, uncommon way.
3. That good fortune and the springtime of life.

4. For you to risk this must suggest.
5. If I fail to meet the deadline or fall short in the particulars.
6. Not having been asked; unquestionably.

2.2

Enter the COUNTESS *and* [LAVATCH] *the clown*

COUNTESS Come on, sir. I shall now put you to the height[1] of
your breeding.

LAVATCH I will show myself highly fed and lowly taught.[2] I know
my business is but to the court.

5 COUNTESS 'To the court'? Why, what place make you special,
when you put off° that with such contempt? 'But to the court'!   *dismiss*

LAVATCH Truly, madam, if God have lent a man any manners
he may easily put it off° at court. He that cannot make a leg,°   *lose it; take it off / bow*
put off's cap, kiss his hand, and say nothing, has neither leg,
10 hands, lip, nor cap, and indeed such a fellow, to say precisely,
were not for the court. But for me, I have an answer will serve
all men.

COUNTESS Marry, that's a bountiful answer that fits all questions.

LAVATCH It is like a barber's chair that fits all buttocks: the pin°-   *pointed*
15 buttock, the quatch°-buttock, the brawn-buttock, or any but-   *fat*
tock.

COUNTESS Will your answer serve fit to all questions?

LAVATCH As fit as ten groats is for the hand of an attorney, as
your French crown[3] for your taffeta punk,° as Tib's rush[4] for   *prostitute*
20 Tom's forefinger, as a pancake[5] for Shrove Tuesday, a morris°   *morris dance*
for May Day, as the nail to his hole, the cuckold to his horn, as
a scolding quean° to a wrangling knave, as the nun's lip to the   *whore*
friar's mouth, nay as the pudding° to his skin.   *sausage*

COUNTESS Have you, I say, an answer of such fitness for all ques-
25 tions?

LAVATCH From beyond your duke to beneath your constable, it
will fit any question.

COUNTESS It must be an answer of most monstrous size that
must fit all demands.

30 LAVATCH But a trifle neither,° in good faith, if the learned   *No, just a trifle*
should speak truth of it. Here it is, and all that belongs to't. Ask
me if I am a courtier. It shall do you no harm to learn.

COUNTESS To be young again, if we could! I will be a fool in
question, hoping to be the wiser by your answer. I pray you, sir,
35 are you a courtier?

LAVATCH O Lord, sir![6]—There's a simple putting off. More,
more, a hundred of them.

COUNTESS Sir, I am a poor friend of yours that loves you.

LAVATCH O Lord, sir!—Thick,° thick, spare not me.   *Quick*
40 COUNTESS I think, sir, you can eat none of this homely° meat.   *plain*

LAVATCH O Lord, sir!—Nay, put me to't, I warrant you.

COUNTESS You were lately whipped, sir, as I think.

LAVATCH O Lord, sir!—Spare not me.

COUNTESS Do you cry 'O Lord, sir!' at your whipping, and 'spare
45 not me'? Indeed, your 'O Lord, sir!' is very sequent[7] to your
whipping. You would answer very well[8] to a whipping, if you
were but bound to't.[9]

2.2 Location: Bertram's palace.
1. Make you display your best manners.
2. Spoiled children were called "better fed than taught."
3. Coin; bald head (from syphilis, the "French disease").
4. Reed twisted into a ring for use in folk marriage, with sexual innuendo.
5. Traditionally eaten on Shrove Tuesday, the day before

the beginning of Lent.
6. A voguish catchphrase that evades an answer by appearing to wonder at the question. *putting off*: evasion.
7. Follows naturally upon (as a plea for mercy).
8. Reply cleverly to; be a fitting recipient of.
9. Required to answer; tied to a whipping post.

LAVATCH   I ne'er had worse luck in my life in my 'O Lord, sir!' I
see things may serve long, but not serve ever.

50   COUNTESS   I play the noble housewife° with the time, to enter-   *good steward (ironic)*
tain it so merrily with a fool.

LAVATCH   O Lord, sir!—Why, there't serves well again.

COUNTESS   An end, sir! To your business: give Helen this,
[*She gives him a letter*]
And urge her to a present° answer back.   *immediate*

55   Commend me to my kinsmen and my son.
This is not much.

LAVATCH   Not much commendation to them?

COUNTESS   Not much employment for you. You understand me.

LAVATCH   Most fruitfully. I am there before my legs.

60   COUNTESS   Haste you again.°   *Exeunt* [*severally*]   *back again*

2.3

Enter [BERTRAM,] LAFEU [*with a ballad*], *and* PAROLES

LAFEU   They say miracles are past, and we have our philosophical persons to make modern and familiar things supernatural
and causeless.[1] Hence is it that we make trifles of terrors,
ensconcing ourselves into° seeming knowledge when we   *sheltering ourselves with*

5   should submit ourselves to an unknown fear.°   *awe of the unknown*

PAROLES   Why, 'tis the rarest argument° of wonder that hath   *best instance*
shot out in our latter° times.   *recent*

BERTRAM   And so 'tis.

LAFEU   To be relinquished of the artists[2]—

10   PAROLES   So I say—both of Galen and Paracelsus.[3]

LAFEU   Of all the learned and authentic Fellows[4]—

PAROLES   Right, so I say.

LAFEU   That gave him out incurable—

PAROLES   Why, there 'tis, so say I too.

15   LAFEU   Not to be helped.

PAROLES   Right, as 'twere a man assured of a—

LAFEU   Uncertain life and sure death.

PAROLES   Just,° you say well, so would I have said.   *Exactly*

LAFEU   I may truly say it is a novelty to the world.

20   PAROLES   It is indeed. If you will have it in showing,° you shall   *demonstrated*
read it in [*pointing to the ballad*] what-do-ye-call there.

LAFEU [*reads*]   'A showing of a heavenly effect in an earthly
actor.'

PAROLES   That's it, I would have said the very same.

25   LAFEU   Why, your dolphin[5] is not lustier.° Fore me, I speak in   *more sportive*
respect°—   *respectfully*

PAROLES   Nay, 'tis strange, 'tis very strange, that is the brief ° and   *short*
the tedious° of it, and he's of a most facinorous° spirit that will   *long / wicked*
not acknowledge it to be the—

30   LAFEU   Very hand of heaven.

PAROLES   Ay, so I say.

LAFEU   In a most weak—

PAROLES   And debile minister° great power, great transcendence,   *feeble agent*

2.3 Location: The King's palace.
1. To make supernatural things, without apparent cause,
seem commonplace and easily explained.
2. Abandoned by the scholars.
3. Galen was a second-century Greek physician, the tra-

ditional medical authority; Paracelsus was a sixteenth-
century Swiss physician who tried to reform Galen's
teachings.
4. Accredited members of the College of Physicians.
5. Punning on "dauphin," heir to the French throne.

which should indeed give us a further use to be made than
35　alone the recov'ry of the king, as to be—
LAFEU　Generally° thankful.　　　　　　　　　　　　　　　　*Universally*

Enter the KING, HELEN, *and attendants*

PAROLES　I would have said it, you say well. Here comes the King.
LAFEU　Lustig,° as the Dutchman says. I'll like a maid the better　　*Frolicsome*
　　whilst I have a tooth in my head.[6]

[*The* KING *and* HELEN *dance*]

40　Why, he's able to lead her a coranto.°　　　　　　　　　　　*running dance*
PAROLES　*Mort du vinaigre*,[7] is not this Helen?
LAFEU　Fore God, I think so.
KING　Go call before me all the lords in court.

[*Exit one or more*]

Sit, my preserver, by thy patient's side,

[*The* KING *and* HELEN *sit*]

45　And with this healthful hand whose banished sense°　　　　*sense of feeling*
Thou hast repealed,° a second time receive　　　　　　　　　*restored*
The confirmation of my promised gift,
Which but attends° thy naming.　　　　　　　　　　　　　　　*awaits*

Enter four LORDS

Fair maid, send forth thine eye. This youthful parcel°　　　*group*
50　Of noble bachelors stand at my bestowing,[8]
O'er whom both sovereign power and father's voice
I have to use. Thy frank election° make.　　　　　　　　　　*free choice*
Thou hast power to choose, and they none to forsake.
HELEN　To each of you one fair and virtuous mistress
55　Fall[9] when love please. Marry, to each but one.
LAFEU [*aside*]　I'd give bay Curtal and his furniture[1]
My mouth no more were broken[2] than these boys',
And writ° as little beard.　　　　　　　　　　　　　　　　　*laid claim to*
KING [*to* HELEN]　　　　　　　　　　　Peruse them well.
Not one of these but had a noble father.
60　HELEN　Gentlemen,
Heaven hath through me restored the King to health.
ALL [*but* HELEN]　We understand it, and thank heaven for you.
HELEN　I am a simple maid, and therein wealthiest
　　That I protest I simply am a maid.—
65　Please it your majesty, I have done already.
The blushes in my cheeks thus whisper me:
'We blush that thou shouldst choose; but, be° refused,　　　*if you are*
Let the white death sit on thy cheek for ever,
We'll ne'er come there again.'
KING　　　　　　　　　　　　　　Make choice and see.
70　Who shuns thy love shuns all his love in me.
HELEN [*rising*]　Now, Dian, from thy altar do I fly,
And to imperial Love, that god most high,
Do my sighs stream.

[*She addresses her to a* LORD]

　　　　　　　　　　　　　Sir, will you hear my suit?
FIRST LORD　And grant it.

6. *whilst . . . head:* so long as I have a taste for pleasure ("sweet tooth"); until I've degenerated into complete senility.
7. Death of the vinegar—a pseudo-French oath.
8. Are in my power to bestow (because they are his wards).
9. Befall, with the suggestion of a sexual "fall."
1. I'd give my dock-tailed bay horse and his trappings.
2. Contained broken teeth; of a boy's voice, "broken" at puberty; of a horse, "broken" to the bit.

HELEN   Thanks, sir. All the rest is mute.°   *I will say no more*

75   LAFEU [*aside*]   I had rather be in this choice than throw
ambs-ace³ for my life.

HELEN [*to another* LORD]   The honour, sir, that flames in your fair eyes,⁴
Before I speak, too threat'ningly replies.
Love make your fortunes twenty times above
Her that so wishes,° and her humble love.   *makes this wish*

SECOND LORD   No better, if you please.

80   HELEN   My wish receive,
Which great Love grant. And so I take my leave.

LAFEU [*aside*]   Do all they deny her?⁵ An they were sons of mine
I'd have them whipped, or I would send them to th' Turk to
make eunuchs of.

85   HELEN [*to another* LORD]   Be not afraid that I your hand should take;
I'll never do you wrong for your own sake.
Blessing upon your vows,° and in your bed   *marriage vows*
Find fairer fortune, if you ever wed.

LAFEU [*aside*]   These boys are boys of ice, they'll none have her.

90   Sure they are bastards to the English, the French ne'er got°   *begot*
'em.

HELEN [*to another* LORD]   You are too young, too happy, and too good
To make yourself a son out of my blood.

FOURTH LORD   Fair one, I think not so.

95   LAFEU [*aside*]   There's one grape° yet. I am sure thy father drunk   *fruit of a noble stock*
wine,⁶ but if thou beest not an ass I am a youth of fourteen. I
have known° thee already.   *found out*

HELEN [*to* BERTRAM]   I dare not say I take you, but I give
Me and my service ever whilst I live

100   Into your guiding power.—This is the man.

KING   Why then, young Bertram, take her, she's thy wife.

BERTRAM   My wife, my liege? I shall beseech your highness,
In such a business give me leave to use
The help of mine own eyes.

KING   Know'st thou not, Bertram,
What she has done for me?

105   BERTRAM   Yes, my good lord,
But never hope° to know why I should marry her.   *expect*

KING   Thou know'st she has raised me from my sickly bed.

BERTRAM   But follows it, my lord, to bring me down
Must answer for your raising? I know her well:

110   She had her breeding° at my father's charge.   *upbringing*
A poor physician's daughter, my wife? Disdain
Rather corrupt° me ever.   *ruin*

KING   'Tis only title° thou disdain'st in her, the which   *rank*
I can build up. Strange is it that our bloods,

115   Of colour, weight, and heat, poured all together,
Would quite confound distinction,⁷ yet stands off °   *separated*
In differences so mighty. If she be
All that is virtuous, save what thou dislik'st—
'A poor physician's daughter'—thou dislik'st

---

3. Two aces (the lowest throw in dice); a joking understatement.
4. The pride of rank that shows in your look.
5. Either Lafeu, standing apart, misunderstands what is
happening, or (less probably) the lords' polite replies are
belied by their evident relief when Helen rejects them.
6. Was red-blooded (wine was supposed to turn directly
into blood).
7. Confuse the effort to distinguish.

120   Of virtue for the name.° But do not so.   *(lack of) a title*
From lowest place when virtuous things proceed,
The place is dignified by th' doer's deed.
Where great additions° swell's, and virtue none,   *titles*
It is a dropsied[8] honour. Good alone°   *in itself*
125   Is good without a name, vileness is so:
The property° by what it is should go,   *quality*
Not by the title. She is young, wise, fair.
In these to nature she's immediate heir,
And these breed honour. That is honour's scorn
130   Which challenges° itself as honour's born   *makes claims for*
And is not like the sire; honours thrive
When rather from our acts we them derive
Than our foregoers. The mere word's a slave,
Debauched° on every tomb, on every grave   *Debased*
135   A lying trophy,° and as oft is dumb   *memorial*
Where dust and dammed° oblivion is the tomb   *stopped-up*
Of honoured bones indeed. What should be said?
If thou canst like this creature as a maid,
I can create the rest. Virtue and she
140   Is her own dower;[9] honour and wealth from me.
    BERTRAM   I cannot love her, nor will strive° to do't.   *attempt*
    KING   Thou wrong'st thyself. If thou shouldst strive to choose—
    HELEN   That you are well restored, my lord, I'm glad.
Let the rest go.
145   KING   My honour's at the stake, which to defeat
I must produce my power. Here, take her hand,
Proud, scornful boy, unworthy this good gift,
That dost in vile misprision° shackle up   *wrongful disdain*
My love and her desert; that canst not dream
150   We, poising us in her defective scale,
Shall weigh thee to the beam;[1] that wilt not know
It is in us° to plant thine honour where   *in our power*
We please to have it grow. Check° thy contempt;   *Restrain*
Obey our will, which travails in° thy good;   *labors for*
155   Believe not thy disdain, but presently
Do thine own fortunes that obedient right
Which both thy duty owes and our power claims,
Or I will throw thee from my care for ever
Into the staggers[2] and the careless lapse°   *fall; ruin*
160   Of youth and ignorance, both my revenge and hate
Loosing upon thee in the name of justice
Without all terms of° pity. Speak. Thine answer. *any concessions to*
    BERTRAM *[kneeling]*   Pardon, my gracious lord, for I submit
My fancy° to your eyes. When I consider   *perceptions; affection*
165   What great creation[3] and what dole° of honour   *portion*
Flies where you bid it, I find that she, which late
Was in my nobler thoughts most base, is now
The praisèd of the King; who, so ennobled,
Is as 'twere born so.

---

8. Unhealthily swollen.
9. *Virtue . . . dower:* Her own marriage gift is virtue and
herself.
1. *We . . . beam:* Adding my weight to her deficient side

of the balance shall raise your (lighter) side. (The King
uses the royal plural.)
2. Confusion (literally, a horse disease).
3. Creating of greatness.

KING   Take her by the hand
170   And tell her she is thine; to whom I promise
         A counterpoise, if not to thy estate
         A balance more replete.[4]
BERTRAM [*rising*]   I take her hand.
KING   Good fortune and the favour of the King
         Smile upon this contract, whose ceremony
175   Shall seem expedient on the now-born brief,[5]
         And be performed tonight. The solemn feast
         Shall more attend upon the coming space,
         Expecting absent friends.[6] As thou lov'st her
         Thy love's to me religious;° else, does err.   *properly devoted*
         [*Flourish.*] *Exeunt* [*all but*] PAROLES *and* LAFEU,
         [*who*] *stay behind, commenting on this wedding*
180   LAFEU   Do you hear, monsieur? A word with you.
PAROLES   Your pleasure, sir.
LAFEU   Your lord and master did well to make his recantation.
PAROLES   Recantation? My lord? My master?
LAFEU   Ay. Is it not a language I speak?
185   PAROLES   A most harsh one, and not to be understood without
         bloody succeeding.° My master?   *consequences*
LAFEU   Are you companion to the Count Roussillon?
PAROLES   To any count, to all counts, to what is man.°   *whatever is manly*
LAFEU   To what is count's man;° count's master is of another   *servant*
190   style.
PAROLES   You are too old, sir. Let it satisfy you,[7] you are too old.
LAFEU   I must tell thee, sirrah, I write 'Man',[8] to which title age
         cannot bring thee.
PAROLES   What I dare too well do I dare not do.[9]
195   LAFEU   I did think thee for two ordinaries° to be a pretty wise   *meals*
         fellow. Thou didst make tolerable vent° of thy travel; it might   *talk passibly*
         pass. Yet the scarves and the bannerets[1] about thee did mani-
         foldly dissuade me from believing thee a vessel of too great a
         burden.° I have now found thee;[2] when I lose thee again I care   *tonnage*
200   not. Yet art thou good for nothing but taking up,[3] and that
         thou'rt scarce worth.
PAROLES   Hadst thou not the privilege of antiquity[4] upon thee—
LAFEU   Do not plunge thyself too far in anger, lest thou hasten
         thy trial, which if—Lord have mercy on thee for a hen! So, my
205   good window of lattice,[5] fare thee well. Thy casement I need
         not open, for I look through thee. Give me thy hand.
PAROLES   My lord, you give me most egregious indignity.
LAFEU   Ay, with all my heart, and thou art worthy of it.
PAROLES   I have not, my lord, deserved it.
210   LAFEU   Yes, good faith, every dram° of it, and I will not bate°   *one-eighth ounce / remit*
         thee a scruple.°   *one-third dram*
PAROLES   Well, I shall be wiser.
LAFEU   E'en as soon as thou canst, for thou hast to pull at a

---

4. *A counterpoise . . . replete:* A dowry equal to, if not
greater than, your own estate.
5. Shall expedite this newly made decree.
6. *The solemn . . . friends:* The wedding reception will be
postponed until relatives and friends can arrive.
7. Don't force me to avenge your insult.
8. I claim myself to be a man.
9. What I have the courage for (fighting), your age

prevents me from doing.
1. Streamers (which remind Lafeu of a ship's pennants).
2. Discovered what you are.
3. Rebuking; arresting; drafting as a soldier.
4. Exemption (from combat) because of age.
5. Paroles is easily seen through despite his affectation;
his fancy "latticework" of scarves suggests a lattice
window.

smack o'th' contrary.[6] If ever thou beest bound in thy scarf and
beaten thou shall find what it is to be proud of thy bondage. I
have a desire to hold° my acquaintance with thee, or rather my   *maintain*
knowledge, that I may say in the default,° 'He is a man I know'.   *in the event*
PAROLES   My lord, you do me most insupportable vexation.
LAFEU   I would it were hell-pains for thy sake, and my poor
doing[7] eternal; for doing[8] I am past, as I will by thee, in what
motion age will give me leave.   *Exit*
PAROLES   Well, thou hast a son shall take this disgrace off me.
Scurvy, old, filthy, scurvy lord. Well, I must be patient. There
is no fettering of authority. I'll beat him, by my life, if I can
meet him with any convenience, an° he were double and dou-   *if*
ble a lord. I'll have no more pity of his age than I would have
of—I'll beat him, an if I could but meet him again.
      Enter LAFEU
LAFEU   Sirrah, your lord and master's married. There's news for
you: you have a new mistress.
PAROLES   I most unfeignedly beseech your lordship to make
some reservation of your wrongs.° He is my good lord; whom I   *restrain your abuse*
serve above is my master.
LAFEU   Who? God?
PAROLES   Ay, sir.
LAFEU   The devil it is that's thy master. Why dost thou garter up[9]
thy arms o' this fashion? Dost make hose of thy sleeves? Do
other servants so? Thou wert best set thy lower part where thy
nose stands. By mine honour, if I were but two hours younger
I'd beat thee. Methink'st thou art a general offence° and every   *public nuisance*
man should beat thee. I think thou wast created for men to
breathe° themselves upon thee.   *exercise*
PAROLES   This is hard and undeserved measure, my lord.
LAFEU   Go to, sir. You were beaten in Italy for picking a kernel
out of a pomegranate,[1] you are a vagabond and no true traveller, you are more saucy with lords and honourable personages
than the commission° of your birth and virtue gives you her-   *warrant*
aldry.° You are not worth another word, else I'd call you knave.   *entitles you*
I leave you.   *Exit*
PAROLES   Good, very good, it is so then. Good, very good, let it
be concealed awhile.
      [*Enter* BERTRAM]
BERTRAM   Undone and forfeited to cares for ever.
PAROLES   What's the matter, sweetheart?
BERTRAM   Although before the solemn priest I have sworn,
I will not bed her.
PAROLES   What, what, sweetheart?
BERTRAM   O my Paroles, they have married me.
I'll to the Tuscan wars and never bed her.
PAROLES   France is a dog-hole, and it no more merits
The tread of a man's foot. To th' wars!
BERTRAM   There's letters from my mother. What th'import is
I know not yet.
PAROLES   Ay, that would be known. To th' wars, my boy, to th' wars!

---

6. *pull . . . contrary:* drink a quantity of the opposite
quality.
7. My poor attempt to vex you.

8. Activity (with sexual suggestion).
9. Tie up (commenting again on Paroles's outfit).
1. *for picking . . . pomegranate:* on the slightest pretext.

He wears his honour in a box unseen°   *(with sexual innuendo)*
That hugs his kicky-wicky° here at home,   *darling*
265 Spending his manly marrow in her arms,
Which should sustain the bound and high curvet°   *leap*
Of Mars's fiery steed. To other regions!
France is a stable, we that dwell in't jades.[2]
Therefore to th' war.
270 BERTRAM   It shall be so. I'll send her to my house,
Acquaint my mother with my hate to her,
And wherefore I am fled, write to the King
That which I durst not speak. His present gift[3]
Shall furnish me to° those Italian fields   *equip me for*
275 Where noble fellows strike. Wars is no strife
To° the dark house and the detested wife.   *Compared to*
PAROLES   Will this *capriccio*° hold in thee? Art sure?   *caprice*
BERTRAM   Go with me to my chamber and advise me.
I'll send her straight away. Tomorrow
280 I'll to the wars, she to her single sorrow.
PAROLES   Why, these balls bound,[4] there's noise in it. 'Tis hard:
A young man married is a man that's marred.
Therefore away, and leave her bravely. Go.
The King has done you wrong, but hush 'tis so.°   *Exeunt*   *but don't say so*

2.4

Enter HELEN *reading a letter, and* [LAVATCH *the*] *clown*

HELEN   My mother greets me kindly. Is she well?
LAVATCH   She is not well,[1] but yet she has her health. She's very
merry, but yet she is not well. But thanks be given she's very
well and wants° nothing i'th' world. But yet she is not well.   *lacks*
5 HELEN   If she be very well, what does she ail
That she's not very well?
LAVATCH   Truly, she's very well indeed, but for two things.
HELEN   What two things?
LAVATCH   One, that she's not in heaven, whither God send her
10 quickly. The other, that she's in earth, from whence God send
her quickly.

Enter PAROLES

PAROLES   Bless you, my fortunate lady.
HELEN   I hope, sir, I have your good will to have
Mine own good fortunes.
15 PAROLES   You had my prayers to lead them° on, and to keep   *(your good fortunes)*
them on have them still.—O my knave, how does my old lady?
LAVATCH   So that you had her wrinkles and I her money, I
would she did[2] as you say.
PAROLES   Why, I say nothing.
20 LAVATCH   Marry, you are the wiser man, for many a man's°   *servant's*
tongue shakes out[3] his master's undoing. To say nothing, to do
nothing, to know nothing, and to have nothing, is to be a great
part of your title,[4] which is within a very little of nothing.
PAROLES   Away, thou'rt a knave.

---

2. Worthless horses; sluts. Paroles considers staying in
France effeminating.
3. Wedding present just bestowed.
4. Are bouncing now (from tennis); that is, that's how it
should be done.

2.4 Location: The King's palace.
1. The dead were said to be well, because in heaven.
2. Perhaps playing on "died."
3. Inadvertently tumbles out.
4. Status; playing on "tittle," "tiny amount."

25 LAVATCH You should have said, sir, 'Before[5] a knave, thou'rt a
        knave'—that's 'Before me,[6] thou'rt a knave'. This had been
        truth, sir.

PAROLES Go to, thou art a witty fool. I have found° thee.   *seen through*

LAVATCH Did you find me in yourself, sir, or were you taught to
30   find me?

PAROLES In[7] myself, knave.

LAVATCH The search, sir, was profitable, and much fool may you
        find in you, even to the world's pleasure and the increase of
        laughter.

35 PAROLES [*to* HELEN] A good knave, i'faith, and well fed.°   *"better fed than taught"*
        Madam, my lord will go away tonight.
        A very serious business calls on him.
        The great prerogative and rite of love,
        Which as your due time claims, he does acknowledge,
40   But puts it off to a compelled restraint:
        Whose want and whose delay is strewed with sweets,
        Which they distil now in the curbèd time,[8]
        To make the coming hour o'erflow with joy,
        And pleasure drown the brim.

HELEN   What's his will else?

45 PAROLES That you will take your instant leave o'th' King,
        And make° this haste as your own good proceeding,   *represent*
        Strengthened with what apology you think
        May make it probable need.[9]

HELEN   What more commands he?

PAROLES That having this obtained, you presently
        Attend° his further pleasure.°   *Await / command*

50 HELEN   In everything
        I wait upon his will.

PAROLES   I shall report it so.

HELEN I pray you.   *Exit* PAROLES [*at one door*]
        Come, sirrah.

                    Exeunt [*at another door*]

2.5

        Enter LAFEU *and* BERTRAM

LAFEU But I hope your lordship thinks not him a soldier.

BERTRAM Yes, my lord, and of very valiant approof.°   *proven valor*

LAFEU You have it from his own deliverance.°   *report*

BERTRAM And by other warranted testimony.

5 LAFEU Then my dial° goes not true. I took this lark for a   *clock*
        bunting.[1]

BERTRAM I do assure you, my lord, he is very great in knowledge,
        and accordingly° valiant.   *correspondingly*

LAFEU I have then sinned against his experience and trans-
10   gressed against his valour—and my state that way is dangerous,[2]
        since I cannot yet find in my heart to repent. Here he comes. I
        pray you make us friends. I will pursue the amity.

---

5. Even in comparison with; in the presence of.
6. An expression like "Upon my soul"; Lavatch insinu-
ates that Paroles is another knave.
7. By (reinterpreted in lines 31–33 by Lavatch). This
speech is not in F, but clearly some such reply should go
here.
8. *whose delay . . . time:* the delay of which multiplies its

sweetness, as distillation intensifies perfumes.
9. May make the need for haste probable.
2.5 Location: The King's palace.
1. I underestimated him (since the bunting looks like a
lark but does not sing).
2. In that respect risks damnation.

Enter PAROLES

PAROLES [*to* BERTRAM]   These things shall be done, sir.

LAFEU [*to* BERTRAM]   Pray you, sir, who's his tailor?[3]

15   PAROLES   Sir!

LAFEU   O, I know him well.[4] Ay, 'Sir', he; 'Sir''s a good workman,
a very good tailor.

BERTRAM [*aside to* PAROLES]   Is she gone to the King?

PAROLES   She is.

20   BERTRAM   Will she away tonight?

PAROLES   As you'll have her.

BERTRAM   I have writ my letters, casketed my treasure,
Given order for our horses, and tonight,
When I should take possession of the bride,

25   End ere I do begin.

LAFEU [*aside*]   A good traveller is something° at the latter end of   *an asset*
a dinner,[5] but one that lies three-thirds and uses a known truth
to pass a thousand nothings with, should be once heard and
thrice beaten. [*To* PAROLES] God save you, captain.

30   BERTRAM [*to* PAROLES]   Is there any unkindness between my
lord and you, monsieur?

PAROLES   I know not how I have deserved to run into my lord's
displeasure.

LAFEU   You have made shift° to run into't, boots and spurs and   *arranged*

35   all, like him that leaped into the custard,[6] and out of it you'll
run again, rather than suffer question for your residence.[7]

BERTRAM   It may be you have mistaken him, my lord.

LAFEU   And shall do so ever, though I took him at's prayers. Fare
you well, my lord, and believe this of me: there can be no

40   kernel in this light nut. The soul of this man is his clothes.
Trust him not in matter of heavy° consequence. I have kept of   *serious*
them tame,[8] and know their natures.—Farewell, monsieur. I
have spoken better of you than you have wit or will[9] to deserve
at my hand, but we must do good against evil.   *Exit*

45   PAROLES   An idle lord, I swear.

BERTRAM   I think not so.

PAROLES   Why, do you not know him?

BERTRAM   Yes, I do know him well, and common speech
Gives him a worthy pass.° Here comes my clog.[1]   *report*

Enter HELEN[, *attended*]

50   HELEN   I have, sir, as I was commanded from you,
Spoke with the King, and have procured his leave
For present parting; only he desires
Some private speech with you.

BERTRAM   I shall obey his will.
You must not marvel, Helen, at my course,

55   Which holds not colour° with the time, nor does   *is not in keeping*
The ministration and requirèd office
On my particular.[2] Prepared I was not
For such a business, therefore am I found

---

3. Mocking Paroles's clothes.
4. Lafeu pretends "Sir" is the tailor's name.
5. When stories are welcome.
6. At the annual Lord Mayor's feast in London, a jester
leaped into an enormous custard pie.
7. Rather than explain how you got there.

8. These kinds of tame animals.
9. The intelligence or intention.
1. Weighty fetter, "ball and chain."
2. *The ministration . . . particular:* The particular duty
incumbent on me (as a husband).

So much unsettled. This drives me to entreat you
60 That presently you take your way for home,
And rather muse° than ask why I entreat you,   *wonder*
For my respects° are better than they seem,   *reasons*
And my appointments° have in them a need   *purposes*
Greater than shows itself at the first view
65 To you that know them not. This to my mother.
        [*He gives her a letter*]
'Twill be two days ere I shall see you, so
I leave you to your wisdom.
HELEN   Sir, I can nothing say
But that I am your most obedient servant.
BERTRAM   Come, come, no more of that.
HELEN   And ever shall
70 With true observance° seek to eke out that   *dutiful service*
Wherein toward me my homely stars° have failed   *humble birth*
To equal my great fortune.
BERTRAM   Let that go.
My haste is very great. Farewell. Hie° home.   *Hurry*
HELEN   Pray sir, your pardon.
BERTRAM   Well, what would you say?
75 HELEN   I am not worthy of the wealth I owe,°   *own*
Nor dare I say 'tis mine—and yet it is—
But like a timorous thief most fain° would steal   *gladly*
What law does vouch mine own.
BERTRAM   What would you have?
HELEN   Something, and scarce so much: nothing indeed.
80 I would not tell you what I would, my lord. Faith, yes:
Strangers and foes do sunder° and not kiss.   *separate*
BERTRAM   I pray you, stay° not, but in haste to horse.   *delay*
HELEN   I shall not break your bidding, good my lord.—
Where are my other men?—Monsieur, farewell.
        Exeunt HELEN [*and attendants at one door*]
85 BERTRAM   Go thou toward home, where I will never come
Whilst I can shake my sword or hear the drum.—
Away, and for our flight.
PAROLES   Bravely. *Coraggio!*°   *Courage*
        Exeunt [*at another door*]

3.1

Flourish of trumpets. Enter the DUKE *of Florence* [*and
the*] *two* [LORDS DUMAINE], *with a troop of soldiers*
DUKE   So that from point to point now have you heard
The fundamental reasons of this war,
Whose great decision° hath much blood let forth,   *process of resolution*
And more thirsts after.
FIRST LORD DUMAINE   Holy seems the quarrel
5 Upon your grace's part; black and fearful
On the opposer.
DUKE   Therefore we marvel much our cousin France
Would in so just a business shut his bosom
Against our borrowing prayers.°   *entreaties for aid*
SECOND LORD DUMAINE   Good my lord,
10 The reasons of our state I cannot yield

3.1 Location: Florence.

But° like a common and an outward man°	*Except / an outsider*
That the great figure° of a council frames	*image*
By self-unable motion;° therefore dare not	*inadequate guess*
Say what I think of it, since I have found	
15 Myself in my incertain grounds° to fail	*conjectures*
As often as I guessed.	

DUKE   Be it his pleasure.

FIRST LORD DUMAINE   But I am sure the younger of our nation,
 That surfeit on° their ease, will day by day   *have had too much of*
 Come here for physic.[1]

DUKE   Welcome shall they be,
20 And all the honours that can fly° from us   *proceed*
 Shall on them settle. You know your places well;
 When better fall,[2] for your avails they fell.
 Tomorrow to the field.   *Flourish. [Exeunt]*

3.2

Enter the COUNTESS [*with a letter,*] *and* [LAVATCH *the*]
clown

COUNTESS   It hath happened all as I would have had it, save that
he comes not along with her.

LAVATCH   By my troth, I take my young lord to be a very melancholy man.

5   COUNTESS   By what observance, I pray you?

LAVATCH   Why, he will look upon his boot and sing, mend° the *adjust*
ruff° and sing, ask questions and sing, pick his teeth and sing. *boot's cuff*
I know a man that had this trick of melancholy sold a goodly
manor for a song.

10   COUNTESS   Let me see what he writes, and when he means to
come.

   [*She opens the letter and reads*]

LAVATCH [*aside*]   I have no mind to Isbel since I was at court.
Our old lings[1] and our Isbels o'th' country are nothing like your
old ling and your Isbels o'th' court. The brains of my Cupid's
15   knocked out, and I begin to love as an old man loves money:
with no stomach.°   *appetite*

COUNTESS   What have we here?

LAVATCH   E'en that you have there.   *Exit*

COUNTESS [*reads the letter aloud*]   'I have sent you a daughter-in-
20   law. She hath recovered° the King and undone me. I have wed- *cured*
ded her, not bedded her, and sworn to make the "not"° eternal. *punning on "knot"*
You shall hear I am run away; know it before the report come.
If there be breadth enough in the world I will hold a long
distance. My duty to you.

25   Your unfortunate son,
           Bertram.'

This is not well, rash and unbridled boy,	
To fly the favours of so good a King,	
To pluck° his indignation on thy head	*pull down*
30 By the misprizing° of a maid too virtuous	*undervaluing*
For the contempt of empire.°	*an emperor*

---

1. Cure (through bloodletting).
2. When better places fall vacant.

3.2 Location: Roussillon, Bertram's palace.
1. Salt cod (slang for "penis").

Enter [LAVATCH *the*] *clown*

LAVATCH O madam, yonder is heavy° news within, between two   *sad*
    soldiers and my young lady.

COUNTESS What is the matter?

35 LAVATCH Nay, there is some comfort in the news, some comfort.
    Your son will not be killed so soon as I thought he would.

COUNTESS Why should he be killed?

LAVATCH So say I, madam—if he run away, as I hear he does.
    The danger is in standing to't;² that's the loss of men, though it
40   be the getting° of children. Here they come will tell you more.   *begetting*
    For my part, I only heard your son was run away.   [*Exit*]

    Enter HELEN [*with a letter,*] *and* [*the*] *two* [LORDS
    DUMAINE]

SECOND LORD DUMAINE [*to the* COUNTESS] Save you, good
    madam.

HELEN Madam, my lord is gone, for ever gone.

45 FIRST LORD DUMAINE Do not say so.

COUNTESS [*to* HELEN] Think upon patience.—Pray you, gentlemen,
    I have felt so many quirks of joy and grief
    That the first face° of neither on the start°   *appearance / suddenly*
    Can woman me unto't.³ Where is my son, I pray you?

FIRST LORD DUMAINE Madam, he's gone to serve the Duke of
50   Florence.
    We met him thitherward,° for thence we came,   *going there*
    And, after some dispatch° in hand at court,   *business*
    Thither we bend again.

HELEN Look on his letter, madam: here's my passport.°   *vagabond's license*
    [*She reads aloud*]

55   'When thou canst get the ring upon my finger, which never
    shall come off, and show me a child begotten of thy body that
    I am father to, then call me husband; but in such a "then" I
    write a "never".'
    This is a dreadful sentence.

COUNTESS Brought you this letter, gentlemen?

60 FIRST LORD DUMAINE   Ay, madam,
    And for the contents' sake are sorry for our pains.

COUNTESS I prithee, lady, have a better cheer.
    If thou engrossest° all the griefs are thine   *monopolize*
    Thou robb'st me of a moiety.° He was my son,   *share*
65   But I do wash his name out of my blood,
    And thou art all my° child.—Towards Florence is he?   *my only*

FIRST LORD DUMAINE Ay, madam.

COUNTESS   And to be a soldier?

FIRST LORD DUMAINE Such is his noble purpose, and—believe't—
    The Duke will lay upon him all the honour
    That good convenience claims.°   *That is suitable*

70 COUNTESS   Return you thither?

SECOND LORD DUMAINE Ay, madam, with the swiftest wing of speed.

HELEN 'Till I have no wife, I have nothing in France.'
    'Tis bitter.

COUNTESS Find you that there?

75 HELEN Ay, madam.

---

2. In standing one's ground (in love and war).   3. Can make me weep like a woman.

SECOND LORD DUMAINE   'Tis but the boldness of his hand,
Haply,° which his heart was not consenting to.   *Perhaps*
COUNTESS   Nothing in France until he have no wife?
There's nothing here that is too good for him
80   But only she, and she deserves a lord
That twenty such rude boys might tend upon
And call her, hourly, mistress. Who was with him?
SECOND LORD DUMAINE   A servant only, and a gentleman
Which I have sometime known.
85   COUNTESS   Paroles, was it not?
SECOND LORD DUMAINE   Ay, my good lady, he.
COUNTESS   A very tainted fellow, and full of wickedness.
My son corrupts a well-derivèd° nature   *nobly born*
With his inducement.
SECOND LORD DUMAINE   Indeed, good lady,
90   The fellow has a deal of that too much,
Which holds him much to have.[4]
COUNTESS   You're welcome, gentlemen.
I will entreat you when you see my son
To tell him that his sword can never win
The honour that he loses. More I'll entreat you
Written to bear along.
95   FIRST LORD DUMAINE   We serve you, madam,
In that and all your worthiest affairs.
COUNTESS   Not so, but° as we change° our courtesies.   *except / exchange*
Will you draw near?   *Exeunt [all but* HELEN]
HELEN   'Till I have no wife I have nothing in France.'
100   Nothing in France until he has no wife.
Thou shalt have none, Roussillon, none in France;
Then hast thou all again. Poor lord, is't I
That chase thee from thy country and expose
Those tender limbs of thine to the event°   *outcome*
105   Of the none-sparing war? And is it I
That drive thee from the sportive court, where thou
Wast shot at with fair eyes, to be the mark
Of smoky muskets? O you leaden messengers°   *(bullets)*
That ride upon the violent speed of fire,
110   Fly with false aim, cleave the still-piecing air[5]
That sings with piercing, do not touch my lord.
Whoever shoots at him, I set him there.
Whoever charges on his forward° breast,   *brave; proud; advancing*
I am the caitiff° that do hold him to't,   *wretch*
115   And though I kill him not, I am the cause
His death was so effected. Better 'twere
I met the ravin° lion when he roared   *ravenous*
With sharp constraint of hunger; better 'twere
That all the miseries which nature owes°   *human nature possesses*
120   Were mine at once. No, come thou home, Roussillon,
Whence honour but of danger wins a scar,[6]
As oft it loses all. I will be gone;
My being here it is that holds thee hence.

---

4. Has all too much persuasive power, which greatly profits him.
5. Air that is constantly repairing itself.
6. *Whence . . . scar:* From where honor at best can win a scar.

Shall I stay here to do't? No, no, although
125 The air of paradise did fan the house
And angels officed all.[7] I will be gone,
That pitiful° rumour may report my flight   *pitying*
To consolate° thine ear. Come night, end day;   *console*
For with the dark, poor thief, I'll steal away.   *Exit*

3.3

Flourish. Enter the DUKE *of Florence,* [BERTRAM,] *a*
drum[mer] *and trumpet*[ers], *soldiers, and* PAROLES

DUKE [*to* BERTRAM]   The general of our horse° thou art, and we,   *cavalry*
Great in our hope, lay° our best love and credence°   *wager / trust*
Upon thy promising fortune.
BERTRAM   Sir, it is
A charge° too heavy for my strength, but yet   *load*
5 We'll strive to bear it for your worthy sake
To th'extreme edge of hazard.°   *limit of danger*
DUKE   Then go thou forth,
And Fortune play upon thy prosperous helm
As thy auspicious mistress.
BERTRAM   This very day,
Great Mars, I put myself into thy file.°   *line of soldiers*
10 Make me but like my thoughts, and I shall prove
A lover of thy drum, hater of love.   *Exeunt*

3.4

Enter the COUNTESS *and* [REYNALDO *her*] *steward* [*with*
a letter]

COUNTESS   Alas! And would you take the letter of her?
Might you not know she would do as she has done,
By sending me a letter? Read it again.
REYNALDO [*reads the*] *letter*[1]   'I am Saint Jaques' pilgrim,[2] thither gone.
5   Ambitious love hath so in me offended
That barefoot plod I the cold ground upon
     With sainted vow my faults to have amended.
Write, write, that from the bloody course of war
     My dearest master, your dear son, may hie.°   *hurry*
10 Bless him at home in peace, whilst I from far
     His name with zealous fervour sanctify.°   *(in prayer)*
His taken° labours bid him me forgive;   *undertaken*
     I, his despiteful Juno,[3] sent him forth
From courtly friends, with camping foes to live,
15   Where death and danger dogs the heels of worth.
He is too good and fair for death and me;
Whom[4] I myself embrace to set him free.'
COUNTESS   Ah, what sharp stings are in her mildest words!
Reynaldo, you did never lack advice° so much   *discretion*
20 As letting her pass so. Had I spoke with her,
I could have well diverted her intents,
Which thus she hath prevented.

---

7. Performed all household tasks.
3.3 Location: Florence.
3.4 Location: Roussillon, Bertram's palace.
1. The letter forms a sonnet.
2. A pilgrim to the shrine of St. James (presumably in

Compostella in Spain).
3. Cruel goddess of marriage (who oppressed Hercules
by assigning him twelve supposedly impossible tasks).
4. Death (but the suggestion "Bertram" may be deliberate).

REYNALDO   Pardon me, madam.
If I had given you this at over-night°   *last night*
She might have been o'erta'en—and yet she writes
Pursuit would be but vain.

25 COUNTESS   What angel shall
Bless this unworthy husband? He cannot thrive
Unless her prayers, whom heaven delights to hear
And loves to grant, reprieve him from the wrath
Of greatest justice. Write, write, Reynaldo,
30 To this unworthy husband of his wife.
Let every word weigh heavy of° her worth,   *emphasize*
That he does weigh too light; my greatest grief,
Though little he do feel it, set down sharply.
Dispatch the most convenient messenger.
35 When haply° he shall hear that she is gone,   *Perhaps when*
He will return, and hope I may that she,
Hearing so much, will speed her foot again,
Led hither by pure love. Which of them both
Is dearest to me I have no skill in sense
40 To make distinction. Provide° this messenger.   *Make ready*
My heart is heavy and mine age is weak;
Grief would have tears, and sorrow bids me speak.   *Exeunt*

3.5

A tucket° afar off. Enter [an] old WIDOW *of Florence, her*   *trumpet call*
*daughter [*DIANA*], and* MARIANA, *with other citizens*
WIDOW   Nay, come, for if they do approach the city we shall
    lose° all the sight.   *miss*
DIANA   They say the French Count has done most honourable
    service.
5 WIDOW   It is reported that he has taken their° greatest com-   *(the Sienese)*
    mander, and that with his own hand he slew the Duke's
    brother. [*Tucket*] We have lost our labour; they are gone a con-
    trary way. Hark. You may know by their trumpets.
MARIANA   Come, let's return° again, and suffice ourselves with   *go home*
10   the report of it.—Well, Diana, take heed of this French earl.
    The honour of a maid is her name,° and no legacy is so rich as   *reputation*
    honesty.°   *chastity*
WIDOW [*to* DIANA]   I have told my neighbour how you have been
    solicited by a gentleman, his companion.
15 MARIANA   I know that knave, hang him! One Paroles. A filthy
    officer° he is in those suggestions° for the young earl. Beware   *agent / solicitings*
    of them, Diana; their promises, enticements, oaths, tokens, and
    all their engines° of lust, are not the things they go¹ under.   *devices*
    Many a maid hath been seduced by them; and the misery is,
20   example, that so terrible shows in the wreck of maidenhood,
    cannot for all that dissuade succession,° but that they are limed   *prevent it recurring*
    with the twigs² that threatens them. I hope I need not to advise
    you further, but I hope your own grace° will keep you where   *virtue*
    you are, though there were no further danger° known but the   *(pregnancy)*
25   modesty which is so lost.
DIANA   You shall not need to fear° me.   *fear for*

3.5 Location: Florence.   2. *they . . . twigs:* other virgins are entrapped (sticky
1. Concealed themselves.   lime was applied to twigs to catch birds).

Enter HELEN [*dressed as a pilgrim*]

WIDOW   I hope so. Look, here comes a pilgrim. I know she will
lie at my house; thither they send one another. I'll question
her.

30   God save you, pilgrim. Whither are you bound?
HELEN   To Saint Jaques le Grand.
Where do the palmers° lodge, I do beseech you?   *pilgrims*
WIDOW   At the 'Saint Francis' here beside the port.°   *city gate*
HELEN   Is this the way?
WIDOW   Ay, marry, is't.
[*Sound of*] *a march, far off*
35   Hark you, they come this way. If you will tarry,
Holy pilgrim, but till the troops come by,
I will conduct you where you shall be lodged,
The rather for I think I know your hostess
As ample° as myself.   *well*
40   HELEN   Is it yourself?
WIDOW   If you shall please so, pilgrim.
HELEN   I thank you, and will stay upon° your leisure.   *await*
WIDOW   You came, I think, from France?
HELEN   I did so.
WIDOW   Here you shall see a countryman of yours
That has done worthy service.
45   HELEN   His name, I pray you?
DIANA   The Count Roussillon. Know you such a one?
HELEN   But by the ear, that hears most nobly of him;
His face I know not.
DIANA   Whatsome'er° he is,   *Whatever kind of man*
He's bravely taken° here. He stole from France,   *highly regarded*
50   As 'tis reported; for the King had married him
Against his liking. Think you it is so?
HELEN   Ay, surely, mere° the truth. I know his lady.   *simply*
DIANA   There is a gentleman that serves the Count
Reports but coarsely of her.
HELEN   What's his name?
DIANA   Monsieur Paroles.
55   HELEN   O, I believe with him:
In argument of praise,[3] or to° the worth   *compared to*
Of the great Count himself, she is too mean°   *lowly*
To have her name repeated. All her deserving°   *Her only merit*
Is a reservèd honesty,° and that   *preserved chastity*
I have not heard examined.°   *questioned*
60   DIANA   Alas, poor lady.
'Tis a hard bondage to become the wife
Of a detesting lord.
WIDOW   I warr'nt, good creature, wheresoe'er she is
Her heart weighs sadly. This young maid might do her
A shrewd turn° if she pleased.   *nasty trick*
65   HELEN   How do you mean?
Maybe the amorous Count solicits her
In the unlawful purpose.
WIDOW   He does indeed,
And brokes° with all that can in such a suit   *bargains*

---

3. As a topic of praise.

Corrupt the tender honour of a maid.
70 But she is armed for him, and keeps her guard
In honestest defence.
MARIANA   The gods forbid else.
            *Enter, [with] drum and colours, [*BERTRAM,] PAROLES,*
            and the whole army
WIDOW   So, now they come.
That is Antonio, the Duke's eldest son;
That, Escalus.
HELEN   Which is the Frenchman?
75 DIANA   He—
That with the plume. 'Tis a most gallant fellow.
I would he loved his wife. If he were honester[4]
He were much goodlier. Is't not
A handsome gentleman?
80 HELEN   I like him well.
DIANA   'Tis pity he is not honest.
Yond's that same knave that leads him to those places.
Were I his lady, I would poison
That vile rascal.
HELEN   Which is he?
DIANA   That jackanapes°   *monkey*
85 With scarves. Why is he melancholy?
HELEN   Perchance he's hurt i'th' battle.
PAROLES [*aside*]   Lose our drum?[5] Well.
MARIANA   He's shrewdly° vexed at something.   *badly*
Look, he has spied us.
WIDOW [*to* PAROLES]   Marry, hang you!
90 MARIANA [*to* PAROLES]   And your courtesy,° for a ring-carrier.°   *bow / go-between*
            *Exeunt [*BERTRAM, PAROLES, *and the army]*
WIDOW   The troop is past. Come, pilgrim, I will bring you
Where you shall host.° Of enjoined penitents[6]   *lodge*
There's four or five to great Saint Jaques bound
Already at my house.
HELEN   I humbly thank you.
95 Please it° this matron and this gentle maid   *If it please*
To eat with us tonight, the charge and thanking
Shall be for me. And to requite you further,
I will bestow some precepts of° this virgin   *advice on*
Worthy the note.
WIDOW *and* MARIANA   We'll take your offer kindly.°   *Exeunt*   *gratefully*

3.6

*Enter [*BERTRAM] *and the [two Captains* DUMAINE]
SECOND LORD DUMAINE [*to* BERTRAM]   Nay, good my lord, put
him to't.° Let him have his way.   *(to the test)*
FIRST LORD DUMAINE [*to* BERTRAM]   If your lordship find him not
a hilding,° hold me no more in your respect.   *worthless wretch*
5 SECOND LORD DUMAINE [*to* BERTRAM]   On my life, my lord, a
bubble.
BERTRAM   Do you think I am so far deceived in him?
SECOND LORD DUMAINE   Believe it, my lord. In mine own direct

---

4. More honorable (and chaste).
5. A military disgrace.
6. Those sworn to a penitential pilgrimage.
3.6 Location: The Florentine camp.

knowledge—without any malice, but to speak of him as° my   *as if he were*
10 kinsman—he's a most notable coward, an infinite and endless
liar, an hourly promise-breaker, the owner of no one good
quality worthy your lordship's entertainment.°   *patronage*
FIRST LORD DUMAINE [*to* BERTRAM]   It were fit you knew him,
lest reposing° too far in his virtue, which he hath not, he might *trusting*
15 at some great and trusty business, in a main danger, fail you.
BERTRAM   I would I knew in what particular action to try him.
FIRST LORD DUMAINE   None better than to let him fetch off° his   *back*
drum, which you hear him so confidently undertake to do.
SECOND LORD DUMAINE [*to* BERTRAM]   I, with a troop of Floren-
20 tines, will suddenly surprise° him. Such I will have whom I am   *ambush*
sure he knows not from the enemy; we will bind and hood-
wink° him so, that he shall suppose no other but that he is   *blindfold*
carried into the laager° of the adversary's when we bring him   *camp*
to our own tents. Be but your lordship present at his examina-
25 tion: if he do not, for the promise of his life and in the highest
compulsion of base fear, offer to betray you, and deliver all the
intelligence° in his power against you, and that with the divine *information*
forfeit of his soul upon oath, never trust my judgement in anything.
30 FIRST LORD DUMAINE [*to* BERTRAM]   O, for the love of laughter,
let him fetch his drum. He says he has a stratagem for't. When
your lordship sees the bottom° of his success in't, and to what   *entirety*
metal this counterfeit lump of ore will be melted, if you give
him not John Drum's entertainment,[1] your inclining° cannot   *partiality*
35 be removed. Here he comes.

     Enter PAROLES

SECOND LORD DUMAINE   O [*aside*] for the love of laughter
[*aloud*] hinder not the honour of his design; let him fetch off
his drum in any hand.°   *case*
BERTRAM [*to* PAROLES]   How now, monsieur? This drum sticks
40 sorely in your disposition.°   *troubles you sorely*
FIRST LORD DUMAINE   A pox on't, let it go. 'Tis but a drum.
PAROLES   But a drum? Is't but a drum? A drum so lost! There
was excellent command: to charge in with our horse° upon our   *cavalry*
own wings° and to rend our own soldiers!   *flank units*
45 FIRST LORD DUMAINE   That was not to be blamed in the command
of the service. It was a disaster° of war that Caesar himself   *an accident*
could not have prevented, if he had been there to command.
BERTRAM   Well, we cannot greatly condemn our success.[2] Some
dishonour we had in the loss of that drum, but it is not to be
50 recovered.
PAROLES   It might have been recovered.
BERTRAM   It might, but it is not now.
PAROLES   It *is* to be recovered. But that the merit of service is
seldom attributed to the true and exact performer, I would have
55 that drum or another, or '*hic iacet*'.[3]
BERTRAM   Why, if you have a stomach,° to't, monsieur. If you   *an inclination*
think your mystery in stratagem° can bring this instrument of   *tactical skill*
honour again into his native quarter,° be magnanimous° in the   *back home / valiant*

---

1. *John Drum's entertainment*: ignominious dismissal   3. Here lies (Latin): Paroles imagines himself dying in an
(proverbial).   attempt to recover the drum.
2. The general success of the battle.

enterprise and go on. I will grace° the attempt for a worthy   *honor*
60   exploit. If you speed° well in it, the Duke shall both speak of it   *succeed*
and extend to you what further becomes his greatness, even to
the utmost syllable of your worthiness.

PAROLES   By the hand of a soldier, I will undertake it.

BERTRAM   But you must not now slumber in it.

65   PAROLES   I'll about it this evening, and I will presently pen down
my dilemmas,[4] encourage myself in my certainty, put myself
into my mortal preparation;[5] and by midnight look to hear further from me.

BERTRAM   May I be bold to acquaint his grace you are gone
70   about it?

PAROLES   I know not what the success will be, my lord, but the
attempt I vow.

BERTRAM   I know thou'rt valiant, and to the possibility° of thy   *utmost capacity*
soldiership will subscribe° for thee. Farewell.   *vouch*

75   PAROLES   I love not many words.   *Exit*

SECOND LORD DUMAINE   No more than a fish loves water. [*To*
BERTRAM] Is not this a strange fellow, my lord, that so confidently seems to undertake this business, which he knows is not
to be done? Damns himself to do, and dares better be damned
80   than to do't.

FIRST LORD DUMAINE [*to* BERTRAM]   You do not know him, my
lord, as we do. Certain it is that he will steal himself into a
man's favour, and for a week escape a great deal of discoveries,[6]
but when you find him out, you have° him ever after.   *understand*

85   BERTRAM   Why, do you think he will make no deed° at all of this   *endeavor*
that so seriously he does addess himself unto?

SECOND LORD DUMAINE   None in the world, but return with an
invention,° and clap upon you two or three probable° lies. But   *tall tale / plausible*
we have almost embosked[7] him. You shall see his fall tonight;
90   for indeed he is not for your lordship's respect.

FIRST LORD DUMAINE [*to* BERTRAM]   We'll make you some sport
with the fox ere we case° him. He was first smoked[8] by the old   *skin*
Lord Lafeu. When his disguise and he is parted, tell me what
a sprat° you shall find him, which you shall see this very night.   *tiny fish*

95   SECOND LORD DUMAINE   I must go look my twigs.° He shall be   *see to my bird trap*
caught.

BERTRAM   Your brother, he shall go along with me.

SECOND LORD DUMAINE   As't please your lordship. I'll leave you.
[*Exit*]

BERTRAM   Now will I lead you to the house, and show you
100   The lass I spoke of.

FIRST LORD DUMAINE   But you say she's honest.°   *chaste*

BERTRAM   That's all the fault. I spoke with her but once
And found her wondrous cold, but I sent to her
By this same coxcomb that we have i'th' wind°   *are stalking*
105   Tokens and letters, which she did re-send,°   *return*
And this is all I have done. She's a fair creature.
Will you go see her?

FIRST LORD DUMAINE   With all my heart, my lord.   *Exeunt*

---

4. I will immediately reflect on my difficulties.
5. Spiritual preparation for death; readying of fatal weapons.
6. *escape . . . discoveries:* largely get away with it.
7. Cornered; run to exhaustion (hunting term).
8. Forced into the open, like a fox smoked from its hole.

3.7

Enter HELEN *and the* WIDOW

HELEN   If you misdoubt° me that I am not she,   doubt
I know not how I shall assure you further
But I shall lose the grounds I work upon.[1]
WIDOW   Though my estate° be fall'n, I was well born,   fortune
5 Nothing acquainted with these businesses,
And would not put my reputation now
In any staining act.
HELEN   Nor would I wish you.
First give me trust° the Count he is my husband,   trust me that
And what to your sworn counsel° I have spoken   secrecy
10 Is so° from word to word, and then you cannot,   true
By° the good aid that I of you shall borrow,   With respect to
Err in bestowing it.
WIDOW   I should believe you,
For you have showed me that which well approves°   confirms
You're great in fortune.
HELEN   Take this purse of gold,
15 And let me buy your friendly help thus far,
Which I will over-pay, and pay again
When I have found it.° The Count he woos your daughter,   succeeded
Lays down his wanton siege before her beauty,
Resolved to carry° her. Let her in fine° consent,   conquer / the end
20 As we'll direct her how 'tis best to bear° it.   manage
Now his important blood° will naught deny   importunate passion
That she'll demand. A ring the County° wears,   Count
That downward hath succeeded in his house
From son to son some four or five descents°   generations
25 Since the first father wore it. This ring he holds
In most rich choice;° yet in his idle° fire   estimation / crazy
To buy his will° it would not seem too dear,   lust
Howe'er repented after.
WIDOW   Now I see the bottom of your purpose.
30 HELEN   You see it lawful then. It is no more
But that your daughter ere she seems as won
Desires this ring; appoints him an encounter;
In fine, delivers me to fill the time,°   keep the appointment
Herself most chastely absent. After,
35 To marry her° I'll add three thousand crowns   As her dowry
To what is passed already.
WIDOW   I have yielded.
Instruct my daughter how she shall persever,
That time and place with this deceit so lawful
May prove coherent.° Every night he comes   fitting
40 With musics of all sorts, and songs composed
To her unworthiness.[2] It nothing steads° us   avails
To chide him from our eaves, for he persists
As if his life lay on't.
HELEN   Why then tonight
Let us essay° our plot, which if it speed°   attempt / succeed

---

3.7 Location: The widow's house, Florence.   2. To my humble daughter; to persuade my daughter to
1. *But . . . upon:* Unless I give up what my plot depends   unworthy deeds.
upon (and reveal my identity to Bertram).

45   Is wicked meaning° in a lawful deed   *intention (Bertram's)*
      And lawful meaning° in a wicked act,   *intention (Helen's)*
      Where both not sin, and yet a sinful fact.³
      But let's about it.   [*Exeunt*]

4.1

Enter [SECOND LORD DUMAINE], *with five or six other soldiers, in ambush*

SECOND LORD DUMAINE   He can come no other way but by this hedge corner. When you sally° upon him, speak what terrible°   *rush / ferocious* language you will. Though you understand it not yourselves, no matter, for we must not seem to understand him, unless°   *except*
5   some one among us, whom we must produce for an interpreter.
INTERPRETER   Good captain, let me be th'interpreter.
SECOND LORD DUMAINE   Art not acquainted with him? Knows he not thy voice?
INTERPRETER   No, sir, I warrant you.
10 SECOND LORD DUMAINE   But what linsey-woolsey¹ hast thou to speak to us again?
INTERPRETER   E'en such as you speak to me.
SECOND LORD DUMAINE   He must think us some band of strangers° i'th' adversary's entertainment.° Now he hath a smack² of   *foreigners / service*
15   all neighbouring languages, therefore we must every one be a man of his own fancy. Not to know what we speak one to another, so° we seem to know, is to know straight° our purpose: *provided / suffices for* choughs'° language, gabble enough and good enough. As for   *crows* you, interpreter, you must seem very politic.° But couch,° ho!   *cunning / hide*
20   Here he comes, to beguile° two hours in a sleep, and then to   *while away* return and swear the lies he forges.
    [*They hide.*] *Enter* PAROLES. [*Clock strikes*]
PAROLES   Ten o'clock. Within these three hours 'twill be time enough to go home. What shall I say I have done? It must be a very plausive° invention that carries it. They begin to smoke°   *plausible / suspect*
25   me, and disgraces have of late knocked too often at my door. I find my tongue is too foolhardy, but my heart hath the fear of Mars before it, and of his creatures, not daring the reports of my tongue.³
SECOND LORD DUMAINE [*aside*]   This is the first truth that e'er
30   thine own tongue was guilty of.
PAROLES   What the devil should move me to undertake the recovery of this drum, being not ignorant of the impossibility, and knowing I had no such purpose? I must give myself some hurts, and say I got them in exploit. Yet slight ones will not
35   carry it. They will say, 'Came you off with so little?' And great ones I dare not give. Wherefore, what's the instance?° Tongue,   *evidence* I must put you into a butter-woman's⁴ mouth, and buy myself another of Bajazet's mute,⁵ if you prattle me into these perils.
SECOND LORD DUMAINE [*aside*]   Is it possible he should know
40   what he is, and be that he is?

---

3. Deed (as Bertram intends it).
4.1 Location: Outside the Florentine camp.
1. Hodgepodge (literally, cloth of mixed linen and wool fibers).
2. Smattering.

3. *my heart . . . tongue:* I am frightened by the god of war and his followers, not daring to do what I have boasted.
4. Proverbially talkative.
5. *of . . . mute:* from the Turkish sultan's servant (whose tongue was cut off to ensure his discretion).

PAROLES I would the cutting of my garments would serve the
turn, or the breaking of my Spanish sword.
SECOND LORD DUMAINE [*aside*] We cannot afford° you so.   *accommodate*
PAROLES Or the baring° of my beard, and to say it was in strat-   *shaving*
45 agem.
SECOND LORD DUMAINE [*aside*] 'Twould not do.
PAROLES Or to drown my clothes, and say I was stripped.
SECOND LORD DUMAINE [*aside*] Hardly serve.
PAROLES Though I swore I leapt from the window of the citadel?
50 SECOND LORD DUMAINE [*aside*] How deep?
PAROLES Thirty fathom.°   *fathom = 6 feet*
SECOND LORD DUMAINE [*aside*] Three great oaths would scarce
make that be believed.
PAROLES I would I had any drum of the enemy's. I would swear
55 I recovered it.
SECOND LORD DUMAINE [*aside*] You shall hear one anon.°   *immediately*
PAROLES A drum now of the enemy's—
    Alarum° within. [*The ambush rushes forth*]   *Call to arms*
SECOND LORD DUMAINE *Throca movousus, cargo, cargo, cargo.*
SOLDIERS [*severally*] *Cargo, cargo, cargo, villianda par corbo,*
60   *cargo.*
    [*They seize and blindfold him*]
PAROLES O ransom, ransom, do not hide mine eyes.
INTERPRETER *Boskos thromuldo boskos.*
PAROLES I know you are the Moscows° regiment,   *Russian*
    And I shall lose my life for want of language.
65 If there be here German or Dane, Low Dutch,
    Italian, or French, let him speak to me,
    I'll discover° that which shall undo the Florentine.   *reveal*
INTERPRETER *Boskos vauvado.*—
    I understand thee, and can speak thy tongue.—
70 *Kerelybonto.*—Sir,
    Betake thee to thy faith,° for seventeen poniards   *Say your prayers*
    Are at thy bosom.
PAROLES   O!
INTERPRETER   O pray, pray, pray!—
    Manka revania dulche?
SECOND LORD DUMAINE *Oscorbidulchos volivorco.*
75 INTERPRETER The general is content to spare thee yet,
    And, hoodwinked[6] as thou art, will lead thee on[7]
    To gather from thee. Haply° thou mayst inform   *Perhaps*
    Something to save thy life.
PAROLES   O let me live,
    And all the secrets of our camp I'll show,
80   Their force, their purposes; nay, I'll speak that
    Which you will wonder at.
INTERPRETER   But wilt thou faithfully?[8]
PAROLES If I do not, damn me.
INTERPRETER   *Acordo linta.*—
    Come on, thou art granted space.°   *breathing space*
    Exeunt [*all but* SECOND LORD DUMAINE *and a* SOLDIER]
    A short alarum within

---

6. Blindfolded; punning on "deceived."   8. Truthfully; loyally (ironic).
7. Will take you elsewhere; will deceive you further.

SECOND LORD DUMAINE   Go tell the Count Roussillon and my brother
85   We have caught the woodcock,[9] and will keep him muffled°   *blindfolded*
        Till we do hear from them.
SOLDIER   Captain, I will.
SECOND LORD DUMAINE   A° will betray us all unto ourselves.   *He*
        Inform on° that.   *Report*
SOLDIER   So I will, sir.
SECOND LORD DUMAINE   Till then I'll keep him dark and safely
90   locked.

Exeunt [severally]

4.2

Enter BERTRAM *and the maid called* DIANA
BERTRAM   They told me that your name was Fontibel.
DIANA   No, my good lord, Diana.
BERTRAM   Titled° goddess,   *Called*
        And worth it, with addition.[1] But, fair soul,
        In your fine frame hath love no quality?
5   If the quick° fire of youth light not your mind,   *vital*
        You are no maiden but a monument.°   *statue*
        When you are dead you should be such a one
        As you are now, for you are cold and stern,
        And now you should be as your mother was
10   When your sweet self was got.°   *begotten*
DIANA   She then was honest.
BERTRAM   So should you be.
DIANA   No.
        My mother did but duty; such, my lord,
        As you owe to your wife.
BERTRAM   No more o' that.
15   I prithee do not strive against my vows.[2]
        I was compelled to her, but I love thee
        By love's own sweet constraint, and will for ever
        Do thee all rights of service.
DIANA   Ay, so you serve us
        Till we serve you.° But when you have our roses,   *(sexually)*
20   You barely° leave our thorns to prick ourselves,   *only; exposed*
        And mock us with our bareness.
BERTRAM   How have I sworn!
DIANA   'Tis not the many oaths that makes the truth,
        But the plain single vow that is vowed true.
        What is not holy, that we swear not by,
25   But take the high'st to witness; then pray you, tell me,
        If I should swear by Jove's great attributes
        I loved you dearly, would you believe my oaths
        When I did love you ill?° This has no holding,[3]   *poorly; irreligiously*
        To swear by him whom I protest to love
30   That I will work against him. Therefore your oaths
        Are words and poor conditions but unsealed,[4]
        At least in my opinion.

9. Proverbially stupid bird.
4.2 Location: The widow's house, Florence.
1. *worth it, with addition:* you more than deserve to be called a goddess; with wordplay on "addition" as an honorific title. The goddess Diana was the patroness of chas-

tity, an "addition" that hardly bodes well for Bertram.
2. Do not quarrel with me about my wedding vows.
3. Consistency; binding power.
4. *words . . . unsealed:* contracts without the validating seal.

BERTRAM   Change it, change it.
　　Be not so holy-cruel. Love is holy,
　　And my integrity ne'er knew the crafts°   *deceptive plays*
35　That you do charge men with. Stand no more off,
　　But give thyself unto my sick desires,
　　Who then recovers. Say thou art mine, and ever
　　My love as it begins shall so persever.
DIANA　　I see that men make toys e'en such a surance⁵
40　That we'll forsake ourselves. Give me that ring.
BERTRAM　　I'll lend it thee, my dear, but have no power
　　To give it from me.
DIANA   Will you not, my lord?
BERTRAM　　It is an honour 'longing to our house,°   *family line*
　　Bequeathèd down from many ancestors,
45　Which were the greatest obloquy° i'th' world   *disgrace*
　　In me to lose.
DIANA   Mine honour's such a ring.
　　My chastity's the jewel of our house,
　　Bequeathèd down from many ancestors,
　　Which were the greatest obloquy i'th' world
50　In me to lose. Thus your own proper wisdom⁶
　　Brings in the champion Honour on my part°   *side*
　　Against your vain assault.
BERTRAM   Here, take my ring.
　　My house, mine honour, yea my life be thine,
　　And I'll be bid° by thee.   *commanded*
55　DIANA　　When midnight comes, knock at my chamber window.
　　I'll order take my mother shall not hear.
　　Now will I charge you in the bond of truth,
　　When you have conquered my yet maiden bed,
　　Remain there but an hour, nor speak to me—
60　My reasons are most strong, and you shall know them
　　When back again this ring shall be delivered—
　　And on your finger in the night I'll put
　　Another ring that, what° in time proceeds,   *whatever*
　　May token° to the future our past deeds.   *betoken*
65　Adieu till then; then, fail not. You have won
　　A wife of° me, though there my hope be done.⁷   *in; through*
BERTRAM　　A heaven on earth I have won by wooing thee.
DIANA　　For which live long to thank both heaven and me.
　　You may so in the end.   [*Exit* BERTRAM]
70　My mother told me just how he would woo,
　　As if she sat in's heart. She says all men
　　Have the like oaths. He had sworn to marry me
　　When his wife's dead; therefore I'll lie with him
　　When I am buried. Since Frenchmen are so braid,°   *deceitful*
75　Marry° that will; I live and die a maid.   *Let those marry*
　　Only, in this disguise I think't no sin
　　To cozen° him that would unjustly win.   *Exit*   *cheat*

---

5. Men treat trifles as if they were such guarantees of   7. My marriage hopes are ruined; my hope of aiding
good faith.   Helen is accomplished.
6. Wisdom in your own affairs.

4.3

Enter the two Captains [DUMAINE] *and some two or three soldiers*

FIRST LORD DUMAINE   You have not given him his mother's letter?

SECOND LORD DUMAINE   I have delivered it an hour since. There is something in't that stings his nature, for on the reading it
5 he changed almost into another man.

FIRST LORD DUMAINE   He has much worthy° blame laid upon   *deserved*
him for shaking off so good a wife and so sweet a lady.

SECOND LORD DUMAINE   Especially he hath incurred the everlasting displeasure of the King, who had even tuned his bounty
10 to sing happiness to him.[1] I will tell you a thing, but you shall
let it dwell darkly° with you.   *secretly*

FIRST LORD DUMAINE   When you have spoken it 'tis dead, and I am the grave of it.

SECOND LORD DUMAINE   He hath perverted a young gentle-
15 woman here in Florence of a most chaste renown,° and this   *reputation*
night he fleshes his will[2] in the spoil of her honour. He hath
given her his monumental° ring, and thinks himself made in   *memorial*
the unchaste composition.°   *bargain*

FIRST LORD DUMAINE   Now God delay our rebellion!° As we are   *stifle our unruliness*
20 ourselves,° what things are we.   *without divine aid*

SECOND LORD DUMAINE   Merely° our own traitors. And as in the   *Absolutely*
common course of all treasons we still° see them reveal them   *always*
selves° till they attain to their abhorred ends, so he that in this   *(their true nature)*
action contrives° against his own nobility, in his proper stream   *plots*
25 o'erflows himself.[3]

FIRST LORD DUMAINE   Is it not meant damnable° in us to be   *meant to be mortal sin*
trumpeters of our unlawful intents? We shall not then have his
company tonight?

SECOND LORD DUMAINE   Not till after midnight, for he is dieted°   *restricted*
30 to his hour.

FIRST LORD DUMAINE   That approaches apace. I would gladly
have him see his company anatomized,° that he might take a   *companion exposed*
measure of his own judgements, wherein so curiously° he had   *carefully*
set this counterfeit.[4]

35 SECOND LORD DUMAINE   We will not meddle with him° till he°   *(Paroles) / (Bertram)*
come, for his presence must be the whip of the other.

FIRST LORD DUMAINE   In the mean time, what hear you of these wars?

SECOND LORD DUMAINE   I hear there is an overture of peace.

40 FIRST LORD DUMAINE   Nay, I assure you, a peace concluded.

SECOND LORD DUMAINE   What will Count Roussillon do then?
Will he travel higher,° or return again into France?   *further*

FIRST LORD DUMAINE   I perceive by this demand you are not altogether of his council.°   *in his confidence*

45 SECOND LORD DUMAINE   Let it be forbid, sir; so should I be a
great deal of his act.[5]

FIRST LORD DUMAINE   Sir, his wife some two months since fled

---

4.3 Location: The Florentine camp.
1. Who had previously readied his generosity to make him happy (with musical metaphor).
2. He feeds his lust (hounds were "fleshed," or rewarded, with a piece of meat from their prey, or "spoil").

3. *in his . . . himself:* dissipates himself outside his appropriate channel.
4. False jewel (Paroles).
5. An accessory to his deeds.

from his house. Her pretence° is a pilgrimage to Saint Jaques   *purpose*
le Grand, which holy undertaking with most austere sancti-
50 mony° she accomplished, and there residing, the tenderness of   *piety*
her nature became as a prey to her grief : in fine,° made a groan   *conclusion*
of her last breath, and now she sings in heaven.
SECOND LORD DUMAINE   How is this justified?°   *verified*
FIRST LORD DUMAINE   The stronger part of it by her own letters,
55 which makes her story true even to the point of her death. Her
death itself, which could not be her office to say is come, was
faithfully confirmed by the rector of the place.
SECOND LORD DUMAINE   Hath the Count all this intelligence?
FIRST LORD DUMAINE   Ay, and the particular confirmations,
60 point from point, to the full arming° of the verity.°   *corroboration / truth*
SECOND LORD DUMAINE   I am heartily sorry that he'll be glad of
this.
FIRST LORD DUMAINE   How mightily sometimes we make us
comforts of our losses.
65 SECOND LORD DUMAINE   And how mightily some other times we
drown our gain in tears. The great dignity that his valour hath
here acquired for him shall at home be encountered° with a   *opposed*
shame as ample.
FIRST LORD DUMAINE   The web° of our life is of a mingled yarn,   *fabric*
70 good and ill together. Our virtues would be proud if our faults
whipped them not, and our crimes would despair if they were
not cherished by our virtues.
        Enter a [SERVANT]
How now? Where's your master?
SERVANT   He met the Duke in the street, sir, of whom he hath
75 taken a solemn leave. His lordship will° next morning for   *intends to leave*
France. The Duke hath offered him letters of commendations
to the King.
SECOND LORD DUMAINE   They shall be no more than needful
there, if they were more than they can commend.[6]
        Enter [BERTRAM]
80 FIRST LORD DUMAINE   They cannot be too sweet for the King's
tartness. Here's his lordship now. How now, my lord, is't not
after midnight?
BERTRAM   I have tonight dispatched sixteen businesses, a
month's length apiece. By an abstract of success:° I have *con-*   *list of items*
géd with° the Duke, done my adieu with his nearest, buried a   *taken leave of*
85 wife, mourned for her, writ to my lady mother I am returning,
entertained my convoy,° and between these main parcels of dis-   *arranged my transport*
patch° affected many nicer° needs. The last was the greatest,   *business / more delicate*
but that I have not ended yet.
90 SECOND LORD DUMAINE   If the business be of any difficulty, and
this morning your departure hence, it requires haste of your
lordship.
BERTRAM   I mean the business is not ended, as fearing to hear of
it hereafter. But shall we have this dialogue between the Fool
95 and the Soldier? Come, bring forth this counterfeit model,° has   *image (of soldiership)*
deceived me like a double-meaning° prophesier.   *ambiguous*
SECOND LORD DUMAINE   Bring him forth.   [*Exit one or more*]
He's sat i'th' stocks all night, poor gallant knave.

6. Even if they were more commendatory than they possibly could be.

BERTRAM   No matter, his heels have deserved it in usurping his
100   spurs[7] so long. How does he carry himself?
SECOND LORD DUMAINE   I have told your lordship already, the
stocks carry him. But to answer you as you would be under-
stood, he weeps like a wench that had shed° her milk. He hath   *spilled*
confessed himself to Morgan, whom he supposes to be a friar,
105   from the time of his remembrance[8] to this very instant° disaster   *present*
of his setting i'th' stocks. And what think you he hath con-
fessed?
BERTRAM   Nothing of me, has a?°   *he*
SECOND LORD DUMAINE   His confession is taken, and it shall be
110   read to his face. If your lordship be in't, as I believe you are,
you must have the patience to hear it.
         Enter PAROLES *[guarded and] blindfolded, with [his]*
         Interpreter
BERTRAM   A plague upon him! Muffled!° He can say nothing of   *Blindfolded*
me.
FIRST LORD DUMAINE *[aside to* BERTRAM*]*   Hush, hush.
115   SECOND LORD DUMAINE *[aside to* BERTRAM*]*   Hoodman[9] comes.
[Aloud] *Porto tartarossa.*
INTERPRETER *[to* PAROLES*]*   He calls for the tortures. What will
you say without 'em?
PAROLES   I will confess what I know without constraint. If ye
120   pinch me like a pasty° I can say no more.   *piecrust*
INTERPRETER   *Bosko chimurcho.*
SECOND LORD DUMAINE   *Boblibindo chicurmurco.*
INTERPRETER   You are a merciful general.—Our general bids
you answer to what I shall ask you out of a note.
125   PAROLES   And truly, as I hope to live.
INTERPRETER *[reads]*   'First demand of him how many horse° the   *horsemen*
Duke is strong.'—What say you to that?
PAROLES   Five or six thousand, but very weak and unserviceable.
The troops are all scattered and the commanders very poor
130   rogues, upon my reputation and credit, and as I hope to live.
INTERPRETER   Shall I set down your answer so?
PAROLES   Do. I'll take the sacrament on't, how and which way
you will.[1]
FIRST LORD DUMAINE[2] *[aside]*   All's one to him.
135   BERTRAM *[aside]*   What a past-saving slave is this!
FIRST LORD DUMAINE *[aside]*   You're deceived, my lord. This is
Monsieur Paroles, the 'gallant militarist'—that was his own
phrase—that had the whole theoric° of war in the knot of his   *theory*
scarf, and the practice in the chape° of his dagger.   *scabbard tip*
140   SECOND LORD DUMAINE *[aside]*   I will never trust a man again for
keeping his sword clean, nor believe he can have everything in
him by wearing his apparel neatly.
INTERPRETER *[to* PAROLES*]*   Well, that's set down.
PAROLES   'Five or six thousand horse,' I said—I will say true—'or
145   thereabouts' set down, for I'll speak truth.
FIRST LORD DUMAINE *[aside]*   He's very near the truth in this.

---

7. Symbolic of knightly valor.   1. According to whatever rite you prefer.
8. As far back as he can recall.   2. F attributes this remark to Bertram.
9. The blindfold player in blindman's buff.

BERTRAM [aside]   But I con him no thanks° for't in the   *feel no gratitude*
nature° he delivers it.   *manner*

PAROLES   'Poor rogues', I pray you say.

150 INTERPRETER   Well, that's set down.

PAROLES   I humbly thank you, sir. A truth's a truth. The rogues
are marvellous poor.

INTERPRETER [reads]   'Demand of him of what strength they are
a-foot.'—What say you to that?

155 PAROLES   By my troth, sir, if I were to die this present hour, I will
tell true. Let me see, Spurio a hundred and fifty; Sebastian so
many;° Corambus so many; Jaques so many; Guillaume,   *the same number*
Cosmo, Lodowick, and Gratii, two hundred fifty each; mine
own company, Chitopher, Vaumond, Bentii, two hundred fifty

160 each. So that the muster file, rotten and sound,[3] upon my life
amounts not to fifteen thousand poll,° half of the which dare   *heads*
not shake the snow from off their cassocks° lest they shake   *cloaks*
themselves to pieces.

BERTRAM [aside]   What shall be done to him?

165 FIRST LORD DUMAINE [aside]   Nothing, but let him have thanks.
[To INTERPRETER] Demand of him my condition, and what
credit I have with the Duke.

INTERPRETER [to PAROLES]   Well, that's set down. [Reads] 'You
shall demand of him, whether one Captain Dumaine be i'th'

170 camp, a Frenchman; what his reputation is with the Duke;
what his valour, honesty, and expertness in wars; or whether he
thinks it were not possible with well-weighing° sums of gold to   *heavy; persuasive*
corrupt him to a revolt.'—What say you to this? What do you
know of it?

175 PAROLES   I beseech you let me answer to the particular of the
inter'gatories.° Demand them singly.   *judicial questions*

INTERPRETER   Do you know this Captain Dumaine?

PAROLES   I know him. A was a botcher's° prentice in Paris, from   *clothes mender*
whence he was whipped for getting the sheriff's fool[4] with

180 child—a dumb innocent° that could not say him nay.   *idiot*

BERTRAM [aside to FIRST LORD DUMAINE]   Nay, by your leave,
hold your hands, though I know his brains are forfeit to the
next tile that falls.[5]

INTERPRETER   Well, is this captain in the Duke of Florence's

185 camp?

PAROLES   Upon my knowledge he is, and lousy.

FIRST LORD DUMAINE [aside]   Nay, look not so upon me: we shall
hear of your lordship anon.

INTERPRETER   What is his reputation with the Duke?

190 PAROLES   The Duke knows him for no other but a poor officer
of mine, and writ to me this other day to turn him out o'th'
band. I think I have his letter in my pocket.

INTERPRETER   Marry, we'll search.

PAROLES   In good sadness,° I do not know. Either it is there, or it   *all seriousness*

195 is upon a file with the Duke's other letters in my tent.

INTERPRETER   Here 'tis, here's a paper. Shall I read it to you?

PAROLES   I do not know if it be it or no.

BERTRAM [aside]   Our interpreter does it well.

---

3. The total roll, sick and able-bodied.   5. I know he's close to sudden death.
4. Mentally retarded girl.

FIRST LORD DUMAINE [*aside*]   Excellently.

200 INTERPRETER [*reads the letter*]   'Dian, the Count's a fool, and full of gold.'

PAROLES   That is not the Duke's letter, sir. That is an advertise-
ment° to a proper maid in Florence, one Diana, to take heed   admonition
of the allurement of one Count Roussillon, a foolish idle boy,
but for all that very ruttish.° I pray you, sir, put it up again.   lecherous

205 INTERPRETER   Nay, I'll read it first, by your favour.

PAROLES   My meaning in't, I protest, was very honest in the
behalf of the maid, for I knew the young Count to be a dangerous and lascivious boy, who is a whale to virginity, and devours
up all the fry° it finds.   tiny fish

210 BERTRAM [*aside*]   Damnable both-sides rogue.

INTERPRETER [*reads*]   'When he swears oaths, bid him drop gold,
and take it.
After he scores he never pays the score.°   bill
Half-won is match well made; match, and well make it.⁶
He ne'er pays after-debts,⁷ take it before.

215 And say a soldier, Dian, told thee this:
Men are to mell° with, boys are not to kiss.   meddle (sexually)
For count° of this, the Count's a fool, I know it,   on account
Who pays before,° but not when he does owe it.   in advance
Thine, as he vowed to thee in thine ear,

220 Paroles.'

BERTRAM [*aside*]   He shall be whipped through the army with
this rhyme in's⁸ forehead.

SECOND LORD DUMAINE [*aside*]   This is your devoted friend, sir,
the manifold linguist and the armipotent° soldier.   mighty-in-arms

225 BERTRAM [*aside*]   I could endure anything before but a cat,⁹ and
now he's a cat to me.

INTERPRETER   I perceive, sir, by the general's looks, we shall be
fain° to hang you.   obliged

PAROLES   My life, sir, in any case! Not that I am afraid to die,

230 but that, my offences being many, I would repent out the
remainder of nature.° Let me live, sir, in a dungeon, i'th' stocks,   my natural life
or anywhere, so I may live.

INTERPRETER   We'll see what may be done, so you confess freely.
Therefore once more to this Captain Dumaine. You have

235 answered to his reputation with the Duke, and to his valour.
What is his honesty?

PAROLES   He will steal, sir, an egg out of a cloister. For rapes and
ravishments he parallels Nessus.¹ He professes° not keeping of   makes a practice of
oaths; in breaking 'em he is stronger than Hercules. He will lie,

240 sir, with such volubility that you would think truth were a fool.
Drunkenness is his best virtue, for he will be swine-drunk, and
in his sleep he does little harm, save to his bedclothes; but they
about him know his conditions,° and lay him in straw. I have   habits
but little more to say, sir, of his honesty. He has everything that

245 an honest man should not have; what an honest man should
have, he has nothing.

FIRST LORD DUMAINE [*aside*]   I begin to love him for this.

---

6. Negotiating a good bargain is half the battle, so be
sure to bargain well.
7. Debts payable after receipt of goods.
8. On his (whores and their customers, when punished
by public whipping, were often made to wear signs indi-

cating their transgressions).
9. A common phobia, but "cat" is also a term of contempt, usually referring to a spiteful or sluttish woman.
1. Centaur who attempted to rape Hercules' wife.

BERTRAM [*aside*] For this description of thine honesty? A pox
upon him! For me, he's more and more a cat.

250 INTERPRETER What say you to his expertness in war?

PAROLES Faith, sir, he's led the drum before the English tragedi-
ans.[2] To belie him I will not, and more of his soldiership I
know not, except in that country he had the honour to be the
officer at a place there called Mile End,[3] to instruct for the

255 doubling of files.[4] I would do the man what honour I can, but
of this I am not certain.

FIRST LORD DUMAINE [*aside*] He hath out-villained villainy so far
that the rarity° redeems him.   *uniqueness*

BERTRAM [*aside*] A pox on him! He's a cat still.

260 INTERPRETER His qualities being at this poor price, I need not
to ask you if gold will corrupt him to revolt.

PAROLES Sir, for a *quart d'écu*[5] he will sell the fee-simple° of   *absolute ownership*
his salvation, the inheritance of it, and cut th'entail from all
remainders,[6] and a perpetual succession for it perpetually.

265 INTERPRETER What's his brother, the other Captain Dumaine?

SECOND LORD DUMAINE [*aside*] Why does he ask him of me?

INTERPRETER What's he?

PAROLES E'en a crow o'th' same nest. Not altogether so great as
the first in goodness, but greater a great deal in evil. He excels

270 his brother for a coward, yet his brother is reputed one of the
best that is. In a retreat he outruns any lackey;[7] marry, in coming on° he has the cramp.   *advancing*

INTERPRETER If your life be saved will you undertake to betray
the Florentine?

275 PAROLES Ay, and the captain of his horse, Count Roussillon.

INTERPRETER I'll whisper with the general and know his pleasure.

PAROLES I'll no more drumming. A plague of all drums! Only
to seem to deserve well, and to beguile the supposition° of that   *judgment*

280 lascivious young boy, the Count, have I run into this danger.
Yet who would have suspected an ambush where I was taken?

INTERPRETER There is no remedy, sir, but you must die. The
general says you that have so traitorously discovered° the secrets   *revealed*
of your army, and made such pestiferous reports of men very

285 nobly held,° can serve the world for no honest use; therefore   *regarded*
you must die.—Come, headsman, off with his head.

PAROLES O Lord, sir!—Let me live, or let me see my death!

INTERPRETER That shall you, and take your leave of all your
friends.

[*He unmuffles* PAROLES]

290 So, look about you. Know you any here?

BERTRAM Good morrow, noble captain.

SECOND LORD DUMAINE God bless you, Captain Paroles.

FIRST LORD DUMAINE God save you, noble captain.

SECOND LORD DUMAINE Captain, what greeting will you° to my   *do you desire*

295 Lord Lafeu? I am for° France.   *off to*

FIRST LORD DUMAINE Good captain, will you give me a copy of
the sonnet you writ to Diana in behalf of the Count Roussillon?

---

2. He's banged the drum to help advertise plays.
3. Where the London citizen militia drilled.
4. Simple drill exercise, in which the men stand in two
rows.

5. Quarter-crown, French coin of small value.
6. Prevent its succession to any future heirs.
7. Footman who runs before his master's coach.

An° I were not a very coward I'd compel it of you. But fare you   *If*
well.   *Exeunt [all but* PAROLES *and the* INTERPRETER]
300 INTERPRETER   You are undone, captain—all but your scarf ; that
has a knot on't yet.
PAROLES   Who cannot be crushed with a plot?
INTERPRETER   If you could find out a country where but women
were that had received so much shame, you might begin an
305 impudent° nation. Fare ye well, sir. I am for France too. We   *a shameless*
shall speak of you there.   *Exit*
PAROLES   Yet am I thankful. If my heart were great
'Twould burst at this. Captain I'll be no more,
But I will eat and drink and sleep as soft
310 As captain shall. Simply the thing I am
Shall make me live.° Who knows himself a braggart,   *sustain me*
Let him fear this, for it will come to pass
That every braggart shall be found an ass.
Rust, sword; cool, blushes; and Paroles live
315 Safest in shame; being fooled, by fool'ry thrive.
There's place and means for every man alive.
I'll after them.   *Exit*

4.4

Enter HELEN, WIDOW, *and* DIANA

HELEN   That you may well perceive I have not wronged you,
One of the greatest in the Christian world
Shall be my surety;° fore whose throne 'tis needful,   *guarantee*
Ere I can perfect mine intents, to kneel.
5 Time was, I did him a desirèd office
Dear almost as his life; which gratitude
Through flinty Tartar's bosom[1] would peep forth
And answer 'Thanks'. I duly am informed
His grace is at Marseilles, to which place
10 We have convenient convoy.° You must know   *suitable transport*
I am supposèd dead. The army breaking,°   *disbanding*
My husband hies him home, where, heaven aiding,
And by the leave of my good lord the King,
We'll be before our welcome.°   *before we're expected*
WIDOW   Gentle madam,
15 You never had a servant to whose trust
Your business was more welcome.
HELEN   Nor you, mistress,
Ever a friend whose thoughts more truly labour
To recompense your love. Doubt not but heaven
Hath brought me up to be your daughter's dower,
20 As it hath fated her to be my motive°   *means*
And helper to a husband. But O, strange men,
That can such sweet use make of what they hate,
When saucy trusting of the cozened° thoughts   *deceived*
Defiles the pitchy night;[2] so lust doth play
25 With what it loathes, for° that which is away.   *in the place of*
But more of this hereafter. You, Diana,

4.4 Location: The widow's house, Florence.
1. Even from a savage's stony heart (Tartars, residents of
central Asia, were considered barbaric by western Europeans).
2. *When . . . night:* When lascivious yielding to deceit
defiles even the black night.

Under my poor instructions yet must suffer
Something in my behalf.

DIANA   Let death and honesty°   *chastity*
Go with your impositions, I am yours,
Upon° your will to suffer.   *At*

30   HELEN   Yet,° I pray you.—   *A little longer*
But with that word° the time will bring on summer,   *("Yet")*
When briers shall have leaves as well as thorns
And be as sweet° as sharp. We must away,   *fragrant*
Our wagon is prepared, and time revives us.

35   All's well that ends well; still the fine's° the crown.   *end*
Whate'er the course, the end is the renown.°   *Exeunt*   *what is remembered*

4.5

Enter [LAVATCH *the*] *clown, old* [COUNTESS], *and* LAFEU

LAFEU   No, no, no, your son was misled with a snipped-taffeta[1]
fellow there, whose villainous saffron[2] would have made all the
unbaked and doughy youth of a nation in his colour. Else, your
daughter-in-law had been alive at this hour, and your son here
5   at home, more advanced by the King than by that red-tailed
humble-bee[3] I speak of.

COUNTESS   I would a° had not known him. It was the death of   *he*
the most virtuous gentlewoman that ever nature had praise for
creating. If she had partaken of my flesh and cost me the
10   dearest groans of a mother I could not have owed her a more
rooted love.

LAFEU   'Twas a good lady, 'twas a good lady. We may pick a
thousand salads ere we light on such another herb.

LAVATCH   Indeed, sir, she was the sweet marjoram of the salad,
15   or rather the herb of grace.°   *rue*

LAFEU   They are not grass,[4] you knave, they are nose-herbs.°   *fragrant plants*

LAVATCH   I am no great Nebuchadnezzar,[5] sir, I have not much
skill in grace.

LAFEU   Whether° dost thou profess thyself, a knave or a fool?   *Which*

20   LAVATCH   A fool, sir, at a woman's service, and a knave at a
man's.

LAFEU   Your distinction?

LAVATCH   I would cozen° the man of his wife and do his service.   *cheat*

LAFEU   So you were a knave at his service indeed.

25   LAVATCH   And I would give his wife my bauble,[6] sir, to do her
service.

LAFEU   I will subscribe° for thee, thou art both knave and fool.   *vouch*

LAVATCH   At your service.

LAFEU   No, no, no.

30   LAVATCH   Why, sir, if I cannot serve you I can serve as great a
prince as you are.

LAFEU   Who's that? A Frenchman?

LAVATCH   Faith, sir, a has an English name, but his phys'namy[7]
is more hotter in France than there.

35   LAFEU   What prince is that?

4.5 Location: Bertram's palace.
1. Silk slashed to show a contrasting lining.
2. Yellow dye, used for pastry; the coward's color.
3. Bumblebee (noisy, colorful, and useless).
4. Misconstruing "grace."

5. In Daniel 4:28–34, the King of Babylon who, lacking
spiritual "grace," went mad and ate "grass."
6. Fool's rod (suggesting "penis").
7. Physiognomy, face (in Elizabethan pronunciation,
punning on "name").

LAVATCH   The Black Prince,[8] sir, alias the prince of darkness, alias the devil.

LAFEU   Hold thee, there's my purse. I give thee not this to sug-
gest° thee from thy master thou talk'st of; serve him still.   *lure*

40 LAVATCH   I am a woodland fellow, sir, that always loved a great
fire, and the master I speak of ever keeps a good fire. But since
he is the prince of the world, let the nobility remain in's court;
I am for the house with the narrow gate,[9] which I take to be
too little for pomp to enter. Some that humble themselves may,
45 but the many will be too chill and tender,[1] and they'll be for
the flow'ry way that leads to the broad gate and the great fire.

LAFEU   Go thy ways. I begin to be aweary of thee, and I tell thee
so before,° because I would not fall out with thee. Go thy ways.   *in advance*
Let my horses be well looked to, without any tricks.

50 LAVATCH   If I put any tricks upon 'em, sir, they shall be jades'
tricks,[2] which are their own right by the law of nature.   *Exit*

LAFEU   A shrewd° knave and an unhappy.   *bitter*

COUNTESS   So a is. My lord that's gone made himself much sport
out of him; by his authority he remains here, which he thinks
55 is a patent° for his sauciness, and indeed he has no pace,° but   *license / restraint*
runs where he will.

LAFEU   I like him well, 'tis not amiss. And I was about to tell you,
since I heard of the good lady's death and that my lord your
son was upon his return home, I moved the King my master to
60 speak in the behalf of my daughter; which, in the minority of
them both, his majesty out of a self-gracious remembrance[3] did
first propose. His highness hath promised me to do it; and to
stop up the displeasure he hath conceived against your son,
there is no fitter matter. How does your ladyship like it?

65 COUNTESS   With very much content, my lord, and I wish it happily effected.

LAFEU   His highness comes post° from Marseilles, of as able   *speedily*
body as when he numbered thirty. A will be here tomorrow, or
I am deceived by him° that in such intelligence° hath seldom   *someone / information*
70 failed.

COUNTESS   It rejoices me that I hope I shall see him ere I die. I
have letters that my son will be here tonight. I shall beseech
your lordship to remain with me till they meet together.

LAFEU   Madam, I was thinking with what manners I might safely
75 be admitted.°   *invited to be present*

COUNTESS   You need but plead your honourable privilege.[4]

LAFEU   Lady, of that I have made a bold charter,[5] but, I thank
my God, it holds yet.

Enter [LAVATCH the] clown

LAVATCH   O madam, yonder's my lord your son with a patch of
80 velvet[6] on's face. Whether there be a scar under't or no, the
velvet knows; but 'tis a goodly patch of velvet. His left cheek is

---

8. Punning on the nickname of Edward III's eldest son, who conquered the French.
9. "Enter in at the strait gate; for it is the wide gate, and broad way that leadeth to destruction, and many there be which go in thereat. Because the gate is strait and the way narrow that leadeth unto life, and few there be that find it" (Matthew 7:13–14; see also Luke 13:24). The devil is called the "prince of this world" in John 12:31 and else-where.

1. Fainthearted and self-indulgent.
2. Contemptible tricks; playing on the sense "tricks played on horses."
3. Recollection prompted by his own graciousness.
4. Privilege due your honor.
5. Made as bold a claim as I dare.
6. Used to cover a battle wound or a facial sore from syphilis.

a cheek of two pile and a half,[7] but his right cheek is worn bare.

LAFEU   A scar nobly got, or a noble scar, is a good liv'ry° of hon-   *uniform*
our. So belike° is that.   *probably*

85   LAVATCH   But it is your carbonadoed[8] face.

LAFEU   [*to the* COUNTESS]   Let us go see your son, I pray you. I
long to talk with the young noble soldier.

LAVATCH   Faith, there's a dozen of 'em, with delicate fine hats,
and most courteous feathers, which bow the head and nod at
90   every man.   *Exeunt*

5.1

Enter HELEN, WIDOW, *and* DIANA, *with two attendants*

HELEN   But this exceeding posting° day and night   *this hasty riding*
Must wear your spirits low. We cannot help it.
But since you have made the days and nights as one
To wear° your gentle limbs in my affairs,   *tire*
5   Be bold° you do so grow in my requital°   *confident / repayment*
As nothing can unroot you.
                    Enter a GENTLE[MAN] *Austringer°*   *keeper of hawks*
                            In happy time!°   *Just at the right time*
This man may help me to his majesty's ear,
If he would spend his power.—God save you, sir.

GENTLEMAN   And you.

10   HELEN   Sir, I have seen you in the court of France.

GENTLEMAN   I have been sometimes there.

HELEN   I do presume, sir, that you are not fall'n
From the report that goes upon your goodness,
And therefore, goaded with most sharp occasions°   *urgent circumstances*
15   Which lay nice° manners by, I put° you to   *scrupulous / urge*
The use of your own virtues, for the which
I shall continue thankful.

GENTLEMAN   What's your will?

HELEN   That it will please you
To give this poor petition to the King,
20   And aid me with that store of power you have
To come into his presence.

GENTLEMAN   The King's not here.

HELEN   Not here, sir?

GENTLEMAN   Not indeed.
He hence removed° last night, and with more haste   *departed*
25   Than is his use.°   *custom*

WIDOW   Lord, how we lose our pains.

HELEN   All's well that ends well yet,
Though time seem so adverse, and means unfit.—
I do beseech you, whither is he gone?

30   GENTLEMAN   Marry, as I take it, to Roussillon,
Whither I am going.

HELEN   I do beseech you, sir,
Since you are like to see the King before me,
Commend° the paper to his gracious hand,   *Present*
Which I presume shall render you no blame,

---

7. The thickest velvet was three-piled; Lavatch invents
an imaginary next best.
8. Slashed (like meat for broiling) in battle or by a surgeon, to treat a syphilitic eruption.
5.1 Location: Marseilles.

35   But rather make you thank your pains for it.
     I will come after you with what good speed
     Our means will make us means.°   *resources will permit*
GENTLEMAN [*taking the paper*]   This I'll do for you.
HELEN   And you shall find yourself to be well thanked,
     Whate'er falls more. We must to horse again.—
40   Go, go, provide.   [*Exeunt severally*]

5.2

*Enter [*LAVATCH*] and* PAROLES[*, with a letter*]
PAROLES   Good Master Lavatch, give my Lord Lafeu this letter.
     I have ere now, sir, been better known to you, when I have held
     familiarity with fresher clothes. But I am now, sir, muddied in
     Fortune's mood, and smell somewhat strong of her strong
5   displeasure.
LAVATCH   Truly, Fortune's displeasure is but sluttish if it smell
     so strongly as thou speakest of. I will henceforth eat no fish of
     Fortune's butt'ring.° Prithee allow the wind.[1]   *prepared by Fortune*
PAROLES   Nay, you need not to stop your nose, sir, I spake but by
10   a metaphor.
LAVATCH   Indeed, sir, if your metaphor stink I will stop my nose,
     or against any man's metaphor. Prithee get thee further.
PAROLES   Pray you, sir, deliver me this paper.
LAVATCH   Foh, prithee stand away. A paper from Fortune's close-
15   stool° to give to a nobleman! Look, here he comes himself.   *toilet*
     Enter LAFEU
     Here is a pur[2] of Fortune's, sir, or of Fortune's cat—but not a
     musk-cat[3]—that has fallen into the unclean fish-pond of her
     displeasure and, as he says, is muddied withal. Pray you, sir,
     use the carp[4] as you may, for he looks like a poor, decayed,
20   ingenious, foolish, rascally knave. I do pity his distress in my
     similes of comfort, and leave him to your lordship.   *Exit*
PAROLES   My lord, I am a man whom Fortune hath cruelly
     scratched.
LAFEU   And what would you have me to do? 'Tis too late to pare
25   her nails now. Wherein have you played the knave with For-
     tune that she should scratch you, who of herself is a good lady
     and would not have knaves thrive long under her? There's a
     quart d'écu for you. Let the justices[5] make you and Fortune
     friends; I am for other business.
30   PAROLES   I beseech your honour to hear me one single word—
LAFEU   You beg a single penny more. Come, you shall ha't. Save
     your word.°   *breath*
PAROLES   My name, my good lord, is Paroles.
LAFEU   You beg more than one word[6] then. Cox my passion!°   *By God's passion*
35   Give me your hand. How does your drum?
PAROLES   O my good lord, you were the first that found me.
LAFEU   Was I, in sooth? And I was the first that lost thee.
PAROLES   It lies in you, my lord, to bring me in some grace,[7] for
     you did bring me out.°   *out of favor*

5.2 Location: Roussillon.
1. Stand downwind of me.
2. Piece of dung; cat's purr; knave (in the card game post
and pair).
3. Civet cat, a source of perfume.

4. Fish often bred in mud ponds; chatterbox.
5. Of the peace, responsible for beggars.
6. Playing on "Paroles," "words."
7. Into some favor (but Lafeu takes "grace" in its religious sense).

40 LAFEU   Out upon thee, knave! Dost thou put upon me at once
both the office of God and the devil? One brings thee in grace,
and the other brings thee out.
           [*Trumpets sound*]
The King's coming; I know by his trumpets. Sirrah, enquire
further after me. I had talk of you last night. Though you are a
45 fool and a knave, you shall eat. Go to, follow.
PAROLES   I praise God for you.   [*Exeunt*]

5.3

Flourish. Enter KING, *old* [COUNTESS], LAFEU, *and attendants*

KING   We lost a jewel of° her, and our esteem°   in / (own) worth
Was made much poorer by it. But your son,
As mad in folly, lacked the sense to know
Her estimation home.°   value to the full
COUNTESS   'Tis past, my liege,
5 And I beseech your majesty to make° it   consider
Natural rebellion done i'th' blade° of youth,   greenness
When oil and fire, too strong for reason's force,
O'erbears it and burns on.
KING   My honoured lady,
I have forgiven and forgotten all,
10 Though my revenges were high[1] bent upon him
And watched° the time to shoot.   vigilantly waited
LAFEU   This I must say—
But first I beg my pardon—the young lord
Did to his majesty, his mother, and his lady
Offence of mighty note, but to himself
15 The greatest wrong of all. He lost a wife
Whose beauty did astonish the survey°   observation
Of richest° eyes, whose words all ears took captive,   most experienced
Whose dear perfection hearts that scorned to serve
Humbly called mistress.
KING   Praising what is lost
20 Makes the remembrance dear. Well, call him hither.
We are reconciled, and the first view shall kill
All repetition.[2] Let him not ask our pardon.
The nature of his great offence is dead,
And deeper than oblivion we do bury
25 Th'incensing relics° of it. Let him approach   infuriating reminders
A stranger, no offender; and inform him
So 'tis our will he should.
ATTENDANT   I shall, my liege.   [*Exit*]
KING [*to* LAFEU]   What says he to your daughter? Have you spoke?
LAFEU   All that he is hath reference° to your highness.   is submitted
30 KING   Then shall we have a match. I have letters sent me
That sets him high in fame.
           Enter BERTRAM [*with a patch of velvet on his left cheek,
           and kneels*]
LAFEU   He looks well on't.
KING [*to* BERTRAM]   I am not a day of season,°   constant weather
For thou mayst see a sunshine and a hail

5.3 Location: Roussillon.   2. Rehearsal of past grievances.
1. To the utmost (like a taut bow).

35   In me at once. But to the brightest beams
Distracted° clouds give way; so stand thou forth.   *Agitated; broken*
The time is fair again.
BERTRAM   My high-repented blames,°   *much-repented faults*
Dear sovereign, pardon to me.
KING   All is whole.°   *healed*
Not one word more of the consumèd time.
40   Let's take the instant by the forward top,³
For we are old, and on our quick'st decrees
Th'inaudible and noiseless foot of time
Steals ere we can effect them. You remember
The daughter of this lord?
45   BERTRAM   Admiringly, my liege. At first
I stuck° my choice upon her, ere my heart   *fixed*
Durst make too bold a herald of my tongue;
Where, the impression of mine eye enfixing,⁴
Contempt his scornful perspective⁵ did lend me,
50   Which warped the line of every other favour,°   *face*
Stained a fair colour° or expressed it stolen,⁶   *complexion*
Extended or contracted all proportions
To a most hideous object. Thence it came
That she° whom all men praised and whom myself,   *(Helen)*
55   Since I have lost, have loved, was in mine eye
The dust that did offend it.
KING   Well excused.
That thou didst love her strikes some scores° away   *debits*
From the great count.° But love that comes too late,   *reckoning*
Like a remorseful° pardon slowly carried,   *compassionate; regretful*
60   To the grace-sender turns a sour offence,
Crying, 'That's good that's gone.' Our rash faults
Make trivial price of° serious things we have,   *Underestimate*
Not knowing them until we know their grave.°   *lose them forever*
Oft our displeasures, to ourselves unjust,
65   Destroy our friends and after weep° their dust.   *mourn over*
Our own love waking° cries to see what's done,   *coming to its senses*
While shameful hate sleeps out the afternoon.
Be this sweet Helen's knell, and now forget her.
Send forth your amorous token for fair Maudlin.°   *Lafeu's daughter*
70   The main consents are had, and here we'll stay
To see our widower's second marriage day.
COUNTESS⁷   Which better than the first, O dear heaven, bless!
Or ere they meet, in me, O nature, cease.⁸
LAFEU [*to* BERTRAM]   Come on, my son, in whom my house's name
75   Must be digested,⁹ give a favour from you
To sparkle in the spirits of my daughter,
That she may quickly come.
      [BERTRAM *gives* LAFEU *a ring*]
               By my old beard
And ev'ry hair that's on't, Helen that's dead
Was a sweet creature. Such a ring as this,

---

3. Let's seize time by the forelock; proverbial for "taking a present opportunity."
4. Once the impression of Lafeu's daughter was implanted in my heart.
5. Distorting optical glass.

6. Declared it artificial.
7. In F, the King speaks these lines.
8. Before they come to resemble one another, let me die.
9. Absorbed (because Maudlin is his only child and will take Bertram's name).

80 The last° that ere I took her leave at court,   *last time*
    I saw upon her finger.[1]
BERTRAM   Hers it was not.
KING Now pray you let me see it; for mine eye,
    While I was speaking, oft was fastened to't.
        [LAFEU *gives him the ring*]
    This ring was mine, and when I gave it Helen
85   I bade her, if her fortunes ever stood
    Necessitied to° help, that by this token   *In need of*
    I would relieve her. Had you that craft to reave° her   *deprive*
    Of what should stead° her most?   *aid*
BERTRAM   My gracious sovereign,
    Howe'er it pleases you to take it so,
    The ring was never hers.
90 COUNTESS   Son, on my life
    I have seen her wear it, and she reckoned it
    At her life's rate.°   *value*
LAFEU   I am sure I saw her wear it.
BERTRAM You are deceived, my lord, she never saw it.
    In Florence was it from a casement thrown me,
95   Wrapped in a paper which contained the name
    Of her that threw it. Noble she was, and thought
    I stood ingaged.[2] But when I had subscribed
    To mine own fortune,° and informed her fully   *admitted my situation*
    I could not answer in that course of honour
00   As she had made the overture, she ceased
    In heavy satisfaction,° and would never   *sad acceptance*
    Receive the ring again.
KING   Plutus° himself,   *god of riches*
    That knows the tinct and multiplying med'cine,[3]
    Hath not in nature's mystery more science°   *expertise*
05   Than I have in this ring. 'Twas mine, 'twas Helen's,
    Whoever gave it you. Then if you know
    That you are well acquainted with yourself,[4]
    Confess 'twas hers, and by what rough enforcement
    You got it from her. She called the saints to surety°   *guarantee*
10   That she would never put it from her finger
    Unless she gave it to yourself in bed,
    Where you have never come, or sent it us
    Upon° her great disaster.   *On the occasion of*
BERTRAM   She never saw it.
KING Thou speak'st it falsely, as I love mine honour,
15   And mak'st conjectural fears to come into me
    Which I would fain° shut out. If it should prove   *gladly*
    That thou art so inhuman—'twill not prove so.
    And yet I know not. Thou didst hate her deadly,
    And she is dead, which nothing but to close
20   Her eyes myself could win me to believe,
    More than to see this ring.—Take him away.
    My fore-past proofs,[5] howe'er the matter fall,°   *befalls*

---

1. See 4.2.60–64.
2. Pledged to her (alternatively, "ungaged," not promised to anyone else).
3. Alchemical elixir for turning other metals into gold.
4. That you know who you are; that you are willing to admit your actions.
5. My evidence already in hand.

Shall tax° my fears of little vanity,°   *accuse / foolishness*
Having vainly feared too little. Away with him.
We'll sift this matter further.
125 BERTRAM   If you shall prove
This ring was ever hers, you shall as easy
Prove that I husbanded her bed in Florence,
Where yet she never was.   [*Exit guarded*]
      Enter the GENTLEMAN [*Austringer with a paper*]
KING   I am wrapped in dismal thinkings.
130 GENTLEMAN   Gracious sovereign,
Whether I have been to blame or no, I know not.
Here's a petition from a Florentine
Who hath for four or five removes come short
To tender it herself.⁶ I undertook it,
135 Vanquished thereto by the fair grace and speech
Of the poor suppliant, who by this° I know   *now*
Is here attending. Her business looks° in her   *shows itself*
With an importing° visage, and she told me   *urgent*
In a sweet verbal brief° it did concern   *summary*
140 Your highness with herself.
KING [*reads*] *a letter* 'Upon his many protestations to marry me
when his wife was dead, I blush to say it, he won me. Now is
the Count Roussillon a widower, his vows are forfeited to me,⁷
and my honour's paid to him. He stole from Florence, taking
145 no leave, and I follow him to his country for justice. Grant it
me, O King! In you it best lies; otherwise a seducer flourishes
and a poor maid is undone.
                          Diana Capilet.'
LAFEU   I will buy me a son-in-law in a fair,⁸ and toll or this.⁹ I'll
150 none of him.
KING   The heavens have thought well on thee, Lafeu,
To bring forth this discov'ry.—Seek these suitors.
Go speedily and bring again the Count.   *Exit one or more*
I am afeard the life of Helen, lady,
Was foully snatched.
      Enter BERTRAM [*guarded*]
155 COUNTESS   Now justice on the doers!
KING [*to* BERTRAM]   I wonder, sir, since wives are monsters to you,
And that° you fly them as you swear them lordship,¹   *since*
Yet you desire to marry.
      Enter WIDOW *and* DIANA
                  What woman's that?
DIANA   I am, my lord, a wretched Florentine,
160 Derivèd° from the ancient Capilet.   *Descended*
My suit, as I do understand, you know,
And therefore know how far I may be pitied.
WIDOW [*to the* KING]   I am her mother, sir, whose age and
      honour
Both suffer under this complaint we bring,
165 And both° shall cease without your remedy.   *(life and honor)*
KING   Come hither, Count. Do you know these women?

---

6. *Who . . . herself:* Who has for four or five changes of   8. Notorious for unreliable merchandise.
royal residence failed to arrive in time to deliver it herself.   9. Pay a tax for the privilege of selling this one (Bertram).
7. His promises have fallen due.   1. As soon as you vow to wed them.

BERTRAM   My lord, I neither can nor will deny
But that I know them. Do they charge me further?

DIANA   Why do you look so strange upon your wife?

BERTRAM   [*to the* KING]   She's none of mine, my lord.

70 DIANA   If you shall marry
You give away this° hand, and that is mine;   (*Bertram's*)
You give away heaven's vows, and those are mine;
You give away myself, which is known mine,
For I by vow am so embodied yours
75 That she which marries you must marry me,
Either both or none.

LAFEU   [*to* BERTRAM]   Your reputation comes too short for my
daughter, you are no husband for her.

BERTRAM   [*to the* KING]   My lord, this is a fond° and desp'rate   *foolish*
creature
80 Whom sometime I have laughed with. Let your highness
Lay a more noble thought upon mine honour
Than for to think that I would sink it here.

KING   Sir, for my thoughts, you have them ill to friend[2]
Till your deeds gain them. Fairer prove your honour
Than in my thought it lies.

85 DIANA   Good my lord,
Ask him upon his oath if he does think
He had not my virginity.

KING   What sayst thou to her?

BERTRAM   She's impudent, my lord,
90 And was a common gamester° to the camp.   *prostitute*

DIANA   [*to the* KING]   He does me wrong, my lord. If I were so
He might have bought me at a common price.
Do not believe him. O behold this ring,
Whose high respect° and rich validity°   *worth / value*
95 Did lack a parallel; yet for all that
He gave it to a commoner o'th' camp,
If I be one.

COUNTESS   He blushes and 'tis hit.°   *that hit the mark*
Of six preceding ancestors, that gem;
Conferred by testament to th' sequent issue°   *following generation*
00 Hath it been owed° and worn. This is his wife.   *owned*
That ring's a thousand proofs.

KING   [*to* DIANA]   Methought you said°   (*perhaps in the letter*)
You saw one here in court could witness it.

DIANA   I did, my lord, but loath am to produce
So bad an instrument. His name's Paroles.

05 LAFEU   I saw the man today, if man he be.

KING   Find him and bring him hither.   [*Exit one*]

BERTRAM   What of him?
He's quoted° for a most perfidious slave   *noted*
With all the spots o'th' world taxed and debauched,
Whose nature sickens but to speak a truth.
10 Am I or° that or this for what he'll utter,   *either*
That will speak anything?

KING   She hath that ring of yours.

BERTRAM   I think she has. Certain it is I liked her

---

2. *you . . . friend*: they are no friends of yours.

And boarded° her i'th' wanton way of youth.   *made advances to*
She knew her distance and did angle for me,
215 Madding° my eagerness with her restraint,   *Maddening*
As all impediments in fancy's° course   *love's*
Are motives° of more fancy; and in fine°   *causes / the end*
Her inf'nite cunning with her modern° grace   *commonplace*
Subdued me to her rate.° She got the ring,   *price*
220 And I had that which my inferior might
At market price have bought.
DIANA   I must be patient.
You that have turned off a first so noble wife
May justly diet° me. I pray you yet—   *starve (of favor)*
Since you lack virtue I will lose a husband—
225 Send for your ring, I will return it home,
And give me mine again.
BERTRAM   I have it not.
KING [*to* DIANA]   What ring was yours, I pray you?
DIANA   Sir, much like the same upon your finger.
230 KING   Know you this ring? This ring was his of late.
DIANA   And this was it I gave him being abed.
KING   The story then goes false you threw it him
Out of a casement?
DIANA   I have spoke the truth.

Enter PAROLES

BERTRAM [*to the* KING]   My lord, I do confess the ring was hers.
235 KING   You boggle shrewdly;[3] every feather starts° you.—   *startles*
Is this the man you speak of ?
DIANA   Ay, my lord.
KING [*to* PAROLES]   Tell me, sirrah—but tell me true, I charge you,
Not fearing the displeasure of your master,
Which on your just proceeding I'll keep off—
240 By° him and by this woman here what know you?   *About*
PAROLES   So please your majesty, my master hath been an hon-
ourable gentleman. Tricks he hath had in him which gentle-
men have.
KING   Come, come, to th' purpose. Did he love this woman?
245 PAROLES   Faith, sir, he did love her, but how?
KING   How, I pray you?
PAROLES   He did love her, sir, as a gentleman loves a woman.
KING   How is that?
PAROLES   He loved her, sir, and loved her not.
250 KING   As thou art a knave and no knave. What an equivocal com-
panion is this!
PAROLES   I am a poor man, and at your majesty's command.
LAFEU [*to the* KING]   He's a good drum,[4] my lord, but a
naughty° orator.   *bad*
DIANA [*to* PAROLES]   Do you know he promised me marriage?
255 PAROLES   Faith, I know more than I'll speak.
KING   But wilt thou not speak all thou know'st?
PAROLES   Yes, so please your majesty. I did go between them, as
I said; but more than that, he loved her, for indeed he was mad
for her and talked of Satan and of limbo and of Furies and I

---

3. You take fright violently; you attempt to evade the point wickedly (or incompetently).

4. Capable only of noise; Lafeu probably also refers to Paroles's earlier adventures.

260 know not what. Yet I was in that° credit with them at that time _so much_
      that I knew of their going to bed and of other motions,° as _proposals_
      promising her marriage and things which would derive me ill
      will to speak of. Therefore I will not speak what I know.
   KING   Thou hast spoken all already, unless thou canst say they
265   are married. But thou art too fine° in thy evidence, therefore _hairsplitting_
      stand aside.—
      This ring you say was yours.
   DIANA   Ay, my good lord.
   KING   Where did you buy it? Or who gave it you?
   DIANA   It was not given me, nor I did not buy it.
   KING   Who lent it you?
270   DIANA   It was not lent me neither.
   KING   Where did you find it then?
   DIANA   I found it not.
   KING   If it were yours by none of all these ways,
      How could you give it him?
   DIANA   I never gave it him.
   LAFEU   [_to the_ KING]   This woman's an easy glove, my lord, she
275   goes off and on at pleasure.
   KING   [_to_ DIANA]   This ring was mine. I gave it his first wife.
   DIANA   It might be yours or hers for aught I know.
   KING   [_to attendants_]   Take her away, I do not like her now.
      To prison with her. And away with him.—
280   Unless thou tell'st me where thou hadst this ring
      Thou diest within this hour.
   DIANA   I'll never tell you.
   KING   [_to attendants_]   Take her away.
   DIANA   I'll put in bail, my liege.
   KING   I think thee now some common customer.° _prostitute_
   DIANA   By Jove, if ever I knew° man 'twas you. _(carnally)_
285   KING   Wherefore hast thou accused him all this while?
   DIANA   Because he's guilty, and he is not guilty.
      He knows I am no maid, and he'll swear to't;
      I'll swear I am a maid, and he knows not.
      Great King, I am no strumpet; by my life,
290   I am either maid or else this old man's° wife. _(Lafeu's)_
   KING   [_to attendants_]   She does abuse our ears. To prison with her.
   DIANA   Good mother, fetch my bail.   [_Exit_ WIDOW]
                              Stay, royal sir.
      The jeweller that owes° the ring is sent for, _owns_
      And he shall surety me.° But for this lord, _be my security_
295   Who hath abused me as he knows himself,
      Though yet he never harmed me, here I quit° him. _acquit; repay; leave_
      He knows himself my bed he hath defiled,
      And at that time he got his wife with child.
      Dead though she be she feels her young one kick.
300   So there's my riddle; one that's dead is quick.° _alive; pregnant_
      And now behold the meaning.
              Enter HELEN _and_ WIDOW
   KING   Is there no exorcist° _conjurer_
      Beguiles the truer office° of mine eyes? _function_
      Is't real that I see?
   HELEN   No, my good lord,

'Tis but the shadow° of a wife you see,   *ghost; imitation*
The name and not the thing.
305 BERTRAM   Both, both. O, pardon!
HELEN O, my good lord, when I was like° this maid   *in the place of*
   I found you wondrous kind. There is your ring.
   And, look you, here's your letter. This it says:
   'When from my finger you can get this ring,
310   And are by me with child,' et cetera. This is done.
   Will you be mine now you are doubly won?
BERTRAM [*to the* KING] If she, my liege, can make me know this clearly
   I'll love her dearly, ever ever dearly.
HELEN If it appear not plain and prove untrue,
315   Deadly divorce step between me and you.—
   O my dear mother, do I see you living?
LAFEU Mine eyes smell onions, I shall weep anon.
   [*To* PAROLES] Good Tom Drum, lend me a handkerchief. So,
   I thank thee. Wait on me home, I'll make sport with thee. Let
320   thy curtsies alone, they are scurvy ones.
KING [*to* HELEN] Let us from point to point this story know
   To make the even° truth in pleasure flow.   *plain*
   [*To* DIANA] If thou be'st yet a fresh uncroppèd flower,
   Choose thou thy husband and I'll pay thy dower.
325   For I can guess that by thy honest aid
   Thou kept'st a wife herself, thyself a maid.
   Of that and all the progress more and less[5]
   Resolvèdly° more leisure shall express.   *So questions are resolved*
   All yet seems well; and if it end so meet,°   *properly*
330   The bitter past, more welcome is the sweet.
      Flourish

Epilogue

The King's a beggar now the play is done.
All is well ended if this suit be won:
That you express content,° which we will pay   *(by applause)*
With strife° to please you, day exceeding° day.   *trying / after*
5   Ours be your patience then, and yours our parts:[1]
  Your gentle hands lend us, and take our hearts.   *Exeunt*

---

5. The course of events, great and small.

Epilogue
1. *Ours . . . parts:* We will wait patiently, like an audience, while you take the active part.

APPENDICES

Early Modern Map Culture

In the early modern period, maps were often considered rare and precious objects, and seeing a map could be an important and life-changing event. This was so for Richard Hakluyt, whose book *The Principal Navigations, Voiages, Traffiques and Discoveries of the English Nation* (1598–1600) was the first major collection of narratives describing England's overseas trading ventures. Hakluyt tells how, as a boy still at school in London, he visited his uncle's law chambers and saw a book of cosmography lying open there. Perceiving his nephew's interest in the maps it contained, the uncle turned to a modern map and "pointed with his wand to all the knowen Seas, Gulfs, Bayes, Straights, Capes, Rivers, Empires, Kingdomes, Dukedomes, and Territories of ech part, with declaration also of their speciall commodities and particular wants, which by the benefit of traffike, and entercourse of merchants, are plentifully supplied. From the Mappe he brought me to the Bible, and turning to the 107 Psalme, directed mee to the 23 and 24 verses, where I read, that they which go downe to the sea in ships, and occupy [work] by the great waters, they see the works of the Lord, and his woonders in the deepe." This event, Hakluyt records, made so deep an impression upon him, that he vowed he would devote his life to the study of this kind of knowledge. *The Principal Navigations* was the result, a book that mixes a concern with the profit to be made from trade and from geographical knowledge with praise for the Christian god who made the "great waters" and, in Hakluyt's view, looked with special favor on the English merchants and sailors who voyaged over them.

In the early modern period, access to maps was far less easy than it is today. Before the advent of printing in the late fifteenth century, maps were drawn and decorated by hand. Because they were rare and expensive, these medieval maps were for the most part owned by the wealthy and the powerful. Sometimes adorned with pictures of fabulous sea monsters and exotic creatures, maps often revealed the Christian worldview of those who composed them. Jerusalem appeared squarely in the middle of many maps (called T and O maps), with Asia, Africa, and Europe, representing the rest of the known world, arranged symmetrically around the Holy City. Because they had not yet been discovered by Europeans, North and South America were not depicted.

Mapping practices changed markedly during the late fifteenth and sixteenth centuries both because of the advent of print and also because European nations such as Portugal and Spain began sending ships on long sea voyages to open new trade routes to the East and, eventually, to the Americas. During this period, monarchs competed to have the best cartographers supply them with accurate maps of their realms and especially of lands in Africa, Asia, or the Americas, where they hoped to trade or plant settlements. Such knowledge was precious and jealously guarded. The value of such maps and the secrecy that surrounded them are indicated by a story published in Hakluyt's *The Principal Navigations*. An English ship had captured a Portuguese vessel in the Azores, and a map was discovered among the ship's valuable cargo, which included spices, silks, carpets, porcelain, and other exotic commercial objects. The map was "inclosed in a case of sweete Cedar wood, and lapped up almost an hundred fold in fine calicut-cloth, as though it had been some incomparable jewell." The value of the map and what explains the careful way in which it was packed lay in the particular information it afforded the English about Portuguese trading routes. More than beautiful objects, maps like this one were crucial to the international race to find safe sea routes to the most profitable trading centers in the East.

In the sixteenth century, books of maps began to be printed, making them more affordable for ordinary people, though some of these books, published as big folio volumes, remained too dear for any but wealthy patrons to buy. Yet maps were increasingly a part of daily life, and printing made many of them more accessible. Playgoers in Shakespeare's audiences must have understood in general the value and uses of maps, for they appear as props in a number of his plays. Most famously, at the beginning of *King Lear,* the old king has a map brought onstage showing the extent of his kingdom. He then points on the map to the three separate parts into which he is dividing his realm to share among his daughters. The map, often unfurled with a flourish on a table or held up for view by members of Lear's retinue, signals the crucial relationship of the land to the monarch. He is his domains, and the map signifies his possession of them. To divide the kingdom, in essence to tear apart the map, would have been judged foolish and destructive by early modern political theorists. Similarly, in *1 Henry IV,* when rebels against the sitting monarch, Henry IV, plot to overthrow him, they bring a map onstage in order to decide what part of the kingdom will be given to each rebel leader. Their proposed dismemberment of the realm signifies the danger they pose. Treasonously, they would rend in pieces the body of the commonwealth.

Maps, of course, had other uses besides signifying royal domains. In some instances, they were used pragmatically to help people find their way from one place to another. A very common kind of map, a portolan chart, depicted in minute detail the coastline of a particular body of water. Used by sailors, these maps frequently were made by people native to the region they described. Many world or regional maps, because they were beautifully decorated and embellished with vivid colors, were used for decorative purposes. John Dee, a learned adviser to Queen Elizabeth and a great book collector, wrote that some people used maps "to beautifie their Halls, Parlers, Chambers, Galeries, Studies, or Libraries." He also spoke of more scholarly uses for these objects. They could, for example, be useful aids in the study of history or geography, enabling people to locate "thinges past, as battels fought, earthquakes, heavenly fyringes, and such occurents in histories mentioned." Today we make similar use of maps, like those included in this volume, when, in reading Shakespeare's plays, we resort to a map to find out where the Battle of Agincourt took place or where Othello sailed when he left Venice for Cyprus.

This edition of the *Norton Shakespeare* includes six maps. Three of them are modern maps drawn specifically to show the location of places important to Shakespeare's plays. They depict London, the British Isles and France, and the eastern Mediterranean. This edition also includes three early modern maps that indicate some of the different kinds of printed maps that people might have seen in Shakespeare's lifetime. The earliest is a map of London that appeared in a 1574 edition of a famous German atlas, *Civitates Orbis Terrarum (Cities of the World),* compiled by George Braun with engravings by Franz Hogenberg. This remarkable atlas includes maps and information on cities throughout Europe, Asia, and North Africa; the first of its six volumes appeared in 1572, the last in 1617. Being included in the volume indicated a city's status as a recognized metropolitan center. In a charming touch, Braun added to his city maps pictures of figures in local dress. At the bottom of the map of London, for example, there are four figures who appear to represent the city's prosperous citizens. In the center, a man in a long robe holds the hand of soberly dressed matron. On either side of them are younger and more ornately dressed figures. The young man sports a long sword and a short cloak, the woman a dress with elaborate skirts. In the atlas, the map is colored, and the clothes of the two young people echo one another in shades of green and red.

At the time the map was made, London was a rapidly expanding metropolis. In 1550, it contained about 55,000 people; by 1600, it would contain nearly 200,000. The map shows the densely populated old walled city north of the Thames River, in the middle of which was Eastcheap, the commercial district where, in Shakespeare's plays about the reign of Henry IV, Falstaff holds court in a tavern. The map also shows that by 1570 London was spreading westward beyond the wall toward Westminster Palace. This medieval structure, which appears on the extreme left side of the map, was where English monarchs resided when in London and where, at the end of *2 Henry IV,* the king dies in the fabled Jerusalem Chamber of the Westminster complex. On the far right of the map, one can see the Tower of London, where Edward IV's young sons were imprisoned by Richard III, an event depicted in Shakespeare's *The Tragedy of King Richard the Third*. The map also indicates the centrality of the Thames to London's commercial life. It shows the river full of boats, some of those on the east side of London Bridge large oceangoing vessels with several masts. South of the river, where many of the most famous London theaters, including Shakespeare's Globe, were to be constructed in the 1590s, there are relatively few buildings. By 1600, this would change, as Southwark, as it was known, came to be an increasingly busy entertainment, residential, and commercial district.

The map of the Christian Holy Lands at the eastern tip of the Mediterranean Sea had extremely wide distribution because it was included in the many editions of the Geneva Bible, an English translation of the Scriptures put together by a group of Puritan scholars working in Geneva in the 1550s. Moderately sized and priced, the Geneva Bible became the most popular Bible in English until the King James version was produced in 1611. Even after that date, many ordinary Protestant readers continued to use the popular Geneva Bible, which underwent refinements, changes, and additions throughout the second half of the sixteenth century, including in 1576 a new translation of the New Testament heavily indebted to the scholarship of the French theologian Théodore de Bèze.

The map included here is from a 1592 edition of this Bible, printed in London by Christopher Barker. The map was placed before Matthew, the first book of the New Testament, and it shows places mentioned in the first four Gospels (Matthew, Mark, Luke, and John), which collectively tell of the life and deeds of Jesus. It indicates, for example, the location of Bethlehem, where he was born; Nazareth, where he spent his youth; and Cana of Galilee, where he turned water into wine at a marriage. It suggests that, to the English reader, this particular territory was overwritten by and completely intertwined with Christian history. Yet in the Mediterranean Sea, on the left of the map, several large ships are visible, and they are reminders of another fact about this region: it was a vigorous trading arena where European Christian merchants did business with local merchants—Christian, Jew, and Muslim—and with traders bringing luxury goods by overland routes from the East. A number of Shakespeare's plays are set in this complex eastern Mediterranean region where several religious traditions laid claim to its territories and many commercial powers competed for preeminence. *Pericles*, for example, has a hero who is the ruler of Tyre, a city on the upper right side of the map. In the course of his wanderings, Pericles visits many cities along the eastern coasts of the Mediterranean. The conclusion of the play, in which the hero is reunited both with his long-lost daughter and the wife he believes dead, has seemed to many critics to share in a sense of Christian miracle, despite the fact of its ostensibly pagan setting. *The Comedy of Errors* and parts of *Othello* and of *Antony and Cleopatra* are also set in the eastern Mediterranean. One of Shakespeare's earliest plays, *The Comedy of Errors*, is an urban comedy in which the protagonists are merchants deeply involved in commercial transactions. It is also the first play in which Shakespeare mentions the Americas in an extended joke in which he compares parts of a serving woman's body to the countries on a map including Ireland, France, and the Americas. In *Othello*, the eastern Mediterranean island of Cyprus is represented as a tense Christian outpost defending Venetian interests against the Muslim Turks. In *Antony and Cleopatra*, Egypt figures as the site of Eastern luxury and also of imperial conquest, an extension of the Roman Empire. Clearly, this region was to Shakespeare and his audiences one of the most complex and most highly charged areas of the world: a site of religious, commercial, and imperial significance.

The map of Great Britain and Ireland comes from a 1612 edition of John Speed's *The Theatre of the Empire of Great Britaine*, an innovative atlas containing individual maps of counties and towns in England and Wales, as well as larger maps that include Scotland and Ireland. Speed was by trade a tailor who increasingly devoted his time to the study of history and cartography. Befriended by the antiquarian scholar William Camden, he eventually won patronage from Sir Fulke Greville, who gave him a pension that allowed him to devote full time to his scholarly endeavors. *The Theatre* was one product of this newfound freedom. The map included here is one of his most ambitious. It shows the entire British Isles, nominated by Speed as "The Kingdome of Great Britaine and Ireland," though at this time Ireland was far from under the control of the English crown and Scotland was still an independent kingdom, despite the fact that James I, a Scot by birth, had tried hard to forge a formal union between England and Scotland. This problem of the relationship of the parts of the British Isles to one another, and England's assertion of power over the others, is treated in *Henry V,* in which officers from Wales, Ireland, and Scotland are sharply delineated yet all depicted as loyal subjects of the English king.

One striking aspect of Speed's map is the balance it strikes between the two capital cities, London on the left, prominently featuring the Thames and London Bridge, and Edinburgh on the right. This would have pleased James, whose interest in his native country Shakespeare played to in his writing of *Macbeth,* based on material from Scottish history. Speed's map acknowledges the claims of the monarch to the territory it depicts. In the upper left corner, the British lion and the Scottish unicorn support a roundel topped with a crown. When James became king of England in 1603, he created this merged symbol of Scottish-English unity. The motto of the Royal Order of the Garter, "Honi soit qui mal y pense" (Shamed be he who thinks ill of it), is inscribed around the circumference. In the bottom left corner of the map, another locus of authority is established. Two cherubs, one holding a compass, the other a globe, sit beneath a banner on which is inscribed the words: "Performed by John Speede." If the territory is the monarch's, the craft that depicts it belongs to the tailor turned cartographer.

Today, maps are readily available from any gasoline station or on the Internet, but in early modern England they were still rare and valuable objects that could generate great excitement in those who owned or beheld them. Along with other precious items, maps were sometimes put on display in libraries and sitting rooms, but they had functions beyond the ornamental. They helped to explain and order the world, indicating who claimed certain domains, showing where the familiar stories of the Bible or of English history occurred, helping merchants find their way to distant markets. As John Dee, the early modern map enthusiast concluded, "Some, for one purpose: and some, for an other, liketh, loveth, getteth, and useth, Mappes, Chartes, and Geographicall Globes."

JEAN E. HOWARD

Ireland, Scotland, Wales, England, and Western France: Places Important to Shakespeare's Plays.

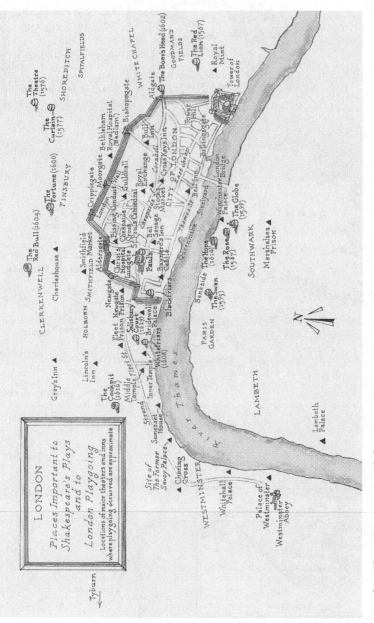

London: Places Important to Shakespeare's Plays and London Playgoing.

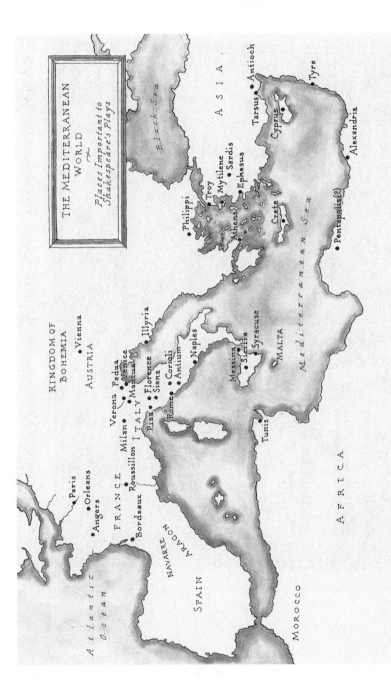

The Mediterranean World: Places Important to Shakespeare's Plays.

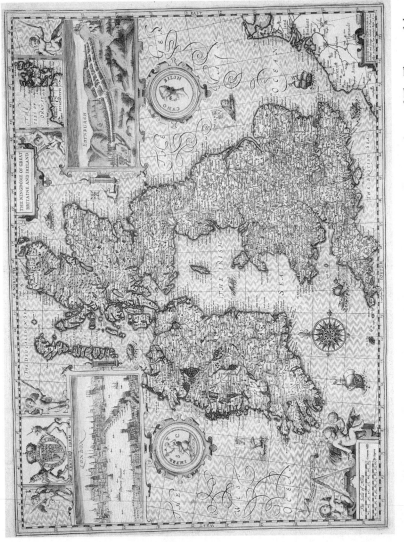

Map of the "Kingdome of Great Britaine and Ireland," from John Speed's 1612 edition of *The Theatre of the Empire of Great Britaine.*

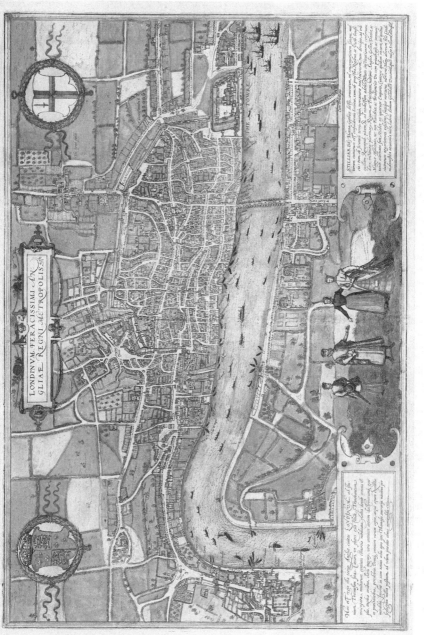

Printed map of London, 1574, taken from a German atlas of European cities by George Braun and Franz Hogenberg.

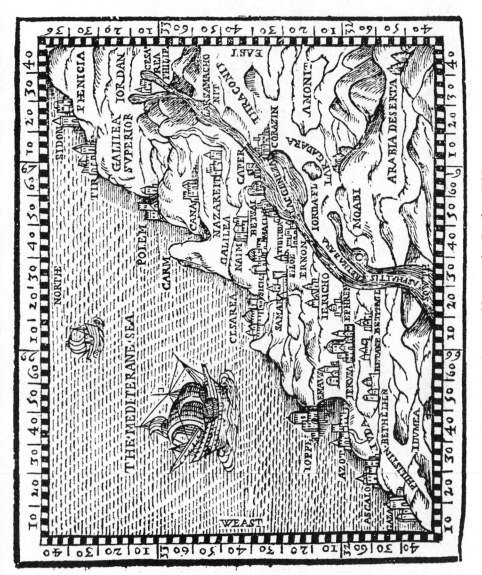

Map of the Holy Land, from the Théodore de Bèze Bible, printed in London, 1592.

Documents

This selection of documents provides a range of contemporary testimony about Shakespeare's character, his work, and the social and institutional conditions under which it was produced. In the absence of newspapers and reviewers, few references to the theater survive. The availability of such hints and fragments as are presented here serves as a mark of Shakespeare's distinction, for the theater was perceived by much of the literate population as ephemeral popular entertainment. The reports of spectators whose accounts we have are more like reviews than any other texts the period has to offer; hence the importance even of brief notes such as Nashe's or Platter's, and the particular value of extended accounts such as those of Simon Forman. The government documents included here offer a vivid glimpse of the institutional procedures by which the theater was regulated. The legal documents—a contract for the construction of a theater modeled on the Globe, and Shakespeare's will—provide the most detailed account available of the material conditions of his life and work. The extracts from criticism and other literary texts show the diversity of contemporary response to his art.

The source for each text is given at the end of the introductory headnote. Additional documents can be found at wwnorton.com/shakespeare.

WS: E. K. Chambers, *William Shakespeare: A Study of Facts and Problems*, 2 vols. (Oxford: Clarendon Press, 1930).
ES: E. K. Chambers, *The Elizabethan Stage*, 4 vols. (Oxford: Clarendon Press, 1923).

Robert Greene on Shakespeare (1592)

[Robert Greene (1560–1592), a prolific author of plays, romances, and pamphlets, attacked Shakespeare in his *Greenes, Groats-worth of Witte, bought with a million of Repentance*. Greene had studied at Cambridge, and his "M.A." was prominently displayed on his title pages. Shakespeare's lack of a university education is clearly one motive for the professional resentment of the following excerpt. Another is probably that Greene was poor and very ill and felt forsaken while writing the *Groats-worth of Witte*; the preface refers to it as his "Swanne-like song," and the narrative is framed as the repentance of a dying man. (Some scholars have held that the posthumously published work contains fabrications by a publisher attempting to capitalize on Greene's name.) The three colleagues Greene addresses are likely to be Christopher Marlowe, Thomas Nashe, and George Peele. The text is that of 1596, as printed in Alexander B. Grosart's *Life and Complete Works in Prose and Verse of Robert Greene*, vol. 12 (New York: Russell and Russell).]

> *To those Gentlemen his Quondam acquaintance,*
> *that spend their wits in making Plaies, R. G.*
> *wisheth a better exercise, and wisdome*
> *to prevent his extremities. . . .*

Base minded men al three of you, if by my miserie ye be not warned: for unto none of you (like me) fought those burres to cleave: those Puppits (I meane) that speake from our mouths, those Anticks garnisht in our colours. Is it not strange that I, to whom they al have beene beholding: is it not like that you, to whome they all have beene beholding, shall (were ye in that case that I am now) be both at once of them forsaken? Yes trust them not: for there is an upstart Crow, beautified with our feathers, that with his *Tygers heart wrapt in a Players hide,*[1] *supposes he is as well able to bumbast out a blanke verse as the best of you: and being an absolute Johannes fac totum,*[2] is in his owne conceit the onely Shake-scene in a countrie. O that I might intreate your rare wits to be imployed in more profitable courses: & let those Apes imitate your past excellence, and never more acquaint them with your admired inventions. I know the best husband[3] of you all will never prove an Usurer, and the kindest of them / all will never proove a kinde nurse: yet whilst you may, seeke you better Maisters; for it is pittie men of such rare wits, should be subject to the pleasures of such rude groomes.

Thomas Nashe on *1 Henry VI* (1592)

[Thomas Nashe (1567–1601), Greene's fellow playwright and pamphleteer, protests the attribution to himself of the *Groats-worth of Witte* in the preface to the 1592 edition of a pamphlet of his own, *Pierce Penilisse; His Supplication to the Devil.* The satire of *Pierce Penilisse* is more general and political than that of the *Groats-worth,* attacking the manners of the middle class. The allusion to the Talbot scenes of *1 Henry VI* (4.2–7) comes in a section subtitled "The defence of Playes." Talbot is supposed to have been played by Richard Burbage, later the leading actor of the Lord Chamberlain's and King's Men. The text is from Ronald B. McKerrow's 1904 edition of Nashe's *Works,* vol. 1 (London: Bullen).]

How would it have joyed brave *Talbot* (the terror of the French) to thinke that after he had lyne two hundred yeares in his Tombe, hee should triumphe againe on the Stage, and have his bones newe embalmed with the teares of ten thousand spectators at least (at severall times), who, in the Tragedian that represents his person, imagine they behold him fresh bleeding.

Francis Meres on Shakespeare (1598)

[Francis Meres (1565–1647) was educated at Cambridge and was active in London literary circles in 1597–98, after which he became a rector and schoolmaster in the country. The descriptions of Shakespeare are taken from a section on poetry in *Palladis Tamia, Wits Treasury,* a work largely consisting of translated classical quotations and exempla. Unlike the main body of the work, the subsections on poetry, painting, and music include comparisons of English artists to figures of antiquity. Meres goes on after the extract below to list Shakespeare among the best English writers for lyric, tragedy, comedy, elegy, and love poetry. The text is from Don Cameron Allen's 1933 edition of the section "Poetrie" (Urbana: University of Illinois).]

From XI

As the Greeke tongue is made famous and eloquent by *Homer, Hesiod, Euripedes, Aeschilus, Sophocles, Pindarus, Phocylides* and *Aristophanes;* and the Latine tongue by *Virgill, Ovid, Horace, Silius Italicus, Lucanus, Lucretius, Ausonius* and *Claudianus:* so the English tongue is mightily enriched, and gorgeouslie invested

---

1. A parody of *Richard Duke of York (3 Henry VI)* 1.4.138: "O tiger's heart wrapped in a woman's hide!" This obvious allusion and the following pun on Shakespeare's name make it certain that Shakespeare is the "crow" described here.
2. Jack-of-all-trades. *conceit:* imagination.
3. Steward.

in rare ornaments and resplendent abiliments by Sir *Philip Sidney, Spencer, Daniel, Drayton, Warner, Shakespeare, Marlow* and *Chapman.*

From XIV

As the soule of *Euphorbus* was thought to live in *Pythagoras:* so the sweete wittie soule of Ovid lives in mellifluous & honytongued *Shakespeare,* witnes his *Venus* and *Adonis,* his *Lucrece,* his sugred Sonnets.

From XV

As *Plautus* and *Seneca* are accounted the best for Comedy and Tragedy among the Latines: so *Shakespeare* among yᵉ English is the most excellent in both kinds for the stage; for Comedy, witnes his *Gẽtlemẽ of Verona,* his *Errors,* his *Love labors lost,* his *Love labours wonne,*[1] his *Midsummers night dreame,* & his *Merchant of Venice:* for Tragedy his *Richard the 2. Richard the 3. Henry the 4. King John, Titus Andronicus* and his *Romeo* and *Juliet.*

As *Epius Stolo* said, that the Muses would speake with *Plautus* tongue, if they would speak Latin: so I say that the Muses would speak with *Shakespeares* fine filed phrase, if they would speake English.

Thomas Platter on *Julius Caesar* (September 21, 1599)

[Thomas Platter (b. 1574), a Swiss traveler, recorded his experience at the Globe playhouse in an account of his travels. The German text is printed in *WS* 2:322.]

Den 21 Septembris nach dem Imbissessen, etwan umb zwey vhren, bin ich mitt meiner geselschaft v̈ber daz wasser gefahren, haben in dem streüwinen Dachhaus die Tragedy vom ersten Keyser Julio Caesare mitt ohngefahr 15 personen sehen gar artlich agieren; zu endt der Comedien dantzeten sie ihrem gebraucht nach gar v̈berausz zierlich, ye zwen in mannes vndt 2 in weiber kleideren angethan, wunderbahrlich mitt einanderen.

On the 21st of September after lunch, about two o'clock, I crossed the water [the Thames] with my party, and we saw the tragedy of the first emperor Julius Caesar acted very prettily in the house with the thatched roof, with about fifteen characters; at the end of the comedy, according to their custom, they danced with exceeding elegance, two each in men's and two in women's clothes, wonderfully together.

[Translated by Noah Heringman]

Gabriel Harvey on *Hamlet, Venus and Adonis,* and *The Rape of Lucrece* (1598–1603)

[Gabriel Harvey (c. 1550–1631), a scholar perhaps best remembered as the particular friend of Spenser, gave the following account of Shakespeare and other contemporaries in a long manuscript note in his copy of Speght's 1598 edition of Chaucer. The date of the note is uncertain, but internal evidence makes it highly unlikely to be later than 1603. The references to Shakespeare are brief but suggestive, and the note is useful both in providing a context for the appreciation of Shakespeare and for its characteris-

---

1. The play—or at least the title—has not survived; a bookseller's record of the title does survive, however.

tically keen assessment of the state of modern literature. The text is from G. C. Moore Smith's edition of *Gabriel Harvey's Marginalia* (Stratford-upon-Avon: Shakespeare Head Press, 1913).]

And now translated Petrarch, Ariosto, Tasso, & Bartas himself deserve curious comparison with Chaucer, Lidgate, & owre best Inglish, auncient & moderne. Amongst which, the Countesse of Pembrokes Arcadia, & the Faerie Queene ar now freshest in request: & Astrophil, & Amyntas ar none of the idlest pastimes of sum fine humanists. The Earle of Essex much commendes Albions England:[1] and not unworthily for diverse notable pageants, before, & in the Chronicle. Sum Inglish, & other Histories nowhere more sensibly described, or more inwardly discovered. The Lord Mountjoy makes the like account of Daniels peece of the Chronicle,[2] touching the Usurpation of Henrie of Bullingbrooke, which in deede is a fine, sententious, & politique peece of Poetrie: as proffitable, as pleasurable. The younger sort takes much delight in Shakespeares Venus, & Adonis: but his Lucrece, & his tragedie of Hamlet, Prince of Denmarke, have it in them, to please the wiser sort. Or such poets: or better: or none.

> Vilia miretur vulgus: mihi flavus Apollo
> Pocula Castaliæ plena ministret aquæ:[3]

quoth Sir Edward Dier, betwene jest, & earnest. Whose written devises farr excell most of the sonets, and cantos in print. His Amaryllis, & Sir Walter Raleighs Cynthia, how fine & sweet inventions? Excellent matter of emulation for Spencer, Constable, France, Watson, Daniel, Warner, Chapman, Silvester, Shakespeare, & the rest of owr florishing metricians. I looke for much, aswell in verse, as in prose, from mie two Oxford frends, Doctor Gager, & M. Hackluit: both rarely furnished for the purpose: & I have a phansie to Owens new Epigrams, as pithie as elegant, as plesant as sharp, & sumtime as weightie as breife: & amongst so manie gentle, noble, & royall spirits meethinkes I see sum heroical thing in the clowdes: mie soveraine hope. Axiophilus[4] shall forgett himself, or will remember to leave sum memorials behinde him: & to make an use of so manie rhapsodies, cantos, hymnes, odes, epigrams, sonets, & discourses, as at idle howers, or at flowing fitts he hath compiled. God knowes what is good for the world, & fitting for this age.

Contract for the Building of the Fortune Theatre (1600)

[This contract was drawn up between Philip Henslowe and Edward Alleyn, partners in the venture, and Peter Street, the carpenter (or general contractor) in charge of the construction. In fact, Alleyn seems to have put up all the money, £440 for the work specified in the contract in addition to £80 for decoration and considerable sums to acquire the lot and surrounding properties. Alleyn faced opposition from residents of the neighborhood, but he had secured the favor of key supporters, so that he was able to proceed with the construction. As the new home of the Lord Admiral's Men, the Fortune did in fact become a center of disturbances, with complaints coming to the Middlesex Bench of assaults, petty thefts, and riotous behavior. Alleyn had been the leading actor of the Lord Admiral's Men, chief competitors of the Lord Chamberlain's Men, and the Fortune was conceived to compete with the Globe, meanwhile replacing the decaying and poorly situated Rose Theatre. The contract's

---

1. By William Warner (1586).
2. *The Ciuile Wars Between the Two Houses of Lancaster and Yorke* (1595).
3. "Let what is cheap excite the marvel of the crowd; for me may golden Apollo minister full cups from the

Castalian fount" (Ovid, *Amores* 1.15.35–36, Loeb translation). These lines also appear on the title page of Shakespeare's *Venus and Adonis* (1592–93).
4. Probably Harvey himself.

descriptions and frequent references to the Globe, given this background, can be seen as providing some of our best evidence on the nature of the Globe itself. The text is reprinted in *ES*, vol. 2.]

'This Indenture made the Eighte daie of Januarye 1599,[1] and in the Twoe and Fortyth yeare of the Reigne of our sovereigne Ladie Elizabeth, by the grace of god Queene of Englande, Fraunce and Irelande, defender of the Faythe, &c. betwene Phillipp Henslowe and Edwarde Allen of the parishe of S[te] Saviours in Southwark in the Countie of Surrey, gentlemen, on thone parte, and Peeter Streete, Cittizen and Carpenter of London, on thother parte witnesseth That whereas the saide Phillipp Henslowe & Edward Allen, the daie of the date hereof, have bargayned, compounded & agreed with the saide Peter Streete ffor the erectinge, buildinge & settinge upp of a new howse and Stadge for a Plaiehouse in and uppon a certeine plott or parcell of grounde appoynted oute for that purpose, scytuate and beinge nere Goldinge lane in the parishe of S[te] Giles withoute Cripplegate of London,[2] to be by him the saide Peeter Streete or somme other sufficyent woorkmen of his provideinge and appoyntemente and att his propper costes & chardges, for the consideracion hereafter in theis presentes expressed, made, erected, builded and sett upp in manner & forme followinge (that is to saie); The frame of the saide howse to be sett square[3] and to conteine ffowerscore foote of lawfull assize everye waie square withoutt and fiftie five foote of like assize square everye waie within, with a good suer and stronge foundacion of pyles, brick, lyme and sand bothe without & within, to be wroughte one foote of assize att the leiste above the grounde; And the saide fframe to conteine three Stories in heighth, the first or lower Storie to conteine Twelve foote of lawfull assize in heighth, the second Storie Eleaven foote of lawfull assize in heigth, and the third or upper Storie to conteine Nyne foote of lawfull assize in heigth; All which Stories shall conteine Twelve foote and a halfe of lawfull assize in breadth througheoute, besides a juttey forwardes in either of the saide twoe upper Stories of Tenne ynches of lawfull assize, with ffower convenient divisions for gentlemens roomes,[4] and other sufficient and convenient divisions for Twoe pennie roomes, with necessarie seates to be placed and sett, aswell in those roomes as througheoute all the rest of the galleries of the saide howse, and with suchelike steares, conveyances & divisions withoute & within, as are made & contryved in and to the late erected Plaiehowse on the Banck in the saide parishe of S[te] Saviours called the Globe; With a Stadge and Tyreinge howse[5] to be made, erected & settupp within the saide fframe, with a shadowe or cover[6] over the saide Stadge, which Stadge shalbe placed & sett, as alsoe the stearecases of the saide fframe, in suche sorte as is prefigured in a plott[7] thereof drawen, and which Stadge shall conteine in length Fortie and Three foote of lawfull assize and in breadth to extende to the middle of the yarde[8] of the saide howse; The same Stadge to be paled in belowe with good, stronge and sufficyent newe oken bourdes, and likewise the lower Storie of the saide fframe withinside, and the same lower storie to be alsoe laide over and fenced with stronge yron pykes; And the saide Stadge to be in all other proporcions contryved and fashioned like unto the Stadge of the saide Plaie howse called the Globe; With convenient windowes and lightes glazed to the saide Tyreinge howse; And the saide fframe, Stadge and Stearecases to be covered with Tyle, and to have a sufficient gutter of lead to carrie & convey the water frome the coveringe of the saide Stadge to fall backwardes; And also all the saide fframe and the Stairecases thereof

---

1. 1600 (New Style).
2. *nere . . . London*: an area then in the northwest suburbs, literally outside Cripplegate and, like the Globe across the water, outside the jurisdiction of a City Council often inimical to the theater.
3. This square shape was unusual; the outlines of comparable theaters of the period were round or polygonal (with more than four sides).
4. Something like the VIP boxes of the present day.

5. "Attiring house," a dressing room and backstage area extending onto the rear of the stage.
6. A roof (known as "the heavens") partially covering the stage, supported by the pillars that also served as versatile pieces of scenery.
7. Plan.
8. *in breadth . . . yarde:* the stage would then extend about 27 feet into the yard, specified earlier as 55 feet square.

to be sufficyently enclosed withoute with lathe, lyme & haire, and the gentlemens roomes and Twoe pennie roomes to be seeled[9] with lathe, lyme & haire, and all the fflowers of the saide Galleries, Stories and Stadge to be bourded with good & sufficyent newe deale bourdes of the whole thicknes, wheare need shalbe; And the saide howse and other thinges beforemencioned to be made & doen to be in all other contrivitions, conveyances, fashions, thinge and thinges effected, finished and doen accordinge to the manner and fashion of the saide howse called the Globe, saveinge only that all the princypall and maine postes of the saide fframe and Stadge forwarde shalbe square and wroughte palasterwise,[1] with carved proporcions called Satiers[2] to be placed & sett on the topp of every of the same postes, and saveinge alsoe that the said Peeter Streete shall not be chardged with anie manner of pay[ntin]ge in or aboute the saide fframe howse or Stadge or anie parte thereof, nor rendringe[3] the walls within, nor seeling anie more or other roomes then the gentlemens roomes, Twoe pennie roomes and Stadge before remembred. Nowe theiruppon the saide Peeter Streete dothe covenant, promise and graunte ffor himself, his executours and administratours, to and with the saide Phillipp Henslowe and Edward Allen and either of them, and thexecutours and administratours of them and either of them, by theis presentes in manner & forme followeinge (that is to saie); That he the saide Peeter Streete, his executours or assignes, shall & will att his or their owne propper costes & chardges well, woorkmanlike & substancyallie make, erect, sett upp and fully finishe in and by all thinges, according to the true meaninge of theis presentes, with good, stronge and substancyall newe tymber and other necessarie stuff, all the saide fframe and other woorkes whatsoever in and uppon the saide plott or parcell of grounde (beinge not by anie aucthoretie restrayned, and haveinge ingres, egres & regres to doe the same) before the ffyve & twentith daie of Julie next commeinge after the date hereof; And shall alsoe at his or theire like costes and chardges provide and finde all manner of woorkmen, tymber, joystes, rafters, boordes, dores, boltes, hinges, brick, tyle, lathe, lyme, haire, sande, nailes, lade, iron, glasse, woorkmanshipp and other thinges whatsoever, which shalbe needefull, convenyent & necessarie for the saide fframe & woorkes & everie parte thereof; And shall alsoe make all the saide fframe in every poynte for Scantlinges[4] lardger and bigger in assize then the Scantlinges of the timber of the saide newe erected howse called the Globe; And alsoe that he the saide Peeter Streete shall furthwith, aswell by himself as by suche other and soemanie woorkmen as shalbe convenient & necessarie, enter into and uppon the saide buildinges and woorkes, and shall in reasonable manner proceede therein withoute anie wilfull detraccion untill the same shalbe fully effected and finished. In consideracion of all which buildinges and of all stuff & woorkemanshipp thereto belonginge, the saide Phillipp Henslowe & Edward Allen and either of them, ffor themselves, theire, and either of theire executours & administratours, doe joynctlie & severallie covenante & graunte to & with the saide Peeter Streete, his executours & administratours by theis presentes, that they the saide Phillipp Henslowe & Edward Allen or one of them, or the executours administratours or assignes of them or one of them, shall & will well & truelie paie or cawse to be paide unto the saide Peeter Streete, his executours or assignes, att the place aforesaid appoynted for the erectinge of the saide fframe, the full somme of Fower hundred & Fortie Poundes of lawfull money of Englande in manner & forme followeinge (that is to saie), att suche tyme and when as the Tymberwoork of the saide fframe shalbe rayzed & sett upp by the saide Peeter Streete his executours or assignes, or within seaven daies then next followeinge, Twoe hundred & Twentie poundes, and att suche time and when as the saide fframe & woorkes shalbe fullie effected & ffynished as is aforesaide, or within seaven daies then next followeinge, thother Twoe hundred and Twentie poundes,

---

9. Coated both on the "ceiling" (a related word) and the walls.
1. Finished in the form of pilasters, ornamental columns in the classical style.

2. Satyrs. *proporcions:* figures.
3. Plastering.
4. Prescribed dimensions of the beams.

withoute fraude or coven.[5] Provided allwaies, and it is agreed betwene the saide parties, that whatsoever somme or sommes of money the saide Phillipp Henslowe & Edward Allen or either of them, or thexecutours or assignes of them or either of them, shall lend or deliver unto the saide Peter Streete his executours or assignes, or anie other by his appoyntemente or consent, ffor or concerninge the saide woorkes or anie parte thereof or anie stuff thereto belonginge, before the raizeinge & settinge upp of the saide fframe, shalbe reputed, accepted, taken & accoumpted in parte of the firste paymente aforesaid of the saide some of Fower hundred & Fortie poundes, and all suche somme & sommes of money, as they or anie of them shall as aforesaid lend or deliver betwene the razeinge of the saide fframe & finishinge thereof and of all the rest of the saide woorkes, shalbe reputed, accepted, taken & accoumpted in parte of the laste pamente aforesaid of the same somme of Fower hundred & Fortie poundes, anie thinge abovesaid to the contrary notwithstandinge. In witnes whereof the parties abovesaid to theis presente Indentures Interchaungeably have sett theire handes and seales. Geoven[6] the daie and yeare ffirste abovewritten.

P S

Sealed and delivered by the saide Peter Streete in the presence of me William Harris Pub[lic] Scr[ivener] And me Frauncis Smyth appr[entice] to the said Scr[ivener]
[*Endorsed:*] Peater Streat ffor The Building of the Fortune.

Augustine Phillips, Francis Bacon, et al. on *Richard II* (1601)

[These extracts from testimony submitted at the Earl of Essex's trial for treason, and related documents, show that some of Essex's supporters had contracted with the Lord Chamberlain's Men to revive *Richard II*, apparently in order to provide a model for the justified deposition of a monarch and thus propitiate the coup in which Essex planned to depose Elizabeth. The play was performed on February 7, and "it was on the same day," according to E. K. Chambers, "that Essex received a summons to appear before the Privy Council. This interrupted his plans for securing possession of the Queen's person and arresting her ministers, and precipitated his futile outbreak of February 8." Augustine Phillips was one of Shakespeare's colleagues in the Lord Chamberlain's Men. Sir Edward Coke was, for a time, chief justice under King James. The last excerpt is a contemporary record of a conversation between the queen and her archivist several months after Essex was executed. The texts are from WS, vol. 2.]

From the Abstract of Evidence

The Erle of Essex is charged with high Treason, namely, That he plotted and practised with the Pope and king of Spaine for the disposing and settling to himself Aswell the Crowne of England, as of the kingdom of Ireland.

From the Examination of Augustine Phillips, February 18, 1601

The Examination of Augustyne Phillypps servant unto the L Chamberlyne and one of hys players taken the xviij[th] of Februarij 1600 upon hys oth

He sayeth that on Fryday last was sennyght or Thursday S[r] Charles Percy S[r] Josclyne Percy and the L. Montegle with some thre more spak to some of the play-

---

5. Deceit.　　　　6. Given.

ers in the presans of thys examinate to have the play of the deposyng and kyllyng of Kyng Rychard the second to be played the Saterday next promysyng to gete them xls. more then their ordynary to play yt. Wher thys Examinate and hys fellowes were determyned to have played some other play, holdyng that play of Kyng Richard to be so old & so long out of use as that they shold have small or no Company at yt. But at their request this Examinate and his fellowes were Content to play yt the Saterday and had their xls. more then their ordynary for yt and so played yt accordyngly

Augustine Phillipps

From the speech of Sir Edward Coke at Essex's trial, February 19

I protest upon my soul and conscience I doe beleeve she should not have long lived after she had been in your power. Note but the precedents of former ages, how long lived Richard the Second after he was surprised in the same manner? The pretence was alike for the removing of certain counsellors, but yet shortly after it cost him his life.

From [Francis Bacon's] "A Declaration of the . . . Treasons . . . by Robert late Earle of Essex"

The afternoone before the rebellion, Merricke,[1] with a great company of others, that afterwards were all in the action, had procured to bee played before them, the play of deposing King Richard the second. Neither was it casuall, but a play bespoken by Merrick. And not so onely, but when it was told him by one of the players, that the play was olde, and they should have losse in playing it, because fewe would come to it: there was fourty shillings extraordinarie given to play it, and so thereupon playd it was. So earnest hee was to satisfie his eyes with the sight of that tragedie which hee thought soone after his lord should bring from the stage to the state, but that God turned it upon their owne heads.

From a Memorandum in the Lambard family manuscript, August 4

. . . so her Majestie fell upon[2] the reign of King Richard II. saying, 'I am Richard II. know ye not that?'

W.L. 'Such a wicked imagination was determined and attempted by a most unkind Gent. the most adorned creature that ever your Majestie made.'

Her Majestie. 'He that will forget God, will also forget his benefactors; this tragedy was played 40tie times in open streets and houses.'

John Manningham on Twelfth Night and Richard III (1602)

[John Manningham (d. 1622) kept a diary during his time as a law student at the Middle Temple, recording the witticisms of his colleagues and a rich variety of anecdotes. The vibrant and boisterous life of the Inns of Court is also illustrated by the Gesta Grayorum (see above). The February entry describes the festivities organized for Candlemas Day at the Middle Temple, while the second recounts an anecdote related to Manningham by one Mr. Touse (this name is difficult to read in the manuscript). As with all the documents in this section, any date before March 25 is assigned to the following year according to our calendar, so that 1601 here becomes 1602 (New Style).

---

1. Sir Gilly Merrick, one of Essex's supporters, was later tried separately for treason.
2. Came across (in reading). The memorandum describes a scene in which the queen is reading over the archives that have been in the keeping of her interlocutor, William Lambard.

The text is from the 1976 edition of Robert Sorlien (Hanover, N.H.: University Press of New England).]

Febr. 1601

2. At our feast wee had a play called "Twelve night, or what you will"; much like the commedy of errores, or Menechmi[1] in Plautus, but most like and neere to that in Italian called Inganni.[2] A good practise in it to make the steward beleeve his Lady widdowe[3] was in Love with him, by counterfayting a letter, as from his Lady, in generall termes, telling him what shee liked best in him, and prescribing his gesture in smiling, his apparraile, &c., and then when he came to practise, making him beleeve they tooke him to be mad.

Marche. 1601

13. . . . Upon a tyme when Burbidge played Rich[ard] 3. there was a Citizen grewe soe farr in liking with him, that before shee went from the play shee appointed him to come that night unto hir by the name of Ri[chard] the 3. Shakespeare, overhearing their conclusion, went before, was intertained, and at his game ere Burbidge came. Then message being brought that Richard the 3[d]. was at the dore, Shakespeare caused returne to be made that William the Conquerour was before Rich[ard] the 3. Shakespeare's name William. (Mr. Touse.)

Letters Patent Formalizing the Adoption of the Lord Chamberlain's Men as the King's Men (May 19, 1603)

[James I issued the warrant ordering this patent shortly after his coronation, enhancing the status of Shakespeare's company. As retainers of the royal household with the title of Grooms of the Chamber, they performed at the court with increasing frequency (177 times between 1603 and 1616) and assisted occasionally with other court functions; but, more important, they acted throughout the kingdom under the authority of the royal patent, whose scope the forceful wording below makes clear. The patent, bearing the Great Seal, was issued May 19 as ordered in the warrant of May 17. There is some evidence to suggest that James was particularly taken with Shakespeare's poetry, and the playwright's valorization of James's ancestry (as originating with Banquo) in *Macbeth* certainly suggests that Shakespeare cultivated his esteem. The text is from *ES*, vol. 2.]

Commissio specialis pro Laurencio Fletcher & Willelmo Shackespeare et aliis[2]   James by the grace of god &c. To all Justices, Maiors, Sheriffes, Constables, hedborowes,[1] and other our Officers and lovinge Subjectes greetinge. Knowe yee that Wee of our speciall grace, certeine knowledge, & mere motion[3] have licenced and aucthorized and by theise presentes[4] doe licence and aucthorize theise our Servauntes Lawrence Fletcher, William Shakespeare, Richard Burbage, Augustyne Phillippes, John Heninges, Henrie Condell, William Sly, Robert Armyn, Richard Cowly, and the rest of theire Assosiates freely to use and exercise the Arte and faculty of playinge

---

1. Source for *The Comedy of Errors.*
2. The two plays with this exact title (1562 and 1592) seem less likely to be "most like" *Twelfth Night* than another Italian play, *Ingannati* (1537), which has characters named Fabio and Malevolti and makes reference to Twelfth Night (Epiphany).
3. Olivia is not a widow in the version of Shakespeare's play that has come down to us, though she is

so described in one of Shakespeare's principal sources for the play.
1. A parish officer similar to a petty constable.
2. *Commissio . . . aliis:* By special commission on behalf of . . . and others.
3. Inclination, desire.
4. The present document.

Comedies, Tragedies, histories, Enterludes, moralls,[5] pastoralls, Stageplaies, and Suche others like as theie have alreadie studied or hereafter shall use or studie, aswell for the recreation of our lovinge Subjectes, as for our Solace and pleasure when wee shall thincke good to see them, duringe our pleasure. And the said Commedies, tragedies, histories, Enterludes, Morralles, Pastoralls, Stageplayes, and suche like to shewe and exercise publiquely to theire best Commoditie,[6] when the infection of the plague shall decrease, aswell within theire nowe usual howse called the Globe within our County of Surrey, as alsoe within anie towne halls or Moute halls[7] or other conveniente places within the liberties and freedome of anie other Cittie, universitie, towne, or Boroughe whatsoever within our said Realmes and domynions. Willinge and Commaundinge you and everie of you, as you tender our pleasure, not onelie to permitt and suffer them herein without anie your lettes hindrances or molestacions during our said pleasure, but alsoe to be aidinge and assistinge to them, yf anie wronge be to them offered, And to allowe them such former Curtesies as hath bene given to men of theire place and quallitie,[8] and alsoe what further favour you shall shewe to theise our Servauntes for our sake wee shall take kindlie at your handes. In wytnesse whereof &c. witnesse our selfe at Westminster the nyntenth day of May

per breve de privato sigillo[9] &c.

Master of the Wardrobe's Account (March 1604)

[This entry offers us a rare glimpse of the players in the entourage of King James, sporting festive regalia in their capacity as Grooms of the Chamber. The royal procession took place March 15, 1604. The text is from *WS*, vol. 2.]

Red Clothe bought of sondrie persons and given by his Majestie to diverse persons against[1] his Majesties sayd royall proceeding through the Citie of London, viz.:— . . .

The Chamber . . .	
Fawkeners[2] &c. &c.	Red cloth
William Shakespeare	iiii yardes di.
Augustine Phillipps	"
Lawrence Fletcher	"
John Hemminges	"
Richard Burbidge	"
William Slye	"
Robert Armyn	"
Henry Cundell	"
Richard Cowley	"

Simon Forman on *Macbeth, Cymbeline,* and *The Winter's Tale* (1611)

[Simon Forman (1552–1611) was a largely self-educated physician and astrologer who rose from humble beginnings to establish a successful London practice. A large parcel of his manuscripts, including scientific and autobiographical material as well as the diary from which this account of the plays is taken, has survived, making his life one of the best-documented Elizabethan lives. These manuscripts provide

5. Morality plays.
6. Advantage.
7. Council chambers.
8. Profession.
9. In sum, from the privy seal.

1. For.
2. Obsolete form of "falconers," very likely the men who trained the falcons used for James's fowl-hunting expeditions. The falconers might owe their place in the retinue to James's well-known passion for hunting.

detailed information about Forman's many sidelines, such as the manufacture of tal-
ismans, alchemy, and necromancy, as well about his sex life. The text is from *WS*,
vol. 2.]

The Bocke of Plaies and Notes therof per formane for Common Pollicie[1]

In Mackbeth at the Glob, 1610 ⟨1611⟩, the 20 of Aprill ♄ (Saturday), ther was
to be observed, firste, howe Mackbeth and Bancko, 2 noble men of Scotland, Ridinge
thorowe a wod, the ⟨r⟩ stode before them 3 women feiries or Nimphes, And saluted
Mackbeth, sayinge, 3 tyms unto him, haille Mackbeth, king of Codon;[2] for thou shalt
be a kinge, but shalt beget No kinges, &c. Then said Bancko, What all to Mackbeth
And nothing to me. Yes, said the nimphes, haille to thee Bancko, thou shalt beget
kinges, yet be no kinge. And so they departed & cam to the Courte of Scotland to
Dunkin king of Scotes, and yt was in the dais of Edward the Confessor. And Dunkin
bad them both kindly wellcome, And made Mackbeth forth with Prince of Northumberland,[3] and sent him hom to his own castell, and appointed Mackbeth to provid
for him, for he would sup with him the next dai at night, & did soe. And Mackebeth
contrived to kill Dunkin, & thorowe the persuasion of his wife did that night Murder the kinge in his own Castell, beinge his guest. And ther were many prodigies seen
that night & the dai before. And when Mack Beth had murdred the kinge, the blod
on his handes could not be washed of by Any meanes, nor from his wives handes,
which handled the bloddi daggers in hiding them, By which means they became both
moch amazed & Affronted. The murder being knowen, Dunkins 2 sonns fled, the on
to England, the ⟨other to⟩ Walles, to save them selves, they being fled, they were supposed guilty of the murder of their father, which was nothinge so. Then was Mackbeth crowned kinge, and then he for feare of Banko, his old companion, that he
should beget kinges but be no kinge him selfe, he contrived the death of Banko, and
caused him to be Murdred on the way as he Rode. The next night, beinge at supper
with his noble men whom he had bid to a feaste to the which also Banco should have
com, he began to speake of Noble Banco, and to wish that he wer ther. And as he
thus did, standing up to drincke a Carouse to him, the ghoste of Banco came and
sate down in his cheier behind him. And he turninge About to sit down Again sawe
the goste of Banco, which fronted him so, that he fell into a great passion of fear and
fury, Utterynge many wordes about his murder, by which, when they hard that Banco
was Murdred they Suspected Mackbet.

Then MackDove fled to England to the kinges sonn, And soe they Raised an
Army, And cam into Scotland, and at Dunston Anyse overthrue Mackbet. In the
meantyme whille Macdovee was in England, Mackbet slewe Mackdoves wife &
children, and after in the battelle Mackdove slewe Mackbet.

Observe Also howe Mackbetes quen did Rise in the night in her slepe, & walke
and talked and confessed all, & the docter noted her wordes.

Of Cimbalin king of England.

Remember also the storri of Cymbalin king of England, in Lucius tyme, howe
Lucius Cam from Octavus Cesar for Tribut, and being denied, after sent Lucius
with a greate Arme of Souldiars who landed at Milford haven, and Affter wer vanquished by Cimbalin, and Lucius taken prisoner, and all by means of 3 outlawes,
of the which 2 of them were the sonns of Cimbalim, stolen from him when they
were but 2 yers old by an old man whom Cymbalin banished, and he kept them as
his own sonns 20 yers with him in A cave. And howe ⟨one⟩ of them slewe Clotan,
that was the quens sonn, goinge to Milford haven to sek the love of Innogen the

---

1. *Common Pollicie:* practical use. Forman's title for
his notes on plays is not printed in Chambers, but
interpolated here from G. Blakemore Evans's transcription in the *Riverside Shakespeare*.

2. Cawdor.
3. Probably Forman's error; Duncan gives Macbeth
the title Thane of Cawdor. Duncan's son Malcolm is
the Prince of Northumberland.

kinges daughter, whom he had banished also for lovinge his daughter,[4] and howe the Italian that cam from her love conveied him selfe into A Cheste, and said yt was a chest of plate sent from her love & others, to be presented to the kinge. And in the depest of the night, she being aslepe, he opened the cheste, & cam forth of yt, And vewed her in her bed, and the markes of her body, & toke awai her braslet, & after Accused her of adultery to her love, &c. And in thend howe he came with the Romains into England & was taken prisoner, and after Reveled to Innogen, Who had turned her self into mans apparrell & fled to mete her love at Milford haven, & chanchsed to fall on the Cave in the wodes wher her 2 brothers were, & howe by eating a sleping Dram they thought she had bin deed, & laid her in the wodes, & the body of Cloten by her, in her loves apparrell that he left behind him, & howe she was found by Lucius, &c.

In the Winters Talle at the glob 1611 the 15 of maye ☿ ⟨Wednesday⟩.

Observe ther howe Lyontes the kinge of Cicillia was overcom with Jelosy of his wife with the kinge of Bohemia his frind that came to see him, and howe he contrived his death and wold have had his cup berer to have poisoned, who gave the king of Bohemia warning therof & fled with him to Bohemia.

Remember also howe he sent to the Orakell of Appollo & the Annswer of Apollo, that she was giltles and that the king was jelouse &c. and howe Except the child was found Again that was loste the kinge should die without yssue, for the child was caried into Bohemia & ther laid in a forrest & brought up by a sheppard And the kinge of Bohemia his sonn maried that wentch & howe they fled into Cicillia to Leontes, and the sheppard having showed the letter of the nobleman by whom Leontes sent a was ⟨away?⟩ that child and the jewells found about her, she was knowen to be Leontes daughter and was then 16 yers old.

Remember also the Rog[5] that cam in all tottered like coll pixci[6] and howe he feyned him sicke & to have bin Robbed of all that he had and howe he cosened the por man of all his money, and after cam to the shep sher[7] with a pedlers packe & ther cosened them Again of all their money And howe he changed apparrell with the kinge of Bomia his sonn, and then howe he turned Courtier &c. Beware of trustinge feined beggars or fawninge fellouss.

Sir Henry Wotton on *All Is True (Henry VIII)* and the Burning of the Globe (1613)

[Sir Henry Wotton (1568–1639), a highly educated poet and essayist, distinguished diplomat, and finally provost of Eton College, wrote to his nephew Sir Edmund Bacon shortly after the burning of the Globe. Chambers includes several other accounts of this incident in *The Elizabethan Stage*, vol. 2, pp. 419ff. The event is also recorded in John Stow's chronicles and was lamented by poets, including (several years later) Ben Jonson, and held up by Puritan divines like Prynne as an intimation of God's wrath. The excerpt below is from the earliest extant text, *Letters of Sir Henry Wotton to Sir Edmund Bacon* (London, 1661), p. 29.]

Now, to let matters of State sleep, I will entertain you at the present with what hath happened this week at the banks side. The Kings Players had a new Play, called *All is true*, representing some principall pieces of the raign of *Henry* 8, which was set forth with many extraordinary circumstances of Pomp and Majesty, even to the matting of the stage; the Knights of the Order, with their Georges and Garter, the Guards with their embroidered Coats, and the like: sufficient in truth within a while to make

---

4. Morgan/Belarius is not banished in the version of the play that comes down to us.
5. Rogue (Autolycus).

6. Probably "colt-pixie," a mischievous sprite or fairy.
7. Sheep shearing.

greatness very familiar, if not ridiculous. Now, King *Henry* making a Masque at the Cardinal, *Wolsey*'s house, and certain Chambers[1] being shot off at his entry, some of the paper, or other stuff wherewith one of them was stopped, did light on the thatch, where being thought at first but an idle smoak, and their eyes more attentive to the show, it kindled inwardly, and ran round like a train, consuming within less then an hour the whole house to the very grounds.

This was the fatal period of that vertuous fabrique, wherein yet nothing did perish, but wood and straw, and a few forsaken cloaks; only one man had his breeches set on fire, that would perhaps have broyled him, if he had not by the benefit of a provident wit put it out with bottle Ale. The rest when we meet.

Ben Jonson on *The Tempest* (and *Titus Andronicus*) (1614)

[This extract from *Bartholomew Fair* contains one of several allusions to Shakespeare in the plays of his associate and sometime rival. The first paragraph alludes to the fashion for revenge plays such as Shakespeare's *Titus Andronicus* and Kyd's *Spanish Tragedy*, at its height roughly twenty-five years before *Bartholomew Fair* was written. The second paragraph refers disapprovingly to *The Tempest* (1613), first produced shortly before *Bartholomew Fair*. The text is that reprinted in WS, vol. 2, from the 1631 edition of Jonson's play (from the play's Induction).]

Hee that will sweare, *Jeronimo*, or *Andronicus* are the best playes, yet, shall passe unexcepted at,[1] heere, as a man whose Judgement shewes it is constant, and hath stood still, these five and twentie, or thirtie yeeres. . . .

If there bee never a *Servant-monster* i' the Fayre; who can helpe it? he[2] sayes; nor a nest of Antiques?[3] Hee is loth to make Nature afraid[4] in his *Playes*, like those that beget *Tales*, *Tempests*, and such like *Drolleries*, to mixe his head with other mens heeles; let the concupisence of *Jigges* and *Dances*, raigne as strong as it will amongst you.[5]

Shakespeare's Will (March 25, 1616)

[Shakespeare probably dictated this will sometime around January 1616. The first draft seems to have been dated in January, and 1616 is the most likely inference for the year (see note 1). The final revision was certainly made on the date given, but no clean copy was prepared, so the manuscript contains a substantial number of insertions and deletions. The text here has been silently emended to assist in ease of reading. Deleted passages have been eliminated; the most significant of these is reproduced in the notes, where significant interlineations are also identified. Most of the altered passages, as Chambers writes, simply "correct slips, make the legal terminology more precise, or incorporate afterthoughts." The revision of the will was occasioned chiefly by the February marriage of Shakespeare's daughter Judith. Our text is adapted from E. A. J. Honigmann and Susan Brock, eds., *Playhouse Wills, 1558–1642* (Manchester: Manchester University Press, 1993). For a facsimile and thorough discussion of the will, see WS 2:169–80.]

1. Small pieces of artillery, used for firing salutes.
1. Uncriticized.
2. The author.
3. Variant spelling of "antics," grotesque or ludicrous representations, or the actors (such as the clowns in *The Tempest*) playing such parts.
4. Make nature afraid by inexact imitation or too much

fantasy.
5. *concupisence . . . you:* a reference to the dance generally incorporated into theatrical performance (see, for example, Platter's account above). Jonson suggests he is refusing to cater to the vulgar taste for more dancing in plays.

Testamentum willelmij Shackspeare
Vicesimo Quinto die martij Anno Regni Domini nostri Jacobi nunc Regis Anglie &c
decimo quarto & Scotie xlixo Annoque domini 1616[1]
In the name of god Amen I William Shackspeare of Stratford upon Avon in the countie of warrwick gentleman in perfect health & memorie god be praysed doe make &
Ordayne this my last will & testament in manner & forme followeing That ys to saye
ffirst I Comend my Soule into the handes of god my Creator hoping & assuredlie
beleeving through thonelie merittes of Jesus Christe my Saviour to be made partaker
of lyfe everlastinge And my bodye to the Earth whereof yt ys made Item I Gyve &
bequeath unto my Daughter Judyth One Hundred & ffyftie poundes of lawfull English money to be paied unto her in manner & forme followeing That ys to saye One
Hundred Poundes in discharge of her marriage porcion[2] within one yeare after my
Deceas with consideracion[3] after the Rate of twoe shillinges in the pound for soe
long tyme as the same shalbe unpaied unto her after my deceas & the ffyftie poundes
Residewe thereof upon her Surrendring of or gyving of such sufficient securitie as
the overseers of this my Will shall like of to Surrender or graunnte All her[4] estate &
Right that shall discend or come unto her after my deceas or that shee nowe hath of
in or to one Copiehold tenemente with thappurtenaunces lyeing & being in Stratford upon Avon aforesaied in the saied countie of warrwick being parcell or holden
of the mannour of Rowington unto my Daughter Susanna Hall & her heires for ever
Item I Gyve & bequeath unto my saied Daughter Judith One Hundred & ffyftie
Poundes more if shee or Anie issue of her bodie be Lyvinge att thend of three Yeares
next ensueing the daie of the Date of this my Will during which tyme my executours
to paie her consideracion from my deceas according to the Rate afore saied And if
she dye within the saied terme without issue of her bodye then my will ys & I doe
gyve & bequeath One Hundred Poundes thereof to my Neece Elizabeth Hall & the
ffiftie Poundes to be sett fourth by my executours during the lief of my Sister Johane
Harte & the use & proffitt thereof Cominge shalbe payed to my saied Sister Jone &
after her deceas the saied l li[5] shall Remaine Amongst the children of my saied Sister Equallie to be Devided Amongst them But if my saied Daughter Judith be lyving
att thend of the saied three Yeares or anie yssue of her bodye then my Will ys & soe
I devise & bequeath the saied Hundred & ffyftie poundes to be sett out by my executours & overseers for the best benefitt of her & her issue & the stock[6] not to be paied
unto her soe long as she shalbe marryed & Covert Baron[7] but my will ys that she shall
have the consideracon yearelie paied unto her during her lief & after her deceas the
saied stock and consideracion to bee paied to her children if she have Anie & if not
to her executours or assignes she lyving the saied terme after my deceas Provided that
if such husbond as she shall att thend of the saied three Yeares be marryed unto
or attaine after doe sufficientle Assure unto her & thissue of her bodie landes
Awnswereable to the porcion by this my will gyven unto her & to be adjudged soe by
my executours & overseers then my will ys that the saied Cl li[8] shalbe paied to such
husbond as shall make such assurance to his owne use Item I gyve & bequeath unto
my saied sister Jone xx li & all my wearing Apparrell to be paied & Delivered within
one yeare after my deceas And I doe Will & devise unto her the house with thappurtenaunces in Stratford wherein she dwelleth for her naturall lief under the yearelie Rent of xii d. Itm I gyve & bequeath unto her three sonns William Harte[9]

---

1. *Testamentum . . . 1616:* The Will of William
Shakespeare (marginal heading). On the twenty-fifth
day of March, in the fourteenth year of the reign of
our lord James now King of England, etc., and of Scotland the forty-ninth, in the year of our Lord 1616.
(The abbreviation for "January" is crossed out in the
manuscript, "March" having been substituted at the
time the will was revised.)
2. The phrase "in discharge of her marriage porcion"
was inserted during the course of revision.

3. Compensation, or interest.
4. Susanna Hall's. (The preceding "All" marks the
beginning of a new sentence.)
5. *l li:* £50.
6. Principal.
7. *Covert Baron:* under the protection of a husband.
8. *Cl li:* £150.
9. A blank in the manuscript. Shakespeare appears to
have forgotten the name of one of his nephews,
Thomas.

hart & Michaell Harte ffyve poundes A peece to be payed within one Yeare after my deceas[1] Item I gyve & bequeath unto her the saied Elizabeth Hall All my Plate (except my brod silver & gilt bole)[2] that I nowe have att the Date of this my Will Itm I gyve & bequeath unto the Poore of Stratford aforesaied tenn poundes to mr Thomas Combe my Sword to Thomas Russell Esquier ffyve poundes & to ffrauncis Collins of the Borough of Warrwick in the countie of Warrwick gentleman thirteene poundes Six shillinges & Eight pence to be paied within one Yeare after my Deceas Itm I gyve & bequeath to Hamlett Sadler xxvi s viii d[3] to buy him A Ringe to William Raynoldes gentleman xxvi s viii d to buy him A Ringe to my godson William Walker xx s in gold to Anthonye Nashe gentleman xxvi s viii d & to mr John Nashe xx vi s viii d & to my fellows John Hemynnges Richard Burbage & Henry Cundell xxvi s viii d A peece to buy them Ringes[4] Item I Gyve Will bequeath & Devise unto my Daughter Susanna Hall for better enabling of her to performe this my will & towardes the performans thereof All that Capitall messuage or tenemente[5] with thappurtenaunces in Stratford aforesaied Called the newe place Wherein I nowe Dwell & twoe messuages or tenementes with thappurtenaunces scituat lyeing & being in Henley streete within the borough of Stratford aforesaied And all my barnes stables Orchardes gardens landes tenementes & hereditamentes[6] Whatsoever scituat lyeing & being or to be had Receyved perceyved or taken within the townes Hamlettes villages ffieldes & groundes of Stratford upon Avon Oldstratford Bushopton & Welcombe or in anie of them in the saied countie of warrwick And alsoe All that Messuage or tenemente with thappurtenaunces wherein one John Robinson dwelleth scituat lyeing & being in the blackfriers in London nere the Wardrobe & all other my landes tenementes & hereditamentes Whatsoever To Have & to hold All & singuler the saied premisses with their Appurtenaunces unto the saied Susanna Hall for & During the terme of her naturall lief & after her Deceas to the first sonne of her bodie lawfullie Issueing & to the heires males of the bodie of the saied first Sonne lawfullie Issueinge & for defalt of such issue to the second Sonne of her bodie lawfullie issueinge & to the heires males of the bodie of the saied Second Sonne lawfullie issueinge & for defalt of such heires to the third Sonne of the bodie of the saied Susanna Lawfullie issueing & of the heries males of the bodie of the saied third sonne lawfullie issueing And for defalt of such issue the same soe to be & Remaine to the ffourth ffyfth sixte & Seaventh sonnes of her bodie lawfullie issueing one after Another & to the heires[7] Males of the bodies of the saied ffourth fifth Sixte & Seaventh sonnes lawfullie issueing in such manner as yt ys before Lymitted to be & Remaine to the first second & third Sonns of her bodie & to their heires males And for defalt of such issue the saied premisses to be & Remaine to my sayed Neece Hall[8] & the heires Males of her bodie Lawfullie yssueing for Defalt of such issue to my Daughter Judith & the heires Males of her bodie lawfullie issueinge And for Defalt of such issue to the Right heires of me the saied William

---

1. *unto . . . deceas*: this passage was inserted at the top of the second page, probably when the will was revised. The following lines, with which the page originally began, are crossed out in the original: "to be sett out for her within one Yeare after my Deceas by my executours with thadvise & direccions of my overseers for her best proffitt untill her Marriage & then the same with the increase thereof to be paied unto her." These lines evidently referred to Judith Shakespeare as unmarried.
2. This parenthetical clause is an insertion, and has sparked some debate about Shakespeare's opinion of Judith's marriage.
3. The "s" stands for "shillings," the "d" for "pence."
4. *to my fellows . . . Ringes*: Shakespeare's "fellows," or colleagues, Heminges, Burbage, and Condell, had worked with him in the Lord Chamberlain's Men and King's Men for many years. Many other wills and documents of the period provide evidence of the practice of wearing mourning rings alluded to here.
5. Residence. *messuage*: dwelling house with its outbuildings or adjoining lands.
6. Heritable property.
7. In addition to the signature near the end, Shakespeare signed the will here, in the bottom right-hand corner of the second page.
8. Susanna Hall's daughter Elizabeth, actually Shakespeare's granddaughter (the sense of "niece" is less restricted in early modern usage). Elizabeth proved to be Susanna's only surviving child, and since Susanna was already thirty-three in 1616, the hypothetical series of seven sons preceding this mention of Elizabeth is doubly remarkable.

Shackspere for ever Itm I gyve unto my wief my second best bed[9] with the furniture Item I gyve & bequeath to my saied Daughter Judith my broad silver gilt bole All the Rest of my goodes Chattelles Leases plate Jewels & household stuffe Whatsoever after my dettes and Legasies paied & my funerall expences discharged I gyve Devise & bequeath to my Sonne in Lawe John Hall gentleman & my Daughter Susanna his wief Whom I ordaine & make executours of this my Last Will & testament And I doe intreat & Appoint the saied Thomas Russell Esquier & ffrauncis Collins gentleman to be overseers hereof And doe Revoke All former wills & publishe this to be my last Will & testament In Witnes Whereof I have here unto put my hand the Daie & Yeare first above Written. / By me William Shakespeare witnes to the publishing hereof Fra: Collyns Julyus Shawe John Robinson Hamnet Sadler Robert Whattcott[1]

Front Matter from the First Folio of Shakespeare's Plays (1623)

[John Heminges and Henry Condell, friends and colleagues of Shakespeare, organized this first publication of his collected (thirty-six) plays. Eighteen of the plays had not appeared in print before, and for these the First Folio is the sole surviving source. Only *Pericles, The Two Noble Kinsmen,* and *Sir Thomas More* are not included in the volume. Four of the first twelve (printed) pages of the Folio are reproduced below in reduced facsimile. They include Jonson's brief address "To the Reader," Droeshout's portrait of Shakespeare, a table of contents, and a list of actors.]

9. This bequest to Shakespeare's wife, Anne, was inserted in the course of his revision of the will. She is not mentioned elsewhere in the will at least partly because, as Shakespeare's widow, she would be guaranteed a certain portion of the estate by law. The appearance of this inserted bequest is nevertheless strange enough to have evoked much speculation.
1. After Shakespeare's death, the will was endorsed here at the bottom of the third page with a Latin inscription indicating that the will had gone to probate before a magistrate on June 22, 1616.

To the Reader.

This Figure, that thou here feeſt put,
    It vvas for gentle Shakeſpeare cut;
Wherein the Grauer had a ſtrife
    with Nature, to out-doo the life :
O, could he but haue dravvne his vvit
    As vvell in braſſe, as he hath hit
His face ; the Print vvould then ſurpaſſe
    All, that vvas euer vvrit in braſſe.
But, ſince he cannot, Reader, looke
    Not on his Picture, but his Booke.

                                B. I.

Mr. WILLIAM

SHAKESPEARES

COMEDIES,
HISTORIES, &
TRAGEDIES.

Publifhed according to the True Originall Copies.

Martin Droeshout sculpsit London.

L O N D O N
Printed by Ifaac Iaggard, and Ed. Blount. 1623.

A CATALOGVE

of the feuerall Comedies, Hiftories, and Tragedies contained in this Volume.

The Workes of William Shakespeare,

containing all his Comedies, Histories, and
Tragedies: Truely set forth, according to their first
ORIGINALL.

The Names of the Principall Actors
in all these Playes.

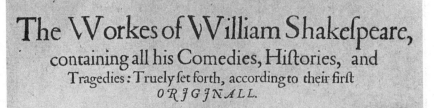

William Shakespeare.	*Samuel Gilburne.*
Richard Burbadge.	*Robert Armin.*
John Hemmings.	*William Ostler.*
Augustine Phillips.	*Nathan Field.*
William Kempt.	*John Underwood.*
Thomas Poope.	*Nicholas Tooley.*
George Bryan.	*William Ecclestone.*
Henry Condell.	*Joseph Taylor.*
William Slye.	*Robert Benfield.*
Richard Cowly.	*Robert Goughe.*
John Lowine.	*Richard Robinson.*
Samuell Crosse.	*Iohn Shancke.*
Alexander Cooke.	*Iohn Rice.*

John Milton on Shakespeare (1630)

[John Milton (1608–1674) was born in London and as a boy might conceivably have seen Shakespeare's company act. This poem first appeared prefixed to the Second Folio of Shakespeare's works in 1632 and again in the 1640 *Poems* of Shakespeare. The text is from the 1645 edition of Milton's *Poems*, as reprinted in *WS*, vol. 2, but the title given is from the Second Folio version.]

An Epitaph on the admirable Dramaticke Poet, W. Shakespeare

> What needs my *Shakespear* for his honour'd Bones,
> The labour of an age in piled Stones,
> Or that his hallow'd reliques should be hid
> Under a star-ypointing[1] *Pyramid?*
> Dear son of memory, great heir of Fame,
> What need'st thou such weak witnes of thy name?
> Thou in our wonder and astonishment
> Hast built thy self a live-long Monument.
> For whilst toth' shame of slow-endeavouring art,
> They easie numbers flow, and that each heart
> Hath from the leaves of thy unvalu'd[2] Book,
> Those Delphick[3] lines with deep impression took,
> Then thou our fancy of itself bereaving,[4]
> Dost make us Marble with too much conceaving;
> And so Sepulcher'd in such pomp dost lie,
> That Kings for such a Tomb would wish to die.

Ben Jonson on Shakespeare (1623–37)

[In addition to numerous allusions to Shakespeare in his plays, Ben Jonson (1573–1637) writes explicitly about his friend, colleague, and rival in a number of places, most significantly in the two commendatory poems prefixed to the First Folio (see above) and in the published extracts from his notebooks entitled *Timber: or, Discoveries; Made upon Men and Matter,* first published in his *Works* of 1640. It is impossible to date the original entries precisely; Chambers's conjecture is that the following entry on Shakespeare was made after 1630. The text is from the authoritative edition by C. H. Herford and Percy Simpson, vol. 8 (Oxford: Clarendon Press, 1952).]

Indeed, the multitude commend Writers, as they doe Fencers, or Wrastlers; who if they come in robustiously, and put for it, with a deale of violence, are received for the *braver-fellowes:* when many times their owne rudenesse is a cause of their disgrace; and a slight touch of their Adversary, gives all that boisterous force the foyle. But in these things, the unskilfull are naturally deceiv'd, and judging wholly by the bulke, thinke rude things greater then polish'd; and scatter'd more numerous, then compos'd: Nor thinke this only to be true in the sordid multitude, but the neater sort of our *Gallants:* for all are the multitude; only they differ in cloaths, not in judgement or understanding.

I remember, the Players have often mentioned it as an honour to *Shakespeare,*

---

1. Pointing to the stars.
2. Invaluable.
3. Reference to Apollo, god of poetry, whose most famous shrine was at Delphi.

4. *our . . . bereaving:* "our imaginations are rapt 'out of ourselves,' leaving behind our soulless bodies like statues"—Isabel MacCaffrey.

that in his writing, (whatsoever he penn'd) hee never blotted out line.[1] My answer hath beene, Would he had blotted a thousand. Which they thought a malevolent speech. [I had not told posterity this,] but for their ignorance, who choose that circumstance to commend their friend by, wherein he most faulted. And to justifie mine owne candor, (for I lov'd the man, and doe honour his memory (on this side Idolatry) as much as any.) Hee was (indeed) honest, and of an open, and free nature: had an excellent *Phantsie*[2]; brave notions, and gentle expressions: wherein hee flow'd with that facility, that sometime it was necessary he should be stop'd: *Sufflaminandus erat*;[3] as *Augustus* said of *Haterius*.[4] His wit was in his owne power; would the rule of it had beene so too. Many times hee fell into those things, could not escape laughter: As when hee said in the person of *Cæsar*, one speaking to him; *Cæsar, thou dost me wrong*. Hee replyed: *Cæsar did never wrong, but with just cause*[5]: and such like; which were ridiculous. But hee redeemed his vices, with his vertues. There was ever more in him to be praysed, then to be pardoned.

John Aubrey on Shakespeare (1681)

[What Chambers calls "the Shakespeare-mythos" was already well under way by the time John Aubrey (1626–1697) collected these anecdotes for the biographies in his *Brief Lives*, first anthologized in 1692. Aubrey's chief sources were prominent figures of the Restoration stage, which had seen increasingly popular revivals and adaptations of *Hamlet*, *The Tempest*, and many other plays of Shakespeare. Numerous actors and critics in the latter part of the seventeenth century helped to "rehabilitate" Shakespeare; if at the time of the Restoration his plays had seemed terribly musty and old-fashioned, by the 1680s his reputation as an author of lasting value was well established, thanks to the enthusiasm of Restoration playgoers. Aubrey's first source, Christopher Beeston, was the son of a one-time member of Shakespeare's company. William Davenant was a formidable entrepreneur as well as a dramatist, and Thomas Shadwell a prolific playwright perhaps best remembered as Dryden's King of Dullness. The text is from Chambers's transcription (*WS*, vol. 2), with a few silent emendations for ease of reading. Some of the material is from the published version of *Brief Lives*, and some of it from manuscript notes apparently used in writing the *Lives*.]

the more to be admired q[uia][1] he was not a company keeper[2]
lived in Shoreditch, wouldnt be debauched, & if invited to
writ; he was in paine.[3]

W. Shakespeare.

M[r]. William Shakespear. *[bay-wreath in margin]* was borne at Stratford upon Avon, in the County of Warwick; his father was a Butcher, & I have been told heretofore by some of the neighbours, that when he was a boy he exercised his father's Trade, but when he kill'd a Calfe, he would doe it in a *high style*, & make a Speech. There was at that time another Butcher's son in this Towne, that was held not at all inferior to him for a naturall witt, his acquaintance & coetanean,[4] but dyed young. This Wm. being inclined naturally to Poetry and acting, came to London I guesse about 18. and was an Actor at one of the Play-houses and did act

---

1. Compare Heminges and Condell's address to the reader in the First Folio: "And what he thought, he uttered with that easinesse, that wee have scarse received from him a blot in his papers."
2. Imagination.
3. "He needed the drag-chain" (adapted from Marcus Seneca's *Controversiae* 4, Preface).
4. Quintus Haterius, Roman rhetorician (d. 26 C.E.).
5. See *Julius Caesar* 3.1.47.

1. Because.
2. "Company keeper" can mean "libertine" or "reveler"; the general sense of the passage is that Shakespeare is "the more to be admired" for his temperance and modesty.
3. The embarrassment ("paine") at being asked to write is presumably due to the same alleged modesty.
4. Contemporary.

exceedingly well: now B. Johnson was never a good Actor, but an excellent Instructor. He began early to make essayes at Dramatique Poetry, which at that time was very lowe; and his Playes tooke well: He was a handsome well shap't man: very good company, and of a very readie and pleasant smooth Witt. The Humour[5] of . . . the Constable in a Midsomersnight's Dreame, he happened to take at Grendon [*In margin,* 'I thinke it was Midsomer night that he happened to lye there'.] in Bucks[6] which is the roade from London to Stratford, and there was living that Constable about 1642 when I first came to Oxon.[7] M[r]. Jos. Howe is of that parish and knew him. Ben Johnson and he did gather Humours of men dayly where ever they came. One time as he was at the Tavern at Stratford super[8] Avon, one Combes an old rich Usurer was to be buryed, he makes there this extemporary[9] Epitaph

> Ten in the Hundred[1] the Devill allowes
> But *Combes* will have twelve, he sweares & vowes:
> If any one askes who lies in this Tombe:
> Hoh! quoth the Devill, 'Tis my John o' Combe.

He was wont to goe to his native Country once a yeare. I thinke I have been told that he left 2 or 300[li] per annum[2] there and therabout: to a sister. [*In margin,* 'V.[3] his Epitaph in Dugdales Warwickshire'.] I have heard S[r] Wm. Davenant and M[r]. Thomas Shadwell (who is counted the best Comœdian we have now) say, that he had a most prodigious Witt, and did admire his naturall parts beyond all other Dramaticall writers. He was wont to say, That he never blotted out a line in his life: sayd Ben: Johnson, I wish he had blotted out a thousand. [*In margin,* 'B. Johnsons Underwoods'.] His Comœdies will remaine witt, as long as the English tongue is understood; for that he handles mores hominum;[4] now our present writers reflect so much upon particular persons, and coxcombeities, that 20 yeares hence, they will not be understood. Though as Ben: Johnson sayes of him, that he had but little Latine and lesse Greek, He understood Latine pretty well: for he had been in his younger yeares a Schoolmaster in the Countrey. [*In margin,* 'from M[r] —— Beeston'.]

S[r] William Davenant Knight Poet Laureate was borne in _____ street in the City of Oxford, at the Crowne Tavern. His father was John Davenant a Vintner there, a very grave and discreet Citizen: his mother was a very beautifull woman, & of a very good witt and of conversation extremely agreable. . . . M[r] William Shakespeare was wont to goe into Warwickshire once a yeare, and did commonly in his journey lye at this house in Oxon: where he was exceedingly respected. I have heard parson Robert D[avenant] say that here M[r] W. Shakespeare here gave him a hundred kisses. Now S[r] Wm. would sometimes when he was pleasant over a glasse of wine with his most intimate friends e.g. Sam: Butler (author of Hudibras) &c. say, that it seemed to him that he writt with the very spirit that Shakespeare,[5] and seemed contented enough to be thought his Son: he would tell them the story as above. in which way his mother had a very light report, whereby she was called a whore.

5. Character, personality.
6. Buckinghamshire.
7. Oxford.
8. Upon.
9. Extemporaneous.
1. 10-percent interest. (Combe is damned because he charges 12 percent on his loans, 2 percent above the maximum allowed for usury not to be a mortal sin.)
2. £300 a year.
3. See.
4. *for that . . . hominum:* because he treats of (general) human manners or customs.
5. A word such as "had" seems to be missing.

TIMELINE

TEXT	CONTEXT
	1558 Queen Mary I, a Roman Catholic, dies; her sister Elizabeth, raised Protestant, is proclaimed queen.
	1559 Church of England is reestablished under the authority of the sovereign with the passage of the Act of Uniformity and the Act of Supremacy.
1562 *The Tragedy of Gorboduc*, by Thomas Norton and Thomas Sackville, is performed; it is the first English play in blank verse.	**1563** The Church of England adopts the Thirty-nine Articles of Religion, detailing its points of doctrine and clarifying its differences both from Roman Catholicism and from more extreme forms of Protestantism.
	1564 William Shakespeare is born in Stratford to John and Mary Arden Shakespeare; he is christened a few days later, on April 23.
	1565 John Shakespeare is made an alderman of Stratford.
	1567 Mary Queen of Scots is imprisoned on suspicion of the murder of her husband, Lord Darnley. Their infant son, Charles James, is crowned James VI of Scotland.
	1568 John Shakespeare is elected Bailiff of Stratford, the town's highest office. Performances in Stratford by the Queen's Players and the Earl of Worcester's men.
	1572 An act is passed that severely punishes vagrants and wanderers, including actors not affiliated with a patron. Performances in Stratford by the Earl of Leicester's men.
	1574 The Earl of Warwick's and Earl of Worcester's men perform in Stratford.
	1576 James Burbage, father of Richard, later the leading actor in Shakespeare's company, builds the Theatre in Shoreditch, a suburb of London.
	1577 The Curtain Theatre opens in Shoreditch.

TEXT	CONTEXT
	1577–1580 Sir Francis Drake circumnavigates the globe.
	1578 Mary Shakespeare pawns her lands, suggesting that the family is in financial distress. Lord Strange's Men and Lord Essex's Men perform at Stratford.
	1580 A Jesuit mission is established in England with the aim of reconverting the nation to Roman Catholicism.
	1582 Shakespeare marries Anne Hathaway.
	1583 The birth of Shakespeare's older daughter, Susanna.
	1584 Sir Walter Ralegh establishes the first English colony in the New World at Roanoke Island in modern North Carolina; the colony fails.
	1585 The birth of Shakespeare's twin son and daughter, Hamnet and Judith. John Shakespeare is fined for not going to church.
	1586 Sir Philip Sidney dies from battle wounds.
1587 Thomas Kyd's *The Spanish Tragedy* (pub. c. 1592) and Christopher Marlowe's *Tamburlaine* (pub. 1590) are performed.	**1587** Mary Queen of Scots is executed for treason against Elizabeth I. Francis Drake defeats the Spanish fleet at Cádiz. John Shakespeare loses his position as an alderman. Philip Henslowe builds the Rose theater at Bankside, on the Thames.
	1588 The Spanish Armada attempts an invasion of England but is defeated.
1589 Robert Greene, *Friar Bacon and Friar Bungay.* Thomas Kyd, *Hamlet* (not extant; perhaps a source for Shakespeare's *Hamlet*). Christopher Marlowe, *The Jew of Malta.*	**1589** Shakespeare is probably affiliated with the amalgamated Lord Strange's and Lord Admiral's Men from about this time until 1594.
1590 Anonymous, *The True Chronicle History of King Leir, and his Three Daughters.*	**1590** James VI of Scotland marries Anne of Denmark, but believes himself to be bewitched on his honeymoon when he cannot consummate the marriage. Witch trials in Scotland.
1591 Shakespeare's *1, 2,* and *3 Henry VI* performed.	**1592** The theatrical manager of the Admiral's Men, Philip Henslowe, begins his diary, continued until 1604, recording his business

TEXT	CONTEXT
	transactions, an important source for theater historians.
1592–1593 *Richard III.* *Venus and Adonis.* *The Comedy of Errors.* *Titus Andronicus.* *The Taming of the Shrew.*	From June 1592 to June 1594, London theaters are shut down because of the plague; acting companies tour the provinces.
1594 Shakespeare dedicates *The Rape of Lucrece* to Henry Wriothesley, Earl of Southampton.	**1594** Roderigo Lopez, Portuguese physician and a Jewish convert to Christianity, is executed on slight evidence for having plotted to poison Elizabeth I.
1594–1596 *A Midsummer Night's Dream.* *Richard II.* *Romeo and Juliet.*	The birth of James VI's first son, Henry. **1595** Shakespeare lives in St. Helen's Parish, Bishopsgate, London. Shakespeare apparently becomes a sharer in (provides capital for) the newly re-formed Lord Chamberlain's Men. The Swan Theatre is built in Bankside. Hugh O'Neill, Earl of Tyrone, rebels against English rule in Ireland. Walter Ralegh explores Guiana, on the north coast of South America.
1596 *King John.* *The Merchant of Venice.* *1 Henry IV.*	**1596** John Shakespeare is granted a coat of arms; hence the title of "gentleman." William Shakespeare's son Hamnet dies.
1597 *The Merry Wives of Windsor.*	**1597** James Burbage builds the second Blackfriars Theatre. But the Lord Chamberlain's Men are not permitted to play in it, so they rent it to boys' companies for a number of years. The landlord refuses to renew the lease on the land under the Theatre in Shoreditch.
1598 *2 Henry IV.* *Much Ado About Nothing.* Ben Jonson, *Every Man in His Humor,* which lists Shakespeare as one of the actors.	**1598** The Edict of Nantes ends the French civil wars, granting toleration to Protestants. Materials from the demolished Theatre in Shoreditch are transported across the Thames to be used in building the Globe Theatre.
1599 *Henry V.* *Julius Caesar.* *As You Like it.*	**1599** The queen's favorite, Robert Devereux, Earl of Essex, leads an expedition to Ireland in March but returns home without permission in October and is imprisoned. Satires and other offensive books are prohibited by ecclesiastical order. Extant copies are gathered and burned. Two notorious satirists, Thomas Nashe and Gabriel Harvey, are forbidden to publish.

TEXT	CONTEXT
1600 *Hamlet.* Michael Drayton and several collaborators, who object to Shakespeare's depiction of Oldcastle-Falstaff in the *Henry IV* plays, write *The First Part of the True and Honorable History of the Life of Sir John Oldcastle, the Good Lord Cobham.*	**1600** The Earl of Essex is suspended from some of his offices and confined to house arrest. The birth of James VI's second son, Charles. The founding of the East India Company. Edward Alleyn and Philip Henslowe build the Fortune Theatre for the Lord Admiral's Men, competing with the Lord Chamberlain's Men at the Globe.
1601 "The Phoenix and the Turtle" published in Robert Chester's *Love's Martyr.* *Twelfth Night.* In the "War of the Theaters," Ben Jonson, John Marston, and Thomas Dekker write a series of satiric plays mocking one another.	**1601** The Earl of Essex leads some gentlemen against Elizabeth I, but the rising is quickly quelled. A few of the rebels, including Shakespeare's patron, the Earl of Southampton, arrange a staging of *Richard II* at the Globe, apparently to incite rebellion. Essex is convicted of treason and beheaded. Shakespeare's father dies.
1602 *Troilus and Cressida.*	**1602** Shakespeare makes substantial real-estate purchases in Stratford. The opening of the Bodleian Library in Oxford.
	1603 Queen Elizabeth dies; she is succeeded by her cousin, James VI of Scotland (now James I of England). Shakespeare's name appears for the last time in Ben Jonson's lists of actors, as a "principal tragedian" in *Sejanus.* Plague closes the London theaters from mid-1603 to April 1604. Hugh O'Neill surrenders in Ireland.
1604 *Measure for Measure.* *Othello.*	**1604** The conclusion of a peace with Spain makes travel across the Atlantic safer, encouraging plans for English colonies in the Americas.
1605 *All's Well That Ends Well.* *King Lear.*	**1605** The discovery of the Gunpowder Plot by some radical Catholics to blow up the Houses of Parliament during its opening ceremonies, when the royal family, Lords, and Commons are assembled in one place. The Red Bull Theatre built.
1606 *Macbeth.* *Antony and Cleopatra.* Ben Jonson, *Volpone.* Anonymous, *The Revenger's Tragedy.*	**1606** The London and Plymouth Companies receive charters to colonize Virginia. Parliament passes "An Act to Restrain Abuses of Players," prohibiting oaths or blasphemy onstage.
1607 *Timon of Athens.* *Pericles.*	**1607** An English colony is established in Jamestown, Virginia. Shakespeare's daughter Susanna marries John Hall. Shakespeare's brother Edmund (described as a player) dies.

TEXT	CONTEXT
1608 *Coriolanus.*	**1608** The King's Men obtain permission to play at the second Blackfriars Theatre, a smaller indoor venue.
1609 *Cymbeline.* Unauthorized publication of the sonnets.	
1610 *The Winter's Tale.* Ben Jonson, *The Alchemist.*	**1610** Henry is made Prince of Wales. Shakespeare probably returns to Stratford and settles there.
1611 *The Tempest.* Francis Beaumont and John Fletcher, *A King and No King.* Publication of the Authorized (King James) Bible.	**1611** Plantation of Ulster in Ireland, a colony of English and Scottish Protestants settled on land confiscated from Irish rebels.
1612 *All Is True (Henry VIII),* with John Fletcher. John Webster, *The White Devil.*	**1612** Prince Henry dies.
1613 *The Two Noble Kinsmen,* with John Fletcher.	**1613** Princess Elizabeth marries Frederick V, Elector Palatine. The Globe Theatre burns down during a performance of *All Is True.*
1614 Ben Jonson, *Bartholomew Fair.* John Webster, *The Duchess of Malfi.*	**1614** Philip Henslowe and Jacob Meade build the Hope Theatre, used both for play performances and as a bearbaiting arena. The Globe Theatre reopens.
1616 Ben Jonson publishes *The Works of Benjamin Jonson,* the first collection of plays by an English author.	**1616** William Harvey describes the circulation of the blood. Shakespeare's daughter Judith marries. Shakespeare dies on April 23.
1623 Members of the King's Men publish the First Folio of Shakespeare's plays.	

Textual Variants

THE TWO GENTLEMEN OF VERONA

CONTROL TEXT: F

F: The Folio of 1623
Fa, Fb: Successive states of F incorporating various print-shop corrections and changes

s.p. PANTHINO [F sometimes refers to Antonio's servant as *Panthino* and sometimes as *Panthion*. Standardized as *Panthino* throughout.]

1.1.26 swam swom **43 doting** eating **65 leave** loue **66 metamorphosed** metamorphis'd **76 a sheep** Sheepe **133 testerned** cestern'd **136 wreck** wrack
1.2.83 o' love O'Loue **97 your** you **99 bauble** babble
1.3.50 O *Pro⟨teus⟩*. Oh **88 father** Fathers
2.1.100 stead steed
2.3.24 moved woman would-woman
2.4.101 worthy worthy a **157 braggartism** Bragadisme **159 makes** make **189 Is it** It is **189 mine** eye, or **mine,** or
2.5.1 Milan *Padua* **35 that** that that
3.1.81 of Verona in *Verona* **269 catalogue** Cate-log **269 conditions** Condition **289 Try** [Fb] thy [Fa] **297 sew** sowe **311 follows** [Fa] follow [Fb] **313 be broken with** be **320 talk** [Fb] take [Fa] **322 villain** [Fb] villanie [Fa] **329 love** [Fb] lone [Fa] **339 hair** [Fb] haires [Fa] **342 last** [Fb; not in Fa]
3.2.14 grievously [Fb] heauily [Fa]
4.1.34 I had been often I often had beene often **44 aweful** awfull **47 An heir, and near** And heire and Neece,
4.2.107 his her
4.3.17 abhors abhor'd
4.4.48 hangman boys Hangmans boyes **54 on end** an end **62 thou** thee **66 to** not **165 beholden** beholding
5.2.7 s.p. JULIA *Pro⟨teus⟩*. **13 s.p. JULIA** *Thu⟨rio⟩*. **18 your** you
5.3.7 Moses *Moyses*
5.4.150 endowed endu'd

THE TAMING OF THE SHREW

CONTROL TEXT: F

s.p. KATHERINE [F's use of *Katerina, Katherina, Katerine, Kate,* and *Katherine* has been standardized throughout.]

s.p. PETRUCCIO [F's use of *Petruchio* has been changed throughout.]
s.p. SLY [F's use of *Beggar* has been changed throughout.]
s.p. BARTHOLOMEW [F's use of *Lady* when Bartholomew is dressed as a woman has been changed throughout.]

Induction 1.13 Breathe Brach **78 s.p. A PLAYER** 2. *Player* **86 s.p. ANOTHER PLAYER** *Sincklo*
Induction 2.2 lordship Lord **51 wi'th'** with **91 Greet** Greece
1.1.3 fore for **13 Vincentio** *Vincentio's* **25 Mi perdonate** *Me Pardonato* **156 captum** captam **232 faith** 'faith **237 your** you
1.2.18 masters mistris **23 Con tutto il cuore ben trovato** Contutti le core bene trobatto **24 ben** bene **24 molto onorato** multo honorata **31 pip** peepe **43 this'** this **70 as is** as **115 me and other more,** me. Other more **167 help me** helpe one **185 Antonio's** *Butonios* **186 his fortune** my fortune **209 ours** yours **263 feat** seeke **278 ben** Been
2.1.8 thee [not in F] **60 Licio** Litio [Licio is four times referred to as *Lisio* and three times as *Litio* in F. Standardized to "Licio" throughout.] **75–76 wooing. Neighbour** wooing neighbors **78 unto you** vnto **240 askance** asconce **322 in me 343 cypress** Cypres **367 Marseilles** Marcellus
3.1.4 this Bianca is, this is **28, 32, 41 Sigeia** . . . *Sigeia* . . . *Sigeia* sigeria . . . Sigeria . . . sigeria **46–48 s.p. HORTENSIO** How . . . yet. [assigned to Lucentio in F] **49 s.p. BIANCA** Lucentio **50 s.p. LUCENTIO** Bian⟨ca⟩. **52 s.p. BIANCA** Hort⟨ensio⟩. **79 change** charge **odd** old **80 s.p. MESSENGER** Nicke.
3.2.16 them [not in F] **29 thy** [not in F] **30 old news** [not in F] **33 hear** heard **51 weighed** Waid **52 half-cheeked** halfe-chekt **84 not** [not in F]
3.3.1 sir, to love sir, Loue **3 I** [not in F] **39 vicar** wench
4.1.22 s.p. CURTIS Gru⟨mio⟩. **75 sleekly** slickely **99 s.p. GRUMIO** Gre⟨mio⟩.
4.2.4 s.p. HORTENSIO Luc⟨entio⟩. **6 s.p. LUCENTIO** Hor⟨tensio⟩. **8 s.p. LUCENTIO** Hor⟨tensio⟩. **13 none** me **31 her** them **72** [ascribed to *"Par."*] **in** me
4.3.63 s.p. HABERDASHER Fel. **81 a** [not in F] **88 like** a like **93 nor cap** neither cap **175 account'st** accountedst

4.4.1 Sir Sirs
4.5.5 he's has 16 except expect 26 t'attend to come
4.6.19 is in 23 so it shall be still so it shall be so 39 where is whether is 79 be [not in F]
5.1.5 master's mistris 43 master's Mistris 56 copintank copataine
5.2.2 done come 38 thee, lad the lad 46 two too 110 wonders a wonder 132 a fiue 136 you're your

The Comedy of Errors

CONTROL TEXT: F

F: The Folio of 1623
F2: Later printing of F (1632) that incorporates various corrections

s.p. EGEON [F's use of *Merchant* and *Father* has been standardized throughout.]
s.p. NELL [F also uses *Luce*. Standardized throughout.]
s.p. ANGELO [F uses both *Angelo* and *Goldsmith* but generally prefers the latter. Standardized throughout.]

1.1.17 seen at seene at any 22 ransom to ransome 38 me happy me; me too [F2] 42 the he 54 mean-born meane 102 upon vp 116 barque backe 123 thee they 143–44 Which . . . disanul, / Against . . . dignity, Against . . . dignity, / Which . . . disanull 151 health helpe
1.2.4 arrival a riuall 40 unhappy vnhappie a 66 clock cooke
2.1.8 mistress Master 12 ill thus 60 thousand hundred 63 come home come 67 thy mistress not not thy mistresse 106 o' a 109 her his 110–11 will / Wear gold, will, / Where gold 111 yet [not in F]
2.2.12 didst did didst 80 men them 98 tiring trying 148 unstained distain'd 175 stronger stranger 186 offered free'd 191 oafs Owles 194 drone Dromio 195 not I I not
3.1.47 pate face aim a name 75 you, sir your sir 89, 91 her your 106 once [not in F] 116 Porcupine *Porpentine*
3.2.1 s.p. LUCIANA Iulia. 4 building buildings ruinous ruinate 16 attaint attaine 21 but not 26 wife wise 46 sister's sister 49 bed bud them thee 57 where when 109 and is 120 her hand the hand
4.1.17 her their 87 she sir she
4.2.6 Of Oh, 30 How? How 47–48 at, / That at / Thus 60 a be I be
4.3.13 redemption from [not in F] 55 you do do 56 and or 60 thou then
4.4.38 to prophesy the prophesie 99 those these 108 his this

5.1.46 much, much much 49 at of 119 point's points 122 death depth 169 s.p. MESSENGER [not in F] 321 bay boy 350 his her 404 ne'er are 407 joy go

Love's Labour's Lost

CONTROL TEXT: Q

F: The Folio of 1623
Q: The Quarto of 1598
Qa, Qb: Successive states of Q incorporating various print-shop corrections and changes

s.p. KING [Q's use of *King, Navarre*, and *Ferdinand* has been standardized throughout.]
s.p. BIRON, LONGUEVILLE, DUMAINE [Q's *Berowne* and *Longauill* (and other spellings) are transliterations of the French, here restored and modernized. "Dumaine" transliterates "Duc de Mayenne," not quite correctly. Rhyme and meter require two syllables.]
s.p. ARMADO [Q's use of *Armado* and *Braggart* has been standardized throughout.]
s.p. MOTE [Q uses either *Boy* or *Page*, which have been replaced throughout. In dialogue and s.d.'s, the name appears as "Moth," meaning "moth" or "mote" (speck). It is pronounced like the latter word, and that sense may be primary; hence the spelling adopted here.]
s.p. PRINCESS [Q more frequently uses *Queene*, but this edition uses "Princess" until she becomes a queen and is addressed as one, at 5.2.708.]
s.p. MARIA, CATHERINE, ROSALINE [In 2.1, they are referred to variously as *Lady*, 2 *Lady* (or *Lady* 2), and 3 *Lady* (or *Lady* 3). For details, see the variants list below and the notes to the text. For interpretation, see the Textual Note and the Introduction.]
s.p. COSTARD [Q generally prefers *Clown* over *Costard*; standardized throughout.]
s.p. JAQUENETTA [Q uses *Maid* more often than *Jaquenetta*; standardized throughout.]
s.p. NATHANIEL [Q's use of *Curate, Nathaniel*, and *Curate Nathaniel* has been standardized throughout.]
s.p. HOLOFERNES [Q uses *Pedant* more often than *Holofernes*; standardized throughout.]
s.p. DULL [Q's use of *Dull, Constable*, and *Anthony* has been standardized throughout.]

1.1.24 three [F] thee 31 pomp [F] pome 62 feast fast 127 s.p. BIRON [In Q, Longueville speaks lines 126–30; Biron's s.p. appears at

line 131.] **184 Señor** Signeour **192 laughing** hearing **211 simplicity** [F] sinplicitie **224–48** [Q prints the King's speech continuously, with Costard's interruptions bracketed.] **247 with, with** Which with **275 s.p. KING** Fer⟨dinand⟩. [F] Ber⟨owne⟩. **1.2.9, 10, 15 Señor** Signeor **91 blushing** blush-in **130 s.p. DULL** Clo⟨wn⟩. **145 Master** [F] M. **2.1.32 Importunes** [F] Importuous **34 visaged** [F] visage **39 Lord Longueville** Longauill. **40 s.p. MARIA** 1. Lady. **44 parts** [F] peerelsse **53 s.p. MARIA** Lad⟨y⟩. **56 s.p. CATHERINE** 2 Lad⟨y⟩. **64 s.p. ROSALINE** [F] 3 Lad⟨y⟩. **88 unpeopled** [F] vnpeeled **113–25 s.p. ROSALINE** [F] Kath⟨erine⟩. **129 of** [F] of, of **189** Non point No poynt **194 Rosaline** Rosalin⟨e⟩ **209 Rosaline** Katherin⟨e⟩ **220–23 s.p. CATHERINE** La⟨dy⟩. **253 s.p. ROSALINE** [F] Lad⟨y⟩. **254 s.p. MARIA** [F] Lad⟨y⟩. 2 **255 s.p. CATHERINE** Lad⟨y⟩. 3 **256 s.p. MARIA** Lad⟨y⟩. **257 s.p. CATHERINE** Lad⟨y⟩.
3.1.11 throat as if throate, if **12 through the nose** through: nose **14 thin-belly** [F] thin-bellies **22 penny** penne **63 salve in the mail** salue, in thee male **131, 134, 136, 138, 142, 144, 159** [Each line in Q starts with "O"; probably a misreading of the s.p. "Bero" as "Ber. O . . ."] **155 guerdon** gardon **165 Junior** Iunios **175 clock** Cloake
4.1.3 s.p. BOYET [F] Forr⟨ester⟩. **50 fit** [Qb] fir [Qa] **64 set's** [Qa] set [Qb] **65 penurious** pernicious **65 was** [Qb] is was [Qa] **72 King's** King **104 suitor** shooter **126 did hit** it did hit [Qb] hid hit [Qa] **132 pin is in** 140 o'th' t'other ath toothen **144 a** [not in Q] **144.1 s.d.** Shout within Shoot with **4.2.11 a 'auld grey doe'** a haud credo **26 of** [not in Q] **33** Dictynna . . . Dictynna Dictisima . . . dictisima **44 'twas** [Qb] was [Qa] **47–48 call** I cald **57 sore 'l'** sorell: **61–96 s.p. HOLOFERNES** Nath⟨aniel⟩. The s.p.'s of Holofernes (lines 61, 71, 76, 80, 86, 96) and Nathaniel (lines 67, 95) are reversed in Q.] **64** pia mater prima-/ter **66 in whom** [F] whom **71 ingenious** ingenous **73** sapit sapis **76 'pierce one'** Person **89–90** Venezia . . . prezia vemchie, vencha, quen non te vnde, que non te perreche **96–98 s.p. HOLOFERNES . . . NATHANIEL** Nath⟨aniel⟩. [In Q, Nathaniel speaks lines 96–111; here, Holofernes delivers lines 96–97, Nathaniel lines 98–111.] **111 singeth** singes **112 apostrophus** apostraphas **113 canzonet** cangent **113 Here are** Nath⟨aniel⟩. Here are. [Q assigns lines 112–13 to Holofernes and, beginning with "Here are," lines 113–19 to Nathaniel. This edition assigns Holofernes all of lines 112–19.] **118–19** domicella—virgin Damosella virgin **120 sir** sir from one mounsier

Berowne, one of the strange Queenes Lordes. **121 s.p. HOLOFERNES** Nath⟨aniel⟩. [Q assigns lines 121–25 to Nathaniel, beginning Holofernes' speech at line 125 with "Sir." This edition assigns the entire speech, lines 121–31, to Holofernes.] **124 writing** written **125 Sir Nathaniel** Ped⟨ant⟩. Sir Holofernes [See line 121 above.] **144** ben bien
4.3.34 wilt [F] will **44 s.p. KING** Long⟨ueville⟩. **54 slop** Shop **70 idolatry** [F] ydotarie **89 I** [not in Q] **104 Wished** [Passionate Pilgrim] Wish. [Dumaine's poem also appears in a poetic collection attributed to Shakespeare, The Passionate Pilgrim (c. 1599).] **108 thorn** [England's Helicon] throne [Dumaine's poem also appears in the collection England's Helicon (1600).] **113 great** [not in Q] **118 true love's** trueloues **142 Faith so** Fayth **151 coaches. In your tears** couches in your teares **172 to . . . by** by . . . to **176 like you** like **178 Joan** [Qb] Loue [Qa] **192 Where** King. Where [Q repeats s.p. "King." (here omitted) after the s.d. "reads the letter."] **204 e'en** and **251 style** Schoole **255 and** [not in Q] **279 Nothing** O nothing **291** [Q follows this line with the twenty-three lines printed here, indented, probably an unrevised version of 4.3.285–91, 292–339.] **333 authors** authour **335 Let** Lets **341 standards** standars **357** Allons, allons! Alone alone
5.1.18 sine 'b' fine **23** insanire in-/famie **25** bone bene **26 Bone?** Bon, fort bon Bome boon for boon **31** Quare Quari **51 wave** [F] wane **59** circum circa vnũ cita **79 choice** chose **88 mustachio** [F] mustachie **100 Nathaniel** Holofernes **101 rendered** [F] rended **102 assistance** assistants **107–08 myself, Judas Maccabeus; and this gallant gentleman, Hector** my selfe, and this Gallant Gentle-/man Iudas Machabeus **129** Allons Alone
5.2.17 been a [F] bin **43 ho! How?** **46 jest; I beshrew** iest, and I beshrow **53, 57 s.p. MARIA** [F] Marg⟨aret⟩. **53 pearls** [F] Pearle **65 hests** deuice **67 pursuivant-like** pert-taunt like **74 wantonness** wantons be **80 stabbed** [F] stable [Q] **89 sycamore** [F] Siccamone **96 they** [F] thy **124 love-suit** Loue-feat **130** [Q follows this line with the two lines printed here, indented, probably an unrevised version of 5.2.131–32.] **133 too** [F] two **147 her** his **151 ne'er** ere **162 ever** [F] euen **217 s.p. ROSALINE** [Before line 216 in Q, which gives Rosaline both lines.] **242–55 s.p. CATHERINE** Maria. **273 Ah, they** They **277** Non point No poynt **309 run over** runs ore **407 affectation** affection **463 zany** [F] saine **482** manège nuage **500 they** [F] thy **513 least** [F] best **516 There** Their **551 s.p. PRINCESS** Lady. **559 this** [F] his

589 **proved** [F] proud 633 **gilt** [F] gift 657 **The party is gone.** [Q centers, italicizes, and fails to attribute this line to Armado or any other character.] 673–74 **on, stir** or stir 696 **s.p. MOTE** [Q's prefix, *"Boy.,"* could refer to Mote or Boyet.] 719 **nimble** humble 745 **strange** straying 752 **them** [not in Q] 760 **the** [F; not in Q] 764 **in** [not in Q] 798 **hermit** herrite 798 [Both Q and F follow this line with the six lines printed here, indented, probably an unrevised version of parts of 5.2.814–31.] 798.2 **rank** rackt 800 A **wife?** [In Q, this begins Catherine's answer to Dumaine (also line 800).] 868 **Ver, begin** [In F, as here, this is part of Armado's speech. In Q, it is separated from Armado's words by a blank line and preceded by "*B.*"] 869 **s.p.** / **s.d. Spring** *[sings] The Song.* [centered in Q] 870, 871 [Lines in reverse order in Q.] 891 **foul** [F] full 903 **s.p. ARMADO** [F; not in Q] 904 **You that way, we this way** [F; not in Q]

A Midsummer Night's Dream

Control text: Q1

F: The Folio of 1623
Q1: The Quarto of 1600
Q2: The Quarto of 1619

Title: A Midsummer Night's Dream [Q1 title page, head title] A mydsomer nighte dreame [Stationers' Register] A Midsommer nightes dream [Q1 running titles]

s.p. THESEUS [Q's use of *Theseus* and *Duke* has been standardized throughout.]
s.p. HIPPOLYTA [Q's use of *Hippolyta* and *Duchess* has been standardized throughout.]
s.p. BOTTOM [Q's use of *Bottom, Pyramus,* and *Clown* has been standardized throughout.]
s.p. FLUTE [Q's use of *Flute* and *Thisbe* has been standardized throughout.]
s.p. ROBIN [Q's use of *Robin* and *Puck* has been standardized throughout.]
s.p. QUINCE [Q's use of *Quince* and *Prologue* has been standardized throughout.]
s.p. SNOUT [Q's use of *Snout* and *Wall* has been standardized throughout.]
s.p. SNUG [Q's use of *Snug* and *Lion* has been standardized throughout.]
s.p. TITANIA [Q's use of *Titania* and *Queen* has been standardized throughout.]
s.p. STARVELING [Q's use of *Starveling* and *Moonshine* has been standardized throughout.]

1.1.4 **wanes** [Q2, F] waues 10 **New** Now 24 **Stand forth Demetrius.** [Q italicizes and

centers on a separate line.] 26 **Stand forth Lysander.** [Q italicizes and centers on a separate line.] 27 **This** This man 136 **low** loue 139 **merit** else, it 159–60 **And . . . son.** / **From . . . leagues.** From . . . leagues? / **And . . . sonne:** 191 **I'd** ile 200 **Helen** Helena 212 **sleights** flights 219 **stranger companies** strange companions
1.2.20 **stones** stormes 64 **s.p. ALL THE REST** *All.*
2.1.7 **moonës** Moons 58 **make room** roome 61 **Fairies** Fairy 78 **Perigouna** Perigenia 79 **Aegles** Eagles 101 **cheer** heere 109 **thin** chinne 158 **the** [not in Q] 190 **slay . . . slayeth** stay . . . stayeth 201 **nor** [F] not 206 **lose** loose
2.2.9 **s.p. FIRST FAIRY** [not in Q] 13 **s.p. CHORUS** [not in Q] 25–30 **Sing . . . with lullaby.** &c. 31–32 **Hence . . . sentinel** [indented as part of the song] 44–45 **comfort . . . Be it** [Q2, F] comfor . . . Bet it 49 **good** [Q2, F] god 53 **is** [Q2, F] it
3.1.44 **s.p. SNOUT** *Sn.* 59 **and** or 71 **Odours, odours.** [F] Odours, odorous 76 **s.p. ROBIN** *Puck.* [F] *Quin⟨ce⟩.* 82 **bristly** brisky 133 **own** [Q2, F] owe 144 **Mote** Moth 145 **s.p. A FAIRY . . . ANOTHER . . . ANOTHER . . . ANOTHER . . .** All Four *Fairies* 148 **apricots** Apricocks 157 **s.p. A FAIRY** *I. Fai.* 157–58 **mortal.** / **ANOTHER** Hail. mortall, haile 159–60 **s.p. ANOTHER . . . ANOTHER** 2. *Fai . . .* 3. *Fai.* 170 **you** of you 182 **love's** louers
3.2.19 **mimic** [F] Minnick 80 **so** [not in Q] 85 **sleep** slippe 137 **s.p. HELENA** [not in Q] 165 **here** heare 202 **is all quite forgot** is all forgot 214 **like** life 221 **passionate** [F; not in Q] 251 **prayers** praise 258 **No, no, sir** [F] No, no 280 **doubt** of doubt 300 **gentlemen** [Q2, F] gentleman 327 **but** [Q2, F] hut 387 **exiled** exile
3.3.14 **shalt** [Q2, F] shat 37 **to** [not in Q]
4.1.19 **courtesy** curtsie 21–22 **Pease-** / **Blossom** Cobwebbe 33 **thee off** thee 38 **all ways** alwaies 52 **flow'rets** flouriets 70 **o'er** or 79 **these five** these, fine 93 **nightës** nights 102 **vanguard** vaward 114 **Seemed** Seeme 125 **this is** [Q2, F] this 170 **in sickness** a sicknesse 188 **found** [Q2, F] fonnd 189 **It** [F] Are you sure / That we are awake? It 199 **let us** [Q2, F] lets 201 **t'expound** expound 203–4 **a patched fool** [F] patcht a foole 208 **ballad** Ballet
4.2.3 **s.p. STARVELING** [F] *Flut⟨e⟩.* 26 **no** [F] not
5.1.34 **our** [F] Or 38 **Egeus** [F] Philostrate 38, 42, 61, 72, 76, 106 **s.p. EGEUS** [F] *Philostrate* 44 **s.p. LYSANDER** [F] *The⟨seus⟩.* 46, 50, 54, 58 **s.p. THESEUS** [F; not in Q] 48, 52, 56 **s.p. LYSANDER** [F; not in Q] 59

strange black strange 189 up in thee [F] now againe 204 wall Moon down [F] used 263 gleams beames 299 prove [Q2, F] yet prooue 306 mote moth 307 warrant warnd 337 s.p. BOTTOM [F] *Lyon.*
5.2.1 lion Lyons 2 behowls beholds 13 we wee 49–50 And . . . blessed / Ever . . . rest. Euer . . . rest, / And . . . blest.

THE COMICAL HISTORY OF THE MERCHANT OF VENICE, OR OTHERWISE CALLED THE JEW OF VENICE

CONTROL TEXT: Q1

F: The Folio of 1623
Q1: The Quarto of 1600
Q2: The Quarto of 1619

s.p. SHYLOCK [Q1's use of *Iew⟨e⟩* has been standardized throughout.]
s.p. LAUNCELOT [Q1's use of *Clo⟨wne⟩* has been standardized throughout.]
s.p. SALERIO [Q1's use of *Salarino* in some s.d.'s and s.p.'s has been standardized throughout.]

Title: The Comical History of the Merchant of Venice, or Otherwise Called the Jew of Venice [after Q half title and Stationers' Register entry] The comicall History of the Mer / *chant of Venice* [Q half title and running title] The most excellent / *Historie of the Mer- chant / of Venice.* With the extreame crueltie of *Shylocke* the *Iewe* / towards the sayd Merchant, in cutting a iust pound / of his flesh: and the obtayning of *Portia* / by the choyse of three / chests. *As it hath been diuers times acted by the Lord / Chamberlaine his Seruants.* / Written by William Shakespeare. [Q title page] The Merchant of Venice [F]

1.1.27 Andrew, decks *Andrew* docks 113 Yet is It is
1.2.51 throstle Trassell
1.3.108 spit spet 121 spat spet
2.2.3–7 Gobbo Iobbe 87 last [Q2] lost 159 a suit [Q2, F] sute
2.4.5 as us
2.5.41 Jew's Iewes
2.6.14 younker younger 24 therein then 58 gentlemen [Q2, F] gentleman
2.7.69 tombs *timber*
2.8.39 Slubber [Q2, F] slumber
2.9.47 chaff [F] chaft
3.1.62 s.p. MAN [not in Q, F] 89 heard [F] heere
3.2.63 s.p. ONE FROM PORTIA'S TRAIN [not in Q, F] 66 ALL [not in Q, F] 67 eyes [F] eye

71 I'll begin it [in Q and F, printed in Roman rather than italic (as the rest of the song), as if not part of the song] 81 vice voyce 93 makes [F] maketh 101 Therefore, thou [Q2] Therefore then thou [Q1, F] 301 thorough through
3.4.23 Hear other things: heere other things 49 Padua Mantua 50 cousin's hands [Q2] cosin hand [Q1] cosins hand [F] 53 traject Tranect 82 my [F] my my
3.5.67 merit it meane it, it 74 for a [F] for
4.1.29 his [Q2, F] this 30 flint [Q2] flints [Q1, F] 50 Mistress Maisters 73 bleat [F] bleake [Q] 74 pines [F] of Pines 99 'Tis [Q2, F] as 121 forfeit forfaiture 127 inexorable inexcrable 225 No, not [Q2, F] Not 392 not [Q2] not to [Q1, F] 395 s.p. GRAZIANO [Q2, F] *Shy⟨locke⟩.* [Q1]
5.1.42 Master Lorenzo! Sola M. *Lorenzo* sola [Q2] & M. *Lorenzo* sola [Q1, F] 47–48 morning. / LORENZO . . . Sweet soul, let's morning sweet soule / Loren⟨zo⟩. Let's 86 Erebus Erobus [F] Terebus [Q] 152 it [Q2, F; not in Q1] 232 my bedfellow [Q2, F] mine bedfellow

THE MERRY WIVES OF WINDSOR

CONTROL TEXT: F

F: The Folio of 1623
Q: The Quarto of 1602

s.p. MASTER/MISTRESS [F uses M. to abbreviate both words. Except at 4.4.24 and 5.5.196, M. occurs in speech prefixes when the reference is clear because either the wife or husband is not onstage, or as an abbreviation for "Mistress" when the husband has an immediately adjacent speech. Standardized throughout.]
s.p. JOHN [F's Ser⟨vant⟩ and 1 Ser⟨vant⟩ have been replaced throughout.]
s.p. ROBERT [F's 2 Ser⟨vant⟩ has been replaced.]
s.p. FALSTAFF [F's use of *Falstaff* and *Sir John* has been standardized throughout.]
Title: A / Most pleasant and / excellent conceited Co- / medie, of Syr *Iohn Falstaffe,* and the / merrie Wiues of *Windsor.* / Entermixed with sundrie / variable and pleasing humors, of Syr *Hugh* / the Welch Knight, Iustice *Shallow,* and his / wise Cousin M. *Slender.* With the swaggering vaine of Auncient *Pistoll,* and Corporall *Nym.* [Q title page] A pleasant conceited Co- / medie, of Syr *Iohn Falstaffe,* and the / merry Wiues of *Windsor.* [Q head title] A *pleasaunt Comedie, of the merry Wiues of Windsor* [Q running title] An excellent & pleasant conceited cōmedie of S^r Io Faulstof and the

merry Wyves of Windesor [Stationers' Register entry]

1.1.16 coad coat 19 cod coate 24 py'r Lady per-lady 28 compromises compremises 39 George *Thomas*. [Perhaps "Geo." in Shakespeare's handwriting could be misread "Tho."] 42 fery ferry 51 s.p. SHALLOW Slen⟨der⟩. 73 Cotswold *Cotsall* 87 Master M. ["M." in dialogue is similarly interpreted throughout unless separately noted, or unless the character in question is obviously female (e.g., "M. Anne").] 117 Garter Gater 119 Fery Ferry 210 contempt content 212 faul' fall
1.2.3 'oman woman [Q] Nurse
1.3.13 lime lyme [Q] liue 19 his mind is not heroic. [not in F] 42 studied her well [Q] Studied her will 46 legion legend 72 o'th' ith' 73 humour [Q] honor 80 stars star 88 this the
1.4.19 whey face wee-face 32 for God's sake [Q; not in F] 39 *un boîtier vert* vnboyteene verd 44–45 *Ma foi, il fait fort chaud! Je m'en vais à la cour. La grande affaire. mai foy, il fait for ehando, Ie man voi a le Court la grand affaires.* 47 *Mets-le à ma pochette. Dépêche mette le au mon pocket, de-peech* 52 and aad 54 *qu'ai-j' que ay ie* 60 *larron* La-roone 77 *baile* ballow 82 your yoe your 106 goodyear good-ier 110–11 Anne— / *Exeunt Doctor* [CAIUS *and* RUGBY] / —asshead *An*-fooles head. [In this edition, "Anne" ("an") serves the double function of proper name and indefinite article.] 139 that I will that wee will
2.1.1 have I haue 21 i'th' with / The 26 O God, that I knew how to [Q] how shall I 28 By my faith Trust me 30 by my faith trust me 51 praised praise 54–55 hundred and fifty psalms hundred Psalms 90 goodman good man 127 Cathayan *Cataian* 169 God bless you, bully rook, God bless you! How now Bully-Rooke 185–86 guest cavaliero guest-Caualeire 187 s.p. FORD Shal⟨low⟩. 188 Brooke [Q] *Broome* 192 mijn'-heers An-heires 201 than then
2.2.2–3 I will retort . . . penny. [not in F] 21 Ay, ay, I I, I, I 22 God [Q] heauen 23–24 you, you you 27 wouldst [Q] would 50 God bless [Q] heauen-blesse 63 rustling rushling 101 O God no, sir [Q; not in F] 139 God bless 'Blesse 155 half, or all all, or halfe 207 exchange enchange 232 spokesmate [Q] assistant 270 God [Q] Heauen 274 God's my life [Q] fie, fie, fie
2.3.16 God bless [Q] 'Blesse 17 God save [Q] 'Saue 25 Galen *Galien* 49 word [Q; not in F] Monsieur Mounseur 70 s.p. PAGE, SHALLOW, *and* SLENDER *All.* 79 patiences patinces [Q] patients [F]

3.1.4 Petty pittie 8 Jeshu pless me [Q] 'Plesse my soule 25 God Heauen 35 God save [Q] 'Saue 36 God pless [Q] 'Plesse 54 pottage porredge 75 By Jeshu [Q; not in F] 88 Give . . . terrestrial—so. [Q; not in F] 93 lads [Q] Lad 95 Afore God [Q] Trust me
3.2.43 By my faith [Q] Trust me 78 s.p. PAGE, CAIUS, *and* EVANS *All.*
3.3.3 Robert *Robin* 33–34 pumpkin Pumpion 51 By the Lord [Q; not in F] 54–55 were, with nature, were not nature 57–58 thee there's [Q] thee. ther's 66 kiln kill 129 s.p. JOHN Ser⟨vant(s)⟩. 139 uncoop vncape 152 what who 163 foolish foolishion 172 Ay, I I, I 173 me you 176 Ay, ay, I I, I: I 192 heartily hartly
3.4.12 s.p. FENTON [not in F] 44 by God be God [Q; not in F] 55 God [Q] Heauen 56 God Heauen 64 Fenton *Fenter*
3.5.7 'Sblood, the [Q] The 14 By the Lord [Q] I should haue beene 53 By the mass [Q] Oh he [Q] be 54 God bless God save [Q] Blesse 73 God [Q] good lucke 74 by [Q] in 78 By the Lord [Q] Yes 104 surge serge
4.1.52 *Genitivo Genitiue* 53 Jenny's Ginyes 57–58 hick . . . hack . . . 'whorum' hic . . . hac . . . *horum* 59 lunatics Lunaties
4.2.4 accoutrement accustrement 46 s.p. MISTRESS PAGE [not in F] 53 s.p. MISTRESS PAGE Mist⟨ress⟩ Ford. 61 Brentford *Brainford* 84 direct direct direct 87 him [not in F] 97 as lief liefe as 100 villains villaine 102 gang gin 108 this is thi is 114 God be Heauen be 125 s.p. PAGE M⟨istress⟩ Ford. 157 not strike strike 167 Jeshu [Q] yea, and no 174 By my troth [Q] Trust me
4.3.1 Germans desire Germane desires 7 them [Q] him 9 house [Q] houses
4.4.6 cold gold 24 s.p. MISTRESS FORD M⟨istress⟩ Ford. 30 trees tree 31 makes make 41 Disguised . . . head [Q; not in F] 59 s.p. MISTRESS FORD Ford. 67 vizors vizards 70 tire tyre [Q] time 77 fery ferry
4.5.35 s.p. SIMPLE Fal⟨staff⟩. 43 Ay, Sir Tike I Sir: like 46 Thou art [Q] Thou are 51 O Lord [Q] Out alas 62–63 cozen Garmombles [Q] Cozen-Iermans 64 Colnbrook *Cole-brooke* 91 O Lord, sir, and [Q] And 97 Brentford *Braineford*
4.6.26 ever euen 38 denote deuote 39 visorèd vizarded
5.1.20 Goliath Goliah
5.2.2 my daughter my 9 struck strooke 10 lights light 11 God Heauen
5.3.11 Hugh Herne
5.5.1 struck stroke 9 foul fault fowle-fault 28 God [Q] Heauen 39, 80, 85 s.p. HOBGOBLIN Pist⟨ol⟩. 46 Bead *Bede* 65 More Mote 78 God [Q] Heauens 113 mate meete 117 By the Lord [not in F] 180

white greene 184 green white 187 *un garçon* oon Garsoon *un paysan* oon pesant 189 green white 196 s.p. MISTRESS PAGE M⟨istress⟩ Page.

MUCH ADO ABOUT NOTHING

CONTROL TEXT: Q

Q: The Quarto of 1600
F: The Folio of 1623
F2: The Folio of 1632

s.p. DON JOHN [Q's use of *John* and *Bastard* has been standardized throughout.]
s.p. DON PEDRO [Q's use of *Pedro* and *Prince* has been standardized throughout.]
s.p. ANTONIO [Q's use of *Old, Antonio,* and *Brother* has been standardized throughout.]
s.p. DOGBERRY [Q's use of *Dogberry* and *Constable* has been standardized throughout.]
s.p. VERGES [Q uses both *Verges* and *Headborough,* but generally prefers the former, standardized throughout.]

1.1.8 Pedro Peter 34–35 bird-bolt Burbolt
1.2.6 event [F2] euents
1.3.3 it [not in Q] 39 brothers [F] bothers 44 on on
2.1.33 bearherd Berrord 39 Peter fore Peter: for . . . heavens 71 a bout about 83, 86, 88 s.p. BALTHASAR *Benedicke*
2.3.22 an [F] and 37 hid-fox kid-foxe 56 s.p. BALTHASAR [not in Q] 124 us of [F] of vs
3.2.24 can cannot 45 s.p. DON PEDRO [F] *Benedicke*
3.3.10, 15 s.p. SECOND WATCHMAN . . . FIRST WATCHMAN [reversed in Q] 24 s.p. FIRST WATCHMAN *Watch 2* 34, 41, 45, 50, 61, 94, 110 s.p. A WATCHMAN *Watch* 78, 85 s.p. FIRST WATCHMAN *Watch* 145, 151 s.p. A WATCHMAN *Watch 2* 154–55 A WATCHMAN Never . . . us. [The speech is assigned to *Conrade* in Q.]
3.4.16 in [F] it
3.5.8 off of
4.1.201 princes left for dead princess (left for dead,)
4.2.1 s.p. DOGBERRY *Keeper* 2, 5 s.p. VERGES *Couley* 4 s.p. DOGBERRY *Andrew* 8, 11, 14, 17, 23, 27, 31, 36, 39, 44, 50, 63, 67 s.p. DOGBERRY *Kemp* 45 s.p. VERGES *Constable* 60 s.p. DOGBERRY *Constable* 61–62 s.p. VERGES Let them be, in the hands— / CONRAD Off, coxcomb! *Couley* Let them be in the hands of Coxcombe.
5.1.16 Bid And 97 an [not in Q]
5.2.41 for [not in Q] 53 maintain maintaind 73 myself. So my self so

5.3.4–11 s.p. CLAUDIO Done . . . dumb [These lines follow the Lord's in Q with no distinct speech prefix] 11 dumb [F] dead 23 s.p. CLAUDIO Lo.
5.4.54 s.p. ANTONIO *Leonato* 96 s.p. BENEDICK *Leonato*

AS YOU LIKE IT

CONTROL TEXT: F

F: The Folio of 1623

s.p. TOUCHSTONE [F's use of *Clowne* has been changed throughout.]
s.p. DUKE FREDERICK [F's use of *Duke* has been changed throughout.]
s.p. SIR OLIVER MARTEXT [F's use of *Oliver* has been changed in 3.3.]
s.p. JAQUES DE BOIS [F's use of *Second Brother* in 5.4 has been changed at lines 140 and 172.]

1.1.10 manège mannage 48, 50 villein . . . villeins villaine . . . villaines 49 Bois Boys 75 Denis Dennis 94 she hee 99 Ardenne Arden [similarly throughout] 138 s.p. OLIVER [not in F]
1.2.3 I [not in F] 69 s.p. CELIA *Ros⟨alind⟩.* 76 Le the 239 shorter taller 256 Rosalind *Rosaline*
1.3.1 Rosalind *Rosaline* 51 likelihood likelihoods 84 Rosalind *Rosaline* 90 Rosalind, lack'st thou then *Rosaline* lacks then 131 we in in we
2.1.49 much must 56 should doe 59 the [not in F]
2.3.16 s.p. ORLANDO [not in F] 30 s.p. ORLANDO *Ad⟨am⟩.* 72 seventeen seauentie
2.4.1 weary merry 39 thy they wound would 43–44 batlet batler 44 chapped chopt 64 you your 69 travel trauaile 78 cot Coate [similarly throughout]
2.5.1 s.p. AMIENS [F has the heading "Song" and no speech prefix.] 32 s.p. ALL [F has no prefix, but the heading "Song." and the phrase "Altogether heere."] 37–39 see . . . weather see. &c. 43 s.p. JAQUES *Amy⟨ens⟩.*
2.7.55 aught but [not in F] 87 comes come 174 s.p. AMIENS [There is no speech prefix in F, but the heading "Song."] 182 Then The 190–93 sing . . . jolly *sing, &c.* 201 master masters
3.2.106 graft graffe 113 a [not in F] 133 her his 216 such [not in F] 222 thy the 328 deifying defying 336 are art
3.3.17 it [not in F] 79 s.p. TOUCHSTONE *Ol⟨iuer⟩.*
3.4.27 a [not in F] 37 puny puisny
3.5.129 I [not in F]

4.1.1 be [not in F] **17 my** by **53 beholden** beholding **66 warr'nt** warne **132 hyena** Hyen **180 it** in
4.2.2 s.p. FIRST LORD Lord. **7 s.p. SECOND LORD** Lord. **10 s.p. LORDS** [not in F, which has the heading "Musicke, Song."]
4.3.96 handkerchief handkercher **141 I'** I **154 his** this
5.2.6 her [not in F] **24 handkerchief** handkercher **28 overcame** ouercome **88 obedience** obseruance **106 I satisfy** I satisfi'd
5.3.14 s.p. BOTH PAGES [not in F, which has the heading "Song."] **17 In** In the **ring** rang **32–37** [F places these lines after 5.3.19.]
5.4.21 your you your **75 to the** to **103 her** his **153 them** him **186 so** [not in F]

TWELFTH NIGHT, OR WHAT YOU WILL

CONTROL TEXT: F

F: The Folio of 1623

s.p. ORSINO [F's use of Duke and Du⟨ke⟩ has been changed throughout.]
s.p. SIR TOBY [F's use of Sir To⟨by⟩, To⟨by⟩, and Tob⟨y⟩ has been standardized throughout.]
s.p. SIR ANDREW [F's use of And⟨rew⟩ and An⟨drew⟩ has been standardized throughout.]
s.p. FESTE [F's use of Clo⟨wne⟩, Clow⟨ne⟩, and Cl⟨owne⟩ has been changed throughout.]

1.1.25 years' heat yeares heate
1.2.14 Arion Orion **48 pray thee** prethee
1.3.44 s.p. SIR ANDREW Ma⟨lvolio⟩. **46 Mary Accost** Mary, accost **83 curl** by coole my **84 me** we **86 housewife** huswife **109 cinquepace** Sinke-a-pace **114 divers-coloured** dam'd colour'd **117 That's** That
1.5.156 'countable comptible **271 County's** Countes
2.2.18 straight [not in F] **29 our** O **30 made of,** made, if
2.3.68 Cathayan Catayan **121 a nayword** an ayword
2.4.50 s.p. FESTE[sings] [not in F] **86 I** it
2.5.103 staniel stallion **109 ay** I **126 born** become **achieve** atcheeues **154 dear** deero
3.1.7 king Kings **61 wise men** wisemens **116 grece** grize
3.2.7 thee the the **57 nine** mine
3.3.36 latchèd lapsed
3.4.23 s.p. OLIVIA Ma⟨lvolio⟩. **65 tang** langer with **153 If** s.p. To⟨by⟩. If **154 You** Yon **179 out** on't **244 virago** firago
4.2.5 in in in **63 to the** the **77 Master** M.

5.1.73 wreck wracke **110 hath** haue **193 pavan** panyn **393 With** [not in F]

TROILUS AND CRESSIDA

CONTROL TEXT: F; OCCASIONALLY, AS NOTED BELOW, Q

F: The Folio of 1623

Q: The Quarto of 1609
Qa, Qb, Fa, Fb: The "b" texts of both Q and F are corrected versions. The change from Qa to Qb is significant: Qb adds a prefatory epistle not found in Qa or in either state of F. See the Introduction and the Textual Note.

Title: Troilus and Cressida [F most running titles] The booke of Troilus and Cresseda [Stationers' Register, 1603], THE history of Troylus and Cressida [Stationers' Register, 1609], THE Historie of Troylus and Cresseida [Qa title page], THE Famous Historie of Troylus and Cresseid [Qb title page], The history of Troylus and Cresseida [Q head title; running titles, all italic], THE TRAGEDIE OF Troylus and Cressida [F title page; initial running titles, all italic]

s.p. PROLOGUE [It is unclear whether the lines of the Prologue in F are actually attributed to a character called "Prologue," as they are in this edition.]
s.p. BASTARD [As in F, Margareton is referred to in the s.p.'s and s.d.'s of 5.8 as Bastard. In F, he is mistakenly referred to in dialogue (at 5.5.7) as Margarelon.]
s.p. PANDARUS [F's occasional use of Pandar in s.p.'s and s.d.'s may be deliberate, but it has been standardized to "Pandarus" throughout.]
s.p. ALEXANDER [F refers to Cressida's servant in 1.2 as Her Man or simply as Man, while Pandarus refers to him in dialogue as Alexander. His name has been standardized to "Alexander" throughout that scene.]
s.p. MAN [Reserved in this edition for the servant of Troilus, who is referred to in the s.p.'s of 3.2 (in this edition as in F) as "Man."]
s.p. SERVANT [Reserved in 3.1 for the servant of Paris and in 5.5 for the servant of Diomedes, both of whom are also referred to in F as Servant]

Pro. **12 barques** Barke **13 freightage** frautage **17 Antenorides** Antenonidus **18 full-filling** fulfilling **19 Spar** Stirre
1.1.0–1.2.215 Enter . . . Hector's, and how he [F in these lines simply reprints Q with a

few errors; therefore its readings and press variants are here treated as without substantive authority. Q is taken as control text; thus variants from Q rather than from F will be noted for these lines. Rejected Q readings are labeled "[Q]" to avoid confusion. See below also 2.2.103–209, 3.3.1–95, and 4.6.0–64.] 29 So, traitor! 'When she comes'? When is she thence? so traitor then she comes when she is thence [Q] 35 askance a scorne [Q] 68 on of you [F] of you [Q] 72 not kin [Fb] kin [Q] 73 care I [F] I [Q] 97 resides [F] reides [Q]

1.2.17 they [F] the [Q] 22 farced sauced [Q] 108 lift [F] liste [Q] 120 the thee [Q] 136 pot [F] por [Q] 137 or [not in Q] 176 a man [F] man [Q] 188 man's [F] mans man [Q] 215 looks and how [At this point, F regains its independent authority and becomes the control text again.] 220 an eye [Q] money 221 comes [Q] come 234 season [Q] seasons 237 date is [Q] dates 243 lie at a [Q] lye at, at a 267 price [Q] prize 272 Then [Q] That

1.3.7 Infects [Q] Infect 18 shames [Q] shame 50 flee fled 53 Retorts Retires 58 th' [Q] the 62 As, Agamemnon, every hand As Agamemnon and the hand 66 On [Q] In 83 masque Maske 84 [ ] [The conjectured missing line is not in Q or F. Some contrast with "Th'unworthiest" (line 83) seems required.] 87 Infixture Insisture 101 fixture fixure 106 primogenity [Q] primogenitiue 117 resides recides 118 their [Q] her 127 it is [Q] is it 156 scaffoldage Scaffolage 159 a-mending a mending 161 seem [Q] seemes 202 calls [Q] call 207 swinge [Q] swing 209 finesse [Q] finenesse 221 heart head 236 great [Q; not in F] acorn accord 240 that the [Q] that he 241 what, repining, the what the repining 260 resty [Q] rusty 262 among [Q] among'st 298 prove [Q] pawne 348 e'en in

2.1.6 then [Q; not in F] 13 thou [Q] you unsifted whinid'st 18 o' thy ath thy 27 foot. An foot, and 42–43 in thy skull [not in F] 45 thrash [Q] thresh 53 ye thus you this 87 bade the [Q] bad the bad thee 96 an [Q] and if 97 a knock he knocke A were [Q] he were 101 your their 106 wit [not in F] 109 peace [Q; not in F] brach Brooch

2.2.9 toucheth [Q] touches 34 reason [Q] reasons 44–45 And . . . reason [Q; lines transposed in F] 47 hare [Q] hard 49 Make [Q] Makes 55 mad [Q] madde made 70 sewer same 89 never fortune [Q] Fortune neuer 103–209 old . . . shriek [F shows no sign of access to manuscript copy in these lines; Q therefore again becomes the control text for this passage.] 110 Ah . . .

ah a . . . a [Q] 119 the [not in Q] 163 But and [Q] 209 [After "shriek," F again becomes the control text.]

2.3.10 ye [Q] thou 14 their [Q] the 16 Neapolitan [Q; not in F] 21 could ha' [Q] could haue 30 prayer [Q] a prayer 32 s.p. PATROCLUS Amen [Q; not in F] 41 Thersites [Q] thy selfe 65 whore and a cuckold [Q] Cuckold and a Whore 66 emulous [Q] emulations 72 faced sent 74 so, lest so, least [Q] of, so [F] 80 you will [Q] will 'tis it is 97–98 his legs . . . flexure [Q] his legge . . . flight 110 on [Q] of 112 unwholesome [Q] vnholdsome 114 come [Q] came 118 tend [Q] tends 122 lunes lines 128 Bring [Fb] ring [Fa] 132 second [Fb]; fecond [Fa] 161 warth [Q] wroth 165 himself [Q] it selfe 208 s.p. AJAX Ulis⟨ses⟩. 209 s.p. ULYSSES Aia⟨x⟩. 211 Farce Force 216 does [Q] do's doth 228 Famed [Q] Fame 230 thine [Q] thy 245 great [Q; not in F] 247 today to Troy to Troy 252 sail . . . hulks [Q] may saile . . . bulkes

3.1.6 notable [Q] noble 16 titles [Q] title 27 thou [Q] thou art 31 visible inuisible 33 not you [Q] you not 36 Cressid [Q] Cressida 39 s.d. HELEN [Q] Helena 52 Will you well, you 66 Ay, faith I faith 77 sweet [Q] sweere 80 I'll lay my life [Q; not in F] 80, 82 dispenser disposer 83 make 's makes [Q] make [F] 85 dispenser's disposer's 104–05 s.p. PANDARUS In . . . so. [Sings] Love [Fb] In . . . so. Pan⟨darus⟩: Love [Fa] [In Fa, Paris continues to speak until the beginning of the song. The song itself is then attributed to Pandarus.] 105 still love, still more [Q] still more 111, 113 O! O! oh ho 115, 116 O! O! O ho 118 ay, faith [Q] I faith yfaith 141 these [Q] this 148 s.p. PARIS [not in F. The line is attributed to Helen.]

3.2.12 Pandar [Q] Pandarus 20 repurèd [Q] reputed 22 tuned [Q] and 30 spirit [Q] spirite sprite 31 as short [Q] so short 64 fears teares 66 safer [Q] safe 71 Nor [Q] Not 109 till now not [Q] not till now 111 grown [Q] grone grow 121 Cunning . . . in my Comming . . . from my 139 speak so [Q] speakes so 157 truth [Q] truths 179 wind or [Q] as Wind, as 180 or [Q] as 186 pain [Q] paines 193–94 with a bed [not in F] 197 pander [Q] and Pander

3.3.1–95 Now . . . virtues [F shows no clear evidence of manuscript authority until "shining" (3.3.95). Q thus becomes the control text in the interim.] 1 you [F; not in Q] 3 your [F; not in Q] 4 come loue [Q] 5 profession possession [Q] 67 use us'd [Q] 95 shining [F] ayming [Q; here F regains its status as control text, though (as elsewhere) some of the variants it retrieved from the manuscript were themselves errors.] **97 givers** [Q] giuer **100–101 To . . . behold itself** [Q; not in F] **105 mirrored** married **107 at** [Q] it at **110 man** [Q] may **111 be** [Q] is **115 they're** th'are [Q] they are [F] **132 fasting** [Q] feasting **156 abject rear** abiect, neere **162 Welcome** the welcome **163 Farewell** [Q] farewels **172 give** goe **177 sooner** [Q] begin to **178 once** [Q] out **192 aught** thought **193 infant** [not in F] **203 his island** her Iland **218 air** [Q] ayre ayrie ayre **237 as** [not in F] **244 a** [Q] he **247 this** [Q] his **260 his presence** [Q] hit presence **make** [Q] make his **286 ye** [Q] you **290 am feared** am sure **4.1.9 wherein** [Q] within **10 e'en** in **17 meet** [Q] meetes **37 'twas** [Q] it was **45 wherefore** [Q] whereof **67 nor less** [Q] no lesse **80 but** not **4.2.4 lull** kill **6 As to** As **12 joys** [Q] eyes **26 Here** [Q] heere Heare **33 Ah . . . capocchia** a *Chipochia* **53 It's** [Q] 'tis **56 Whoa** Who **57 you are** [Q] y'are **67 Diomedes'** [Q] *Diomeds* **68 so concluded** [Q] concluded so **74 secrecies** secrets **4.3.5 Ah, ah** [Q] Ah, ha **26 force** orce **30 I'll** [Q] Ile I will **4.4.3 us** [not in F] **9 own** [Q; not in F] **4.5.4 violenteth** [Q] no lesse **9 dross** [Q] crosse **11 Ah a ducks** [Q] ducke **14 you** [not in F] **23 strained** [Q] strange **40 one** [Q] our **47 Distasted** [Q] Distasting **48 s.p. AENEAS** *Aeneas within* **56 When** [Q] Troy⟨lus⟩. When [F attributes the line to Troilus rather than, as here, to Cressida.] **77 gifts . . . flowing** guift . . . Flawing **79 novelty** [Q] nouelties **82 afeard** [Q] affraid **119 usage** vsage [Q] visage [F] **122 zeal** seale **thee** [Q; not in F] **123 In** [Q] I **132 you** [Q] my **144 s.p. DEIPHOBUS** *Dio⟨medes⟩.* **4.6.0–64 Enter . . . game.** [F in this passage shows no sign of manuscript influence and repeats several suspicious or erroneous Q readings. F is therefore here regarded as a mere reprint, and Q is taken as control text.] **38 s.p. MENELAUS** *Patr⟨oclus⟩.* [Q] **44 not** [F] nor [Q] **49 too** then [Q] **60 accosting** a coasting [Q] **64 Exeunt** *Exennt* [F; not in Q. F here regains its access to manuscript authority and hence its status as control text.] **71 they** [Q; not in F] **75 s.p. ACHILLES** *Aga⟨memnon⟩.* **94 breath** [Q] breach **4.7.28 could** [Q] could'st **72 th'advancèd** [Q] thy aduanced **147 have** [Q; not in F] **168 you** [Q] thee **5.1.5 botch** batch **24 cur, no** [Q] curre **58 sprites** [Q] spirits **68 sewer** sure **84 it: that** it, that it

5.2.3 your [Q] you **10 sing** [Q] finde **11 clef** [Q] Cliff life **13 s.p. CRESSIDA** *Cal⟨chas⟩.* **22 forsworn** [Q] a forsworne **27 do** [Q] doe not **40 prithee** [Q] pray thee **41 all hell's** [Q] hell **57 la lo** **72 ha't** [Q] haue't **83–84 s.p. DIOMEDES As . . . thee. CRESSIDA** Nay . . . withal As . . . thee. *Dio⟨medes⟩:* Nay . . . me. *Cres⟨sida⟩:* He . . . withal [F makes "As I kiss thee" the end of Cressida's preceding speech and attributes "Nay . . . me" to Diomedes and "He . . . withal" to Cressida. Here, "As I kiss thee" is attributed to Diomedes, and both "Nay . . . me" and the succeeding line, "He . . . withal," to Cressida.] **84 doth take** [Q] rakes **90 one's** [Q] on's one **103 s.p. TROILUS** *Ther⟨sites⟩:* you [Q] me **114 said** [Q] say **122 th'attest** [Q] that test **136 a** [Q] he **139 be sanctimonies** [Q] are sanctimonie **144 Bifold** [Q] By foule **161 e'en be** be **167 as I** I Cressid [Q] *Cressida* **173 sun** [Q] Fenne **5.3.4 in** [Q] gone **5 all** [Q; not in F] **21 give much, to use** count giue much to as **47 mother** [Q] Mothers **75 sire** sir **85 do** [Q] doth **87 dolours** [Q] dolour **92 Yet** [Q] yes **106 o' these** o'th's **5.4.8 stale** [Q] stole **10 proved not** not proou'd **5.5.6 Polydamas** [Q] *Polidamus* **7 Margareton** *Margarelon* **11 Cedius** *Cedus* **12 Thoas** *Thous* **17 Go** [Q] Coe **24 strawy** [Q] straying **47 brave** [not in F] **5.6.7 the** thy **13 Ha** [Q; not in F] **5.7.6 arms** [Q] arme **5.8.3 horned Spartan** hen'd sparrow **8–9 am bastard begot** [Q] am a Bastard begot **5.9.7 dark'ning** [Q] darking **13 and** [Q; not in F] **15 retire** [Q] retreat **16 sound** [Q] sounds **20 bait** [Q] bed **5.11.7 smite** smile **12 fear of** [Q] feare, of **17 their** [Q] there **20 Cold** Coole

Measure for Measure

Control text: F

F: The Folio of 1623

s.p. MISTRESS OVERDONE [F's use of *Bawd* has been changed throughout.]
s.p. POMPEY [F's use of *Clown* has been changed throughout.]

1.1.8 But this But that **51 leavened** a leauen'd **1.2.17 wast** was't **31 pil'd . . . pilled** pil'd . . . pil'd **75 you?** [In F, a short exchange follows between Pompey and Mistress Overdone, which the preceding dialogue apparently was meant to replace: printed in this edition as

Additional Passage A.] **102 bonds** words **113 morality** mortality **145 fourteen** nin-teene **166 thy** the
1.3.10 a witless witlesse **27 More mocked** becomes More mock'd **43 T'allow in** To do in
1.4.5. sisterhood Sisterstood
2.1.12 your our **21–23 What . . . on thieves?/What's . . . seizes.** what's . . . ceizes;/What . . . on theeves? **21 law** Lawes **34 execute** executed **39 vice** Ice **205 spay** splay
2.2.25 God save 'Save 98 raw now **101 ere** here **119 Split'st** splits **164 prayer is crossed** prayers crosse **166 God save** 'Save
2.3.42 law Loue
2.4.4 God heauen **9 seared** feard **12 in** for **17 now the** not the **45 God's** heauens **48 moulds** meanes **53 or** and **75 craftily** crafty **76 me be** be **94 all-binding law** all-building-Law **112 Ignominy** Ignomie
3.1.29 sire fire **38 in** yet in **51 me . . . them** them . . . me **67 Though** Through **89 enew** emmew **92, 95 precise** prenzie **121 dilated** delighted **130 penury** perjury **169 falsify** satisfie **265 on** and **280 eat, array** eate away **294 Free from** From or as **356 ungenerative** generatiue **413 not** now **450 it** as it **451 inconstant** constant **494 Make my** Making
4.1.1 s.p. BOY Song. **6 though** but **51 and so** and **58 their** these **72 tilth's** Tithes **93–94 s.p. PROVOST** Duke.
4.2.81 unlisting vnsisting **100 s.p. DUKE** Pro⟨vost⟩. **111 s.p. PROVOST** The letter [centered on a separate line]
4.3.13 Forthright Forthlight **81 yonder** yond
4.4.4 redeliver reliver
4.5.6 Flavio's Flavia's **8 Valentinus** Valencius
5.1.13 me your we your **167 her face** your face **237 even to** to **367 wast** was't **415 confiscation** confutation **532 that's meet** that meete

Additional Passage **Very well met** Very well met, and well come

ALL'S WELL THAT ENDS WELL

COPY TEXT: F

F: The Folio of 1623

s.p. COUNTESS [also called *Mother, Lady, Old Lady*]
s.p. HELEN [occasionally called *Hellena* in F, although *Hellen* is the more common form]
s.p. LAVATCH [changed from *Clowne*]
s.p. REYNALDO [changed from *Steward*]

s.p. LAFEU [occasionally called *old Lafew*]
s.p. BERTRAM [standardized from *Bertram, Count*, and *Rossillion*]
s.p. FIRST and SECOND LORD DUMAINE [standardized from F's *French E.* and *French G., Captaine E.* and *Captaine G., Lord E.*, and *1 Lord E*]

1.1.50 not [not in F] **63 Farewell.** Farwell **121 got** goe
1.2.18 Roussillon *Rosignoll*
1.3.37 madam— Madam **46 Poisson** *Poysam* **78 ere** ore **100 Dian no** [not in F] **155 loneliness** louelinesse **161 to th'other** tooth to th'other **186 intenable** intemible **200 to find** not to finde
2.1.3 gain all, gaine, all: **41 with his cicatrice** his sicatrice, with **60 fee see 61 bought** brought **139–40 denied [. . .]** denied. **143 fits** shifts **154 impostor** Impostrue **161 coacher** torcher **172 nay** ne **191 heaven** helpe
2.2.26 beyond below **35 I pray you** La⟨dy⟩. I pray you **53 An end, sir!** To And end sir to
2.3.59 these those **62 s.p. ALL** [but **HELEN** *All.* **89 her** heere **92 s.p. HELEN** La⟨dy⟩. **121 when** whence **126 it is** is is **133 word's a slave** words, a slaue **134 grave** graue: **276 detested** detected
2.4.14 fortunes fortune **31 s.p. PAROLES In myself, knave.** [not in F]
2.5.25 End And **43 wit** [not in F] **46 not** [not in F]
3.1.17 nation nature **23 to the** to'th the
3.2.8 sold hold **19 s.p. COUNTESS** [*reads the letter aloud*] A Letter. **41 heard** heare **110 cleave** moue **still-piecing** still-peering
3.4.4 s.p. REYNALDO [not in F, which has *"Letter."*] **18 s.p. COUNTESS** [not in F]
3.5.5 greatest great'st **17 their** these **30 you** [not in F] **63 warr'nt** write **82 those places** these places
3.6.32 his this **33 ore** ours **98 s.p. SECOND LORD DUMAINE** Cap⟨tain⟩. G. **101, 108 s.p. FIRST LORD DUMAINE** Cap⟨tain⟩. E.
3.7.19 Resolved Resolue **46 wicked act** lawfull act
4.1.1 s.p. SECOND LORD DUMAINE 1. Lord E. **38 mute** Mule **59 SOLDIERS** [*severally*] All. **83 art** are
4.2.39 toys e'en such a surance rope's in such a scarre
4.3.80 FIRST LORD DUMAINE Ber⟨tram⟩. **84 apiece;** a peece, **114 s.p. FIRST LORD DUMAINE** [not in F] **115 s.p. SECOND LORD DUMAINE** Cap⟨tain⟩. G. **122 s.p. SECOND LORD DUMAINE** Cap⟨tain⟩. G. **134 s.p. FIRST LORD DUMAINE** [not in F] **155 die** liue **157 Guillaume** Guiltan **188 lordship** Lord **242–43 bedclothes; but they** about

him bed-cloathes about him: but they 262
quart d'écu Cardceue
4.4.16 you, mistress your Mistris 31 that the
4.5.3 Else [not in F] 7 a I 16 grass hearbes
33 name maine 41 since sure 42 the
nobility his Nobilitie
5.2.21 similes smiles 27 under her vnder 34
one [not in F]

5.3.27 s.p. ATTENDANT *Gent⟨leman⟩*. 51
Stained Scorn'd 60 grace-sender great
sender, 72 s.p. COUNTESS [not in F] 102
Plutus *Platus* 115 conjectural connec-
turall 141 s.p. KING [not in F] 156 since
sir, 184 them. Fairer them fairer: 198
gem; Iemme 218 inf'nite cunning insuite
comming 220 my any 310 are is

General Bibliography[*]

There is a huge and ever-expanding scholarly literature about Shakespeare and his culture. This general list and the lists that accompany the individual plays and the poems in this volume are only a small sampling of the available resources. Journals devoted to Shakespeare studies include *Shakespeare Bulletin, Shakespeare Jahrbuch* (Germany), *Shakespeare Quarterly, Shakespeare Studies,* and *Shakespeare Survey* (England); other journals, such as *English Literary History, English Literary Renaissance, Renaissance Quarterly, Representations,* or *Studies in English Literature,* also frequently publish essays on Shakespeare's works. The categories below are only approximate; many of the texts could properly belong in more than one category.

Guides and Companions to Shakespeare Studies

Callaghan, Dympna, ed. *A Feminist Companion to Shakespeare.* Malden, Mass.: Blackwell, 2000.

De Grazia, Margreta, and Stanley Wells, eds. *The Cambridge Companion to Shakespeare.* Cambridge, Eng.: Cambridge University Press, 2001.

Drakakis, John, ed. *Alternative Shakespeares.* 2nd ed. London: Routledge, 1985.

Dutton, Richard, and Jean E. Howard, eds. *A Companion to Shakespeare's Works,* I: *The Tragedies.* Malden, Mass.: Blackwell, 2003.

———, eds. *A Companion to Shakespeare's Works,* II: *The Histories.* Malden, Mass.: Blackwell, 2003.

———, eds. *A Companion to Shakespeare's Works,* III: *The Comedies.* Malden, Mass.: Blackwell, 2003.

———, eds. *A Companion to Shakespeare's Works,* IV: *Poems, Problem Comedies, Late Plays.* Malden, Mass.: Blackwell, 2003.

Hattaway, Michael, ed. *The Cambridge Companion to Shakespeare's History Plays.* Cambridge, Eng.: Cambridge University Press, 2002.

Hawkes, Terence, ed. *Alternative Shakespeares, Volume 2.* London: Routledge, 1996.

Hodgdon, Barbara, and W. B. Worthen, eds. *A Companion to Shakespeare and Performance.* Malden, Mass.: Blackwell, 2005.

Jackson, Russell, ed. *The Cambridge Companion to Shakespeare on Film.* 2nd ed. Cambridge, Eng.: Cambridge University Press, 2007.

Kasten, David Scott, ed. *A Companion to Shakespeare.* Malden, Mass.: Blackwell, 1999.

Kinney, Arthur F. *Shakespeare by Stages: An Historical Introduction.* Malden, Mass.: Blackwell, 2003.

Leggatt, Alexander, ed. *The Cambridge Companion to Shakespearean Comedy.* Cambridge, Eng.: Cambridge University Press, 2002.

McDonald, Russ, ed. *The Bedford Companion to Shakespeare: An Introduction with Documents.* 2nd ed. Houndmills, Basingstoke: Palgrave Macmillan, 2001.

———, ed. *Shakespeare: An Anthology of Criticism and Theory, 1945–2000.* Malden, Mass.: Blackwell, 2004.

McEachern, Claire, ed. *The Cambridge Companion to Shakespearean Tragedy.* Cambridge, Eng.: Cambridge University Press, 2002.

[*]Edited by Holger Schott Syme, Department of English, University of Toronto.

Schoenfeldt, Michael. *A Companion to Shakespeare's Sonnets*. Malden, Mass.: Blackwell, 2006.

Smith, Emma, ed. *Shakespeare's Comedies: A Guide to Criticism*. Malden, Mass.: Blackwell, 2003.

———, ed. *Shakespeare's Histories: A Guide to Criticism*. Malden, Mass.: Blackwell, 2003.

———, ed. *Shakespeare's Tragedies: A Guide to Criticism*. Malden, Mass.: Blackwell, 2003.

Wells, Stanley, and Lena Cowen Orlin, eds. *Shakespeare: An Oxford Guide*. Oxford: Oxford University Press, 2003.

Wells, Stanley, and Sarah Stanton, eds. *The Cambridge Companion to Shakespeare on Stage*. New York: Cambridge University Press, 2002.

Shakespeare's World

Social, Political, and Economic History

Amussen, Susan Dwyer. *An Ordered Society: Gender and Class in Early Modern England*. New York: Columbia University Press, 1993.

Archer, Ian W. *The Pursuit of Stability: Social Relations in Elizabethan London*. New York: Cambridge University Press, 1991.

Ariès, Philippe, and Georges Duby, general eds. *A History of Private Life*, Volume III: *Passions of the Renaissance*. Ed. Roger Chartier. Trans. Arthur Goldhammer. Cambridge, Mass.: Belknap Press, 1989.

Armitage, David, and Michael J. Braddick, eds. *The British Atlantic World, 1500–1800*. New York: Palgrave Macmillan, 2002.

Barry, Jonathan, ed. *The Tudor and Stuart Town: A Reader in English Urban History, 1530–1688*. London: Longman, 1990.

Barry, Jonathan, and Christopher Brooks. *The Middling Sort of People: Culture, Society and Politics in England, 1550–1800*. Houndmills, Basingstoke: Palgrave Macmillan, 1994.

Barthelmey, Anthony Gerard. *Black Face, Maligned Race: The Representation of Blacks in English Drama from Shakespeare to Southerne*. Baton Rouge: Louisiana State University Press, 1987.

Beier, A. L. *Masterless Men: The Vagrancy Problem in England, 1560–1640*. New York: Methuen, 1985.

Beier, A. L., and Roger Finlay, eds. *London 1500–1700: The Making of the Metropolis*. New York: Longman, 1986.

Ben-Amos, Ilana Krausman. *Adolescence and Youth in Early Modern England*. New Haven: Yale University Press, 1994.

Bridenbaugh, Carl. *Vexed and Troubled Englishmen, 1590–1642*. New York: Oxford University Press, 1976.

Brigden, Susan. *New Worlds, Lost Worlds: The Rule of the Tudors, 1485–1603*. New York: Viking, 2001.

Burgess, Glenn. *The Politics of the Ancient Constitution: An Introduction to English Political Thought, 1603–1642*. University Park: Pennsylvania State University Press, 1993.

Capp, Bernard S. *When Gossips Meet: Women, Family, and Neighbourhood in Early Modern England*. Oxford: Oxford University Press, 2003.

Clark, Alice. *Working Life of Women in the Seventeenth Century*. Introduction by Amy Louise Erickson. 1968. New York: Routledge, 1992.

Clay, C. G. A. *Economic Expansion and Social Change: England 1500–1700*. 2 vols. New York: Cambridge University Press, 1984.

Cressy, David. *Birth, Marriage, and Death: Ritual, Religion, and the Life-Cycle in Tudor and Stuart England*. Oxford: Oxford University Press, 1997.

Cruickshank, Charles Greig. *Elizabeth's Army.* 2nd ed. Oxford: Clarendon, 1966.

Elliot, John Huxtable. *The Old World and the New, 1492–1650.* New York: Cambridge University Press, 1970.

Ellis, Steven G. *Tudor Ireland: Crown, Community, and the Conflict of Cultures, 1470–1603.* London: Longman, 1985.

Elton, G. R. *England Under the Tudors.* 3rd ed. New York: Routledge, 1991.

———. *The Tudor Revolution in Government: Administrative Changes in the Reign of Henry VIII.* Cambridge, Eng.: Cambridge University Press, 1959.

Emmison, F. G. *Elizabethan Life.* Chelmsford: Essex County Council, 1970.

Erickson, Amy Louise. *Women and Property in Early Modern England.* New York: Routledge, 1993.

Finlay, Roger. *Population and Metropolis: The Demography of London, 1580–1650.* Cambridge, Eng.: Cambridge University Press, 1981.

Fletcher, Anthony. *Gender, Sex, and Subordination in England, 1500–1800.* New Haven: Yale University Press, 1995.

Fletcher, Anthony, and John Stevenson, eds. *Order and Disorder in Early Modern England.* New York: Cambridge University Press, 1985.

Gaskill, Malcolm. *Crime and Mentalities in Early Modern England.* New York: Cambridge University Press, 2000.

Gittings, Clare. *Death, Burial and the Individual in Early Modern England.* London: Croom Helm, 1984.

Gowing, Laura. *Common Bodies: Women, Touch and Power in Seventeenth-Century England.* New Haven: Yale University Press, 2003.

Griffiths, Paul. *Youth and Authority: Formative Experiences in England, 1560–1640.* Oxford: Clarendon, 1996.

Griffiths, Paul, Adam Fox, and Steve Hindle, eds. *The Experience of Authority in Early Modern England.* New York: St. Martin's, 1996.

Guy, John A. *Queen of Scots: The True Life of Mary Stuart.* Boston: Houghton Mifflin, 2004.

———, ed. *The Reign of Elizabeth I: Court and Culture in the Last Decade.* Cambridge, Eng.: Cambridge University Press, 1995.

———. *Tudor England.* New York: Oxford University Press, 1988.

Heal, Felicity, and Clive Holmes. *The Gentry in England and Wales, 1500–1700.* Basingstoke: Macmillan, 1994.

Herrup, Cynthia B. *The Common Peace: Participation and the Criminal Law in Seventeenth-Century England.* New York: Cambridge University Press, 1987.

Hindle, Steve. *The State and Social Change in Early Modern England, c.1550–1640.* New York: St. Martin's, 2000.

Hirst, Derek. *Authority and Conflict: England, 1603–1658.* Cambridge, Mass.: Harvard University Press, 1986.

Ingram, Martin. *Church Courts, Sex, and Marriage in England, 1570–1640.* New York: Cambridge University Press, 1987.

James, Mervyn. *Society, Politics and Culture: Studies in Early Modern England.* New York: Cambridge University Press, 1986.

King, John N. *Tudor Royal Iconography: Literature and Art in an Age of Religious Crisis.* Princeton: Princeton University Press, 1989.

Kishlansky, Mark A. *A Monarchy Transformed: Britain 1603–1714.* New York: Penguin Books, 1996.

Klein, Joan Larsen. *Daughters, Wives, and Widows: Writings by Men about Women and Marriage in England, 1500–1640.* Urbana: University of Illinois Press, 1992.

Lake, Peter, with Michael Questier. *The Anti-Christ's Lewd Hat: Protestants, Papists and Players in Post-Reformation England.* New Haven: Yale University Press, 2002.

Laslett, Peter. *The World We Have Lost: Further Explored.* 3rd ed. New York: Scribner, 1984.

Levin, Carole. *The Heart and Stomach of a King: Elizabeth I and the Politics of Sex and Power.* Philadelphia: University of Pennsylvania Press, 1994.

Lockyer, Roger. *The Early Stuarts: A Political History of England, 1603–1642.* 2nd ed. London: Longman, 1999.

MacCaffrey, Wallace T. *Elizabeth I: War and Politics, 1588–1603.* Princeton: Princeton University Press, 1992.

Manning, Roger B. *Village Revolts: Social Protest and Popular Disturbances in England, 1509–1640.* Oxford: Clarendon, 1988.

Matar, Nabil I. *Islam in Britain, 1558–1685.* New York: Cambridge University Press, 1998.

———. *Turks, Moors, and Englishmen in the Age of Discovery.* New York: Columbia University Press, 1999.

Mendelson, Sara Heller, and Patricia Crawford. *Women in Early Modern England, 1550–1720.* Oxford: Clarendon, 1998.

Moody, T. W., F. X. Martin, and F. J. Byrne, eds. *A New History of Ireland,* Volume 3: *Early Modern Ireland, 1534–1691.* Oxford: Oxford University Press, 2001.

Mukerji, Chandra. *From Graven Images: Patterns of Modern Materialism.* New York: Columbia University Press, 1983.

Neale, J. E. *Elizabeth I and Her Parliaments, 1559–1581.* London: Cape, 1971.

———. *Queen Elizabeth I.* London: Pimlico, 1998.

Nichols, John, ed. *The Progresses and Public Processions of Queen Elizabeth.* 3 vols. London: J. Nichols, 1823.

Palliser, D. M. *The Age of Elizabeth: England under the Later Tudors, 1547–1603.* 2nd ed. New York: Longman, 1992.

Parry, J. H. *The Age of Reconnaissance: Discovery, Exploration, and Settlement, 1450 to 1650.* New York: Praeger, 1969.

Pearson, Lu Emily Hess. *Elizabethans at Home.* Stanford: Stanford University Press, 1967.

Peck, Linda Levy. *Court Patronage and Corruption in Early Stuart England.* Boston: Unwin Hyman, 1990.

Peters, Christine. *Women in Early Modern Britain, 1450–1640.* New York: Palgrave Macmillan, 2004.

Pocock, J. G. A. *The Ancient Constitution and the Feudal Law: Study of English Historical Thought in the Seventeenth Century—A Reissue with a Retrospect.* Rev. ed. New York: Cambridge University Press, 1987.

Rappaport, Steve. *Worlds within Worlds: Structures of Life in Sixteenth-Century London.* New York: Cambridge University Press, 1989.

Sharpe, J. A. *Crime in Early Modern England, 1550–1750.* 2nd ed. New York: Longman, 1999.

———. *Early Modern England: A Social History, 1550–1760.* 2nd ed. London: Arnold, 1997.

Slack, Paul. *The Impact of Plague in Tudor and Stuart England.* Boston: Routledge and Kegan Paul, 1985.

———. *Poverty and Policy in Tudor and Stuart England.* New York: Longman, 1988.

———, ed. *Rebellion, Popular Protest, and the Social Order in Early Modern England.* New York: Cambridge University Press, 1984.

Stone, Lawrence. *The Causes of the English Revolution, 1529–1642.* New York: Routledge, 2002.

———. *The Crisis of the Aristocracy, 1558–1641.* Oxford: Clarendon, 1965.

———. *The Family, Sex and Marriage in England, 1500–1800.* New York: Harper & Row, 1979.

Thirsk, Joan. *Economic Policy and Projects: The Development of a Consumer Society in Early Modern England.* Oxford: Clarendon, 1978.

Thomas, Keith. *Religion and the Decline of Magic: Studies in Popular Beliefs in Sixteenth and Seventeenth Century England.* New York: Scribner, 1971.

Underdown, David. *Fire from Heaven: Life in an English Town in the Seventeenth Century.* London: HarperCollins, 1992.

———. *Revel, Riot, and Rebellion: Popular Politics and Culture in England, 1603–1660.* Oxford: Clarendon, 1985.

Williams, Penry. *The Later Tudors: England, 1547–1603.* New York: Oxford University Press, 1995.

Wrightson, Keith. *Earthly Necessities: Economic Lives in Early Modern Britain.* New Haven: Yale University Press, 2000.

———. *English Society, 1580–1680.* London: Hutchinson, 1982.

Yates, Frances Amelia. *Astraea: The Imperial Theme in the Sixteenth Century.* London: Routledge and Kegan Paul, 1975.

Zagorin, Perez. *Rebels and Rulers, 1500–1660.* 2 vols. New York: Cambridge University Press, 1982.

Intellectual and Religious History

Armitage, David. *The Ideological Origins of the British Empire.* New York: Cambridge University Press, 2000.

Baker, Herschel Clay. *The Race of Time: Three Lectures on Renaissance Historiography.* Toronto: University of Toronto Press, 1967.

Barkan, Leonard. *Nature's Work of Art: The Human Body as Image of the World.* New Haven: Yale University Press, 1975.

Bossy, John. *Christianity in the West, 1400–1700.* New York: Oxford University Press, 1985.

Bouwsma, William James. *John Calvin: A Sixteenth-Century Portrait.* New York: Oxford University Press, 1988.

Cassirer, Ernst. *The Individual and the Cosmos in Renaissance Philosophy.* Trans. Mario Domandi. Philadelphia: University of Pennsylvania Press, 1972.

Clark, Stuart. *Thinking with Demons: The Idea of Witchcraft in Early Modern Europe.* New York: Oxford University Press, 1997.

Collinson, Patrick. *The Birthpangs of Protestant England: Religion and Cultural Change in the Sixteenth and Seventeenth Centuries.* New York: St. Martin's, 1988.

———. *The Elizabethan Puritan Movement.* New York: Oxford University Press, 1990.

———. *The Religion of Protestants: The Church in English Society, 1559–1625.* Oxford: Clarendon, 1982.

Doran, Susan, and Christopher Durston. *Princes, Pastors, and People: The Church and Religion in England, 1500–1700.* Rev. ed. New York: Routledge, 2003.

Duffy, Eamon. *The Stripping of the Altars: Traditional Religion in England, c. 1400–c. 1580.* 2nd ed. New Haven: Yale University Press, 1992.

Gadd, Ian, and Alexandra Gillespie, eds. *John Stow (1525–1605) and the Making of the English Past.* London: British Library, 2004.

Haigh, Christopher. *English Reformations: Religion, Politics, and Society under the Tudors.* New York: Oxford University Press, 1993.

Hill, Christopher. *Society and Puritanism in Pre-Revolutionary England.* New York: Schocken Books, 1964.

Houlbrooke, Ralph A. *Death, Religion, and the Family in England, 1480–1700.* New York: Oxford University Press, 1998.

Kelly, Henry Ansgar. *Divine Providence in the England of Shakespeare's Histories.* Cambridge, Mass.: Harvard University Press, 1970.

Kilroy, Gerard. *Edmund Campion. Memory and Transcription.* Aldershot, Eng.: Ashgate, 2005.

Klaits, Joseph. *Servants of Satan: The Age of the Witch Hunts.* Bloomington: Indiana University Press, 1985.

Kristeller, Paul Oskar. *Renaissance Thought: The Classic, Scholastic, and Humanistic Strains.* New York: Harper & Row, 1961.

Levao, Ronald. *Renaissance Minds and Their Fictions: Cusanus, Sidney, Shakespeare.* Berkeley: University of California Press, 1985.

Levin, Harry. *The Myth of the Golden Age in the Renaissance.* Bloomington: University of Indiana Press, 1969.

Levy, Fred Jacob. *Tudor Historical Thought*. San Marino, Calif.: Huntington Library Press, 1967.

MacCulloch, Diarmaid. *The Later Reformation in England, 1547–1603*. 2nd ed. New York: Palgrave, 2001.

———. *The Reformation*. New York: Viking, 2004.

Mack, Peter, ed. *Renaissance Rhetoric*. New York: St. Martin's, 1994.

Marotti, Arthur F. *Religious Ideology and Cultural Fantasy: Catholic and Anti-Catholic Discourses in Early Modern England*. Notre Dame, Ind.: University of Notre Dame Press, 2005.

Marshall, Peter. *Beliefs and the Dead in Reformation England*. London: Oxford University Press, 2002.

Oldridge, Darren, ed. *The Witchcraft Reader*. London: Routledge, 2001.

Patterson, Annabel M. *Reading Holinshed's* Chronicles. Chicago: University of Chicago Press, 1994.

Popkin, Richard H. *The History of Skepticism from Erasmus to Spinoza*. Berkeley: University of California Press, 1979.

Sharpe, James. *Instruments of Darkness: Witchcraft in England 1550–1750*. New York: Penguin Books, 1996.

Shuger, Debora Kuller. *Habits of Thought in the English Renaissance: Religion, Politics, and the Dominant Culture*. Berkeley: University of California Press, 1990.

Sonnino, Lee A. *A Handbook to Sixteenth-Century Rhetoric*. London: Routledge and Kegan Paul, 1968.

Strong, Roy. *The Cult of Elizabeth: Elizabethan Portraiture and Pageantry*. London: Thames and Hudson, 1977.

———. *The English Icon: Elizabethan & Jacobean Portraiture*. New York: Pantheon Books, 1969.

Walsham, Alexandra. *Providence in Early Modern England*. New York: Oxford University Press, 1999.

Watt, Tessa. *Cheap Print and Popular Piety, 1560–1649*. New York: Cambridge University Press, 1991.

Wind, Edgar. *Pagan Mysteries in the Renaissance*. Rev. and enl. ed. London: Oxford University Press, 1980.

Woolf, D. R. *Reading History in Early Modern England*. New York: Cambridge University Press, 2000.

———. *The Social Circulation of the Past: English Historical Culture, 1500–1730*. New York: Oxford University Press, 2003.

Cultural History and Early Modern Cultural Studies

Aers, David, Bob Hodge, and Gunther Kress. *Literature, Language, and Society in England, 1589–1680*. Totowa, N.J.: Barnes & Noble Books, 1981.

Agnew, Jean-Christophe. *Worlds Apart: The Market and the Theater in Anglo-American Thought, 1550–1750*. New York: Cambridge University Press, 1986.

Andersen, Jennifer, and Elizabeth Sauer, eds. *Books and Readers in Early Modern England: Material Studies*. Philadelphia: University of Pennsylvania Press, 2001.

Bakhtin, Mikhail. *Rabelais and His World*. Trans. Hélène Iswolsky. Rev. ed. Bloomington: Indiana University Press, 1984.

Baldwin, Thomas Whitfield. *William Shakespere's Small Latine & Lesse Greeke*. Urbana: University of Illinois Press, 1944.

Barkan, Leonard. *The Gods Made Flesh: Metamorphosis & the Pursuit of Paganism*. New Haven: Yale University Press, 1986.

Barker, Francis. *The Tremulous Private Body: Essays on Subjection*. New York: Methuen, 1984.

Baron, Sabrina Alcorn, ed. *The Reader Revealed*. Washington, D.C.: Folger Shakespeare Library, 2001.

Bartels, Emily Carroll. *Spectacles of Strangeness: Imperialism, Alienation, and Marlowe.* Philadelphia: University of Pennsylvania Press, 1993.

Beilin, Elaine V. *Redeeming Eve: Women Writers of the English Renaissance.* Princeton: Princeton University Press, 1987.

Blank, Paula. *Broken English: Dialects and the Politics of Language in Renaissance Literature.* New York: Routledge, 1996.

Bloom, Gina. *Voice in Motion: Staging Gender, Shaping Sound in Early Modern England.* Philadelphia: Pennsylvania University Press, 2007.

Bray, Alan. *Homosexuality in Renaissance England.* Rev. ed. New York: Columbia University Press, 1995.

Brayman Hackel, Heidi. *Reading Material in Early Modern England: Print, Gender, and Literacy.* New York: Cambridge University Press, 2005.

Briggs, Julia. *This Stage-Play World: Texts and Contexts, 1580–1625.* 2nd ed. New York: Oxford University Press, 1997.

Bristol, Michael D. *Carnival and Theater: Plebeian Culture and the Structure of Authority in Renaissance England.* New York: Methuen, 1985.

Brotton, Jerry. *Trading Territories: Mapping the Early Modern World.* London: Reaktion Books, 1997.

Brown, Pamela Allen. *Better a Shrew than a Sheep: Women, Drama, and the Culture of Jest in Early Modern England.* Ithaca, N.Y.: Cornell University Press, 2003.

Burke, Peter. *Popular Culture in Early Modern Europe.* New York: New York University Press, 1978.

Burt, Richard, and John Michael Archer, eds. *Enclosure Acts: Sexuality, Property, and Culture in Early Modern England.* Ithaca, N.Y.: Cornell University Press, 1994.

Bushnell, Rebecca W. *A Culture of Teaching: Early Modern Humanism in Theory and Practice.* Ithaca, N.Y.: Cornell University Press, 1996.

Buxton, John. *Elizabethan Taste.* London: Macmillan, 1963.

Caldwell, John. *The Oxford History of English Music.* New York: Oxford University Press, 1991.

Carroll, William C. *Fat King, Lean Beggar: Representations of Poverty in the Age of Shakespeare.* Ithaca, N.Y.: Cornell University Press, 1996.

Clegg, Cyndia Susan. *Press Censorship in Elizabethan England.* New York: Cambridge University Press, 1997.

———. *Press Censorship in Jacobean England.* New York: Cambridge University Press, 2001.

Cox, John D. *The Devil and the Sacred in English Drama, 1350–1642.* New York: Cambridge University Press, 2000.

Crane, Mary Thomas. *Framing Authority: Sayings, Self, and Society in Sixteenth-Century England.* Princeton: Princeton University Press, 1993.

Crawford, Julie. *Marvelous Protestantism: Monstrous Births in Post-Reformation England.* Baltimore: Johns Hopkins University Press, 2005.

Cressy, David. *Literacy and the Social Order: Reading and Writing in Tudor and Stuart England.* New York: Cambridge University Press, 1980.

De Grazia, Margreta, Maureen Quilligan, and Peter Stallybrass, eds. *Subject and Object in Renaissance Culture.* New York: Cambridge University Press, 1996.

Diehl, Huston. *Staging Reform, Reforming the Stage: Protestantism and Popular Theater in Early Modern England.* Ithaca, N.Y.: Cornell University Press, 1997.

Dolan, Frances E. *Dangerous Familiars: Representations of Domestic Crime in England, 1550–1700.* Ithaca, N.Y.: Cornell University Press, 1994.

———. *Whores of Babylon: Catholicism, Gender, and Seventeenth-Century Print Culture.* Ithaca, N.Y.: Cornell University Press, 1999.

Eisenstein, Elizabeth L. *The Printing Press as an Agent of Change: Communications and Cultural Transformations in Early-Modern Europe.* 2 vols. New York: Cambridge University Press, 1979.

Ferguson, Margaret W. *Dido's Daughters: Literacy, Gender, and Empire in Early Modern England and France*. Chicago: University of Chicago Press, 2003.

Ferguson, Margaret W., Maureen Quilligan, and Nancy J. Vickers, eds. *Rewriting the Renaissance: The Discourses of Sexual Difference in Early Modern Europe*. Chicago: University of Chicago Press, 1986.

Fisher, Will. *Materializing Gender in Early Modern English Literature and Culture*. New York: Cambridge University Press, 2006.

Fleming, Juliet. *Graffiti and the Writing Arts of Early Modern England*. Philadelphia: University of Pennsylvania Press, 2001.

Frye, Susan. *Elizabeth I: The Competition for Representation*. New York: Oxford University Press, 1993.

Fumerton, Patricia. *Cultural Aesthetics: Renaissance Literature and the Practice of Social Ornament*. Chicago: University of Chicago Press, 1991.

———. *Unsettled: The Culture of Mobility and the Working Poor in Early Modern England*. Chicago: University of Chicago Press, 2006.

Gillies, John. *Shakespeare and the Geography of Difference*. New York: Cambridge University Press, 1994.

Goldberg, Jonathan. *James I and the Politics of Literature: Jonson, Shakespeare, Donne, and Their Contemporaries*. Baltimore: Johns Hopkins University Press, 1983.

———. *Writing Matter: From the Hands of the English Renaissance*. Stanford: Stanford University Press, 1990.

———, ed. *Queering the Renaissance*. Durham, N.C.: Duke University Press, 1994.

Greenblatt, Stephen. *Learning to Curse: Essays in Early Modern Culture*. New York: Routledge, 1990.

———. *Renaissance Self-Fashioning: From More to Shakespeare*. Chicago: University of Chicago Press, 1980.

———, ed. *New World Encounters*. Berkeley: University of California Press, 1993.

———, ed. *Representing the English Renaissance*. Berkeley: University of California Press, 1988.

Grout, Donald Jay, and Hermine Weigel Williams. *A Short History of Opera*. 4th ed. New York: Columbia University Press, 2003.

Hall, Kim F. *Things of Darkness: Economies of Race and Gender in Early Modern England*. Ithaca, N.Y.: Cornell University Press, 1995.

Harris, Jonathan Gil. *Foreign Bodies and the Body Politic: Discourses of Social Pathology in Early Modern England*. New York: Cambridge University Press, 1998.

Harvey, Elizabeth D., ed. *Sensible Flesh: On Touch in Early Modern Culture*. Philadelphia: University of Pennsylvania Press, 2003.

Haselkorn, Anne M., and Betty S. Travitsky, eds. *The Renaissance Englishwoman in Print: Counterbalancing the Canon*. Amherst: University of Massachusetts Press, 1990.

Helgerson, Richard. *Forms of Nationhood: The Elizabethan Writing of England*. Chicago: University of Chicago Press, 1992.

Henderson, Katherine Usher, and Barbara F. McManus. *Half Humankind: Contexts and Texts of the Controversy About Women in England, 1540–1640*. Urbana: University of Illinois Press, 1985.

Hendricks, Margo, and Patricia Parker, eds. *Women, "Race," and Writing in the Early Modern Period*. New York: Routledge, 1994.

Hillman, David, and Carla Mazzio, eds. *The Body in Parts: Fantasies of Corporeality in Early Modern Europe*. New York: Routledge, 1997.

Hoeniger, F. David. *Medicine and Shakespeare in the English Renaissance*. Newark: University of Delaware Press, 1992.

Huizinga, Johan. *The Autumn of the Middle Ages*. Trans. Rodney J. Payton and Ulrich Mammitzsch. Chicago: University of Chicago Press, 1996.

Hull, Suzanne W. *Chaste, Silent & Obedient: English Books for Women, 1475–1640*. San Marino, Calif.: Huntington Library, 1982.

Hutson, Lorna. *The Usurer's Daughter: Male Friendship and Fictions of Women in Sixteenth-Century England*. New York: Routledge, 1994.

Javitch, Daniel. *Poetry and Courtliness in Renaissance England*. Princeton: Princeton University Press, 1978.

Jones, Ann Rosalind, and Peter Stallybrass. *Renaissance Clothing and the Materials of Memory*. New York: Cambridge University Press, 2000.

Jordan, Constance. *Renaissance Feminism: Literary Texts and Political Models*. Ithaca, N.Y.: Cornell University Press, 1990.

Knapp, Jeffrey. *Shakespeare's Tribe: Church, Nation, and Theater in Renaissance England*. Chicago: University of Chicago Press, 2002.

Laqueur, Thomas Walter. *Making Sex: Body and Gender from the Greeks to Freud*. Cambridge, Mass.: Harvard University Press, 1990.

MacDonald, Joyce Green. *Women and Race in Early Modern Texts*. New York: Cambridge University Press, 2002.

Magnusson, Lynne. *Shakespeare and Social Dialogue: Dramatic Language and Elizabethan Letters*. New York: Cambridge University Press, 1999.

Manley, Lawrence. *Literature and Culture in Early Modern London*. New York: Cambridge University Press, 1995.

Marcus, Leah S. *The Politics of Mirth: Jonson, Herrick, Milton, Marvell, and the Defense of Old Holiday Pastimes*. Chicago: University of Chicago Press, 1986.

McJannet, Linda. *The Sultan Speaks: Dialogue in English Plays and Histories about the Ottoman Turks*. New York: Palgrave Macmillan, 2006.

Meron, Theodor. *Bloody Constraint: War and Chivalry in Shakespeare*. New York: Oxford University Press, 1998.

Miller, David Lee, Sharon O'Dair, and Harold Weber, eds. *The Production of English Renaissance Culture*. Ithaca, N.Y.: Cornell University Press, 1994.

Montrose, Louis. *The Subject of Elizabeth: Authority, Gender, and Representation*. Chicago: University of Chicago Press, 2006.

Neill, Michael. *Issues of Death: Mortality and Identity in English Renaissance Tragedy*. Oxford: Clarendon, 1997.

Netzloff, Mark. *England's Internal Colonies: Class, Capital, and the Literature of Early Modern English Colonialism*. New York: Palgrave Macmillan, 2003.

Orlin, Lena Cowen. *Private Matters and Public Culture in Post-Reformation England*. Ithaca, N.Y.: Cornell University Press, 1994.

———, ed. *Material London, ca. 1600*. Philadelphia: University of Pennsylvania Press, 2000.

Parry, Graham. *The Golden Age Restor'd: The Culture of the Stuart Court, 1603–42*. New York: St. Martin's, 1981.

Paster, Gail Kern. *The Body Embarrassed: Drama and the Disciplines of Shame in Early Modern England*. Ithaca, N.Y.: Cornell University Press, 1993.

———. *Humoring the Body: Emotions and the Shakespearean Stage*. Chicago: University of Chicago Press, 2004.

Paster, Gail Kern, Katherine Rowe, and Mary Floyd-Wilson, eds. *Reading the Early Modern Passions: Essays in the Cultural History of Emotion*. Philadelphia: University of Pennsylvania Press, 2004.

Patterson, Annabel M. *Censorship and Interpretation: The Conditions of Writing and Reading in Early Modern England*. Madison: University of Wisconsin Press, 1984.

Peck, Linda Levy. *Consuming Splendor: Society and Culture in Seventeenth-Century England*. New York: Cambridge University Press, 2005.

Platt, Peter G. *Reason Diminished: Shakespeare and the Marvelous*. Lincoln: University of Nebraska Press, 1997.

Pollard, Tanya. *Drugs and Theater in Early Modern England*. New York: Oxford University Press, 2005.

Sanders, Eve Rachele. *Gender and Literacy on Stage in Early Modern England*. New York: Cambridge University Press, 1998.

Sawday, Jonathan. *The Body Emblazoned: Dissection and the Human Body in Renaissance Culture*. New York: Routledge, 1995.

Schoenfeldt, Michael C. *Bodies and Selves in Early Modern England: Physiology and Inwardness in Spenser, Shakespeare, Herbert, and Milton*. New York: Cambridge University Press, 1999.

Schwyzer, Philip. *Literature, Nationalism, and Memory in Early Modern England and Wales*. New York: Cambridge University Press, 2004.

Shapiro, James. *Shakespeare and the Jews*. New York: Columbia University Press, 1996.

Sharpe, Kevin, and Peter Lake, eds. *Culture and Politics in Early Stuart England*. Stanford: Stanford University Press, 1993.

Sherman, William H. *John Dee: The Politics of Reading and Writing in the English Renaissance*. Amherst: University of Massachusetts Press, 1995.

Shuger, Debora. *Censorship and Cultural Sensibility: The Regulation of Language in Tudor-Stuart England*. Philadelphia: University of Pennsylvania Press, 2006.

Simon, Joan. *Education and Society in Tudor England*. Cambridge, Eng.: Cambridge University Press, 1966.

Singh, Jyotsna G. *Colonial Narratives/Cultural Dialogues: 'Discoveries' of India in the Language of Colonialism*. New York: Routledge, 1996.

Smith, Bruce R. *The Acoustic World of Early Modern England: Attending to the O-Factor*. Chicago: University of Chicago Press, 1999.

———. *Homosexual Desire in Shakespeare's England: A Cultural Poetics*. Chicago: University of Chicago Press, 1994.

Smuts, R. Malcolm. *Court Culture and the Origins of a Royalist Tradition in Early Stuart England*. Philadelphia: University of Pennsylvania Press, 1987.

Stallybrass, Peter, and Allon White. *The Politics and Poetics of Transgression*. Ithaca, N.Y.: Cornell University Press, 1986.

Traub, Valerie, M. Lindsay Kaplan, and Dympna Callaghan, eds. *Feminist Readings of Early Modern Culture: Emerging Subjects*. New York: Cambridge University Press, 1996.

Turner, Henry S. *The English Renaissance Stage: Geometry, Poetics, and the Practical Spatial Arts 1580–1630*. New York: Oxford University Press, 2006.

Turner, James Grantham, ed. *Sexuality and Gender in Early Modern Europe: Institutions, Texts, Images*. New York: Cambridge University Press, 1993.

Wall, Wendy. *Staging Domesticity: Household Work and English Identity in Early Modern Drama*. New York: Cambridge University Press, 2002.

Watson, Robert N. *The Rest Is Silence: Death as Annihilation in the English Renaissance*. Berkeley: University of California Press, 1994.

Whigham, Frank. *Ambition and Privilege: The Social Tropes of Elizabethan Courtesy Theory*. Berkeley: University of California Press, 1984.

Woodbridge, Linda. *Vagrancy, Homelessness, and English Renaissance Literature*. Urbana: University of Illinois Press, 2001.

———. *Women and the English Renaissance: Literature and the Nature of Womankind, 1540 to 1620*. Urbana: University of Illinois Press, 1984.

Shakespeare's Generic, Literary, and Theatrical Contexts

Alpers, Paul. *What Is Pastoral?* Chicago: University of Chicago Press, 1996.

Altman, Joel. *The Tudor Play of Mind: Rhetorical Inquiry and the Development of Elizabethan Drama*. Berkeley: University of California Press, 1978.

Barish, Jonas. *The Antitheatrical Prejudice*. Berkeley: University of California Press, 1981.

Bate, Jonathan. *Shakespeare and Ovid*. Oxford: Clarendon, 1993.

Bates, Catherine. *The Rhetoric of Courtship in Elizabethan Language and Literature*. New York: Cambridge University Press, 1992.

Beckwith, Sarah. *Signifying God: Social Relation and Symbolic Act in the York Corpus Christi Plays.* Chicago: University of Chicago Press, 2001.

Belsey, Catherine. *The Subject of Tragedy: Identity and Difference in Renaissance Drama.* New York: Methuen, 1985.

Bevington, David M. *From "Mankind" to Marlowe: Growth of Structure in the Popular Drama of Tudor England.* Cambridge, Mass.: Harvard University Press, 1962.

———. *Tudor Drama and Politics: A Critical Approach to Topical Meaning.* Cambridge, Mass.: Harvard University Press, 1968.

Bly, Mary. *Queer Virgins and Virgin Queans on the Early Modern Stage.* New York: Oxford University Press, 2000.

Bowers, Fredson Thayer. *Elizabethan Revenge Tragedy, 1587–1642.* Princeton: Princeton University Press, 1940.

Braden, Gordon. *Renaissance Tragedy and the Senecan Tradition: Anger's Privilege.* New Haven: Yale University Press, 1985.

Bruster, Douglas. *Drama and the Market in the Age of Shakespeare.* New York: Cambridge University Press, 1992.

Bullough, Geoffrey, ed. *Narrative and Dramatic Sources of Shakespeare.* 8 vols. New York: Columbia University Press, 1957–75.

Butler, Martin. *Theatre and Crisis, 1632–1642.* New York: Cambridge University Press, 1984.

Carroll, William C. *The Metamorphoses of Shakespearean Comedy.* Princeton: Princeton University Press, 1985.

Cartwright, Kent. *Theatre and Humanism: English Drama in the Sixteenth Century.* New York: Cambridge University Press, 1999.

Clubb, Louise George. *Italian Drama in Shakespeare's Time.* New Haven: Yale University Press, 1989.

Cohen, Walter. *Drama of a Nation: Public Theater in Renaissance England and Spain.* Ithaca, N.Y.: Cornell University Press, 1985.

Crewe, Jonathan. *Trials of Authorship: Anterior Forms and Poetic Reconstruction from Wyatt to Shakespeare.* Berkeley: University of California Press, 1990.

Danson, Lawrence. *Shakespeare's Dramatic Genres.* New York: Oxford University Press, 2000.

Dawson, Anthony B., and Paul Yachnin. *The Culture of Playgoing in Shakespeare's England: A Collaborative Debate.* New York: Cambridge University Press, 2001.

Dillon, Janette. *Language and Stage in Medieval and Renaissance England.* New York: Cambridge University Press, 1998.

Felperin, Howard. *Shakespearean Romance.* Princeton: Princeton University Press, 1972.

Finkelpearl, Philip J. *John Marston of the Middle Temple: An Elizabethan Dramatist in His Social Setting.* Cambridge, Mass.: Harvard University Press, 1969.

Gardiner, Harold C. *Mysteries' End: An Investigation of the Last Days of the Medieval Religious Stage.* New Haven: Yale University Press, 1946.

Halasz, Alexandra. *The Marketplace of Print: Pamphlets and the Public Sphere in Early Modern England.* New York: Cambridge University Press, 1997.

Harbage, Alfred. *Shakespeare and the Rival Traditions.* New York: Macmillan, 1952.

Hardison, O. B. *Christian Rite and Christian Drama in the Middle Ages: Essays in the Origin and Early History of Modern Drama.* Baltimore: Johns Hopkins University Press, 1965.

Heinemann, Margot. *Puritanism and Theatre: Thomas Middleton and Opposition Drama under the Early Stuarts.* New York: Cambridge University Press, 1980.

Honan, Park. *Christopher Marlowe: Poet & Spy.* New York: Oxford University Press, 2005.

Honigmann, E. A. J., ed. *Shakespeare and His Contemporaries: Essays in Comparison.* Manchester: Manchester University Press, 1986.

———, ed. *Shakespeare's Impact on His Contemporaries.* London: Macmillan, 1982.

Howard, Jean E. *Theater of a City: The Places of London Comedy, 1598–1642.* Philadelphia: University of Pennsylvania Press, 2007.

Hunter, G. K. *John Lyly: The Humanist as Courtier.* Cambridge, Mass.: Harvard University Press, 1962.

Jones, Emrys. *The Origins of Shakespeare.* Oxford: Clarendon, 1977.

———. *Scenic Form in Shakespeare.* Oxford: Clarendon, 1971.

Kastan, David Scott, and Peter Stallybrass, eds. *Staging the Renaissance: Reinterpretations of Elizabethan and Jacobean Drama.* New York: Routledge, 1991.

Kermode, Lloyd Edward, Jason Scott-Warren, and Martine van Elk, eds. *Tudor Drama Before Shakespeare, 1485–1590: New Directions for Research, Criticism, and Pedagogy.* New York: Palgrave Macmillan, 2004.

Kolve, V. A. *The Play Called Corpus Christi.* Stanford: Stanford University Press, 1966.

Leggatt, Alexander. *Citizen Comedy in the Age of Shakespeare.* Toronto: University of Toronto Press, 1973.

———. *Introduction to English Renaissance Comedy.* Manchester: Manchester University Press, 1999.

Levin, Harry. *Shakespeare and the Revolution of the Times: Perspectives and Commentaries.* New York: Oxford University Press, 1976.

Levith, Murray J. *Shakespeare's Italian Settings and Plays.* Basingstoke: Macmillan, 1989.

Lomax, Marion. *Stage Images and Traditions: Shakespeare to Ford.* New York: Cambridge University Press, 1987.

Martindale, Charles, and A. B. Taylor, eds. *Shakespeare and the Classics.* New York: Cambridge University Press, 2004.

Masten, Jeffrey. *Textual Intercourse: Collaboration, Authorship, and Sexualities in Renaissance Drama.* New York: Cambridge University Press, 1997.

McLuskie, Kathleen. *Renaissance Dramatists.* New York: Harvester Wheatsheaf, 1989.

McMillin, Scott. *The Elizabethan Theatre and the Book of Sir Thomas More.* Ithaca, N.Y.: Cornell University Press, 1987.

McMillin, Scott, and Sally-Beth MacLean. *The Queen's Men and Their Plays.* New York: Cambridge University Press, 1998.

McMullan, Gordon, and Jonathan Hope, eds. *The Politics of Tragicomedy: Shakespeare and After.* New York: Routledge, 1991.

Miola, Robert S. *Shakespeare's Reading.* New York: Oxford University Press, 2000.

———. *Shakespeare's Rome.* New York: Cambridge University Press, 1983.

Newcomb, Lori Humphrey. *Reading Popular Romance in Early Modern England.* New York: Columbia University Press, 2002.

Norbrook, David. *Poetry and Politics in the English Renaissance.* London: Routledge and Kegan Paul, 1984.

Orgel, Stephen. *The Illusion of Power: Political Theater in the English Renaissance.* Berkeley: University of California Press, 1975.

Peters, Julie Stone. *Theatre of the Book, 1480–1880: Print, Text, and Performance in Europe.* New York: Oxford University Press, 2000.

Riggs, David. *Ben Jonson: A Life.* Cambridge, Mass.: Harvard University Press, 1989.

———. *The World of Christopher Marlowe.* London: Faber and Faber, 2004.

Rose, Mark. *Shakespearean Design.* Cambridge, Mass.: Belknap Press, 1972.

Rose, Mary Beth. *The Expense of Spirit: Love and Sexuality in English Renaissance Drama.* Ithaca, N.Y.: Cornell University Press, 1988.

Salingar, Leo. *Dramatic Form in Shakespeare and the Jacobeans: Essays.* New York: Cambridge University Press, 1986.

———. *Shakespeare and the Traditions of Comedy.* New York: Cambridge University Press, 1974.

Schwyzer, Philip. *Archaeologies of English Renaissance Literature.* New York: Oxford University Press, 2007.

Shapiro, James. *Rival Playwrights: Marlowe, Jonson, Shakespeare.* New York: Columbia University Press, 1991.

Snyder, Susan. *The Comic Matrix of Shakespeare's Tragedies:* Romeo and Juliet, Hamlet, Othello, *and* King Lear. Princeton: Princeton University Press, 1979.

Spivack, Bernard. *Shakespeare and the Allegory of Evil: The History of a Metaphor in Relation to His Major Villains.* New York: Columbia University Press, 1958.

Thomas, Vivian. *The Moral Universe of Shakespeare's Problem Plays.* New York: Routledge, 1991.

Vickers, Brian, ed. *English Renaissance Literary Criticism.* New York: Oxford University Press, 1999.

Vitkus, Daniel. *Turning Turk: English Theater and the Multicultural Mediterranean, 1570–1630.* New York: Palgrave Macmillan, 2003.

Weimann, Robert. *Shakespeare and the Popular Tradition in the Theater: Studies in the Social Dimension of Dramatic Form and Function.* Ed. Robert Schwartz. Baltimore: Johns Hopkins University Press, 1978.

Whitney, Charles. *Early Responses to Renaissance Drama.* New York: Cambridge University Press, 2006.

Woolf, Rosemary. *The English Mystery Plays.* Berkeley: University of California Press, 1972.

The Playing Field: Theaters, Actors, Patrons, and the State

Astington, John H. *English Court Theatre, 1558–1642.* Cambridge, Eng.: Cambridge University Press, 1999.

———, ed. *The Development of Shakespeare's Theater.* New York: AMS Press, 1992.

Barroll, J. Leeds. *Politics, Plague, and Shakespeare's Theater: The Stuart Years.* Ithaca, N.Y.: Cornell University Press, 1991.

Beckerman, Bernard. *Shakespeare at the Globe, 1599–1609.* New York: Macmillan, 1962.

Bentley, Gerald Eades. *The Jacobean and Caroline Stage.* 7 vols. Oxford: Clarendon, 1941–68.

———. *The Profession of Dramatist in Shakespeare's Time, 1590–1642.* Princeton: Princeton University Press, 1971.

———. *The Profession of Player in Shakespeare's Time, 1590–1642.* Princeton: Princeton University Press, 1984.

Berry, Herbert. *Shakespeare's Playhouses.* Illustrated by C. Walter Hodges. New York: AMS Press, 1987.

Bradbrook, M. C. *The Rise of the Common Player: A Study of Actor and Society in Shakespeare's England.* Cambridge, Mass.: Harvard University Press, 1962.

Chambers, E. K. *The Elizabethan Stage.* 4 vols. Oxford: Clarendon, 1923.

———. *The Mediaeval Stage.* 2 vols. Oxford: Clarendon, 1903.

Clare, Janet. *Art Made Tongue-Tied by Authority: Elizabethan and Jacobean Dramatic Censorship.* 2nd ed. Manchester: Manchester University Press, 1999.

Cook, Ann Jennalie. *The Privileged Playgoers of Shakespeare's London: 1576–1642.* Princeton: Princeton University Press, 1981.

Cox, John D., and David Scott Kastan, eds. *A New History of Early English Drama.* New York: Columbia University Press, 1997.

Dessen, Alan C. *Elizabethan Stage Conventions and Modern Interpreters.* Cambridge, Eng.: Cambridge University Press, 1984.

———. *Recovering Shakespeare's Theatrical Vocabulary.* New York: Cambridge University Press, 1995.

Dessen, Alan C., and Leslie Thomson. *A Dictionary of Stage Directions in English Drama, 1580–1642.* New York: Cambridge University Press, 1999.

Dillon, Janette. *The Cambridge Introduction to Early English Theatre.* New York: Cambridge University Press, 2006.

Dutton, Richard. *Licensing, Censorship and Authorship in Early Modern England: Buggeswords.* Houndmills, Basingstoke: Palgrave Macmillan, 2000.

————. *Mastering the Revels: The Regulation and Censorship of English Renaissance Drama*. London: Macmillan, 1991.

Dutton, Richard, Alison Findlay, and Richard Wilson, eds. *Region, Religion, and Patronage: Lancastrian Shakespeare*. Manchester: Manchester University Press, 2003.

Erne, Lukas. *Shakespeare as Literary Dramatist*. New York: Cambridge University Press, 2003.

Foakes, R. A. *Illustrations of the English Stage, 1580–1642*. Stanford: Stanford University Press, 1985.

Gair, W. Reavley. *The Children of Paul's: The Story of a Theatre Company, 1553–1608*. New York: Cambridge University Press, 1982.

Greg, W. W., ed. *Dramatic Documents from the Elizabethan Playhouses: Stage Plots: Actor's Parts: Prompt Books*. 2 vols. Oxford: Clarendon, 1931.

Gurr, Andrew. *Playgoing in Shakespeare's London*. 3rd ed. New York: Cambridge University Press, 2004.

————. *The Shakespeare Company, 1594–1642*. New York: Cambridge University Press, 2004.

————. *The Shakespearian Playing Companies*. Oxford: Clarendon, 1996.

————. *The Shakespearean Stage, 1574–1642*. 3rd ed. New York: Cambridge University Press, 1992.

Gurr, Andrew, and John Orrell. *Rebuilding Shakespeare's Globe*. London: Weidenfeld & Nicolson, 1989.

Harris, Jonathan Gil, and Natasha Korda, eds. *Staged Properties in Early Modern Drama*. New York: Cambridge University Press, 2002.

Hattaway, Michael. *Elizabethan Popular Theatre: Plays in Performance*. London: Routledge and Kegan Paul, 1982.

Henslowe, Philip. *Henslowe's Diary*. Ed. R. A. Foakes. 2nd ed. New York: Cambridge University Press, 2002.

Hodges, C. Walter. *The Globe Restored: A Study of the Elizabethan Theatre*. New York: Norton, 1973.

Holland, Peter, and Stephen Orgel, eds. *From Performance to Print in Shakespeare's England*. New York: Palgrave Macmillan, 2006.

————, eds. *From Script to Stage in Early Modern England*. Houndmills, Basingstoke: Palgrave Macmillan, 2004.

Ingram, William. *The Business of Playing: The Beginnings of Adult Professional Theater in Elizabethan London*. Ithaca, N.Y.: Cornell University Press, 1992.

Kernan, Alvin. *Shakespeare, the King's Playwright: Theater in the Stuart Court, 1603–1613*. New Haven: Yale University Press, 1995.

King, T. J. *Shakespearean Staging, 1599–1642*. Cambridge, Mass.: Harvard University Press, 1971.

Knutson, Roslyn Lander. *Playing Companies and Commerce in Shakespeare's Time*. Cambridge, Eng.: Cambridge University Press, 2001.

————. *The Repertory of Shakespeare's Company, 1594–1613*. Fayetteville: University of Arkansas Press, 1991.

Laroque, François. *Shakespeare's Festive World: Elizabethan Seasonal Entertainment and the Professional Stage*. New York: Cambridge University Press, 1991.

Lopez, Jeremy. *Theatrical Convention and Audience Response in Early Modern Drama*. New York: Cambridge University Press, 2002.

MacIntyre, Jean. *Costumes and Scripts in the Elizabethan Theatres*. Edmonton: University of Alberta Press, 1992.

Milling, Jane, and Peter Thomson, eds. *The Cambridge History of British Theatre*, Vol. 1: *Origins to 1660*. New York: Cambridge University Press, 2004.

Mulryne, J. R., and Margaret Shewring, eds. *Shakespeare's Globe Rebuilt*. New York: Cambridge University Press, 1997.

Munro, Lucy. *Children of the Queen's Revels: A Jacobean Theatre Repertory*. New York: Cambridge University Press, 2005.

Palfrey, Simon, and Tiffany Stern. *Shakespeare in Parts.* Oxford: Oxford University Press, 2007.

Shapiro, Michael. *Children of the Revels: The Boy Companies of Shakespeare's Time and Their Plays.* New York: Columbia University Press, 1977.

Smith, Irwin. *Shakespeare's Blackfriars Playhouse: Its History and Its Design.* New York: New York University Press, 1964.

Stern, Tiffany. *Making Shakespeare: From Stage to Page.* New York: Routledge, 2004.

———. *Rehearsal from Shakespeare to Sheridan.* Oxford: Clarendon, 2000.

White, Paul Whitfield, and Suzanne Westfall, eds. *Shakespeare and Theatrical Patronage in Early Modern England.* New York: Cambridge University Press, 2002.

Wickham, Glynne. *Early English Stages, 1300 to 1660.* 4 vols. New York: Routledge, 2002.

Wickham, Glynne, Herbert Berry, and William Ingram, eds. *English Professional Theatre, 1530–1660.* New York: Cambridge University Press, 2000.

Shakespeare's Life

Alexander, Peter. *Shakespeare's Life and Art.* New ed. New York: New York University Press, 1961.

Bate, Jonathan. *The Genius of Shakespeare.* London: Picador, 1997.

Bradbrook, M. C. *Shakespeare: The Poet in His World.* New York: Columbia University Press, 1978.

Chambers, E. K. *William Shakespeare: A Study of Facts and Problems.* 2 vols. Oxford: Clarendon, 1930.

Duncan-Jones, Katherine. *Ungentle Shakespeare: Scenes from His Life.* London: Arden Shakespeare, 2001.

Eccles, Mark. *Shakespeare in Warwickshire.* Madison: University of Wisconsin Press, 1961.

Edwards, Philip. *Shakespeare: A Writer's Progress.* New York: Oxford University Press, 1986.

Fraser, Russell A. *Shakespeare, The Later Years.* New York: Columbia University Press, 1992.

———. *Young Shakespeare.* New York: Columbia University Press, 1988.

Greenblatt, Stephen. *Will in the World: How Shakespeare Became Shakespeare.* New York: Norton, 2004.

Greer, Germaine. *Shakespeare.* New York: Oxford University Press, 1986.

Honan, Park. *Shakespeare: A Life.* New York: Oxford University Press, 1998.

Honigmann, E. A. J. *Shakespeare: The Lost Years.* 2nd ed. Manchester: Manchester University Press, 1998.

Hotson, Leslie. *Shakespeare Versus Shallow.* Boston: Little, Brown, and Company, 1931.

Levi, Peter. *The Life and Times of William Shakespeare.* New York: Macmillan, 1988.

Matus, Irvin Leigh. *Shakespeare, The Living Record.* Houndmills, Basingstoke: Macmillan, 1991.

Reese, M. M. *Shakespeare: His World and His Work.* Rev. ed. London: Edward Arnold, 1980.

Sams, Eric. *The Real Shakespeare: Retrieving the Early Years, 1564–1594.* New Haven: Yale University Press, 1995.

Schmidgall, Gary. *Shakespeare and the Poet's Life.* Lexington: University Press of Kentucky, 1990.

Schoenbaum, Samuel. *Shakespeare's Lives.* New ed. New York: Oxford University Press, 1991.

———. *William Shakespeare: A Compact Documentary Life.* Rev. ed. New York: Oxford University Press, 1987.

Shapiro, James. *A Year in the Life of William Shakespeare: 1599.* New York: Harper-Collins, 2005.

Taylor, Gary. *Reinventing Shakespeare: A Cultural History, from the Restoration to the Present.* New York: Weidenfeld & Nicolson, 1989.

Thomson, Peter. *Shakespeare's Professional Career.* New York: Cambridge University Press, 1992.

Wells, Stanley. *Shakespeare: A Life in Drama.* New York: Norton, 1995.

———. *Shakespeare: For All Time.* London: Macmillan, 2002.

Wood, Michael. *In Search of Shakespeare.* London: BBC, 2003.

Critical Approaches

Classics of Shakespeare Criticism

Barber, C. L. *Shakespeare's Festive Comedy: A Study of Dramatic Form and Its Relation to Social Custom.* Princeton: Princeton University Press, 1959.

Bradley, A. C. *Shakespearean Tragedy: Lectures on* Hamlet, Othello, King Lear, Macbeth. 3rd ed. New York: St. Martin's Press, 1992.

Coleridge, Samuel Taylor. *Coleridge on Shakespeare: The Text of the Lectures of 1811–12.* Ed. R. A. Foakes. Charlottesville: University Press of Virginia, 1971.

———. *Shakespearean Criticism.* 2 vols. Ed. T. M. Raysor. 2nd ed. New York: Dutton, 1969.

Eliot, T. S. "Shakespeare and the Stoicism of Seneca." *Selected Essays, 1917–1932.* New ed. New York: Harcourt, Brace, 1950.

Empson, William. *The Structure of Complex Words.* 3rd ed. London: Chatto & Windus, 1977.

Frye, Northrop. *Fools of Time: Studies in Shakespearean Tragedy.* Toronto: University of Toronto Press, 1967.

———. *A Natural Perspective: The Development of Shakespearean Comedy and Romance.* New York: Columbia University Press, 1965.

Hazlitt, William. *Characters of Shakespear's Plays.* London, 1817.

Johnson, Samuel. *Samuel Johnson on Shakespeare.* Ed. H. R. Woudhuysen. New York: Penguin, 1989.

Jones, Ernest. *Hamlet and Oedipus.* New York: Norton, 1949.

Kermode, Frank, ed. *Four Centuries of Shakespearian Criticism.* 1965. New York: Avon, 1965.

Knight, G. Wilson. *The Wheel of Fire: Interpretations of Shakespearean Tragedy, with Three New Essays.* 4th ed. New York: Harper & Row, 1977.

Kott, Jan. *Shakespeare Our Contemporary.* Trans. Boleslaw Taborski. Garden City, N.Y.: Anchor Books, 1966.

Morgann, Maurice. *Shakespearean Criticism.* Ed. Daniel A. Fineman. Oxford: Clarendon, 1972.

Spurgeon, Caroline F. E. *Shakespeare's Imagery, and What It Tells Us.* New York: Macmillan, 1935.

Tillyard, E. M. W. *Shakespeare's History Plays.* London: Chatto and Windus, 1944.

Vickers, Brian, ed. *Shakespeare: The Critical Heritage.* 6 vols. London: Routledge and Kegan Paul, 1974–1981.

General Studies

Barton, Anne. *Essays, Mainly Shakespearean.* New York: Cambridge University Press, 1994.

Bloom, Harold. *Shakespeare: The Invention of the Human.* New York: Riverhead Books, 1998.

Burckhardt, Sigurd. *Shakespearean Meanings*. Princeton: Princeton University Press, 1968.

Garber, Marjorie. *Shakespeare After All*. New York: Pantheon, 2004.

Hibbard, G. R. *The Making of Shakespeare's Dramatic Poetry*. Toronto: University of Toronto Press, 1981.

Honigmann, E. A. J. *Myriad-Minded Shakespeare: Essays on the Tragedies, Problem Comedies, and Shakespeare the Man*. 2nd ed. New York: St. Martin's Press, 1998.

Jones, John. *Shakespeare at Work*. New York: Oxford University Press, 1995.

Nuttall, A. D. *Shakespeare the Thinker*. New Haven: Yale University Press, 2007.

Ryan, Kiernan. *Shakespeare*. 3rd ed. New York: Palgrave Macmillan, 2001.

Language and Style

Baxter, John. *Shakespeare's Poetic Styles: Verse into Drama*. London: Routledge and Kegan Paul, 1980.

Blake, N. F. *Shakespeare's Language: An Introduction*. New York: St. Martin's Press, 1983.

Cercignani, Fausto. *Shakespeare's Works and Elizabethan Pronunciation*. New York: Oxford University Press, 1981.

Clemen, Wolfgang. *Shakespeare's Soliloquies*. Trans. Charity Scott Stokes. New York: Methuen, 1987.

———. *The Development of Shakespeare's Imagery*. New York: Hill and Wang, 1962.

Danson, Lawrence. *Tragic Alphabet: Shakespeare's Drama of Language*. New Haven: Yale University Press, 1974.

Donawerth, Jane. *Shakespeare and the Sixteenth-Century Study of Language*. Urbana: University of Illinois Press, 1984.

Edwards, Philip, Inga-Stina Ewbank, and G. K. Hunter, eds. *Shakespeare's Styles: Essays in Honour of Kenneth Muir*. New York: Cambridge University Press, 1980.

Gross, Kenneth. *Shakespeare's Noise*. Chicago: University of Chicago Press, 2001.

Hope, Jonathan. *Shakespeare's Grammar*. London: Arden Shakespeare, 2003.

Houston, John Porter. *Shakespearean Sentences: A Study in Style and Syntax*. Baton Rouge: Louisiana State University Press, 1988.

Hussey, S. S. *The Literary Language of Shakespeare*. 2nd ed. New York: Longman, 1992.

Kökeritz, Helge. *Shakespeare's Pronunciation*. New Haven: Yale University Press, 1953.

Mahood, M. M. *Shakespeare's Wordplay*. London: Methuen, 1957.

McDonald, Russ. *Shakespeare and the Arts of Language*. New York: Oxford University Press, 2001.

———. *Shakespeare's Late Style*. New York: Cambridge University Press, 2006.

Miriam Joseph, Sister. *Shakespeare's Use of the Arts of Language*. New York: Columbia University Press, 1947.

Palfrey, Simon. *Late Shakespeare: A New World of Words*. Oxford: Clarendon, 1997.

Parker, Patricia. *Literary Fat Ladies: Rhetoric, Gender, Property*. New York: Methuen, 1987.

———. *Shakespeare from the Margins: Language, Culture, Context*. Chicago: University of Chicago Press, 1996.

Partridge, Eric. *Shakespeare's Bawdy: A Literary & Psychological Essay and a Comprehensive Glossary*. 3rd ed. New York: Routledge, 1991.

Trousdale, Marion. *Shakespeare and the Rhetoricians*. Chapel Hill: University of North Carolina Press, 1982.

Vickers, Brian. *The Artistry of Shakespeare's Prose*. London: Methuen, 1968.

———. "Shakespeare's Use of Rhetoric." *A New Companion to Shakespeare Studies*. Ed. Kenneth Muir and S. Schoenbaum. Cambridge, Eng.: Cambridge University Press, 1971. 83–98.

Wright, George T. *Shakespeare's Metrical Art*. Berkeley: University of California Press, 1988.

Young, David. *The Action to the Word: Structure and Style in Shakespearean Tragedy.* New Haven: Yale University Press, 1990.

Psychoanalytic Criticism

Adelman, Janet. *Suffocating Mothers: Fantasies of Maternal Origin in Shakespeare's Plays, Hamlet to* The Tempest. New York: Routledge, 1992.

Armstrong, Philip. *Shakespeare in Psychoanalysis.* New York: Routledge, 2001.

Berger, Harry Jr. *Making Trifles of Terrors: Redistributing Complicities in Shakespeare.* Stanford: Stanford University Press, 1997.

Charnes, Linda. *Notorious Identity: Materializing the Subject in Shakespeare.* Cambridge, Mass.: Harvard University Press, 1993.

Enterline, Lynn. *The Rhetoric of the Body from Ovid to Shakespeare.* Cambridge, Eng.: Cambridge University Press, 2000.

Fineman, Joel. *Shakespeare's Perjured Eye: The Invention of Poetic Subjectivity in the Sonnets.* Berkeley: University of California Press, 1986.

Freedman, Barbara. *Staging the Gaze: Postmodernism, Psychoanalysis, and Shakespearean Comedy.* Ithaca, N.Y.: Cornell University Press, 1991.

Garber, Marjorie. *Coming of Age in Shakespeare.* New York: Methuen, 1981.

——. *Shakespeare's Ghost Writers: Literature as Uncanny Causality.* New York: Methuen, 1987.

Girard, René. *A Theater of Envy: William Shakespeare.* New York: Oxford University Press, 1991.

Holland, Norman N. *Psychoanalysis and Shakespeare.* New York: Octagon, 1966.

Lupton, Julia Reinhard, and Kenneth Reinhard. *After Oedipus: Shakespeare in Psychoanalysis.* Ithaca, N.Y.: Cornell University Press, 1993.

Marshall, Cynthia. *The Shattering of the Self: Violence, Subjectivity, and Early Modern Texts.* Baltimore: Johns Hopkins University Press, 2002.

Mazzio, Carla, and Douglas Trevor, eds. *Historicism, Psychoanalysis, and Early Modern Culture.* New York: Routledge, 2000.

Pye, Christopher. *The Regal Phantasm: Shakespeare and the Politics of Spectacle.* New York: Routledge, 1990.

——. *The Vanishing: Shakespeare, the Subject, and Early Modern Culture.* Durham, N.C.: Duke University Press, 2000.

Schwartz, Murray M., and Coppélia Kahn, eds. *Representing Shakespeare: New Psychoanalytic Essays.* Baltimore: Johns Hopkins University Press, 1982.

Skura, Meredith Anne. *The Literary Use of the Psychoanalytic Process.* New Haven: Yale University Press, 1981.

——. *Shakespeare the Actor and the Purposes of Playing.* Chicago: University of Chicago Press, 1993.

Wheeler, Richard P. *Shakespeare's Development and the Problem Comedies: Turn and Counter-Turn.* Berkeley: University of California Press, 1981.

Zimmerman, Susan, ed. *Erotic Politics: Desire on the Renaissance Stage.* New York: Routledge, 1992.

Feminism, Gender Studies, and Queer Studies

Bamber, Linda. *Comic Women, Tragic Men: A Study of Gender and Genre in Shakespeare.* Stanford: Stanford University Press, 1982.

Barker, Deborah, and Ivo Kamps, eds. *Shakespeare and Gender: A History.* New York: Verso, 1995.

Boose, Lynda E. "The Father and the Bride in Shakespeare." *PMLA* 97 (1982): 325–47.

Callaghan, Dympna. *Shakespeare Without Women: Representing Gender and Race on the Renaissance Stage.* New York: Routledge, 2000.

———. *Women and Gender in Renaissance Tragedy: A Study of* King Lear, Othello, The Duchess of Malfi, *and* The White Devil. Atlantic Highlands, N.J.: Humanities Press International, 1989.

Chedgzoy, Kate, ed. *Shakespeare, Feminism and Gender.* Houndmills, Basingstoke: Palgrave Macmillan, 2001.

Dash, Irene G. *Wooing, Wedding, and Power: Women in Shakespeare's Plays.* New York: Columbia University Press, 1981.

DiGangi, Mario. *The Homoerotics of Early Modern Drama.* New York: Cambridge University Press, 1997.

Dusinberre, Juliet. *Shakespeare and the Nature of Women.* 3rd ed. New York: Palgrave Macmillan, 2003.

Erickson, Peter. *Patriarchal Structures in Shakespeare's Drama.* Berkeley: University of California Press, 1985.

French, Marilyn. *Shakespeare's Division of Experience.* New York: Summit Books, 1981.

Garner, Shirley Nelson, and Madelon Sprengnether, eds. *Shakespearean Tragedy and Gender.* Bloomington: Indiana University Press, 1996.

Goldberg, Jonathan. *Sodometries: Renaissance Texts, Modern Sexualities.* Stanford: Stanford University Press, 1992.

Howard, Jean E., and Phyllis Rackin. *Engendering a Nation: A Feminist Account of Shakespeare's English Histories.* New York: Routledge, 1997.

Jardine, Lisa. *Still Harping on Daughters: Women and Drama in the Age of Shakespeare.* 2nd ed. New York: Columbia University Press, 1989.

Kahn, Coppèlia. *Man's Estate: Masculine Identity in Shakespeare.* Berkeley: University of California Press, 1981.

———. *Roman Shakespeare: Warriors, Wounds, and Women.* New York: Routledge, 1997.

Korda, Natasha. *Shakespeare's Domestic Economies: Gender and Property in Early Modern England.* Philadelphia: University of Pennsylvania Press, 2002.

Lenz, Carolyn, Ruth Swift, Gayle Greene, and Carol Thomas Neely, eds. *The Woman's Part: Feminist Criticism of Shakespeare.* Urbana: University of Illinois Press, 1980.

Neely, Carol Thomas. *Broken Nuptials in Shakespeare's Plays.* New Haven: Yale University Press, 1985.

———. *Distracted Subjects: Madness and Gender in Shakespeare and Early Modern Culture.* Ithaca, N.Y.: Cornell University Press, 2004.

Newman, Karen. *Fashioning Femininity and English Renaissance Drama.* Chicago: University of Chicago Press, 1991.

Novy, Marianne. *Love's Argument: Gender Relations in Shakespeare.* Chapel Hill: University of North Carolina Press, 1984.

———, ed. *Women's Re-Visions of Shakespeare: On the Responses of Dickinson, Woolf, Rich, H.D., George Eliot, and Others.* Urbana: University of Illinois Press, 1990.

Orgel, Stephen. *Impersonations: The Performance of Gender in Shakespeare's England.* New York: Cambridge University Press, 1996.

Shapiro, Michael. *Gender in Play on the Shakespearean Stage: Boy Heroines and Female Pages.* Ann Arbor: University of Michigan Press, 1994.

Shepherd, Simon. *Amazons and Warrior Women: Varieties of Feminism in Seventeenth Century Drama.* New York: St. Martin's, 1981.

Traub, Valerie. *Desire and Anxiety: Circulations of Sexuality in Shakespearean Drama.* New York: Routledge, 1992.

———. *The Renaissance of Lesbianism in Eary Modern England.* New York: Cambridge University Press, 2002.

Wayne, Valerie, ed. *The Matter of Difference: Materialist Feminist Criticism of Shakespeare.* Ithaca, N.Y.: Cornell University Press, 1991.

Historical Approaches: Materialism, New Historicism, and Cultural Materialism

Archer, John Michael. *Citizen Shakespeare: Freemen and Aliens in the Language of the Plays.* New York: Palgrave Macmillan, 2005.

Arnold, Oliver. *The Third Citizen: Shakespeare's Theater and the Early Modern House of Commons.* Baltimore: Johns Hopkins University Press, 2007.

Belsey, Catherine. *Shakespeare and the Loss of Eden: The Construction of Family Values in Early Modern Culture.* New Brunswick, N.J.: Rutgers University Press, 1999.

Berry, Ralph. *Shakespeare and Social Class.* Atlantic Highlands, N.J.: Humanities Press International, 1988.

Bristol, Michael D. *Shakespeare's America, America's Shakespeare.* New York: Routledge, 1990.

Bruster, Douglas. *Shakespeare and the Question of Culture: Early Modern Literature and the Cultural Turn.* New York: Palgrave Macmillan, 2003.

Cox, John D. *Shakespeare and the Dramaturgy of Power.* Princeton: Princeton University Press, 1989.

Dollimore, Jonathan. *Radical Tragedy: Religion, Ideology, and Power in the Drama of Shakespeare and His Contemporaries.* 3rd ed. New York: Palgrave Macmillan, 2004.

Dollimore, Jonathan, and Alan Sinfield, eds. *Political Shakespeare: Essays in Cultural Materialism.* 2nd ed. Ithaca, N.Y.: Cornell University Press, 1994.

Dubrow, Heather, and Richard Strier, eds. *The Historical Renaissance: New Essays on Tudor and Stuart Literature and Culture.* Chicago: University of Chicago Press, 1988.

Eagleton, Terry. *William Shakespeare.* Malden, Mass.: Blackwell, 1986.

Greenblatt, Stephen. *Hamlet in Purgatory.* Princeton: Princeton University Press, 2001.

———. *Shakespearean Negotiations: The Circulation of Social Energy in Renaissance England.* Berkeley: University of California Press, 1988.

Hadfield, Andrew. *Shakespeare and Republicanism.* New York: Cambridge University Press, 2005.

Hawkes, Terence. *Meaning by Shakespeare.* New York: Routledge, 1992.

———. *That Shakespeherian Rag: Essays on a Critical Process.* New York: Methuen, 1986.

Holderness, Graham, ed. *The Shakespeare Myth.* Manchester: Manchester University Press, 1988.

———, ed. *Shakespeare's History Plays: Richard II to Henry V.* Houndmills, Basingstoke: Palgrave Macmillan, 1992.

Howard, Jean E. *The Stage and Social Struggle in Early Modern England.* New York: Routledge, 1994.

Howard, Jean E., and Scott Cutler Shershow, eds. *Marxist Shakespeares.* New York: Routledge, 2001.

Howard, Jean E., and Marion F. O'Connor, eds. *Shakespeare Reproduced: The Text in History and Ideology.* New York: Methuen, 1987.

Jardine, Lisa. *Reading Shakespeare Historically.* New York: Routledge, 1996.

Jordan, Constance. *Shakespeare's Monarchies: Ruler and Subject in the Romances.* Ithaca, N.Y.: Cornell University Press, 1997.

Kamps, Ivo, ed. *Materialist Shakespeare: A History.* New York: Verso, 1995.

Kastan, David Scott. *Shakespeare After Theory.* London: Routledge, 1999.

———. *Shakespeare and the Shapes of Time.* Hanover, N.H.: University Press of New England, 1982.

Mallin, Eric S. *Inscribing the Time: Shakespeare and the End of Elizabethan England.* Berkeley: University of California Press, 1995.

Marcus, Leah S. *Puzzling Shakespeare: Local Reading and Its Discontents.* Berkeley: University of California Press, 1988.

Maus, Katharine Eisaman. *Inwardness and Theater in the English Renaissance.* Chicago: University of Chicago Press, 1995.

Montrose, Louis. *The Purpose of Playing: Shakespeare and the Cultural Politics of the Elizabethan Theatre.* Chicago: University of Chicago Press, 1996.

Mullaney, Steven. *The Place of the Stage: License, Play, and Power in Renaissance England.* Chicago: University of Chicago Press, 1988.

Orgel, Stephen. *The Authentic Shakespear: and Other Problems of the Early Modern Stage.* New York: Routledge, 2002.

Patterson, Annabel. *Shakespeare and the Popular Voice.* Malden, Mass.: Blackwell, 1989.

Rackin, Phyllis. *Stages of History: Shakespeare's English Chronicles.* Ithaca, N.Y.: Cornell University Press, 1990.

Siemon, James R. *Word Against Word: Shakespearean Utterance.* Amherst: University of Massachusetts Press, 2002.

Sinfield, Alan. *Shakespeare, Authority, Sexuality: Unfinished Business in Cultural Materialism.* New York: Routledge, 2006.

Tennenhouse, Leonard. *Power on Display: The Politics of Shakespeare's Genres.* New York: Methuen, 1986.

Weimann, Robert. *Author's Pen and Actor's Voice: Playing and Writing in Shakespeare's Theatre.* Ed. Helen Higbee and William West. New York: Cambridge University Press, 2000.

Wells, Robin Headlam. *Shakespeare, Politics, and the State.* Houndmills, Basingstoke: Palgrave Macmillan, 1986.

Wilson, Richard. *Secret Shakespeare: Studies in Theatre, Religion and Resistance.* Manchester: Manchester University Press, 2004.

———. *Will Power: Essays on Shakespearean Authority.* Detroit: Wayne State University Press, 1993.

Postcolonial Criticism, Race, and Ethnicity

Alexander, Catherine M. S., and Stanley Wells, eds. *Shakespeare and Race.* New York: Cambridge University Press, 2000.

Cartelli, Thomas. *Repositioning Shakespeare: National Formations, Postcolonial Appropriations.* New York: Routledge, 1999.

de Sousa, Geraldo U. *Shakespeare's Cross-Cultural Encounters.* Houndmills, Basingstoke: Palgrave Macmillan, 2002.

Floyd-Wilson, Mary. *English Ethnicity and Race in Early Modern Drama.* New York: Cambridge University Press, 2003.

Hendricks, Margo. " 'Obscured by dreams:' Race, Empire, and Shakespeare's A Midsummer Night's Dream." *Shakespeare Quarterly* 47 (1996): 37–60.

Hulme, Peter. *Colonial Encounters: Europe and the Native Caribbean, 1492–1797.* New York: Methuen, 1986.

Knapp, Jeffrey. *An Empire Nowhere: England, America, and Literature from Utopia to The Tempest.* Berkeley: University of California Press, 1992.

Loomba, Ania. *Gender, Race, Renaissance Drama.* Manchester: Manchester University Press, 1989.

Loomba, Ania, and Martin Orkin, eds. *Post-colonial Shakespeares.* New York: Routledge, 1998.

Maley, Willy. *Nation, State, and Empire in English Renaissance Literature: Shakespeare to Milton.* New York: Palgrave Macmillan, 2003.

Vaughan, Virginia Mason. *Performing Blackness on English Stages, 1500–1800.* New York: Cambridge University Press, 2005.

Other Philosophical and Theoretical Approaches

Booth, Stephen. *King Lear, Macbeth, Indefinition, and Tragedy.* New Haven: Yale University Press, 1983.

Cavell, Stanley. *Disowning Knowledge in Seven Plays of Shakespeare.* Updated ed. New York: Cambridge University Press, 2003.

Engle, Lars. *Shakespearean Pragmatism: Market of His Time.* Chicago: University of Chicago Press, 1993.

Evans, Malcolm. *Signifying Nothing: Truth's True Contents in Shakespeare's Text.* Athens: University of Georgia Press, 1986.

Felperin, Howard. *The Uses of the Canon: Elizabethan Literature and Contemporary Theory.* New York: Oxford University Press, 1990.

Goldberg, Jonathan. *Shakespeare's Hand.* Minneapolis: University of Minnesota Press, 2003.

Grady, Hugh. *The Modernist Shakespeare: Critical Texts in a Material World.* Oxford: Clarendon, 1991.

———. *Shakespeare, Machiavelli, and Montaigne: Power and Subjectivity from Richard II to Hamlet.* Oxford: Oxford University Press, 2002.

Grady, Hugh, and Terence Hawkes, eds. *Presentist Shakespeares.* New York: Routledge, 2006.

Hawkes, Terence. *Shakespeare in the Present.* New York: Routledge, 2002.

Knapp, Robert S. *Shakespeare—The Theater and the Book.* Princeton: Princeton University Press, 1989.

Lukacher, Ned. *Daemonic Figures: Shakespeare and the Question of Conscience.* Ithaca, N.Y.: Cornell University Press, 1994.

Lupton, Julia Reinhard. *Citizen-Saints: Shakespeare and Political Theology.* Chicago: University of Chicago Press, 2005.

Parker, Patricia, and Geoffrey Hartman, eds. *Shakespeare and the Question of Theory.* New York: Methuen, 1985.

Pechter, Edward. *What Was Shakespeare?: Renaissance Plays and Changing Critical Practice.* Ithaca, N.Y.: Cornell University Press, 1995.

Rabkin, Norman. *Shakespeare and the Problem of Meaning.* Chicago: University of Chicago Press, 1981.

Schalkwyk, David. *Speech and Performance in Shakespeare's Sonnets and Plays.* Cambridge, Eng.: Cambridge University Press, 2002.

Textual Criticism and Bibliography

Allen, Michael J. B., and Kenneth Muir, eds. *Shakespeare's Plays in Quarto: A Facsimile Edition of Copies Primarily from the Henry E. Huntington Library.* Berkeley: University of California Press, 1981.

Blayney, Peter W. M. *The First Folio of Shakespeare.* Washington, D.C.: Folger Library Publications, 1991.

———. *The Texts of* King Lear *and Their Origins.* Vol. 1: *Nicholas Okes and the First Quarto.* New York: Cambridge University Press, 1982.

Bowers, Fredson. *On Editing Shakespeare.* Charlottesville: University Press of Virginia, 1966.

Brooks, Douglas A. *From Playhouse to Printing House: Drama and Authorship in Early Modern England.* New York: Cambridge University Press, 2000.

De Grazia, Margreta. "Homonyms Before and After Lexical Standardization." *Deutsche Shakespeare-Gesellschaft West* (Jahrbuch 1990): 143–56.

———. *Shakespeare Verbatim: The Reproduction of Authenticity and the 1790 Apparatus.* New York: Oxford University Press, 1991.

De Grazia, Margreta, and Peter Stallybrass. "The Materiality of the Shakespearean Text." *Shakespeare Quarterly* 44 (1993): 255–83.

Erne, Lukas, and Margaret Jane Kidnie, eds. *Textual Performances: The Modern Reproduction of Shakespeare's Drama.* New York: Cambridge University Press, 2004.

Franklin, Colin. *Shakespeare Domesticated: The Eighteenth-Century Editions.* Brookfield, Vt.: Gower Publishing Company, 1991.

Hinman, Charlton, ed. *The First Folio of Shakespeare.* 2nd ed. New York: Norton, 1996.

———. *The Printing and Proof-Reading of the First Folio of Shakespeare.* 2 vols. Oxford: Clarendon, 1963.

Honigmann, E. A. J. *The Stability of Shakespeare's Text.* London: E. Arnold, 1965.

Ioppolo, Grace. *Dramatists and Their Manuscripts in the Age of Shakespeare, Jonson, Middleton and Heywood: Authorship, Authority and the Playhouse.* New York: Routledge, 2006.

———. *Revising Shakespeare.* Cambridge, Mass.: Harvard University Press, 1991.

Irace, Kathleen O. *Reforming the "Bad" Quartos: Performance and Provenance of Six Shakespearean First Editions.* Newark: University of Delaware Press, 1994.

Jackson, MacDonald P. *Defining Shakespeare: Pericles as Test Case.* New York: Oxford University Press, 2003.

Kastan, David Scott. *Shakespeare and the Book.* New York: Cambridge University Press, 2001.

Lesser, Zachary. *Renaissance Drama and the Politics of Publication: Readings in the English Book Trade.* New York: Cambridge University Press, 2004.

Maguire, Laurie E. *Shakespearean Suspect Texts: The "Bad" Quartos and Their Contexts.* New York: Cambridge University Press, 1996.

Maguire, Laurie E., and Thomas L. Berger, eds. *Textual Formations and Reformations.* Newark: University of Delaware Press, 1998.

Marcus, Leah S. *Unediting the Renaissance: Shakespeare, Marlowe, Milton.* New York: Routledge, 1996.

McKerrow, Ronald B. *Prolegomena for the Oxford Shakespeare: A Study in Editorial Method.* Oxford: Clarendon, 1939.

McLeod, Randall, ed. *Crisis in Editing: Texts of the English Renaissance.* New York: AMS Press, 1994.

———. "UN *Editing* Shak-speare." *SubStance* 33/34 (1982): 26–55.

———[as Random Cloud]. "The Psychopathology of Everyday Art." *The Elizabethan Theatre IX.* Ed. G. R. Hibbard. Port Credit, Ontario: P. D. Meany, 1986. 100–68.

Murphy, Andrew. *Shakespeare in Print: A History and Chronology of Shakespeare Publishing.* New York: Cambridge University Press, 2003.

———, ed. *The Renaissance Text: Theory, Editing, Textuality.* Manchester: Manchester University Press, 2000.

Pollard, Alfred W. *Shakespeare's Folios and Quartos: A Study in the Bibliography of Shakespeare's Plays, 1594–1685.* London: Methuen, 1909.

Seary, Peter. *Lewis Theobald and the Editing of Shakespeare.* Oxford: Clarendon, 1990.

Taylor, Gary, and Michael Warren, eds. *The Division of the Kingdoms: Shakespeare's Two Versions of* King Lear. Oxford: Clarendon, 1986.

Urkowitz, Steven. *Shakespeare's Revision of* King Lear. Princeton: Princeton University Press, 1980.

Vickers, Brian. *Shakespeare, Co-Author: A Historical Study of Five Collaborative Plays.* New York: Oxford University Press, 2002.

Walker, Alice. *Textual Problems of the First Folio:* Richard III, King Lear, Troilus & Cressida, 2 Henry IV, Hamlet, Othello. Cambridge, Eng.: Cambridge University Press, 1953.

Wells, Stanley. *Re-Editing Shakespeare for the Modern Reader.* New York: Oxford University Press, 1984.

Wells, Stanley, and Gary Taylor. *Modernizing Shakespeare's Spelling.* Oxford: Clarendon, 1979.

———. *William Shakespeare: A Textual Companion.* Oxford: Clarendon, 1987.

Werstine, Paul. "A Century of 'Bad' Shakespeare Quartos." *Shakespeare Quarterly* 50 (1999): 310–33.

———. "Narratives about Printed Shakespeare Texts: 'Foul Papers' and 'Bad' Quartos." *Shakespeare Quarterly* 41 (1990): 65–86.

Williams, George Walton. *The Craft of Printing and the Publication of Shakespeare's Works.* Washington, D.C.: Folger Shakespeare Library, 1985.

Wilson, J. Dover. *The Manuscript of Shakespeare's "Hamlet" and the Problems of Its Transmission: An Essay in Critical Bibliography.* 2 vols. New York: Macmillan, 1934.

Shakespeare and Performance

Aebischer, Pascale. *Shakespeare's Violated Bodies: Stage and Screen Performance.* New York: Cambridge University Press, 2003.

Aebischer, Pascale, Edward J. Esche, and Nigel Wheale, eds. *Remaking Shakespeare: Performance Across Media, Genres, and Cultures.* New York: Palgrave Macmillan, 2003.

Bartholomeusz, Dennis. *"Macbeth" and the Players.* Cambridge, Eng.: Cambridge University Press, 1969.

Barton, John. *Playing Shakespeare.* London: Methuen, 1984.

Bate, Jonathan, and Russell Jackson, eds. *Shakespeare: An Illustrated Stage History.* New York: Oxford University Press, 1996.

Berger, Harry Jr. *Imaginary Audition: Shakespeare on Stage and Page.* Berkeley: University of California Press, 1989.

Berry, Francis. *The Shakespeare Inset: Word and Picture.* London: Routledge and Kegan Paul, 1965.

Berry, Ralph. *Changing Styles in Shakespeare.* Boston: Allen & Unwin, 1981.

Bevington, David M. *Action Is Eloquence: Shakespeare's Language of Gesture.* Cambridge, Mass.: Harvard University Press, 1984.

———. *This Wide and Universal Theater: Shakespeare in Performance, Then and Now.* Chicago: University of Chicago Press, 2007.

Branam, George Curtis. *Eighteenth-Century Adaptations of Shakespearean Tragedy.* Berkeley: University of California Press, 1956.

Bratton, Jacky, and Julie Hankey, gen. eds. The Shakespeare in Production Series. Cambridge, Eng.: Cambridge University Press, 1996–.

Brennan, Anthony. *Onstage and Offstage Worlds in Shakespeare's Plays.* New York: Routledge, 1989.

———. *Shakespeare's Dramatic Structures.* Boston: Routledge and Kegan Paul, 1986.

Brown, Ivor. *Shakespeare and the Actors.* London: Bodley Head, 1970.

Brown, John Russell. *Shakespeare and the Theatrical Event.* Houndmills, Basingstoke: Palgrave Macmillan, 2002.

———. *Shakespeare's Dramatic Style: Romeo and Juliet, As You Like It, Julius Caesar, Twelfth Night, Macbeth.* London: Heinemann, 1970.

Bulman, James C., ed. *Shakespeare, Theory, and Performance.* New York: Routledge, 1996.

Calderwood, James. *Shakespearean Metadrama: The Argument of the Play in* Titus Andronicus, Love's Labour's Lost, Romeo and Juliet, A Midsummer Night's Dream, *and* Richard II. Minneapolis: University of Minnesota Press, 1971.

Carlisle, Carol Jones. *Shakespeare from the Greenroom: Actors' Criticisms of Four Major Tragedies.* Chapel Hill: University of North Carolina Press, 1969.

Cohn, Ruby. *Modern Shakespeare Offshoots.* Princeton: Princeton University Press, 1976.

Dean, Winton. "Shakespeare in the Opera House." *Shakespeare Survey* 18 (1965): 75–93.

Dobson, Michael. *The Making of the National Poet: Shakespeare, Adaptation and Authorship, 1660–1769.* Oxford: Clarendon, 1992.

————, ed. *Performing Shakespeare's Tragedies Today: The Actor's Perspective*. New York: Cambridge University Press, 2006.

Downer, Alan S. *The Eminent Tragedian William Charles Macready*. Cambridge, Mass.: Harvard University Press, 1966.

Duffin, Ross W. *Shakespeare's Songbook*. New York: Norton, 2004.

Foulkes, Richard, ed. *Shakespeare and the Victorian Stage*. New York: Cambridge University Press, 1986.

Goldman, Michael. *Acting and Action in Shakespearean Tragedy*. Princeton: Princeton University Press, 1985.

Hirsch, James E. *The Structure of Shakespearean Scenes*. New Haven: Yale University Press, 1981.

Hogan, Charles Beecher, ed. *Shakespeare in the Theatre, 1701–1800*. 2 vols. Oxford: Clarendon, 1952–57.

Holland, Peter. *English Shakespeares: Shakespeare on the English Stage in the 1990's*. New York: Cambridge University Press, 1997.

Homan, Sidney, ed. *Shakespeare's "More Than Words Can Witness": Essays on Visual and Nonverbal Enactment in the Plays*. Lewisburg, Pa.: Bucknell University Press, 1980.

————, ed. *When the Theater Turns to Itself: The Aesthetic Metaphor in Shakespeare*. Lewiston, Pa.: Bucknell University Press, 1981.

Hoenselaars, Ton, ed. *Shakespeare's History Plays: Performance, Translation and Adaptation in Britain and Abroad*. Cambridge, Eng.: Cambridge University Press, 2004.

Howard, Jean E. *Shakespeare's Art of Orchestration: Stage Technique and Audience Response*. Urbana: University of Illinois Press, 1984.

Jones, Emrys. *Scenic Form in Shakespeare*. Oxford: Clarendon, 1971.

Kennedy, Dennis. *Looking at Shakespeare: A Visual History of Twentieth-Century Performance*. 2nd ed. New York: Cambridge University Press, 2001.

————, ed. *Foreign Shakespeare: Contemporary Performance*. New York: Cambridge University Press, 1993.

Marshall, Gail, and Adrian Poole, eds. *Victorian Shakespeare*. New York: Palgrave Macmillan, 2003.

McGuire, Philip C. *Speechless Dialect: Shakespeare's Open Silences*. Berkeley: University of California Press, 1985.

McGuire, Philip C., and David A. Samuelson. *Shakespeare: The Theatrical Dimension*. New York: AMS Press, 1979.

Mooney, Michael E. *Shakespeare's Dramatic Transactions*. Durham, N.C.: Duke University Press, 1990.

Mowat, Barbara A. *The Dramaturgy of Shakespeare's Romances*. Athens: University of Georgia Press, 1976.

Odell, George Clinton Densmore. *Shakespeare from Betterton to Irving*. 2 vols. New York: Scribner, 1920.

Parsons, Keith, and Pamela Mason, eds. *Shakespeare in Performance*. London: Salamander, 1995.

Poel, William. *Shakespeare in the Theater*. London: Sidgwick and Jackson, 1913.

Rosenberg, Marvin. *The Masks of King Lear*. Berkeley: University of California Press, 1972.

Rosenberg, Marvin, et al. *Clamorous Voices: Shakespeare's Women Today*. London: Women's Press, 1988.

Rutter, Carol, gen. ed. The Shakespeare in Performance Series. Manchester: Manchester University Press, 1982–.

Shattuck, Charles H. *Shakespeare on the American Stage*, vol. 1: *From the Hallams to Edwin Booth*. Washington, D.C.: Folger Shakespeare Library, 1976.

————. *Shakespeare on the American Stage*, vol. 2: *From Booth and Barrett to Sothern and Marlowe*. Washington, D.C.: Folger Shakespeare Library, 1987.

———. *The Shakespeare Promptbooks: A Descriptive Catalogue.* Urbana: University of Illinois Press, 1965.

Slater, Ann. *Shakespeare, the Director.* Totowa, N.J.: Barnes & Noble Books, 1982.

Smallwood, Robert, ed. *Players of Shakespeare.* 6 vols. New York: Cambridge University Press, 1985–2004.

———, gen. ed. The Shakespeare at Stratford series. London: Arden Shakespeare, 2002– .

Speaight, Robert. *Shakespeare on the Stage: An Illustrated History of Shakespearian Performance.* London: Collins, 1973.

———. *William Poel and the Elizabethan Revival.* Cambridge, Mass.: Harvard University Press, 1954.

Spencer, Hazelton. *Shakespeare Improved: The Restoration Versions in Quarto and On the Stage.* Cambridge, Mass.: Harvard University Press, 1927.

Styan, J. L. *The Shakespeare Revolution: Criticism and Performance in the Twentieth Century.* New York: Cambridge University Press, 1977.

———. *Shakespeare's Stagecraft.* Cambridge, Eng.: Cambridge University Press, 1967.

———. "Sight and Space: The Perception of Shakespeare on Stage and Screen." *Shakespeare, Pattern of Excelling Nature: Shakespeare Criticism in Honor of America's Bicentennial.* Ed. David Bevington and Jay L. Halio. Newark: University of Delaware Press, 1978.

Thompson, Marvin and Ruth, eds. *Shakespeare and the Sense of Performance.* Newark: University of Delaware Press, 1989.

Trewin, J. C. *Shakespeare on the English Stage, 1900–1964.* London: Barrie and Rockliff, 1964.

Wells, Stanley. *Royal Shakespeare: Four Major Productions at Stratford-upon-Avon.* Manchester: Manchester University Press, 1977.

———, ed. *Shakespeare in the Theatre: An Anthology of Criticism.* New York: Oxford University Press, 1997.

Worthen, William B. *Shakespeare and the Authority of Performance.* New York: Cambridge University Press, 1997.

———. *Shakespeare and the Force of Modern Performance.* New York: Cambridge University Press, 2003.

Shakespeare on Film

Ball, Robert Hamilton. *Shakespeare on Silent Film: A Strange Eventful History.* London: Allen & Unwin, 1968.

Burt, Richard, and Lynda E. Boose, eds. *Shakespeare the Movie: Popularizing the Plays on Film, TV, and Video.* New York: Routledge, 1997.

———. *Shakespeare the Movie II: Popularizing the Plays on Film, TV, Video, and DVD.* New York: Routledge, 2003.

Bristol, Michael D. *Big-Time Shakespeare.* New York: Routledge, 1996.

Buchanan, Judith. *Shakespeare on Film.* New York: Pearson Longman, 2005.

Buchman, Lorne Michael. *Still in Movement: Shakespeare on Screen.* New York: Oxford University Press, 1991.

Bulman, J. C., and H. R. Coursen, eds. *Shakespeare on Television: An Anthology of Essays and Reviews.* Hanover, N.H.: University Press of New England, 1988.

Burnett, Mark Thornton, and Ramona Wray, eds. *Shakespeare, Film, Fin de Siècle.* New York: St. Martin's, 2000.

Burt, Richard. *Shakespeare After Mass Media.* New York: Palgrave Macmillan, 2002.

Cartelli, Thomas, and Katherine Rowe, eds. *New Wave Shakespeare on Screen.* Malden, Mass.: Polity Press, 2007.

Crowl, Samuel. *Shakespeare at the Cineplex: The Kenneth Branagh Era.* Athens: Ohio University Press, 2003.

———. *Shakespeare and Film.* New York: Norton, 2008.

Davies, Anthony, and Stanley Wells, eds. *Shakespeare and the Moving Image: The Plays on Film and Television.* New York: Cambridge University Press, 1994.

Donaldson, Peter S. *Shakespearean Films/Shakespearean Directors.* Boston: Unwin Hyman, 1990.

Henderson, Diana E. *Collaborations with the Past: Reshaping Shakespeare Across Time and Media.* Ithaca, N.Y.: Cornell University Press, 2006.

———. *A Concise Companion to Shakespeare on Screen.* Malden, Mass.: Blackwell, 2007.

Hindle, Maurice. *Studying Shakespeare on Film.* New York: Palgrave Macmillan, 2007.

Kliman, Bernice W. *Hamlet: Film, Television, and Audio Performance.* Madison, N.J.: Fairleigh Dickinson University Press, 1988.

Lehmann, Courtney. *Shakespeare Remains: Theater to Film, Early Modern to Postmodern.* Ithaca, N.Y.: Cornell, 2002.

Lehmann, Courtney, and Lisa S. Starks, eds. *Spectacular Shakespeare: Critical Theory and Popular Cinema.* Madison, N.J.: Fairleigh Dickinson University Press, 2002.

Rothwell, Kenneth S. *A History of Shakespeare on Screen: A Century of Film and Television.* 2nd ed. Cambridge, Eng.: Cambridge University Press, 2004.

Glossary

STAGE TERMS

"Above" The gallery on the upper level of the *frons scenae*. In open-air theaters, such as the Globe, this space contained the lords' rooms. The central section of the gallery was sometimes used by the players for short scenes. Indoor theaters such as Blackfriars featured a curtained alcove for musicians above the stage.

"Aloft" See *"Above."*

Amphitheater An open-air theater, such as the Globe.

Arras See *Curtain.*

Cellerage See *Trap.*

Chorus In the works of Shakespeare and other Elizabethan playwrights, a single individual (not, as in Greek tragedy, a group) who speaks before the play (and often before each act), describing events not shown on stage as well as commenting on the action witnessed by the audience.

Curtain Curtains, or arras (hanging tapestries), covered a part of the *frons scenae,* thus concealing the discovery space, and may also have been draped around the edge of the stage to conceal the open area underneath.

Discovery space A central opening or alcove concealed behind a curtain in the center of the *frons scenae.* The curtain could be drawn aside to "discover" tableaux such as Portia's caskets, the body of Polonius, or the statue of Hermione. Shakespeare appears to have used this stage device only sparingly.

Doubling The common practice of having one actor play multiple roles, so that a play with a large cast of characters might be performed by a relatively small company.

Dumb shows Mimed scenes performed before a play (or before each act), summarizing or foreshadowing the plot. Dumb shows were popular in early Elizabethan drama; although they already seemed old-fashioned in Shakespeare's time, they were employed by writers up to the 1640s.

Epilogue A brief speech or poem addressed to the audience by an actor after the play. In some cases, as in *2 Henry IV,* the epilogue could be combined with, or could merge into, the jig.

Forestage The front of the stage, closest to the audience.

Frons scenae The wall at the back of the stage, behind which lay the players' tiring-house. The *frons scenae* of the Globe featured two doors flanking the central discovery space, with a gallery "above."

Gallery Covered seating areas surrounding the open yard of the public amphitheaters. There were three levels of galleries at the Globe; admission to these seats cost an extra penny (in addition to the basic admission fee of one penny to the yard), and seating in the higher galleries another penny yet. In indoor theaters such as Blackfriars, where there was no standing room, gallery seating was less expensive than seating in the pit; indeed, seats nearest the stage were the most expensive.

Gatherers Persons employed by the playing company to take money at the entrances to the theater.

Groundlings Audience members who paid the minimum price of admission (one penny) to stand in the yard of the open-air theaters; also referred to as "understanders."

Heavens The canopied roof over the stage in the open-air theaters, protecting the players and their costumes from rain. The "heavens" would be brightly decorated with sun, moon, and stars, and perhaps the signs of the zodiac.

Hut A structure on the top of the cover over the stage, where stagehands produced the effects of thunder and lightning and operated the machinery by which gods, such as Jupiter in *Cymbeline,* descended through the trapdoor in the "heavens."

Jig A song-and-dance performance by the clown and other members of the company at the conclusion of a play. These performances were frequently bawdy and were officially banned in 1612.

Lords' rooms Partitioned sections of the gallery "above," where the most prestigious and expensive seats in the public playhouses were located. These rooms were designed not to provide the best view of the action on the stage below, but to make their privileged occupants conspicuous to the rest of the audience.

Open-air theaters Unroofed public playhouses in the suburbs of London, such as The Theatre, the Rose, and the Globe.

Part The character played by an actor. In Shakespeare's theater, actors were given a roll of paper called a "part" containing all of the speeches and all of the cues belonging to their character. The term "role," synonymous with "part," is derived from such rolls of paper.

Patrons Important nobles and members of the royal family under whose protection the theatrical companies of London operated; players not in the service of patrons were punishable as vagabonds. The companies were referred to as their patrons' "Men" or "Servants." Thus the name of the company to which Shakespeare belonged for most of his career was first the Lord Chamberlain's Men, then was changed to the King's Men in 1603, when James I became their patron.

Pillars The "heavens" were supported by two tall painted pillars or posts near the front of the stage. These occasionally played a role in stage action, allowing a character to "hide" while remaining in full view of the audience.

Pit The area in front of the stage in indoor theaters such as Blackfriars, where the most expensive and prestigious bench seating was to be had.

Posts See *Pillars.*

Proscenium The space of the transparent "fourth wall," which divides the actors from the orchestra and audience in the standard modern theater. The stages on which Shakespeare's plays were first performed had no proscenium.

Rearstage The back of the stage, farthest from the audience.

Repertory The stock of plays a company had ready for performance at a given time. Companies generally performed a different play each day, often more than a dozen plays in a month and more than thirty in the course of the season.

Role See *Part.*

Sharers Senior actors holding shares in a joint-stock theatrical company; they paid for costumes, hired hands, and new plays, and they shared profits and losses equally. Shakespeare was not only a longtime "sharer" of the Lord Chamberlain's Men but, from 1599, a "housekeeper," the holder of a one-eighth share in the Globe playhouse.

Tiring-house The players' dressing (attiring) room, a structure located at the back of the stage and connected to the stage by two or more doors in the *frons scenae.*

Trap A trapdoor near the front of the stage that allowed access to the "cellarage" beneath and was frequently associated with hell's mouth. Another trapdoor in the "heavens" opened for the descent of gods to the stage below.

"Within" The tiring-house, from which offstage sound effects such as shouts, drums, and trumpets were produced.

Yard The central space in open-air theaters such as the Globe, into which the stage projected and in which audience members stood. Admission to the yard in the public theaters cost a penny, the cheapest admission available.

TEXTUAL TERMS

Aside See *Stage direction.*

Autograph Text written in the author's own hand. With the possible exception of a few pages of the collaborative play *Sir Thomas More,* no dramatic works or poems written in Shakespeare's hand are known to survive.

Canonical Of an author, the writings generally accepted as authentic. In the case of Shakespeare's dramatic works, only two plays that are not among the thirty-six plays contained in the First Folio, *Pericles* and *The Two Noble Kinsmen,* have won widespread acceptance into the Shakespearean canon. (This sense of "canonical" should not be confused with the use of "the canon" to denote the entire body of literary works, including but not limited to Shakespeare's, that have traditionally been regarded as fit objects of admiration and study.)

Catchword A word printed below the text at the bottom of a page, matching the first word on the following page. The catchword enabled the printer to keep the pages in their proper sequence. Where the catchword fails to match the word at the top of the next page, there is reason to suspect that something has been lost or misplaced.

Compositor A person employed in a print shop to set type. To speed the printing process, most of Shakespeare's plays were set by more than one compositor. Compositors frequently followed their own standards in spelling and punctuation. They inevitably introduced some errors into the text, often by selecting the wrong piece from the type case or by setting the correct letter upside down.

Conflation A version of a play created by combining readings from more than one substantive edition. Since the early eighteenth century, for example, most versions of *King Lear* and of several other plays by Shakespeare have been conflations of quarto and First Folio texts.

Control text   The text upon which a modern edition is based.

Dramatis personae   A list of the characters appearing in the play. In the First Folio such lists were printed at the end of some but not all of the plays. The editor Nicholas Rowe (1709) first provided lists of dramatis personae for all of Shakespeare's dramatic works.

Exeunt / Exit   See *Stage direction*.

Fair copy   A transcript of the "foul papers" made either by a scribe or by the playwright.

Folio   A bookmaking format in which each large sheet of paper is folded once, making two leaves (four pages front and back). This format produced large volumes, generally handsome and expensive. The First Folio of Shakespeare's plays was printed in 1623.

Foul papers   An author's first completed draft of a play, typically full of blotted-out passages and revisions. None of Shakespeare's foul papers is known to survive.

Licensing   By an order of 1581, new plays could not be performed until they had received a license from the Master of the Revels. A separate license, granted by the Court of High Commission, was required for publication, though in practice plays were often printed without license. From 1610, the Master of the Revels had the authority to license plays for publication as well as for performance.

Manent / Manet   See *Stage direction*.

Memorial reconstruction   The conjectured practice of reconstructing the text of a play from memory. Companies touring in the provinces without access to promptbooks may have resorted to memorial reconstruction. This practice also provides a plausible explanation for the existence of the so-called bad Quartos.

Octavo   A bookmaking format in which each large sheet of paper is folded three times, making eight leaves (sixteen pages front and back). Only one of Shakespeare's plays, *Richard Duke of York* (3 *Henry VI*, 1595), was published in octavo format.

Playbook   See *Promptbook*.

Press variants   Minor textual variations among books of the same edition, resulting from corrections made in the course of printing or from damaged or slipped type.

Promptbook   A manuscript of a play (either foul papers or fair copy) annotated and adapted for performance by the theatrical company. The promptbook incorporated stage directions, notes on properties and special effects, and revisions, sometimes including those required by the Master of the Revels. Promptbooks are usually identifiable by the replacement of characters' names with actors' names.

Quarto   A bookmaking format in which each large sheet of paper is folded twice, making four leaves (eight pages front and back). Quarto volumes were smaller and less expensive than books printed in the folio format.

Scribal copy   A transcript of a play produced by a professional scribe (or "scrivener"). Scribes tended to employ their own preferred spellings and abbreviations and could be responsible for introducing a variety of errors.

Speech prefix (s.p.)   The indication of the identity of the speaker of the following line or lines. Early editions of Shakespeare's plays often use different prefixes at different points to designate the same person. On occasion, the name of the actor who was to play the role appears in place of the name of the character.

Stage direction (s.d.) The part of the text that is not spoken by any character but that indicates actions to be performed onstage. Stage directions in the earliest editions of Shakespeare's plays are sparse and are sometimes grouped together at the beginning of a scene rather than next to the spoken lines they should precede, accompany, or follow. By convention, the most basic stage directions were written in Latin. "Exit" indicates the departure of a single actor from the stage, "exeunt" the departure of more than one. "Manet" indicates that a single actor remains onstage, "manent" that more than one remains. Lines accompanied by the stage direction "aside" are spoken so as not to be heard by the others onstage. This stage direction appeared in some early editions of Shakespeare plays, but other means were also used to indicate such speech (such as placing the words within parentheses), and sometimes no indication was provided.

Stationers' Register The account books of the Company of Stationers (of which all printers were legally required to be members), recording the fees paid for permission to print new works as well as the fines exacted for printing without permission. The Stationers' Register thus provides a valuable if incomplete record of publication in England.

Substantive text The text of an edition based upon access to a manuscript, as opposed to a derivative text based only on an earlier edition.

Variorum editions Comprehensive editions of a work or works in which the various views of previous editors and commentators are compiled.

ILLUSTRATION ACKNOWLEDGMENTS

General Introduction Plague death bill: By permission of the Folger Shakespeare Library • Webbe: By permission of the British Library • Amman: Spencer Collection, The New York Public Library, Astor, Lenox and Tilden Foundation • *Swetnam* title page: By permission of The Huntington Library, San Marino, California • Pope as Antichrist: By permission of the Folger Shakespeare Library • de Heere: The National Museum of Wales • Armada portrait: By kind permission of Marquess of Tavistock and Trustees of the Bedford Estate • Boaistuau: By permission of The Huntington Library, San Marino, California • Mandeville: By permission of the Houghton Library, Harvard University • Funeral procession: Additional Ms. 35324, folio 37v. By permission of the British Library • Gheeraerts: By permission of the Trustees of Dulwich Picture Gallery • van den Broek: Fitzwilliam Museum, University of Cambridge • Swimming: Bodleian Library, University of Oxford, 4° G.17.Art • Panorama of London: By permission of the British Library • Tarleton: Harley 3885, folio 19. By permission of the British Library • Hanging: Pepys Library, Magdalene College, Cambridge • Syphilis victim: By permission of The Huntington Library, San Marino, California • *Spanish Tragedy* title page: By permission of the Folger Shakespeare Library • Stratford-upon-Avon: By permission of City of York Libraries • Cholmondeley sisters: Tate Gallery, London • Alleyn: By permission of the Trustees of Dulwich Picture Library • *If You Know Not Me* title page: By permission of The Huntington Library, San Marino, California • van der Straet: By permission of the Folger Shakespeare Library

The Shakespearean Stage Braun and Hogenburg: 8.Tab.c.4. Bk.1.pl.1. By permission of the British Library • Hollar: Guildhall Library, Corporation of London • Interior of the "new" Globe: Courtesy of The International Shakespeare Globe Center Ltd. Photo: John Tramper • Exterior of the "new" Globe: Courtesy of The International Shakespeare Globe Center Ltd. Photo: Richard Kalina • *Frons scenae* of the "new" Globe: Courtesy of The International Shakespeare Globe Center Ltd. Photo: Richard Kalina • Oliver: The Burghley House Collection. Photograph: Courtauld Institute of Art • Peacham: Reproduced by permission of the Marquess of Bath, Longleat House, Warminster, Wiltshire, Great Britain. Photograph: Courtauld Institute of Art • de Witt: University Library, Utrecht, MS 842, f.132r • Middle Temple Hall: The Benchers of the Honorable Society of the Middle Temple, London • Hollar: Guildhall Library, Corporation of London

Shakespearean Comedy Kempe: By permission of the Folger Shakespeare Library • Terence: Internet Shakespeare Editions, University of Victoria

The Two Gentlemen of Verona Brathwaite: By permission of the Folger Shakespeare Library • Oliver: Powis Castle Estate (National Trust). Photograph: Courtauld Institute • Whitney: By permission of the Folger Shakespeare Library

The Taming of the Shrew Rowlands: C151e6(1). By permission of the British Library • Brushfield: By permission of the Folger Shakespeare Library • Flötner: Bancroft Library, University of California, Berkeley

The Comedy of Errors Merchant: Reproduced by permission of The Huntington Library, San Marino, California • Terence: Chapin Library of Rare Books, Williams College • Hollar: By permission of the Folger Shakespeare Library

Love's Labour's Lost Hill: Bodleian Library, University of Oxford, Douce M 399 • Turberville: Reproduced by permission of The Huntington Library, San Marino, California • Quarto extract: Reproduced by permission of The Huntington Library, San Marino, California • Folio extract: *The Norton Facsimile of the First Folio of Shakespeare*

A Midsummer Night's Dream Corrozet: By permission of the Houghton Library, Harvard University • Wither: By permission of the Houghton Library, Harvard University • Magnus: Bodleian Library, University of Oxford, H 4 12 Art

The Merchant of Venice Braun and Hogenburg: 8 Tab.c.4, Bk. 1 pl. 43. By permission of the British Library • Amman: Spencer Collection, The New York Public Library, Astor, Lenox and Tilden Foundation. Photo: Robert D. Rubic

The Merry Wives of Windsor Cuckold: By permission of the Floger Shakespeare Library • Elizabeth I: © British Museum • Skimmington: By permission of the Folger Shakespeare Library

Much Ado About Nothing Peacham: By permission of the Folger Shakespeare Library • Dekker: By permission of the Folger Shakespeare Library • Wither: By permission of the Houghton Library, Harvard University

As You Like It Robin Hood: The Trustees of the National Library of Scotland • Bonasone: All rights reserved. The Metropolitan Museum of Art, Gift of Philip Hofer, 1933 (33.77.5) • Weindler: Bancroft Library, University of California, Berkeley

Twelfth Night Stubbes: By permission of the Folger Shakespeare Library • Amman: Spencer Collection, The New York Public Library, Astor, Lenox and Tilden Foundation

Troilus and Cressida Whitney: By permission of the Folger Shakespeare Library • 1609 Quarto: Reproduced by permission of The Huntington Library, San Marino, California • Chapman title page: By permission of the Folger Shakespeare Library

Measure for Measure Whitney: By permission of the Folger Shakespeare Library • Amman: Audio-Visual Archives, Special Collections and Archives, University of Kentucky Libraries

All's Well That Ends Well Whitney: By permission of the Folger Shakespeare Library • Whitney: By permission of the Folger Shakespeare Library • Flötner: Ashmolean Museum, University of Oxford

Early Modern Map Culture Speed: © British Library/HIP/Art Resource, NY • Braun and Hogenberg: HIP/Art Resource, NY. Museum of London, London, Great Britain

Contemporary Documents First Folio front matter: *The Norton Facsimile of the First Folio of Shakespeare,* 2nd ed. (1996)

THE HOUSE OF LANCASTER

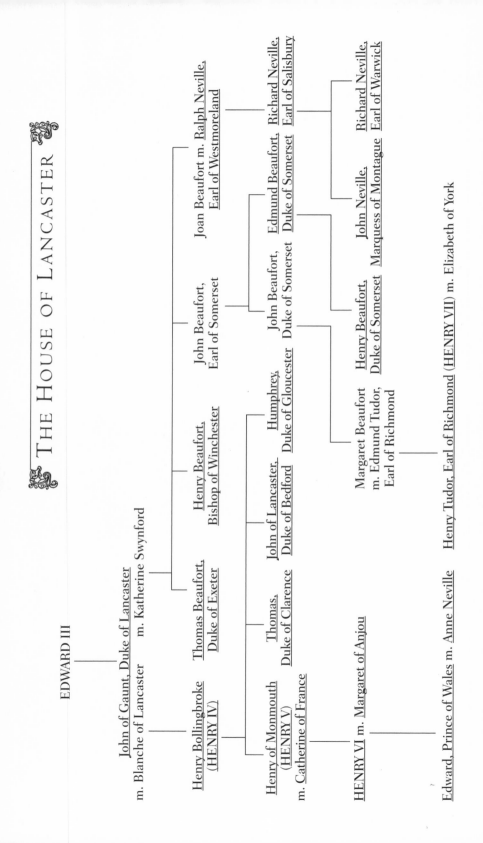

THE HOUSE OF YORK

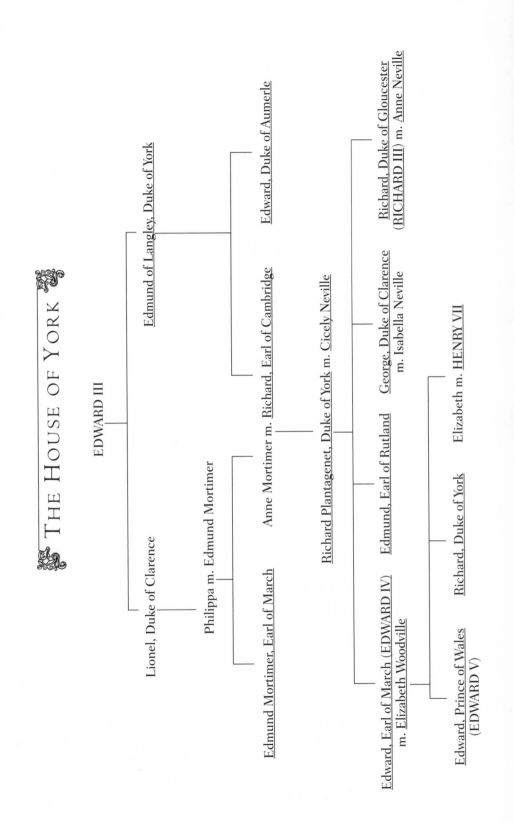

EDWARD III

Lionel, Duke of Clarence

Edmund of Langley, Duke of York

Philippa m. Edmund Mortimer

Edward, Duke of Aumerle

Anne Mortimer m. Richard, Earl of Cambridge

Edmund Mortimer, Earl of March

Richard Plantagenet, Duke of York m. Cicely Neville

George, Duke of Clarence
m. Isabella Neville

Richard, Duke of Gloucester
(RICHARD III) m. Anne Neville

Edmund, Earl of Rutland

Edward, Earl of March (EDWARD IV)
m. Elizabeth Woodville

Richard, Duke of York

Elizabeth m. HENRY VII

Edward, Prince of Wales
(EDWARD V)

Tudors (1485–1603) and Stuarts (1603–1714)

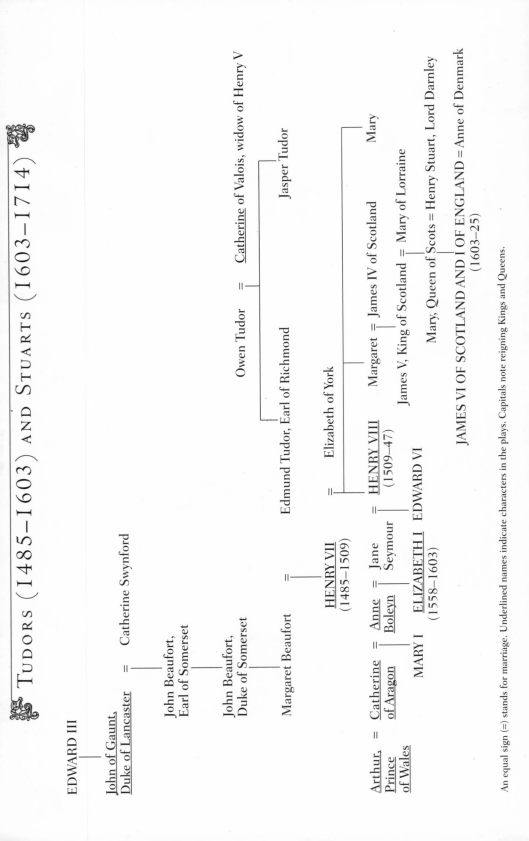

EDWARD III

John of Gaunt, = Catherine Swynford
Duke of Lancaster

John Beaufort,
Earl of Somerset

John Beaufort,
Duke of Somerset

Owen Tudor = Catherine of Valois, widow of Henry V

Margaret Beaufort

Jasper Tudor

Edmund Tudor, Earl of Richmond = Elizabeth of York

HENRY VII
(1485–1509)

HENRY VIII
(1509–47)

Margaret = James IV of Scotland   Mary

James V, King of Scotland = Mary of Lorraine

Arthur, = Catherine = Anne = Jane   ELIZABETH I
Prince   of Aragon   Boleyn   Seymour   (1558–1603)
of Wales

MARY I   EDWARD VI

Mary, Queen of Scots = Henry Stuart, Lord Darnley

JAMES VI OF SCOTLAND AND I OF ENGLAND = Anne of Denmark
(1603–25)

An equal sign (=) stands for marriage. Underlined names indicate characters in the plays. Capitals note reigning Kings and Queens.